THE COMPLETE
P E E R A G E

G.E. Cokayne (G.E.C.) Clarenceaux King of Arms, 1825–1911. (College of Arms)

THE COMPLETE
PEERAGE

OR A HISTORY OF THE HOUSE OF LORDS AND ALL ITS MEMBERS FROM THE EARLIEST TIMES

BY G.E.C.

REVISED AND MUCH ENLARGED

EDITED BY

PETER W. HAMMOND

VOLUME XIV

ADDENDA & CORRIGENDA

SUTTON PUBLISHING

First published in the United Kingdom in 1998 by
Sutton Publishing Limited · Phoenix Mill
Thrupp · Stroud · Gloucestershire GL5 2BU

Reprinted 1998

British Library Cataloguing in Publication Data
A catalogue record for this book is available from the British Library

ISBN 0 7509 0154 3

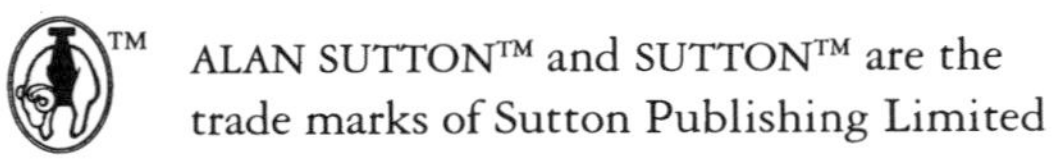

Typeset in 10/12pt Garamond.
Typesetting and origination by
Sutton Publishing Limited.
Printed in Great Britain by
WBC Limited, Bridgend, Mid-Glamorgan.

THIS VOLUME IS DEDICATED TO ALL PREVIOUS EDITORS OF

THE COMPLETE PEERAGE

CONTENTS

PREFACE viii

INTRODUCTION
A BRIEF HISTORY OF *THE COMPLETE PEERAGE* x

CORRECTIONS AND ADDITIONS 1

TITLE INDEX TO VOLUME XIII CORRECTIONS 857

PREFACE

The second edition of *The Complete Peerage* was published over forty-nine years, from 1910 to 1959, and in that time many corrections and possible additions were suggested to the various editors. These accumulated, and the present volume was first promised in 1959 in the preface to volume XII, part 2 of *The Complete Peerage*, 'if financial resources permit'. Unfortunately financial resources did not permit, and the corrections that had accumulated over nearly fifty years were all deposited in the House of Lords Record Office. These papers consisted of volumes annotated by Doubleday (editor 1920–41), but probably also included annotations by Vicary Gibbs (editor 1910–26, who seems to have shared corrections with Doubleday) and other members of staff. There are letters sent to the editors and many other papers, including a draft of part of a correction volume by R.S. Lea, last (acting) editor, and an outline of the peers created from 1939–67, prepared by R.S. Lea with additions by Mr Christopher Dobson, lately Librarian, House of Lords. From these I have extracted all factual corrections (omitting merely illustrative notes on the grounds of space) and additions, and added to them all corrections of which I was aware, as well as corrections and additions brought to my notice by historians and genealogists.

This volume brings the previous ones up to date. It includes the above corrections and additions, as well as information on all hereditary peers (and their wives) who have succeeded since the previous volumes were published, usually to the end of 1995 but occasionally after this date. The original plan of the second edition of *The Complete Peerage* was to stop at the year 1900 but, fortunately, in practice all editors included events after this, so that the task of bringing the history of the peerage up to date was less than it would otherwise have been. Also included here are peers created since 1939, when volume XIII, Peerage Creations 1901–38, was published. Only hereditary peers are included and, because they are in previous volumes, the Lords of Appeal in Ordinary, but not other life peers, as they are included in Professor W.D. Rubinstein's excellent *Biographical Dictionary of Life Peers* (1991). The new entries only include basic genealogical information on each peer. With the availability of *Who's Who* and the *Dictionary of National Biography*, both of which barely existed when G.E.C. began work, the need for full information was lessened to a large extent and to include it would have meant delaying the production of this volume even more. The real purpose of this book as part of the history of the hereditary peerage has, I hope, been fulfilled by the information included. In the belief that it is of great interest, and to fulfil the wish of Geoffrey White (editor 1941–59) and the trustees, I have also included a brief history of *The Complete Peerage* and the Trust which published it for many years. This is drawn largely from the surviving records of the Trust, also in the House of Lords Record Office.

The ideal course would have been to re-edit volumes I–IV (at least) as Doubleday and Geoffrey White believed should be done, but that was not possible at this stage, although the possibility of producing a third edition of *The Complete Peerage* is being investigated, and I therefore hope that this volume is an acceptable compromise. Succeeding generations of peers have been added to the entries for that peerage, corrections are arranged in the same order as the main volumes, i.e. A–Z by title and to the point on the page to which they refer, with the reference following immediately in square brackets. More extensive information is given in a new note following the correction or addition. Corrections to existing notes are given at the end of corrections to the text on the page. New peers created after 1938 have been added in chronological order of creation, with a cross reference to the main entry where necessary, following the pattern of volume XIII to which they have been added. There is a name and title index to the peers in this section at the end of the volume.

The corrections are given in good faith on the authority of the often distinguished genealogist or historian sending them. Others have been checked where possible or where it appeared advisable. Because there are so many, it is not possible to list separately everyone who has helped, they are named at the point at which their information is used, and thereby gratefully thanked. Thanks for extensive help are due to very many people, some of whom have passed beyond any except posthumous acknowledgement, although on behalf of Geoffrey White (who recorded in a letter that he wished to do so in any future volume) I would like to record particular thanks to the late C. Roy Hudleston for his many contributions.

I would also like to record my grateful thanks for his help to Mr David Johnson, Clerk of the Records, House of Lords, for allowing me to use the records of the Complete Peerage Trust, and for the considerable help and kindness that he and his staff showed me over very many months, also to Lord Cullen of Ashbourne for lending me his grandfather's (G.E.C.'s) set of the *Complete Peerage* and to Mr Christopher Gibbs for lending me volumes from a set of the *Complete Peerage* annotated by his great uncle Vicary Gibbs. I further wish to thank: the Chapter of the College of Arms for allowing me to have a photograph of the portrait of G.E.C., in the room of Clarenceux King of Arms; Sir Malcolm Innes of Edingight, the Lord Lyon King of Arms, for help with Scots peerages; Mr D.L. Jones, Librarian, House of Lords, for allowing me to use R.S. Lea's manuscript list of peerage creations and to look at the J.H. Round papers and to the late Mr Lea himself for his permission to use his manuscript and for much help with personal knowledge of previous editors; Eric J. Thompson, who as he knows well was responsible for first bringing to my attention the documents in the House of Lords Record Office and encouraging this work, as well as for drawing my attention to numerous necessary corrections; Mr Howard Shearring, for sharing the depressing task of checking the daily obituary notices over a period; Dr Rosemary Horrox for so much help with late medieval corrections; Professor Lorraine Attreed for suggestions and additions; Professor W.D. Rubinstein for giving me copies of his notes on new hereditary peers; Lynda Pidgeon and Canon Brian Carne for help with the St John family; Mr Brice M. Clagett of Maryland, USA, for his many suggestions and corrections and Dr Neil D. Thompson of Salt Lake City for his help with the Mortimers of Chirk; Dr Robert Hetherington for his very many notes and letters, my only regret is that I was unable to make full use of all of his information and Mr Philip Daykin for sharing with me his knowledge of the Tony and Daubeney families. Finally, but of course by no means least, I wish to thank Gillian Clegg for a great deal of work on the peers since 1900, making finishing the volume before the end of the century possible, and my wife Carolyn for this, for preparing the index, for work on corrections to other volumes and for much else besides. Without her help and encouragement this book would never have been finished.

Working on this book has been arduous but rewarding. In a work of this nature it is too much to hope that errors have not been introduced, as well as corrected, although every effort has been made to avoid this. For remaining errors and inconsistencies I can only apologise and ask scholars to inform me of them.

Peter Hammond
December 1997

INTRODUCTION

A BRIEF HISTORY OF *THE COMPLETE PEERAGE*

The Complete Peerage is one of those books which it is difficult to imagine as not existing. Its thirteen volumes are indispensable for research in many fields, including as they do a full historical and genealogical account of all peerages created in these islands since the Conquest. It is unique in that previous Peerages had only covered one country, England, Scotland or Ireland, and it is thus so very much more useful. It is now in its second edition, published over forty-nine years, from 1910 to 1959, although in a sense it has only just been finished. The last volume, number XIV, to bring it up to date, give corrections and additions and, if possible, include an index, was originally abandoned in 1960 as impossible to finance. The idea of publication was only revived about ten years ago. The second edition had a publishing history fraught with difficulty and as will be seen, it is a miracle that it was ever completed.

The first edition of *The Complete Peerage* (this edition omitted the definite article) was written, single-handedly, in eight volumes over the years 1884–98, by G.E. Cokayne, who appeared only by his initials G.E.C. on the title page. G.E.C. was a herald, he entered the College of Arms in 1859 and progressed to the office of Clarenceux King of Arms, in which office he died in 1911. He was an indefatigable genealogist, known for the ability to expound the family history of the school friends of his sons as soon as they were introduced and for his industry right up until his death. Before he started work on the *Peerage* he already had much published work to his credit, notably in *The Genealogist*.[1] He worked on the *Peerage* by himself, although of course he sought and received the help of friends, notably the redoubtable J.H. Round,[2] with whom he was on very good terms and who gave him considerable help. It is, however, a remarkable *tour de force*, and much of what G.E.C. wrote covering the seventeenth century onwards (the area in which his strength as a genealogist lay) remains in the current edition.[3]

There appear to be no surviving papers setting out how and when G.E.C. first thought of the idea of a 'complete peerage'.[4] As noted above, no one else had thought of such a book, or at least had not carried it out. Publication began as a supplement (probably paid for by G.E.C.) to the journal *The Genealogist* in 1884. Only the first two volumes appeared thus, in volumes I–V of the New Series, 1884–9. The official reason for stopping was so that publication could be speeded up, but it seems possible that it was taking up too much space or was costing too much. It seems that G.E.C. paid for the subsequent publication of the book himself, each volume costing some £130 to £140 to produce, for 300 copies of each. It was completed in volume VIII with a list of addenda and corrigenda, and with an index compiled by G.E.C.'s nephew the Hon. Vicary Gibbs, son of his sister. Each individual volume cost £1 1*s* 0*d* to subscribers and £1 10*s* 6*d* after publication.

It had been clear soon after the publication of the first edition that another would be called for. There had been considerable demand for copies of each volume from the first; by 1898 only one copy of volume I was left in stock, and by 1909 sets had been unavailable for nearly ten years and genealogists had 'paid £50 for a copy'.[5] Cokayne had been carefully annotating copies of the *Peerage* since publication (there are several such sets in existence) and Vicary Gibbs had begun to collect materials for a new edition from around 1895.[6] Gibbs was by profession a banker; he was a partner in the family business of Anthony Gibbs & Sons and had been MP for St Albans between 1892 and 1904, resigning his seat on a point of principle and losing a subsequent by-election. He was also a genealogist in his own right, had published articles in *The Genealogist* and had supplied information to G.E.C. for the first edition of *The Complete Peerage*. Thus, with the blessing of G.E.C., work on a new edition, with Vicary Gibbs as editor, was in hand by 1908.

The first volume was published in 1910 and was received with universal acclaim. G.E.C. died in August 1911 so he only saw this first volume, but it is pleasant to think that he saw what was being made of his great work. His own copy of volume I still exists.[7] It is not now known how long it was originally thought that publication would take, but as by 1916 volume IV had appeared (i.e. four volumes in six years), then the planned twelve volumes would have taken about twenty years. Gibbs set the course which the volumes were to follow from then on. He edited the first two volumes alone and the following two with the 'assistance of H. Arthur Doubleday', as the title page has it. They included much new information and some new research, particularly on the pre-fifteenth-century peerages, but in some ways these first four volumes were really mostly G.E.C.'s work with added notes by Gibbs. He was responsible for many fascinating sidelights on peers, particularly the eighteenth- and nineteenth-century holders of titles – his reading of memoirs was obviously enormous. However, the one distinctive feature of his editing is the greatly increased number of notes, many of them distinguished by his particularly acerbic sense of humour. He was always reluctant to let the Whigs escape without censure, for example. His influence continued even after he finally gave up editorial control in 1926, as notes with his initials appended appeared in all subsequent volumes and he frequently wrote to Doubleday in the 1920s sending him new notes, corrections or additions culled from his reading. He died in 1932.[8]

Volumes I–IV (and probably the first version of volume V) were produced entirely at Gibbs' expense. However, in about 1919 (the exact date is unclear, later references are ambiguous), with rising costs and increasing ill health, he ceased paying all expenses and was forced to hand over the direction of the enterprise to H.A. Doubleday, who had been associated with him from the beginning, as Assistant from 1910, Assistant Editor from 1916 and Joint Editor from 1920. Doubleday was a typical Victorian in his capacity for hard work and certainly towards the end of his life did little else than work on the latest volume of the *Peerage*, usually at least six days a week and about ten hours a day, although as he commented, 'As my sole interest in life is the Complete Peerage, this is no hardship'.[9] He had been co-founder of the *Victoria County History* and general editor from 1901 to 1903 and afterwards, in 1907–8, founded his own publishing firm, firstly as Doubleday & Co. and later as the St Catherine's Press, this originally in Belgium. The latter subsequently published all volumes of the *Peerage*, although not by then under Doubleday's immediate control. It was as founder of the St Catherine's Press that he was first associated with *The Complete Peerage*, as at Gibbs' request he devised the type, format and layout. Doubleday had an excellent eye for these as well as for paper and binding, and indeed a legendary eagle eye for proof errors.[10]

That the work did not come to a halt when Gibbs withdrew financial support was entirely due to Doubleday. He continued the work, financed by various means (see below), with co-editors, one of whom was the noted antiquarian and philanthropist, Lord Howard de Walden (who died in 1946). Together, these two produced volumes VI–X and XIII, but throughout, from 1920 to 1941 when he died, Doubleday was editor-in-chief and he was the power that drove the work on. He was also a scholar; he was, for example, one of the few witnesses called to give evidence to the Select Committee on Peerages in Abeyance in 1926, which accepted many of his views in their final report.[11] As a scholar he immediately increased the amount of research carried out, particularly on the earlier peerages and their antecedents, and under him the book really ceased to be a second edition and became more of a new work. He was determined that the greatly increased amount of published research available, in particular published records, should be used to make *The Complete Peerage* a valuable and useful work of reference, not just a 'Peerage'. His great ambition throughout the rest of his life was to re-edit the first four volumes to the standard of those he was bringing out. He did reprint them all (incorporating minor amendments) in the 1920s,[12] perhaps in 1926 when volume V was reprinted. This volume had originally been published in 1921 (probably financed by Gibbs) in an unfinished form, with some of the 'G' peers omitted and reserved for volume VI. It is likely that it was produced thus to placate the subscribers, who may have been protesting about the five-year period when nothing had been published, although no one should have been surprised that work slowed down during the First World War. These reprints were an expensive exercise, and also meant increased delays in producing the next volume. Plans to increase the amount of detail meant too that the plans to complete the work in twelve volumes were becoming increasingly unrealistic.

The major problem faced by Doubleday during his editorship was not the content of the volumes but raising the money to pay for them. According to Geoffrey White, Gibbs had spent about £60,000 on the first four volumes,[13] and costs had increased enormously during the war. With the withdrawal of funding by Vicary Gibbs, it was necessary to find the money to continue the enterprise. Doubleday was not a wealthy man and as his colleagues said, the only thing that saved the *Peerage* was his refusal to admit defeat.[14] At first he raised money by means of loans from his friends and some money was raised in America and Canada as the result of an appeal for a research fund. This was obviously an unsatisfactory way of proceeding and in 1921 it was suggested by Viscount Cowdray, the wealthy building contractor and philanthropist, that capital should be raised by the issue of debentures by a private company. The Genealogical Publishing Company was therefore founded in 1922 for this purpose and some £16,400 was raised. Viscount Cowdray himself took up ten debentures of £100 each, Granville Proby (Clerk, afterwards Principal Clerk, in the House of Lords and a strong supporter of the enterprise), took thirty-two while Howard de Walden took no less than sixty-seven, with subsequent loans of more than £3,000. The debenture holders voluntarily gave up their holdings in 1936, and frequently waived their rights to interest before this.[15]

With the help of these debentures Doubleday's friends were repaid their loans and work proceeded with the aid of the rest of the money. However, by 1926 this was exhausted and the problem began again. One of the reasons for the rapidity with which money ran out was that several office staff were deemed necessary to help the enterprise, which meant staff salaries. Doubleday himself, a firm believer in the value of what he was doing, was paid £1,500 per annum from 1926, although he and all the staff voluntarily agreed to a reduction in 1932 – Doubleday went down to £1,200. The total office expenses in around 1932 were nearly £3,500 per annum.[16] To compound his financial problems, after he took control Doubleday insisted on having 3,500 copies of all volumes printed. In comparison, only 1,500 copies of volumes I to IV were published.[17] Not all of the sets of sheets were bound up, and in those days of low rents the sheets did not cost a great deal to store, but this was still many copies more than the numbers sold on publication (or given away as complimentary copies), which was about 800–900 copies. Probably very few copies were sold after the first year of publication, for example in 1938/9 the sales appear to have been two sets and one copy of volume 9.[18]

While Vicary Gibbs was still paying for the publication, each volume was produced on handmade paper ('writing paper' as they described it) as well as on ordinary paper, 'so that readers who know any further details can write them in the margins'.[19] This must have cost a great deal and caused problems when deciding how many copies to bind up, but the practice was stopped with volume IV. Another practice caused problems until the publication of the last volume. This was the adherence to the principle of supplying the original subscribers (who had paid £42 for the whole set) with each volume free as it came out, and the original 'volume by volume' subscribers with each one for 1 guinea, despite the enormous increase in costs over the years. The only way to buy the *Peerage* was to subscribe, agreeing to buy the whole set from the beginning or from when the subscription was started. Enormous energy was put into tracing subscription sets which slowly became separated from the original subscriber as time went on and subscribers died. In theory, no one was allowed to cancel a subscription. The price to new subscribers had risen to 3½ guineas per volume by 1921 (you could subscribe for a whole set for £30 in 1924), but the price did not rise again until 1959, when it went up to 5 guineas. None of these prices really reflected the costs: prices had risen four times by 1921 (when volume V was first published) and they continued to rise, notably after the Second World War.[20] There was also a consistent refusal to sell single volumes, but to sell sets only, a policy which was maintained right until after the publication of volume XII, part 2, in 1959.[21] Some subscribers voluntarily increased their payments, but not all, and some subscribers who were alive after the Second World War demanded, and received, their volumes for 1 guinea. The cost of this policy must have been many thousands of pounds. The volumes were not priced to make a profit from the beginning and the whole enterprise most certainly never did; the sales for 1924–37 brought in £7,459 against expenses for 1920–40 of approximately £72,000.[22]

In 1926, when the available money ran out again, a generous benefactor was found in the person of Sir Harry Mallaby-Deeley, a business man, who covenanted to pay no less than £32,500 over the next few years. This lasted until the end of 1934, and although Lord Leverhulme gave £2,500 in 1935, in November of 1936 Doubleday was writing to Lord Mersey, one of the members of a recently formed Executive and Finance Committee, saying that unless he could acquire more funds *The Complete Peerage* would 'have to be abandoned'. In July 1937 he was writing to Mersey again, rather pathetically expressing his heartfelt thanks for an anonymous cheque for £5,000, which had 'saved the work from collapse'.[23] The anonymous cheque was in fact from Sir Julien Cahn, sportsman and philanthropist. In 1938, however, a saviour appeared in the form of Lord Nuffield, who gave £50,000 which, if all had gone well, would have been enough to finish the work. Doubleday was overjoyed, as may be imagined.[24]

Following this very generous gift, a trust, the Complete Peerage Trust, was formed to oversee both the work and the expenditure of the funds, and remained in being until the early 1960s. The original Trustees were the Duke of Norfolk, Viscounts Halifax and Mersey (all of whom had been in a list of 'Patrons' of the enterprise), Lord Howard de Walden and Granville Proby, but not Doubleday. There had been a committee in existence before this (not the Executive and Finance Committee mentioned above, although with some of the same members), consisting mostly of *ex officio* worthies such as the Lord Chancellor, the President of the Society of Antiquaries and the Provost of Eton, but it seems never to have met.[25]

A change of policy was seen with the formation of the Trust. The original plan was for the *Peerage* to stop at 1900, a sensible policy when it was thought that the second edition would be completed within fifteen or twenty years, but becoming increasingly difficult to justify as time went on. In practice, the editors did include details of peers who had succeeded after this, albeit with the final rubric at the end 'who, as a peer, is outside the scope of this work' or in footnotes, but this did nothing to meet the lack of entries for the many peers created after 1900. In the hope that a volume giving such entries would sell well and bring in more subscribers (particularly peers), volume XIII, 'Peers Created 1900 to 1938' was published in 1940. This was the only volume of the set that, at that time, could be purchased separately. This volume also had the advantage that Lord Nuffield was one of those included, which gave an excuse for appendixes on 'The ancestry of Viscount Nuffield' and 'Lord Nuffield's gifts of £25,000 and upwards', a rather nice way of saying thank you. Unfortunately, the volume did not sell particularly well and was one of those remaindered in the 1960s.

Despite the problems, volumes continued to appear about every three to four years throughout the 1920s and '30s: volume VI in 1926, volume VII in 1929, volume VIII in 1932 and volume IX in 1936. Lord Howard de Walden had agreed to act as co-editor with Doubleday after the resignation of Gibbs, and they had worked together on the next five volumes. De Walden, the 8th Baron of that title, was among very much else, a historian, genealogist and antiquarian. Apart from his great generosity to the *Peerage* (perhaps overall to the extent of about £10,000), the enterprise undoubtedly benefited from his talents and his associations. He and Doubleday seem to have got on well together. In volume VI they had as a colleague Major Duncan Warrand. He was also a genealogist (he had been genealogical editor of the *Victoria County History*) and was recruited chiefly to work on medieval Scots pedigrees. He does not seem to have been an easy colleague and his association with the work was ended shortly after the publication of volume VI by his resignation on the grounds of ill health.

Volume X, the last volume in the original series with which Doubleday was associated, was delayed by his final illness and by the Second World War, not being published until 1945.[26] Doubleday himself died in March 1941, having struggled on with the work after he became ill in 1938. He worked on the *Peerage* very nearly until his death, having done virtually nothing else for many years. His sole interest in life was indeed *The Complete Peerage*.

Joining Doubleday and Howard de Walden on the title page of volume X was Geoffrey White, who had been appointed Editor-in-Chief by the Trustees in 1941, having been Doubleday's assistant since early 1938. White had been producing work for the *Peerage* from 1929 at least. He was the son of a wine merchant and had been a historian and genealogist for many years, and was Vice President of the Society of Genealogists for eleven years, until his death. He was an expert in the Anglo-Norman period, and together with Lewis Loyd and Charles Clay he increased the coverage of this period. He proved to be an excellent editor. He was appointed at a salary of £600 per annum, rather lower than Doubleday had enjoyed.[27] The Trust was in fact quite a generous employer; salaries were increased regularly and appeals for more money on compassionate grounds (in one case for a five-month back tax demand) were usually answered positively. Its attitude to the staff was very paternalistic in fact. The small staff of four or five included White, R.S. Lea before and then after the war, Miss Ethel Stokes until her death, Shenton, the Secretary, who died in harness in 1958, and Arthur Yeames, who had a background in the classics and who retired through ill health in 1945, to be replaced by Michael Hughes, a historian, who died in 1952. There was also Mrs Fox the cleaner, who worked for them for many years, receiving just over £62 a year.[28]

The work of producing the volumes was immeasurably more difficult during the Second

World War (although work never ceased); the manuscripts from the British Museum and Public Record Office were stored in Wales, for example. The war interrupted the succession of editors too, as Robert Lea, the staff member who was the Trustees' first choice as editor following Doubleday's death, had refused the position, because he had already volunteered for the forces. He was in fact already in his forties and had served in the First World War. Lea himself felt that White was the better man for the post of editor, on the grounds of his experience and expertise.[29] One of White's advantages as new editor was that he was well over military age: he was sixty-eight in 1942. Lea's departure left a gap in the staff, and another blow was the death of one of the most regular contributors and long-term associates, Miss Ethel Stokes, who was killed in the blackout. White's flat (rented by the Trust and also the headquarters of *The Complete Peerage*) suffered minor bomb damage.[30]

Despite these problems, volume X was published in 1945 and the next volume followed in 1949. Problems in production now included the difficulty of obtaining paper to print on – it was rationed for several years after the war. Fortunately Doubleday had purchased a sufficient quantity before the war for volume X. None of this was left for volume XI in 1949, however, and, as well as the problems of persuading the authorities that *The Complete Peerage* was a suitable recipient of scarce resources, they had difficulty in acquiring the gilt for the top. They had to agree to use bronze in the end, which has not lasted as well.[31]

Other difficulties were caused by the fact that those who had been involved with the *Peerage* from the 1920s were becoming older and by 1949 the Trustees reported that two of their number, Lord Howard de Walden and Granville Proby, had died (in 1946 and 1947 respectively). In November 1949 they elected the House of Lords' Librarian, Charles Clay, and Hon. Geoffrey Gibbs (cousin to Vicary Gibbs) in their places. With the publication of volume XII in 1953, it was reported that because of the much fuller treatment of the early descents of peerages from Doubleday's tenure as editor onwards, the original plan of completing the work in twelve volumes had been changed. Accordingly, this volume had been numbered XII, part 1. The last volume could not be numbered XIII as that had already been published.[32] The calculations of the amount of space the second edition would occupy, made at the beginning from G.E.C.'s original volumes, were in fact remarkably accurate considering the difficulties of such a calculation.

The old perennial problem of money was also raising its head. The money given by Lord Nuffield was running out faster than had been allowed for in 1938. It had naturally been invested and the income and carefully calculated fractions of the capital had been spent in the subsequent years. However, the cost of paper, printing and binding had increased greatly since the war and capital was draining faster than had been expected. No economies could be made in the main contents of each volume, but the size of the appendixes was reduced drastically and some of those promised from the beginning, such as (most unfortunately) those on baronies by writ and on feudal Irish baronies, were abandoned. More important in the eyes of many was the announcement in volume XII, part 1, that the publication of an index to the work would not now take place. This news caused a stir and letters appeared in *The Times* signed by all the heralds and kings of arms and a number of eminent historians who protested against this decision in no uncertain terms. The Trustees had naturally considered all the implications, not least the potential size of the index and the cost of staff time to produce it. The plain fact was that the Trust did not have the money to pay for an index.[33]

The situation was so bad that the Trust did not have enough money to pay for the last volume of the main series, taking the peerage to Zouche. It was very fortunate in receiving gifts for general expenses, notably from Sir Geoffrey Ellis, the peerage lawyer, and a large enough grant from the Pilgrim Trust specifically to publish volume XII, part 2. Without these gifts it was, as the Trustees said, 'doubtful whether the publication of this volume could have been achieved'.[34] Very little money indeed was left after the volume was published in 1959, not even enough to publish a 'slim' volume of the corrections and additions accumulated since the first volume was published in 1910 and a list of newly created peers since 1938, which was half promised by the Trustees in their preface to the last volume. As said above, the price of the last volume was set at 5 guineas, which was a slightly more realistic price than before. Given that the total edition cost £4,880 for 1,500 copies (only 806 were bound) and that they expected to sell about 700 copies at this price to subscribers (plus the 100 or so copies to original subscribers at £1.05 each), it was still not very realistic though. A change of policy at this time to allow the sale of single copies was too late to make any difference to the finances of the Trust.[35]

Following the publication of that last volume, the Trust virtually ceased operations. Geoffrey White, who was by now in his eighty-seventh year (and losing his eyesight) retired in the middle of 1959. He went to live in the Charterhouse and died ten years later in his ninety-sixth year.[36] Robert Lea, his deputy for the last few years, was appointed acting editor for the winding-up period. Lea was an excellent genealogist, with a great facility for summarising clearly the most complicated work. He too would have been an excellent editor.[37] He had prepared the list of newly created peers and made a start on drawing up the final list of corrections which he offered to prepare for publication, but this offer was refused. Both of these manuscripts are still in existence and (with his permission, just before he died in his ninety-eighth year in 1995) use has been made of them in the present volume.

With the retirement of White and the publication of the 'Zouche' volume, the Complete Peerage Trust ran down its activities and Lea made arrangements for the closure of the office, for the sale of the furniture and even for the sale of the editors' reference library, accumulated over forty years or more. As part of the closing-down process the Trustees considered their stock of volumes. As already said, Doubleday had great confidence in the numbers that would be sold and had 3,500 copies printed (against 1,500 of the original printing by Gibbs for volumes I–V). This was maintained by White, although only 1,500 were printed of the last volume. Most of these books were stored as loose sheets, not bound up. The cost of storing these was mounting and it was decided that only 50 sets of bound books would be kept and 350 sets of the loose sheets.[38] At the time, given the state of the Trust's finances, this was probably sensible but it was a most unfortunate decision in the long term. The Trust was then slowly wound down, having achieved, so far as was within its power, its sole object, the publication of *The Complete Peerage*.

REFERENCES

1. G. Ambrose Lee, 'The Late Clarenceux King of Arms', *Genealogist* (1912), vol. 28, pp. 150–1.
2. The extent of G.E.C.'s help from Round is shown in G.E.C.'s letters to him, Univ. of London, I.H.R., MS 628, 1883–1908. I am grateful to Mr W.R. Powell for copies of his transcripts of these letters.
3. See, for example, Francis, 2nd Baron Godolphin, in volume V (1926 reprint), which is identical to the corresponding entry in the first edition volume IV, p. 49, with the corrections called for in volume VIII.
4. Geoffrey White thought that G.E.C. started work on the first edition around 1870, *Geneal. Mag.*, vol. 9, 1942, p. 253. The Cokayne Papers, in the Northampton Record Office (NRO), where they were deposited by his grandson, the present Lord Cullen of Ashbourne, give no help in this matter.

5. *Daily Express*, 15 July 1909; *Daily Chronicle*, 3 Dec. 1909. The *Chronicle* thought that it had only fetched as much as £35. In 1904 Francis Edwards, the bookseller, sold a set, described as rare, for £35 (NRO, C 806).
6. For fifteen years, he said in the preface to volume I, published in 1910.
7. This volume is now NRO, C 877. G.E.C. left his 'dear nephew' his interleaved copy of *The Complete Peerage* and his copyright (NRO, C 581).
8. *Dictionary of National Biography* (*DNB*), under Vicary Gibbs; *Complete Peerage* (1898), vol. VIII, p. 252; Card Index with the Complete Peerage Trust papers in the House of Lords Record Office (HLRO).
9. HLRO, CP 43, letter from Doubleday to Lord Mersey, 23 May 1938.
10. H.A. Doubleday: 1867–1941 (a commemorative booklet published by his friends, 1942), p. 31. *The Complete Peerage* is in fact set in 12 pt Caslon, a typeface which Doubleday considered particularly attractive. As a person, Doubleday was apparently slightly self-important, with a love of controversy and good food (R.S. Lea, personal communication). He had been a sportsman in his youth.
11. Report of the Select Committee on Peerages in Abeyance (Sumner Report), HMSO, House of Lords, 189, 190 (1927), pp. 113–23; for acceptance of his views, H.A. Doubleday: 1867–1941, pp. 10–11.
12. Volumes I–IV seem to have been reprinted in the mid-1920s (see HLRO, CP 16, for various estimates of costs). Evidence of the reprinting may be seen at various points in these volumes, e.g. in volume I, where the last four lines of the entry on the 4th Earl of Abercorn were rewritten to correct the mistaken statement in the first printing that the earl died when re-embarking for France after the battle of the Boyne.
13. G.H. White, *Geneal. Mag.*, vol. 9, 1942, p. 255.
14. *The Complete Peerage* (1945), vol. X, p. vii.
15. *The Complete Peerage* (1936), vol. IX, pp. i–ii. A full list of the debenture holders is on p. ii.
16. HLRO, CP 7 and CP 16.
17. HLRO, CP 16, memorandum by H.A. Doubleday of around 1922–4. It is possible that more than 1,500 copies of volumes I–IV were printed (even though Doubleday seemed sure of the figure), as there are now no surviving records from before 1922, and because of the reprints of volumes I–IV.
18. HLRO, CP 62, letter of Granville Proby to Lord Mersey, 27 Mar. 1941. When volume XII, part 2, was published, 800 copies were distributed to subscribers, HLRO, Trust Minutes, memo by Sir Charles Clay, 22 July 1958. For numbers sold in 1938/9, see HLRO, CP 24 and CP 25 (1939/40).
19. *Daily Express*, 15 July 1909. There exists a piece of the special paper inscribed by G.E.C.: 'paper for my copy of the new edition'.
20. HLRO, Complete Peerage Trust, Correspondence with Sir Charles Clay 1939–52: letter from Miss Steele, Secretary of the Trust to St Catherine's Press, 17 August 1953; *The Complete Peerage*, (1926), vol. V, p. vii. The subscription price of £42 per set in 1910 seems odd, but appears to be correct.
21. *The Complete Peerage* (1959), vol. XII, part 2, p. viii.
22. HLRO, Complete Peerage Trust Papers 1933–61, Sir Charles Clay, letters of 1956–8; HLRO, CP 62; HLRO, CP 45, letter of Lord Mersey to Lord Aldenham, 15 Mar. 1940.
23. HLRO, CP 42, Doubleday to Lord Mersey, 20 Nov. 1936 and 18 July 1937.
24. HLRO, CP 43, Doubleday to Lord Mersey, 14 June 1938.
25. *The Complete Peerage* (1936), vol. IX, p. ii; (1940), vol. XIII, p. iii; HLRO, Complete Peerage Trust (a deed box), bundle of letters, 1937. The 'Committee' had fourteen members, but probably never met as a committee; the Executive and Finance Committee had eleven members, again including such men as the Archbishop of Canterbury and the Lord Chancellor.
26. The estimated cost of this volume in 1941 was £1,220 for 3,500 copies, of which 1,000 were to be bound, HLRO, CP 46, letter of Lord Mersey to Lord Howard de Walden, 2 Sep. 1941.
27. *Who Was Who*, 1961–1970 (1979), under Geoffrey Henllan White; HLRO, CP 7 (White as Assistant to Doubleday); HLRO, CP 45, Lord Mersey to the Duke of Norfolk, 30 Apr. 1941 (for White's salary); White's letter of acceptance, letter of 3 May 1941. His salary had risen to £900 by 1957.
28. Tax demand, HLRO, CP 48, letter of 27 Nov. 1943.
29. *The Complete Peerage* (1945), vol. X, pp. vii–viii; offering editorship to Lea or White, HLRO, Trust Minutes, 9 Apr. 1941; Lea's letter regarding the editorship, HLRO, CP 45, 23 Apr. 1941; memo by Lord Mersey to Lewis Loyd, 1 Apr. 1941, saying Doubleday thought Lea was the best man to succeed him, HLRO, CP 46. Lea was originally a schoolmaster after leaving Oxford in 1921 (Rugby School Registers, 1911–1946, 1957), and joined the staff of *The Complete Peerage* in Jan. 1936 (HLRO, CP 7), for 6 months' unpaid work to learn historical research. He stayed on after the death of Doubleday's brother, Archibald, as a staff member, and rejoined them in 1945 after his war service (HLRO, CP 50, Lord Mersey to Lea, Sep. 1945).
30. *The Complete Peerage* (1945), vol. 10, p. vii.

31. Appeal for paper, HLRO, CP 53; substitute for gilding, HLRO, CP 54, White to Lord Mersey, 31 May 1949. 'Bronze' was used for subsequent volumes too.

32. *The Complete Peerage* (1953), vol. XII, part 1, p. ix.

33. *The Times*, 30 Nov. 1953 and 2 Jan. 1954; HLRO, CP 59, memo by Sir Charles Clay, 18 Jan.; HLRO, Trust Minutes, 5 May 1954.

34. *The Complete Peerage* (1959), vol. XII, part 2, p. viii.

35. Cost of vol. XII, part 2, HLRO, Complete Peerage Trust (deed box), envelope addressed to Miss K.L. Steele, 1960. Printing alone cost £898 (for 1,500 copies), compared with £788 for vol. XI in 1949 and £669 for vol. X in 1945 (for 3,500 copies each).

36. White died on 6 Mar. 1969, within three weeks of his 96th birthday, obituary, *Geneal. Mag.*, vol. 16, 1969, p. 113; *The Times*, 8 Mar. 1969, p. 10. With regard to the former obituary, it should be noted that White was elected Vice President of the Society of Genealogists in 1958, not 1960 (*Geneal. Mag.*, vol. 12, 1958, p. 504). White, as a person, was a very kindly man, easy to get on with and (apparently) much preferring a quiet life to engaging in controversy, unlike Doubleday (R.L. Lea, personal communication).

37. After the Complete Peerage Trust was wound up he went to work for the History of Parliament Trust, contributing to the volumes covering 1715–74.

38. HLRO, Complete Peerage Trust Papers 1933–1961, letter to Sir Charles Clay, 4 May 1961; Secretary of the Trustees to Sir Geoffrey Gibbs (a Trustee), 21 June 1960. There were larger quantities of bound volumes for numbers X, XII, part 2, and XIII; these were remaindered (I am grateful to Mrs Rosemary Pinches for this information). The loose sheets were subsequently destroyed too.

APPENDIX: J.H. ROUND AND H.A. DOUBLEDAY

Among many others, the great J.H. Round gave a considerable amount of help to the editors of the second edition of *The Complete Peerage*, directly and indirectly. Mr W.H. Powell, author of a forthcoming biography of Round (and to whom I owe much of the information in the following note), has shown that there are many references to his works, or contributions by him, in the complete work – well over a thousand in fact.

Doubleday and Round were indeed friends for many years, they were associated closely when Doubleday published (and edited) the *Victoria County History*, to which Round was a major contributor. Doubleday also published Round's *Commune of London* and *Studies in Peerage and Family History*. It was natural, therefore, that Round's association with *The Complete Peerage* should continue with the second edition. All seems to have gone fairly amicably until 1919, when any active participation by Round ceased abruptly. This was probably due entirely to a major quarrel between Doubleday and Round. It seems to have begun with Doubleday making changes to Round's work on Darcy, for volume IV and to have reached a climax with Doubleday's (mild) criticisms of Round in vol. 4, Appendix H, 'Earldoms and Baronies in History and in Law, and the Doctrine of Abeyance'. Round took these very much amiss and published a very harsh criticism of Doubleday's work in the *English Historical Review* ("'Barons' and 'Peers'", vol. 33, 1918, pp. 453–71), accusing him of inaccuracy and plagiarism. It was so extreme that Doubleday threatened to sue Round, the *E.H.R.* and Longman's, the publisher. The quarrel was ended by a limited apology in *E.H.R.* and the publication by Doubleday of a pamphlet (*Dr Round's "'Barons' and 'Peers'"; a Reply* by H.A. Doubleday, n.d.) in which he ably defended himself. When Doubleday reprinted volume IV in the 1920s he changed some of the references to Round slightly, and deleted others. This quarrel ended Round's connection with *The Complete Peerage*, but naturally not the use of his works.

ABBREVIATIONS

Abbreviations used in previous volumes have been used where possible, including original county names. No new county names are used. New, or less familiar, abbreviations used in this volume are as follows:

The Geneal.: *The Genealogist* (the new American journal, founded in 1980)

Geneal. Mag.: *The Genealogist's Magazine*

J. Med. Hist.: *The Journal of Medieval History*

R.A.C., Cirencester: Royal Agricultural College, Cirencester

R.M.A., Woolwich: Royal Military College, Woolwich

R.M.C., Sandhurst: Royal Military College, Sandhurst

WW1: First World War, 1914–18

WW2: Second World War, 1939–45

VOLUME I

page x,
line 11, after 'Victoria' add '22 Jan. 1901'

page xvii,
line 33, after 'Reginaldo de Grey' add '(of Wilton)'

page xviii,
line 4, For 'Thome Willelmi de Creistok' read 'Thome filio Willelmi de Greistok' G.W.W.

page xxii,
line 32, Nicolas is speaking of the admission of a writ 'at the Bar of the House of Lords' while Watson attempts to convict him of error by assuming that he is speaking of the case in 1616 'before the Commissioners for the office of Earl Marshal'. I have often wondered what was the exact admission spoken of by Nicolas, but I have always assumed that he was speaking of the Ros case fought out in 1805–6 'at the bar of the House of Lords' (Cruise, 48–51), though I have not been able to refer to it. The probable reason why this writ would then be put in was that it summoned Robert de Ros *de Werke* and William de Ros de *Imgmanthorpe*. This last is believed to have been William de Ros *of Belvoir*, and to have been summoned also as *de Hamlake* (see Courthope, in error; G.E.C. is correct here), for the question of *styles* was an important point in 1805–6, and as three of the Ros family were summoned in 1294, this writ would certainly have been cited. G.W.W. seems to be wrong in believing that the 1294 writs have not 'ever been brought forward in any case' for they were adduced in the Mowbray case, Roger de Mowbray having been then summoned, and admitted, if I remember correctly. Again, it is true that the 1294 writs are 'not even mentioned in *Lords Reports*, vol. i, p. 208, 'but three of them *are* mentioned – and not even questioned – in *Lords Reports*, vol. iii, pp. 87, 89! After a long search I have found passages in the Third Report, pp. 230, 235, which *may* be what Nicolas refers to (for he speaks of the 'last' report). On p. 230 they speak of Greystock's summons in 1294 as 'to a Council' and on p. 235 they say that T. de Furnivall was 'summoned to Parliament . . . in the 22d of Edward I, (if the Summons remaining on Record of that Year was a Summons to Parliament).' J.H.R.

page xxxiii,
line 2, for 'inherited' read 'borne'

ABBOTS LANGLEY

page 1,
line 2, for '1753' read '1756'

ABERCORN

page 2,
line 3, for '6th' read '5th'
line 20, for '5th' read '6th'

page 3,
line 25, for 'in Scotland' read '21 Aug. at Paisley'
after '*bur.*' add 'there'

page 5,
line 2, after 'da.' add 'and coh.'
line 3, for 'Hester' read 'Bridget'
line 34, after 'da.' add 'and coh.'

page 6,
line 9, after 'obtained' add 'On 22 Jan. 1683/4 a warrant issued to create him BARON HAMILTON OF BELLAMONT, co. Dublin [I.], but the patent never passed the Great Seal' (*Cal. S. P. Dom., 1683–4*, p. 234; *cf. Hist. MSS. Com.*, Ormonde MSS., N.S., vol. vii, p. 183)
line 12, for '2 Sep.' read '2 Dec.'
line 16, after '*m.*' add 21 Jan. 1683/4' (*Hist. MSS. Com.*, Ormonde MSS., N.S., vol. vii, p. 183)

page 10,
line 16, for '4th' add 'and yst.'
line 17, after 'Earl Howe' add 'being only da.'
line 18, delete from 'She' to '1848.' and replace by 'He *d.* at 61 Green Str., Grosvenor Sq., of pneumonia, 3, and was *bur.* 7 Jan. 1913 at Baronscourt. His widow, who was *b.* 23 July 1848, and was Lady in Waiting to Queen Alexandra, *d.* at her house in Park Str., W. 10, and was *bur.* 15 May 1929, at Baronscourt.'
line 19, line to read as follows

DUKEDOM [I.]
III.
MARQUESSATE [G.B.]
IV
EARLDOM and BARONY [S.]
XII.
} 1913

3, 4 and 12. JAMES ALBERT EDWARD (HAMILTON), DUKE OF ABERCORN [1868], &c., 1st s. and h.;

line 21, after 'Eton' add 'after 1885 *styled* MARQUESS OF HAMILTON'
line 26, delete ']' and replace by 'He *d.* 12 Sep. 1953. His widow *d.* 18 Jan. 1958.'
lines 27–8, delete all detail and replace as follows

DUKEDOM [I.]
IV.
MARQUESSATE [G.B.]
V
EARLDOM and BARONY
XIII.
} 1953

4, 5 and 13. JAMES EDWARD (HAMILTON), DUKE OF ABERCORN [1868], &c., 1st s. and h., *b.* 29 Feb. 1904, for whom King Edward VII stood sponsor. *Styled* LORD PAISLEY until 1913, MARQUESS OF HAMILTON 1913–53; ed. at Eton. He *m.* at St. Martin-in-the-Fields, 9 Feb.

1928, Mary Cathleen, only da. of Henry William (CRICHTON), VISCOUNT CRICHTON, by Mary Cavendish, 5th da. of Hugh Lupus (GROSVENOR), 1st DUKE OF WESTMINSTER. He *d.* 4 June 1979. His widow *d.* 1990.

DUKEDOM [I.] V. MARQUESSATE [G.B.] VI EARLDOM and BARONY XIV	1979	5, 6 and 14. JAMES (HAMILTON), DUKE OF ABERCORN [1868], &c., 1st s. and h., *b.* 4 July 1934. Ed. at Eton and R.A.C., Cirencester. He *m.*, 20 Oct. 1966, Alexandra Anastasia, eldest da. of Col. Harold Pedro Joseph PHILLIPS of Checkendon Court, Reading.

[James Harold Charles, Marquis of Hamilton, 1st s. and h. ap., b. 19 Aug. 1969.]

ABERCROMBIE

page 11,
line 3, for '*d. v.p.*' read 'was living 1 Jan. 1644/45' (*Scots Peerage*, vol. ix, p. 4)
line 13, delete 'Crichton'
line 14, after 'Forfar' add 'From her he obtained a divorce, apparently on 13 Mar. 1662/63' (*Scots Peerage*, vol. ix, p. 5)
line 14, after '1663' add 'after 18 Oct.'

ABERCROMBY OF ABOUKIR AND TULLIBODY

page 13,
line 18, after 'V.A.' add 'She *d.* at Camperdown House, near Dundee, 8 Dec. 1915. He *d.* in London, 30 Oct. 1917, aged 79.'

V. 1917 5. JOHN (ABERCROMBY), BARON ABERCROMBY OF ABOUKIR AND TULLIBODY, br. and h., *b.* 15 Jan. 1841. He *m.*, 26 Aug. 1876, his cousin Adele Wilhelmina Marika, da. of Chevalier Charles VON HEIDENSTERN. This marriage was diss. by divorce in 1879. He *d. s.p.m.* 7 Oct. 1924, when his title became *extinct*.

ABERDARE OF DUFFRYN

page 14
line 9, after 'LYNDHURST' add 'He *d.* at 83 Eaton Sq., London S.W. 20, and was *bur.* 23 Feb. 1929 at Mountain Ash, Glamorgan, aged 78. His widow *d.* 8 and was *bur.* 11 Feb. 1932 at Mountain Ash afsd.'

[HENRY LYNDHURST BRUCE, 1st s. and h. ap., *b.* 25 May 1881; ed. at Winchester from 1894; matric. at Oxford (New Coll.) 1899; Capt. 3rd Battn. Royal Scots 1906; he served in WW1 and was *k.* in action near Ypres, 14 Dec. 1914, aged 33; [aa] *m.*, 11 Oct. 1906 at the Registry Office for St. Geo., Han. Sq., in Mount Str., Midx., Camilla Antoinette, da. of Reynold CLIFFORD.[b] He *d.* as abovesaid, in 1914. Will pr. Feb. 1915, at £37,564 gross, and £3,284 net. His widow *m.*, 9 Aug. 1917, at St. Paul's, Knightsbridge, Brig. John Meredyth Jones Evans, M.C.]

note ([aa]) For a list of peers and sons of peers who served in WW1, see vol. viii, Appendix F.

note ([b]) The lady was a 'Gibson girl' on the Vaudeville stage, i.e. a young woman chosen because her features recalled the type of female beauty which the American artist Gibson affected. She first acted in London in 1904 and continued to play after her marriage. V.G.

III. 1929 3. CLARENCE NAPIER (BRUCE), BARON ABERDARE OF DUFFRYN; 2nd but 1st surv. s. and h., *b.* 2 Aug. 1885 at Duffryn; ed. Winchester from 1898; matric. at Oxford (New Coll.) 1903; Barrister at Law, Inner Temple, 1911; he served in WW1 in Glamorgan Yeomanry, 2nd Life Guards, 61st Division Head Quarters, and Guards Machine Gun Regt.; Capt. 1918; in WW2 in Home Guard; Major 1943; Prior of Priory for Wales, O.St.J., 1948 to death; appointed C.B.E., 1949; G.B.E., 1954. He *m.* 1stly, 12 Dec. 1912, Margaret Bethune, only da. of Adam BLACK of Hurstmonceux, Sussex, by Mary, eld. da. of James Henry SMITH of Maidstone, Kent. She *d.* 8 Feb. 1950. He *m.* 2ndly, 12 Sep. 1957, Griselda Harriet Violet Finetta Georgina, only da. of Dudley Francis Amelius HERVEY (son of the Rev. Charles Amelius HERVEY, 5th son of the 1st MARQUESS OF BRISTOL) by Griselda Mary Theophila yst. da. of Col. Sir Edward FitzGerald CAMPBELL, Bart. He *d.* in a motor accident in Yugoslavia, 4, and was *bur.* 8 Oct. 1957 at Mountain Ash, Glamorgan. His widow *d.* 1980.

IV. 1957 4. MORYS GEORGE LYNDHURST (BRUCE) BARON ABERDARE OF DUFFRYN, eld. s. and h. by 1st wife, *b.* 16 June 1919; ed. Winchester from 1932; matric. at Oxford (New Coll.) 1940; Lieut. Welsh Guards, 1940; Capt. 1942; Prior of Priory for Wales, O.St.J., 1958. He *m.*, 1 June 1946, Maud Helen Sarah, only da. of Sir John Lindsay DASHWOOD 10th Bart. by Helen Moira, da. of Lieut. Col. Vernon EATON, Royal Canadian Horse Artillery.

[ALISTAIR JOHN LYNDHURST BRUCE, 1st s. and h. ap., *b.* 2 May 1947; ed. Eton from 1960; matric. at Oxford (Ch. Ch.) 1971. He *m.*, 1971, Elizabeth Mary Culbert, da. of John FOULKES.]

ABERDEEN (County of)

page 14
replace entry by,

EARLDOM [S.] I. 1682 1. SIR GEORGE GORDON, of Haddo, co. Aberdeen, Bart. [S.], 2nd son of Sir John G. by Mary, da. of William FORBES of Tolquhoun, *b.* 3 Oct. 1637; *suc.* his eldest br. in the Baronetcy and estate of Haddo in 1665. He became an Advocate 7 Feb. 1668, M.P. for co. Aberdeen 1669–74, 1678, and 1681-2, P.C. 1678, one of the Lords of Session 1 June 1680, President 1 Nov. 1681, and having been made HIGH CHANCELLOR [S.] 1 May 1682, was, on 30 Nov. 1682, *cr.* LORD HADDO, METHLICK, TARVES, and KELLIE, VISCOUNT OF FORMATINE, and EARL OF ABERDEEN [S.].([c]) In June 1684 he resigned office, and though at the Revolution he was imprisoned in Edinburgh Castle for refusing to take the oath of allegiance to William III, he took it subsequently to Queen Anne. In Mar. 1707/8 he, being suspected of complicity with the abortive invasion of Scotland by the French, in the Jacobite interest, was compelled to give a bond for his appearance if called upon before 8 Nov. 1708.([d]) He *m.* (cont. 1671)

Anne, 1st da. of George LOCKHART, of Torbrecks, by Anne, da. of Sir James LOCKHART, of Lee. In 1672 she became h. to her br., William L. She was *bur.* 19 July 1707, at Methlick. He *d.* 20 Apr. 1720, at Kellie, in his 83rd year. Will dat. 5 May 1706.

page 15,
line 14, for '12 Oct.' read '23 Apr.[da]'
note [da] *Hist. MSS. Com.*, House of Lords MSS., N.S., vol. viii, p. 179.
line 27, after 'year' add ', and was *bur.* at St. Cuthbert's, in that City'

page 16,
note [d], line 2, for 'twelve' read '13' (after page 17)
line 1, '1883' add '; the Duke of Buccleugh [S.], K.G. 1897'
line 2, for 'twelve' read 'thirteen'
line 8, at end add 'The case of the Earl of Rosebery [S.] seems to be unique, for he was made K.T. in 1895, having already been made K.G. in 1892.'

page 18,
line 11, after '1857' add '[for further detail see vol. xiii, p. 209]. He *d.* 7 Mar. and was *bur.* at Haddo, 12 Mar. 1934. His widow *d.* 18 Apr. 1939.'
line 12, line to read as follows

MARQUESSATE II. EARLDOM [S.] VIII. — 1934

2 and 8. GEORGE (GORDON), MARQUESS OF ABERDEEN AND TEMAIR [U.K.], EARL OF ABERDEEN, &c., s. and h. ap., *b.* 20 Jan. 1879.

line 13, after 'Midx.' add '*styled* LORD HADDO 1879–1934
line 16, for ']' read 'His wife *d.* 5 Jan. and was *bur.* 7 Jan. 1937 at Haddo. He *m.* 2ndly, 21 Dec. 1940, Sheila, widow of Capt. James William Guy INNES, R.N., of Maryculter House, Kincardineshire, and da. of Lieut. Col. John Foster FORBES of Rothiemay. She *d.* 12 Mar. 1949. He *d. s.p.* 6 Jan. 1965.'

MARQUESSATE III. EARLDOM [S.] IX. — 1965

3 and 9. DUDLEY GLADSTONE GORDON (GORDON), MARQUESS OF ABERDEEN AND TEMAIR, &c., br. and h., *b.* 6 May 1883; ed. at Harrow. He *m.* 1stly, 25 Apr. 1907, Cécile Elizabeth, eldest da. of George James DRUMMOND of Swaylands House, Penshurst, Kent. She *d.* 17 Sep. 1948. He *m.* 2ndly, 17 June 1949, Margaret Gladys, only da. of Lieut. Col. Reginald George MUNN of East Grinstead. He *d.* 16 Apr. 1972. His widow *d.* 1990.

MARQUESSATE IV. EARLDOM [S.] X. — 1972

4 and 10. DAVID GEORGE IAN ALEXANDER (GORDON), MARQUESS OF ABERDEEN AND TEMAIR, &c., 1st s. and h., *b.* 21 Jan. 1908; ed. at Harrow and Oxford (Balliol Coll). He *m.*, 29 Apr. 1939, Beatrice Mary June, only da. of Arthur Paul BOISSIER, headmaster of Harrow Sch. He *d.* 13 Sep. 1974. His widow was living 1995.

MARQUESSATE V. EARLDOM [S.] XI.	1974	5 and 11. ARCHIBALD VICTOR DUDLEY (GORDON), MARQUESS OF ABERDEEN AND TEMAIR, &c., br. and h., *b.* 9 July 1913; ed. at Harrow. He *d.* unm. 7 Sep. 1984.
MARQUESSATE VI. EARLDOM [S.] XII.	1984	6 and 12. ALASTAIR NINIAN JOHN (GORDON), MARQUESS OF ABERDEEN AND TEMAIR, &c., br. and h., *b.* 20 July 1920; ed. at Harrow. He *m.*, 24 Feb. 1950, Anne, eldest da. of Lieut. Col. Gerald BARRY, M.C., of Great Witchingham, Norwich.

[ALEXANDER GEORGE, *styled* EARL OF HADDO, s. and h. ap., *b.* 31 Mar. 1955; ed. at Harrow. He *m.*, 1981, Joanna Clodagh, da. of Major Ian George Henry HOULDSWORTH.]

ABERDELGY

page 18,
delete all detail

ABERGAVENNY

page 20,
note (e), add 'See vol. viii, p. 677, pedigree *sub* LINCOLN'

page 21,
line 9, for 'Bohon' read 'Bohun'

page 22,
line 1, after 'abovenamed' add ,' being da. of MILES OF GLOUCESTER, 1st EARL OF GLOUCESTER'
line 27, after 'PEMBROKE' add ', by Isabel, *suo jure* COUNTESS OF PEMBROKE'

page 24,
line 7, for 'unm.' read '*s.p.*'

page 26,
line 8, after 'pr.' add '1411'

page 27,
line 15, for '5th' read '13th'

page 28,
line 28, for 'about 1490' read 'shortly before 20 Sep. 1492'

page 31,
lines 6–9, delete from '(whose' to '[1475–6]' and replace by 'who *d.* Sep. 1485 (will dat.

23 Sep. 1485, pr. 12 Sep. 1486), and before that, widow of Robert BASSETT, Lord Mayor of London (1475–6), who *d.* between 11 May and 27 July 1484, and before that widow of Richard NAYLOR,(c) citizen of London, who was *bur.* at St. Martin's, Outwich, London (will dat. 18 July, and pr. 22 Aug. 1483)'

note (e), before 'There' add 'There was an earlier John Stokker, who *d.* 1464, and it is possible that he and not the J.S. of the text was her husband and, if so, her 1st husband.'

page 33,
line 4, after '2ndly' add 'before 21 Dec. 1495' (William Brett's will of that date, *P.C.C.*, 34 Vox)
line 5, after 'gentleman' add 'by Anne, or Amy, da. and coh. of William ROSMODERES, of Cornwall' [*Ex inform.* Philip H. Blake, Canterbury; *cf. Visit. of Kent*, 1619, Harl. Soc., p. 211]
line 6, for '1515' read '3 Aug. 1516 (her mother's will of that date)' [*Ex inform.* Philip H. Blake, *Canterbury Wills and Admons, 1396–1558*, Brit. Rec. Soc., p. 64]
line 10, after '*d.*' add 'June' ['this Sunday morning', *L. and P. Hen. VIII*, vol. viii, no. 960]
lines 13–14, after '1586' add '(ca)'
note (ca) These dates are from Dugdale, see vol. ii, pp. v–vi.
note (c), line 2, after 'names.' add 'However, see vol. ii, p. 19, note (b) and corrections to that note, below.'

page 35,
line 17, after 'Midx' add 'by Elizabeth, da. of Sir Griffith DWNN'

page 36,
note (c), after 'nothing' add 'When Leonard Dacre claimed the Barony the award was not produced by either party and no reference was made to it in the hearing of the case by the Commissioners.'

page 37,
line 23, after 1601 add '(ax)'
note (ax) A Bill preferred by Lord Bergavenny's father 'to assure a jointure to Mary, daughter of Lord Buckhurst, whom Henry Nevill, his eldest son, intendeth to marry' is ascribed in *Cal. S. P. Dom., 1581–90*, p. 639, to the year 1589.'

page 38,
line 9, after 'BERGAVENNY' add 'or ABERGAVENNY'
line 10, delete from 'He' to 'Parl'
line 20, after 'BERGAVENNY' add 'or ABERGAVENNY'

page 40,
line 15, for 'who was' read 'which Edward was yr.'
line 20, delete from 'bapt.' to '1737'

page 41,
line 17, for '1552' read '1535'

page 44,
line 19, after 'net.' add 'He *d.* at Eridge Castle, 12, and was *bur.* 16 Dec. 1915 at Eridge Green in his 90th year.'
line 20, line to read as follows

MARQUESSATE. II.
EARLDOM. VI.
BARONY XII } 1915

2 and 6. REGINALD WILLIAM BRANSBY (NEVILL), MARQUESS OF ABERGAVENNY, &c., 1st s. and h.,

line 21, after '1853' add '*styled* EARL OF LEWES 1876–1915'
line 22, for ']' read 'He *d.* unm. at Cheadle Royal, Cheshire 13, and was *bur.* privately at Eridge, 17 Oct. 1927.'

MARQUESSATE. III.
EARLDOM. VII.
BARONY XXIII } 1927

3 and 7. HENRY GILBERT RALPH (NEVILL), MARQUESS OF ABERGAVENNY, &c., b. and h., *b.* 2 Sep. 1854. He *m.* 1stly, 12 Sep 1876, Violet, eldest da. of Col. Henry Dorrien STREATFEILD of Chiddingstone Castle, Kent. She *d.* 25 Dec. 1880. He *m.* 2ndly, 20 Oct. 1886, Maud Augusta, da. of William BECKETT. She *d.* 15 July 1927 and he *m.* 3rdly, 18 Oct. 1928, Mary Frances, widow of Henry Charles HARDINGE, 3rd VISCOUNT HARDINGE, and da. of Ralph NEVILLE, br. of 1st Marquess of Abergavenny. He *d.* 10 Jan. 1938, being thrown from his horse while hunting.

MARQUESSATE. IV.
EARLDOM. VIII.
BARONY XXIV } 1938

4 and 8. GUY TEMPLE MONTACUTE (LARNACH-NEVILL *formerly* NEVILL), MARQUESS OF ABERGAVENNY, &c., nephew and h., being 1st s. and h. of Guy Montacute NEVILL (*d.* 10 Aug. 1920), by Alice, da. of Thomas Scurr WOMERSLEY, 3rd s. of the 1st Marquess. He was *b.* 15 July 1883. He *m.*, 30 Oct. 1909, Isabel Nellie, only child and heir of James Walker LARNACH of Brambletye, Sussex by his wife Lady Isabella Lettice Theodosia, da. of Richard Edmund St. Lawrence (BOYLE), 9th Earl of Cork and Orrery. He assumed by deed poll, 17 June 1919, the surname of LARNACH-NEVILL instead of NEVILL for himself and his wife only. She *d.* 5 Nov. 1953. He *d.* 29 Mar. 1954.

MARQUESSATE. V.
EARLDOM. IX.
BARONY XXV } 1954

5 and 9. JOHN HENRY GUY (NEVILL), MARQUESS OF ABERGAVENNY, EARL OF LEWES [U.K.], EARL OF ABERGAVENNY, VISCOUNT NEVILL [G.B.], and LORD ABERGAVENNY [E.], 1st s. and h., *b.* 8 Nov. 1914; ed. at Eton and Cambridge (Trin. Coll.). He *m.*, 4 Jan. 1938, Mary Patricia, 4th da. of Major John Fenwick HARRISON of King's Walden Bury, Hitchin, Herts.

[HENRY JOHN MONTAGUE NEVILL, *styled* EARL OF LEWES, *b.* 2 Feb. 1948; ed. at Eton, *d.* 2 Apr. 1965.]

ABINGDON

page 49,
lines 25–6, delete from 'Lieut. Col.' to '1880'
line 33, after 'She' add ', who' and after '1867' add ', *d.* 16 Sep. 1942. He *d.* at Oaken Holt, Oxford, 10, and was *bur.* 14 Mar. 1928 at Abingdon.'
line 42, after 'Baron.' add 'He *d.* *v.p.* from heart failure 24 Sep. 1919. His widow *d.* 21 Dec. 1933.'

VIII. 1928 8. MONTAGU HENRY EDMUND CECIL (BERTIE), EARL OF ABINGDON, &c., s. and h., *b.* 2 Nov. 1887. Succeeded his distant cousin as EARL OF LINDSEY 2 Jan. 1938. For further details and for subsequent Earls of Abingdon see *sub* LINDSEY.

ABINGER

page 51,
lines 38–9, delete from 'He' to 'work.'

V. 1903 5. SHELLEY LEOPOLD LAURENCE (SCARLETT), BARON ABINGER, cousin and h., being s. and h. of Leopold James Yorke Campbell SCARLETT of Parkhurst, Surrey (21 Oct. 1888), by Bessie Florence, da. and coh. of Edward GIBSON, which Leopold was s. and h. of Peter Campbell SCARLETT (*d.* 15 July 1881), by his 1st wife Frances Sophia Mostyn, 2nd da. and coh. of Edmund LOMAX of Parkhurst, Surrey, 3rd s. and the 1st Baron Abinger. He was *b.* 1 Apr. 1872. He *m.*, 8 Aug. 1899, Lila Lucy Catherine Mary, widow of Kammerherr Carl Emmanuel DE GEIJER, only da. of Rt. Hon. Sir William Arthur WHITE. He *d. s.p.* in London, 23, and was *bur.* 26 May 1917 at Brookwood Cemetery. His widow *d.* 7 June 1941.

VI. 1917 6. ROBERT BROOKE CAMPBELL (SCARLETT), BARON ABINGER, br. and h., *b.* 8 Jan. 1876; ed. at Wellington. He *m.*, 26 June 1917, at Roupell Park Wesleyan Chapel, Tulse Hill, and afterwards at the French Consulate, Bedford Sq., Jean Marguerite (Madame DE SERIGNAC), da. of Edouard JAPY of Beaucourt near Belfort, France, and widow of Adolphe STEINHEIL of Paris. He *d. s.p.* 10 June 1927. His widow *d.* 17 July 1954.

VII. 1927 7. HUGH RICHARD (SCARLETT), BARON ABINGER, br. and h., *b.* 25 Nov. 1878. He *m.*, 15 Oct. 1913, Marjorie Ursula, 2nd da. of John MCPHILLAMY of Blair Atholl, Bathurst, New South Wales. He *d.* 21 July 1943. His widow *d.* 17 Sep. 1965.

VIII. 1943 8. JAMES RICHARD (SCARLETT), BARON ABINGER, eldest s. and h., *b.* 28 Sep. 1914; ed. at Eton and Cambridge (Magdalene Coll.). He *m.*, 4 Apr. 1957, Isla Carolyn, only da. of Vice-Adm. James William RIVETT-CARNAC of Fornham House, Bury St. Edmunds.

[JAMES HARRY SCARLETT, 1st s. and h. ap., *b.* 28 May 1959.]

page 52,
line 2, for 'Inverlochie' read 'Inverlochy'
line 2, for 'Kingussie' read 'Fort William'

ABOYNE

page 54
line 4, after 'h.' add 'by 2nd wife, was *b.* 1669–70; adm. Douai, 10 Apr. 1681, aged 11.'
line 7, for '3rd' read '1st'

ACTON OF ALDENHAM

page 55,
line 13, delete 'on petition'
line 22, delete from 'He' to 'work' and replace by 'His widow *d.* at Aldenham, 3 Apr. 1923.'

II. 1902 2. RICHARD MAXIMILIAN (DALBERG-ACTON), BARON ACTON OF ALDENHAM, s. and h., *b.* in Bavaria, 7 Aug. 1870; ed. at Oxford (Magdalen Coll.). He was declared a British subject by Act of Parliament 1911 and assumed the name and arms of Lyon by Royal Licence 1919. He *m.*, 7 June 1904, Dorothy, only child of Thomas Henry LYON, of Appleton Hall, Cheshire. She *d.* at Aldenham Park, Bridgenorth, co. Salop., after a long illness, 17 Mar. 1923. He *d.* 16 June 1924.

III. 1924 3. JOHN EMERICH HENRY (DALBERG-ACTON), BARON ACTON OF ALDENHAM, 1st s. and h., *b.* 15 Dec. 1907; ed. at Downside, Sandhurst and Cambridge (Trin. Coll.). He *m.*, 25 Nov. 1931, Daphne, only da. of Robert John (STRUTT), 4th BARON RAYLEIGH. He *d.* 23 Jan. 1989. His widow was living 1995.

IV. 1989 4. RICHARD GERALD (DALBERG-ACTON), BARON ACTON OF ALDENHAM, 1st s. and h., *b.* 30 July 1941; ed. at St. George's Coll. Salisbury, Rhodesia and Oxford (Trin. Coll.). He *m.* 1stly, 28 Aug. 1965, Hilary Juliet Sarah, 2nd da. of Dr Osmond Laurence Charles COOKSON of Perth, W. Australia. She *d.* 1973. He *m.* 2ndly, 1974, Judith Garfield, da. of Sir Garfield TODD, sometime Prime Minster of S. Rhodesia. This marriage was diss. by divorce in 1987 and he *m.* 3rdly, 1988, Patricia, only da. of M. Morey NASSIF, of Cedar Rapids, Iowa, U.S.A.

[JOHN CHARLES FERDINAND HAROLD DALBERG-ACTON, s. and h. ap., *b.* 19 Aug. 1966; ed. at Winchester and Oxford (Balliol Coll.).]

ADDINGTON

page 57,
line 11, for 'Mar.' read '26 Feb.'
line 13, after '79' add ', and was *bur.* at Addington.'
line 23, after 'afsd.' add 'He *d.* of heart failure at Addington Manor, 14, and was *bur.* 18 June 1915 at Addington. His widow *d.* 2 Dec. 1933.'
line 24, line to read as follows

III. 1915 3. JOHN GELLIBRAND (HUBBARD), BARON ADDINGTON, s. and h., *b.* at 23 Cadogan Place, 7 June 1883; ed. at Eton and Oxford (Ch. Ch.). He *d.* unm. 20 June 1966.

line 27, delete ']' and replace by 'etc'

IV. 1966 4. RAYMOND EGERTON (HUBBARD), BARON ADDINGTON, br. and h., *b.* 11 Nov. 1884; ed. at Eton and Oxford (Magdalen Coll.). He *m.*, 11 Nov. 1926, Margaret Favre, da. of William MACCALLUM and widow of Edward Marriott GIBSON. She *d.* 16 Jan. 1963. He *d. s.p.* 17 Aug. 1971.

V. 1971 5. JAMES (HUBBARD), BARON ADDINGTON, kinsman and h., being s. of John Francis HUBBARD (*d.* 3 June 1953), by 3rd wife Betty Riversdale, da. of Horace WEST; which John Francis was s. of Cecil John HUBBARD (*d.* 10 Mar. 1926), by Helen Jane, da. of Arthur Macdonald RITCHIE; which Cecil John was 3rd s. of 1st Baron. He was *b.* 3 Nov. 1930; ed. at Eastbourne Coll. and Chadacre Agric. Inst. He *m.*, 7 Oct. 1961, Alexandra Patricia, da. of Norman Ford MILLAR. This marriage was diss. by divorce in 1974. He *d.* 26 June 1982. His widow was living 1995.

[DOMINIC BRYCE HUBBARD, s. and h. ap., *b.* 24 Aug. 1963; ed. at Hewett Comp. Sch., Norwich and Aberdeen Univ.]

AGHRIM

page 58,
line 2, for '1677' read '1676'

AILESBURY

page 58,
in margin, for '1664' read '1665'
line 7, after 'London' add 'and was *bap.* there 19 Mar. 1626/27'
line 10, for '1661' read '1660'
line 11, for '1663/4' read '1664/5'

page 59,
line 11, for 'Groom' read 'Lord'

page 64,
line 29, for '30' read '29'
lines 30–1, delete from 'Lieut. Col.' to 'Hon. Col.'

page 66,
line 18, after 'Str.' add 'He *d.* at Tottenham House, Savernake Forest, 10, and was *bur.* 15 Mar. 1911, in St. Katherine's church there.'
line 19, line to read as follows

MARQUESSATE. VI. EARLDOM X. } 1911

6 and 7. GEORGE WILLIAM JAMES CHANDOS (BRUDENELL-BRUCE), MARQUESS OF AILESBURY, &c., only s. and h.; *b.* 21 May 1873; ed. at Westminster; *styled* EARL OF CARDIGAN 1894-1935. [For further information see pages 66–7.] His first wife Caroline Sydney Anne *d.* 5 May 1941. He *m.* 2ndly, 21 Feb. 1945, Mabel Irene, da. of John Samuel LINDSAY of Wrexham. She *d.* 26 June 1954. He *m.* 3rdly, 9 July 1955, Alice Maude Emily, da. of Capt. John Forbes PINHEY and widow 1stly of Col. John Henry Arthur BOYCE, 2ndly of Col. Francis Byrne JOHNSON, and 3rdly of Col. Rowland MONEY. She *d.* 9 Feb. 1960. He *d.* 4 Aug. 1961.

page 67,
line 2, delete ']'
lines 3–4, delete all detail and replace by

MARQUESSATE. VII. EARLDOM. XI. } 1961

7 and 8. CHANDOS SYDNEY CEDRIC (BRUDENELL-BRUCE), MARQUESS OF AILESBURY, &c., s. and h., *b.* 26 Jan. 1904; *styled* VISCOUNT SAVERNAKE 1904–11, and EARL OF CARDIGAN 1911–61; ed. at Eton and Oxford (Ch. Ch.) He *m.* 1stly, 5 July 1924, Joan Houlton, da. of Stephen SALTER of Pondwell House, Ryde, Isle of Wight. She *d.* 24 July 1937. He *m.* 2ndly, 11 Mar. 1944, Joyce Frances, da. of Charles WARWICK-EVANS, and formerly wife of Peter QUENNELL. This marriage was diss. by divorce in 1948. He *m.* 3rdly, 20 Feb. 1950, Jean Frances Margaret, da. of John Addison WILSON of Bodicote, Banbury, Oxon., and widow of Sqn. Ldr. Richard WILLIAMSON. He *d.* 15 July 1974. His widow was living 1995.

MARQUESSATE. VIII. EARLDOM. XII. } 1974

8 and 9. MICHAEL SYDNEY CEDRIC (BRUDENELL-BRUCE), MARQUESS OF AILESBURY, &c., 1st s. and h.; *b.* 31 Mar. 1926; ed. at Eton. He *m.* 1stly, 17 Mar. 1952, Edwina Sylvia de Winton, yr. da. of Lieut. Col. Sir Ernest Edward de Winton WILLS, 4th Bart. This marriage was diss. by divorce in 1961 and he *m.* 2ndly, 10 July 1963, Juliet Adrienne Lethbridge, da. of Edward Hilary Lethbridge KINGSFORD. This marriage was diss. by divorce in 1974 and he *m.* 3rdly, 1974, Caroline Elizabeth, da. of Cmdr. Owen Francis MacTier WETHERED, R.N., and formerly wife of Simon ROMILLY. This marriage was diss. by divorce in 1992.

[DAVID MICHAEL JAMES BRUDENELL-BRUCE, *styled* EARL OF CARDIGAN, s. and h., *b.* 12 Nov. 1952; ed. at Eton, Rannoch and R.A.C., Cirencester. He *m.*, 1980, Rosamund Jane, eldest da. of Capt. W.R.M. WINKLEY of Wyke Champflower Manor, Bruton, Somerset.]

AILSA

page 68,
line 23, after 'India' add 'He *d.* 9 Apr. 1938. His widow *d.* 9 Dec. 1945.'
line 24, line to read as follows

IV. 1938 4. ARCHIBALD (KENNEDY), MARQUESS OF AILSA [U.K.], &c., s. and h. by 1st wife.

line 25, after 'Midx.' add '*styled* EARL OF CASSILIS from 1872. Ed. at Eton, Cambridge (Trin. Coll.) and Edinburgh Univ.

line 29, for ']' read 'She *d.* 29 Oct. 1939. He *d. s.p.* 27 Feb. 1943.'

V. 1943 5. CHARLES (KENNEDY), MARQUESS OF AILSA, &c., br. and h., *b.* 10 Apr. 1875. Ed. at Eton and R.A.C., Cirencester. He *m.* 1stly, 15 Dec. 1925, Constance Barbara, da. of Edward CLARKE of Avishays, Chard and widow of Adm. Sir John Erskine Kennedy BAIRD. She *d.* 3 Nov. 1931. He *m.* 2ndly, 26 Apr. 1933, Helen Ethel, da. of James MCDOUALL of Logan and widow of Richard John CUNNINGHAME, M.C., of Hensol, Stewartry of Kirkcudbright. He *d. s.p.* 1 June 1956. His widow *d.* 17 Feb. 1959.

VI. 1956 6. ANGUS (KENNEDY), MARQUESS OF AILSA, &c., br. and h., *b.* 28 Oct. 1882; ed. at Eton. He *m.*, 28 Jan. 1922, Gertrude Millicent, yr. da. of Gervas Weir COOPER of Wordwell Hall, Bury St. Edmunds. He *d.* 31 May 1957. His widow *d.* 25 Aug. 1957.

VII. 1957 7. ARCHIBALD DAVID (KENNEDY), MARQUESS OF AILSA and BARON AILSA [U.K.], also EARL OF CASSILIS and LORD KENNEDY [S.], s. and h., *b.* 3 Dec. 1925; ed. at Nautical Coll., Pangbourne. He *m.*, 7 Apr. 1954, Mary, yst. da. of John BURN of Amble, Northumberland. He *d.* 7 Apr. 1994. His widow was living 1995.

VIII. 1994 8. ARCHIBALD ANGUS CHARLES (KENNEDY), MARQUESS OF AILSA and BARON AILSA [U.K.], also EARL OF CASSILIS and LORD KENNEDY [S.], s. and h., *b.* 13 Sep. 1956. He *m.*, 1979, Dawn Leslie Anne, only da. of David A. KEEN of Paris. This marriage was diss. by divorce in 1989.

AIREY

page 69,

line 11, for '1838–47' read '1847–51'

line 12, after '53' add 'Mil. Sec. to the Cmdr.-in-Chief, 1852–4'

AIRLIE

page 70,

lines 3–4, delete from 'of the same' to 'of Seton'

lines 9–10, delete from 'Helen' to '1486' and substitute ', 2ndly, before May 1478, Helen widow of William (DOUGLAS), 2nd EARL OF ANGUS [S.], by Margaret, da. of Sir William HAY of Yester. She was living 20 Nov. 1486.'

line 11, for 'about 1504' read 'shortly'

line 11, after '1504' add ', being dead three and a half years before 2 May 1508. [*Scots Peerage*, vol. 1, p. 70; vol. 9, p. 7]'

lines 15–16, for '(GRAHAM)' read '2nd LORD GRAHAM, [S.], by Helen, da. of William (DOUGLAS), 2nd EARL OF ANGUS [S.].'

line 20, for '8th' read '7th'

line 20, for 'Isobel' read 'Margaret'
line 25, for '1st' read '3rd'
line 25, for 'da.' read 'sister'
line 26, after '[S.]' add 'da. of Adam HEBURN, MASTER OF HAILES.'
note ([d]), line 1, after 'note' add 'Isobel Forbes, who surv. him.'
note ([d]), line 5, after 'note' add 'Moreover, James, the 5th Lord, writes to his son, 11 June 1606, "God took my lord my guidsir [i.e. grandfather] and my father (of good memory) from me of 5 years old and the whole friends and name in one day" (*Hist MSS. Com.*, Var. Coll., vol. v, p. 245). Although the words 'one day' must not be taken literally, yet they plainly show that the writer's father and grandfather died at about the same time. V.G.'

page 71,
line 3, after 'Katherine' add '([ax])'
note ([ax]) Katherine Campbell *m.* 2ndly as his 2nd wife David (Lindsay), 9th Earl of Crawford [S.], and *d.* 1 Oct. 1578.

page 73,
line 13, for '1799' read '1699'

page 74,
line 13, after '1stly' add 'on or before 31 May 1748'
line 32, after 'Marylebone' add 'and was *bur.* in the Canongate, Edinburgh.'
note ([a]), line 6, for 'F' read 'E'

page 75,
line 12, for 'was living 1909' read '*d.* in York Terrace, Regent's Park, 5, and was *bur.* 11 Jan. 1920 at Cortachy afsd.'
line 18, after '1885' add '–1900'
line 34, after 'OGILVY OF' add 'ALITH AND'
line 36, after 'Tipperary' add 'Ed. at Eton. Lieut. 10th Hussars, served in WW1 from 1914 (Despatches, M.C.). He *m.*, 17 July 1917, at St. George's, Hanover Sq., Alexandra Marie Bridget, 2nd da. of Thomas William (COKE), 3rd EARL OF LEICESTER OF HOLKHAM, by Alice Emily, 2nd da. of Luke (WHITE), 2nd Baron Annaly. He *d.* 28 Dec. 1968. His widow *d.* 1984.

EARLDOM [S.] VIII. BARONY XIV. } 1968 — 8 and 14. DAVID GEORGE PATRICK COKE (OGILVY), EARL OF AIRLIE, &c., 1st s. and h., *b.* 17 May 1926; ed. at Eton. He *m.*, 23 Oct. 1952, Virginia Fortune, da. of John Barry RYAN of Newport, Rhode Island, U.S.A.

[DAVID JOHN OGILVY, 1st s. and h. ap., *styled* LORD OGILVY from 1958, *b.* 9 Mar. 1958; ed. at Eton and Oxford (Ch. Ch.). He *m.* 1stly, Geraldine Theodora Gabriel, eldest da. of Vere Harold Esmond (HARMSWORTH), 3rd VISCOUNT ROTHERMERE. This marriage was diss. by divorce in 1990. He *m.* 2ndly, 1991, Tarka, da. of John KINGS of Austin, Texas, U.S.A.]

AIRTH

page 77,
note (c), line 16, for 'MONTEITH' read 'MENTEITH'

ALBANY

page 78,
line 28, for '(Erskine)' read '9th'
line 29, for 'da.' read 'only surv. child and h.'

page 79,
line 2, after 'da. and h. of' add 'John FRASER of Zouch Fraser, s. and h. of'
line 17, after '*m.*' add '1stly, Joan (?DOUGLAS). He *m.* 2ndly' [*Scots Peerage*, vol. v, p. 342, note]
line 18, delete '1st da. and coh.' and substitute '*suo jure* COUNTESS OF LENNOX [S.], 1st da. and h. of line'
line 26, for 'either' read 'probably'
line 26, delete 'or 1459'
line 31, after '1410' add 'On 4 May 1414 he had a disp. from the Antipope Benedict to *m.* Eupheme, *suo jure* COUNTESS OF STRATHEARN [S.], but the marriage did not take place. See that title.'
line 34, after 'Castle' add 'On 5 Sep. 1415 he had a disp. from the Antipope Benedict to *m.* Eupheme, COUNTESS OF STRATHEARN [S.], who had been contracted to his elder brother Robert, but neither marriage took place. See that title.'

page 80,
lines 22–4, delete from '1st' to '[S.]' and replace by '2nd wife Margery SUTHERLAND, da. of Alexander SUTHERLAND of Dunbeath'. [Andrew MacEwen, *The Geneal.*, vol. 2, 1981, p. 52.]

page 82,
line 5, after '*d. s.p.*' add 'or *s.p.s.*(aa)'
note (aa) The Emperor Charles V writing to the Bishop of Badajoz, 20 Dec. 1521, mentions that the Pope will be unlikely to grant the Duke a dispensation (presumably for a marriage), especially as he has children by his present wife, 'la fille de Boulogne'. (*L. and P. Hen. VIII*, vol. iii, p. 801)

page 84,
note (c), lines 20–1, delete from 'but' to 'Albanie'
lines 22–3, delete from 'He' to 'Salmon' and substitute 'By his 2nd wife, a Miss Salmon, he had a large family who all repudiated the Sobieski-Stuart fraud (*ex inform.* C.L. Berry). A discussion of an annotated pedigree of the Allan family and the 'Sobieski-Stuarts' appeared in *N&Q*, vol. 197, pp. 428, 455, 470 and 511; vol. 199, p. 209. See also *N&Q*, vol. 157, pp. 435 and 452; vol. 177, pp. 265, 320, 357 and 369.'
line 24, for 'Stuart Hay' read 'Manning'

page 85,
line 6, for '£2000 *p.a*' read '£1,600 *p.a.* in Oct. 1807'. (*Hist. MSS. Com.*, Fortescue MSS., vol. ix, p. 163)

line 11, for 'Alberstroff' read 'Albestroff'
line 11, delete '(i)'
line 12, delete 'Camlachie and'
line 13, for '1st da. by his 3rd wife' read 'da'. [He only *m.* once, see Godfrey Iredell, *Geneal. Mag.*, vol. 23, 1989, p. 137.]
note (g), insert at beginning 'See Henrietta Taylor, *Prince Charlie's Daughter* (1950).'
note (h), lines 1–2, delete from 'Gen.' to 'Prince'
note (i), delete all detail

page 86,
line 1, for 'Johnson' read 'Johnston'
line 3, for '6' read '7'
line 3, after 'unm.' add '(aa)
note (aa) By Prince Ferdinand de Rohan, Archbishop of Cambrai (br. of the famous Cardinal de Rohan of the diamond necklace scandal), she had 3 illegit. children, (1) Aglaé, *b.* 1780–1, and (2) Marie, *b.* 1782–2, both of whom presumably *d.* young; (3) Charles Edward Stuart, so-called Count Roehenstart [?Rohan Stuart], *b.* 1784, perhaps on 11 June. From 1801–5 he lived in the household of Prince Alexander of Wurtemberg, where he became major-domo; after service in the Napoleonic wars he eventually went to Scotland. He *m.* 1stly, Marie Antoinette Sophie Barbuoni, who *d.* in 1821 and was *bur.* at Marylebone. He *m.* 2ndly, in 1826, Louisa Constance Smith, known as 'Madame Stuart'. He *d. s.p.* 28 Oct. 1854 as the result of a stage coach accident near Stirling, aged 70, and was *bur.* in Dunkeld Cath. M.I. See Henrietta Taylor, *op. cit.*, pp. 47–8 *et passim* and Appendix I.
line 11, after 'SAXONY' add '[see note (ax) to vol. iii, p. 451, below *sub* CORNWALL]'
line 25, for 'Living 1909' read 'She *d.* when on a visit to her s., 1 Sep. 1922.'
note (b), line 6, after 'V.G.' add 'For her will see C.L. Berry, *N&Q.*, vol. 194, 1949, pp. 502–3.'

page 87,
line 2, after 'SAXONY' add '[see note (ax) to vol. iii, p. 451, below]'
line 14, after 'Denmark.' add 'He was struck from the roll of the Order of the Garter on 13 May 1915. His name was removed from the roll of Peers of the United Kingdom by Order of the King in Council, 28 May 1919(ax). He *d.* at Coburg, 6 Mar. 1954. His widow *d.* at Coburg, 3 Oct. 1970.'
lines 15–17, delete all detail and replace as follows

III. *1954* 3. JOHANN LEOPOLD WILHELM ALBERT FERDINAND VICTOR, DUKE OF SAXE-COBURG AND GOTHA, who but for the abovementioned Order in Council, would have been *H.R.H.* the DUKE OF ALBANY, EARL OF CLARENCE AND BARON ARKLOW [U.K.]. 1st s. and h., *b.* at the Castle of Callenburg, near Coburg, 2 Aug. 1906; renounced his rights to the Duchy of Saxe-Coburg and Gotha. He *m.* 1stly Baroness Feodora Maria Alma Margarete, 1st da. of Baron Bernhard VON DER HORST, and formerly wife of Baron Wolf Sigismund Pergler VON PERGLAS. She was *b.* 7 July 1905. His marriage was diss. by divorce in 1962 (she *d.* 23 Oct. 1991) and he *m.* 2ndly, 3 May 1962, Maria Theresa Elizabeth, da. of Max REINDL and formerly wife of Werner MULLER. He *d.* 4 May 1972. His widow was still living 1995.

IV. *1972* 4. ERNST LEOPOLD EDUARD WILHELM JOSIAS, who but for the abovementioned Order in Council, would have been *H.R.H.* the DUKE OF ALBANY, &c., 1st s. and h. by 1st wife, *b.* 14 Jan. 1935. He *m.* 1stly, 4 Feb. 1961, Ingeborg, da. of Richard HENIG of Herrenberg, Wurttemberg. She was *b.* 1 July 1938. The marriage was diss. by divorce in 1963 and he *m.* 2ndly, 29 May 1963, Gertrude Maria Monika, da. of Hermann Horst PFEIFFER. This marriage was in turn diss. by divorce in 1985 and he *m.* 3rdly, 20 Jan. 1986, Sabine Margarete, da. of Alfred Carl BILLER. In the titular Duke of Albany is vested the right to petition under the Titles Deprivation Act, 1917, for the restoration of his peerages.[ay]

[*PRINCE* HUBERTUS RICHARD ERNST LEOPOLD, 1st s. and h. ap. by 1st wife, *b.* 8 Dec. 1961.]

note [ax] For bearing arms against Great Britain in WW1.
note [ay] See Burke's *Peerage*, 1953, pp. cli–cliii.

ALBEMARLE

page 87,
line 16, delete 'said to have been'
note [a], line 7, after 'Albemarle' add 'V.G.'

page 90,
line 21, after '183' add 'see Ruvigny, *Jacobite Peerage*, p. 3'

page 91,
note [c], delete all detail and replace by 'He had one posthumous da., Cristine Marie Jacqueline Henriette, *b.* 29 May 1703 at Bagnols afsd., who was *bap.* 22 May 1711 at St. Germain-en-Laye. She became a nun. V.G.
note [d], delete from 'No' to 'husband' and replace by 'The story is confirmed, or at any rate repeated by Saint Simon, who however confuses this Col. Mahony with Lieut. Gen. David Mahony, who *m.* Charlotte Bulkeley, widow of Charles O'Brian, but for the attainder, 5th Viscount Clare [I.]'

page 95,
line 6, for '67' read '77'
line 7, delete from '*d. s.p.*' to '85' and replace by 'who was *b.* 20 Sep. 1774 at Wingerworth, co. Derby, and *bap.* there the same day, *d. s.p.* 13 Oct. 1862 at Twickenham, aged 88, and was *bur.* 22 Oct. at Wingerworth.'
lines 16–17, delete from 'having' to '1849' and replace by '23 July 1849'

page 96,
lines 7 & 8, for 'Dundrum' read 'Dundurn'
line 11, for 'living 1909' read '*d.* 5 Apr. 1917.'
line 19, delete from 'She' to '1861' and replace by 'He *d.* 12 Apr. 1942. His widow, who was *b.* 9 Jan. 1861, *d.* 7 June 1943.'
line 20, line to read as follows

IX. 1942 9. WALTER EGERTON GEORGE LUCIAN (KEPPEL), EARL OF ALBERMARLE, &c., 1st s. and h., *b.* 28 Feb. 1882; from 1894 *styled* VISCOUNT BURY; ed. at Eton 1895–9.

line 25, for ']' read 'at Innsbruck, Tyrol, and was *bur.* Quidenham, Norfolk, 24 Mar. 1928. He *m.* 2ndly, 24 Feb. 1931, at the Scots Church, St. Columba, Pont Str., Chelsea, Diana Cicely, da. of John GROVE of Allan House, S. Kensington. He *d.* 14 July 1979. His widow was living 1995.

X. 1979 10. RUFUS ARNOLD ALEXIS (KEPPEL), EARL OF ALBEMARLE, &c., grandson and h., being s. of Derek William Charles KEPPEL (*d.* 8 Nov. 1968), by 2nd wife Marina, yr. da. of COUNT SERGE ORLOFF DAVIDOFF, which Derek William Charles was 1st s. of 9th Earl of Albermarle. He was *b.* 16 July 1965; ed. at St. Christopher Sch., Letchworth, Chelsea Sch. of Art and Central Sch. of Art.

ALBION

page 97,
note ([a]), line 4, after 'V.G.' add 'The patent [I.], dat. 21 June 1634, whereby Sir Edmund Plowden was granted by Wentworth, then Lord Lieut., the province of New Albion, i.e. the whole of New Jersey with the adjacent islands, contains this clause; "To have, hold, possess, exercise, and enjoy the said title, addition, dignity, and privilege of EARL PALATINE, or the office of Governor of the region, island and premises, unto the said Edmund Plowden, Knight, his heirs and assigns forever. To be holden of us, our heirs and successors, *as of our Crown of Ireland*, in Capite." See *Montgomeryshire Coll.*, Powys-land Club, vol. xxi, pp. 320–7, where the patent is recited in full.'

ALDBOROUGH

page 98,
line 18, for '1715' read '1716'

ALDEBURGH OR ALDBROUGH

page 102,
line 2, for 'his wife' read 'He *m.*, before 1364, Elizabeth, who'

ALDENHAM

page 104,
line 2, for '1891–1907' read '1890 till his death'
lines 10–11, delete from 'He' to 'work.'

II. 1907 2. ALBAN GEORGE HENRY (GIBBS), BARON ALDENHAM, 1st s. and h., *b.* 23 Apr. 1846; ed. at Eton and Oxford (Ch. Ch.). He *m.*, 18 Feb. 1873, Bridget, 6th surviving da. of Rt. Hon. Alexander James Beresford BERESFORD-HOPE by his wife Lady Mildred Arabella, eldest da. of James Brownlow William (GASCOYNE-CECIL), 2nd MARQUESS OF SALISBURY. She *d.* 27 Feb. 1896. He *d.* 9 May 1936.

III. 1936 3. GERALD HENRY BERESFORD (GIBBS), BARON ALDENHAM, s. and h., *b.* 9 Jan. 1879; ed. Eton and Oxford (Ch. Ch.). He *m.*, 9 May 1905, Lillie Caroline, eldest da. of Rev. William Thomas HOULDSWORTH. He *d. s.p.* 21 Mar. 1939. His widow *d.* 1 Sep. 1950.

BARONY. IV. 1939
BARONY. II. 1935

4 and 2. WALTER DURANT (GIBBS), BARON HUNSDON and BARON ALDENHAM, cousin and h., being 1st s. of HERBERT COKAYNE GIBBS (*d.* 22 May 1935), by Anna Maria, 4th da. and co. of Richard DURANT of High Canons, Herts, which Herbert Cokayne was 4th son of 1st Baron Aldenham and 1st Baron Hunsdon of Hunsdon. He was *b.* 11 Aug. 1888; ed. at Eton and Cambridge (Trin. Coll.). He *m.*, 6 Nov. 1919, Beatrix Elinor, da. of Herbert Woodfield PAUL and widow of Algernon Hyde VILLIERS. He *d.* 30 May 1969. His widow *d.* 1978.

[VICARY PAUL GIBBS, 1st s. and h. ap., *b.* 11 Feb. 1921; ed. at Eton; *m.*, 19 Sep. 1942, Jean Francis, da. of Capt. Angus Valdimar HAMBRO, M.P., of Milton Abbas, Dorset. He *d. v.p. s.p.m.* 20 Sep. 1944, being *k.* in battle at Nijmegen. His widow *m.* 2ndly, 29 May 1946, Rev. Hon. Andrew Charles Victor ELPHINSTONE. His widow was living 1995.]

BARONY. V.
BARONY. III. } 1969

5 and 3. ANTHONY DURANT (GIBBS), BARON HUNSDON and BARON ALDENHAM, 2nd but 1st surviving s. and h., *b.* 18 May 1922; ed. at Eton and Oxford (Ch. Ch.). He *m.*, 16 July 1947, Mary Elizabeth, only da. of Walter Parkyns TYSER of Gordonbush, Brora, Sutherland. He *d.* 25 Jan. 1986. His widow was living 1995.

BARONY. VI.
BARONY. IV. } 1986

6 and 4. VICARY TYSER (GIBBS), BARON HUNSDON and BARON ALDENHAM, eldest s. and h., *b.* 9 June 1948; ed. at Eton, Oxford (Oriel Coll.) and R.A.C., Cirencester. He *m.*, 1980, Josephine Nicola, elder da. of John FELL of Lower Bourne, Farnham, Surrey.

[HUMPHREY WILLIAM FELL, s. and h. ap., *b.* 31 Jan. 1989.]

ALEXANDER

page 105,
line 18, for '1801' read '1800'

ALFORD

page 106,
line 3, for '1745' read '1754'

ALINGTON OF CRICHEL

page 109,
lines 20–1, delete from 'He' to 'work'

II. 1904 2. HUMPHREY NAPIER (STURT), BARON ALINGTON OF CRICHEL, s. and h., *b.* 20 Aug. 1859; ed. at Eton 1873–7 and at Oxford (Ch. Ch.). He *m.*, 29 June 1883, Feodorovna, da. of Charles Philip (YORKE), 5th EARL OF HARDWICKE. He *d.* in London 30 July, and was *bur.* 6 Aug. 1919 at Moor Crichel, Wimborne, Dorset. His widow *d.* 27 June 1934 and was *bur.* in Witchampton Church, co. Dorset.

[GERARD PHILIP MONTAGU NAPIER STURT, 1st s. and h. ap., *b.* 9 Apr. 1893; Capt. Coldstream Guards, *d. v.p.* at Crichel House, near Wimborne, of wounds received in action in the early part of WW1, 11, and was *bur.* 14 Nov. 1918 at Crichel.]

III. 1919 3. NAPIER GEORGE HENRY (STURT), BARON ALINGTON OF CRICHEL, 2nd but only surv. s. and h., *b.* 4 Nov. 1896. He *m.*, 27 Nov. 1928, Mary Sibell, 1st da. of Anthony (ASHLEY-COOPER), 9th EARL OF SHAFTESBURY at St. Margaret's, Westm. She *d.* 2 Aug. 1936. He *d. s.p.m.* 17 Sep. 1940 when his title became *extinct*.

ALLANSON

page 110,
line 3, for 'EARLDOM' read 'BARONY'

ALLEN

page 111,
line 25, for '1845' read '1846'

ALMOND

page 112,
line 9, for 'CLARENDON' read 'CALLENDAR'

ALNWICK

page 113,
line 7, for '1652' read '1659'
line 8, for '1794' read '1784'

ALTAMONT

page 113,
line 19, for 'MONTEAGLE' read 'MOUNT EAGLE'

ALTHAM

page 116,
note (b), (cont. from page 115), line 20, after 'of' add 'Sir', after 'I'Anson' add '4th Bart.', and after 'Tunbridge' add 'Kent, by Mary, only surv. da. of John BANKES, of Kingston Hall, Dorset. She was *b.* 23 Aug. 1727 at New Bounds'

ALTRIE

page 118,
line 2, after '*m.*' add '(cont. 24 May 1566)'
lines 3–4, for '1 July and 26 Sep. 1592' read '18 Mar. and 19 May 1596'
note (a), delete all detail and replace by '*Scots Peerage*, vol. i, p. 159; vol. ix, p. 10'

ALVERSTONE

page 120,
line 12, after 'Southampton.' add 'On his resignation of the Chief Justiceship owing to ill health he was *cr.* 24 Nov. 1913, VISCOUNT ALVERSTONE of Alverstone, co. Southampton.'
line 16, after '(b)' add 'He *d. s.p.m.s.*, aged nearly 72, of dropsy, after a long illness, at his seat, Winterfold, Cranleigh, Surrey, 15, and was *bur.* 18 Dec. 1915 at Norwood, when the Barony and Viscountcy became *extinct.*'

AMHERST OF HOLMESDALE, &c.

page 121,
line 20, for '1717' read '1716/7'

page 122,
line 10, for '1722' read '1722/3'
line 11, after 'Kent' add 'M.I.'

page 124,
line 14, after 'Lincoln.' add 'He *d. s.p.*, aged 74, from an operation for an infection of the throat undergone three months before, at Montreal Park, 14, being cremated 16, at Golders Green, and his ashes *bur.* at Riverhead, 18 Aug. 1910. His widow *m.* 3rdly, 16 Dec. 1914, *H.S.H.* PRINCE JEAN SAPIENA-KODENSKI and *d.* 27 Apr. 1933.'

EARLDOM. IV. BARONY V. } 1910 4 and 5. HUGH (AMHERST), EARL AMHERST OF ARRACAN, &c., br. and h., *b.* 30 Jan. 1856. He *m.*, 2 Jan. 1896, Eleanor Clementina ST. AUBYN. He *d.* 7 Mar. and was *bur.* 12 Mar. 1927 at Golders Green Cemetery. His widow *d.* 17 Sep. 1960.

EARLDOM. V. BARONY VI. } 1927 5 and 6. JEFFERY JOHN ARCHER (AMHERST), EARL AMHERST OF ARRACAN, &c., s. and h., *b.* 13 Dec. 1896; ed. at Eton and R.M.C., Sandhurst. He *d.* unm. 4 Mar. 1993 when his titles became *extinct.*

AMHERST OF HACKNEY

page 125,
lines 9–10, delete from 'He' to 'work' and replace by 'His widow *d.* at Foulden Hall, Norfolk, 2 Nov. 1919.'

II. 1909 2. MARY ROTHES MARGARET, BARONESS AMHERST OF HACKNEY, da. and h. under the special rem., *b.* 25 Apr. 1857. She *m.*, 2 Sep. 1885, Lord William CECIL (*b.* 2 Nov. 1854), 3rd s. of 3rd Marquess of Exeter. She *d.* in London, 22, and was *bur.* 26 Dec. 1919, at Stowlaughton Church, Suffolk. Her widower *m.* 2ndly, 16 Aug. 1924, Violet Maud, da. of Percy FREER, and formerly wife of Herbert Oswald COLLYER. Lord William *d.* 16 Apr. 1943.

[WILLIAM AMHERST CECIL, 1st s. and h. ap., *b.* 30 June 1886. He *m.*, 14 Apr. 1910, Gladys, da. and h. of Henry Charles BAGGALLAY of Heatherhurst Grange, Frimley, Surrey. He was Capt. Gren. Gds., served in WW1, and *d. v.p. s.p.* 16 Sep. 1914, being *k.* in action at the battle of the Aisne. His widow *d.* 30 May 1947.]

III. 1919 3. WILLIAM ALEXANDER EVERING (CECIL), BARON AMHERST OF HACKNEY, grandson and h., being 1st s. of William Amherst CECIL by Gladys abovesaid. He was *b.* 31 May 1912; ed. at Eton and Cambridge (Trin. Coll.). He *m.*, 14 Sep. 1939, Margaret Eirene Clifton, yst. da. of Brig. Gen. Howard Clifton BROWN of Holmbush, Faygate, Sussex. He *d.* 22 July 1980. His widow was living 1995.

IV. 1980 4. WILLIAM HUGH AMHERST (CECIL), s. and h., *b.* 28 Dec. 1940; ed. at Eton. He *m.*, 30 Mar. 1965, Elizabeth, da. of Hugh Humphrey MERRIMAN of Hazel Hall, Peaslake, Surrey.

[HUGH WILLIAM AMHERST, s. and h. ap., *b.* 17 July 1968.]

AMPTHILL

page 126,
line 3, for '1664' read '1665'

line 25, for 'Living 1909' read 'She *d.* 22 Feb. 1927.'
line 33, after '1874.' add 'He *d.* 7 July 1935. His widow *d.* 12 Dec. 1957.'

III. 1935 3. JOHN HUGO (RUSSELL), BARON AMPTHILL, 1st s. and h., *b.* 4 Oct. 1896. He *m.*, 1stly, at St. Jude's, Kensington, 18 Oct. 1918, Christabel Hulme, da. of Col. John HART(c). This marriage was diss. by divorce in 1937, she *d.* 1976. He *m.* 2ndly, 22 Feb. 1937, Sibell Faithfull, da. of Thomas Wilkinson LUMLEY. She *d.* 13 Sep. 1947. He *m.* 3rdly, 24 July 1948, Adeline Mary Constance, eldest da. of Canon Henry Evelyn HONE, Vicar and Rural Dean of Godalming. He *d.* 3 June 1973. His widow was living 1995.

IV. 1973 4. GEOFFREY DENIS ERSKINE (RUSSELL), BARON AMPTHILL, 1st s. and h., *b.* 15 Oct. 1921; ed. at Stowe. He *m.* 1stly, 20 July 1946, Susan Mary Sheila, yr. da. of Charles John Frederick WINN of Nostell Priory, Wakefield. This marriage was diss. by divorce in 1971 and he *m.* 2ndly, 1972, Elizabeth Anne Marie, da. of Claude Henri MALLON of Paris.

[DAVID WHITNEY ERSKINE RUSSELL, s. and h. ap., *b.* 27 May 1947; ed. at Stowe. He *m.*, 1980, April McKenzie, yst. da. of Paul ARBON of New York.]

note (c) In Apr. 1922 he was petitioning for divorce on account of her adultery, misconduct being alleged as early as Nov. 1918, within a month of their wedding. On 15 Oct. 1921 she gave birth to a male child, of which the petitioner, by affidavit, disclaimed the paternity. After a divorce of 1923 was overturned on appeal in 1924, his wife petitioned on behalf of her son seeking a declaration of legitimacy. This was granted, 1925. Following the death of 3rd Baron Ampthill, the succession of his son was allowed on the grounds that his declared legitimacy brought him within the terms of the patent as heir male of the body (H.L. 147–1, 1976).

ANCASTER

page 129,
line 28, for '1743' read '1733'

page 130,
line 25, delete from 'She' to '1846.' and replace by 'He *d.*, aged 80, at Grimsthorpe, 24, and was *bur.* 30 Dec. 1910, at Edenham. His widow, who was *b.* 22 Mar. 1846, *d.*, aged nearly 75, at Normanton Park, Stamford, 16, and was *bur.* 21 Mar. 1921 at Edenham.'
line 26, line to read as follows

II. 1910 2. GILBERT (HEATHCOTE-DRUMMOND-WILLOUGHBY), EARL OF ANCASTER, &c., 1st s. and h.,

line 29, after '1889' add 'From 1892 *styled* LORD WILLOUGHBY DE ERESBY'
line 31, delete '(__)' to ']' and replace by 'Marie Louise, da. of the Hon. George PARSONS, of Columbia, Ohio, U.S.A. He *d.* 19 Sep. 1951. His widow *d.* 12 Dec. 1953.'

III. 1951 3. GILBERT JAMES (HEATHCOTE-DRUMMOND-WILLOUGHBY), EARL OF ANCASTER, LORD WILLOUGHBY DE ERESBY, BARON AVELAND and a Baronet, 1st s. and h., *b.* 8 Dec. 1907; ed. at Eton and Cambridge (Magdalene Coll.). He *m.*, 27 July 1933, Nancy Phyllis Louise, only da. of Waldorf (ASTOR), 2nd VISCOUNT ASTOR. She *d.* 1975. He *d.* 29 Mar. 1983 when the Earldom of Ancaster and the Barony of Aveland became *extinct*. The Baronetcy of Heathcote was inherited by a distant cousin. He was *suc.* in the Barony of Willoughby de Eresby by his da. Nancy Jane Marie. See that title.

[TIMOTHY GILBERT HEATHCOTE-DRUMMOND-WILLOUGHBY, *styled* Lord Willoughby de Eresby, s. and h. ap., *b.* 19 Mar. 1936; ed. at Eton. He disappeared at sea between Cap Ferrat and Corsica, 19 Aug. 1963.]

ANCRAM

page 132,
line 7, delete 'only s. by 2nd wife' and replace by '1st s. by 2nd wife, *b.* 6 Aug. 1624 at Richmond, Surrey and *bap.* there 8 Sep.'

ANGLESEY

page 132,
line 34, delete 'VILLIERS OF'

page 133,
line 7, delete 'VILLIERS OF'
note (d), line 7, for 'the' read 'to'

page 134,
line 4, for 'Early in 1660' read 'He'
lines 4–5, delete from 'Was' to 'was' and replace by '16 Feb. 1659/60; P.C. [E.] 31 May 1660, and [I.] Dec. 1660'

page 135,
line 15, for '14' read '13'
line 20, after 'Henrietta' read 'Maria'
note (c), line 1, after '*m.*' add '25'
line 1, after 'Phipps' add 'of St. Giles in the Fields, who *d.* 1 Feb. 1729/30 and'
line 2, delete '1765' and replace by '1767. She *d.* 18 Jan. 1735/6'

page 136,
note (f), line 3, add at end 'This James *d.* 5 Jan. 1760'

page 137,
line 17, after 'of' add 'Ballynamony, afterwards'
lines 17–18, delete from 'whose' to '1771' and replace by 'who *d.* 27 Oct. 1795. Will dat. 28 Oct 1791 to 29 Aug. 1794, pr. 19 Dec. 1795. She *d.* 26 Feb. 1777 at Bath, Somerset, and was *bur.* with her 1st husband. Will dat. 12 Dec. 1776, pr. 31 May 1777'

page 141,
line 4, delete from 'was' to '1909' and replace by '*d.* 22 May 1931.'
lines 14–15, delete from 'He' to 'work' and replace by 'His widow *m.* 2ndly, 11 Dec. 1909, at the Rom. Cath. Church of the Assumption, Warwick Str., W., John Francis Grey GILLIAT, of Honington Hall, co. Warwick. She *d.* 20 Feb. 1962.'

VI. 1905 6. CHARLES HENRY ALEXANDER (PAGET), MARQUESS OF ANGLESEY, &c., cousin and h., being 1st s. and h. of Alexander Victor PAGET (*d.* 26 Oct. 1896), by Hester Alice, 2nd da. of Wellington Henry (STAPLETON-COTTON), 2nd VISCOUNT COMBERMERE, which Alexander Victor was 3rd s. (2nd by 2nd wife) of 2nd Marquess of Anglesey. He was *b.* 14 Apr. 1885; ed. at Eton and R.M.C., Sandhurst. He *m.*, 3 Aug. 1912, Lady Victoria Marjorie Harriet, 1st da. of Henry John Brinsley (MANNERS), 8th DUKE OF RUTLAND. She *d.* 3 Nov. 1946. He *d.* 21 Feb. 1947.

VII. 1947 7. GEORGE CHARLES HENRY VICTOR (PAGET), MARQUESS OF ANGLESEY, &c., s. and h., *b.* 8 Oct. 1922; ed. at Eton. He *m.*, 16 Oct. 1948, Elizabeth Shirley Vaughan, only da. of Charles Langbridge MORGAN by his wife Hilda VAUGHAN.

[CHARLES ALEXANDER VAUGHAN PAGET, *styled* Earl of Uxbridge, 1st s. and h. ap., *b.* 13 Nov. 1950; ed. at Eton, Oxford (Exeter Coll.) and Sussex Univ. He *m.*, 1986, Georgeanne Elizabeth Elliott, da. of Col. John Alfred DOWNES, M.C., of Whittlesford, Cambridgeshire.]

ANGUS

page 145,
line 21, after 'He' add 'apparently'

page 146,
line 21, for 'of Chilham, or of Dover' read 'Richard DE DOUVRES, of Chilham, Kent'
note ([h]), line 2, after 'V.G.' add 'See also G.S. Moriarty, "The First House of De Douvres or De Chilham", in *The New England Hist. and Gen. Reg.*, vol. cv, 1951, pp. 39–40; *cf.* vol. xii, part 2, p. 298, *sub* WAKE.'

page 147,
note ([c]), delete all detail

page 149,
line 23, for '. . . . .' read 'Joan'
page 150,
line 12, after '1332' add 'In 1338 he *suc. de jure* (according to modern doctrine) to the Barony of Kyme on the death *s.p.* of his maternal uncle William, 2nd Lord Kyme.'

page 151,
note ([a]), line 1, after 'Alienor' add '*de jure* (according to modern doctrine), Baroness Kyme'

line 4, after 'Tailboys' add '*de jure* 6th Lord Kyme'
line 5, after '1436/7' add 'See Kyme'

page 153,
line 32, after '*d.*' add '*s.p. legit.*(c)'
note (c) In *Scots Peerage*, vol. ix, p. 11, it is stated of William, a bastard s. of this Earl, that he "is the only known son of Earl Thomas". Douglas, followed by the *Complete Peerage*, gives him a son Thomas, Earl of Angus from 1361 to 1377, but his statement is founded on wrong premises.
lines 34–5, delete all detail

page 154,
line 1, for 'XVII. 1377. 4.' read 'XVI. 1361. 3'
line 21, for 'XVIII' read 'XVII'

page 155,
lines 8–9, delete from 'William' to '1423' and replace by 'Sir William GRAHAM (grandfather of Patrick, 1st LORD GRAHAM [S.]), who *d.* 1424'
line 12, for 'XIX' read 'XVIII'
line 16, for '1435' read '1436'
line 16, for '1425' read '3 Dec. 1414' [Neil Thompson and Charles Hansen, *The Geneal*, vol. 6, 1986, pp. 103, 156.]
line 17, for 'only' read '1st'
lines 17–18, delete from 'Yester' to 'Yester' and replace by 'Locherworth and Yester by his wife Alice (bb)'
note (bb) *Scots Peerage*, vol. viii, p. 424; vol. ix, p. 164. Douglas gives as his wife Jean Giffard, she was, however, his mother.
line 20, for 'XX', read 'XIX'
line 24, for 'XXI' read 'XX'

page 156,
line 12, for 'XXII' read 'XXI'
line 21, for 'only' read '1st'
line 23, for '2nd' read '1st'
line 32, after '*Etc*' add '(c)'
note (c) This lady nowhere appears upon record as Countess of Angus. On 6 and 28 Nov. 1505 she is referred to in civil actions as the spouse of Sir John Ramsay of Trarinzean (the *forfeited* Lord Bothwell [S.], and the fact that she is called Lady Bothwell in the abovementioned charter of 1 June 1501 does not point to her having married him before that date, but, as stated in the *Scots Peerage* (vol. ii, p. 459) that name was applied to her on account of the lands settled on her by Angus having included the Lordship of Bothwell. It is a strange coincidence that she should afterwards have married a man who had been Lord Bothwell, but a lady who was held so lightly by the marriage tie is a cause of trouble to genealogists. Anyhow, she was separated from Ramsay also before Feb. 1507/8, when he had another wife. She was still alive as late as Dec. 1543. V.G.

page 157,
line 9, delete '29' [A letter, dat. 23 Nov. [1513], from Thomas, Lord Darcy, to Wolsey

announces, though possibly in error, the death of the Earl at St. Ninian's, *L. and P. Hen. VIII*, vol. i, pp. 703–4]

line 11, for 'before Mar. 1487/8' read 'after July 1485 and before 31 Jan. 1488/9' [Thompson and Hansen, *The Geneal.*, vol. 5, 1984, p. 239.]

line 13, after '[S.]' add 'by Elizabeth, da. of Alexander (LINDSAY), 4th Earl of Crawford [S.]'

line 15, for 'XXIII' read 'XXII'

line 33, for '1526/7' read '1527/28'

page 158,

line 8, for '1593' read '31 Jan. 1593/4'

line 11, for 'XXIV' read 'XXIII'

line 15, for '10 Sep. 1547' read 'Aug. 1552'

line 17, delete 'or Elizabeth'

line 17, for 'Laird' read 'Younger'

line 18, for 'Clydesdale' read 'Samuelston'

line 22, for 'XXV' read 'XXIV'

line 23, for '1585' read '1586'

page 159,

line 2, after 'divorced' add '12 July'

line 5, for '1584' read 'Mar. 1584/5'

line 6, for 'Alexander' read 'William'

lines 9–10, for 'before July 1592' read probably in May 1590'

line 10, for 'July' read 'probably 16 June'

line 11, delete from 'was' to '1611' and replace by '*d.* shortly before Mar. 1610'

line 12, for 'XXVI' read 'XXV'

line 26, for 'XXVII' read 'XXVI'

page 160,

line 2, for '7th' read '4th'

line 6, for 'XXVIII' read 'XXVII'

line 7, for '17 June' read '14 June'

page 162,

line 1, for '1643' read '1633'

ANNALY OF ANNALY AND RATHCLINE

page 162,

line 10, for 'Andrew' read 'Peter'

note (b), line 1, after 'Dublin' add 'br. of this Peter'

lines 2–3, delete from 'most' to 'question' and replace by '1st cousin of the Elizabeth in the text and often confused with her.'

page 163,

line 7, after '58.' add 'His widow *d.* 22 Jan. 1915.'

line 15, delete from 'She' to '1862.' and replace by 'He *d.* at his residence, Holdenby House, Northants, 15, and was *bur.* 19 Dec. 1922 at Holdenby. His widow, who was *b.* 6 Aug. 1862, *d.* 27 Jan. 1944.'

lines 16–17, delete all detail and replace by

IV. 1922 4. LUKE HENRY (WHITE), BARON ANNALY OF ANNALY AND RATHCLINE, s. and h., *b.* 7 Aug. 1885; ed. at Charterhouse. Major 11th Hussars, served in WW1. He *m.*, 9 Apr. 1919, Lavinia Emily, 2nd da. of Charles Robert (SPENCER), 6th EARL SPENCER, by Margaret, 2nd da. of Edward Charles (BARING), 1st LORD REVELSTOKE. She, who was *b.* 29 Sep. 1899, *d.* 9 May 1955. He *d.* 4 May 1970.

V. 1970 5. LUKE ROBERT (WHITE), BARON ANNALY OF ANNALY AND RATHCLINE, s. and h., *b.* 15 Mar. 1927; ed. at Eton and Cambridge (Trin. Coll.). He *m.* 1stly, 23 July 1953, Lady Marye Isabel, eldest da. of John Digby Thomas (PEPYS), 7th EARL OF COTTENHAM. She, who was born 18 Oct. 1934, *d.* 4 June 1958. This marriage was diss. by divorce in 1956. He *m.* 2ndly, 26 Jan. 1960, Jennifer Margaret, only da. of Rupert Sausmarez CAREY of East Hoe Manor, Hambledon, Hampshire. This marriage was diss. by divorce in 1967 and he *m.* 3rdly, 1984, Mrs Beverley Elizabeth HEALY, da. of William MAXWELL. He *d.* 30 Sep 1990. His widow was living 1995.

VI. 1990 6. LUKE RICHARD (WHITE), BARON ANNALLY AND RATHCLINE, s. and h., *b.* 29 June 1954; ed. at Eton, R.M.C., Sandhurst and R.A.C., Cirencester. He *m.*, 1983, Caroline Nina, yr. da. of Col. Robert Hugh Garnett, of Hope Bowdler Court, Church Stretton, Shropshire.

[LUKE HENRY WHITE, s. and h. ap., b. 20 Sep. 1990]

ANNANDALE AND HARTFELL

page 165,
line 2, after 'Cockpool' add 'who *d.* 22 May 1605'
line 3, for '5th' read '4th'
line 14, after 'London' add '22'
line 25, for 'Isabel' read 'Mary'
note (b), line 3, after 'V.G.' add 'See *sub* STORMONT [1621], as to his being named 3rd remainder man in the limitation of that Viscountcy [S.]'

page 166,
lines 11–12 delete 'of his body'
line 19, after '1672' add 'at Leith, aged 47, and was apparently *bur.* 30 July in the Greyfriars, Edinburgh'

page 167,
line 3, after '1718' add '(aa)'
note (aa) See *Hist. MSS. Com.*, Stuart MSS, vol. vii, p. 616.
line 8, after '*m.*' add '1 Dec. (lic. London, 29 Nov.) 1731, at St. Benet, Paul's Wharf (being *styled* merely Charlotte Vanlo).'
line 10, after 'afsd.(c)' add 'She was *bur.* in Bristol Cath., 29 Nov. 1762' [*The Bristol Cathedral Register, 1669–1837*, ed. C. Roy Hudleston, 1933, p. 31]

page 168

EARLDOM [S.] VII. | 1985 | 5. PATRICK ANDREW WENTWORTH HOPE (JOHNSTONE), EARL OF ANNANDALE AND HARTFELL, LORD JOHNSTONE [S. 1662] (*c*), of Annandale and of that ilk, *b.* 19 Apr. 1941; ed. at Stowe and R.A.C. Cirencester. Chief of Clan Johnstone. He *m.*, 1969, Susan, only da. of Col. Walter John Macdonald ROSS, of Castle Douglas, Kirkcudbrightshire.

[DONALD PATRICK WENTWORTH JOHNSTONE, Master of Annandale and Hartfell, *styled* LORD JOHNSTONE, s. and h. ap., was *b.* 13 Oct. 1971, ed. at Stowe.]

note ([c]) His claim to the title was recognised by the Committee for Privileges on the grounds that a charter of 23 April 1662 acted as a new grant of the Earldom of Annandale and Hartfell and Barony of Johnstone to a new series of heirs, redirecting the titles to the heirs male of the body of James Johnston, 1st Earl of Annandale and Hartfell (as opposed to the grant of 1661 which was to heirs male). Failing heirs male of the body the remainder was to heirs female of his body and their heirs male of their body. With the death of George, 4th Marquess of Annandale the heirs male of the body of James, 1st Earl of Annandale and Hartfell became extinct. The petitioner descended from Lady Anne Hope Johnstone, eldest heir female of the body of James, 1st Earl and daughter of James, 3rd Earl of Hoptoun, grandson of the elder daughter of William, 1st Marquess of Annandale, mother of claimant (1), p. 168. The Committee for Privileges decision meant that there were two Earldoms of Annandale and Hartfell existing at the same time, 1662–1792, with different destinations. The petitioners claim to the peerage undoubtedly created in 1661 was reserved. See *Report of the Committee for Privileges*, HMSO, 228–I, 1985; G.W. Iredall, *Genealogists Magazine*, vol. 22, 1986, pp. 54–6.

ANNESLEY OF CASTLEWELLAN

page 170,

line 9, for 'Robert' read 'Richard'

note ([d]), cont. from page 169, line 6, for 'is' read 'in'

page 172,

line 22, for 'pr. Aug.' read 'dat. 5 Aug. 1907, pr. 31 July'

lines 22–3, delete from 'His' to 'work.' and replace by 'His widow *d.* 9 Oct. 1941.'

EARLDOM [I.] VI. BARONY [I.] VII. | 1908 | 6 and 7. FRANCIS (ANNESLEY), EARL ANNESLEY OF CASTLEWELLAN, &c., s. and h. by 1st wife, *b.* at Castlewellan 25 Feb. and baptised there 28 Mar. 1884; *styled* VISCOUNT GLERAWLY from 1884; ed. at Eton 1897–8 and Cambridge (Trin. Hall); Sub-Lieut., R.N.V.R., and served in the Flying Corps in WW1. He left England for France in an aeroplane 6 Nov. 1914 and was never seen again. He *m.*, 14 Feb. 1909, Evelyn Hester, 1st da. of Alfred Edward Miller MUNDY, of Shipley Hall, co. Derby, being only child by 1st wife, Ellen Mary, yst. da. of Charles Rowland PALMER-MOREWOOD, of Alfreton Hall, co. Derby, and formerly wife of Capt.

Hugh Robert Edward HARRISON. She *m.* 3rdly, 15 May 1919, Guy AYLWIN, who *d.* 31 May 1957. She *d.* 16 June 1947.

EARLDOM [I.] VII.
BARONY [I.] VIII. } 1914

7 and 8. WALTER BERESFORD (ANNESLEY), EARL ANNESLEY OF CASTLEWELLAN, &c., cousin and h., being s. and h. of William Octavius Beresford ANNESLEY (*d.* 20 July 1875), by Caroline, da. of John MEARS of Bagshot, co. Surrey, 6th s. of 3rd Earl Annesley by his 2nd wife. He was *b.* 10 Feb. 1861. He *m.* 1stly, 21 June 1893, Maud Fleming, da. of Haynes Bingham HIGGINSON of Rock Ferry, Cheshire. She *d.* 2 July 1923. He *m.* 2ndly, 23 Jan. 1924, Mabel Frances, da. of John BURNETT and formerly wife of Petrus AGANOOR. She *d.* 10 July 1931. He *d.* 7 July 1934.

EARLDOM [I.] VIII.
BARONY [I.] IX. } 1934

8 and 9. BERESFORD CECIL BINGHAM (ANNESLEY), EARL ANNESLEY OF CASTLEWELLAN, &c., s. and h., *b.* 4 Apr. 1894. He *m.* 1stly, 30 July 1921, at the Register Office, Prince's Row, Buckingham Palace Rd., Edith Constance, only da. of Major Albemarle Alexander RAWLINSON, divorced wife of Richard Frederick John (LE POER TRENCH), LORD KILCONNEL (eld. s. of the EARL OF CLANCARTY). This marriage was diss. by divorce in 1941 and she *d.* 7 July 1950. He *m.* 2ndly, 7 Dec. 1945, Josephine Mary, da. of Philip BRANDELL of New York City and widow of Capt. George John Seymour REPTON. He *d. s.p.* 29 June 1957. His widow *d.* 1977.

EARLDOM [I.] IX.
BARONY [I.] X. } 1957

9 and 10. ROBERT (ANNESLEY), EARL ANNESLEY OF CASTLEWELLAN, &c., distant cousin and h. male, being s. and h. of Arthur Albert O'Donel Valentia ANNESLEY by Elizabeth Mary, da. Embertus VAN OOMS of the Netherlands, s. and h. of Arthur Adolphus Annesley (*d.* 4 May 1887), by Martha, da. of Edmund AUSTIN, 2nd s. and h. of James Annesley (d. 29 Sep. 1859), by Clementine, da. of BARON DE BROCKHAUSEN of Prussia, which James was 1st s. of Robert ANNESLEY (*d.* 21 Apr. 1825), by Mary Anne, da. of James GANDON of Canon Brook, 2nd s. of 2nd Earl Annesley. He was *b.* 20 Feb. 1900. He *m.*, 19 Apr. 1922, Nora, yst. da. of Walter HARRISON of Sapperton, Gloucestershire. He *d.* 21 Feb. 1979. His widow *d.* 1992.

EARLDOM. [I.] X.
BARONY. [I.] XI. } 1979

10 and 11. PATRICK (ANNESLEY) EARL ANNESLEY OF CASTLEWELLAN, &c., s. and h., *b.* 12 Aug. 1924; *styled* VISCOUNT GLERAWLY 1957–79; ed. at Strode's Gram. Sch., Egham. He *m.*, 21 June 1947, Catherine, only da. of John BURGESS of Edinburgh.]

ANSON

page 172,
line 34, for 'Wirkworth' read 'Wirksworth'

ANTRIM

page 175,
line 16, after '1635' add 'before the 12th'
line 28, after 'h.,' add '([ea])'

note ([ea]) As to his narrow escape of losing his father's estates, see note *sub* JERMYN OF ST. EDMUNDSBURY [1643]
line 30, for '1685' read '[I.] May 1686'

page 178,
line 37, after 'class' add 'He *d.* at his seat Glenarm Castle, co. Antrim, 19 July 1918. His widow *d.* 2 Apr. 1949.'
line 38, line to read as follows

XII. 1918 7. RANDAL MARK KERR (MCDONNELL), EARL OF ANTRIM and VISCOUNT DUNLUCE [I.], *b.* 10 Dec. 1878, at St. James's Palace, Midx. From 1878 *styled* VISCOUNT DUNLUCE. Ed. at Eton 1892–6.

line 39, for 'Lancashire' read 'Lancaster'
line 42, for ']' read 'He *d.* 15 June 1932. His widow *d.* 1974'

XIII. 1932 8. RANDAL JOHN SOMERLED (MCDONNELL), EARL OF ANTRIM, &c., s. and h., *b.* 22 May 1911; ed. at Eton and Oxford (Ch. Ch.). He *m.*, 11 May 1934, Angela Christina, yst. da. of Sir Mark SYKES, 6th Bart. He *d.* 26 Sep. 1977. His widow *d.* 1984.

XIV. 1977 9. ALEXANDER RANDAL MARK (MCDONNELL), EARL OF ANTRIM, &c., s. and h., *b.* 3 Feb. 1935; ed. at Downside and Oxford (Ch. Ch.). He *m.* 1stly, 9 Feb. 1963, Sarah Elizabeth Anne, 2nd da. of St. John Bernard Vyvyan HARMSWORTH of Valley Holme, Horsted Keynes, Sussex. This marriage was diss. by divorce in 1974 and he *m.* 2ndly, 1977, Elizabeth, da. of Michael Moses SACHER.

[RANDAL ALEXANDER ST. JOHN MCDONNELL, s. and h. ap., *b.* 2 July 1967.]

AP ADAM

page 180,
note ([e]), delete all detail

ARBUTHNOTT

page 184,
line 28, for 'about 1660' read '17 Oct. 1658'
line 37, for 'in 1684' read '(cont. 29 Oct. 1684), as his 2nd wife'
lines 37–8, delete from 'Bart.' to '1692' and replace by '1st Bart., who *d.* Nov. 1708. She *d.* Oct. and was *bur.* 4 Nov. 1692'

page 186,
line 15, delete '; unm. in 1909'; after ([a]), add 'He *d.* in Edinburgh, 24 May 1914.'

XII. 1914 12. WILLIAM (ARBUTHNOTT), VISCOUNT ARBUTHNOTT, &c., br. and h., *b.* 24 Oct. 1849. He *d.* unm. 8 Nov. 1917.

XIII. 1917 13. WALTER CHARLES WARNER (ARBUTHNOTT), VISCOUNT ARBUTHNOTT, &c., cousin and h., being s. of Walter (*d.* 5 Jan. 1891), by Anna Maria, yst. da. of Brook Taylor OTTLEY of Delaford, co. Dublin, which Walter was 2nd s. of 8th VISCOUNT ARBUTHNOTT. He was *b.* 22 Oct. 1847. He *m.*, 15 Jan. 1878, Emma Marion Hall, da. of Rev. John Hall PARLBY of Manaton, Devon. He *d.* 9 Aug. 1920. His widow *d.* 27 Jan. 1930.

XIV. 1920 14. JOHN OGILVY (ARBUTHNOTT), VISCOUNT ARBUTHNOTT, &c., 2nd but 1st surviving s. and h., *b.* 15 Sep. 1882. He *m.*, 6 June 1914, Dorothy, yst. da. of Adm. Charles Lister OXLEY of Ripon, Yorks. He *d. s.p.* 17 Oct. 1960. His widow *d.* 1990.

XV. 1960 15. ROBERT KEITH (ARBUTHNOTT), VISCOUNT ARBUTHNOTT, &c., kinsman, being 2nd s. of John Campbell ARBUTHNOTT (*d.* 20 May 1923), by Jeannie Sinclair, da. of Robert HAMILTON, which John Campbell Arbuthnott was s. of Lieut. Col. Hugh Arbuthnott (*d.* 5 Feb 1866), by Susannah Morrison, da. of John CAMPBELL, which Hugh ARBUTHNOTT was 3rd s. of 8th Viscount Arbuthnott. He was *b.* 21 Aug. 1897; ed. at Fettes and R.M.C., Sandhurst. He *m.*, 10 Jan. 1924, Ursula, da. of Sir William COLLINGWOOD of Dedham Grove, Colchester. He *d.* 15 Dec. 1966. His widow *d.* 1989.

XVI. 1966 16. JOHN CAMPBELL (ARBUTHNOTT), VISCOUNT ARBUTHNOTT, &c., eldest s. and h., *b.* 26 Oct. 1924; ed. at Fettes and Cambridge (Gonville and Caius Coll.). He *m.*, 3 Sep. 1949, Mary Elizabeth Darley, elder da. of Cmdr. Christopher Bernard OXLEY, R.N., of Morley, Ware, Herts.

[JOHN KEITH OXLEY ARBUTHNOTT, Master of Arbuthnott, *b.* 18 July 1950; ed. at Fettes and N. Scotland Coll. of Agric., Aberdeen. He *m.*, 1974, Jill Mary, eldest da. of Capt. Colin FARQUHARSON of Whitehouse, Alford, Aberdeenshire.]

ARCEDEKNE

page 187,
line 12, for '13 Feb. 1370/1' read '30 Oct. 1371'
note (e), delete all detail
page 188,
line 1, after 'Lucy' add (ax)
note (ax) See LUCY (of Newington).

ARDEE

page 189,
note (a), line 6, for 'Edward, 2nd' read 'William, 3rd'
line 19, for 'father's' read 'great-grandfather's'

ARDGLASS

page 192,
line 6, for 'only' read '1st'
line 25, after '*m.*' add 'after 20 Dec. 1617' [*Letters of John Chamberlain*, American Phil. Soc., vol. ii, p. 122]

page 193,
line 14, for 'Notts' read 'co. Stafford'
line 35, after 'Catherine' add 'widow of Richard PRICE, of Greencastle, co. Down (admon. granted to her, 25 Nov. 1670), and'

page 194,
lines 5–7, delete from 'this' to '1734'
line 9, for '1714' read '1715'
note ([a]), lines 4–9, delete from 'It' to 'said' and replace by 'No such writ was, however, issued. Neither the 1st nor the 2nd Lord Cromwell ever had a barony by writ descendible to heirs general (see those titles as to Dugdale's mis-statements on the subject), but Thomas was *cr.* Baron Cromwell by patent, 9 July 1536, and'

ARDILAUN OF ASHFORD

page 194,
line 20, in margin under '1880' add 'to 1915'
line 28, delete from 'She' to '1850.' and replace by 'He *d. s.p.*, aged 74, at St. Anne's afsd. 20, and was *bur.* 23 Jan. 1915, at All Saints, Rahemy, co. Dublin, when the Barony became *extinct*, but the Baronetcy devolved on his nephew. Will dat. 25 Feb. 1902, pr. Apr. 1915. His widow, who was *b.* 27 Aug. 1850, *d.* at 42 St. Stephen's Green, Dublin, 13, and was *bur.* 17 Dec. 1925, at Rahemy, co. Dublin.'

ARGENTINE

page 196,
note ([b]), add at end 'J.H. Round said that he could trace the Argentines back at Wymondeley to *temp.* Henry I.'
note ([e]), line 12, delete from 'and' to 'volume'

page 197,
line 12, after 'Joan' add 'da. of Thomas FitzEustace'
line 13, delete 'his wife'

ARGYLL

page 198,
line 4, after 'by' add ', as is said,([aa])'
note ([aa]) There is no proof of this marriage. According to *Scots Peerage*, vol. ix, p. 18, he probably *m.* Mariota of the Isles, da. of Sir Donald, Lord of the Isles and Ross, as on 13 Feb. 1419/20, being betrothed, they had a Papal disp. to marry.
line 5, for '(SOMERVILLE), 3rd LORD SOMERVILLE' read '(SOMERVILLE), 2nd LORD SOMERVILLE [S.]'
line 7, after '1440' add 'probably before 1439'

page 199,
lines 29–30, delete from 'in' to '(b)' and replace by '9 Oct. 1529' [*Scots Peerage*, vol. ix, p. 20]
note (b), delete all detail

page 200,
line 3, for 'before 26 Mar.' read 'after 27 Aug.'
line 9, delete from 'before' to 'Maclean' and replace by '(cont. 12 Mar. [?1545/46]), before 23 Jan. 1546/7, Catherine, da. of Hector Maclean of Doward'
line 13, for '27' read '22'
line 14, for 'Dec. 1567' read '26 Nov. 1566'
line 16, after '1595' add 'She also *d.* shortly before 1595'
note (a), delete all detail and replace by '*Reg. Mag. Sig.* [S.], 1513–46, nos. 826–7; *cf. Hist. MSS. Com.*, 11th Rep., part vi, p. 53'

page 201,
line 2, after '*d. s.p.*' add 'he had, however, a posthumous son who *d.* at birth, 30 June 1574' [*Cal. S. P.* [S.], vol. v, p. 13]
line 5, for '*d. s.p.*' read '*d. s.p.s.*'
line 23, for 'May 1571' read '13 Jan. (when the banns were read in Dunottar Church)'

page 202,
line 9, for '8th' read '6th'

page 205,
line 9, after '1stly' add '(cont. 29 Mar.)'
line 20, after 'wife' add 'was *bap.* 25 July 1658 in the Canongate'

page 206,
note (c), line 4, after 'life"' add 'In a newsletter dated Edinburgh, 27 May 1704 it is stated that "on Tuesday last the body of the late Duke of Argyll was privately taken away from the Church of Duddeston, as were the gathered remains of the body of his father, who was beheaded here in 1685 . . . Both were removed to the West Highlands" (*i.e.* Inverary).'

page 208,
line 18, after 'Sherifmuir' add 'There is a warrant from the *titular* James III, dat. Urbino 10 Mar. 1717/18 for *cr.* him Baron and Earl in the Kingdom of England' [*Stuart Papers at Windsor Castle*, H.M.S.O., vol. 6, 1939, pp. 132–3.]

page 210,
line 9, for 'Mar.' read 'Feb.'
line 18, for 'officer' read 'Marshal'

page 211,
line 29, after '*b.*' add '3 Apr.'
line 37, for '1852–5' read 'Jan. 1853 to Nov. 1855'

page 212,
line 16, after 'She' add ', who was *b.* 12 Apr. 1843,'

line 22, after 'personalty.' add 'His widow *d.* in Cadogan Sq., Chelsea, 24, after a long illness, and was *bur.* at Iona, 30 Dec. 1925.'

page 213,
line 16, delete from 'She' to '1848' and replace by 'He *d. s.p.*, aged 68, from double pneumonia, at Kent House, Cowes, 2 May 1914. A memorial service was held at Westm. Abbey (the King and Queen being present), 8 May, and he was *bur.* 15 May 1914 at Kilmuir. His widow, who was *b.* 18 Mar. 1848, *d.* 3 Dec. 1939.

DUKEDOM [U.K.] III.
DUKEDOM [S.] X.
EARLDOM [S.] XIX
1914

3, 10 and 19. NIALL DIARMID (CAMPBELL), DUKE OF ARGYLL [U.K. 1892], &c., nephew and h., being s. and h. of Archibald CAMPBELL (*d.* 29 Mar. 1913), by Janey Sevilla, 3rd da. of James Henry CALLENDAR of Craigforth, Stirling, 2nd s. of 8th Duke of Argyll. He was *b.* 16 Feb. 1872; ed. at St. George's Ascot, Charterhouse and Oxford (Ch. Ch.). He *d.* unm. 20 Aug. 1949.

DUKEDOM [U.K.] IV.
DUKEDOM [S.] XI.
EARLDOM [S.] XX.
1949

4, 11 and 20. IAN DOUGLAS (CAMPBELL), DUKE OF ARGYLL [U.K. 1892], &c., 1st cousin once removed, being s. and h. of Douglas Walter Campbell (*d.* 5 Jan. 1926), by his 1st wife, Aimée Marie Suzanne, da. of John LAWRENCE of New York, s. of Walter CAMPBELL (2 May 1889), by Olivia Rowlandson, da. of John Clarkson MILNS of Asory House, Bute, which Walter was 3rd s. of the 8th Duke of Argyll. He was *b.* 18 June 1903; ed. at Milton, Mass., U.S.A. and Oxford (Ch. Ch.). He *m.* 1stly, 12 Dec. 1927, Janet Gladys, only da. of William Maxwell (AITKEN), 1st BARON BEAVERBROOK. This marriage was diss. by divorce in 1934 and she *d.* 1988. He *m.* 2ndly, 23 Nov. 1935, Louise Hollingsworth Morris, only da. of Henry CLEWS of Chateau La Napoule, Alpes Maritimes, France, and formerly wife of Hon. Andrew Nicholas Armstrong VANNECK. This marriage was diss. by divorce in 1951 and she *d.* in 1970. He *m.* 3rdly, 22 Mar. 1951, Margaret, only da. of George Hay WHIGHAM, and formerly wife of Charles SWEENY. This marriage was diss. by divorce in 1963 and she *d.* in 1993. He *m.* 4thly, 15 June 1963, Mathilda Coster, da. of Stanley MORTIMER of Lichfield, Conn. U.S.A. and formerly wife of Professor Clemens HELLER of Paris Univ. He *d.* 7 Apr. 1973. His widow was living 1995.

DUKEDOM [U.K.] V.
DUKEDOM [S.] XII.
EARLDOM [S.] XXI.
1973

3, 12 and 21. IAN (CAMPBELL), DUKE OF ARGYLL [U.K. 1892], &c., 1st s. and h., *b.* 28 Aug. 1937; ed. at Le Rosey, Trin. Coll. Glenalmond and McGill Univ., Canada. He *m.*, 4 July 1964, Iona Mary, only da. of Sir Ivar Iain (COLQUHOUN) of Luss, 8th Bart.

[TORQUIL IAN CAMPBELL, *styled* MARQUESS OF LORNE, s. and h., *b.* 29 May 1968; ed. at Glenalmond and R.A.C., Cirencester.]

ARLINGTON

page 218,
line 4, for 'soon after Mar. 1664/5' read '16 Apr. 1666, at Moor Park, Herts. (the residence of his wife's br.-in-law, Lord Ossory)' [*cf. Mem. Lady Fanshawe*, 1907, p. 562]
line 16, for '3rd' read '4th'

ARMAGH

page 218,
line 25, for '1644' read '1693'

ARMSTRONG OF GRASSIDE

page 218,
In margin, for '1890' read '1900'

ARRAN (in Scotland)

page 220,
lines 10–11, delete from '(she' to 1468,' and replace by 'certainly before Apr. 1474, and probably in Feb. or Mar. 1473/4' [see vol. vi, *sub* HAMILTON, p. 255]

ARRAN (in Ireland)

page 222,
line 2, for '24 May 1579' read '6 Dec. 1580' [*Scots Peerage*, vol. ix, p. 103]

page 223,
line 18, after 'Morton' add 'His s. James became, in 1615, Lord Ochiltree [S.]'

page 224,
line 14, for '1559' read '1599'

page 225,
line 23, for 'before' read 'between 4 and'
note (c), line 5, after 'p. 4.' add 'This Earldom of Arran was ostensibly offered for sale in Apr. 1994. The vendor was not heir male of the body of the grantee, and there can be no question of this dignity being involved. The title sold was probably no more than a feudal barony.'
note (d), line 1, before 'His' add '"Lord Arran's match is concluded with Mrs Ferrars, but the solemnity is to be deferred till Lord Ossory's return from sea". Letter of 4 June 1673 to Theophilus, Earl of Huntingdon, *Hist. MSS. Comm.*, Hastings MSS., part III, p. 164.'

page 226,
line 2, for '1881' read '1681'
line 4, after 'ap.' add '*b.* 16 Mar. 1681/2 in London, was'

page 227,
line 12, after '1703' add 'at Newtowngore, co. Mayo'
line 24, for '(__)' read 'Joanna'

page 229,
line 17, for 'Freshfield' read 'Freshford'
line 43, delete from 'He' to 'work.' and replace by 'His widow *d*., at 50 Eaton Sq., 12, and was *bur*. 16 Nov. 1921 in Windsor Cemetery.'

VIII. 1901 6. ARTHUR JOCELYN CHARLES (GORE), EARL OF ARRAN, &c., s. and h., *b*. 14 Sep. 1868. He *m*. 1stly, 16 Aug. 1902, Maud Jacqueline Marie Beauclerk, only da. of 3rd BARON HUYSSEN VAN KATTENDYKE of Kattendyke, Zeeland, Holland. She *d*. 6 Mar. 1927. He *m*. 2ndly, 17 Dec. 1929, Lilian Constance, da. of Joseph QUICK of Twickenham and widow of Francis BROWNE of Pycroft Place, Chertsey. He *d*. 19 Dec. 1958. His widow *d*. 25 Jan. 1961.

IX. 1958 7. ARTHUR PAUL JOHN JAMES CHARLES (GORE), EARL OF ARRAN, &c., elder s. and h., *b*. 31 July 1903; ed. at Winchester and Oxford (New Coll.). He *d*. unm. 28 Dec. 1958.

X. 1958 8. ARTHUR STRANGE KATTENDYKE DAVID ARCHIBALD (GORE), EARL OF ARRAN, &c., br. and h., *b*. 5 July 1910; ed. at Eton and Oxford (Balliol Coll.). He *m*., 11 June 1937, Fiona Bryde, eldest da. of Sir Iain COLQUHOUN of Luss, 7th Bart. He *d*. 23 Feb. 1983. His widow was living 1995.

XI. 1983 9. ARTHUR DESMOND COLQUHOUN (GORE), EARL OF ARRAN, &c., s. and h., *b*. 14 July 1938; ed. at Eton and Oxford (Balliol Coll.). He *m*., 1974, Eleanor, elder da. of Bernard VAN CUTSEM.

page 231,
note (b), line 1, before 'The' add 'There is no contemporary evidence to show that Roger was considered Earl of Arundel (see *Handbook of British Chronology*, 1986, p. 449).'

ARUNDEL

page 233,
line 17, after 'Bigod' add 'probably by his 2nd wife, Alice, s. and coh. of William de Tosny, Lord of Belvoir, da. of Robert de Tosny of the same' [B.L. Cott. MS. Titus CVIII, f. 71, *ex inform*. Ethel Stokes. See NORFOLK.]

page 237,
lines 19–20, for 'of Mold (*de Monte alto*)' read 'de Mohaut'
line 23, for '152' read '253'

page 239,
line 7, for 'before 23 Nov.' read 'shortly before 20 Sep.' [*Cal. Fine Rolls, 1272–1307*, vol. i, p. 169]
lines 29–30, delete '[2nd BARON BUTLER [I.]]'
line 30, after 'da.' add 'and h.'

page 240,
lines 19–20, for 'was living in 1300' read '*d.* shortly before 1 Apr. 1292'

page 242,
line 12, delete 'AND SUSSEX'
line 24, for '3 Sep.' read '19 Mar.'

page 243,
line 16, for 'in' read 'on 12 Apr.' [*Cal. Pat. Rolls, 1364–67*, pp. 237–8]

page 244,
line 8, for 'in 1346' read 'before 1347([ca])'
note ([ca]) He appears to have been the illegit. s. of his parents. The Arundell property was settled by fine, Trin., 1347 (Case 287/43/401), on Richard, the XIVth Earl, for life, with remainders successively to Eleanor, da. of Henry de Lancaster the elder, late Earl of Lancaster, and the heirs male of the bodies of the said Richard and Eleanor. *If no h. male shall be so begotten*, then to Richard de Arundel the younger, in tail mail, and the right heirs of the Earl successively. Another fine, All Souls, 1354 (*Idem*, 287/45/505) makes a similar entail but adds (after Richard de Arundel the younger), John and Thomas, brothers of the said Richard de Arundell the younger, in tail mail successively, before the right heirs of the Earl. The aforesaid John was grandfather of the XVIIIth Earl of Arundel.
note ([b]), line 1, for '3' read '2'
line 4, for '(2)' read 'and'
line 7, for '(3)' read '(2)'
note ([d]), (cont. from page 243, line 7), after 'Eleanor' add 'See also *Reg. of John de Trillek, Bishop of Hereford*, Cantilupe Soc., pp. 56–8, where another Papal disp., 6 July 1345, appears for the Earl's 2nd marriage. In this the 1st marriage is ignored and his son by Isabel Dispencer is spoken of as begotten in fornication. It is also stated (pp. 58–9) that, in answer to the Pope's request, the Bishop of Chichester excused himself from taking part in the dispensation, which shows that the bishop disapproved of the annulling of the 1st marriage.'

page 245,
line 8, for '1382/3' read '1392/3'

page 246,
line 13, after 'Perez' add 'da. of Pedro ESTERES' [See note *sub* EXETER [1444]]
line 17, after '*s.p.*' add '*legit.*' [The Earl in his will makes detailed provisions for his son John and appoints his wife Beatrice as guardian for the boy, who presumably was illegit., see Canterbury and York Soc., *Chichele Register*, vol. 42, 1937, pp. 71–3.]
line 22, for '(1437)' read '(1439)'

line 23, for '(1442/3)' read '(1443/4)'

note ([d]), line 10, after '*post*' add 'Another sister, Alice, *m.* John (Cherleton), 4th Lord Cherleton, *feudal* Lord of Powis, and *d. s.p. legit.* presumably before her brother's death in 1415. She was the mother of Bishop Henry Beaufort's illegit. da. Joan, wife of Sir Edward Stradling (*Studies in Medieval Hist. presented to F.M. Powicke*, ed. Hunt, Pantin and Southern, p. 425, note 5).' [*Ex inform.* K.B. McFarlane]

page 247,
line 22, for 'about 1430' read '10 June 1429'
line 23, after '*d.*' add '9 Aug.'
line 24, after '*d.*' add '1'

page 248,
line 14, after 'STAFFORD' add 'of Southwick, Wilts'
line 14, after 'da.' add 'and h.'
line 15, for 'Robert LOVELL' read 'Sir Robert LOVELL (yr. s. of John, 5th LORD LOVELL (of Titchmarsh)'

page 249,
line 12, for 'Countess of Salisbury' read 'COUNTESS OF SALISBURY'
lines 19–21, delete from 'It' to 'till' and replace by 'He was sum.' [no Parl. sat July 1471]
note ([d]), delete all detail

page 250,
line 12, after 'h.' add '*styled* LORD MAUTRAVERS'
line 30, for '(1533/4) 25 Hen VIII' read '(1532/3), 24 Hen.VIII'
line 31, after 'MAUTRAVERS' add 'taking his seat, 7 Feb. following'

page 251,
line 19, after '1stly' add 'after 25 Jan. 1524/5'
line 22, for '1532' read '1542'

page 255,
line 9, for 'Francis' read 'James'

page 258,
line 10, for '21 Mar. 1639/40' read '13 Apr. 1640'
line 24, after '1673/4' add 'of the stone, at Arundel House and was *bur.* at Arundel.([b])'
note ([b]) *Lives of Lady Anne Clifford and of her Parents*, Roxburghe Club, 1916, p. 160, where it is also stated that "part of her jointure was the castle and barony of Greystock, in Cumberland".
line 28, for '1627/8' read '1626/7'

page 259,
lines 15–16, for '17 Feb. 1358/9' read 'shortly before 4 Aug. 1357' [*Cal. Pat. Rolls, 1354–58*, vol. x, p. 595]
line 19, for '1364/5' read '1363/4'

page 260,
line 11, for '1387' read '1385'

ARUNDELL OF TRERICE

page 261,
In margin, for '1664' read '1665'

page 262,
line 3, for '1663/4' read '1664/5'

ARUNDELL OF WARDOUR

page 263,
line 19, after 'Margaret' add 'only'
line 20, delete 'Sir'

page 265,
line 5, after 'da.' add 'and eventually coh.'

page 267,
line 1, after 'widow' add ', who was *b.* 1781,'
line 39, delete from 'He' to 'work' and replace by 'His widow *d.* 24 Oct. 1934.'

XIII. 1906 13. EVERARD ALOYSIUS (ARUNDELL), BARON ARUNDELL OF WARDOUR, br. and h., *b.* 6 Sep. 1834; ed. at London Univ.; ordained priest of the Church of Rome 1862. He *d.* unm. 11 July 1907.

XIV. 1907 14. EDGAR CLIFFORD (ARUNDELL), BARON ARUNDELL OF WARDOUR, cousin and h., being 2nd but 1st surv. s. of Theodore ARUNDELL by his cousin Louisa, 2nd da. of John HUSSEY, of Nash Court, Dorset, which Theodore (*d.* 21 Aug. 1868) was 1st s. of Henry Raymond Arundell (*d.* 1886), 2nd but 1st surv. s. of Thomas Raymond Arundell, of Ashcombe, Wilts. (*d.* 18 Jan. 1829), by Elizabeth Mary Anne, da. of Sir Edward SMYTHE, Bart., which Thomas was 2nd s. of James Everard ARUNDELL, 3rd s. of Henry, 6th Lord Arundell. He was *b.* 20 Dec. 1859. He *m.*, 28 Nov. 1895, Ellen, da. of John THATCHER, widow of J. Melbourne EVANS. He *d. s.p.* 8 Dec. 1921, at his residence, Fiddington, Somerset. His widow *d.* 22 July 1935.

XV. 1921 15. GERALD ARTHUR (ARUNDELL), BARON ARUNDELL OF WARDOUR, next and yst. br. and h., *b.* 11 Dec. 1861; ed. at Stonyhurst Coll. He *m.*, 9 Jan. 1906, Ivy Florence Mary, only da. of Capt. W.F. SEGRAVE. He *d.* 30 Mar. 1939.

XVI. 1939 16. JOHN FRANCIS (ARUNDELL), BARON ARUNDELL OF WARDOUR, only s. and h., *b.* 18 June 1907; ed. at Stonyhurst Coll. and Oxford (New Coll.). Lieut. 4th Battn. Wilts Regt. He *d.* unm. 25 Sep. 1944, being *k.* in action, when his title became *extinct*.

ASCOTT

page 268,
line 7, for 'HERTFORD' read 'Bucks.'

ASHBOURNE

page 268,
line 25, after 'Law' add 'by Elizabeth Mary, da. of John MAYNE, Barrister-at-Law'
line 26, after 'Dublin.' add 'He *d.*, aged 76, in London, 22, being cremated at Golders Green Crematorium, 26, and his ashes placed in Mount Jerome Cemetery, Dublin, 28 May 1913. His widow *d.* at Lincoln House, Basil Str., S.W., 21 Mar. 1926.
lines 27–9, delete all detail

II. 1913 2. WILLIAM (GIBSON), BARON ASHBOURNE, 1st s. and h. ap., *b.* 16 Dec. 1868 at 20 Upper Pembroke Str., Dublin; ed. at Harrow, Dublin (Trin. Coll.) and Oxford (Merton Coll.). He *m.*, 7 Jan. 1896, Marianne, da. of Henri Roger Conquerré DE MONBRISON. He *d. s.p.* 21 Jan. 1942. His widow *d.* 17 Aug. 1953.

III. 1942 3. EDWARD RUSSELL (GIBSON), BARON ASHBOURNE, nephew and h., being 1st s. and h. of Edward Graves Mayne GIBSON (*d.* 26 Apr. 1928), by Mary Phillips, da. of Henry Russell GREG, of Lode Hill, Cheshire, he being 3rd s. of the 1st Baron Ashbourne. He was *b.* 1 June 1901; ed. at R.N.C.s, Osborne and Dartmouth, and Cambridge (Gonville and Caius Coll.). He *m.*, 20 July 1929, Reta Frances Manning, elder da. of Ernest Manning HAZELAND of Hong Kong. He *d.* 3 Sep. 1983. His widow was living 1995.

IV. 1983 4. EDWARD BARRY GREYNVILLE (GIBSON), BARON ASHBOURNE, s. and h., *b.* 28 Jan. 1933; ed. at Rugby. He *m.*, 25 Mar. 1967, Yvonne Georgina, da. of Major Gordon William HAM of Malin, co. Donegal.

[EDWARD CHARLES D'OLIER GIBSON, s. and h. ap., *b.* 31 Dec. 1967.]

ASHBROOK

page 269,
lines 19–20, for '9 Mar. 1766' read '20 Mar. 1766 at Northmoor, Oxon.'

page 270,
lines 36–7, delete from 'He' to 'work'

VIII. 1906 8. ROBERT THOMAS (FLOWER), VISCOUNT ASHBROOK, &c., br. and h., *b.* 1 Apr. 1836. He *m.*, 18 July 1866, Gertrude Sophia, da. of Rev. Sewell HAMILTON of Bath. She *d.* 8 Nov. 1911. He *d.* 9 Mar. 1919.

IX. 1919 9. LLOWARCH ROBERT (FLOWER), VISCOUNT ASHBROOK, &c., 1st s. and h., *b.* 9 July 1870. He *m.*, 14 Feb. 1899, Gladys Lucille Beatrice, da. of Gen. Sir George Wentworth Alexander HIGGINSON. He *d.* 30 Aug. 1936. His widow *d.* 18 June 1968.

X. 1936 10. DESMOND LLOWARCH EDWARD (FLOWER), VISCOUNT ASHBROOK, &c., s. and h., *b.* 9 July 1905; ed. at Eton and Oxford (Balliol Coll.). He *m.*, 8 Nov. 1934, Elizabeth, elder da. and coheir of Capt. John EGERTON-WARBURTON of Arley Hall, Cheshire.

[MICHAEL LLOWARCH WARBURTON, s. and h. ap., *b.* 9 Dec. 1935; ed. at Eton and Oxford (Worcester Coll.). He *m.*, 1971, Zoë Mary, yst. da. of Francis H.A. ENGLEHEART of The Priory, Stoke-by-Nayland, Suffolk.]

ASHBURNHAM

page 271,
line 6, for '30 May' read '20 May'
line 10, after 'Brecon' add 'by Alice, da. of Thomas BOND, of Ogbourne St. George and Aldbourne, Wilts'
note (d), delete all detail and replace by 'This Walter was s. and h. of Canon Frederick Vaughan (who *d.* 1663 and was *bur.* in Salisbury Cath.), by Francis, da. of William Daniell of Preshute, Wilts.' [*Ex inform.* George R. Brigstocke]

page 275,
line 13, after '£5,900.' add 'He *d. s.p.m.s.* in a hotel in Paris, 15, and was *bur.* 23 Jan. 1913 at Ashburnham.'

EARLDOM. VI. BARONY VIII. } 1913 6 and 8. THOMAS (ASHBURTON), EARL OF ASHBURNHAM [1730], VISCOUNT ST. ASAPH [1730], and BARON ASHBURNHAM [1689], next surv. br. and h., being 5th s. of the 4th Earl; *b.* 8 Apr. 1855. He *m.*, 10 June 1903, Maria Elizabeth, da. of W.H. ANDERSON, of Frederickton, New Brunswick. He *d. s.p.*, 12, and was *bur.* at Ashburnham, 15 May 1924, when all his titles became *extinct.*

note (a), line 1, delete 'and (1909) h. presumptive,'
line 4, after 'V.G.' add 'He *d. s.p.* 12 Apr. 1912.'

ASHBURTON

page 276,
line 13, after 's. and h.' add '(ba)'
note (ba) His elder br. *d. v.p.* in Apr. 1783.

page 278,
line 26, after '(b)' add 'He *d.* 27 Mar. 1938. His widow, who was *b.* 1885, in the U.S.A, *d.* 31 Mar. 1959.'

VIII. 1938 6. ALEXANDER FRANCIS ST. VINCENT (BARING), BARON ASHBURTON, &c., s. and h., *b.* 7 Apr. 1898; ed. at Eton and R.M.C., Sandhurst. He *m.*, 17 Nov. 1924, Doris Mary Thérèse, eldest da. of Lewis (HARCOURT), 1st VISCOUNT HARCOURT. She *d.* 1981. He *d.* 12 June 1991.

IX. 1991 7. JOHN FRANCIS HARCOURT (BARING), BARON ASHBURTON, &c., elder s. and h., *b.* 2 Nov. 1928; ed. at Eton and Oxford (Trin. Coll.). He *m.* 1stly, 25 Nov. 1955, Susan Mary, eldest da. of Sir Robert Burnham (RENWICK), 1st BARON RENWICK. This marriage was diss. by divorce in 1984 and he *m.* 2ndly, 1987, Mrs Sarah CREWE, da. of John George SPENCER-CHURCHILL.

[MARK FRANCIS ROBERT BARING, 1st s. and h. ap., *b.* 17 Aug. 1958; ed. at Eton and Oxford (Ch. Ch.). He *m.*, 1983, Miranda Caroline, 2nd da. of Capt. Charles St. John Graham MONCRIEFF of Easter Elcho, Rhynd, Perth.]

ASHCOMBE OF DORKING

page 279,
line 6, after 'Common' add 'and *bap.* at St. Peter's, Eaton Sq.'
line 15, after 'Surrey.' add 'He *d.* at 17 Princes Gate, London, 26 Feb. and was *bur.* 2 Mar. 1917 at Ranmore, near Dorking, Surrey.'
line 16, line to read as follows

II. 1917 2. HENRY (CUBITT), BARON ASHCOMBE OF DORKING AND OF BODIAM CASTLE, 3rd([d]) but 1st surv. s. and h., *b.* at 17 Prince's Gate afsd.,'

line 24, for ']' read 'and *d.* 7 Mar. 1945. He *d.* 27 Oct. 1947.'

III. 1947 3. ROLAND CALVERT (CUBITT), BARON ASHCOMBE OF DORKING AND OF BODIAM CASTLE, 4th but 1st surv. s. and h., *b.* 26 Jan. 1899; ed. at Eton and R.M.C., Sandhurst. He *m.* 1stly, 16 Nov. 1920, Sonia Rosemary, da. of Lieut. Col. George KEPPEL. This marriage was diss. by divorce in 1947, and she *d.* in 1986. He *m.* 2ndly, 6 Aug. 1948, Idina Joan, only da. of Col. Robert Edward MYDDELTON of Chirk Castle, co. Denbigh, and formerly wife of John Charles Trueman MILLS. She *d.* 9 Oct. 1954. He *m.* 3rdly, 2 July 1959, Jean, da. of Charles Tuller GARLAND of Moreton Hall, Moreton Morrell, Warwickshire, and formerly wife of (1) Arthur Turberville SMITH-BINGHAM, (2) Sir Robert George Maxwell THROCKMORTON, 11th Bart., (3) Greville Pollard BAYLISS. He *d.* 28 Oct. 1962. His widow *d.* 1973.

IV. 1962 4. HENRY EDWARD (CUBITT), BARON ASHCOMBE OF DORKING AND OF BODIAM CASTLE, 1st s. and h., *b.* 31 Mar. 1924; ed. at Eton. He *m.* 1stly, 12 Sep. 1955, Ghislaine, only da. of Cornelius William DRESSELHUYS of Long Island, U.S.A., and formerly wife of Major Denis James ALEXANDER. This marriage was diss. by divorce in 1968 and he *m.* 2ndly, 1973, Virginia, yr. da. of Peter Alexander Rupert (CARRINGTON), 6th BARON CARRINGTON. This marriage was diss. by divorce in 1979 and he *m.* 3rdly, 1979, Mary Elizabeth, da. of Dr Henry Davis CHIPPS of Lexington, Kentucky, U.S.A. and widow of Geoffrey Mark DENTON-BROCKLEHURST of Sudeley Castle, Winchcombe, Gloucestershire.

ASHTON

page 280,
line 19, for 'Ashton afsd.' read 'Lancaster'

page 281,
line 7, after 'York.' add 'He *d. s.p.* 27 May 1930 when his title became *extinct*.'

ASHTOWN

page 282,
line 28, add at end 'She *d.* 2 Sep. 1945. He *d.* 20 Mar. 1946.'
line 30, after '1895.' add 'Ed. at Eton, R.M.C., Sandhurst and Oxford (Magdalen Coll.); Lieut. K.R.R.C., *d.* unm. and *v.p.*, of wounds received in action, 16 Nov. 1916.'

IV. 1946 4. ROBERT POWER (TRENCH), BARON ASHTOWN, 2nd, but 1st surv. s. and h., *b.* 27 Apr. 1897; ed. at Eton. He *m.* 1stly, 20 Oct. 1926, Geraldine Ida, 4th da. of Sir Henry Foley (GREY), 7th Bart. This marriage was diss. by divorce in 1938 and she *d.* 11 Oct. 1940. He *m* 2ndly, 27 June 1950, his cousin Oonah Anne, elder da. of Brig. Gen. Lewis Frederick GREEN-WILKINSON by his wife Sarah May, sister of the 3rd Baron. He *d. s.p.* 3 Nov. 1966.

V. 1966 5. DUDLEY OLIVER (TRENCH), BARON ASHTOWN, br. and h., *b.* 11 July 1901; ed. at Wellington and R.M.C., Sandhurst. He *m.* 1stly, 1 Dec. 1932, Ellen Nancy, yr. da. of William GARTON of Brixedone, Bursledon, Hants. She *d.* 10 Mar. 1939. He *m.* 2ndly, 28 Nov. 1955, Sheelah Adrienne Sarah, his cousin and sister-in-law, yr. da. of Brig. Gen. Lewis Frederick GREEN-WILKINSON by his wife Sarah May, sister of the 3rd Baron. She *d.* 9 July 1963. He *m.* 3rdly, 27 Jan. 1966, Frances Natalie, da. of Major Hermon BARKER-HAHLO of St. Martin, Guernsey and widow of James Fenwick DE SALES LA TERRIERE of Dunalastair, Perthshire. She *d.* in 1979. He *d. s.p.m.* 19 Aug. 1979.

VI. 1979 6. CHRISTOPHER OLIVER (TRENCH), BARON ASHTOWN, kinsman and h., being s. of Algernon Oliver TRENCH (*d.* Dec. 1955), by Muriel Dorothy, eldest da. of Frank THORNE of Weston-super-Mare, which Algernon Oliver Trench was 3rd s. of William Cosby Trench (*d.* 12 Mar. 1944), by Frances Elizabeth, only da. of Walter Taylor Newton Shawe TAYLOR of Castle Taylor, co. Galway, which William Cosby Trench was br. of 3rd Baron Ashtown. He was *b.* 23 Mar. 1931 and *d.* unm. 27 Apr. 1990.

VII. 1990 7. NIGEL CLIVE COSBY (TRENCH), BARON ASHTOWN, kinsman and h., being s. of Clive Newcombe TRENCH (*d.* 24 Feb. 1964), by Kathleen Maud Marion, 2nd da. of Major Ivar MCIVOR, which Clive Newcombe Trench was 3rd s. of Cosby Godolphin Trench (*d.* 9 Dec. 1925), by Maria, eldest da. of Sir Richard MUSGRAVE, 4th Bart., which Cosby Godolphin Trench was 2nd s. of the 2nd Baron Ashtown. He was *b.* 27 Oct. 1916; ed. at Eton and Cambridge (Corpus Christi Coll.). He *m.*, 1 Dec. 1939, Marcelle Catherine, yst. da. of Johan Jacob Clotterbrooke Patyn VAN KLOETINGE of Zeist, Netherlands. She *d.* in 1994.

[RODERICK NIGEL GODOLPHIN TRENCH, s. and h. ap., *b.* 17 Nov. 1944; ed. at Eton and Stanford Univ., U.S.A. He *m.* 1stly, 27 June 1967, Janet Merle, yr. da. of Harold HAMILTON-FAULKNER of Redwood City, California, U.S.A. She *d.* in 1971. He *m.* 2ndly, 1973, Susan Barbara, da. of Lewis Frank DAY of Cooden, Sussex and formerly wife of Michael R.J. WRIGHT.]

ASTLEY

page 283,
line 27, after 'WOLVEY' add 'of Wolvey, co. Warwick, by his wife Alice'
note ([d]), delete all detail

page 284,
line 2, delete from 'Alice' to 'Toni' and replace by 'by his 2nd wife, Alice, sister and h. of Ralph (DE TONI), Lord Tony, da. of Ralph DE TOENI VII'

ASTON OF FORFAR

page 289,
note ([a]), lines 1–3, delete from '"Died' to 'watchmaker"' and replace by 'against a list of deaths (p. 146), March 25, Lord Aston, Baron Forfar of Scotland; he was a few years ago cook to Sir [Charles] Mordaunt, Bart., when the title descended to him; he is succeeded by Mr Walter Aston, a watchmaker.'

ATHBOY

page 290,
note ([b]), delete all detail

ATHENRY

page 294,
lines 25–6, delete from 'According' to 'Galway' and replace by 'He *m.* ?2ndly, Joan or Margaret, an illegit. da. of Sir Roger O'SHAUGHNESSY, of Gortinchigorie, co. Galway, by Honora (a professed nun, whom he afterwards *m.*), da. of Murrough (O'BRIEN), 1st EARL OF THOMOND [I.]' [See *Cal. Pat. Rolls, 1603–17* [I.], pp. 300–1]
line 30, after '1615' add '([e])'
note ([e]), delete all detail and replace by 'According to the *Pat. and Close Rolls* [I.], vol. iii, p. 593, he had special livery of his father's lands, 9 Feb. 1630/1. This cannot be understood if he was old enough to have sat in Parliament in 1613 and 1615, nor how he can have sat in Parliament if his father did not in fact die in 1614.'

page 296,
line 6, after '1stly' add 'in or before 1675 ([aa])'
note ([aa]) In the Abbey of Athenry is a monument to Brigid and Mary, daughters of the 13th Lord, by his 1st wife, "they died in their infancy in 1676 and 1677". V.G.'

ATHLONE

page 302,
line 33, after '1830' add 'William Gambier *m.*, 2ndly, 5 July 1831, Annabel Frances, 2nd da. of Charles Garth COLLETON, of Haines Hill, Wilts, and *d.* 5 Dec. 1860.'
line 35, for '22' read '20'
line 36, after 'Hague' add 'and *bap.* 30 Mar. 1822'

ATHLUMNEY OF SOMERVILLE AND DOLLARDSTOWN

page 304,

line 8, after 'Conservative' add 'He *m.* at the Guards Chapel, 30 July 1919, Margery, da. of Henry BOAN of Australia. He *d. s.p.* at Somerville, co. Meath, 8, and was *bur.* at Kentstown, 10 Jan. 1929, when his two Baronies became *extinct* and the Baronetcy became *dormant*. His widow *d.* 10 July 1946.'

ATHOLL

page 305,

line 16, after 'unm.' add 'and was *bur.* there in the graveyard of the Franciscans'

line 17, after 'Fernelith' add 'or Forneleth' [This is the Gaelic *Forbhflaith*, meaning 'perfect princess' (*Scots Peerage*, vol. ix, p. 26)]

lines 30–1, delete from 'da.' to 'Dover' and replace by 'sister and h. of Richard DE DOUVRES of Chilham, Kent (*d.* 1265–6), da. of Richard DE DOUVRES of the same (living 1247)'

note (c), delete all detail and replace by 'This Richard de Douvres was s. and h. of Richard Fitzroy (*d.* 1245–6), by Rose (*d.* 1264–5), da. and h. of Foubert de Douvres, all of Chilham afsd., which Richard last named was bastard s. of King John: see G.J. Turner in *Genealogist*, N.S., vol. xxii, pp. 105–10, and G.A. Moriarty, "The First House of De Douvres or De Chilham", in *The New England Hist. and Gen. Reg.*, vol. cv, 1951, pp. 39–40; *cf.* vol. xii, part 2, p. 298, note (a), *sub* WAKE.'

page 306,

line 1, delete from 'who' to '1307' and replace by 'who *d.* between Apr. 1310 and June 1311'

line 2, delete from 'Feb.' to '*bur.*' and replace by '18 Mar. 1291/2 and was *bur.* 24 Mar. near the altar of St. Edward' [*Scots Peerage*, vol. ix, p. 27]

note (a), line 3, for '1483' read '1433'

page 307,

line 5, before 'EARL' add 'sometimes *styled*'

line 19, delete from 'h.' to '4th' and replace by 'coh. of Alexander COMYN, Sheriff of cos. Wigtown and Aberdeen (yr. s. of Alexander, 6th EARL OF BUCHAN [S.]), and niece and h. of line of John, 7th'

page 308,

line 13, for '1361' read '18 July 1356' [*Cal. Pat. Rolls, 1354–6*, p. 419]

page 309,

note (e), (cont. from page 308, line 19), after 'Sussex' add 'by whom she had been abducted, shortly before 15 Feb. 1383/4. See G.W. Watson, "Philippe de Strabolgy; a Fourteenth Century Abduction", in *Genealogist*, N.S., vol. xxix, pp. 1–11.'

page 310,

line 9, after 'MENTEITH' add 'of Rusky'

line 14, for 'before Nov. 1347' read 'as his second wife (post nuptial dispute, 9 Nov. 1347)'

line 14, for '4th' read '5th'
line 27, delete 'Hugh Dacre' and replace by 'between 8 Oct.1354 and 1 July 1355, Hugh (DE DACRE), 4th LORD DACRE, who *d.* 24 Dec. 1383. She *d.* before 1 Jan. 1369/70. See that title.'

page 311,
line 7, after 'John' add '(RANDOLPH), 3rd'
line 7, for '6th' read '4th'
line 8, after 'Margaret' add 'da. of Sir David'
line 8, delete from 'She' to '1387'

page 313,
line 18, for '1518' read '1518/19' [Andrew MacEwen, *The Geneal.*, vol. 2, 1981, p. 52.]
line 28, for 'da.' read 'granddaughter and h. of line'

page 314,
line 28, for '3rd' read '4th'
line 31, for '6 Oct. 1580' read '27 Oct. 1582'
line 36, for 'Aug. and Oct.' read '26 Aug. and 8 Oct.'
line 37, for 's' read '1st s. and h.'
line 37, after 'Buchan' add '(2nd but 1st surv. s. of John (STEWART), 3rd EARL OF BUCHAN [S.])' [*Scots Peerage*, vol. ii, p. 269, vol. ix, p. 48]
line 38, for 'John' read 'James'
line 39, for 'only' read '1st'

page 315,
lines 5–6, delete 'Capt. Peter Rollock' and replace by 'before 11 Feb. 1633/4, Capt. Peter ROLLO (yst. s. of Sir Walter ROLLO of Petmady and Lawton)'
line 8, for '1609' read '1613'
line 9, for 'coh.' read 'h. of line'
line 10, delete from 'or' to '1626' and replace by 'July 1627'
line 30, for 'At' read 'After' and delete 'in 1660'
line 32, for '1663 to 1676' read '1661 to 1665'

page 316,
line 1, for '17' read '7'

page 317,
line 31, for '18 July 1687' read '26 Dec. 1688'
page 318,
line 7, for 'the' read 'a'
line 8, for '18' read '10'

page 321,
line 21, for '16th' read '17th'

line 23, after 'there' add '11 Oct. follg.'
line 24, after 'widow' add 'who was *b*. 3 Feb. 1761'
line 24, after '1842' add 'at Dunkeld, aged 81, and was *bur*. there 13 Oct.'

page 322,
line 7, for '9' read '17'
line 27, for '9 or 14' read '7 or 14'

page 323,
line 1, after 'Castle.' add 'Ed. at Eton 1853–6.'
line 11, after 'She' add ', who was *b*. 11 June 1844,'
line 12, after 'Blair' add 'He *d*. at Blair Castle, Blair Atholl, 20, and was *bur*. 23 Jan. 1917 with his wife.'
line 15, line to read as follows

DUKEDOM [S.] VIII.
MARQUESSATE [S.] IX.
EARLDOM [S.] XXXVI.
1917

8 or 15. JOHN GEORGE (STEWART-MURRAY), DUKE OF ATHOLL [1703], &c., 2nd but 1st surv. s. and h.,'

line 16, after 'Perth' add 'from 1871 *styled* MARQUESS OF TULLIBARDINE; ed. at Eton.'
line 26, for ']' read 'He *d. s.p.* 16 Mar. 1942. His widow *d*. 21 Oct. 1960.'

DUKEDOM [S.] IX.
MARQUESSATE [S.] X.
EARLDOM [S.] XXXVII.
1942

9 or 16. JAMES THOMAS (STEWART-MURRAY), DUKE OF ATHOLL, &c., br. and h., *b*. 18 Aug. 1879. Ed. at Eton. He *d*. unm. 8 May 1957.

DUKEDOM [S.] X.
MARQUESSATE [S.] XI.
EARLDOM [S.] XXXVIII.
1957

10 or 17. GEORGE IAIN (STEWART-MURRAY), DUKE OF ATHOLL, &c., remote cousin and h., being 1st s. and h. of George Anthony MURRAY (*d*. Apr. 1945), by Angela, 3rd da. of Weetman Harold Miller (PEARSON), 2nd VISCOUNT COWDRAY, he being s. and h. of George Evelyn Pemberton Murray (*d*. 30 Mar. 1947), by Muriel Mildred Elizabeth, eldest da. of Philip Beresford HOPE, he being s. and h. of George Herbert Murray (*d*. 4 Apr. 1936), by Helen Mary, 1st da. of John (MULHOLLAND), 1st BARON DUNLEATH, he being s. and h. of Rev. George Edward Murray (*d*. 14 Sep. 1854), by Penelope Francis Elizabeth Pemberton, da. of Brig. Gen. AUSTIN, he being s. and h. of Rt. Rev. George Murray, Bishop of Sodor and Man (*d*. 16 Feb. 1860), by Lady Sarah Maria, da. of Robert Auriol (HAY-DRUMMOND), 10th EARL OF KINNOULL, he being 2nd s. and h. of Rt. Rev. George MURRAY, Bishop of St. David's

(*d.* 1803), by Anne Charlotte, da. of Lieut. Gen. Francis GRANT, which George MURRAY was 2nd s. of the 3rd Duke of Atholl. He was *b.* 19 June 1931; ed. at Eton and Oxford (Ch. Ch.).

ATON

page 324,
note (g), line 1, after 'Kildare' add '[Lord Vescy]'

page 325,
line 16, for 'She *d.* before' read 'She *d.* between 13 Sep. 1349 and'
line 16, delete (second) 'before' and replace by 'between 29 Sep. and'
note (d), delete all detail
note (h), line 3, after 'f.123d)' add 'She was a da. of Michael (de Poynings), 1st Lord Poynings. See that title.

page 326,
note (b), line 7, after '214).' add 'For a discussion of his ancestry, see W.L. Sheppard, *Geneal. Mag.*, vol. 17, 1972, pp. 86–8 and 219.'

AUBIGNY

page 327,
line 15, after 'Elizabeth' add 'widow of Alexander (__)'

page 330,'
note (c), lines 3–4, delete from 'Evelyn' to 'effeminacy'

AUCKLAND

page 336,
line 26, after 'Kent.' add 'She *d.* 28 Mar. 1931.'
line 29, after '-Maine;' add 'ed. at Eton 1872–6;'
line 32, for 'Eustace' read 'Eustacie'
line 33, after 'ARKWRIGHT.' add 'He *d.* at Bournemouth, 31 July 1917. His widow, who was *b.* 25 June 1871, *d.* 22 Apr. 1955.'
line 34, after '1892.' add 'Lieut. K.R.R.C., *d.* unm. 2 Mar. 1915, being *k.* in action.'

VI. 1917 6. FREDERICK COLVIN GEORGE (EDEN), BARON AUCKLAND [1793], &c., 2nd but 1st s. and h., *b.* 21 Feb 1895; ed. at Malvern Coll. and Camborne Sch. of Mines. He *m.* 1stly, 2 June 1917, Susan Livingstone, da. of Augustus Griffin HARTRIDGE of Jacksonville, Florida, U.S.A. This marriage was diss. by divorce in U.S.A. in 1925. He *m.* 2ndly, 25 Apr. 1939, Mrs Constance Caroline HART-FAURE, da. of Benno HART of San Francisco, U.S.A. He *d. s.p.m.*, being *k.* in an air raid on London, 16 Apr. 1941. His widow *d.* 23 Dec. 1946.

VII. 1941 7. GEOFFREY MORTON (EDEN), BARON AUCKLAND, &c., cousin and h., being s. and h. of George EDEN (*d.* 14 June 1924), by Amy Violet, 3rd da. of Col.

Charles Rowley HAY-DRUMMOND, which George was 2nd s. of 4th Baron Auckland. He was *b.* 17 Feb. 1891; ed. at Eton. He *m.*, 30 Apr. 1919, Dorothy Ida, yst. da. of Rev. Francis Clyde HARVEY, Vicar of Hailsham, Sussex. He *d. s.p.m.* 21 June 1955. His widow *d.* 24 July 1964.

VIII. 1955 8. TERENCE (EDEN), BARON AUCKLAND, &c., br. and h., *b.* 3 Nov. 1892; ed. at Eton. He *m.*, 12 Sep. 1925, Evelyn Vane, 3rd da. of Col. Arthur William Henry HAY-DRUMMOND of Cromlix. He *d.* 14 Sep. 1957. His widow *d.* 1971.

IX. 1957 9. IAN GEORGE (EDEN), BARON AUCKLAND, &c., 1st s. and h., *b.* 23 June 1926; ed. at Blundells. He *m.*, 28 Aug. 1954, Dorothy Margaret, yr. da. of Henry Joseph MANSER of Eastbourne, Sussex.

[ROBERT IAN BURNARD EDEN, s. and h. ap., *b.* 25 July 1962; ed. at Blundells. He *m.*, 1986, Geraldine, da. of (__).]

AUDLEY

page 337,
line 2, after 'fitz Orm' add 'of Darlaston, Staffs.'
line 14, add at end 'She was *bur.* in Hulton Abbey'

page 338,
lines 4–5, delete from 'often' to 'Salisbury' and replace by 's. and h. of Ela, *suo jure* COUNTESS OF SALISBURY'
line 13, after '1273' add 'before 7 Nov.' [*Cal. Fine Rolls, 1272–1307*, vol. 1, p. 14]
line 14, delete from 'in' to [LORD DEIVILL]' and replace by '(pardon for marrying without lic., 5 Feb. 1275/6), before 8 May 1275, Sir John D'EIVILLE, of Egmanton, Notts, etc.'
line 16, after 'Lucy' add 'da. of John DE ROS, yr. s. of Robert DE ROS, 1st LORD ROS of Helmsley)'
line 21, for '11 Edw. I' read ', before 12 Nov.'
line 28, delete from '(sometimes' to 'Salisbury)'

page 339,
line 6, for 'between 8 July and 14 Dec.' read 'shortly before 21 Nov.'
line 38, delete 'da. of PIERS DE JOINVILLE' and replace by '1st da. and h. of Sir Piers DE GENEVILLE (2nd but 1st surv. s. and h. ap. of Geoffrey, 1st LORD GENEVILLE)'
line 40, after 'Isabel' add '(c)'
(c) In a ped. of Touchet, dat. 1597, apparently prepared for George, 1st Earl of Castlehaven [I.] (who *d.* 1617), this Isabel is said to have been da. of Robert, Lord Fitzwalter. See *Genealogist*, N.S., vol. xxxvi, p. 15. Roger, 5th Lord Strange (of Knokyn), was not *b.* till *circa* 1326 and *m.*, as a child, in or before 1338. See that title.
line 40, for 'Baron' read 'LORD'
note (b), delete all detail

page 340,
line 19, after 'dat.' add 'and pr.'

lines 28–30, delete from '21 Dec.' to 'was' and replace by '20 Oct. 1403 to 26 Aug. 1407, the writs being,'

page 341,
line 1, after 'TUCHET?)' add 'According to modern doctrine, which was not then invented, the issue to him of a writ would probably be regarded as terminating the *abeyance* (then unknown) in the Barony of Audley'
lines 18–22, delete from 'of Thomas' and replace by 'of Edmund (DE HOLLAND), 4th EARL OF KENT, by Constance, widow of Thomas (LE DESPENCER), 2nd s. of 5th LORD DESPENCER and sometime EARL OF GLOUCESTER, da. of Edmund (of Langley), 1st DUKE OF YORK'
note (e), delete all detail and replace by 'See vol. iv, note *sub* DESPENCER [1375], and vol. vii, note *sub* KENT [1400]

page 342,
line 19, for 'in or before 1483' read '(cont. 25 Oct. 1480, to marry before Christmas)'
line 20, after 'da.' add 'and h.'
line 21, for 'coh.' read '(in her issue) h.'
line 30, after 'GRIFFIN' add *de jure* (according to modern doctrine) 9th LORD LATIMER'
note (f), line 3, after 'Wilts.' add 'John Daccombe, of Steepleton, Dorset, in his will dat. 6 July 1562, leaves 'to my daughter Lady Audley, 40 ewes' (Crisp, *Somerset Wills*, 6th ser. p. 74).'
note (f), line 8, after 'V.G.' add 'Lord Audley had a wife living, 1 Apr. 1537 (*L. and P. Hen. VIII*, vol. xii, part 1, p. 356).'

page 343,
line 3, after '1stly' add 'before 30 Aug. 1538' [*L. and P. Hen. VIII*, vol. xiii, part 2, p. 84]
line 13, after 'widow' add 'who appears to have *m.* Stephen BAGOT. Sir Gilbert Gerrard, in his will dat. 1592, refers to Elizabeth, Lady Audley, now wife of Stephen Bagot Esq. V.G.'

page 346,
between lines 10 and 11 add

XXII. 1937 22. MARY THICKNESSE-TOUCHET, 1st da. of George Edward THICKNESS-TOUCHET above named, *suo jure* BARONESS AUDLEY, succeeding to the title on the death of her younger sister, 17 May 1937. She was *b.* 13 Aug. 1858. She *d.* unm. 27 May 1942.

XXIII. 1942 23. THOMAS PERCY HENRY (TOUCHET-JESSON), LORD AUDLEY, distant cousin and h., being s. and h. (by Thomas JESSON), of Charlotte Anne (*d.* 1 Mar. 1912), yst. but only child to leave issue, of John Nicholas THICKNESSE-TOUCHET (*d.* 21 July 1861), by Elizabeth Montgomery, da. of John Henry BLENNERHASSET, of Tralee, co. Kerry, which John was 2nd s. of the 20th Lord Audley. He was *b.* 15 Sep. 1913; ed. at Lancing Coll. He *m.* 1stly, 15 Nov. 1952, June Isabel, only da. of Lieut. Col. Reginald CHAPLIN, and formerly wife of Rudolph Edgar Francis DE TRAFFORD. This marriage was diss. by divorce in 1957 and she *d.* in 1977. He *m.* 2ndly, 26 Apr. 1962, Sarah Millicent Hermione,

2nd da. of Rt. Hon. Sir Winston Leonard Spencer CHURCHILL and formerly wife of Vic Oliver of Vienna, and of Anthony Beauchamp. He *d. s.p.* 3 July 1963. His widow *d.* in 1982.

XXIV. 1963 24. ROSINA LOIS VERONICA, *born* TOUCHET-JESSON, sister and h., *b.* 10 July 1911. She *m.*, 24 Apr. 1943, John Archibald Joseph, yr. s. of Bernard MACNAMEE of Glasgow. He *d.* 1969. She *d. s.p.* 24 Oct. 1973.

XXV. 1973 25. RICHARD MICHAEL THOMAS (SOUTER), LORD AUDLEY, cousin and h., being s. of Sir Charles Alexander SOUTER (*d.* 9 Jan. 1958), by Charlotte Dorothy JESSON, which Charlotte Dorothy Jesson was 2nd da. of Charlotte Anne by Thomas JESSON – which see in the lineage of the 23rd Baron. He was *b.* 31 May 1914; ed. at Uppingham. He *m.*, 18 Oct. 1941, Lily Pauline, da. of Dallas Louis ESKELL of Exmouth, Devon.

note (e), after '241' add '*cf.* White, in vol. x, Appendix K, p. 123'

page 347,
line 19, after 'Longespée' add '(s. and h. ap. of Ela, *suo jure* COUNTESS OF SALISBURY)'
line 34, after 'MORTIMER' add '1st LORD MORTIMER'
lines 34–5, delete from 'Margaret' to 'FIENNES' and replace by '(__)'
note (e), line 4, after 'V.G.' add 'The mother of Isolt must be an earlier wife of Edmund Mortimer than Margaret de Fiennes, since Isolt married Hugh, Lord Audley *circa* 1288 and Margaret married Edmund in 1285 (see *post*, vol. ix, p. 283, note (m)).' [*Ex inform.* Lindsay L. Brook]

AUDLEY OF WALDEN

page 348,
line 21, after 'Attorney' add 'Gen.'
line 22, for '1530' read '1526–31'
note (a), line 8, for '1344' read '1348'

page 349,
line 9, after '?Margaret' add 'or Elizabeth,(ba)'
note (ba) An indenture of sale by Sibilla Newdigate to Sir Thomas Audley, Lord Chancellor, and Elizabeth his wife is dat. 4 Nov. (1537) 29 Hen. VIII (*Close Rolls*, part iii, no. 67). V.G.
note (a), lines 14–15, delete from 'He' to 'which' and replace by 'On 3 Apr 1542 he had lic. to found Magdalene Coll., Cambridge, on the site of the older Buckingham Coll. (*L. and P., Henry VIII*, vol. 17, p. 158) This'

page 351,
note (d), after 'the pedigree' add 'For further comments on the parentage of Countess Judith, see M.L. Bierbriar, *Geneal. Mag.*, vol. 19, 1978, pp. 176, 257; G.R. Tibbetts, *op. cit.* p. 257.'

AUMALE

page 353,

note ([d]), delete all detail and replace by 'William le Meschin, Lord of Copeland, br. of Ranulph, 1st Earl of Chester, yr. s. of Rannulf, Vicomte of the Bessin, *m.* Cicely de Rumilly, Lady of Skipton, da. and h. of Robert de Rumelli, of Harewood and Skipton, co. York (see ped. of Lisle in vol. viii, between pp. 48 and 49), and had 3 daughters and coheirs. (1) Alice, Lady of Skipton, who *m.* 1stly, William fitz Duncan, s. of Duncan II, King of Scots. See Clay, *Early Yorks Charters*, vol. vii, pp. 9–10. They had one s., William, 'the Boy of Egremont', who *d.* in the King's ward after 1155, leaving his 3 sisters his coheirs: (i) Cicely, as in the text; (ii) Amabel, Lady of Copeland (called in the *Pipe Rolls* and elsewhere, *Comitissa de Couplanda*), who *m.* Reynold de Lucy (see vol. iii, pp. 247–8, *sub* Lucy); (iii) Alice de Rumilly, Lady of Allerdale, who *m.* 1stly, Gilbert Pipard, Sheriff of cos. Gloucester and Hereford, and 2ndly, Robert de Courtenay, Sheriff of Cumberland and *d. s.p.* (see vol. ix, pp. 527–8, *sub* Pipard). Alice, Lady of Skipton, *m.* 2ndly, Alexander FitzGerold. (2) Avice, Lady of Harewood, who *m.* 1stly, William de Courcy III, 2ndly, William Paynell, of Drax, co. York, and 3rdly, William de Percy of Rougemont, in Harewood, co. York (see vol. x, p. 319, *sub* Paynel, and p. 439, *sub* Percy). (3) Maud, *m.* 1stly, Philip de Belmeis, of Tong, Salop., and 2ndly, Hugh de Mortimer, of Wigmore, co. Hereford (see vol. ix, p. 271, note ([e]), *sub* Mortimer (of Wigmore), and vol. xii, part 2, pp. 930–1, *sub* Zouche.)'

AVANDALE

page 359,

line 19, for '1356/7' read '1357/8'

line 20, for 'AVONDALE' read 'AVANDALE'

AVEBURY

page 360,

line 12, after 'London' add 'He *d.* from heart failure, 28 May 1913, at his seat, Kingsgate Castle, Kent. His widow *d.* 11 Mar. 1947.'

line 13, delete all detail and replace as follows

II. 1913. 2. JOHN BIRKBECK (LUBBOCK), BARON AVEBURY, &c., 1st s. and h. by 1st wife, *b.* 4 Oct. 1858; ed. at Eton. He *d.* unm. 26 Mar. 1929.

III. 1929. 3. JOHN (LUBBOCK), BARON AVEBURY, &c., nephew and h., being s. and h. of Harold Fox Pitt LUBBOCK (*k.* in action 4 Apr. 1918), by Dorothy Charlotte, da. of Henry William (FORSTER), Lord Forster, which Harold was 4th s. of the 1st Baron Avebury. He was *b.* 13 May 1915; ed. at Eton and Oxford (Balliol Coll.). He *m.* 1stly, 24 Feb. 1938, Cecily Kathleen, da. of Dr Nathaniel Alexander Knox SPARROW. This marriage was diss. by divorce in 1945 and he *m.* 2ndly, 31 July 1946, Diana Mary Margaret Westcott, yr. da. of Capt. Edward Westcott KING, formerly of Malaya. This marriage was diss. by divorce in 1955 and he *m.* 3rdly, 22 Dec. 1955, Betty Gay, da. of William Oscar INGHAM of Poulton-le-Fylde, Lancs and formerly wife of (—) GOODE. He *d. s.p.m.* 21 June 1971. His widow was living 1995.

IV. 1971. 4. ERIC REGINALD (LUBBOCK), BARON AVEBURY, &c., cousin and h., being s. and h. of Maurice Fox Pitt LUBBOCK (*d.* 26 Apr. 1957), by Mary Katharine Adelaide, 1st da. of Arthur Lyulph (STANLEY), 5th Baron Stanley of Alderley, which Maurice was 6th s. of the 1st Baron Avebury. He was *b.* 29 Sep. 1928; ed. at Upper Canada Coll., Harrow and Oxford (Balliol Coll.). He *m.* 1stly, 2 Sep. 1953, Kina Maria, only da. of COUNT JOSEPH HENRY O'KELLY DE GALLAGH. This marriage was diss. by divorce in 1983 and he *m.* 2ndly, 1985, Lindsay Jean, da. of Gordon Neil STEWART.

[LYULPH AMBROSE JONATHAN LUBBOCK, 1st s. and h. ap., *b.* 15 June 1954. He *m.*, 1977, Susan Carol MACDONALD.]

AVENDALE

page 361,
line 10, for 'AVONDALE' read 'AVANDALE'

AVONDALE

page 361,
line 15, for 'AVONDALE' read 'AVANDALE'
between lines 15 and 16 insert 'See also "AVANDALE, AVENDALE, or AVONDALE"'

AVONMORE

page 363,
line 5, after 'K.C.B.' add 'by Mary Anne, 3rd da. of Sir Giles ROOKE, a Judge of the Court of Common Pleas'
line 6, after 'widow' add ', who was *b.* in 1825,'

page 364,
line 2, after 'Canada.' add 'He *d. s.p.m.* 3 Sep. 1910 when his honours became *dormant*. His widow *d.* at 64 West Cliff Rd., Bournemouth, 17 Jan. 1917.'

AXILHOLM

page 364,
lines 5–7, delete all detail

AYLESFORD

page 365,
line 3, for '1708' read '1707'

page 367,
line 8, before 'CHARLES' add '8.'
line 11, for '1855' read '1885'
note (b), line 15, after 'who' add 'though separated by deed'
note (b), line 28, after 'Lords' add 'In 1811 the Judges, in answer to a question put to them by the Committee for Privileges, replied "that the presumption of legitimacy arising from the birth of a child during wedlock, the husband and wife not being proved to be impotent, and having opportunities of access to each other during the period in which a child could be begotten and born in the course of nature, may be rebutted by circumstances inducing a contrary presumption." A long-winded way of watering down the old maxim for nothing, which goes some way to justify the subsequent decisions of the Lords. The valuable doctrine may now be rendered, "The father of the child is the man who married the mother, unless there is ground for suspecting somebody else." V.G.'

page 368,
line 2, for 'Ella' read 'Marcella'
line 3, for 'Charles' read 'Capt. James Wingfield'
line 4, after 'Cork.' add 'He *d.* at Packington Hall, near Tamworth, Staffs, 16, and was *bur.* 20 Sep. 1924 at Great Packington. His widow *d.* 1939.'
line 12, after '1885.' add 'He *d. v.p.m.s.* 14 Sep. 1914, being *k.* in action in WW1 at Soupin, France. His widow *d.* 4 Aug. 1952.'

IX. 1924. 9. HENEAGE MICHAEL CHARLES (FINCH), EARL OF AYLESFORD, &c., grandson and h., being s. of the abovementioned Heneage Greville, *b.* 31 Oct. and *bap.* 7 Dec. 1908 in the Chapel Royal, St. James; ed. at Eton. He *m.*, 18 Apr. 1940, Pamela Elizabeth, elder da. of Col. Charles John COVENTRY of Worcester and formerly wife of Lieut. Cmdr. James George Greville DUGDALE, R.N. He *d. s.p.*, being *k.* in action, 28 May 1940. His widow *d.* in 1990.

X. 1940. 10. CHARLES DANIEL (FINCH-KNIGHTLY), EARL OF AYLESFORD, &c., uncle and h. male, being 2nd s. of the 8th Earl of Aylesford, *b.* 23 Aug. 1886. He assumed the additional name of Knightley in 1912. He *m.*, 7 Feb. 1918, Aileen Jane Chartres, only da. of William McCormac BOYLE of Armagh, N. Ireland. He *d.* 20 Mar. 1958. His widow *d.* in 1977.

XI. 1958. 11. CHARLES IAN (FINCH-KNIGHTLEY), EARL OF AYLESFORD, &c., 1st s. and h., *b.* 2 Nov. 1918; ed. at Oundle. He *m.*, 21 Mar. 1946, Margaret Rosemary, only da. of Major Austin Arnold TYER of Tunstall, Wadhurst. She *d.* in 1989.

[CHARLES HENEAGE FINCH-KNIGHTLEY, *styled* LORD GUERNSEY, *b.* 27 Mar. 1947; ed. at Oundle and Cambridge (Trin. Coll.). He *m.*, 1971, Penelope Anstice, yr. da. of Kenneth Arnold Gibbs CRAWLEY.]

AYLMER

page 370,
line 26, for 'only s. and h.' read '1st s. and h. by 1st wife'

line 27, before 's.' add '2nd'
lines 33–4, delete from 'and' to 'work.'

VIII. 1901. 8. MATTHEW (AYLMER), LORD AYLMER, &c., 1st s. and h., *b.* 28 Mar. 1842. He *m.*, 20 Oct. 1875, Amy Gertrude, 2nd da. of John YOUNG of Montreal. He *d.* 11 June 1923. His widow *d.* 14 Sep. 1935.

IX. 1923. 9. JOHN FREDERICK WHITWORTH (AYLMER), LORD AYLMER, &c., s. and h., *b.* 23 Apr. 1880. He *m.*, 3 July 1928, Emma Gertrude, 4th da. of Colin BLACK of Victoria, British Columbia. He *d. s.p.* 1970. His widow *d.* 1977.

X. 1970. 10. KENNETH ATHALMAR (AYLMER), LORD AYLMER, &c., br. and h., *b.* 23 June 1883. He *m*, 25 Sep. 1924, Eleanor Katherine, 3rd da. of John Francis ROGERS of Swanington, Norfolk. She *d.* 1970. He *d. s.p.* 1 May 1974.

XI. 1974. 11. BASIL UDOLPHUS (AYLMER), LORD AYLMER, &c., br. and h., *b.* 20 May 1886. He *m.*, 1stly, 28 Feb. 1916, Bessie Irving, da. of Joseph WATSON of Westward Park, Wigtown. She *d.* 12 Nov. 1956. He *m.* 2ndly, 3 Oct. 1960, Helen Cooper, da. of Thomas HOGG of Toronto, Canada, and widow of Frederick Gordon RISEBOROUGH. He *d.* 13 Mar. 1977. His widow was living 1995.

XII. 1977. 12. HUGH YATES (AYLMER), LORD AYLMER, &c., cousin and heir male, being s. and h. of Arthur Lovell AYLMER, (*d.* 1961), by Georgina Henrietta Emmeline, da. of Lieut. Col. James Fielding SWEENEY, which Arthur was 1st s. and h. of Henry Lovell Aylmer, (*d.* 3 June 1882), by his cousin Isabella, 1st da. of 7th Baron Aylmer, which Henry was 1st s. and h. of Major Gen. Henry Aylmer, (*d.* 31 Mar. 1904), by Charlotte Louisa, da. of John GWATKIN of Parc Behan, Cornwall, which Henry was 2nd s. of Adm. John Aylmer abovenamed by his 2nd wife Frances, 2nd da. of Rev. Thomas Horner PEARSON. He was *b.* 5 Feb. 1907; ed. at Minneapolis, Minnesota, U.S.A. He was *m.*, 12 Aug. 1939, Althea, 1st da. of Lieut. Col. John TALBOT. He *d. s.p.m.* 6 Dec. 1982. His widow was living 1995.

XIII. 1982. 13. MICHAEL ANTHONY (AYLMER), LORD AYLMER, &c., cousin and h. male, being only s. and h. of Christopher AYLMER, (*d.* 6 Feb. 1955), by his 1st wife Marjorie Marianne Ellison, da. of Percival Ellison BARBER of Sheffield, which Christopher was 1st s. and h. of Lieut. Col. Frederick Arthur Aylmer, (*d.* 29 Mar. 1918), by Constance Isabella, da. of Charles William GRENFELL, M.P., of Taplow Court, co. Buckingham, which Frederick was 2nd s. of Major Gen. Henry Aylmer abovenamed. He was *b.* 27 Mar. 1923; ed. privately and at Cambridge (Trin. Hall). He *m.*, 5 May 1950, COUNTESS MADDALENA SOFIA MARIA GABRIELLA CECILIA STEFANIA FRANCESCA, only da. of COUNT ARBENO ATTEMS DI SANTA CROCE of Italy by his wife Sofie, eldest da. of PRINCE MAXIMILIAN KARL FRIEDRICH ZU LÖWENSTEIN-WERTHEIM-FREUDENBERG.

[ANTHONY JULIAN AYLMER, s. and h. ap., *b.* 10 Dec. 1951; ed. at Westminster and Cambridge (Trin. Hall). He *m.*, 1990, Belinda Rosemary, only da. of Major Peter Henry PARKER.]

BADENOCH

page 371,
line 14, for 'STRATHNAVON read 'STRATHAVON'

BADLESMERE

page 372,
lines 1–4, delete from 'by' to 'FitzBernard' [See vol. v, p. 403, note (b)]
line 4, for 'attended' read 'was excused from service in'
line 20, for 'vii' read '8th'
lines 21–2, delete from '(yr.' to 'HERTFORD)'
note (c), delete all detail

page 373,
line 4, delete from 'GRANSON to '22' and replace by 'GRANDISON.(b). He *d. s.p.* 7'
line 5, for '24' read '23'
line 6, after '*abeyance*' add 'Will dat. at Hambleton, 4 Dec. 1337, pr. at Lincoln, 20 June 1338.'
line 6, for 'May' read '27 Apr.'
lines 25–6, delete from 'that' to 'Oxford' and replace by "That, for the baronies [of Bolebec, Sandford and Badlesmere], they are wholly in your Majesty's hand, to dispose at your own pleasure" [See vol. iv, Appendix H, p. 711]

BAGOT OF BAGOT'S BROMLEY

page 374,
line 20, delete '1728' and replace by '1728/9 and *bap.* 16 Mar. at Blithfield'
line 24, after '1760' add 'at Wroxton, co. Oxford'
line 28, delete from 'pr.' to 'again' and replace by 'dat. 11 June 1796 to 29 Aug. 1798, pr. 15'
line 29, after '76' add 'and was *bur.* there 11 Feb.'
line 32, after 'Westm.' add 'School'

page 375,
line 6, after 'Ruthyn' add 'and was *bur.* 21 Aug. at Blithfield'
line 7, after '82' add 'Will dat. 22 Oct. 1852 to 1 Feb. 1856, pr. 15 Apr. 1857'
line 14, after '1851' add 'at St. James's, Westm.'
line 17, delete from 'in' to '75' and replace by 'at 34 Princes Gdns., S. Kensington, aged 75, and was *bur.* at Blithfield. Will dat. 26 July 1880, pr. 31 May 1887.'
line 18, after 'heart' add 'and was *bur.* at Blithfield. Will dat. 28 Dec. 1893 to 2 Oct. 1894, pr. 12 Feb. 1895.'
line 25, after 'Hall;' add 'ed. at Eton 1871–3;'
line 28, after 'U.S.A.' add 'He *d. s.p.m.* 23 Dec. 1932 at Blithfield. His widow *d.* 21 Feb. 1958.'

V. 1932. 5. GERALD WILLIAM (BAGOT), BARON BAGOT OF BAGOT'S BROMLEY, &c., distant cousin and h., being 4th s. and h. male of Henry BAGOT (*d.* 30 Nov. 1877), by his 2nd wife, Eleanor, da. of Edward Sacheverell CHANDOS-POLE of Radbourne Hall, co. Derby, Henry being 3rd s. of the Rt. Rev. Richard BAGOT, Bishop of Bath and Wells (*d.* 15 May 1854), by Lady Harriet, da. of George Bussy (VILLIERS), 4th EARL OF JERSEY, which Richard was 3rd s. of the 1st Baron Bagot. He was *b.* 13 May 1866; ed. at Haileybury Coll. He *d.* unm. 5 Apr. 1946.

VI. 1946. 6. CARYL ERNEST (BAGOT), BARON BAGOT OF BAGOT'S BROMLEY, &c., cousin and h., being s. and h. of Rev. Lewis Richard Charles BAGOT (*d.* 13 Feb. 1922), by Coelia Cator, 4th da. of Rev. Henry JODRELL, which Lewis was 1st s. and h. of Rev. Charles Walter BAGOT (*d.* 10 Sep. 1886), by Mary, 2nd da. of Lieut. Gen. John CHESTER, Charles Walter being the 4th s. of the 1st Baron Bagot. He was *b.* 9 Mar. 1877; ed. at Radley Coll. He *m.* 1stly, 6 Feb. 1911, Margaret, da. of James MACMENEMY. She *d.* 10 Aug. 1937. He *m.* 2ndly, Nancy Constance, da. of Francis Aldborough SPICER of Sydney, Australia. He *d. s.p.* 5 Aug. 1961. His widow *m.* 2ndly, 19 Sep. 1965, George Kenneth WHITEHEAD of Greenbank, Bury, Lancs; this marriage was diss. by divorce in 1972. His widow was living 1995.

VII. 1961. 7. HARRY ERIC (BAGOT), BARON BAGOT OF BAGOT'S BROMLEY, &c., cousin and h., being 1st s. and h. of Charles Frederick Heneage BAGOT (*d.* 2 June 1939), by his 1st wife Florence Eleanor, eldest da. of Vice-Adm. Henry Bagot (3rd s. of the 1st Baron Bagot), Charles being 4th s. of Charles Walter BAGOT above mentioned. He was *b.* 4 Feb. 1894; ed. at Marlborough. He *m.* 1stly, 11 July 1951, Kathleen Elizabeth Saddler, widow of Noel Murray PUCKLE of Melbourne, Australia. She *d.* in 1972. He *m.* 2ndly, 1972, Mary Frances, da. of Lieut. Col. George Frederick HIBBERT and widow of Lieut. Col. Albert Claud HEWITT. He *d. s.p.* 20 June 1973. His widow was living 1995.

VIII. 1973. 8. REGINALD WALTER (BAGOT), BARON BAGOT OF BAGOT'S BROMLEY, &c., brother and h., *b.* 24 Aug. 1897; ed. at Wellington. He *m.* 1stly, 1922, Winifred Gwyneth BOWEN. This marriage was diss. by divorce in 1934 and he *m.* 2ndly, 1934, Millicent Brenda, only da. of Henry White BOWDEN of Great Missenden, Bucks. He *d. s.p.* 2 Oct. 1979. His widow *d.* 1980.

IX. 1979. 9. HENEAGE CHARLES (BAGOT), BARON BAGOT OF BAGOT'S BROMLEY, &c., half-brother and h., being s. of Charles Frederick Heneage BAGOT by his 2nd wife Alice Lorina, da. of Thomas FARR of Ceylon and Chittlehamholt Manor, Chulmleigh, Devon. He was *b.* 11 June 1914; ed. at Harrow. He *m.*, 29 Nov. 1939, Muriel Patricia Moore, yst. da. of Maxwell James Moore BOYLE of Tullyvin House, co. Cavan.

[CHARLES HUGH SHAUN BAGOT, s. and h. ap., *b.* 23 Feb. 1944; ed. at Abbotsholme. He *m.*, 1986, Mrs Sally A. Stone, da. of D.G. BLUNDEN of Farnham, Surrey.]

BALCARRES

page 376,
line 18, for '1640/1' read '1641/2'
line 20, in margin, for '1641' read '1642'
note ([d]), lines 1–2, delete 'note' to 'Holme' and replace by 'vol. v, Appendix E'

BALFOUR OF BURLEIGH

page 380,
line 9, after '*m.*' add '(cont. 12 July 1591)'
line 10, for '(__)' read 'William'
line 14, for 'settl. Sep.' read 'cont. 30 Aug.'

page 381,
line 4, for 'a girl' read 'Janet Thomson, his sister's governess'

page 382,
line 24, after 'Blackheath.' add 'He *d.* at Cadogan Sq. Chelsea, 6, and was *bur.* 11 July 1921 at Clackmannan. His widow *d.* 28 Feb. 1931.'
line 26, after 'Edinburgh' add 'He was ed. at Eton 1893–7, Capt. Argyll and Sutherland Highlanders, served in the S. African War, 1900–2, and in WW1, being *k.* in action, *v.p.* and unm., 26 Aug. 1914, at Le Cateau.'

VII. 1921. 7. GEORGE JOHN GORDON (BRUCE), LORD BALFOUR OF BURLEIGH, 2nd but 1st surv. s. and h., *b.* 18 Oct. 1883; MASTER OF BURLEIGH from 1914; ed. at Eton 1896–1900. Fought in WW1. He *m.*, 2 June 1919, Violet Dorothy Evelyn, yr. da. of Richard Henry DONE of Tarporley, Cheshire. He *d.* 4 June 1967. His widow *d.* 1976.

VIII. 1967. 8. ROBERT (BRUCE), LORD BALFOUR OF BURLEIGH, 1st s. and h., *b.* 6 Jan. 1927; ed. at Westminster. He *m.* 1stly, 1971, Jennifer, da. of E.S. MANASSEH and formerly wife of John Brittain CATLIN. This marriage was diss. by divorce in 1993 and he *m.* 2ndly, 1993, Dr Janet, da. of Dr Frank MORGAN.

BALFOUR (of Glenawley)

page 383,
line 11, after '2ndly' add 'June 1604, in the Old Kirk of Aberdeen'
line 13, for '6th' read '7th'
line 14, after 'Walter' add 'BRYSON, or'
line 15, after 'Perth' add 'From him she obtained a decree of divorce, 24 Mar. 1620'

BALGONIE

page 384,
line 3, for 'ROTHES' read 'LEVEN'

BALGOWAN

page 384,
line 5, for '1818' read '1814'

BALLINASLOE

page 384,
line 16, for '1800' read '1801'

BALLIOL

page 386,
note ([c]), delete all detail

page 387,
line 4, for 'Having' read 'He'
lines 5–8, delete from 'coh.' to 'and' and replace by 'h. of Richard DE DOUVRES, of Chilham, Kent (*d.* 1265–6), da. of Richard DE DOUVRES, of the same (living 1247), by Maud *suo jure* COUNTESS OF ANGUS [S.], da. and h. of Malcolm, 6th EARL OF ANGUS [S.], which Richard last named was s. and h. of Richard FITZROY (*d.* 1245–6, a natural s. of King John), by Rose (*d.* 1264–5), da. and h. of Foubert DE DOUVRES, also of Chilham afsd.([ax]) Having acquired that Lordship in her right, he'
note ([ax]) See G.J. Turner, in *Genealogist*, N.S., vol. xxii, pp. 105–10, and G.J. Moriarty, "The First House of De Douvres or De Chilham", in *New England Hist. and Gen. Reg.*, vol. cv, 1951, pp. 39–40, *cf.* vol. xii, part 2, p. 298, note ([a]), *sub* WAKE.

BALLYHIGUE

page 388,
lines 20–2, delete all detail. [This Barony, which it was supposed might have been *cr.* by James II when in exile, was in fact a French creation of Louis Philippe, dat. 18 Nov. 1839.]

BALLYMORE

page 389,
line 2, for '*Littelton*' read '*Lyttleton*'

BALLYSHANNON

page 389,
line 8, for 'FOLIOT' and '*Foliot*' read 'FOLLIOTT' and '*Folliott*'
line 9, for '1619' read '1620' and for '1630' read '1716'

BALMERINOCH

page 390,
line 6, for '21 Mar. 1588' read 'after 10 Apr. 1589' [*Scots Peerage*, vol. ix, p. 33]
line 9, for '21 June' read 'May, certainly before 2 June' [*Scots Peerage*, vol. ix, p. 33]

page 391,
line 9, delete from '16' to 'Cramond' and replace by '15 Feb. 1671/2 at Holyroodhouse' [Canongate Reg.]
line 11, for '7' read '12'

between lines 15 and 16 insert

[James ELPHINSTONE, 1st s. and h. ap., by 1st wife, *b.* before 3 Mar. 1672/3, *d. v.p.*, probably in infancy([aa])]

[(__) ELPHINSTONE, MASTER OF BALMERINO, younger, 2nd but 1st surv. s. and h. ap., by 1st wife, *d. s.p.* and *v.p.* before 6 Mar. 1697/8([aa])]

note ([aa]), *Scots Peerage*, vol. ix, p. 34.

lines 16–17, delete 'from '2nd to 1704' and replace by 'after 1704, 3rd but 1st surv. s. and h. ap., by 1st wife'
line 20, for '3rd' read '4th'
line 25, after 'year' add 'and was *bur.* 9 Jan. at Restalrig'
line 27, after '*bur.*' add '27 Sep.'

BALTIMORE

page 394,
note ([b]), lines 2–5, delete from 'There' to 'note.' and replace by 'Longford, the county usually assigned to the creation contains a very obscure place of the name Baltimore (see Hamill Kenny, *Maryland Historical Mag.*, vol. xlix, 1954, pp. 116–21), and it is possible that this was the source. It remans possible, however, that Baltimore in co. Cork, then a place of considerable note, was meant.'

page 394,
line 15, for '(__)' read 'Mary'
lines 16–18, delete from 'He' to 'Lows' and replace by 'He m. 2ndly, about 1666, Jane, widow of Henry SEWELL, M.D., da. of Vincent Lowe, by his wife, Anne, da. of Henry Cavendish of Tutbury, co. Stafford.' [See *Maryland Genealogies*, vol. 1, 1980, p. 139; "Lowe of Denby, County Derby, England and Maryland", G. Rodney Crowther, *National Genealogical Society Quarterly*, vol. 51, 1963, pp. 37–9, *ex inform.* Brice M. Clagett, Maryland.]'
line 20, for '(__),' read '(__)'
line 21, after '4thly' add '1712,'

BALTINGLASS

page 396,
line 23, after '*m.*' add 'before 27 July 1568' [*Cal. Pat. and Close Rolls* [I.], vol. i, p. 544]
line 25, after '*m.*' add 'before June 1588'
line 26, for '1621' read 'Jan. 1621/2'
line 27, for 'Monkton' read 'Monkstown' and after 'ent.' add 'Sir Gerald *d.* 19 Aug. 1634.'
note ([c]), line 1 (on p. 397), after 'reports' add 'under date 8 Feb. 1596/7' and after 'Lord' add 'of'

page 398,
line 15, delete 'about 1670' and replace by 'and was *bur.* 25 Apr. 1666 at Thornborough, Bucks.'

line 17, delete from '*bap.*' to '1619' and replace by '*b.* 9 Jan. 1618/9 and *bap.* 26 Jan.'
line 21, in margin, for '1670' read '1666'
note (b), line 4, after 'V.G.' add 'See also George Sherwood, *Geneal. Mag.*, vol. 9, 1942, pp. 467–8.'

BALVAIRD

page 399,
lines 6–7, delete from 'but' to 'h.' and replace by 's.'
line 8, for '(__)' read 'Sir William'
line 15, after '*m.*' add '(cont. 30 Apr. 1628)'
line 17, after 'Edzell' add 'She was living 19 Mar. 1638/9' [*Hist. MSS. Com.*, Laing MSS., vol. i, p. 202]
line 17, after '1644' add 'aged about 47. Will reg. at St. Andrews, 22 June 1653.'

BANBURY

page 400,
line 6, for 'Mary' read 'Katherine' [M.I. Westm. Abbey]
page 402,
note (a), line 28, add at end 'Lieut. Col. R.W.E. Knollys, I.A. retd., writing to *The Times*, 27 Mar. 1935, "as representative of the eldest branch of the Knollys family and claiming to be heir male of William first Earl of Banbury" emphasised nine facts which he said tended to refute the alleged "contemporary inference" as to Edward and Nicholas being the sons of the fourth Lord Vaux'.

page 406,
line 29, after '1798' add 'and was *bur.* 2 Apr. in Winchester Cath.'

BANDON

page 408,
line 38, for '26 Nov.' read '30 Nov.'
line 39, for '4 Oct.' read '6 Oct.'

page 409,
line 28, after '67' add 'Will dat. 17 Jan. 1874, pr. 20 Apr. 1877.'
line 38, after '1853.' add 'He *d.* at 23 Prince's Gdns., S.W., 18 May 1924. His widow *d.* 29 June 1942.'

V. 1924. 5. PERCY RONALD GARDNER (BERNARD), EARL OF BANDON, VISCOUNT BERNARD [1800] VISCOUNT and BARON BANDON [1793], all in the Peerage of Ireland, cousin and h., being 1st s. of Ronald Percy Hamilton BERNARD (*d.* 2 Feb. 1921), by Lettice Mina, yr. da. of Capt. Gerald Cecil Stewart PAGET, which Ronald Percy Hamilton Bernard was 1st s. of Percy Brodrick Bernard by Isabel Emma Beatrice, da. of John Newton LANE of King's Bromley Manor, Staffs., which Percy Brodrick Bernard was 1st s. of Charles Brodrick Bernard (*d.* 31 Jan. 1890), by Jane Grace Freke, sister of George Patrick Percy (CARBERRY), 7th Baron Carberry, which Charles Brodrick Bernard was 2nd s. of 2nd Earl. He was *b.* 30 Aug. 1904; ed. at Wellington and R.A.F. Coll., Cranwell. He *m.* 1stly, 28 Feb. 1933, Mabel Elizabeth, 2nd da. of Raymond Playfair of Nairobi, at Nairobi Cath. This marriage was diss. by divorce in 1946 and she *m.* 2ndly, 1965, Sir Reginald HOLCROFT, 2nd Bart. He *m.* 2ndly, 2 Oct. 1946, Lois, da. of Francis RUSSELL of Victoria, Australia and formerly wife of Sqn. Ldr. Frederick Arthur WHITE. He *d. s.p.m.* 8 Feb. 1979, whereupon his titles became *extinct*. Hs widow was living 1995.

BANDON BRIDGE

page 410,
lines 4 & 5, for 'BANDONBRIDGE' and 'BANDONBRIDGE' read 'BANDON BRIDGE' and BANDON BRIDGE'
line 6, for 'KYBALMEAKY' read 'KINALMEAKY'
line 8, '*Boyle*' read '*Bernard*'

BANFF

page 410,
line 11, before 'Walter' delete 'Sir' and after 'O' add (who *d.* between 14 Feb. 1626/7 and 10 May 1628)'
line 25, after '*m.*' add '(cont. 12 Aug. and 2 Sep. 1648)'

page 411,
line 4, after 'with her' add 'and 12 days later obtained an award against him of 2,000 marks *p.a.*'

BANGOR

page 413,
line 34, after 'She' add 'who was *b.* 11 Feb. 1805' and for '76' read '75'
line 36, after 'London.' add 'Ed. at Eton 1841–2.'

page 414,
line 8, after '[I.]' add 'He *d.*, aged 82, at Castle Ward, 23, and was *bur.* 27 Feb. 1911 at Ballycutter, near Strangford.'
line 8, after 'She' add ', who,'
line 9, after '1828' add ', *d.*, aged 90, at Beechwood, Killiney, Co. Dublin, 11, and was *bur.* 15 Jan. 1919 at Ballyculter in that County.'
line 10, line to read as follows

VI. 1911. 6. MAXWELL RICHARD CROSBIE (WARD), VISCOUNT BANGOR, &c., 3rd, but only surv. s.[a] and h.,'

line 11, after '1868' add 'ed. at Harrow and R.M.A., Woolwich'
line 13, for ']' read 'He *d.* 17 Nov. 1950. His widow *d.* 1972.'

VII. 1950. 7. EDWARD HENRY HAROLD (WARD), VISCOUNT BANGOR, &c., s. and h., *b.* 5 Nov. 1905; ed. at Harrow and R.M.A., Woolwich. He *m.* 1stly, 29 Apr.

1933, Elizabeth, eldest da. of Thomas BALFOUR of Wrockwardine Hall, Wellington, Salop. This marriage was diss. by divorce in 1937, and he *m.* 2ndly, 14 Aug. 1937, May Kathleen, da. of William B.O. MIDDLETON of Shanghai. This marriage was diss. by divorce in 1947 and she *d.* 9 May 1969. He *m.* 3rdly, 12 Nov. 1947, Leila Mary, 2nd da. of David Rimington HEATON of Downderry, Torpoint, Cornwall. This marriage was diss. by divorce in 1951 and she *d.* 23 Feb. 1959. He *m.* 4thly, 1951, Marjorie Alice, da. of Peter BANKS of St. Leonards-on-Sea, Sussex, and formerly wife of Reginald Forbes SIMPSON. She *d.* in 1991. He *d.* 8 May 1993.

VIII. 1993. 8. WILLIAM MAXWELL DAVID (WARD), VISCOUNT BANGOR, &c., s. and h. by 3rd wife, *b.* 28 Sep. 1948; ed. at St. Edward's Sch., Oxford and Univ. Coll., London. He *m.*, 1976, Sarah Mary Malet, da. of Brig. Hilary Anthony HAYES and formerly wife of Anthony John BRADFORD of Lisbon, Portugal.

BANTRY

page 414,
line 26, for '1693' read '1672'
line 29, for '1679' read '1681'
line 30, for 'OF TYRCONNELL' read 'and DUKE OF TYRCONNEL [I.]'
page 415,
line 3, for 'TYRCONNELL' read 'TYRCONNEL'

page 416,
line 21, after '1854.' add 'Ed. at Eton 1868–70.'
lines 27–8, for 'and was living 1910' read '*d.* 5 Feb. 1942.'

BARD OF DRUMBOY

page 416,
line 35, for '1660' read '1667'

BARDOLF

page 417,
lines 13–14, delete from 'In' to 'he' and replace by 'He'
notes ([e]) and ([f]), delete all detail

page 418,
lines 6–8, delete from 'da.' to 'VAUD' and replace by 'a grandson'
line 9, for '1328' read '1329' and for '46' read '47'
line 13, in margin, for '1328' read '1329' [Writ for *Inq. p.m.*, 30 Dec. 1329, vol. 7, p. 174]
line 14, for '1311/2' read '1312/3'
note ([a]), lines 15–17, delete from 'was 'to 'text' and replace by 'seems unlikely to have been da. of William, Seigneur de Grandson, by Blanche of Savoie, as suggested previously. See, for example, *Europaische Stammtafeln*, vol. 11, table 154.' [*Ex inform.* Brice M. Clagett, Maryland, U.S.A.]

page 419,
lines 3–4, delete from 'brought' to 'and'
line 4, for '1360' read '5 Feb. 1360/1' [*Cal. Close Rolls*, *1360–64*, pp. 160–1]
line 10, after '*m.*' add 'after 10 Feb. 1365/6' [*Cal. Close Rolls*, *1364–68*, p. 263.]
line 12, after 'Moleyns' add '(1st s. and h. ap. of John DE MOLEYNS)'
line 12, delete from 'da.' to 'ROKESLEY' and replace by 'whose parentage is unknown'
line 14, delete '(1385) 9 Ric.II' and replace by '(1384) 9 Ric. II at Wallingford, pr. 21 Mar. 1385/6'
note (b), line 7, for 'Advincla' read 'Advincula'

BARFLEUR

page 421,
line 12, for 'Oxford' read 'Orford'

BARGANY

page 421,
line 15, after 'by' add 'his 2nd wife'
line 16, after 'Jean' add '(*m.*, 1596)'
page 422,
line 7, for 'Elliott' read 'Alyth'
line 19, for 'in 1662' read '(cont. 23 Aug. 1662)'
line 22, for '1676' read 'Sep. 1677'

page 423,
line 1, after '1stly' add 'about 1694'

BARHAM

page 423,
line 21, for 'and' read 'in'

BARNARD

page 427,
line 9, after 'She' add ', who' and after '1861' add ', *d.* of bronchial pneumonia, 14, and was *bur.* 18 Mar. 1918 in Staindrop Church. He *d.* at Raby Castle, 28, and was *bur.* 31 Dec. 1918 at Staindrop.'
lines 16–17, delete all detail and replace as follows

[HENRY CECIL VANE, 1st s. and h. ap., *b.* 19 Sep. 1882; ed. at Eton 1895–1900, and Oxford (Ch. Ch.); A.D.C. to Governor of Madras, 1903–7. He *m.*, 25 Aug. 1914, Enid Victoria Rachel, da. of Anthony Mildmay Julian (FANE), 13th EARL OF WESTMORLAND. Major, Yorks. Hussars, he fought in WW1, and *d. v.p. s.p.* 9 Oct. 1917. His widow *m.* 2ndly, 1 Sep. 1922, Major Herbert Broke TURNOR, M.C., and *d.* 9 Sep. 1969.]

X. 1918. 10. CHRISTOPHER WILLIAM (VANE), BARON BARNARD OF BARNARD'S CASTLE, 2nd but 1st surv. s. and h., *b.* 28 Oct. 1888; ed. at Eton and Cambridge (Trin. Coll.). He *m.*, 14 Oct. 1920, Sylvia Mary, only da. of Herbert STRAKER of Hartforth Grange, Richmond, Yorks. He *d.* 19 Oct. 1964. His widow *d.* 1993.

XI. 1964. 11. HARRY JOHN NEVILLE (VANE), BARON BARNARD OF BARNARD'S CASTLE, 1st s. and h., *b.* 21 Sep. 1923; ed. at Eton and Durham Univ. He *m.*, 8 Oct. 1952, Lady Davina Mary, eldest da. of David George Brownlow (CECIL), 6th MARQUESS OF EXETER. This marriage was diss. by divorce in 1992.

[HENRY FRANCIS CECIL VANE, s. and h. ap., *b.* 11 Mar. 1959; ed. at Eton and Edinburgh Univ.]

BARRETT

page 431,
line 2, in margin, for '[I.]' read '[S.]'

BARRINGTON

page 433,
note (b), lines 12–13, delete from 'See' to 'volume'

page 434,
lines 25–6, delete from 'Isabella' to 'Seymour' and replace by 'Maria Susannah, da. and coh. of John SIMPSON, of Bradley Hall, co. Durham' [*Ex inform.* Michael Maclagan]
line 31, after 'Midx.' add 'Ed. at Eton *circa* 1837–41.'
note (a), line 1, after 'He' add 'was s. of the Rev. Robert Morritt, by Alice his wife, and'

BARRINGTON OF ARDGLASS and BARRINGTON OF NEWCASTLE

page 435,
lines 16–17, delete from 'He' to 'work.'

IX. 1901. 9. WALTER BULKELEY (BARRINGTON), VISCOUNT BARRINGTON OF ARDGLASS, &c., s. and h., *b.* 20 Apr. 1848; ed. at Eton 1857–63. He *m.* 1stly, 26 Apr. 1870, Mary Isabella, 2nd da. of Rev Richard BOGUE, Vicar of Denbury, Devon. She *d.* 16 Nov. 1903. He *m.* 2ndly, 19 Jan. 1905, Charlotte Mary Leycester, elder da. of Major George Montagu STOPFORD, and widow of John Arden BIRCH. He *d.* 12 Sep. and was *bur.* 15 Sep. 1933 at Shrivenham, Berks. His widow *d.* 22 and was *bur.* 25 Oct. 1935 at Shrivenham afsd.

X. 1933. 10. WILLIAM REGINALD SHUTE (BARRINGTON), VISCOUNT BARRINGTON OF ARDGLASS, &c., 1st s. and h., *b.* 23 July 1873; ed. at Cambridge (Trin. Hall). He *d.* unm. 4 Oct. 1960.

XI. 1960. 11. PATRICK WILLIAM DAINES (BARRINGTON). VISCOUNT BARRINGTON OF ARDGLASS and BARON BARRINGTON OF NEWCASTLE [I. 1720], also

BARON SHUTE OF BECKET [U.K. 1880], nephew and h., being s. and h. of Walter Bernard Louis BARRINGTON (*d.* 12 May 1959), by Eleanor Nina, da. of Sir Thomas William SNAGGE, which Walter was 2nd s. of the 9th Viscount. He was *b.* 29 Oct. 1908; ed. at Eton and Oxford (Magdalen Coll.). He *d.* unm. 6 Apr. 1990, when his titles became *extinct*.

BARROGILL

page 435,
line 24, for '1886' read '1866'

BARRY

page 444,
line 5, after 'wife' add 'lic. Cloyne, 1703'
line 7, after '84' add 'She was living, 16 Dec. 1709'

page 446,
note (a), line 6, delete from 'See' to 'work'

BASING OF BASING BYFLEET AND OF HODDINGTON

page 450,
line 21, for '1862' read '1882'
line 25, after '1904.' add 'He *d.* at Hoddington House afsd., 8, and was *bur.* 12 Apr. 1919 at Upton Grey.'
line 26, delete and replace as follows

III. 1919. 3. JOHN LIMBREY ROBERT (SCLATER-BOOTH), BARON BASING OF BASING BYFLEET AND OF HODDINGTON [1887], s. and h., *b.* 3 Dec. 1890; ed. at Eton and R.M.C., Sandhurst. He *m.*, 27 Feb. 1924, at Holy Trinity, Brompton, Mary Alice Erle, yr. da. of Lieut. Col. Richard Erle BENSON. He *d. s.p.m.* 2 Oct. 1969. His widow *d.* 1970.

IV. 1969. 4. GEORGE LUTLEY (SCLATER-BOOTH), BARON BASING OF BASING BYFLEET AND OF HODDINGTON [1887], cousin and h., being s. of Charles Lutley SCLATER-BOOTH (*d.* 23 Jan. 1931), by Ellen Geraldine, yst. da. of George JONES of Mitton Manor, Staffs. and widow of William Tudor FRERE, which Charles Lutley Sclater-Booth was 2nd s. of 1st Baron. He was *b.* 7 Dec. 1903; ed. at Winchester. He *m.* 1stly, 16 Mar. 1938, Jeannette, da. of Neil Bruce MACKELVIE of New York. This marriage was diss. by divorce in 1944 and she *d.* 17 Nov. 1957. He *m.* 2ndly, 18 July 1951, Cynthia, da. of Charles W. HARDY of Salt Lake City, Utah, U.S.A. and widow of Carl H. BEAL of Los Angeles, California, U.S.A. She *d.* 1982. He *d.* 18 Sep. 1983.

V. 1983. 5. NEIL LUTLEY (SCLATER-BOOTH), BARON BASING OF BASING BYFLEET AND OF HODDINGTON [1887], s. and h., *b.* 16 Jan. 1939; ed. at Eton and Harvard Univ. He *m.*, 16 Sep. 1967, Patricia Ann, da. of George Bryan WHITFIELD of New Haven, Conn., U.S.A.

[STUART ANTHONY WHITFIELD SCLATER-BOOTH, s. and h. ap., *b.* 18 Dec. 1969; ed. at The Collegiate Sch.]

APPENDIXES

APPENDIX A

page 459,
line 39, add at end 'It may be mentioned in this connection that there is some evidence that in 1484/5 the Earl of Nottingham, afterwards Marquess of Berkeley, was assuming the title of Viscount Carlow, or Catherlough [I.]. See note *sub* Berkeley [1463], vol. ii, p. 134, note (b)'

APPENDIX D

page 473,
line 29, after 'Maynard' add '(8a). In Apr. 1640 Henry Frederick Howard, *styled* Lord Mautravers, s. and h. ap. of the Earl of Arundel, afterwards (1644), Earl of Norfolk, was sum. by writ, in what was erroneously considered to have been his father's Barony, as Lord Mowbray, being on the 16th placed at the upper end of the Baron's bench (that is, allowed the precedence of that ancient Barony). As he was not the coheir to that Barony, the writ cannot have determined the *abeyance* in that dignity and operated to create a new Barony. See vol. ix, *sub* MOWBRAY [1640] and NORFOLK [1646].'

after line 47 add

(10) In 1680 the issue of William, 1st s. of 2nd BARON WILLOUGHBY OF PARHAM became *extinct* and the Barony devolved *de jure* on the issue of Ambrose, the 2nd son. However, it was erroneously supposed to have devolved onto the descendants of Thomas, the 5th son, who was therefore summoned by writ, taking his seat 21 Oct. 1680. This thereby created a Barony by writ, accorded the precedence of the original (1546/7) which descended to his son and to Hugh Willoughby, who died unm. 21 Jan. 1765 when the Barony then fell into *abeyance* between his two sisters and coheirs. See below, *sub* Willoughby of Parham.

APPENDIX E

page 477,
lines 1–2, for '10 July 1854' read '13 Aug. 1857'

APPENDIX F

page 480,
line 7, for 'May' read 'Apr.'
line 36, for 'Liddal' read 'Liddall' and for 'Amounderness' read 'Amoundernesse'

page 482,
insert between lines 14 and 15 '1689/90. 10 Mar. James (DRUMMOND), Earl of Perth [S.], *cr.* BARON CONCRAIG, VISCOUNT BARGILL, EARL OF STOBHALL, MARQUESS OF DRUMMOND and DUKE OF PERTH [S.]. He did not assume this title until 24 Sep. 1701. His s. and h. ap. was *attainted*, *v.p.* in 1716. Issue male of the grantee *extinct* 1760.'

note (d), line 4, for '1689' read '1692'

page 483,
lines 8–9, delete all detail. The Barony of Ballyhigue, which it was supposed might have been created by James II when in exile, was in fact a French creation of Louis Philippe on 18 Nov. 1839.
line 16, for '4' read '5' and after 'Powis [E.]' add 'Perth [S.]'
line 21, for '5' read '8'
line 23, delete 'Ballyhigue [I.]'
line 24, for '21 or 25' read '23 or 26' and after 'Powis' add 'Perth'
line 34, delete all detail
note ([b]), delete all detail

page 484,
lines 1–3, delete all detail

page 485,
line 16, for 'Middelton' (twice) read 'Middleton'. This creation was probably made at an earlier date by James II but Lord Middleton did not assume his new title until 24 Sep. 1701. See vol. x, note *sub* PERTH [1675].
line 18, after '*cr.*' add 'Viscount Clermount and' and for '*s.p.m.s.*' read 'unm.'
insert between lines 33 and 34 '1718. Archibald (Campbell), Earl of Islay [S.], afterwards Duke of Argyll [S.]. A warrant, dat. 10 Mar. 1717/8 for creating him an Earl [E.] is preserved among the Stuart Papers' [*Hist. MSS. Com.*, Stuart MSS., vol. vi, pp. 132–3]

page 487,
lines 10–11, delete from 'between' to 'Mar.'. This creation was probably was probably made at an earlier date by James II but Caryll did not assume his title until 24 Sep. 1701. See vol. x, note *sub* PERTH [1675].
line 21, for '28 Sep.' read '9 Dec.'
line 29, after '1717' add 'with rem. to James Oglethorpe, his br., and the heirs male of his body.'

page 488,
line 3, for '[__]' read 'Matthew'

APPENDIX G

page 490,
no. 2, delete all detail. Despite the Report of the Committee for Privileges in 1928, there is no evidence that the Countess of Salisbury was considered *temp.* Henry VIII, to hold any Barony of Montagu. Her son Henry Pole was probably *cr.* Lord Montagu *circa* 1514, shortly after his mother's restoration to the Earldom of Salisbury (only), and he was presumably sum. in that Barony in 1529. See vol. viii, *sub* MONTAGU [*circa* 1514], and Apps B and E in that vol.

no. 3, delete all detail. The Earl of Wiltshire and Ormond had been *cr.* Viscount Rochford but held no Barony of that name. His s. George Boleyn was a Baron, as Lord Rochford, before 15 July 1530 and was presumably sum. in that Barony in 1532/3. See those titles and vol. ix, Appendix B, p. 18.

no. 4, for 'Jan. 1533/4' read '5 Feb. 1532/3'

no. 5, for 'Jan. 1533/4' read '17 Feb. 1532/3'

no. 6, for 'Mar.' read '5 Jan.'

no. 7, for 'Mar.' read '5 Jan.'

no. 8, for 'Mar.' read '5 Jan.'

note (d), delete all detail
note (e), delete all detail. Round has confused the (non-existent) Barony of Rochford with that of Ormond, to which the Earl of Wiltshire and Ormond was coh.

page 491,
no. 15, for 'Feb.' read '28 Jan.'

no. 16, for 'Feb.' read '5 Jan.'

no. 17, for 'Feb.' read '31 Jan.'

no. 18, for 'Feb.' read '31 Jan.'

notes (a) to (c), for Dugdale's lists of Summonses, see vol. ii, pp. v–vi.
note (c), lines 3–5, delete from 'must' to 'Essex' and replace by '*d.* 12 June 1585'. See, however, vol. ix, Appendix B, p. 11.

page 492,
no. 27, for 'Feb.' read '7 Mar.'
[This was really a new Barony, but he was allowed the precedency of 1299, on the assumption that the ancient Barony of Strange (of Knokyn) was vested in his father.]

no. 28, for 'Feb.' read '21 Mar.'

no. 31, delete 'D'ERESBY' and for 'Oct.' read '3 Nov.'

no. 33, for 'Oct.' read '3 Nov.'

no. 34, for 'HUNDSON' read 'HUNSDON'
no. 38, for 'May 1641' read '1640–1'.
[The date of the writ is not known but he took his seat 14 May 1641.]

no. 39, for 'June 1641' read '3 Nov. 1640'

no. 40, for 'Mar. 1678/9' read '14 Jan. 1677/8'

Between nos 40 and 41 insert '40a. ROBERT LEKE, s. and h. ap. of Nicholas, Earl of Scarsdale, sum. as LORD DEINCOURT, 22 Oct. 1680'

no. 41, for 'Mar. 1679/80' read '1 Nov. 1680'

page 495,
no. 92, for 'AMSHERST' read 'AMHERST'

VOLUME 2

page ii,
line 10, for '*a.*' read '*b.*'

BASSETT (of Drayton)

page 1,
note (b), line 3, for '1144' read 'between 16 Sep. 1144 and 29 May 1147' [W.T. Reedy, *Bassett Charters, 1120–1250*, Pipe Roll Soc., N.S., vol. 50, 1995, p. xxxii. p. 26]

page 3,
line 3, for '1353, before 5 Apr.' read 'on the Wed. or Sat. before Palm Sunday (i.e. 13 or 16 Mar.) 1353. Writ for *Inq. p.m.* 1 Apr. (1353), 27 Edw. III. [*Cal. Inq. p.m.*, vol. x, no. 92]

BASSETT (of Sapcote)

page 6,
line 10, for '(__)' read 'Elizabeth de Colville' [Reedy, *op. cit.*, p. xxxvii]

BASSETT

page 7,
line 6, delete '[LORD COLVILLE]'

BASSETT (of Weldon)

page 9,
note (d), line 1, after 'etc.' add '*m.* Beatrice and'

BATEMAN OF SHOBDON

page 15,
line 16, delete 'was living 1910' and replace by '*d.* 1918'
line 17, line to read as follows

III. 1901. 3. WILLIAM BATEMAN (SPENCER-HANBURY), BARON BATEMAN, s. and h., *b.* 30 Sep. 1856; ed.'

lines 20–1, delete from 'Having' to 'work.]' and replace by 'He *d. s.p.* 4 Nov. 1931 when his title became *extinct*.

BATH

page 16,
line 7, for '12' read '18'
lines 7–8, delete from 'became' to '1491' and replace by 'had special livery of his father's lands, without proof of age, 29 Mar. 1491. See FITZWARIN'
line 8, for '1492' read '1491', and after '1536' add 'by writs directed *Johanni Bourchier de FitzWaren*'
line 23, for 'in 1542' read '22 Sep. 1545'

page 17,
line 4, after '2ndly' add 'before 25 May 1524' [*L. and P. Hen. VIII*, vol. iv, part 1, p. 154]
line 22, for '1556' read '1556/7'
line 34, after '1587' add 'till after 1614'

page 19,
line 15, for '1644' read '1643/4'
line 26, after 'creation' add 'From him she obtained a separation by a decree of the Court of Arches, 13 June 1661, on account of his cruelty and desertion. See MIDDLESEX.'
note (b), lines 3–5, delete from 'the' to '(See' and replace by 'this very early example of someone bearing more than one Christian name may be surpassed by one Robert Browne Trappes, s. of Robert Trappes, citizen and mercer of London, by Dorothy Browne. Robert Trappes probably died before Nov. 1576 (will dat. 29 Oct. 1576 and pr. 21 Mar. 1576/7, PCC Doughty). Robert B.T. is mentioned in the will of his aunt, dat. 20 Feb. 1586/7, PCC Spencer. (See also' [*Ex inform.* Robert Browne]

page 20,
note (c), line 8, after '193' add 'See Round, *Family Origins*, pp. 130–69, for exposure of this concocted descent.'

page 21,
line 27, after '2ndly' add '(cont. 1690)(f)'
note (f), For particulars of the marriage articles see *Hist. MSS. Com.*, House of Lords MSS., N.S., vol. vi, pp. 249–50.

page 26,
line 31, delete 'was living 1910' and replace by '*d.* 31 Oct. 1915.'

page 27,
line 5, after '[S.]' add 'She, who was *b.* 28 Feb. 1869, at Walton Hall, co. Lancs., *d.* 29 May, and was *bur.* at Longbridge Deverill, Warminster, Wilts., 2 June 1928. He *d.* 9 June 1946.'
line 6, after 'WEYMOUTH' add '1896–1916'
line 7, after '1895.' add '2nd Lieut. Royal Scots Greys, *d.* unm. and *v.p.*, being *k.* in action, while serving with the 2nd Dragoons (R. Scots Greys), 13 Feb. 1916.'

VI. 1946. 6. HENRY FREDERICK (THYNNE), MARQUESS OF BATH, &c., 2nd but only surv. s. and h., *b.* 26 Jan. 1905; *m.* 1stly, 27 Oct. 1927, Daphne Winifred Louise Vivian, 1st da. of George Crespigny Brabazon (VIVIAN), 4th BARON VIVIAN. This marriage was diss. by divorce in 1953 (she *m.* 2ndly, 1953, Major Alexander Wallace FIELDING; they were div. in 1978 and he *d.* 1991; she was still living 1995), and he *m.* 2ndly, 15 July 1953, Virginia Penelope, da. of Alan Leonard Romaine PARSONS of Broxbourne, co. Hertford and formerly wife of David Pax TENNANT. He *d.* 30 June 1992. His widow was still living 1995.

VII. 1992. 7. ALEXANDER GEORGE (THYNNE), MARQUESS OF BATH, &c., 2nd but 1st surv. s. and h., *b.* 6 May 1932; ed. at Eton and Oxford (Ch. Ch.); *m.*, 9 May 1969, Anna, da. of Laszlo Izsak GYARMATHY of Los Angeles, California, U.S.A.

[CEAWLIN HENRY LASZLO THYNNE, *styled* VISCOUNT WEYMOUTH, s. and h. ap., *b.* 6 June 1974; ed. at Kingsdown Comp. Sch., Bedales, Cambridge Coll., Richmond Univ., Virginia, U.S.A. and Univ. Coll., London.]

BATHURST OF BATTLESDEN, and BATHURST OF BATHURST

page 30,
line 21, delete '1834' and replace by 'till his death'

page 31,
line 2, for '1823–34' read 'Jan. 1828 to Nov. 1830'

page 32,
line 16, after '£238,149.' add 'His widow *d.* 1, and was *bur.* at Cirencester, 5 Mar. 1927.'
line 21, after 'Eton' add 'and Oxford (Ch. Ch.)'
line 23, after 'LISTER.' add 'He *d.* 21 Sep. 1943. His widow, who was *b.* 12 Oct. 1871, *d.* 30 Dec. 1965.'
lines 17–18, delete all detail and replace as follows

[ALLEN ALGERNON BATHURST, 1st s. and h. ap., *b.* 3 Aug. 1895; *styled* LORD APSLEY; ed. at Eton; *m.*, 28 Feb. 1924, at St. Paul's Knightsbridge, Viola Emily Mildred, 1st da. of Capt. Bertram Charles Christopher MEEKING of Richings Park, co. Buckingham by Viola, 1st da. of John FLETCHER of Saltoun. He was *k.* on active service in Malta, *v.p.*, 17 Dec. 1942. His widow *d.* 20 Jan. 1966.]

VIII. 1943. 8. HENRY ALLEN JOHN (BATHURST), EARL BATHURST [1772], &c., grandson and h., being 1st s. of Allen Algernon BATHURST and Viola Emily Mildred abovenamed. He was *b.* 1 May 1927; ed. at Eton, Ridley Coll., Canada and Oxford (Ch. Ch.); *m.*, 20 Mar. 1959, Judith Mary, only da. of Amos Christopher NELSON of Colne, co. Lancaster. This marriage was diss. by divorce in 1976 and he *m.* 2ndly, 1978, Gloria Wesley, only da. of Harold Edward

CLARRY of Vancouver, British Columbia, Canada and widow of David RUTHERSTON.

[ALLEN CHRISTOPHER BERTRAM BATHURST, *styled* LORD APSLEY, 1st s. and h. ap. by 1st wife, *b.* 11 Mar. 1961; *m.*, 1986, Hilary Jane, yr. da. of John F. GEORGE of Albury, Surrey.]

BATTERSEA OF BATTERSEA AND OVERSTRAND

page 33,
line 8, delete 'living 1909' and replace by '*d.* 22 Nov. 1931, at Overstrand.'

BAVENT

page 34,
line 10, after 'Hawise' add 'da. of William (DE MONTAGU), 2nd LORD MONTAGU, by Elizabeth, da. of Sir Piers DE MONTFORT, of Beaudesert, co. Warwick[aa]'

note [aa] See vol. ix, p. 82, note [f], *sub* MONTAGU [1316]. In the *Close Rolls*, under date 13 Feb. 1371/2 (*Cal. Close Rolls, 1369–74*, pp. 431–2), there is a sworn statement of one William Stile, to the effect that this Hawise had owned to forging two seals bearing the arms of her husband and affixing them to documents purporting to entail certain manors on her. Stile further states that she had consented that her son John should become a Friar Minor, and that this John had gone to France and received the order of knighthood and had told Stile that he thought not ever to come to England, but to go to Assisi and take orders as he was bound to do. It does not appear from the above whether Hawise and John were then alive. V.G.

BAYNING

page 37,
line 37, for '1624' read '1634' and for 'Herts' read 'Suffolk'

BEACONSFIELD

page 38,
line 19, delete from 'is' to '1789' and replace by 'was *b.* presumably in Exeter, 11, and *bap.* 14 Nov. 1792 at St. Sidwell's there' [John McLeod, *Geneal. Mag.*, vol. 24, 1993, p. 345.]

page 40,
line 1, for 'Feb. 1874' read 'Mar. 1874'
line 13, for 'Carmanton' read 'Carnanton'

BEAUCHAMP

page 43,
line 25, for 'living 1909' read '*d.* at Sunningdale, 11 May 1935.'

page 44,
line 4, after 'She' add ', who'
line 5, after 'Chester' add ', *d.* 28, and was *bur.* 31 July 1936 at Eccleston, near Chester. He *d.* 15 Nov. 1938.'
lines 6–7, delete and replace as follows

VIII. 1938. 8. WILLIAM (LYGON), EARL BEAUCHAMP, [1815], VISCOUNT ELMLEY, BARON BEAUCHAMP OF POWYK, 1st s. and h., *b.* 3 July 1903 at Madresfield. *Styled* VISCOUNT ELMLEY till 1938. He was ed. at Eton and Oxford (Magdalen Coll.); *m.*, 16 June 1936, Else, da. of Viggo SCHIWE and widow of Direktor C.P. DORNONVILLE DE LA COUR of Copenhagen. He *d. s.p.* 3 Jan. 1979 when all his titles became *extinct.*

BEAUCHAMP (of Bletsoe)

page 44,
line 34, for 'living 26 Oct. 1351' read 'aged 20 and more at her father's death, 27 Sep. 1359'

page 45,
line 2, after 'Blackfriars' add (aa)
note (aa) *Test. Vet.*, pp. 103–4. This will shows that his grandfather was Sir Walter Beauchamp.
line 3, after 'B' add 'by his 1st wife (__)(ax)
note (ax) Roger Beauchamp *m.* 2ndly, Joan, da. and h. of Sir Walter Clopton, widow of Sir Walter Walcot of Gunton, Norfolk (*Hist. Parl, 1386–1421*, vol. ii, p. 154). Joan cannot have been mother of his h., who was *b.* in 1362, since Sir Walter did not die until 1366 (Rye, *Norfolk Families*, 1911, p. 971)
line 4, after '*d. v.p.*' add '1373/4' [his wife was granted letters of admin., 15 May 1374, Harl. Soc., *Visit. Suffolk, 1561*, N.S., vol. 2, p. 23]
line 5, after 'was' add '*b.* at Bletsoe, *bap.* 14 Aug. 1362, and was'
line 6, for '1374' read '1384'
line 8, for 'a knight' read 'knighted by 18 Feb. 1393'
line 8, after 'Ireland' add 'in 1399, M.P. for Beds.'
line 9, delete all detail and replace by 'He *m.* Mary (__). He *d.* 13 May 1406, will dat. 1406, PCC 11 March.'
line 13, for 'about 1412' read 'Apr. 1412. Will dat. 21 Feb. 1412, pr. 10 Dec. 1414' [*Test. Vet.*, p. 178]
line 16, after 'unm.' '1420' [V.C.H., *Wiltshire*, vol. 9, p. 79]

BEAUCHAMP OF POWICK

page 47

note ([a]), line 1, after 'page' add 'He had already been sum. to Parl., 3 Mar. 1446/7, the day Parl. was dissolved.'

BEAUCHAMP (of Somerset)

page 50,

note ([a]), line 9, for '1383' read '14 Sep. 1368' [*Cal. Close Rolls, 1369–74*, p. 331]

line 20, after 'daughters' add 'Col. Ulric Oliver Thynne claimed the Barony of Beauchamp of Somerset in 1924, as one of the coh. of the 12th Duke of Somerset. His petition was rejected by the Committee for Privileges, 29 July 1924, on the grounds that there was no proof that either John Beauchamp (*d.* 1336) or his s. (from whom Col. Thynne descended) could be shown to have actually sat following their writs of summons, see *Barony of Beauchamp*, 1925 (HL 189), pp. 145–52.'

BEAUCHAMP (of Warwick)

page 50,

line 12, for '1344' read '1348'

page 51,

between lines 6 and 7 add

BEAUCLAIRE

In the Royal Warrant assigning arms to Charles Beauclerk, then Earl of Burford, afterwards 1st Duke of St. Albans, 17 Jan. 1676/7, the King declares his pleasure to give to James, yr. br. of the said Charles, the "Title and Appellation of LORD BEAUCLAIRE", with the place and precedence of the eldest son of an Earl, but no patent for this creation appears to have passed the Great Seal. See SAINT ALBANS.

line 8, for '1550' read '1549'

BEAUFORT

page 51,

lines 11–15, delete from 'is' to 'related' and replace by 'was promised, or granted, shortly before 10 Jan. 1644/5, privately, by Charles I, the Earldom of Glamorgan. Though a bill to this effect, according to which he was to be *cr.* BARON BEAUFORT, of Caldicot Castle, co. Monmouth, and EARL OF GLAMORGAN, reached the Signet Office early in 1645, no patent passed the Great Seal before 31 Jan. 1645/6, and the creation must be regarded as incomplete. See WORCESTER, Marquessate, under which title the circumstances of the case are fully related.'

page 53,
line 7, after '16)' add 'in the chapel of the manor house'
line 15, after 'Will' add 'dat. 7 July 1711'
line 29, for '1638' read '1688'
line 30, after 'Badminton' add 'M.I.'
line 36, after 'Badminton' add 'M.I.'
line 37, after '1711' add 'in the Duke of Leeds Chapel'

page 54,
line 8, after 'Will' add 'dat. 3 Feb. 1721/2'
line 22, delete from 'Will' to '1745' and replace by 'M.I. Will dat. 7 June 1744, pr. 8 Mar. 1744/5'

page 55,
line 4, for 'Will pr.' read 'M.I. Will dat. 20 Aug. 1750 to 27 May 1754, pr. 30.'
line 5, for 'pr.' read 'dat. 11 May 1785 to 25 June 1795, pr. 30'
line 20, for 'pr.' read 'dat. 21 June 1789 to 11 Sep. 1800, pr. 2'

page 56,
line 4, for 'Hall' read 'Hay'

page 57,
line 1, after 'widow' add ', who was *b.* 3 Mar. 1800,'
line 23, after '1847.' add 'Ed. at Eton 1860–4.'
line 30, after '1864.' add 'He *d.* at Badminton, 24, and was *bur.* there, 30 Nov. 1924. He took no active part in politics, nor indeed in any public life, outside his own county. Will pr. Feb. 1925 gross £541,843, net £169,763. His widow *d.* 11 Oct. 1945.'
lines 31–2, delete all detail and replace as follows

X. 1924. 10. HENRY HUGH FITZROY (SOMERSET), DUKE OF BEAUFORT, &c., s. and h., *b.* 4 Apr. 1900. *Styled* from birth MARQUESS OF WORCESTER; ed. at Eton and R.M.C., Sandhurst; *m.* at St. Margaret's, Westm., 14 June 1923, Victoria Constance Mary, 1st da. of Adolphus Charles, 1st MARQUESS OF CAMBRIDGE. He *d. s.p.* 5 Feb. 1984 when the Baronies of Botetourt [E. 1305] and Herbert [E. 1461] fell into *abeyance* between the descendants of his sister Blanche Linnie, and he was *suc.* in his other titles by his distant cousin. His widow *d.* 1987.

XI. 1984. 11. DAVID ROBERT (SOMERSET), DUKE OF BEAUFORT, MARQUESS OF WORCESTER [1642], EARL OF WORCESTER [1514], BARON HERBERT OF RAGLAND, CHEPSTOW AND GOWER [1506], distant cousin and h. being 2nd but 1st surv. s. and h. of Henry Robert Somers FitzRoy de Vere SOMERSET (*d.* 27 Feb. 1965), by Bettine Violet, 2nd. da. of Major Charles Edward MALCOLM, which Henry Robert was 1st s. of Henry Charles Somers Augustus Somerset (*d.* 25 Nov. 1945), by Katherine, da. of William Ameleus Aubrey de Vere (BEAUCLERK), 10th DUKE OF ST. ALBANS, which Henry Charles was only s. and h. of Henry Richard Charles SOMERSET (*d.* 10 Oct. 1932), by Isabelle Caroline, da. and coh. of Charles Somers (COCKS), 3rd EARL SOMERS, which Henry Richard was 2nd s. of the 8th Duke of Beaufort. He was *b.* 23 Feb. 1928; ed. at Eton; *m.*,

5 July 1950, Caroline Jane, only da. of Henry Frederick (THYNNE), 6th MARQUESS OF BATH.

[HENRY JOHN FITZROY SOMERSET, *styled* MARQUESS OF WORCESTER from 1984, 1st s. and h. ap.; *b.* 22 May 1952; ed. at Eton; *m.*, 1987, Tracy Louise, yr. da. of Peter Alistair WARD.]

BEAULIEU

page 58,
lines 24–5, delete from 'Her' to 'husband' and replace by 'She'
line 25, after 'Midx.' add 'and was *bur.* 28 Dec. at Warkton, Northants'
line 26, for '2' read '14' and for 'Beaulieu' read 'Warkton afsd.'

page 59,
line 3, after '1787' add 'and was *bur.* 10 July at Warkton, afsd.'
lines 6–7, for '*Montagu Douglas Scott*' and '*Douglas Scott Montagu*' read '*Montagu-Douglas-Scott*' and *Douglas-Scott-Montagu*'
note ([b]), line 1, for 'iv' read 'xii'

BEAUMONT

page 60,
line 7, after '(1305)' add '(yr. s. of Alexander, 6th EARL OF BUCHAN [S.])'
line 15, after 'at' add 'Bannockburn, 24 June 1314, and'

page 61,
lines 12–16, delete all detail and replace by 'Margaret, da. of John (DE VERE), 7th EARL OF OXFORD, by Maud, sister and coh. of Giles (DE BADLESMERE), 2nd LORD BADLESMERE, da. of Bartholomew, 1st LORD BADLESMERE. He *d.* 25 July 1369 [*Inq. p.m.*, vol. 12, no. 321] and was *bur* in Sempringham Priory, co. Lincoln. His widow *m.*, as his 2nd wife, Sir Nicholas LOVAIN, of Penshurst, Kent, who *d. s.p.m.* in 1375. Will dat. at Poplar, 20 Sep. 1375, pr. at Southwark, 25 Nov. follg. She *m.* 3rdly, John (DEVEREUX), 1st LORD DEVEREUX, who *d.* 22 Feb. 1392/3 and was *bur.* in the Church of the Grey Friars, London. She *d.* 15 June 1398 and was *bur.* with him. See DEVEREUX.'

page 62,
line 9, after 'BEAUMONT' add '([ca])'
note ([ca]), He was one of a group of 4 sons-in-law, 5 sons and 4 grandsons of Ralph, 1st Earl of Westmorland, who all sat together in the House of Lords. For similar cases see note *sub* BOYLE OF KINALMEAKY. V.G.

page 64,
line 1, after 'wife' add 'between 28 Nov. 1508 and 10 Apr. 1509'
line 3, after '1537' add 'pr. 6 Nov. follg.'

page 66,
line 5, after '49' add 'and was *bur.* in the family vault in Carlton parish church.'
line 6, delete from 'is' to 'York.' and replace by 'who became a Roman Catholic in 1872, *d.* 16, and was *bur.* 18 Mar. 1916, with her husband.'
line 8, after 'Midx.' add '; ed. at Eton 1862–3.'
line 17, delete 'living 1910' and replace by '*d.* 16 Mar. 1910.'
line 32, for 'living 1910' read ', who was *b.* 8 Oct. 1864, at Bosworth Hall, Rugby, *d.* 19, and was *bur.* 22 Jan. 1937 at Carleton, Yorks.'
line 36, after '[1432]' add 'She *m.*, 5 Sep. 1914, Bernard Edward (FITZALAN-HOWARD), 3rd BARON HOWARD OF GLOSSOP. See that title.'

XII. 1971. 12. MILES FRANCIS (FITZALAN-HOWARD), LORD BEAUMONT, s. and h., *b.* 21 July 1915. *Suc.* his father as Lord Howard of Glossop, 1972 and his distant cousin as Duke of Norfolk, 1975. See *sub* NORFOLK.

BECKETT

page 68,
line 14, for 'CHUTE OF BECKETT' read 'SHUTE, of Beckett'

BEDFORD

page 68,
line 27, delete from 'BEAUMONT' to '*Pauper*' and replace by 'MEULAN, *styled* also "le Pauvre"'
line 28, for 'Normandy' read 'France, and 1st EARL OF LEICESTER'

page 69,
line 1, after 'and' add 'is alleged to have been'
line 8, after 'ENGUERRAND DE COUCY' add '*de jure* 4th LORD GYNES'
note (a), after 'D' add 'It is very doubtful if Hugh was ever *cr.* Earl of Bedford. See G.H. White, *Trans.* R.H.S., 4th ser., vol. xiii, pp. 77–82. The recent (1955) edition of the *Gesta Stephani* (Medieval Texts) does not throw any light on the question.'

page 70,
lines 2–3, delete from 'this' to '1379' and replace by 'She *d.* 5 Oct. 1382. See GYNES.'

page 71,
line 12, after 'England' add '"from the time of his return to England (*i.e.* 1425) and as long as he should remain there." In his absence the office was to be held by Duke Humphrey.' [*Rot. Parl.*, vol. 4, pp. 174–5]
line 15, delete from 'Lord' to 'death'

page 72,
line 11, delete from '15 Sep.' to 'Repos', at' and replace by '*legit.* 14 Sep. 1435 in the castle

of' [See Charles de Beaurepaire, *Bibliothèque de l'Ecole des Chartes*, vol. 34, p. 343. Bedford is said to have been survived by his natural son. See RICHMOND.]

note (g), line 3, delete from 'note' to '[1692]' and replace by 'Vol. vii, Appendix G'

page 73,
between line 2 and 3 add

GEORGE OF WINDSOR, 3rd and yst. s. of King EDWARD IV, *b.* Mar. 1476/7 at Windsor, appears to have been *designated* (he was never so *cr.*) DUKE OF BEDFORD. He *d.* about two years later, *circa* Mar. 1479, and was *bur.* at Windsor.

line 11, for 'Elected' read 'Nom.'
line 30, after 'Spain' add 'She predeceased him(ee)'
note (ee) Sir Richard Wingfield's will, dat. 5 Apr. 1525, provides for obits. for Dame Katherine, Duchess of Bedford and Buckingham, his late wife (*Hist. MSS. Com.*, Cecil MSS., vol. xiii, p. 11).
note (d), delete all detail
note (f), line 4, after 'V.G.' add 'See also Gladys Scott Thomson, *Two Centuries of Family History*, 1930).

page 74,
line 26, for '1540' read '1539'
note (a), line 1, for 'that of' read 'those of Parr and'
line 2, for 'thereto' read 'to the latter'
line 3, add at end 'See note *sub* William, MARQUESS OF NORTHAMPTON, relating to his creation as Baron Parr.'

page 75,
line 18, for '1555, and again 16 July 1605' read '1556, admon. 16 July 1605' [*Ex inform.* R.M. Glencross]
line 27, for '1 Mar.' read '5 Jan.'

page 76,
line 26, after 'M.I.' add 'originally at Watford but removed in 1907 to Chenies'

page 78,
line 14, after 'only' add 'surv.'
line 17, after '*b.*' add '1587 or' and after '1593' add '(aa)'
note (aa) Although 1593 is the accepted date, a Francis, s. of Sir William Russell, was *bap.* 19 Oct. 1587 at Watford. *Cf. Cal. S. P. For.*, Apr.–Dec. 1587, p. 388. This can only refer to the future Earl or to an unrecorded elder br. of the same name, who must have *d.* an infant. The Earl's parents were married at Watford, 18 Feb. 1584/5, and no record of any Russell baptism appears in the Watford Par. Reg. for 1593.

page 79,
line 1, after '*d.*' add 'at her house at Chiswick'

page 81,
line 26, after 'pr.' add 'dat. 24 Feb. 1700/1. Admon. to his widow, 15'

page 87,
line 27, for 'living 1910' read '*d.* of heart failure following influenza at 33 Dover Sq., 12, and was *bur.* 17 Apr. 1920 at Chenies.'

page 88,
line 7, after '1888' add 'at Barrackpore, India'
lines 8–9, delete from '(__)' to 'G.C.B.' and replace by 'by Sophie, da. of Charles LANDER, Consul-Gen. at the Dardenelles (during the Crimean War) [*ex inform.* M.J. Beaver, of Eton Coll.]. She, who was *b.* 26 Sep. 1865, at Stockbridge, Hants., *d.* (presumably) 22 Mar. 1937, having left Woburn by aeroplane that day and was never seen again. He *d.* 27 Aug. 1940.'
lines 11–12, delete all detail and replace as follows

DUKEDOM. XIV. EARLDOM. XVIII. } 1940 — 12 and 16. HASTINGS WILLIAM SACKVILLE (RUSSELL), DUKE OF BEDFORD, &c., only s. and h., *b.* 21 Dec. 1888, *styled* MARQUESS OF TAVISTOCK from 1893. He was ed. at Oxford (Balliol Coll.); served in WW1 as private in the 10th Battn. Middlesex Regt. He *m.*, 21 Nov. 1914, Louisa Crommelin Roberta Jowitt, yr. da. of Robert Jowitt WHITWELL of Thornbury Lodge, Oxford. He *d.* 9 Oct. 1953. His widow *d.* 2 Oct. 1960.

DUKEDOM. XV. EARLDOM. XIX. } 1953 — 13 and 17. JOHN ROBERT (RUSSELL), DUKE OF BEDFORD, &c., 1st s. and h., *b.* 24 May 1917; *m.* 1stly, 6 Apr. 1939, Clare Gwendolyn, yst. da. of Ernest John BRIDGMAN and formerly wife of Major Kenneth Chamney Walpole HOLLWAY, M.C. She *d.* 1 Sep. 1945 and he *m.* 2ndly, 12 Feb. 1947, Lydia, 3rd da. of John Reginald Lopes (YARDE-BULLER), 3rd BARON CHURSTON and widow of Capt. Ian Archibald de Hoghton LYLE. This marriage was diss. by divorce in 1960 and he *m.* 3rdly, 4 Sep. 1960, Nicole Charlotte Pierette, da. of Paul SCHNEIDER of Neuilly, Seine, France and formerly wife of Henri MILINAIRE.

[HENRY ROBIN IAN RUSSELL, *styled* MARQUESS OF TAVISTOCK, 1st s. and h. ap. by 1st wife, was *b.* 21 Jan. 1940; ed. at Le Rosey and Harvard Univ.; *m.*, 20 June 1961, Henrietta Joan, only da. of Henry Frederic TIARKS of Marbella, Malaga, Spain.]

BEKE

page 89,
note ([d]), line 1, delete from 'apparently' to 'FitzJohn'
line 2, after '1287' add 'She was da. of John FitzMatthew, by Margaret, da. of Thomas de Berkeley, of Berkeley, co. Gloucester. See FITZJOHN (of Stokenham).'

BELASYSE OF WORLABY

page 90,
line 16, for 'Halstead' read 'Hawstead'

BELHAVEN AND STENTON

page 93,
line 17, delete from 'was' to '1666' and replace by '*d.* 1695/6'

page 94,
line 6, after 'Marion' add '(*m.* 17 Mar. 1652/3), da. of John'; after 'DENHOLM' add 'of Muirhouse'
line 6, for 'In 1696' read 'On 10 Nov. 1695'
line 23, after '*m.*' add '(cont. 5 Feb. 1696/7)'
line 24, after 'She' add '*d.* 17 Aug. and'
note ([b]), line 1, for '2nd' read '3rd'
line 2, after 'was' add '2nd'

page 95,
line 5, after 'John H., of Udston' add '*b.* 1567, *d.* before 1627'
line 11, after 's. and h.' add '*d. v.p.* 1616'
line 12, after '2nd s.' add '*d.* 1632'
line 14, after 'h.' add '*d.* before 1673'
line 17, after 'h.' add '*d. circa* 1689'
line 21, after 'h.' add 'living 1695'
lines 25–7, delete 'John H. of Udston, s. and h.' [*i.e.* John H. (living 1695) was father of Alexander.]
[Corrections to this pedigree were supplied by George Hamilton, of 46 London Wall.]

page 97,
line 29, delete 'was living 1910' and replace by 'who was *b.* 1 Mar. 1856, at 121 Wellington Str., Glasgow, *d.* 9 Nov. 1940.'

page 98,
line 7, after 'RICHMOND.' add 'He *d. s.p.s.* at Wishaw House, 31 Oct. 1920, and was *bur.* in Cambusnethan Cemetery, Lanarkshire. His widow *d.* 26, and was *bur.* at Cambusnethan afsd., 30 Sep. 1932.'
line 9, after '1883' add '; ed. at Eton 1897–9 and R.M.C., Sandhurst.'
line 13, after '1880.' add 'Fought in WW1, being *k.* in action, *v.p. s.p.*, 31 Mar. 1918. His widow *d.* 26 Sep. 1932.'

XI. 1920. 11. ROBERT EDWARD ARCHIBALD (HAMILTON later UDNY-HAMILTON), LORD BELHAVEN AND STENTON [S. 1647], nephew and h., being s. and h. of Archibald William HAMILTON (*d.* 5 Jan. 1886), by Elizabeth Anne, da. of W. BILLYARD of Sydney, N.S.W., which Archibald was 4th s. of William John abovementioned. He was *b.* 8 Apr. 1871; assumed name and arms of UDNEY, 1934, on *suc.* to the Udney estates. He *m.* 1stly, 15 Nov. 1898, Kathleen Gonville, da. of Col. Sir Benjamin Parnell BROMHEAD, Bart. She *d.* 1 Dec. 1935 and he *m.* 2ndly, 25 Mar. 1938, Sheila de Hautville, only da. of Major Algernon George PEARSON. He *d.* 26 Oct. 1950. His widow *d.* 20 Sep. 1962.

XII. 1950. 12. ROBERT ALEXANDER BENJAMIN (UDNY-HAMILTON, later HAMILTON), LORD BELHAVEN AND STENTON, only s. and h., *b.* 16 Sep.

1903; ed. Eton and R.M.C., Sandhurst; *m.* 1stly, 4 Feb. 1926, Heather Mildred Carmichael, da. of Lieut. Col. Richard Carmichael BELL, D.S.O. This marriage was diss. by divorce in 1941 (in the Scottish Courts, she *d.* 1992, having *m.* 2ndly.) and he *m.* 2ndly, 21 Mar. 1942, Cyrilla Mary, da. of Raymond Louis BINNS. He *d.* 10 July 1961. His widow *m.* 2ndly, 25 June 1969, Denis Beaumont VALE. He *d.* 10 July 1961. His widow was still living 1995.

XIII. 1961. 13. ROBERT ANTHONY CARMICHAEL (HAMILTON), LORD BELHAVEN AND STENTON, only s. and h., *b.* 27 Feb. 1927; ed. at Eton; *m.*, 27 Sep. 1952, Elizabeth Ann, da. of Col. Arthur Henry MOSELEY, D.S.O. of Warawee, New South Wales, Australia. This marriage was diss. by divorce in 1973 and he *m.* 2ndly, 1973, Rosemary, da. of Sir Herbert Geraint WILLIAMS, Bart., M.P., formerly wife of Sir Ian John Auld MACTAGGART, Bart. This marriage was in turn diss. by divorce in 1986 (she *d.* 1992) and he *m.* 3rdly, 1986, Malgorzata Maria, da. of Tadeusz Pobog HRUZIK-MAZURKIEWICZ of Krakow, Poland.

[FREDERICK CARMICHAEL ARTHUR HAMILTON, MASTER OF BELHAVEN, *b.* 27 Sep. 1953; ed. at Eton; *m.* 1stly, 1981, Elizabeth Anne, da. of S.V. TREDINNICK of Wisborough Green, Sussex. This marriage was diss. by divorce and he *m.* 2ndly, 1991, Philippa Martha Gausel (Mrs COLLINS), da. of Sir Rowland John Rathbone WHITEHEAD, Bart.]

BELLAMONT

page 98,
between lines 18 and 19 insert

BELLAMONT

See HAMILTON OF BELLAMONT, Barony (HAMILTON), a warrant for which issued 22 Jan. 1683/4.

BELLENDEN OF BROUGHTON

page 99,
line 20, for '1707' read 'shortly before 5 Nov. 1706 at his lodgings in Paterson's Land, near the Canongate foot, and was *bur.* in the Abbey Church.'
line 22, for '1707' read '1706'
note (b), line 1, before '"The' add '*Hist. MSS. Com.*, Laing MSS., part 2, p. 139.'

BELLEW

page 101,
line 2, after '(DE BELLA ACQUA)' add 'of Kirklington, Notts.'
lines 10–11, delete from 'Ladreina' to 'Cleveland' and replace by '1stly, Ladereyne, sister and coh. of Sir Piers DE BRUS III, of Skelton and Danby in Cleveland (who *d.* 18 Sep. 1272), 4th da. of Sir Piers DE BRUS II, of the same, by Hawise, sister and (in her

issue) coh. of William de Lancaster, Lord of Kendal (*d.* 29 Nov. 1246), 1st da. of Sir Gilbert FitzRoger FITZREINFRID, Lord of Kendal. She *d.* before 3 Dec. 1293. He *m.*, 2ndly, Isabel, by whom he had a s. and h., William, who surv. him.' See notes *sub* FAUCONBERGE [1295], FITZHENRY [1309] and LANCASTER (Barony). See also *Yorks. Deeds*, vol. 8, Yorks. Arch. Soc., 1940, p. 135

line 12, after 'co-heirs' add '(to the inheritance of his 1st wife)' and after 'Miles Stapleton' add '[2nd and 1st LORDS STAPLETON]'

lines 13–14, after 'FitzHenry' add '[1st LORD FITZHENRY]'

BELLEW OF BARMEATH

page 103,

line 33, after 'and' add 'ultimately'

page 104,

line 2, after '65' add 'and was *bur.* at Bad Mannheim'

line 2, after 'Will' add 'dat. 19 Dec. 1891, pr. 25 Sep. 1895'

line 3, after '70' add 'and was *bur.* there.'

line 9, after '1883' add 'at All Saints Rom. Cath. Church, Barton-upon-Irwell, co. Lancaster'

line 12, after 'SHREWSBURY.' add 'She was *b.* 27 Mar. 1856. He *d.* 15, at Barmouth Castle, aged 56, and was *bur.* 18 July 1911, at Barmouth. His widow *d.* at Weysprings, Haslemere, 29 Dec. 1934.'

IV. 1911. 4. GEORGE LEOPOLD BRYAN (BELLEW later BRYAN), BARON BELLEW OF BARMEATH, br. and h., *b.*, 22 Jan. 1857. Assumed the name of BRAND, 13 Oct. 1880. He *m.*, 9 Apr. 1927, Mrs Elaine Carlisle, widow of Herbert LLOYD-DODD, of Johannesburg, S. Africa, da. of John Benjamin LEACH, of Simonstown, S. Africa. He *d. s.p.*, in London, 15 June 1935. His widow *d.* 1973.

V. 1935. 5. EDWARD HENRY (BELLEW), BARON BELLEW OF BARMEATH, nephew and h., being 1st s. and h. of Richard Eustace BELLEW (8 Feb. 1933), by his 1st wife Ada Kate, 2nd da. of Henry Parry GILBEY, of Stanstead, which Richard Eustace was 4th s. of the 2nd Baron Bellew. He was *b.* 6 Feb. 1889; ed. at Oratory Sch. and Cambridge (Trin. Hall.). He *m.*, 20 July 1912, Barbara Helen Mary, only da. of Sir Henry FARNHAM-BURKE, Garter King of Arms. She *d.* 23 Oct. 1967. He *d. s.p.* 8 Aug. 1975.

VI. 1975. 6. BRYAN BERTRAM (BELLEW), BARON BELLEW OF BARMEATH, br. and h., *b.* 11 June 1890; ed. at Cambridge (Trin. Hall); *m.*, 17 Dec. 1918, Jeannie Ellen Agnes, only da. of James Ormsby JAMESON of Dollond, Clonsilla, co. Dublin. She *d.* 1973. He *d.* 7 Sep. 1981.

VII. 1981. 7. JAMES BRYAN (BELLEW), BARON BELLEW OF BARMEATH, s. and h., *b.* 5 Jan. 1920; *m.* 1stly, 11 June 1942, Mary Elizabeth, 1st da. of Rev. Edward Eustace HILL of West Malling, Kent. She *d.* 1978 and he *m.* 2ndly, 1978, Gwendoline, da. of Charles Redmond CLAYTON-DAUBENEY of Bridgwater, Somerset and formerly wife of Major P. HALL.

[BRYAN EDWARD BELLEW, 1st s. and h. ap. by 1st wife, was *b.* 19 Mar. 1943; ed. at Eton and R.M.A., Sandhurst; *m.*, 18 Apr. 1968, Rosemary Sarah, 1st da. of Major Reginald Kilner Brasier HITCHCOCK of Mayfield, Sussex.]

note ([b]), line 2, after '1874' add 'at Fermoy Barracks, from the discharge of his revolver, and was *bur.* at Fermoy.'

BELLOMONT

page 105,
line 14, for 'Meath' read 'Eastmeath'

page 108,
line 16, for '1716' read '1766'

page 109,
line 6, after '*m.*' add '6 Feb. 1733/4'

page 110,
line 5, after 'ap.' add '*b.* 1 May 1778'
line 5, after '*d. v.p.*' add '16 Apr. 1786 at Toulouse in his 8th year, and was *bur.* 10 May at Coote Hill.'

BELMORE

page 112,
line 6, after 'year' add ', and was *bur.* 7 Jan. 1904 at Edwardston, Suffolk.'
line 21, after 'Brighton.' add 'He *d.* at his residence Castle Coole, Inniskillen, 6, and was *b.* 9 Apr.1913 at Derryvullen, co. Fermanagh. His widow *d.* at midnight at Castle Coole, 5, and was *bur.* 8 Oct. 1919 with her husband.'
line 22, line to read as follows

V. 1913. 5. ARMAR (LOWRY-CORRY), EARL BELMORE, &c., s. and h., *b.* 5 May 1870, *styled* from birth VISCOUNT CORRY; ed. at Winchester and Cambridge (Trin. Hall.). He *d.* unm. and *s.p.* 12 Feb. 1948.

VI. 1948. 6. CECIL (LOWRY-CORRY), EARL BELMORE, &c., only surv. br. and h., *b.* 20 Mar. 1873; ed. at Wellington. He *d.* unm. and *s.p.* 2 Mar. 1949.

VII. 1949. 7. GALBRAITH ARMAR (LOWRY-CORRY), EARL BELMORE, &c., cousin and h., being s. and h. of Adrian LOWRY-CORRY (*d.* 12 Feb. 1921), by Geraldine, 4th da. of William Thomas HARTCUP of Eastwood, Old Catton, Norfolk, which Adrian was 5th s. of Adm. Armar LOWRY-CORRY (*d.* 1 Aug. 1919), by Kate Elizabeth, da. of Capt. James BULLEN, which Armar was 2nd s. of the 3rd Earl Belmore. He was *b.* 14 Apr. 1913; ed. at Lancing and R.M.C., Sandhurst; *m.*, 18 Feb. 1939, Gloria Anthea, da. of Herbert Bryant HARKER of Melbourne, Australia. He *d.* 20 July 1960. His widow *m.* 2ndly, 23 Nov. 1963, Col. Robert James Thompson IRWIN, M.C.

VIII. 1960. 8. JOHN ARMAR (LOWRY-CORRY), EARL BELMORE, &c., s. and h., *b.* 4 Sep. 1951; *m.*, 1984, Mary Jane, 2nd da. of John Charles Edmund Carson (MEADE), 6th EARL OF CLANWILLIAM.

[JOHN ARMAR GALBRAITH LOWRY-CORRY, *styled* VISCOUNT CORRY, 1st s. and h. ap., was *b.* 2 Nov. 1985.]

BELPER

page 113,
line 12, after '1840' add 'at St. Helen's House, Derby, and'
line 21, for 'She' read 'He *d.* at Kingston Hall, near Derby, 26, and was *bur.* 30 July, at Kingston. His widow, who'
line 22, after '1852' add , *d.* at Swaffham Prior House, Cambridge, 2 Aug. 1922.'
lines 23–4, delete all detail and replace as follows

III. 1914. 3. ALGERNON HENRY (STRUTT), BARON BELPER, 3rd but 1st surv. s.,[d] *b.* 6 May 1883; Lieut. 2nd Life Guards, etc. He *m.*, 26 Apr. 1911, at St. Margaret's, Westm., Eva Isabel Marian, 3rd da. of Henry Campbell (BRUCE), 2nd LORD ABERDARE, by Constance Mary, only da. of Hamilton BECKETT. She was *b.* 17 June 1892 and *d.* 1987. The marriage was diss. by divorce in 1922 and he *m.* 2ndly, 12 July 1923, Angela Mariota, yr. da. of Alfred Douglas TOLLEMACHE of Ipswich, Suffolk. He *d.* 20 Mar. 1956. His widow *m.* 2ndly, 2 Oct. 1958, Rev. Harry Norman TOLLEMCHE (*formerly* WRIGLEY). His widow was still living 1995.

IV. 1956. 4. ALEXANDER RONALD GEORGE (STRUTT), BARON BELPER, 1st s. and h., *b.* 23 Apr. 1912; ed. at Harrow and R.M.C., Sandhurst; *m.*, 15 Nov. 1940, Zara Sophie Kathleen Mary, yr. da. of Sir Harry Stapleton MAINWARING, Bart. This marriage was diss. in 1949.

[RICHARD HENRY STRUTT, s. and h. ap.; *b.* 24 Oct. 1941; ed. at Harrow and R.A.C., Cirencester; *m.*, 22 Oct. 1966, Jennifer Vivian, da. of Capt. Peter WINSER. This marriage was diss. by divorce and he *m.* 2ndly, 1980, Judith Mary (Mrs DE JONGE), da. of James TWYNAM of Faringdon, co. Oxford.]

BENEDERALOCH

page 115,
line 11, for '1861' read '1681'

BERKELEY

page 124,
line 11, for 'began' read 'is said to have begun' [Lord Berkeley wrote to the then editor in 1924, expressing his opinion that the castle was not begun till about 45 years later]

page 125,
note ([a]), line 6, for '1st' read '2nd'

page 126,
line 16, after 'John' add 'FITZGILBERT, *styled* also JOHN THE'

page 127,
line 2, after 'John' add 'FITZGILBERT, *styled* also JOHN THE'
line 13, delete from 'Rohese' to 'DOVER' and replace by 'Rose, da. and h. of Foubert DE DOUVRES' [see *Genealogist*, N.S., 1906, vol. xxii, pp. 107–8]

page 129,
line 6, for 'Eudes' read 'Eon'
line 7, delete from 'Milicent' to 'Bergavenny' and replace by 'Millicent, sister and coh. of George DE CAUNTELO, Lord of Abergavenny, da. of William DE CAUNTELO, of Calne, co. Wilts. and Aston Cantlow, co. Warwick.'
line 8, for '5' read '6'

page 130,
lines 9–10, delete from 'da.' to 'Joinville' and replace by '*de jure suo jure* (according to modern doctrine) BARONESS GENEVILLE, da. and h. of Sir Piers DE GENEVILLE (2nd but 1st surv. s. and h. ap. of Geoffrey, 1st LORD GENEVILLE.'
line 24, for 'da.' read '1st sister of the whole blood and'

page 131,
line 9, delete from 'only' to 'sole' and replace by '*de jure suo jure* (according to modern doctrine) BARONESS LISLE (of Kingston Lisle) and BARONESS TYEYS, da. and'
line 13, for '20 Mar. 1391/2' read 'between May and Sep. 1392'
line 16, for '1415' read '1415/6, pr. 1417'
note ([c]), line 1, for '12th' read '13th'

page 132,
line 26, for 'da.' read 'elder da. and h.'

page 133,
line 13, for '1468' read '1467'

page 135,
line 2, for 'Thomas' read 'John'
note ([c]), line 17, (on page 136). Line 17, after '(Courthope)' add 'See also Doubleday, in vol. ix, Appendix B, pp. 12–15, who regards the issue of a summons as tantamount to a restoration rather than a creation.'

page 137,
line 1, for 'was in' read 'held a'
line 4, after '1523' add 'On 9 July 1528 Thomas, Duke of Norfolk, became a trustee for his cousin Thomas Berkeley, who is then described as "Lord Berkeley, Mowbray and Segrave"([ax]).'
note ([ax]) *Ante*, vol. ix, Appendix G, p. 57. For the assumption between 1485 and 1698, by

successive Lords Berkeley of the *style* of Lord Mowbray and Segrave, to which Baronies they were coheirs only, see *idem*, pp. 56–7 *et passim* where the whole subject is discussed.

page 139,
line 12, after '*bur.*' add 'these, being removed 50 years later to'
line 16, after 'h.' add 'was *bap.* 23 Apr. 1627 at St. James's, Clerkenwell'
note (e), line 1, after 'Charles' add '*b.* 26 Aug. 1623'

page 140,
lines 22–3, delete from 'of' to '1695' and replace by 'General of the United Provinces of the Netherlands, 1689–94'

page 142,
note (c), line 2, for '1884' read '1844'
line 3, after 'p. 278.' add 'For a modern account see Hope Costley White, *Mary Cole*, 1961.

page 144,
line 7, for 'FITZHARDINGE' read 'RAWDON'
line 14, after '1827' add 'and was *bap.* 28 Mar. at Brighthelmston, Sussex'
line 24, after '1865' add 'at Ixelles'
line 26, after '*m.*' add '1stly'
line 29, after 'Berks.' add 'He *m.* 2ndly, 7 Nov. 1924, Mrs Lowell Lloyd, da. of John LOWELL of Boston, U.S.A., at the Register Office, Princes Row. He *d. s.p.* 15 Jan. 1942 when his titles became *extinct* or *dormant*.'

page 147,
line 17, after 'Regt.' add 'He *d.* 7 Oct. 1949. She *d.* 4 Dec. 1964 when the Barony fell into *abeyance* between her two daughters. This was terminated in favour of her elder da. on 5 Apr. 1967.'

XVII. 1967. 17. MARY LALLE FOLEY, *suo jure* BARONESS BERKELEY [1421], eld. da., *b.* 9 Oct. 1905. In 1951 assumed the additional surname of BERKELEY. She *d.* unm. 17 Oct. 1992.

XVIII. 1992. 18. ANTHONY FITZHARDINGE (GUETERBOCK), BARON BERKELEY [1421], nephew and h., being only s. and h. of Cynthia Ella, 2nd da. of Mary Lalle FOLEY-BERKELEY abovenamed, by Brig. Ernest Adolphus Leopold GUETERBOCK, yst. s. of Alfred GUETERBOCK of Bowdon, Cheshire. He was *b.* 20 Sep. 1939; ed. at Eton and Cambridge (Trin. Coll.); *m.*, 10 July 1965, Diana Christine, 1st da. of Eric William John TOWNSEND of East Molesey, Surrey.

[THOMAS FITZHARDINGE GUETERBOCK, 1st s. and h. ap., was *b.* 5 Jan. 1969; ed. at St. Paul's.]

BERKELEY OF STRATTON

page 148,
line 13, for '1672' read '1672/3'

page 149,
lines 15–16, for 'being then probably about 16' read '*b.* 16 May 1697' [Diary of John, Lord Berkeley of Stratton, 16 May 1761 and 16 May 1767, Brownlow papers, Lincs. R.O. *Ex inform.* Dr Stephen Farrell.]

BERKSHIRE

page 150,
line 21, for '7 Feb.' read '5 Feb.'

BERMINGHAM

page 152,
lines 13–14, for 'as his 2nd' read 'probably as his 4th'
line 14, for 'before 1402–3' read '(lic. 24 Dec. 1398)' [*P.C.C.*, 366a, Chichele Register, part 1]

BERNERS

page 153,
line 12, delete 'Sir'
lines 19–20, for 'Boston, co. Lincoln' read 'Ashwellthorpe, Norfolk'
note (e), line 8, for '*cr.* Earl FitzWarine' read 'Lord FitzWarin'
note (f), line 3, after '*s.p.m.*' add '*recte* 6 Aug. 1412. [*Cal. Inq. p.m.*, vol. 20, p. 217.]

page 154,
line 8, for '1519' read '1520'
line 9, for 'in 1520 was' read 'on 28 Nov. was app.' and after 'Calais' add '(ba)'
note (ba) He was relieved of the office 25 Oct. 1526, but reappointed 27 Mar. 1531, and held it until his death, *L. and P. Hen. VIII*, vol. iv, nos 2,518–9, 2,546, 2,597; vol. v, no. 166 [48]
line 11, delete from 'whose' to 'was'

page 158,
lines 37–8, delete from 'is' to 'living' and replace by '*d.* at Ashwellthorpe, Norwich, 18, and was *bur.* there 22 Aug. 1917 aged 81.'

page 159,
line 1, line to read as follows

XIII. 1917. 13. RAYMOND ROBERT (TYRWHITT-WILSON), LORD BERNERS, 2nd but 1st surv. s. and h.,

line 3, for ']' read 'He *d.* unm. 5 Sep. 1918.'

XIV. 1918. 14. GERALD HUGH (TYRWHITT), LORD BERNERS, &c., nephew and h., being s. and h. of Hugh Tyrwhitt (*d.* 26 Oct. 1907), by Julia Mary, da. of William Orme FOSTER, which Hugh was 3rd s. of Emma Harriet, *suo jure*

Baroness Berners. He was *b.* 18 Sep. 1883; ed. at Eton; assumed by Royal lic. the name of WILSON, 31 Mar. 1919. He *d.* unm. 19 Apr. 1950, when his Baronetcy became *extinct*.

XV. 1950. 15. VERA RUBY TYRWHITT, *suo jure* BARONESS BERNERS, being da. of Rupert TYRWHITT (*d.* 3 Aug. 1940), by Louise Isabel Frances, 1st da. of Walter Fox Williamson WELLS, which Rupert was 5th s. of Emma Harriet, *suo jure* Baroness Berners. She was *b.* 25 Dec. 1901; *m.*, 2 Aug. 1927, Harold WILLIAMS, 2nd s. of William WILLIAMS. She *d.* 20 Feb. 1992 when the Barony fell into *abeyance* between her two daughters.(aa)

note (aa) These are, (1) Pamela Vivien, *b.* 30 Sep. 1929, *m.*, 1 Mar. 1952, Michael Joseph Sperry Kirkham of Parwich Lees, co. Derby, and has issue, and (2) Rosemary Tyrwhitt, *b.* 20 July 1931, *m.*, 8 June 1959, Kelvin Alexander Pollock, s. of Kelvin Clayton Pollock, of Rochester, Kent.

BERTRAM

page 162,

line 10, for '(__)' read 'Robert' [*Hist. of Northumberland*, Northumberland Co. Hist. Committee, vol. xi, p. 77]

note (d), line 2, after 'matter.' add 'The "barony" of Bertram was later assumed by the Cavendishes, Dukes of Newcastle, see *post*, vol. ix, p. 523 (*cf.* Round, *Family Origins*, p. 189).'

BERWICK-UPON-TWEED

page 163,

line 11, after 'forfeited.' add '(aa)'

note (aa) Or possibly as early as 1 Aug. 1689, see Godfrey W. Iredell, *Geneal. Mag.*, vol. 20, 1981, pp. 147–51. See also vol. xii, part 2, Appendix H, by A.J. Wagner.

page 167,

line 21, delete from 'on' to 'yacht' and replace by 'in the Holland House Hotel'

note (a), delete all detail.

BERWICK OF ATTINGHAM

page 168,

line 13, after 'DUBOCHET' add 'a Swiss clockmaker in Mayfair, by Amelia his wife.'

page 169,

line 16, for 'living (1911)' read '*d.* 7 Feb. 1934.'

line 17, after 'Conservative.' add 'He *m.*, 30 June 1919, Edith Teresa, da. of William HULTON of Venice. He *d.* 12 June 1947.'

IX. 1947. 9. CHARLES MICHAEL WENTWORTH (NOEL-HILL), BARON BERWICK OF ATTINGHAM, cousin and h., being only s. of the Rev. Charles NOEL-HILL (18 Nov. 1911), by Edith Mary, 1st da. of Rev. Riou George BENSON, which Charles was only s. of Charles Arthur Wentworth Harwood NOEL-HILL (*d.* 2 June 1853), by Catherine Mary, 1st da. of Charles Marsh ADAMS, of the Abbey, Shrewsbury, which Charles was 4th s. of the 4th Baron Berwick. He was *b.* 4 Mar. 1897. He *d.* unm. and *s.p.* 27 Jan. 1953, when his title became *extinct.*

BESSBOROUGH

page 170,
line 10, for 'pr.' read 'dat. 11 Aug. 1724, pr. 11 Dec.' and after 'Fiddown' add 'co. Kilkenny'
line 27, after 'afsd.' add 'M.I.'
line 35, after '79' add 'M.I. Will dat. 3 Nov. 1753, pr. 23 Aug. 1758'

page 171,
line 16, after '88' add 'M.I. to both there'
line 17, for 'pr. May' read 'dat. 14 Sep. 1785 to 23 Sep. 1786, pr. 18 July'
line 29, after 'Wimbledon' add 'and *bap.* there 25 July'
line 32, after 'Gloucester' add 'Admon. 28 June 1846'

page 172,
line 4, after 'Marylebone.' add 'Ed. at Harrow.'
line 22, after 'year' add 'M.I. to both there'

page 173,
line 4, after 'marriage' add 'M.I.'
line 7, after '70' add 'M.I.'
line 10, after '71' add 'M.I.'

page 174,
line 4, line to read as follows

EARLDOM [I.] VIII. BARONY [I.] IX.	1906	8 and 9. EDWARD (PONSONBY), EARL OF BESSBOROUGH, &c., 1st s. and h., *b.* 1 Mar. 1851.

lines 12–13,delete from 'Having' to 'work]' and replace by 'She *d.* at Pilltown, 11, and was *bur.* there 15 Oct. 1919. He *d.* at Birmingham, 1, and was *bur.* 7 Dec. 1920 at Pilltown.'

EARLDOM [I.] IX. BARONY [I.] X.	1920	9 and 10. VERE BRABAZON (PONSONBY), EARL OF BESSBOROUGH, &c., 1st s. and h., *b.* 27 Oct. 1880. He was *cr.*, 2 June 1937, EARL OF BESSBOROUGH [U.K.] [for further details see vol. xiii, p. 582]. He *d.* 10 Mar. 1956. His widow *d.* 1979.
EARLDOM [U.K.] II. EARLDOM [I.] X. BARONY [I.] XI.	1956	2, 10 and 11. FREDERICK EDWARD NEUFLIZE (PONSONBY), EARL OF BESSBOROUGH [I.], &c., also Earl of Bessborough in the peerage of the U.K., 1st and only surv. s. and h., *b.* 29 Mar. 1913; ed. at Eton and Cambridge (Trin. Coll.); *m.*, 29 Sep. 1948, Mary, da. of Charles A. MUNN. He *d.* *s.p.m.* 5 Dec. 1993

when the Earldom of Bessborough [U.K.] became *extinct* but he was *suc.* in his other titles by his cousin.

EARLDOM [I.] XI. BARONY [I.] XII.	1993	11 and 12. ARTHUR MOUNTIFORT LONGFIELD (PONSONBY), EARL OF BESSBOROUGH [I.], &c., cousin and h., being s. of Cyril Miles Brabazon PONSONBY (*d.* 28 Sep. 1915, being *k.* in action in France), by Rita Narcissa, 1st da. of Lieut. Col. Mountifort John Courtanay LONGFIELD of Castle Mary, Cloyne,

co. Cork, which Cyril Miles Brabazon was 2nd s. of 8th Earl of Bessborough. He was *b.* 11 Dec. 1912; ed. at Harrow and Cambridge (Trin. Coll.); *m.* 1stly, 28 July 1939, Patricia, da. of Col. Fitzhugh Lee MINNIGERODE of Virginia, U.S.A. She *d.* 12 Sep. 1952 and he *m.* 2ndly, 20 Sep. 1956, Anne Marie, da. of Major Gen. Sir Rudolph Carl SLATIN Pasha (BARON VON SLATIN), G.C.V.O., K.C.M.G., formerly wife of PRINCE GEORGE GALITZINE. This marriage was diss. by divorce in 1963 and he *m.* 3rdly, 17 Dec. 1963, Madeleine Lola Margaret, only da. of Major Gen. Laurence Douglas GRAND of Iver, co. Buckingham.

[MILES FITZHUGH LONGFIELD PONSONBY, *styled* VISCOUNT DUNCANNON, 1st s. and h. ap. by 1st wife, was *b.* 16 Feb. 1941; ed. at Harrow and Cambridge (Trin. Coll.); *m.*, 1972, Alison Marjorie, 3rd da. William STOREY of Great Bealings, Suffolk.]

BEVERLEY

page 175,
line 12, for '1751' read '1750/1'

BIDDEFORD

page 176,
lines 22–3, delete all detail
between lines 25 and 26 insert as under

BIDEFORD

i.e. GRANVILLE OF KILKHAMPTON AND BIDEFORD, Barony (*Granville*), *cr.* 1661, with the EARLDOM OF BATH, which see; *extinct* 1711.

BIRMINGHAM

page 179,
line 5, for '1664' read '1643/4'

BLACKBURN

page 180,
note (b), line 10 (on page 181), for 'under the Act of their creation in 1876' read 'under a royal warrant dated 22 Dec. 1876.'

BLAKENEY

page 182,
line 10, for '1672' read '1671' [*Corrections and Additions to the D.N.B.*, 1966, p. 27]

BLANTYRE

page 184,
line 3, for 'Margaret' read 'Marie'
line 4, after 'Rowallan' add 'by Sara, da. of (__) BRISBANE'
line 4, after '*m.*' add 'in terms of disposition, 14 May 1644'
line 5, after 'BRISBANE' add 'younger of Bishopstown'
line 10, after 'Houston' add 'He *d.*, apparently in May 1676, in Bute, certainly before 1690, probably of the smallpox' [*Scots Peerage*, vol. ix, p. 38]
line 11, for '[1670?]' read '1676?'

page 186,
note (a), between lines 2 and 3 insert 'Archibald (Kennedy), 3rd Marquess of Ailsa, and *d.* 26 July 1888. His 4th da., Gertrude, *b.* 11 Nov. 1849, *m.*'
line 3, for '26 June 1888' read '25 Apr. 1935'

BLARNEY

page 186,
line 15, for '*extinct* 1770' read '*forfeited* 1691'

BLAYNEY

page 187,
line 8, delete from 'of the' to 'which'
line 21, after '1640/1' add 'aged 16'
line 26, delete '[U.K.]'

BLESINGTON

page 190,
line 28, delete '1648'
line 29, for '18' read '8' and after '1662' read 'aged 17'

page 191,
line 9, for 'Rose' read 'after 1695, Penelope Rose, 4th and yst.'
line 10, for 'Charles' read 'Richard'

page 192,
line 22, after '*d. s.p.m.*' add '*s.*'
note (c), delete all detail and replace by 'On the death of William (Stewart), Earl of Blesington, in 1769, the estates which he had inherited from his mother, *i.e.* those in cos. Kildare and Wicklow, and the manor of Silchester, Hants. went to Charles Dunbar,

as nearest heir general of Archbishop Michael Boyle. The Donegal estates went to Sir Annesley Stewart, who inherited the Baronetcy. The Tyrone estates were left to the testator's widow for life, with remainder in tail male successively to Adm. John Forbes, and William and James Stewart, elder brothers of Sir Annesley abovenamed (who, however, pre-deceased the testator without issue), and ultimate remainder to the Earl's "own right heirs". On the death of Adm. Forbes, *s.p.m.* in 1796, Luke (Gardiner), Viscount Mountjoy, claimed the estates under that remainder, and after a contest with the Earl of Granard, had them awarded to him.'

BLETSO OR BLETSOE

page 193,
line 13, for 'BLETSHO' read 'BLETSO'
line 15, for 'BLETSHO' read 'BLETSO'

BLOUNT

page 195,
lines 12–14, delete from 'Julian' to '1328' and replace by 'Juliane, *de jure* (according to modern doctrine) *suo jure* BARONESS LEYBURN, widow of John (DE HASTINGES), 3rd LORD HASTINGS (who *d.* 20 Jan. 1324/5), da. and h. of Thomas DE LEYBURN (s. and h. ap. of William, 1st LORD LEYBURN) by Alice, sister and h. of Robert (DE TONI), 1st LORD TONY, da. of Ralph DE TONY VII, of Flamstead, Herts. He *d.* 17 Aug. 1328' [See vol. vii, *sub* LEYBURN]
line 16, after '*d. s.p.*' add '25 Aug.'

page 196,
line 3, after 's' add 'and h.'
line 5, for 'and 'da. of' read 'who was h. of his br.'
line 13, for 'VERDON' (twice) read 'VERDUN'
line 21, after 'HUSEE' add '(s. and h. ap. of Henry, 2nd LORD HUSEE)'
line 22, delete from '*d.*' to '1349' and replace by '*d. v.p.* before 10 Feb. 1345/6'
line 24, after '1383' add 'She *d.* in or before 1377'. See HUSEE.'
note (e), line 4, add 'This John was ancestor of the Lords Mountjoy. See that title.'

BLYTHSWOOD

page 198,
line 12, delete 'living 1911' and replace by '*d.* from the affect of an operation at Dunally Lodge, Shepperton on Thames, 23, and was *bur.* 28 Mar. 1922 at Inchinnan afsd.'
lines 13–14, delete from 'He' to 'work' and replace by

II. 1908. 2. SHOLTO (CAMPBELL, later DOUGLAS-CAMPBELL, later CAMPBELL), BARON BLYTHSWOOD, br. and h. under the spec. rem., *b.* 28 June 1839; ed. at Cambridge (Trin. Coll.); ordained Priest; *m.*, 1889, Violet Mary, da. of Gen. Lord Alfred PAGET. She *d.* 1908. He *d. s.p.* 30 Sep. 1916.

III. 1916. 3. BARRINGTON BULKELEY (CAMPBELL, later DOUGLAS-CAMPBELL, later CAMPBELL), BARON BLYTHSWOOD, br. and h. under the spec. rem., *b.* 18 Feb. 1845. He *m.*, 7 July 1869, Mildred, da. of Sir Joseph HAWLEY, Bart. She *d.* 1902. He *d.* at Douglas Support, Coatsbridge, 13, and was *bur.* 15 Mar. 1918 at Inchinnan afsd.

IV. 1918. 4. ARCHIBALD (CAMPBELL, later DOUGLAS-CAMPBELL, later CAMPBELL), BARON BLYTHSWOOD, 1st s. and h., 25 Apr. 1870; ed. at Eton. He *m.*, 25 July 1895, Evelyn, da. of John FLETCHER of Saltoun. He *d. s.p.m.*, at Blythswood House, 14, and was *bur.* at Inchinnan, Renfrewshire, 18 Nov. 1929.

V. 1929. 5. BARRINGTON SHOLTO (DOUGLAS-CAMPBELL), BARON BLYTHSWOOD, br. and h., *b.* 15 July 1877; ed. at Eton. He *d.* unm. 3 Mar. 1937.

VI. 1937. 6. LEOPOLD HENRY (DOUGLAS-CAMPBELL later CAMPBELL), BARON BLYTHSWOOD, br. and h., *b.* 5 Mar. 1881; ed. at Eton and Cambridge (Trin. Coll.); ordained Priest. He *m.*, 22 July 1908, Mabel, da. of E.C. DUMBLETON. He *d.* 8 Feb. 1940.

VII. 1940. 7. PHILIP ARCHIBALD (DOUGLAS-CAMPBELL), BARON BLYTHSWOOD, s. and h., *b.* 19 Feb. 1919; ed. at Eton and Cambridge (Trin. Coll.). He *d.* unm. Sep. 1940 when his title became *extinct*.

BOHUN

page 201,
line 22, after '*m.*' add '1stly'
line 24, after '1445/6' add 'He *m.* 2ndly, before 16 June 1450, Blanche' [*Cal. Papal Reg.*, vol. x, p. 488]

BOLEBEC

page 203,
line 3, for '1245' read '1485'
lines 5–6, delete '(1462–1625)'
lines 8–12, delete from 'Isabel' to 'successors([c])' and replace by 'Isabel, da. and h. of Walter de Bolebec, Lord of Whitchurch, Bucks. *m.*, as his 1st wife, Aubrey (de Vere), 2nd Earl of Oxford (who *d. s.p. legit.* in 1214), and *d. s.p.* 1206–7. Isabel, da. of Hugh and sister of Walter de Bolebec abovenamed, coh. to her niece, Isabel. Countess of Oxford, and widow of Henry de Nonant, *m.* Robert (de Vere), 3rd Earl of Oxford (who *d.* 1221), br. and h. of Aubrey. She *d.* 3 Feb. 1244/5, being ancestress of those later Earls of Oxford, who, from Tudor times, adopted the *style* of Viscount or Baron Bolebec, or Bulbeck'
note ([a]), delete all detail and replace by 'When the 14th Earl of Oxford *d. s.p.* in 1526, leaving sisters and coheirs, the Bolebec lands were among those which passed to his 2nd cousin and h. male, John, the 15th Earl, but were sold, with other family estates, by Edward the 17th Earl, in 1580–1. See *V.C.H. Bucks.*, vol. 3, pp. 444–5. On the death of the latter's s. Henry, the 18th Earl, in 1625, the alleged Barony of

Bolebec was one of the Baronies claimed by his 2nd cousin and h. male, Robert de Vere, and by his next h. of the whole blood, Robert, Lord Willoughby de Eresby. The judges did not question the existence of the Baronies of Bolebec, Sandford and Badlesmere, but declared that in strictness of law they had reverted to Henry VIII in 1526 and were at his disposal. As the Crown had not conferred the titles on anyone, the House of Lords, in 1626, informed the King, Charles I, that they were "wholly in [his] Majesty's hand to dispose of at [his] own pleasure". In spite of this decision, the 19th Earl's s. Aubrey, the 20th Earl, continued to assume the titles of Lord Bolebec, Sandford and Badlesmere. According to modern doctrine, if these had been peerage dignities, they would have fallen into *abeyance* on the death of the 14th Earl in 1526; but the doctrine of *abeyance* had not yet come into being. Actually Bolebec was only a territorial barony, Sandford was held by grand serjeanty and the 14th Earl was only a coheir of Badlesmere. For a list of peerage titles assumed by peers see vol. v, Appendix F.'

note ([b]), lines 2–4, delete from 'It' to 'family'

note ([c]), delete all detail and replace by 'For the origin of the family of Bolebec see Loyd, *Origins of some Anglo-Norman Families*, Harl. Soc., p. 17.'

BOLINGBROKE

page 203,

lines 18–19, for 'Sir John REDE, of Odington' read 'John READ, of Boddington'

page 205,

line 13, delete from 'was' to '1702'

note ([a]), line 2, after 'Univ.' add 'The evidence for his going to Eton is in a letter he wrote later (BL, Add. MS. 34,196, f. 2).' [*Ex inform.* Canon Brian Carne]

page 207,

line 5, after 'Oct. 1718' add 'aged 38, and was *bur.* at Bucklebury afsd.'

line 18, for '1734' read '21 Dec. 1732 and *bap.* 17 Jan. 1732/3 at St. George's, Hanover Sq.'

line 19, for 'Feb. 1748/9' read '26 Nov. 1748' [*Ex inform.* Canon Brian Carne]

page 208,

line 18, for '18 Dec.' read '11 Dec.' [M.I.]

page 209,

line 11, for 'is alleged to' read 'claimed' [No proof of any marriage has been found.]

line 11, delete '([b])'

line 12, for 'G.W.' read 'Charles([b])', for '(__)' read 'Mary' and delete 'of Netherby'

note ([b]), delete all detail of original note and replace by 'This Charles was probably a s. of Moses Medex, a Dutchman, who was granted letters of denization in 1802. Mary is said to have been a near relative of the Grahams of Netherby but it has not been possible to establish her place in the ped. of that family. Four children were born of this association, of whom only one, Ellen Rose St. John, living in 1922, survived infancy. *Ex inform.* C. Roy Hudleston; *cf. Corrigenda* to note ([c]) below.'

line 17, after 'mistress' add '([c])'

note ([c]) They lived together in Bath as 'Mr and Mrs Wilson'. A s., Henry Mildmay, was *b.* to this Miss Howard, 5 Dec. 1882, and another s., Charles Reginald, on 14 Nov. 1885. Nine days after their marriage a still born da. was *b.* 14 Jan. 1893. It is said that in 1885 Lord Bolingbroke revealed to Miss Howard the facts about Ellen Medex and suggested that their son, Henry Mildmay afsd., should be brought up as Ellen's son in the hope that he might be able to claim the title. In peerages subsequent to this appeared a statement that Lord Bolingbroke had *m.* Ellen Medex in 1869 and had had issue by her, Henry Mildmay and Charles Reginald. [*Ex inform.* C. Roy Hudleston]

line 19, delete from 'is' to 'Park' and replace by '*d.* 22 Feb. 1940.'

line 20, for 'HENRY VERNON' read 'VERNON HENRY'

lines 25–6, delete from 'has' to 'been' and replace by 'was not'

line 26, after 'disputed.' add 'and his claim was admitted by the Committee for Privileges in 1922. He *m.*, 15 June 1950, Valezina, da. of Frederick William FROHAWK of Sutton, Surrey. This marriage was annulled in 1952. He *d. s.p.* 1 May 1974.'

VII. 1974. 7. KENNETH OLIVER MUSGRAVE (ST. JOHN), VISCOUNT BOLINGBROKE, &c., distant cousin and h. being 2nd but 1st surv. s. and h. of Geoffrey Robert ST. JOHN, by his 1st wife, Gwendolen Isobel, da. and h. of Herbert George OKEDEN, of Stutton House, Suffolk, which Geoffrey was s. and h. of Henry Percy St. John (*d.* 9 Sep. 1921), by Maud Louisa, da. of Pascoe Charles GLYN, which Henry was 1st s. and h. of Rev. Maurice William Ferdinand St. John, (18 Feb. 1914), by Charlotte Lucy Hamilton, da. of John DALYELL, which Maurice was s. of Ferdinand ST. JOHN (*d.* 10 Oct. 1865), by Selina Charlotte, da. of Col. Maurice St. Leger KEATINGE which Ferdinand was s. by his 2nd wife of the 3rd Viscount Bolingbroke. He was *b.* 22 Mar. 1927; ed. at Eton; *m.*, 1953, Patricia Mary, da. of B.J. MCKENNA of Christchurch, New Zealand. This marriage was diss. by divorce in 1972 and he *m.* 2ndly, 1972, Jainey Anne, da. of Alexander Duncan MCRAE of Timaru, New Zealand. This marriage was in turn diss. by divorce in 1987.

[HENRY FITZROY ST. JOHN, 1st s. and h. ap. by 1st wife, was *b.* 18 May 1957.]

BOLTON

page 210,
line 28, for 'May' read 'July'

page 213,
line 11, after '*m.*' add '1stly'

page 214,
line 13, for 'Catharine' read 'Catherine' and for 'Charles' read 'Frances' [G.S. Parry, *N&Q.*, 11th ser., vol. viii, 1913, p. 393.]

note (a), lines 1–12, from 'He' to '1837)' refer to the 4th Duke.

page 215,
line 9, for '1559' read '1539'

lines 17–18, for 'da. of (__) Munn' read 'presumably da. of Mary Nunn, widow (? of Richard Nunn)' [*Ex inform.* E.G. Bolton]

note (c), delete all detail

page 216,
line 6, for '1740' read '1746'

page 217,
line 31, after 'Castle' add ', and *d.* 22 June 1919. He *d.* at Bolton Hall, Wensleydale, 14, and was *bur.* 17 Oct. 1922 in the Mausoleum at Bolton Hall afsd.'

V. 1922. 5. WILLIAM GEORGE ALGAR (ORDE-POWLETT), BARON BOLTON OF BOLTON CASTLE, only s. and h., *b.* at Bolton Hall, 21 Aug. 1869; ed. at Eton 1883–7, and R.M.C., Sandhurst. He served in WW1 as Lieut. Col. 5th Battn. Yorks. Regt. He *m.*, at St. George's, Hanover Sq., 6 June 1893, Elizabeth Mary, 1st da. of Edward (GIBSON), 1st LORD ASHBOURNE. She, who was *b.* 1871, *d.* 9 Dec. 1943. He *d.* 11 Dec. 1944.

[WILLIAM PERCY ORDE-POWLETT, 1st s. and h. ap., *b.* 7 Apr. 1894. Served in WW1 as 2nd Lieut. 1st Battn. Yorks Regt., *d. v.p.* and unm., being *k.* in action 17 May 1915.]

VI. 1944. 6. NIGEL AMYAS (ORDE-POWLETT), BARON BOLTON OF BOLTON CASTLE, 2nd but only surv. s. and h., *b.* 26 Mar. 1900. He *m.*, 11 June 1928, Victoria Mary, da. of Montague VILLIERS, of Helmsley, Yorks. She *d.* 1 Nov. 1933. He *d.* 15 June 1963.

VII. 1963. 7. RICHARD WILLIAM ALGAR (ORDE-POWLETT), BARON BOLTON OF BOLTON CASTLE, 1st s. and h., *b.* 11 July 1929; ed. at Eton and Cambridge (Trin. Coll.); *m.*, 31 July 1951, Christine Helene, 1st da. of Cecil George Wilfred (WELD-FORESTER), 7th BARON FORESTER. This marriage was diss. by divorce in 1981 and he *m.* 2ndly, 1981, Masha Anne, only da. of Major Francis Edward HUDSON of Bedale, co. York. This marriage was in turn diss. by divorce and he *m.* 3rdly, 1991, Lavinia (Mrs FENTON), da. of William Edward WRIGHT.

[HARRY ALGAR NIGEL ORDE-POWLETT, 1st s. and h. ap. by 1st wife, was *b.* 14 Feb. 1954; ed. at Eton; *m.*, 1977, Philippa, da. of Major Peter L. TAPLEY of Wanstead, Essex.]

BONVILLE

page 218,
line 25, after '*m.*' add 'by June 1414,' and after 'Margaret' add 'da. of Reynold GREY, 3rd LORD GREY of Ruthyn, s. of Reynold, 2nd LORD GREY by his 2nd wife Joan' [*Cal. Close Rolls, 1413–19*, pp. 136, 197–200]

page 219,
line 2, after 'CAMOYS add '3rd LORD CAMOYS'
line 6, for '18' read '28'
line 16, after '1475' add '(cont. 18 July 1474), as his 2nd wife'
line 18, delete '6' and for 'before 2 June 1530' read '12 May 1529'
line 20, for '6 May 1527' read '6 Mar. 1527/8'
in right margin, for '1495' read '1475'

BORTHWICK

page 222,
line 15, for 'before' read 'between 15 Dec. 1530 and' [*Scots Peerage*, vol. ix, p. 39]
line 18, for 'Mar' read '27 Feb.'
line 20, for 'before 1544' read '(cont. 28 May 1538)'
line 21, after '*d.*' add '28 Mar.'

page 223,
line 5, for '1582' read '(cont. 26 Oct. 1582)'
line 9, after '1602' add 'was of full age, July 1612'
lines 21–2, delete from 'between' to '1675' and replace by 'Nov. 1674'
lines 26–7, in margin delete 'or 1675'

page 224,
line 1, for 'next br.' read 'yst. s.'

page 226,
line 25, for 'living 1911' read '*d.* 17 Feb. 1917, at Sevenoaks, Kent, aged 82.'
line 35, delete '*extinct* or'
line 36, for 'living 1911' read '*m.* 2ndly, 8 Jan. 1916; Alfred William Maitland FITZROY, *styled* EARL OF EUSTON, later 8th DUKE OF GRAFTON. He *d.* 10 Jan. 1930. She *d.* 3 Oct. 1961.'

XXI. 1986. 21. JOHN HENRY STUART (BORTHWICK), LORD BORTHWICK, recognised, 1986, by Lord Lyon as *de jure* LORD BORTHWICK, following recognition, 26 July 1944, by the Lyon Court as BORTHWICK OF BORTHWICK and in that surname, as descended from John Borthwick, of Crookston, 2nd s. of Sir William B., *cr.* 1452 LORD BORTHWICK (see above),(c) being s. and h. of Henry Borthwick of Borthwick, 16th of Crookston (*b.* 23 July 1868, *d.* 27 May 1937), by Melena Florence, 4th da. of James Thomas PRINGLE, Capt., R.N. He was *b.* 13 Sep. 1905; ed. at Fettes; *m.*, 8 Jan. 1938, Margaret Frances, da. of Alexander Campbell CORMACK of Edinburgh.

[JOHN HUGH BORTHWICK, MASTER OF BORTHWICK, 1st s. and h. ap., was *b.* 14 Nov. 1940; ed. at Gordonstoun; *m.*, 1974, Adelaide, only da. of Archy BIRKMYRE of Comrie, Perthshire.]

note (c) See *Burke's Landed Gentry*, 18th edn., vol. 2, 1969, pp. 55–6.

BOSTON

page 228,
line 8, after '1802' add ', ed. at Eton 1814–17'
line 17, for 'living 1911' read '*d.* 20 Dec. 1927.'
line 24, for 'Portlamel' read 'Porthamel'
lines 27–8, delete from 'She' to '1911' and replace by 'His widow *d.* 16 Feb. 1929.'
line 36, after 'She' add ', who' and after '1870' add ', *d.* at Monkshatch Compton, Guildford, 10, and was *bur.* there 13 Jan. 1938. He *d. s.p.* 16 Sep. 1941.'

VII. 1941. 7. GREVILLE NORTHEY (IRBY), BARON BOSTON, nephew and h., being s. and h. of Cecil Saumarez IRBY (*b.* 21 Feb. 1935), by Florence Augusta, da. of Clement Upton Cottrell DORMER, of Rousham, co. Oxon., which Cecil was 2nd s. of the 5th Baron Boston. He was *b.* 24 Aug. 1889; *m.* 1stly, 29 Sep. 1913, Constance Beryl, 1st da. of William Richard LESTER of Alderley, Llandudno, co. Carnarvon. This marriage was diss. by divorce in 1954 (she *d.* 17 Jan. 1969) and he *m.* 2ndly, 6 Feb. 1954, Irene Frances, da. of Francis HOLT of Ewell, co. Surrey and widow of Harry MILLS. He *d. s.p.m.* 16 Sep. 1958. His widow *d.* 1987.

VIII. 1958. 8. CECIL EUSTACE (IRBY), BARON BOSTON, br. and h., *b.* 14 July 1897; ed. at Eton and R.M.C., Sandhurst. He *d.* unm. 12 Oct. 1972.

IX. 1972. 9. GERALD HOWARD BOTELER (IRBY), BARON BOSTON, distant cousin and h., being 1st s. and h. of Leonard Paul IRBY (*d.* 26 Nov. 1936), by Ethel Maud, 1st da. and coh. of William John Casberd BOTELER, Capt., R.N., of Taplow, co. Buckingham and Eastry, co. Kent, which Leonard Paul was 2nd s. of Leonard Howard Loyd Irby (*d.* 14 May 1905), by his 1st wife Geraldine Alicia Mary, da. of Rev. J.B. MAGENIS, which Leonard Howard Loyd was 4th s. of Frederick Paul IRBY, Rear Adm. (*d.* 24 Apr. 1844), 3rd s. by his 2nd wife Frances, 2nd da. of Ichabod WRIGHT of Mapperley Hall, co. Nottingham, which Frederick Paul was 2nd s. of 2nd Baron Boston. He was *b.* 29 Aug. 1897; *m.* 1stly, 14 Aug. 1926, Katherine Gertrude, da. of Capt. C.M.H. EDWARDS. This marriage was diss. by divorce in 1931 and he *m.* 2ndly, 8 Feb. 1936, Erica Nelly, da. of T.H. HILL. He *d.* 17 Feb. 1978. His widow *d.* 1990.

X. 1978. 10. TIMOTHY GEORGE FRANK BOTELER (IRBY), BARON BOSTON, only s. and h. by 2nd wife, *b.* 27 Mar. 1939; ed. at Clayesmore Sch., Dorset and Southampton Univ.; *m.*, 1967, Rhonda Anne, da. of Ronald Albert BATE of Balgowlah, New South Wales, Australia.

[GEORGE WILLIAM EUSTACE BOTELER IRBY, 1st s. and h. ap., *b.* 1 Aug. 1971.]

line 40, for 'Llandidan' read 'Llanidan'

BOTELER OF BRANTFIELD

page 229,
line 30, for '1647' read 'living 'July 1661' [*N&Q*, vol. 200, 1955, p. 345]

BOTELER, BOTILER OR BUTILLER (of Warrington)[ax]

page 230,
lines 2–15, delete all detail and replace as follows

BARONY BY WRIT I. 1295 1. WILLIAM LE BOTELER,[a] s. and h. of Amory LE BOTELER, of Warrington,[b] co. Lancaster by Aline

(? da. and h. of Stephen DE UPTON, of Upton, co. Warwick), *suc.* his father between 20 Nov. 1233 and 4 Sep. 1235,[ba] came of age about 1245, Sheriff of co. Lancaster and Governor of Lancaster Castle 1259. On 8 June (1294) 22 Edw. I, was sum. to attend the King wherever he might be,[bb] being excused 6 days later from serving in the French wars in Gascony, and was sum. to Parliament 23 June (1295) 23 Edw I, 26 Aug. (1295) 24 Edw. I, and 6 Feb. (1298/9) 27 Edw. I,[c] by writs directed *Willelmo le Butiller* and *Willelmo le Botiller de Werington*, whereby he may be held to have become LORD LE BOTILLER[d]. He *d.* between 1301 and the middle of 1304.

[Though none of his descendants (who were settled at Warrington, Bewsey and elsewhere) were sum. to Parl., his grandson, William le Boteler, of Bewsey (*m.* Sybil, and *d.* 1329), and his great grandson, Sir William le Boteler (Knight of the Shire, *m.* Elizabeth, and *d.* 1380), were sum. to attend the King in various campaigns down to 1335; and his great grandson, Sir John le Boteler (Knight of the Shire, *m.* Alice, and *d.* 1400), was one of the King's Commissioners in the Scrope and Grosvenor trial in 1386, being *styled Baro de Weryngton*.[da]]

note [ax] The arms of the Botelers of Warrington were azure, a bend between six covered cups, or.

note [a], delete all detail and replace by 'The name was derived from the office of Butler, which devolved on the family of Boteler of Warrington after the extinction of the male issue of Robert le Boteler, Butler to Ranulph de Gernon, Earl of Chester. This Robert, who founded the Abbey of Pulton, co. Chester before 1153, was possibly brother, but more probably cousin, of Richard *Pincerna*, the ancestor of the Botelers of Warrington referred to in the next note.'

note [b], as before

note [ba] *V.C.H., Lancs.*, vol. iii, p. 319b.

note [bb] As to this not being a summons to Parl., see Preface to vol. i, p. xxii.

notes [c], and [d], as before

note [da] For the descent of this family see *V.C.H., Lancs.*, vol. i, pp. 341–9.

BOTELER (of Wem)

page 232,

line 14, after '*m.*' add '1stly'

line 16, after 'Piedmont' add 'He *m.* 2ndly, before 1355, Joan, 1st da. of John (DE SUDELEY), 2nd LORD SUDELEY by Eleanor DE SCALES, presumably da. of Roland, 2nd LORD SCALES. By her he had a s. Thomas who, eventually, on the death *s.p.* in 1379 of his mother's yr. sister Margery, *suc.* his maternal uncle as 4th LORD SUDELEY.[ba]'

note [ba] See W.L. Sheppard, *Geneal. Mag.*, vol. 13, 1960, pp. 173–4, and Col. F.R. Twemlow, *Manor of Tyrley*, Staffs. Rec. Ser., pp. 41–2; also vol. xii, part 1, *sub* SUDELEY [1379], where note [c], p. 418, has been corrected.

line 16, after '1361' add 'She *d.* before Aug. 1367 when her s. Thomas abovenamed was her representative.

lines 23–5, delete from 'between' to 'who' and replace by '(lic. Coventry and Lichfield, 27 Sep. 1369, to marry in the chapel of the manor of Sir Nicholas Burnell at Acton Burnell, Salop), Robert DE FERRERS (yr. s. of Robert, 3rd LORD FERRERS (of Chartley), being only s. by his 2nd wife, Joan DE LA MOTE, of Willisham, Suffolk). He' [See FERRERS (of Chartley)]

line 30, for '(1380–1) 4 Ric. II' read '24 or 31 Dec. 1380'

page 233,
line 11, after 'Ferrers' add 'aged 8 in 1380'
note ([a]), line 4, after 'Nevill' add '(yr s. of Ralph, 1st Earl of Westmorland)'

BOTETOURT

page 233,
line 13, for 'whose parentage is unknown' read 'bastard s. of Edward I' [Hailes Chron., in BM Cott. MS. Cleopatra, D III, f. 51, *ex inform.* A.R. Wagner]

page 234,
line 8 of pedigree, two other sisters, Maud and Agnes, who were nuns, are here omitted, see vol. xii, part 2, note *sub* ZOUCHE (of Mortimer etc.) [1399].
line 11 of pedigree, for '*d. s.p.*' read '*d. s.p.m.*' [Joyce and Sir Adam Peshall had two daughters and coheirs who married and left issue. These were (i) Joan, wife of Sir William Birmingham, and (ii) Margaret, wife of Sir Richard Mytton (Canon Bridgeman, "Hist. of Weston-under-Lizard", in *Staffs. Hist. Coll.*, William Salt Arch. Soc., N.S., 1899, vol. ii, pp. 89–95, and ped. opp. p. 98). *Ex inform.* Walter G. Davis.]

page 235,
line 18, after 'under' add 'Will, as Lord of Weologh, pr. 1386 at Lambeth'
line 24, after '*d. v.p.*' add '21 Sep.'

page 236,
line 6, for 'pr.' read 'dat. 26 July 1766, pr. 10' [An abstract of his will is given in *Misc. Gen. et Her.*, vol. ii, p. 232]

BOTHWELL

page 237,
line 2, after 'RAMSAY' add 'of Trarinzean'
line 18, delete 'shortly' and for '15--' read '1505'
line 18, delete 'Kennedy([b])' and after 'Janet' add '([b]) 2nd wife of Archibald (DOUGLAS), 5th EARL OF ANGUS [S.], whom she left about 1499, and before that 1st wife, or possibly mistress, of Sir Alexander GORDON (who was slain at Flodden, 9 Sep. 1513), da. of John (KENNEDY), 2nd LORD KENNEDY [S.], by his 2nd wife, Elizabeth, widow of Nicholas (HAY) 2nd EARL OF ERROLL [S.], da. of Alexander (SETON, otherwise GORDON), 1st EARL OF HUNTLY [S.]. From her he was apparently soon divorced.'
line 20, after 'Livingston' add 'said to be a da. of (__) LIVINGSTON of East Wemyss'
line 26, after '(HOME)' add '1st'
line 28, delete from 'in' to 'he' and replace by 'apparently shortly after 6 Dec. 1482, and'
line 29, after 'England' add 'in 1483'
note ([b]), delete from 'She' to 'IV' and replace by 'In or about 1499 she became the mistress of James IV, by which King she was the mother of James Stewart, *cr.* (as an infant) Earl of Moray [S.] in 1501). For the explanation of her being referred to as the Lady Bothwell before 1505, see *Scots Peerage*, vol. ii, p. 459. See also Angus [1462] and *Addenda* above'

page 239,
from line 9 to line 5 on page 240, delete all detail. This article on James (HEPBURN), 4th EARL OF BOTHWELL, is superseded by that in vol. x, pp. 97–100, *sub* Orkney.

page 240,
line 6, for 'Francis Stewart' read 'Francis (STEWART), 2nd LORD DARNLEY [S.]'
line 7, for 'John S.' read 'John, 1st Lord Darnley [S.] (so *cr*. 1562)'
line 8, after 'V' add ')' and after '(HEPBURN)' add '3rd'
line 10, delete ')' and after 'father' add 'as 2nd LORD DARNLEY [S.]'
line 18, for '12 July 1592' read '21 July 1593'

page 241,
lines 1–2, delete from 'in' to '1614' and replace by '4 Nov. 1613' [*N&Q*, vol. 193, 1948, p. 206]
note (a), line 7, after 'Worcester' add 'He left 3 other sons and one illegit. son' [*Scots Peerage*, vol. ii, pp. 171–2; *N&Q*, *op. cit.*, pp. 205–6]

BOTREAUX

page 242,
line 2, for 'DAUBENY' read 'DAUBENEY [2nd LORD DAUBENEY]' and for '1st' read '2nd'
lines 11–12, delete from '4 Sep.' to '1458' and replace by 'dead by 7 Dec. 1411' [*Cal. Close Rolls, 1409–13*, p. 247]
line 19, after 'Notts.' add 'She was living 20 July 1415' [*Hist. MSS. Com.*, Hastings MSS., part 1, p. 287]
line 22, after 'as' add '20 July'

page 243,
line 2, for '14' read '18'
line 8, for '1468' read '17 Jan. 1468/9 at Salisbury'
line 10, for '1463' read '18 May 1464'
line 20, for '1511' read '1 May 1509'
line 21, for 'between 1528 and 1531/2' read 'before 10 July 1533'
line 29, for '1545' read '1543/4'

page 244,
line 19, for '5' read '26'

page 245,
lines 20–1, delete from 'and' to 'HUNGERFORD,' [this Barony was not claimed in 1871]

BOURCHIER

page 246,
line 32, after 'plague' add '*c*. 18 May' [Michael Jones, *Essex Arch. and Hist.*, vol. 26, 1995, p. 145. Thanks are due to Professor Jones for drawing my attention to his article].

page 247,
line 1, after 'h.' add', was *b.* 12 Mar. 1329' [Jones, *op. cit.*]
line 4, after 'France;' add 'a captive in France 1371 until 1375 [Jones, *op. cit.*]
line 5, after '1379' add 'may have been' [Jones, *op. cit.*]
line 14, after 'Burgundy.' add 'On crusade in Prussia 1390–1.' [Jones, *op. cit.*, p. 153]
line 16, for 'Elizabeth' read 'Maud' [Jones, *op. cit.*, p. 155, note 11]
line 25, for '(—)' read 'probably da. of John LOVEY, citizen and mercer of London' [*Essex Feet of Fines*, vol. 3, pp. 195, 201. *Ex inform.* Dr W.E. Church]

page 248,
line 1, for '26 Nov. 1431' read '1430, writ of *diem clausit extr.* issued 26 Jan.1430/1'(ax)
note (ax) See "John Benet's Chronicle", *Camden Miscellany*, vol. xxiv, p. 185, note 38.
note (b), line 1, add at beginning, 'See that title'

page 249,
line 4, after 'm.,' add '?1stly Isobel, da. of John (DE VERE), EARL OF OXFORD and ?2ndly' [See corrections to vol. v, p. 138, note (b), below]
lines 8–9, delete from 'being' to '1471' and replace by 'before 26 June 1480' [See ESSEX, vol. v, p. 138]
lines 9–10, delete from 'Sir' to '3rdly'
line 10, for '1480' read 'in or after 1483'
line 22, delete 'OF KENDAL'

page 250,
line 1, for '1570' read '1571'
line 2, for 'and soon afterwards his' read 'His'
line 4, for '1570' read '1571'
line 19, in margin for '1647' read '1646'

BOURKE OF BRITTAS

page 253,
line 13, after 'Italy.(d)' add 'His widow was living at St. Germain-en-Laye, 10 Oct. 1718' [*Hist. MSS. Com.*, Stuart MSS., vol. vii, p. 371]

BOURKE OF CLANMORIES

page 254,
note (c), line 2, for '1657' read '1658'

BOYD

page 261,
line 3, after 'Ochiltree' add 'by Eupheme, da. of (__) Wallace'

page 262,
line 35, for '1628' read '1629'

page 263,
lines 13–14, for '*d.* Mar. 1654' read 'was *bur.* 13 Mar. 1653/4 in the chancel of the church at Cottingham, co. York'

BOYLE OF KINALMEAKY

page 264,
note (c), line 13, after 'Berners' add 'Humphrey Bourchier, his grandson also sat in Parliament with his uncles as Lord Cromwell (see vol. iii, p. 554, *sub* CROMWELL [1467])'

BOYNE

page 269,
line 11, line to read as follows

IX. 1907. 9. GUSTAVUS WILLIAM (HAMILTON-RUSSELL), VISCOUNT BOYNE, &c., 2nd but 1st surv. s.(b)

lines 16–17, delete from 'Having' to 'work.]' and replace by 'He *d.* 18 Jan. 1942. His widow *d.* 1978.'

[GUSTAVUS LASCELLES HAMILTON-RUSSELL, 1st s. and h. ap., *b.* 18 Oct. 1907; ed. at Eton and Cambridge (Magdalene Coll.); *m.*, 20 Jan. 1931, Joan Verena, da. of Sir Harry Lloyd VERNEY. She *d.* 1 Apr. 1938. He served in WW2 and was *k.* in action, *v.p.*, June 1940.]

X. 1942. 10. GUSTAVUS MICHAEL GEORGE (HAMILTON-RUSSELL), VISCOUNT BOYNE, &c., grandson and h., being s. and h. of Gustavus Lascelles HAMILTON-RUSSELL and Joan Verena abovenamed. He was *b.* 10 Dec. 1931; ed. at Eton and R.M.A., Sandhurst; *m.*, 11 Apr. 1956, Rosemary Anne, 2nd da. of Major Sir Dennis Frederic Bankes STUCLEY, Bart.

[GUSTAVUS MICHAEL STUCLEY HAMILTON-RUSSELL, s. and h. ap., was *b.* 27 May 1965; ed. at Harrow and R.A.C., Cirencester; *m.*, 1991, Lucy, da. of George POTTER of Bunbury, Cheshire.]

BRABOURNE

page 270,
line 29, for 'living 1911' read '*d.* at Parham, Pulborough, 7 Jan. 1929.'

page 271,
line 9, delete from 'He' to 'work' and replace by 'His widow *d.* 19 May 1949.'

[RICHARD EDWARD WENTWORTH KNATCHBULL-HUGESSON, 1st s. and h. ap., *b.* 24 Aug. 1881, *d. v.p.* 3 May 1883.]

III. 1909. 3. WYNDHAM WENTWORTH (KNATCHBULL-HUGESSON), BARON BRABOURNE, 2nd but only surv. s. and h., *b.* 21 Sep. 1885; ed. at Eton 1899–1900; served in WW1, *d.* unm., being *k.* in action 11 Mar. 1915.

IV. 1915. 4. CECIL MARCUS (KNATCHBULL-HUGESSON), BARON BRABOURNE, and a Baronet, uncle and h., being 2nd s. of the 1st Baron Brabourne, *b.* 27 Nov. 1863; ed. at Cambridge (King's Coll.); *m.*, 8 Nov. 1893, Helena Regina Frederica, da. of Hermann VON FLESCH BRUNNINGEN, Imperial Councillor, of Vienna. She *d.* 15 Nov. 1919. He *d.* at sea, 15 Feb. 1933.

V. 1933. 5. MICHAEL HERBERT RUDOLF (KNATCHBULL-HUGESSON, later KNATCHBULL), BARON BRABOURNE, s. and h., *b.* 8 May 1895; assumed the name (only), 29 June 1919, of KNATCHBULL. He *m.*, 22 Jan. 1919, Doreen Geraldine, 3rd da. of George Ulick (BROWNE), 6th MARQUESS OF SLIGO. He *d.* 23 Feb. 1939. His widow *d.* 1979.

VI. 1939. 6. NORTON CECIL MICHAEL (KNATCHBULL), BARON BRABOURNE, &c., 1st s. and h., *b.* 11 Feb. 1922; ed. at Eton and R.M.A., Sandhurst. He was *k.* on active service, unm., 15 Sep. 1943, being shot after recapture in Italy.

VII. 1943. 7. JOHN ULICK (KNATCHBULL), BARON BRABOURNE, &c., br. and h., *b.* 9 Nov. 1924; ed. at Eton and Oxford (Brasenose Coll.); *m.*, 26 Oct. 1946, Patricia Edwina Victoria, 1st da. of Louis Francis Albert Victor Nicholas (MOUNTBATTEN), 1st EARL MOUNTBATTEN OF BURMA, K.G.[ax]

note [ax] She *suc.* to her father's Earldom under the spec. rem. on his death by assassination, 27 Aug. 1979. See below, *sub* MOUNTBATTEN, Earldom, [1947].

[NORTON LOUIS PHILIP KNATCHBULL, *styled* LORD ROMSEY, 1st s. and h. ap., *b.* 8 Oct. 1947; ed. at Gordonstoun and Univ. of Kent; *m.*, 20 Oct. 1979, Penelope Meredith, only da. of Reginald EASTWOOD of Palma da Mallorca, Spain.]

BRADESTON

page 273,

line 17, after 'Agnes' add 'widow of John MAUDUIT, of Somerford Mauduit, Wilts., Broughton, Oxon., etc. (*d.* 21 Aug. 1347), and described as sister of Robert DE WALKINGTON and William DE ROTHER' [See vol. viii, p. 553, *sub* MAUDUIT]

line 17, after '*d.*' add '25'

line 18, after '*d. s.p.m.*' add '31 Aug.'

BRADFORD

page 276,

line 21, after 'She' add ', who was *b.* 20 Aug. 1790,'

page 277,
line 11, after 'Tickhill.' add 'He *d.* 2, in London, aged nearly 70, and was *bur.* 6 Jan. 1915 at Weston Park, Shropshire. His widow *d.* 22, and was *bur.* 25 Aug. 1936 at St. Andrew's, Weston-under-Lizard, near Wolverhampton.'
line 12, line to read as follows

EARLDOM. IX. BARONY. VI.	1915	5 and 6. ORLANDO (BRIDGEMAN), EARL OF BRADFORD, &c., 1st s. and h., *b.*

line 18, for ']' read 'She *d.* 16 Apr. 1949. He *d.* 21 Mar. 1957.'

EARLDOM. X. BARONY. VII.	1957	6 and 7. GERALD MICHAEL ORLANDO (BRIDGEMAN), EARL OF BRADFORD, &c., only s. and h., *b*, 29 Sep. 1911; ed. at Harrow and Cambridge (Trin. Coll.); *m.*, 31 Oct. 1946, Mary Willoughby, 1st da. of Lieut. Col. Thomas Hassard MONTGOMERY of Cadogan House, Shrewsbury. He *d.* 30 Aug.

1981. His widow *d.* 1986.

EARLDOM. XI. BARONY. VIII.	1981	7 and 8. RICHARD THOMAS ORLANDO (BRIDGEMAN), EARL OF BRADFORD, &c., 1st s. and h., *b.* 3 Oct. 1947; ed. at Harrow and Cambridge (Trin. Coll.); *m.*, 1979, Joanne Elizabeth, 1st da. of Benjamin MILLER.

[ALEXANDER MICHAEL ORLANDO BRIDGEMAN, *styled* VISCOUNT NEWPORT, 1st s. and h. ap., *b.* 6 Sep. 1980.]

BRAMWELL OF HEVER

page 279,
line 4, after '1808;' add 'ed. at Dr Reddy's Sch., Camberwell and then at Dr May's Acad., Enfield, then a clerk in his father's bank for 6 years.' [See Charles Fairfield, *A Memoir of Lord Bramwell*, 1899]

BRASSEY OF BULKELEY

page 282,
line 19, after '; Sq.' add 'He *d.* at his residence in Park Lane, 23, aged 82, and was *bur.* 27 Feb. 1918, at Catsfield, Battle, Sussex. His widow *d.* 20 and was *bur.* 23 Feb. 1934, at Golders Green Cemetery.'
line 20, line to read as follows

II. 1918. 2. THOMAS ALLNUTT (BRASSEY), EARL BRASSEY [1911], VISCOUNT HYTHE OF HYTHE [1911], and BARON BRASSEY OF BULKELEY [1886], s. and h. by 1st wife, *b.* 7 Mar. 1863; ed. at Eton and Oxford (Balliol Coll.);

line 27, for ']' read 'He *d. s.p.* 12, and was *bur.* 16 Nov. 1919, at Catsfield, afsd., when all his honours became *extinct*. His widow *d.* 22 Feb. 1951.'

BRAYBROOKE

page 283,
line 21, for 'Genoa' read 'Geneva'
line 22, for 'July' read 'and *bap.* 29 June'

page 286,
lines 17–18, delete from 'was' to 'work.' and replace by '*d.* at Little Hadham Place, Herts, 18, aged 88, and was *bur.* 23 Mar. 1914, at Littlebury, Essex.'

VI. 1902. 6. LATIMER (NEVILLE), LORD BRAYBROOKE, &c., br. and h., *b.* 22 Apr. 1827; ed. at Cambridge; ordained Priest. He *m.*, 2 June 1853, Lucy Frances, da. of John Thomas LE MARCHANT. He *d.* 12 Jan. 1904. His widow *d.* 6, and was *bur.* 9 Dec. at Littlebury afsd.

VII. 1904. 7. HENRY (NEVILLE), LORD BRAYBROOKE, &c., 1st s. and h., *b.* 11 July 1855; ed. at Cambridge (Magdalene Coll.). He *m.* 1stly, 3 Nov. 1898, Emilie Pauline, yst. da. of Antoine GONIN, of Condeminié, Maçon. She *d.* 20 Oct. 1912, at Heydon, Royston, Herts., after several months' illness. He *m.* 2ndly, 18 Sep. 1917, at St. James's Church, Sussex Gdns., Dorothy Edith, yst. da. of Sir George LAWSON, K.C.B. He *d.* 9 Mar. 1941. His widow *d.* 1973.

VIII. 1941. 8. RICHARD HENRY CORNWALLIS (NEVILLE), LORD BRAYBROOKE, &c., 1st s. and h., by 2nd wife, *b.* 13 July 1918. He *d.* unm. 23 Jan. 1943, being *k.* in action.

IX. 1943. 9. HENRY SEYMOUR (NEVILLE), LORD BRAYBROOKE, &c., cousin and h., being s. and h. of Rev. Grey NEVILLE (*d.* 28 Dec. 1920), by Mary Peele, da. of the Rev. Canon Francis SLATER, which Grey was 2nd s. of the 6th Lord Braybrooke. He was *b.* 5 Feb. 1897; *m.* 1stly, 1 Mar. 1930, Muriel Evelyn, da. of William Charles MANNING of Newmarket, co. Suffolk, and widow of Euan Curle CARTWRIGHT. She *d.* 16 June 1962 and he *m.* 2ndly, 2 Sep. 1963, Angela Mary, da. of William Herbert HOLLIS and widow of John REE. She *d.* 1985. He *d.* 12 Feb. 1990.

X. 1990. 10. ROBIN HENRY CHARLES (NEVILLE), LORD BRAYBROOKE, BARON OF BRAYBROOKE, only s. and h., *b.* 29 Jan. 1932; ed. at Eton and Cambridge (Magdalene Coll.); *m.*, 29 July 1955, Robin Helen, only da. of Thomas Adolph BROCKHOFF of Sydney, New South Wales, Australia. This marriage was diss. by divorce in 1974 and he *m.* 2ndly, 1974, Linda, 2nd da. of Arthur NORMAN of Saffron Waldon, co. Essex.

BRAYE

page 287,
line 7, for 'writ' read 'writs'

line 8, after '*m.*' add 'before 21 Mar. 1500/1, when they had a grant of the dissolved Priory of Newenham, Beds.'

page 288,
pedigree, line 1, after '*m.*' add '1stly' and after '1573' add '2ndly. William (Knollys), Earl of Banbury (*d.* 1632)'

page 290,
line 4, for 'is' read 'was'
line 6, after 'Lancaster.' add 'He *d.* 1, and was *bur.* in the family vault, Stamford Park, Rugby, 6 July 1928. His widow *d.* 25 Nov. 1935.'
line 7, line to read as follows

VI. 1928. 6. ADRIAN VERNEY (VERNEY-CAVE), LORD BRAYE, 1st s. and h., *b.* 11 Oct. 1874, *m.*'

line 10, for ']' read 'He *d.* 12 Feb. 1952. His widow *d.* 7 July 1955.'

VII. 1952. 7. THOMAS ADRIAN (VERNEY-CAVE), LORD BRAYE, 1st s. and h., *b.* 26 July 1902; *m.*, 3 Feb. 1934, Dorothea, da. of Daniel Charles DONOGHUE of Philadelphia, U.S.A. He *d.* 19 Dec. 1985. His widow *d.* 1994.

VIII. 1985. 8. MARY PENELOPE, *suo jure* BARONESS BRAYE, only child and h., *b.* 29 Sep. 1941; *m.*, 1981, as his 2nd wife, Lieut. Col. Edward Henry Lancelot AUBREY-FLETCHER, s. of Major Sir Henry Lancelot AUBREY-FLETCHER, Bart.

BREADALBANE

page 290,
line 19, for 'only' read '1st'

page 293,
line 7, after '1stly' add '(lic. Nottingham, 17 Apr. 1685)'
line 14, for 'Abbey' read 'Palace'

page 294,
line 9, after 'Preston' add 'co. Kircudbright, by Elizabeth, da. of William HAIRSTANES of Craigs, in that co.'

page 295,
pedigree, line 2, for 'only' read 'eld.'

page 296,
line 19, for '1852' read '1844'

page 298,
line 2, after 'Albany.' add 'He *d.* at the Central Station Hotel, Glasgow, 19, and was

bur. 24 Oct. 1922, at Finlarig, Kellin, when the Marquessate and his other peerages of the U.K. became *extinct*. His widow *d.* 10 May 1932.'

EARLDOM [S.] VIII. 1922. 8. IAIN EDWARD HERBERT HERBERT (CAMPBELL), EARL OF BREADALBANE AND HOLLAND, &c. [S.], nephew and h. being s. of Ivan CAMPBELL (*d.* 16 Mar. 1917), by Margaret Elizabeth Diana, da. of James Charles Herbert Welbore Ellis (AGAR), 3rd EARL OF NORMANTON, which Ivan was 2nd s. of 6th Earl of Breadalbane. He was *b.* 14 June 1885 and *d.* unm. in a nursing home in Bournemouth, Hants., 10, and was *bur.* 14 May 1923 in the Mausoleum of Finlarig Castle, Perthshire.

IX. 1923. 9. CHARLES WILLIAM (CAMPBELL), EARL OF BREADALBANE, &c., distant cousin and h. male, being s. of Major Gen. Charles William CAMPBELL (*d.* 1894), by Gwynnedd, only da. of William Edward BRINCKMAN, which Charles William was 1st s. of Charles William C. (*d.* 18 June 1861), by Charlotte Olympia Cockburn, da. of John CAMPBELL of Kinloch, which Charles William was 1st s. of John C. (*d.* 12 Mar. 1823), by Janet, da. of William BUTTER of Edinburgh, which John was 3rd s. of Colin C. (*d.* 2 Oct. 1791), by his 2nd wife Susanna, da. of Rev. Duncan CAMPBELL, which Colin was 1st s. of Robert Campbell (*b.* 10 Aug. 1737), by Susanna, da. of James MENZIES of Culdares, which Robert was 1st s. of William CAMPBELL of Glenfalloch (*d. circa* 1621), by Jean, da. of Sir Colin CAMPBELL of Ardkinglas, which William was 5th s. of Sir Robert CAMPBELL, 3rd Baronet of Glenorchy. He was *b.* 11 June 1889; *m.*, 10 Aug. 1918, Armorer Romer, da. of Romer WILLIAMS of Newnham Hall, Daventry, co. Northampton and widow of Capt. Eric NICHOLSON. He *d.* 5 May 1959. His widow *d.* 1987.

X. 1959. 10. JOHN ROMER BORELAND (CAMPBELL), EARL OF BREADALBANE, &c., s. and h., *b.* 28 Apr. 1919; ed. at Eton and R.M.C., Sandhurst; *m.*, 2 Nov. 1949, Coralie, only da. of Charles ARCHER.

BRENTFORD

page 300,
line 12, for '*Vane*' read '*Kielmansegge*'
line 13, for '1730' read '1725'

BRERETON

page 301,
note (e), line 8, after 'Brereton' add 'See also *N&Q*, vol. 193, 1948, p. 261 for possible descendants of Mary, sister of William, 2nd Lord Brereton.'

BREWES

page 302,
line 15, for 'MOELES or MULES' read 'MOELS' and after 'Somerset 'add 'by Hawise, widow of John DE BOTREAUX, yr. da. and coh. of James DE NEWMARCH, of Cadbury afsd. [See MOELS.]'

line 16, for 'William' read 'Robert' and delete '[LORD ROS]

lines 17–18, delete 'shortly before' and after '1290/1' add 'at Findon, West Sussex, and was *bur.* at Sele Priory 15 Jan.'

note (b), line 3, after 'Lord' add 'The evidence for this filiation is discussed by Eugene Stratton, *The Geneal.*, vol. 6, 1985, pp. 85–9.

note (g), add at end 'See MULTON (of Gilsland)'

note (j), line 1, before 'Writ' add 'Eastry Letters IV, sheet 18, no. 102, Muniments of the Dean and Chapter of Canterbury Cathedral.' [*Ex inform.* Robert Edmunds, as are succeeding corrections and additions on page 303.]

page 303,

line 8, for 'The name of his 1st wife is unknown' read 'He *m.* 1stly, Agnes.'

line 14, after 'Aline' add '(probably in fact the younger da., aged about 8 in 1298)' [Breviate of Domesday, PRO E164/1, f. 17v]

note (e), line 1, before 'Genealogists' add 'A charter, granted by William de Breuse, gives the name Agnes.'

note (i), line 9, after 'Breuwosa.' add 'BL, Harl. MS. 152, f. 11; PRO C71/4 m. 4, for further references to this William in 1306 and 1311. According to *Flores Historiarum*, Rolls Ser., 1890, vol. 3, p. 344, he *d.* in 1320.'

page 304,

line 3, after 'Bohun' add 'of Midhurst, Sussex'

line 5, after '1324' add '(probably 11 May in a chapel in St. Benet's Abbey, Holme, Norfolk)' [John Harvey, *William Worcestre, Itineraries*, 1969, pp. 222, 223]

page 305,

lines 7–8, delete from 'da.' to 'Norwich' and replace by 'da. of John (LA WARRE), 2nd LORD LA WARRE, by Jean, sister and coh., eventually sole h. of Thomas (DE GRELLE), 1st LORD GRELLE, 1st da. of Sir Robert DE GRELLE, lord of Manchester' [See LATIMER [1334]]

lines 10–11, delete from 'became' to '1378/9(g)' and replace by '*m.* 2ndly, in or before 1328, Warin (LE LATIMER), 2nd LORD LATIMER, who *d.* 13 Aug. 1349. She *d.* 9 Aug. 1361.'

note (g), [this Katherine was not wife of Robert DE BEUSE, *d. circa* 1325. See correction note to vol. vii, p. 765]

page 308,

line 3, for 'Werthorpe' read 'Weaverthorpe'

line 6, for 'his wife' read 'widow of Sir Henry HUSEE, of Harting, Sussex, etc. (*d.* 27 Aug. 1290)' [See vol. vii, p. 3, note (b), *sub* HUSEE]

line 13, for 'before 13 Sep. 1337' read '*circa* Aug. 1334'

line 15, for 'JOINVILLE' read 'GENEVILLE'

line 16, after 'Salop' add '2nd but 1st surv. s. and h. ap. of Geoffrey, 1st LORD GENEVILLE'

line 17, for 'Werthorpe' read 'Weaverthorpe'

note (c), line 1, after 'Winterthorpe' add '(now Weaverthorpe)'

line 3, delete 'It has now disappeared.'

note (e), delete all detail and replace by 'Loyd and Stenton, *Hatton's Book of Seals*, no. 363'

page 309,
line 3, for 'whose name is unknown' read 'Joan, whose parentage is unknown'

page 310,
lines 9–11, delete from 'and' to 'issue' and replace by 'sister and h. of John (DE SAY), 4th LORD SAY, da. of William, 3rd LORD SAY, by Beatrice, da. and (in her issue) h. of Thomas, 1st LORD BREWOSE'

BRIDGEWATER

page 311,
line 13, for 'Sir Philip' read 'Hugh' and after '*d. s.p.*' add '8, and was *bur.* in Dorset, 12'

page 312,
line 2, delete 'about 1601' and replace by 'between 27 June 1602 and'

BRIDPORT

page 317,
line 21, for '1761' read '21 Aug. 1758' [See Maud Wyndham, *Chron. of the 18th Century*, vol. ii, 1924, p. 278] and after 'Mary' add 'then aged 54'
note ([d]), delete all detail

page 319,
line 10, line to read as follows

VISCOUNTCY II. BARONY [I.] IV. } 1904 — 2 and 4. ARTHUR WELLINGTON ALEXANDER NELSON (HOOD), VISCOUNT BRIDPORT OF CRICKET ST. THOMAS AND OF BRONTE, BARON BRIDPORT, 1st s. and h., *b.*

lines 16–18, delete from 'Having' to 'work]' and replace by 'She *d.* at Merstham, Surrey, 12 Oct. 1922. He *d.* at Lancrosse Vale, Guernsey, 28 Mar., and was *bur.* 1 Apr. 1924 at Vale Cemetery, Guernsey.'

[ALEXANDER JOHN NELSON HOOD, 1st s. and h. ap., *b.* 13 Aug. 1876, *d.* 31 Aug. 1877.]

[MAURICE HENRY NELSON HOOD, 2nd s. and h. ap., *b.* 16 Jan. 1881; *m.* 19 Nov. 1908, Ethel Rose, eld. da. of Charles KENDALL of Wokingham. He served in WW1 in the R.N.D. and was *k.* in action at Gallipoli, *v.p.*, 4 June 1915. His widow *d.* 17 Apr. 1931 at Eastbourne.]

VISCOUNTCY III. BARONY [I.] V. } 1922 — 3 and 5. ROWLAND ARTHUR HERBERT NELSON (HOOD), VISCOUNT BRIDPORT OF CRICKET ST. THOMAS, &c., grandson and h., being only s. and h. of Maurice Henry Nelson HOOD and Ethel Rose abovenamed. He was *b.* 22 May 1911; ed. at R.N.C., Dartmouth; *m.*, 11 July 1934, Pamela Aline Mary, only da. of Charles J. BAKER. This marriage was diss. by divorce in 1945 and he *m.*

2ndly, 2 Jan. 1946, Sheila Jeanne Agatha, only da. of Johan Hendrik VAN MEURS of London and widow of Wing Cmdr. James Hayward LITTLE, D.F.C. He *d.* 25 July 1969. His widow *m.* 3rdly, 1988, Alexei V. HAIEFF. She was still living 1995.

VISCOUNTCY IV. BARONY [I.] VI. } 1969 — 4 and 6. ALEXANDER NELSON (HOOD), VISCOUNT BRIDPORT OF CRICKET ST. THOMAS, &c., 2nd but 1st surv. s. and h., *b.* 17 Mar. 1948; ed. at Eton and the Sorbonne; *m.*, 1972, Linda Jacqueline, da. of Lieut. Col. Vincent Rudolph PARAVICINI of Nutley Manor, Basingstoke, Hants. This marriage was diss. by divorce in 1979 and he *m.* 2ndly, 1979, Nina, da. of Curt LINCOLN, formerly wife of Phillip MARTYN and widow of Jochen RINDT.

[PEREGRINE ALEXANDER NELSON HOOD, s. and h. ap. by 1st wife, *b.* 30 Aug. 1974.]

BRISTOL

page 321,
line 7, after 'Madrid' add 'and *bap.* there 6 Nov. (O.S.)' [*Hist. MSS. Com.*, Portland MSS., vol. ix, p. 131]

page 325,
line 24, for 'Governor' read 'Lieut.-Gov.'

page 326,
line 23, for '18' read '17'

page 329,
lines 19–20, delete from 'He' to 'work]' and replace by 'His widow *d.* at St. George's Hosp., Hyde Park Corner, having been knocked down and fatally injured by a motor car, 25, aged 83, and was *bur.* 29 Jan. 1927, at Ickworth.'

MARQUESSATE IV. EARLDOM. XI. } 1907 — 4 and 8. FREDERICK WILLIAM FANE (HERVEY), MARQUESS OF BRISTOL, &c., nephew and h., being 2nd but 1st surv. s. and h. of Augustus Henry Charles HERVEY (*d.* 28 May 1875), by Marian, yst. da. of William P. HODNETT and widow of Ashton BENYON of Stetchworth Park, Camb., which Augustus was 2nd s. of the 2nd Marquess of Bristol. He was *b.* 8 Nov. 1863; ed. at Tonbridge Gram. Sch.; *m.*, 6 Dec. 1896, Alice Frances Theodora, da. of George Edward WYTHES of Copped Hall, Epping, Essex. He *d.* 24 Oct. 1951. His widow *d.* 15 Sep. 1957.

MARQUESSATE V. EARLDOM. XII. } 1951 — 5 and 9. HERBERT ARTHUR ROBERT (HERVEY), MARQUESS OF BRISTOL, &c., br. and h. (being 5th s. of the afsd. Augustus), *b.* 10 Oct. 1870; ed. at Clifton; *m.* 1stly, 29 Oct. 1914, Jean Alice Elaine, da. of Douglas Mackinnon Baillie Hamilton (COCHRANE), 12th EARL OF DUNDONALD. This marriage was diss. by divorce in 1933 (she *d.* 5 Jan. 1955) and he *m.* 2ndly, 15 Dec. 1952, Dora Frances Emblin, only da. of George MARSHALL and widow of Don Pedro DE ZULUETA. She *d.* 27 Mar. 1953. He *d.* 5 Apr. 1960.

MARQUESSATE VI. EARLDOM. XIII. } 1960 — 6 and 10. VICTOR FREDERICK COCHRANE (HERVEY), MARQUESS OF BRISTOL, &c., s. and h., *b.* 6 Oct. 1915; ed. at Eton and R.M.C., Sandhurst; *m.* 1stly, 6 Oct. 1949, Pauline Mary, da. of Herbert Coxon BOLTON. This marriage was diss. by divorce in 1959 (she was still living 1995) and he *m.* 2ndly, 23 Apr. 1960, Lady Anne Juliet Dorothea Maud, da. of William Henry Laurence Peter (WENTWORTH-FITZWILLIAM), 8th EARL FITZWILLIAM. This marriage was in turn diss. by divorce in 1972 and he *m.* 3rdly, 1974, Yvonne Marie, only da. of Anthony SUTTON of Farnborough Park, Kent. He *d.* 10 Mar. 1985. His widow was still living 1995.

MARQUESSATE VII. EARLDOM. XIV. } 1985 — 7 and 11. FREDERICK WILLIAM JOHN AUGUSTUS (HERVEY), MARQUESS OF BRISTOL, &c., s. and h. by 1st wife, *b.* 15 Sep. 1954; *styled* EARL JERMYN till 1985; ed. at Harrow; *m.*, 1984, Francesca, da. of Douglas H. FISHER of Marbella, Spain and formerly wife of Phillip JONES of U.S.A. This marriage was diss. by divorce in 1987.

BRITTANY

page 330,
line 9, for '*s.p.*' read 'unm.'
lines 13–18, delete all detail (see *sub* RICHMOND)

BROMLEY

page 331,
line 6, for '1707' read '1733'

BROOKE

page 334,
line 3, after 'unm.' add '19 Nov. 1658 at Chiswick, Midx., and was *bur.* 21 Dec. at Warwick'
line 5, after '*b.*' add '4 Jan. 1638/9 and *bap.* 24 Jan. at Warwick'
line 10, after 'Somerset' add 'and was *bur.* 20 Mar. at Warwick'
line 11, delete from 'Will' to '1677' and replace by 'Will dat. 14 Nov. 1667 to 24 Nov. 1674, pr. 2 June 1677'
line 12, after '*d.*' add '3' and after '1690/1' add 'and was *bur.* 19 Feb. at Breamore afsd.'
line 20, after '*d.*' add '20' and after '1705' add 'and was *bur.* 3 Oct. at Warwick'
line 21, after 'year' add 'and was *bur.* in St. Mary's, Warwick'

page 335,
line 8, for 'pr.' read 'dat. 1 Feb. 1725/6, pr. 8 July'

page 336,
line 9, for 'pr.' read 'dat. 23 May 1770 to 2 Sep. 1771, pr. 23'
line 10, for 'whose' read 'who *d.* suddenly in 1797 at the house of his mistress in Cleveland Str., aged towards 70. His' [*Farrington Diary*, ed. Greig, 6 Feb. 1806]

line 17, after 'sponsors.' add 'Ed. at Eton 1753–4.'
page 337,
line 12, after 'Lane' add 'and was *bur.* 12 May at Warwick'
line 14, for '78' read '77'
line 23, after 'Chester' add 'and at Eton till 1796'

page 338,
line 29, after '1893.' add 'Ed. at Eton 1867.'
line 36, after '(a) add 'He *d.* aged nearly 71, at Cliffe House, Beer, Devon, 15, and was *bur.* 19 Jan. 1924, at Warwick. His widow *d.* 26 July 1938.'
line 37, line to read as follows

EARLDOM. VI. BARONY. XIII. } 1924 6 and 13. LEOPOLD GUY FRANCIS MAYNARD BROOKE (GREVILLE), EARL BROOKE OF WARWICK CASTLE, [1746], &c., 1st s. and h.,

line 40, after 'sponsors' add '*styled* LORD BROOKE from 1893 to 1924.'

page 339,
line 6, for ']' read 'He *d.* 31 Jan. 1928. His widow *d.* 10 Feb. 1943.'

EARLDOM. VII. BARONY. XIV. } 1928 7 and 14. CHARLES GUY FULKE (GREVILLE), EARL BROOKE OF WARWICK CASTLE, &c., 1st s. and h., *b.* 4 Mar. 1911; ed. at Eton; *m.* 1stly, 11 July 1933, Rose, da. of David Cecil BINGHAM. This marriage was diss. by divorce in 1938 (she *d.* 1982) and he *m.* 2ndly, 19 Feb. 1942, Mary Kathleen, 1st da. of Percy Clifford HOPKINSON of Kingston Gorse, Sussex and formerly wife of Harold Edward BELL. This marriage was in turn diss. by divorce in 1949 and he *m.* 3rdly, 25 Nov. 1963, Janine, da. of Georges Detry DE MARÈS. He *d.* 20 Jan. 1984. His widow was still living 1995.

EARLDOM. VIII. BARONY. XV. } 1984 8 and 15. DAVID ROBIN FRANCIS GUY (GREVILLE), EARL BROOKE OF WARWICK CASTLE, &c., s. and h., *b.* 15 May 1934; ed. at Eton; *m.* 1stly, 28 June 1955, Sarah Anne, da. of Alfred Chester BEATTY of Wittersham, Kent. This marriage was diss. by divorce in 1967. He *d.* 20 Jan. 1996. His widow was still living 1995.

EARLDOM. IX. BARONY. XVI. } 1996 9 and 16. GUY DAVID (BROOKE), EARL BROOKE OF WARWICK CASTLE, &c., s. and h., *styled* LORD BROOKE 1984–96, *b.* 30 Jan. 1957; ed. at Eton; *m.*, 1981, Susan McKinley, da. of George William McKinley WILSON of Melbourne, Australia and formerly wife of Nicholas Sydney COBBOLD.

[CHARLES FULKE CHESTER GREVILLE, s. and h. ap., was *b.* 27 July 1982.]

BROUGHAM

page 339,
line 22, after 'Eleanor' add '(*d.* 31 Dec. 1839)'

page 342,
line 31, after 'Bart.' add 'She *d.* after an operation at 36 Chesham Place, S.W.17, 17 Dec. 1925. He *d.* suddenly at Chesham Place afsd. 24 May 1927.'

page 343,
line 5, after '1884.' add 'This marriage was dissolved in 1919 and he *m.* 2ndly at Budapest, the BARONESS HENGELMÜLLER, da. of BARON HENGELMÜLLER VON HENGERVAR, former Austro-Hungarian ambassador to the U.S.A. He *d.* 4 May 1927.'

IV. 1927. 4. VICTOR HENRY PETER (BROUGHAM), BARON BROUGHAM AND VAUX OF BROUGHAM AND OF HIGHMEAD CASTLE, grandson and h., being 1st s. by 1st wife of Henry BROUGHAM and Diana Isabel abovesaid, *b.* 23 Oct. 1909. He *m.*, 21 Apr. 1931, Violet Valerie, younger da. of Major Gerald FRENCH, at St. Margaret's, Westm. This marriage was diss. by divorce in 1934 and he *m.* 2ndly, 3 June 1935, Jean, da. of Brig. Gen. Gilbert Burrell Spencer FOLLETT, D.S.O. This marriage was in turn diss. by divorce in 1942 (she *d.* 1992) and he *m.* 3rdly, 4 June 1942, Edith Ellaline, da. of Leonard TEICHMAN and formerly wife of Richard Vaughan HART-DAVIS. He *d.* 20 June 1967. His widow was still living 1995.

[JULIAN HENRY PETER BROUGHAM, 1st s. and h. ap. by 1st wife, was *b.* 5 Oct. 1932. He *d.* unm. and on active service in Malaya, 8 May 1952.]

V. 1967. 5. MICHAEL JOHN (BROUGHAM), BARON BROUGHAM AND VAUX OF BROUGHAM AND OF HIGHMEAD CASTLE, 2nd but 1st surv. s, 1st s. by 2nd wife, *b.* 2 Aug. 1938; ed. at Lycée Jaccard, Lausanne, and Millfield Sch.; *m.* 1stly, 20 July 1963, Olivia Susan, only da. of Rear Adm. Gordon Thomas Seccombe GRAY, D.S.C. of Midhurst, Sussex. This marriage was diss. by divorce in 1967 and he *m.* 2ndly, 1969, Catherine Jill, 1st da. of William GULLIVER. This marriage was in turn diss. by divorce in 1981.

[CHARLES WILLIAM BROUGHAM, s. and h. ap. by 2nd wife, *b.* 9 Nov. 1971.]

BROUNCKER

page 345,
line 5, for 'Ragland' read 'Oxford'

BROWNLOW

page 350,
line 14, after 'She' add ', who' and after '(c)' add ', *d.* after a long illness at 8 Carlton House Terrace, 16, and was *bur.* 19 Mar. 1917. He *d. s.p.*, at Belton, 17, and was *bur.* there 22 Mar. 1921 when the Earldom of Brownlow and Viscountcy of Alford became *extinct* and the Barony of Brownlow of Belton, together with his Baronetcy devolved on his distant cousin.'

BARONY. V. } 1921. 5. ADELBERT SALUSBURY COCKAYNE (CUST), BARON BROWNLOW OF BELTON [1776], also a Baronet, distant cousin and h., being 2nd s. of Henry Francis COCKAYNE-CUST (*d.* 5 Apr. 1884), by Sara Jane, 4th da. of Isaac COOKSON, widow of Major Sidney Robert STREATFEILD, which Henry Francis was 1st s. and h. of Rev. Henry Cockayne CUST (*d.* 19 May 1861), by Anna Maria, eldest da. of Francis (NEEDHAM), 1st EARL OF KILMOREY, Henry being 2nd s. of the 1st Baron Brownlow. He was *b.* 14 Sep. 1867; *m.*, 5 Oct. 1895, Maud, da. of Capt. S. BUCKLE. He *d.* 19 Apr. 1927. His widow *d.* 19, in London and was *bur.* 22 Sep. 1936 at Belton, Grantham.

VI. 1927. 6. PEREGRINE FRANCIS ADELBERT (CUST), BARON BROWNLOW OF BELTON, &c., s. and h., *b.* 27 Apr. 1899; ed. at Eton and R.M.C., Sandhurst; *m.* 1stly, 18 Oct. 1927, Katharine Hariot, yr. da. of Brig. Gen. Sir David Alexander KINLOCH, Bart. She *d.* 27 Nov. 1952 and he *m.* 2ndly, 10 Dec. 1954, Dorothy, yr. da. of Thomas Sarsfield Kent POWER of Norfolk, Virginia, U.S.A. and formerly wife of 1stly, Harry Ester Reynolds HALL, 2ndly of David Field (BEATTY), 2nd EARL BEATTY and 3rdly of John Gordon BARAGWANATH. She *d.* 11 May 1966 and he *m.* 3rdly, 14 May 1969, Leila, only da. of Major Phillip Guy REYNOLDS, D.S.O., widow of George Miles (WATSON), 2nd BARON MANTON and formerly wife of John Dane PLAYER. He *d.* 28 July 1978. His widow *d.* 1983.

VII. 1978. 7. EDWARD JOHN PEREGRINE (CUST), BARON BROWNLOW OF BELTON, &c., 2nd but 1st surv. s. and h. by 1st wife, *b.* 25 Mar. 1936; ed. at Eton; *m.*, 31 Dec. 1964, Shirlie Edith, 2nd da. of John Paske YEOMANS of Upton on Severn, co. Worcester.

[PEREGRINE EDWARD QUINTIN CUST, s. and h., *b.* 9 July 1974.]

BRUCE OF KINLOSS

page 352,
line 3, after 'unm.' add 'a day or two after 10'
line 15, after '*d.*' add '20 Oct.'
line 19, after '*d.*' add '16 Dec.'
note ([a]), line 1, after 'in' add '*Hist. MSS. Com.*, Portland MSS., vol. ix, pp. 53–8, and in'

BRUN

page 356,
line 5, for 'before' read 'between 6 Feb. 1362/3 (when she had lic. to marry whom she would) and'
note ([e]), add at beginning 'See HAUDLO'

BRUS

page 359,
line 12, for 'before 12 May 1275' read '3 May 1273 at Hoddam, in the diocese of Glasgow([e])'
note ([e]), delete all detail and replace by 'G.O. Sayles, *Scot. Hist. Rev.*, vol. xxv, 1928, pp. 386–9'

BRYAN

page 360,
line 3, after '1stly' add '?Isobel([da]), 2ndly,'
note ([da]) For this earlier marriage see *Scots Peerage*, vol. 6, p. 290, (*cf.* vol. ix, p. 167, note ([c]), *sub* MORAY). This Isobel was mother of Thomas Randolph, Earl of Moray.

page 361,
line 6, for '30' read '40'
lines 16–18, delete from 'He appears' to 'wife' and replace by 'He *m.* 1stly, Joan (living 12 Apr. 1348), said to be da. of Sir John DE CARREU, of Carew, co. Pembroke'
line 18, after '*m.*' add '2ndly'
line 19, delete from 'presumably' to 'wife'
note ([d]), delete all detail and replace by '*Cal. Papal Letters*, vol. 3, p. 272; *Collect. Topog. et Geneal.*, vol. 3, pp. 250–5. See also vol. 5, p. 463, *sub* FITZPAYN.
note ([e]), delete all detail and replace by '*Cal. Close Rolls, 1349–54*, p. 191.'
note ([h]), l. 2, delete 'de Ros' and replace by 'Devereux'

page 362,
line 2, after '1386,' add '(will dat. 7 July 1383)' [*Collect. Topog. et Geneal.*, vol. 3, pp. 253–4]
line 3, for '8 July 1387' read '20 May 1409' [*Cal. Close Rolls, 1409–13*, p. 501]

page 363,
line 10, after '1517' add 'She *m.* 2ndly, David SOCHE, who appears to have *d.* in 1526' [*L. and P. Hen. VIII*, vol. xi, p. 90]

BUCCLEUGH

page 365,
note ([a]), lines 7–10, delete from 'Fraser' to 'But' and replace by 'The 2nd Earl, however, executed a bond of tailzie, 14 June 1650 (recorded in the Books of Council and Session, 24 June following), whereby he assigned his honours and estates into the hands of the Barons of the Exchequer for a new infeftment in favour of himself and the heirs male of his body, whom failing the eldest heirs female of his body, whom failing the heirs female of his sister Jean (see *Scots Peerage*, vol. ii, p. 236; vol. ix, p. 46). It must be assumed that such a new infeftment was obtained, for'

page 368,
line 5, after 'She' add ', who was *b.* 24 May 1701 in London,'

page 370,
line 2, after '*bur.*' add '3 Dec.'
line 26, after 'throat' add 'and was *bur.* 11 Sep. at Warkton afsd.'
line 27, after 'year' add 'and was *bur.* 27 May at Warkton'
lines 27–8, delete from 'Both' to 'afsd.'
line 33, for '11' read 'early in'
line 34, after '*bur.*' add '12'

page 371,
line 7, after 'and' add '(it is said)'

page 372,
line 31, after '76.' add 'He *d.* at Montagu House, Whitehall, 5, aged 83, and was *bur.* 10 Nov. 1914, in St. Mary's Chapel, Dalkeith.'

page 373,
line 3, line to read as follows

DUKEDOM [S.] VII. EARLDOM [S.] X. BARONY [S.] XI.	1914	7, 10 and 11. JOHN CHARLES (MONTAGUE-DOUGLAS-SCOTT), DUKE OF BUCCLEUGH, &c., 2nd but 1st surv. s. and h.,

line 5, after 'Abbey' add 'From 1886 *styled* Earl of Dalkeith'
line 10, for ']' read 'He *d.* 19, at Bowhill, Selkirk, and was *bur.* 22 Oct. 1935 in the Buccleugh Memorial Chapel at St. Mary's Episcopal Church in Dalkeith. His widow *d.* 7 Aug. 1954.'

DUKEDOM [S.] VIII. EARLDOM [S.] XI. BARONY [S.] XII.	1935	8, 11 and 12. WALTER JOHN (MONTAGUE-DOUGLAS-SCOTT), DUKE OF BUCCLEUGH, &c., 1st s. and h., *b.* 30 Dec. 1894; *styled* EARL OF DALKEITH from 1914; ed. at Eton and Oxford (Ch. Ch.). He *m.*, 21 Apr. 1921, Vreda Esther Mary, 1st da. of Major William Frank LASCELLES. He *d.* 4 Oct. 1973. His widow *d.* 1993.

DUKEDOM [S.] IX. EARLDOM [S.] XII. BARONY [S.] XIII.	1973	9, 12 and 13. WALTER FRANCIS JOHN (MONTAGUE-DOUGLAS-SCOTT), DUKE OF BUCCLEUGH, &c., s. and h., *b.* 28 Sep. 1923; *styled* EARL OF DALKEITH from 1935; ed. at Eton and Oxford (Ch. Ch.); *m.*, 10 Jan. 1953, Jane, only da. of John MCNEILL of Druimavuie, Appin, Argyll.

[RICHARD WALTER JOHN MONTAGUE-DOUGLAS-SCOTT, 1st s. and h. ap., *styled* EARL OF DALKEITH; *b.* 14 Feb. 1954; ed. at Eton and Oxford (Ch. Ch.); *m.*, 1981, Elizabeth Marion Frances, yst. da. of Peter Francis Walter (KERR), 12th MARQUESS OF LOTHIAN.]

line 16, for '6000' read '60,000'
line 27, for 'possessing' read 'which possessed in the 18th century'
line 28, after 'avenues' add 'said to be'

BUCHAN

page 375,
line 23, after '(1305)' add 'probably by Joan, sister of William LE LATIMER'

page 377,
line 15, for 'the' read 'Alexander (STEWART), 11th'

page 378,
line 1, after 'James I' add '[S.]'

page 379,
line 3, for '1 Mar. 1466/7' read '27 Mar. 1459' [*Scots Peerage*, vol. ii, p. 266; vol. ix, p. 47; *Genealogist*, N.S., vol. xxv, p. 165]
lines 5–6, delete from 'between' to '1500' and replace by 'in 1499'
line 12, for 'in' read '5 Apr.'
line 21, for 'Mary, only child' read 'Elizabeth, illegit. da.' [*Scots Peerage*, vol. ix, p. 47]
line 22, after 'James IV' add 'Shortly after 12 Sep. 1546 he divorced her on the ground that she had cohabited before the marriage with a man related in the 4th degree to the Master. Elizabeth surv. him and on this ground an attempt, abandoned in 1549, was made by his next br., James STEWART, to establish the bastardy of Christian, the Master's da. by his 2nd wife.' [*Idem*]
line 24, after 'widow' add '*m.*, after 16 Dec. 1549, George BARCLAY of that Ilk and'
line 28, after 'abovenamed' add 'was *b.* 1547–8'

page 380,
line 2, after '*m.*' add '6 Oct. 1552' [*Scots Peerage*, vol. ix, p. 48.]
line 9, after 's. and h.' add 'was *b.* perhaps in or about Nov. 1565 and' [*Reg. P.C.* [S.], vol. i, p. 396]
line 17, for 'before 1617' read '18 June 1615' [*Scots Peerage*, vol. ix, p. 48]
line 30, delete '20 Aug. 1628' and after 'Holyrood' add 'and was *bur.* 20 Aug. 1628 at Auchterhouse' [*Idem*]

page 381,
line 4, after '*m.*,' add 'shortly after 11 Apr. 1655'
lines 11–12, delete from ', where' to '1695' and replace by '. He *m.*, 4 Sep. 1683, at the Chapel in Duke's Place, St. James's, Marjory, widow of William (DOUGLAS), 9th EARL OF MORTON [S.], da. of (__) FOULIS. She *d.* before 19 Feb. 1689/90. He *d. s.p.*, a prisoner at Stirling, in 1695'
line 34, for 'Frances' read 'Anne'

page 382,
line 15, after '1739' read 'in Lady Huntingdon's Chapel at Bath'

page 384,
line 12, after 'Coventry.' add 'He *d.* 16, in London, and was *bur.* 19 Apr. 1934 in Dryburgh Abbey. His widow *d.* as the result of an accident, 29 Jan. 1943.'
lines 13–14, delete all detail and replace as follows

XXIX. 1934. 15. RONALD DOUGLAS STUART MAR (ERSKINE), EARL OF BUCHAN, &c., s. and h., *b.* 6 Apr. 1878. *Styled* LORD CARDROSS after 1898. He *d.* unm. 18 Dec. 1960.

XXX. 1960. 16. DONALD CARDROSS FLOWER (ERSKINE), EARL OF BUCHAN, [1469], LORD AUCHTERHOUSE, [1469], LORD CARDROSS [1606], also BARON ERSKINE OF RESTORMEL CASTLE [U.K., 1806], distant cousin and h. male, he being s. and h. of Montague (ERSKINE), 6th BARON ERSKINE, he being descended from Thomas Erskine, 1st Baron Erskine, 3rd s. of Henry David Erskine, 10th Earl of Buchan. He was *b.* 3 June 1899; ed. at Charterhouse and R.M.C., Sandhurst. He *suc.* his father as BARON ERSKINE in 1957. He *m.*, 5 Jan. 1927, Christina, da. of Hugh WOOLNER and adop. da. of Lloyd Harry BAXENDALE of Newbury, Berks. He *d.* 26 July 1984. His widow *d.* 1994.

XXXI. 1984. 17. MALCOLM HARRY (ERSKINE), EARL OF BUCHAN, &c., 2nd but 1st surv. s. and h.,[ba] *b.* 4 July 1930; *styled* LORD CARDCROSS 1960–84; ed. at Eton; *m.*, 21 Feb. 57, Hilary Diana Cecil, only da. of Sir Ivan McLannahan Cecil POWER, Bart.

note [ba] David Stuart Erskine, 1st s. and h. ap. was *b.* 20 June 1928, and *d.* 1 Feb. 1933.

[HENRY THOMAS ALEXANDER ERSKINE, 1st s. and h. ap. *styled* LORD CARDROSS, was *b.* 31 May 1960; *m.*, 1987, Charlotte Catherine Lucinda, da. of Hon. Matthew Henry BEAUMONT.]

BUCKHURST

page 385,
line 30, for '[1671]' read '[1761]' and after 'CANTELUPE' add '[1761]'
line 31, for '[1299]' read '[1570]'

BUCKINGHAM

page 388,
note (c), line 1, for 'He' read 'On 29 Aug. 1442 he was "made Captain of Calais by the name of the earl of Buckingham" and' (Nicholas, *Proc. and Ord. of the Privy Council*, vol. v, p. 209)
line 9, after 'Northampton' add 'See vol. v, *sub* ESSEX'

page 389,
line 13, for '*d. v.p.*, being slain' read 'was wounded, fighting' [See vol. xii, part 1, note *sub* WILTSHIRE [1470]]
line 14, after '1455' add 'He, who was living, 17 Dec. 1457 and (presumably) 19 Jan. 1457/8, *d. v.p. circa* 1459' [*Idem*]
line 17, delete 'posthumous and'
line 33, after 'present' add 'as LORD GREAT CHAMBERLAIN, so app. 28 June 1483' [See vol. x, Appendix F, pp. 62–3]
note (c), lines 2–3, delete from 'A' to 'them'

page 391,
line 5, for '4th' read '3rd'
line 11, for '1530' read '1530/1' [*Inq. p.m.*, 1 Mar. 1531/2, 23 Henry VIII]
line 11, for '(__)' read 'Anne' [*Lincs. Pedigrees*, Harl. Soc., vol. 1, 1902, p. 43]
note (c), lines 3–9, delete from 'The' to 'red' [refers to Henry Stafford, Earl of Wilts.], and

replace by 'Henry, *styled* Earl of Stafford, *m.*, shortly after 20 Oct. 1518, when the marriage covenant is dated. His wife was da. of Sir Richard Pole, K.G., by Margaret, Countess of Salisbury. See STAFFORD, vol. xii, part 1, p. 184.

page 392,
line 21, for '1616' read 'Jan. 1615/6'

page 395,
note ([c]), line 15, for 'killed' read 'mortally wounded' and for 'Mar.' read 'Jan.'

page 397,
note ([d]), line 2, after 'Court [I.]' add 'It was probably this lady, or possibly her predecessor, who *m.* Capt. James Leith, of Harthill, co. Aberdeen, who *d.* in the King's Bench, early in Apr. 1780, aged 91. See *Newcastle Courant*, 26 Apr. 1780.' [*Ex inform.* C. Roy Hudleston]

page 398,
line 21, for 'May 1708' read '20 May 1707'

BUCKINGHAMSHIRE (BUCKINGHAM)

page 402,
line 16, after 'Stepney' add '(reg. at Twickenham)' [and so possibly *b.* there]

page 405,
line 19, after 'Catherine' add '3rd'
line 20, after 'Bombay' add 'being 1st da. by his 2nd wife, Catherine Emily, only da. of Lieut. Col. T. MACMAHON'

page 406,
line 5, after '1867.' add 'He *d.* 15 Jan. 1930 at Hampden House, Great Missenden. His widow *d.* at Fordell House, Inverkeithing, Fife, 26, and was *bur.* 30 Mar. 1937 at Fordell, afsd.'
lines 6–7, delete all detail and replace as follows

XXI. 1930. 8. JOHN HAMPDEN (HOBART-HAMPDEN-MERCER-HENDERSON later MERCER-HENDERSON), EARL OF BUCKINGHAMSHIRE, &c., s. and h., *b.* 16 Apr. 1906; ed. at Eton. He obtained a Royal lic. to use the surnames of MERCER-HENDERSON alone in 1938. He *d.* unm. 2 Jan. 1963.

XXII. 1963. 9. VERE FREDERICK CECIL (HOBART-HAMPDEN), EARL OF BUCKINGHAMSHIRE, &c., distant cousin, being 2nd but only surv. s. and h. of Arthur Ernest H.-H. (*d.* 18 June 1952), by his 1st wife, Henrietta Louisa, only da. of Rev. Thomas Orme FETHERSTONHAUGH, which Arthur Ernest was 2nd but 1st surv. s. (1st by 2nd wife) and h. of Charles Edward HOBART-HAMPDEN (*d.* 25 Sep. 1913), by his 2nd wife Lucy Pauline, da. of John WRIGHT of Lenton Hall, Notts., which Charles Edward was 4th s. of the 6th Earl of Buckinghamshire. He was *b.* 17 May 1901; ed. at St.

Lawrence Coll., Ramsgate, Kent; *m.*, 1972, Margot Macrae, da. of John Storey RODGER of New South Wales, Australia and widow of F.C. Bruce HITTMAN, M.D. of Sydney, Australia. He *d. s.p.* 19 Apr. 1983. His widow was still living 1995.

XXIII. 1983. 10. GEORGE MILES (HOBART-HAMPDEN), EARL OF BUCKINGHAMSHIRE, &c., distant cousin and h., being s. and h. of Cyril Langel H.-H., by Margaret, only da. of George Hilborne JOLIFFE, which Cyril Langel was 1st s. of Ernest Miles H.-H. (*d.* 1 May 1949), by Marie Hélène, 1st da. of Rev. Louis LANGEL, which Ernest Miles was 3rd s. of George Augustus HOBART-HAMPDEN (*d.* 8 Dec. 1899), by Jane, 1st da. of Sir John Wither AWDRY of Notton House, Wilts., which George Augustus was 5th s. of 6th Earl of Buckinghamshire. He was *b.* 15 Dec. 1944; ed. at Clifton, Exeter Univ. and London Univ.; *m.*, 27 July 1968, Susan Jennifer, da. of Raymond W. ADAMS of Halesowen, co. Worcester. This marriage was diss. by divorce and he *m.* 2ndly, 1975, Alison Wightman, da. of William FORREST of Edinburgh and formerly wife of D.A. WISHART of Edinburgh.

BUCKINGHAM

page 410,
line 34, after 'widow' add 'who was *b.* 29 Sep. 1847, at 15 Charlotte Sq., Edinburgh'

BULKELEY

page 413,
note (d), line 2 (on page 414), for '*Warner*' read '*Warren*'

BULMER

page 414,
line 19, for 'He *m.*' read 'He appears to have *m.* 1stly, (__). He *m.* 2ndly'
page 416,
line 5, after 'SUTTON' add '[3rd LORD SUTTON OF HOLDERNESS]'

BURDETT-COUTTS

page 420,
line 17, in margin, below '1871' add 'to 1906'
line 36, for 'is' read 'was'

page 421,
line 2, after '92' add 'when the Barony became *extinct*'
line 4, after net.' add 'He *d.* 28 July 1921.'

BURFORD

page 421,
line 19, for '1673' read '1676'

BURGH

page 422,
note ([b]), line 3, for 'a' read 'b'
line 10, after 'Parliament' add 'See, however, notes *sub* CHEYNE [1487] and Dinham [1467]'

page 423,
lines 2–3, delete from 'Anne' to 'BUCKINGHAM' and replace by 'Elizabeth, da. of Sir John CHIDIOK, of Chidiok, Dorset'

page 424,
between lines 18 and 19 add

VII. 1916. 7. ALEXANDER HENRY (LEITH), LORD BURGH, *b.* 27 July 1866, *suc.* as Lord Burgh on the termination of the *abeyance* in his favour, 5 May 1916, [see vol. xiii, p. 220.]

VIII. 1926. 8. ALEXANDER LEIGH HENRY (LEITH), LORD BURGH, 1st s. and h., *b.* 16 May 1906. [for further details see vol. xiii, p. 220] He *d.* 26 May 1959.

IX. 1959. 9. ALEXANDER PETER WILLOUGHBY (LEITH), 1st s. and h., *b.* 20 Mar. 1935; ed. at Harrow and Cambridge (Magdalene Coll.). He *m.*, 29 Aug. 1957, Anita Lorna, da. of Frederick Charles ELDRIDGE of Gillingham, Kent.

[ALEXANDER GREGORY DISNEY LEITH, s. and h. ap., *b.* 16 Mar. 1958; *m.* Catherine Mary, da. of David PARKES.]

line 21, for '1787' read '1784'
note ([e]), line 11, for 'Kenworth' read 'Kenworthy'
line 12, after 'V.G.' add 'The *abeyance* was terminated by the issue of a writ of summons to Parliament, 5 May 1916, to Col. Henry Leith Alexander abovenamed. See vol. xiii, p. 220.'

BURGHCLERE

page 425,
line 15, after '1864' add 'He *d. s.p.m.* at his residence in Charles St., Berkeley Sq., 6, and was *bur.* 10 May 1921, at Stansted, Essex. At his death his peerage became *extinct*. His widow *d.* 28 Sep. 1933, at Green Str., Park Lane.'

BURGHERSH

page 427,
line 6, for '(__)' read 'Henry'
line 7, after 'PICHARD' add 'citizen and vintner of London'
line 25, for '7' read 'by 16 Apr.' [*Cal. Pat. Rolls, 1413–16*, p. 192, *ex inform* Dr Rosemary Horrox] and for '14' read '18'

line 27, for '23' read '22'

page 428,
line 2, delete '18'
line 16, for 'June' read 'Jan.'
line 17, for '1449' read '1448/9'
note ([a]), line 10, for 'about 1490' read 'shortly before 20 Sep. 1492' [See WARWICK]

BURGHLEY

page 428,
line 24, after 'Richard C.' add '([b])'
note ([b]) Richard Cecil was s. of David Cecil, who *d.* Oct. 1535. See Burghley's Diary, in *Hist. MSS. Com.*, Cecil MSS., vol. xiii, p. 141.
line 23, after 'Northants' add '([c])'
note ([c]) On 9 Sep. 1586 Burghley claimed Northants for his native country, where he was "no new planted or feathered gentleman" and later made the same claim for Lincolnshire, with which he was connected through his mother. V.G.

page 429,
line 20, for 'Sep.' read 'July'
line 24, for '1543/4' read '1542/3([da])'
note ([da]) According to his Diary (see note ([b]) above) she *d.* 1542/3 and not 1543/4 as sometimes stated.
line 26, after 'Off.),' add '([db])'
note ([db]) According to his Diary he *m.* 21 Dec. 1546.

BURLINGTON

page 431,
line 28, in margin for '1694' read '1698'

page 434,
line 11, after 'William' add '(ed. at Eton from 1796),'

BURNELL

page 434,
line 32, for 'shortly before 28 Nov. 1353' read '16 May 1353' [*Inq. p.m.*, vol. 11, no. 489]

page 435,
line 2, after 'Maud' add '(*m.* 1315) widow of John (LOVEL), 2nd LORD LOVEL'
line 5, delete 'a minor' and replace by 'aged 23' [see *Inq. p.m.* on Sir John Haudlo, vol. 8, no. 667, p. 491]
lines 18–19, delete from 'Phillipe' to 'STAFFORD' and replace by '(__)'
line 19, after 'EARL' add 'OF'
line 20, for '22 May' read '21 Apr.'

line 21, after 'BOTETOURT' add 'and BARONESS ZOUCHE (of Mortimer) &c.,'
line 23, for '1408 or 1409' read 'before 29 Jan. 1407/8'
line 23, after 'Joan' add '*de jure suo jure* (according to modern doctrine) BARONESS DEVEREUX'
line 24, after 'FITZWALTER' delete '(d)' and add 'sister and h. of John, 2nd LORD DEVEREUX'
line 25, for 'Maud' read 'Margaret'
line 27, delete '1390 and'
line 29, before '11' add '10 or'
line 32, after '1417' add 'at Wesley, pr. 6 Feb. 1420/1 in the Palace of the Archbishop of Canterbury'
note (d), delete all detail
note (f), line 3, delete from '; he' to '1415' and replace by 'she *m.* 2ndly, *circa* 1425, Sir Thomas Kerdeston and *d.* before Apr. 1440; he *d. v.p.* 23 Sep. 1415 of disease at the siege of Harfleur'
line 2, after 'Elizabeth' add 'da. of Michael de la Pole, 2nd Earl of Suffolk,'
lines 6–7, delete from 'and' to 'Shrewsbury'

BURNELL OF EAST WITTENHAM

page 436,
line 9, for '1611' read '1610/1'

BURNTISLAND

page 438,
line 5, after 'WEMYSS,' add 'only'

BURTON OF RANGEMORE &c.

page 440,
lines 2–3, delete from 'who' to work' and replace by 'His widow *d.* 21 Jan. 1931.'

II. 1909. 2. NELLIE LISA BAILLIE, *suo jure* BARONESS BARON BURTON OF BURTON-ON-TRENT AND RANGEMORE, only child and h. under the special remainder of 1897. She was *b.* 27 Dec. 1873; *m.* 1stly, 31 Jan. 1894, Col. James Evan Bruce BAILLIE of Dochfour, co. Inverness, M.P. He *d.* 6 May 1931 and she *m.* 2ndly, 25 July 1932, Major William Eugene MELLES, 1st s. of Joseph William MELLES of Gruline, Isle of Mull. He *d.* 20 Feb. 1953. She *d.* 28 May 1962.

[GEORGE EVAN MICHAEL BAILLIE, 1st s. and h. ap., *b.* 19 Dec. 1894; ed. at Eton; *m.*, 15 Nov. 1923, Maud, 1st da. of Victor Christian William (CAVENDISH), 9th DUKE OF DEVONSHIRE. He *d. v.m.* on active service, 6 June 1941.]

III. 1962. 3. MICHAEL EVAN VICTOR (BAILLIE), BARON BURTON OF BURTON ON TRENT AND OF RANGEMORE, grandson and h., being 1st s. and h. of

George Evan Michael BAILLIE and Maud, abovenamed. He was *b.* 27 June 1924; ed. at Eton; *m.*, 28 Apr. 1948, Elizabeth Ursula Forster, 1st da. of Capt. Anthony Forster WISE. This marriage was diss. by divorce in 1977 (she *d.* 1993) and he *m.* 2ndly, 1978, Coralie Denise, da. of Claud R. CLIFFE.

[EVAN MICHAEL RONALD BAILLIE, 1st s. and h. ap. by 1st wife; *b.* 19 Mar. 1949; ed. at Harrow; *m.*, 1970, Lucinda, 1st da. of Robert LAW of Haverhill, Suffolk.]

BUTE

page 440,
line 23, delete from 'concurred' to 'Revolution,'

page 441,
line 21, after 'She' add 'who was *b.* 12 Jan. 1691/2'

page 443,
line 12, for '1766' read '1776'

page 444,
line 13, after '1767' add 'in Grosvenor Sq., Midx.; ed. at Eton 1775–9, adm. as a nobleman at Cambridge (St. John's Coll.), 27 May 1784, M.A. 1787.'
line 31, after 'Eton' add '1806–10'

page 445,
line 29, for 'living 1912' read '*d.* in London, 15 Jan. 1932.'

page 446,
line 13, after '1905.' add 'K.T. 1922'
line 17, after '1880.' add 'He *d.* 25 Apr. 1947. His widow *d.* 16 May 1947.'
lines 18–19, delete all detail and replace as follows

MARQUESSATE. V. EARLDOM [S.] VIII. } 1947

5 and 8. JOHN (CRICHTON-STUART), MARQUESS OF BUTE, &c., s. and h., *b.* 4 Aug. 1907. *Styled* EARL OF DUMFRIES from birth; *m.*, 26 Apr. 1932, Eileen Beatrice, yr. da. of Bernard Arthur William Patrick Hastings (FORBES), 8th EARL OF GRANARD, K.P. He *d.* 14 Aug. 1956. His widow *d.* 1993.

MARQUESSATE. VI. EARLDOM [S.] IX. } 1956

6 and 9. JOHN (CRICHTON-STUART), MARQUESS OF BUTE, &c., 1st s. and h., *b.* 27 Feb. 1933; ed. at Ampleforth and Cambridge (Trin. Coll.); *m.*, 19 Apr. 1955, Beatrice Nicola Grace, only da. of Wolstan Beaumont Charles WELD-FORESTER, Lieut. Cmdr., R.N. This marriage was diss. by divorce in 1977 (she was still living 1995) and he *m.* 2ndly, 1978, Jennifer, da. of John

Brougham HOME-RIGG and formerly wife of Gerald PERCY. He *d.* 21 July 1993. His widow was still living 1995.

MARQUESSATE. VII. EARLDOM [S.] X. } 1993 — 7 and 10. JOHN COLUM (CRICHTON-STUART), MARQUESS OF BUTE, &c., 1st s. and h., *b.* 25 Apr. 1958; *styled* EARL OF DUMFRIES till 1993; ed. at Ampleforth; *m.*, 1984, Carolyn, da. of Bryson WADDELL. This marriage was diss. by divorce in 1993.

[JOHN BRYSON CRICHTON-STUART, *styled* LORD MOUNT STUART, *b.* 21 Dec. 1989.]

BUTLER

page 447,
lines 27–8, delete from 'and was' to 'in that co.' and replace by '(g)'
note (g) He was not founder of Cockersand Abbey, see William Farrer, *Chartulary of Cokersand Abbey*, Chetham Soc., 1898, p. 353.

page 448,
line 3, delete 'and h.'
line 4, after 'Edlington' add 'co. York', for 'Newborough' read 'Narborough' and for '&c., co. York' read 'co. Leicester, &c.,'

page 451,
line 16, for '17' read '14'

BYRON

page 454,
line 5, after '1614;' add 'matric. Cambridge (Trin. Coll.) Easter 1615, as a Fell. Com., M.A. 1618;'
line 22, after 1638' add 'and was *bur.* at Hucknall Torkard, Notts.'

page 455,
line 1, after '1638' add 'and was *bur.* at Hucknall Torkard afsd.'
line 24, for '(__)' read 'Sir Richard' and after 'STYDOLPH' add '(*d.* 13 Feb. 1676/7) of Norbury, Surrey, 1st Bart.'
line 30, for '4th' read '5th(d)'
note (d) All of his elder brothers William, Richard, John and Ernestus *d. v.p.* as infants.

page 456,
line 7, after '*bur.*' add '7 Apr.'
line 18, after '1722.' add '(aa)'
note (aa) Of his three elder brothers of the half-blood who were sons of the 2nd wife, (1) George, *b.* 1 Oct. 1707, *d. v.p.* 6 and was *bur.* 8 July 1719 at Hucknall, (2) William, *b.* 6 July 1709, *d. v.p.* a few days later, and was *bur.* at Hucknall, (3) William Henry, *b.* 23 Oct. 1710, *d. v.p.* shortly after and was *bur.* at Hucknall.
line 24, after 'Norfolk' add 'by Elizabeth his wife'

line 25, after 'Str.' add 'and was *bur.* 16 July at Besthorpe. Will dat. 4 Jan. 1785 to 21 June 1787, pr. 15 July 1788'

line 25, after '*bur.*' add '10 June'

note (e), delete all detail and replace by 'By her he had two sons: (1) William, *b.* 7 June 1748, *d. v.p.*, and was *bur.* 7 May 1749. (2) William, *b.* 27 Oct. 1749; ed. at Eton 1763–6; M.P. for Morpeth 1774; *m.*, 1771, Juliana Elizabeth (who *d.* 18 Mar. 1788), 2nd da. of his uncle Vice-Adm. John Byron, by Sophia, da. of John Trevannion of Carhays, Cornwall and *d.* 22, being *bur.* 26 June 1776 at Twickenham. Admon. 8 July 1776. They had an only s. William, *b.* 6 May 1772, who *d.* unm. in his grandfather's lifetime, being *k.* 31 July 1794, at the siege of Calvi, in Corsica. V.G.'

page 457,

line 20, after '1792' add 'at Elemore Hall, co. Durham and *bap.* 10 Aug. at Seaham'

note (d), lines 5–10, delete from 'The' to 'malice' and replace by 'When note (d) was written the editor [Vicary Gibbs] had not read *Astarte*, pub. in 1905 by the 2nd Earl Lovelace. After doing so, the editor finds it impossible to doubt the criminality of the relations existing between Lord Byron and his half-sister.'

page 458,

line 27, delete from 'and' to '(1912)' and replace by 'she *d.* 28 May 1912 at Thrumpton and was *bur.* there 1 June aged 88.'

page 459,

line 1, for 'widow of T. BROADHEAD' read 'Broadhead'

lines 1–2, delete from '52' to 'W' and replace by '9 Wedderburn Rd., Hampstead'

line 2, for 'RADNALL' read 'RADMALL'

line 3, add at end 'He *d.* at Thrumpton Hall afsd., 30 Mar., aged 61, and was *bur.* 3 Apr. 1917, at Thrumpton.'

X. 1917. 10. FREDERICK ERNEST CHARLES (BYRON), BARON BYRON OF ROCHDALE, br. and h., *b.* 26 Mar. 1861; ed. at Oxford (Exeter Coll.). Ordained priest 1889, vicar of Thrumpton. He *m.*, 31 Jan. 1921, at St. James', Bury St. Edmunds, Anna Ismay Ethel, eld. da. of the Rev. Lord Charles Edward FITZROY (4th s. of Augustus Charles Lennox (FITZROY), 7th DUKE OF GRAFTON), by Ismay Mary Helen Augusta, da. of Charles (FITZROY), 3rd LORD SOUTHAMPTON. He *d. s.p.* 6 June 1949. His widow *d.* 14 Apr. 1966.

XI. 1949. 11. RUPERT FREDERICK GEORGE (BYRON), BARON BYRON OF ROCHDALE, distant cousin and h., being s. and h. of Wilfred BYRON (*d.* Nov. 1936), by his cousin Sylvia Mary, da. of the Rev. Charles Thomas MOORE, which Wilfred was 2nd s. of the Rev. William BYRON (*d.* 17 May 1907), by his 1st wife Mary Elizabeth, da. of Sir Richard Torin KINDERSLEY, which William was 4th s. of the 7th Baron Byron. He was *b.* 13 Aug. 1903; *m.*, 29 July 1931, Pauline Augusta, da. of T.J. CORNWALL of Wagin, Western Australia. He *d. s.p.m.* 1 Nov. 1983. His widow *d.* 1993.

XII. 1983. 12. RICHARD GEOFFREY GORDON (BYRON), BARON BYRON OF ROCHDALE, distant cousin and h. male, being s. and h., of Richard BYRON (*d.* 1 Aug. 1939), by Mabel Mackenzie, da. of Charles Albert WINTER, which Richard was s. and h. of John Byron (*d.* 13 Aug. 1895), by Susan Amelia Graves, da. of Edward CHIAPPINI of Capetown, which John was s. and h. of the Rev. John Byron (*d.* 6 Dec. 1878), by Mary, da. of William RICHARDSON, of Leatherhead, Surrey, which John was 3rd s. of Rear Adm. Richard Byron (*d.* 2 Sep. 1837), by Sarah, da. of James SYKES, which Richard was 1st s. and h. of the Rev. Richard BYRON (*d.* 5 Nov. 1811), by Mary, da. of Richard FARMER, which Richard was 3rd s. of the 4th Lord Byron. He was *b.* 3 Nov. 1899; ed. at Eton; *m.* 1stly, 8 Aug. 1926, Margaret Mary, only da. of Francis Gerald STEUART of Winchester, Hants. This marriage was diss. by divorce in 1946 and he *m.* 2ndly, 8 Aug. 1946, Dorigen Margaret, only da. of Percival Kennedy ESDAILE. She *d.* 1985. He *d.* 15 June 1989.

[RICHARD NOEL BYRON, 1st s. and h. ap., was *b.* 5 Jan. 1948; ed. at Wellington. He was *k.* in an air accident, *v.p.* and unm., 1985.]

XIII. 1989. 13. ROBERT JAMES (BYRON), BARON BYRON OF ROCHDALE, 2nd but 1st surv. s. and h., *b.* 5 Apr. 1950; ed. at Wellington and Cambridge (Trin. Coll.); *m.*, 1979, Robyn Margaret, da. of John MCLEAN of Hamilton, New Zealand.

[CHARLES RICHARD GORDON BYRON, s. and h. ap., was *b.* 28 July 1990.]

CADOGAN

page 461,
line 7, for 'John (or William) MUNTER' read 'Jacob MUNSTERS'
line 13, after '*b.*' add 'in Amsterdam'
note (d), delete all detail and replace by 'He had advocated Atterbury being "thrown to the lions", who revenged himself by the following lines:

By fear unmoved, by shame unawed
Offspring of hangman and of bawd
Ungrateful to the ungrateful men who grew by
A bold, bad, boist'rous, blust'ring, bloody, booby'

page 462,
line 13, after 'Mary,' add '1st'
line 15, after 'She' add 'who was *b.* 23 Feb. 1758'

page 463,
line 23, after '1810,' add 'ed. at Eton *circa* 1824–8'

page 464,
line 11, after 'K.C.B.' add 'He *d.*, aged 74, in London after an operation, 6, and was *bur.* 10 Mar. 1915, at Culford. Will dat. 24 Feb. 1914, pr. Apr. 1915, at £354,207 gross, and £260,043 net. His widow *d.* 23 Feb. 1960.'

line 24, after 'LAMBTON' add 'She *d.* 17 Sep. 1942.'
line 25, line to read as follows

EARLDOM. VII. BARONY. VIII. } 1915 — 6 and 8. GERALD OAKLEY (CADOGAN), EARL CADOGAN [1800], &c., 3rd s. and eventual h.,

line 28, after '(d)' add 'From 1908 *styled* VISCOUNT CHELSEA'
line 29, for ']' read 'He *d.* 4 Oct. 1933 in a London Nursing Home. His widow *d.* 1973.'

EARLDOM. VIII. BARONY. IX. } 1933 — 7 and 8. WILLIAM GERALD CHARLES (CADOGAN), EARL CADOGAN, &c., s. and h., *b.* 13 Feb. 1914; ed. at Eton and R.M.C., Sandhurst. He *m.*, 11 June 1936, Primrose Lilian, yst. da. of John Reginald Lopes (YARDE-BULLER), 3rd LORD CHURSTON at Holy Trinity Ch., Sloane Str. This marriage was diss. by divorce in 1960 (she *d.* 1970). He *m.* 2ndly, 13 Jan. 1961, Cecilia Margaret, yst. da. of Lieut. Col. Henry Kellerman HAMILTON-WEDDERBURN.

[CHARLES GERALD JOHN CADOGAN, *styled* VISCOUNT CHELSEA from 1937; *b.* 24 Mar. 1937; ed. at Eton; *m.*, 6 June 1963, Philippa Dorothy Bluet, 2nd da. of Gerard Vernon (WALLOP), 9th EARL OF PORTSMOUTH. She *d.* 1984 and he *m.*, 1989, Jennifer Jane Greig, da. of J.E.K. RAE. This marriage was diss. by divorce and he *m.* 2ndly, 1994, Dorothy Ann, yr. da. of Dr W.E. SHIPSEY.]

page 465,
lines 4–7, delete from 'The Rt.' to '*whole.*'

CAHER

page 465,
line 15, after 'Eske,' add '(*d.* 1513)'
line 16, after 'Catherine,' add '(*d.* 1512)'
line 20, after 'KILDARE [I.]' add '(da)'
note (da), In Clonmel Church there is an M.I. to the ancestors of the 1st Baron, which concludes with a request to pray for the souls of Thomas and Eleanor Butler who had erected it in 155? (*sic*). According to the account in vol. i of the *Association for the Preservation of the Memorials of the Dead in Ireland*, 1888, pp. 239–40, this Eleanor was the Baron's 1st wife, and was therefore living at least as late as 1550; but if so he must have married Ellen very late in his life. V.G.
note (b), line 2, after '63).' add 'The grant of the dignity is dat. 10 Nov. 34 Hen. VIII (1542) in *Cal. Pat. Rolls* [I.], vol. i, pp. 94–5.'
note (d), line 2, delete from 'preceded' to 'and'
line 3, add at end 'For a discussion on whether such a remainder also applied to the Earldom of Ormond (1328), see vol. x, p. 117, note (k)'

page 468,
line 12, after 'Christian' add '5th'
line 13, for 'by' read 'being 4th and yst. da. by his 2nd wife'

CAILLY

page 470,
line 7, in margin, for '1317' read '1316'
line 9, for '4 Mar. 1308/9' read '26 Oct. 1309'
line 11, for 'Margaret, his wife' read 'Catherine, da. of John DE HEDERSETE and sister to John DE NORWICH to whose grandson John her issue ultimately became heirs.'

CAIRNS

page 471,
lines 9–10, delete 'living 1912' and replace by '*d.* 29 Oct. 1919.'
line 13, after 'Coll.' add 'and at Eton, 1875/6'
line 16, after 'Olivia' add 'Elizabeth'
line 22, delete 'Both living 1912' and replace by 'He *d.* 18 Nov. 1944. She *d.* 20 June 1951.'

page 472,
lines 4–5, delete from 'He' to 'work'

IV. 1905. 4. WILFRED DALLAS (CAIRNS), EARL CAIRNS, &c., br. and h., *b.* 28 Nov. 1865; *m.*, 12 July 1894, Olive, 4th da. of John Patteson COBBOLD of Ipswich, co. Suffolk. He *d.* 23 Oct. 1946. His widow *d.* 19 Sep. 1952.

[HUGH WILFRED JOHN CAIRNS, *styled* VISCOUNT GARMOYLE, 1st s. and h., ap.; *b.* 9 June 1907. He *m.*, 2 June 1936, Barbara Elizabeth, yr. da. of Capt. Arden FRANKLYN, of New Place, Shedfield, Hants. He *d. v.p. s.p.*, of wounds received in action in Egypt, July 1942. His widow *m.* 2ndly, 28 Oct. 1948, Sir John Nicholson HOGG. Both living 1995.]

V. 1942. 5. DAVID CHARLES CAIRNS), EARL CAIRNS, &c., 2nd but 1st surv. s. and h., *b.* 3 July 1909; *m.*, 16 Apr. 1936, Barbara Jeanne Harrisson, yst. da. of Sydney Harrisson BURGESS of Altrincham, Cheshire. He *d.* 21 Mar. 1989. His widow was still living 1995.

VI. 1989. 6. SIMON DALLAS (CAIRNS), EARL CAIRNS, &c., 1st s. and h., *b.* 27 May 1939; ed. at Eton and Cambridge (Trin. Coll.); *m.*, 4 Feb. 1964, Amanda Mary, only da. of Major Edgar Fitzgerald HEATHCOAT-AMORY.

[HUGH SEBASTIAN CAIRNS, *styled* VISCOUNT GARMOYLE, 1st s. and h. ap.; *b.* 26 Mar. 1965; ed. at Eton and Edinburgh Univ.; *m.*, 1991, Juliet, only da. of Andrew Eustace PALMER of Little Missenden, co. Buckingham.]

CAITHNESS

page 472,
line 9, delete all following to page 476, line 3 and replace by vol. x, Appendix A.

page 476,
line 4, after 'MALISE' add '8th'
line 10, after 'his' add 'grand'
lines 13–15, delete from '1stly' to 'Maud' and replace by 'perhaps *circa* 1325–8, Marjory (or Mary),'
line 15, after 'Hugh' add '4th' and after 'ROSS' add '[S.]'

page 477,
line 19, delete from '*suc.*' to '1427' and replace by '(living 4 Jan. 1433/4) by (__) da. and h. of Duncan CAIRNS of that ilk.'

page 478,
line 12, after 'STEWART' add '(illegit. s. of Alexander (STEWART) 11th EARL OF MAR [S.])'
line 12, before 'Earl' add '3rd'
lines 16–17, for 'apparently early in 1480' read 'between Martinmas and Whit-Sunday 1480'
line 26, for 'Mary' read 'Margaret' and for William' read 'Gilbert' [*Acta Dom.Conc.*, vol. xxiii, p. 101]

page 479,
line 20, after 'ap.' add 'was 20 years of age or "thereby" on 8 Nov. 1563' [*Scots Peerage*, vol. ix, p. 51]
line 25, for '1573' read '"by famine and vermin" Sep. 1575' [*Scots Peerage*, vol. ii, p. 340]

page 480,
line 11, delete from 'between' to '1634' and replace by '(cont. 17 and 25 Dec. 1633)'

page 483,
line 26, after 'coh.' add '(c)'
note (c) Her eldest sister *m.* Adam 2nd Earl of Camperdown, and the 2nd *m.* Robert, 2nd Baron Carew.
line 28, after 'She' add 'who was *b.* 27 Feb. 1827,'

page 484,
line 35, after 'above.' add 'He *d.* unm. 30 May 1914.'

XXXVIII. 1914. 18. NORMAN MACLEOD (SINCLAIR, *later* BUCHAN), EARL OF CAITHNESS, &c., br. and h., *b.* 4 Apr. 1862; ed. at Cambridge (Trin. Hall); *m.*, 21 Dec. 1893, Lilian, 2nd da. of Higford HIGFORD of Aldermaston Court, Berks. She *d.* 11 Aug. 1933. After succession to the Auchmacoy estates, 18 Apr. 1910, as heir of his grand uncle, James Buchan, he (1911) assumed the name and arms of BUCHAN. He *d. s.p.m.* 25 Mar. 1947.

XXXIX. 1947. 19. JAMES RODERICK (SINCLAIR), EARL OF CAITHNESS, &c., nephew and h. male, being s. and h. of the Rev. Charles Augustus SINCLAIR (*d.* 9 Mar. 1944), by Mary Ann, 2nd da. of the Rev. Edward HARMAN, which Charles was 3rd s. of the 16th Earl of Caithness. He was *b.* 29 Sep. 1906; ed. at Marlborough; *m.* 1stly, 29 Apr. 1933, Grizel Margaret, only da. of Sir George MILLER-CUNNINGHAM, K.B.E. of Leithenhopes, co. Peebles. She *d.* 2 Sep. 1943 and he *m.* 2ndly, 17 Aug. 1946, Madeleine Gabrielle, 3rd da. of Herman Edward DE PURY and widow of Capt. George Wareing Drewry ORMEROD of Tyldesley, co. Lancaster. He *d.* 8 May 1965. His widow *m.* 3rdly, 1977, David Frederick EWEN. He *d.* 1986. She *d.* 1990.

XL. 1965. 20. MALCOLM IAN (SINCLAIR), EARL OF CAITHNESS, &c., s. and h. by 2nd wife, *b.* 3 Nov. 1948; ed. at Marlborough and R.A.C., Cirencester; *m.*, 1975, Diana Caroline, da. Major Richard Lovel COKE, D.S.O., M.C. She *d.* 1994.

[ALEXANDER JAMES RICHARD SINCLAIR, *styled* LORD BERRIEDALE, s. and h. ap.; *b.* 26 Mar. 1981.]

CALDECOT CASTLE

page 485,
line 7, for 'CALDECOT' read 'CALDICOT'

CALEDON

page 486,
line 3, after 'Eton' add '1790–6'
line 17, after 'Ed.' add 'at Eton *circa* 1824–8 and'
line 37, after '51(d)' add 'Will dat. 10 Aug. 1896.'
line 38, delete from 'is' to 'living' and replace by '*d.* 6 Oct. 1939.'

page 487,
line 3, after 'Westm.' add 'Ed. at Eton 1899–1903, and at Cambridge (Trin. Coll.)'
line 4, after 'Guards.' add 'Fought in WW1. He *d.* unm. 10 July 1968.'

VI. 1968. 6. DENIS JAMES (ALEXANDER), EARL OF CALEDON, &c., nephew and h., being s. and h. of Herbrand Charles ALEXANDER (*d.* 6 May 1965), by his 1st wife Millicent Valla, da. of Sir Henry Bayly MEREDYTH, Bart., which Herbrand was 2nd s. of the 4th Earl of Caledon. He was *b.* 10 Apr. 1920; ed. at Eton and R.M.C., Sandhurst; *m.*, 6 Apr. 1943, Ghislaine, only da. of Cornelius Willem DRESSELHUYS of Long Island, U.S.A. This marriage was diss. by divorce in 1948 and he *m.* 2ndly, 31 Dec. 1952, Anne Louise, da. of BARON NICHOLAS WERNER ALEXANDER DE GRAEVENITZ. She *d.* 20 July 1963 and he *m.* 3rdly, 4 Aug. 1964, Marie Elisabeth Burton, da. of Major Richard Burton ALLEN of Ballachulish, Argyll and formerly wife of Major Hon. Ian Maxwell ERSKINE. He *d.* 20 May 1980. His widow was still living 1995.

VII. 1980. 7. NICHOLAS JAMES (ALEXANDER), EARL OF CALEDON, &c., s. and h. by his 2nd wife, *b.* 6 May 1955; ed. at Gordonstoun; *m.* 1stly, 1979, Wendy Catherine, da. of Spiro Nicholas COUMANTAROS of Athens. This marriage was diss. by divorce in 1985 and he *m.* 2ndly, 1989, Henrietta Mary Alison, 1st da. of John Francis NEWMAN.

[FREDERICK JAMES ALEXANDER, *styled* VISCOUNT ALEXANDER, s. and h. ap. by 2nd wife, was *b.* 15 Oct. 1990.]

CALLAN

page 487,
line 25, after '1751;' add 'ed. at Eton 1767–9, adm. as a Fell. Com. at Cambridge (Trin. Hall.) 2 Apr. 1770, but did not graduate;'

CALLENDAR

page 489,
line 5, after '1659([a])' add 'aged 67'
line 17, for '3rd' read '2nd'
line 26, after '[S.]' add 'and a minor in 1674.' [See vol. viii, p. 30, note ([c]), *sub* LINLITHGOW]

CALTHORPE

page 490,
line 11, after '1749' add 'Ed. at Eton 22 Apr. 1762–7 and at Oxford (Oriel Coll.).'

page 491,
line 17, after 'Eton' add '1839–41'
line 27, delete '([d])'
lines 30–1, delete from 'He' to 'work'
line 31, delete from 'is' to 'living' and replace by '*d.* at 38 Grosvenor Sq., 9, and was *bur.* at Elvetham, Hants., 12 Mar. 1925.'
after line 31 add

[WALTER GOUGH-CALTHORPE, only s. and h. ap., *b.* 3 May 1873; ed. at Eton 1887–91 and at Oxford (Ch. Ch.); *d.* unm. and *v.p.*, 21 Dec. 1906, of consumption, at San Moritz.]

VII. 1910. 7. SOMERSET JOHN (GOUGH-CALTHORPE), BARON CALTHORPE, yst. and only surv. br., *b.* 23 Jan. 1831; *m.*, 28 Jan. 1862, Eliza Maria, da. of Frederick CHAMIER, Capt., R.N., and widow of Capt. Frederick CREWE. He *d.* at Wordlands Vale, Isle of Wight, 16, and was *bur.* 21 Nov. 1912, at St. John's, Perry Bar, Birmingham. His widow *d.* 26 Aug. 1919.

VIII. 1912. 8. SOMERSET FREDERICK (GOUGH-CALTHORPE), BARON CALTHORPE, 1st s. and h., *b.* 23 Dec. 1862; *m.*, 22 July 1891, Mary, 1st da. of Ogden Hoffman BURROWS of Newport, U.S.A. He *d.* 6 July 1940. His widow *d.* 2 July 1940.

[FREDERICK SOMERSET GOUGH-CALTHORPE, 1st s. and h. ap., *b.* 27 May 1892. Served in WW1. He *m.*, 5 Sep. 1922, Rose Mary Dorothy, only da. of Leveson William VERNON-HARCOURT, at St. Paul's Church, Knightsbridge. He *d. v.p.* 19 Nov. 1935. His widow *m.* 2ndly, 12 Aug. 1949, Lieut. Col. Guy Alexander Ingram DURY.]

IX. 1940. 9. RONALD ARTHUR SOMERSET (GOUGH-CALTHORPE), BARON CALTHORPE, grandson, being 1st s. and h. of Frederick abovesaid, *b.* 22 June 1924; served in WW2, *k.* in a flying accident, and *d.* unm. 9 Oct. 1945.

X. 1945. 10. PETER WALDO SOMERSET (GOUGH-CALTHORPE), BARON CALTHORPE, br. and h., *b.* 13 July 1927; ed. at Stowe; *m.*, 6 June 1956, Saranne Francis, only da. of James Harold ALEXANDER of Eton Park, Dublin. This marriage was diss. by divorce in 1971 (she *d.* 1984) and he *m.* 2ndly, 1979, Elizabeth Sibyl, da. of James YOUNG of Guildford, Surrey.

note ([d]), delete all detail

CAMBRIDGE

page 494,
line 9, for '1361' in right margin read '1385'
line 29, for 'only sister' read 'elder sister and coh., being eventually in her issue, h.'
line 29, after 'da.' add 'and, in her issue, coh.'
note ([c]), line 4, after '(*Courthope*)' add 'The date of 1 May 1414 rests solely on the authority of Courthope. It seems more likely that the Earl was invested on 16 May, see vol. xii, part 2, p. 904, note ([e]).'

page 495,
line 2, delete '*attainted* and' [Neither the sentence passed on the Earl in August nor the confirmation passed in Parliament in November were attainders. See T.B. Pugh, *Henry V and the Southampton Plot*, 1988, p. 134]
line 8–13, delete from 'On' to 'uncle.([c])' and replace by 'He succeeded to the title of DUKE OF YORK on the death of his uncle. There is no evidence that he ever assumed the title of EARL OF CAMBRIDGE.([c])
note ([c]), line 4, after 'Duke' see 'See vol. xii, part 2, p. 905, note ([h]).'

page 499,
note ([c]), lines 12–18, delete from 'He' to '1912' and replace by 'He *m.*, 25 Nov. 1885, Rosa Frederica, divorced wife of Frank Wigsell Arkwright, of Sanderstead Court, Surrey, yr. of the two das. of William Baring, of Norman Court, Hants. He *d.* 2 Sep. 1907. (2) Adolphus Augustus Frederick FitzGeorge, *b.* 30 Jan. 1846.

Lieut., R.N., Mar. 1859; Capt., retd. Jan. 1893; Rear Adm. 1896; K.C.V.O. 1904. He *m.* 1stly, 1895, Sophia Jane, da. of Thomas Holden, of Winestead Hall, Hull. She *d.* 3 Feb. 1920. He *m.* 2ndly, 28 Oct. 1920, Margarita Beatrice, da. of John Watson, of Waresley Court, co. Worcs. He *d.* 17 Dec. 1922, at 20 Eccleston Sq., Pimlico, aged 76. (3) Augustus Charles Frederick FitzGeorge, *b.* 12 June 1847; extra A.D.C. to the Prince of Wales 1871–6 and A.D.C. to the same 1895–6; Col. late 11th Hussars; retd. 1900; K.C.V.O. 1904; *d.* unm. 30 Oct. 1933.

CAMDEN

page 501,
line 1, after '10' add 'and was *bur.* 17 at Seale afsd.'; after '1779' add 'aged 54'
line 2, after 'Sq.,' add 'and was *bur.* 26 Apr. at Seale ,'

page 502,
line 11, for 'before 27 Feb. 1766' read 'between 1756 and 1759'
line 13, after '81' add 'and was *bur.* at Seale'
line 17, after 'Eton' add '*circa* 1810–15'

page 503,
line 26, after 'Midx.' read 'Ed. at Eton 1885–90 and at Cambridge (Trin. Coll.).'
line 29, after 'Marion' add '1st'
line 30, for 'by' read 'being only da. by his 1st wife' and for 'H.D.' read 'Henry Dourien'
line 31, add at end 'He *d.* 14 Dec. 1943. His widow *d.* 4 July 1952.'
lines 32–3, delete all detail and replace as follows

MARQUESSATE. V. EARLDOM. BARONY. VI. } 1943

5 and 6. JOHN CHARLES HENRY (PRATT), MARQUESS CAMDEN [1812], &c., only s. and h., *b.*12 Apr. 1899. *Styled* EARL OF BRECKNOCK till 1943; ed. at Eton and R.M.C., Sandhurst. He *m.*, 19 Oct. 1920, at St. Margaret's, Westm., Marjorie, only da. of Col. A.G. JENKINS of Wherwell Priory, Andover. This marriage was diss. by divorce in 1941 and he *m.* 2ndly, 31 Jan. 1942, Averil, 1st da. of Col. Henry Sidney STREATFEILD, formerly wife of John Prescott HALLETT. She *d.* 1977 and he *m.* 3rdly, 1978, Rosemary Cecil, da. of Brig. Hanbury PAWLE, formerly wife of Grp. Capt. Peter Wooldridge TOWNSEND and John DE LASZLO. He *d.* 22 Mar. 1983. His widow was still living 1995.

MARQUESSATE. VI. EARLDOM. BARONY. VII. } 1983

6 and 7. DAVID GEORGE EDWARD HENRY (PRATT), MARQUESS OF CAMDEN, &c., 1st s. and h. by 1st wife, *b.* 13 Aug. 1930; ed. at Eton. He *m.*, 20 Apr. 1961, Virginia Ann, only da. of Francis Harry Hume FINLAISON of Windsor Berks. This marriage was diss. in 1985.

[JAMES WILLIAM JOHN PRATT, *styled* EARL OF BRECKNOCK, s. and h. ap., *b.* 11 Dec. 1965; ed. at Eton.]

CAMERON

page 505,
line 21, for '1745' read '1748'

CAMOYS

page 506,
line 12, for '1279' read '1276–9' [*Coram Rege Roll*, 2 Edw. II, *rot.* 76]
line 15, after 'Paynel' add '[1st LORD PAYNEL]'
line 19, for '1311' read '1310/1'

page 507,
line 6, after 'William [' add '1st' and for 'William DE ROS' read 'Robert DE ROS'
line 7, delete '[LORD ROS]'
note (i), line 2, after 'Richard' add '3rd Lord Foliot. She *d. s.p.*'
lines 2–4, delete from 'but' to 'Hastings'

page 508,
note (g), line 1, for '*a.*' read '*d.*'

page 509,
line 27, delete from 'is' to 'living' and replace by '*m.* 2ndly, 3 Sep. 1914, Sir Evelyn RUGGLES-BRISE, who *d.* 18 Aug. 1935. She *d.* 29 Nov. 1928.(c)
line 29, after 'afsd.' add 'He was ed. at the Oratory Sch. and Oxford (Balliol Coll.).'
line 31, after 'SHERMAN.' add 'She *d.* 21 Nov. 1961. He *d.* 3 Aug. 1968.'

VII. 1968. 6. RALPH ROBERT WATTS (STONOR), LORD CAMOYS, s. and h., *b.* 5 July 1913. He *m.*, 14 July 1938, Mary Jeanne, da. of Major Herbert Marmaduke Joseph STOURTON. He *d.* 9 Mar. 1976. His widow *d.* 1987.

VIII. 1976. 7. RALPH THOMAS CAMPION GEORGE SHERMAN (STONOR), LORD CAMOYS, 1st s. and h., *b.* 16 Apr. 1940; ed. at Eton and Oxford (Balliol Coll.); *m.*, 11 June 1966, Elisabeth Mary Hyde, only da. of Sir William Stephen Hyde PARKER, Bart.

[RALPH WILLIAM ROBERT THOMAS STONOR, s. and h. ap., *b.* 10 Sep. 1974; ed. at Eton.]

page 511,
line 2, after 'K.G.' add 'probably by his 2nd wife Elizabeth PERCY.(ax)'
note (ax) Her brass in Trotton shows that she had at least one son by Sir Thomas, and Roger's age of 22 in the inquisition of 1428 is compatible with his being her son. He inherited the entailed estates after the death of Hugh Camoys, his nephew of the half-blood. For inheritance by the half-blood see T.F.T. Plunkett *Concise History of the Common Law*, 1940, p. 647, note 5. [*Ex inform.* K.B. Mcfarlane]

page 512,
line 3, for 'Finally, in' read 'In'
line 9, delete 'appears to have' and after '1stly' add 'before 3 Mar. 1437/8,(da)'
note (da) There is a grant of this date by the feofees of Roger, Lord de Camoys, to Lady Isobel his wife, *Hist. MSS. Com.*, Hastings MSS., part 1, p. 273.

line 10, after '*d.*' add 'between 28 Mar.(ea) and'

note (ea) A general release to Roger Lord de Camoys and Isobel his wife is of this date. *Hist. MSS. Com.*, Hastings MSS., part 1, p. 273.

line 15, after 'cohabited' add 'He was living 9 Aug. 1473, when he remitted all action outstanding against William Lord Hastings on that day [BL Harl. MSS. 3881, f. 18. *Ex inform.* K.B. Mcfarlane]

CAMPBELL

page 512,

line 24, for '1445' read 'before 27 Apr. 1427' [J.R.N. Macphail, *Highland Papers*, vol. ii, Scottish History Soc., 1916, p. 153, and note (2); *ex inform.* Colin Campbell of Belmont, Mass.]

line 27, delete from 'She' to Aug.' and replace by 'She was living Feb. 1419/20 when they had a licence for a portable altar'. [*Scots Peerage*, vol. ix, p. 18]

page 513,

line 1, delete '1430' and for 'before 12 Mar. 1439/40' read 'Papal disp. 17 Jan. 1422/23' [*Scots Peerage*, vol. ix, p. 18]

CAMPDEN

page 515,

top line, for 'CAMDEN' read 'CAMPDEN'

page 516,

top line, for 'CAMDEN' read 'CAMPDEN'

page 517,

top line, for 'CAMDEN' read 'CAMPDEN'

CAMPERDOWN

page 518,

line 6, after 'h.' add '(ax)'

note (ax) In the *Gentleman's Mag.*, 1803, vol. 50, p. 381, is a reference to the "Hon. Captain Duncan of the Guards, eldest son of the Lord Viscount Duncan" who had died at sea and was buried in Malta. *The Times*, 9 Jan. 1803, says that he died 7 Jan. This is presumably the third son.

line 20, after 'Eton' add '*circa* 1824–8'

line 28, after 'widow' add 'who was *b.* 16 Mar. 1821'

line 35, after 'Eton' add '1853–9'

page 519,

line 2, after 'Unionist.' add 'He *d.* unm. at his res. at Shipston-on-Stour, 5, and was *bur.* 10 June 1918, at Long Compton, co. Warwick. Will dat. 9 Oct. 1916, lodged in Register House, Edinburgh, June 1918, pr. Oct. follg. at £432,115 gross.

EARLDOM. VI. VISCOUNTCY V. } 1918 4 and 5. GEORGE ALEXANDER PHILIPS (HALDANE-DUNCAN), EARL OF CAMPERDOWN, VISCOUNT CAMPERDOWN OF LUNDIE, BARON DUNCAN OF LUNDIE, br. and h., *b.* 9 May 1845. An engineer of Boston, Mass., U.S.A. He *m.*, 4 Feb. 1888, Laura, da. of John DOVE, of Andover, Mass., U.S., and widow of J.A. BLANCHARD. She *d.* 17 Aug. 1910. He *d. s.p.* 5 Dec. 1933, in Boston, when his titles became *extinct*. He was *bur.* 23 Dec. at Lundie, Angus.

CANNING

page 519,
line 28, after 'at' add 'Hyde Abbey, near Winchester and then at Eton, 1783–7'

page 520,
line 21, after 'Eton' add '*circa* 1824–8'
note (d), line 1, for '*b.* 1801' read '25 Apr. 1801' and for 'in' read '25 Apr.'
line 2, after 'Pitt' add '*b.* Dec. 1802' and for 'in' read 'Sep.'

APPENDIXES

APPENDIX B

page 534,
It proved impossible to revise either the Introduction to the Appendix or update the lists of Knights. See *The Knights of the Garter*, 1348–1939 [n.d.], by Edmund Fellowes, for a partial update.
note (a), lines 1–2, delete from 'the' to 'information'
line 3, add at end 'In Jan. 1348 mantles and garters were issued for the king and twelve companions at Eltham, P.R.O. E 101, Wardrobe Accts., 391/15, 21–3 Edw. III.'

page 535,
lines 2–3, for 'nothing known of him later' read 'apparently *d.* in 1353, since on 3 July of that year payment was made to Monsignor Nicole d'Auberchicourt of £200 owed by the Countess of Hainault for the services of Monsignor Sansset d'Auberchicourt his brother.' [*Cart. des Comtes de Hainault*, vol. I, p. 770]

page 536,
no. 49, delete from 'between' to '1376' and replace by 'on All Saints Day, 1375'

page 542,
no. 184, for 'July' read 'Sep.'

page 546,
no. 238, after '1489' add '[See vol. xii, p. 684, note (h)]'

page 547,
line 10, delete *
line 23, after 'Sovereign' add 'In consequence of the numerous attainders which had taken place in this reign it was decided at a Chapter of the Order held 9 May 1540 "to consult the Sovereign whether the names of traitors should continue written with the rest, or be blotted out as they deserved; for though they ought to have their names abolished yet the books would look ugly. The King chose a middle course, ordering that opposite such names should be written in the margin, 'Vah! Proditor'" V.G.'

page 548,
no. 294, for '6 May' read '7 May([a])'
note ([a]) See *L. and P. Henry VIII*, vol. v, p. 96.

page 576,
nos. 754, 767 and 769: before these entries add * and add footnote *. These knights were removed from the Roll and their insignia removed from the Garter Chapel, on the authority of the King, as Sovereign of the Order, on 14 May 1915.

page 578,
nos. 792 and 797: before these entries add * and add footnote *. See note on p. 576.

page 579,
nos. 814 and 822: before these entries add * and add footnote *. See note on p. 576.

page 580,
no. 827: before the entry add * and add footnote *. See note on p. 576.
note ([a]), line 2, after '529.' add 'On becoming King he ceased to be an ordinary Knight, but after his abdication was reinstated with the precedence of his original position. The same procedure was followed with his other Orders.'

page 581,
line 8, add at end 'See also note on pp. 576, 578, 579 and 580.'

page 582,
line 32, for '1585/6' read '1584/5'

page 589,
line 33, for 'four' read 'three' [The 5th Duke was nominated but never installed.]

page 594,
line 22, for 'Joan, wife' read 'Philippe, widow'
line 23, for '2ndly Hugh [Lord] Burnell' read '3rdly, Edward Duke of York'
lines 23–4, delete from 'She' to '1409'

APPENDIX C

page 599,
line 3, delete all detail
line 29, insert new line following, to read 'Adam Everingham, of Birkin, cousin of Sir Adam de E. of Laston, summoned 1309–15.' [See vol. v, p. 187, note ([f])]

APPENDIX D

page 603,
line 6, after 'offices' add 'See also "The Great Officers of State", Geoffrey H. White, *Geneal. Mag.*, vol. 11, 1954, pp. 500–2, 530–4.'

page 604,
line 40, for 'II' read 'I' and delete '(his uncle)'
line 41, for '*in fee*' read 'for life'

page 608,
line 21, for '1559' read '1558/9'

page 609,
line 18, For the agreement as to the holders of the office at present, drawn up in 1912, see G.J. Townsend, *History of the Great Chamberlainship of England*, 1934, pp. 19, 112–14.

page 615,
It was reluctantly decided not to revise the lists of non-hereditary great offices for the present volume. The policy of previous editors to restrict most of the lists to peers also seemed difficult to defend. The comprehensive lists in the *Handbook of British Chronology*, 3rd edn., ed. E.B. Fryde *et al.*, 1986, pp. 69–204, which, moreover, include the Scots and Irish officers, are therefore recommended.

APPENDIX F

page 651,
lines 14–15, for 'two Earldoms' read 'one Earldom'
line 15, delete 'and Kent (*Nevill*)'
line 19, for 'two Dukedoms' read 'one Dukedom' and delete 'and'
line 20, delete 'Gloucester' and for 'two brothers' read 'eldest brother'
line 21, after 'enobled' add 'Two peerages were created on 1 Nov., the Earldom of Kent (*Nevill*) and the Dukedom of Gloucester on the King's other brother.'

page 653,
line 26, for '14' read '12', for '8' read '6' and delete 'Carnavon'
line 27, delete from '(*Brydges*)' to '(*Watson*)'
lines 30, 31, for '*' read '+' in all cases.
line 32, after 'peerages' add 'He created two Earldoms on 9 Oct., *i.e.* Carnavon (*Brydges*) and Rockingham (*Watson*).'
Footnote, for '*' read '+'.

page 655,
For peerages created at the time of the coronations of GEORGE VI (12 May 1937) and ELIZABETH II (2 June 1953), see vol. xiii, pp. 580–94 and p. 806 below.

APPENDIX G

page 656,
For a complete list of the Lords Lieutenant appointed by JAMES II see *42nd Report of the Deputy Keeper of the Public Records*, pp. 722–9.

VOLUME 3

CANTERBURY

page 2,
line 7, after '*d.*' add 'in childbed'
line 8, after 'PURVES' add 'of Purves, co. Berwick.'

page 3,
line 8, after 'WALPOLE' add 'He *d.* at Seething Hall, near Norwich, 19, and was *bur.* 23 Feb. 1914, at Bergh Apton, Norfolk. His widow *d.* 1935.'
lines 9–10, delete all detail and replace as follows

V. 1914. 5. HENRY FREDERICK WALPOLE (MANNERS-SUTTON), VISCOUNT CANTERBURY and BARON BOTTESFORD, only s. and h., *b.* 8 Apr. 1879. He *d.* unm. in London after a short illness, 22, and was *bur.* 26 Oct. 1918, at Burgh Apton, Norwich.

VI. 1918. 6. CHARLES GRAHAM (MANNERS-SUTTON), VISCOUNT CANTERBURY, and BARON BOTTESFORD OF BOTTESFORD, cousin and h., being 2nd s. of Graham Edward Henry MANNERS-SUTTON (*d.* 30 May 1888), by Charlotte Laura, da. of Lieut. Col. F. L'Estrange ASTLEY, which Graham Edward Henry was 2nd s. of 3rd Viscount Canterbury. He was *b.* 23 Jan. 1872; *m.*, 15 Jun. 1903, Ethelwyn, da. of Charles HINDLE. He *d. s.p.m.* 26 Feb. 1941 when his titles became *extinct.*

CAPELL OF HADHAM

page 5,
line 11, for 'Hill' read 'Hall'
line 24, after 'Nov.)' add 'at Watford, Herts'

page 6,
line 1, after 'who' add 'was *bap.* 23 Mar. 1610/11 at Watford and who'
line 3, after '51' add 'M.I. (kneeling effigy), at Watford'

CARBERY

page 9,
line 16, after 'Northants' add 'by (__), da. of Sir (__) Corbet'

page 10,
line 10, after 'Eton' add '1778–81' and after '1784' add 'adm. there as a nobleman, 5 May.'

page 11,
line 32, delete 'was living 1913' and replace by '*d.* 22 Feb. 1932.'
line 41, delete 'and was living 1913' and replace by ', who *d.* 12 May 1939. She *d.* 6 Feb. 1949.'

page 12,
lines 1–2, delete all detail and replace as follows

X. 1898. 10. JOHN (EVANS-FREKE, *later* CARBERRY) BARON CARBERY [I. 1715], also a Baronet [I. 1768], 1st s. and h., *b.* 20 May 1892. By Deed Poll, 23 Nov. 1921, he changed his name to John Evans CARBERRY. He *m.*, 7 July 1913, at Paddington Parish Church, José, da. of Evelyn James METCALFE. She divorced him, 12 Dec. 1919, in Dublin, and *m.*, 15 Feb. 1922, at St. Marylebone Register Office, and later at the Parish Church, Capt. O.B.J. Montfort BEBB. He *m.* 2ndly, 1922, Maiä Ivy, da. of Alfred ANDERSON of Nairobi, Kenya. She *d.* 12 Mar. 1928. He *m.* 3rdly, July 1930, June Weir, da. of (__) MOSLEY. He *d. s.p.m.* 25 Dec. 1970. His widow *d.* 1980.

XI. 1970. 11. PETER RALFE HARRINGTON (EVANS-FREKE), BARON CARBERY [I.], &c., nephew and h., being s. and h. of Ralfe EVANS-FREKE (*d.* 23 May 1969), 2nd s. of the 9th Baron, by his 1st wife Vera, da. of C. Harrington MOORE. He was *b.* 20 Mar. 1920; ed. at Downside; *m.*, 27 Dec. 1941, Joyzelle Mary, da. of Herbert BINNIE of Sydney, New South Wales.

[MICHAEL PETER EVANS-FREKE, 1st s. and h. ap., *b.* 11 Oct. 1942; ed. at Downside; *m.* 9 Sep. 1967, Claudia Janet Elizabeth, da. of Capt. Percy Lionel Cecil GURNEY of Penshurst, Kent.]

CARDIGAN

page 14,
line 14, for '1708/9' read '1707/8'
line 19, after '*d.*' add 'of a bleeding at the nose'

page 15,
line 7, delete from 'the' to 'issue' and replace by 'da.'
line 9, for '16' read '13'
line 10, for 'Walton' read 'Warkton'
line 11, after '([a])' add 'and was *bur.* 9 June at Warkton afsd.'
line 19, after 'Midx' add 'Ed. at Eton from *circa* 1747;'
line 23, for '23' read '21' and for 'Walton' read 'Warkton'

page 16,
line 13, for '1809' read '1807'
note ([a]), line 10, after 'Earl' add 'However, Robert King, 2nd Earl of Kingston, was tried for

murder before his peers in the Irish House of Lords in 1798. He was acquitted. See vol. vii, p. 299.'

page 17,
line 25, delete 'was living 1912' and replace by '*d.* at Deane Park, 25, aged 90, and was *bur.* 28 May 1915. Will pr. Aug. 1915, £16,425 gross, £9,199 net.'

CARDROSS

page 19,
line 8, for '3 Dec.' add '8 Dec. 1625'
lines 8–9, delete from 'soon' to '1625' and replace by '18 Apr. 1626' [*Scots Peer.*, vol. ix, p. 52]
line 27, after '1625' add 'and *d.* May 1653'
line 29, after '*d.*' add 'and was *bur.* in Holyrood Church, 25 July'
line 29, after '44.' add 'The warrant to *bur.* his widow in Holyrood is dat. 28 Dec. 1696.' [*Ibid.*]

page 20,
line 8, after 'year' add 'and was *bur.* at Holyrood'

CARDWELL OF ELLERBECK

page 20,
line 21, after '1838' add 'and Bencher 1868'

CAREW

page 21,
line 23, after 'Dublin;' add 'ed. at Eton *circa* 1798–1803;'

page 22,
line 11, after 'Eton' add '*circa* 1829–35'
line 18, after 'widow' add 'who was *b.* 16 Nov. 1823'
line 27, after 'West' add 'She *d.* 28 Sep. 1922. He *d.* 29 Apr. 1923 at 28 Belgrave Sq. London.'

IV. 1923. 4. GEORGE PATRICK JOHN (CAREW), BARON CAREW, &c., br. and h., *b.* 1 Feb. 1863; *m.*, 5 Oct. 1888, Maud Beatrice, 2nd da. of John Summons RAMSAY. He *d. s.p.* 21 Apr. 1926. His widow *d.* 17 July 1955.

V. 1926. 5. GERALD SHAPLAND (CAREW), BARON CAREW, &c., cousin and h., being s. and h. of Shapland Francis CAREW (*d.* 6 June 1892), by Hester Georgiana, da. of Howe Peter (BROWNE), 2nd MARQUESS OF SLIGO, which Shapland was 2nd s. of the 1st Baron. He was *b.* 26 Apr. 1860; *m.*, 21 Apr. 1904, Catherine, da. of Thomas CONOLLY, M.P., of Castletown. He *d.* 3 Oct. 1927. His widow *d.* 20 Mar. 1947.

VI. 1927. 6. WILLIAM FRANCIS (CAREW, later CONOLLY-CAREW), BARON CAREW, &c., 1st s. and h., *b.* 23 Apr. 1905; ed. at Wellington; by Deed Poll, 25 Mar. 1938, took the name of CONOLLY-CAREW for himself and his descendants; *m.*, 3 June 1937, Lady Sylvia Gwendoline, da. of Ian Colin (MAITLAND), 15th EARL OF LAUDERDALE. She *d.* 1991. He *d.* 27 June 1994.

VII. 1994. 7. PATRICK THOMAS (CONOLLY-CAREW), BARON CAREW, &c., s. and h., *b.* 6 Mar. 1938; ed. at Harrow and R.M.A., Sandhurst; *m.*, Celia Mary, yr. da. of Col. Guy CUBITT, D.S.O. of Effingham, Surrey.

[WILLIAM PATRICK CONOLLY-CAREW, s. and h. ap., *b.* 27 Mar. 1973.]

CARGILL

page 23,
lines 1–2, for '22 Oct. 1716' read '10 Mar. 1689/90'

CARHAMPTON

page 24,
line 23, for '1783' read '1785'

CARLANSTOWN

page 25,
lines 18–19, delete all detail
note ([b]), line 8, after 'family."' add 'Both the newspaper and Justin Browne are wrong: Edward Luttrell was the legit. son of Southcote Hungerford Luttrell, of Saunton Court, Devon and had no descent from the Earls of Carhampton. See Sir H.C. Maxwell-Lyte's *History of Dunster*, pp. 527–8 and 539–40. V.G.'

CARLETON OF ANNER

page 26,
line 6, after 'adm.' add 'Trin. Coll., Dublin, 7 Apr. 1755, and'

CARLINGFORD

page 27,
line 29, for '21' read '26'

page 28,
line 21, for 'Suggenhill' read 'Sugnal'
note ([d]), line 7 (on page 29), after 'Viscount' add 'i.e. Viscount Magennis of Iveagh'

page 29,
line 10, for '2' read '1'

CARLISLE

page 33,
line 2, after '*s.p.*' add '*s.*'
line 3, after 'father' add '21 Nov.'
line 13, for 24 Oct. 1637' read '27 Sep. 1637'
note ([a]), line 1, before 'She' add 'In a letter from Chamberlain to Carleton dated 28 Nov. 1618 it is mentioned that "Viscount Doncaster has a son", which son *d.* an infant in Dec. follg., his burial being recorded on the 19th.' [*Cal. S. P. Dom.*, vol. ix, 1611–18, p. 598]

page 34,
note ([b]), line 2, for '1659' read '1658'

page 35,
line 5, for '([a]) his wife' add 'Carey, his 2nd([a])'
line 24, for 'Cumberland' read 'co. York'
line 27, for '*b.* 1694' read '*bap.* 14 Aug. 1693 at Watford, Herts;'
line 27, for 'Eton, and at' read 'Eton, 1706–7, adm. 2 May 1711 as a Fell. Com.'
note ([a]), after 'Price' add 'On 8 Oct. 1669, Lady Clifford mentions that Lord Morpeth "and his lady, who was one of the younger daughters to Sir William Uvedale by his second wife Victoria Carey, and widow to one of the Berkeleys who was killed at sea in the late wars" had come to stay with her on that day. See *Lives of Lady Anne Clifford and her Parents*, privately printed (1916) for presentation to the Roxburghe Club, p. 140.'

page 36,
line 6, after 'at' add 'her home in Priory Gdns.'
line 19, after 'Eton' add '12 May 1754–6'
line 19, after 'and' add 'adm. as a Fell. Com. about Mich. 1764'

page 37,
line 5, after 'Eton' add '1785–90'

page 38,
line 8, after 'Eton' add '*circa* 1813–18'

page 39,
line 4, after 'Eton' add '1857–61'
line 15, delete 'living 1912' and replace by '*d.* at her residence in Kensington Palace Gdns., 12, and after cremation was *bur.* 18 Aug. 1921, at Lanercost. Will pr. Apr. 1922 at £180,406 gross and £106,902 net.'

line 16, line to read as follows

XIII. 1901. 10. CHARLES JAMES STANLEY (HOWARD), EARL OF CARLISLE, &c., s. and h., *b.* 8 Mar. 1867, at 122 Park Str.; *styled* VISCOUNT MORPETH 1889–1911;

lines 23–4, delete from 'Having' to 'work'
line 26, delete 'was living 1912]' and replace by '*d.* 9 Dec. 1957.'

XIV. 1912. 11. GEORGE JOSSLYN L'ESTRANGE (HOWARD), EARL OF CARLISLE, &c., s. and h., *b.* 6 Jan. 1895; *m.* 1stly, 17 Jan. 1918, Bridget Helen (*suo jure* Baroness Ruthven of Freeland),([d]) 1st da. of Walter Patrick (HORE-RUTHVEN), *de jure* (apparently) 10th BARON RUTHVEN. This marriage was diss. by divorce in 1947 (she *m.* 2ndly, 13 Aug. 1947, as his 2nd wife, Walter Turner (MONCKTON), 1st VISCOUNT MONCKTON OF BRENCHLEY (who *d.* 9 Jan. 1965); she *d.* 17 Apr. 1982) and he *m.* 2ndly, 15 Aug. 1947, Esme Mary SHRUBB, yr. da. of Charles Edward IREDELL, M.D. He *d.* 17 Feb. 1963. His widow was still living 1995.

XV. 1963. 12. CHARLES JAMES RUTHVEN (HOWARD), EARL OF CARLISLE, &c., BARON DACRE OF GILLESLAND [1661] and BARON RUTHVEN OF FREELAND [S. 1651], s. and h., *b.* 21 Feb. 1923, at 64 Pont Str., Chelsea, *bap.* 29 Apr. 1923 at Lanercost Abbey; ed. at Eton; *suc.* to the Barony of Ruthven of Freeland, 17 Apr. 1982; *m.*, 3 Oct. 1945, Ela Hilda Aline, da. of Wentworth Henry Canning (BEAUMONT), 2nd VISCOUNT ALLENDALE.

[GEORGE WILLIAM BEAUMONT HOWARD, *styled* VISCOUNT MORPETH, MASTER OF RUTHVEN, 1st s. and h. ap., *b.* 15 Feb. 1949; ed. at Eton and Oxford (Balliol Coll.).]

note ([a]), line 1, before 'He' add 'His parliamentary service was not continuous, he was returned unopposed for East Cumberland on his father's death, 24 Apr. 1879; defeated at the General Election, 5 Apr. 1880. Elected at a by-election, 26 Feb. 1881. In 1885, due to redistribution, East Cumberland division ceased to exist' (*ex inform.* C.R. Hudleston).
line 4, for 'is' read 'was'

note ([d]) This question was resolved by decision of the Lyon Court, 1947, as a result of a petition by Bridget Helen Ruthven to be heir of line and heir tailzie of the 1st Lord Ruthven of Freeland. On the death of her father *s.p.m.* she, therefore, *suc.* to this title. See also vol. xi, Appendix H and vol. xiii, p. 323, *sub* Ruthven of Gowrie.

CARLOW

page 40,
line 7, after 'co.' add ', *b.* at Portarlington; adm. Trin. Coll., Dublin, 9 July 1732, aged 19.'

CARLYLE

page 41,
line 19, after 'CAITHNESS' add '[S.]'

page 42,
line 7, after 'LOTHIAN).' add 'He inhibited her in 1593'

CARMICHAEL

page 43,
line 20, after '1636' add 'and again 1641'
line 27, for '1 Nov. 1603' read '(cont. dat. 1 Nov. 1603)' and after 'WILKIE' add 'Burgess of Lanark,'
line 28, for 'Nov.' read 'Dec.'

CARNARVON

page 44,
line 10, after 'Alice' add '(ba)'
note (ba) She was a Roman Catholic recusant.
line 25, for '1625' read '1624/5' and after 'Sophia' add 'at the Earl of Montgomery's lodgings in the Cock-Pit'
line 28, for '1650' read '1653'
line 29, for '*d.* shortly before 7' read 'was *bur.* 6'
line 30, after 'age.' add '(ca)'
note (ca) The Wing Parish register contains an inexplicable entry "Burials 1643. The Right honorable ladie Agnes Dormor Countes of Carnarvene, June ye ii". [Register examined for Vicary Gibbs by the then Vicar, the Rev. Francis Tatham.]

page 45,
line 26, for '19' read '9'

page 46,
line 18, after 'Hants' add 'Ed. at Eton, Jan. 1753–9'
line 19, after '(a)' add 'matric. at Glasgow Univ. 1762,'
line 27, for '1st' read '2nd'
line 34, after 'Sq.;' add 'ed. at Eton 1782–9'

page 47,
line 10, after 'Eton' add '*circa* 1812–17'
line 21, after 'Eton' add '1844–8'

page 48,
line 11, for '1858' read '1856'
line 11, delete 'was living 1912' and replace by '*d.* at Portofino, 1, and was *bur.* in the private chapel of Highclere Park, 8 Feb. 1929.'

line 16, after 'Eton' add '1879–82' and after 'Newbury' add '1890'

line 19, after 'BOYER' add 'He *d.* 5 April, in Cairo, Egypt, from the effects of a mosquito bite, following his successful excavation of the tomb of the Pharaoh Tutankhamen, and was *bur.* 30 Apr. 1923 on Beacon Hill, near Highclere. Will dat. 29 Oct. 1919 to 3 Apr. 1923, pr. May 1923, at £398,925 gross, and £274,376 net. His widow *m.* 19 Dec. 1923 at St. George's Register Office, London, as his 2nd wife, Lieut. Col. Ian Onslow Dennistoun, M.V.O., late Gren. Guards (*d.* 22 May 1938), whose 1st wife had divorced him. She *d.* 1969.

lines 21–2, delete all detail and replace as follows

XI. 1923. 6. HENRY GEORGE ALFRED MARIUS VICTOR FRANCIS (HERBERT), EARL OF CARNARVON [1793], &c., s. and h., *b.* 7 Nov. and *bap.* 17 Dec. 1898, at the Chapel Royal, St. James Palace; ed. at Eton; Lieut. 7th Hussars; *m.* 1stly, 17 July 1922 at St. Margaret's, Westm., Catherine Tredick, 1st da. of J. WENDELL, of New York, and Sandridgebury, Sandridge, Herts. This marriage was diss. by divorce in 1936 (she *d.* 1977) and he *m.* 2ndly, 1 Sep. 1939, Ottilie Ethel, da. of Eugene LOSCH of Vienna and formerly wife of Edward Frank Willis JAMES of West Dean Park, Sussex. She *d.* 1975. He *d.* 22 Sep. 1987.

XII. 1987. 7. HENRY GEORGE REGINALD MOLYNEUX (HERBERT), EARL OF CARNARVON, &c., only s. and h., *b.* 19 Jan. at Lancaster Gate, London, and *bap.* 20 Apr. 1924, at Highclere; ed. at Eton; *m.*, 7 Jan. 1956, Jean Margaret, 1st da. of Oliver Malcolm WALLOP of Big Horn, Wyoming, U.S.A.

[GEORGE REGINALD OLIVER MOLYNEUX HERBERT, *styled* LORD PORCHESTER, 1st s. and h. ap., *b.* 10 Nov. 1956; ed. at Eton and Oxford (St. John's Coll.); *m.*, 1989, Jayne, 1st da. of Kenneth A. WILBY of Cheshire.]

CARNEGIE

page 49,
lines 1–4, for 'CARNEGY' read 'CARNEGIE'
line 7, for 'CARNEGY' read 'CARNEGIE'

CARNWATH

page 49,
line 15, after '1636.' add 'P.C. [S.] June 1638; subscribed the Covenant, 22 Sep. 1638.'
line 16, after 'CARNWATH' add 'BARON DALZELL and LIBERTON'

page 50,
line 12, after 'who,' add 'on 15 Sep. 1633 had, as s. of Sir Robert DALZELL, a lic. to pass the seas, and'
line 16, after '1637' add ', tocher 2,000 pounds Scots'
line 27, after 'in' add 'Jan.' [*Scots Peerage*, vol. ix, p. 54]
line 34, after '1659.' add 'Capt. of a Company in the Guards 1686; Lieut. Col. 1691.'

page 51,
line 24, after 'Margaret,' add '(b)'
note (b) "The grandfather of this Lady Carnwath was one Vincent, a carrier in Oliver Cromwell's time. She is a well bred cheerful woman and wants for conversation in matters of low life", (Diary of the 1st Earl of Egmont, 29 Apr. 1744).

page 52,
line 26, for 'CORNELL' read 'CARNELL'
line 32, after 'Blachford' add '(?Becford)' [*Scots Peerage*, vol. ix, p. 55]

page 53,
line 5, for '93rd' read '83rd'
line 39, line to read as follows

XII. 1910. 12. RONALD ARTHUR (DALZELL), EARL OF CARNWATH [S.], 2nd(a) but 1st surv. s. and h.,

page 54,
lines 2–3, delete from 'Having' to 'work]' and replace by 'He *d. s.p.* 11 July 1931.

XIII. 1931. 13. ARTHUR EDWARD (DALZELL), EARL OF CARNWATH [S.], uncle and h., being 2nd s. of Robert Alexander George DALZELL (*d.* 19 Oct. 1878), by Sarah Bushby, da. of Capt. John HARRIS, R.N., which Robert was 4th s. by his 2nd wife of the 6th Earl. He was *b.* 3 June 1883; *m.*, 4 Dec. 1902, Muriel Wyndham, da. of Col. Norton KNATCHBULL. He *d. s.p.m.*(ax) 9 Mar. 1941 when his Earldom became *extinct* or *dormant.*

note (ax) His only s. Arthur Robert Lancelot, was *b.* 11 Mar. 1907 and *d.* 28 Feb. 1909.

CARPENTER OF KILLAGHY

page 54,
line 37, after '1722,' add 'at Leyton, Essex(c)'
note (c) She is described in the register as "of St. Andrews Undershaft, London".

page 55,
line 1, after 'London.' add 'by Mary, da. of John CROKES (?COOKES) of co. Worcester' [*ex inform.* R.M. Glencross]

CARRICK [SCOTLAND]

page 55,
line 25, after '*m.*' add 'Isabel or' [*Scots Peerage*, vol. ix, p. 55]

page 56,
line 20, for '16 Mar. and 19 Oct.' read '13 Apr. and 8 Sep.' [See *ante sub* BRUS vol. ii, p. 360, see also WALEYS.]

page 57,
line 5, after 'IRELAND' add 'Though the expedition ended in failure and his own death he gained several victories over the English, notably against the Earl of Ulster at Conyers, 10 Sep. 1315, over Roger Mortimer (afterwards Earl of March) at Kenlis, co. Kildare, 6 Dec. of the same year, and over Edmund Butler the Justiciar [I.], at Ardskull, co. Kildare, 20 Jan. 1315/16.'
line 6, after 'Atholl' and after 'Mar' add '[S.]'
line 22, after 'sister' add 'and (in her issue) h.'

page 59,
line 15, delete '*cr.* 1469'

CARRICK [Orkney, Scotland]

page 60,
line 5, after '*d. s.p.m.*' add '*legit.*'
line 6, after 'and' add '3 Mar.'

CARRICK [Ireland]

page 61,
line 12, after '1779.' add 'Adm. Trin. Coll., Dublin, 16 June 1795'
line 19, after '58' add 'and was *bur.* at Thomastown'
line 35, line to read as follows

VI. 1901. 6. CHARLES HENRY SOMERSET (BUTLER), EARL OF CARRICK [1748] &c., 2nd cousin and h., being only s. of

page 62,
lines 6–7, delete from 'Having' to 'work'
line 7, for 'was living 1912.]' read '*d.* 1915.'

VII. 1909. 7. CHARLES ERNEST ALFRED FRENCH SOMERSET (BUTLER), EARL OF CARRICK, &c., 1st s. and h., *b.* 15 Nov. 1873 [for further detail see vol. xiii, p. 165, *sub* BARON BUTLER]. He *d.* 2 Nov. 1931 in Florida.

VIII. 1931. 8. THEOBALD WALTER SOMERSET HENRY (BUTLER), EARL OF CARRICK, &c. [I.], Baron Butler [U.K.], 1st s. and h., *b.* 23 May 1903 [for further detail see vol. xiii, p. 165, *sub* BARON BUTLER and in the present volume, *infra*]. He *d.* 31 July 1957.

IX. 1957. 9. BRIAN STUART THEOBALD SOMERSET CAHER (BUTLER), EARL OF CARRICK and VISCOUNT IKERRIN [I.] and BARON BUTLER [U.K.], 1st s. and h., *b.* 17 Aug. 1931; ed. at Downside; *m.*, 25 Aug. 1951, Mary Belinda, 1st da. of David TURVILLE-CONSTABLE-MAXWELL of Bosworth Hall, Rugby. This marriage was diss. by divorce in 1976 (she *d.* 1993) and he *m.* 2ndly, Gillian Irene, da. of Leonard GRIMES. He *d.* 5 Oct. 1992. His widow was still living 1995.

X. 1992. 10. DAVID JAMES THEOBALD SOMERSET (BUTLER), EARL OF CARRICK, &c., only s. and h., *b.* 9 Jan. 1953; ed. at Downside; *m.*, 1975, Philippa Janice Victoria, yr. da. of Wing Cmdr. Leonard Victor CRAXTON of Milford on Sea, Lymington, Hants.

[ARION THOMAS PIERS HAMILTON BUTLER, *styled* VISCOUNT IKERRIN, s. and h. ap., *b.* 1 Jan. 1975.]

line 11, for '1771' read '1791'

between lines 14 and 15 add as follows

CARRINGTON or KERINGTON

i.e. "RAMSAY AND CARRINGTON", Barony [S.] (*Ramsay*), *cr.* 1633, see DALHOUSIE, Earldom [S.], under the 1st Earl.

CARRINGTON OF BULCOT LODGE

page 62,
line 21, after 'M.P.' add '*b.* 1707' and after 'Mary' add '(*d.* 4 Apr. 1780)'

page 63,
line 18, after 'ed.' add 'at Eton 1805–11, and'

page 64,
line 20, after 'Eton' add '1856–61'

page 65,
line 7, after 'Sq.' add 'He *d. s.p.m.s.*, at Daws Hill House, High Wycombe, 13, and was *bur.* 16 June 1928 at Mulsoe, Bucks, when the Marquessate of Lincolnshire, the Earldom of Carrington and the Viscountcy of Wendover became *extinct*, and the Baronies devolved on his brother. His widow, who was a Lady of the Bedchamber to Queen Alexandra 1911–25, *d.* at Burnt Norton, Campden, co. Gloucester, 6, and was *bur.* 10 Oct. 1934, at Mulsoe.'
line 11, after 'Eton.' add 'Lieut. Royal Horse Guards, *d. v.p.* and unm. of wounds received in action in WW1, 19 May 1915.'

IV. 1928. 4. RUPERT CLEMENT GEORGE (CARRINGTON), BARON CARRINGTON OF UPTON, [G.B.], BARON CARRINGTON OF BULCOT LODGE [I.], br. and h., *b.* 18 Dec. 1852; *m.*, 23 Mar. 1891, Edith, 1st da. of John HORSEFALL of Widgiewa, New South Wales, Australia. She *d.* 26 Jan. 1908. He *d.* 11 Nov. 1929 in London.

V. 1929. 5. RUPERT VICTOR JOHN (CARRINGTON), BARON CARRINGTON OF UPTON, &c., s. and h., *b.* 20 Dec. 1891; *m.*, 25 May 1916, Sybil Marion, da. of Charles Robert William (COLVILLE), 2nd VISCOUNT COLVILLE. He *d.* 19 Nov. 1938. His widow *d.* 30 Sep. 1946.

VI. 1938. 6. PETER ALEXANDER RUPERT (CARRINGTON), BARON CARRINGTON OF UPTON, &c., only s. and h., *b.* 6 June 1919; ed. at Eton and R.M.C., Sandhurst; *m.*, 25 Apr. 1942, Ion, yr. da. of Lieut. Col. Sir Francis Kennedy MCCLEAN of Henley on Thames, co. Oxford.

[RUPERT FRANCIS JOHN CARRINGTON, s. and h. ap., *b.* 2 Dec. 1948; ed. at Eton and Bristol Univ.; *m.*, 1989, Daniela, da. of Flavio DIOTALLEVI of Madrid.]

CARRINGTON OF WOTTON

page 66,
line 12, after '1621.' add 'Adm. Gray's Inn 10 Mar. 1673/4'

page 67,
line 4, after 'Anne' add '(aa)'
note (aa) Her sister was the well-known Lady Nithsdale, who by her courage and resource saved her husband's life.
line 27, after '1667,' add 'at Hinchingbrooke, Hunts.'

CARYLL

page 70,
line 4, for 'A few months after' read 'After'
line 5, for '8 and 28 Mar.' read '16 Sep. and 17 Oct.'
line 10, for 'Dominicans' read 'Benedictines'
note (a), line 1, before 'For' add 'His peerage was in accordance with the directions in the Testament of James II.'

CARYSFORT

page 71,
line 22, for '*d. s.p.m.*' read '*d. s.p.m.s.* (she had a s. who *d.* in his first year)'

page 73,
line 11, after 'Eton' add '1847–55'
line 22, for 'was living 1912' read '*d.*, aged 80, at Cleveland, Stoke Poges, 13, and was *bur.* 17 Jan. 1918, at Elton afsd. Will pr. Mar. 1918 at £352,135 gross.'

CASEWICK

page 73,
line 29, for '1858' read '1868'

CASSILIS

page 74,
note (a), line 1, for '*maie*' read '*male*'

page 75,
line 3, after 'but' add 'allowed to return to Scotland early in 1543 and, failing to surrender himself, his three sureties and kinsmen, being in great peril of their lives, wrote 11 Dec. 1544, imploring him to do so. He was' [*L. and P. Hen. VIII*, vol. xix, part 2, pp. 439–40]
line 4, after '1545' add 'P.C. [S.], attending meetings of that body at Stirling 28 and 30 June 1545.'
line 6, for '1554' read '30 Jan. 1553/4 till his death.'
line 23, after '*m.*,' add '(fa)'
note (fa) On 10 July 1546 he was contracted to Jean, 2nd da. of James (Hamilton), 2nd Earl of Arran, but the marriage did not take place. [*Scots Peerage*, vol. ii, p. 473.]

page 76,
line 2, for '1575' read 'probably between Michaelmas 1574 and Apr. 1575' [*Scots Peerage*, vol. ix, p. 56]
line 10, after '1615' add 'aged 40'
line 22, after 'office.' add 'Baillie of Carrick, 1656.'

page 77,
line 20, after '1697/8' add '(post nuptial contract 9 Nov. 1698) [*Scots Peerage*, vol. ix, p. 57]

page 78,
line 1, after 'Notts.' add ', by Isabella, da. and coh. of Sir Francis BOTELER of Hatfield Woodhall, Herts.'

CASTLECOMER

page 82,
line 8, for '1701/2' read '1700/1'
line 12, after 'NEWCASTLE' add '2nd'
line 18, after '1717.' add 'Ed. at Eton, 1728, matric. Oxford (Ch. Ch.); M.A. 1735/6.'

CASTLE COOTE

page 84,
line 8, after '1754.' add 'Ed. at Eton, 1767–71; adm. as a Fell. Com. at Trin. Coll., Dublin, 7 July 1772; B.A. Dublin 1776.'
line 19, after '1793.' add 'Ed. at Harrow; adm. Trin. Coll., Dublin, 10 July 1811.'
line 21, for 'Bart.' read 'Kt.(ca)'
note (ca) He is *styled* a Baronet in a false pedigree. V.G.

CASTLE DONINGTON

page 85,
line 5, for '*Granard*' read '*Forbes*'
line 25, for '1603' read '1703'

CASTLEHAVEN

page 86,
line 9, after '1601.' add 'By deed dated 1 June 1610, he assigned to his eldest s. his whole estate in Ireland in consideration of an annuity or life charge of £500 English for life. On 12 June 1608 he wrote from Clerkenwell, to the Lord Treasurer (Salisbury) asking for the command of a company in a force about to be sent to Ireland, and mentioned that he had served in Ireland, the Low Countries and France.' [*Cal. Pat. and Close Rolls* [I.], 1–16 Jac. I, p. 195.]
line 17, after '1611,' add '(ca)'
note (ca) A grant to "George Tuchet, Lord Audley, and Elizabeth his wife" is dated 12 Mar. 1610/1 [*sic*]. *Cal. Pat. Rolls* [I.], 1–16 Jac. I, p. 222.'
line 26, for 'only' read '1st(cb)'
note (cb) He had a younger brother of the whole blood, Sir Ferdinando Tuchet, knighted before 1 June 1610. He was living 17 Oct. 1615. *Cal. Pat. Rolls* [I.], 1–16 Jac. I, pp. 195, 222.

page 87,
line 8, for 'BARON AUDLEY OF HELY' read 'BARON AUDLEY OF HELY'

page 88,
line 21, after '*bur.*' add '13 Aug.'

CASTLEMAINE

page 90,
note (b), line 1, before 'For' add 'He had been converted to Rom. Catholicism about 1670.'

page 91,
line 7, after 'and' add 'was ed. at Trin. Coll., Dublin'

page 93,
line 4, after '1761' add 'in Dublin; adm. Trin. Coll., Dublin, 4 Aug. 1779'
line 21, after '1767' add 'in co. Westmeath; adm. Trin Coll., Dublin, 28 July 1784'
line 28, after 'Dublin' add '; adm. Trin. Coll., Dublin, 14 June 1808'

page 94,
line 19, after '1873' add 'He *d.* 6 July 1937 in London, aged 74. His widow *d.* 14 Nov. 1955.'

VI. 1937. 6. ROBERT ARTHUR (HANDCOCK), BARON CASTLEMAINE OF MOYDRUM [I.], &c., br. and h., *b.* 19 Apr. 1864; *m.*, 16 Jan. 1894, Ethel Violet, da. of Col. Sir Edmond BAINBRIDGE, K.C.B. She *d.* 13 July 1934. He *d. s.p.* 31 May 1954.

VII. 1954. 7. JOHN MICHAEL SCHOMBERG STAVELEY (HANDCOCK), BARON CASTLEMAINE OF MOYDRUM, &c., distant cousin and h., being s. and h. of

Robert John H. (*d.* 26 Sep. 1951), by Eleanor Annie Esther, 1st da. of Jones Hodder STAVELEY, of Glanduff Castle, Charlville, co. Cork, which Robert was 2nd s. of Robert John HANDCOCK (*d.* 10 Apr. 1902), by Caroline Emily Louisa, da. of Gen. Henry PESTER, which Robert was 2nd s. of the 3rd Baron. He was *b.* 10 Mar. 1904; *m.*, 8 Oct. 1930, Rebecca Ellen, da. of William T. SOADY. He *d.* 31 July 1973. His widow *d.* 1978.

VIII. 1973. 8. ROLAND THOMAS JOHN (HANDCOCK), BARON CASTLEMAINE OF MOYDRUM, &c., s. and h., *b.* 22 Apr. 1943; *m.* 1stly, 1969, Pauline Anne, 1st da. of John Taylor BAINBRIDGE Burstow, co. Surrey. This marriage was diss. by divorce and he *m.* 2ndly, 1988, Lynne Christine, da. of Major Justin Michael Gurney.

[RONAN MICHAEL EDWARD HANDCOCK, s. and h. ap. by 2nd wife, *b.* 27 Mar. 1989.]

CASTLEMARTIN

page 94,
line 32, for '1821' read '1827'

CASTLEROSSE

page 95,
line 22, for 'May' read 'Apr.'

CASTLE STEWART

page 96,
line 19, after '(d)' add 'On 26 Sep. 1628/9, under the designation of Sir Andrew Stewart, he had a grant, as an undertaker in the province of Ulster, of 3,000 acres, in the Barony of Duncannon, co. Tyrone.'

page 99,
line 6, after 'Gloucester.' add 'Adm. Trin. Coll., Dublin, Nov. 1828, aged 18.'
line 7, for 'da.' read 'sister'
line 25, after 'Cookstown.' add 'He *d. s.p.m.* 5 June 1914, at his residence, Stuart Hall, Stewartstown, co. Tyrone, aged 77. Will pr. Nov. 1914, at £15,229.'

EARLDOM AND VISCOUNTCY [I.] VI.
BARONY [I.] XIV.
1914.
6 and 14. ANDREW JOHN (STUART), EARL CASTLE STEWART, &c. [I.], cousin and h., being 2nd s. and h. of Canon Andrew Godfrey STUART (*d.* 19 Sep. 1889), who was 4th s. of the 2nd Earl, by his 1st wife, Catherine Anne, da. of Richard (WINGFIELD), 5th VISCOUNT POWERSCOURT. He was *b.* 21 Dec. 1841. He *m.*, 23 Sep. 1876, Emma Georgiana Diana, da. of Gen. Arthur STEVENS of the 26th Madras N.I. He *d.* in Gledstanes Rd., W. Kensington, 7 Nov. 1921. His widow *d.* 5 Dec. 1949.

[ANDREW JOHN STUART, *styled* VISCOUNT STUART, 1st s. and h. ap., *b.* 27 Dec. 1880; ed. at Oxford (Corpus Christi Coll.). He was *k.* in action, 25 Sep. 1915, *v.p.* and unm., in France.]

EARLDOM AND VISCOUNTCY [I.] VII.
BARONY [I.] XV.
} 1921.

7 and 15. ARTHUR (STUART), EARL CASTLE STEWART, &c., 3rd but 1st surv. s.(b) Ed. at Charterhouse, Cambridge (Trin. Coll.) and Univ. of Paris; served in WW1. He *m.*, at St. Margaret's, Westm., Eleanor May, 1st da. of S.R. GUGGENHEIM, of New York, U.S.A. He *d.* 5 Nov. 1961. His widow *d.* 1992.

[DAVID ANDREW NOEL STUART, *styled* VISCOUNT STUART, 1st s. and h. ap., *b.* 7 Oct. 1921; ed. at Eton; served in WW2, *d. v.p.* and unm., being *k.* in action 10 Nov. 1942.]

[ROBERT JOHN OCHILTREE STUART, *styled* VISCOUNT STUART, 2nd s. and h. ap., *b.* 12 Dec. 1923; ed. at Eton; served in WW2, *d. v.p.* and unm., dying of wounds received in action, 17 Sep. 1944.]

EARLDOM AND VISCOUNTCY [I.] VIII.
BARONY [I.] XVI.
} 1961.

8 and 16. ARTHUR PATRICK AVONDALE (STUART), EARL CASTLE STUART, &c., 3rd but 1st surv. s. and h., *b.* 18 Aug. 1928; ed. at Eton and Cambridge (Trin. Coll.); *m.*, 20 Dec. 1952, Edna, William Edward FOWLER, of Harborne, Birmingham.

[ANDREW RICHARD CHARLES STUART, *styled* VISCOUNT STUART, s. and h. ap., *b.* 7 Oct. 1953; ed. at Millfield; *m.*, 1973, Annie Yvette, da. of Robert LE POULAIN of St. Malo, Brittany, France.]

note (b) The 2nd s., Robert Sheffield STUART, *b.* 1 May 1886, who *m.*, Constance Evelyn Nancy, yst. da. of Capt. Edward William Dunlo CROKER of Ballynagarde, co. Limerick, was *k.* in action, *v.p. s.p.*, 2 Nov. 1914. His widow *m.* 2ndly, 1 Jan. 1920, Charles Gordon Lee EVERSON. She *d.* 12 Oct. 1964.

CASTLETOWN

page 101,
line 22, for '21' read '23'

page 102,
line 2, after 'widow' add 'who was *b.* 1810,'
line 14, after CONYNGHAM' add 'He *d. s.p.* at Grantstown Manor, Abbey Leix, Queen's co., 29 May 1937 when his Barony became *extinct*.'
line 14, after 'She' add 'who' and after '1853' add ', *d.* at Doneraile Court, Doneraile, 11, and was *bur.* there 14 Mar. 1927.'

page 103,
note (b), line 12, for 'Dalwellington' read 'Dalmellington'

CATHCART

page 104,
line 18, for '1603' read '15 May 1602'
line 23, after '-garet' add '1st'

page 105,
line 26, for 'before that' read 'afterwards' and after 'Capt.' add 'Joseph'
lines 32–3, delete from 'For' to 'death' and replace by 'As she declined to make over her property to him, he kept her a prisoner in Castle Nugent in co. Meath for 16 years, when she was released by his death in a duel'

page 106,
line 4, after 'A.D.C.' add 'to Lord Stair at Dettingen, 16 June (N.S.) 1743 and'
line 5, after 'Apr.' add '11 May N.S.)'
line 7, after 'br.' add 'Schaw'
line 20, after '*d.*' add 'of consumption'
line 21, after '*d.*' add 'also of consumption'
line 26, for 'Glasgow' read 'matric. at Glasgow Univ. 1772'

page 107,
line 11, for '9' read '3'
line 29, after 'Gartside' add 'Cottage'
line 30, after 'year' add 'and was *bur.* at Paisley Abbey'
line 32, after 'Eton' add 'from 1791'

page 108,
line 7, after 'Eton' add '1793'
line 33, for '1460?' read '1452?'

page 109,
line 9, line to read as follows

EARLDOM AND VISCOUNTCY. IV.
BARONY [S.] XIII.
} 1905.

4 and 13. ALAN (CATHCART), EARL CATHCART, &c., 1st s. and h., *b.* 16 Mar. 1856, at Thornton le Street, co. York; *styled* LORD GREENOCK 1859–1905;

line 10, after 'Eton' add '1870–2' and for 'sometime' read '2nd'
line 11, after '(1879–82)' add 'Lieut.'
lines 13–14, delete from 'Having' to 'work.]'

EARLDOM AND VISCOUNTCY. V. BARONY [S.] XIV. } 1911. 5 and 14. GEORGE (CATHCART), EARL CATHCART, &c., next surv. br. and h., being the 3rd s. of the 3rd Earl, was *b.* 26 June 1862. He *m.*, 6 Jan. 1919, at Holy Trinity, Chelsea, Vera Estelle, widow of Henry de Grey WATER, sometime Capt. of the 4th Dragoon Guards, da. of John FRASER of Capetown. From her he obtained a divorce decree nisi, 23 Feb. 1922. He *d.* 19 Nov. 1927 in London.

EARLDOM AND VISCOUNTCY. VI. BARONY [S.] XV. } 1927. 6 and 15. ALAN (CATHCART), EARL CATHCART, &c., only s. and h., *b.* 22 Aug. 1919; ed. at Eton and Cambridge (Magdalene Coll.); *m.* 1stly, 10 July 1946, Rosemary Clare Marie Gabrielle, yr. da. of Air Commodore Sir Henry Percy SMYTH-OSBOURNE, C.M.G. of Exbourne, North Devon. She *d.* 1980, and he *m.* 2ndly, 1984, Marie Isobel, da. of William Joseph FRENCH and widow of Sir Thomas Brian WELDON, Bart.

[CHARLES ALAN ANDREW CATHCART, *styled* LORD GREENOCK, s. and h. ap., *b.* 30 Nov. 1952; ed. at Eton; *m.*, 1981, Vivien Vlare, da. of Francis Desmond McInnes SKINNER of Snetterton, Norfolk.]

CATHERLOUGH

page 109,
lines 23–5, delete all detail
line 35, for '1670' read '1682'

page 110,
lines 1–2, for '15 Feb. 1714/5, with the' read '12 Apr. 1715, see' and delete 'which see'

CAUNTELO

page 113,
line 12, after '1337/8' add 'and da. of Sir Humphrey de Littlebury'

page 115,
line 7, after 'Maud' add ', da. and h. of Sir Philip Neville of Scotton'
line 7, after '1375' add 'He was murdered in his house at Scotton, and his wife was indicted together with many others but acquitted' [See *Some Sessions of the Peace in Lincolnshire*, by Rosamund Sillern, Lincs. Rec. Soc., vol. xxx, 1937.]

page 116,
line 14, after 'Essex' add '(ca)'
note (ca) For the knighting in 1596 of Oliver Lambart see 'p. 400 *infra*, note (a).
line 15, for '1594' read '1599'

page 117,
line 6, after 'Cavan' add '6 Mar. 1626/7'
line 6, for 'John' read 'Richard'
line 18, after 'h.,' add '*b.* at ?Lanatherick, in England,'
line 21, after 'estates.' add 'Adm. Trin. Coll., Dublin, 10 Sep. 1641, aged 16.'

page 118,
line 30, after '1718,' add 'at Maryborough; adm. Trin. Coll., Dublin, 14 Nov. 1740, aged 21,'

page 119,
line 19, for '27' read '25'
line 20, after 'Clifton 'add 'aged 73, and was *bur.* 2 Mar. in Bristol Cath.'

page 120,
line 1, after 'Midx.' add 'and was *bur.* in the General Cemetery, Harrow Rd.'
line 11, after '1789.' add 'Ed. at Eton from *circa* 1803.'
line 12, after 'Sarah' add 'only'
line 18, after '2nd' add '([a])'
note ([a]) An elder br., *b.* 4 Nov. 1812, *d.* 1813.
line 21, after 'Eton' add '1829 to *circa* 1833'

CAVAN

page 121,
line 8, before 'FREDERICK' add '10 and 11.'
line 13, after 'Eton' add '1879–84, and at R.M.A., Sandhurst; matric. at Oxford (Ch. Ch.) 1883.'
line 17, after '1910' add 'He served with marked distinction in WW1 and was in command of the Guards Division and XIV Corps, twice mentioned in despatches; C.B. 1915 for services in the field, temp. Lieut. Gen., receiving the Cross of a Commander of the Legion of Honour, Sep. 1915. Rep. Peer [I.], Sep. 1915; K.P. July 1916.'
line 17, after '*m.*,' add '1stly'
line 19, for 'H.' read 'Henry'
line 20, after 'Marylebone' add 'and *d.* of heart failure at Wheathamstead House afsd., 15 June 1920. He *m.* 2ndly, at St. Mark's, N. Audley Str., 27 Nov. 1922, Hester Joan, widow of Capt. A.E. MULHOLLAND, Irish Guards (*k.* in action 1 Nov. 1914), 5th da. of Francis Edmund (CECIL), 5th EARL OF STRAFFORD, by Emily Georgiana, eldest da. of Lord Frederick KERR. He *d.* 28 Aug. 1946. His widow *d.* 1976.'

EARLDOM [I.] XI. BARONY [I.] XII. } 1946

11 and 12. HORACE EDWARD SAMUEL SNEADE (LAMBART), EARL OF CAVAN, &c., br. and h., *b.* 25 Aug. 1878; ed. at Oxford (Magdalen Coll.); Clerk in Holy Orders; *m.*, 9 July 1907, Audrey Kathleen, da. of Alfred Basil LODER of Aldwickbury, co. Hertford. She *d.* 8 Apr. 1942. He *d.* 9 Dec. 1950.

EARLDOM [I.] XII. BARONY [I.] XIII. } 1950 — 12 and 13. MICHAEL EDWARD OLIVER (LAMBART), EARL OF CAVAN, &c., s. and h., *b.* 29 Oct. 1911; ed. at Radley; *m.*, 10 Apr. 1947, Essex Lucy, da. of Henry CHOLMONDELEY of Shotton Hall, Shrewsbury. He *d. s.p.m.* 17 Nov. 1988. His widow was still living 1995.

EARLDOM [I.] XIII. BARONY [I.] XIV. } 1988 — 13 and 14. ROGER CAVAN (LAMBART), EARL OF CAVAN, &c., distant cousin and h., being s. of Frederick Cavan LAMBART (*d.* 13 May 1963), by his 2nd wife Audrey May (still living in 1995), da. of Albert Charles DUNHAM, which Frederick Cavan was s. of Major Charles Edward Kilcoursie LAMBART (*d.* 5 June 1916, being *k.* in action), by his 2nd wife Florence Marion, da. of Frederick Mancesseh BRANDON, which Charles Edward Kilcoursie was 4th s. of Major Frederick Richard Henry Lambart (*d.* 19 Aug. 1888), by Catherine Adeline Maxwell, da. of Walter H. GILL, which Frederick Richard Henry was 2nd s. of Oliver William Matthew LAMBART, Cmdr., R.N. (*d.* 28 Apr. 1863), by Anne Elizabeth, 2nd da. of George W. WILLES, Capt., R.N., which Oliver William Matthew was 2nd s. of 7th Earl of Cavan, 1st s. by his 2nd wife. He was *b.* 1 Sep. 1944; ed. at Wilson's Sch., Wallington, Surrey.

CAVERTON

page 122,
lines 12 and 13, for 'CAVERTOUN' read 'CAVERTON'
line 14, for 'ROXBURGH' read 'ROXBURGHE'

CAWDOR

page 122,
line 20, after '1753;' add 'ed. at Eton 19 Apr. 1763–7;'

page 123,
line 6, delete '([a])'
line 11, after 'London;' add 'ed. at Eton from *circa* 1803'
line 13, for '([b])' read '([a])'
line 15, for '([c])' read '([b])'
line 22, after 'day.' add '([c])'
line 29, after 'Eton' add '*circa* 1829–34'
note ([a]), read ([c])
note ([b]), read ([a])
note ([c]), read ([b])

page 124,
line 13, after 'Eton' add '1860–4'
line 26, for 'was living 1913' read ', who was *b.* 20 Jan. 1844, *d.* 2 Sep. 1926 and *bur.* at Stackpole, Pembroke.'
line 27, line to read as follows

EARLDOM. IV. BARONY. V. } 1911 — 4 and 5. HUGH FREDERICK VAUGHAN (CAMPBELL), EARL CAWDOR OF CASTLEMAINE, &c., 1st s. and h., *b.* 21 June 1870; *styled* VISCOUNT EMLYN 1898–1911; ed. at Eton 1884–9;

page 125,
lines 1–3, delete from 'Having' to 'work.]' and replace by 'He *d.* (having been an invalid for some years) at a nursing home at Kingston, 7, and was *bur.* 10 Jan. 1914, at Cleriton, co. Pembroke. She *d.* 26 July 1945.'

EARLDOM. V. BARONY. VI. } 1914 — 5 and 6. JOHN DUNCAN VAUGHAN (CAMPBELL), EARL CAWDOR, &c., 1st s. and h., *b.* 17 May 1900. He *m.*, 16 May 1929 at Aldenham Church, Wilma Mary, eld. da. Vincent Cartwright VICKERS of Edge Grove, Aldenham, Herts. This marriage was diss. by divorce in 1961 (she *d.* 1982) and he *m.* 2ndly, 29 June 1961, Elizabeth Topham, da. of John Topham RICHARDSON of Merstham, Surrey and widow of Major Sir Aleaxander Penrose Gordon CUMMING, Bart., M.C. He *d.* 9 Jan. 1970. His widow *d.* 1985.

EARLDOM. VI. BARONY. VII. } 1970 — 6 and 7. HUGH JOHN VAUGHAN (CAMPBELL), EARL CAWDOR, &c., 1st s. and h., *b.* 6 Sep. 1932; ed. at Eton and Oxford (Magdalen Coll.); *m.*, 19 Jan. 1956, Cathryn, 2nd da. of Major Gen. Sir William Robert Norris HINDE, D.S.O., of Salisbury, Wilts. This marriage was diss. by divorce in 1979 (she was still living in 1995) and he *m.* 2ndly, 1979, COUNTESS ANGELIKA, da. of COUNT PROKOP LAZANSKY VON BUKOWA. He *d.* 20 June 1993. His widow was still living 1995.

EARLDOM. VII. BARONY. VIII. } 1993 — 7 and 8. COLIN ROBERT VAUGHAN (CAMPBELL), EARL CAWDOR, &c., s. and h., *b.* 30 June 1962; ed. at Eton and Oxford (St. Peter's Coll.).

CESSFORD

page 125,
lines 21, 22 and 24, for 'CESSFURD' read 'CESSFORD'
line 22, for 'CAVERTOUN' read 'CAVERTON'

CHANDOS

page 126,
line 35, after 'Oxon.' add '*Inq. p. m.* at Marlborough, 13 Oct. (1607), 7 Jac. I.'
line 38, after '1586.' add 'Adm. as an Ancient of Gray's Inn, 2 Feb. 1591/2.([d])'
note ([d]), A statement of the many oppressions committed by him, and of his insolent and contemptuous demeanour towards the Council of the Marches of Wales, is in *Cal. S. P. Dom., 1547–80*, p. 545, under date Apr. 1577.

note ([a]), line 2, after 'CHAUNDOS' add 'The third lord writing in 1588, spells the family name "Brugges"'

page 127,
note ([b]), line 3, after 'V.G.' add 'Regarding Dugdale's *Summonses*, see Introduction to vol. ii.'

page 128,
line 2, before 's.' add '2nd but 1st surv' and after 'h.,' add '([ax])'
note ([ax]) His elder br. Robert *d. v.p.* an infant before 20 June 1611. At that date his father wrote to Robert, Earl of Salisbury, thanking him for "giving his name to his son who lived not long to enjoy it". (*Cal. S. P. Dom., 1611–18*, p. 217)

page 129,
line 3, after '*b.*' add '2' ['Lady Chandos' Register', *Geneal. Mag.*, vol. 10, 1948, p. 257]
lines 7–8, for 'before 1673' read '4 May 1665' [*op.cit.*]
line 8, after 'Elizabeth' add '(*b.* 5 Feb. 1642/3)' [*op.cit.*]
line 15, after 'SUDELEY' add '4th but 1st surv.'
note ([a]), line 3, after '1686.' add 'He did not return to England till Dec. 1687.'

page 130,
line 18, for '16' read '18' [*op. cit.*, p. 349]
line 19, after '([c])' add ', who was *b.* 3 Nov. 1693' [*op. cit.*, p. 349]

page 131,
line 2, after 'widow' add 'who was *b.* 3 Nov. 1693 and' and for '18' read '19' [*op. cit.*, p. 348]
line 5, for '1703' read '15 Jan. 1702/3' [*op. cit.*, p. 341]
line 10, for '8' read '7' [*op. cit.*, p. 309]
line 15, after 'male' add '*b.* 17 Jan. 1707/8 and was' [*op. cit.*, p. 342]
line 25, for 'about 28' read '18'
line 27, for 'SAVILE' read 'SAVILLE'

page 132,
line 1, for '12' read '9' [*op. cit.*, p. 350]
line 2, for 28' read '18' [*op. cit.*, p. 351]
line 15, for '11' read '14' [*op.cit.*, p. 307]
line 27, for '14' read '17' [*op. cit.*, p. 351]

page 133,
line 3, after 'ELLETSON' read '(Lieut. Gov. of Jamaica, *d.* 28 Nov. 1775)'

CHARLEMONT

page 135,
line 5, after '[I.]' add '12 June'

page 138,
line 4, after '1794.' add '([ax])'
note ([ax]) There is apparently no record of any such admission.

page 139,
line 26, for 'was living 1913' read '*d.* at Bath, 7, and was *bur.* 11 Mar. 1925 at South Ascot.'
line 38, after '1830' add 'at Loy House, Cookstown; ed. in Germany'

page 140,
line 2, delete '*s.p.m.*(a)' and after '1888.' add 'He *d. s.p.m.*(a) suddenly at his residence, Drumcairne, co. Tyrone, 4 July 1913, aged 83.'

VISCOUNTCY [I.] VIII. BARONY [I.] XII. 1913

8 and 12. JAMES EDWARD GEALE (CAULFEILD), VISCOUNT CHARLEMONT, &c., nephew and h., being s. and h. of Marcus Piers Francis CAULFEILD (*d.* 15 Apr. 1895), by Louisa Gwyn, 4th da. of Robert Griffith Williams BULKELEY, which Marcus was 2nd s. of Edward Houston CAULFIELD abovesaid. He was *b.* 12 May 1880; ed. at Winchester; *m.* 1stly, 26 Nov. 1914, Evelyn Fanny Charlotte, da. of Edmund Charles Pendleton HULL of Park Gate House, Ham Common, co. Surrey. This marriage was diss. by divorce in Apr. 1940 (she was *k.* by enemy action 14 Oct. 1940) and he *m.* 2ndly, 25 July 1940, Hildegarde, da. of Rodolphe STOCK-COTELL of Malstapel, Ruiselede, Belgium. He *d. s.p.* 30 Aug. 1949. His widow *d.* 22 Jan. 1969.

VISCOUNTCY [I.] IX. BARONY [I.] XIII. 1949

9 and 13. CHARLES EDWARD ST. GEORGE (CAULFEILD), VISCOUNT CHARLEMONT, &c., distant cousin and h., being s. and h. of Hans St. George C. (*d.* 14 Feb. 1899), by Emily Bertha, da. of Edward JAMES, of Edgebaston, which Hans was s. and h. of the Rt. Rev. Charles C., Bishop of Nassau, (*d.* 4 Sep. 1862), by Grace Anne, da. of Sir Richard Bligh ST. GEORGE, Bart., which Charles was s. and h. of the Rev. Hans C. (*d.* June 1854), by Anne, da. of John ROTHE, of Bloomhill, co. Kilkenny, which Hans was s. and h. of the Rev. Charles C., by Margaret, da. of Hans Widman WOOD of Rosmead, West Meath, which Charles was 2nd s. of the Rev. Charles CAULFEILD abovesaid, 2nd s. of the 2nd. Viscount Charlemont. He was *b.* 12 July 1887; *m.*, 2 Sep. 1911, Mabel, 1st da. of James Frederick William HAWTHORN. He *d. s.p.m.* 18 Jan. 1964. His widow *d.* 15 Feb. 1965.

VISCOUNTCY [I.] X. BARONY [I.] XIV. 1964

10 and 14. ROBERT TOBY ST. GEORGE (CAULFEILD), VISCOUNT CHARLEMONT, &c., cousin and h., being 2nd s. of Henry St. George C. (*d.* 22 May 1943), by Jane, da. of William GOLDSMITH, which Henry was the 2nd s. of James C. (*d.* 4 May 1861), by Eliza, da. of Basil GREY, which James was 2nd s. of the Rev. Hans CAULFEILD (*d.* 1854) abovesaid, descended from the 2nd Viscount Charlemont. He was *b.* 30 Sep. 1881; ed. at Von Schultz Gram. Sch., Bundaberg, Australia. He *d.* unm. 26 Nov. 1967.

VISCOUNTCY [I.] XI. BARONY [I.] XV. 1967

11 and 15. CHARLES ST. GEORGE (CAULFEILD), VISCOUNT CHARLEMONT, &c., br. and h., *b.* 1884; *m.*, 24 Nov. 1915, Lydia Clare, da. of Charles James KINGSTON of Aramac, Queensland, Australia. He *d. s.p.m.* 18 Nov. 1971. His widow *d.* 1973.

VISCOUNTCY [I.]
XII.
BARONY [I.]
XVI. } 1971

12 and 16. RICHARD WILLIAM ST. GEORGE (CAULFEILD), VISCOUNT CHARLEMONT, &c., br. and h., *b.* 13 Mar. 1987; *m.*, 7 Oct. 1914, Dorothy Laura, only da. of Frank GILES. She *d.* 18 May 1961. He *d. s.p.m.* 18 June 1979.

VISCOUNTCY [I.]
XIII.
BARONY [I.]
XVII. } 1979

13 and 17. CHARLES WILBERFORCE (CAULFEILD), VISCOUNT CHARLEMONT, &c., distant cousin, being 1st s. and h. of Charles Hans C. (*d.* 2 Nov. 1950), by Ethel Jessie, da. of D.G.R. MANN, of Ottawa, which Charles was 1st s. and h. of the Rev. Hans C. (*d.* 10 Dec. 1874), by Rachel, da. of Thomas READE, of Callan, co. Kilkenny, which Hans was 1st s. and h. of the Rev. Wilberforce C. (*d.* 27 Apr. 1872), by Catherine, da. of E. BUTLER, which Wilberforce was 3rd s. of the Rev. Hans CAULFEILD (*d.* 1854), abovementioned, descended from the 2nd Viscount. He was *b.* 10 Mar. 1899; *m.*, 24 Sep. 1930, Dorothy Jessie, da. of Albert A. JOHNSTON of Ottawa, Canada. He *d. s.p.* 14 Sep. 1985. His widow was living 1995.

VISCOUNTCY [I.]
XIV.
BARONY [I.]
XVIII. } 1985

14 and 18. JOHN DAY (CAULFEILD), VISCOUNT CHARLEMONT, &c., nephew and h., being s. and h. of Eric St. George CAULFEILD (*d.* 1975), by Edith Evelyn, da. of F.W. DAY, which Eric was 2nd s. of the abovesaid Charles Hans (*d.* 2 Nov. 1950). He was *b.* 19 Mar. 1934; *m.* 1stly, 15 Aug. 1964, Judith Ann, da. of James E. DODD. She *d.* 1971 and he *m.* 2ndly, 1972, Janet Evelyn, da. of Orville R. NANCEKIVELL of Mount Elgin, Ontario, Canada.

[JOHN DODD CAULFEILD, s. and h. ap. by 1st wife, *b.* 15 May 1966.]

CHARLETON

page 140,
line 9, for 'CHARLETON' read 'HOWARD OF CHARLETON'

CHARLEVILLE

page 140,
line 19, for 'LUNN' read 'LUM'
line 21, after '"nobilis"' add '"aged 14"'

page 141,
line 18, after 'Earl.' add 'Adm. Trin. Coll., Dublin, 11 Oct. 1781, aged 17.'
line 30, after 'who' add 'was *b.* 22 Dec. 1762 and'

page 142,
line 3, after '1801.' add 'Ed. at Eton, 1814 to *circa* 1819.'
line 11, after 'she' add 'who was *b.* Aug. 1801'
line 15, after 'forest;' add 'ed. at Eton *circa* 1836–40'
line 25, after 'forest.' add 'Ed. at Eton 1865–7.'

note ([b]), line 3, after '1834)' add 'It appears that from an action brought in the Queen's Bench 20 Nov. 1849, against his son Lord Tullamore, that in 1848 Lord Charleville was in greatly embarrassed circumstances and that his goods had been seized in execution by his creditors.'

CHATHAM

page 143,
line 27, for '1719' read '1705'

page 144,
line 11, after 'Foundation' add '1719–26'
line 14, after 'Horse' add ', afterwards 1st Dragoon Guards'
note ([b]), line 3, for '1st Dragoon' read 'Royal Horse'

page 145,
line 11, after 'COBHAM' add 'and Countess TEMPLE, 1749'

page 147,
line 6, after 'Abbey.' add '([ax])'
note ([ax]) Thomas Grenville in a letter to his br., Lord Grenville, dated 9 Jan. 1808, writes that she was "much disordered in her senses". (*Hist. MSS. Com.*, Fortescue MSS., vol. ix, p. 171)
note ([a]), line 1, for 'the Hon.' read 'Lady'

CHAUNDOS

page 148,
line 11, for 'POINTZ' read '(DE POINTZ), 2nd' and delete from 'of' to 'Somerset'
line 12, for 'da.' read 'sister and (in her issue) h. of'
line 13, after 'Gloucester,' read 'da. of John D'ACTON' of the same'

page 149,
line 14, delete from 'of' to 'BRIENE]' and replace by '[1st LORD BRYAN]'

page 149,
note ([i]), line 6, delete '[*sic*]'

page 150,
lines 1–2, delete from ', Margaret' to '1406' and replace by 'Elizabeth'
note ([a]), line 1, before 'Margareta' add 'Thomas Berkeley married three times: (1) Juliana (__), (2) Elizabeth Chaundos, and (3) Margaret (__). His two das. were by his 2nd wife. That the sister of John Chaundos was called Elizabeth is shown by his *Inq. p.m.* (see note ([i]) on p. 149), see also Henry Barkly, *Trans. B.G.A.S.*, vol. 17, 1892–3, pp. 123, 124.). Thomas' 3rd wife *d.* 1406,'

page 151,
line 8, for 'Harefield' read 'Hasfield, co. Gloucester'

CHAURCES

page 154,
note (d), lines 1 and 2, for 'Dinan' read 'Dinham'
line 5, after '*d. s.p.*' add ', see also *ante* vol. ii, note *sub* BASSET (of Drayton) [1343].'

CHAWORTH

page 155,
line 15, after 'Charles I.' add 'Constable of Bristol Castle for life, 1 Apr. 1616.'

CHEDWORTH

page 157,
line 4, for 'pr.' read 'dat. 14 Feb. 1740/1, pr. 24'
line 6, after '14' add ', and was *bur.* 24' and delete 'and was *bur.*'
line 8, for '1714' read '1714/15'
line 14, for 'pr.' read 'dat. 15 Feb. 1752, pr. 16 Feb.'
line 15, for '1715' read '1715/16'
line 17, for 'pr.' read 'dat. 23 Sep. pr. 11'
line 19, for 1715' read '1715/16. Adm. Lincoln's Inn 1 Aug. 1732'
line 21, for 'pr.' read 'dat. 5 June 1769, pr. 11 Dec.'
line 24, after 'HOWE,' add '(*d.* 3 June 1770),'
line 25, after 'Frances,' add '(*d.* 17 Feb. 1778),'
line 26, after 'Oxford' add '; matric. 29 Oct. 1772'
line 29, for 'pr.' add 'dat. 18 July to 10 Sep. 1804, pr. 13 Nov.'

CHELMSFORD

page 159,
line 2, for '1837,' read '1827; ed. at Eton *circa* 1840–4;'
line 21, for 'was living 1913' read '*d.* in Onslow Sq. S.W., 25 Feb., and was *bur.* 2 Mar. 1926 at Brompton Cemetery'
line 22, line to read as follows

III. 1905
VISCOUNTCY
I. 1921

1. and 3. FREDERIC JOHN NAPIER (THESIGER), BARON CHELMSFORD, 1st s. and h., *b.* 12 Aug. 1868.

line 23, after 'Winchester' add 'from 1881', after 'and' add 'matric.', and after 'Oxford,' add '1887'
line 27, after '1909.' add 'He was *cr.*, 3 June 1921, VISCOUNT CHELMSFORD of Chelmsford, co. Essex. Viceroy of India, 1916–21.'
lines 31–2, delete from 'Having' to 'work.]' and replace by '[for further detail see vol. xiii, p. 349]. His widow *d.* 24 Sep. 1957.'

VISCOUNTCY II. BARONY. IV.	1933	2 and 4. ANDREW CHARLES GERALD (THESIGER), VISCOUNT CHELMSFORD, &c., 2nd but 1st surv. s. and h., *b.* 25 July 1903 [for further detail see vol. xiii, p. 349]. He *d.* 27 Sep. 1970. His widow *d.* 1978.
VISCOUNTCY III. BARONY. V.	1970	3 and 5. FREDERIC JAN (THESIGER), VISCOUNT CHELMSFORD, &c., s. and h., *b.* 7 Mar. 1931; *m.*, 16 Aug. 1938, Clare Rendle, da. of Dr George Rendle ROLSON of Crofts, Haslemere, co. Surrey.

[FREDERIC CORIN PIERS THESIGER, s. and h. ap., *b.* 6 Mar. 1962.]

CHERLETON

page 161,
line 7, for 'da. of Piers DE JOINVILLE.' read '*de jure*, *suo jure* (according to modern doctrine), BARONESS GENEVILLE, da. and h. of Sir Piers de GENEVILLE (2nd but 1st surv. s. and h. ap. of Geoffrey, 1st LORD GENEVILLE)'
line 23, after '(FITZALAN),' add '11th or 4th'
line 36, after 'da.' add 'and (in her issue), coh.'
line 37, after '(FITZALAN)' add '10th or 3rd'

page 162,
line 1, after 'da.' add 'and h.[?]'

CHESHAM

page 163,
line 5, after 'Eton' add '1829–32'
line 16, after 'Eton' add '1863–6'
line 24, after 'death.' add 'Inspector Gen. of Imperial Yeomanry [G.B.], 1902–4'
line 37, line to read as follows

IV. 1907. 4. JOHN COMPTON (CAVENDISH), BARON CHESHAM, 2nd,(b) but only surv. s. and h., *b.* 13 June 1894,

lines 38–9, delete from 'Having' to 'work.]' and replace by 'He *m.* 1stly, 17 Aug. 1915, Margot, da. of John Layton MILLS of Tansor Court, Oundle, co. Northampton. This marriage was diss. by divorce in 1937 (she *d.* 1985), and he *m.* 2ndly, 20 Oct. 1938, Marion Caher, da. of Daniel Charles DONOGHUE of Philadelphia, U.S.A. and formerly wife of Theobald Walter Somerset Henry (BUTLER), 8th EARL OF CARRICK. He *d.* 26 Apr. 1952. His widow *d.* 1973.'

V. 1952. 5. JOHN CHARLES COMPTON (CAVENDISH), BARON CHESHAM, s. and h., *b.* 18 June 1916; ed. at Eton; *m.*, 28 Sep. 1937, Mary Edmunds, 4th da. of

David Gregory MARSHALL of Fen Ditton, co. Cambridge. He *d.* 23 Dec. 1989. His widow was living 1995.

VI. 1989. 6. NICHOLAS CHARLES (CAVENDISH), BARON CHESHAM, 1st s. and h., *b.* 7 Nov. 1941; ed. at Eton; *m.*, 4 Nov. 1965, Susan Donne, 1st da. of Frederick Guy BEAUCHAMP, M.D. This marriage was diss. by divorce in 1969 and he *m.* 2ndly, 1973, Suzanne Adrienne, 1st da. of Alan Gray BYRNE of Sydney, New South Wales, Australia.

[CHARLES GRAY COMPTON CAVENDISH, 1st s. and h. ap. by 2nd wife, *b.* 11 Nov. 1974; ed. at King's Sch., Parramatta and Durham Univ.]

note ([b]), line 2, after 'Maidenhead,' add 'ed. at Eton 1891–6, and R.M.C., Sandhurst,'

CHESTER

page 164,
line 35, delete from 'da.' to 'who' and replace by '(__)'

page 165,
lines 1–2, delete from '(by' to 'queror''
line 15, for '23, and *d.*' read 'three days (?24) before he *d.*'
line 16, after 'afsd.' add 'He was *bur.* in the cemetery of St. Werburg, but his body was afterwards removed to the Chapter House by Earl Ranulph le Meschin.' [Ormerod, *Cheshire*, ed. Helsby, vol. i, p. 15]

page 166,
line 15, for 'about 1129' read '17 or 27 Jan. 1128/9' [*Rec. Soc. Lancs. and Cheshire*, M.V. Taylor (ed.), vol. lxiv, 1912, p. 90]
note ([d]), for 'note *sub* LINCOLN.' read 'vol. vii, Appendix J, and additional note.'

page 167,
line 11, after '16' add '(?17)'
line 16, after 'Kevelioc' add '(?Machynlleth)'
line 20, after 'Simon' add 'DE MONTFORT' and for 'Leeke' read 'Leek'
line 21, after 'Stafford,' add '30 June' [*Annales Cestrienses*, pp. 28, 125; *Rec. Soc. Lancs. and Cheshire*, *op. cit.*, p. 96]
line 21, after '([d])' add 'and was *bur.* at St. Werburg's, Chester' [Ormerod, *Cheshire*, Helsby (ed.), vol. i, pp. 29, 49]
line 25, for ') in Powys, about 1172' read 'in Powys), Salop, about 1170 or 1172'
line 27, for ') in Powys' read ' in Powys), Salop.,'

page 168,
line 20, for '1220, when he' read '1220. He'
line 21, for 'Chartley Castle and the' read 'in 1225, having already begun', and for 'both co. Stafford' read 'co. Stafford, in 1214 before he left for Jerusalem.' [Ormerod, *Cheshire*, Helsby (ed.), vol. i, p. 34; *Annales Cestrienses*, pp. 54, 127]

lines 31–4, delete from 'of the' to 'DAVID I' and replace by 'widow of the King's s. Geoffrey, EARL OF RICHMOND and DUKE OF BRITTANY, da. and h. of Conan, 3rd EARL OF RICHMOND and DUKE OF BRITTANY by Margaret of SCOTLAND, da. of Henry, 4th EARL OF HUNTINGDON, s. of DAVID I of SCOTLAND.'

line 37, for '28 Oct.' read 'shortly before 27 Oct.' [See vol. iv, p. 661, note ([d]). He may have *d.* 26 Oct., see *Rec. Soc. Lancs. and Cheshire*, vol. xlviii, p. 146, note §.]

line 38, after 'pomp' add 'in the Chapter House'

page 169,

line 19, for 'Darnal' read 'Darnhall, co. Chester'

note ([a]), line 6, for 'Alice' read 'Agnes' [*V.C.H. Lancs.*, vol. i, pp. 3, 222]

note ([e]), lines 1–2 (page 170), delete from 'but' to 'lands' and replace by 'but the court at Westminster, while recognising the right of *esnecia*, allowed the King to make arrangements to extinguish the Earldom.'

line 3 (page 170), after '–132' add '; see also R Stewart Brown, 'End of the Norman Earldom of Chester', *Eng. Hist. Review*, vol. 35, 1920, pp. 26–51, and "Abeyance of Title as Illustrated by the Earldom of Chester Case", *Genealogist*, N.S., vol. xxxvi, 1920, pp. 169–73' and delete 'V.G.'

page 173,

line 22, for '9 Aug.' read '16 Sep.'

page 179,

after line 11, add 'For subsequent Earls of Chester and Dukes of Cornwall, see vol. 13 p. 117 and below, pp. 657 and 800'

CHESTERFIELD

page 180,

line 8, after 'ham.' add 'He bought this peerage for £10,000, which judging from the payments made by Lords Teynham, Houghton, &c., seems to have been the standard price of a Barony *temp.* James I, "Winwood has bargained with Sir Philip Stanhope to pay £10,000 to be made a Baron, Sir William Cope having dallied too long about it." (Letter of J. Chamberlain to Dudley Carleton, 12 Oct. 1616.) See *infra*, p. 247, note ([e]), and vol. xii, part 1, p. 680, note ([d]).

note ([c]), line 1, for 'child' read 'son'

page 182,

line 6, for 'Wellingborough' read 'Buxton'

line 7, after '1665' add 'and was *bur.* on the 18th at Wellingborough'

line 9, after 'She' add 'who was *b.* 1653 at Wing'

note ([a]), line 16, after 'jealous' add 'and treated her ill because he was in love with Barbara Villiers, Lady Castlemaine,'

line 17, after 'sacrament' add ', but the story is probably untrue, for her death was officially ascribed to the plague'

page 183,
lines 11–12, for 'apparently his only child' read 'second da.' [See vol. vii, p. 112, note (a) *sub* Kendal.]
line 13, for 'Sep.' read 'Apr.'
line 19, after '1773.' add '(ga)'
note (ga) He left £500 to Elizabeth de Bouchet, the mother of his natural s. "as some small reparation of the injury he did her".
note (e), lines 2–6, delete from 'The' to '*quietus*.'

page 184,
line 11, after 'Mansfield,' add 'his predecessor in title being one of the godfathers,'

page 185,
line 1, for '1809' read '1807'
line 6, after 'Eton' read '1817–22'
line 17, after 'Eton' add '1845–7'

page 187,
line 7, for 'was living 1912' read '*d.* at 26 Eaton Gdns., Chelsea, in her 96th year, 26 Apr. and was *bur.* 1 May 1923 at Holme Lacey. Will pr. July 1923, gross £10,701, net £9,815.'
line 11, after 'Eton' add '1868–9'
line 11, after '1877' add 'Barrister-at-Law, Asst. Private Sec. to the Chancellor of the Exchequer, 1886;'
line 13, after '(a)' add 'nom. K.G. 1 Jan. 1915; Master of the Horse under the Coalition Ministry, 1915–22.'
line 17, after 'Yorks.' add 'He *d.* 24 Jan. 1933 in London. His widow *d.* 30 Nov. 1957.'

XI. 1933. 11. HENRY ATHOLE (SCUDAMORE-STANHOPE), EARL OF CHESTERFIELD, &c., br. and h., *b.* 29 May 1855. Served in the R.N. (Capt., R.N.). He *d.* unm. 2 Nov. 1935 at Bournemouth.

XII. 1935. 12. EDWARD HENRY (SCUDAMORE-STANHOPE), EARL OF CHESTERFIELD [1628] and BARON STANHOPE OF SHELFORD [1616], also a Baronet [1807], nephew and h., being s. and h. of Evelyn Theodore SCUDAMORE-STANHOPE, *d.* 9 Nov. 1925), by Julia Dasha, yst. da. of John Gerald POTTER, which Evelyn was 5th s. of the 9th Earl. He was *b.* 9 Feb. 1889. He *m.*, 1stly, 17 Sep. 1915, Lorna Marie, da. of William Henry LEVER, of Wellington, New Zealand. This marriage was diss. in 1925 and he *m.* 2ndly, 28 Oct. 1931, Angela Domitilla, da. of Francis Patrick HOPKINS. He *d. s.p.m.* 2 Aug. 1952 when his titles devolved onto the 7th Earl of Stanhope, his h. male and the Baronetcy became *extinct*. See STANHOPE, vol. xii, part 1. His widow *d.* 5 July 1952.

CHETWYND

page 188,
lines 27–8, delete from 'before' to '1738/9,' and replace by 'shortly after 25 July 1716 (date of signing of marriage articles), Esther, da. and h. of Richard KENT (who

d. before 25 July 1716), of The Close, New Sarum, co. Wilts, by his wife, da. and h. of (__) FITZJAMES of Chalford. She *d.* 10 June 1741, aged 41 years.' [*Ex inform.* Major Anthony Crofton]

line 28, after 'Ingestrie' add 'M.I.'

page 190,

line 13, for 'CAMPBELL, of Sanderlands, Scotland' read 'Frederick CAMPBELL of Shawfield and Sanderlands, Scotland, by his 1st wife Eleanor, 1st da. of Francis 8th EARL OF WEMYSS.'

lines 15–16, delete from 'He' to 'work'

line 18, after 'Sq.,' add 'ed. at Eton 1872–8'

line 19, after 'Regt.' add 'A journalist.'

line 22, after '1900' add 'She *d.* 28 Apr. 1955.'

VIII. 1911. 8. GODFREY JOHN BOYLE (CHETWYND), VISCOUNT CHETWYND OF BEARHAVEN, &c., nephew and h., being 2nd s. of Henry Weyland CHETWYND (*d.* 27 Nov. 1893), by Julia Bosville, da. of Duncan DAVIDSON, which Henry Weyland was 3rd s. of the 6th Viscount. He was *b.* 3 Oct. 1863; *m.* 12 Apr. 1893, Hilda, da. of BARON GEORGE VON ALVENSLEBEN RUSTEBERG. This marriage was diss. by divorce and he *m.* 2ndly, 10 Feb. 1904, Mary, 3rd da. of William George (EDEN), 4th BARON AUCKLAND. She *d.* 22 Jan. 1925. He *d.* 22 Mar. 1936 in San Angelo, Texas.

IX. 1936. 9. ADAM DUNCAN (CHETWYND), VISCOUNT CHETWYND OF BEARHAVEN, &c., s. and h., *b.* 14 Nov. 1904; ed. at Eton and Oxford (New Coll.). He *m.* 1stly, 30 Apr. 1928, Joan Gilbert, formerly wife of Victor Alexander Charles FINDLAY, da. of Herbert Alexander CASSON of Tyn-y-Coed, Arthog, co. Merioneth. This marriage was diss. by divorce in 1951 (she *d.* 1979) and he *m.* 2ndly, 17 Jan. 1952, Dorothea Marianne, da. of Lieut. Col. Angus Colin DUNCAN-JOHNSTONE of Hermitage, Berks. He *d.* 12 June 1965. His widow *d.* 1990.

X. 1965. 10. ADAM RICHARD JOHN CASSON (CHETWYND), VISCOUNT CHETWYND OF BEARHAVEN, &c., s. and h., *b.* 2 Feb. 1935; ed. at Eton; *m.*, 19 Feb. 1966, Cecilia Grace, 1st da. of Alexander Robert RAMSAY, Cmdr., R.N.V.R., of Salisbury, Rhodesia. This marriage was diss. by divorce in 1974 (in Rhodesia) and he *m.* 2ndly, 1975, Angela May, only da. of Jack Payne MCCARTHY of Apsley, Nottingham.

[ADAM DOUGLAS CHETWYND, 1st (twin) s. and h. ap. by 1st wife, *b.* 26 Feb. 1969.]

CHEYLESMORE

page 191,

lines 17–18, delete from 'He' to 'work'

III. 1902. 3. HERBERT FRANCIS (EATON), BARON CHEYLESMORE, br. and h., *b.* 25 Jan. 1848; *m.* 14 July 1892, Elizabeth Richardson, 1st da. of Francis Ormond FRENCH of New York, U.S.A. He *d.* in a motor accident, 29 July 1925. His widow *d.* 15 Sep. 1945.

IV. 1925. 4. FRANCIS ORMOND HENRY (EATON), BARON CHEYLESMORE, 1st s. and h., *b.* 19 June 1893; ed. at Eton and Cambridge (Trin. Coll.). He *m.* 1stly, 18 Mar. 1916, Leonora Mary, da. of Erskine PARKER of Tasmania. This marriage was diss. by divorce in 1927 and he *m.* 2ndly, July 1929, Pearl Margaret, da. of A.J. SUNDBERG. He *d. s.p.* 21 Apr. 1985. At his death his title became *extinct.*

note ([b]), lines 3–4, for 'was living 1912' read 'She *d.* 15 Apr. 1934.'

CHEYNE

page 192,
line 6, for 'Lord' read '2nd BARON' and after 'CHIDIOCKE' add '6th LORD FITZPAYN'
note ([c]), line 4, for 'Mutterd' read 'Montreuil'

page 193,
line 9, for '1738' read '1728'
line 12, for '1639' read '1639/40'
line 13, for '1639' read '1640' and for '1728' read '1737'
note ([b]), after 'Crispe' add 'and *d. v.p.* and *s.p.*'

CHICHESTER

page 194,
line 34, for '1537' read '1546/7'

page 197,
lines 17–19, delete from 'He' to 'work'

IX. 1902. 5. FRANCIS GODOLPHIN (PELHAM), EARL OF CHICHESTER, &c., br. and h., *b.* 18 Oct. 1844; ed. at Cambridge. He *m.*, 4 Aug. 1870, Alice Carr, da. of George Carr (GLYNN), 1st BARON WOLVERTON. He *d.* 14 Nov. 1926. His widow *d.* 1, at Falmer, Sussex, and was *bur.* 6 Feb. 1934 at Stanmer.

X. 1905. 6. JOCELYN BRUDENELL (PELHAM), EARL OF CHICHESTER, &c., s. and h., *b.* 21 May 1871; ed. at Cambridge (Trin. Coll.); *m.*, 17 May 1898, Ruth, 1st da. of Francis William BUXTON, etc. He *d.* 14, of pneumonia at Stanmer Park and was *bur.* 26 Nov. 1926 at Stanmer. His widow *d.* 8 Feb. 1865.

XI. 1926. 7. FRANCIS GODOLPHIN HENRY (PELHAM), EARL OF CHICHESTER, &c., 1st s. and h., *b.* 23 Mar. 1905. He *d.* unm. 22 Nov. 1926 of pneumonia at Stanmer Park, Lewes, Sussex.

XII. 1926. 8. JOHN BUXTON (PELHAM), EARL OF CHICHESTER, &c., br. and h., *b.* 12 June 1912; *m.*, 27 Mar. 1940, Ursula, da. of Walter DE PANNWITZ of Hautekamp, Bennbrock, Holland. He was *k.* on active service, 21 Feb. 1944. His widow *m.* 2ndly, 8 May 1957, Ralph Gunning HENDERSON of Argentina. This marriage was diss. by divorce in 1971. She *d.* 1989.

XIII. 1944. 9. JOHN NICHOLAS (PELHAM), EARL OF CHICHESTER, &c., only s. and h., *b.* (posthumously) 14 Apr. 1944; ed. at Stanbridge Earls Sch., Romsey, Hants. He *m.*, 1975, June Marijke (Mrs HALL), da. of Grp. Capt. E.D. WELLS of Marbella, Spain.

page 198,
line 22, after '[I.]' add 'July'

CHISLEHURST

page 200,
line 12, after '1789' add '; *extinct* 1890'

CHOLMONDELEY

page 203,
line 16, for '1736' read '1 Mar. 1735/6' [*Recog. Rolls of Chester*, 9 Geo. II]

page 204,
line 10, after 'Northants.' add 'Ed. at Eton 19 Sep. 1758–65.'

page 205,
line 5, after 'MALPAS;' add 'ed. at Eton *circa* 1804–7;'

page 207,
line 3, after 'Sq.' add 'He *d.* at Cholmondeley Castle 16 Mar. from injuries caused by a fall in the hunting field 28 Feb. preceding and was *bur.* 20 Mar. 1923, in the private burial ground at Cholmondeley. His widow *d.* 25 Oct. 1938'
lines 4–5, delete all detail and replace as follows

MARQUESSATE. V.
EARLDOM. VIII.
VISCOUNTCY. [I.] X.
BARONY. IX.
1923

5, 8, 9, and 8. GEORGE HORATIO CHARLES (CHOLMONDELEY), MARQUESS OF CHOLMONDELEY, &c., 1st s.[a] and h., *b.* 19 May 1883, in Charles Str. afsd.; *styled* EARL OF ROCKSAVAGE 1884–1923; ed. at Eton 1896–8; joined 9th Lancers 1901; Lieut. 1905; served in the S. African War as Railway Staff Officer 1899–1901.[b] A.D.C. to the Viceroy of India. He served in WW1 as Capt. 9th Lancers.[c] Joint Hereditary GREAT CHAMBERLAIN to Edward VIII and Elizabeth II (1952–66). He *m.*, 6 Aug. 1913, Sybil Rachel Betty Cecile, only da. of Sir Edward SASSOON, 2nd Bart. of Sandgate, by Aline Caroline, da. of BARON GUSTAVE DE ROTHSCHILD. She was *b.* 30 Jan. 1894. He *d.* 16 Sep. 1968. His widow *d.* 1989.

MARQUESSATE. VI.
EARLDOM. IX.
VISCOUNTCY. [I.] XI.
BARONY. X.
1968

6, 9, 10 and 9. GEORGE HUGH (CHOLMONDELEY), MARQUESS OF CHOLMONDELEY, &c., s. and h., *b.* 24 Apr. 1919; ed. at Eton and Cambridge (Magdalene Coll.); *m.*, 14 June 1947, Lavinia, only da. of Col. John LESLIE of Brancaster, Norfolk. He *d.* 13 Mar. 1990. His widow was living 1995.

MARQUESSATE. VII. EARLDOM. X. VISCOUNTCY. [I.] XII. BARONY. XI.	1990	7, 10, 11 and 10. DAVID GEORGE PHILIP (CHOLMONDELEY), MARQUESS OF CHOLMONDELEY, &c., s. and h., *b.* 27 June 1960; ed. at Eton and the Sorbonne; joint hereditary LORD GREAT CHAMBERLAIN.

note ([a]), line 2, for 'widow' read 'divorced wife'
note ([b]), For a list of peers and their heirs ap. who served in this war see vol. iii, Appendix B.
note ([c]), For a list of peers and their sons who served in this war see vol. viii, Appendix F.

CHURCHILL OF WHICHWOOD

page 208,
line 31, after '1876–81;' add 'ed. at Eton 1878–9, and R.M.C., Sandhurst;'
line 32, after 'Guards' add '1884–9'
line 33, after '–1905;' add 'Master of the Buckhounds 1900–1; acting LORD GREAT CHAMBERLAIN at the Coronation of Edward VII; one of the Conservative Whips in the House of Lords. Prince of the Holy Roman Empire. Held the Red Eagle of Prussia 1st Class, The Crown of Italy and other foreign orders.'

page 209,
line 1, after '*m.*' add '1stly'
line 4, after 'Midx.' add 'From her he obtained a divorce in 1927. She *d.* 25 Dec. 1938. He *m.*, 2ndly, at St. Columba's Church, Pont Str., S.W., 29 Aug. 1927, Christine, eld. da. of William SINCLAIR. He *d.* of pneumonia, 3 Jan. 1934, at Langlee House, Roxburghshire. His widow *m.* 2ndly, 12 June 1937, Lieut. Col. Ralph Heyeard ISHAM. This marriage was diss. by divorce in 1938 (he *d.* 13 June 1955) and she *m.* 3rdly, 6 Nov. 1939, Sir Lancelot OLIPHANT, K.C.M.G. He *d.* 2 Oct. 1965. She *d.* 1972.
line 5, line to read as follows

VISCOUNTCY II. BARONY. IV.	1934	2 and 4. VICTOR ALEXANDER (SPENCER), VISCOUNT CHURCHILL, BARON CHURCHILL OF WHICHWOOD, 2nd but 1st surv.([a]) s. and h., *b.*

line 8, for ']' read 'He was ed. at Eton; *m.* 1stly, 15 July 1916, Katherine Emily, da. of Robert BEAVEN and formerly wife of Stanley Venn ELLIS, Capt., R.N. She *d.* 1 Dec. 1943 and he *m.* 2ndly, 19 Oct. 1949, Joan, 1st da. of Joseph Baron BLACK of Belfast. She *d.* 12 May 1957. He *d.* 21 Dec. 1973.

VISCOUNTCY III. BARONY. V. } 1973 3 and 5. VICTOR GEORGE (SPENCER), VISCOUNT CHURCHILL, &c., br. and h., being only s. by 2nd wife, *b.* (posthumously) 31 July 1934; ed. at Eton and Oxford (New Coll.).

CHURSTON

page 210,
line 10, after 'wife,' add '(he was ed. at Eton 1837–41),'
line 11, after '1846;' add 'ed. at Eton 1855–63;'
lines 19–20, for 'was living 1912' read '*d.* at Churston Court, Churston Ferrers, 1, and was *bur.* 4 Oct. 1924, at Churston Ferrers. Will pr. gross £2,519, net £2,345.'
lines 21–2, lines to read as follows

III. 1910. 3. JOHN REGINALD LOPES (YARDE-BULLER), BARON CHURSTON OF CHURSTON FERRERS AND LUPTON &c., 1st s. and h., *b.* 9 Nov. 1873; ed. at Winchester from 1887; 2nd Lieut. 1st Battn. Scots Guards, 1896, Lieut. 1898, Capt. 1902; served in the S. African War[a]

line 24, after '1904–6' add 'M.V.O. 1903'
line 27, after 'She' add ', who was *b.* 26 Aug. 1884,'
lines 28–9, delete from 'Having' to 'work.]' and replace by 'This marriage was diss. by divorce in 1928. He *d.* 19 Apr. 1930. His widow *d.* 20 Oct. 1960.'

IV. 1930. 4. RICHARD FRANCIS ROGER (YARDE-BULLER), BARON CHURSTON OF CHURSTON FERRERS AND LUPTON, &c., 1st s. and h., *b.* 12 Feb. 1910; ed. at Eton. He *m.* 1stly, 5 Jan. 1933, Elizabeth Mary, 2nd da. of Lieut. Col. William Baring DU PRE, of Wilton Park, Beaconsfield, Bucks. This marriage was diss. by divorce in 1943 (she *d.* 23 Sep. 1951) and he *m.* 2ndly, 31 Mar. 1949, Sandra, da. of Percy NEEDHAM, and formerly wife of, 1stly, Claud Harold Bertram Arthur GRIFFITHS and 2ndly of Jack DUNFEE. She *d.* 1979 and he *m.* 3rdly, 1981, Olga Alice Muriel, illegit. da. of Lionel Walter (ROTHSCHILD), 2nd BARON ROTHSCHILD by Marie Barbara, da. of Maximilian FREDENSON, formerly wife of Bryce Evans BLAIR. He *d.* 9 Apr. 1991. His widow *d.* 1992.

V. 1991. 5. JOHN FRANCIS ROGER (YARDE-BULLER), BARON CHURSTON OF CHURSTON FERRERS AND LUPTON, &c., only s. and h., *b.* 29 Dec. 1934; ed. at Eton; *m.*, 1973, Alexandra Joanna, only da. of Anthony CONTOMICHALOS.

[BENJAMIN FRANCIS ANTHONY YARDE-BULLER, s. and h. ap., *b.* 13 Sep. 1974; ed. at Eton.]

CLANBRASSIL

page 212,
line 4, for '*d. s.p.*' read '*d. s.p.s.*' [*Conway Letters ... 1642–84*, M.H. Nicolson (ed.), 1930, p. 302]

page 213,
line 3, after '1730' add '([ax])'
note ([ax]) *Gent. Mag.*, vol. 2, 1732, p. 726, has an entry: "Lady of Ld. Vt. Limerick of Ireland 30 Apr. 1732 – of a son."
line 17, for 'CLANBRASSILL' read 'CLANBRASSIL'
line 18, for '1693' read '1692'

CLANCARE

page 214,
line 3, for 'MacCormach' read 'MacCormac'
line 4, after 'MORE' add '; he had a grant of English liberty, 12 Feb. 1555/6;'
line 18, after '*s.p.*' add 'before 1588'

CLANCARTY

page 214,
line 26, for 'but' read 'and in 1644 was a Commissioner from that party to the King, a truce having been agreed on. After the resumption of hostilities he'
note ([c]), line 1, after '*m.*,' add 'in Mar. 1588'

page 215,
line 14, for '3' read 'off Lowestoft, 2,'
line 15, after 'widow' add 'who was *b.* at Kreny, in Denmark'
note ([e]), line 1, before 'James' add 'Charles (WESTON), 3rd Earl of Portland,'
line 2, after 'and' add 'the three last'

page 217,
line 11, after '1707.' add 'On 18 Feb. 1711/12 he was living at Hamburg in banishment'
line 11, after '11' add 'or 13'
line 20, after '1685.' add 'brought up as a Protestant and ed. at St. Paul's Sch.' [Diary of first Earl of Egmont, 7 Dec. 1735]
line 21, after 'man-of-war' add ', the Solebay,'
note ([d]), for '1715' read '1724–5'

page 218,
line 1, after 'Joanna' add '(with a fortune of £30,000)'

page 220,
line 17, for '4 and 5' read '5 and 4'
line 26, after 'Eton' add '1883–7'
line 35, delete from '(in 1908' to 'Gardens.)' and replace by 'He *d.* at Dunlo Lodge, Taplow, Bucks, 18 Feb. 1929. His widow *d.* 1974.'

page 221,
lines 1–3, delete all detail and replace as follows

EARLDOM [I.] X.
VISCOUNTCY [U.K.] V. } 1929

6 and 5. RICHARD FREDERICK JOHN DONOUGH (LE-POER TRENCH), EARL OF CLANCARTY, &c., 1st s. and h., by 1st wife, *b.* 27 Dec. 1891, at Upper Hare Park, Bottisham, co. Cambridge; *styled* LORD KILCONNEL 1891–1929; ed. at Repton. He *m.*, 28 Oct. 1915, Edith Constance, da. of Major Albemarle Alexander RAWLINSON. From her he obtained a decree of divorce, 9 May 1918 (she *d.* 7 July 1950), and he *m.* 2ndly, 12 Mar. 1919, Cora Maria Edith, 1st da. of H.H. SPOONER of Thornton Hall, Surrey.(ax) He *d. s.p.m.s.* 5 June 1971. His widow *d.* 1993.

EARLDOM [I.] XI.
VISCOUNTCY [U.K.] VI. } 1971

7 and 6. GREVILLE SYDNEY ROCHFORT (LE-POER TRENCH), EARL OF CLANCARTY, &c., br. and h., being 4th s. by 1st wife, *b.* 10 Dec. 1902; ed. at R.N.C.s, Osborne and Dartmouth; *m.*, 26 July 1926, Beatrice Georgiana, yst. da. of Capt. James Gordon MILLER of Thulow Hall, Thurlow, Suffolk. He *d. s.p.* 15 Sep. 1975. His widow *d.* 1979.

EARLDOM [I.] XII.
VISCOUNTCY [U.K.] VII. } 1975

8 and 5. WILLIAM FRANCIS BRINSLEY (LE-POER TRENCH), EARL OF CLANCARTY, &c., br. and h., being 1st s. by 2nd wife, *b.* 18 Sep. 1911; ed. at Nautical Coll., Pangbourne; *m.* 1stly, 6 June 1940, Diana Joan, yr. da. of Sir William Robert YOUNGER, Bart. This marriage was diss. by divorce in 1947 and he *m.* 2ndly, 16 June 1961, Wilma Dorothy Millen, da. of S.R. VERMILYEA of U.S.A. and formerly wife of William Burke BELKNAP. This marriage was in turn diss. by divorce in 1969 and he *m.* 3rdly, 1974, Mildred Alleyn (Mrs SPONG), da. of R. BENSUSAN. She *d.* 1975 and he *m.* 4thly, 1976, Mary Agnes, da. of E. RADONICICH and widow of Frank M. BEASLEY, Cmdr., R.N.

note (ax) Their only son, William John Hervey Le Poer Trench, was *b.* 6 Mar. and *d.* 5 May 1926.

CLANCONNELL

page 221,
line 13, for 'Tyrconnel,' read 'Tyrconnel. On 12 Apr. 1562 he murdered his cousin Brien (O'NEILL), EARL OF TYRONE. He'

page 222,
line 20, after '["Omey"]' add '"for his life only". In the same petition he asks for "Authority" to legitimate his son, Sir Arthur O'Neill.'
line 24, for 'Sep.' read 'shortly before Aug.'
line 27, after 'HUNTLY' add 'She was living Apr. 1590.'
line 28, after '1597' add '(ga)'
note (ga) As "Sir Art. Oneyle" he appears in a list of "doubtful men in Ireland" Dec. 1589.

CLANDEBOYE

page 222,
line 32, after 'Ayrshire,' add '(who *d.* 30 May 1608)', after 'Janet' add '(living 16 Dec. 1616)' and for '(__)' read 'James'
note (g), line 1, after 'occasion' read ', in 9 May 1583,'

page 223,
line 1, for 'Weshiels' read 'Westshiels'
line 8, after '[I.]' add 'On 20 Apr. 1629 he had a part of the late dissolved Abbey of Bangor, co. Down.
line 12, after 'SMITH' add 'From her he was divorced, she *d.* in 1625'
line 14, after '*d.*' add '24'
line 15, after '84.' add '*Inq. p.m.* at Killyleagh, co. Down.'

CLANMORRIS

page 226,
line 15, after '1796' add 'in co. Mayo; adm. Trin. Coll., Dublin, 7 June 1813.'

page 227,
line 3, after 'Eton' add '1866–9'
line 3, after '1875' add '–8; A.D.C. to the Viceroy of Ireland, 1876–8'
line 7, after 'Piccadilly' add 'He *d.* 4 Nov. 1916 at Bangor Castle, co. Down, aged 64. His widow *d.* 14 Feb. 1941.'
line 8, line to read as follows

VI. 1916. 6. ARTHUR ROBERT MAURICE (BINGHAM), BARON CLANMORRIS OF NEWBROOK [I.], 1st s. and h., *b.* at Bangor Castle,

line 9, after 'Eton' add '1893–7;'
line 10, for 'Sometime Capt. 5th Lancers' read 'Lieut, 5th Lancers, 1900, Capt. 1905; served in the S. African War, 1899–1902; Queen's Medal with 5 clasps and King's Medal with 2 clasps(aa)'
note (aa) For a list of peers and heirs ap. of peers who served in this war, see Appendix B of this volume.
line 10, after 'Zealand' add ', 1904–7'
line 12, for ']' read 'He *d.* 24 June 1960. His widow *d.* 3 June 1969.'

VII. 1960. 7. JOHN MICHAEL WARD (BINGHAM), BARON CLANMORRIS OF NEWBROOK [I.], s. and h., *b.* 3 Nov. 1908; ed. at Cheltenham; *m.*, 28 July 1934, Madeleine Mary, 1st da. of Clement EBEL, of Cuckfield, Sussex. She *d.* 16 Feb. 1988. He *d.* 6 Aug. 1988.

VIII. 1988. 8. SIMON JOHN WARD (BINGHAM), BARON CLANMORRIS OF NEWBROOK, s. and h., *b.* 25 Oct. 1937; ed. at Downside and Cambridge (Queens' Coll.); *m.*, 1971, Gisella Maria, only da. of Sandor ZVERKÓ of Budapest.

CLANRANALD

page 227,
line 25, after 'Bouvinot,' add 'and' [i.e. it was Penelope who was widow of Alan Macdonald]

CLANRICARDE

page 228,
note (e), line 3, after 'Burtchaell).' add 'He was unable to speak English, and had to take an interpreter with him when going to England with a view to being made an Earl.'

page 229,
line 1, after '1stly' add 'at ?Modreeny (Modrujime)(aa)'
note (aa) Depositions of witnesses of the marriage, dat. 5 Oct. 1544, are given in *Cal. Pat. and Close Rolls* [I.], vol. i, p. 504.
line 2, after 'Grany,' add 'wife or' and after '(__)' add 'O'MALAGHLIN or'
line 3, after '2ndly,' add 'during the lifetime of his 1st wife (alleging that his first marriage had not been good'
line 12, after 'O'MELAGHLIN' add 'MACCOGHLAN'
line 19, after '1548,' add 'before 6 Oct.'
line 25, for 'Gille or Cecilia, widow' read 'Julia, widow of Edmund (BUTLER), 1st BARON DUNBOYNE [I.] (*d.* May 1567), and before that of Cormac MCCARTHY REAGH, chieftain of Carbery, and of Gerald (FITZMAURICE), 14th BARON OF KERRY AND LIXNAW [I.] (*d.* July 1550), da. of' [See *Irish Genealogist*, vol. ii, 1947, p. 136.]
note (e), line 1, after 'wives' add ', and when aged 80 and upwards, about Jan. 1615/16, as "Margaret, Dowager Countess of Clanrickard" made a deposition. (*Cal. Pat. Rolls, Chancery* [I.], 1–16 Jac. I, pp. 300–1).'

page 230,
line 1, delete from 'of' to 'DUNBOYNE,'
line 5, for 'wife,' read 'wife. At Athenry 9 Dec. 1577, a decree was issued establishing his legitimacy. He'
line 7, for 'He' read 'During 1572 he was in rebellion but in Nov. sued for pardon, and in May 1589 is described as fighting with great gallantry against the rebel Irish,(aa) and'
note (aa) *State Papers* [I.], 1588–92, p. 186. V.G.
line 13, after 'h.' add ', *b.* about 1570'
note (d), delete all detail and replace by 'At the Earl's instance with a view to establishing his legitimacy which had been impugned by his brother Sir Thomas Bourke, who alleged that he had been born before his parent's marriage, his mother deposed in July 1604, when aged 72, that "she had been married about 38 years ago to Ulick the late Earl in the parish church of Athenrie, and that when about two years married she had issue Richard and Mary both deceased, and the Richard the present Earl who was born about six years after marriage.", his brother

Richard thus being born *circa* 1566 and dying an infant. This statement would make Earl Richard to have been born about 1570, and more or less confirm his age as given at his matriculation. (*Cal. Pat. Rolls, Chancery* [I.], 1–16 Jac. I, p. 47)'

page 231,
line 2, after '1604–16;' add 'adm. Gray's Inn 6 Mar. 1609/10;' and after '1616' add ', and Lord Lieut. of that co.'
line 25, for '1657' read '1658'

page 232,
line 8, for 'July 1657' read '29 Apr. 1658' [Thurloe, *State Papers*, ed. T. Birch, vol. i, 1742, p. 734; B.M. Landsdowne MS. 823, f. 55, *ex inform.* G.T. Hales. Brit Mus.]
line 16, for '1657' read '1658'
line 24, after '1668.' add 'His widow was living 10 Aug. 1667.(e)'
note (e), This is the date of an M.I. erected by her in memory of her husband in the Franciscan monastery at Meelick (*Memorials of the Dead in Ireland*, vol. i, 1888, p. 39).

pages 233–4,
line 18 (page 233) and lines 1–3 (page 234), delete from 'He' to 'WARWICK.'
note (a), lines 1–3 (page 234), delete from 'as' to 'statement' and replace by 'but this is wrong, see vol. xii, part 2, p. 416, note (c).'

page 236,
line 9, after 'Midx.; add 'ed. at Eton 1753–8;'
line 31, after '1744.' add 'Ed. at Eton 2 July 1754–8; Ensign 1st Foot Guards 30 July 1762.'

page 237,
line 12, for '2' read '3'
line 14, after 'Hants.' add 'Ed. at Eton 1814 to *circa* 1818.'
line 16, for '13 Dec.' read '4 July'

page 238,
line 7, after 'Eton' add '1840–3'
line 15, for '3' read '4'

page 239,
line 5, after '(a)' add 'He *d.*, aged 83, at his home in Hanover Sq., 12, and was *bur.* 15 Apr. 1916, in Highgate Cemetery. At his death the Marquessate of Clanricarde and Barony of Somerhill became *extinct*, but the Earldom became merged in the Marquessate of Sligo, which see.'

CLANWILLIAM

page 239,
line 13, after '1744,' add 'adm. Trin. Coll., Dublin, 30 Apr. 1760,'

line 25, after 'year' add ', and was *bur*. in the churchyard of Preston Church, which contains an M.I.'

page 240,
line 2, after '1766.' add 'Ed. at Eton 1783–85.'

page 241,
line 3, for '1786' read '1766'
line 18, for 'Hollywood' read 'Holywood'
lines 21–2, delete from 'He' to '1912' and replace by 'His widow *d*. at Hallgrove, Bagshot, 1, and was *bur*. 3 Apr. 1925, at Wilton, Salisbury.'
line 30, after '37.' add 'His widow *d*. 21 Apr. 1951'

EARLDOM AND VISCOUNTCY. V. BARONY [U.K.] III. } 1907

5 and 3. ARTHUR VESEY (MEADE), EARL OF CLANWILLIAM, &c., 2nd but 1st surv. s. and h., *b*. 14 Jan. 1873; ed. at Eton 1887–90; *m*., 27 Apr. 1909, da. of Russell Maule STEPHENSON and widow Oliver HOWARD. She *d*. 2 June 1952. He *d*. 23 Jan. 1953.

EARLDOM AND VISCOUNTCY. VI. BARONY [U.K.] IV. } 1953

6 and 4. JOHN CHARLES EDMUND CARSON (MEADE), EARL OF CLANWILLIAM, &c., s. and h., *b*. 6 June 1914; ed. at Eton; *m*., 1 Dec. 1948, Catherine, yst. da. of Arthur Thomas LOYD, of Lockinge, Wantage, Berks. He *d*. 30 Mar. 1989. His widow was living 1995.

EARLDOM AND VISCOUNTCY. VII. BARONY [U.K.] V. } 1989

7 and 5. JOHN HERBERT (MEADE), EARL OF CLANWILLIAM, &c., cousin and h., being 2nd s. of Adm. Herbert MEADE-FETHERSTONHAUGH, (*d*. 27 Oct. 1964), by Margaret Isobel Frances, 1st da. of Rt. Rev. Edward Carr GLYN, Bishop of Peterborough, which Arthur was 3rd s. of 4th Earl of Clanwilliam. He was *b*. 27 Sep. 1919; ed. at R.N.C., Dartmouth; *m*., 1956, Maxine, only da. of James Adrian HAYDEN-SCOTT of Isère, France, and formerly wife of Michael John Willson LEVIEN.

[PATRICK JAMES MEADE, *styled* LORD GILLFORD, s. and h. ap., *b*. 28 Dec. 1960; *m*., 1989, Serena Emily, adop. da. of Lieut. Col. Brian Joseph LOCKHART of Maungersbury, co. Gloucester.]

CLARE

page 242,
line 28, after 'elder,' add 'and aunt and h. of Walter (GIFFARD), 2nd EARL OF BUCKINGHAM,'

page 246,
line 27, after 'da.' add 'and h.'
note (c), line 1, delete ', who'
lines 2–3, delete from ', was' to 'Hertford'

page 247,
line 11, after 'Haughton,' add '"being between the years of 9 and 10" when on 19 Apr. 1605 he was at Dunkirk with his father, who had accompanied the Earl of Hertford on an Embassy to the Archduke.'
line 18, for '12' read 'until that Prince's death 6 Nov. 1612.'
note (c), line 2, after 'of' add 'Sir'
lines 2–3, delete from '[2nd' to 'WELLE],' and replace by 'For Robert de Welle, see *Knights of Edw. I*, vol. T–Z, pp. 176–7.'

page 248,
line 1, after 'Margaret,' add 'who *d.* Mar. or Apr. 1613,'

page 255,
line 6, after 'Commoner)' add '6 June'

page 256,
line 14, for '2' read '3'

page 257,
line 7, after 'with 'add 'her 1st cousin'
line 8, after 'in' add 'July'
line 9, after 'Midx.' add 'by Anne, da. of Maurice CROSBIE, Dean of Limerick, and sister of William CROSBIE, 4th and last BARON BRANDON [I.].'

CLARENCE

page 257,
line 24, for '9 Sep.' read '15 Aug.(aa)'
note (aa) "Die Jovis xv die Augusti. Isto die fuerunt nupcie Leonelli filii Regis et filie Comitis Ultonie et tenuit Rex convivium in Turrim [sic] Londonie" (P.R.O., Wardrobe Book of Edward III., L.T.R. Misc. Books, no. 204, p. 56).

page 258,
line 22, for '1411' read '1412'
line 24, for '1389' read '1388'

page 259,
note (f), after 'p. 230' add ', see also Canterbury and York Society, *Chichele Register*, vol. 42, 1937, pp. 293–6.'

page 260,
line 9, for '1472' read 'Mich. 1470 to 1477'

line 23, after 'Anne' add '*suo jure* Countess of Warwick, sister and (eventually) coh. (sole h. of the whole blood) of Henry (BEAUCHAMP), DUKE and EARL OF WARWICK'

note ([a]), lines 1–2, delete from 'at' to 'done'

CLARENDON

page 265,

line 3, after '1662;' add 'a Lord Proprietor of Carolina 1683,' [See note *sub* 1st Earl Craven.]

line 10, for 'in 1629' read '4 Feb. 1631/2' [*ex inform.* Canon Brian Carne. See also *Eng. Hist. Rev.*, vol. 32, pp. 405–7]

line 12, for 'six' read 'five'

page 267,

line 1, for 'before 1674' read '19 Oct. 1670'

page 268,

line 4, after 'Westm.,' add 'ed. at Eton 1702–6'

page 269,

line 14, for 'St. John's' read 'Eton 1725 and adm. as a Fell. Com., 5 Apr. 1728 at Queen's'

page 270,

line 7, after 'CLARENDON' add 'and took his seat 31 Oct. 1776' [not 13 Oct. as misprinted in the Journal of the House of Lords]

line 20, after 'ed.' add 'at Eton 3 Sep. 1764–70; adm. as a nobleman 10 Apr. 1771'

line 21, after 'bridge' add 'M.A. 1773'

line 26, for 'from 1771 and' read '1766–74; adm. 5 Feb. 1774 as a student at Lincoln's Inn; and 13 Apr. follg. as a Fell. Com.'

page 271,

line 17, after 'who' add 'was *b.* 23 Nov. 1759, *m.* 17 Apr. 1798 and'

line 17, after 'Theresa,' add '(*d.* 12 Jan. 1856)'

page 272,

line 21, after 'C.S.I.' add 'He *d.*, aged 68, at The Grove, Watford, 2, and was *bur.* 8 Oct. 1914. Will pr. Mar. 1915, at £26,409 gross, and £21,609 net. His widow *d.* 9, in London and was *bur.* 12 Mar. 1935 also at The Grove.'

line 22, line to read as follows

X. 1914. 6. GEORGE HERBERT HYDE (VILLIERS), EARL OF CLARENDON, &c., s. and h.

line 23, after 'Midx.' add 'Ed. at Eton 1891–3; A.D.C. to Lord Lieut. of Ireland, 1902–5.'

line 27, for ']' read 'He *d.* 13 Dec. 1955. His widow *d.* 6 Feb. 1963'

[GEORGE HERBERT ARTHUR EDWARD HYDE, *styled* LORD HYDE, 1st s. and h. ap., *b.* 6 May 1906; ed. at Eton and Oxford (Trin. Coll.); *m.*, 18 Apr. 1932, Marion Feodorovna Louise, 1st da. of Frederic (GLYN), 4th BARON WOLVERTON. He *d. v.p.*, being *k.* in a shooting accident at De Beers estate near Kimberley, South Africa, 27 Apr. 1935. His widow *d.* 1970.]

XI. 1955. 7. GEORGE FREDERICK LAURENCE (HYDE), EARL OF CLARENDON, &c., grandson and h., being s. and h. of the abovesaid George Herbert Arthur Edward HYDE and Marion Feodorovna Louise abovesaid. He was *b.* 2 Feb. 1933; ed. at Eton; *m.*, 1974, Jane Diana, da. of Edward William DAWSON of Salisbury, Wilts.

[GEORGE EDWARD LAURENCE HYDE, *styled* LORD HYDE, s. and h. ap., *b.* 12 Feb. 1976.]

CLARINA

page 273,
line 21, after '1773.' add 'Adm. Trin. Coll., Dublin, 12 Apr. 1790.'
line 25, after 'Barbados,' add '26, and was *bur.* there at St. Michael's, 27'

page 274,
line 3, after 'Marylebone' add 'Ed. at Eton 1843–4.'
line 5, after '1881' add '–6'
line 24, after '56' add 'He *d.* 13 Oct. 1922 at Lawday House, Farnham, Surrey. Will pr. Sep. 1923 at £34,270.'
line 25, line to read as follows

VI. 1922. 6. EYRE NATHANIEL (MASSEY), BARON CLARINA OF ELM PARK [I. 1800], only s. and h. by 1st wife, *b.* 8 Feb. 1880,

line 29, for ']' read 'He *d. s.p.m.* 4 Nov. 1952 when his title became *extinct*. His widow *d.* 12 May 1961.'

CLAVERING

page 274,
line 39, after 'He' add 'was excused 14 June 1294 from attendance on the King in Gascony, and'

page 275,
line 6, for 'Margery' read 'Margaret, da. of Sir Alan' and after 'ZOUCHE' add 'of Ashby, co. Leicester'
line 11, after 'wars.' add 'He was excused 14 June 1294 from attendance on the King in Gascony. He had livery of his father's lands 29 May 1310.'
line 25, for '16 Jan. 1307/8' read 'shortly before 21 Nov. 1307' [See vol. xii, part 2, p. 155, note (a), *sub* UFFORD.]
note (a), delete all detail

CLERMONT

page 276,
line 24, after '1722;' add 'adm. Trin. Coll., Dublin, 8 Jan. 1738/9, aged 18;'

page 280,
line 4, for 'Dunkirk' read 'Dundalk'
line 17, for 'was *b*. about 1641' read '*b*. 1640, and *bap*. 17 Nov. of that year at St. Margaret's, Westm.,'
line 27, after '([c])' add 'about 1663 she became a Rom. Cath., her husband being received into that Church about 1670.'

CLEVELAND

page 283,
line 26, after '1731/2' add 'at Lady Nottingham's house in Bloomsbury Sq.'

page 285,
line 5, for 'Burmiston' read 'Burnaston'

page 286,
line 6, for 'Staincross' read 'Staindrop'
line 15, for '1699' read '1698'
line 31, for '1699' read '1698'

CLIFDEN

page 289,
line 7, after 'Midx.' add ', as his 1st wife.'
line 8, after 'She' add 'who was *b*. 14 July 1833, and was one of the Ladies of the Bedchamber to Queen Victoria, 1867–72, extra Lady thereafter,'
line 12, after 'Eton' add '1877–80'
line 27, for 'is now (1912) living' read '*d*. 17 May 1914. Will pr. Aug. 1914, at £9,400 gross.'
line 38, after 'CAREY' add 'She *d*. at Lanhydrock, 19, and was *bur*. there 22 Jan. 1921. He *d*. 19 and was also *bur*. there, 22 July 1930.'

page 290,
line 2, after 'Str.,' add 'ed. at Eton 1894–9; matric. at Oxford (Ch. Ch.) 1899;'
line 3, after '1906,' add 'when he was unseated on petition'
line 4, after '1908' add 'Served in WW1 as Capt. Coldstream Guards; despatches. He *d. v.p.* and unm. 30 Sep. 1915 of wounds received in action.'

VII. 1930. 7. FRANCIS GERALD (AGAR-ROBARTES), VISCOUNT CLIFDEN OF GOWRAN [1781], &c., 2nd surv. s. and h., *b*. 14 Apr. 1883; ed. at Eton and Oxford (Ch. Ch.). He *d*. unm. 15 July 1966.

VIII. 1966. 8. ARTHUR VICTOR (AGAR-ROBARTES), VISCOUNT CLIFDEN OF GOWRAN [1781], and LORD CLIFDEN, BARON OF GOWRAN [1776], in the peerage of Ireland, also BARON MENDIP [G.B. 1794], and BARON ROBARTES OF LANHYDROCK AND TRURO [U.K. 1869], 3rd and only surv. br. and h., *b.* 9 June 1887; ed. at Eton and Oxford (Brasenose Coll.); *m.* 1stly, 17 Nov. 1920, Patience Mary, only da. of Arthur Francis BASSET. This marriage was diss. by divorce in 1945 (she *d.* 31 Dec. 1956) and he *m.* 2ndly, 29 Jan. 1948, Margaret, da. of Ray CARTER of St. Louis, U.S.A., formerly wife of John THURSBY and widow of John Eaton MONINS of Ringwould, Kent. He *d. s.p.m.* 22 Dec. 1974 when under the spec. rem. he was *suc.* in the Barony of Mendip by his distant cousin Shaun James Christian Welbore Ellis (AGAR), 6th EARL OF NORMANTON (which see). His other titles became *extinct.*

note (f), delete all detail

CLIFFORD

page 291,
line 8, after 'da.' add 'and h.'
line 12, after 'without' add 'royal' and after '1315,' add 'Sir'
line 13, delete from '[WELLE' to '1320;' [See vol. xii, part 2, p. 440, note (b), *sub* WELLES.]
lines 15–16, after 'dated' add 'He was living 29 Aug. 1326.'
line 31, after 'MUSGRAVE' add '[1st LORD MUSGRAVE]'
note (d), after '"c"' add 'For the Richard de Welle whom Maud Clifford married, see Harleian Soc., *Knights of Edw. I*, vol. T–Z, pp. 176–7.'

page 292,
line 1, for '1342' read '1344'
lines 2–3, delete from 'aged' to 'death' and replace by '*b. circa* 1330' [*Cal. Fine Rolls, 1337–47*, p. 417]
line 11, for '10 July 1333' read 'and *bap.* at Brougham, Westmorland, 20 July 1333;(ba)'
note (ba) *Fourth Report*, D.K. Pub. Rec., Appendix 2, p. 133. His godfathers were Sir Ralph de Bethune and Sir Roger de Leyburn, *Cal. Inq. p.m.*, vol. x, no. 202. V.G.
line 12, after 'III,' add 'and did homage 14 Dec. follg.,'
line 31, after 'Germany' add ', i.e. in Prussia, when fighting under Thomas of Woodstock against the Lithuanians'

page 293,
note (a), line 1, before 'There' add 'He (John) was present in Parl. before he was sum., 24 July 1455, being then still under age (J. Enoch Powell and Keith Wallis, *The House of Lords in the Middle Ages*, 1968, p. 459)

page 294,
line 3, after 'slain.' add 'He was not yet 26 when he was *k.*, being the 4th Lord Clifford in succession to come to a violent end.'
line 6, for 'William' read 'Henry'

page 296,
note ([c]), line 1, for 'da.' add '4th da. and 6th child'
line 2, for '1661' read '1660/1, in Lincoln's Inn Fields'

page 299,
line 29, for 'only' read '1st([ba])'
note ([ba]) A younger br., Sydney Russell, *d.* 22 Jan. 1838 of a putrid sore throat at Kirkby Mallory, aged 10.

page 301,
line 1, after '([a])' add 'Ed. at Eton 1869–72.'
line 2, after '1894' add 'of consumption'
line 13, for 'was living 1912' read '*m.* 2ndly, 7 Apr. 1913, Arthur Roy STACK of Glenapp Castle, Ballantrae, Ayr. He *d.* 12 Dec. 1915 and she *m.* 3rdly, 22 Sep. 1922, George Vernon TATE. He *d.* 30 Sep. 1955. She *d.* 1979.
lines 14–16, delete all detail and replace as follows

XXVI. 1909. 26. EDWARD SOUTHWELL (RUSSELL), LORD DE CLIFFORD [1299], s. and h., *b.* 31 Jan. 1907. He *m.*, 11 Mar. 1926, at Marylebone Church, Dorothy Evelyn, da. Ferdinand Richard Holmes MEYRICK, M.D. This marriage was diss. by divorce in 1973 (she *d.* 1987) and he *m.* 2ndly, 1973, Mina Margaret, only da. of George Edward SANDS. z 3 Jan. 1982. His widow was still living 1995.

XXVII. 1982. 27. JOHN EDWARD SOUTHWELL (RUSSELL), LORD DE CLIFFORD [1299], 1st s. and h., *b.* 8 June 1928; ed. at Eton and R.A.C., Cirencester; *m.*, 27 June 1959, Bridget Jennifer, yst. da. of Duncan ROBERTSON of Llantisilio, Llangollen, co. Denbigh.

CLIFFORD OF LANESBOROUGH

page 302,
line 14, for '1663/4' read '1664/5'

CLIFFORD OF CHUDLEIGH

page 305,
line 23, after '*d.*' add '8, and was *bur.*'

page 307,
line 20, after 'Bart.' add 'He *d.* 19, and was *bur.* 22 July, 1916 at Ugbrooke Park. His widow *d.* at Ugbrooke, 24, and was *bur.* there 28 Jan. 1921.'

X. 1916. 10. WILLIAM HUGH (CLIFFORD), BARON CLIFFORD OF CHUDLEIGH, br. and h., *b.* 17 Dec. 1858; *m.* 1stly, 1886, Catherine Mary, da. of R. BASSETT. She *d.* Mar. 1943 and he *m.* 2ndly, 29 May 1943, Grace Muriel, da. of W. St. Clair MUNRO of Glasgow. He *d.* 5 July 1943. His widow *d.* 18 Feb. 1963.

XI. 1943. 11. CHARLES OSWALD HUGH (CLIFFORD), BARON CLIFFORD OF CHUDLEIGH, 1st s. and h., *b.* 24 Apr. 1887; *m.* 1stly, 6 Nov. 1917, Dorothy, only da. of Alfred Joseph HORNYOLD. She *d.* 3 Dec. 1918 and he *m.* 2ndly, 3 Jan. 1940, Clare Mary, da. of Capt. Jasper Graham MAYNE, of Chagford, co. Devon, grand da. of Sir Frederick WELD, G.C.M.G., and widow of Charles Struthers White OGILVIE. He *d. s.p.m.* 1 Feb. 1962. His widow *d.* 1975.

XII. 1962. 12. LEWIS JOSEPH HUGH (CLIFFORD), BARON CLIFFORD OF CHUDLEIGH, br. and h., *b.* 7 Feb. 1889; *m.* 1stly, 1914, Amy, da. of John Arthur WEBSTER, M.D. She *d.* 15 Jan. 1926 and he *m.* 2ndly, 14 Dec. 1934, Mary Elizabeth, da. of Rt. Hon. Sir Adrian KNOX, P.C., K.C.M.G., Chief Justice of the Commonwealth of Australia. He *d.* 27 Aug. 1964.

XIII. 1964. 13. LEWIS HUGH (CLIFFORD), BARON CLIFFORD OF CHUDLEIGH, only s. and h., *b.* 13 Apr. 1916; ed. at Beaumont Sch. and Oxford (Hertford Coll.); *m.*, 29 Jan. 1945, Katharine Vavasseur, 2nd da. of Cecil Vavasseur (FISHER), 2nd BARON FISHER. He *d.* 17 Mar. 1988. His widow was still living 1995.

XIV. 1988. 14. THOMAS HUGH (CLIFFORD), BARON CLIFFORD OF CHUDLEIGH, 1st s. and h., *b.* 17 Mar. 1948; ed. at Downside; *m.*, 1980, Muriel Suzanne, da. of Major Campbell AUSTIN of Muff, co. Donegal.

[ALEXANDER THOMAS HUGH CLIFFORD, 1st s. and h. ap., *b.* 24 Sep. 1985.]

note ([a]), line 4., for 'h.' read 'coh.'
line 5, after 'Tateshale' add '[3rd Lord Tateshal]'

CLIFTON

page 308,
line 13, for 'da. of Sir John PLAIZ' read '*de jure suo jure* (according to modern doctrine) BARONESS PLAIZ, da. and h. of Sir John PLAIZ [5th LORD PLAIZ]'
note ([a]), delete all detail

page 309,
note ([d]), line 7, after '1614' add '(although this date cannot be correct since the Earl of March was not so *cr.* until 1619' [See vol. xi, p. 608, *sub* LENNOX.]
line 9, after 'throate"' add 'On 18 Nov. 1618 the goods and chattels of Gervase Lord Clifton, felon, were granted to [his son-in-law], Esme Lord Aubigny'
note ([f]), for 'June' read 'July' *Scots Peerage*, vol. 5, p. 359.

page 310,
line 18, for '1667' read '1668'
line 29, after 'Dec.,' add '(her da. Mary was *b.* 7 May 1662)' [See KILDARE [1664].]

page 311,
line 14, for ', on' read 'was still there 12 Aug. 1708. On', and after '1712,' add 'he'

page 312,
line 16, after '1900' add 'etc. She was called to the Bar by Lincoln's Inn in 1926. She *d.* unm. 5 July 1937 when her title was inherited by her cousin Esme Ivo (BLIGH), 9th Earl of DARNLEY, which see.'

CLINTON

page 314,
note (e), line 4, after 'V.G.' add 'See W.L. Sheppard, *Geneal. Mag.*, vol. 16, 1971, pp. 550–1, for arguments that the second wife may not have existed.'

page 315,
line 2, after 'VI' add 'Will dat. 1423' [Canterbury and York Society, *Chichele Register*, vol. 42, 1937, pp. 266–9]
line 11, after 'Elizabeth,' add 'sister and h. of Philip Limbury,' [See DARCY, pp. 53–4.]
line 13, after 'FITZWARIN' add '[6th LORD FITZWARIN]'
line 14, after '(BOTREAUX)' add '2nd', and after 'da.' add 'and coh.'
line 15, after 'LO' add 'of Newton St. Lo, Wilts'

page 316,
line 2, for '(__)' read '*circa* 29 Oct. 1431 Joan, da. of Sir Edmund Ferrers, of Chartley, by Ellen, Lady of Castle Bromwich, and 2nd da. and coh. of Thomas Roche, of Castle Bromwich.' [See chart pedigree of Ferrers of Chartley, vol. v, between pp. 320 and 321.]
line 4, after 'HUNGERFORD' add '2nd s. of Sir Edmund Hungerford by Margery Burnell, his wife,'
line 5, after 'HEVENINGHAM' add '(*d.* 20 Mar. 1498/9)'
lines 18–19, delete from 'not' to '*ch'r.*(e)' and replace by 'never sum. to Parl.'
note (a), line 2, for 'p. 167' read 'pp. 167 *et seq.*, particularly p. 183'
note (e), delete all detail

page 317,
line 6, delete from 'never' to 'Parl.' and replace by 'sum. to the Parl. of 1515'
line 20, for '1616' read '1615'
note (c), delete all detail and replace by 'The first writ to Lord Clinton was addressed to *Clynton de Clynton, ch'r*, the clerks evidently being ignorant of his Christian name (PRO, C54/382 (LP.i(2), 3464(2))). He was present in Parl. regularly from 19 Nov. 1515 till the end of the session on 22 Dec.'

page 319,
line 1, for '1749' read '1746'
line 23, for '4th s.' read '(*b.* 19 Oct. 1709), 14th s., being 4th s. of 2nd mar.'
note (b), line 3, after '*Baronagium.*' add 'She was styled Lady Clinton in a deed of 1757 (*ex inform.* Lord Harrowby, from a deed in the Harrowby archives).'

page 321,
line 26, for '1751' read '1746'

page 322,
line 24, after 'Harrow' add 'and at Eton, 1802'
line 29, after 'Sussex,' add 'who *d.* 8 Apr. 1840'

page 323,
line 2, after 'Eton' add '*circa* 1806–9'
line 17, after 'Eton' add '1846–52'
line 28, for '2nd' read '3rd'
line 33, for 'was living 1913' read '*d.* 19, at Heathermount, Crowthorne and was *bur.* 23 Jan. 1930, at Huish Church, North Devon.'
line 34, line to read as follows

XXI. 1904. 21. CHARLES JOHN ROBERT (HEPBURN-STUART-FORBES-TREFUSIS), LORD CLINTON [1299], 1st. s. and

lines 9–10, delete from 'Having' to 'work.]', after 'She' add ', who' and after 'Antrim' add ', *d.* 27 Aug. 1953. He *d.* 5 July 1957, when his title fell into *abeyance* between his two das., Harriet, wife of Major Henry Nevile FANE and Fenella, wife of the John Herbert BOWES-LYON, 2nd s. of the 14th Earl of STRATHMORE.'

* * * * * *

XXII. 1965. 22. GERARD NEVILE MARK (FANE, later FANE-TREFUSIS), LORD CLIFFORD [1299], from 18 Mar. 1965 when the *abeyancy* was terminated in his favour. He was great-grandson and eventual h. male of the 21st Baron, being only s. of Capt. Charles NEVILE (*d.* 21 May 1940), by Gladys Mabel, da. of Sir Gerald LOWTHER, Bart., which Charles was 1st s. of the abovesaid Harriet. He was *b.* 7 Oct. 1934; took, 1959, the additional surname of TREFUSIS. He *m.*, 18 July 1958, Nicola Harriette, 1st da. of Major Charles Robert Purdon COOTE of Ballyclough Castle, co. Cork.

[CHARLES PATRICK ROLLE FANE-TREFUSIS, s. and h. ap., *b.* 21 Mar. 1962; *m.*, 1992, Rosanna, yr. da. of Alexander John Rennie IZAT of Berwick upon Tweed.]

CLIVE

page 326,
line 6, after '*bur.*' add '30th'
line 7, for 'pr.' read 'dat. 24 Nov. 1773 pr. 13' and after 'widow' add 'who was *bap.* 1735'

CLONBROCK

page 327,
line 32, after 'Eton' add '*circa* 1819–22'

page 328,
line 11, after 'Eton' add '1846–52'

line 18, for 'She' read 'He *d.* after a long illness in Dublin, 14 May 1917. His widow *d.* 5 Sep. 1928.'

line 19, delete all detail and replace as follows

V. 1917. 5. ROBERT EDWARD (DILLON), BARON CLONBROCK [I. 1790], only s. and h., *b.* 21 May 1869. He *d.* unm. 1 Nov. 1926 when his title became *extinct.*[ax]

note [ax] His heir presumptive, his uncle, Col. Robert Dillon, *d.* 19 Apr. 1923. Col. Dillon's only s. was *k.* in the S. African war.

CLONCURRY

page 329,

line 11, for 'ed. at' read 'adm.' and after 'Dublin' add '17 Oct. 1789'

note [b], after 'Somerset' add ', and *d.* 12 June 1857, having had by Mr Sanford a da., Anna Horatia Caroline, who *m.* the 2nd Baron Methuen'

page 330,

line 20, after 'Gardens.' add 'He *d.* at Lyons, co. Kildare, 12 Feb. 1928.'

BARONY [I.] V. BARONY [U.K.] IV.	1928	5 and 4. FREDERICK (LAWLESS), BARON CLONCURRY [I. and U.K.], and a Baronet [I.], br. and h., *b.* 20 Apr. 1847; ed. at Eton. He *d.* unm. at Maretimo, Blackrock, co. Dublin, 18, and was *bur.* 20 July 1929 at Lyons, co. Kildare, when his titles and his Baronetcy became *extinct.*

note [a], line 2, after '1805' add 'ed. at Eton *circa* 1818–22.'

CLONMELL

page 331,

line 9, delete from 'and' to 'Dublin,' and replace by 'adm. Trinity Coll., Dublin, 16 Apr. 1756, scholar'

page 332,

line 7, after 'at' add 'his seat'

line 13, after 'Eton' add '1832 to *circa* 34; an officer' and delete 'Sub Lieut.'

line 18, after 'afsd.' add 'ed. at Eton 1850–4'

page 333,

line 10, after 'burgh;' add 'ed. at Eton 1861–5;'

line 21, after 'afsd.' add 'Ed. at Eton 1890–5.'

line 22, after 'Estelle' add '[a]'

note [a] Her father having died leaving her without means, she was trained for the stage and acted in the provinces till shortly before her marriage.

line 22, after 'Rugby' add ', a tenant farmer. He *d. s.p.m.* at Williton, West Somerset, 18, and was cremated at Woking, 21 Nov. 1928; his ashes were scattered on the hills of his Warwickshire estate. Will pr. 1929, net £4,020.'

VIII. 1928. 8. DUDLEY ALEXANDER CHARLES (SCOTT), EARL OF CLONMELL [1793], VISCOUNT CLONMELL [1789] and BARON EARLSFORT OF LISSON EARL [1784], all in the peerage of Ireland, uncle and h., being 3rd s. of Charles Grantham SCOTT abovesaid. He was *b.* 26 May 1853; *m.*, 7 Aug. 1908, Rose Clare, da. of G. CUTTING of New York. He *d. s.p.* 16 Jan. 1935 at Tonbridge Wells, when his titles became *extinct*.

CLONTARFF

page 334,
note (c), line 2 (on page 335), after '1540.' add 'On 12 Sep. preceding the Lord Deputy had reported to the King that Rawson "would be much missed out of the parliament and council here" and further that he was "very aged, and not likely long to charge the King" with his pension.'

page 335,
line 12, for 'Ingram' read 'Ellis'

COBHAM

page 338,
line 10, after 'Mary' add ', sister of Thomas [LORD BREWOSE or BREWES], da. of Sir Piers de BREWES, of Tetbury'

page 341,
line 30, for '*d. s.p.*' read '*d. s.p.s.*'

page 342,
line 40, after 'Eton' add '1852–60'

page 343,
line 9, after 'House.' add 'He *d.* 9 June 1922, at his residence Hagley Hall, Stourbridge. His widow *d.* 28 Jan. and was *bur.* 2 Feb. 1937 at Hagley.'
line 10, line to read as follows

IX. & XI. 1922. 9. JOHN CAVENDISH (LYTTELTON), VISCOUNT COBHAM, &c., 1st s. and h., *b.* 23 Oct. 1881;

line 11, after 'Eton' add '1894–1900; second' and delete 'sometime'
line 11, after '1902' add 'Queen's Medal, 3 clasps'
line 12, after 'Colony' add '1905–8'
line 13, after '1910.' add 'He served in WW1 as Major, Worcestershire Yeomanry.(ba)
note (ba) For a list of peers and their sons who served in this war, see vol. viii, Appendix F.
line 15, after 'Colony.' add 'He *d.* 31 July 1949. His widow *d.* 28 Feb. 1966.'

X. & XII. 1949. 10. CHARLES JOHN (LITTLETON), VISCOUNT COBHAM, &c., s. and h., *b.* 8 Aug. 1909; ed. at Eton and Cambridge (Trin. Coll.); *m.*, 30 Apr. 1942,

Elizabeth Alison, yr. da. of John Reeder MAKEIG-JONES of Ottery St. Mary, Devon. He *d.* 20 Mar. 1977. His widow *d.* 1986.

XI. & XIII. 1977. 11. JOHN WILLIAM LEONARD (LITTLETON), VISCOUNT COBHAM, &c., 1st s. and h., *b.* 5 June 1943; ed. at Eton, Christ's Coll., New Zealand and R.A.C., Cirencester; *m.*, 1974, Penelope Ann, 1st da. of Roy COOPER of Knutford, Cheshire.

page 344,

note (b), after 'sitting.' add '"Johan, Sire de Cobehoun" was described as a baron in 1377, being a member of the Council to act during the King's minority, but see vol. iv, p. 277, note (c).'

page 345,

line 1, after '1407/8' add 'at Bradelegh (?Bradleigh Priory)'

line 9, after '*d.*' add 'September'

line 10, after 'BRAYBROKE' add '(M.P. for Kent in 1404)'

line 21, for '25' read '14'

note (b), line 2, after '387.' add 'There was, however, at Dunster Castle an inventory of the goods of Sir John Cobham taken at Bradelegh on 20 Jan., 9 Hen. IV (1407/8). It mentions the carriage of his corpse from Bradelegh to Cobham for burial.'

note (d), line 2, after 'V.G.' add 'Oldcastle was Joan Cobham's first husband after she inherited the Cobham estates. Sir Reynold Braybrooke was described as "lord of Cobham" in papal indults in May 1405, although his wife's grandfather was still alive.'

page 348,

line 2, after 'Boleyn.' add 'Deputy of Calais, 17 June 1544.'

line 22, after 'Cobham.' add 'By the Parl. of 33 to 35 Hen. VIII she had assurance of certain lands on the site of the dissolved college of Cobham, in lieu of jointure. V.G.

line 26, after 'travel' add ', having, 4 June 1541, "a pass into the parts beyond the sea, for his further increase of virtue and learning." In 1543 he was studying in Padua. He was back in England in the spring of 1553/4 when he was in trouble for his share in Wyatt's rebellion, but was pardoned 24 Mar. 1553/4.'

lines 28–9, delete from '5 Nov.' to 'Eliz.;' and replace by '1559' [*Hist. of Parl., 1509–1558*, vol. i, p. 512.]

line 36, after '*m.*' add '(he had been affianced, presumably to her, before 4 June 1541)' [*L. and P. Hen. VIII*, vol. xvi, p. 434]

page 349,

line 10, after 'Ports,' add 'Sep.'

line 21, after '1601)' add '(fa)'

note (fa) This was apparently post nuptial, for in a letter of 4 May 1601, from Geo. Whitton to Dudley Carleton it is stated that "my Lord of Cobham is married to the Countess".

line 24, after 'trial,' add '(fb)'

note (fb) However, letters in *Hist. MSS. Com.*, Salisbury MSS., part xv, from her, both to Cecil and to the Privy Council urging them "For God's sake move the King to pity" and alleging that her "dear Lord" had been drawn in by Sir Walter Raleigh, make it clear that she did her utmost to save his life. Possibly their separation was due simply to the fact that he was always a prisoner. V.G.

note ([b]), line 2, after 'literature' add 'His London house was in Blackfriars. His will is printed in full in *Cal. S. P. Dom., 1595–7*, pp. 363–4.'

note ([e]), line 2, for 'King' read 'Fox' and after 'cubs"' add '(i.e. the King and his sons)'

page 351,
after line 5 add as follows

For the termination of the "*abeyance*" of this Barony in 1916 see vol. xiii, p. 231.

page 352,

line 16, after '1stly' add '(by May 16 1367)' [P.R.O. *De Banco Rolls*, Hilary, 18 Ric. II, CP40/536, *ex inform*. Nicholas Macmichael]

line 19, for '1393–4' read '8 Feb. 1393/4' [*Genealogist*, vol. xxix, 1913, p. 205]

line 20, after 'wife' add ', of age 10 June 1393' [*op.cit.*]

line 21, after '*m.*' add ', before Mich. 1395' [*op.cit.*]

line 23, for '31' read '12'

line 24, for '*d.* 1451' read '*m.* 2ndly, William Clifford (Sheriff of Kent 1402–3 and 1434–5), who *d.* in Lent 1438. She *d.* 8 Oct. 1440.' [*op.cit.* pp. 207–8]

note ([a]), line 2, after 'V.G.' add 'It is possible that this 'Elizabeth' is in fact Eleanor, only da. of Reynold Cobham, see *Genealogist*, vol. xxix, 1913, p. 207.'

page 353,

line 19, for '£2900' read '£2,000'

line 24, after 'at' add 'the Archbishop's Palace,'

line 31, after 'John,' add '4th' and after 'Ferrers' add '(of Chartley)'

page 354,

line 4, after 'MAUTRAVERS' add '(s. and h. ap. of John, 1st LORD MAUTRAVERS),'

line 27, for 'Rayal' read 'Bay Hall, Pembury, Kent.'

line 32, after '([d])' add 'pr. 1446' [P.C.C. Wills, 142 Stafford. V.G.]

note ([a]), line 1, after 'Ela' add '(?Millicent)'

page 355,

lines 4–5, delete from 'Sir' to 'BEAUMONT' and replace by 'Thomas Fauconer, London Mercer and Alderman' [S.J. Payling, "A Disputed Mortgage", in *Rulers and Ruled in Late Mediaeval England*, Rowena Archer and Simon Walker (eds.), 1955, p. 123]

line 7, for '(1441–2) 20 Hen. VI' read 'before 20 Sep. 1428' [*Cal. Fine Rolls, 1422–30*, p. 235]

line 11, delete from 'before' to '1460' and replace by 'some time between 20 Nov. 1466 and 26 Apr. 1471,([b])'

line 13, for 'Reynold' read 'Thomas'

lines 18–21, delete from 'He' to 'WESTMORLAND' and replace by 'He *m.*, before 5 Nov. 1438, Elizabeth, widow of Walter, 7th Lord Fitzwalter, who *d. s.p.m.*, 25 Nov.

1431, and was *bur.* in Dunmow Priory. She, who had *m.* previously William MASSY, King's esquire (who was living 16 May 1425), was da. to Sir John CHIDIOK, of Chidiock, Dorset [5th LORD FITZPAYN], by Alianore, da. and h. of Sir John FITZWARIN, of Caundle Haddon, Dorset, Isle Brewers, Somerset, &c. She *d.* 14 June 1464, and was *bur.* in Dunmow Priory.'

line 21, for '*s.p.m. legit.*,' read '26 Apr.'

lines 22–4, delete from 'His' to '1472.'

note (b), delete all detail and replace by 'See vol. xii, part 2, p. 550, notes (c) and (d).'

COGAN

page 357,

note (h), line 2, for '1314/5' read '1315'

line 7, for 'intoxicated' read 'poisoned'

page 360,

line 1, after 'Salop' add '[5th LORD FITZWARIN]'

COLBORNE

page 361,

line 12, after 'later,' add 'being found dead in her bed after influenza,'

COLCHESTER

page 361,

line 24, for 'in 1728' read '*circa* 1735'

page 363,

line 6, after 'Eton' add '1855–8'

line 14, for 'She' read 'He *d. s.p.*, aged 77, at Brighton, 26 Feb. and was *bur.* 3 Mar. 1919, at Forest Row, Sussex, when the Barony became *extinct*. His widow, who' and after '1846' add ', *d.* at Tunbridge Wells, 10, and was *bur.* at Forest Row, 12 Nov. 1927'

COLEPEPER OF THORESWAY

page 363,

lines 27–9, delete from 'only' to 'Southfleet' and replace by 's. of Thomas COLEPEPER of Wysell by 1st wife Anne, da. of Sir Stephen SLANEY, Lord Mayor of London.' [*Sussex Arch. Colls.*, vol. xlvii, p. 66.]

page 364,

line 15, for 'before 1635' read 'by lic. date 12 Jan. 1630/1 at Wantage, Kent.'

page 365,

lines 1–2, for 'before 13 Sep. 1660' read 'first proclamation of the marriage 3 Aug. 1659,'

line 3, for 'Zealand' read 'Holland'
line 4, after 'who' add 'was *b.* at The Hague in Holland and *bap.* in the French Church there 12 Jan. 1634,'

COLERAINE

page 367,
line 12, for '17' read '27'

page 368,
line 7, after 'Driffield,' add '4 Feb.'
line 11, after '*bur.*' add '28 Dec.'
line 16, after 'England,' add '16 Jan. 1795,'

page 369,
line 6, for 'Eton' read 'Dr Fountaine's Sch. in Marylebone and at Eton 15 Oct. 1764–9,'
line 11, after '1799.' add 'Capt. Commissary of the Corps of Royal Artillery Drivers, 1806–8.'

page 370,
line 1, after 'afsd.,' add '7 Apr.'

COLERIDGE

page 371,
note (d), line 2, for '1878' read '1870'

page 372,
lines 3–4, for 'was living 1913' read '*d.* 27 May 1933 at Hyde Park Gate, London.'
line 7, after 'Eton' add '1865–70'

page 373,
line 3, after 'abovenamed' add 'He *d.* at The Chanter's House, Ottery St. Mary, Devon, 4, and was *bur.* 7 Sep. 1927 at Ottery St. Mary. His widow *d.* 2 Apr. 1940.'
line 4, line to read as follows

III. 1927. 3. GEOFFREY DUKE (COLERIDGE), BARON COLERIDGE OF OTTERY ST. MARY [1875], s. and h., *b.* 23 July 1877, at

line 5, after 'Eton' add '1890–6'
line 9, for ']' read 'He *d.* 27 Mar. 1955. His widow *d.* 25 Apr. 1957.'

IV. 1955. 4. RICHARD DUKE (COLERIDGE), BARON COLERIDGE OF OTTERY ST. MARY, 1st s. and h., *b.* 24 Sep. 1905; ed. at R.N.C.s, Osborne and

Dartford; *m.*, 28 Aug. 1936, Cecilia Rosamund, 1st da. of Adm. Sir William Wordsworth FISHER, G.C.B., G.C.V.O. He *d.* 20 May 1984. His widow *d.* 1991.

V. 1984. 5. WILLIAM DUKE (COLERIDGE), BARON COLERIDGE OF OTTERY ST. MARY, 1st s. and h., *b.* 18 June 1937; ed. at Eton and R.M.A., Sandhurst; *m.*, 17 Feb. 1962, Everild Tania Judy, only da. of Lieut. Col. Beauchamp HAMBROUGH of Nairobi, Kenya. This marriage was diss. by divorce in 1977 and he *m.* 2ndly, 1977, Pamela, da. of George William BAKER.

[JAMES DUKE COLERIDGE, s. and h. ap. by 1st wife, *b.* 5 June 1967.]

COLLINGWOOD

page 375,
line 26, for '1750' read '1748'
line 29, for 'almost every post' read 'several of the posts'

page 376,
line 17, for '59' read '61'
note (b), delete all detail (on page 376), and from 'trained' to '*Nelson*).' on page 377, and replace by 'He has been underestimated in the past as an Admiral, but recent work has shown that he was in many ways the equal of Nelson. See Piers Mackesy, *The War in the Mediterranean, 1803–10*, 1957, and C.H.H. Owen (ed.), *The Private Correspondence of Vice-Admiral Lord Collingwood*, Naval Records Soc., 1957.' [Thanks are due to Capt. Hugh Owen, R.N. (retd.), for this information on Admiral Collingwood.]
line 4 (on page 376), after 'Whig' add 'He tried, unsuccessfully, to get a special remainder of his title in favour of one of his daughters.'

COLUMBIERS

page 378,
line 23, after '[' add '2nd'

page 379,
line 1, after '[' add '1st'

COLVILL

page 380,
line 25, for '24' read '26'

page 381,
line 11, after '1630.' add 'She *m.* 2ndly, 27 Jan. 1622, Laurence Mercer of Aldie' [*Scots Peerage*, vol. ix, p. 59]

page 384,

line 20, for 'in Bath Abbey' read '15 Mar. in Bristol Cath.'
page 385,
line 26, after 'husband' add 'M.I. to both at St. Peter's, Eaton Sq. Her'
line 28, line to read as follows

VISCOUNTCY. II. BARONY [S.] XI. } 1903 — 2 and 11. CHARLES ROBERT WILLIAM (COLVILLE), VISCOUNT COLVILLE OF CULROSS, LORD COLVILLE OF CULROSS [S.], s. and h.,

lines 36–7, delete from 'Having' to 'work.]' and replace by 'He *d.* at Danegate House, Eridge Green, Sussex, 25, and was *bur.* at Chiddingstone, Kent, 29 Mar. 1928. His widow *d.* 14 Dec. 1943.'

VISCOUNTCY. III. BARONY [S.] XII. } 1928 — 3 and 12. CHARLES ALEXANDER (COLVILLE), VISCOUNT COLVILLE OF CULROSS, &c., 1st s. and h., *b.* 26 May 1888; Cmdr., R.N., served at Jutland, despatches. He *m.*, 21 May 1931, Kathleen Myrtle, 1st da. of Brig. Gen. Henry Richmond GALE of Bardsea Hall, co. Lancaster. He *d.* in a flying accident, on active service, Mar. 1945. His widow *d.* 1986.

VISCOUNTCY. IV. BARONY [S.] XIII. } 1945 — 4 and 13. JOHN MARK ALEXANDER (COLVILLE), VISCOUNT COLVILLE OF CULROSS, &c., 1st s. and h., *b.* 19 July 1933; ed. at Rugby and Oxford (New Coll.); *m.*, Oct. 1958, Mary Elizabeth, only da. of Col. Mostyn Hird Wheeler WEBB-BOWEN of Beccles, co. Suffolk. This marriage was diss. by divorce in 1973 and he *m.* 2ndly, 1974, Margaret Birgitta, da. of Major Gen. Cyril Henry NORTON, C.B., D.S.O. and formerly wife of John Andrew (DAVIDSON), 2nd VISCOUNT DAVIDSON.

[CHARLES MARK TOWNSHEND COLVILLE, MASTER OF COLVILLE, 1st s. and h. ap. by 1st wife, *b.* 5 Sep. 1959; ed. at Rugby and Durham Univ.]

note (b), line 1, for 'She' read 'Ruby Streatfield'

COLVILL OF OCHILTREE

page 386,
line 10, for 'Euphemia' read '25 Feb. 1655/6 in the Kirk of Carnock, Eupheme'
line 13, for 'Balniblae' read 'Balmedie'

COMBERMERE

page 389,
line 21, after 'Will' add 'dat. 8 July 1862,'
line 24, after 'at' add 'Bridgetown,'
line 32, after '*d.*' add 'as the result of an accident,' and after '*bur.*' add '5 Dec.'
line 33, after 'Wrenbury.' add 'Will dat. 30 Nov. 1887 to 20 Feb. 1888, pr. 17 Feb. 1892.'

note (e), line 2, after '1802,' add 'at Gort, co. Galway,'

page 390,
line 8, for 'of the 2 daughters' read 'da.'
line 13, for 'was living 1913' read ', who was *b.* 22 Aug. 1847, *d.* 17, and was *bur.* 30 Sep. 1930 at Wrenbury, Cheshire.'
line 17, for '. A Conservative.' read 'at Dover; ed. at Harrow. He *m.* 1stly, 30 Oct. 1913, at Holy Trinity, Chelsea, Hazel Louisa, yr. da. of Henry de Courcy AGNEW, by Ethel Anne, da. of Captain Thomas William GOFF, of Oakport, co. Roscommon. This marriage was dissolved in 1916. He *m.* 2ndly, in London, 1 Jan. 1927, Constance Mary Katherine, yst. da. of Lieut. Col. Sir Francis Dudley DRUMMOND, K.B.E. She *d.* 29 June 1968. He *d.* 8 Feb. 1969.'

V. 1969. 5. MICHAEL WELLINGTON (STAPLETON-COTTON), VISCOUNT COMBERMERE OF BHURTPORE, &c., 1st s. and h., *b.* 8 Aug. 1929; ed. at Eton and King's Coll., London; *m.*, 4 Feb. 1961, Pamela Elizabeth Jill, 1st da. of Rev. Robert Gustavus COULSON of Sapperton, Cirencester, co. Gloucester.

[THOMAS ROBERT WELLINGTON STAPLETON-COTTON, s. and h. ap., *b.* 30 Aug. 1969.]

COMPTON

page 389,
line 26, after '1537/8' add '(or possibly 14 July 1544(ba))'
note (ba) This date was given in a contemporary hand in a Bible dated 1529. It also stated that his godmother was Queen Katherine, his godfathers Lord Chancellor "Wreysley" and the Bishop of Winchester, Doctor "Thyrleby". This Bible was lot 486 in Sotheby's sale, 21 July 1953. [*Ex inform.* Philip Blake, Mystoke House, Canterbury]

CONCRAIG

page 393,
line 2, for '1696' read '1689/90'

CONGLETON

page 395,
line 3, for 'was living 1913' read '*d.* 22 Jan. 1931.'
lines 4–6, delete all detail and replace as follows

V. 1906. 5. HENRY BLIGH FORTESCUE (PARNELL), BARON CONGLETON [1841], 1st s. and h., *b.* 6 Sep. 1890, at Anneville, Clonmell; matric. Oxford (New Coll.) 1909. Lieut. 2nd Battn. Gren. Guards, fought in WW1, *d.* unm., being *k.* in action, 18 Nov. 1914.

VI. 1914. 6. JOHN BROOKE MOLESWORTH (PARNELL), BARON CONGLETON, br. and h., *b.* 16 May 1892; ed. at R.N.C., Osborne and McGill Univ. He *m.*, 6 Apr. 1918, at St. Mark's, North Audley Str., Edith Mary Palmer, 2nd da. of Robert Jared Bliss HOWARD by Margaret Charlotte, *suo jure* Lady Strathcona and Mount Royal. He *d.* 21 Dec. 1932. His widow *m.* 2ndly, Flt. Lieut. Alfred Eric Rowland ALDRIDGE (*d.* 11 June 1950) and *d.* 1979.

[HARRY DOUGLAS PARNELL, 1st s. and h. ap., *b.* 14 Dec. 1920, *d.* 7 Jan. 1928.]

VII. 1932. 7. WILLIAM JARED (PARNELL), BARON CONGLETON, 2nd but 1st surv. s. and h., *b.* 3 Aug. 1925; ed. at Eton; *d.* unm., as the result of a motor accident, 12 Oct. 1967.

VIII. 1967. 8. CHRISTOPHER PATRICK (PARNELL), BARON CONGLETON, br. and h., *b.* 11 Mar. 1930; ed. at Eton and Oxford (New Coll.); *m.*, 19 Nov. 1955, Anne Hedi, 1st da. of Gustav Adolf SOMMERFELT, of Oslo, Norway.

[JOHN PATRICK CHRISTIAN PARNELL, 1st s. and h. ap., *b.* 17 Mar. 1959; *m.*, 1985, Marjorie-Anne, only da. of John HOBDELL of Cobham, Surrey.]

CONINGSBY

page 395,
line 13, after 'Court,' add '(aa)'
note (aa) For the devolution of this estate see vol. v, p. 147, note (f).

CONNAUGHT

page 398,
line 3, after 'SAXONY' add '(ax)'
note (ax) For the title "Duke of Saxony", to which, in fact, he had no right, see *The Greville Memoirs*, vol. iv, 1938, pp. 432–3, *ex inform.* Eric J. Thompson.
line 31, after 'C.I.' add 'She *d.* 14, and was *bur.* 19 Mar. 1917, at Windsor the body having been cremated at Golders Green the preceding day. Will pr. Aug. 1917 at £125,611. He *d.* at Bagshot Park, Surrey 16 Jan. 1942, and was *bur.* at Windsor.'
line 33, after 'Saxony' add '(ax)'

page 399,
line 4, after 'Oxford' add 'He *m.*, 15 Oct. 1913, at the Chapel Royal, St. James's Palace, *H.H.* PRINCESS ALEXANDRA VICTORIA ALBERTA EDWINA LOUISE, *suo jure* DUCHESS OF FIFE (see vol. v, *sub* FIFE), 1st da. and coh. of Alexander William George (DUFF), 1st DUKE OF FIFE, by *H.R.H.* PRINCESS LOUISE, PRINCESS ROYAL, 1st da. of KING EDWARD VII. He *d. v.p.* 12 Sep. 1938, at Belgrave Sq., London. His widow *d.* 26 Feb. 1959, at Avenue Rd., London and was cremated at Golders Green Crematorium.

II. 1942. 2. ALASTAIR ARTHUR, DUKE OF CONNAUGHT AND STRATHEARN, EARL OF SUSSEX, &c., grandson and h., *b.* 9 Aug. 1914, at Mount St. London; *styled* EARL OF MACDUFF, 1917–42. He *d.* unm. on active service, at Govt. House, Ottawa, 26 Apr. 1943, when his titles became *extinct*.

CONNEMARA

page 399,
line 11, after '1827' add 'in co. Meath'
line 12, for 'at' read 'adm.' and after 'Dublin' add '14 Oct. 1845, aged 18'

CONSTABLE

page 399,
line 30, for '1721' read '1718'

CONWAY

page 400,
line 23, for 'before 30 Dec. 1619' read 'in 1613/14 after '13 Mar.(ca)'
note (ca) In a letter of 13 Mar. 1613/14 Graye Conyers writes to his father Francis C. that "Sir Edward Conway is to marry a grocer's widow in London, she is worth £5000 or £6000; she is lame and in years".

page 401,
line 12, after '*d.*' add 'at Ragley'

page 402,
line 1, after '1682/3' add 'when he was peremptorily removed from office'
line 5, after 'Quakeress' add 'in 1677 was *b.* in Dec. 1631, at Kensington House (now Kensington Palace) and'
line 6, after 'Will' add 'dat. 30 June 1673(ax)'
note (ax) This is given in full with a codicil after she became a Quaker in *Conway Letters*, M.H. Nicolson (ed.), 1930, pp. 480–1.
line 7, after '2ndly' add 'late in 1679'
line 13, for '*d. s.p.*' read '*d. s.p.s.*'
line 15, after 'pr.' add '11'
line 20, after '1679' add 'ed. at Eton till 1698,'
note (a), line 1, before 'See' add 'In accordance with her expressed wish she was *bur.* "without ceremony or display.'
line 4, after 'C.,' add '*b.* 6' and after '1658/9' add '*d.* of smallpox 14,'
note (b), line 1, before 'He' add 'Particulars of his will are given in *Hist. MSS. Com.*, Hastings MSS., part 1, pp. 321–2.'

CONYERS

page 404,
lines 7–8, delete from 'is' to 'VII' and replace by 'bore the title of LORD CONYERS from at least 26 Feb. 1505' [*Cal. Pat. Rolls, 1494–1509*, p. 420]
line 12, after '1509.' add 'Sometime Constable of Barnard's Castle.'

page 405,
line 2, after 'divorce.' add 'Sometime Constable of Barnard's Castle.'
line 4, after '1538' add ',(ax) charged with great debts.'
note (ax) On 24 May 1538 he signed a letter to Cromwell with a very tremulous hand.
line 6, after 'h.' add ', a minor at his father's death and a ward of his mother during his minority.(ay) Steward of Richmondshire and Keeper of Galtres Forest, 1543.'
note (ay) In *Pat. Roll*, 31 Hen. VIII, p. 6, m. 5 (5 May 1539), the minority of "George [*sic*] Lord Coniers, the King's ward" is mentioned, "George" being presumably a clerical error for "John". He was ward of his mother by 1538, *L. and P. Hen. VIII*, vol. xiii, part 1, pp. 504–5.
line 6, after '1544' add 'at Leith by the Earl of Hertford after the burning of Edinburgh. He had livery of his father's lands 14 June 1544'
line 9, for '*temp*. Edward VI' read '1551/2'
line 14, after '(b)' add 'His wife was living 23 July 1544.'

page 408,
line 14, for '*d*. 10 Apr. 1786, aged 63' read 'who was *b*. 7 Feb. 1756, *d*. 2 Aug. 1791 at Valenciennes, aged 35'

page 409,
line 20, for 'was living 1913' read '*d*. 12, and was *bur*. 16 Nov. 1921 in Brompton Cemetery.'

page 410,
line 4, after 'sponsors.' add 'For further particulars see "YARBOROUGH," Earldom.'

CONYNGHAM

page 411,
line 17, for '22 May 1787' read '22, aged 57, and was *bur*. 24 May 1787 (M.I. Clifton Church, Bristol).'

page 413,
line 10, after 'Dublin.' add 'Ed. at Eton *circa* 1809–13.'

page 414,
line 7, after 'Westm.' add 'Ed. at Eton *circa* 1837–41.'
line 28, after 'Eton' add '1871–4'
line 29, after '1880–2.' add 'Knight of the Order of St. John of Jerusalem; Vice-Adm. of Ulster.'

line 40, for 'was living 1913' read '*d.* 8 July 1939.'

page 415,
line 15, after 'peerage' add 'Ed. at Eton 1896–9; served in S. African War, 1902.(ax)'
note (ax) For a list of peers and their heirs ap. who served in this war, see Appendix B in this volume.
line 15, after 'Conservative.' add 'He *d.* unm. 9 Nov. 1918.'

MARQUESSATE [I.] VI.
EARLDOM AND VISCOUNTCY [I.] VII.
BARONY [I.] VIII.
1918

6 and 8. FREDERICK WILLIAM BURTON (CONYNGHAM), MARQUESS CONYNGHAM, &c., br. and h., *b.* 24 June 1890; ed. at Winchester. He served in WW1 as Lieut., Irish Horse.(ay) He *m.*, 28 Nov. 1914, in London, Bessie Alice, da. of William Andrew TOBIN of Australia. Early in 1918 he deserted her, and in May 1921, she who was *b.* in Australia, obtained a divorce in the Irish Court on the grounds of his misconduct. She *m.*, 2ndly, 7 June 1922, Alfred Baldwin RAPER (*b.* 8 May 1889), M.P. for East Islington, s. of Walter RAPER, of Gerrards Cross, Bucks. He *m.*, 2ndly, 8 May 1922, in London, Antoinette, el. da. of J.W.H. THOMPSON of Bratton House, Wincanton, Somerset. She *d.* 1966. He *m.* 3rdly, 1966, Stella, 1st da. of Francis Barallier THOMPSON and widow of Robert Newton TORY. He *d.* 1 Apr. 1974. His widow *d.* 1985.

note (ay) For a list of peers and their sons who served in this war see vol. viii, Appendix F.

MARQUESSATE [I.] VII.
EARLDOM AND VISCOUNTCY [I.] VIII.
BARONY [I.] IX.
1974

7 and 9. FREDERICK WILLIAM HENRY FRANCIS (CONYNGHAM), MARQUESS OF CONYNGHAM, &c., s. and h., *b.* 13 Mar. 1924; ed. at Eton; *m.* 1stly, 29 Apr. 1950, Eileen Wren, only da. of Capt. Clement Wren NEWSAM of Beauparc, co. Meath. This marriage was diss. by divorce in 1970 and he *m.* 2ndly, 1971, Elizabeth Ann, yr. da. of Frederick Molyneux HUGHES of Fareham, Hants., and formerly wife of David Sutherland RUDD. This marriage was in turn diss. by divorce and he *m.* 3rdly, 1980, Daphne Georgina Adelaide, 1st da. of R.C. ARMOUR, and formerly wife of C.P.V. WALKER of Nairobi, Kenya. She *d.* 1986 and he *m.* 4thly, 1987, Emma Christianne Annabel, only da. of Denys Martin AGNEW.

[HENRY VIVIAN PIERPOINT CONYNGHAM, *styled* VISCOUNT SLANE 1951–74, EARL OF MOUNT CHARLES from 1974, s. and h. ap. by 1st wife, *b.* 23 May 1951; ed. at Harrow; *m.*, Juliet Ann, yr. da. of Robert KITSON of Morval, Cornwall. This marriage was diss. by divorce in 1985 and he *m.* 2ndly, 1985, Lady Iona Charlotte, yst. da. of John (GRIMSTON), 6th EARL OF VERULAM.]

CORBET

page 417,
line 15, after 'Alice' add 'de Orreby' [See P.W. Montague-Smith, *N&Q*, vol. 199, p. 188.]

line 30, after 'LEYBURN]' add '(of Berwick)' and after '*d.*' add '6 Oct.'

note (f), line 1, after 'Joan,' add 'sister and h. of Alan (de Plugenet), 2nd Lord Plugenet,' and after 'Alan,' add '1st Lord'

page 418,

note (a), line 6, after 'Cornwall.' add 'It is possible, however, that John C. left male issue. See Patrick Montague-Smith, 'Corbets, Barons of Caus and of Leighton', *N&Q*, vol. 199, 1954, pp. 188–9. He there cites an *Inq. p. m.* of Mary, Lady Ros in 1403/4 where the heir to the Orreby estates was found to be Richard Corbet of Leighton, great-great-grandson of Peter Corbet and his wife Alice de Orreby. This information does not appear in the published *Inq. p.m.* of 1393/4 when she died (vol. 17, nos 513–22), but see also *Cal. Pat. Rolls*, 1401–5, p. 325, of 4 Nov. 1403.'

CORK

page 418,

lines 22–3, delete from 'before' to '*&c.*)' and replace by 'before 15 Jan. 1394/5' [See below, vol. xii, part 2, p. 900 and note (i).]

page 420,

line 16, after '*d. s.p.s.*' add 'in childbed'

page 421,

line 16, for '1663/4' read '1664/5'

page 425,

line 30, after 'Eton' add '1842–6' and after '1847' add ', BA'

page 426,

lines 4–7, delete all detail and replace as follows

XI. 1904. 10. CHARLES SPENCER CANNING (BOYLE), EARL OF CORK [1620], &c., s. and h., *b.* 24 Nov. 1861, at 1 Grafton Str., Midx.; *styled* VISCOUNT DUNGARVAN until 1904; ed. at Eton 1875–8; served in the S. African War 1900–2.(c) He *m.*, 21 Nov. 1918, Mrs Rosalie GRAY, da. of William Waterman DE VILLIERS of Romsey, Hants. He *d. s.p.* in London, 25, and was *bur.* 27 Mar. 1925 at Marston, Somerset. He left unsettled property of gross value of £68,000, with net personalty of £62,371. His widow *d.* 15 Mar. 1930 at Seamore Court, London W1.

XII. 1925. 11. ROBERT JOHN LASCELLES (BOYLE), EARL OF CORK, &c., br. and h., *b.* 8 Nov. 1864; *m.*, 30 Apr. 1890, Josephine Catherine, da. of Joseph P. HALE of San Francisco, California, U.S.A. He *d. s.p.* 13 Oct. 1934, at Pau, France. His widow *d.* 2 Apr. 1953.

XIII. 1934. 12. WILLIAM HENRY DUDLEY (BOYLE), EARL OF CORK, &c., distant cousin and h., being 2nd s. of Col. Gerald Edmund BOYLE (*d.* 28 Dec. 1927), by his 1st wife Lady Elizabeth Teresa, da. of Charles Christopher

(PEPYS), 1st EARL OF COTTENHAM, which Gerald was 1st s. and h. of John BOYLE (*d.* 6 Dec. 1874), by Cecilia, da. of Lord Henry FITZGERALD by his wife Charlotte, BARONESS ROS, which John was 3rd s. of the 8th Earl of Cork. He was *b.* 30 Nov. 1873; *m.*, 24 July 1902, Lady Florence Cecilia, da. of William Coutts (KEPPPEL), 7th EARL OF ALBEMARLE. She *d.* 30 June 1963. He *d. s.p.* 19 Apr. 1967.

XIV. 1967. 13. PATRICK REGINALD (BOYLE), EARL OF CORK, &c., nephew and h., being s. and h. of Reginald Courtenay BOYLE (*d.* 16 Feb. 1946), by Violet, da. of Arthur FLOWER, of Princes Gate, which Reginald was 4th s. of Col. Gerald Edmund BOYLE abovesaid. He was *b.* 7 Feb. 1910; ed. at Harrow and R.M.C., Sandhurst; *m.* 1stly, 28 Jan. 1952, Dorothy Kate, only da. of Robert RAMSDEN of Maltham, co. York and formerly wife, 1stly, of MARQUESS DEMETRIO IMPERIATI DI FRANCAVILLA and 2ndly of G.F. SCELSI. She *d.* 1978 and he *m.* 2ndly, 1978, Mary Gabrielle, only da. of Louis GINNETT and widow of Kenneth McFarlane WALKER.

CORNEWALL

page 426,
line 21, for '3' read '7'

CORNWALL

page 427,
line 5, for 'BRIENT' read 'BRIEN,' and delete 'DE BRETAGNE'
line 6, after 'Eudes,' add 'a' and delete 'PENTHIEVRE'
lines 7–8, delete from 'Onguen' to Brittany' and replace by 'Orguern, whose parentage is unknown'
line 9, after 'Alan' add 'the Red'
lines 16–17, delete from 'He' to 'Italy' [See vol. x, p. 782, note (d).]

page 428,
lines 15–16, after 'William' delete from 'SEIGNEUR' to 'BELLÊME and replace by 'TALVAS (5th son of William de Bellême, *seigneur* of Alençon and Bellême)'

page 429,
line 10, after 'da.' add 'and (in her issue)'
line 11, for 'Beatrice' read '?Mabel' [see Douglas Richardson, *The Geneal.*, vol. 9, 1988, p. 226]
line 17, after '*d. s.p.m.*' add '*s. legit.*(ba)'
note (ba) The das. of Reynold are discussed in W.L. Sheppard, *Amer. Geneal.*, vol. 29, 1953, pp. 13–17.

page 430,
line 21, for '21 Aug.' read '30 May'

page 431,
line 11, after 'Isabel' add '*suo jure* COUNTESS OF PEMBROKE'
line 14, for '22' read '23'

page 433,
line 3, after '5 Dec. 1250' add '(ba)'
note (ba) N. Denholm-Young, *Richard of Cornwall*, 1947, p. 112, suggests he was *b.* 1 Jan. 1349/50.

page 434,
line 17, for '1309' read 'at Berkhamstead, 3 Nov. 1307' [N. Denholm-Young, *History and Heraldry*, 1965, p. 128 and note 6]
note (c), line 1, for 'only da. and h.' read 'eldest da.'
line 4, after 'marriage.' add 'For persuasive evidence that Gaveston had two das., the second, Amy, being *b.* after 6 Jan. 1312, see J.G. Hunt, *Amer. Geneal.*, vols 35, 1959, pp. 100–6; 37, 1961, pp. 45–7; 40, 1964, p. 25.

page 435,
lines 5–7, delete from 'He' to 'degree' and replace by 'He had a dispensation, 11 Oct. 1334, to *m.* Maria de Lara or de la Cerda, da. of Fernando de Espana or de la Cerda, Seigneur de Lara, by Juana called Columbina, da. and eventual heiress of Juan Nunes de Lara, Seigneur de Lara, but he did not marry her.' [*Papal Letters*, vol. ii, p. 413; *cf. Cal. Pat. Rolls, 1334–8*, p. 33.]
note (d), line 1, for '1406' read '140b'
line 2, for 'on the same day' read 'in the same Parliament'

page 436,
line 16, for '10 Sep.' read '7 Sep.(e)'
note (e), A clandestine marriage had taken place earlier, see Karl P. Wentersdorf, *J. Med. Hist.*, vol. 5, 1979, pp. 217–18.

page 437,
line 29, for '1386' read '1387'

page 439,
line 2, for '1 Sep.' read '31 Aug.'

page 440,
line 9, for 'Sir Richard WYDEVILE' read 'Richard (WYDEVILE), 1st EARL RIVERS'
line 18, for '18 July' read '8 July'
line 19, for 'same' read 'former' and after 'pleasure' add 'and the latter to himself and his heirs'
line 25, for '1473' read 'probably early 1476'

page 441,
line 7, for '10' read 'about 8'
line 8, for '9' read 'early'

page 443,
line 16, for '1510' read '1511'

page 446,
line 31, after 'Eleanora,' add 'who *d.* 7 May 1718 at St. Germain-en-Laye'

page 447,
line 8, for 'Feb.' read 'Sep.'
line 20, for 'by proxy' read 'papal dispensation to be married by proxy and without publication of banns, dat. 10 Sep. 1718,'
line 21, after 'Clementina,' add '3rd and yst.'

page 448,
line 14, after 'Britain' add ', High Steward of Exeter 29 Oct. 1715.'

page 451,
line 12, after 'SAXONY' add '(ax)'
note (ax) For this title of Duke of Saxony, to which he was not in fact entitled, see *The Greville Memoirs*, vol. iv, 1938, pp. 432–3, *ex inform.* Eric J. Thompson.

page 452,
line 26, after 'SAXONY' add '(ax), page 451'

page 453,
between lines 6 and 7, add 'For subsequent Dukes of Cornwall see vol. xiii and below pp. 657 and 800'

CORNWALLIS

page 455,
line 3, after 'Fields;' add 'ed. at Eton till 1717; adm. as nobleman, 9 Nov. 1717 to Cambridge (Clare Coll.);'
line 17, after 'Eton' add 'Jan. 1753 to Dec. 1754'
line 18, after 'Turin' add ', adm. as a nobleman at Clare Hall, Cambridge, 31 Dec. 1755, but did not take a degree'
line 18, after 'Ensign' add '1st Regt. of Foot Guards, now'

page 457,
line 4, for 'and' read '1782–91; adm. as a nobleman 2 Oct. 1792'
line 25, for 'and' read 'Jan. 1753–60; matric. 23 Oct. 1760'
line 27, for 'at the Temple' read 'and was adm. to Lincoln's Inn, 23 Dec. 1761'

page 458,
line 13, after 'Eton' add '1789–94' and after 'and' add 'adm. as a Fell. Com.'
line 7, after 'Cambridge' add '12 Apr. 1796'

COTTENHAM

page 460,
line 10, after 'Elizabeth,' add '2nd'
line 14, after 'widow,' add 'who was *b.* 2 Nov. 1801,' and for '65' read '67'
line 18, after 'Eton' add '1838–42'
line 24, after 'ed' add 'at Eton *circa* 1838–41 and'
line 26, after 'Selina' add 'only'
line 30, for 'was living 1913' read '*d.* at 94 Queens Gate, 27 Feb. 1919.'

page 461,

line 1, after 'Eton' add '1887–90'

line 6, after 'Eridge' add 'Will pr. July 1913, at £8,655 gross and £3,615 net. He *m.* 2ndly, 16 Aug. 1916, Patricia, da. of John Humphrey BURKE, of Galway. He *d.* 22 Apr. 1919. His widow *d.* 26 Mar. 1962.'

lines 7–8, delete all detail and replace as follows

V. 1919. 5. KENELM CHARLES FRANCIS (PEPYS), EARL OF COTTENHAM, &c., 1st s. and h., *b.* 13 May 1901, at 4 Egerton Gdns., Brompton; *styled* VISCOUNT CROWHURST until 1919; ed. at Eton and Oxford; Lieut. 2nd. Battn. Coldstream Guards. He *d.* unm. 29 Dec. 1922 of pneumonia at Park Gate, Battle, Sussex and was *bur.* 2 Jan. 1923 at Tandridge in Surrey.

VI. 1922. 6. MARK EVERARD (PEPYS), EARL OF COTTENHAM, &c., br. and h., *b.* 29 May 1903; *m.*, 19 Jan. 1927, Sybil Venetia, only da. of Capt. John Vickris TAYLOR of North Aston Manor, Oxford. This marriage was diss. by divorce in 1939. He *d. s.p.m.* 19 July 1943.

VII. 1943. 7. JOHN DIGBY THOMAS (PEPYS), EARL OF COTTENHAM, &c., br. and h., *b.* 14 June 1907; ed. at Eton and R.M.C., Sandhurst; *m.*, 3 Oct. 1933, Lady Angela Isobel Nellie, only da. of Guy Temple Montacute (NEVILL), 4th MARQUESS OF ABERGAVENNY. He *d.* 12 May 1968. His widow *d.* 1980.

VIII. 1968. 8. KENELM CHARLES EVERARD DIGBY (PEPYS), EARL OF COTTENHAM, &c., s. and h., *b.* 27 Nov. 1948; ed. at Eton; *m.*, 1975, Sarah, yr. da. of Samuel Richard Le Hunte LOMBARD-HOBSON, Capt., R.N.

[MARK JOHN HENRY PEPYS, *styled* VISCOUNT CROWHURST, 1st s. and h. ap., *b.* 11 Oct. 1983.]

COTTESLOE

page 462,

line 4, after 'Eton' add '1842–8'

line 12, after '£2500' add 'He *d.*, aged 88, at Swanbourne House, 13, and was *bur.* there 17 Apr. 1918.'

lines 13–14, lines to read as follows

III. 1918. 3. THOMAS FRANCIS (FREMANTLE), BARON COTTESLOE OF SWANBOURNE AND HARDWICK [1874], &c., 1st s. and h., *b.* 5 Feb. 1862, at 22 Chesham Place; ed. at Eton, matric. at Oxford (Balliol Coll.) 1881, B.A. 1885,

line 15, after '1901–3' add 'Lieut. Col. Bucks Battn. Oxford and Bucks L.I.

line 17, for ']' read 'She *d.* 4 Apr. 1956. He *d.* 19 July 1956.'

[THOMAS FRANCIS HALFORD FREMANTLE, 1st s. and h. ap., *b.* 20 Jan. 1897; ed. at Eton; served in WW1, *d.* unm. 17 Oct. 1915 of wounds received in action.]

IV. 1956. 4. JOHN WALGRAVE HALFORD (FREMANTLE), BARON COTTESLOE OF SWANBOURNE AND HARDWICK, 2nd but 1st surv. s. and h., *b.* 2 Mar. 1900; ed. at Eton and Cambridge (Trin. Coll.); *m.* 1stly, 16 Feb. 1926, Lady Elizabeth, only da. of James Edward (HARRIS), 5th EARL OF MALMESBURY. This marriage was diss. by divorce in 1944 and he *m.* 2ndly, 26 Mar. 1959, Gloria Jean Irene Dunn, adop. da. of W.E. HILL of Barnstaple, North Devon. He *d.* 22 Apr. 1994. His widow was living 1995.

V. 1994. 5. JOHN TAPLING (FREMANTLE), BARON COTTESLOE OF SWANBOURNE AND HARDWICK, 1st s. and h., *b.* 22 Jan. 1927; ed. at Eton; *m.*, 26 Apr. 1958, Elizabeth Ann, 1st da. of Lieut. Col. Henry Shelley BARKER of Walcote House, Rugby, co. Warwick.

[THOMAS FRANCIS HENRY FREMANTLE, s. and h. ap., *b.* 17 Mar. 1966; ed. at St. Edmund's Sch., Oxford and R.A.C., Cirencester.]

COURTENAY

page 465,
note (c), line 3, after 'William' add '(de Reviers or de Vernon) 5th'

page 468,
line 16, for 'Nov.' read 'May'
line 25, after '1700;' add 'adm. Trin. Coll., Dublin, 27 June 1716, aged 17;'

COURTOWN

page 468,
line 39, after '1731;' add 'adm. Trin. Coll., Dublin, 27 Feb. 1747/8;'

page 469,
line 15, delete from 'sometime' to 'Guards' and replace by 'ed. at Eton 1779–81; Ensign in Coldstream Guards. 8 Dec. 1780, Lieut. and Capt. 17 Sep. 1788–91'
note (b), line 1, after 'title,' add '(which appears to have been taken from his estate by that name in Cheshire),'

page 470,
line 15, after 'Eton' add '*circa* 1834–9'
line 20, after 'House' add 'He *d.* there 28 Nov. 1914, aged 90.'
lines 21–2, lines to read as follows

VI. 1914. 6. JAMES WALTER MILLES (STOPFORD), EARL OF COURTOWN, &c., 1st s. and h., *b.* 3 Mar. 1853, at 34 Cavendish Sq., Marylebone; *styled* VISCOUNT STOPFORD 1858–1914; ed. at Eton 1866–71,

line 34, for ']' read 'He *d.* suddenly at 7 Chesham Place, S.W. 18, and was *bur.* 21 July 1933 at the City of Westm. Cem., Hanwell, aged 80. His widow *d.* 15, and was *bur.* 19 Mar. 1934 at Westm. Cem. afsd.'

VII. 1933. 7. JAMES RICHARD NEVILLE (STOPFORD), EARL OF COURTOWN, &c., 1st s. and h., *b.* 16 Sep. 1877. He *m.*, 26 Apr. 1905, at Trinity Church, Brompton, Cicely Mary, yr. da. of John Arden BIRCH, by Charlotte Mary Leycester (who shortly before had become Viscountess BARRINGTON [I.]), 1st da. of Major George Montagu STOPFORD. He *d.* 25 Jan. 1957. His widow *d.* 1973.

VIII. 1957. 8. JAMES MONTAGU BURGOYNE (STOPFORD), EARL OF COURTOWN, &c., 1st s. and h., *b.* 24 Nov. 1908; ed. at Eton; *m.* 1stly, 1 Aug. 1934, Christina Margaret, 3rd da. of Adm. John Ewen CAMERON of Alnwick, Northumberland. This marriage was diss. by divorce in 1946 and he *m.* 2ndly, 23 Feb. 1951, Patricia, 3rd da. of Harry Stephen WINTHROP of Auckland, New Zealand. He *d.* 23 July 1975. His widow was living 1995.

IX. 1975. 9. JAMES PATRICK MONTAGU BURGOYNE (STOPFORD), EARL OF COURTOWN, &c., 1st s. and h., *b.* 19 Mar. 1954; ed. at Eton, Berkshire Coll. of Agric. and R.A.C., Cirencester; *m.*, 1985, Elisabeth Dorothy, yr. da. of Ian Rodger DUNNETT of Broad Campden, co. Gloucester.

[JAMES RICHARD IAN MONTAGU STOPFORD, *styled* VISCOUNT STOPFORD, s. and h. ap., *b.* 30 Mar. 1988.]

COVENTRY

page 472,
line 1, for '1670' read '1666 and probably about 1660' [See will of her father]
line 17, after '1691' add 'at Badminton'
line 22, for 'pr.' read 'dat. 28 May 1734 to Dec. 1761, pr. 10'
line 24, after '1702;' add 'ed. at Eton from 1710;'

page 475,
line 21, after 'Anne' add '1st'
line 25, after 'widow' add 'who was *b.* 15 June 1812' and for '33' read '29'
line 31, after 'Eton' add '1851–5'

page 476,
line 7, after 'Abbey' add 'He *d.* 13 Mar. 1930. His widow *d.* 16, at Croome Court and was *bur.* 17 Mar. 1930 in the family vault in Croome Church.'
line 9, after 'Eton' add '1879–84 and at Cambridge (Trin. Coll.)'
line 15, after 'California.' add 'He *d. v.p.* 8 Aug. 1927. His widow *d.* 8 Nov. 1948.'

XII. 1930. 10. GEORGE WILLIAM REGINALD VICTOR (COVENTRY), EARL OF COVENTRY, &c., grandson and h., being 1st s. and h. of George William COVENTRY and Virginia Lee abovesaid. He was *b.* 10 Sep. 1900; *m.*, 17 Sep. 1921, Hon. Nesta Donne, 1st da. of Owen Cosby (PHILIPPS), 1st and last BARON KYLSANT He *d.* May 1940, being *k.* in action at Givenchy. His widow *m.* 2ndly, 17 Jan. 1953, Major Terrance Vincent FISHER-HOCH. He *d.* 1978. She was still living 1995.

XIII. 1940. 11. GEORGE WILLIAM (COVENTRY), EARL OF COVENTRY, &c., only s. and h., *b.* 25 Jan. 1934; ed. at Eton and R.M.A., Sandhurst; *m.* 1stly, 22 Mar. 1955, Marie Farquhar, da. of William Sherman MÉDARD of St. Louis, U.S.A. This marriage was diss. by divorce in 1963 and he *m.* 2ndly, 1969, Ann, da. of Frederick William James CRIPPS, of Bickley, Kent. This marriage was in turn diss. by divorce in 1975 and he *m.* 3rdly, 1980, Valerie Ann BIRCH. This marriage was also diss. by divorce in 1988 and he *m.* 4thly, 1992, Rachel Wynne, da. of Jack MASON.

[EDWARD GEORGE WILLIAM OMAR COVENTRY, *styled* VISCOUNT DEERHURST, s. and h. ap. by 1st wife, *b.* 24 Sep. 1957.]

page 477,
line 21, after '*d.*' add 'of gangrene in the toes'
line 25, after '1653' add 'at her father's house in Aldersgate Str., London' [*Lives of Lady Anne Clifford*, Roxburghe Club, 1916.]

page 478,
line 3, after 'Croome' add ', and *bap.* there on the 17th' [His next br., Thomas, *b.* 27 Aug. 1659 at Croome, *d.* there, an infant, 17 June 1660. See *Lives of Lady Anne Clifford*, Roxburghe Club, 1916.]
line 24, for 'COWALL' read 'COWAL'

page 479,
line 6, after '1773;' add 'ed. at Eton 1783–9; entered the Army as Ensign 4th Regt. 31 Aug. 1790;'

page 481,
line 17, for '1850' read '1847–51'

COWLEY

page 482,
line 6, for 'was living 1913' read ', who was *b.* July 1839, *d.* 9 Nov. 1932.'
line 12, after 'Eton' add '1880–1. He served with the Imperial Yeomanry in the S. African War, 1899–1900(ax)'
note (ax) For a list of peers and their heirs ap. who served in this war, see Appendix B in this volume.
line 21, after 'Place' add ', and from him she obtained a divorce in 1913. She *m.* 3rdly, 25 July 1914, Major Grey William DUBERLEY, who was *k.* in WW1, 13 Mar. 1915. She *d.* 29 Nov. 1952. He *m.* 3rdly, 19 Jan. 1914, Clare Florence Mary, da. of Sir Francis George STAPLETON, Bart., formerly wife of Major Geoffrey Charles BUXTON. He *d.* at his residence, Chippenham, Wilts., 15, and was *bur.* 18 Jan. 1919 at Chippenham. His widow *d.* 8 May 1949.'
lines 22–3, delete all detail and replace as follows

EARLDOM. IV. BARONY. V. } 1919 — 4 and 5. CHRISTIAN ARTHUR (WELLESLEY), EARL COWLEY, &c., only s. and h. by 1st wife, *b.* 25 Dec. 1890; *styled* VISCOUNT DANGAN 1895–1919. He *m.*, 23 Feb. 1914, May PICARD, "an American showgirl playing in 'The Girl'". This marriage was diss. by divorce in 1933 (she *d.* 3 June 1946) and he *m.* 2ndly, 1933, Mrs Mary Elsie HIMES. He *d.* 29 Aug. 1962. His widow was living 1995.

[MICHAEL WELLESLEY, *styled* VISCOUNT DANGAN, 1st s. and h. ap., *b.* 24 May 1915, *d.* 13 Feb. 1922.]

EARLDOM. V. BARONY. VI. } 1962 — 5 and 6. DENIS ARTHUR (WELLESLEY), EARL COWLEY, &c., 2nd but 1st surv. s. and h., *b.* 25 Dec. 1921; *m.* 1stly, 16 Nov. 1944, Elizabeth Anne, yr. da. of Lieut. Col. Pelham Rawstorn PAPILLON, of Crowhurst Park, Sussex and widow of Flt. Lieut. Stephen Alers HANKEY. This marriage was diss. by divorce in 1950 and he *m.* 2ndly, 11 July 1950, Annette Nancy Doughty, da. of Major J.J. O'HARA of Northumberland and formerly wife of Lieut. Arthur SIMMONDS and before that widow of (__). She *d.* 29 Oct. 1959 as the result of a motor accident and he *m.* 3rdly, 15 Feb. 1961, Janet Elizabeth Mary, da. of Ramiah Doraswamy AIYAR of Ystrad, Denbigh. He *d.* 23 Mar. 1968. His widow *m.* 2ndly, 1976, Piers DIXON. This marriage was diss. by divorce in 1981. She was still living 1995.

EARLDOM. VI. BARONY. VII. } 1968 — 6 and 7. RICHARD FRANCIS (WELLESLEY), EARL COWLEY, &c., only s. and h., *b.* 12 June 1946; ed. at Eton; *m.*, 1971, Maria Della, yr. da. of Enrique BUENANO of Buenos Aires, Brazil. He *d.* 13 Dec. 1975. His widow *m.* 2ndly, 1980, as his 2nd wife, Major Robin James Stirling BULLOCK-WEBSTER. She was still living 1995.

EARLDOM. VII. BARONY. VIII. } 1975 — 7 AND 8. GARRET GRAHAM (WELLESLEY), EARL COWLEY, &c., uncle and h., being 3rd s. of the 4th Earl. He was *b.* 30 July 1934; ed. at Harvard Univ. and Univ. of Southern California; *m.* 1stly, 16 Sep. 1960, Elizabeth Susanne, da. of Bayes LENNON of Georgia, U.S.A. This marriage was diss. by divorce in 1966 and he *m.* 2ndly, 1968, Isabelle O'BREADY of Sherbrooke, Quebec, Canada. This marriage was in turn diss. by divorce in 1981 and he *m.* 3rdly, 1981, Paige DEMING.

[GARRET GRAHAM WELLESLEY, *styled* VISCOUNT DANGAN, s. and h. ap. by 1st wife, *b.* 30 Mar. 1965; *m.*, 1990, Claire, only da. of Peter W. BRIGHTON of Stow Bridge, Norfolk.]

COWPER

page 484,
line 2, for 'in' read '8 Nov.'
line 5, after '1723/4' add ', aged 38'
line 15, for 'James' read 'Thomas'

page 485,
line 4, after 'present;' add 'ed. at Eton Jan. 1753–6'
line 16, after '68' add '(c)'
note (c) On 30 Sep. 1820 her daughter-in-law, Lady Cowper, wrote that "instead of dying she is going to marry a young apothecary, one Michelette, a *tres mauvais sujet.*" However, this undesirable union seems never to have taken place.

page 486,
line 13, after 'Sq.;' add 'ed. at Eton, *circa* 1818–23;'

page 487,
line 30, after '68' add 'Will pr. July 1913, £243,913 gross, £239,339 net.'

CRAGSIDE

page 488,
line 14, after '1887.' add '*Extinct* 1900.'

CRAMOND

page 488,
line 19, after '*m.*,' add '27 Nov. 1594,'

CRANBROOK

page 494,
line 1, line to read as follows

II. 1911. 2. JOHN STEWART (GATHORNE-HARDY *formerly* (1839–78) HARDY), EARL OF CRANBROOK, VISCOUNT CRANBROOK OF HEMSTED, &c., 1st s. and h., *b.* 22 Mar. 1839; *styled* LORD MEDWAY 1892–1906;

line 3, after 'Eton' add '1851–7'
line 6, for 'was living 1913' read '*d.* 20 Feb. 1931 at Wilbraham Place, London.'
lines 6–8, delete from 'Having' to 'work.]'

III. 1911. 3. GATHORNE (GATHORNE-HARDY), EARL OF CRANBROOK, &c., 1st s. and h., *b.* 18 Dec. 1870. He *m.*, 25 Apr. 1899, at Holy Trinity, Sloane Str., Lady Dorothy Montagu, yst. da. of David (BOYLE), 7th EARL OF GLASGOW. She was *b.* 14 Mar. 1879 at Shewalton, co. Ayr. He *d.* 23 Dec. 1915. His widow *d.* 17 Mar. 1968.

IV. 1915. 4. JOHN DAVID (GATHORNE-HARDY), EARL OF CRANBROOK, &c., 1st s. and h., *b.* 15 Apr. 1900 at 27 Cranley Gdns., London; ed. at Eton and R.M.A., Woolwich; *m.* 7 Oct. 1926, Bridget Cicely, da. of Rupert D'Oyley CARTE, by his wife Lady Dorothy Milner, 3rd da. of John Stewart (GATHORNE-HARDY),

2nd EARL OF CRANBROOK. This marriage was diss. by divorce in 1931 (she *d.* 1985) and he *m.* 2ndly, 26 July 1932, Fidelity, da. of Hugh Exton SEEBOHM of Hitchen, co. Hertford. He *d.* 22 Nov. 1978. His widow was living 1995.

V. 1978. 5. GATHORNE (GATHORNE-HARDY), EARL OF CRANBROOK, &c., 1st s. and h., *b.* 20 June 1933; ed. at Eton and Cambridge (Corpus Christi Coll.); *m.*, 9 May 1967, Caroline, only da. of Col. Ralph George Edward JARVIS of Doddington Hall, Lincoln.

[JOHN JASON GATHORNE-HARDY, *styled* LORD MEDWAY, 1st s. and h. ap., *b.* 26 Oct. 1968; ed. at Woodbridge Sch. and Oxford (Pembroke Coll.).]

CRANSTOUN

page 495,
line 16, after '2ndly' add '(cont. 7 Apr.)'

page 497,
line 21, after 'widow' add ', who was *b.* 7 Nov. 1790,' and after '1858' add ', and was *bur.* in Arnos Vale Cemetery.'

CRANWORTH OF LETTON

page 499,
line 5, after 'at' add 'Eton 1841–8 and at Trin. Coll.'
line 11, for '*d.*' read 'who was *b.* 1836, *d.* in childbed'
line 17, for 'was living 1913' read '*d.* 3 Apr. 1934.'
lines 18–19, lines to read as follows

II. 1902. 2. BERTRAM FRANCIS (GURDON), BARON CRANWORTH OF LETTON AND CRANWORTH, 2nd, but 1st surv. s. and h. by 2nd wife, *b.* 13 June 1877, at 9 Oxford Sq., Hyde Park; ed. at Eton 1890–6 and at Cambridge (Trin. Coll.), 2nd Class Law Tripos and B.A. 1899.

line 20, after '(d)' add 'Lieut. Reserve of Officers 1909.'
lines 23–4, delete from 'Having' to 'work.]' and replace by 'He *d.* 4 Jan. 1964. His widow *d.* 1966.'

[ROBERT BRAMPTON GURDON, s. and h. ap., *b.* 21 June 1904. He *m.*, 20 Jan. 1932, Hon. Daisy Yoskyl Consuelo, 1st da. of Weetman Harold Miller (PEARSON), 2nd VISCOUNT COWDRAY. He *d. v.p. s.p.* July 1942, being *k.* in action.]

III. 1964. 3. PHILIP BERTRAM (GURDON), BARON CRANWORTH OF LETTON AND CRANWORTH, grandson and h., being yr. but 1st surv. s. and h. of Robert Brampton GURDON and Daisy Yoskyl Consuelo abovesaid. He was *b.* 24 May 1940; ed. at Eton and Cambridge (Magdalene Coll.); *m.*, 18 Jan. 1968, Frances Henrietta, twin da. of Lord William MONTAGU-DOUGLAS-SCOTT, M.C., of Beechwood, Melrose, co. Roxburgh.

[SACHA WILLIAM ROBIN GURDON, 1st s. and h. ap., *b.* 12 Aug. 1970.]

page 505, CRAVEN
line 3, after 'Sq.;' add 'ed. at Eton 1781–6;'
line 23, after 'Eton' add '*circa* 1822–7'

page 506,
line 12, for 'was living 1913' read '*d.* at Ashdown Park, Berks., 9, and was *bur.* 14 Nov. 1924 at Ashdown Park Chapel.'
line 17, after '1868.' add 'Ed. at Eton 1882–4. Extra'
line 18, after 'Ireland' add '1890–2'
line 22, after 'Inverness.' add 'He was drowned at Cowes, 9, and was *bur.* 14 July 1921 at Hamstead Marshall. His widow *d.* 19 May 1961.'
lines 23–4, delete all detail and replace as follows

EARLDOM. VI. BARONY. XI. } 1921

5 and 11. WILLIAM GEORGE BRADLEY (CRAVEN), EARL OF CRAVEN, &c. s. and h., *b.* at Combe Abbey 31 July, and *bap.* 26 Aug. 1897 at Binley; *styled* VISCOUNT UFFINGTON 1897–1921; Lieut. 3rd Battn. Hampshire Regt., and was wounded when serving therewith in WW1. He *m.*, 14 Oct. 1916 (both then aged 19), Mary Williamina, da. of William GEORGE, Town Clerk of Invergordon. He *d.* 15 Sep. 1932 of peritonitis at Pau, France. His widow *d.* 1974.

EARLDOM. VII. BARONY. XII. } 1932

6 and 12. WILLIAM GEORGE BRADLEY (CRAVEN), EARL OF CRAVEN, &c., only s. and h., *b.* 8 Sep. 1917; ed. at Downside and Northamptonshire Inst. of Agric.; *m.* 1stly, 3 May 1939, Irene, yst. da. of Ferdinand Richard Holmes MEYRICK, M.D. This marriage was diss. by divorce in 1954 and he *m.* 2ndly, 25 Sep. 1954, Elizabeth Gwendolen Teresa, only da. of Robert Sholto JOHNSTONE-DOUGLAS of Mayfield, East Sussex. He *d.* 27 Jan. 1965. His widow *m.* 2ndly, 27 July 1966, Kenneth Harmood BANNER of Pevensey, Sussex. She was still living 1995.

EARLDOM. VIII. BARONY. XIII. } 1965

7 and 13. THOMAS ROBERT DOUGLAS (CRAVEN), EARL OF CRAVEN, &c., 1st s. and h., by 2nd wife, *b.* 24 Aug. 1957. He *d.* unm. 22 Oct. 1983.

EARLDOM. IX. BARONY. XIV. } 1983

8 and 14. SIMON GEORGE (CRAVEN), EARL OF CRAVEN, &c., br. and h., *b.* 16 Sep. 1961; *m.*, 1988, Teresa Maria Bernadette, da. of Arthur John DOWNES of Clane, co. Kildare. He *d.* 30 Aug. 1990 as the result of a motor accident. His widow was living 1995.

EARLDOM. X. BARONY. XV.	1990	9 and 15. BENJAMIN ROBERT JOSEPH (CRAVEN), EARL OF CRAVEN, &c., only s. and h., *b.* 13 June 1989.

CRAWFORD

page 508,
line 5, after 'Bridge.' add 'In 1392 he was severely wounded at Grasclune, by a Highlander.'

page 509,
line 4, after '([a])' add 'He held the Shrievality of Banff, which he alienated to the Earl of Moray.'

page 511,
line 17 of pedigree, for 'John, 9th Lord L.' read 'Robert, 9th Lord L.'

page 513,
line 2, for '2nd' read '1st'
line 3, for 'STRATHERN' read 'STRATHEARN [S.]'
line 10, after '*m.*' add ', before 12 June 1480'
line 26, for 'Nichola' read 'Nichole'

page 515,
line 19, for 'Balthyock' read 'Balthayock'
line 20, for '1549' read '1549/50'
line 21, for '1549' read '1550'

page 517,
line 12, for 'From her he was divorced' read 'She was suing for divorce from him in 1610, which she obtained either then or at any rate before 1618.'

page 519,
line 20, for '1596' read 'about 1611'

page 520,
line 26, delete ', in his 81st year'

page 522,
line 18, for '2nd s.' read '5th but 2nd surv. s.'
line 21, for '1738' read '1739'

page 523,
line 14, for '7th' read '6th'

page 524,
line 33, after 'Eton' add '*circa* 1824–8'

page 525,
line 15, after 'Eton' add '1860–2'
line 28, after 'net' add 'His widow *d.* 15, in London and was *bur.* in Balcarres Chapel, Fife, 15 Jan. 1934.'
lines 29–30, lines to read as follows

XXVII. 1913. 27. DAVID ALEXANDER EDWARD (LINDSAY), EARL OF CRAWFORD, &c., s. and h., *b.* 10 Oct. 1871 at Dun Echt; *styled* LORD BALCARRES 1880–1913; ed. at Eton 1860–2;

page 526,
lines 4–5, delete from 'Having' to 'work.]' and replace by 'He *d.* 8 Mar. 1940. His widow *d.* 8 Jan. 1947.'

XXVIII. 1940. 28. DAVID ALEXANDER ROBERT (LINDSAY), EARL OF CRAWFORD, &c., 1st s. and h., *b.* 20 Nov. 1900; ed. at Eton and Oxford (Magdalen Coll.). He *m.*, 9 Dec. 1925, at St. Margaret's, Westm., Mary, 3rd da. of Lord Richard CAVENDISH (br. of the 9th DUKE OF DEVONSHIRE). He *d.* 13 Dec. 1975. His widow was living 1995.

XXIX. 1975. 29. ROBERT ALEXANDER (LINDSAY), EARL OF CRAWFORD, &c., 1st s. and h., *b.* 5 Mar. 1927; ed. at Eton and Cambridge (Trin. Coll.); *cr.* 24 Jan. 1975, a Life Peer as BARON BALNIEL of Pitcorthie, co. Fife. He *m.*, 27 Dec. 1949, Ruth Beatrice, da. of Leo MEYER-BECHTLER of Zurich.

[ANTHONY ROBERT LINDSAY, *styled* LORD BALNIEL, 1st s. and h., *b.* 24 Nov. 1958; ed. at Eton and Edinburgh Univ.; *m.*, 1989, Nicola, yst. da. of Anthony BICKET of Derwas, Dolwen, North Wales.]

CRAWSHAW OF CRAWSHAW

page 526,
line 23, add at end 'His widow *d.* 26 June 1917.'
line 24, line to read as follows

II. 1908. 2. WILLIAM (BROOKS), BARON CRAWSHAW OF CRAWSHAW, 1st s. and h., *b.* 16 Oct. 1853;

lines 28–30, delete from 'Having' to 'work.]' and replace by 'She *d.* 1 Oct. 1914. He *d.* suddenly at Whatton, Loughborough, co. Leics., 19, and was *bur.* 22 Jan. 1929 at Long Whatton.'

III. 1929. 3. GERALD BEACH (BROOKS), BARON CRAWSHAW OF CRAWSHAW, 1st s. and h., *b.* 1 Apr. 1884; ed. at Oxford (Ch. Ch.); *m.*, 4 Mar. 1930, Marjory

Sheila, only da. of Lieut. Col. Percy Robert CLIFTON of Clifton Hall. Nottingham. He *d.* 21 Oct. 1946. His widow *d.* 5 Sep. 1964.

IV. 1946. 4. WILLIAM MICHAEL CLIFTON (BROOKS), BARON CRAWSHAW OF CRAWSHAW, 1st s. and h., *b.* 25 Mar. 1933; ed. at Eton and Oxford (Ch. Ch.).

CREMORNE

page 528,
line 6, for '2nd' read '3rd and yst., being 2nd surviving'

CRETING

page 532,
note (c), line 2, after 'da.' add 'and h.'

CREWE

page 536,
line 5, for '1893' read '1894'
line 17, for '1893' read '1894'
line 25, for 'since May 1911' read 'May 1911 to May 1915' and for '22 June' read '3 July'
line 27, after '(b)' add 'Lord Pres. of the Council in the Coalition Cabinet, 30 May 1915.'
line 28, for '3rd' read '4th'
line 34, after 'Epsom' add 'He *d.* 20 June 1945 when his titles became *extinct*.'

between lines 34 and 35 add as follows

line 35, for 'GEORGE RICHARD' read 'RICHARD GEORGE'
line 38, after 'sponsor' add 'He *d. v.p.* at Crewe House, Curzon Str., 31 Mar. 1922, aged 11, and was *bur.* 4 Apr. 1922 at Barthomley, near Crewe'

CRICHTON

page 537,
note (b), line 19, after 'created' add 'no, or'

page 539,
line 30, after '1457)' add '(e)'
note (e) *Cal. Papal Reg.*, vol. XI, p. 330.

page 540,
line 20, for 'after 'read 'in'

line 24, after '1538/9' add 'P.C. [S.] attending the meetings of that body 28 June and 31 Oct. 1545.[aa])

note [aa] James V, writing two letters in his favour to Pope Paul III on the Kal. Jan. 1539, calls him "William Lord Santher", and "William Lord of Santher".

page 541,
after line 34 add as follows

CRICHTON[c]

Viscountcy assumed as the *style* of the s. and h. ap. of the Earls of Erne, see that title.

note [b], line 6, after '86).' add 'The jewels, debts and goods of Robert Creichton, felon, were granted 16 July 1612, to Thomas Creichton.'

note [c] Sometimes Creighton.

page 542,
line 3, for '*Hooa*' read '*Hood*'

CROFTON OF MOTE

page 543,
line 32, delete from 'He' to 'work'

IV. 1912. 4. ARTHUR EDWARD LOWTHER (CROFTON), BARON CROFTON OF MOTE, nephew and h., being s. and h. of Charles St. George LOWTHER (*d.* 2 Feb. 1895), by Teresa Augusta, 3rd da. of Daniel BUNBURY-TIGHE, of Rossana, co. Wicklow, which Charles was 2nd s. of the 2nd Baron Crofton. He was *b.* 7 Aug. 1866; *m.*, 14 Apr. 1893, Jessie Castle, da. of James HEWITSON and widow of Neville PADDON. She *d.* at Mote Park, Roscommon, 19 Jan. 1923. He *d.* 15 June 1942.

[EDWARD CHARLES CROFTON, s. and h. ap., *b.* 18 Jan. 1896. He *m.*, 5 Mar. 1925, Cecilia Mabel, widow of Alexander Francis MACDONALD and da. of John T. DAY of Hayswood, Streatham Park. He *d. v.p.* 25 Nov. 1936.]

V. 1942. 5. EDWARD BLAISE (CROFTON), BARON CROFTON OF MOTE, grandson and h., being 1st s. and h. of Edward Charles CROFTON and Cecilia Mabel abovenamed. He was *b.* 31 May 1926; *m.* 1stly, 10 June 1948, Ann, 1st da. of Grp. Capt. Charles Herbert TIGHE of Ballina Park, co. Wicklow. This marriage was diss. by divorce in 1963 and he *m.* 2ndly, 19 Dec. 1964, Mary, 1st da. of Major James Irvine Hatfield FRIEND of Northdown, Thanet, Kent and formerly wife of Robert Thomas Francis FLACH. He *d.* 13 June 1974. His widow was living 1995.

VI. 1974. 6. CHARLES EDWARD PIERS (CROFTON), BARON CROFTON OF MOTE, 1st s. and h., *b.* 27 Apr. 1949; *m.*, 1976, Maureen Jacqueline, da. of Stanley James BRAY of Taunton, Somerset. He *d. s.p.* 27 June 1989. His widow was living 1995.

VII. 1989. 7. GUY PATRICK GILBERT (CROFTON), BARON CROFTON OF MOTE, br. and h., being 3rd but 2nd surv. s., *b.* 17 June 1951; ed. at Theresianistische Akad. and Midhurst Gram. Sch.; *m.*, 1985, Gillian Susan BURROUGHS, only da. of Harry Godfrey Mitchell BASS of Reedham, Norfolk.

[EDWARD HARRY PIERS CROFTON, 1st s. and h. ap., *b.* 23 Jan. 1988.]

CROFTS OF SAXHAM

page 544,
line 13, for '(living 1645)' read '(*d.* 1648)'
line 14, for 'da.' read 'da. and coh.' [*Visit. of Oxford*, Harl. Soc., vol. 5, pp. 268–9]

CROMARTIE or CROMARTY

page 545,
line 21, after '1stly' add '(cont. 6 July),'
line 24, for '[I.]' read '[S.]'

page 547,
line 6, for '16th' read '17th'
line 20, for 'following' read '1849'

page 548,
lines 14–15, for 'Sutherland Tower, Torquay' read 'Stafford House, St. James'
line 22, for '1st' read '3rd'

page 549,
line 1, for '*abeyance*' read '"*abeyance*"'
lines 5–6, delete from 'was' to '1913' and replace by '*d.* 20 Nov. 1926.'
line 8, for '*abeyance*' read '"*abeyance*"'
line 14, after '1860.' add 'He *d.* 31 July 1949. She *d.* 20 May 1962.'
lines 15–17, delete all detail and replace as follows

VII. 1962. 4. RODERICK GRANT FRANCIS (BLUNT-MACKENZIE, *later* MACKENZIE), EARL OF CROMARTIE, &c., 1st s. and h., *b.* 24 Oct., and *bap.* 2 Dec. 1904, at Adderbury Church, Oxon.; *styled* VISCOUNT TARBAT till 1962; ed. at Charterhouse and R.M.C., Sandhurst; discontinued, 1979, name of BLUNT; recognised as Chief of Clan Mackenzie by Lord Lyon. He *m.* 1stly, 11 Mar. 1933, Dorothy (Mrs PORTER), da. of Grant Butler DOWNING of Kentucky, U.S.A. This marriage was diss. by divorce in 1945 and he *m.* 2ndly, 30 Jan. 1947, Olga, da. of Stuart LAURANCE formerly wife of Peter MENDOZA. This marriage was in turn diss. by divorce in 1962 (she was still living 1995) and he *m.* 3rdly, 1 Dec. 1962, Lilias Janet Garvie, da. of Emeritus Prof. J. Walter MACLEOD of Edinburgh and formerly wife of Lieut. Col. D.S. RICHARD. He *d.* 13 Dec. 1989. His widow was living 1995.

VIII. 1989. 5. JOHN RUARIDH BLUNT GRANT (BLUNT-MACKENZIE, *later* MACKENZIE), EARL OF CROMARTIE, &c., s. and h., *b.* 12 June 1948; ed. at Rannoch Sch. and Strathclyde Univ.; discontinued, 1962, use of Christian name and surname of BLUNT; recognised by Lord Lyon as Chief of Clan Mackenzie. He *m.* 1stly, 1973, Helen, da. of John MURRAY. This marriage was diss. by divorce in 1983 and he *m.* 2ndly, 1985, Janet Clare, da. of Christopher James HARLEY of Strathpeffer, Ross-shire.

[COLIN RUARIDH MACKENZIE, *styled* VISCOUNT TARBAT, 1st s. and h. ap., *b.* 7 Sep. 1987.]

note ([a]), line 10, after 'V.G.' add 'Round's view is now generally accepted. The Select Committee on Peerages in Abeyance in 1926 came to no conclusion on whether peerages other than baronies in fee were capable of *abeyance*, see Geoffrey Ellis, *Earldoms in Fee*, 1963, p. 91, note 1.

CROMER

page 550,

line 18, after 'VESCI.' add 'He *d.* in London 29 Jan., and was *bur.* 3 Feb. 1917, at Bournemouth.' and for 'She' read 'His widow'

line 19, after 'Sq.' add ', and *d.* 4 Mar. 1933.'

line 20, line to read as follows

II. 1917. 2. ROWLAND THOMAS (BARING), EARL OF CROMER, &c., 1st s. and h. by 1st wife, *b.* 29 Nov. 1877; *styled* VISCOUNT ERRINGTON 1892–1917;

line 21, after 'Service' add '1902–6, 2nd Sec. 1906' and after 'Affairs' add '1907–11. Served in WW1 as 2nd Lieut. Gren. Guards, A.D.C. on Personal Staff;([ca]) A.D.C. to the Viceroy of India 1915. Held the Order of St. Anne of Russia of the 2nd Class. He *d.* 13 May 1953. His widow *d.* 5 Nov. 1961.'

note ([ca]) For a list of peers and sons of peers who served in this war, see vol. viii, Appendix F.

III. 1953. 3. GEORGE ROWLAND STANLEY (BARING), EARL OF CROMER, &c., s. and h., *b.* 28 July 1918; ed. at Eton and Cambridge (Trin. Coll.); *m.*, 10 Jan. 1942, Esmé Gabrielle, yr. da. of Esmond Cecil (HARMSWORTH), 2nd VISCOUNT HARMSWORTH. He *d.* 1991. His widow *m.*, 2ndly, 1993, as his 2nd wife, Reinier Gerrit Anton VAN DER WOUDE. They were both still living 1995.

IV. 1991. 4. EVELYN ROWLAND STANLEY (BARING), EARL OF CROMER, &c., 1st s. and h., *b.* 3 June 1946; ed. at Eton; *m.* 1stly, 1971, Plern, da. of Dr Charanpat Isarangkul na AYUDHYA of Thailand. This marriage was diss. by divorce in 1992 and he *m.* 2ndly, 1993, Shelley Hu, da. of Hu Guo-qin of Shanghai.

[ALEXANDER ROWLAND HARMSWORTH BARING, *styled* VISCOUNT ERRINGTON, s. and h. ap. by 1st wife, *b.* 5 Jan. 1994.]

CROMLIX

page 550,
line 32, for '1717' read '1718'

CROMWELL

page 552,
line 6, after 'William,' add '(who *d.* 18 Dec. 1360),'
line 7, after 'and' add '(eventual)'
line 9, after '1419.' add 'Her will dat. 14 Sep. 1416 to 14 Sep. 1417 is preserved at Penshurst.' [An English copy of her will in French is given in *Hist. MSS. Com.*, De L'Isle and Dudley MSS., vol. 1, pp. 204–6.]
line 27, after 'Joan,' add '*de jure suo jure* (according to modern doctrine) Baroness GREY (of Rotherfield)'
line 30, for '1454/5' read '1455/6'

page 553,
line 21, after 'He' add 'was living 15 Oct. 1335, and'

page 554,
line 4, for '25' read '26'
after line 20 add

* * * * * *

VI. 1923. 5. ROBERT GODFREY WOLSELEY (BEWICKE-COPLEY), LORD CROMWELL, *suc.* as Lord Cromwell on the termination of the *abeyance* in his favour, 16 July 1923.(d) He was *b.* 23 May 1893; ed. at Eton; *m.*, 12 Feb. 1925, at Ampney Crucis Church, Glos., Freda Constance, da. of Major Frederick William Beresford CRIPPS, of Waterton House, Cirencester. He *d.* 21 Oct. 1966. His widow *d.* 1979.

VII. 1966. 6. DAVID GODFREY (BEWICKE-COPLEY), LORD CROMWELL, s. and h., *b.* 29 May 1929; ed. at Eton and Cambridge (Magdalene Coll.); *m.* Doris Vivian, yst. da. of Hugh de Lisle PENFOLD, of South Africa. He *d.* 18 Aug. 1982. His widow was living in 1995.

VIII. 1982. 7. GODFREY JOHN (BEWICKE-COPLEY), LORD CROMWELL, 1st s. and h., *b.* 4 Mar. 1960; ed. at Eton and Cambridge; *m.*, 1990, Elizabeth, da. of John HAWKSLEY.

note (c), line 4 (on page 555), after 'Benstead.' add 'This *abeyance* was terminated in 1923, see above and vol. xiii, p. 388.'

note (d) The Barony of Cromwell was claimed in 1922 by Selina Frances, da. and coh. of Sir Charles Watson-Copley, Bart., the senior h. of Maud, 2nd da. of Ralph, 1st Lord Cromwell [1375]. The Committee for Privileges reported on 10 Mar. 1922 in favour of the claim but Selina Frances (who had *m.* Brig. Gen. Sir Robert Calverley Alington Bewicke-Copley in 1886) *d.* 27 June 1923. Her only surv. s. and h. was therefore *sum.* in her place.

page 556,
line 7, for 'July' read '29 June'
line 12, after 'Trent' add 'and Steward of Whitby both'
line 14, after 'Wells.' add 'Constable of Leeds Castle, Kent, Jan. 1538/9.'

page 557,
line 17, after '(e)' add 'On 29 Sep. 1544 he had exemption from attending the King in the War.'

page 558,
line 2, for 'before 1538' read 'between 17 July and 3 Aug. 1537' [*L. and P. Hen. VIII*, vol. xii, part 2, pp. 113, 232. V.G.]
line 10, delete 'before'

page 559,
line 11, after '1704,' add 'as his 1st wife,'
line 12, for '*d.*' read '*m.* 2ndly a da. of ?Secretary Blathwayt and *d.* of apoplexy'
line 25, for BANDEN read 'BRANDEN'

CROSS OF BROUGHTON IN FURNESS

page 560,
line 23, after 'Furness' add 'He *d.* there, 8, aged 90, and was *bur.* 10 Jan. 1914, at Broughton. Will pr. Apr. 1914 at £91,617 gross, £79,299 net.'
line 29, after '1855' add 'She *d.* 8 Nov. 1946.'

page 561,
line 1, line to read as follows

II. 1914. 2. RICHARD ASSHETON (CROSS), VISCOUNT CROSS OF BROUGHTON IN FURNESS, grandson and h., being only s. and h.

line 4, for ']' read 'He *m.*, 11 Feb. 1918, at St. Mark's, Audley Str., Maud Evelyn, da. of Major Gen. Inigo JONES, C.V.O., C.B., of Kelston Park, Somerset. He *d.* 14, and was *bur.* 17 Mar. 1932 at Broughton in Furness. His widow *m.* 2ndly, 18 Apr. 1944, Guy Hope COLDWELL, who *d.* 10 Oct. 1948. She *d.* 1976.'

III. 1932. 3. ASSHETON HENRY (CROSS), VISCOUNT CROSS OF BROUGHTON IN FURNESS, 1st s. and h., *b.* 7 May 1920; ed. at Shrewsbury and Cambridge (Magdalene Coll.); *m.* 1stly, 12 Jan. 1952, Patricia Mary, 1st da. of Edward Pearson HEWITSON of Windermere, Westmorland. This marriage was diss. by divorce in 1957 and he *m.* 2ndly, 1972, Mrs Victoria WEBB. This marriage was in turn diss. by divorce in 1977 and he *m.* 3rdly, 1983, Patricia, widow of John ROSSITER. This marriage was also diss. by divorce in 1987.

CULLEN

page 561,
line 24, after 'Mary,' add '(*d.* 8 Jan. 1648/9)'

page 564,
line 13, after 'Eton' add '*circa* 1725'

page 565,
line 18, for '1695' read '1698'

CUMBERLAND

page 566,
line 6, for '1631' read '1650'
note (b), line 3, after 'others,"' add 'In a Report on the English nobility which internal evidence shows to have been written between July and Nov. 1538, he is described as "a man of 50 years, of good power, without discretion or conduct", *L. and P. Hen. VIII*, vol. xiii, part 2, p. 280.'

page 567,
line 3, for '(1541)' read '(3 Apr. 1542, on payment of £2,490)'
line 5, after 'Marches' add 'till 1537' and for '–28' read '–27'
line 19, after '1542;' add 'on 9 May 1543 he had livery of his father's lands;'
line 28, delete from 'in' to 'Oswald' and replace by 'after 21 Aug. 1554 at Kirkoswald,'
note (d), line 1, before 'See' add 'The date is that of a letter from William, Lord Dacre, to the Earl of Shrewsbury, asking him to approach the Earl of Cumberland as to whether "he will be contente to tayke my said dowghter with one thousande poundes"'. (Cod. Tenison 696 [Shrewsbury Papers, vol. iii, Lambeth Palace Library, f. 39]; *ex inform.* H. Ince Anderton)'

page 568,
line 21, for '29 Dec. 1605' read '13 Mar. 1605/6'
line 25, for '22' read '24'
line 26, for '7' read '11'

page 569,
lines 4–5, for 'aged 1 in 1585' read '*b.* 10 Apr. 1584,'
line 5, for 'early in Dec. 1589' read 'an infant, 10 or 11 Dec. 1584,'
line 7, after '*b.*' add '21 Sep. 1585'
line 12, for 'in' read '13 Oct.'
line 16, after 'Lieut.' add 'of that co. and of Northumberland jointly with the Earl of Dunbar'
line 19, after 'Hughes' add '(or HEWES, who *d.* 27 Mar. 1587 at North Mimms, Herts.)'
line 26, after 'only' add 'surv.' and after 'h.' add '(aa)'
note (aa), His older br., George, *d.* an infant.

page 570,
line 8, after 'also' add 'in the same house'
line 13, for 'RUPRECHT' read 'RUPPRECHT'

page 571,
note (b), line 2, after 'was' add 'ed. at Eton and later'
line 5, after '[I.]' add 'and *d.* at Somerset House about 1740'

page 572,
line 15, for '2nd' read '3rd'

page 573,
note (b), line 10, after 'Hinchinbrooke.' add 'The contemporary attitude towards concubinage is illustrated by the following extract from the Diary of the 1st Earl of Egmont under date 15 Jan. 1738/9. "This week Miss Williams, a player, was complimented in the Green room by her fellow comedians for the honour done her by the Duke of Cumberland in taking her for a mistress."'

page 574,
note (a), line 24, after 'V.G.' add 'The question of her identity is discussed in *Princess or Pretender*, 1939, by Mary Prendered and J. Mallett.'

page 577,
line 12, after 'occurred.' add 'He was struck from the Roll of the Order of the Garter on 13 May 1915. His name was removed from the roll of Peers of Great Britain and of Ireland by Order of the King in Council, 28 Mar. 1919.(ax)'
note (ax) For bearing arms against Great Britain.
line 16, add at end 'He *d.* at Gmunden, 14 Nov. 1923. His widow *d.* there, 26 Feb. 1933.'
lines 22–3, delete all detail and replace as follows

VIII. 1923. 4. *H.R.H.* ERNEST AUGUSTUS CHRISTIAN GEORGE, DUKE OF BRUNSWICK-LUNEBERG, PRINCE OF GREAT BRITAIN AND IRELAND, 3rd and only surv. s. and h., *b.* at Penzing, near Vienna, 17 Nov. 1887, who but for the abovementioned Order in Council, in which he was named an enemy of the United Kingdom, would have been DUKE OF CUMBERLAND AND TIVIOTDALE [G.B.], also EARL OF ARMAGH [I.]. He *m.*, 24 May 1913, at Berlin, *H.R.H.* PRINCESS VICTORIA LOUISE ADELDEID MATHILDE CHARLOTTE, only da. of *H.I.M.* WILHELM II, GERMAN EMPEROR and KING OF PRUSSIA. He *d.* at Schloss Marienburg, near Nordstemmen, 30 Jan. 1953. His widow *d.* 11 Dec. 1980.

IX. 1953. 5. *H.R.H.* ERNST AUGUST GEORG WILHELM CHRISTIAN LUDWIG FRANZ JOSEF NIKOLAUS, DUKE OF BRUNSWICK-LUNEBERG, PRINCE OF GREAT BRITAIN AND IRELAND, who but for the abovementioned Order in Council would have been DUKE OF CUMBERLAND, &c., 1st s. and h., *b.* 18 Mar. 1914; ed. Oxford (Univ. Coll.); *m.* 4 Sep. 1951, *H.H.* PRINCESS ORTRUD BERTHA ADELHEID HEDWIG, 2nd da. of *H.H.* PRINCE ALBERT OF SCHLESWIG-HOLSTEIN-SONDERBURG-GLUCKSBURG. She *d.* 6 Feb. 1980 and he *m.* 2ndly, 17 July 1981, Monika, da. of Georg Friedrich, COUNT OF SOLMS-LAUBACH. He *d.* 9 Dec. 1987. His widow was still living 1995.

X. 1987. 6. *H.R.H.* ERNST AUGUST ALBERT PAUL OTTO RUPPRECHT BERTHOLD FRIEDRICH FERDINAND CHRISTIAN LUDWIG, PRINCE OF GREAT BRITAIN AND IRELAND, who but for the abovementioned Order in Council would have been DUKE OF CUMBERLAND, &c., 1st s. and h., *b.* 26 Feb. 1954; ed. at Salem, R.A.C., Cirencester and Univ. of Guelph, Canada. He *m.*, 30 Aug. 1981, Chantal, da. of Johann Gustav HOCHULI, of Zurich, Switzerland. In the titular Duke of Cumberland and Tiviotdale is vested the right to petition under the Titles Deprivation Act, 1917, for the restoration of his peerages.[d]

[*H.R.H.* PRINCE ERNST AUGUST ANDREAS PHILIPP KONSTANTIN MAXIMILIAN ROLF STEPHAN LUDWIG RUDOLF, 1st s. and h. ap., *b.* 19 July 1983.]

note ([d]), Act, 7&8 Geo. V, *cap.* 47. See Burke's *Peerage*, 1953, pp. cli–cliii.

page 578,
line 23, after 'Eton' add '1846–52'

CURZON OF KEDLESTON

page 580,
line 19, after '*b.*' add 'at Kedleston Hall, co. Derby' and after 'Eton 'add '1872–8'

page 581,
line 2, for '–89' read '–98'
note ([a]), No Irish Peerages have been created since 1922, with the passing of the Irish Free State Act, nor, perhaps, are any more such creations likely.

page 582,
line 5, after '([a])' add 'Lord Privy Seal in the Coalition Cabinet 30 May 1915. He *suc.* his father as 5th Baron Scarsdale, 23 Mar. 1916. He was *cr.* 28 June 1921 MARQUESS CURZON.' and after '*m.*' add '1stly'
line 9, after '£11,000' add 'He *m.*, 2ndly, 2 Jan. 1917, in the private chapel in Lambeth Palace, Grace Elvina, G.B.E., widow of Alfred DUGGAN, of Buenos Aires, and 1st da. of J. Monroe HINDS, sometime U.S.A. Minister at the Court of Brazil. He *d. s.p.m.* at 1 Carlton House Terrace after an operation, 20, and was *bur.* 26 Mar. 1925 at Kedleston, the funeral service having been held at Westm. Abbey. At his death his Marquessate, Earldom and the Barony of Curzon of Kedleston [I.] became *extinct*. [For his other peerages see vols. xi, p. 522 and xiii, p. 354.] His widow *d.* 29 Jan. 1958.'

CURZON OF PENN

page 583,
line 15, after 'wife,' add '*b.* 31 Jan. 1757,'
note ([c]), line 2, for 'fusileers' read 'fusiliers'

CUTTS

page 584,
line 2, for 'at Steinkirk' read 'in the English defeat at Enghien or Steinkirk, 24 July 1692'
note ([b]), line 2, delete from 'the' to 'Guard.' and replace by '*i.e.* the Gentlemen at Arms.'

APPENDIXES

APPENDIX A

page 589,
line 7, for '1230' read '1239'
between lines 12 and 13 add as follows

1241 CHESTER, Earldom, surrender of William de Forz and his wife of all her share in the inheritance of John late Earl of Chester, by charter 16 Oct. 1241 [for full particulars see "The End of the Norman Earldom of Chester", by R Stewart Brown, *Eng. Hist. Review*, Jan. vol. 35, 1920, pp. 26–51].

page 590,
between lines 19 and 20 add as follows

1524 KENT, Earldom. Sir Henry Grey, who *suc.* as Earl of Kent in 1524, did not assume the Earldom, but he did not formally resign it. His s. *d. v.p.* and his grandson, Reynold, was M.P. for Weymouth 1563–7. The Crown must have acquiesced in the resignation of the Earldom or Reynold would not have been allowed to take his seat in the House of Commons.

line 20, for '1640' read '1639'

APPENDIX B

page 592,
between lines 33 and 34 add as follows

BINGHAM, see CLANMORRIS

page 593,
between lines 18 and 19 add as follows

CLANMORRIS, Arthur Maurice Bingham, 1st son of 5th Baron

page 594,
between lines 16 and 17 add as follows

FITZHERBERT, Francis Edward, nephew and h. ap. of Fitzherbert (Stafford-Jerningham), 11th Lord Stafford

page 595,
line 26, for 'Sandford' read 'Sanford'

page 596,
between lines 12 and 13 add as follows

ROTHERHAM, Stuart-Lund *Holland*, 1st s. of the 1st Baron Rotherham.

APPENDIX C

page 606,
line 12, after '9517).' add '(b)'

note (b) The name Charles begins to occur in the records of Winchester and Southampton almost immediately after the visit of Charles V to those cities in 1523; *ex inform.* Henry Newbolt, Salisbury, 1913.

page 607,
line 25, for 'We' read 'Roger de Mowbray's dapifer in 1140 was named George [Stenton, *First Century of English Feudalism*, p. 72] and we'

page 615,
line 33, after 'name.' add 'Maria occurs as a man's name in the 16th century, see below, p. 622, lines 4, 5. The names Martin, Philpot, Will and Rawlyn may also be added to names used by both sexes, see addition to p. 617 below.'

page 617,
line 5, after 'pieces.' add 'In the Miscellaneous Deeds in the City of Exeter the following unusual women's names occur: Aumeye, Blandeva, Dewnys [Dionys], Edevia, Elisoba, Emmoba, Gesiana, Gilda, Giliana, Gonilda, Lyvena, Martyne, Mawyte [Maud], Maysanda, Miralda, Parva Rosa, Paschasia, Philpota, Rawlyn, Savra, Sonotta, Urith, Willa, Yllaria. Doubtless some of these occur in Latin MSS., and have been Latinised by adding a terminal "a".'

page 620,
line 30, after 'century.' add 'In Develly's *Parish Records*, among the Bishop's transcripts at Wells, the following rare Christian names occur: Cressela, Jenarivale, Andronicus, Aramirsing, Oineri, Sabrene, Exponsoi and Eponforus.'

APPENDIX G

page 640,
between lines 20 and 21 add as follows

KILMAINE, Mary, 2nd wife of the 3rd Baron, 1873

page 644,
line 2, for '10' read '19'

APPENDIX H

page 646,
between lines 13 and 14 add as follows

James Cuffe 22 Nov. 1797 *cr.* Lord Tyrawley of Ballinrobe

line 21, for '21 Mar.' read '4 Apr.'
line 42, for '6 Aug.' read '30 Aug.'

VOLUME 4

DACRE

page 1,
note ([c]), line 5, for 'Aude' read 'Ada'.

page 2,
line 15, after 'MULTON' add '*de jure suo jure* (according to modern doctrine), BARONESS MULTON'.
line 16, before 'da.' add 'presumably'

page 3,
line 8, for '*v.p.*' read 'soon after 1331'
note ([e]), line 1, before 'Randolf' add '*Feet of Fines*, case 138, file 100, no. 43. See *Genealogist*, N.S., vol. xxxiii, p. 133.'

page 5,
note ([a]) line 1, before 'The' add 'His brother Hugh was indicted in 1376 for the murder, with Sir Hugh Harrington.' [Simon Walker, *The Lancastrian Affinity, 1361–1399*, 1990, p. 157.]

page 7,
line 10, for '1353' read '1453'

page 10,
line 4, after 'Castle;' add 'was apparently at the Field of the Cloth of Gold in 1520;'
line 15, after '([d])' add 'had livery of his lands 11 May 1537 and'
line 20, after '1536,' add 'while still under age and a ward of the King,'

page 11,
lines 8–9, delete from ', and' to 'Eliz.' [There are no writs for Elizabeth till 1586, these are Dugdale forgeries.]

page 14,
line 2, for '16 May' read '11 Aug.'
note ([b]), line 4, after '1672/3.' add 'The date in Lysons is probably an error for 1674. Phillimore's *Marr. Reg. for Middlesex*, vol. iii, p. 6, gives 11 Aug. 1674.'

page 17,
line 7, after 'WILMOT' add 'of Farnborough in that co.'
line 23, for 'Benjamin' read 'Bury' and for '6th' read '5th'

page 18,
between lines 8 and 9 add as follows

XXVII. 1970. 27. RACHEL LEILA, 1st da. of Thomas Henry (BRAND), 4th VISCOUNT HAMPDEN, 26th LORD DACRE, *suc.* to the Barony on the termination in 1970 of the *abeyance* caused by the death of Viscount Hampden on 17 Oct. 1965 (see HAMPDEN below). She was *b.* 24 Oct. 1929; *m.*, 26 July 1951, William, 3rd s. of Charles Cospatrick Archibald (DOUGLAS-HOME), 13th EARL OF HOME (*d.* 28 Sep. 1992).

[JAMES THOMAS ARCHIBALD DOUGLAS-HOME, s. and h. ap., *b.* 16 May 1952; *m.*, 1979, Christine, da. of William STEPHENSON of Royston, Herts.]

page 19,
note (f), line 2, for '70' read 'over 80'
line 9 (on page 20), after '2115.' add 'For a full discussion of those present at this coronation see Anne F. Sutton and P.W. Hammond, *The Coronation of Richard III*, 1983, pp. 270–3 and pp. 303 *et seq.*'

page 20,
note (f), line 1, after the second 'Dacre' add '(this may possibly have been Thomas Fiennes)'

page 21,
line 5, delete 'or 1472'

page 22,
line 15, after 'at' add 'his seat'

page 23,
lines 11–12, delete from ', who' to 'Eliz'
note (d), lines 1–3, delete from 'a writ' to 'Parl.' and replace by 'although no Parliament was summoned in that year (1473–4). A Parliament was summoned on 20 Nov. 1477 (17 Edw. IV) but no writs seem to exist for this. To the Parliament of 22 Edw. IV' and delete 'first'

page 24,
line 3, after 'of' add 'of Croglin, co. Cumberland and' [See B.L. Harl. Charters 77 F 1 and 77 H 37.]
line 18, after 'Musqueteers.' add '(da)'
note (da) On 5 Dec. 1595 he wrote from Liège to his eldest and dearly beloved da., Eleanor, asking her to appeal to the Queen that "their house may be restored to its ancient state" and authorising her to say that "he and his son are departed the King of Spain's domains having already some months past left his pension and service" (*Hist. MSS. Com.*, Hatfield House MSS., part xiii, p. 547). On 8/18 July 1599 he was still in Liège, and had sent for his son (?Francis) to be with him. V.G.

page 26,
line 2, for 'of Derwentwater' read 'of Fallantire, Cumberland,(aa)'

note ([aa]), See H.H.E. Craster, *History of Corbridge* (vol. x of the *History of Northumberland*, 1914), p. 285 and pedigree opposite p. 280. Dorothy had been previously contracted to marry a son of her kinsman Sir George Radcliff of Dilston, Northumberland, Kt., but this child marriage does not appear to have been carried out. She sold her Derwentwater property 25 Apr. 1577 and 22 Aug. 1578 after her marriage to Francis Dacre.

DAGWORTH

page 27,
note ([e]), line 4, for '17 Nov. 1260' read 'by Jan. 1265/6' [*Excerpta e. Rot. Finium*, vol. 2, 1836, p. 433]

page 28,
line 17, after 'ORMOND' add '[I.]'

DALHOUSIE

page 32,
line 37, delete from 'She' to 'M.D.' [The statement in R. Douglas, *Peerage of Scotland*, ed. J.P. Wood, 1813, that she *m.* 3rdly is erroneous.]

page 33,
lines 16–19, delete from 's.' to 'Earl' and replace by '1st and possibly only s. of John RAMSAY (2nd s. of William 1st Earl of Dalhousie), by Marjorie SPENCE, his wife.([aa]) He was *bap.* 2 Dec. 1660 at Dundee.'
note ([aa]) He is generally supposed to have been the son of another John Ramsay who was 2nd son of George, 2nd Earl of Dalhousie.

page 34,
line 5, for '3rd' read '1st'
line 25, after '1788' add 'as Cornet in the 3rd Dragoon Guards'

page 35,
line 6, for 'in' read '11 Ainsley Place'

page 38,
line 19, after 'Eton' add '1892–5'
line 27, after 'Rutland' add 'He *d.* suddenly at Brechin Castle, co. Forfar, 23 Dec. 1928. His widow *d.* 23 May 1960.'
lines 28–9, delete all detail and replace as follows

EARLDOM [S.] XV.
BARONY [S.] XVI.
BARONY [U.K.] IV.
1928

15 and 16. JOHN GILBERT (RAMSAY), EARL OF DALHOUSIE, &c., s. and h., *b.* 25 July 1904; *styled* LORD RAMSAY till 1928; ed. at Oxford (Ch. Ch.). He *d.* unm. 3 May 1950.

EARLDOM [S.] XVI. BARONY [S.] XVII. BARONY [U.K.] V.	1950	16 and 17. SIMON (RAMSAY), EARL OF DALHOUSIE, &c., br. and h., *b.* 17 Oct. 1917. He *m.*, 26 June 1940, Margaret Elizabeth Mary, 2nd da. of Brig. Gen. Archibald STIRLING of Keir, Perthshire.

[JAMES HUBERT RAMSAY, *styled* LORD RAMSAY, 1st s. and h. ap., *b.* 17 Jan. 1948; ed. at Ampleforth; *m.*, 1973, Marilyn Davina, da. of Major Sir David Henry Butter, K.C.V.O., M.C.]

DALLING

page 41,
line 21, after 'ilk' add '(who *d.* between 2 Jan. 1608/9 and Feb. 1610)'

DAMORY

page 45,
line 8, after '*d.*' add 'being *b.* 16 Sep. 1295 at Tewkesbury,'
lines 8–9, delete from 'with' to 'Ware' and replace by 'at the Convent of the Minoresses without Aldgate'

DANBY

page 49,
line 7, for '1607/15' read '1607–14/15'

DARCY

page 50,
note ([c]), line 4, for '1186' read '1185'

page 58,
line 10, after 'KILDARE' add '[I.]'
line 11, after 'ULSTER' add '[I.]'

page 60,
line 3, for 'MENILLE' read 'MEINILL'
line 9, after 'Notton,' add 'in Royston Parish,'
note ([a]), line 7, for 'both the 3rd and 4th' read 'the 3rd–4th degrees'

page 62,
line 17, for 'Henes' read 'Heynings'

page 63,
line 14, after 'da.' add '(it is said)'

page 67,
note (e), line 3, after '*d. v.p.*' add '26 July 1469, being slain at Edgecote Field'

page 68,
line 5 of chart, under 'Lord Conyers' add 'disp. to marry 4 Nov. 1528'
last line of note: after 'field.' add 'For the crown claim to West Harlsey, see also *V.C.H. Yorks., W. Riding*, vol. 1, 1914, pp. 437–8.'

page 73,
line 4, after 'KERRY' add 'She *d.* 29 Apr. and was *bur.* 2 May 1929, at Welshpool.'
line 6, after '1892' add '*d.* unm. 13 Oct. 1916.'

XV. 1929. 17. MERVYN HORATIO (HERBERT), LORD DARCY [1344], 2nd but only surv. s. and h., *b.* 7 May 1904, *k.* in action, Mar. 1943 [for further detail see POWIS].

XVI. 1943. 18. DAVINA MARCIA (HERBERT), BARONESS DARCY, *b.* 10 July 1938; *m.*, 1 Mar. 1960, Rupert George INGRAMS, who *d.* in a motor accident, 28 Feb. 1964.

[CASPAR DAVID INGRAMS, s. and h. ap., *b.* 5 Jan. 1962.]

page 73,
line 18, after '1509' add 'till his death'

page 74,
line 2, after '1513;' add 'apparently present at the Field of the Cloth of Gold (1520);'

page 76,
line 14, after 'Margaret' add '(*m.* 30 Jan. 1575/6)' [Aston Register]

page 77,
line 17, after '*bap.*' add '(12 Apr. 1607)'
line 18, for '1625,' read '1626,(da)'
note (da) Not in 1624 as in the M.I.: John, s. and h. ap. of John, Lord Darcy, was *bap.* at Aston 4 July 1626 (Register), he *d. trimestris*, and was *bur.* with his mother (M.I.).
note (e), line 1, after 'had' add 'by his 1st wife'

page 78,
line 5, after 'her' add ', 28 Oct.'
line 7, after 'of' add 'Sir'
line 8, after 'Elizabeth' add '(living 22 Sep. 1545)(ba)'
note (ba), She *m.* as her 3rd husband, John (Bourchier), Earl of Bath.

page 79,
line 17, after '*m.*' add '(aa)'
note (aa) On 4 Mar. 1582/3 Lord Paget wrote "Lord Percy and Lord Darcy, are suitors for the hand of Lady Kitson's daughter, who prefers Lord Percy." In those days the young lady's preference was not usually the deciding factor in a marriage. V.G.

DARLINGTON

page 80,
line 26, after 'Mary,' add '(living 29 Apr. 1744)'
line 36, after 'being' add 'nominally'
line 38, after 'MUND' add '(but actually da. of Ernst August, Elector of Hanover),'
lines 39–40, delete from 'who' to 'to' and replace by 'who was the Elector's mistress'

page 81,
lines 1–2, delete all detail
lines 6–9, delete from 'The ' to '(b)'
line 11, after 'life.' add 'She was naturalised by a private Act of Parliament, 8 Geo. I (1721–3) (b).'
note (b), delete all detail and replace by 'The stories that Sophia Charlotte was mistress of George I were demolished in Ragnild Hatton, *George I, Elector and King*, 1978, pp. 23–4, 134–5.' [Thanks are due to William A. Reitweissner of Washington, U.S.A. for drawing my attention to this book.]

DARNLEY

page 84,
line 10, after '*d.*' add 'in childbed'
line 28, for 'in' read 'at St. Anne's'
line 37, for 'and' read '1775–84; matric. at' and after 'Oxford' add '16 Nov. 1784'

page 85,
line 9, after 'Eton' add '1805–11'
line 20, after 'Eton' add '*circa* 1839–43'
line 32, after 'Eton' add '1864–70'

page 86,
line 14, after 'Eton' add '1872–7'
line 18, after 'Australia' add 'He *d.* of heart failure at Puckle Hill House, Cobham, Kent, 10, and was *bur.* there 14 Apr. 1927. His widow *d.* 30 Aug. 1944.'
line 19, line to read as follows

IX. 1927. 9. ESME IVO (BLIGH), EARL OF DARNLEY, &c., 1st s. and h., *b.* 11 Oct. 1886. On the death, 5 July 1937, of his cousin, Elizabeth Adeline Mary, *suo jure* BARONESS CLIFTON OF LEIGHTON BROMSWOLD [1608] (see that title above), he *suc.* to that title. He *m.* 1stly, 25 June 1912, Daphne Rachel, da. of Alfred John MULHOLLAND. This marriage was diss. by divorce in 1920 and he *m.* 2ndly, 11 Oct. 1923,

Nancy, 1st da. of Capt. Archibald Glen KIDSTON. This marriage was in turn diss. by divorce in 1936 and he *m.* 3rdly, 4 Nov. 1940, Rosemary, da. of Edmund Basil POTTER of Witherslack, co. Westmorland. He *d.* 29 May 1955. His widow *m.* 2ndly, 18 Apr. 1963, Pierre TRANRESEST of Vaux Sous Chevremont, Belgium (he *d.* 1968). His widow was still living 1995.

X. 1955. 10. PETER STUART (BLIGH), EARL OF DARNLEY, &c., LORD CLIFTON OF LEIGHTON BROMSWOLD, s. and h., *b.* 1 Oct. 1915; ed. at Eton and R.M.C., Sandhurst. he *d.* unm. 15 June 1980.

XI. 1980. 11. ADAM IVO STUART (BLIGH), EARL OF DARNLEY, &c., half-brother and h., being 2nd s. by 3rd wife, *b.* 8 Nov. 1941; ed. at Harrow and Oxford (Ch. Ch.); *m.*, 14 Oct. 1965, Susan Elaine, yst. da. of Sir Donald Forsyth ANDERSON.

[IVO DONALD STUART BLIGH, *styled* LORD CLIFTON OF RATHMORE, s. and h. ap., *b.* 17 Apr. 1968; ed. at Marlborough and Edinburgh.]

DARTMOUTH

page 89,
line 19, after '1754;' add 'took his seat 31 May 1754'

page 90,
note (b), line 1, for 'Reynolds' read 'Lawrence'

page 91,
line 16, after 'Eton' read '*circa* 1835–41'
line 23, after 'Patshull' add ', dat. 17 June 1885 to 17 Sep. 1890, pr. 7 Sep. 1891'
line 25, after 'Will' add 'dat. 2 July 1896, pr. 5 Feb. 1901,'
line 32, after 'Eton' add '1865–9'

page 92,
line 2, after 'She' add ', who'
line 3, after '1849.' add '*d.* 28 Dec. 1929 and was *bur.* 2 Jan. 1930 at Patshull, Wolverhampton. He *d.* 11 Mar. 1936 at Patshull House.'
line 4, line to read as follows

EARLDOM. VII. BARONY. IX. } 1936 7 and 8. WILLIAM (LEGGE), EARL OF DARTMOUTH, &c., 1st s. and h., *b.* 22 Feb. 1881 at 55 Manchester Str.; *styled* VISCOUNT LEWISHAM 1891–1936; ed. at Eton 1894–9 and at Oxford (Ch. Ch.) 1900; executed the office of GREAT CHAMBERLAIN, 1928–36;

line 8, for ']' read 'He *d. s.p.m.s.* 28 Feb. 1958. His widow *d.* 26 June 1963.'

[WILLIAM LEGGE, s. and h. ap., *styled* VISCOUNT LEWISHAM, was *b.* 23 Jan. 1913, served in WW2 and *d.* unm. and *v.p.* Oct. 1942, being k. in action at El Alamein.]

EARLDOM. VIII. BARONY. X.	1958	8 and 9. HUMPHREY (LEGGE), EARL OF DARTMOUTH, &c., br. and h., *b.* 14 Mar. 1888; ed. at H.M.S. Britannia, Dartmouth; *m.*, 10 Apr. 1923, Roma Ernestine, 2nd da. of Sir Ernest Burford HORLICK, Bart. He *d.* 16 Oct. 1962. His widow was still living 1995.

EARLDOM. IX. BARONY. XI.	1962	9 and 10. GERALD HUMPHREY (LEGGE), EARL OF DARTMOUTH, &c., s. and h., *b.* 26 Apr. 1924; ed. at Eton. He *m.* 1stly, 21 July 1948, Raine, da. of Alexander George MCCORQUODALE of Newbury, Berks. This marriage was diss. by divorce in 1976 and he *m.* 2ndly, 1986, Gwendoline May, da.

of Charles René SEGUIN.

[WILLIAM LEGGE, *styled* VISCOUNT LEWISHAM, 1st s. and h. by 1st wife, *b.* 23 Sep. 1949; ed. at Eton and Oxford (Ch. Ch.).]

DARTREY

page 92,
line 29, after 'Emily,' add '3rd'
line 36, after '1827;' add 'ed. at Eton *circa* 1829–34'

page 93,
line 14, after 'Eton' add '1855–7'
line 21, after '(c)' add 'He *d.* at Dartrey afsd. 14 June 1920. His widow *m.* 2ndly, 29 Apr. 1933 John Townshend (ST AUBYN), 2nd LORD ST. LEVAN; she *d.* in London, 7, and was *bur.* 10 Feb. 1938 at St. Michael's Mount, Cornwall.'

III. 1920. 3. ANTHONY LUCIUS (DAWSON), EARL OF DARTREY, &c., br. and h., *b.* 12 May 1855; *m.*, 2 Oct. 1878, Mary Frances, *suo jure* BARONESS DE ROS (see that title). He *d. s.p.m.* 9 Feb. 1933 when his titles became *extinct*.

DAUBENEY

page 93,
note (d), after 'V.G.' add 'Much work has been done recently on the origins of this family. Wagner, *English Geneal.*, 1983, p. 72, touches on it, and Philip Daykin has shown that Sir Ralph D'Aubigné given here was 3rd in descent from William (Brito) D'Aubigné and Cecily Bigod (referred to by Wagner) and yst. of the three sons of Ralph D'Aubigné of Mont Sorel. His eldest brother William carried away the Breton lands of Mont Sorel and Landal; Sir Ralph inherited the English lands only.'

page 97,
line 5, after 'THWENG,' add '[4th LORD THWENG]'

page 98,
line 12, after '*m.*' add 'after 26 June 1386' [*Cal. Pat. Rolls, 1385–89*, p. 223]

page 104,
line 3, for '1492/3' read '1493'

page 105,
line 2, delete from 'was' to 'him' and replace by '*m.* 2ndly, Lord Leonard GREY between 18 Feb. 1509/10 and Easter 1514 (when Lord Leonard Grey and Elizabeth his wife quit claimed the Daubeney manor of Bramshill, Hants., to Henry 2nd Lord Daubeney). Lord Leonard Grey, afterwards VISCOUNT GRANE [I.], who *d. s.p.*, was executed on Tower Hill 28 July 1541. She, who was living 26 June 1515, was *bur.* with her 1st husband.[aa]'

note [aa] *Cal. Inq. P. M.*, Hen. VII, vol. iii, no. 529; *L. and P. Hen. VIII*, vol. ii, no. 627; *V.C.H. Hants*, vol. 4, pp. 35 note 94. In the latter reference it is wrongly suggested that the Elizabeth referred to was probably the widow of William Essex. For this latter Elizabeth (living 1518), da. and h. of Thomas Rogers, and her husband Sir William Essex (*d.* 13 Aug. 1548) who together sold Bramshill to Giles, 1st Lord Daubeney in May 1499, see *Cal. Close Rolls, 1485–1500*, no. 1130; *Cal. Pat. Rolls, 1494–1508*, p. 482; *Visit. Berks.*, Harl. Soc., vol. i, pp. 7, 24; *V.C.H. Berks.*, vol. iv, pp. 105, 171, 255, 535; *Genealogist*, N.S., vol. xv, p. 261. It is clear that the only Elizabeth who, in 1514, could both be wife of Grey and have an interest in Bramshill was the widow of Giles, 1st Lord Daubeney. This supposition is confirmed by a pedigree of Grey, Lord of Wexford and Viscount Grany in Ireland in Harl. MS. 1425, f. 135. (*Ex inform* Edward Stewart Grey).

line 7, after '[b]' add 'He was apparently present at the Field of the Cloth of Gold in 1520.'

DE BLAQUIERE

page 110,
line 9, after 'Montreal.' add 'He *d. s.p.m.s.* 28 July 1920 when his Barony became *extinct*.'
line 11, after 'Canada.' add 'Ed. at Winchester from 1903.'
line 11–12, delete from 'He' to '1915' and replace by 'He served in WW1 and *d.* unm. and *v.p.*, being *k.* in action 10 Mar. 1915.'
between lines 12 and 13 add as follows

[ALAN BOYLE DE BLAQUIERE, 2nd s. and h. ap., *b.* 28 Mar. 1895. Served in WW1 and *d.* unm. and *v.p.*, as Sub-Lieut., R.N., Jan. 1917 in the Laurentic, off the coast of Ireland.]

note [a], lines 1–2, delete from 'His' to 'cadet' and for 'h. ap.' read 'sons'
line 3, after '1941–' add '1918'

DECIES

page 111,
line 11, delete 'ed.' and replace by 'admitted', and after 'Dublin;' add '18 Dec. 1759'

page 112,
line 6, after 'Dublin;' add 'adm. Trin. Coll., Dublin, 21 Oct. 1789 and'
line 21, for 'was living 1915' read '*d.* 27 Feb. 1941.'
line 24, after 'Eton' add '1878–81'
lines 31–3, delete from 'His' to 'work' and replace by 'His widow *d.* 4 Apr. 1939.'

V. 1910. 5. JOHN GRAHAM HOPE DE LA POER (HORSLEY-BERESFORD), BARON DECIES, br. and h., *b.* 5 Dec. 1866; ed. at Eton; *m.* 1stly, 7 Feb. 1911, Helen Vivien, da. of George Jay GOULD of New York. She *d.* 3 Feb. 1931 of heart failure and he *m.* 2ndly, 25 May 1936, Elizabeth Wharton, da. of Joseph Wilhelm DREXEL, of Philadelphia. He *d.* 31 Jan. 1944.(d) His widow *d.* June 1944.

VI. 1944. 6. ARTHUR GEORGE MARCUS DOUGLAS DE LA POER (BERESFORD), BARON DECIES, only s. and h., *b.* 24 Apr. 1915; *m.* 1stly, 21 Oct. 1937, Anne Christina Margo, da. of Sidney Walter TREASURE of Victoria, Australia. She *d.* 28 Mar. 1945. He *m.* 2ndly, 12 Sep. 1945, Diana, da. of Wing Cmdr. George TURNER-CAIN, of Wells, Norfolk and widow of Major David GALSWORTHY. He *d.* 7 Nov. 1992. His widow was still living 1995.

VII. 1992. 7. MARCUS HUGH TRISTRAM DE LA POER (BERESFORD), BARON DECIES, only s. and h., *b.* 5 Aug. 1948; ed. at St. Columba's Coll. and Dublin. He *m.* 1stly, 1970, Sarah Jane, da. of Col. Basil GUNNELL. This marriage was diss. by divorce in 1974 and he *m.* 2ndly, Edel Jeanette, da. of Vincent Ambrose HENDRON of Dublin.

[ROBERT MARCUS DUNCAN DE LA POER BERESFORD, s. and h. ap. by his 1st wife, *b.* 14 July 1988.]

note (d), line 1, for 'He and his' read 'His other'

DE FREYNE

page 114,
line 25, after '1786;' add 'Adm. Trin. Coll., Dublin, 3 June 1806, aged 18'

page 115,
line 12, after '1788;' add 'adm. Trin. Coll., Dublin, 4 June 1806' and delete '(Trin Coll.), Dublin'

page 116,
line 10, for 'was living 1915' read '*d.* at 48 Queen's Gate, S.W., 20, and was bur. at Kensal Green, 22 Feb. 1923.'
line 11, line to read as follows

V. 1913. 5. ARTHUR REGINALD (FRENCH), BARON DE FREYNE OF COOLAVIN, 1st s. and h. by 1st wife, *b.* 3 July 1879

lines 13–14, delete from 'Having' to 'work' and replace by '[for further detail see note (b)]. His widow *d.* 1962.'

VI. 1915. 6. FRANCIS CHARLES (FRENCH), BARON DE FREYNE OF COOLAVIN, half-brother and h., being 1st s. by 2nd wife, *b.* 15 Jan. 1884. He *m.*, 28 Feb. 1916 at the Brompton Oratory, Lina Victoria, yr. of the twin daughters of Sir John ARNOTT, Bart. He *d.* 24, and was *bur.* Clooshamble, French Park, co. Roscommon, 28 Dec. 1935. His widow *d.* 1974.

VII. 1935. 7. FRANCIS ARTHUR JOHN (FRENCH), BARON DE FREYNE OF COOLAVIN, only s. and h., *b.* 3 Sep. 1927; *m.* 1stly, 30 Jan. 1954, Shirley Ann, da. of Douglas Rudolph POBJOY of Woodmancote, co. Glos. This marriage was diss. by divorce in 1978 and he *m.* 2ndly, 1978, Sheelin Deirdre, da. of Col. Henry Kane O'KELLY of co. Wicklow, widow of William Walker STEPHENSON.

[FULKE CHARLES ARTHUR JOHN FRENCH, 1st s. and h. ap. by 2nd wife, *b.* 21 Apr. 1957; *m.*, 1986, Julia Mary, da. of James H. WELLARD.]

DEINCOURT

page 118,
note (b), line 2, delete from 'Aincourt' to 'normand'
note (c), line 4, for '1186' read '1185'

page 120,
note (d), line 3, after '17)' add 'Trevor Faulds, *The Thurgarton Cartulary*, 1994, pp. xcviii, cxv, suggests that he was a distant cousin of Edmund, 1st Lord. His arguments are unconvincing.

page 122,
note (c), line 5, for 'ferra' read 'fra'

page 124,
line 11, delete from 'da.' to 'of' and replace by '*de jure suo jure* (according to modern doctrine) Baroness Grey (of Rotherfield), da. and h. of Robert, 4th LORD GREY (of Rotherfield),'
note (g), delete all detail

page 125,
line 1, delete 'Rotherfield, Oxon'

page 129,
line 13, after 'SUDELEY' add 'and 1st BARON SUDELEY'
note (a), after 'm. 27.' add 'In an indenture between her and Thomas Deyncourt, dated 7 Mar. 1458, she is described as 'Alese, Lady Lovell and Deyncourt (*Hist. MSS. Com.*, De L'Isle Papers, vol. 1, 1925, p. 19.)

DEIVILLE

page 131,
line 2, for 'June 1242' read 'Jan. 1243/4'

page 132,
line 17, after '*d.*' add '*s.p.*' and after '(i)' add 'She *d.* about Apr. 1276' [*Cal. Inq. p.m.*, vol. 2, no. 196]

DELAMERE

page 137,
line 30, after 'Midx.' add 'ed. at Eton 1883–6; member of Legislative Council East African Protectorate'

page 138,
line 2, after '1914–' add '1918'
line 6, add at end 'He *m.* 2ndly, 28 May 1928, Gwladys Helen, 1st da. of Rupert Evelyn BECKETT and formerly wife of Sir Charles Markham, Bart. He *d.* 13 Nov. 1931. His widow *d.* 22 Feb. 1943.'
lines 7–8, delete all detail and replace as follows

IV. 1931. 4. THOMAS PITT HAMILTON (CHOLMONDELEY), BARON DELAMERE OF VALE ROYAL, 1st s. and h., *b.* 19 Aug. 1900 at Vale Royal. Ed. at Eton; *m.* 1stly, 14 June 1924, Phyllis Anne, 1st da. of Lord George William MONTAGUE-DOUGLAS-SCOTT, O.B.E., of Ancrum, Roxburghshire (she *d.* 1978). This marriage was diss. by divorce in 1944 and he *m.* 2ndly, 15 June 1944, Ruth Mary Clarisse, yr. da. of Wilfred William (ASHLEY), 1st and last BARON MOUNT TEMPLE and formerly wife of Capt. Alec Stratford CUNNINGHAM-REID and of Major Ernest Laurie GARDNER. This marriage was in turn diss. by divorce and he *m.* 3rdly, 26 Mar. 1955, Diana, yr. da. of Seymour CALDWELL of Hove, Sussex, formerly wife of Gilbert de Previle COLVILE, previously widow of Sir Henry John Delves BROUGHTON, Bart. He *d.* 13 Apr. 1979.

V. 1979. 5. HUGH GEORGE (CHOLMONDELEY), BARON DELAMERE OF VALE ROYAL, only s. and h. by 1st wife, *b.* 18 Jan. 1934; ed. at Eton and Cambridge (Magdalene Coll); *m.*, 11 Apr. 1964; Ann Willoughby, da. of Sir Patrick Muir RENNISON, G.C.M.G. of Mayfield, Sussex, formerly wife of Michael Patrick TINNÉ.

[THOMAS PATRICK GILBERT CHOLMONDELEY, s. and h. ap., *b.* 19 June 1968.]

DE LA WARR

page 151,
note (h), line 15, after 'amplius"' add '(the descent given in this *Inq. p.m.* is incorrect, it should read John s. of Richard (Griffin), s. of Elizabeth (Latimer, not Thomas Griffin), da. of Katherine (La Warr, not Warin Latimer), sister of John, father of Roger, father of Thomas. See also vol. vii, p. 457, note (b))'

page 153,
line 14, for 'Lisle' read 'widow of Gerard DE LISLE (s. and h. ap. of Warin, 2nd LORD LISLE), da. of Sir Michael DE LA POLE'

page 155,
lines 6–7, delete 'sometimes called'
line 7, after 'Margaret' add '*suo jure* BARONESS BOTREAUX'
line 8, delete 'sometimes called'
line 9, after 'widow' add '*m.* 2ndly, probably before 1 Nov. 1476, as his 2nd wife, Nicholas LEVENTHORP' [Marshall Kirk, *New Engl. Gen. and Hist. Reg.*, vol. 150, pp. 91–3]

page 156,
line 8, after '1513' add ', present at the Field of the Cloth of Gold'
line 13, after 'Eleanor,' add '3rd'
line 17, after 'widow' add '(who was *b. circa* 1476)'
line 20, after 'wife' add ', *b.* in Hampshire.(ca)'
note (ca) See note (d), below.
line 26, for 'a few years later' read 'in Mar. 1539/40' and for 'that service' read 'the surrender to the Crown of his wife's lands at Halnaker,'
line 27, after 'Etc.' add '(d)'
note (d) On 8 Nov. 1539 his wife wrote from Halnaker to Cromwell that she perceived from his letter that the King had forgiven her husband his offences. She adds that the King wishes to have "Halfnakyd" [Halnaker] and asks him to see that the land they shall have in exchange may be good. Ten days later Lord de la Warr writes that a valuation has been made of Halfnakyd, and expresses a wish to have the Nunnery of Horweld [*i.e.*, Wherwell], Hants, which stands "in exchange" (*L. and P. Hen. VIII*, vol. xiv, part 2, pp. 190–1). The grant of Wherwell is dated 24 Mar. (1539/40) 31 Hen. VIII (*Patent Roll*, part 4, m. 4) V.G.
line 33, for '1536' read '16 Jan. 1541/2'

page 160,
line 13, for 'Mary' read 'Katherine' [M.I., Westm. Abbey]

page 161,
line 3, after 'dies' add '(at Port le Have, Nova Scotia)' [N. Currer Briggs, *Geneal. Mag.*, vol. 18, 1976, p. 289]
lines 12–13, delete from '*d.*' to '1677)' and replace by 'She was living 17 Nov. 1676.' [P.R.O., Chancery Proceedings, C.8 893/87]
line 20, for 'da.' read 'only da. and h.' and for 'WILD read 'WILDE'
line 20, after '-Law' add ', by Anne, da. of Sir Thomas Harries, Bart. (*cr.* 1613) of Tong Castle, Salop.'

page 162,
line 5, after '1693.' add 'Ed. at Eton 1707.'

page 163,
line 10, for '1771' read '1767–94'
line 16, for '1771' read '1767–74'

page 165,
line 16, for 'was living 1915' read '*d.* at Easter Duddingstone, 19 July 1929.'
line 18, after 'Kensington.' add 'Ed. at Eton 1882–3'
line 25, for 'They were living 1915' read 'She *d.* 21 May 1953. He *d.* (as BARON JEFFREYS), 19 Dec. 1960.'
line 29, delete '*or* 1572],(b)'
line 34, after '1914–' add '1918'
note (b), delete all detail

page 166,
line 5, after 'actress.' add 'She *d.* 8 Aug. 1930.'
line 8, after 'adultery' add 'She *m.* as his 2nd wife, 18 Apr. 1922, at St. James Cath. Church, Spanish Place, John William DENNIS, M.P. for Deritend Division of Birmingham (who was *b.* 16 May 1865). He (Gilbert) *d.* of pneumonia at Messina, 16 Dec. 1915. She *d.* 1963.'
lines 9–11, delete all detail and replace as follows

EARLDOM. IX.
BARONY. XXIV. } 1915

9 and 14. HERBRAND EDWARD DUNDONALD BRASSEY (SACKVILLE), EARL DE LA WARR, &c., s. and h., by 1st wife, *b.* at Normanhurst, Sussex, 20 June, and *bap.* 9 Aug. 1900, at Withyam; *styled* LORD BUCKHURST till 1915; ed. at Eton and Oxford (Magdalen Coll.). He *m.*, 31 Dec. 1920, at St. Alban's Church, Brook Str., Holborn, Helena Diana, only surv. da. of Capt. Gerard LEIGH. She *d.* 29 Mar. 1966. He *m.* 2ndly, 1 Mar. 1968, Sylvia Margaret, D.B.E., da. of William HARRISON of Liverpool and widow of David Patrick Maxwell (FYFFE), 1st EARL OF KILMUIR. He *d.* 28 Jan. 1976. His widow *d.* 1992.

EARLDOM. X.
BARONY. XXV. } 1976

10 and 15. WILLIAM HERBRAND (SACKVILLE), EARL DE LA WARR, &c., s. and h., *b.* 16 Oct. 1921; ed. at Eton; *m.*, 18 May 1946, Anne Rachel, da. of Geoffrey Charles DEVAS, M.C., of Maidstone, Kent. He *d.* 9 Feb. 1988. His widow was still living 1995.

EARLDOM. XI.
BARONY. XXVI. } 1988

11 and 16. WILLIAM HERBRAND (SACKVILLE), EARL DE LA WARR, &c., 1st s. and h., *b.* 10 Apr. 1948; ed. at Eton; *m.*, 1978, Anne Pamela, 1st da. of Arthur Edmund LEVESON, O.B.E., of Ropley, Hants., formerly wife of Adrian John Charles (HOPE), EARL OF HOPETOUN.

[WILLIAM HERBRAND THOMAS SACKVILLE, *styled* LORD BUCKHURST, 1st s. and h. ap., *b.* 13 June 1979.]

DE L'ISLE AND DUDLEY OF PENSHURST

page 166,
line 26, after 'Eton' add '*circa* 1814–18'

page 167,
line 12, after 'Eton 'add '*circa* 1840–3'

line 27, for 'was living 1915' read '*d.* 3 Nov. 1926.'
line 30, after 'Place;' add 'ed. at Eton 1867–72 and Cambridge (Trin. Coll);'
line 30, for 'Capt.' read 'Major' and after 'Brigade' add 'retiring 1891'
note ([a]), (cont. from page 166), line 10, for 'H' read 'A'

page 168,
line 5, after '1861.' add 'He *d.* in London *s.p.*, 24, aged 69, and was *bur.* at Penshurst 28 Dec. 1922. Will pr. £66,008 gross. His widow *d.* 19 July 1958.'

IV. 1922. 4. ALGERNON (SIDNEY), BARON DE L'ISLE AND DUDLEY, br. and h., *b.* 11 June 1854. He *d.* unm. 18 Apr. 1945.

V. 1945. 5. WILLIAM (SIDNEY), BARON DE L'ISLE AND DUDLEY, br. and h., being 4th s. of the 2nd Baron, *b.* 19 Aug. 1859; *m.*, 5 Dec. 1905, Winifred Agneta Yorke, 2nd da. of Roland Yorke BEVAN. He *d.* 18 June 1945. His widow *d.* 11 Feb. 1959.

VI. 1945. 6. WILLIAM PHILIP (SIDNEY), BARON DE L'ISLE AND DUDLEY, s. and h., *b.* 23 May 1909; ed. at Eton and Cambridge (Magdalene Coll.). He was *cr.* VISCOUNT DE L'ISLE of Penshurst in the co. of Kent, 12 Jan. 1956 and *suc.* to the Baronetcy of Castle Goring on the death of his distant kinsman Sir Sidney Patrick SHELLEY, 25 July 1965. H *m.* 1stly, 8 June 1940, Jacqueline Corinne Yvonne, da. of John Standish Surtees Prendergast (VEREKER), Field Marshal, 6th VISCOUNT GORT. She *d.* 15 Nov. 1962 and he *m.* 2ndly, 24 Mar. 1966, Margaret Eldrydd, da. of Major Gen. Thomas Herbert SHOUBRIDGE, C.B., C.M.G., D.S.O., widow of Col. Wilfred Russell (BAILEY), 3rd BARON GLANUSK. He *d.* 5 Apr. 1991. His widow was still living 1995.

VISCOUNTCY. II. BARONY. VII. } 1991 2 and 7. PHILIP JOHN ALGERNON (SIDNEY), VISCOUNT DE L'ISLE, &c., s. and h. by 1st wife, *b.* 21 Apr. 1945; ed. at Tabley House; *m.*, 1980, Isobel Tresyllian, yst. da. of Sir Edmund Gerald COMPTON, G.C.B., K.B.E.

[PHILIP WILLIAM EDMUND SIDNEY, s. and h. ap., *b.* 2 Apr. 1985.]

DELORAIN

page 169,
line 23, for 'Fenwick' read 'FENWICKS'
line 24, for 'pr. 1740' read 'dat. 3 Aug. 1739, pr. 18 and 21 Feb. 1739/40'
line 26, after 'Midx.' add 'Both the Earl and Countess are *bur.* in the church of Great Haseley, Oxon.' and for 'pr. June 1794' read 'dat. 12 Jan. 1789, cod. 15 Apr. 1793, pr. 13 June 1794'

page 170,
line 8, after '([a])' add 'He was *bur.* in the church of Great Haseley, Oxon.'

DELVIN

page 173,
lines 5–6, delete from 'of' to 'of' and after 'Robert' add '(PRESTON)'
line 22, after 'Marian,' add '(fa)'
note (fa), She *m.* 2ndly, before 16 Feb. 1554/5, when they had pardon for alienating certain lands, Edward FitzSimon, of Dublin (*Cal. Pat. and Close Rolls* [I.], vol. i, p. 326). V.G.
line 24, after 'lands.' add 'He had pardon as "Richard Nugent Baron of Delven" 26 Sep. 1549, and in Dec. of that year was a member of the Irish Council. On 10 Nov. 1552 he had a grant from the Crown in consideration of his good and faithful service, of the Priory of the Holy Island in the Annaly, and of the late religious house of Granard of the same.' [*Cal. Pat. and Close Rolls* [I.], vol. i, p. 268. V.G.]

page 174,
line 1, after '*m.*' add 'shortly after 4 June 1543,(ax)'
note (ax) It appears from a letter of that date, by Sir Anthony St. Leger, that he was then aged 20 and unm., but as his eldest s. came of age in 1565, he must have been married soon after (*L. and P. Hen. VIII*, vol. xviii, part 1, p. 377). V.G.
line 1, after 'Navan,' add '(ay)'
note (ay) The statement that he married Elizabeth, widow of Thomas Nangle, appeared also in the 1st edition of this work, drawn from Lodge, but is possibly incorrect. Thomas Nangle was living 1561, *i.e.*, two years after the death of Lord Delvin who is supposed to have married his widow, but *d.* before 7 July 1562, when his s. and h., Patrick, had livery of his lands. It is possible that Elizabeth may have been not the widow, but the divorced wife of Nangle when Delvin married her; or it may be that Nangle married Delvin's widow and not *vice versa*, but in that case she was not the mother of Nangle's children. V.G.
line 21, after '1610,' add '(?1611),(e)'
note (e) The date of 1611 appears from a letter from the Privy Council for her surrender of certain lands, dated 27 Oct. 1610, and her surrender of the same is dated 15 Feb. 1610/1. [*Cal. Pat. and Close Rolls* [I.], 1–16 Jac. I, p. 191]

DE MAULEY

page 175,
line 16, after 'Midx.;' add 'ed. at Harrow;'

page 176,
line 8, after 'Eton' add '*circa* 1828–32'
line 21, after 'Unionist.' add 'He *d.* unm. suddenly, near Ramsbury, 13, and was *bur.* 24 Apr. 1918 at Little Faringdon, Berks.'

IV. 1918. 4. MAURICE JOHN GEORGE (PONSONBY), BARON DE MAULEY OF CANFORD, br. and h., *b.* 7 Aug. 1846; ed. at Oxford (Ch. Ch.); *m.*, 29 Dec. 1875, Madeleine, yst. da. of Thomas Charles (HANBURY-TRACY), 2nd BARON SUDELEY. She *d.* 28 Jan. 1938. He *d.* 15 Mar. 1945.

V. 1945. 5. HUBERT WILLIAM (PONSONBY), BARON DE MAULEY OF CANFORD, 2nd but 1st surv. s., *b.* 21 July 1878; *m.*, 11 Oct. 1920, Elgiva Margaret, da. of Cospatrick DUNDAS. He *d.* 13 Sep. 1962. His widow *d.* 1987.

VI. 1962. 6. GERALD JOHN (PONSONBY), BARON DE MAULEY OF CANFORD, 1st s. and h., *b.* 19 Dec. 1921; ed. at Eton and Oxford (Ch. Ch.); *m.*, 16 Nov. 1954, Helen Alice, da. of Charles William Sholto DOUGLAS, of Malmesbury, Wilts and widow of Lieut. Col. Brian Lynch Leslie Abdy COLLINS, O.B.E., M.C.

DE MONTALT

page 176,
line 34, after '1727' add ', in Dublin; ed. by Dr Thompson; adm. as a Fell. Com., aged 17, at Trin. Coll., Dublin, 4 Dec. 1744'

page 177,
line 10, for '10 June 1791' read '5 Dec. 1793'

DENBIGH

page 178,
line 2, for '7 Sep. 1534' read '1532 or 1533'

page 180,
line 25, after '2ndly,' add 'about Apr. 1673' and after 'da.' add 'and coh.[ba]'
note [ba] See *Hist. MSS. Com.*, Hastings MSS., part ii, p. 162, letter of Lucy, Dow. Countess of Huntingdon, and will of her sister, Elizabeth Carey, *P.C.C.* Hale 3.

page 182,
line 16, after 'Eton,' add '*circa* 1807–10'
line 29, after 'Eton,' add '*circa* 1836–40'

page 183,
line 1, after '*d.*' add '*s.p.*'
line 12, for '1662' read '1622'
line 18, after '1914–' add '1918' and after '*m.*' add '1stly'
line 22, after 'She' add 'who'
line 23, after 'Devon.' add '*d.* at Newnham Paddox afsd., 8, aged 59, and was *bur.* 11 Dec. 1919, at Newnham. He *m.* 2ndly, 12 Feb. 1928, in the Crypt Chapel at the Westm. Cath., Kathleen, yst. da. of Thomas Addis EMMET of New York. He *d.* 25 Nov. 1939. His widow *d.* 13 Feb. 1952.'

page 184,
lines 3–4, delete from 'Charles' to 'C.M.G.' and replace by 'John SOMERS-COCKS. He *d. v.p.* 10 Jan. 1937. His widow *d.* 6 May 1937.'

X. 1937. 10. WILLIAM RUDOLPH STEPHEN (FEILDING), EARL OF DENBIGH, &c., grandson and h., being 1st s. and h. of Rudolph Edmund Aloysius abovesaid, *b.* 17 Apr. 1912; Oratory Sch., Caversham, Reading, Berks.; *m.*, 17 May 1940, Verena Barbara, da. of William Edward PRICE of Cropston, Leicester and widow of Lieut. Col. Thomas Paget Fielding JOHNSON. He *d.* 31 Dec. 1966. His widow was still living 1995.

XI. 1966. 11. WILLIAM RUDOLPH MICHAEL (FEILDING), EARL OF DENBIGH, &c., only s. and h., *b.* 2 Aug. 1943; ed. at Eton; *m.*, 2 Sep. 1965, Caroline Judith Vivienne, da. of Lieut. Col. Geoffrey COOKE of Sunningdale, Berks.

[ALEXANDER STEPHEN RUDOLPH FEILDING, *styled* VISCOUNT FEILDING, s. and h. ap., *b.* 4 Nov. 1970.]

DENHAM OF DOVEDALE

page 184,
line 15, for 'and' read '1788–95; adm. 23 June 1796 as a pensioner'
line 17, after 'and,' add '23 June 1798,'

page 186,
line 3, after 'Eton,' add '1818 to *circa* 1822'

page 187,
line 4, after 'Bradford.' add 'She *d.* 2 June 1954. He *d.* 24 June 1954.'
lines 5–6, delete all detail and replace as follows

IV. 1954. 4. THOMAS (DENMAN), BARON DENMAN OF DOVEDALE [1834], s. and h., *b.* 2 Aug. 1905, at Paddockhurst, Worth, Sussex. Ed. at Eton and Cambridge (Trin. Coll.). He *d.* unm. 21 Mar. 1971.

V. 1971. 5. CHARLES SPENCER (DENMAN), BARON DENMAN OF DOVEDALE, also a Baronet [U.K. 1945], cousin and h., being 1st s. and h. of Richard Douglas DENMAN (*cr.* Baronet 1945, *d.* 22 Dec. 1957), by his 2nd wife May Radley, da. of James SPENCER of Greystoke, Penrith, which Richard was 2nd s. of Richard DENMAN, yr. br. of the 3rd Baron Denman. He was *b.* 7 July 1916; *m.*, 11 Sep. 1943, Sheila Ann, eldest twin da. of Col. Algernon Bingham Anstruther STEWART, D.S.O.

[RICHARD THOMAS STEWART DENMAN, 1st s. and h. ap., *b.* 4 Oct. 1946; ed. at Milton Abbey; *m.*, 1984, Lesley Jane, da. of John STEVENS of Hinckley, co. Leics.]

DERAMORE OF BELVOIR

page 188,
line 36, after 'Richmond.' add 'Ed. at Eton 1879–82'

page 189,
line 6, after '1884.' add 'She *d.* 26 Oct. 1901 and he *m.* 2ndly, 26 June 1907, Blanche Violet, 1st da. of Col. Philip SALTMARSHE of Saltmarshe, co. Yorks. He *d. s.p.m.* 1, at Heslington Hall, York, and was *bur.* 6 Apr. 1936 at Heslington. His widow *d.* 1972.'

IV. 1936. 4. GEORGE NICHOLAS (DE YARBURGH-BATESON), BARON DERAMORE OF BELVOIR, br. and h., *b.* 20 Nov. 1870. He *m.*, 12 Dec. 1900, at St. Nicholas, Coney Str., York, Muriel Katherine, yst. da. of Arthur GREY (formerly DUNSCOMBE), of Sutton Hall, Easingwold, Yorks. He *d.* 4 Nov. 1943. His widow *d.* 21 Mar. 1960.

V. 1943. 5. STEPHEN NICHOLAS (DE YARBURGH-BATESON), BARON DERAMORE OF BELVOIR, 1st s. and h., *b.* 18 May 1903; ed. at Harrow and Cambridge (St. John's Coll.); *m.*, 14 May 1929, Nina Marion, 1st da. of Alastair MACPHERSON-GRANT. He *d. s.p.m.* 23 Dec. 1964. His widow *d.* 1979.

VI. 1964. 6. RICHARD ARTHUR (DE YARBURGH-BATESON), BARON DERAMORE OF BELVOIR, br. and h., *b.* 9 Apr. 1911; ed. at Harrow and Cambridge (St. John's Coll.); *m.*, 28 Aug. 1948, Janet Mary, 1st da. of John WARE of Askham in Furness, co. Yorks.

DE RAMSEY OF RAMSEY ABBEY

page 189,
line 30, after 'Eton' add '1861–3'

page 190,
line 2, after 'She' add ', who'
line 3, after 'Midx.' add '*d.* suddenly at Haveringland Hall, near Norwich, 2, and was *bur.* 9 Dec. 1920 at Ramsey. He *d.* of pneumonia at 5 Belgrave Sq., 8 May 1925. Will pr. £144,610 gross, £100,600 net.'
line 7, after '1914–' add '1918'
line 11, after '1914,' add 'in London,'
line 12, after 'Ellen' add 'Harriet'
line 13, after '1884' add 'at Drumoland Castle, co. Clare. He *d.* 22, from illness contracted in WW1 and was *bur.* 26 Oct. 1915, at Ramsey Abbey. His widow *m.* 2ndly, 6 Mar. 1925, Nobile Riccardo ASSANTI.

III. 1920. 3. AILWYN EDWARD (FELLOWES), BARON DE RAMSAY OF RAMSEY ABBEY, grandson and h., being s. and h. of Coulson Churchill abovenamed, *b.* 16 Mar. 1910; ed. at Oundle; *m.*, 27 July 1937, Lilah Helen Suzanne, da. of Francis Anthony LABOUCHERE. She *d.* 1987. He *d.* 31 Mar. 1993.

IV. 1993. 4. JOHN AILWYN (FELLOWES), BARON DE RAMSAY OF RAMSEY ABBEY, 1st s. and h., *b.* 27 Feb. 1942; ed. at Winchester and Essex Coll. of Agric.; *m.* 1stly, 1973, Phyllida Mary, yr. da. of Philip Athelstan FORSYTH, of

Wickhambrook, Suffolk. This marriage was diss. by divorce in 1983 and he *m.* 2ndly, 1984, Alison Mary, 2nd da. of Sir Archibald BIRKMYRE, Bart.

[FREDDIE JOHN FELLOWES, 1st s. and h. ap. by 1st wife, *b.* 31 May 1978; ed. at Eton.]

DERBY

page 192,
line 4, for 'PEVERIL' read 'PEVEREL'
note ([e]), for 'PEVERIL' read 'PEVEREL'

page 193,
note ([e]), line 14, after 'Robert.' add 'It appears, however, that this whole charter is a fabrication by Vincent. Apart from giving the wrong name to the Earl, the charter is nearly identical to one of Robert de Stafford for Bordesley Abbey (Harl. Charter 56D.50, printed in *Staffs. Collections*, William Salt Soc., vol. ii, p. 259, *ex inform.* Lewis Loyd). This charter being the sole evidence for the marriage of Earl William, it now does not appear whom he did marry.

page 194,
line 1, after 'him,' add 'and *m.* 2ndly, Adam DE PORT, Lord of Basing, who *d.* 1213.' [See vol. x, Appendix G, pp. 96–7.]

page 196,
line 1, after 'Agnes' add '(?Alice)'

page 197,
line 10, for 'da. and' read '*suo jure* COUNTESS OF PEMBROKE, da. and eventually'
line 11, for '(DE CLARE)' read '(FITZGILBERT)'
line 14, for 'GALWEYE read 'GALLOWAY'

page 199,
line 44, for 'Nov.' read 'about Oct.' [See Leyburne.]

page 203,
line 26, after '([b])' add 'This John, who apparently had possession of Chartley, was summoned as Lord Ferrers (of Chartley) from 1298/9' [See vol. v, p. 307, *sub* FERRERS]
line 31, after 'have' add 'usually' and after 'Lancaster' add ', although he is known to have used the title Earl of Derby itself at least once'
note ([c]), line 2, after '108)' add 'In the Assize Roll 1059 (Yorks, m. 32, 8 Edw. I (1279/80)), appears the following: Edmundus Comes Derb. summonitus fuit ad respondendum domini Regis de placito quo warranto tenet Osingwad et Hoby que sunt de antiquo domenico corone domisie Regis' (*ex inform.* W. Pailly Baildon)

page 206,
line 3, for '1471–85' read '1472 until just before the coronation of Richard III (6 July

1483), and after 21 Sep. 1484, until the end of that reign' [Sutton and Hammond, *Coronation of Richard III*, 1983, pp. 251–2; Michael Jones, in Rosemary Horrox, *Richard III and the North*, 1986, p. 49, note 85]

note (e), line 6 (on page 207), for 'W.H.W.' read 'W.H.B.'

page 207,

line 7, after 'Alice,' add '*suo jure* COUNTESS OF SALISBURY'

line 9, for '1482 (before Nov.)' read 'before Oct. 1473' [See vol. x, p. 827, note (g).]

line 12, after 'da.' add 'and (eventually) h.'

page 208,

lines 11–12, for 'WIDVILLE' read 'WYDEVILL'

line 13, for '*suo jure*' read '*de jure suo jure* (according to modern doctrine)'

page 209,

line 4, after 'Mary,' add '*de jure suo jure* (according to modern doctrine), BARONESS BOTREAUX, HUNGERFORD and MOLEYNS,'

line 7, after 'date,' add '(aa)'

note (aa) The will mentions "Mr John Veysy Clerk Dean of the most honourable chapel" [*i.e.* St. George's, Windsor], who was appointed 28 Sep. 1515, and "Hugh Bishop of Exeter" who *d.* 25 June 1519, and the will must therefore have been made between these dates. (*ex inform.* R.M. Glencross)

line 9, after '1550.' add '(ba)'

note (ba) According to Dugdale's Visit. of Lancs., 1664 (Chetham Soc., vol. 88, p. 282) the widow of Thomas Stanley, 2nd Earl of Derby, married 2ndly, John Radcliffe, Lord FitzWalter, father of Robert, Earl of Sussex.

line 10, after '1550/1' add '[Will printed in *Hist. MSS Com.*, Hastings MSS., part 1, p. 315.]

note (a), after 'Garlickhithe.' add 'John Stowe, *Survey of London*, ed. C.L. Kingsford, 1908, vol. 2, p. 249. However, the indenture of covenant for the marriage of the Earl is dated 17 Dec. 1505, see *Hist. MSS. Com.*, Hastings MSS., part 1, p. 306. V.G.'

page 210,

note (b), line 9, after 'Derby.' add 'In a Report on the English nobility, which internal evidence shows to have been written between July and Nov. 1538, he is described as "The greatest of power and land, young, and a child in wisdom, and half a fool." (*L. and P. of Hen. VIII*, vol. xiii, part 2, p. 280)'

page 213,

line 2, after 'wife,' add 'clandestinely, in Russell House, Strand (disp. from the Archbishop 21 Oct. 1600)'

page 214,

line 5, for '65' read '81'

line 7, after '1607,' add '(ax)'

note (ax) This should possibly be 1606, because a letter dated 14 Feb. 1605/6 was written to

Lord Darcy appointing him proxy for the King for the christening of the Earl of Derby's son.

page 215,
line 3, after '(b)' add 'and was naturalised, taking the oath before the Lord Keeper 29 Jan. 1628/9'
line 16, after 'who' add 'was *b.* at Kreny in Denmark, and'

page 217,
line 14, for 'Hayton' read 'Huyton'
note (a), line 2, for 'Scaresbig' read 'Scaresbrick'

page 218,
line 10, after 'Eton' add '6 Sep. 1764–70'
line 11, after 'Cambridge' add 'as a Fell. Com. 1 Feb. and again as a nobleman 15 Dec.,'

pge 219,
line 11, after 'Eton' add '1789–92'
line 12, after 'Cambridge' add 'as a nobleman 4 July' and after '1792,' add 'matric. 1793,'

page 220,
line 3, after 'Eton' add '*circa* 1809–14'

page 221,
line 22, after 'Eton' add '1853–4'
line 44, for 'was living 1915' read '*d.*, in Upper Brook Str., 17, aged 82, and was *bur.* at Knowsley 21 Apr. 1922. Will pr. July 1922, £58,302 gross, net £53,340.'

page 222,
line 1, line to read as follows

XXVI. 1908. 17. EDWARD GEORGE VILLIERS (STANLEY), EARL OF DERBY, &c., 1st s. and h., *b.* 4 Apr. 1865, at 23 St. James Sq.; *styled* LORD STANLEY 1893–1908;

lines 18–19, delete from 'Having' to 'work' and replace by 'He *d.* 4 Feb. 1948. His widow *d.* 23 July 1957.'

[EDWARD MONTAGU CAVENDISH STANLEY, 1st s. and h. ap., *b.* 9 July 1894, at 36 Great Cumberland Place, Midx., *styled* LORD STANLEY; ed. at Eton and Oxford (Magdalen Coll.); *m.*, 17 July 1917, in the Guards Chapel, Wellington Barracks, Sybil, 1st da. of Henry Arthur (CADOGAN), *styled* VISCOUNT CHELSEA, by Mildred Cecilia Harriet, 3rd da. of Henry Gerard (STURT), 1st LORD ALINGTON. She was *b.* 7 Jan. 1893. He served in WW1 as a Lieut. 3rd Battn. Gren. Guards.(c) He *d. v.p.* 16 Oct. 1938. His widow *d.* 21 June 1969.]

XXVII. 1948. 18. EDWARD JOHN (STANLEY), EARL OF DERBY, &c., grandson and h., being 1st s. and h. of Edward Montagu Cavendish abovenamed. He was *b.* 21 July 1918; ed. at Eton and Oxford (Magdalen Coll.); *m.* 22 July 1948, Lady Isobel, yst. da. of Henry MILLES-LADE, sister of the 4th EARL SONDES. She *d.* 1990. He *d. s.p.* 21 Apr. 1994.

XXVIII. 1994. 19. EDWARD RICHARD WILLIAM (STANLEY), EARL OF DERBY, &c., nephew and h. male, being 1st s. and h. of Hugh Henry Montague STANLEY, (*d.* 1971), by Mary Rose, 2nd da. of Charles Francis BIRCH of Rhodesia, which Hugh was 3rd s. of the 17th Earl of Derby. He was *b.* 10 Oct. 1962; ed. at Eton and R.A.C. Cirencester.

note (c), lines 1–3, delete from 'His' to 'Guards'

DERWENT OF HACKNESS

page 223,
line 18, after 'Eton,' add '1841–5'
line 26, after '£21,000.' add 'He *d.* 1 Mar. 1916.'
line 27, line to read as follows

II. 1916. 2. FRANCIS (VANDEN-BEMPDE-JOHNSTONE), BARON DERWENT OF HACKNESS, 1st s. and h.,(c) *b.* 26 May 1851,

page 224,
line 3, for ']' read 'He *d. s.p.m.* at Hackness Hall, Scarborough, 20, and was *bur.* 23 Apr. 1929, at Hackness.'

III. 1929. 3. GEORGE HARCOURT (VANDEN-BEMPDE-JOHNSTONE), BARON DERWENT OF HACKNESS, nephew and h., being 2nd s. of Edward Henry V-B-J (*d.* 29 Apr. 1903), by Evelyn Mary, da. of Leopold George Frederick (AGAR-ELLIS), 5th VISCOUNT CLIFDEN, which Edward Henry was 2nd s. of the 1st Baron Derwent. He was *b.* 22 Oct. 1899; ed. at Charterhouse and Oxford (Merton Coll.); *m.*, 21 Dec. 1929, COMTESSE SABINE CZAYKOWSKA, da. of Gen. D. ILIESCO She *d.* 18 May 1941. He *d. s.p.* 12 Jan. 1949.

IV. 1949. 4. PATRICK ROBIN GILBERT (VANDEN-BEMPDE-JOHNSTONE), BARON DERWENT OF HACKNESS, br. and h., *b.* 26 Oct. 1901; ed. at Charterhouse and R.M.C., Sandhurst; *m.*, 7 Dec. 1929, Marie-Louise Henriette, da. of Albert PICARD of Paris, formerly wife of Brig. Philip Stafford MYBURGH, C.B.E., D.S.O., M.C. She *d.* 1985. He *d.* 2 Jan. 1986.

V. 1986. 5. ROBIN EVELYN LEO (VANDEN-BEMPDE-JOHNSTONE), BARON DERWENT OF HACKNESS, only s. and h., *b.* 30 Oct. 1930; ed. at Winchester and Oxford (Clare Coll.); *m.*, 12 Jan. 1957, Sybille Marie Louise, da. of VICOMTE DE SIMARD DE PITRAY, of Paris.

[FRANCIS PATRICK HARCOURT VANDEN-BEMPDE-JOHNSTONE, s. and h. ap., *b.* 23 Sep. 1965; ed. at Eton and Edinburgh; *m.*, 1990, Cressida, da. of Christopher BOURKE.]

note ([c]), line 1, after '1914–' add '1918'

DERWENTWATER

page 224,
line 11, for 'Wenby' read 'Whenby'

page 225,
line 5, after '3rdly' add '(by lic.)'
line 23, after 'h.' add ', *b.* about 1713'
line 28, for '1732' read '28 Jan. 1731/2'
note ([d]), line 1, before 'Anne' add 'Though this will was proved, John cannot have been 19 years of age when it was made if he was born in wedlock, which there is no reason to doubt, so it was clearly bad.'

page 226,
line 26, after '23' add 'and *bap.* 25'

DESART

page 227,
line 8, after 'London,' add '*b.* Apr. 14 1683 in Burntchurch, co. Kilkenny,'

page 228,
line 6, for '; ed. at' read 'in co. Kilkenny; adm. Trin. Coll.'
line 7, for 'Univ.' read '13 Aug. 1747'
line 28, after 'Clifton' add ', and was *bur.* in Clifton Old Churchyard'

page 229,
line 4, delete 'JOHN'
line 24, after 'Eton' add '1856–9'

page 230,
line 3, for 'was living 1916' read '*d.* 29 June 1933.'
line 19, after '1913' add 'and K.P. in 1919'
line 22, after 'She' add 'who'
line 23, after 'Hall' add ', *d.* at Hawkhurst Court Sussex, 19, and was *bur.* 23 Sep. 1927, at Kirdford Church, near Petworth. He *d. s.p.m.* 4, and was *bur.* 7 Nov. 1934, at Kirdford afsd. when all his honours became *extinct.*' [See vol. xiii, p. 104 for quotation from an obituary.]

DE SAUMAREZ

page 231,
line 25, for 'Kirkshill' read 'Creskeld [Kirskill]'
line 33, after 'Eton,' add '1853–6 and afterwards at'

line 38, after 'Ayr.' add 'She *d.* 17, and was *bur.* 20 Jan. 1933 at Barham, Suffolk. He *d.* at Saumarez, 25, aged 93, and was *bur.* 28 Apr. 1937.'

page 232,
line 1, line to read as follows

V. 1937. 5. JAMES ST. VINCENT BROKE (SAUMAREZ), BARON DE SAUMAREZ [1831], s. and h., *b.* 29 Nov. 1889

line 2, after 'Guernsey;' add 'ed. at Harrow and Cambridge (Trin. Coll.);'
line 5, for ']' read 'He *d.* 16 Jan. 1969. His widow *d.* 1985.'

[PHILIP ST. VINCENT SAUMAREZ, 1st s. and h. ap., *b.* 17 Nov. 1917. He *d.* unm. and *v.p.* 15 Dec. 1935.]

VI. 1969. 6. JAMES VICTOR BROKE (SAUMAREZ), BARON DE SAUMAREZ, 2nd but 1st surv s. and h., *b.* 28 Apr. 1924; ed. at Eton and Cambridge (Magdalene Coll.); *m.*, 28 Apr. 1953, Joan Julia, da. of Douglas Raymond CHARLTON of Holland-on-Sea, Essex. He *d.* 20 Jan. 1991. His widow was still living 1995.

VII. 1991. 7. ERIC DOUGLAS (SAUMAREZ), BARON DE SAUMAREZ, 1st (twin) s. and h., *b.* 13 Aug. 1956; ed. at Milton Abbey, Nottingham Univ. and R.A.C., Cirencester; *m.* 1stly, 1982, Christine Elizabeth, yr. da. of Bernard Neil HALIDAY, O.B.E. This marriage was diss. by divorce in 1990 and he *m.* 2ndly, 1991, Susan, da. of Joseph HEARN.

DESMOND

page 235,
note (d), line 9, for 'in 1287' read '18 July 1287 at Rathmore'

page 237,
line 1, for '1393' read '1293'

page 240,
lines 3–4, for 'FITZ MORICE of Kerry' read '(FITZ MAURICE), 2nd Baron of KERRY AND LIXNOR'

page 242,
line 6, for 'ROOS' read 'ROS' (twice)

page 244,
line 19, after 'ORMOND' add '[I.]'

page 247,
line 6, after '(b)' add 'On 27 Oct. 1447 he had an indult from Pope Nicholas V for a portable altar.'
line 16, after '*m.*' add '(disp. to *m.* though within the prohibited degrees, 22 Aug. 1455)'

note (f), line 1, before 'In' add 'The disp. of 1455 confirms the corrections of her Christian name and parentage as given in the text, which differ from those in the 1st edition of this work.'

page 248,
line 1, after '(a)' add 'With the Lords Killeen and Kildare and others he founded a fraternity of St. Nicholas in 1465' [See vol. vii, p. 250, *sub* Killeen.]

page 251,
line 23, after '1538/9.' add '(f)'
note (f) In this petition he alleges that his cousin James FitzMaurice, the 12th Earl, was a bastard, as there had been no lawful marriage between his parents Maurice and Joan abovenamed. V.G.
note (c), after 'counsell."' add 'He was at the English Court 20 July 1538 when the Earl of Ormond wrote that "the young man now with the King is never likely to come by his inheritance" owing to the power which his successor in title, James of Desmond, had acquired from the support of the Lord Deputy (Lord Leonard Grey, Viscount Grane).'

page 252,
line 4, after 'authorities,' add 'in Mar. 1537/8,(ba) and had pardon for all offences, 17 July 1540,'
note (ba) "James FitzJohn of Desmond has taken oath of obedience." Letter from William Wise, in Dublin, to the Lord Privy Seal (Cromwell), 26 Mar. 1538. V.G.
note (e), line 3, after 'Mary).' add 'A similar grant to "Donald M'Cartie, otherwise called Lord M'Cartie More and Lady Ellene M'Cartie, daughter of the said Donald and [who is] the Countess of Desmond" is dated 12 Feb. 1555/6' (*Cal. Pat. and Close Rolls* [I.], vol. i, p. 340).

page 253,
line 30, after 'pension' add 'of £200 *p.a.* early in that year,(f)'
note (f) On 10 Feb. 1585/6 she wrote from Dyryloskaubath to Burghley and Walsingham setting forth the miserable poverty of himself and 5 children.
line 31, after 'clothes."' add 'On 8 Feb. 1597/8 she had pardon.'

page 257,
line 11, after '*d. s.p.m.*' add 'intestate'

DESPENCER

page 261,
line 17, after '*d.* ' add '*s.p.*'

page 265,
line 16, after '*d.* ' add '*s.p.m.*'

page 273,
line 12, after 'Katherine,' add 'yst.' and for 'GRANDSON' read 'GRANDISON'

line 13, for 'GRANDSON' read 'GRANDISON'

page 274,
note (e), line 10, for '(co. Bucks.)' read '(co. Hants.)'

page 275,
line 6, after 'dine' add 'afsd'

page 281,
line 12, delete 'in 1420'
note (f), line 2, delete 'anno domini 1420' [This phrase is part of the next entry, *ex inform.* Dr Rosemary Horrox.]

page 282,
line 7, for '7 Oct.' read 'by 16 Apr.' [*Cal. Pat. Rolls, 1413–16*, p. 192, *ex inform.* Dr Rosemary Horrox]

page 284,
line 26, after 'Eton,' add '1725'

page 287,
note (c), lines 17–18, delete from 'It' to 'that' and for 'the' read 'The'
lines 18–19, delete from 'or' to 'was' and replace by 'of Simon'

page 291,
line 3, for 'ROOS' read 'ROS' (twice)

page 292,
line 16, after 'of' add 'Fen'

page 293,
line 3, for 'MOUNTAGUE' read 'OF MONTAGU'

DE TABLEY

page 295,
line 3, after 'in' add 'the apartment of her father at'
line 9, after 'who' add 'was *b.* 17 July 1802, and'
note (b), line 3, delete from ', and' to 'GREY'

page 296,
line 2, after '-BARRY,' add 'of Marbury Hall, Cheshire, and Fota Island, co. Cork (*d.* 1857)'
line 11, for '1848–54' read '1847–51'
line 14, for 'Peever' read 'Peover'

DEVEREUX

page 298,
line 20, after '*d.* ' add '*s.p.m.*'

page 300,
line 6, for 'sometimes called' read '3rd'

page 301,
line 2, for 'sometimes called' read '5th'

DE VESCI

page 307,
line 5, for 'ed. at the Univ. of Dublin' read 'adm. Trin. Coll., Dublin, 2 June 1753'
line 15, after 'Dublin;' add 'ed. Harrow; adm. Trin. Coll., Dublin, 13 Oct. 1788, aged 17;'
note (b), line 1, delete from 'See' to 'for' and replace by 'See DE TABLEY for comments and a reference to'

page 308,
line 8, after 'Midx.' add '; ed. at Eton 1858–1;'
line 10, after '1876;' add 'served in the Egyptian Campaign 1882;'
lines 18–19, delete from '(c)' to 'work' and replace by 'see below.'
line 21, for 'was living 1916' read '*d.* 18 June 1939.'

V. 1903. 5. IVO RICHARD (VESEY), VISCOUNT DE VESCI OF ABBEY LEIX, &c., nephew and h., being the 2nd s. of Capt. Eustace VESEY (d. 18 Nov. 1886), by Constance Mary, 3rd da. of Beilby Richard (LAWLEY), 2nd BARON WENLOCK, which Eustace was 2nd s. of the 3rd Viscount de Vesci. He was *b.* 15 Dec. 1881; served in WW1 as Capt. Irish Guards. He *m.* 1stly, 24 Apr. 1906, Georgiana Victoria, da. of Gerald Edward WELLESLEY. This marriage was diss. by divorce in 1919 (she *d.* 22 Apr. 1930) and he *m.* 2ndly, 15 May 1920, Francis Lois, 2nd da. of Sir Cecil Edmund LISTER-KAYE, Bart. and widow of William Edward (PARSONS), 5th EARL OF ROSSE. He *d. s.p.* 16 Aug. 1958. His widow *d.* 1984.

VI. 1958. 6. JOHN EUSTACE (VESEY), VISCOUNT DE VESCI OF ABBEY LEIX, &c., nephew and h., being s. and h. of Lieut. Col. Thomas Eustace VESEY (*d.* 1 Feb. 1946), by Cecily Kathleen, da. of Valentine Charles (BROWNE), 5th EARL OF KENMARE, which Thomas Eustace was 4th s. of the 3rd Viscount de Vesci. He was *b.* 25 Feb. 1919; ed. at Eton and Cambridge (Trin. Coll.); *m.*, 20 May 1950, Susan Anne, da. of Ronald Owen Lloyd ARMSTRONG-JONES, M.B.E., Q.C., of Llanwnda, Caernarvon. He *d.* 13 Oct. 1983. His widow *d.* 1986.

VII. 1983. 7. THOMAS EUSTACE (VESEY), VISCOUNT DE VESCI OF ABBEY LEIX, &c., s. and h., *b.* 8 Oct. 1955; ed. at Eton and Oxford (Univ. Coll.); *m.*, 1987, Sita-Maria Arabella, da. of Brian DE BREFFNY, of Castletown Cox, co. Kilkenny.

[DAMIAN BRIAN JOHN VESEY, 1st s. and h. ap., *b.* 1985.]

note (c), lines 1–2, delete from 'Ivo' to 'Guards'

DEVON

page 313,
line 1, after 'Reynold' add 'DE DUNSTANVILLE'
line 2, for '. . .' read 'Beatrice'

page 315,
line 10, delete 'and h.' and for 'DE BEAUMONT' read 'DE DUNSTANVILLE'
line 11, after 'Reynold,' add 'DE DUNSTANVILLE'

page 323,
line 16, delete '[LORD LE DESPENSER]'

page 324,
line 12, after '1345' add '(?1340)' [See G.W. Watson, *Genealogist,* N.S., vol. xxxiv, p. 29.]
line 20, after 'lands.' add 'He attended the tournament held at Lichfield, 9 Apr. 1347, as one of the knights of the King's Chamber.' [P.R.O., E 101 Wardrobe Acts, 21–3 Edw. III, 391/15, *ex inform.* John Brownbill]
line 22, for '1314/5' read '27 Sep. 1314'

page 325,
line 5, after 'Elizabeth' add 'da. of John (DE VERE or VEER), Earl of Oxford, by Maud, widow of Robert FITZPAYN and 2nd da. of Bartholomew LORD BADLESMERE'
line 6, for '23 Sep.' read 'Aug. or Sep.'
line 18, for 'da.' read '*suo jure* COUNTESS OF KENT, da. and (eventually) h.'
note (c), delete all detail and replace by 'For her 2nd and 3rd marriages, see Mowbray, vol. ix, p. 383.'

page 326,
line 2, after '1419' add ', pr. 1419' [Lambeth Wills, 328 Chichele]
line 10, after 'Alienor,' add 'yr and (eventually) coh.'
line 11, after '1413/4' add 'but was presumably dead by 1425 when Richard Duke of York, the s. of her sister Anne became the Mortimer heir'
line 26, for '1422/3' read '1432/3' [R. Griffiths, *Henry VI,* 1981, p. 92, note 92]

page 327,
line 1, after 'da.' add 'and (eventually) coh.'
line 5, after '(1466–7)' add 'his widow *d.* Nov. 1449. She is probably *bur.* in Colyton Church, Devon.' [Lady Radford, *Trans. Devon Assoc.*, vol. 67, 1935, p. 294. Thanks are due to Professor Lorraine Attreed for drawing my attention to this reference; *Arch.*, vol. 48, 1884, pp. 157–64.]
line 12, for '*d.* unm.' read '*m.* after 9 Sep. 1456, Marie, illegit. da. of Charles, COUNT OF MAINE, br. of René, DUKE OF ANJOU, (also KING OF JERUSALEM etc.), s.

of Louis II, DUKE OF ANJOU by Yolande, da. of JOHN, KING OF ARAGON. She was still living 1470.[ax] He *d.s.p.*

note [ax] See Ralph Griffiths, *The Reign of King Henry VI*, 1981, p. 802 and note 175 and *King and Country*, 1991, p. 25. She is said to have been married by 1470 to the Seigneur d'Auricher. This may possibly be a corruption of Lord Devonshire. See *Les Valois*, by Patrick Kerrebrouck, *et al.*, 1990, p. 317 and note 28 (for her living 1470). She is probably the 'Countasse of Devonshire' referred to by Warkworth (*Chronicle*, p. 19), as being captured with Queen Margaret (her cousin) after the battle of Tewkesbury in 1471. Thanks are due to Professor Griffiths for discussing this matter with me.

page 328,

lines 31–2, for 'between May 1471 and Aug. 1472' read '5 May 1471, after the battle of Tewkesbury' *{Paston Letters,* James Gairdner (ed.), vol. 3, 1875; *Cal. Pat. Rolls, 1467–77,* p. 374}

page 330,

line 9, for '(WYDEVILLE)' read '(WYDEVILL), 1st EARL RIVERS,'

line 39, after '1525' add '–38'

page 331,

line 12, after 'therein.' add '[aa]'

note [aa] In a report on the English nobility, which internal evidence shows to have been written between July and Nov. 1538, he is still being stated to be "36, lusty and strong of power, specially beloved, diseased often with the gout, and next unto the Crown of any man in England." *(L. and P. Hen. VIII*, vol. xiii, part 2, pp. 279–80)

line 15, for 'being taken prisoner' read 'having, with Lord Montagu, been imprisoned in the Tower 4 Nov.'

line 22, after '*s.p.*' add '[ca]'

note [ca] According to a letter of Lord Lisle to Cromwell in 1538, "she died or she came to the age of 14" *(L. and P. Hen. VIII*, vol. xiii, part 1, p. 119)

line 26, for 'years, but her' read 'months, but had pardon for all offences committed before 1 July 1539, on 21 Dec. 1539. On 22 Mar. 1539/40, 31 Hen. VIII, she had an annuity of £163 15*s* 11*d* from her late husband's lands. On 10 Apr. 1540 her release from the Tower was anticipated shortly.[cb]

note [cb] *Patent Rolls,* part 7, m. 21; part 5, m. 21. On 10 Apr. 1540 Marillac, the French Ambassador, wrote from London to Montmorency that they say she will soon come out of the Tower, though her s. and the nephew of Cardinal Pole are to remain lest they should some day trouble the Crown. *(L. and P. Henry VIII,* vol. xv, p. 207). V.G.

line 27, after 'Waiting' add 'in 1555'

note [b], line 2, after 'Cornwall.' add 'The ceremony of his degradation took place at Windsor, 15 Dec. 1538. V.G.'

note [d], after 'young' add ', by 6 Mar. 1527–8. See Will of Cecill (Gray), Marquess Dorset where his br. Edward is called Lord Courtney' (*P.C.C.* 22 Jankyn)

page 332,

line 24, for '1644' read '1644/5'

page 337,
line 10, for 'da.' read 'yr. of the 2 daughters'

page 338,
line 21, delete from 'He' to 'work'
after line 34 add as follows

XXXIII. 1904. 24. CHARLES PEPYS (COURTENAY), EARL OF DEVON, grandson and h., being s. and h. of Henry Reginald and Evelyn abovenamed, *b.* 14 July 1870; served in WW1(b) as Major, Devonshire Regt., relinquishing his commission 24 Mar. 1915. He *d.* unm. at Powderham, 4, and was *bur.* there 8 Feb. 1927.

XXXIV. 1927. 25. HENRY HUGH (COURTENAY), EARL OF DEVON, br. and h., *b.* 1 Aug. 1872. Clerk in Holy Orders. He *d.* unm. at Powderham, 8, and was *bur.* there 13 Feb. 1935.

XXXV. 1935. 26. FREDERICK LESLIE (COURTENAY), EARL OF DEVON, br. and h., *b.* 31 Aug. 1875; ed. at Oxford (Exeter Coll.); Clerk in Holy Orders; *m.*, 9 Jan. 1907, Marguerite, da. of John SILVA, of Itchen Abbas, co. Hants. He *d.* at Windsor 19 June 1935. His widow *d.* 4 May 1950.

XXXVI. 1935. 27. CHARLES CHRISTOPHER COURTENAY (COURTENAY), EARL OF DEVON, 2nd but 1st surv. s. and h., *b.* 13 July 1916; ed. at Winchester and R.M.C., Sandhurst; *m.*, 29 July 1939, Sybil Venetia, da. of Capt. John Vickris TAYLOR of North Aston Manor, co. Oxford.

[HUGH RUPERT COURTENAY, s. and h. ap., *styled* LORD COURTENAY, *b.* 5 May 1942; ed. at Winchester and Oxford (Magdalen Coll.); m., 1967, Diana Frances, da. of Jack WATHERSTON of Jedburgh, Roxburghshire.]

note (b), lines 1–2, delete from 'Charles' to '1915.'

DEVONSHIRE

page 340,
line 4, after 'da.' add 'and coh.(aa)' and after 'KEIGHLEY, add 'of Inskip, co. Lancs. and'
note (aa) The other coh., Catherine, *m.* Thomas Worsley of Bootle, co. Lancs. On the partition Keighley was allotted to the Cavendish share.
line 5, after 'CARUS' add 'of Kirby Lonsdale, Westmorland,' [Chetham Soc., vol. 81, p. 60]
line 6, after '1566.' add 'She d. in Feb. 1598 and was *bur.* at Ault Hucknall, co. Derby. M.I.'
note (b), line 1, after 'Cavendish,' add 'who *d. v.p.* and unm. in Jan. 1617/18,'

page 344,
line 13, after '1707–10;' add 'he took his seat 23 Oct. 1707;'

page 347,
line 2, after '1stly' add 'by spec. lic.;'
line 4, for '1757' read 'and *bap.* 12 July 1757 at Wimbledon'

page 348,
note ([a]), line 13, after 'friendships."' add 'As the Duke's mistress, she bore him two illegit. children in his first wife's lifetime. They were known as Caroline and Augustus Clifford, of whom the latter became a Capt. R.N. and married, 20 Oct. 1813, Elizabeth, 2nd da. of Lord John Townshend. In 1811 Capt. Clifford, when quartered at Portsmouth, was foolish enough to claim the precedence of a Duke's son.

page 350,
line 6, for 'Holkar' read 'Holker'

page 351,
lines 8–9, delete from 'He' to 'work'

DUKEDOM IX. EARLDOM XIII. } 1908 — 9 and 12. VICTOR CHRISTIAN WILLIAM (CAVENDISH), DUKE OF DEVONSHIRE, &c., nephew and h., being 1st s. of Lieut. Col. Edward CAVENDISH (*d.* 18 May. 1891), by Emma Elizabeth, 4th da. of the Rt. Hon. William LASCELLES, which Edward was 3rd s. of the 7th Duke of Devonshire. He was *b.* 31 May 1868; ed. at Cambridge (Trin. Coll.); *m.*, Lady Evelyn, da. of Henry Charles Keith (FITZMAURICE), 5th MARQUESS OF LANSDOWNE. He *d.* 6 May 1938. His widow *d.* 2 Apr. 1960.

DUKEDOM X. EARLDOM XIV. } 1938 — 10 and 13. EDWARD WILLIAM SPENCER (CAVENDISH), DUKE OF DEVONSHIRE, &c., 1st s. and h., *b.* 6 May 1895; he served in WW1([b]) as Lieut. Derbyshire Yeomanry; A.D.C. Personal Staff; K.G. He *m.*, 21 Apr. 1917, at St. Etheldreda's Church, Hatfield, Herts, Mary Alice, yr. of the 2 daughters of James Edward Herbert (GASCOYNE-CECIL) MARQUESS OF SALISBURY, by Cecily Alice, 2nd da. of Arthur Saunders William Fox (GORE) 5th EARL OF ARRAN. He *d.* 26 Nov. 1950. His widow, who was *b.* 29 July 1895, *d.* 1988.

[WILLIAM JOHN ROBERT CAVENDISH, *styled* MARQUESS OF HARTINGTON, 1st s. and h. ap., *b.* 10 Dec. 1917, at 29 Arlington Str., S.W.; ed. at Eton; *m.*, 6 May 1944, Kathleen, 2nd da. of Joseph P. Kennedy, U.S. Ambassador at the Court of St. James. He *d. v.p. s.p.*, being k. in action in Belgium, 10 Sep. 1944. His widow d. in a flying accident in France 13 May 1948.]

DUKEDOM XI. EARLDOM XV. } 1950 — 11 and 14. ANDREW ROBERT BUXTON (CAVENDISH), DUKE OF DEVONSHIRE, &c., 2nd and only surv. s. and h., *b.* 2 Jan. 1920; ed. at Eton and Cambridge (Trin. Coll.); *m.*, 19 Apr. 1941, Deborah Vivien, yst. da. of David Bertram Ogilvy (FREEMAN-MITFORD), 2nd BARON REDESDALE.

[PEREGRINE ANDREW MORNY CAVENDISH, *styled* MARQUESS OF HARTINGTON, 2nd and 1st surv. s. and h., *b.* 27 Apr. 1944; ed. at Eton and Oxford (Exeter Coll.); m., 28 June 1967, Amanda Carmen, da. of Cmdr. Edward HEYWOOD-LONSDALE, R.N.]

note ([b]), lines 1–3, delete from 'Victor' to 'Staff.'

page 352,
line 8, for 'Holkar' read 'Holker' and for 'Westmorland' read 'co. Lancaster'

DIGBY

page 352,
line 21, for '9 June 1641' read '3 Nov. 1640'

page 353,
line 15, after 'Co.' add '11 May'

page 356,
lines 25–30, for 'Melbury, Lampford' read 'Melbury Sampford'
line 40, for 'She' read 'He *d.* 11 May 1920. His widow, who'
line 41, after 'Kensington' add ', *d.* at a nursing home 28 Nov. and was *bur.* at Minterne co. Dorset, 1 Dec. 1928.

page 357,
lines 1–3, delete all detail and replace as follows

BARONY. VIII. BARONY. XI. } 1920 — 5 and 11. EDWARD KENELM (DIGBY), BARON DIGBY OF SHERBOURNE, &c., 1st s. and h., *b.* 1 Aug. 1894, at 39 Belgrave Sq., Midx. He served in WW1, 1914–18 as Lieut. in the Coldstream Guards.([a]) He *m.*, 1 July 1919, Constance Pamela Alice, yst. da. of Henry Campbell (BRUCE), 2nd BARON ABERDARE. He *d.* 29 Jan. 1964. His widow *d.* 1978.

BARONY. IX. BARONY [I.]. XII. } 1964 — 6 and 12. EDWARD HENRY KENELM (DIGBY), BARON DIGBY OF SHERBOURNE, &c., only s. and h., *b.* 24 July 1924; *m.*, 18 Dec. 1952, Dione Marian, yr. da. of Rear Adm. Robert St. Vincent SHERBROOKE, V.C., C.B., D.S.O., of Oxton Hall, co. Notts.

[HENRY NOEL KENELM DIGBY, 1st s. and h. ap., *b.* 6 Jan. 1954; ed. at Eton; *m.*, 1980, Susan, da. of Peter WATTS.]

DILLON

page 361,
note ([b]), line 9, after 'gentlemen.' add '(*The Jerningham Letters*, vol. i, pp. 365–6. The wording and capitalisation of the quotation is not entirely accurate, although only in minor matters.)'

page 363,
line 10, after '*m.*' add '1stly'
line 12, after 'She' add 'who'
line 13, after 'Canada' add ', *d.* at Ditchley, 6 June 1925. He *m.* 2ndly, at St. Martin-in-the-Fields, 15 June 1926, Margaret Louisa Everard, da. of the Rev. Henry Edward Browne FFOLKES and widow of the Rev. John Erasmus PHILLIPS. He

d. s.p.m.s. at Ditchley, 18, and was bur. 22 Dec. 1932 at Enstone. His widow *d.* 12 July 1954.'

line 20, add at end 'This marriage was diss. by divorce in 1912 and he *m.* 2ndly, 9 Sep. 1913, Kathleen Clare, 2nd da. of James AITCHISON of Strathavon, Lanarkshire. He *d. v.p. s.p.m.* 7, at Boulogne, and was *bur.* 10 Feb. 1923 at Enstone, Oxford. His widow *m.* 2ndly, 1924, Lieut. Cmdr. Robert Francis LEE-DILLON, R.N. (*d.* 24 Feb. 1954) and *d.* 29 Dec. 1950.

XVIII. 1932. 18. ARTHUR HENRY (LEE-DILLON), VISCOUNT DILLON OF COSTELLO GALLEN, nephew and h., being 1st s. and h. of Conrad Adderley DILLON (*d.* 4 Nov. 1901), by Ellen Tousia, 1st da. of Sir Henry William DASHWOOD, Bart., which Conrad was 2nd s. of the 16th Viscount Dillon. He was *b.* 5 Jan. 1875; *m.*, 5 Jan. 1907, Hilda, 3rd da. of the Rt. Hon. Sir John Tomlinson BRUNNER, Bart. and widow of Charles Harold BROADBENT. He *d. s.p.* in Oxford 25 May 1934. His widow *d.* 23 May 1966.

XIX. 1934. 19. ERIC FITZGERALD (DILLON), VISCOUNT DILLON OF COSTELLO GALLEN, br. and h., *b.* 4 Apr. 1981; *m.*, 4 June 1907, Nora Juanita Muriel, da. of Brig. Gen. Charles Edward BECKETT, C.B., of Dewlish, Dorchester. He *d.* 6 Apr. 1946. His widow *d.* 9 Sep. 1962.

XX. 1946. 20. MICHAEL ERIC (DILLON), VISCOUNT DILLON OF COSTELLO GALLEN, only s. and h., *b.* 13 Aug. 1911; ed. at Eton and R.M.C., Sandhurst; *m.*, 4 Dec. 1939, Irène Marie France, yr. da. of René Merandon DU PLESSIS of Whitehall. Mauritius. He *d.* 30 Nov. 1979. His widow was still living 1995.

XXI. 1979. 21. CHARLES HENRY ROBERT (DILLON), VISCOUNT DILLON OF COSTELLO GALLEN, 1st s. and h., *b.* 18 Jan. 1945; ed. at Downside; *m.*, 1972, Mary Jane, da. of John YOUNG of Birtle, co. Lancs. He *d.* 15 Sep. 1982. His widow was still living 1995.

XXII. 1982. 22. HENRY BENEDICT CHARLES (DILLON), VISCOUNT DILLON OF COSTELLO GALLEN, only s. and h., *b.* 6 Jan. 1973.

DINEVOR

page 364,

line 27, after '*d. s.p.m.*' add '*s.*'

line 34, for 'Pendoyton' read 'Pendoylan'

line 39, after 'Denbigh.' add '(a)'

note (a) It seems possible that the wife of Robert Wilson was in fact an illegit. half-sister of Cecil, Baroness Dinevor. See *Surprising Life and Adventures of Mary Anne Talbot, otherwise John Taylor*, "as narrated by herself to the Editor of the Scientific Museum", pub. by Robert S. Kirby in his *Wonderful Museum*, 1804, also M.M. Dowie (ed.), *Women Adventurers*, 1893.

page 366,

line 10, line to read as follows

VII. 1911. 7. WALTER FITZURYAN (RICE, *later* RHYS), BARON DINEVOR, only s. and h., b. 17 Aug. 1873; ed. at Eton 1887–92;

lines 17–18,delete from 'Having' to 'work' and replace by 'He *d.* 8 June 1956. His widow *d.* 1 Apr. 1959.'

VIII. 1956. 8. CHARLES ARTHUR URYAN (RHYS), BARON DINEVOR, 1st s. and h., *b.* 21 Sep. 1899; ed. at Eton and R.M.C., Sandhurst; *m.*, 29 Sep. 1934, Hope Mary Woodbine, da. of Charles Woodbine PARISH and formerly wife of Capt. Arthur Granville SOAMES. He *d.* 15 Sep. 1962. His widow *d.* 1980.

IX. 1962. 9. RICHARD CHARLES URYAN (RHYS), BARON DINEVOR, only s. and h., *b.* 19 June 1935; ed. at Eton and Cambridge (Magdalene Coll.); *m.*, 7 Jan. 1959, Lucy Catherine King, da. of Sir John Knewstub Maurice ROTHENSTEIN, C.B.E., of Newington, Warborough, co. Oxford.

[HUGO GRIFFITH URYAN RHYS, s. and h. ap., *b.* 19 Nov. 1966.]

DINGWALL

page 367,
line 30, after '*d. s.p.m.*,' add 'intestate,'

page 369,
line 12, after 'Earl' add 'and, subsequently, see LUCAS OF CRUDWELL, Barony [E.]'

DINHAM

page 374,
line 13, for 'MOELES' read 'MOELS [4th LORD MOELS]'

page 376,
line 9, after 'Alianore,' add 'said to be'

page 377,
line 13, for 'Eythorpe' read 'Eythrope'

page 379,
line 30, after 'Elizabeth,' add '*de jure suo jure* (according to modern doctrine) BARONESS FITZWALTER'

page 380,
line 2, delete 'sometimes called'
line 3, for 'his wife' read 'da. of Sir John CHIDIOK of Chideok, Dorset [5th LORD FITZPAYN]'
line 5, after '2ndly,' add '(lic. 26 Mar. 1488)' [Lambeth, Morton 1, f. 13]
line 6, for 'BROOK' read 'WILLOUGHBY DE BROKE'

page 381,
line 12, after 'Moone):' add 'she *m.* 3rdly, before 10 Jan. 1506/7, as 2nd wife, Sir Thomas Brandon, K.G., of Duddington, Northants, who *d.* 27 Jan., and was *bur.* 29 Jan. 1509/10 in the Church of the Black Friars by Ludgate' [See also vol. v, p. 510.]
line 14, after 'Zouche' add 'of '(Harringworth)'

page 382,
note (b), line 21, after 'Dynaunt"' add 'The 1283 visit was held to be vital to the petitioners case because it was agreed for him that the meeting at Shrewsbury was a trial of David ap Griffiths as a peer by his fellow peers, and that therefore a summons to that trial proved the recipient to be a peer.'

DINORBEN

page 383,
line 12, after 'unm.' add 'of epilepsy, to fits of which he had been subject,'
line 18, after 'ALBANY' add '[S.]'
line 27, for 'STRATHERNE' read 'STRATHEARN'

DOCKWRA

page 387,
line 10, delete from 'was' to '1568.' and replace by '2nd s. of Edmund D. of Thatcham, Berks, by Dorothy, da. of John GOLDING, of Belchamp St. Paul, Essex; *bap.* 30 Apr. 1564 at Thatcham.'
note (a), line 4, for 'before 1642' read '22 Sep. 1634'

page 388,
line 2, after '1627.' add 'On 4 Aug. 1628 he had a grant as an undertaker of 2747 acres in the territory of Ranelagh, co. Wicklow.'
line 3, after 'Derwent' add ', co. York, by Anne only da. of Sir Thomas BOYNTON of Barmston in Holderness'
line 5, after '[I.].' add '(aa)'
note (aa) Richard, 1st Earl of Cork, in a letter to Lord Dorchester, dated 28 June 1631, refers to her as "this noble distressed lady, the widow of the lord Docwra . . . who served long and died very poor". See *Cal. S. P.* [I.], vol. 252, no. 83. V.G.

DONEGALL

page 392,
line 24, after '[I.]' add 'by Elizabeth da. of Francis Lumley of Passage, co. Waterford'
note (c), line 1, before '"The' add 'Between 1795 and the date of the marriage there was no Private Act or entry in the Lords' Journals referring to the marriage.' [*ex inform.* R.M. Glencross]

page 393,
line 17, after '(c)' add 'on 12 June 1845 the Earl of Shaftesbury reported from the Committee for Privileges that George Hamilton, Marquess of Donegal had made out his claim as a Temporal Peer of Ireland.'
line 24, after 'K.C.B.,' add '(*d.* 1 Aug. 1858),'

page 394,
line 14, after 'Dublin,' add '27 Dec. 1820,'

page 395,
line 3, after '*nil.*(a)' add 'His widow *d.* 8 Oct. 1952.'
lines 4–7, delete all detail and replace as follows

MARQUESSATE [I.] VI. EARLDOM [I.] X. } 1904

6 and 10. EDWARD ARTHUR DONALD ST. GEORGE HAMILTON (CHICHESTER), MARQUESS OF DONEGALL, &c., only s. and h., by 3rd wife, *styled* EARL OF BELFAST till 1904, *b.* 7 Oct. 1903, at 11 Ovington Sq., Chelsea; his father than aged over 80. He was ed. at Eton and Oxford (Ch. Ch.); *m.* 1stly, Gladys Jean, yr. da. of Capt. Christian COMBE of Strathconan, Carnock, Ross and Cromarty. This marriage was diss. by divorce in 1968 and he *m.* 2ndly, 17 Aug. 1968, Maureen, da. of Major Geoffrey SCHOLFIELD, M.C. of Birkdale, co. Lancs. and formerly wife of Douglas MCKENZIE. He *d. s.p.* 24 May 1975. His widow was still living 1995.

MARQUESS [I.] VII. EARLDOM [I.] XI. } 1975

7 and 11. DERMOT RICHARD CLAUDE (CHICHESTER), MARQUESS OF DONEGALL, &c., also BARON TEMPLEMORE [1831], distant cousin and h. male, being descended from Arthur Chichester, 1st BARON TEMPLEMORE (which see), 1st s. and h. of Lord Spencer Stanley CHICHESTER, 2nd s. of the 1st Marquess of Donegal. He was *b.* 18 Apr. 1916; ed. at Harrow and R.M.C., Sandhurst; *m.*, 16 Sep. 1946, Lady Josceline Gabrielle, da. of William (LEGGE), 7th EARL OF DARTMOUTH.

[ARTHUR PATRICK CHICHESTER, *styled* EARL OF BELFAST, s. and h. ap., *b.* 9 May 1952; ed. at Harrow; *m.*, 1989, Caroline Mary, da. of Major Christopher Roland PHILIPSON of Saffron Walden, Essex.]

DONERAILE

page 395,
line 30, after '1695' add 'in England'
line 32, for 'Mary' read 'Elizabeth'

page 396,
line 2, for 'Thomas MAINWARING' read 'James MANWARING.(ax)'
note (ax) Mary Mohun was never owned by her father, but her parents were never divorced, so she must be regarded as legitimate, see H.C. Maxwell-Lyte's *History of Dunster*,

1909, pp. 493–4. By his will, dated 23 Mar. 1710, Lord Mohun left £100 to Elizabeth his "pretended daughter" by his first wife.

line 4, after '1733/4.' add 'He was *bur.* 17 Mar. at Kirk Ghrint, Lezayre, I.O.M.' [*ex inform.* C.R. Hudleston]

page 399,
line 10, after '(a)' add 'He *d.* unm. 7 Sep. 1941.'

VISCOUNTCY [I.] XI. BARONY [I.] VII. } 1941 — 7. HUGH (ST. LEGER), VISCOUNT DONERAILE, &c., br. and h., *b.* 6 Aug. 1869; *m.*, 18 Dec. 1919, Mary Isobel, 1st da. of Francis MORICE of Gisborne, New Zealand. He *d. s.p.* 18 Dec. 1956. His widow *d.* 1976.

VISCOUNTCY [I.] XII. BARONY [I.] VIII. } 1956 — 8. ALGERNON EDWARD (ST. LEGER), VISCOUNT DONERAILE, &c., cousin and h., being s. and h. of Richard William ST. LEGER (*d.* 20 Mar. 1925), by Matilda Emma, da. of Samuel Higgins BURROUGHS, which Richard William was 1st s. of John Gillis St. Leger (*d.* 17 Jan. 1867), by Charlotte Anne, 2nd da. of William Slade GULLY of Trevennan House, Tregony, Cornwall, which John Gillis was 3rd s. of Col. Richard ST. LEGER (*d.* 30 Dec. 1840), by his 1st wife Anne, 1st da. of Charles BLAKENEY of Holywell, co. Roscommon, which Richard was 2nd s. of the 1st Viscount Doneraile. He was *b.* 10 June 1878; *m.*, 27 Nov. 1919, Sylvia Stephenson, da. of Alexander MITCHELL, of Jarrow-on-Tyne, co. Durham. He *d.* 18 Nov. 1957.

VISCOUNTCY [I.] XIII. BARONY [I.] IX. } 1957 — 9. RICHARD ST. JOHN (ST. LEGER), VISCOUNT DONERAILE, &c., only s. and h., *b.* 29 Oct. 1923; *m.*, 1945, Melva Jean, da. of George W. CLIFTON of St. Louis, Missouri, U.S.A. He *d.* in 22 Oct. 1983. His widow was still living 1995.

VISCOUNTCY [I.] XIV. BARONY [I.] X. } *1983* — *10.* RICHARD ALLEN (ST. LEGER), VISCOUNT DONERAILE, &c., 1st s. and h., *b.* 17 Aug. 1946; ed. at Orange Coast Coll., California, U.S.A.; *m.*, 1970, Kathleen Mary, da. of Nathaniel SIMCOX of Mallow, co. Cork. He has not yet established his claim to his titles which are accordingly *dormant*.

[NATHANIEL WARHAM ROBERT ST. JOHN ST. LEGER, s. and h. ap., *b.* 13 Sep. 1971.]

DONINGTON

page 400,

III. 1920. 3. GILBERT THEOPHILUS CLIFTON (ABNEY-HASTINGS, afterwards RAWDON-HASTINGS afterwards CLIFTON-HASTINGS-CAMPBELL), BARON DONINGTON [U.K. 1888], 2nd br. and h. male, *b.* 29 May

1859; *m.*, 12 July 1894, Maud Kemble, da. of Sir Charles Edward HAMILTON. He *d.* 31 May, in Eaton Sq., and was *bur.* 3 June 1927 at Ashby de la Zouch, when his peerage became extinct.

DONOUGHMORE

page 401,
line 15, for '(8!)' read '(81)' and after 'Eton,' add '1767–72; adm. Student Lincoln's Inn, 13 June 1770; matric.'
line 16, after 'Oxford,' add '6 July' and for 'Dublin' read 'Trin. Coll., Dublin, *circa* 1773'

page 402,
line 23, after 'Eton' add '1767–73; adm. Student Lincoln's Inn 13 June 1770; matric.'
line 24, after 'Coll.)' add '8 Nov.' and after 'Dublin' add 'B.A. 1775, M.A. 1780'

page 403,
line 1, after 'Army' add 'as Cornet 18th Light Dragoons, May'
line 26, after '1787;' add 'adm. Trin. Coll., Dublin, 2 May 1803, aged 16;'

page 404,
line 3, after 'Margaret,' add '7th'
line 32, after 'Eton 'add '1861–4'

page 405,
line 2, for 'Kilmainham' read 'Kilmanahan'
line 3, after '£14,500' add 'His widow *d.* at Sidmouth 27 Apr. 1924.'
line 13, after 'Eton' add '1889–93' and after 'Oxford' add '2nd Class Mod. Hist. and B.A. 1897; Private Sec. to Gov. of Hong Kong 1899–1901;'
line 19, add at end 'She *d.* 22 Feb. 1944. He *d.* 19 Oct. 1948.'
lines 20–1, delete all detail and replace as follows

EARLDOM AND VISCOUNTCY [I.] VII.
BARONY [I.] VIII.
} 1948

7 and 8. JOHN MICHAEL HENRY (HELY-HUTCHINSON), EARL OF DONOUGHMORE OF KNOCKLOFTY, &c., 1st s. and h., *b.* 12 Nov. 1902; styled VISCOUNT SUIRDALE till 1948. He was ed. at Winchester and Oxford (Magdalen Coll.); *m.*, 27 July 1925, Dorothy Jean, 1st da. of John Beaumont HOTHAM of Milne Graden, Coldstream, co. Berwick. He *d.* 12 Aug. 1981. His widow was still living 1995.

EARLDOM AND VISCOUNTCY [I.] VIII.
BARONY [I.] IX.
} 1981

8 and 9. RICHARD MICHAEL JOHN (HELY-HUTCHINSON), EARL OF DONOUGHMORE OF KNOCKLOFTY, &c., 1st s. and h., *b.* 8 Aug. 1927; ed. at Winchester and Oxford (New Coll.); *m.*, 1 Nov. 1951, Sheila, da. of Frank Frederick PARSONS.

[JOHN MICHAEL JAMES HELY-HUTCHINSON, *styled* VISCOUNT SUIRDALE, 1st s. and h. ap., *b.* 7 Aug. 1952; ed. at Harrow; *m.*, 1977, Marie-Claire, da. of Gerard van den DREISSCHE.]

DORCHESTER

page 407,
line 22, after 'Dorset;' add 'adm. Trin Coll., Dublin, 16 Feb. 1734/5;'

page 408,
line 16, after 'Eton 'add '25 May 1755–63' and after 'admitted' add 'as a Fell. Com. 14 Nov.'
line 27, after 'Joyce,' add '(*d.* Dec. 1611)'
line 31, after '1600;' add 'from Sep. 1603 to Dec. 1605 he was Comptroller of the Household to the Earl of Northumberland;[ba]'
note [ba] His close relations with that Earl led to his being suspected of previous knowledge of the Gunpowder Plot, 5 Nov. 1605, and from 23rd of that month he was under restraint in the Bailiff's house at Westminster until 13 Dec. when he was released on parole. On 6 Nov. 1606 he was still not allowed to take his place in the House of Commons. For a list of the peers suspected of concern in that plot see note *sub* 2nd Viscount Montagu.
note [a], line 1, after 'John,' add '*b.* 25 June 1744; ed. at Eton 1755–61; adm. Cambridge (Trin. Coll.), 20 Apr. 1762,'

page 409,
line 11, after '1607,' add 'at the Temple Church' [He wrote to her father 3 Nov. 1607, announcing his marriage there.]
note (c), line 3, after 'London.' add 'He had a son by his 1st wife, *b.* on Ascension Day 1609 in London, who must have *d.* in infancy. See his letter of 26 May 1609 (*Cal. S. P. Dom., 1602–10*, p. 515).'

page 410,
line 25, after 'chester.' add 'He took his seat in the House of Lords 11 Apr. 1826.'

page 411,
line 2, after 'Hussars.' add 'He took his seat in the House of Lords 3 May 1833.'
line 4, after '64' add ', and was *bur.* at Nately Scures'
line 14, after 'Liberal' add '(he took his seat in the House of Lords 8 Feb. 1876)'
line 31, after '*Leir.*' add 'He *d.* 1933.'
line 32, after 'issue.' add 'She *d.* at Greywell Hill afsd., 2, aged 78, and was *bur.* 7 Mar. 1925 at Nately Scures, Hants. Will pr. £10,647 gross, £10,496 net.'
line 33, line to read as follows

VI. 1925. 2. DUDLEY MASSEY PIGOTT (CARLETON), BARON DORCHESTER [1899], 2nd[c] but 1st surv. s. and h.,

page 412,
line 2, after 'Reserve.' add 'Served in WW1 as Staff Capt.'

line 5, for ']' read 'He *d. s.p.m.* 20 Jan. 1963 when his Barony became *extinct*.

DORMER OF WYNG

page 412,
line 20, after 'Etc.' add '1603.' and for 'about St. James's tide 1590' read 'before 1577, probably at Cowdray'
line 26, after 'DORMER,' add '(*b.* 10 Sep. 1580),'
line 29, after '*d. v.p.*,' add 'before 26'

page 413,
line 16, for '1651' read '23 Oct. 1656' [F.G. Lea, *History of Thame*, 1883, p. 514.]
line 24, after '1761' add 'in New Bond Str.'
line 41, after 'Abbey' add '([a])'
note ([a]) Though *bur.* in the Abbey he appears to have been a Roman Catholic.

page 415,
line 8, for 'was living 1916' read '*d.* 18 Sep. 1919.'
line 16, after 'Cairo.' add 'He *d. s.p.m.s.* in his 58th year at Varenne in Italy, 9 Feb. 1920.'

XIV. 1920. 14. CHARLES JOSEPH THADDEUS (DORMER), BARON DORMER OF WYNG, br. and h., *b.* 24 Feb. 1864; ed. at Oscott; joined the Britannia as cadet 1877; naval attaché to Embassy at Tokyo 1906–8; Gent. Usher to the King, 1919 till his death. He *m.* 17 Feb. 1903, Caroline May, da. of Col. Sir Spencer CLIFFORD. He *d.* suddenly in his garden at Grove Park afsd., 4, and was *bur.* 8 May 1922 at Hampton-on-the-Hill afsd.

XV. 1922. 15. CHARLES WALTER JAMES (DORMER), BARON DORMER OF WYNG and a Baronet, 1st s. and h., *b.* 20 Dec. 1903; ed. at The Oratory Sch. and R.M.C., Sandhurst; *m.*, 19 Feb. 1944, Lady Maureen Thérèse Josephine, da. of Arthur Edward Joseph (NOEL), 4th EARL OF GAINSBOROUGH. He *d. s.p.m.* 27 May 1975. His widow *m.* 2ndly, 1982, Peregrine Edward Launcelot FELLOWES and was still living 1995.

XVI. 1975. 16. JOSEPH SPENCER PHILLIP (DORMER), BARON DORMER OF WYNG, br. and h., *b.* 4 Sep. 1914; ed. at Ampleforth and Oxford (Ch. Ch.).

DORSET

page 416,
note ([a]), lines 4–5, delete from 'He' to 'exist.' and replace by 'The authority for this statement was probably no. 457, *Liber Evidentiarum B* in the Episcopal Registry, Salisbury, a manuscript begun soon after 1308.'

page 417,
line 3, for '1411' read '1412'
line 11, for '28 (or 18) Aug. 1441' read '28 Aug. 1442'
note ([b]), delete all detail and replace by '*Report on the Dignity of a Peer*, vol. v, p. 238.'

page 418,
line 14, for 'appears to have' read 'may have'
line 20, for 'Thomas' read 'Henry'
line 25, for '20 Sep.' read '30 Aug.'
note ([g]), after 'See' add 'Sutton and Hammond, *Coronation of Richard III*, 1983, p. 314. For'

page 419,
line 3, for '6 Apr.' read 'Mar.' and for '12 Apr. 1530' read '12 May 1529.'
lines 4–5, for '"Marquess of Dorset, Lady' read 'Lady Cecill, Marquess'
line 5, for 'May 1527' read 'Mar. 1527/8'
note ([a]), after '631.' add 'The date given by Nicolas is wrong, as are the words 'Marquess of Dorset, Lady'. The registered copy of the will actually says "Lady Cecill Marquess Harrington and Bonville", doubtless omitting by accident the words "of Dorset, Lady".' (*P.C.C.* Jankyn 22)

page 420,
line 5, for '6 Oct. 1535' read '17 Nov. 1539.'
line 7, for '1300' read '1299'
line 12, after 'year;' add 'had livery of his father's lands 12 July (1538), 30 Hen. VIII;([d])'
note ([d]) In a report on the English nobility, which internal evidence shows to have been written between July and Nov. 1538, he is described as "26, young, lusty and poor, of great possessions but which are not in his hands, many friends of great power, with little or no experience, well learned, and a great wit". (*L. and P. Hen. VIII*, vol. xiii, part 2, p. 280). V.G.
note ([c]), delete all detail and replace by *L. and P. Hen. VIII*, vol. xiv, part 2, p. 187.

page 421,
line 4, after 'repudiated.' add '([aa])'
note ([aa]) On 9 July 1539 she wrote from Downely, her br. the Earl of Arundel's house in Sussex, to Cromwell signing her letter "K. Arundell", from which it may be presumed that the repudiation took place before this date. V.G.
line 12, for '1554' read '1553/4'
line 13, delete 'and the Marquessate of Dorset'
line 14, after '*extinct*,' add 'the Marquessate of Dorset falling under attainder,'
note ([c]), line 5, after '1295.' add 'In a lic. to alienate lands dat. 1546, he is described as "Henry Marquess of Dorset, Lord Ferrers of Groby, Harrington, Bonolde [Bonville] and Asteldy [Astley]". (*L. and P. Hen. VIII*, vol. xxi, part 1, p. 78)'
line 6, after 'Porter,' add '(who *d.* about 3 Sep. 1571)'

page 422,
line 19, for 'between 26 June 1582 and' read '2'
line 20, after '1585/6' add '([fa])'
note ([fa]) See 'Extracts from a 17th Century Notebook', *Genealogist*, N.S., vol. xxxiv, p. 82.
note ([c]), after '*Her.*,' add '(4th ser.)'

page 423,
line 2, after '1589;' add 'Chief Butler of England and Wales, 12 Dec. 1590;'
line 8, after '1601' add ',(aa) 4 Feb. 1603/4 and 5 Feb. 1604/5' [For his colleagues in 1604 and 1605, see vol. vii, p. 605, note (e). *sub* Lennox]
note (aa) His colleagues were the Earls of Worcester and Nottingham.
line 22, after 'Sussex,' add 'Aug.'
note (c), after '1608' add ', he having made a declaration of her misconduct on 27 Dec. of that year to the Archbishop of Canterbury and the Lord Chancellor'
note (d), after '*Biog.*' add ', see letter of John Chamberlain 3 Mar. 1608/9 (*Cal. S. P. Dom., 1603–10*, p. 495)'

page 426,
note (d), line 1, after 'Middleton' add '[*sic*, actually Middlesex],'

page 427,
line 4, after '1706' add ', he received his writ of summons 9, and took his seat 19 Jan. 1707/8'

page 430,
line 10, after '1843' add 'at under £50,000'

DOUGLAS

page 435,
line 26, for '*Avondale*' read '*Avendale*'
note (c), delete all detail and replace by 'She was probably da. of Henry, 1st Earl, killed 1400. See Andrew MacEwen, *The Geneal.*, vol. 2, 1981, p. 51.'

page 436,
line 7, after *m.*' add '*per verba de praesenti*, she being then, as alleged in the disp. granted to her later, when she *m.* his br., not yet 12 years of age,'
line 13, for '26' read '27'

page 437,
line 3, for 'disp. 26' read 'for which they incurred sentence of excommunication but were absolved by disp. 27'
line 8, after 'NEVILL,' add 'sister and (eventually) h. of Henry (DE HOLLAND) 2nd DUKE OF EXETER,'
lines 9–10, for '2nd' read '1st' and delete from 'John' to 'SALISBURY' and replace by Edmund EARL OF STAFFORD'

page 441,
line 26, after 'school' add ', and apparently also at Eton 1763–7'

page 443,
line 2, after 'Eton' add '1785–91'
line 7, after 'London.' add 'Ed. at Eton 1785–92; matric. at Oxford (Ch. Ch.) 30 Apr. 1793, B.A. 1797, M.A. 1803; Fellow of All Souls Coll., Oxford, 1803–34;'

DOVER

page 446,
line 10, after '1620,' add 'matric. Cambridge (St John's Coll.) 1624;'
line 21, after '[I.],' add '6th'
note (e), line 2, after '1655)' add ', at St. Paul's, Covent Garden 23–30 Apr. 1655,'

page 448,
note (a), line 6, after 'work.' add 'The *Royal Reporter* (vol. v, p. 159), says "A very valuable servant of the Crown. He is at once able, well instructed, diligent, upright. Among all the King's foreign Ministers, he is the only one of whom he has a right to boast".'

DOWNE

page 450,
line 9, after 'Elizabeth,' add '(who *m.* 2ndly, Sir Thomas Peniston and *d.* 19 Sep. 1638),'

page 452,
line 21, after 'Louisa,' add '(who *d.* before June 1731)'
line 23, after '*d. v.p.*,' add '29 July or'
line 24, after '1727;' add 'ed. at Eton 1742;'

page 453,
line 14, after '1764;' add 'ed. at Eton 1776–81;'

page 454,
line 18, after 'York,' add 'her cousin'
line 19, after 'who' add 'was *b.* 13 Apr. 1831, and'
line 24, after 'Eton' add '1858–62'
line 32, after '1900;' add 'twice mentioned in despatches;'

page 455,
lines 1–2, delete from 'and' to '(b)'
line 11, after 'DENING.' add 'He *d.* at Dingley Hall afsd., 21, and was *bur.* 25 Jan. 1924 at Wykeham Abbey. Will pr. gross £233,999, net £123,420. His widow *m.* 2ndly, 15 Apr. 1931, the Rev. Arthur Maxwell BURY (who *d.* 29 Dec. 1936) at St. Lawrence's Church, Chobham, Surrey. She *d.* 23 Jan. 1958.'
lines 12–13, lines to read as follows

X. 1924. 9. JOHN (DAWNAY), VISCOUNT DOWNE [I.], 1st s. and h., *b.* 23 May 1872, at 41 South Str., Park Lane; ed. at Eton 1885–90; entered the 10th Hussars 1891, Adjt. 1898–1901, Capt. 1899–1904; retired 1904; served in S. Africa 1899–1901 (despatches, Queen's Medal, 7 clasps)

line 18, for ']' read 'He *d.* 1, and was *bur.* 4 Dec. 1931 at Wykeham Abbey, Yorks. His widow *d.* 23 Mar. 1957.'

XI. 1931. 10. RICHARD (DAWNAY), VISCOUNT DOWNE, 1st s. and h., *b.* 16 May 1903; ed. at Eton; *m.*, 28 Oct. 1928, Margaret Christine, da. of Christian BAHNSEN of Pasale, New Jersey, U.S.A. He *d.* 8 Dec. 1965. His widow *d.* 1967.

XII. 1965. 11. JOHN CHRISTIAN (DAWNAY), VISCOUNT DOWNE, 1st s. and h., *b.* 8 Sep. 1937; ed. at Eton and Oxford (Ch. Ch.); *m.*, 16 Sep. 1965, Alison Diana, 1st da. of Ian Francis Henry SCONCE, O.B.E., of Brasted, Kent.

[RICHARD HENRY DAWNAY, s. and h. ap., *b.* 9 Apr. 1967.]

note ([b]), delete all detail

DOWNES OF AFGHANVILLE

page 455,
line 32, after 'Castle;' add 'Adm. Trin. Coll., Dublin, 9 July 1768,'
line 33, delete 'Dublin Univ.,'

page 456,
line 17, after '1788;' add 'adm. Trin. Coll., 26 Jan. 1803;'
line 33, after 'Hants.' add '(*d.* 1844),'

DOWNSHIRE

page 458,
line 15, after '1789–93;' add 'ed. at Eton 1767–70;'

page 460,
line 19, after 'beth' add '2nd'
line 22, for 'was living 1916' read ', who was *b.* 26 Jan. 1843, *d.* 12, aged 76, and was *bur.* 16 Jan. 1919, at Easthampstead Park. Will pr. Feb. 1919 at £15,968.'
line 30, after '1874.' add 'Ed. at Eton 1885–7.'
line 36, for 'She' read 'He *d.* at his seat, Easthampshire Park, Berks., after a short illness, 29 May, and was *bur.* there 3 June 1918. His widow, who'
line 37, after 'afsd.' add ', *d.* 2 Feb. 1959.'

page 461,
lines 1–5, delete all detail and replace as follows

VII. 1918. 7. ARTHUR WILLS PERCY WELLINGTON BLUNDELL TRUMBULL SANDYS (HILL), MARQUESS OF DOWNSHIRE [1789], &c., 1st s. and h., *b.* at Downshire House, Belgrave Sq., 7 Apr., and *bap.* 15 May 1894, at Easthampstead, the Duke of Connaught being sponsor; *styled* EARL OF HILLSBOROUGH till 1918; ed. at Eton. Served in WW1 as Lieut. Berks. Yeomanry.([a]) He *m.*, 23 July 1953, Noreen, da. of William BARRACLOUGH, widow of (__) GRAY-MILLER and of Major Walter FOX, previously wife of (__) ALLEN. She *d.* 1983. He *d.* 28 Mar. 1989.

VIII. 1989. 8. ARTHUR ROBIN IAN (HILL), MARQUESS OF DOWNSHIRE, &c., nephew and h., being s. and h. of Capt. Arthur Francis Henry HILL (*d.* 25 Dec. 1953), by Ishabel Wilhelmina Sheila, yst. da. of Col. Stewart MACDOUGALL of Lunga, Argyll, which Arthur Francis was 2nd s. of the 6th Marquess of Downshire. He was *b.* 10 May 1929; ed. at Eton; *m.* 1stly, 5 Oct. 1957, Juliet Mary, 2nd da. of Col. Cecil George Wilfred (WELD-FORESTER), 7th BARON FORESTER. She *d.* 1986 and he *m.* 2ndly, 1989, Mrs Diana Marion HIBBERT, 2nd da. of the Rt. Hon. Sir Ronald Hibbert CROSS, Bart., K.C.M.G., K.C.V.O.

[ARTHUR FRANCIS NICHOLAS WILLS HILL, *styled* EARL OF HILLSBOROUGH, 1st s. and h. ap. by 1st wife, *b.* 4 Feb. 1959; *m.*, 1990, Diana Jane, da. of Gerald Leeson BUNTING of North Allerton, Yorks.]

DROGHEDA

page 462,
line 18, after '1603' add 'till his death'

page 464,
line 1, after '(a)' add 'who was *b.* 10 and *bap.* 17 Feb. 1651/12 at Halstead, Essex' [Lanhydrock, Cornwall, Parish Register]

page 465,
line 7, after '*d.*' add '3 or' and after '*bur.*' add '8,'

page 467,
line 11, for '*circa* 1837–41' read '1836–42'
line 12, after 'Dublin,' add 'adm. 7 Nov. 1842'
line 40, for 'was living 1916' read '*d.* at Pinner, Midx. 21 Feb. 1924.'

page 468,
lines 1–2, lines to read as follows

EARLDOM [I.]
X.
VISCOUNTCY [I.]
XII. } 1908 10 and 12. HENRY CHARLES PONSONBY (MOORE), EARL OF DROGHEDA, &c., only s. and h., *b.* 21 Apr. 1884, in Sussex Sq., Brighton; ed. at Eton 1897–1901, and Cambridge (Trin. Coll.); ent. the Foreign Office, 1907. He was *cr.* BARON MOORE of Cobham, co. Surrey [U.K.], 30 Jan. 1954.

lines 4–5, delete from 'Having' to 'work.]' and replace by 'She obtained a divorce in 1922, and *m.* 2ndly, 31 Aug. 1932, Guilermo DE LOUDA, a member of a wealthy S. American family. She *d.* 18 Mar. 1966. He *m.* 2ndly, at the Kensington Register Office, 22 June 1922, Olive Mary, da. of George MEATYARD of Kensington, and formerly Lady Victor PAGET.(a) She *d.* 24 Nov. 1947. He *d.* 22 Nov. 1957.'

note (a), Formerly a light comedy actress, her stage name being Olive May.

EARLDOM [I.] XII. VISCOUNTCY [I.] XIII. BARONY [U.K.] II.	1957	11 and 13. CHARLES GARRETT PONSONBY (MOORE), EARL OF DROGHEDA, &c., only s. and h., *b.* 23 Apr. 1910; ed. at Eton and Cambridge (Trin. Coll.); *m.*, 16 May 1935, Joan Eleanor, da. of William Henry CARR. She *d.* 16 Dec. 1989. He *d.* 24 Dec. 1989.
EARLDOM [I.] XIII. VISCOUNTCY [I.] XIV. BARONY [U.K.] III.	1989	12 and 14. HENRY DERMOT PONSONBY (MOORE), EARL OF DROGHEDA, &c., only s. and h., *b.* 13 Jan. 1937; ed. at Eton and Cambridge (Trin. Coll.); *m.* 1stly, 15 May 1968, Eliza, da. of Stacey Barcroft LLOYD, of Philadelphia, U.S.A. This marriage was diss. by divorce in 1972 and he *m.* 2ndly, 1978, Alexandra, da. of Sir Nicholas HENDERSON, G.C.M.G., K.C.V.O.

[BENJAMIN GARRETT HENDERSON PONSONBY MOORE, *styled* VISCOUNT MOORE, 1st s. and h. ap. by 2nd wife, *b.* 21 Mar. 1983.]

DRUMMOND

page 470,
line 28, after 'whatsoever.' add 'P.C. [S.], sitting at a meeting of that body 28 June 1545.'

page 471,
note (b), line 1, for 'The' read 'James Drummond, the' and delete 'James Drummond,'

page 473,
line 1, for '1701' read '10 Mar. 1689/90'
note (b), line 2, after 'DORSET.' add 'The Ranulf Higden continuator commented, "Statuit eum appelari Marchionem Dubliniae; marchis est major comite et minor duce", see *Polychronicon*, Rolls Series, vol. ix, p. 72, *sub* 1385.'

DUCIE

page 474,
line 26, after 'M.I.' add 'Will dat. 3 Aug. 1738, pr. 10 May 1750, Glos. Probate Registry'

page 476,
line 6, after 'Eton' add '1790–1'
line 7, after 'Coll.)' add 24 Mar.'

page 477,
line 5, for '1840' read '1841'
line 11, after 'Julia' read '1st and only surv.'
line 13, after 'She' add ', who was *b.* 1 Oct. 1827,'
line 14, for 'at' read 'from' and after 'Tortworth' add 'Court at Falfield, Glos. He *d.* 23 Oct. 1921 at Tortworth Court and was *bur.* with her. Will pr. Jan. 1922 at £196,877 gross.'

line 17, for 'lives' read 'lived'

line 20, after 'Astrop.' read 'He *d. v.p. s.p.* of bronchial pneumonia at 37 Park Lane, 28 Feb. and was *bur.* 4 Mar. 1920 at Tortworth.'

EARLDOM. IV. BARONY. VII. } 1921 4 and 7. BERKELEY BASIL (MORETON), EARL OF DUCIE, &c., br. and h., *b.* 18 July 1834; ed. at Rugby, Oxford (Magdalen Coll.) and the R.A.C., Cirencester. Post Master Gen., Queensland, 1885; Colonial Sec. and Min. of Public Instruction 1886–8; *m.* 13 Oct. 1862, Emily Eleanor, da. of John KENT, Commr. of Crown Lands in Queensland. She *d.* 7 June 1921. He *d.* 7 Aug. 1924.

EARLDOM. V. BARONY. VIII. } 1924 5 and 8. CAPEL HENRY BERKELEY REYNOLDS (MORETON), EARL OF DUCIE, &c., 1st s. and h., *b.* 16 May 1875; *m.*, 1 Aug. 1903, Maria Emma, da. of Frederick BRYANT of Maryborough, Queensland, Australia. He *d. s.p.* 17 June 1952. His widow *d.* 5 June 1958.

EARLDOM. VI. BARONY. IX. } 1952 6 and 9. BASIL HOWARD (MORETON), EARL OF DUCIE, &c., nephew and h., being s. and h. of Algernon Howard MORETON (*d.* 23 June 1951), by Annie, da. of Robert BELL of Rockhampton, Queensland, which Algernon Howard was 2nd s. of the 4th Earl of Ducie. He was *b.* 15 Nov. 1917; *m.*, 15 Apr. 1950, Alison May, 1st da. of Leslie Aitken BATES of Pialba, Queensland. He *d.* 12 Nov. 1991. His widow was still living 1995.

EARLDOM. VII. BARONY. X. } 1991 7 and 10. DAVID LESLIE (MORETON), EARL OF DUCIE, &c., 1st s. and h., *b.* 20 Sep. 1951; ed. at Cheltenham, London and Wye Coll.; *m.*, 1975, Helen, da. of M.L. DUCHESNE of Bristol.

[JAMES BERKELEY MORETON, *styled* LORD MORETON, s. and h. ap., *b.* 6 May 1981.]

DUDHOPE

page 479,

note (a), line 14, after 'V.G.' add 'As agreed by the House of Lords in 1952 and 1953, see below *sub* DUNDEE.'

DUDLEY

page 479,

note (d), delete all detail

note (e), line 3, after '1341/2' add '(*d.* on Friday before 23 Nov. 1359)'

page 480,

line 5, after 'da.' add 'and h.' and after 'BETTESHORNE add 'of Betteshorne, Hants.'

page 481,
note (f), line 4, after 'p. 578' add 'and vol. xvii, part 1, p. 301'

page 482,
line 8, after '1556,' add '(aa)'
note (aa) As early as 1539 he had made proposals of marriage to Cicely, widow of Thomas, 5th Lord Berkeley, but though his suit was supported by the Lord Privy Seal (Cromwell), and the King, the lady made him "a very light answer that she was not minded to marry". V.G.

page 486,
between lines 7 and 8 add as follows

XII. 1916. 12. FERDINANDO DUDLEY WILLIAM LEA (SMITH), LORD DUDLEY, *b.* 4 Apr. 1872. [For details of his ancestry and claim to the title see note (a) below. See also vol. xiii, p. 221.] He *m.*, 3 Feb. 1904, Sybil Augusta, da. of Rev. Canon Henry COVENTRY, Rector of Severn Stoke, co. Worcester. He *d.* 5 Dec. 1936. His widow *d.* 5 Nov. 1958.

XIII. 1936. 13. FERDINANDO DUDLEY HENRY (SMITH), LORD DUDLEY, 1st s. and h., *b.* 18 June 1910; ed. at Repton; *m.*, July 1941, Kirsten Laura Hedvig, da. of Lars Anton ALBRECHTSEN of Vibsig, Denmark. This marriage was diss. by divorce, 1965. He *d. s.p.* 19 Apr. 1972.

XIV. 1972. 14. BARBARA AMY FELICITY SMITH, sister and h., *suo jure* BARONESS DUDLEY. She was *b.* 23 Apr. 1907; *m.* 1stly, 22 Aug. 1929, Guy Raymond Hill WALLACE of Astley, co. Worcs. He *d.* Mar. 1967 and she *m.* 2ndly, 1980, Charles Anthony Cross HAMILTON.

[JIM ANTHONY HILL, 1st s. and h. ap. by 1st husband, *b.* 9 Nov. 1930; ed. at Lancing; *m.*, 16 June 1962, Nicola Jane, da. of Lieut. Col. Philip William Edward Leslie DUNSTERVILLE of Hitcham, Suffolk.]

line 22, delete 'of Germany'

page 487,
line 2, after '*Holy*' add '*Roman*'

page 488,
line 23, for 'May' read 'Jan.(ca)'
note (ca) May is the month usually given, but in *Memorials of Twickenham*, by R.S. Cobbett (1872), it is given as Jan. and is followed by a burial for 15 Mar. 1810, so it seems that Jan. is more likely to be right. V.G.
line 27, for 'from 1765' read '25 Apr. 1765–9'

DUDLEY OF DUDLEY CASTLE

page 490,
line 14, for 'only child' read '1st da.'

page 491,
line 2, for 'was living 1916' read '*d.* 2 Feb. 1929.'
line 6, after 'Eton 'add '1881–4'
line 8, after '1902;' add 'served as D.A.A.G., Imperial Yeomanry in the S. African War, 1899–1900;[aa]'
note ([aa]) For a list of Peers and their heirs who served in this war, see vol. iii, Appendix B.
line 13, after 'Service.' add 'She was drowned while bathing in Camus Bay, co. Galway, 26 June, and was *bur.* 2 July 1920, at Witley, co. Worcs. He *m.* 2ndly, at the British Consulate, Paris, 30 Apr. 1924, Gertrude, da. of John MILLAR, and widow of Lionel MONCKTON. She *d.* in an accident in Kent 21 July 1930. He *d.* 29 June and was *bur.* 2 July 1932 in the grounds of Himley Castle.'
line 14, line to read as follows

IV. 1932. 3. WILLIAM HUMBLE ERIC (WARD), EARL OF DUDLEY OF DUDLEY CASTLE, &c., s. and h.,

line 17, for '1914–' read '1914–18' and for ']' read 'He *m.* 1stly, 8 Mar. 1919, Lady Rosemary Millicent, da. of Cromartie (LEVESON-GOWER), 4th DUKE OF SUTHERLAND, K.G. She *d.* 21 and was *bur.* 25 July 1930 at Himley Hall afsd. He *m.* 2ndly, 25 Feb. 1943, Frances Laura, 2nd da. of Guy Lawrence CHARTERIS formerly wife of Walter Francis David (LONG), 2nd VISCOUNT LONG. This marriage was diss. by divorce in 1954 and he *m.* 3rdly, 17 July 1961, Grace Maria, da. of Dr Michael KOLIN of Saint Jacob, Dubrovnik, formerly wife of PRINCE STANISLAUS RADZIWILL. He *d.* 26 Dec. 1969. His widow was still living 1995.

V. 1969. 4. WILLIAM HUMBLE DAVID (WARD), EARL OF DUDLEY OF DUDLEY CASTLE, &c., 1st s. and h., *b.* 5 Jan. 1920; ed. at Eton and Oxford (Ch. Ch.); *m.* 1stly, 10 Jan. 1946, Stella, 1st da. of Dr Don Miguel Angel CARCANO, K.B.E., Argentine Ambassador at the Court of St. James 1942–6. This marriage was diss. by divorce in 1961 and he *m.* 2ndly, 24 Aug. 1961, Maureen, da. of James SWANSON.

[WILLIAM HUMBLE DAVID JEREMY WARD, *styled* VISCOUNT EDNAM, 1st s. and h. ap. by 1st wife, *b.* 27 Mar. 1947; ed. at Eton and Oxford (Ch. Ch.); *m.* 1stly, 1972, Sarah Mary, da. of Sir Alastair Francis Stuart COATS, Bart. This marriage was diss. by divorce in 1976 and he *m.* 2ndly, 1976, Debra Louise, da. of George Robert PINNEY. This marriage was in turn diss. in 1980.]

DUFFERIN

page 492,
line 6, for '*b.* 1726' read '*bap.* 7 July 1726 at Killyleagh'
line 17, after '1755;' add 'in 1794 raised 33rd Regt. of Light Dragoons, Col. of Royal North Down Militia;'
note ([d]), lines 1–2, for '31 Jan. 1785' read '30 Jan. 1786'

page 493,
line 6, delete '28 Mar. 1865'
line 7, after 'Down' add ', 28 Mar. and was *bur.* 5 Apr. at Killyleagh.'
line 9, after '1758' add 'at Ballyleigh'
lines 15–16, delete from '18' to afsd.' and replace by 'in Dublin, 18, aged 81, and was *bur.* 27 Nov. 1839, at Ballyleigh.'
lines 16–17, delete from 'July' to 'Antrim' and replace by 'at Red Hall, co. Antrim, the seat of David Stewart KER (her son-in-law), 28 July, aged 63, and was *bur.* 3 Aug. 1843, at Killyleagh.'
line 24, for 'Sir' read 'Col.' and delete 'Bart.'

page 494,
line 8, after 'Eton' add '*circa* 1839–43'

page 495,
lines 13–15, delete from 'and' to 'work' and replace by '*d.* 25 and was *bur.* 28 Oct. 1936 at Clandeboye.'
line 19, after 'AVA' add 'Ed. at Eton 1876–8.' and after 'India.' add 'He served in S. Africa as extra A.D.C. to Major Gen. Ian Hamilton 1899–1900, and'
line 20, delete 'He'
after line 21 add as follows

MARQUESSATE. II. EARLDOM. II. BARONY. VI. } 1902

2 and 6. TERENCE JOHN TEMPLE (HAMILTON-TEMPLE-BLACKWOOD), MARQUESS OF DUFFERIN AND AVA, &c., 2nd surv. s. and h., *b.* 16 Mar. 1866; *m.*, 16 Oct. 1893, Florence, da. of John H. DAVIS of New York. He *d. s.p.m.* of double pneumonia at a nursing home in Carlton Rd., Putney, 7, and was *bur.* 11 Feb. 1918, in Putney Vale Cemetery. His widow *m.* 2ndly, 11 Dec. 1919, at Christ Church, Down Str., Richard George Penn (CURZON), 4th EARL HOWE. She *d.* 14 Apr. 1925.

MARQUESSATE. III. EARLDOM. III. BARONY. VII. } 1918

3 and 7. FREDERICK TEMPLE (HAMILTON-TEMPLE-BLACKWOOD), MARQUESS OF DUFFERIN AND AVA, &c., br. and h., *b.* 26 Feb. 1875; *m.*, 20 June 1908, Brenda, da. of Major Robert WOODHOUSE, of Bishop's Stortford, co. Hertford. He *d.* 21 July 1930. His widow *m.* 2ndly, 28 Jan. 1932, Henry Charles Somers Augustus SOMERSET (he *d.* 25 Nov. 1945). She *d.* 17 July 1946.

MARQUESSATE. IV. EARLDOM. IV. BARONY. VIII. } 1930

4 and 8. BASIL SHERIDAN (HAMILTON-TEMPLE-BLACKWOOD), MARQUESS OF DUFFERIN AND AVA, &c., s. and h., *b.* 6 Apr. 1909; *m.*, 3 July 1930, Maureen Constance, 2nd da. of Arthur GUINNESS at St. Margaret's, Westm. He *d.* 25 Mar. 1945, being *k.* in action. His widow (after two more marriages) was still living in 1995.

MARQUESSATE. V. EARLDOM. V. BARONY. IX. } 1945 5 and 9. SHERIDAN FREDERICK TERENCE (HAMILTON-TEMPLE-BLACKWOOD), MARQUESS OF DUFFERIN AND AVA, EARL OF DUFFERIN, EARL OF AVA, VISCOUNT CLANDEBOYE and BARON CLANDEBOYE, all in the peerage of the United Kingdom, BARON DUFFERIN AND CLANEBOYE OF BALLYLEIDY AND KILLYLEAGH in the peerage of Ireland, and a Baronet, only s. and h., *b.* 9 July 1938; ed. at Eton and Oxford (Ch. Ch.); *m.*, 21 Oct. 1964, Serena Belinda Rosemary Lindy, da. of Grp. Capt. Loel Evelyn Bulkeley GUINNESS, O.B.E., of Lausanne, Switzerland. He *d. s.p.* 29 May 1988 when all his titles became *extinct* except for the Barony of Dufferin and Claneboye, also his Baronetcy [I.], which became *dormant*. They were probably inherited by his distant cousin. His widow was still living 1995.

BARONY. X. } *1988* *10*. FRANCIS GEORGE (BLACKWOOD), BARON DUFFERIN AND CLANEBOYE OF BALLYLEIDY AND KILLYLEAGH [I.] and a Baronet, distant cousin and heir, being descended from Sir Hugh Martin BLACKWOOD, 1st Baronet Blackwood [U.K.], (see Baronetcies), (*d.* 14 Dec. 1832) by his 2nd wife, Eliza, 4th da. of Capt. Martin WAGHORN, R.N., which Sir Hugh was 7th s. of Sir John BLACKWOOD, 2nd Baronet of Blackwood of Ballyleidy [I.], see above. He was *b.* 20 May 1916. He *m.*, 1940, Margaret, da. of Hector KIRKPATRICK, of Lindfield, N.S.W. He never established his claim to the peerage. He *d.* 1991. His widow was living 1995.

BARONY. XI. } *1991* *11*. JOHN FRANCIS (BLACKWOOD), BARON DUFFERIN AND CLANEBOYE, [I.], &c., 1st s. and h., was *b.* 18 Oct. 1944; ed. at Barker Coll., Hornsby, and Univ. of N.S.W.; *m.*, 1971, Annette Kay, da. of Harold GREENHILL of Sydney, N.S.W. He has not yet established his claim to the peerage.

[FRANCIS SENDEN BLACKWOOD, s. and h. ap., was *b.* 6 Jan. 1979]

note (b), line 1, delete from 'Terence' to '1866'

DUFFUS

page 497,
line 18, after 'Sweden' add 'by Charlotte Regina his wife'
line 19, after 'widow' add ', who was *b.* at Charlescrane in Sweden, but professing the Protestant religion, was naturalised 24 Feb. 1708/9. She'

page 498,
line 5, for 'in the army' read 'ent. the army as Ensign in the 68th Regiment May 1762'

DUMFRIES

page 501,
line 14, after 'year' add 'from a fall in the street at Edinburgh and was *bur.* at St. Cuthbert's there'
line 14, after '73' add 'and was *bur.* at Hendon, Midx.'

DUNALLEY OF KILBOY

page 502,
line 8, after '1743' add ', adm. Trin. Coll., Dublin, 3 June 1760'
line 17, after 'Kilboy.' add 'Adm. Trin. Coll., Dublin, 19 June 1792, aged 17.'

page 503,
line 13, after 'R.A.' add 'He *d.* 5 Aug. 1927. His widow *d.* 18 May 1929.'
line 14, line to read as follows

V. 1927. 5. HENRY CORNELIUS O'CALLAGHAN (PRITTIE), BARON DUNALLEY OF KILBOY [I.], 1st s. and h.,

line 15, for '1914–' read '1914–18'
line 19, for ']' read 'He *d.* 3 May 1948. His widow *d.* 4 Apr. 1967.'

VI. 1948. 6. HENRY DESMOND GRAHAM (PRITTIE), BARON DUNALLEY OF KILBOY, 1st s. and h., *b.* 14 Oct. 1912; *m.*, 23 Apr. 1947, Mary Philippa, Major Philip Plantagenet CARY. He *d.* 26 June 1992. His widow was still living 1995.

VII. 1992. 7. HENRY FRANCIS CORNELIUS (PRITTIE), BARON DUNALLEY OF KILBOY, 1st s. and h., *b.* 30 May 1948; ed. at Gordonstoun and Dublin (Trin. Coll.); *m.*, 1978, Sally Louise, da. of Ronald VERE of Heaton Chapel, Cheshire.

[JOEL HENRY PRITTIE, s. and h. ap., *b.* 29 Apr. 1981.]

DUNBAR

page 505,
line 28, after '1214' add '(probably before 1208)' [See Andrew B.W. MacEwan, *The Geneal.*, vol. 9, 1988, pp. 229–30.]

page 506,
lines 7–8, delete from 'Walter' to '[S.]' and replace by 'William de BRUS by Christina, da. of (__) (and Earl Patrick's stepsister)' [MacEwan, *op. cit.*, pp. 231, 236]
line 21, delete '[?Fraser]'
note ([a]), lines 2–5, delete from 'She' to 'Dunbar' and replace by 'She was probably the da. of John FitzRobert of Warkworth, co. Northumberland, by Ada, da. of Hugh de Baliol of Barnard Castle (and sister of John de Baliol), see MacEwan, *op. cit.*, pp. 231–6.'

page 508,
line 7, delete from 'in' to 'EARLDOM' and replace by ', on the death of the Earl, his brother-in-law, assumed the title of EARL'
line 8, after '[S.]' add 'some time after 1346'

page 510,
line 17, for 'Mar.' read 'Aug.'

page 511,
line 10, after 'Scotland;' add 'Lord Lieut. of cos. Northumberland, Cumberland and Westmorland, jointly with the Earl of Cumberland, Oct. 1607;'
note (d), line 1, for '[S.]' read '[E.]'

page 513,
line 2, for 'West' read 'East'

DUNBARTON

page 515,
line 28, after '(e)' add 'On 24 Jan. 1709 he was received into the Church of England by Abp. Tenison in his Chapel at Lambeth.(f)'
note (f) The form of the service is given in Lambeth MSS. 933, f. 61. See E.F. Carpenter, *Thomas Tenison, Archbishop of Canterbury: His life and times*, 1948, pp. 73–6 (*ex inform*. G. Johnson).

DUNBOYNE

page 516,
line 11, after '[I.].' add 'He sat in the parl. [I.] of 1541, which proclaimed Henry VIII King of Ireland.'
line 15, for '1551, Cecilia, or Gille' read '27 July 1551, Julia'

page 517,
line 19, after 'h.' add '(ax)'
note (ax) On 6 May 1613, a King's letter issued for a commission of enquiry into the allegations of Peter Butler, a son of the 2nd Baron Dunboyne, that his (Peter's) elder brother John (abovenamed) had married Elinor, da. of the Baron of Caher, and had begotten an illegit. son, called Edmond, by Joan Fitzpatrick, and having died without legit. issue the said Peter had been entitled to the Barony of Dunboyne and his father's and brother's lands, but that by an inquisition taken without his knowledge it was found that the said Edmond was s., and h. to the said John, and being under age, his wardship was granted to the Baron of Dunboyne, his pretended grandfather (*Cal. Pat. Rolls* [I.], 1–16 Jac. I, p. 327).
line 20, after 'abovenamed.' add 'After his father's death his wardship was granted to his grandfather, the 2nd Baron. He had livery of his said grandfather's lands 16 Dec. 1625.'

page 519,
line 15, for 'VII' read 'VI'
line 22, after 'widow' add 'who was *b*. 1764'

page 520,
line 30, for 'was living 1916' read '*d*. at Greendale, Clyst St. Mary, Exeter, 15 June 1919.'
line 41, for 'was living 1916' read '*d*. 11 Jan. 1927.'

page 521,
line 1, line to read as follows

XVII. 1913. 17. FITZWALTER GEORGE PROBYN (BUTLER), BARON DUNBOYNE [I.], 1st s. and h. ap., *b.* 20 Mar. 1874.

line 4, for '1914–' read '1914–18'
lines 4–5, delete from 'Having' to 'work]' and replace by 'He *m.*, 26 July 1915, Dora Isolde Butler, 1st da. of Francis Fitzpatrick TOWER, O.B.E. He *d.* 9 May 1945. His widow *d.* 1977.'

XVIII. 1945. 18. PATRICK THEOBALD TOWER (BUTLER), BARON DUNBOYNE [I.], only s. and h., *b.* 27 Jan. 1917; ed. at Winchester and Cambridge (Trin. Coll.); *m.*, 29 July 1950, Anne Marie, da. of Sir Victor Alexander Louis MALLET, G.C.M.G., C.V.O.

[JOHN FITZWALTER BUTLER, s. and h. ap., *b.* 31 July 1951; ed. at Winchester and Cambridge (Trin. Coll.); *m.*, 1975, Diana Caroline, da. of Sir Michael Sanigear WILLIAMS, K.C.M.G.]

DUNDAS

page 522,
line 15, after 'Edinburgh;' add 'ed. at Eton Jan. 1753–6'

DUNDEE

* * * * * *

page 523,
after line 12 add

VISCOUNTCY [S.] IV. 1952; EARLDOM [S.] II. 1953. 2 and 4. HENRY JAMES (SCRYMGEOUR-WEDDERBURN), EARL OF DUNDEE, VISCOUNT OF DUDHOPE, LORD SCRYMGEOUR, and LORD INVERKEITHING all in the peerage of Scotland,(ax) was *b.* 3 May 1902; ed. at Winchester and Oxford (Balliol Coll.). He was *cr.*, 30 July 1954, BARON GLASSARY, of Glassary, co. Argyll [U.K.], with the usual rem. He *m.*, 30 Oct. 1946, Patricia Katherine, yr. da. of Herbert Andrew MONTAGUE-DOUGLAS-SCOTT, widow of 1stly, Lieut. Col. Walter Douglas FALKNER M.C. and 2ndly, of Lieut. Col. David SCRYMGEOUR-WEDDERBURN, D.S.O., (yr. br. of the Earl). He *d.* 29 June 1983. His widow was still living 1995.

EARLDOM [S.] III. VISCOUNTCY. V. BARONY. II. 1983. 3, 5. and 2. ALEXANDER HENRY (SCRYMGEOUR-WEDDERBURN), EARL OF DUNDEE [S.], &c., only s. and h. He was *b.* 5 June 1949; ed. at Eton and St Andrews Univ.; *m.*, 1979, Siobhan Mary, da. of David LLEWELLYN.

[HENRY DAVID SCRYMGEOUR-WEDDERBURN, *styled* LORD SCRYMGEOUR, was *b.* 20 June 1982.]

note ([ax]) On 31 July 1952 it was resolved by the House of Lords that Henry James Scrymgeour-Wedderburn of Wedderburn and Birkhill, Hereditary Royal Standard Bearer of Scotland was entitled of right to the dignities of Viscount Dudhope and Lord Scrymgeour [S.], as heir male (collateral) of Sir John Scrymgeour of Dudhope, who was so *cr.*, 15 Nov. 1641, with rem. to his heirs male whatsoever. On 20 May 1953 it was further resolved by the House of Lords that he was also entitled of right to the dignities of Earl of Dundee and Lord Inverkeithing [S.] as h. male (collateral) of John (Scrymgeour), 2nd Viscount Dudhope, who was so *cr.*, 8 Sep. 1660, with rem. to his heirs male whatsoever. See above, *sub* DUDHOPE, pp. 478, note "c" and 479, note "a".

page 525,
line 8, for '21 Dec. 1717' read '14 June 1718'
note ([c]), line 12, after 'V.G.' add 'For a discussion of possible heirs male to the Viscountcy of Dundee, see L.G.H. Horley, *N&Q.*, vol. 189, 1945, pp. 146–8.'

DUNDONALD

page 526,
note ([b]), for 'II' read 'I'

page 531,
line 3, after 'Harriet,' add '1st'
line 4, after 'Emma' add 'Mary'
line 12, after 'Eton' add '1866–9'
line 22, after 'Mawn.' add 'She, who was a Lady of Grace of the Order of St. John of Jerusalem, *d.* 17 at 5 Cadogan Sq., Chelsea and was *bur.* 19 Jan. 1924 at Llanddulas, Denbighshire. He *d.* 12, at Wimbledon Park and was *bur.* 16 Apr. 1935 at Achnaba Church, Argyllshire.
lines 23–6, delete all detail and replace as follows

XIII. 1935. 13. THOMAS HESKETH DOUGLAS BLAIR (COCHRANE), EARL OF DUNDONALD, &c., 1st s. and h., *b.* 21 Feb. 1886, 50 Eaton Place.; *styled* LORD COCHRANE till 1958; ed. at Eton; served in WW1 as Capt. Scots Guards, and was wounded.([d]) Rep. Peer [S.], 1941–55. He *d.* unm. 23 May 1958.

XIV. 1958. 14. IAN DOUGLAS LEONARD (COCHRANE), EARL OF DUNDONALD, &c., nephew and h., being s. and h. of Douglas Robert Hesketh Roger COCHRANE (*d.* 19 May 1942), by Enid Marion, da. of Miles Leonard DAVIS, which Douglas Robert was 2nd s. of the 12th Earl of Dundonald. He was *b.* 6 Dec. 1918; ed. at Wellington and R.M.C., Sandhurst; *m.* 1stly, 30 Jan. 1960, Aphra Farquhar, da. of Cmdr. George FEATHERSTONEHAUGH, R.N.R. She *d.* 1978 and he *m.* 2ndly, Ann Margaret, da. of Sir Joseph Welsh Park HARKNESS, C.M.G. and formerly wife of C.F.E. STAIB. He *d.* 4 Oct. 1986. His widow was still living 1995.

XV. 1986. 15. IAIN ALEXANDER DOUGLAS BLAIR (COCHRANE), EARL OF DUNDONALD, &c., only s. and h., *b.* 17 Feb. 1961; ed. at Wellington and R.A.C., Cirencester; *m.*, 1987, M. Beatrice L., da. of Adolphus RUSSO of Gibralter.

[ARCHIE IAIN THOMAS BLAIR COCHRANE, *styled* LORD COCHRANE, s. and h. ap., *b.* 14 Mar. 1991.]

note ([c]), line 1, after 'Cochrane,' add 'later *cr.* Cochrane of Cults,'

DUNFERMLINE

page 532,
line 14, after '1608;' add 'on 27 Jan. 1604/5 he had a grant of denization; on 12 Feb. 1604/5 he was discharged of the custody of Charles Duke of York, with an attestation that the Prince was in perfect health;'
line 16, for '1609' read '1609/10'
line 25, after 'Margaret,' add '(then aged 15),'
line 28, after '*bur.*' add '9 July'
line 31, after '1659,' add 'at Fyvie'
lines 33–4, delete 'young and' and after '*v.p.*' add 'of the plague in 1605, aged little more than 1 year, and was *bur.* at Dalgety.'
note ([a]), for '*baine*' read '*bairne*'

page 533,
line 1, after '1642;' add 'Gent. of the Bedchamber *circa* 1644; Keeper of the Privy Seal in reversion 1646, succeeding to that office on the death of the Earl of Roxburghe 1649/50 with a pension of £1,000 *p.a.*;'
line 9, for '*b.* 13 June 1640' read '*bap.* 13 June 1640 at Dunfermline'
line 10, delete from 'being' to '1672.' and replace by 'before 8 Aug. 1660 when his br. Alexander is *styled* LORD FYVIE.([ax])'
note ([ax]) See *Reg. P.C.* [S.], 3rd ser., vol. i, p. 56, *cf.* A.M.W. Stirling, *Fyvie Castle*, 1928, p. 234, and *Cal. S. P. Dom., 1671–2*, p. 95.
line 12, for '12 June 1642' read '*bap.* 12 June 1642 at Dunfermline'
lines 26–7, for '4 Mar. 1694/5' read 'at Fyvie, in 1707, when she made a disposition of her lands to George Seton of Barns, and 1 June 1709, when she stood Godmother at a Christening.'
note ([b]), line 2 (on page 534), after 'him.' add 'He is again mentioned in a letter from Mar to Straiton dated 2 Oct. 1718, "Lord Dunfermline shall be taken care of as soon as it is in our power".' (*Hist. MSS. Com.*, Stuart MSS., vol. vii, p. 350)

page 534,
line 24, after '1838,' add 'at Minto House'
line 25, after 'Mary,' add '1st'
line 26, after 'BRYDONE' add ', of Lemmel House, co. Berwick.'

DUNGANNON

page 536,
line 12, after '1704–6' add 'being ordered beyond the sea [Catalonia] in command of it Dec. 1705.'

DUNLEATH OF BALLYWALTER

page 541,
line 23, for 'Eton. Sometime' read 'Eton 1867–71, R.M.A., Woolwich and Oxford (Balliol Coll.).' and after 'R.E.' add '1874–8'
line 24, after 'Rifles' add '1890–6'
note (b), line 2, for 'succession' read 'estate'
note (c), line 1, after 'Eton' add '1866–71 and Oxford (Balliol Coll.). He'
line 2, for 'and *d. s.p.*' read 'by his 1st wife, Frances, da. of the Rev. Peter Hordern. He *d. s.p.* and *v.p.* of typhoid fever,'

page 542,
line 2, add at end 'He *d.* 22 Mar. 1931. His widow *d.* 23 July 1935.'
line 4, after 'Monkstown.' add 'Ed. at Eton 1896–1901; matric. Oxford (Ch. Ch.) 1902; joined Irish Guards 1906, Lieut. 1909.'
line 11, for 'was living 1916.' read '*m.* 2ndly, 27 Nov. 1922, Field Marshal Frederick Rudolph (LAMBART), 10th EARL OF CAVAN, who *d.* 28 Aug. 1946.'
after line 11 add as follows

III. 1931. 3. CHARLES HENRY GEORGE (MULLHOLLAND), BARON DUNLEATH OF BALLYWALTER, 2nd but 1st surv. s. and h., *b.* 19 Aug. 1886; Capt. 11th Hussars, served in WW1, wounded Nov. 1914, mentioned in despatches, D.S.O. He *m.* 1stly, 26 Feb. 1920, Sylvia Henrietta, da. of Sir Arthur Douglas BROOKE, Bart. She *d.* 19 May 1921 and he *m.* 2ndly, 23 Aug. 1932, Henrietta Grace, 2nd. da. of Most Rev. Charles Frederick D'ARCY, Archbishop of Armagh and Primate of all Ireland. He *d.* 20 July 1956. His widow *d.* 20 Mar. 1969.

IV. 1956. 4. CHARLES EDWARD HENRY JOHN (MULHOLLAND), BARON DUNLEATH OF BALLYWALTER, only s. and h. by 2nd wife, *b.* 23 June 1933; ed. at Eton and Cambridge (Trin. Coll.); *m.*, 5 Dec. 1959, Dorinda Margery, da. of Lieut. Gen. Arthur Ernest PERCIVAL, of Ware, Herts. He *d. s.p.* 9 Jan. 1993. His widow was still living 1995.

V. 1993. 5. MICHAEL HENRY (MULHOLLAND), BARON DUNLEATH OF BALLYWALTER, also a Baronet [1945], cousin and h., being s. and h. of Sir Henry George Hill MULHOLLAND, 1st Baronet (*d.* 5 Mar. 1971), by Sheelah, da. of Sir Arthur Douglas BROOKE, Bart., which Henry George was 3rd s. of the 2nd Baron Dunleath. He was *b.* 15 Oct. 1915; ed. at Eton and Cambridge (Pembroke Coll.); *m.* 1stly, 21 Mar. 1942, Rosemary, da. of Major David Alfred William KER of Donaghdee, co. Down. They were divorced in 1949 and he *m.* 2ndly, 29 June 1949, Elizabeth, twin da. of Laurence B. HYDE of Bexhill-on-Sea, Sussex.

[BRIAN HENRY MULHOLLAND, s. and h. ap. by 2nd wife, *b.* 25 Sep. 1950; ed. at Eton; *m.*, 1976, Mary Joan, da. of Major Robert John Fuller WHISTLER of Camberley, Surrey.]

note (b), lines 1–3, delete from 'Two' to '(2)' and replace by 'His younger br. also fought,'

DUNMORE

page 545,
line 29, after 'Eton' add '1854–7'

page 546,
line 3, for 'was living 1916' read '*d.* 28 Nov. 1943.'
line 4, line to read as follows

EARLDOM [S.] VIII. BARONY IV.	1907	8 and 4. ALEXANDER EDWARD (MURRAY), EARL OF DUNMORE, &c., s. and h.,

line 7, after 'sponsors.' add '*styled* VISCOUNT FINCASTLE till 1908; ed. at Eton 1885–8;'
lines 15–16, delete from 'Having' to 'work]' and replace by 'He *d.* 29 Jan. 1962. His widow *d.* 9 Feb. 1966.'

[EDWARD DAVID MURRAY, *styled* VISCOUNT FINCASTLE, s. and h. ap., *b.* 3 Apr. 1908; ed. at Winchester; *m.*, 26 Apr. 1938, Pamela Kate, 1st da. of Roland Hermon (HERMON-HODGE), 2nd BARON WYFOLD. He *d. v.p.* June 1940, being *k.* in action. His widow *m.* 2ndly, 27 June 1944, Capt. Follett Watson BELL.]

EARLDOM [S.] IX. BARONY V.	1962	9 and 5. JOHN ALEXANDER (MURRAY), EARL OF DUNMORE, &c., grandson and h., being s. of Edward David and Pamela Kate abovenamed, *b.* 3 Apr. 1939; ed. at Eton; *m.*, 8 Dec. 1967, Anne Augusta, da. of Thomas Clouston WALLACE, of Dounby, Orkney. He *d. s.p.* 12 Aug. 1980. His widow was still living 1995.

EARLDOM [S.] X. BARONY VI.	1980	10 and 6. REGINALD ARTHUR (MURRAY), EARL OF DUNMORE, &c., distant cousin, being s. and h. of Arthur Charles MURRAY (*d.* 5 Sep. 1964), by his 1st wife Susan Maud, da. of Edward RICHARDS of Tasmania, which Arthur Charles was 2nd s. of Reginald Augustus Frederick Murray

(*d.* 5 Sep. 1925), by his 1st wife Jane Louisa Otway, da. of Henry Bayles FORD of Melbourne, Australia, which Reginald Augustus was s. of Verginius Murray (*d.* 25 Dec. 1861), by Elizabeth Alicia, da. of Col. Charles POITIERS, which Verginius was 2nd s. of Lieut. Col. Alexander MURRAY (*d.* July 1842), by Deborah, da. of Robert HUNT, which Alexander was 2nd s. of the 4th Earl of Dunmore. He was *b.* 17 July 1911; *m.*, 1948, Patricia Mary, da. of Frank COLES of Robingana, West Tamar, Tasmania. He *d. s.p.* 14 Jun. 1981. His widow *m.* 2ndly, 1984, Geoffrey Howard FITZE. She was still living 1995.

EARLDOM [S.] XI. BARONY VII.	1981	11 and 7. KENNETH RANDOLPH (MURRAY), EARL OF DUNMORE, &c., br. and h., *b.* 6 June 1913; *m.*, 1938, Margaret Joy, da. of P.D. COUSINS of Burnie, Tasmania.

[MALCOLM KENNETH MURRAY, *styled* VISCOUNT FINCASTLE, 1st s. and h. ap., *b.* 17 Sep. 1946; *m.*, 1970, Joy Anne, da. of A. PARTRIDGE of Launceston, Tasmania.]

DUNRAVEN AND MOUNT EARL

page 548,
line 28, after '1826–9;' add 'adm. Trin. Coll., Dublin, 17 Nov. 1831;'

page 549,
line 9, for 'was living 1916' read '*d.* at her home in Seymour Str., Portman Sq., 30 Oct. 1917.'
line 25, after 'She' add 'who,' and after '1841' add '*d.* after a long illness at Kenry House, Putney Vale, 21, and was *bur.* 28 Sep. 1916, at Adare, co. Limerick. Admon. Nov. 1916, £1,956 gross and £1,783 net. He *d. s.p.m.* 14 June 1926 when the Barony of Henry became *extinct* but he was *suc.* in his other titles by his cousin.

V. 1926. 5. WINDHAM HENRY (WYNDHAM-QUIN), EARL OF DUNRAVEN AND MOUNT-EARL, VISCOUNT MOUNTEARL, VISCOUNT ADARE and BARON ADARE, all in the peerage of Ireland, cousin and h. being s. and h. of Windham Henry W-Q (*d.* 24 Aug. 1865), by Caroline, 3rd da. of Rear Adm. Sir George TYLER, K.H., which Windham Henry was 2nd s. of the 2nd Earl of Dunraven. He was *b.* 7 Feb. 1857; *m.*, 7 July 1885, Lady Eva Constance Aline, da. of Richard Southwell (BOURKE), 6th EARL OF MAYO. She *d.* 19 Jan. 1940. He *d.* 23 Oct. 1952.

VI. 1952. 6. RICHARD SOUTHWELL WINDHAM ROBERT (WYNDHAM-QUIN), EARL OF DUNRAVEN AND MOUNT-EARL, &c., 1st s. and h., *b.* 18 May 1887; ed. at Winchester; *m.* 1stly, 20 Oct. 1915, Helen Lindsay, da. of John SWIRE of Harlow, Essex. They were divorced in 1932 (she *d.* 1 Jan. 1962), and he *m.* 2ndly, 7 Mar. 1934, Nancy, da. of Thomas Burke YUILLE of Halifax County, Virginia, U.S.A. He *d.* 28 Aug. 1965. His widow *d.* 1994.

VII. 1965. 7. THADY WINDHAM THOMAS (WYNDHAM-QUIN), EARL OF DUNRAVEN AND MOUNT-EARL, &c., s. and h. by 2nd wife, *b.* 27 Oct. 1939; ed. at Le Rosey; *m.*, 15 Feb. 1969, Geraldine, da. of Air Commodore Gerard Ward MCALEER of Wokingham, Berks.

DUNSANDLE AND CLANCONAL

page 550,
line 4, after 'Henrietta,' add '(who *m.* 5 July 1780 and *d.* 6 Mar. 1852)'
line 5, after '1782' add 'in Dublin; adm. Trin. Coll., Dublin, 7 Oct. 1799'
line 21, after 'Dublin.' add 'He inherited none of the estates.'
line 28, after 'Eton' add '1863–6'

DUNSANY

page 551,
lines 32–3, delete from 'by' to 'DARTOIS' and replace by 'probably by Elizabeth, da. of John BRUNE' [See vol. x, *sub* Dunsany, pp. 599, 600.]

page 552,
line 19, after '1541' add ', which proclaimed Henry VIII King of Ireland'

page 553,
line 7, after 'learning,' add '(aa)'
note (aa) In 1591 he was apparently the only man available to translate for the English Govt. a letter written in Erse by the Primate of Ireland.
line 24, after 'death.' add 'He was ed. at Trin. Coll., Dublin.'
note (d), line 5, before 'The' add 'The wardship of his s. was granted to George Erskine, 19 Oct. 1603 (*Cal. Pat. Rolls, Chancery* [I.], 1–16 Jac. I, p. 6), which is odd *if* Lord Dunsany did die on 15 Dec. It is not known how reliable is the latter date.'

page 554,
line 21, for 'Suggenhill' read 'Suggenhall (now Sugnall)'
note (c), line 13 (on page 555), after 'general' add '(in the case of Howth as long as the title lasted, the Earldom became *extinct* with the death of the 4th Earl 9 Mar. 1909 and no heir general has claimed the Barony)'

page 556,
line 32, after '1916.' add 'Will pr. June 1916 at £344,954 gross and £61,204 net.'
line 35, after 'Eton' add '1892–4 and R.M.C., Sandhurst'
line 37, for '1914–' read '1914–18'
note (a), line 1, after 'Plunkett,' add '*b.* 15 Nov. 1848; ed. at Eton 1862–5 and Oxford (Ch. Ch.)'

page 557,
line 5, add at end 'He *d.* 25 Oct. 1957. His widow *d.* 1970.'
lines 6–7, delete all detail and replace as follows

XIX. 1957. 19. RANDALL ARTHUR HENRY (PLUNKETT), LORD DUNSANY [I.], s. and h., *b.* 25 Aug. 1906, at Portobello House, Dublin. He was ed. at Eton; *m.* 1stly, 23 Aug. 1938, Vera, yst. da. of Dr. Genesio DE SÀ SOTTOMAJOR of Sao Paulo, Brazil and formerly wife of Ivar BRYCE. They were divorced in 1947 and he *m.* 2ndly, 8 Oct. 1947, Sheila Victoria Katrin, da. of Sir Henry Erasmus Edward PHILIPPS, Bart. and widow of Major John Frederick (FOLEY), BARON DE RUTZEN.

[EDWARD JOHN CARLOS, s. and h. ap., *b.* 10 Sep. 1939; ed. at Eton and Slade Sch. of Fine Art; *m.*, 1982, Maria Alice Villela DE CARVALHO.]

DURHAM

page 560,
note (a), line 1, for 'the Russian Embassy' read 'our Embassy in Russia'

page 561,
line 7, add at end 'He *d. s.p.* 18 Sep. 1928. His widow *d.* 28 Oct. and was *bur.* 25 Nov. at Buckminster Church, Grantham 25 Nov. 1931.'

IV. 1928. 4. FREDERICK WILLIAM (LAMBTON), EARL OF DURHAM, &c., twin br. and h., *b.* 19 June 1855; *m.* Beatrix, da. of John BULTEEL of Pamflete, Ivybridge, Devon. 31 Jan. 1929. His widow *d.* 28, and was *bur.* 30 Apr. 1937 at Fence Houses, co. Durham.

V. 1929. 5. JOHN FREDERICK (LAMBTON), EARL OF DURHAM, &c., 1st s. and h., *b.* 7 Oct. 1884; ed. at Eton; *m.* 1stly, 12 Nov. 1919, Diana Mary, da. of Granville Richard Frederick FARQUHAR of Dalton Hall, Beverley, Yorks. She *d.* 28 Aug. 1924 and he *m.* 2ndly, 4 Mar. 1931, Hermione, da. of Sir George BULLOUGH, Bart. He *d.* 4 Feb. 1970. His widow *d.* 1990.

VI. 1970. 6. ANTHONY CLAUD FREDERICK (LAMBTON), EARL OF DURHAM, &c., 1st s. and h. by 1st wife, *b.* 10 July 1922; *m.*, 10 Aug. 1942, Belinda Bridget, da. of Major Douglas BLEW-JONES of Westward Ho!, North Devon. He disclaimed his peerages for life, 23 Feb. 1970, on the death of his father, retaining the courtesy title of VISCOUNT LAMBTON.

[EDWARD RICHARD LAMBTON, *styled* LORD DURHAM, s. and h. ap., *b.* 19 Oct. 1961; *m.*, 1983, Christabel Mary, yst. da. of Roderick MCEWAN of Colomell, Ayrshire.]

DYSART

page 562,
line 12, for 'June 1636' read '28 Sep. 1626 (when his da. Elizabeth was *bap.*)'
lines 14–15, delete from 'was' to *d. s.p.m.*' and replace by '*d.* 2 Aug. 1649.(c) He *d. s.p.m.*(d) between Jan. and 28 May 1654.'
note (c), delete all detail and replace by 'Coffin plate from Petersham Church at Ham House.'
note (d), delete all detail and replace by 'Two letters from Hyde to Nicholas in Jan. 1654 show that he was then living at Antwerp, and a letter of condolence from King Charles written on 28 May of that year suggests that he died shortly before that date. Charles' letter was [in the 1920s] in the possession of Lady Tollemache.'

page 563,
line 2, after 'line.(a)' add 'She was *bap.* 28 Sep. 1626.'
line 6, for 'before 22 May 1651,(c)' read '1648'
line 7, delete 'probably in 1647'
note (c), delete all detail

page 564,
line 8, for 'HESIGE read 'HENEAGE'
line 9, after 'DEVONSHIRE' add 'by a Mrs Heneage'

page 566,
line 11, after '*m.*,' add '(aa)'
note (aa) The marriage, which took place without his father's consent, was very unhappy. During the first 18 years of it the parties only cohabited for broken periods, in all not more than 3 years. He appears to have treated her brutally and to have deprived her of

the ordinary comforts suited to her station in life. In March 1847 the Court of Arches, satisfied "that wilful violence had been used upon the wife from which she had an undeniable right to be protected", pronounced a legal separation.

line 28, after 'Marylebone.' add 'Ed. at Eton 1834–8.'

note ([c]), after 'horse dealing.' add 'An action was brought against him unsuccessfully in 1852 (Jarrett *v.* Tollemache) at the Kingston Assizes, which sought to establish that Elizabeth Alford, a domestic servant, who had been Lord Huntingtower's mistress from 1843 to 1848, had been married to him in Scotland during that period. Lord H. in his evidence stated "In 1842 I was bankrupt, in 1844 I was insolvent". The jury found that the evidence before them did not establish the marriage to their satisfaction.'

page 567,
line 9, after 'Leicester.' add 'She *d.* 23 Dec. 1917. He *d. s.p.* 22 Nov. 1935 when his niece *suc.* to the Earldom and Barony and his distant cousin to the Baronetcy.

X. 1935. 10. WENEFRYDE AGATHA GREAVES SCOTT, niece and h. of line, *suo jure* COUNTESS OF DYSART, &c., being only da. of Agnes Mary Manners Tollemache (who *m.*, 4 Feb. 1882, Charles Norman Lindsay Tollemache SCOTT of Bosworth Park, co. Leics., and *d.* 27 July 1912), which Agnes Mary was 2nd but only surv. da. of William Lionel Felix and Katherine Elizabeth Camilla abovenamed. She was *b.* 13 Nov. 1889; *m.*, 4 Jan. 1913, Major Owain Edward Whitehead GREAVES. He *d.* 18 Feb. 1941. She *d.* 2 Jun. 1975.

XI. 1975. 11. ROSAMUND AGNES GREAVES, 1st da. and h., *suo jure* COUNTESS OF DYSART, &c., *b.* 15 Feb. 1914.

APPENDIXES

APPENDIX D

page 576,
note ([a]), after 'V.G.' add 'See G.H. White, "King Stephen's Earldoms", *Trans. R. Hist. Soc.*, vol. xiii, 1930, pp. 51–82.'

page 577,
line 21, delete from '["The' to 'Pauper."' and replace by 'It seems most unlikely that Hugh was ever *cr.* Earl of Bedford.' [See White, *op. cit.*, pp. 77–82.]

APPENDIX F

page 584,
line 7, for 'Wishart-Baillie-Cochrane' read 'Cochrane-Wishart-Baillie'

APPENDIX G

page 589,
note (b), after '*Journal*' add 'The name of Edmund Dunch, "Lord Burnell of East Wittenham" (see vol. ii, p. 436, *sub* BURNELL OF EAST WITTENHAM), does not appear.'

page 603,
line 22, after 'Church' add 'co. Lincoln'

page 606,
note (c), line 1, for 'Sholay' read 'Showley'

page 608,
line 10, for 'M.P. for Midx.' read 'of Henley Park in Ash, Surrey (*d.* 1650)'

page 624,
note (a), line 3, 'for twelve Peers' read 'eleven Peers or sons of Peers'

APPENDIX H

page 660,
line 10, for '1335/6' read '1334/5'
note (b), after '376.' add 'However, against the argument that no man except an Earl was entitled to the third penny may be set the case of Simon de St. Liz to whom the Eschaetors of Hunts. and Cambridge were ordered to pay again the third penny in 1248 (*Cal. Close Rolls, 1247–51*, p. 79).'

page 667,
line 15, for 'On the death of Alice in 1375' read 'After the death of Joan, da. of Alice, by about 1377,'
line 16, for 'was' read 'seems to have been'

CHART I

page 668,
line 9, for '1228' read '1226/7'
line 21, after 'Stafford' add 'She *d.* 1438.'

CHART V

page 672,
line 8, after 'Lancaster,' add '(Edmund is called Earl of Derby in Assize Roll 8 Edw. I, see DERBY)'

page 678,
line 7, after 'III' add '1337/8'
line 19, after 'II' add '(1381/2)'
line 23, after 'later' add '(1385)'

page 696,
note ([c]), after '312a.' add 'A dispute between Lord Grey of Codnor and Henry Lord Beaumont as to precedence arose in 1405, see *Proc. Privy Council*, vol. ii, p. 105.'

page 700,
note ([d]), before 'Compare' add 'There is now no doubt that Lord Say was so *created* in Feb. 1446/7, see vol. xi, Appendix I.'

page 725,
line 31, for '1777' read '1481 and 1777'
line 39, for '1603' read '1601/2'

page 730,
line 24, for 'seven' read 'eight'
note ([a]), after '459.' add 'In addition *Willelmo Hastinges militi, domino Hastynges*, had a grant of lands 17 Feb. 1461/2 and is said to have lately been raised to the rank of a baron. See vol. vi, pp. 370–1.'

page 743,
note ([a]), for '1695/6' read '1694/5' and after '522b.' add 'See also vol. xii, part 2, p. 694.'

APPENDIX I

page 761,
note ([b]), line 7, after '113).' add 'J. Keelan, *Family History*, vol. 14, NS. No. 85, 1985, pp. 3–7 rather unconvincingly argues that William Peverel was in fact a s. of William I.

page 767,
line 3, after 'Essex.' add '(Stephen's confirmation of this grant is now B.L. Egerton Ch. 2213F, and speaks of Robert as Earl of Nottingham, *ex inform.* G. Johnson.)'

VOLUME 5

EBURY OF EBURY MANOR

page 4,
line 6, add at end 'He *d.* 13 Nov. 1918. His widow *d.* 18 Dec. 1923.'
line 7, line to read as follows

III. 1918. 3. ROBERT VICTOR (GROSVENOR), BARON EBURY [1857], 1st s. and h., *b.* 28 June 1868;

line 11, for ']' read 'He *d. s.p.* 5 Nov. 1921. His widow *d.* 20 Oct. 1927.'

IV. 1921. 4. FRANCIS EGERTON (GROSVENOR), BARON EBURY, br. and h., *b.* 8 Sep. 1883; *m.*, 21 July 1902, Mary Adela, da. of John GLASSON. He *d.* 15 May 1932. His widow *d.* 13 Oct. 1960.

V. 1932. 5. ROBERT EGERTON (GROSVENOR), BARON EBURY, s. and h., *b.* 8 Feb. 1914; *m.* 1stly, 1 July 1933, Anne, da. of Major Herbert Walter ACLAND-TROYTE, M.C. This marriage was diss. by divorce 1941 (she *d.* 1982) and he *m.* 2ndly, 21 Nov. 1941, Denise Margaret, 2nd da. of John Reginald (YARDE-BULLER), 3rd BARON CHURSTON. This marriage was in turn diss. by divorce 1954 and he *m.* 3rdly, 12 Oct. 1954, Sheila Winifred, da. of Arthur Edward DASHFIELD of Oxford. He *d.* 5 May 1957 in a motor racing accident. His widow was still living 1995.

VI. 1957. 6. FRANCIS EGERTON (GROSVENOR), BARON EBURY, s. and h. by his 1st wife, *b.* 8 Feb. 1934; ed. at Eton; *m.* 1stly, 10 Dec. 1957, Gillian Elfrida Astley Elfin, da. of Martin Roland SOAMES. This marriage was diss. by divorce 1962 and he *m.* 2ndly, 8 Mar. 1963, Kyra, da. of L.L. ASLIN. This marriage was in turn diss. by divorce 1973 and he *m.* 3rdly, 1974, Suzanne Jean, da. of Graham SUCKLING of Tai Tapu, New Zealand.

[JULIAN FRANCIS MARTIN GROSVENOR, 1st s. and h. ap. by 1st wife, *b.* 8 June 1959; ed. at Gordonstoun; *m.*, 1987, Danielle, 6th da. of Theo ROSSI of Sydney, Queensland, Australia.]

ECHINGHAM

page 5,
line 11, after 'before him' add ', before 24 Aug. 1325' [*Hist. MSS. Com.*, De L'Isle and Dudley MSS., vol. 1, p. 138]
note (g), line 2, after 'no. 1).' add ', who on 30 Mar. 1333 was lord of the manor of Echingham and rector of Hurst Monceux (*H.M.C.*, De L'Isle and Dudley MSS., vol. 1, p. 141).'

EDINBURGH

page 7,
line 20, after 'Saxony' add '(ca)'
note (ca), For the title Duke of Saxony to which he was not in fact entitled, see *The Greville Memoirs*, vol. iv, 1938, pp. 432–3. [*ex inform.* Eric J. Thompson]

page 8,
line 13, for 'was living 1917' read '*d.* 25 Oct. 1920.'
[after line 17]

* * * * * *

VI. 1953. 1. *H.R.H.* PHILIP, PRINCE OF THE UNITED KINGDOM OF GREAT BRITAIN AND NORTHERN IRELAND, only s. of *H.R.H.* PRINCE ANDREW OF GREECE AND DENMARK. See below, p. 786.

EFFINGHAM

page 9,
line 20, for 'BOUGHTON' read 'BROUGHTON'

page 15,
line 15, after 'year' add 'and was *bur.* in Preston Churchyard'

page 16,
line 9, after 'Unionist.' add 'He *d.* unm. 6 May 1927.'

EARLDOM. IX. BARONY. XV. } 1927 5 and 15. GORDON FREDERICK HENRY CHARLES (HOWARD), EARL OF EFFINGHAM, &c., cousin and h., being 1st s. and h. of Capt Frederick Charles HOWARD (*d.* 26 Oct. 1893), by Constance Eleanora Caroline, 1st da. of George James (FINCH), 11th EARL OF WINCHELSEA, which Frederick Charles was 2nd s. of the 2nd Earl of Effingham. He was *b.* 18 May 1873; *m.* 1stly, 26 Jan. 1904, Rosamund Margaret, da. of Edward Harrison HUDSON of Scarborough. This marriage was diss. by divorce 1914 (she *d.* 25 Dec. 1957) and he *m.* 2ndly, 17 Jan. 1924, Madeleine, da. of William D. FOSHAY and widow of James P. KELCHER of San Francisco, California. He *d.* 7 July 1946. His widow *d.* 27 June 1958.

EARLDOM. X. BARONY. XVI. } 1946 6 and 16. MOWBRAY HENRY GORDON (HOWARD), EARL OF EFFINGHAM, &c., *b.* 29 Nov. 1905; ed. at Lancing; *m.* 1stly, 28 Oct. 1938, Manci Maria Malvina, da. of Ferenz Joseph GERTLER. This marriage was diss. by divorce 1946 and he *m.* 2ndly, 12 Aug. 1952, Gladys Irene, da. of Capt. William FREEMAN, Merchant Navy, formerly wife of Frederick Charles KERRY. This marriage was in turn diss. by divorce 1971 and he *m.* 3rdly, 1972, Mabel Suzanne Mingay, da. of Maurice Jules-Marie LE PEN of Paris and widow of Wing Cmdr. Francis Talbot CRAGG.

EGERTON OF TATTON

page 17,
lines 22–3, delete from ',([c])' to 'work'
line 26, for 'was living 1917' read '*d.* 15 Sep. 1931.'

III. 1909. 3. ALAN DE (TATTON), BARON EGERTON OF TATTON, *b.* 19 Mar. 1845; *m.*, 13 June 1867, Anna Louisa, da. of Simon Watson TAYLOR, of Erlestoke Park, co. Wilts. He *d.* 9 Sep. 1920. His widow *d.* 22 Dec. 1933.

IV. 1920. 4. MAURICE (EGERTON), BARON EGERTON OF TATTON, 3rd but only surv. s. and h., *b* 4 Aug. 1874. Served in WW1 as Lieut. Com., R.N.V.R.([c]) He *d.* unm. 30 Jan. 1958 when his Barony became *extinct.*

note ([c]), delete from 'Alan' to 'R.N.V.R.'

EGLINTON

page 18,
line 11, for 'Lord of Lorne' read '2nd LORD LORNE [S.]'

page 27,
lines 4–5, delete from '3rd' to '[I.]' and replace by '2nd EARL OF YARBOROUGH, by Anderson Horsley Maria Adelaide, 2nd da. of Cornwallis (MAUDE), 3rd VISCOUNT HAWARDEN [I.]'
line 18, after 'Australia' add 'He *d.* 10 Aug. 1919. His widow *d.* 6 Oct. 1923.'
line 19, line to read as follows

XVI. 1919. 16. ARCHIBALD SEATON (MONTGOMERIE), EARL OF EGLINTON, &c., 1st s. and h., *b.* 23 June 1880, at Redburn, Irvine, co. Ayr; *styled* LORD MONTGOMERIE 1892–1919;
line 26, for ']' read 'This marriage was diss. by divorce 1922 (she *d.* 10 May 1962) and he *m.* 2ndly, 16 Aug. 1922, Marjorie, da. of Thomas Walker MCINTYRE and widow of Guy VERNON. He *d.* 22 Apr. 1945. His widow *d.* 7 Dec. 1963.

XVII. 1945. 17. ARCHIBALD WILLIAM ALEXANDER (MONTGOMERIE), EARL OF EGLINTON, &c., only s. and h. by 1st wife, *b.* 16 Oct. 1914; ed. at Eton and Oxford (New Coll.); *m.*, 10 Nov. 1938, Ursula Joan, 1st da. of Ronald Bannatyne WATSON. He *d.* 21 Apr. 1966. His widow *d.* 1987.

XVIII. 1966. 18. ARCHIBALD GEORGE (MONTGOMERIE), EARL OF EGLINTON, &c., only s. and h., *b.* 27 Aug. 1939; ed. at Eton; *m.*, 7 Feb. 1964, Marion Carolina, John Henry DUNN-YARKER of Chateau de la Tour de Peilz, Vaud, Switzerland.

[HUGH ARCHIBALD WILLIAM MONTGOMERIE, *styled* LORD MONTGOMERIE, s. and h. ap., *b.* 24 July 1966; *m.*, 1991, S. Alexandra, 1st da. of Neil REDPATH.]

EGMONT

page 32,
line 9, for 'was living 1917. read '*d.* 1 June 1932.'
lines 29–30, delete from 'living' to 'work' and replace by '*d.* 6 Nov. 1926.'

IX. 1910. 9. CHARLES JOHN (PERCEVAL), EARL OF EGMONT, &c., br. and h., *b.* 29 June 1858; *m.*, 15 June 1890, Florence, da. of George GIBSON, M.D. He *d. s.p.* 10 Jan. 1929 when his titles all became *dormant*. His widow *d.* 31 Dec. 1954.

X. 1939. 10. FREDERICK GEORGE MOORE (PERCEVAL), EARL OF EGMONT, &c., distant cousin and h. male, being s. and h. of Frederick Joseph Trevelyan PERCEVAL, *de jure* 10th EARL OF EGMONT, but who *d.* (in a motor accident) 16 May 1932, before establishing his claim to the titles, by Cecilia, da. of James Burns MOORE, of Montreal, Canada, which Frederick Joseph was 1st s. and h. of George Drummond Ince Perceval (*d.* 19 Jan. 1920), by Marianne, da. of Edward BAXTER, which George was 2nd s. of Frederick James Perceval (*d.* 22 July 1861), by his 2nd wife Emma, 2nd da. of Ralph GILBERT, which Frederick James was 2nd s. of Rt. Hon. Spencer PERCEVAL, Chancellor of the Exchequer and First Lord of the Treasury (*d.* 11 May 1812, being assassinated in the Lobby of the House of Commons), by Jane, 2nd da. of Lieut. Gen. Sir Thomas Spencer WILSON, Bart., which Spencer was 7th s. of the 2nd Earl of Egmont. He was *b.* 14 Apr. 1914; *m.*, 31 Aug. 1932, Ann Geraldine, da. of Douglas Gerald MOODY, of Calgary, Alberta, Canada.

[THOMAS FREDERICK GERALD PERCEVAL, *styled* VISCOUNT PERCEVAL, 1st and only surv. s. and h. ap., *b.* 17 Aug. 1934.]

EGREMONT

page 34,
line 20, for 'Sometime afterwards' read 'On 31 Oct. or 1 Nov.'
note (d), line 3., after '*sqq.*' add 'See also R.A. Griffiths, *Speculum*, vol. xliii, 1968, pp. 622, 623–4.'

page 35,
line 5, after '(c)' add 'He was apparently never formally recognised as Lord Egremont.'
line 11, for 'before 21 Mar. 1496/7' read 'after '30 May 1505' [*Y.A.S.*, MS. 282, f. 103v. *Ex inform.* Drs Rosemary Horrox and Henry Summerson]
line 12, delete '(e)'
note (e), delete all detail

ELDON

page 40,
line 23, after '[I.].' add 'She *d.* 30 Aug. 1921. He *d.* 10 Aug. 1926.'

page 41,
lines 2–3, for 'was living 1917' read '*d.* 3 Dec. 1946.'

line 3, line to read as follows

IV. 1926. 4. JOHN (SCOTT), EARL OF ELDON, &c., grandson and h. being

line 5, for ']' read 'He *m.* at Brompton Oratory, 10 Apr. 1934, Magdalen Mary Charlotte, 1st da. of Thomas Alexander (FRASER), 14th BARON LOVAT. She *d.* 1969. He *d.* 20 Oct. 1976.'

V. 1976. 5. JOHN JOSEPH NICHOLAS (SCOTT), EARL OF ELDON, &c., 1st s. and h., *b.* 24 Apr. 1937; ed. at Ampleforth and Oxford (Trin. Coll.); *m.*, 1961, Claudine, yst. da. of COUNT VON MONTJOYE-VAUFREY of Vienna.

[JOHN FRANCIS THOMAS MARIE JOSEPH COLUMBA FIDELIS, *styled* VISCOUNT ENCOMBE, s. and h. ap., *b.* 9 July 1962.]

ELGIN

page 44,
line 4, after 'Haddington' add ', by Mary, da. of Lord Robert MANNERS.'

page 46,
line 6, line to read as follows

EARLDOM [S.] X. BARONY III. } 1917 10 and 3. EDWARD JAMES (BRUCE), EARL OF ELGIN, &c., 1st s. and h., *b.* 8 June 1881 at Broomhall;

lines 10–11, delete from 'Having' to 'work]' and replace by 'He *m.*, 5 Jan. 1921, Katherine Elizabeth, 1st da. of Thomas Horatio Arthur Ernest (COCHRANE), 1st BARON COCHRANE OF CULTS. He *d.* 27 Nov. 1968. His widow *d.* 1989.

EARLDOM [S.] XI. BARONY IV. } 1968 11 and 4. ANDREW DOUGLAS ALEXANDER THOMAS (BRUCE), EARL OF ELGIN, &c., 1st s. and h., *b.* 17 Feb. 1924; ed. at Eton and Oxford (Balliol Coll.); *m.*, 27 Apr. 1959, Victoria Mary, da. of Major Dudley George USHER, of Kilchrenan, co. Argyll.

[CHARLES EDWARD BRUCE, *styled* LORD BRUCE, 1st s. and h., *b.* 19 Oct. 1961.]

ELIBANK

page 46,
line 20, delete 'M.A. Oxford 1605;'

page 49,
line 15, after '1844.' add 'He *d.* 20 Feb. 1927. His widow *d.* 22 Oct. 1936.'

line 28, after 'Edinburgh' add '*d. v.p. s.p.* at Elibank, 13, and was *bur.* 17 Sep. 1920 at Darnhall, Eddleston when his Barony became *extinct*. His widow *d.* from the apparently accidental discharge of her gun when shooting near her house, 27 Sep. 1929, and was *bur.* at Darnhall afsd.'

BARONY [S.] XI. VISCOUNTCY. II. } 1920 11 and 2. CHARLES GIDEON (MURRAY), VISCOUNT ELIBANK, &c., 3rd but 1st surv. s., *b.* 7 Aug. 1877; *m.*, 23 Jan. 1908, Ermine Mary Katherine, da. of Henry Robert MADOCKS of Glanywern, Denbigh [for further detail see vol. xiii, p. 152]. He *d.* 11 Mar. 1951. His widow *d.* 22 Mar. 1955.

BARONY [S.] XII. VISCOUNTCY. III. } 1951 12 and 3. ARTHUR CECIL (MURRAY), VISCOUNT ELIBANK, &c., br. and h., *b.* 27 Mar. 1879; *m.*, 3 July 1931, Faith Celli, da. of Francis H. STANDING. She *d.* 16 Dec. 1942. He *d. s.p.* 5 Dec. 1962 when his Viscountcy became *extinct*, but he was *suc.* in his Barony and Baronetcy by a distant cousin.

XIII. 1962. 13. JAMES ALASTAIR FREDERICK CAMPBELL (ERSKINE-MURRAY), LORD ELIBANK [S. 1643], and a Baronet [S. 1628], distant cousin and h., being s. and h. of James Robert ERSKINE-MURRAY (*d.* 12 Feb. 1927), by Alleine Frederica Florinda, da. of Major Gen. G.F. GILDEA, C.B., which James Robert was 1st s. of Alexander Erskine ERSKINE-MURRAY (*d.* 17 Dec. 1907), by Helen, da. of Robert PRINGLE, W.S., of Symington, which Alexander was 1st s. of James MURRAY (*d.* 17 Feb. 1844), by Isabella, da. of James ERSKINE of Aberdona, which James was 2nd s. of the 7th Baron Elibank by his 2nd wife. He was *b.* 23 June 1902; ed. at Harrow and R.M.C., Sandhurst and Glasgow Univ. He *d.* unm. 2 June 1973.

XIV. 1973. 14. ALAN D'ARDIS (ERSKINE-MURRAY), LORD ELIBANK, cousin and h., being s. and h. of Robert Alan ERSKINE-MURRAY (*d.* 21 Aug. 1939), by Eileen Mary, da. of John Percy MACMANUS of Piersfield House, co. Westmeath, which Robert Alan was br. to James Robert abovenamed. He was *b.* 31 Dec. 1923; ed. at Bedford Sch. and Cambridge (Peterhouse Coll.); *m.*, 1962, Valerie Sylvia, da. of Herbert William DENNIS

[ROBERT FRANCIS ALAN ERSKINE-MURRAY, MASTER OF ELIBANK, 1st s. and h. ap., *b.* 10 Oct. 1964; ed. at Harrow.]

ELLENBOROUGH

page 50,
line 17, for 'Unerigge' read 'Ewanrigg'

page 52,
line 21, after 'Elizabeth' add ', widow of Charles Nevinson HOWARD, VISCOUNT ANDOVER,'

page 53,
note ([a]), lines 5–6, for 'who committed suicide when she left him' read 'from whom she was divorced in 1842. In 1841 she went through a form of marriage with a Greek named Spiridon Theotoky. After this she lived with an Albanian brigand named Xristodolous, following which she' [For the complicated marital adventures of Jane Digby see Mary Lovell, *A Scandalous Life*, 1995].

page 54,
line 6, for 'was living 1917' read '*d.* 17 May 1932.'
lines 13–14, delete from 'He' to 'work' and replace as follows

V. 1902. 5. EDWARD DOWNES (LAW), BARON ELLENBOROUGH [1802], distant cousin and h., being 1st s. and h. of Henry Spencer LAW (*d.* 15 July 1885), by Dorothea Anne, 1st da. of Col. John Staunton ROCHFORT of Clogrenane, co. Carlow, which Henry Spencer was 3rd s. of the 1st Baron Ellenborough. He was *b.* 9 May 1841; *m.*, 19 Dec. 1906, Hermione, da. of E.W.H. SCHENLEY. He *d. s.p.* 9 Dec. 1915. His widow *d.* 26 Aug. 1942.

VI. 1915. 6. CECIL HENRY (LAW), BARON ELLENBOROUGH [1802], br. and h., *b.* 25 Nov. 1849; *m.*, 22 July 1884, Alice Caroline, da. of John Harvey ASTELL, M.P., of Woodbury Hall, co. Beds. She *d.* 3 Nov. 1916. He *d.* 22 and was *bur.* 26 Jan. 1931 at Dorchester Cemetery,'

VII. 1931. 7. HENRY ASTELL (LAW), BARON ELLENBOUGH [1802], s. and h., *b.* 11 July 1889; served in WW1 as Capt. King's Own Yorks. L.I.([a]) He *m.*, 31 Jan. 1923, Helen Dorothy, da. of Harry William LOVATT. He *d.* 19 May 1945. His widow was still living 1995.

VIII. 1945. 8. RICHARD EDWARD CECIL (LAW), BARON ELLENBOROUGH, 1st s. and h., *b.* 14 Jan. 1926; ed. at Eton and Cambridge (Magdalene Coll.); *m.*, 9 Oct. 1953, Rachel Mary, da. of Major Ivor Mathews HEDLEY.

[RUPERT EDWARD HENRY LAW, 1st s. and h. ap., *b.* 28 Mar. 1955; *m.*, 1981, Grania Janet Gray, da. of Thomas Gray (BOARDMAN), BARON BOARDMAN, a Life Peer.]

note ([a]), lines 1–4, delete from 'Edward' to 'L.I.'

ELLESMERE

page 56,
line 13, for 'was living 1917' read '*d.* 23, and was *bur.* 28 Sep. 1926 at Worsley, co. Lancaster.'
line 14, line to read as follows

IV. 1914. 4. JOHN FRANCIS GRANVILLE SCROPE (EGERTON), EARL OF ELLESMERE, &c., s. and h., *b.* 14 Nov. 1872 at Bridgewater House; *styled* VISCOUNT BRACKLEY till 1914;

lines 21–2, delete from 'Having' to 'work]' and replace by 'He *d.* 24 Aug. 1944. His widow *d.* 1972.'

V. 1944. 5. JOHN SUTHERLAND (EGERTON), EARL OF ELLESMERE and VISCOUNT BRACKLEY, s. and h., *b.* 10 May 1915; ed. at Eton and Cambridge (Trin. Coll.). On the death, 1 Feb. 1963, of his distant cousin George Granville (SUTHERLAND-LEVESON-GOWER), 5th DUKE OF SUTHERLAND, &c., he *suc.* to all his dignities, except for the Earldom of Sutherland. See SUTHERLAND (Dukedom), *cr.* 1833. He *m.*, 29 Apr. 1939, Lady Diana Evelyn, da. of Alan Ian (PERCY), 8th DUKE OF NORTHUMBERLAND. She *d.* 1978 and he *m.* 2ndly, 1979, Evelyn Mary, da. of Major Robert MOUBRAY.

ELPHINSTONE

page 59,
line 11–13, delete from 'William' to 'OXFURD' and replace by 'Charles MAITLAND, LORD HALTON (afterwards 3rd EARL OF LAUDERDALE), by Elizabeth, da. of Richard LAUDER of Halton, Edinburgh.'
note (b), line 3, for '1680' read '1680/1'
note (c), line 1, for 'His next elder' read 'His eldest br. John was *b.* and *d.* 29 June 1703, the third' and for 'eldest' read '2nd br. John'
line 2, for 'Archibald' read 'Gilbert'

page 61,
lines 36–7, for 'was living' read '*d.* 16 Mar. 1922.'

page 62,
line 10, after 'Forfar.' add 'He *d.* 28 Nov. 1955. His widow *d.* 8 Feb. 1961.'
lines 11–12, delete all detail and replace as follows

BARONY [S.] XVII. BARONY [U.K.] III. } 1955 17 and 3. JOHN ALEXANDER (ELPHINSTONE), LORD ELPHINSTONE, &c., s. and h., *b.* 22 Mar. 1914. He was ed. at Eton and Oxford (Ch. Ch.). He *d.* unm. 15 Nov. 1975.

BARONY [S.] XVIII. BARONY [U.K.] IV. } 1975 18 and 4. JAMES ALEXANDER (ELPHINSTONE), LORD ELPHINSTONE, &c., nephew and h., being 1st s. and h. of Rev. Andrew Charles Victor ELPHINSTONE, by Jean Frances, 4th da. of Angus Valdimar HAMBRO of Milton Abbas, co. Dorset, which Andrew Charles was br. of 17th Lord Elphinstone. He was *b.* 22 Apr. 1953; Eton and R.A.C., Cirencester; *m.*, 1978, Willa Mary Gabriel, da. Major George David CHETWODE.

[ALEXANDER MOUNTSTUART ELPHINSTONE, MASTER OF ELPHINSTONE, 1st s. and h. ap., *b.* 15 Apr. 1980.]

ELY

page 65,
line 17, after 'wife' add '; *b.* in co. Wexford, adm. Trin. Coll., Dublin, 21 Feb. 1731/2, aged 18'
line 35, after 'under' add '(c)'
note (b), line 1, after 'Nicholas' add 'by respectively (possibly), Miss A.M. Phillips, a Dublin actress, and by Mary Heron, his housekeeper (Mount Loftus Papers, document no. 83, draft marriage settlement of Nicholas, 22 Mar. 1758, Ms. Catalogue by Dr Hetherington, now in the National Library of Ireland; Bettina Grattan-Bellew, *J. Kilkenny Arch. Soc.*, no. 25, 1977, p. 24, *ex inform.* Dr Robert Hetherington).'
line 4, after 'V.G.' add 'The aforesaid Grant shows an unusual interest in, and respect for, heraldry. The attitude of the 1st Viscount is also shown by his son (the 1st Earl) obtaining a grant of arms on the occasion of his marriage and changing his name. (Gen. Office of Ireland, no. 103, pp. 49 and 50, 19 July 1736, Hetherington catalogue no. 46).'
note (c), He appears to have been feeble, both physically and mentally, possibly as the result of a blow on the head when young (Mount Loftus documents 134 and 151 in MS. catalogue by Dr Hetherington).'

page 66,
line 16, after '1745,' add '(settlement 12 Feb. 1744/5)' [Mount Loftus papers, Hetherington catalogue, no. 58]
line 29, after '1738;' add 'adm. Trin. Coll., Dublin, 13 Aug. 1755;'
line 30, after '1759;' add 'Hon. LL.D. Trin. Coll., 1766;'

page 69,
line 18, after 'Sussex.' add 'He *d. s.p.* 18 Dec. 1925. His widow *d.* 1 Aug. 1931.'

MARQUESSATE [I.] VI.
EARLDOM [I.] VIII.
VISCOUNTCY [I.] XIII.
1925

6. GEORGE HERBERT (LOFTUS), MARQUESS OF ELY, &c., br. and h., *b.* 19 Apr. 1854; *m.* 1stly, 29 Apr. 1884, Emily Harriet, da. of Major Arthur VANDELEUR, of Ralahine, co. Clare. She *d.* 27 Nov. 1886 and he *m.* 2ndly, 7 June 1902, Ethel Beatrice Lemprière, da. of Nigel John Davies GRESLEY, of Hobart, Tasmania. She *d.* 23 Oct. 1927. He *d.* 10 Apr. 1935.

MARQUESSATE [I.] VII.
EARLDOM [I.] IX.
VISCOUNTCY [I.] XIV.
1935

7. GEORGE HENRY WELLINGTON (LOFTUS), MARQUESS OF ELY, &c., 2nd but 1st surv. s. and h., being s. by 2nd wife, *b.* 3 Sep. 1903; ed. at Lancing; *m.*, 5 Sep. 1928, Thea Margaret Gordon, da. of Lars GRONVOLD of Tvedestrand, Norway. He *d.* 31 May 1969. His widow was still living 1995.

MARQUESSATE [I.] VIII.
EARLDOM [I.] X.
VISCOUNTCY [I.] XV.
1969

8. CHARLES JOHN (TOTTENHAM), MARQUESS OF ELY, &c., distant cousin and h., being 1st s. and h. of George Leonard TOTTENHAM (*d.* 9 June 1928), by Cecile Elizabeth, 3rd da. of James Salkeld BURRA of Bockhanger, Kennington. Kent, which George was 2nd s. of Major Charles Robert Worsley T. (*d.* 31 Oct.

1923), by his 1st wife Dorothea Anne, da. of Leonard CORNWALL, of Brownstown House, co. Meath, which Charles Robert was 1st s. of Charles John T. (*d.* 17 Dec. 1878), by Isabella, da. of Cornwallis (MAUDE), 3rd VISCOUNT HAWARDEN, which Charles John was 1st s. of Robert Ponsonby TOTTENHAM (which name he resumed, from LOFTUS, *d.* 26 Apr. 1850), by Alicia, da. of Cornwallis (MAUDE), 1st VISCOUNT HAWARDEN, which Robert Ponsonby was 2nd s. of the 1st Marquess of Ely. He was *b.* 30 May 1913; *m.* 1stly, 23 June 1938, Katherine Elizabeth, da. of Lieut. Col. W.H. CRAIG of Kingston, Ontario, Canada. She *d.* 1975, and he *m.* 2ndly, 1978, Elspeth Ann, da. of P.T. HAY.

[CHARLES JOHN TOTTENHAM, *styled* VISCOUNT LOFTUS, *b.* 2 Feb. 1943; ed. at Trin. Coll. Sch. and Toronto Univ.; *m.*, 1969, Judith Marvell, da. of Dr J.J. PORTER, of Calgary, Alberta, Canada.]

EMLY OF TURVOE

page 70,
line 31, after 'Kilfane.' add 'She *d.* 5 Sep. 1925. He *d. s.p.* 24 Nov. 1932 when his title became *extinct*.'

ENGAINE

page 75,
line 4, after 'da.' add '(?by his 1st wife)'

ENNISKILLEN

page 82,
line 24, after '1768' add 'in co. Fermanagh'
line 25, after '1803;' add 'adm. Trin. Coll., Dublin, 16 Aug. 1785;'

page 84,
line 7, after '1852.' add 'He *d.* 28 Apr. 1924. His widow *d.* 30 Jan. 1937.'
line 8, line to read as follows

V. 1924. 5. JOHN HENRY MICHAEL (COLE), EARL OF ENNISKILLEN, Etc. 2nd[b] but 1st surv. s. and h., *b.* 10 Sep. 1876, at 24 Arlington Str. Midx., *styled* VISCOUNT COLE 1886–1924;

line 15, for ']' read 'This marriage was diss. by divorce in 1931 (she *d.* 15 Aug. 1937) and he *m.* 2ndly, 4 May 1932, Mary Cicely, da. of Hugh NEVILL, and widow of Major Thomas SYERS. He *d. s.p.m.s.* 19 Feb. 1963. His widow *d.* 18 July 1963.'

[MICHAEL GALBRAITH LOWRY COLE, *styled* VISCOUNT COLE, s. and h. ap., *b.* 25 Nov. 1921; ed. at Eton. He *d. v.p.* unm. 26 Aug. 1956.]

VI. 1963. 6. DAVID LOWRY (COLE), EARL OF ENNISKILLEN, &c., nephew and h., being 1st s. of Galbraith Lowry Egerton COLE (*d.* 6 Oct. 1929), by Lady Eleanor, da. of Gerald William (BALFOUR), 2nd EARL OF BALFOUR, which Gerald was 3rd s. of 4th Earl of Enniskillen and br. of the 5th Earl. He was *b.* 10 Sep. 1918; ed. at Eton; *m.* 1stly, 31 July 1940, Sonia Mary, da. of Major Thomas SYERS (see above). This marriage was diss. by divorce in 1955 (she *d.* 1982), and he *m.* 2ndly, 7 May 1955, Nancy Henderson, da. of Dr John Alexander MACLENNAN of Bridgeport, Connecticut, U.S.A. He *d.* 30 May 1989. His widow was still living 1995.

VII. 1989. 7. ANDREW JOHN GALBRAITH (COLE), EARL OF ENNISKILLEN, &c., only s. and h. by 1st wife, *b.* 28 Apr. 1942; ed. at Eton; *m.*, 3 Oct. 1964, Sarah Francis Caroline, da. of Major Gen. John Keith EDWARDS of Nairobi, Kenya.

ERDINGTON

page 90,
note (b), line 10, for '5 July 1394' read '4 May 1386' [*ex inform.* G.W. Watson]

ERNE OF CROM CASTLE

page 93,
line 20, for 'was living 1919' read '*d.* 23 Mar. 1924.'

page 94,
line 3, for 'was living 1919' read ' She *m.* 2ndly, Apr. 1918, Col. Algernon Francis STANLEY, D.S.O. He *d.* 10 Feb. 1962. She *d.* 14 Jan. 1959.'
line 4, line to read as follows

EARLDOM, &c. [I.] V.
BARONY [I.] VI. } 1914 5 and 6. JOHN HENRY GEORGE (CRICHTON), EARL OF ERNE OF CROM CASTLE, &c., grandson and h.,

lines 9–10, delete from 'Having' to 'work]' and replace by 'He *m.*, 15 July 1931, Lady Davidema Katherine Cynthia Mary Millicent, yr. da. of Victor Alexander George Robert (LYTTON), 2nd EARL OF LYTTON. He *d.* 23 May 1940 in France of wounds received. His widow *m.* 2ndly, 28 Aug. 1945, Col. Christopher Montague WOODHOUSE, D.S.O., O.B.E., M.P. She was still living 1995.

EARLDOM, &c. [I.] VI.
BARONY [I.] VII. } 1940 6 and 7. HENRY GEORGE VICTOR JOHN (CRICHTON), EARL OF ERNE OF CROM CASTLE, &c., only s. and h., *b.* 9 July 1937; ed. at Eton; *m.*, 5 Nov. 1958, Camilla Margaret, 1st da. of Wing Cmdr. Owen George Endicott ROBERTS. This marriage was diss. by divorce in 1980 and he *m.* 2ndly, 1980, Anna Carin, da. of (__) BJORCK, formerly wife of (__) ROBERTS.

ERROLL

page 100,
line 21, after 'Bristol' add 'and was *bur.* 4 May in Bristol Cath.'

page 102,
line 3, after '46' add 'and was *bur.* in the vault of the Compton family at Minstead in that co. M.I.'

page 103,
line 24, after '1849.' add 'He *d.* 8 July 1927. His widow *d.* 12 Oct. 1934.'
line 25, line to read as follows

XXI. 1927. 21. VICTOR ALEXANDER SERELD (HAY), EARL OF ERROLL, &c., 1st s. and h., *b.* 17 Oct.

line 27, after 'sponsors;' add '*styled* LORD KILMARNOCK 1891–1927;'
line 32, for ']' read 'He *d.* 20 Feb. 1928. His widow *m.* 2ndly, 27 June 1935, Major James Frank GRESHAM. He *d.* 19 May 1944. She *d.* 18 Jan. 1957.'

XXII. 1928. 22. JOSSLYN VICTOR (HAY), EARL OF ERROLL, LORD HAY OF ERROLL, and HEREDITARY CONSTABLE all in the peerage of Scotland, *also* BARON KILMARNOCK [U.K. 1831], 1st s. and h., *b.* 11 May 1901; *m* 1stly, 22 Sep. 1923, Lady Idina, da. of Gilbert George Reginald (SACKVILLE), 8th EARL DE LA WARR. This marriage was diss. by divorce in 1930 (she *d.* 5 Nov. 1955) and he *m.* 2ndly, 8 Feb. 1930, Edith Mildred Mary Agnes, da. of Richard Watson MAUDE of Cleveland, co. Yorks. and widow of (__), RAMSAY-HILL She *d.* 13 Oct. 1939. He *d. s.p.m.* 24 Jan. 1941, being *k.* near Nairobi, Kenya, when he was *suc.* in his Barony of Kilmarnock by his br. (see KILMARNOCK below) and in his other titles by his da.

XXIII. 1941. 23. DIANA DENYSE HAY, da. and h. by 1st wife, *suo jure* COUNTESS OF ERROLL, LADY HAY, and HEREDITARY CONSTABLE OF SCOTLAND. She was *b.* 5 Jan. 1926; *m.* 1stly, 19 Dec. 1946, Sir Rupert Iain Kay MONCREIFFE of the Ilk, Bart. He *d.* 27 Feb. 1985. This marriage was diss. by divorce in 1964 and she *m.* 2ndly, 27 Nov. 1964, Major Raymond Alexander CARNEGIE. She *d.* 16 May 1978.

XXIV. 1978. 24. MERLIN SERELD VICTOR GILBERT (HAY), EARL OF ERROLL, &c., 1st s. and h., *b.* 20 Apr. 1948; ed. at Eton and Cambridge (Trin. Coll.). He *suc.* his father as Baronet [N.S. 1685], 1985; *m.*, 1982, Isabelle Jacqueline Laline, da. of Thomas Sidney Astell HOHLER, M.C., of Wolverton Park, Basingtoke, co. Hants.

[HARRY THOMAS WILLIAM HAY, *styled* LORD HAY, s. and h. ap., *b.* 8 Aug. 1984.]

ERSKINE

page 108,
line 14, after 'Dumfries.' add '([c])'

note (c), On 12 July 1826 there appeared before the Lord Mayor of London a woman in needy circumstances claiming to be Lady Erskine. She was presumably an impostor.

page 110,
line 5, for 'was living 1919' read '*d.* 2 Mar. 1922.'
line 6, line to read as follows

VI. 1913. 6. MONTAGU (ERSKINE), BARON ERSKINE OF RESTORMEL CASTLE, 1st s. and h., 13 Apr. 1865, in Portland Place

line 11, for ']' read 'She *d.* 3 Dec. 1936 at Spratt Hall, co. Northampton. He *d.* 9 Feb. 1957.'

VII. 1957. 7. DONALD CARDROSS FLOWER (ERSKINE), BARON ERSKINE OF RESTORMEL CASTLE, s. and h., *b.* 3 June 1899; ed. at Charterhouse and R.M.C., Sandhurst. On the death of his distant cousin, 15th Earl of Buchan, 18 Dec. 1960, he *suc.* him as 16th Earl of Buchan [for further detail see that title, above].

ESHER

page 111,
line 19, after 'James's.' add 'He *d.* 22 Jan. 1930. His widow *d.* 7 Feb. 1940.'
line 20, line to read as follows

VISCOUNTCY. III. BARONY. III. } 1930 3. OLIVER BALIOL SYLVAIN (BRETT), VISCOUNT ESHER, 1st s. and h., *b.* 23 Mar. 1881; ed. at Eton;

line 24, for ']' read 'He *d.* 8 Oct. 1963. His widow *d.* 22 July 1965.'

VISCOUNTCY. IV. BARONY. IV. } 1963 4. LIONEL GORDON BALIOL (BRETT), VISCOUNT ESHER, s. and h., *b.* 18 July 1913; ed. at Eton and Oxford (New Coll.); *m.*, 22 Oct. 1935, Helena Christian Olive, 1st da. of Col. Ebenezer John Lecky PIKE, C.B.E., M.C., of Arundel, Sussex.

[CHRISTOPHER LIONEL BALIOL BRETT, 1st s. and h. ap., *b.* 23 Dec. 1936; ed. at Eton and Oxford (Magdalen Coll.); *m.*, 28 Feb. 1962, Camilla Charlotte, yst. da. of Sir Horace Anthony Claude RUMBOLD, Bart., C.B., C.M.G. This marriage was diss. by divorce in 1970 and he *m.* 2ndly, 1971, Valerie HARRINGTON.]

ESSEX

page 113,
note (c), delete all detail and replace by 'The family of Geoffrey de Mandeville probably derive their name from Manneville (Seine-Maritime, arrondissement Dieppe, canton Bacquville, now in the combined commune of Le Thil-Manneville), or perhaps Colmesnil-Manneville, in the same departement and arrondissement, but canton Offranville. See L.C. Loyd, *The Origins of Some Anglo-Norman*

Families, 1951, p. 57 (for the Mandevilles of Earl's Stoke, pp. 57–8); K.S.B. Keats-Rohan, *Medieval Prosopography*, vol. 14, 1993, p. 8.'

page 116,
note (e), line 1, before 'This' add 'Or possibly because he was illegitimate' (J.C. Holt, in *The Anarchy of King Stephen's Reign*, ed. E. King, 1994, p. 298, note 24)

between pages 116 and 117,
pedigree, line 3, under 'Geoffrey de Say' add '(see SAY)'

page 117,
lines 6–7, delete from 'said' to 'Henry II' and replace by 'probably bastard da. of Eustace IV, COUNT OF BOULOGNE (*d.* 1153)'
note (f), line 9, after 'parentage' add 'For evidence on her probable parentage see Charles Evans, *Geneal. Mag.*, vol. 15, 1965, p. 186.'

page 127,
line 8, delete '(DE BEAUMONT)'

page 133,
note (f), line 1, for 'Baillol' read 'Balliol'
line 5 (on page 134), for 'Baillol' read 'Balliol' (twice)'

page 137,
note (c), line 1, after 'VI' add '(1432/3)'

page 138,
line 15, after '*m.*' add '?1stly Isobel, da. of John (DE VERE), EARL OF OXFORD(ba) and ?2ndly'
note (ba) The evidence for this 1st marriage is in some glass formerly in the east window of the Lady Chapel in Canterbury Cath. (Thomas Willement, *Heraldic Notices of Canterbury Cathedral*, 1827, Appendix, p. 162.). This glass showed the arms of Henry Earl of Essex and his sons and near relatives, a shield almost certainly meant for William Bourchier has Bourchier impaling Vere.
line 16, for '(WIDEVILE)' read '(WYDVILL)'
line 18, for 'after 12 Feb.' read 'by 8 Feb. 1479/80'
line 18, after '2ndly' add 'before 26 June 1480'
line 26, for 'Coronation of' read 'Coronations of Richard III and'
note (c), lines 1–2, delete from ': he' to '*Rolls*).' and replace by '*Cal. Fine Rolls, 1471–85*, no. 517. In addition, Ann Wydvill had definitely married her 2nd husband by 26 June 1480 (*Privy Purse Expenses*, p. 157), so that William was dead by then. The date of William's death is still in some doubt in that Henry, Earl of Essex and William his son were pardoned on 2 July 1482 and William's name appears on the Commission of the Peace 12 Feb. 1482/3. These may have been errors for the Earl of Essex's other sons, John or Thomas. Thanks are due to Dr Rosemary Horrox for discussing this matter.'

page 139,
line 10, for 'elder' read 'yr.'

page 140,
line 15, after 'Dorothy' add '(aa)'
note (aa) The indenture of covenant for this marriage is dated 1 July 1536 (*Hist. MSS. Com.*, Hastings MSS, part 1, p. 313).
line 32, for 'Mary' read 'Katherine' [M.I., Westm. Abbey]

page 141,
note (d), after 'Leicester.' add 'See vol. vii, p. 551, *sub* Leicester.'

page 150,
line 9, for 'was living 1920' read '*d.* 28 July 1920.'
line 10, line to read as follows

XXVIII. 1916. 8. ALGERNON GEORGE DE VERE (CAPELL), EARL OF ESSEX, &c., 1st s. and h.

line 12, after 'Mayfair;' add '*styled* VISCOUNT MALDEN 1892–1916;'
lines 17–18, delete from 'Having' to 'work]' and replace by 'This marriage was diss. by divorce in 1926 (she *d.* 30 Oct. 1955) and he *m.* 2ndly, 10 Feb. 1926, Alys Montgomery, da. of Robert Hayes FALKINER and formerly wife of Ernest SCOTT-BROWN. This marriage was in turn diss. by divorce in 1950 and he *m.* 3rdly, 10 Dec. 1950, Zara Mildred CARLSON, of Los Angeles, California. This marriage was diss. by divorce in 1957 and he *m.* 4thly, 1957, Christine Mary, da. of George Frederick DAVIS of Handsworth Wood, co. Warwick. He *d.* 8 Dec. 1966. His widow *d.* 1985.

XXIX. 1966. 9. REGINALD GEORGE DE VERE (CAPELL), EARL OF ESSEX, &c., only s. and h. by 1st wife, *b.* 9 Oct. 1906; ed. at Eton and Cambridge (Magdalene Coll.); *m.* 1stly, 2 Mar. 1937, Mary Reeve, da. of F. Gibson WARD of Rosemount, Bermuda and widow of Col. George Aston STRUTT. This marriage was diss. by divorce in 1957 and he *m.* 2ndly, 6 Nov. 1957, Nona Isobel, da. of David Wilson MILLER of Christchurch, New Zealand and widow of Francis Sydney SMYTHE of Colgate, Sussex. He *d.* 18 May 1981. His widow was still living 1995.

X. 1981. 10. ROBERT EDWARD DE VERE (CAPELL), EARL OF ESSEX, &c., distant cousin and h., being 2nd s. of Charles Horatio Algernon CAPELL (*d.* 14 Oct. 1924), by his 2nd wife Alice Mabel, da. of James CURRIE, which Charles Horatio was 2nd s. of Capt. Algernon Henry Champagne Capell, R.N. (*d.* 21 Nov. 1886), by Caroline, 2nd da. of Adm. Sir Charles PAGET, K.C.B., which Algernon Henry was 2nd s. of John Thomas CAPELL (*d.* 5 Mar. 1819), by Caroline, 1st da. of Henry Bayly (PAGET), 1st EARL OF UXBRIDGE, which John was 2nd s. of the 4th Earl of Essex by his 2nd wife. He was *b.* 13 Jan. 1920. His claim to the Earldom and other titles was admitted by the Committee for Privileges, 1989; *m.*, 3 Jan. 1942, Doris Margaret, da. of George Frederick TOMLINSON of Morecombe, co. Lancs.

[FREDERICK PAUL DE VERE CAPELL, *styled* VISCOUNT MALDEN, s. and h. ap., *b.* 29 May 1944; ed. at Lancaster Royal Gram. Sch., Didsbury Coll. of Ed. and Northern Sch. of Music.]

EU

page 153,
line 8, after 'Tréport' add 'He probably *m.* a 2nd wife, Helisende, parentage unknown.'
line 11, delete from 'He' to '([e])'
note ([b]), line 7, after 'Ralph.' add 'The "mother of William d'Ow" is almost certainly not the mother of Count William of Eu.'
note ([e]), delete all detail

page 154,
lines 1–5, delete from 'In' to '([a])'
line 7, after 'He' add 'possibly'
lines 8–14, delete from 'At' to 'afterwards.' and replace by 'He *d. circa* 1095 or 1096.'
note([a]), delete all detail
note([f]), delete all detail and replace by 'It seems probable that William of Ow who rebelled against William Rufus was not identical to Count William of Eu. The most reliable Chroniclers, *e.g.* the strictly contemporary Ordericus Vitalis and Florence of Worcester only call the rebel "William d'Owe" or "William d'Ou", never "Count William" and the judicial combat at which William the rebel was defeated took place on the Octave of the Ephiphany, *i.e.* 15 January 1096. Count William *d.* on 2 Jan. This could of course have been in the following year, although if Count William did marry Helisende as a 2nd wife, she was a widow by Feb. 1096 (Guibertus, Abbas Novigentinus, *De Vita sua*, lib. ii, cap. 5). She could not therefore have married William the rebel, because if he died on 2 Jan. it must have been 1097. See E.C. Waters, "The Counts of Eu", *Yorks. Arch. Top. Assoc. Journal*, vol. ix, 1886, p. 271–3.'

EVERINGHAM

page 185,
note ([b]), line 17, for 'MENILLE' read 'MEINILL'

page 193,
line 3 of pedigree, delete '2' above 'Methley'

EXETER

page 199,
line 11, for 'CORNWAILLE' read 'CORNWALL'
note ([f]), line 1, for 'Cornewaille' read 'Cornwall'
note ([g]), line 1, for 'Cornewaille' read 'Cornwall'

page 200,
line 2, for 'Cornewaille' read 'Cornwall'
line 3, for 'Fownhope' read 'Fanhope'
line 4, for 'Millbrook' read 'Milbroke'

page 208,
line 13, after '1424/5)' add 'and was *bur.* in the Collegiate Church at Stoke-by-Clare' [*ex inform.* G.W. Watson]

page 211,
line 2, after 'afsd.' add 'at the north end of the High Altar.([ba])'
note ([ba]) See Gough, *Sepulchral Monuments*, vol. 2, part 3, 1796, plate 54 and pp. 155–6.

page 218,
line 18, after '2ndly' add 'after '22 Dec. 1614' [*Cal. State Papers Dom.*, vol. ix, 1611–18, p. 263]

page 224,
line 22, after '1879.' add 'K.G. at Coronation 12 May 1937. He *d.* 6 Aug. 1956. His widow *d.* 1973.'
lines 23–4, delete all detail and replace as follows

MARQUESSATE. VII. EARLDOM XV. } 1956 6 and 15. DAVID GEORGE BROWNLOW (CECIL), MARQUESS OF EXETER, &c., 1st s. and h., *b.* 9 Feb. 1905 at Burghley House. He was ed. at Eton and Cambridge (Magdalene Coll.); *m.* 1stly, 10 Jan. 1929, Lady Mary Theresa, 4th da. of John Charles (MONTAGU-DOUGLAS-SCOTT), 7th DUKE OF BUCCLEUGH. This marriage was diss. by divorce in 1946 (she *d.* 1984) and he *m.* 2ndly, 12 Dec. 1946, Diana Mary, da. of Arnold HENDERSON, O.B.E., and widow of Lieut. Col. David Walter Arthur William FORBES, M.C. He *d. s.p.m.s.* 21 Oct. 1981.([c]) His widow *d.* 1982.

note ([c]), His only s. and h. ap. was *b.* 1 June 1933 and *d.* 6 July 1934.

MARQUESSATE. VIII. EARLDOM XVI. } 1981 7 and 16. WILLIAM MARTIN ALLEYNE (CECIL), MARQUESS OF EXETER, &c., br. and h., *b.* 27 Apr. 1909; *m.* 1stly, 17 Jan. 1934, Edith Lilian, da. of Aurel Csanady DE TELEGD of Budapest, Hungary. She *d.* 29 Mar. 1954 and he *m.* 2ndly, 3 Sep. 1954, Lillian Jane, 1st da. of Roy Peter Kopf JOHNSON of Milwaukee, Wisconsin, U.S.A. He *d.* 12 Jan. 1988. His widow was still living 1995.

MARQUESSATE. IX. EARLDOM XVII. } 1988 8 and 17. WILLIAM MICHAEL ANTHONY (CECIL), MARQUESS OF EXETER, &c., only s. and h., *b.* 1 Sep. 1935; ed. at Eton; *m.* 1967, Nancy Rose, da. of Lloyd Arthur MEEKER of Loveland, Colorado, U.S.A. This marriage was diss. by divorce in 1993.

[ANTHONY JOHN CECIL, *styled* LORD BURGHLEY, s. and h. ap., *b.* 9 Aug. 1970; ed. at Eton and Oxford.]

EXMOUTH

page 226,
line 26, after '(c)' add 'He *d.* unm. 16 Aug. 1922.'

VI. 1922. 6. HENRY EDWARD (PELLEW), VISCOUNT EXMOUTH, &c., distant cousin and h., being 1st s. of the Very Rev. George PELLEW, Dean of Norwich (*d.* 13 Oct. 1866), by Frances, 2nd da. of Henry (ADDINGTON), 1st VISCOUNT SIDMOUTH, which George was 3rd s. of the 1st Viscount Exmouth. He was *b.* 26 Apr. 1828; ed. at Cambridge (Trin. Coll.); *m.* 1stly, 5 Oct. 1858, Eliza, da. of Hon. Judge William JAY of New York. She *d.* 22 Dec. 1869 and he *m.* 2ndly, 14 May 1873, Augusta, yst. da. of Hon. Judge William JAY aforenamed. She *d.* 24 Jan. 1917. He *d.* 4 Feb. 1923.

VII. 1923. 7. CHARLES ERNEST (PELLEW), VISCOUNT EXMOUTH, &c., 2nd but only surv. s. and h. by 1st wife, *b.* 11 Mar. 1863; admitted to British Nationality, 1931. He *m.* 1stly, 1886, Margaret, da. of Prof. C.F. CHANDLER. She *d.* 3 May 1922 and he *m.* 2ndly, 12 May 1923, Mabel, da. of Richard GRAY of San Francisco, California, U.S.A. He *d.* 7 June 1945. His widow *d.* 28 Mar. 1949.

VIII. 1945. 8. EDWARD IRVING POWNOLL (PELLEW), VISCOUNT EXMOUTH, &c., distant cousin and h., being s. and h. of Pownoll William PELLEW (*d.* 12 Mar. 1872), by Mary Elizabeth, da. of Rev. John Armstrong BAGNEL, which Pownoll was 1st s. of Rev. Edward PELLEW (*d.* 29 Aug. 1869), by Marianne, da. of Stephen WINTHROP, M.D., which Edward was 4th s. of the 1st Viscount Pellew. He was *b.* 3 May 1868; *m.*, 1902, Frances, da. of Alfred Wells EDWARDS. He *d.* 19 Aug. 1951. His widow *d.* 1963.

IX. 1951. 9. POWNOLL IRVING EDWARD (PELLEW), VISCOUNT EXMOUTH, &c., only s. and h., *b.* 28 May 1908; ed. at Oundle; *m.*, 2 Jan. 1938, Maria Luisa, da. of Luis DE URQUIJO, MARQUES DE AMURRIO of Madrid and widow of Don Gonzalo ALVAREZ-BUILLA Y ALVERA. He *d.* 2 Dec. 1970. His widow was still living 1995.

X. 1970. 10. PAUL EDWARD (PELLEW), VISCOUNT EXMOUTH, &c., 1st s. and h., *b.* 8 Oct. 1940; ed. at Downside; *m.*, 10 Dec. 1964, Maria Krystina, da. of Don Recaredo DE GARAY Y GARAY of Madrid. This marriage was diss. by divorce in 1974 and he *m.* 2ndly, 1975, Rosemary Frances, da. of Francis Harold SCOONES and formerly wife of Murray de Vere (BEAUCLERK), EARL OF BURFORD, *later* 14th DUKE OF ST. ALBANS.

[EDWARD FRANCIS PELLEW, 1st s. and h. ap. by 1st wife, *b.* 30 Oct. 1978.]

EYRE

page 227,
line 11, after '1720' add 'in co. Cork'

FAIRFAX

page 234,
line 16, after '1917.' add 'He *m.*, 19 Jan. 1922, Maud Wishart, da. of James MCKELVIE of East Grinstead, Sussex. He *d.* 4 Oct. 1939. His widow *m.* twice more and *d.* 1973.'

XIII. 1939. 13. THOMAS BRIAN MCKELVIE (FAIRFAX), LORD FAIRFAX OF CAMERON, 1st s. and h., *b.* 14 May 1923; ed. at Eton; *m.*, 17 Apr. 1951, Sonia Helen, yr. da. of Capt. Cecil Bernard GUNSTON, M.C. He *d.* 8 Apr. 1964. His widow was still living 1995.

XIV. 1964. 14. NICHOLAS JOHN ALBERT (FAIRFAX), LORD FAIRFAX OF CAMERON, 1st s. and h., *b.* 4 Jan. 1956; ed. at Eton; *m.* 1982, Annabel Ruth, 1st da. of Henry Lester Louis MORRISS.

[EDWARD NICHOLAS THOMAS FAIRFAX, 1st s. and h. ap., *b.* 20 Sep. 1984.]

note (b), line 1, for 'case' read 'cases'
line 3, for 'was 'read 'were'
line 4, after '1658' add 'and James (Stewart), 1st (4th) Lord Ochiltree' and for 'that title' read 'those titles'

page 235,
line 14, for '1620' read '1630'
line 16, for '28' read '18'

FALCONER

page 238,
line 24, after 'He' add 'was a Colonel in the Dutch service and'
line 25, for 'a lady of that country' read 'Rembertina Maria, da. of Burgomaster IDIKINGS of Groningen'

FALKIRK

page 239,
before line 1 add as follows

FALKIRK

i.e. '"Falkirk", Viscountcy [S.] (GRAEME), *cr.* 1760 by the titular James III with the BARONY OF NEWTON and the EARLDOM OF ALFORD [S.]. See ALFORD, Earldom, *extinct* 1773.

FALKLAND

page 245,
line 15, after 'LUCAS. add 'She *d.* 17 Nov. 1920. He *d.* 10 Jan. 1922.'
line 16, line to read as follows

XIII. 1922. 13. LUCIUS PLANTAGENET (CARY), VISCOUNT OF FALKLAND, &c., 1st s. and h., *b.* 23 Sep. 1880 at 119 Sloane Str. Chelsea; MASTER OF FALKLAND 1886–1922;

line 24, for ']' read 'She *d.* 4 May 1954. He *d.* 24 July 1961.'

XIV. 1961. 14. LUCIUS HENRY CHARLES PLANTAGENET (CARY), VISCOUNT OF FALKLAND, &c., 1st s. and h., *b.* 25 Jan. 1905; ed. at Eton; *m.* 1stly, 14 Oct. 1926, Joan Sylvia, da. of Capt. Charles Bonham SOUTHEY, of Frinton-on-Sea, Essex. This marriage was diss. by divorce in 1933 and he *m.* 2ndly, 9 Aug. 1933, Constance Mary, da. of Capt. Edward BERRY. This marriage was in turn diss. by divorce in 1958 and he *m.* 3rdly, 24 Apr. 1958, Charlotte Anne, da. of Bevil GRANVILLE of Wellesbourne, co. Warwick. He *d.*16 Mar. 1984.

XV. 1984. 15. LUCIUS EDWARD WILLIAM PLANTAGENET (CARY), VISCOUNT OF FALKLAND, &c., only s. and h., *b.* 8 May 1935; ed. at Wellington; *m.*, 26 Apr. 1962, Caroline Anne, da. of Lieut. Cmdr. George Gerald Augustin Francis BUTLER, D.S.C., R.N., of Ashton Keynes, co. Wilts. This marriage was diss. by divorce in 1990 and he *m.* 2ndly, 1990, Nicole, da. of Milburn MACKEY.

[LUCIUS ALEXANDER PLANTAGENET CARY, MASTER OF FALKLAND, 1st s. and h. ap. by 1st wife, *b.* 1 Feb. 1963; ed. at Westminster, Loretto and R.M.A., Sandhurst; *m.*, 1993, Linda, da. of Raymond PURL, of Colorado City, U.S.A.]

FALMOUTH

page 247,
line 11, after 'at' add 'the Bear Inn' [*Farley's Bristol Journal*, 9 Feb., *ex inform.* C.R. Hudleston]

page 249,
line 26, for 'was living 1920' read '*d.* 29 Dec. 1953.'
line 27, line to read as follows

IX. 1918. 8. EVELYN HUGH JOHN (BOSCAWEN), VISCOUNT FALMOUTH, &c., 1st s. and h., *b.* 5 Aug. 1887,

line 29, for 'Scots' read 'Coldstream'

page 250,
lines 6–8, delete from 'Having' to 'work]' and replace by 'He *d.* 18 Feb. 1962. His widow *d.* 1985.'

[EVELYN FREDERICK VERE BOSCAWEN, 1st s. and h. ap., *b.* 25 Aug. 1916; ed. at Eton and Cambridge (Magdalene Coll.). He *d.* 21 May 1940, being *k.* in action.]

X. 1962. 9. GEORGE HUGH (BOSCAWEN), VISCOUNT FALMOUTH, &c., 2nd but 1st surv. s. and h., *b.* 31 Oct. 1919; ed. at Eton and Cambridge (Trin. Coll.); *m.*, 9 May 1953, Beryl Elizabeth Price, 1st da. of Arthur Harold BROWNE of West Peckham, Kent.

[EVELYN ARTHUR HUGH BOSCAWEN, 1st s. and h. ap., *b.* 13 May 1955; ed. at Eton and R.A.C., Cirencester; *m.*, 1977, Lucia Caroline, 1st da. of Ralph William VIVIAN-NEAL of Poundisford Park, Taunton, Somerset.]

FALVESLE

page 251,
line 2, after 'SAY' add '[4th LORD SAY]'
line 5, after 'SAY' add '[5th LORD SAY]'
line 6, after 'BREWOSE' add '[3rd LORD BREWOSE]'
line 9, after '[' add '1st'
note (a), line 3, for '*Almain*' read '*French*'

page 252,
lines 4–5, for '1392 or 1393' read 'soon after 23 Nov. 1392'
line 8, after 'HERON' add '[1st LORD HERON or LORD SAY]'

FANE

page 253,
line 12, for 'Sturton' read 'Stuston'
note (d), line 2, after 'Margaret' add '2nd'
line 3, delete from 'de' to 'Burford' and replace by '(de Mortimer), 1st Lord Mortimer (of Richard's Castle)'

FARNHAM

page 258,
line 26, after 'h.;' add 'pensioner at Trin. Coll., Dublin, 6 May 1738;'

page 259,
line 11, after '1779.' add 'His widow was *bur.* 1 June 1795 at Clifton, Bristol.' [*ex inform.* C.R. Hudleston]

page 260,
line 18, after '1767;' add 'Fell. Com. Trin. Coll., Dublin, 27 Oct. 1783;'
line 27, after 'Orders.' add 'Fell. Com. Trin. Coll., Dublin, 7 Nov. 1791, aged 17;'

lines 33–4, delete from 'admitted' to '1817' and replace by 'Pensioner, Trin. Coll., Cambridge, 27 Apr. 1818 and Fell. Com. Trin. Coll., Dublin, 5 Oct. 1820'

page 262,
line 6, after '1878.' add 'He *d.* 5 Feb. 1957. His widow *d.* 1 Feb. 1964.'
line 7, after '1905.' add 'M.P. for King's Lynn, 1935–42. He *m.*, 15 Oct. 1930, Angela Susan, da. of Capt. Marshall Owen ROBERTS. He *d. v.p.* Dec. 1942 of wounds received in action. His widow *m.* twice more and *d.* 10 Apr. 1953 in an air accident.'

XII. 1957. 12. BARRY OWEN SOMERSET (MAXWELL), BARON FARNHAM, grandson and h., being 1st s. and h. of Somerset Arthur and Angela Susan abovenamed, *b.* 7 July 1931; ed. at Eton and Harvard Univ.; *m.*, 19 Jan. 1959, Diana Marion, 1st da. of Nigel Eric Murray GUNNIS of Branden, Sissinghurst, Kent.

FARRER

page 263,
line 11, for 'was living 1920' read '*d.* 2 Sep. 1931.'
line 24, after 'Limerick.' add 'He *d.* 12 Apr. 1940.
line 25, line to read as follows

III. 1940. 3. CECIL CLAUDE (FARRER), BARON FARRER OF ABINGER, 1st and h. by 1st wife, *b.* 8 May 1893

line 27, for ']' read 'He *m.*, 30 Sep. 1919, Evelyn Hilda Perry, 1st da. of Edward Tipping CROOK of Woodlands Hall, Bridgenorth, co. Salop. He *d. s.p.* 11 Mar. 1948.

IV. 1948. 4. OLIVER THOMAS (FARRER), half-brother and h., being 2nd s., 1st by 2nd wife, *b.* 5 Oct. 1904; ed. at Westminster and Cambridge (Trin. Coll.); *m.*, 23 Oct. 1931, Katharine, yst. da. of Walter (RUNCIMAN), 1st VISCOUNT RUNCIMAN. He *d. s.p.* 24 Jan. 1954. His widow was still living 1995.

V. 1954. 5. ANTHONY THOMAS (FARRER), BARON FARRER OF ABINGER, nephew and h., being s. and h. of Noel Maitland FARRER (*d.* 7 May 1929), by Mabel Elizabeth, da. of Ralph ELLIOT, which Noel was 3rd s. of the 1st Baron Farrer. He was *b.* 22 Apr. 1910; *m.*, 1931, Florence Elizabeth FLORIO. He *d. s.p.* 16 Dec. 1964 when the Barony and the Baronetcy became *extinct*. His widow, who *m.* 2ndly, was still living 1995.

FAUCONBERG

page 267,
line 11, after 'Lancaster.' add 'M.I. in Lancaster Church.'
note ([a]), line 3, for '1825' read '5 May 1825 in Paris' [*ex inform.* C.R. Hudleston]

FAUCONBERGE

page 270,
line 9, delete '[LORD ROS]'

page 271,
line 3, for 'Ralph' read 'Randolph'
line 4, after 'Durham,' add '[1st LORD NEVILLE]'
lines 4–5, delete from 'and' to 'Essex' and replace by 'Robert (FITZROGER), 1st LORD FITZROGER'

page 274,
line 2, for 'GRAUNSON' read 'GRANDISON'
line 4, after 'Etc.' add '4th LORD' and for 'GRAUNSON' read 'GRANDISON'
line 5, for 'GRAUNSON' read 'GRANDISON'

page 278,
note (c), line 1 (on page 279), for 'Graunson' read 'Grandison'
line 3, for 'Graunson' read 'Grandison'

page 284,
note (h), line 3, delete 'captured at Southampton and'

page 286,
note (a), line 7, for '10 Sep.' read '15 Sep.'

page 287,
line 14, after '(c)' add 'She *d.* 17 Nov. 1926.'

FELTON

page 290,
line 7, delete from 'of' to 'DE' and replace by '[1st LORD STRANGE OF KNOKIN], by Alienore, da. of Eble de MONTZ and widow of Stephen' [See STRANGE.]

page 292,
line 6, after '2ndly' add 'in or before Nov. 1367,' [*Cal. Inq. p.m.*, vol. 11, p. 74]
line 7, after 'Etc.' add '[2nd LORD KERDISTON]'
line 8, after '1361)' add 'da. (or ?widow) of COBOLD'

FERMANAGH

page 295,
line 21, after 'BAKER' add '(*d.* Aug. 1700)'
line 23, after 'year' add 'M.I.'
line 27, after '*b.*' add '18 Mar.'

line 28, for '18 Mar. 1683' read '20 Mar. 1683 at St. Mary Abbot's'
line 32, after 'Essex' add '(*d.* in Little Chelsea, late in Mar. 1727)'

page 296,
line 4, for '*circa* 1712' read '1 Feb. 1713/14 at Baddow'
line 14, for 'about 79' read '77'
note ([a]), line 1, after 'John' add '*b.* 30 Apr. 1711 in Cecil Str., London,'
line 2, for 'in' read 'at Clapham, Surrey, and was *bur.* at Middle Claydon, 26'
line 3, after 'only' add 'She was *b.* 2 Apr. 1716.'

FERMOY

page 298,
line 20, for 'James BUTLER, of Dunboyne' read 'Piers (BUTLER), EARL OF OSSORY AND ORMOND [I.]'

page 303,
after line 16 add as follows

III. 1920. 3. JAMES BOOTHBY BURKE (ROCHE), BARON FERMOY [I.], br. and h., *b.* 28 July 1852. He *m.*, 22 Sep. 1980, Frances, 1st da. of F. WORK of New York. This marriage was diss. by divorce 1891. She *d.* Jan 1947. He *d.* at Artillery Mansions, Westm. 30 Oct. and *bur.* 3 Nov. 1920, in St. Marylebone Cemetery, Finchley.

IV. 1920. 4. EDMUND MAURICE BURKE (ROCHE), BARON FERMOY [I.], 1st s. and h., *b.* 15 May 1885; *m.*, 17 Sep. 1931, Ruth Sylvia, da. of Col. William Smith GILL, C.B., V.D., of Bieldside, co. Aberdeen. He *d.* 8 July 1955. His widow *d.* 1993.

V. 1955. 5. EDMUND JAMES BURKE (ROCHE), BARON FERMOY., only s. and h., *b.* 20 Mar. 1939; ed. at Eton and R.M.A., Sandhurst; *m.*, 22 June 1964, Lavinia Frances Elizabeth, da. of Capt. John PITMAN of Malmesbury, co. Wilts. He *d.* 19 Aug. 1984. His widow was still living 1995.

VI. 1984. 6. PATRICK MAURICE BURKE (ROCHE), BARON FERMOY, 1st s. and h., *b.* 11 Oct. 1967; ed. at Eton.

note ([b]), delete all detail

FERRERS

page 307,
line 19, after 'FERRERS' add '([ca])'
note ([ca]) None of his descendants appear to have been summoned to Parliament.

page 311,
line 17, after '([d])' add 'He was at the tournament held on 9 Apr. 1347 at Lichfield as

one of 11 knights of the King's Chamber.' [P.R.O., E 101 Wardrobe Accounts, 391/15, 21–3 Edw. III, *ex inform.* John Brownbill]

page 313,
line 16, after 'LESTRAUNGE' add '[3rd LORD STRANGE],'

page 317,
line 8, after 'Gloucester' add '[4th LORD SUDELEY]'

page 320,
Pedigree chart,
generation 3: for 'Margaret' read 'Joan'
generation 6: for 'le Botiller of Wem' read 'le Boteler, 3rd Lord Boteler of Wem'

page 325,
line 13, for 'BOURGCHIER' add ', *styled* LORD BOURCHIER'
line 15, for '(WIDEVILE)' read '(WYDEVILL)'

page 333,
Pedigree, lines 17–20, delete from 'still' to 'wick' and replace by 'became *extinct* on the death *s.p.* of the only surv. son Marmion Edward Ferrers, 24 Aug. 1884.'

page 340,
lines 1–2, delete from 'having' to 'work.([a])' and replace by 'succeeded him.'

XI. 1912. 11. WALTER KNIGHT (SHIRLEY), EARL FERRERS, &c., distant cousin and h., being s. and h. of Rev. Prof. Walter Waddington SHIRLEY (*d.* 20 Nov. 1866), by Philippa Frances Emelia, da. of Samuel KNIGHT of Impington Hall, co. Cambs., which Walter was s. and h. of Rev. Walter Augustus Shirley, Bishop of Sodor and Man (*d.* 21 Apr. 1847), by Maria, da. of William WADDINGTON of St. Rémy, Normandy, which Walter was s. of Rev. Walter Shirley, by Alice, da. of Sir Edward NEWENHAM, which Walter was s. of Rev. Walter SHIRLEY (*d.* 7 Apr. 1786), by Henrietta Maria, da. of John PHILLIPS of Swords, co. Dublin, which Walter was 4th and yst. br. of the 4th Earl Ferrers. He was *b.* 5 June 1864; *m.*, 9 July 1890, Mary Jane, da. of Robert MOON. He *d.* 2, and was *bur.* 5 Feb. 1937 at Staunton Harold, Ashby de la Zouche, co. Leicester. His widow *d.* 10 Feb. 1944.

XII. 1937. 12. ROBERT WALTER (SHIRLEY), EARL FERRERS, &c., 1st s. and h., *b.* 7 July 1894; *m.*, 28 Feb. 1922, Hermione Justice, da. of A. Noel MORLEY, of Lychwood, Worpleston, Surrey. He *d.* 11 Oct. 1954. His widow *d.* 16 July 1969.

XIII. 1954. 13. ROBERT WASHINGTON (SHIRLEY), EARL FERRERS, &c., s. and h., *b.* 8 June 1929; ed. at Winchester and Cambridge (Magdalene Coll.); *m.*, 21 July 1951, Annabel Mary, da. of Brig. William Greenwood CARR, D.S.O., of Ditchingham Hall, Norfolk.

[ROBERT WILLIAM SASWALO SHIRLEY, *styled* VISCOUNT TAMWORTH, s. and h. ap., *b.* 29 Dec. 1952; ed. at Ampleforth; *m.*, 1980, Susannah Mary, yst. da. of Charles Edward William SHEEPSHANKS of Arthington Hall, Otley, co. Yorks.]

note (a), delete all detail

page 345,
note (d), line 4, after 'Whitchurch' add '[2nd Lord Strange]'

page 349,
line 17, after 'Etc.' add '2nd LORD NORWICH,'
line 21, after 'Angus' add '[S.]'

page 353,
note (a), line 8, for 'Ponynges' read 'Poynings. However, her seal on a grant of hers (Dugdale MS. 15 f. 66, Merevale Abbey), has a shield of Ferrers impaling on a chief two mullets pierced, presumably for St. John, as used by Poynings.'

page 355,
line 2, for 'sometimes called' read '5th'

page 357,
line 4, after 'da.' add 'and in her issue'

page 358,
line 1, delete 'D'ARUNDELLE'
line 2, after 'Thomas,' add '12th or 5th' and after 'Richard,' add '11th or 4th'

page 359,
line 2, after 'Warwick' add '[4th LORD ASTLEY],'

page 361,
line 4, for '(b)' read '*circa* 1455(ba)'
note (ba), Her 1st son Thomas was aged 37 or more in 1492.

FEVERSHAM OF DOWNTON

page 366,
line 20, after '*d. s.p.m.s.*' add 'add at his seat, Burford, Wilts.' [*Farley's Bristol Journal*, 25 June 1763, *ex inform.* C.R. Hudleston]

FEVERSHAM OF DUNCOMBE PARK

page 368,
line 34, line to read as follows

EARLDOM. II. BARONY IV. } 1915 2 and 4. CHARLES REGINALD WILLIAM (DUNCOMBE), EARL OF FAVERSHAM OF RYEDALE, &c., grandson and h., being only s. and h.

page 369,
lines 7–9, delete from Having' to 'h.([b])]' and replace by 'He *d.* 24 Aug. 1937. She *d.* 25 July 1964.'

EARLDOM. III. BARONY V. } 1915 3 and 5. CHARLES WILLIAM SLINGSBY (DUNCOMBE), EARL OF FAVERSHAM, &c., 1st s. and h., *b.* 2 Nov. 1906; ed. at Eton; *m.* at York Minster, 9 May 1936, Lady Anne Dorothy, da. of Edward Frederick Lindley (WOOD), 1st EARL OF HALIFAX. He *d. s.p.m.* 4 Sep. 1963 when his Earldom and Viscountcy became *extinct*, but he was *suc.* in his Barony by his distant cousin. His widow was still living 1995.

VI. 1963. 6. CHARLES ANTHONY PETER (DUNCOMBE), BARON FEVERSHAM OF DUNCOMBE PARK, distant cousin, being s. of Anthony John DUNCOMBE (*d.* 20 Nov. 1949), by Gioranna Georgina Valerie, da. of Major C.E. Irvine MCNALTY, which Anthony John was 1st s. of Wilfred Arthur Duncombe-Anderson (*d.* 13 Oct. 1952), by Margaret Louise, 1st da. and coh. of Francis Foljambe ANDERSON, which Wilfred Arthur was 2nd s. of Frederick William Duncombe (*d.* 6 Feb. 1878), by Lady Katherine, da. of Archibald (ACHESON), 3rd EARL OF GOSFORD, which Frederick William was 3rd s. of Arthur DUNCOMBE, by his 1st wife Delia, yst. da. and coh. of John Wilmer FIELD of Heaton Hall. co. Yorks., which Arthur was 3rd s. of 1st Baron Feversham. He was *b.* 3 Jan. 1945; ed. at Eton; *m.* 1stly, 12 Sep. 1966, Shannon, yst. da. of Sir Thomas Arthur Wyness FOY. She *d.* 1976, and he *m.* 2ndly, 1979, Pauline, da. of John ALDRIDGE of Newark, co. Notts.

[JASPAR ORLANDO SLINGSBY DUNCOMBE, 1st s. and h. ap. by 1st wife, *b.* 14 Mar. 1968.]

note ([b]), delete all detail

FFRENCH

page 370,
line 23, after '1813;' add 'Fell. Com. Trin. Coll., Dublin, 5 July 1832;'
line 26, after 'afsd.' add 'She *d.* 6 Mar. 1908.'

page 371,
line 3, after 'Kerry.' add 'She *d.* 7 May 1944. He *m.* 2ndly, 8 June 1951, Catherine Elizabeth, yst. da. of Rt. Hon. Sir Christopher John NIXON, Bart. He *d. s.p.m.s.* 4 Mar. 1955. His widow *d.* 25 July 1960.

after line 5 add as follows

VII. 1955. 7. PETER MARTIN JOSEPH CHARLES JOHN MARY (FFRENCH), BARON FFRENCH OF CASTLE FFRENCH, nephew and h., being 1st s. and h. of

John Martin Valentine Joseph FFRENCH (*d.* 7 May 1946), by Sophia, yst. da. of Giovanni BRAMBILIA of Como, Italy, which John Martin was 2nd s. of the 5th Baron Ffrench. He was *b.* 2 May 1926, *m.*, 5 Aug. 1954, Katherine Sonia, 2nd da. of Digby Coddington CAYLEY of Bury St. Edmunds, Suffolk. He *d.* 30 Jan. 1986. His widow was still living 1995.

VIII. 1986. 8. ROBERT JOHN PETER CHARLES MARIO (FFRENCH), BARON FFRENCH OF CASTLE FFRENCH, only s. and h., *b.* 14 Mar. 1956; ed. at Ampleforth and Blackrock, co. Dublin; *m.*, 1987, Döthe Marie-Louise, da. of Capt. Wilhelm SCHAUER of Zurich. Switzerland.

FIFE

page 373,
line 11, for 'STRATHERN' read 'STRATHEARN'
lines 11–12, delete from 'Maud' to 1228' and replace by 'Margaret, da. of Roger DE TOSNY by Constance, da. of Raoul, VICOMTE DE BEAUMONT. He *d. s.p.* 1229 or 1230 and was *bur.* in the Abbey of Culross.' [See G.W. Watson, *Misc. Gen. et Herald.*, 5th ser., vol. vii, pp. 329–32.]
line 19, delete from 'about' to '1291.' and replace by 'probably soon after 25 July 1297. She was living in Feb. 1294/5.'
line 28, after 'wife' add 'Alice da. of Hugh de Lusignan (LE BRUN), Count of LA MARCH and ANGOULÉME'

page 380,
line 9, for 'was living 1925' read '*d.* 4 Jan. 1931.'
after line 9 add as follows

DUKEDOM. II. } 1912 2. *H.H.* PRINCESS ALEXANDRA VICTORIA ALBERTA EDWINA LOUISE DUFF, 1st da., *suo jure* DUCHESS OF FIFE and COUNTESS MACDUFF by virtue of the spec. rem. She was *b.* 17 May 1891; *m.*, 15 Oct. 1913, Major Gen. *H.R.H.* ARTHUR FREDERICK PATRICK ALBERT, PRINCE OF THE UNITED KINGDOM, K.G., &c., only s. of Field Marshal *H.R.H.* PRINCE ARTHUR, 1st DUKE OF CONNAUGHT, K.G., Etc. (see CONNAUGHT). He *d.* 12 Sep. 1938. She *d. s.p.s.* 26 Feb. 1959.

III. 1959. 3. JAMES GEORGE ALEXANDER BANNERMAN (CARNEGIE), DUKE OF FIFE and EARL MACDUFF, under the spec. rem., also EARL OF SOUTHESK, &c., being s. and h. of *H.H.* PRINCESS MAUD ALEXANDRA VICTORIA GEORGINA BERTHA, 2nd da. and coh. of Alexander William George (DUFF), 1st DUKE OF FIFE (which see), by Charles Alexander (CARNEGIE), 8th EARL OF SOUTHESK. *Suc.* his aunt as DUKE OF FIFE, 26 Feb. 1959 and his father as EARL OF SOUTHESK, 16 Feb. 1992. He was *b.* 23 Sep. 1929; ed. at Gordonstoun and R.A.C., Cirencester; *m.*, 11 Sep. 1956, Caroline Cicely, 1st da. of Henry Evelyn Alexander (DEWAR), 3rd BARON FORTEVIOT.

[DAVID CHARLES CARNEGIE, *styled* EARL OF MACDUFF, s. and h. ap., *b.* 3 Mar. 1961; ed. at Eton and Cambridge (Pembroke Coll.), R.A.C., Cirencester and Edinburgh Univ.; *m.*, 16 July 1987, Caroline Ann, da. of Martin BUNTING.]

FINCH

page 381,
line 13, for 'WALLER' read 'WALKER'

FINGALL

page 388,
line 13, for '12 Apr. 1808' read '12 Mar. 1808 at Clifton' [*Farley's Bristol Journal*, 19 Mar., *ex inform*. C.R. Hudleston]
line 14, for 'at Bristol' read 'in Trenchard St., Bristol' [*Cath. Rec. Soc.*, vol. iii, p. 324, where she is called Henrietta Plunkett]

page 389,
line 33, after 'Limerick.' add 'He *d.* 12 Nov. 1929 at Killeen Castle, co. Meath. His widow *d.* 28 Oct. 1944.'

page 390,
line 1, line to read as follows

EARLDOM [I.] XII. BARONY [U.K.] V. } 1929 — 12 and 5. OLIVER JAMES HORACE (PLUNKETT), EARL OF FINGALL, [1628], and BARON KILLEEN [1426?], in the Peerage of Ireland, also BARON FINGALL OF WOOLHAMPTON LODGE [1831], 1st s. and h.

line 2, after '1896.' add 'Ed. at Downside and R.M.C., Sandhurst.'
line 3, for ']' read 'He *m.* at Brompton Oratory, 1stly, 17 June 1926, Jessica, yr. da. of Allan HUGHES of Lynch, Allerford, Somerset. She *d.* 14 Apr. 1965 and he *m.* 2ndly, 4 May 1966, Clair Hilda, da. of Henry Robert SALMON of Ballarat, Victoria, Australia and widow of Frank RICHARDSON of Ballarat afsd. He *d. s.p.* 5 Mar. 1984 when his titles became *extinct*. His widow was still living 1995.

FITTON

page 391,
line 9, for 'May' read 'Apr.'
note ([d]), line 3, for 'patent' read 'writ'

FITZALAN

page 393,
note ([d]), lines 12–13, delete from 'br.' to '52),' and replace by 'living 1242'.
line 13, after '521.).' add 'See also C.T. Clay, "Origins of the FitzAlans of Bedale", *Yorks. Arch. Soc. J.*, vol. xxx, 1931, pp. 281–90; *Early Yorks. Families*, Yorks. Arch. Soc., Rec. Ser., vol. 135, 1973, p. 27.'

page 397,
pedigree, line 7, after 'Rotherfield' add '1st Lord Grey (of Rotherfield)'

line 8, after 'Joan' add '*de jure suo jure* (according to modern doctrine), Baroness Ingham'

line 9, after 'Bicker' add '3rd Lord Ingham'

line 10, after 'Bedale' add '4th Lord Ingham' and after 'Wormegay' add '4th Lord Bardolf'

line 11, after 'Bedale' add '5th Lord Ingham'

FITZBERNARD

page 403,
line 20, after 'Ulster' add '[I.]'
line 24, after 'temer' add '[LORD MORTIMER]'

FITZHARDINGE

page 408,
note (d), line 3, after 'Abbey' add ', also Charles (Weston), 3rd Earl of Portland, whose burial place is not known.'

FITZHUGH

page 420,
line 6, after 'AUDELEYE' add 'of Stratton'

page 432,
pedigree, line 8, after 'Felton' add '(s. and h. ap. of John (Melton) *de jure* 8th Lord Lucy)'

FITZJOHN

page 437,
pedigree, line 4, for '*d.* 1 Jan. 1324/5' read '*d.* shortly before 8 Jan. 1324/5' and after 'Crumbwelle' add '[1st Lord Cromwell]'

page 444,
line 17, after 'da.' add 'and h.'

FITZPAYN

page 464,
line 5, for 'Ponynges' read 'Poynings'
line 7, for 'sometimes called Lord Ponynges' read '3rd LORD POYNINGS'
note (c), line 2, for PONYNGES' read 'POYNINGS'
note (e), line 3, for 'Ponynges' read 'Poynings'
note (h), line 1, for 'Ponynges' read 'Poynings'
note (i), line 1, for 'Ponynges' read 'Poynings'
line 2, for 'PONYNGES' read 'POYNINGS'

page 469,
note (h), line 11, after 'no. 288).' add 'For a discussion of the St. John lands, see W.L. Sheppard, *Geneal. Mag.*, vol. 19, 1977, pp. 130–3.'

FITZWALTER

page 472,
line 14, delete 'William (LONGESPEE), EARL OF SALISBURY' and replace by '(__)'
note (g), before '*Liber*' add 'According to Bowles this Ida was da. of William (Longespee), Earl of Salisbury and after 'p. ii).' add 'but see vol. xii, part 1, p. 111, *sub* SOMERY.'

page 474,
line 5, after 'BALLIOL' add 'KING OF SCOTLAND (1292–6),'
line 20, after '1296)' add 'da. of Sir Piers DE MONTFORT, of Beaudesert, co. Warwick,' [See LISLE, vol. viii, p. 71.]
note (f), after 'Priory).' add 'She left a da. and (eventually) sole h., Christian, who *m.* William (Marshal), 1st Lord Marshal. See that title, also note (j) below.

page 475,
line 6, after 'Lincoln,' add '[1st LORD WELLES],'

page 479,
line 2, after 'Alianore,' add 'sister and (in her issue) h. of Sir Nicholas DE DAGWORTH [2nd LORD DAGWORTH],'
line 6, for '2nd' read '3rd'

page 483,
line 13, after 'Dorset,' add '[5th LORD FITZPAYN],'

page 484,
line 6, after 'Surrey' add '[5th LORD COBHAM]'

page 492,
after line 3 add as follows

XVII. 1924. 20. HENRY FITZWALTER (PLUMPTRE), LORD FITZWALTER [1295], s. and h. of John Bridges PLUMPTRE [see note (c), page 493 (from page 492), lines 3–6], *suc.* on the termination of the *abeyance* in his favour 30 Sep. 1924. He was *b.* 12 Dec. 1860; *m.* 1stly, 26 Apr. 1892, Maude Dora Gertrude, da. of Capt. Thomas Carpendale BAIRD. of Flatfields, Ayrshire. She *d.* 4 May 1893 and he *m.* 2ndly, 1 Feb. 1908, Emily Harriet Jemima, 1st da. of Capt Thomas Carpendale BAIRD afsd. He *d. s.p.* 12 Sep. 1932 when his barony again became *dormant*. His widow *d.* 15 Jan. 1951.

XVIII. 1953. 21. FITZWALTER BROOK (PLUMPTRE), LORD FITZWALTER, nephew and h., in whose favour the *abeyance* was terminated, 28 May 1953, being s. and h. of George Beresford PLUMPTRE (*d.* 28 Apr. 1934), by Mary Augusta, 2nd da. of Rev. Henry Western PLUMPTRE of Eastwood, co. Notts., which

George was 4th s. of John Bridges PLUMPTRE abovenamed. He was *b.* 15 Jan. 1914; ed. at Diocesan Coll., Capetown and Cambridge (Jesus Coll.); *m.*, 29 Sep. 1951, Margaret Melesina, 3rd da. of Herbert William DEEDES of Hythe, Kent.

[JULIAN BROOK PLUMPTRE, 1st s. and h. ap., *b.* 18 Oct. 1952; ed. at Radley and London (Wye Coll.); *m.*, 1988, Alison, da. of I.M.T. QUINEY.]

note ([c]), line 3 (on page 493), for 'Plumtre' read 'Plumptre' (twice)
line 4 (on page 493), for 'Plumtre' read 'Plumptre'

FITZWARIN

page 498,
line 6, after the first 'of' add 'Hatch,' and delete '[LORD BEAUCHAMP]'

page 500,
line 6, after 'da.' add 'and coh.'

page 508,
line 4, for '2 Jan. 1448/9' read '22 May 1449' [*Cal. Close Rolls, 1447–54*, p. 106]

page 509,
line 11, for 'Eythorpe' read 'Eythrope'

FITZWILLIAM

page 514,
note ([g]), line 4, after 'Huntercombe' add '[1st Lord Huntercombe]'
line 13, after 'Lancastre,' add '[1st Lord Lancastre],'

page 519,
line 14, for 'Robert' read 'Richard'
line 16, after '1169–70' add '(see Lacy pedigree, vol. vii, p. 677)'

page 526,
line 3, line to read as follows

EARLDOM, Etc. V.
EARLDOM [I.] VII.
BARONY [I.] IX.
} 1902

5, 7 and 9. WILLIAM CHARLES DE MEURON (WENTWORTH-FITZWILLIAM), EARL FITZWILLIAM OF NORBOROUGH, grandson and h.

line 8, after 'Woodhouse;' add '*styled* VISCOUNT MILTON 1877–1902;'
lines 21–2, delete from 'Having' to 'work([d])' and replace by 'He *d.* 15 Feb. 1943. His widow *d.* 15 Mar. 1967.'

EARLDOM, Etc. VI. EARLDOM [I.] VIII. BARONY [I.] X. } 1943

6, 8 and 10. WILLIAM HENRY LAURENCE PETER (WENTWORTH-FITZWILLIAM), EARL FITZWILLIAM OF NORBOROUGH [1746], &c., only s. and h., *b.* 31 Dec. 1910; *styled* VISCOUNT MILTON till 1943; *m.* at St. Patrick's Cath., Dublin, 19 Apr. 1933, Olive Dorothea, yr. da. of Rt. Rev. Benjamin John PLUNKETT, D.D. He *d. s.p.* in a flying accident, 13 May 1948.

EARLDOM, Etc. VII. EARLDOM [I.] IX. BARONY [I.] XI. } 1948

7, 9 and 11. ERIC SPENCER (WENTWORTH-FITZWILLIAM), EARL FITZWILLIAM OF NORBOROUGH, &c., distant cousin and h., being s. and h. of Sir William Charles WENTWORTH-FITZWILLIAM (*d.* 17 Apr. 1925), by Constance Anne, da. of Henry BROCKLEHURST, which William Charles was 4th s. of 6th Earl FitzWilliam. He was *b.* 4 Dec. 1883; ed. at Eton and Cambridge (Trin. Coll.); *m.*, 1912, Jessica Gertrude, da. of R.F. ROWLANDS. This marriage was diss. by divorce in 1917. He *d. s.p.* 3 Apr. 1952.

EARLDOM, Etc. VIII. EARLDOM [I.] X. BARONY [I.] XII. } 1952

8, 10 and 12. WILLIAM THOMAS GEORGE (WENTWORTH-FITZWILLIAM), EARL FITZWILLIAM OF NORBOROUGH, &c., distant cousin and h., being s. and h. of George Charles WENTWORTH-FITZWILLIAM (*d.* 8 Dec. 1935), by Daisy Evelyn, da. of Charles Stephen LYSTER, which George Charles was s. of George WENTWORTH-FITZWILLIAM (*d.* 4 Mar. 1874), by Alice Louisa, 2nd da. of Gen. George ANSON, which George was 3rd s. of 5th Earl FitzWilliam. He was *b.* 28 May 1904; ed. at Eton and Cambridge (Magdalene Coll.); *m.*, 3 Apr. 1956, Joyce Elizabeth Mary, 1st da. of Col. Phillip Joseph LANGDALE, O.B.E., of Houghton Hall, co. Yorks. and formerly wife of Henry Edmund (FITZALAN-HOWARD), 2nd VISCOUNT FITZALAN OF DERWENT. He *d. s.p.* 21 Sep. 1979 when all his titles became *extinct*. His widow was still living 1995.

note ([d]), delete all detail.

page 528,
lines 25–6, delete from 'He' to '1705' and replace by 'He *d.* 25 Feb. 1704/5. Will dat. 24 Apr. 1704. Admon. with will 7 Apr. 1705.'

FOLEY

page 538,
lines 16–17, delete from 'was' to 'work' and replace by '*d.* 21 Jan. 1968.'

VIII. 1905. 6. FITZALAN CHARLES JOHN (FOLEY), BARON FOLEY OF KIDDERMINSTER, br. and h., *b.* 27 Sep. 1852. He *d.* unm. at Ruxley Lodge, Claygate, 14, and was *bur.* 21 Feb. 1918, in Kensal Green Cemetery.

IX. 1918. 7. GERALD HENRY (FOLEY), BARON FOLEY OF KIDDERMINSTER, distant cousin, being s. and h. of Henry St. George FOLEY (*d.* 13 Apr. 1903), by Lady Mary Adelaide, yst. da. of James Charles Herbert Welbore Ellis (AGAR), 3rd EARL OF NORMANTON, which Henry was 1st s. of Gen. Sir St. George Gerald FOLEY, K.C.B. (*d.* 24 Jan. 1897), by Augusta Selina, da. of Henry Charles STURT of Crichel House, Wimbourne, Dorset, which St. George was 3rd s. of 3rd Baron Foley. He was *b.* 15 Apr. 1898; *m.* at the Registry Office, Marylebone, on 24 May 1922, Mrs Minoru BARRIE, da. of Henry GREENSTONE, of South Africa, mine-owner. He *d.* 3 Apr. 1927. His widow *d.* 18 Apr. 1968.

X. 1927. 8. ADRIAN GERALD (FOLEY), BARON FOLEY OF KIDDERMINSTER, s. and h., *b.* 9 Aug. 1923; *m.*, 23 Dec. 1958, Patricia, da. of Joseph ZOELLNER of Pasadena, California, U.S.A. and formerly wife of Minoe de Uribe MEEK. This marriage was diss. by divorce in 1971 and he *m.* 2ndly, 1972, Ghislaine, da. of Cornelius DRESSELHUYS of The Hague, Holland and formerly wife of 1stly Major Denis James ALEXANDER (*later* 6th EARL OF CALEDON), and 2ndly of Henry Edward (CUBITT), 4th BARON ASHCOMBE.

[THOMAS HENRY FOLEY, s. and h. ap. by 1st wife, *b.* 1 Apr. 1961.]

note (b), delete all detail.

FOLIOT

page 538,
note (f), line 9, (on page 539), after 'uncertain.' add 'see also Charles Clay, *Lincs. Hist. and Arch.*, 1966, pp. 5–28.'

page 541,
line 14, after 'Hastinges' add ', yr. s. of John (de Hastinges), 1st Lord Hastinges'
line 15, after 'Camoys' add ', yr. s. of Ralph (de Camoys), 1st Lord Camoys'

FORBES

page 544,
line 29, after 'Gille' add '(or Egidia)' and for (KEITH), 1st EARL MARISCHAL' read 'KEITH'

page 545,
line 1, delete '[S.]' and 'da. of Sir James HAMILTON' [See vol. viii, p. 475, *sub* MARISCHAL.]
line 10, after 'Margaret,' add 'sister and h. of James, 2nd LORD BOYD [S.]'

page 547,
lines 22–3, delete from 'He' to '1648.'

page 549,
lines 30–1, delete from 'He' to 'work'

XXI. 1914. 21. ATHOLL MONSON (FORBES), LORD FORBES [S.], br. and h., being

6th s. by 1st wife of 19th Lord, *b.* 15 Feb. 1841; *m.*, 19 Sep. 1876, Margaret Alice, yst. da. of Sir William DICK-CUNYNGHAM, 8th Bart., by Susan, 3rd da. of James ALSTON-STEWART. He *d.* 31 Jan. 1916. His widow *d.* 6 Feb. 1943.

XXII. 1916. 22. ATHOLL LAURENCE CUNYNGHAM (FORBES), LORD FORBES [S.], 1st s. and h., *b.* 14 Sep. 1882, at Wimbledon. Ed. at Winchester, matric. at Oxford (Ch. Ch.) 1912. Fought in WW1, 1914–18, as Capt. in Grenadier Guards. Rep. Peer [S.] 1917–24. He *m.*, 13 Oct. 1914, Mabel, 2nd. da. of Thomas Francis (ANSON), 3rd EARL OF LICHFIELD, by Mildred, 7th da. of Thomas William (COKE), 2nd EARL OF LEICESTER. He *d.* 26 Nov. 1953. Hs widow, who was *b.* 18 July 1882, *d.* 1972.

XXIII. 1953. 23. NIGEL IVAN (FORBES), LORD FORBES [S.], 1st s. and h., *b.* 19 Feb. 1918, in London, MASTER OF FORBES 1918–53; ed. at Harrow and R.M.C., Sandhurst; *m.*, 23 May 1942, Rosemary Katherine, da. of Gustavus William (HAMILTON-RUSSELL), 9th VISCOUNT BOYNE.

[MALCOLM NIGEL FORBES, MASTER OF FORBES, 1st s. and h. ap., *b.* 6 May 1946; ed. at Eton and Aberdeen Univ; *m.* 1stly, 20 Jan. 1969, Carole Jennifer Andrée, da. of Norman Stanley WHITEHEAD, of Aberdeen. This marriage was diss. by divorce in 1982 and he *m.* 2ndly, 1988, Jennifer Mary, da. of Ian Peter WHITTINGTON of Tunbridge Wells, Kent and widow of (__) GRIBBON.]

note ([d]), delete all detail.

FORESTER

page 554,
line 33, line to read as follows

VI. 1917. 6. GEORGE CECIL BEAUMONT (WELD-FORESTER), BARON FORESTER OF WILLEY PARK [1821], 1st s. and h., *b.* 9 Sep. 1867;

page 555,
lines 2–3, delete from 'Having' to 'work]' and replace by 'He *d.* 10 and was *bur.* at Brosely, Wenlock, Shropshire, 13 Oct. 1932. His widow *d.* 1 Apr. 1948.'

VII. 1932. 7. CECIL GEORGE WILFRED (WELD-FORESTER), BARON FORESTER OF WILLEY PARK, 1st s. and h., *b.* 12 July 1899; *m.* at St. Margaret's, Westm., 2 June 1931, Marie Louise Priscilla, da. of Col. Sir Herbert Charles PERROTT, Bart. He *d.* 4 Jan. 1977. His widow *d.* 1988.

VIII. 1977. 8. GEORGE CECIL BROOKE (WELD-FORESTER), BARON FORESTER OF WILLEY PARK, s. and h., *b.* 20 Feb. 1938; ed. at Eton and R.A.C., Cirencester; *m.*, 14 Jan. 1967, Elizabeth Catherine, 2nd da. of Charles John (LYTTELTON), 10th VISCOUNT COBHAM.

[CHARLES RICHARD GEORGE WELD-FORESTER, s. and h. ap., *b.* 8 July 1975.]

FORRESTER

page 559,
line 17, after 'Kent' add 'and was *bur.* at Goudhurst, Kent, 10 Dec. 1808' [*ex inform.* Dr J.R. Thomson]

FORTESCUE

page 562,
line 3, line to read as follows

EARLDOM. IV. BARONY. VI. } 1905 — 4 and 6. HUGH (FORTESCUE), EARL FORTESCUE, &c., s. and h., *b.* 16 Apr. 1854; *styled* VISCOUNT EBRINGTON 1861–1905;

lines 11–12, delete from 'having' to 'work(b)]' and replace by 'She *d.* 12 and was *bur.* 16 July 1929 at Filleigh. He *d.* 29 Oct., at Castle Hill, and was *bur.* 1 Nov. 1932 at Filleigh afsd.'

EARLDOM. V. BARONY. VII. } 1932 — 5 and 7. HUGH WILLIAM (FORTESCUE), EARL FORTESCUE, &c., 1st s. and h., *b.* 14 June 1888; *styled* VISCOUNT EBRINGTON 1905–32; served in WW1(b) as Capt. 2nd Dragoons (Royal Scots Greys), wounded Feb. 1915. He *m.*, 8 Feb. 1917, Margaret Helen, 1st da. of Wentworth Canning Blackett (BEAUMONT), 1st VISCOUNT ALLENDALE. She *d.* 10 June 1958. He *d. s.p.m.s.* 14 June 1958.

[HUGH PETER FORTESCUE, *styled* VISCOUNT EBRINGTON, s. and h. ap., *b.* 9 Dec. 1920; ed. at Eton and R.M.C., Sandhurst. He *d. v.p.* unm. 17 July 1942, being *k.* in action at El Alamein.]

EARLDOM. VI. BARONY. VIII. } 1958 — 6 and 8. DENZIL GEORGE (FORTESCUE), EARL FORTESCUE, &c., br. and h., *b.* 13 June 1893; ed. at Eton and Oxford (New Coll.); served in WW1 as 2nd Lieut. Royal North Devon Hussars and in WW2. He *m.* 1stly, 10 June 1920, Marjorie Ellinor, da. of Col. Charles William TROTTER. This marriage was diss. by divorce in 1941 (she *d.* 9 July 1964) and he *m.* 2ndly, 8 Aug. 1941, Sybil Mary, yr. da. of Henry Charles (HARDINGE) 3rd VISCOUNT HARDINGE and formerly wife of Hugh Napier (DOUGLAS-PENNANT), 4th BARON PENRHYN. He *d.* 1 June 1977. His widow *d.* 1985.

EARLDOM. VII. BARONY. IX. } 1977 — 7 and 9. RICHARD ARCHIBALD (FORTESCUE), EARL FORTESCUE, &c., 1st s. and h. by 1st wife, *b.* 14 Apr. 1922; ed. at Eton and Oxford (Ch. Ch.); *m.* 1stly, 24 Oct. 1949, Penelope Jane, yr. da. of Robert Evelyn HENDERSON. She *d.* 28 May 1959 and he *m.* 2ndly, 3 Mar. 1961, Margaret Anne, da. of Charles Michael STRATTON of Evenley, co. Northants. This marriage was diss. by divorce in

1987 and he *m.* 3rdly, 1989, Carolyn Mary, da. of Major Clement Walter Rowland HILL and formerly wife of Richard LOCKWOOD. He *d.* 7 Mar. 1993. His widow was still living 1995.

EARLDOM. VIII. BARONY. X.	1993	8 and 10. CHARLES HUGH RICHARD (FORTESCUE), EARL FORTESCUE, &c., 1st s. and h. by 1st wife, *b.* 10 May 1951; ed. at Eton; *m.*, 1974, Julia, 1st da. of Air Commodore John Adam SOWREY.

note ([b]), lines 1–3, delete from 'His' to 'Hussars.'

FRANKFORT

page 566,
line 19, for 'was living 1925' read '*d.* 10 Mar. 1936.'
line 20, line to read as follows

IV.	1902.	4. WILLIAM JOHN HORACE (DE MONTMORENCY), VISCOUNT FRANKFORT DE MONTMORENCY, &c., 2nd([b]) but 1st surv. s. and h.,

lines 28–30, delete from 'Having' to '1925' and replace by 'His widow *d.* 13 Dec. 1946.'

FRENE

page 573,
line 9, after 'Margaret,' add '*de jure* COUNTESS OF SALISBURY,'
line 15, after 'LESTRAUNGE,' add '[1st LORD STRANGE]'

FURNIVALLE

page 582,
line 8, delete 'his wife' and replace by 'da. and h. of Matthew DE LA MARE' [See MONTFORT.]

page 590,
line 20, after 'Richard' add '(FITZALAN), 10th or 3rd'

page 594,
line 13, after 'Kerry.' add 'This marriage was diss. by divorce in 1931 (he *d.* 31 Dec. 1968) and she *m.* 2ndly, 23 Feb. 1932, William Herbert Shelley DENT, M.C. She *d. s.p.m.* 24 Dec. 1968 when her Barony again fell into *abeyance*, between her two das.([c]) Her widower *d.* 31 Dec. 1968.

note ([c]), These are 1. Rosamund Mary (Sister Ancilla, O.S.B.), *b.* 3 June 1933, who has renounced her right to the Barony, and 2. Patricia Mary, *b.* 4 Apr. 1935; *m.* 1stly, 25 Aug. 1956, Capt. Thomas Hornsby. This marriage was diss. by divorce in 1963 and she *m.* 2ndly, 1970, Roger Thomas John Bence.

GAGE

page 598,
line 29, for 'Torrington' read 'Toddington'

page 599,
lines 3–7, delete all detail and replace as follows

VISCOUNTCY, Etc. [I.] VI. BARONY [G.B.] V. } 1912 6 and 5. HENRY RAINALD (GAGE),[b] VISCOUNT GAGE OF CASTLE ISLAND, &c., only s. and h., *b.* 30 Dec. 1895; adm. to Oxford (Ch. Ch.) 1915; served in WW1 as Capt. Coldstream Guards[c] and in WW2; K.C.V.O., 1939. He *m.* 1stly, 26 Feb. 1931, Hon. Alexandra Imogen Clair, yr. da. of William Henry (GRENFELL), 1st and last BARON DESBOROUGH. She *d.* 3 Jan. 1969 and he *m.* 2ndly, 1971, Diana, da. of Col. Rt. Hon. Lord Richard Frederick CAVENDISH, C.B., C.M.G., formerly wife of Robert John Graham BOOTHBY and widow of Lieut. Col. Ian DOUGLAS-CAMPBELL-GRAY He *d.* 27 Feb. 1982. His widow *d.* 1992.

VISCOUNTCY, Etc. [I.] VII. BARONY [U.K.] VI. } 1982 7 and 6. GEORGE JOHN ST. CLERE (GAGE), VISCOUNT GAGE OF CASTLE ISLAND, &c., 1st s. and h., *b.* 8 July 1932; ed. at Eton; *m.* 1stly, 1971, Valerie Ann, da. of Joseph E. DUTCH of Horam, Sussex. This marriage was diss. by divorce in 1975 and he *m.* 2ndly, 1990, Deirdre Melina Jane, da. of Thomas James SIMMONS. He *d. s.p.* 30 Nov. 1993. His widow was still living 1995.

VISCOUNTCY, Etc. [I.] VIII. BARONY [U.K.] VII. } 1993 8 and 7. HENRY NICHOLAS (GAGE), VISCOUNT GAGE OF CASTLE ISLAND, &c., br. and h., *b.* 9 Apr. 1934; ed. at Eton and Oxford (Ch. Ch.); *m.*, 1974, Lady Diana Adrienne, da. of David Field (BEATTY), 2nd EARL BEATTY.

[HENRY WILLIAM GAGE, 1st s. and h. ap., *b.* 1975.]

GAINSBOROUGH

page 603,
line 10, after 'JERNINGHAM' add 'He *d.* 17 Apr. 1926. His widow *d.* 17 Nov. 1937.'
line 11, line to read as follows

X. 1926. 4. ARTHUR EDWARD JOSEPH (NOEL), EARL OF GAINSBOROUGH, &c., 1st s. and h. by 2nd wife;

line 13, after 'Hants.' add '; *styled* VISCOUNT CAMPDEN till 1926.'
line 15, for ']' read 'He *d.* 27 Aug. 1927. His widow *d.* 1970.'

XI. 1927. 5. ANTHONY GERARD EDWARD (NOEL), EARL OF GAINSBOROUGH,

VISCOUNT CAMPDEN OF CAMPDEN and BARON BARHAM OF BARHAM COURT AND TESTON and BARON NOEL OF RIDLINGTON, also a Baronet [1781], s. and h., *b.* 24 Oct. 1923; *m.*, 23 July 1947, Mary, 1st da. of John Joseph STOURTON of Wadhurst, Sussex.

[ANTHONY BAPTIST NOEL, *styled* VISCOUNT CAMPDEN, 1st s. and h. ap., *b.* 16 Jan. 1950; ed. at Ampleforth and R.A.C., Cirencester; *m.*, 1972, Sarah Rose, 1st da. of Col. Thomas Foley Churchill WINNINGTON.]

GALLOWAY

page 608,
lines 28–9, delete from 'He' to 'work'
note (c), delete all detail

page 609,
after line 2 add as follows

XI. 1901. 11. RANDOLPH HENRY (STEWART), EARL OF GALLOWAY, &c., br. and h., *b.* 14 Oct. 1836; ed. at Harrow; joined the Black Watch and served in the Crimean War and in the Indian Mutiny. He *m.*, 3 June 1891, Amy Mary Pauline, da. of Anthony John CLIFFE of Bellevue, co. Wexford. He *d.* at Cumloden, 7, and was *bur.* 11 Feb. 1920, at Challoch, Newton Stewart. His widow *d.* 25 June 1942.

XII. 1920. 12. RANDOLPH ALGERNON RONALD (STEWART), EARL OF GALLOWAY, &c., 1st s. and h., *b.* 1 Nov. 1892. Ed. at Harrow and R.M.C., Sandhurst; served in WW1(ax) as Lieut. in the Scots Guards, taken prisoner in 1914. He *m.*, 14 Oct. 1924, Philippa Fendall, yr. da. of Jacob WENDELL, of New York, U.S.A. She *d.* 1974. He *d.* 13 June 1978.

XIII. 1978. 13. RANDOLPH KEITH REGINALD (STEWART), EARL OF GALLOWAY, &c., s. and h., *b.* 14 Oct. 1928; ed. at Harrow; *m.*, 1975, Lily May, da. of Andrew MILLER of Duns, co. Berwick. and formerly wife of (__) BUDGE.

note (ax) His yr. br., Keith Anthony Stewart, *b.* 8 Sep. 1894, also served in this war and was *k.* in action, 9 May 1915 as Lieut. in the Black Watch. For a list of peers and their sons who served in this war, see vol. viii, Appendix F.

GALWAY

page 613,
line 3, after '1692' add '(ax)'
note (ax) In Apr. 1692 he is already called Lord Galway, for though the patent of the Viscountcy did not come till Nov., the royal warrant for it is dated Mar. 1691/2 (*Treas. Cal.*, vol. ix, p. 1662).

page 614,
note (d), after '252).' add 'In a list of M.P.s compiled in 1754–6 for Sir James Lowther (later

1st Earl of Lonsdale) in the Lonsdale archives appears "Lord Gallway", member for Pontefract, against whose name is a note, "Wm Mellish Comr. of Excise is his father in law" (*ex inform.* C. Roy Hudleston). This may point to an earlier marriage than that to Elizabeth, particularly if her baptismal date in the text is correct, given the birth date of the 3rd Viscount.'

page 616,
line 17, after 'Serlby.' add 'He *d.* 7 Mar. 1931.'
line 18, line to read as follows

XII. 1931. 8. GEORGE VERE ARUNDELL (MONCKTON-ARUNDELL), VISCOUNT GALWAY, &c., only s. and h., *b.* 24 Mar. 1882;

line 26, for ']' read 'He *d.* 27 Mar. 1943. His widow *d.* 1983.'

XIII. 1943. 9. SIMON GEORGE ROBERT (MONCKTON-ARUNDELL), VISCOUNT GALWAY, &c., only s. and h., *b.* 11 Nov. 1929; ed. at Eton; *m.*, 4 Nov. 1953, Lady Teresa Jane, da. of Edward Henry Charles James (FOX-STRANGWAYS), 7th EARL OF ILCHESTER. He *d. s.p.* 1 Jan. 1971 when the Barony of Monckton of Serlby [U.K. 1887] became *extinct*, but he was *suc.* in his other titles by his distant cousin. His widow *m.* 2ndly, 1972, Mark AGNEW. She *d.* 1989.

XIV. 1971. 10. WILLIAM ARUNDELL (MONCKTON-ARUNDELL), VISCOUNT GALWAY and BARON OF KILLARD, both in the peerage of Ireland, distant cousin and h., being s. and h. of William Henry MONCKTON (*d.* 19 Mar. 1900), by Rose Ethel, da. of Henry VATCHER of Rosemount, Jersey, which William Henry was 1st s. of Edmund Gambier MONCKTON (*d.* 7 Oct. 1872), by Arabella Martha, da. of Rev. John ROBINSON, which Edmund was 4th s. of 5th Viscount Galway. He was *b.* 24 Sep. 1894; ed. at Eton and Cambridge (Trin. Coll.); *m.*, 1939, Joan, da. of Major G.A. WILLIAMS of Purbrook, co. Hants. She *d.* 1973. He *d. s.p.* 15 Aug. 1977.

XV. 1977. 11. EDMUND SAVILE (MONCKTON-ARUNDELL), VISCOUNT GALWAY, &c., br. and h., *b.* 11 Sep. 1900; ed. at Charterhouse and Cambridge (Trin. Coll.); *m.*, 20 Apr. 1927, Kathleen Joyce, yr. da. of James MUSGRAVE. She *d.* 1975. He *d. s.p.m.* 30 Jan. 1980.

XVI. 1980. 12. GEORGE RUPERT (MONCKTON-ARUNDELL), VISCOUNT GALWAY, &c., distant cousin and h., being 2nd but only surv. s. of Philip Marmaduke MONCKTON (*d.* 4 Oct. 1965), by Lavender, da. of W.J. O'HARA of St. Albans, co. Herts., which Philip Marmaduke was s. of Marmaduke John Monckton (*d.* 4 Apr. 1922), by Kathleen Swan, da. of Dep. Surg. Gen. James BROWNE, M.D., which Marmaduke John was 3rd s. of Edmund Gambier MONCKTON abovenamed. He was *b.* 13 Oct. 1922; *m.*, 12 Oct. 1944, Fiona Margaret, da. of Capt. Percival Walter de Putron TAYLOR of Sooke, British Columbia, Canada.

[JOHN PHILIP MONCKTON-ARUNDELL, s. and h. ap., *b.* 8 Apr. 1952; ed. at Univ. of

West Ontario; *m.*, 1980, Deborah Kathleen, da. of A. Bruce HOLMES of Ottawa, Canada. This marriage was diss. by divorce in 1992.]

GARDNER

page 618,
line 15, for '23' read '29'
lines 23–4, delete from '1' to 'Jamaica' and replace by '31 Dec. 1808 at Bath' [*ex inform.* Capt. Hugh Owen]

page 620,
note (b), line 7, after 'V.G.' add 'The title is still *dormant* (1995), being claimed by Julian Gardner, grandson of Alan Legge Gardner abovenamed.'

GARVAGH

page 624,
line 22, for 'was living 1925' read '*d.* 17 May 1926.'
line 23, line to read as follows

IV. 1915. 4. LEOPOLD ERNEST STRATFORD GEORGE (CANNING), BARON GARVAGH [I.], only child and h., *b.* 21 July 1878;

line 29, for '(__)' read 'Bayley'
lines 30–1, delete from 'Having' to 'work.]' and replace by 'He *d.* 16 July 1956. His widow *d.* 1982.'

V. 1956. 5. ALEXANDER LEOPOLD IVOR GEORGE (CANNING), BARON GARVAGH, s. and h., *b.* 6 Oct. 1920; ed. at Eton and Oxford (Ch. Ch.); *m.*, 12 July 1947, Edith Christine, yr. da. of Jack H. COOPER of Worplesdon, Surrey. This marriage was diss. by divorce in 1973 and he *m.* 2ndly, 1974, Cynthia, da. of Eric Ernest Falk PRETTY, C.M.G.

[SPENCER GEORGE STRATFORD DE REDCLIFFE CANNING, s. and h. ap., *b.* 12 Feb. 1953; *m.*, 1979, Julia Margery Morison, 1st da. of Col. F.C.E. BYE.]

GAUNT

page 627,
line 8, after 'KERDESTONE' add '[1st LORD KERDESTON]'

GENEVILLE

page 629,
line 3, after '*m.*' add ', 4 Aug. 1252 at Woodstock' [P.R.O., E.101 349/17, containing costs of the Queen's gifts.]

GERARD OF GERARD'S BROMLEY

page 635,
line 4, for 'Wimersley' read 'Winmarleigh'

GERARD OF BRYN

page 638,
line 20, line to read as follows

III. 1902. 3. FREDERIC JOHN (GERARD), BARON GERARD OF BRYN, only s. and h., *b.* 10 Nov. 1883, at

lines 26–7, delete from 'Having' to 'work]' and replace by 'He *d.* 12 Feb. 1953. His widow *d.* 6 Apr. 1954.'

IV. 1953. 4. ROBERT WILLIAM FREDERICK ALWYN (GERARD), BARON GERARD OF BRYN, only s. and h., *b.* 23 May 1918; ed. at Ampleforth. He *d.* unm. 11 July 1992.

V. 1992. 5. ANTHONY ROBERT HUGO (GERARD), BARON GERARD OF BRYN, distant cousin and h., being 1st s. and h. of Major Rupert Charles Frederick GERARD, by Huguette, da. of Hugo REISS, which Rupert was 1st s. of Lieut. Col. Charles Robert Tolver Michael Gerard, by his 1st wife Aimée Gwendolyn, yr. da. of Sir Rupert Havelock CLARKE, Bart., which Charles was 1st s. of Robert Joseph GERARD-DICCONSON (*d.* 16 Sep. 1918), by Eleanor, 2nd da. of William John BANKES of Rosemount, Ross-shire, which Robert was 2nd s. of 1st Baron Gerard. He was *b.* 3 Dec. 1949; ed. at Harvard; *m.*, 1976, Kathleen, 1st da. of Dr Bernard RYAN of New York.

[RUPERT BERNARD CHARLES GERARD, 1st s. and h. ap., *b.* 17 Dec. 1981.]

GIFFARD

page 642,
note (c), line 10, after '19' add 'and *Cal. Close Rolls, 1268–72*, pp. 294–5]'

page 643,
line 1, after 'NEVILLE,' add '(father of Hugh, 1st LORD NEVILLE of Essex)'

page 644,
note (c), line 13, after 'Osbert' add 'or Osbern'

GIFFORD

page 655,
lines 18–20, delete from 'was living' to 'work' and replace by '*d.* 14 Feb. 1947.'

IV. 1911. 4. EDGAR BERKELEY (GIFFORD), BARON GIFFARD OF ST. LEONARD'S, br. and h., *b.* 8 Mar. 1857; *m.* 1stly, 26 Nov. 1879, Mary, da. of John OSBOURNE, Q.C. She *d.* 15 Aug. 1913 and he *m.* 2ndly, 5 June 1918, Anne Maud, 2nd da. of Lieut. Col. William AITCHISON of Drummore, Musselburgh, Midlothian. He *d. s.p.m.* at Shrivenham House, Berks., 29 Jan., and was *bur.* 2 Feb. 1937 at North Nibley, Glos. His widow *d.* 24 Feb. 1956.

V. 1937. 5. CHARLES MAURICE ELTON (GIFFORD), BARON GIFFARD OF ST. LEONARD'S, nephew and h., being s. and h. of Maurice Raymond GIFFORD (*d.* 1 July 1910), by Marguerite, da. of Capt. Cecil THOROLD of Boothby Hall, Grantham, co. Lincs., which Maurice was 4th s. of 2nd Baron Gifford. He was *b.* 4 Mar. 1899; *m.*, 5 Mar. 1939, Ellice Margaret, 2nd da. of Arthur Wigram ALLEN of Sydney, New South Wales, Australia. He *d.* 16 Apr. 1961. His widow *d.* 1990.

VI. 1961. 6. ANTHONY MAURICE (GIFFORD), BARON GIFFARD OF ST. LEONARD'S, only s. and h. *b.* 1 May 1940; ed. at Winchester and Cambridge (King's Coll.); *m.*, 22 Mar. 1965, Katherine Ann, da. of Dr Max MUNDY.

[THOMAS ADAM GIFFORD, s. and h. ap., *b.* 1 Dec. 1967.]

GLANUSK

page 660,

line 18, for 'was living 1925' read '*d.* 18 and was *bur.* 20 Apr. 1935 at Crickhowell, co. Brecon.'

line 19, line to read as follows

II. 1906. 2. JOSEPH HENRY RUSSELL (BAILEY), BARON GLANUSK OF GLANUSK PARK, 1st s. and h., *b.* 26 Oct. 1864;

lines 27–9, delete from 'Having' to 'work]' and replace by 'He *d.* 11 Jan. 1928. His widow *d.* 19 Apr. 1938.'

III. 1928. 3. WILFRED RUSSELL (BAILEY), BARON GLANUSK OF GLANUSK PARK, 1st s. and h., *b.* 27 June 1891; *m.* 1stly, 27 Feb. 1919, Victoria Mary Enid Ann Vera, da. of Lieut. Col. Frank DUGDALE, C.V.O. This marriage was diss. by divorce in 1939 and he *m.* 2ndly, 17 Mar. 1942, Margaret Eldrydd, da. of Major Gen. Thomas Herbert SHOUBRIDGE. He *d. s.p.m.* 12 Jan. 1948. His widow *m.* 2ndly, 24 Mar. 1966, William Philip (SIDNEY), 1st VISCOUNT DE L'ISLE. She was still living 1995.

IV. 1948. 4. DAVID RUSSELL (BAILEY), BARON GLANUSK OF GLANUSK PARK, cousin and h., being 1st s. of Herbert Crawshay BAILEY (*d.* 13 Apr. 1936), by Kathleen Mary, yr. da. of Sir Shirley Harris SALT, Bart., which Herbert was 4th s. of 1st Baron Glanusk. He was *b.* 19 Nov. 1917; ed. at Eton; *m.*, 25 Jan. 1941, Lorna Dorothy, da. of Capt. Ernest Courtenay Harold Norman ANDREWS of Southsea, co. Hants.

[CHRISTOPHER RUSSELL BAILEY, s. and h. ap., *b*. 18 Mar. 1942; ed. at Eton and Cambridge (Clare Coll.); *m*., 1974, Frances Elizabeth, da. of Air Chief Marshal Sir Douglas Charles LOWE, G.C.B., D.F.C.]

GLASGOW

page 664,
lines 23–4, for 'was living 1925' read '*d*. 22 Apr. 1931.'

page 665,
line 5, line to read as follows

VIII. 1915. 8. PATRICK JAMES (BOYLE), EARL OF GLASGOW, &c., 1st s. and h., *b*. 18 June 1874, in Edinburgh; *styled* VISCOUNT KELBURN 1890–1915;

lines 9–10, delete from 'Having' to 'work]' and replace by 'He *d*. 14 Dec. 1963. His widow *d*. 1977.'

IX. 1963. 9. DAVID WILLIAM MAURICE (BOYLE), EARL OF GLASGOW, &c., s. and h., *b*. 24 July 1910; ed. at Eton; *m*. 1stly, 4 Mar. 1937, Dorothea, da. of Sir Archibald Moir Park LYLE, Bart., M.C. This marriage was diss. by divorce in 1962 and he *m*. 2ndly, 6 Mar. 1962, Ursula Vanda Maud, yr. da. of Geoffrey Crespigny Brabazon (VIVIAN), 4th BARON VIVIAN, formerly wife, 1stly, of Major Philip Alexander Clement BRIDGEWATER and 2ndly of Sir William Fane WRIXON-BECHER, Bart. She *d*. 1984. He *d*. 8 June 1984.

X. 1984. 10. PATRICK ROBIN ARCHIBALD (BOYLE), EARL OF GLASGOW, &c., only s. and h. by 1st wife, *b*. 30 July 1939; ed. at Eton and Sorbonne; *m*., 1975, Isabel Mary, adop. da. of George Douglas JAMES.

[DAVID MICHAEL DOUGLAS BOYLE, *styled* VISCOUNT OF KELBURN, s. and h. ap., *b*. 15 Oct. 1978.]

GLEAN O'MALLUN

page 667,
lines 4–5, delete from 'between' to '1640.([b])' and replace by '1 May 1639.([a])'
note ([a]), line 1, before 'The' add 'According to '*Le Grand Théatre Sacré du Duché de Brabant*, 1734, vol. 1, p. 211, a memorial then in the nave of the Church of St. Gudule in Brussels gave his date of death and that of his wife Marie as 1 Feb. 1641.'
note ([b]), continue on from note ([a]).

GLENCAIRN

page 669,
line 6, after 'Anne,' add 'sister of Alexander, 1st LORD MONTGOMERIE [S.],'

GLENGALL

page 679,
line 11, for 'JEFFEREYS' read 'JEFFERYES'

GLOUCESTER

page 683,
line 2, after '1047)' add '([ax])'
note ([ax]) As to this see H.W.C. Davis, *Regesta Regum Anglo-Normannorum*, vol. i, no. 45, and Introduction, p. xxiii.

page 688,
line 16, delete '(DE BEAUMONT)'

page 689,
line 5, after 'Mabel,' add '(*d.* 1198)'

page 692,
line 21, for '*comté*' read 'the city and country of Evreux ("*civitatem Evroicensem et Ebroicinum*")'
note ([g]), before '"Omnibus' add 'See charter dated at Le Goulet in May 1200 in J.J. Vernier, *Receuil de Facsimiles de Chartes Normandes*, Soc. Hist. Norm., 1919, no. 16. Amaury is described in the charter itself as Earl of Gloucester.'

page 693,
lines 8–9, delete from 'In' to 'Normandy,' and replace by 'By 24 Mar. 1263/4 he had'
note ([a]), after 'clxxiv.' add 'The seal illustrated by Vernier (see note ([g]) on previous page) is inscribed SIGILLUM.AMAL . . . . TIS.EBROICENSIS. It is possible that both this seal and that illustrated in Stapleton have "Earl of Gloucester" on one side and "Count of Evreux" on the other.
note ([e]), delete all detail and replace by 'On that day as Count of Evreux he was at the King's Court at Westminster.' (*Registrum Antiquissimum . . . of Lincoln*, vol. i, p. 140, C.W. Foster (ed.), Lincs. Rec. Soc., vol. xxvii)

page 700,
line 10, for '(DE QUINCY)' read 'DE QUINCY'
line 11, delete 'EARL OF WINCHESTER'
note ([h]), line 29 (on page 701), for 'John' read 'Bartholomew'
line 35 (on page 701), for 'See MOWBRAY' read 'Roese's date of *b.* is probably later than 1252, since she was app. under 15 years of age in 1270, see vol. ix, p. 377, note ([f]), *sub* MOWBRAY.'
page 719,
line 20, for 'Ralph de Stafford, Lord Stafford' read 'Ralph (DE STAFFORD), 1st EARL OF STAFFORD.'
line 22, for '6th' read '7th'
note ([k]), line 2 (on page 720), for 'Murimuth' read 'Robert of Avesbury'

page 722,
note (l), after '*masculis*' add '*de corpore suis*'

page 741,
line 15, for 'probably' read 'possibly'
line 18, for '12 July 1472' read 'before 6 June 1474' [*Cal. Pat. Rolls, 1467–78*, p. 455]
line 24, for '1473' read 'probably early 1476'
note (f), line 8 (on page 742), delete from 'but' to 'authority' and replace by 'Angelo Raine (ed.), *York Civic Records*, vol. ii, 1941, pp. 71–2.)'

page 742,
line 2, for '31 Mar.' read 'early Apr.'

page 743,
line 7, for 'of scarlet fever' read 'probably of smallpox'
note (c), before 'As' add 'See W.P. MacArthur, *British Med. J.*, vol. 1, 24 Mar. 1928, pp. 502–3. MacArthur further believes that the death was further complicated by tonsillitis.'

VOLUME 6

INTRODUCTION

page viii,
line 7, for 'R.G. Glencross' read 'R.M. Glencross'

GORDON

page 4,
line 18, for 'dension' read 'pension'

GORGES

page 12,
line 3, for '1330' read '1326' and after 'Peche' add '[1st LORD PECCHE],'
note (b), delete all detail and replace by 'See vol. x, p. 343, note (e).'

page 16,
line 17, for '1645' read 'before 20 Dec. 1634' [*ex. inform.* C.T.C. Andrew]

GORMANSTON

page 19,
line 6, after 'HARINGTON,' add '(s. and h. ap. of John 1st LORD HARINGTON), sister and coh. of John (DE MULTON), 2nd LORD MULTON,'

page 26,
line 40, for 'was living 1925' read '*d.* 9 Apr. 1932.'

page 27,
line 1, line to read as follows

VISCOUNTCY [I.] XV. BARONY [I.] XVIII. BARONY [U.K.] III.	1907	15, 18 and 3. JENICO EDWARD JOSEPH (PRESTON), VISCOUNT GORMANSTON, &c., 1st s. and h., *b.* 16 July 1879,

lines 6–7, delete all detail and replace by 'He *d.* 7 Nov. 1925. His widow *m.* 2ndly, 11 Aug. 1934, John Black ATKINS, who *d.* 16 Mar. 1954. She *d.* 28 Mar. 1964.'

VISCOUNTCY [I.] XVI. BARONY [I.] XIX. BARONY [U.K.] IV.	1925	16, 19 and 4. JENICO WILLIAM RICHARD (PRESTON), VISCOUNT GORMANSTON, &c., 1st s. and h., *b.* 7 Oct. 1914; *m.*, 18 Feb. 1939, Pamela, da. of Capt. Edward Dudley HANLY. He *d.* 9 June 1940, being *k.* in action. His widow *m.* 2ndly, 23 Dec. 1943, Maurice Bernard O'CONNOR, who *d.* 9 Feb. 1961. She *d.* 1975.
VISCOUNTCY [I.] XVII. BARONY [I.] XX. BARONY [U.K.] V.	1940	17, 20 and 5. JENICO NICHOLAS DUDLEY (PRESTON), VISCOUNT GORMANSTON, &c., only s. and h., *b.* 19 Nov. 1939; ed. at Downside; *m.*, 1974, Eva LANDZIANOWSKI. She *d.* 1984.

[JENICO FRANCIS TARA PRESTON, 1st s. and h. ap., *b.* 30 Apr. 1974.]

GORT

page 29,
line 19, for 'S.M.' read 'Starling Meux'
line 20, after 'Lancers.' add 'She *d.* 27 Dec. 1933.'
line 21, line to read as follows

VI. 1902. 6. JOHN STANDISH SURTEES PRENDERGAST (VEREKER), VISCOUNT GORT, &c., 1st s. and h.

line 24, after '(b)' add 'Field Marshal, C.I.G.S., 1937–9.'
lines 28–9, delete from 'Having' to 'work.]' and replace by 'This marriage was diss. by divorce in 1925. She *d.* 5 Oct. 1940. He was *cr.*, 8 Feb. 1946, VISCOUNT GORT of Hamsterley, co. Durham [U.K.]. He *d. s.p.m.s.* 31 Mar. 1946 when his Viscountcy [U.K.] became *extinct* but he was *suc.* in his other titles by his br. and h. male.

[CHARLES STANDISH VEREKER, s. and h. ap., *b.* 23 Feb. 1912; ed. at Cambridge (Trin. Coll.); *m.*, 21 Apr. 1938, Yvonne Francis, da. of Major Geoffrey Arthur BARNETT. He *d. v.p. s.p.* 26 Feb. 1941.]

VII. 1946. 7. STANDISH ROBERT GAGE PRENDERGAST (VEREKER), VISCOUNT GORT [1816] and BARON KILTERTON OF GORT [1810], in the peerage of Ireland, br. and h., *b.* 12 Feb. 1888; ed. at Harrow and Cambridge (Trin. Coll.); *m.*, 11 June 1921, Bessy, da. of Aubone Alfred SURTEES, of Dinsdale Manor, co. Durham. She *d.* 1972. He *d. s.p.* 21 May 1975.

VIII. 1975. 8. COLIN LEOPOLD PRENDERGAST (VEREKER), VISCOUNT GORT, &c., distant cousin and h., being s. of Cmdr. Leopold George Prendergast VEREKER, R.N.R. (*d.* 16 Dec. 1937), by Helen Marjorie, 1st da. of Colin CAMPBELL, which Leopold George was 2nd s. of Capt. Foley Charles

Prendergast VEREKER, R.N. (*d.* 24 Oct. 1900), by Ellen Amelia, da. of Rev. Henry Michael Mydleton WILSHERE, which Foley Charles was 2nd s. of 4th Viscount Gort. He was *b.* 21 June 1916; *m.* 4 July 1946, Bettine Mary Mackenzie, da. of Godfrey GREEN, formerly wife of Arthur Henry JARAND.

[FOLEY ROBERT STANDISH PRENDERGAST VEREKER, 1st s. and h. ap., *b.* 24 Oct. 1951; ed. at Harrow; *m.*, 1979, Julie Denise, da. of D.W. JONES of Ballasalla, Isle of Man.]

GOSCHEN

page 30,
line 26, line to read as follows

II. 1907. 2. GEORGE JOACHIM (GOSCHEN), VISCOUNT GOSCHEN, 1st s. and h., *b.* 15 Oct. 1866, at St. Leonards-on-Sea

lines 33–4, delete from 'Having' to 'work.]' and replace by 'She *d.* 11 July 1943. He *d. s.p.m.s.* 24 July 1952.
after line 34 add as follows

[George Joachim Goschen, only s. and h. ap., *b.* 18 Nov. 1893; ed. at Eton and Oxford (Ch. Ch.). Fought in WW1([d]) as Lieut. in the East Kent Regt., his father's regiment. He *d. v.p.* 19 Jan. 1916 of wounds received on the 7th, in Mesopotamia.]

III. 1952. 3. JOHN ALEXANDER (GOSCHEN), VISCOUNT GOSCHEN, nephew and h., being 2nd s. of William Henry GOSCHEN (*d.* 16 June 1943), by Geraldine Elizabeth, da. of Rt. Hon. John William MELLOR, P.C., K.C., which William was 2nd s. of 1st Viscount Goschen. He was *b.* 7 July 1906; ed. at Eton; *m.*, 21 Nov. 1934, Hilda Violet Ursula, yr. da. of Col. St. Leger Henry JERVIS, D.S.O. This marriage was diss. by divorce in 1949 and he *m.* 2ndly, 18 Aug. 1955, Alvin Moyanna Lesley, yr. da. of Harry ENGLAND of Durban, South Africa. He *d.* 22 Mar. 1977. His widow was still living 1995.

IV. 1977. 4. GILES JOHN HARRY (GOSCHEN), VISCOUNT GOSCHEN, s. and h., *b.* 16 Nov. 1965; *m.*, 1991, Sarah, yr. da. of A.G. HORSNAIL of Westbury on Trim, Bristol.

note ([d]), lines 1–3, delete from 'He' to 'Mesopotamia.'

GOSFORD

page 33,
line 11, after 'Alexandra.' add 'She *d.* 3 Mar. 1944.'
line 12, line to read as follows

EARLDOM [I.]
V.
VISCOUNTCY, Etc. [I.]
VI.
} 1922 5 and 6. ARCHIBALD CHARLES MONTAGU BRABAZON (ACHESON), EARL OF GOSFORD, &c., 1st s. and h.,

line 3, after 'Marylebone;' add '*styled* LORD ACHESON till 1922;'
line 18, delete from 'was' to 'Officers' and replace by 'Brevet Major (Temp. Lieut. Col.)'.
lines 21–2, delete from 'Having' to 'work.]' and replace by 'This marriage was diss. by divorce in 1928 (she *d.* 7 Sep. 1965) and he *m.* 2ndly, 1 Oct. 1928, Beatrice, da. of Arthur CLAFIN of Southampton, New York, U.S.A. and formerly wife of Robert P. BREESE He *d.* 20 Mar. 1954. His widow *d.* 1967.

EARLDOM [I.] VI.
VISCOUNTCY, Etc. [I.] VII. } 1954

6 and 7. ARCHIBALD ALEXANDER JOHN STANLEY (ACHESON), EARL OF GOSFORD, &c., s. and h., *b.* 14 Jan., and *bap.* 21 July 1911, at the Guards' Chapel, Wellington Barracks, Queen Alexandra being one of the sponsors. Ed. at Harrow and Cambridge (Trin. Coll.); *m.* 1stly, 14 Dec. 1935, Francesca Augusta Maria, 1st da. of Francesco CAGIATI, of Rome. This marriage was diss. by divorce in 1960 and he *m.* 2ndly, 21 Sep. 1960, Cynthia Margaret, da. of Capt. Henry Cave WEST, M.C., and widow of James Pringle DELIUS. He *d.* 17 Feb. 1966. His widow was still living 1995.

EARLDOM [I.] VII.
VISCOUNTCY, Etc. [I.] VIII. } 1966

7 and 8. CHARLES DAVID ALEXANDER JOHN SPARROW (ACHESON), EARL OF GOSFORD, &c., only s. and h., *b.* 13 July 1942; ed. at Harrow Sch. and Royal Acad. Sch.; *m.*, 1983, Lynette REDMOND of Sydney, Australia.

note ([d]), delete all detail

GOUGH

page 36,
line 6, after '1919.' add 'His widow *d.* 30 July 1943.'
line 7, line to read as follows

IV. 1919. 4. HUGH WILLIAM (GOUGH), VISCOUNT GOUGH OF GOOJERAT AND OF LIMERICK, &c., only s. and h., *b.* 22 Feb. 1892, at

lines 12–13, delete from 'Having' to 'work.]' and replace by 'He *m.*, 12 Nov. 1935, at the Royal Military Chapel, Wellington Barracks, Margaretta Elizabeth, da. of Sir Spencer MARYON-WILSON, Bart. He *d.* 4 Dec. 1951. His widow *d.* 1977.'

V. 1951. 5. SHANE HUGH MARYON (GOUGH), VISCOUNT GOUGH OF GOOJERAT AND OF LIMERICK, &c., only s. and h., *b.* 26 Aug. 1941; ed. at Winchester.

note ([c]), line 4, for 'first 'read 'second'

page 37,
line 1, for 'Lyne' read 'Lyme'

GOXHILL

page 42,
note (h), line 4, for 'vol. ii' read 'vol. iii'
line 4 (on page 43), for 'vol. ii' read 'vol. iii'

GRAFTON

page 50,
line 24, line to read as follows

VIII. 1918. 8. ALFRED WILLIAM MAITLAND (FITZROY), DUKE OF GRAFTON, &c., yr. and only surv. s. and h.,

note (e), delete all detail

page 51,
lines 7–8, delete from 'Having' to 'work.]' and replace by 'He *d.* 10 Jan. 1930. His widow *d.* 3 Oct. 1961.'

[WILLIAM HENRY ALFRED FITZROY, only s. and h. ap., *b.* 24 July 1884; *styled* VISCOUNT IPSWICH 1912–18; *m.* 27 Sep. 1913, Auriol Margaretta, only child of Major James BROUGHAM, of Woodland Hall, Lancs., and Potterspury House, Northants. He fought in WW1, as Lieut. Coldstream Guards, later in the R.A.F., and was *k.* flying in Wiltshire, 23, and was *bur.* 29 Apr. 1918, at Euston. His widow *m.* 2ndly, 28 Oct. 1929, at St. Mary's Church, Whittlebury, co. Northampton, Lieut. Col. Gavin Robert Vernon HUME-GORE, M.C. She *d.* 7 Feb. 1938.]

IX. 1930. 9. JOHN CHARLES WILLIAM (FITZROY), DUKE OF GRAFTON, &c., grandson and h., being s. and h. of William Henry Alfred and Auriol Margaretta abovenamed, *b.* 1 Aug. 1914; *styled* EARL OF EUSTON 1918–30. Ed. at Cambridge (Trin. Coll.). He *d.* unm. 4 Aug. 1936 at Euston Hall, of pneumonia, when the Earldom and Barony of Arlington and the Viscountcy of Thetford, all in the peerage of England, fell into *abeyance* (in so far as any Earldom may be said to be in *abeyance*; see the spec. rem. for these peerages, *sub* ARLINGTON) between his two sisters.(a) He was *suc.* in his other titles by his distant cousin.

X. 1936. 10. CHARLES ALFRED EUSTON (FITZROY), DUKE OF GRAFTON, &c., distant cousin and h., being 1st s. of Rev. Charles Edward FITZROY (*d.* 27 Aug. 1911), by Ismay Mary Helen Augusta, da. of Charles Henry (FITZROY), 4th BARON SOUTHAMPTON, which Charles Edward was 3rd s. of 7th Duke of Grafton. He was *b.* 4 June 1892; ed. at Wellington and R.M.C., Sandhurst; *m.* 1stly, 24 Jan. 1918, Lady Doreen Maria Josepha Sydney, 2nd da. of Sydney Charles (BUXTON), 1st and last EARL OF BUXTON. She *d.* 28 July 1923 and he *m.* 2ndly, 6 Oct. 1924, Lucy Eleanor, da. of Sir George Stapylton BARNES, K.C.B., K.C.S.I., of Cobham, Surrey. She *d.* 11 Sep. 1943 and he *m.* 3rdly, 18 July 1944, Rita Emily, da. of John Ralph Stockley CARR-ELLISON and widow of Lieut. Cmdr. John Thurburn CURRIE, R.N. She *d.* 1970. He *d.* 11 Nov. 1970.

XI. 1970. 11. HUGH DENIS CHARLES (FITZROY), DUKE OF GRAFTON, &c., 1st s. and h. by 1st wife, *b.* 3 Apr. 1919; ed. at Eton and Cambridge (Magdalene Coll.); *m.*, 12 Oct. 1946, Anne Fortune, da. of Capt. Evan Cadogan Eric SMITH.

[JAMES OLIVER CHARLES FITZROY, *styled* EARL OF EUSTON, *b.* 13 Dec. 1937; ed. at Eton and Cambridge (Magdalene Coll.); *m.*, 1972, Lady Clare Amabel Margaret, da. of Peter Francis Walter (KERR), 12th MARQUESS OF LOTHIAN.]

note ([a]), before 'A' add 'These are: (1) Margaret Jane, *b.* 27 Apr. 1916, *m.*, 10 Oct. 1936, Gen. Sir Eustace John Blois NELSON, K.C.V.O, D.S.O., M.C. (he *d.* 1993), and (2) Mary Rose, *b.* (posthumously), 7 Sep. 1918, *m.*, 3 Nov. 1945, Francis Trelawney WILLIAMS (he *d.* 1977). This marriage was diss. by divorce in 1952.'

GRANARD

page 55,
line 18, after 'Oct.' add '([ea])'
note ([ea]) On 2 Oct. 1678, Lord Conway wrote to his wife, "my Neece will be marryed to my Lord Granard's eldest Sonne, I beleeve upon the 28 of November" [*Conway Letters*, p. 442]. V.G.

page 56,
line 23, after '1778.' add '([fa])'
note ([fa]) *Farley's Bristol Journal*, 30 May 1778, has "On Tuesday last died at Brockley Court Somerset, the Countess Dowager of Granard" [*ex inform.* C.R. Hudleston]. This is exactly one week later.

page 59,
line 21, after 'U.S.A. 'add 'He *d.* 10 Sep. 1948. His widow *d.* 1972.'
line 22, delete all detail and replace as follows

EARLDOM [I.] IX. BARONY [U.K.] IV. } 1948 9 and 4. ARTHUR PATRICK HASTINGS (FORBES), EARL OF GRANARD, &c., s. and h., *b.* 10 Apr. 1915, *styled* VISCOUNT FORBES until 1948; ed. at Eton and Cambridge (Trin. Coll.); *m.*, 29 July 1949, Marie Madeleine Eugène, yst. da. of Jean Maurel, of Millau, Aveyron, France and formerly wife of PRINCE HUMBERT DE FAUCIGNY LUCINGE. She *d.* 1990. He *d. s.p.m.* 19 Nov. 1992.

EARLDOM [I.] X. BARONY [U.K.] V. } 1992 10 and 5. PETER ARTHUR EDWARD HASTINGS (FORBES), EARL OF GRANARD, &c., nephew and h., being s. and h. of John FORBES, by Joan, 3rd da. of A. Edward SMITH of Sallins, co. Kildare. He was *b.* 15 Mar. 1957; ed. at Eton; *m.*, 1980, Nora Ann Noreen, da. of Robert MITCHELL of Portarlington, co. Leix.

[JONATHAN PETER HASTINGS FORBES, *styled* VISCOUNT FORBES, 1st s and h. ap., *b.* 24 Dec. 1981.]

GRANDISON

page 60,
line 17, delete 'Archbishop of York'
note (g), line 3, after 'York' add '[*sic*]'

page 68,
line 7, after 'Northwood,' (second occurrence) add '[2nd LORD NORTHWODE],'
line 8, after 'Northwood,' add '[3rd LORD NORTHWODE],'

page 74,
line 13, for 'co. Leitrim' read 'co. Limerick'

page 75,
line 7, for '1st' read '5th'

page 76,
line 25, delete from 'on' to '1676/7' and replace by '20 May 1673 at Lambeth Chapel' [See TYRONE, vol. xii, part 2, p. 144.]

page 77,
line 19, delete '*circa*'

page 78,
line 23, after 'Regiment' add ', who *d.* 1777'

GRANE

page 79,
note (c), line 3, for 'sons' read 'brothers-in-law and her stepson'
line 4, after 'State' add '(his sister Elizabeth had married Gerald 9th Earl of Kildare, whose five brothers and his son by his first marriage were sent to London by Lord Leonard). See Kildare'.

page 80,
line 3, after 'month.' add 'He *m.* 1stly, between 18 Feb. 1509/10 and Easter 1514, Elizabeth, widow of Giles (DAUBENEY), 1st or 10th LORD DAUBENEY, da. of Sir John ARUNDELL of Lanherne, Cornwall, by his 2nd wife Katherine, 1st da. and coh. of Sir John CHIDIOCK. She, who was living 26 June 1515, was *bur.* with her 1st husband in Westm. Abbey, M.I. He is said to have *m.* 2ndly, Eleanor, widow of Charles (SOMERSET), 1st EARL OF WORCESTER (*d.* 19 Apr. 1526), da. of Edward (SUTTON), 2nd LORD DUDLEY, by Cicely, da. of Sir William WILLOUGHBY.(aa) She pres. *d. s.p.* before 24 May 1532.(ab)
note (aa) See addendum *sub* Daubeney in this present volume, also Worcester, vol. xii, part 2, p. 850.

note ([ab]) When he had "Communication with [Elizabeth, widow of Gilbert (Tailboys), 1st Lord Tailboys] in the way of marriage" (*L. and P. Hen. VIII*, vol. v, no. 1049, see also vol. xii, part 1, note *sub* Tailboys [1529]).

GRANTLEY

page 87,
line 14, after '[I.].' add 'She *d.* 11 May 1942. He *d.* 5 Aug. 1943.'
line 15, line to read as follows

VI. 1943. 6. RICHARD HENRY BRINSLEY (NORTON), BARON GRANTLEY OF MARKENFIELD, 2nd but 1st surv. s. and h. by 1st wife,

line 17, for ']' read 'He *m.*, 3 Apr. 1919, Jean Mary, 1st da. of Brig. Gen. Sir David Alexander KINLOCH, Bart. She *d.* 16 Jan. 1945. He *d.* 17 July 1954.'

VII. 1954. 7. JOHN RICHARD BRINSLEY (NORTON), BARON GRANTLEY OF MARKENFIELD, only s. and h., *b.* 30 July 1923; ed. at Eton and Oxford (New Coll.); *m.*, 18 Jan. 1955, Lady Deirdre Elizabeth Freda, da. of William Francis (HARE), 5th EARL OF LISTOWEL.

[RICHARD WILLIAM BRINSLEY HARE, 1st s. and h. ap., *b.* 30 Jan. 1956; ed. at Ampleforth and Oxford (New Coll.).]

GRANVILLE

page 93,
note ([i]), line 3 (on page 93), for 'Francis' read 'George' and for '5th' read '8th'

page 96,
lines 9–10, for 'was living 1925' read '*d.* 12 Nov. 1938.'
line 23, after '1876.' add 'He *d. s.p.* 21 July 1939. His widow *d.* 12 June 1955.'

EARLDOM. VII. VISCOUNTCY. IV. } 1939 4. WILLIAM SPENCER (LEVESON-GOWER), EARL GRANVILLE, &c., br. and h., *b.* 11 July 1880; made K.G. 1952; *m.*, 24 May 1916, Lady Rose Constance, da. of Claude George (BOWES-LYON), 14th EARL OF STRATHMORE. He *d.* 25 June 1953. His widow *d.* 17 Nov. 1967.

EARLDOM. VIII. VISCOUNTCY. V. } 1953 5. GRANVILLE JAMES (LEVESON-GOWER), EARL GRANVILLE, &c., only s. and h., *b.* 6 Dec. 1918; ed. at Eton; *m.*, 9 Oct. 1958, Doon Aileen, yr. da. of Brinsley Sheridan Bushe PLUNKET. He *d.* 31 October 1996. His widow was living 1996.

EARLDOM. IX. VISCOUNTCY. VI. } 1996 6. GRANVILLE GEORGE FERGUS (LEVESON-GOWER), EARL GRANVILLE, &c., 1st s. and h., *b.* 10 Sep. 1959; *styled* LORD LEVESON 1959–96.

GRAVES

page 98,
lines 20–2, delete from 'was living' to 'work' and replace by '*d.* 16 May 1926.'

V. 1904. 5. HENRY CYRIL PERCY (GRAVES), BARON GRAVES OF GRAVESEND, cousin and h., being the 1st s. and h. of Henry Richard GRAVES (*d.* 29 Apr. 1882), by Henrietta WELLESLEY, which Henry Richard was 2nd s. of the 2nd BARON GRAVES; *b.* 10 Sep. 1847. He *m.* 11 Oct. 1870, Elizabeth Ellen, da. of Henry CRAVEN of Wickham Hall, Kent. She *d.* 5 Jan. 1914. He *d.* 13 Jan. 1914.

VI. 1914. 6. CLARENCE PERCY RIVERS (GRAVES), BARON GRAVES OF GRAVESEND, only s. and h., *b.* 16 Oct. 1871. He *m.* 7 Feb. 1903, his cousin, Mary Ada Isobel, 3rd da. of Edward Corbett PARKER, by Georgiana Louisa Alice, 2nd da. of Henry Richard GRAVES, 3rd s. of the 2nd Baron. He *d. s.p.m.* 1 Mar. 1937. His widow *d.* 7 Jan. 1962.

VII. 1937. 7. HENRY ALGERNON CLAUDE (GRAVES), BARON GRAVES OF GRAVESEND, distant cousin and h., being s. and h. of Claude Thomas GRAVES (*d.* 1898), by Georgina, da. of Capt. (__) HILL, which Claude was 3rd s. of Henry Richard GRAVES abovenamed. He was *b.* 3 Oct. 1877; *m.*, 1909, Vera Blanche Neville, da. of Alfred Neville SNEPP. This marriage was diss. by divorce in 1922 (she *d.* 20 May 1953). He *d.* 6 Nov. 1963.

VIII. 1963. 8. PETER GEORGE WELLESLEY (GRAVES), BARON GRAVES OF GRAVESEND, only s. and h., *b.* 21 Oct. 1911; ed. at Harrow; *m.*, 28 May 1960, Winifred Ruby, da. of Alfred MOULE and widow of Warde MORGAN. She *d.* 1992. He *d. s.p.m.* 6 June 1994.

IX. 1994. 9. EVELYN PAGET (GRAVES), BARON GRAVES OF GRAVESEND, distant cousin and h., being s. and h. of Alweyn Montague GRAVES (*d.* 30 Aug. 1956), by Kathleen Eleanor Cowley PRIEST, which Alweyn was 2nd s. of Adolphus Edward Paget GRAVES (*d.* 5 Aug. 1931), by his 2nd wife Katherine Louisa, 2nd da. of Col. Henry Constantine Evelyn WARD, which Adolphus Edward was 5th s. of Henry Richard GRAVES abovenamed. He was *b.* 17 May 1926; *m.*, 13 Mar. 1957, Marjorie Ann, da. of Dr Ernest Sidney HOLDER of Wallingford, co. Berks.

[TIMOTHY EVELYN GRAVES, 1st s. and h. ap., was *b.* 27 Mar. 1960.]

note (b), delete all detail

GRAY

page 106,
line 1, line to read as follows

XX. 1918. 20. JAMES MACLAREN STUART (GRAY), LORD GRAY [S.], 1st and only surv s. and h., *b.* 4 June 1864; Master of Gray 1895–1918;

lines 4–5, delete from 'Having' to 'work([a])]'

XXI. 1919. 21. ETHEL EVELEEN GRAY, *suo jure* BARONESS GRAY [S.], sister and h., *b.* 16 Jan. 1866; *m.*, 23 July 1888, Henry Tufnell CAMPBELL of Brownswood, Enniscorthy, co. Wexford (maternal grandson of the 9th Earl of Lindsay). By Roy. Lic., 24 Apr. 1920, he assumed the name of Gray before that of Campbell and the name of Gray after that of Campbell, together with the arms of Gray alone, for his issue. He *d.* 31 Jan. 1945. She *d.* 2 Oct. 1946.

[LINDSAY STUART CAMPBELL-GRAY, MASTER OF GRAY, 1st s. and h. ap., *b.* 4 May 1894; *m.*, 8 July 1930, Doreen McClymont, 1st da. of Cyril TUBBS of Thedden Grange, Alton, co. Hants. He *d. v.p.* 7 Sep. 1945. His widow *d.* 11 May 1948.]

XXII. 1946. 22. ANGUS DIARMID IAN (CAMPBELL-GRAY), LORD GRAY, grandson and h., being s. of Lindsay Stuart and Doreen abovenamed, *b.* 3 July 1931; *m.* 1stly, 5 Sep. 1959, Patricia Margaret, da. of Capt. Philip Sylvester ALEXANDER of Lismore, co. Waterford. She *d.* 1987 and he *m.* 2ndly, 1994, Cilla, da. of (__) and widow of Paul BLACK.

[ANDREW GODFREY DIARMID STUART CAMPBELL-GRAY, MASTER OF GRAY, s. and h. ap. by 1st wife, *b.* 3 Sep. 1964; *m.*, 1993, Hon. Lucy, da. of Rodney (ELTON), 2nd BARON ELTON.]

note ([a]), delete all detail

GREENWICH

page 107,
line 7, delete '23 July 1742' and replace by '10 June 1747'

GREVILLE OF CLONYN

page 117,
line 34, for 'was living 1925' read '*d.* 15 Sep. 1942.'

page 118,
line 6, for 'was living 1925' read '*d.* 15 Sep. 1942.'
line 7, line to read as follows

III. 1909. 3. CHARLES BERESFORD FULKE (GREVILLE), BARON GREVILLE OF CLONYN, 2nd but only surv. s. and h.,

lines 13–14, delete from 'Having' to 'work.]' and replace by 'He *d.* 14 May 1952. His widow *d.* 1 Oct. 1959.'

IV. 1952. 4. RONALD CHARLES FULKE (GREVILLE), BARON GREVILLE OF CLONYN, only s. and h., *b.* 11 Apr. 1912; ed. at Eton and Oxford (Magdalen Coll.). He *d.* unm. 9 Dec. 1987 when his title became *extinct*.

GREY

page 122,
lines 20–1, for 'was living 1925' read '*d.* 22 Sep. 1944.'
line 22, line to read as follows

V. 1917. 5. CHARLES ROBERT (GREY), EARL GREY, &c., only s. and h., *b.* 15 Dec. 1879; *styled* VISCOUNT HOWICK 1894–1917;

lines 29–30, delete from 'Having' to 'work.]' and replace by 'She *d.* 15 July 1958. He *d. s.p.m.* 2 Apr. 1963.

VI. 1963. 6. RICHARD FLEMING GEORGE CHARLES (GREY), EARL GREY, &c., distant cousin and h., being 1st s. of Albert Harry George Campbell GREY (*d.* 1942 on active service), by Vera Helen Louise, da. of William HARDING, which Albert Harry was 1st s. of George Archibald Grey (*d.* 1952), by his 1st wife Margery Berridge Stuart, da. of Wilfred CAMPBELL, of City View, Ottawa, which George Archibald was s. of Francis William Grey (*d.* July 1939), by Jessie Macleod, da. of Charles ROLLAND, SEIGNEUR OF S. MARIE DE MANOIR, Quebec, which Francis William was 5th s. of Adm. George GREY, Bath King of Arms (*d.* 3 Oct. 1891), by Jane Frances, da. of Gen. Sir Patrick STUART, which George was 4th s. of 2nd Earl Grey. He was *b.* 4 Mar. 1939; *m.*, 26 Mar. 1966, Margaret Ann, 1st da. of Henry G. BRADFORD, of Ashburton, co. Devon. This marriage was diss. by divorce in 1974 and he *m.* 2ndly, 1974, Stephanie Caroline, da. of Donald Gaskell BROWN, of Newton Ferrers, Plymouth and formerly wife of Neil Leicester DENHAM, Surg. Cmdr. R.N.

GREY (of Codnor)

page 126,
line 22, after 'TYES' (2nd occurrence), add ', 2nd LORD TYES'

page 129,
line 16, after 'His' add '1st'
line 17, after '(k)' add 'He *m.* 2ndly, Elizabeth da. of Gerald (FITZGERALD), 5th EARL OF KILDARE.' and after '(l)' add 'His widow *m.* in 1432 James (BUTLER), 4th EARL OF ORMOND.'

page 131,
line 19, delete '1474, Margaret' and replace by '1458–9, Margaret, one of the 3 das. of Sir Ralph Moton.'
note (i), line 2, after '"b"' add ', and *Hist. MSS. Comm.*, De L'Isle and Dudley MSS., vol. 1, p. 192. According to the *Visitation of Leicestershire* (Harl. Soc., vol. ii, p. 58), her sister Anne *m.* William Grymsby of Drakeboro, and her sister Elizabeth *m.* Rafe Pole of Radbourne, but no mention is there made of Margaret or her marriage. Their father is there called Reginald Motton.'

page 132,
line 2, delete '1496' and replace by '18 Apr. 1495' [*Cal. Inq. p. m.*, Hen. VII, vol. iii, nos. 477, 571]
line 10, for '5th' read '4th'

page 133,
after line 4 add

* * * * * *

VIII. 1989. 8. CHARLES LEGH SHULDHAM (WALKER, *later* (1926) CORNWALL-LEGH), LORD GREY (of Codnor), for whom the *abeyance* in the Barony of Grey was terminated, 30 Oct. 1989, he being a descendant of Lucy Lenthall, see above.[aa] He was *b.* 10 Feb. 1903; ed. at King's Sch., Bruton and Oxford (Hertford Coll.); *m.*, 8 Feb. 1930, Dorothy Catherine Whitson, 1st da. of John Whitson SCOTT of Seal, Sevenoaks, co. Kent. She *d.* 1993.

[RICHARD HENRY CORNWALL-LEGH, s. and h. ap., *b.* 14 May 1936; ed. at Stowe; *m.*, 1974, Joanna Storm, 7th da. of Major Sir Kenelm Henry Ernest CAYLEY, Bart.]

note [aa] A claim to be one of the coheirs to the Barony of Grey of Codnor was first presented in 1926. The petitioner (the father of the present peer) died in 1934 before the case could be heard by the Committee for Privileges, the petition was presented again in 1935 and later referred to the Committee by the King, Edward VIII, in November 1936. It was not actually heard by the Committee until 1989, when they agreed that there were good reasons to overrule the recommendation of the 1926 Select Committee on Peerages in Abeyance that no *abeyance* should be terminated if the first *abeyance* had occurred more than 100 years before the presentation of the petition, as was certainly the case here. See Reports of the Committee for Privileges, 1989, HL Papers 59 and 59-1.

Note, line 11, after 'Rotherfield).' add 'However, John de Grey, Bishop of Norwich (brother of Hawise, ancestress of the Greys of Rotherfield), granted land in Sandiacre to William "fil Roberti" in July of the 3rd year of John (1201), which seems to show some connection between the Greys of Rotherfield and those descended from Henry Grey of Grays Thurrock. See I.H. Jeayes, *Derbyshire Charters*, 1906, nos. 2769, 2770.'

line 23, after 'Hawise,' add 'possibly' and after 'Fleming' add 'but more probably da. of Geoffrey (FitzPiers), 3rd Earl of Essex. See Mohun.'

GREY (of Powis)

page 140,
line 7, delete 'widow of Sir Roger VAUGHAN, kt.,[d] and'
line 8, delete 'or Audley'
line 9, after '30' add 'His widow *m.* 2ndly, Sir Roger VAUGHAN, Kt.,[d] and'
line 10, delete 'His widow'

page 142,
note (h), line 16 (on page 143), after 'Cherleton.' add 'For Elizabeth see Francis Jones, "The Dynasty of Powys", *Cymmrod. Soc., Trans.*, 1958, pp. 123–32 (particularly p. 32, note 31).'

GREY (of Rotherfield)

page 145,
line 1, delete 'his wife' and replace by 'da. of Walter FITZROBERT, of Woodham Walter, Essex.' [See CLINTON, vol. iii, p. 313.]

page 146,
note (f), line 18, after 'furred.' add 'At the tournament in Lichfield, 9 Apr. 21 Edw. III (1347), occurs the name (with 10 others) of John Grey (P.R.O., E 101 Wardrobe Accts, 21–3 Edw. III, 391/15, *ex inform.* John Brownbill). This John Grey is perhaps also more likely to be John Grey of Rotherfield.'

page 148,
note (e), line 1, after 'Poynings' add '[1st LORD POYNINGS]'

page 149,
line 12, after '4thly,' add '(lic. 20 Dec. 1398)'

GREY (of Rougemont)

page 151,
line 2, for '1449' read '1450'

GREY (of Ruthin)

page 153,
line 10, after '*m.*' add ', by 1311' [*Cal. Pat. Rolls*, *1307–13*, p. 401, cited in R.I. Jack, 'The Greys of Ruthin', PhD thesis, London, 1961, p. 429]
line 12, for (DE VALENCE)' read 'DE VALENCE, sometimes *styled*'

page 154,
line 11, for '25 Oct. 1348 and 4 May 1350' read '6 Jan. 1349 and 6 Feb. 1350'
note (e), delete all detail and replace by '*Records of Harrold Priory*, ed. G.H. Fowler, Beds. Hist. Record Soc., vol. 17, 1935, p. 156; PRO, E403/349, cited by Jack, *op. cit.*

page 155,
lines 5–6, delete from 'Sir' to 'LESTRAUNGE]' and replace by 'John LESTRAUNGE of Blackmere [2nd LORD STRANGE]
note (c), delete all detail and replace by 'The filiation of Eleanor is proved by the deposition of William Alnwick in 1408 (College of Arms MS., Proc. in Cur. Mar. I 227). Also, this lady Eleanor had a br., Hamon (*Cal. Pat. Rolls, 1381–5*, p. 33); Eleanor, da. of Roger Lestrange of Knockin, also suggested as her father, did not. See Jack, *op. cit.*'

page 157,
line 20, for 'Weyfford' read 'Weysford [*i.e.* Wexford]' [See PEMBROKE [1307] and subsequently.]

page 158,
line 5, after 'Warwick' add '[4th LORD ASTLEY],'; after 'wife' add '(see ASTLEY)' and for '18 Oct.' read '30 Sep.'

page 159,
line 5, after 'John' add 'of Gaunt'

page 161,
lines 18–19, delete from 'and' to 'PALMER' and replace by 'of Edward NEVILLE of Bentworth, Hants., by Margaret, da. of Sir Francis PALMES' [See *V.C.H. Hants*, vol. 4, p. 69.]

page 165,
lines 8–11, delete from 'He' to 'work'

XXIV. 1912. 24. CECIL TALBOT (CLIFTON), LORD GREY (of Ruthin) [1312], br. and h., being the 2nd surv. s.; *b.* 9 Jan. 1862. He was a ranch holder, of Northfields, Montana, U.S.A. He *d.* unm. 21, at Melrose House, Fownhope, co. Hereford and was *bur.* there 23 May 1934, when his Barony fell into *abeyance* between his nephew, s. of his 1st sister, and his 2nd sister. It was called out of *abeyance* in 1940 after the death without issue of the latter.(da)

XXV. 1940. 25. JOHN WYKEHAM (BUTLER-BOWDEN), LORD GREY (of Ruthin) [1312], nephew and h., being only s. and h. of Ella Cicely Mary, 1st da. of BERTHA LELGARDE, *suo jure* BARONESS GREY (of Ruthin) and Augustus Wykeham CLIFTON abovenamed. He was *b.* 25 Oct. 1883; ed. at Mount St. Mary's Coll., Spinkhill. He *d.* unm. 25 Oct. 1963 when the Barony again fell into *abeyance*, between the representatives of the sisters of BERTHA LLGARDE, *suo jure* BARONESS GREY (of Ruthin), abovenamed.(db)

note (da) These sisters were 1. Ella Cicely Mary, *b.* 22 Nov. 1856, *m.*, 30 July 1879, Lancelot George Butler-Bowdon of Barlborough House, Chesterfield, co. Derby. He *d.* 12 Sep. 1909. She *d.* 2 July 1912, and 2. Lelgarde Harry Florence, *b.* 16 Feb. 1870, *m.*, 11 June 1895, Sir Alan Henry Bellingham, Bart. He *d.* 9 June 1921. She *d. s.p.* 15 Oct. 1939.

note (db) These sisters were: (1) Edith Maud, Countess of Loudoun (see that title); (2) Victoria Mary Louisa, who *m.* John Forbes Stratford Kirwan, and died leaving issue; (3) Frances Augusta Constance, who *m.* Charles (Marsham), 4th Earl of Romney (see that title); (4) Barbara (only da. of Barbara, Baroness Grey by her 2nd husband), *m.* John (Yarde-Buller), 2nd Baron Churston (see that title). See also note (a), p. 164.

note (d), delete all detail

GREY (of Wilton)

page 171,
note (f), before 'All' add '"Carta Stephanie de Segrave cum Emma de Cauz nuper uxore

Johannis de Segrave filii dicti Stephanie ad totam vitam eiusdem Emme nomis dotis de tota terra sua de Henlawe" (Segrave Cartulary, Harl. MS. 4748, f. 6d).'

page 176,
line 12, delete all detail and replace by 'apparently da. of Sir Richard DE LA VACHE(ca)'
note (ca) In the de Bonis Roll, 22 Hen. VI, no 408, Reynold de Grey of Wilton sued Margaret, late wife of Richard de Grey, for lands and rents in Shenley by virtue of a fine of 1 Edw. II, by which they were settled on Richard de la Vache for life with remainder to Matthew son of Richard and the heirs of his body, remainder to Richard, brother of Matthew and the heirs of his body, which failing to Maud, sister of Richard, and Reynold de Grey claimed as heir.'

page 186,
line 20, after '(f)' add 'of which county he was Lieut. in or before 1570,'

GREYSTOKE

page 196,
line 17, after 'John' add 'of Gaunt'
line 19, after 'BOTILLER,' add '[3rd LORD LE BOTILLER],'

page 199,
line 6, after 'FERRERS' add '(s. and h. ap. of William LORD FERRERS (of Groby))'

GRIFFIN

page 202,
line 1, delete 'GRIFFIN see POWIS'

GRIMTHORPE

page 208,
lines 1–2, delete from 'He was' to 'work'

II. 1905. 2. ERNEST WILLIAM (BECKETT), BARON GRIMTHORPE, 5th Bart., nephew and h. under the spec. rem., being the eld. s. of the 3rd and only s. to leave issue of Sir Edmund Beckett, 4th Bart., *b.* 25 Nov. 1856; *m.* 4 Oct. 1883, Lucy. only child of William Tracy LEE, of New York U.S.A. She *d.* 9 May 1891. He *d.* 11 May 1917.

III. 1917. 3. RALPH WILLIAM ERNEST (BECKETT), BARON GRIMTHORPE, only s. and h., *b.* 4 May 1891; matric. Oxford (Univ. Coll.) 1891. Served in WW1(a) as Lieut. Yorks. Hussars. He *m.* 1stly, 3 Sep. 1914, at St. Martin's York, Mary, da. of Lieut. Col. Mervyn Henry ARCHDALE. This marriage was diss.

by divorce in 1945 (she *d.* in an accident 28 Apr. 1962) and he *m.* 2ndly, 25 Mar. 1945, Angela, yst. da. of Edward Hubert COURAGE, of Kirkby Fleetham Hall, Bedale, co. York and formerly wife of David Cecil Lycett GREEN, Lieut. Cmdr., R.N. He *d.* 22 Feb. 1963. His widow *d.* 1992.

IV. 1963. 4. CHRISTOPHER JOHN (BECKETT), BARON GRIMTHORPE, 1st s. and h. by 1st wife, *b.* 16 Sep. 1915; ed. at Eton; *m.*, 17 Feb. 1954, Lady Elizabeth, 2nd da. of Lawrence Roger (LUMLEY), 11th EARL OF SCARBOROUGH, K.G.

[EDWARD JOHN BECKETT, 1st s. and h. ap., *b.* 20 Nov. 1954; *m.*, 1992, Carey Elizabeth (Mrs MCEWAN), yr. da. of Robin GRAHAM.]

note (a), lines 1–7, delete from 'Ernest' to 'Archdale'

GROSVENOR

page 209,
note (d), line 1 (on page 210), after 'and' add 'his wife' and for 'as' read 'in'

pages 211–18, for GUILDFORD read 'GUILFORD'

page 213,
line 33, after '1732' add 'in Albemarle St.'

page 217,
line 17, for 'his *d.* in 1861' read '1855'
note (d), line 1, before 'His' add 'When he was succeeded by the Rev. L.M. Humbert.'

page 218,
lines 23–4, for 'was living 1925' read '*d.* 13 May 1935.'
line 34, after 'VINCENT.' add 'She *d.* 8 Dec. 1947. He *d.* 9 Nov. 1949.'

[FRANCIS GEORGE NORTH, *styled* LORD NORTH, 1st s. and h. ap., *b.* 15 June 1902; *m.*, 9 June 1927, Joan Louise, 1st da. of Sir Merrik Raymond BURRELL, Bart. He *d. v.p.* in an accident, 25 Aug. 1940. His widow *m.* 2ndly, 25 June 1947, Charles Harman HUNT.]

XI. 1949. 9 and 11. EDWARD FRANCIS (NORTH), EARL OF GUILFORD, &c., grandson and h., being s. and h. of Francis NORTH, *styled* LORD NORTH by Joan Louise, both abovenamed. He was *b.* 22 Sep. 1933; ed. at Eton; *m.*, 15 Sep. 1956, Osyth Vere Napier, da. of Cyril Napier LEESON of Trottiscliffe, West Malling, Kent.

[PIERS EDWARD BROWNLOW NORTH, *styled* LORD NORTH, s. and h. ap., *b.* 9 Mar. 1971; *m.*, 1994, Michèle, da. of Gilbert Desvaux DE MARIGNY of Curepipe, Mauritius.]

GUILLAMORE

page 219,
line 6, after '1780' add 'aged 16'

page 220,
lines 20–2, delete from 'He was' to 'work'

VI. 1918. 6. FREDERICK STANDISH (O'GRADY), VISCOUNT GUILLAMORE, &c., br. and h. being 6th and yst. s.(c) of the 2nd Viscount, *b.* 20 Apr. 1847, at Cahir Guillamore, co. Limerick; *m.* 1stly, 1881, Mary Theresa Burdett, da. of William James COVENTRY. She *d.* 12 Jan. 1910, and he *m.* 2ndly, 28 Mar. 1911, Gertrude Lily, da. of John LANGFORD of Draycott, Sudbury. He *d. s.p.m.* 11 Oct. 1927. His widow *d.* 1952.

VII. 1927. 7. HUGH HAMON MASSY STANDISH (O'GRADY), VISCOUNT GUILLAMORE, &c., distant cousin and h., being 2nd s. of Hugh Hamon Massy Standish O'GRADY (*d.* 9 Dec. 1859), by Selina Maria, 1st da. of William Henry HUTCHINSON of Rockforest, co. Tipperary, which Hugh Hamon was 1st s. of Waller O'GRADY (*d.* 9 June 1849), by Grace Elizabeth, 1st da. of Hugh (MASSY), 3rd LORD MASSY, which Waller was 2nd s. of 1st Viscount Guillamore. He was *b.* 5 July 1860; *m.*, 27 Mar. 1890, Mary Margaret Frances, da. of Vere HUNT of High Park, co. Tipperary. He *d. s.p.* 13 June 1930. His widow *d.* 23 Sep. 1930.

VIII. 1930. 8. RICHARD STANDISH (O'GRADY), VISCOUNT GUILLAMORE, &c., cousin and h., being 1st s. of James Waller Standish O'GRADY (*d.* 23 May 1898), by Ada Catherine, da. of William Cunningham BRUCE (2nd s. of Sir William BRUCE, Bart.), which James Waller was 2nd s. of Waller O'GRADY and Grace Elizabeth abovenamed. He was *b.* 9 Aug. 1867. He *d.* unm. Nov. 1943.

IX. 1943. 9. STANDISH BRUCE (O'GRADY), VISCOUNT GUILLAMORE, OF CAHIR GUILLAMORE and BARON O'GRADY OF ROCKBARTON, both in the Peerage of Ireland, br. and h., *b.* 17 Mar. 1869. He *d.* unm. and *s.p.* 15 Oct. 1955 when his titles became *extinct.*

GWYDIR

page 223,
line 22, line to read as follows

V. 1909. 5. WILLOUGHBY MERRICK CAMPBELL (BURRELL), BARON GWYDIR, &c., only s. and h., by 1st wife

page 224,
line 2, after 'of' add 'James'
lines 6–7, delete from 'Having' to 'work'
line 9, delete ']'

GYNES

page 225,
line 3, for 'of David EARL OF HUNTINGDON' read 'of Alan, Lord of Galloway'

HADDINGTON

page 233,
lines 14–15, for 'in the summer of' read 'before 13 Aug.' [*The Blair Papers*, M.V. Hay (ed.), p. 87]

page 236,
line 3, after '7' add ', and was *bur.* 12'

page 238,
lines 19–20, delete from 'He' to 'work'
note ([b]), lines 1–4, delete from 'His' to 'Montreal'

page 239,
after line 2 add as follows

XII. 1917. 12. GEORGE (BAILLIE-HAMILTON), EARL OF HADDINGTON [S.], &c., grandson and h., being s. and h. of George BAILLIE-HAMILTON, *styled* LORD BINNING, by Katherine his wife, both abovenamed. He was *b.* 18 Sep. 1894; ed. at Eton. Served in WW1 as Lieut. 2nd Dragoons (Royal Scots Greys). He *m.* 10 Oct. 1923, at the Roman Catholic Archbishop's Palace, Montreal Canada, Sarah, sister of Marian, Countess of Minto, and yst. da. of George William COOK, of Westmount, Montreal. He *d.* 17 Apr. 1986. His widow was still living 1995.

XIII. 1986. 13. JOHN GEORGE (BAILLIE-HAMILTON), EARL OF HADDINGTON, &c., s. and h., *b.* 21 Dec. 1941; ed. at Ampleforth; *m.* 1stly, 1975, Prudence Elizabeth, da. of Andrew Rutherford HAYLES, of Bowerchalke, Wilts. This marriage was diss. by divorce in 1981 and he *m.* 2ndly, 1984, Jane, da. of John HEYWORTH of Burford, co. Oxford.

[GEORGE EDMUND BALDRED BAILLIE-HAMILTON, *styled* LORD BINNING, s. and h. ap., *b.* 27 Dec. 1985.]

HALDON

page 241,
line 6, for 'Whichdon' read 'Whitchurch'
lines 15–16, for 'was living 1925' read '*d.* 2 May 1926.'
line 17, line to read as follows

III. 1903. 3. LAWRENCE WILLIAM (PALK), BARON HALDON [1880], &c., 1st s. and h., *b.* 13 July 1869;

lines 23–4, delete from 'Having' to 'work.]' and replace by 'She *d.* 26 Nov. 1928 and he *m.* 2ndly, 25 Jan. 1929, Edith Castle, da. of William Ball BIGGS of Clifton, Bristol and widow of E.C. BRIGHTMAN of Cotham Park, Bristol. She *d.* 1 May 1930. He *d.* 12 Jan. 1933.'

IV. 1933. 4. LAWRENCE EDWARD BROOMFIELD (PALK), BARON HALDON [1880], and a Baronet [1782], only s. and h.; ed. at Beaumont Sch. Served in WW1 as 2nd Lieut. Royal Engineers. He was *b.* 13 May 1896. He *d.* unm. and *s.p.* 16 Aug. 1938.

V. 1938. 5. EDWARD ARTHUR (PALK), BARON HALDON, &c., distant cousin and h., being 4th s. of 1st Baron Haldon. He was *b.* 1854; *m.*, 18 July 1883, Charlotte Frances, da. of Rev. Sir Frederick SHELLEY, Bart. She *d.* 12 Jan. 1931. He *d. s.p.* 11 Jan. 1939 when his Barony became *extinct* but he was *suc.* in the Baronetcy by his distant cousin.

HALIBURTON

page 242,
line 24, for 'Paragon' read 'Polygon'

HALIFAX

page 246,
line 2, for '12 May 1688' read '18 Feb. 1687/8'

page 247,
line 19, after 'Coll.)' add 'admitted as a pensioner, aged 17, 14 Feb.'

HALIFAX OF MONK BRETTON

page 250,
line 4, after 'Yorks.' add 'He *d.* 19 Jan. 1934.'
line 5, line to read as follows

III. 1934. 3 and 1. EDWARD FREDERICK LINDLEY (WOOD), VISCOUNT HALIFAX OF MONK BRETTON, 4th and yst.([a]) but 1st surv. s. and h.,

line 11, after '([b])' add 'He was *cr.* BARON IRWIN of Kirby Uderdale, co. York, 22 Dec. 1925, and EARL OF HALIFAX, 11 July 1944. See vol. xiii, p. 415.'
line 16, for ']' read 'He *d.* 23 Dec. 1959. His widow *d.* 2 Feb. 1976.

EARLDOM. II. VISCOUNTCY. IV. } 1959 2 and 4. CHARLES INGRAM COURTENAY (WOOD), EARL OF HALIFAX, &c., 1st s. and h., *b.* 3 Oct. 1912; ed. at Eton and Oxford (Ch. Ch.); *m.*, 25 Apr. 1936, Ruth Alice Hannah, da. of Capt. Rt. Hon. Neil James Archibald PRIMROSE. He *d.* 19 Mar. 1980. His widow was still living 1995.

EARLDOM. III. V. } 1980 3 and 5. CHARLES EDWARD PETER NEIL (WOOD), EARL OF HALIFAX, &c., only s. and h., *b.* 14 Mar. 1944; ed. at Eton and Oxford (Ch. Ch.); *m.*, 1976, Camilla, da. of Charles YOUNGER of Gledswood, Melrose, co. Roxburgh and formerly wife of Richard Eustace Parker BOWLES.

[JAMES CHARLES WOOD, *styled* LORD IRWIN, s. and h. ap., *b.* 24 Aug. 1977.]

HALSBURY

page 252,

line 4, after '(b)' add 'His widow *d.* 22 Dec. 1927.'

line 5, line to read as follows

I. 1921. 2. HARDINGE GOULBURN (GIFFARD), EARL OF HALSBURY, &c., only s. and h., *b.* 20 June 1880, *styled* LORD TIVERTON from 1898; ed.

line 11, for ']' read 'He *d.* 15 Sep. 1943, in an internment camp in France. His widow *d.* 1973.'

III. 1943. 3. JOHN ANTHONY HARDINGE (GIFFARD), EARL OF HALSBURY, &c., only s. and h., *b.* 4 June 1908, at 4 Ennismore Gdns. He was ed. at Eton; *m.* 1stly, 1 Oct. 1930, in Falkland Palace Chapel, Ismay Catherine, 1st da. of Lord Ninian CRICHTON-STUART, of Kellie Castle, Arbroath, Angus. This marriage was diss. by divorce in 1936 (she *d.* 1989) and he *m.* 2ndly, 12 Dec. 1936, Elizabeth Adeline Faith, da. of Major Harry Crewe GODLEY. She *d.* 1983.

[ADAM EDWARD GIFFARD, s. and h. ap. by 1st wife, *b.* 3 June 1934; ed. at Stowe and Cambridge (Jesus Coll.); *m.*, 1 Aug. 1963, Ellen, da. of Brynjolf HOVDE and formerly wife of Matthew HUXLEY. This marriage was diss. by divorce and he *m.* 2ndly, 1976, Joanna Elizabeth, da. of Frederick Harry COLE.]

note (d), delete all detail

HAMBLEDEN

page 253,

line 22, line to read as follows

II. 1913. 2. WILLIAM FREDERICK DANVERS (SMITH), VISCOUNT HAMBLEDEN, only s. and h., *b.* 12 Aug. 1868,

page 254,

lines 5–6, delete from 'Having' to 'work.]' and replace by 'He *d.* at Greenlands, Henley on Thames, 16 and was *bur.* 19 June 1928 at Hambledon. His widow *d.* 11 Oct. 1955.'

III. 1928. 3. WILLIAM HENRY (SMITH), VISCOUNT HAMBLEDEN, 1st s. and h., *b.* 25 July 1903; ed. at Eton and Oxford (New Coll.); *m.*, 26 Sep. 1928, at Salisbury Cathedral, Lady Patricia, da. of Reginald (HERBERT), 15th EARL OF PEMBROKE AND MONTGOMERY. He *d.* 31 Mar. 1948. His widow *d.* 1994.

IV. 1948. 4. WILLIAM HERBERT (SMITH), VISCOUNT HAMBLEDON, 1st s. and h., *b.* 2 Apr. 1930; ed. at Eton; *m.* 1stly, 21 Feb. 1955, Donna Maria Carmela ATTOLICO DI ADELFIA, da. of COUNT BERNARDO ATTOLICO. This marriage was diss. by divorce in 1988 and he *m.* 2ndly, 1988, Mrs Lesley WATSON.

[WILLIAM HENRY BERNARD SMITH, 1st s. and h. ap. by 1st wife, *b.* 18 Nov. 1955; *m.*, 1983, Sara Suzanne, da. of Joseph F. ANLAUF of Palos Verdes Estates, California, U.S.A.]

note ([a]), delete all detail

HAMILTON

page 270,
line 7, for 'in' read 'at Chalfont St. Peter, 14 Sep.'

page 275,
line 17, delete '([e])'
line 18, for 'Napoleon II' read 'Napoleon III'
note ([e]), delete all detail

page 276,
line 6, for 'was living 1925' read '(he *d.* 23 June 1925). She *d.* 10, at Archrannie, Brodick, Arran, and was *bur.* 13 Feb. 1934 at Brodick afsd.'

page 277,
line 6, after '1878.' add 'He *d.* 16 Mar. 1940 and was *suc.* in his titles by his 1st s. and h. but in the Earldom of Selkirk and the Baronies of Daer and Shortcleugh in the peerage of Scotland by his 2nd s., George Nigel. See *sub* SELKIRK. His widow *d.* 12 Jan. 1951.'
lines 7–9, delete all detail and replace as follows

XIV. 1940. 14. DOUGLAS (DOUGLAS-HAMILTON), DUKE OF HAMILTON, &c., 1st s. and h., *b.* 3 Feb. 1903, at 71 Eccleston Sq., Pimlico; *styled* MARQUESS OF DOUGLAS AND CLYDESDALE 1903–40; ed. at Eton and at Oxford (Ch. Ch.). He *m.*, 2 Dec. 1937, Lady Elizabeth Ivy, da. of Alan Ian (PERCY), 8th DUKE OF NORTHUMBERLAND. He *d.* 30 Mar. 1973. His widow was still living 1995.

XV. 1973. 15. ANGUS ALAN DOUGLAS (DOUGLAS-HAMILTON), DUKE OF HAMILTON, &c., 1st s. and h., *b.* 13 Sep. 1938; ed. at Eton and

Oxford (Balliol Coll.); *m.*, 1972, Sarah Jane, da. of Sir Walter SCOTT, Bart. This marriage was diss. by divorce in 1987 and he *m.* 2ndly, 1988, Jillian, da. of (__) ROBERTSON and formerly widow of 1stly Martin PAGE and 2ndly of Edward HULTON.

[ALEXANDER DOUGLAS DOUGLAS-HAMILTON, *styled* MARQUESS OF DOUGLAS AND CLYDESDALE, 1st s. and h., *b.* 31 Mar. 1978.]

HAMILTON OF BELLAMONT

page 277,
line 28, for 'Sep.' read 'Dec.'
lines 31–2, delete from ', where' to 'omitted' and replace by '.'

HAMILTON OF DALZELL

page 278,
line 24, after 'Liberal.' add 'She *d.* 3, at Dalzell, Motherwell, and was *bur.* 6 May 1933 at Dalzell afsd. He *d. s.p.* 23 June 1952.'

III. 1952. 3. JOHN D'HENIN (HAMILTON), BARON HAMILTON OF DALZELL, nephew and h., being s. of Leslie d'Henin HAMILTON (*d.* 29 Oct. 1914), by Amy Cecile, 1st da. of Col. Horace RICARDO, C.V.O., which Leslie was 3rd s. of 1st Baron Hamilton. He was *b.* 1 May 1911; ed. at Eton and R.M.C., Sandhurst; *m.*, 4 Mar. 1935, Rosemary Olive, 1st da. of Major Sir John Spencer COKE, K.C.V.O. He *d.* 31 Jan. 1990. His widow *d.* 1993.

IV. 1990. 4. JAMES LESLIE (HAMILTON), BARON HAMILTON OF DALZELL, 1st s. and h., *b.* 11 Feb. 1938; ed. at Eton; *m.*, 29 Mar. 1967, Ann Anastasia Corinna Helena, yr. da. of Sir Pierson John Dixon, G.C.M.G., C.B.

[GAVIN GOULBURN HAMILTON, 1st s. and h. ap., *b.* 8 Oct. 1968; ed. at Eton and Buckingham Univ.]

HAMPDEN

page 288,
line 26, line to read as follows

III. 1906. 3. THOMAS WALTER (BRAND), VISCOUNT HAMPDEN OF GLYNDE, &c., 1st s. and h., *b.* 29 Jan. 1869;

page 289,
lines 2–3, delete from 'Having' to 'work.([a])' and replace by 'She *d.* 7 Mar. 1951. He *d.* 4 Sep. 1958.'

IV. 1958. 4. THOMAS HENRY (BRAND), VISCOUNT HAMPDEN OF GLYNDE, and LORD DACRE [1321], 1st s. and h., *b.* 30 Mar. 1900; ed. at Eton. He *m.* 26 July 1923, at St. Margaret's, Westm., Leila, 1st da. of Lieut. Col. Frank SEELY, of Ramsdale Park, Nottingham. He *d. s.p.m.* 17 Oct. 1965 when he was *suc.* in his Viscountcy by his 1st surv. br., but the Barony of Dacre fell into *abeyance* between his two das., until it was terminated in favour of the elder. See *sub* DACRE above. His widow *d.*, aged 96, 27 Oct. 1996.

V. 1965. 5. DAVID FRANCIS (BRAND), VISCOUNT HAMPDEN OF GLYNDE, br. and h., *b.* 14 June 1902; ed. at Eton and Cambridge (Trin. Coll.); *m.*, 14 July 1936, Imogen Alice, da. by his 2nd wife of Walter FitzUryan (RHYS), 7th BARON DYNEVOR He *d.* 4 Sep. 1975. His widow was still living 1995.

VI. 1975. 6. ANTHONY DAVID (BRAND), VISCOUNT HAMPDEN OF GLYNDE, s. and h., *b.* 7 May 1937; ed. at Eton; *m.*, 1969, Caroline Fiona, da. of Capt. Claude PROBY. This marriage was diss. by divorce in 1988 and he *m.* 2ndly, 1993, Mrs Sally SNOW.

[FRANCIS ANTHONY BRAND, 1st s. and h. ap. by 1st wife, *b.* 17 Sep. 1970.]

note (a), delete all detail

HAMPTON

page 291,
line 1, line to read as follows

IV. 1906. 4. HERBERT STUART (PAKINGTON), BARON HAMPTON OF HAMPTON LOVETT AND WESTWOOD, &c., 2nd(a) but 1st surv. s. and h., *b.* 15 May 1883; ed. at Wellington and R.M.C., Sandhurst.

lines 3–4, delete from 'Having' to 'work.]' and replace by 'He *d.* unm. 30 Oct. 1962.'

V. 1962. 5. HUMPHREY ARTHUR (PAKINGTON), BARON HAMPTON OF HAMPTON LOVETT AND WESTWOOD, &c., yst. and only surv. br. being 4th son of the 3rd Baron; ed. at H.M.S. Britannia and R.N.C., Greenwich. Served as Lieut. R.N. in WW1. He *m.*, 26 Mar. 1913, Grace Dykes, 3rd da. of Rt. Hon. Sir Albert SPICER, Bart. She *d.* 18 May 1959. He *d.* 17 Feb. 1974.

VI. 1974. 6. RICHARD HUMPHREY RUSSELL (PAKINGTON), BARON HAMPTON OF HAMPTON LOVETT AND WESTWOOD, s. and h., *b.* 25 May 1925; *m.*, 25 Oct. 1958, Jane Elizabeth Farqhuharson, da. of Thomas Frank ARNOTT, O.B.E., of Bovey Tracy, co. Devon.

[JOHN HUMPHREY ARNOTT PAKINGTON, s. and h. ap., *b.* 24 Dec. 1964.]

note (b), lines 1–2, delete from 'His' to 'R.N.'

HARBERTON

page 295,
line 6, line to read as follows

VII. 1912. 7. ERNEST ARTHUR GEORGE (POMEROY), VISCOUNT HARBERTON, &c., 1st s. and h., *b.* 1 Dec.;

lines 8–9, delete from 'Having' to 'work.]' and replace by 'He *m.*, 1 Mar. 1932, Fairlie, da. of Col. Charles D'Oyley HARMAR of Ramridge, Andover, Hants. He *d. s.p.* 22 Apr. 1944. His widow *d.* 13 Jan. 1945.'

VIII. 1944. 8. RALPH LEGGE (POMEROY), VISCOUNT HARBERTON, &c., only br. and h., *b.* 31 Dec. 1869; ed. Oxford (Balliol Coll.); served in the South African War, also in WW1 as Capt. 1st Regt. of Cavalry (Special Reserve).([a]) He *m.*, 25 June 1907, Mary Katharine, da. of Arthur William LEATHAM, of Smallfield, Surrey. He *d.* 4 July 1956. His widow *d.* 1971.

IX. 1956. 9. HENRY RALPH MARTYN (POMEROY), VISCOUNT HARBERTON, &c., s. and h., *b.* 12 Oct. 1908; ed. at Eton. He *d.* unm. 25 May 1980.

X. 1980. 10. THOMAS DE VAUTORT (POMEROY), VISCOUNT HARBERTON, &c., br. and h., *b.* 19 Oct. 1910; ed. at Eton; *m.* 1stly, 2 Feb. 1939, Nancy Ellen, da. of C.A. PENOYER of San Francisco, California, U.S.A. This marriage was diss. by divorce in 1946 and he *m.* 2ndly, 4 Sep. 1950, Paula Stafford, da. of Wilfred Sydney BAKER, of Stoke, Plymouth, co. Devon. She *d.* 1971 and he *m.* 3rdly, Wilhelmine Vilma, da. of Heinrich WAHL and widow of Sir Alfred BUTT, Bart.

note ([a]), lines 1–3, delete from 'His' to 'Reserve)'

HARBOROUGH

page 295
line 32, after '*d. s.p.s.*' add '([e])'
note ([e]) His only son was educated at Eton, 1728–9 and appears in the school list as "Lord Sherard". He *d. v.p.*, presumably in 1729 or 30.

page 296,
line 22, after 'h.' add '*b.* 22 Aug.' [*Verney Letters*, vol. ii, p. 240]

page 297,
line 29, for '(__) ADAMS' read '?Thomas ADAMS of Whatton (Northants)'

HARDINGE

page 304,
line 29, for 'was living 1925' read '*d.* 31 Oct. 1954.'

lines 33–5, delete all detail and replace as follows

IV. 1924. 4. CARYL NICHOLAS CHARLES (HARDINGE), VISCOUNT HARDINGE OF LAHORE AND KINGS NEWTON [1846], 2nd but 1st surv. s. and h., *b.* 25 Dec. 1905; ed. at Harrow and R.M.C., Sandhurst; *m.*, 15 Sep. 1928, Margaret Elizabeth Arnot, da. of Hugh Percy FLEMING, of Wynyards, Rockcliffe, Ottawa, Canada. He *d.* 13 June 1979. His widow *d.* 1993.

V. 1979. 5. HENRY NICHOLAS PAUL (HARDINGE), VISCOUNT HARDINGE OF LAHORE AND KINGS NEWTON, only s. and h., *b.* 15 Aug. 1929; ed. at Harrow; *m.* 1stly, 13 Oct. 1955, Zoë Ann, da. of Hartland de Montarville MOLSON, Senator of Canada, O.B.E., Montreal, Quebec, Canada. This marriage was diss. by divorce in 1982 (she married 2ndly, 1983, Christopher Mark Henry MURRAY, St. Aubin, Jersey, Channel Islands, and was still living in 1995) and he *m.* 2ndly, 1982, BARONESS FLORENCE ELIZABETH, da. of BARON HAROLD VON OPPENHEIM, of Cologne. He *d.* 16 July 1984. His widow *m.* 2ndly, 1993, Martin Graham SHELLEY, of St. Boswells, co. Roxburgh. She was still living 1995.

VI. 1984. 6. CHARLES HENRY NICHOLAS (HARDINGE), VISCOUNT HARDINGE OF LAHORE AND KINGS NEWTON, 1st s. and h., *b.* 25 Aug. 1956; ed. at McGill Univ.; *suc.* his distant cousin as 7th Baronet [U.K. 1801], 1986; *m.*, 1985, Julie Therese, da. of Keith SILLETT, of Sydney, Australia.

page 304,
note ([b]), line 2 (cont. from page 304), after '1914' add 'See vol. xiii, p. 128'

HARDWICKE

page 310,
lines 4–6, delete from 'He was' to 'work'

VII. 1904. 7. JOHN MANNERS (YORKE), EARL OF HARDWICKE, &c., uncle and h., being the 2nd s. of the 4th Earl. He was *b.* 30 Oct. 1840; entered the Navy and served in the Baltic in 1854, and in the Crimea 1854–5, and commanded the Coastguard at Folkestone 1870–4. He *m.* 9 Jan. 1869, Edith Mary, yr. da. of Alexander Haldane OSWALD, of Auchencruive, co. Ayr. He *d.* 13, at 52 Rutland Gate and was *bur.* 18 Mar. 1909, at Hamble, South Hants. His widow *d.* 27 and was *bur.* 31 July 1930 in Hamble afsd.

VIII. 1909. 8. CHARLES ALEXANDER (YORKE), EARL OF HARDWICKE, &c., 1st s. and h., *b.* 11 Nov. 1869. Served in WW1([a]) as Lieut. R.N.V.R. He *m.* 27 Apr. 1911, Ellen, da. of James RUSSELL, of New Zealand. This marriage was diss. by divorce in 1927 (she *d.* 16 Feb. 1968) and he *m.* 2ndly, 20 Aug. 1930, Mary Radley, da. of Edward Robert TWIST of Liverpool. He *d. s.p.m.* 1 Feb. 1936. His widow *m.* 2ndly, 5 July 1938, W.E.L. JENNINGS of Nyasaland. She *d.* 16 July 1938.

IX. 1936. 9. PHILIP GRANTHAM (YORKE), EARL OF HARDWICKE, &c., nephew and h., being s. of Alfred Ernest Frederick YORKE (*d.* 6 Nov. 1933), by Gladys Dunlop, da. of Andrew Vans Dunlop BEST, which Alfred Ernest was 2nd s. of 7th Earl of Hardwicke. He was *b.* 9 Apr. 1906; ed. at Eton and R.M.C., Sandhurst; *m.*, 12 June 1934, Sarah Katharine, 3rd. da. of Rt. Hon. Sir Francis Oswald LINDLEY, P.C., G.C.M.G., C.B., C.B.E. She *d.* 8 Nov. 1965 and he *m.* 2ndly, 1970, Enid Munnick, da. of Pieter GRUNWALD of S. Africa and formerly wife of Roy BOULTING. He *d.* 31 Dec. 1974. His widow was still living 1995.

[PHILIP SIMON PROSPERO LINDLEY RUPERT YORKE, *styled* VISCOUNT ROYSTON, s. and h. ap., *b.* 20 Apr. 1938; ed. at Eton and MacGill Univ., Montreal; *m.*, 20 Nov. 1968, Virginia Anne, 1st da. of Geoffrey LYON of Hambledon, Godalming, co. Surrey. He *d.* 1 Jan. 1973. His widow *d.* 1988.]

X. 1974. 10. JOSEPH PHILIP SEBASTIAN (YORKE), EARL OF HARDWICKE, &c., grandson and h., being only s. and h. of Philip Simon Prospero Lindley Rupert YORKE and Virginia Anne abovesaid. He was *b.* 3 Feb. 1971.

note ([a]), lines 1–7, delete from 'He' to 'R.N.V.R.'

HAREWOOD

page 313,
line 24, for 'Earl' read 'the Earl of'
line 31, after '1859.' add 'He *d.* 6 and was *bur.* 10 Oct. 1929 at Harewood. His widow *d.* 5 May 1943.'
line 32, line to read as follows

EARLDOM. VI. BARONY. VII. } 1929 6. HENRY GEORGE CHARLES (LASCELLES), EARL OF HAREWOOD, &c., 1st s. and h., *b.* 9 Sep. 1892; *styled* VISCOUNT LASCELLES 1892–1929;

page 314,
line 2, for '([a])]' read 'He *d.* 24 May 1947. His widow *d.* 28 Mar. 1965.'

EARLDOM. VII. BARONY. VIII. } 1947 7. GEORGE HENRY HUBERT (LASCELLES), EARL OF HAREWOOD, &c., *b.* 7 Feb. and *bap.* 25 Mar. 1923, in the presence of George V and Queen Mary; ed. at Eton and Cambridge (King's Coll.); *m.*, 29 Sep. 1949, Maria Donata Nanetta Paulina Gustava Wilhelmina Marion, da. of Erwin STEIN. This marriage was diss. by divorce in 1967 and he *m.* 2ndly, 1967, Patricia Elizabeth, da. of Charles TUCKWELL of Sydney, Australia.

[DAVID HENRY GEORGE LASCELLES, *styled* VISCOUNT LASCELLES, 1st s. and h. by 1st wife, *b.* 21 Oct. 1950; ed. at Westminster; *m.* 1stly, 12 Feb. 1979, Margaret Rosalind, da. of Edgar Frank MESSENGER. This marriage was diss. by divorce in 1989 and he *m.* 2ndly, 11 Mar. 1990, Diane Jane, da. of John Prince HOWSE.]

note ([a]), delete all detail

HARINGTON

page 316,
line 3, after 'MULTON,' add '2nd LORD MULTON (of Egremont),'
line 4, after 'MULTON,' add '1st LORD MULTON (of Egremont), by Eleanor da. of Richard (DE BURGH), EARL OF ULSTER,'

page 317,
line 19, after 'K.G.,' add 'of Chalgrove, Beds., by Margaret, da. and h. of Ralph BEAUPEL, of Knowstone, Devon.'

page 318,
line 11, after 'DEVON' add 'by Maud, said to be the da. of Thomas (CAMOYS), 3rd LORD CAMOYS

page 320,
line 8, after 'SALISBURY' add 'by Anne, *suo jure* COUNTESS OF SALISBURY, da. and h. of Thomas (MONTAGUE), 4th EARL OF SALISBURY'

HARLECH

page 323,
line 22, line to read as follows

III. 1904. 3. GEORGE RALPH CHARLES (ORMESBY-GORE), BARON HARLECH, 2nd but 1st surv. s. and h.,

lines 29–31, delete from 'Having' to 'work.]' and replace by 'He *d.* 8 May 1938. His widow *d.* 25 Apr. 1950.'

IV. 1938. 4. WILLIAM GEORGE ARTHUR (ORMSBY-GORE), BARON HARLECH, s. and h., *b.* 11 Apr. 1885. Served in WW1, till 1915, as Staff Capt. and A.D.C. Personal Staff; *m.*, 12 Apr. 1913, Lady Beatrice Edith Mildred, 1st da. of James Edward Hubert (GASCOYNE-CECIL), 4th MARQUESS OF SALISBURY. He *d.* 14 Feb. 1964.

[OWEN GERARD CECIL ORMSBY-GORE, 1st s. and h. ap., *b.* 30 July 1916 and *d. v.p.* and unm. 3 Oct. 1935.]

V. 1964. 5. WILLIAM DAVID (ORMSBY-GORE), BARON HARLECH, 2nd but 1st surv. s. and h., *b.* 20 May 1918; ed. at Eton and Oxford (New Coll.); *m.* 1stly, Sylvia, da. of Hugh Lloyd THOMAS, C.M.G., C.V.O. She was *k.* in a motor accident 30 May 1967 and he *m.* 2ndly, 11 Dec. 1969, Pamela, da. of Ralph F. COLIN of New York City. He *d.* 26 Jan. 1985 as the result of a motor accident. His widow was still living 1995.

[JULIAN HUGH ORMSBY-GORE, 1st s. and h. ap., *b.* 23 Dec. 1940; ed. at Eton and McGill Univ, Montreal, Canada. He *d. v.p.* 1974.]

VI. 1985. 6. FRANCIS DAVID (ORMSBY-GORE), BARON HARLECH, 2nd but only surv. s. and h., *b.* 13 Mar. 1954; *m.*, 1986, Amanda Jane, da. of Alan Thomas GRIEVE of Stoke Lodge, Ludlow, Shropshire.

[JASSET DAVID CODY ORMSBY-GORE, s. and h. ap., *b.* 1 July 1986.]

note (b), lines 2–3, delete from '; and' to 'Staff'

HARRINGTON

page 329,
lines 14–15, delete from 'He was' to 'work.(b)'

IX. 1917. 9. DUDLEY HENRY EDEN (STANHOPE), EARL OF HARRINGTON, &c., br. and h. male, being 5th and only surv. s. of the 7th Earl, *b.* 13 Jan. 1859; *m.*, 26 Apr. 1883, Kathleen, da. of Joseph Carter WOOD of Falcourt, Sussex. He *d.* 13 Nov. 1928. His widow *d.* 6 Aug. 1949.

X. 1928. 10. CHARLES JOSEPH LEICESTER (STANHOPE), EARL OF HARRINGTON, &c., 1st and only surv. s. and h., *b.* 9 Oct. 1887. Served in WW1,(b) Lieut. 15th Hussars. He *m.*, 23 Apr. 1919, Margaret Trelawney, 2nd da. of Major H.H.D. SEATON of Bulford, Salisbury. He *d.* 16 Nov. 1929 as the result of a hunting accident. His widow *m.* twice more and *d.* 15 Sep. 1952.

XI. 1929. 11. WILLIAM HENRY LEICESTER (STANHOPE), EARL OF HARRINGTON, &c., 2nd but 1st surv. s. and h.,(c) *b.* 24 Aug. 1922; ed. at Eton and R.M.C., Sandhurst. On 15 Aug. 1967, on the death *s.p.* of James Richard (STANHOPE), 7th EARL OF STANHOPE and 13th EARL OF CHESTERFIELD, and as the only surv. male heir of a yr. br. (of the half-blood) of Philip 1st EARL OF CHESTERFIELD he inherited the Viscountcy of Stanhope of Mahon and the Barony of Stanhope of Elvaston [1717] in accordance with the spec. rem. to those dignities. [See STANHOPE, vol. xii, part 1, pp. 230 and 232, note (d).] He *m.* 1stly, 5 Feb. 1942, Eileen, da. of Sir John Foley GREY, Bart. This marriage was diss. by divorce in 1947 and he *m.* 2ndly, 24 Jan. 1947, Ann Theodora, da. of Major Richard Arenbourg Blennerhassett CHUTE, of Doneen, Patrickswell, co. Limerick. This marriage was in turn diss. by divorce in 1962 and he *m.* 3rdly, 14 Oct. 1964, Priscilla Margaret, da. of Archibald Edward CUBITT of Dedington, co. Oxford.

[CHARLES HENRY LEICESTER STANHOPE, *styled* VISCOUNT PETERSHAM, 1st s. and h. by 1st wife, *b.* 20 July 1945; ed. at Eton; *m.* 1stly, 14 Sep. 1966, Virginia Alleyne Freeman, da. of Capt. Harry Freeman JACKSON, of Mallow, co. Cork. He *m.* 2ndly, 1984, Anita Robsahm, da. of Robin Robsahm FUGLESANG of Laycock, Wilts. and formerly wife of Michael John James George Robert (HOWARD), 21st EARL OF SUFFOLK.]

note ([a]), line 6, after 'V.G.' add 'It still exists though it is no longer a private house.'
note ([b]), lines 1–2, delete from 'Dudley' to 'Hussars (2)' and replace by 'His only br.,'
line 3, after 'Stanhope' add 'also served in WW1 as'
note ([c]) His 1st s., Charles, was *b.* 19 and *d.* 23 Jan. 1921.

HARRIS OF SERINGAPATAM

page 329,
line 25, for 'Cumberland' read 'Essex'

page 331,
line 11, after 'C.I.' add 'She *d.* 12 Feb. 1930 at Faversham, of heart failure. He *d.* 24 at Belmont, Faversham, Kent and was *bur.* 29 Mar. 1932 at Throwley, Faversham.'
line 12, line to read as follows

V. 1932. 5. GEORGE ST. VINCENT (HARRIS), BARON HARRIS OF SERINGAPATAM AND MYSORE AND OF BELMONT, only s. and h., *b.* 3 Sep. 1889;

line 16, for ']' read 'His wife *d.* 1981. He *d.* 16 Oct. 1984.'

VI. 1984. 6. GEORGE ROBERT JOHN (HARRIS), BARON HARRIS OF SERINGAPATAM AND MYSORE AND OF BELMONT, only s. and h., *b.* 17 Apr. 1920; ed. at Eton and Oxford (Ch. Ch.).

HARROWBY

page 331,
note ([c]), line 3, for '(*d.* Dec. 1771)' read '(*bur.* 6 Dec. 1721)'
line 5, for 'living' read 'rector of'

page 332,
line 1, after 'Holborn;' add 'ed. at Eton;'
line 8, after 'widow' add '(who was *bap.* 12 May 1739)' [Guildhall MSS., 6667/9]
line 10, for '75' read '?65'
line 13, after 'at' add 'Harrow and'
line 18, for 'Jan.' read '4 Dec.'
line 19, for '1805' read '1804'
note ([b]), line 6, for 'BATH' read 'BATHURST'
note ([d]), for 'The estate of' read 'His portrait as a boy at Harrow is at' and after 'Stafford' add 'which estate'

page 333,
lines 1–2, delete from '2nd' to 'BRIDGEWATER and replace by '3rd wife Susannah, 3rd da. of Alexander (STEWART), 6th EARL OF GALLOWAY [S.]'
line 4, for 'House' read 'Hall'

page 334,
line 1, after 'Frances,' add '2nd'
line 18, after '3rd' add 'but 1st surv. da.'
line 22, after '1917' add 'and was *bur.* at Sandon'
note (c), lines 2–6, from 'He' to '107)' refers to the 2nd Earl.

page 335,
line 9, after 'ORDE' add 'by his 2nd wife Margaret, eldest da. of William Beckford, of Fonthill'
line 12, after 'widow' add ', who was *b*, 22 Oct. 1838,'
line 23, for 'Oxford' read 'Bucks'
line 25, add at end 'She *d.* 27 Mar. 1956. He *d.* 30 Mar. 1956.'
line 26, line to read as follows

EARLDOM. VI. BARONY. VII. } 1956 — 6 and 7. DUDLEY (RYDER), EARL OF HARROWBY, &c., only s. and h., *b.* 11 Oct. 1892, at 3 Grosvenor Place, *styled* VISCOUNT SANDON 1900–56

line 32, for '(c)]' read 'She *d.* 1974. He *d.* 7 May 1987.'

EARLDOM. VII. BARONY. VIII. } 1987 — 7 and 8. DUDLEY DANVERS GRANVILLE COUTTS (RYDER), EARL OF HARROWBY, &c., s. and h., *b.* 20 Dec. 1922 at 10 Upper Belgrave Str. 19 Jan. 1923, and *bap.* at St. Peter's, Eaton Sq.; ed. at Eton; *m.*, 14 June 1949, Jeannette Rosalthé, yr. da. of Capt. Peter JOHNSTON-SAINT.

[DUDLEY ADRIAN CONROY RYDER, *styled* VISCOUNT SANDON, s. and h. ap., *b.* 18 Mar. 1951; ed. at Eton, Univ. of Newcastle upon Tyne and Oxford (Magdalen Coll.); *m.*, 1977, Sarah Nichola Hobhouse, da. of Capt. Anthony Denys Phillpotts PAYNE of Marnhull, co. Dorset. She *d.* 29 Dec. 1994.]

note (a), delete all detail
note (c), delete all detail

HASTANG

page 338,
line 30, after 'da.' add 'and coh.'

page 339,
note (e), line 2, delete ', between two wyverns'

page 342,
lines 13–14, delete from 'and' to 'Warwick' and replace by 'before that of John DE STRADLING or STRATTELINGES, da. and h. of John DE WALTON, of Little Wellesbourne and Walton Deyville, co. Warwick, by his wife Isabel'

note (h), before 'In' add 'C. L'Estrange Ewen, *Observations on the L'Estranges*, 1946, pp. 4–8; *V.C.H. Warwick*, vol. 5, pp. 195–6; Warwick, *Feet of Fines*, 1284–1435, Dugdale Soc., no. 1093'

HASTINGS

page 345,
line 4, for '4th' read 'sister and coh. of John the Scot, 10th EARL OF HUNTINGDON, 3rd da. of David of Scotland, 9th EARL OF HUNTINGDON'

page 347,
line 25, for '(DE VALENCE)' read 'DE VALENCE, sometimes *styled*'

page 349,
line 4, after 'Alianore,' add 'sister and coh. of William MARTIN [2nd LORD MARTIN]'
line 6, after 'MARTIN' add 'by Eleanor, da. of Sir Reynold FITZPIERS'
line 7, after '*d.*' add '*s.p.* and'

page 350,
line 3, for 'da.' read '*de jure suo jure* (according to modern doctrine) BARONESS LEYBURN, da. and h.'
line 4, after 'Kent,' add '(s. and h. ap. of William, 1st LORD LEYBURN)' and for 'coh.' read 'h.'
line 5, after 'TONI,' add '[1st LORD TONI]'
line 9, after 'Gloucester,' add '[1st LORD BLOUNT]'
line 14, delete '31 Oct.' and ', or 2'
note (g), line 2, after '1' add 'gives these separate dates for her death, but see vol. vii, *sub* Leyburn.

page 351,
line 1, after 'HASTINGES,' add 'and *de jure* LORD LEYBURN'

page 353,
line 10, after 'Norfolk,' add '[3rd LORD FOLIOT]'
line 11, after 'FOLIOT,' add '[2nd LORD FOLIOT]'

page 356,
line 10, for 'England' read 'Ireland'

page 369,
line 17, for 'was living 1925' read '*d.* 19 Feb. 1957.'
line 18, line to read as follows

XXI. 1904. 6. ALBERT EDWARD DELAVAL (ASTLEY), LORD HASTINGS, 1st s. and h., *b.* 24 Nov. 1882;

lines 25–6, delete from 'Having' to 'work.]' and replace by 'He *d.* 18 Jan. 1956. His widow *d.* 1975.'

XXII. 1956. 7. EDWARD DELAVAL HENRY (ASTLEY), 1st s. and h., *b.* 14 Apr. 1912; ed. at Eton; *m.*, 7 July 1954, Catherine Cecilia Rosaline Ratcliffe, yr. da.

of Capt. Harold Virgo HINTON of Walton-in-Gordano, co. Somerset, formerly wife of Vernon William COATS.

[DELAVAL THOMAS HAROLD ASTLEY, 1st s. and h. ap., *b.* 25 Apr. 1960; ed. at Radley and Hatfield Coll., Durham; *m.*, 1987, Veronica, 1st da. of Richard SMART of Chester.]

note (c), delete all detail

HASTINGS (of Hastings)

page 370,
line 4, after 'Alice,' add 'living 1 Feb. 1455/6,'
note (i), line 2 (on page 371), after 'Parliament.' add 'He is referred to as "dominus Hastynges" in a letter of Anne, Duchess of Buckingham appointing him seneschal of Oakham on 12 July, 1 Edw. IV (see *Sir Christopher Hatton's Book of Seals*, 1950, no. 23).'

page 373,
line 20, after 'Alice,' add '*suo jure* COUNTESS OF SALISBURY'
note (f), line 12, after '449)' add 'The date of Lord Hasting's death was questioned by Alison Hanham in *Eng. Hist. Review.*, vol. lxxxvii, 1972, p. 236, where she suggested that it was in fact a week later, on 22 June. This revision was questioned by several authors, who showed that the traditional date is correct. For a review of the controversy, see Lorraine Attreed, *The Ricardian*, vol. v, 1979, pp. 41–50.'
line 13, after 'who' add 'possibly'

page 374,
line 5, after '*m.*,' add 'after 6 Nov. 1472,(ba)'
note (ba) Date of indenture of marriage covenants, *Hist. MSS. Com.*, Hastings MSS., part I, p. 303.

page 381,
line 31–3, delete from ', which' to 'work'

page 382,
line 1, after 'Gilbert' add 'see under DONINGTON' in the present volume'
note (a), add at end 'See below, p. 452.' [*sub* Loudoun]

HATCH

page 393,
line 10, after 'John' add '(or Richard)' [See vol. xii, part 1, p. 630, *sub* Talbot.]

HATHERTON

page 395,
line 33, after 'Penkridge.' add 'He *m.* 2ndly, 27 May 1922, Lettice Mina, da. of Gerald

PAGET and widow of Lieut. Col. Ronald BERNARD. She *d.* 19 Feb. 1923. He *d.* 24 Aug. 1930, at Teddesley Park, Penkridge afsd.

line 34, line to read as follows

IV. 1930. 4. EDWARD ROWLEY CHARLES (LITTLETON), BARON HATHERTON, 1st s. and h., *b.* 6 Aug. 1868;

page 396,
line 2, for '([a])]' read 'He *d.* 10 Nov. 1944. His widow *d.* 6 Jan. 1947.'

V. 1944. 5. EDWARD THOMAS WALHOUSE (LITTLETON), BARON HATHERTON. 1st s. and h., *b.* 13 Aug. 1900; ed. at R.N.C.s, Osborne and Dartmouth; served in WW1 as Naval Cadet.([a]) He *m.* 1stly, 5 Sep. 1925, Ida Gwendolene, da. of Robin LEGGE and formerly wife of Capt. Henry Burton TATE. This marriage was diss. by divorce in 1951 (she *d.* 1969) and he *m.* 2ndly, 11 Jan. 1952, Kathleen May, da. of Clarence Ernest Orlando WHITECHURCH, of Esher, co. Surrey and formerly wife of Major Oscar WESTENDARP. He *d. s.p.m.* 13 Nov. 1969. His widow *d.* 1983.

VI. 1969. 6. JOHN WALTER STUART (LITTLETON), BARON HATHERTON, br. and h., *b.* 9 Aug. 1906; ed. at Cranleigh; *m.* 1stly, 6 Nov. 1932, Nora Evelyn, da. of R.C. SMITH of Edgbaston, Birmingham. She *d.* May 1955 and he *m.* 2ndly, Mary Alice, da. of John ROBERTS, of Ruthin, co. Denbigh. He *d. s.p.m.* 27 June 1973. His widow was still living 1995.

VII. 1973. 7. THOMAS CHARLES TASMAN (LITTLETON), BARON HATHERTON, br. and h., *b.* 7 Oct. 1907; *m.*, 7 Apr. 1933, Ann Scott, da. of Thomas MCLEOD, Lieut. Cmdr., R.N. He *d. s.p.m.* 28 Sep. 1985. His widow *d.* 1994.

VIII. 1985. 8. EDWARD CHARLES (LITTLETON), BARON HATHERTON, distant cousin and h., being only s. of Mervyn Cecil LITTLETON, by Margaret Ann, da. of Frank SHEEHY, which Mervyn Cecil was s. of Charles Christopher Joscelyn LITTLETON (*d.* 12 Mar. 1950), by his 1st wife Aline Beatrix, 2nd da. of Sir Frederick HERVY-BATHURST, Bart., which Charles Christopher was 3rd s. of 3rd Baron Littleton. He was *b.* 24 May 1950; *m.*, 1974, Hilda Mary, da. of Rodolfo ROBERT of San José, Costa Rica.

[THOMAS EDWARD HATHERTON, s. and h. ap., *b.* 7 Mar. 1977.]

note ([a]), lines 1–2, delete from 'His' to 'brothers' and replace by 'His two brothers also served'

HAUDLO

page 401,
line 16, after 'Bruyn' add '[3rd Lord Bruyn],'

HAUSTED

page 404,
lines 14–15, delete from 'She' to 'Denshanger.([l])'
note ([l]), delete note number and run note as first part of note ([m]). Alter as follows
line 1, for 'He' read 'A John Cope'
line 4, after 'no. 23).' add 'This John Cope, said to have married Elizabeth Haudlo, could not have done so; he must have been a young man when he went to Ireland in the service of the King's Justiciar in 1379 (*Cal. Pat. Rolls, 1377–9*, p. 384).'

HAWARDEN

page 411,
line 19, delete from 'admitted' to '1744;'

page 412,
lines 28–9, delete from 'He was' to 'work'
note ([d]), delete all detail

page 413,
after line 4 add as follows

V. 1905. 5. ROBERT HENRY (MAUDE), VISCOUNT HAWARDEN, and BARON DE MONTALT OF HAWARDEN [I.], 1st cousin and h., being 1st s. and h. of the Very Rev. Robert William Henry MAUDE, Dean of Clogher, by Martha Elizabeth Mary, eld. da. of Francis Aldborough PRITTLE and half-sister of 3rd BARON DUNELLY, which Robert was 3rd and yst. s. of the 2nd VISCOUNT, *b.* 24 June 1842; *m.*, 15 Dec. 1881, Caroline Anna Mary, da. of Arthur OGLE. He *d.* 6 Sep. 1908. His widow *d.* 15 Mar. 1930.

VI. 1908. 6. ROBERT CORNWALLIS (MAUDE), VISCOUNT HAWARDEN, &c., only s. and h., *b.* 6 Sep. 1890; ed. at Oxford (Ch. Ch.). Fought in WW1 and was mortally wounded 25, and *d.* unm and *s.p.* 27 Aug. 1914, at Landécies and was *bur.* there the same day.

VII. 1914. 7. EUSTACE WYNDHAM (MAUDE), VISCOUNT HAWARDEN, &c., 1st cousin and h., being only s. of Ludlow Eustace MAUDE, by Clara Louisa, da. of the Rev. Wyndham Carlyon MADDEN, which Ludlow was 2nd s. of the afsd. Robert (father of the 5th Viscount. He was *b.* 20 Sep. 1877. He *m.* 17 Nov. 1920, Marion, 1st da. of Albert Leslie WRIGHT, of Butterley Hall, Derby. He *d.* 6 Apr. 1958. His widow *d.* 1974.

VIII. 1958. 8. ROBERT LESLIE EUSTACE (MAUDE), VISCOUNT HAWARDEN, &c., 1st s. and h., *b.* 26 Mar. 1926; ed. at Winchester and Oxford (Ch. Ch.); *m.*, 28 Sep. 1957, Susannah Caroline Hyde, da. of Major Charles Phillips GARDNER of Shanklin, Isle of Wight. He *d.* 6 Sep. 1991. His widow was still living 1995.

IX. 1991. 9. ROBERT CONNAN WYNDHAM LESLIE (MAUDE), VISCOUNT HAWARDEN, &c., 1st s. and h., *b.* 23 May 1961; ed. at St. Edmund's Sch., Canterbury and R.A.C., Cirencester.

HAWKE

page 415,
line 32, add at end 'He *d. s.p.* in a nursing home at Edinburgh 10 Oct. 1938. His widow *d.* 25 and was *bur.* 29 Jan. 1936 at Norwood.'

VIII. 1938. 8. EDWARD JULIAN (HAWKE), BARON HAWKE OF TOWTON, br. and h., *b.* 16 Feb. 1873; *m.*, 9 Oct. 1900, Frances Alice, 2nd da. of Col. John Randle WILMER. He *d.* 4 Sep. 1939. His widow *d.* 8 July 1959.

IX. 1939. 9. BLADEN WILMER (HAWKE), BARON HAWKE OF TOWTON, 1st s. and h., *b.*, 31 Dec. 1901; ed. at Winchester and Cambridge (King's Coll.); *m.*, 1 Nov. 1934, Ina Mary Faure, 1st da. of Henry Faure WALKER of Highley Manor, Balcombe, co. Sussex. He *d. s.p.m.* 5 July 1985. His widow was still living 1995.

X. 1985. 10. JULIAN STANHOPE THEODORE (HAWKE), BARON HAWKE OF TOWTON, br. and h., *b.* 19 Oct. 1904; ed. at Eton and Cambridge (King's Coll.); *m.* 1stly, 17 Feb. 1933, Angela Margaret Griselda, da. of Capt. Edmund William BURY. This marriage was diss. by divorce in 1946 (she *d.* 1984) and he *m.* 2ndly, 22 May 1947, Georgette Margaret, da. of George Spence DAVIDSON. He *d.* 19 Aug. 1992. His widow was still living 1995.

XI. 1992. 11. EDWARD GEORGE (HAWKE), BARON HAWKE OF TOWTON., only s. and h. by 2nd wife, *b.* 25 Jan. 1950; ed. at Eton; *m.*, 1993, Bronwen, da. of William T. JAMES.

HAWKESBURY

page 417,
line 17, line to read as follows

V. 1907. 2. ARTHUR WILLIAM DE BRITO SAVILE (FOLJAMBE), EARL OF LIVERPOOL [1905], VISCOUNT HAWKESBURY OF KIRKHAM AND OF MANSFIELD, BARON HAWKESBURY OF HAZELBEACH AND OF OLLERTON [1893], 1st s. and h., being only s. by 1st wife,

lines 30–1, delete from 'Having' to 'work.]' and replace by 'He *d. s.p.* 15 May 1941. His widow *d.* 25 May 1948. For 3rd and subsequent Earls of Liverpool, see below *sub* LIVERPOOL.'

HAY

page 420,
line 15, for 'PENWARDINE' read 'PEDWARDINE'

line 18, for 'PENWARDINE' read 'PEDWARDINE'

HEADFORT

page 428,
line 21, for 'was living 1925' read '*d.* 16 July 1926.'
line 32, for 'was living 1925' read '*d.* 25 Feb. 1928.'

page 429,
line 3, after '([a])' add 'He *d.* 29 Jan. 1943. His widow *d.* 17 Aug. 1958.'
lines 4–5, delete all detail and replace as follows

MARQUESSATE [I.] V. VISCOUNTCY, Etc. [I.] VI. } 1943 5 and 6. TERENCE GEOFFREY THOMAS (TAYLOUR), MARQUESS OF HEADFORT, &c., 1st s. and h., *b.* 1 May 1902, *styled* EARL OF BECTIVE from birth until 1943. Ed. at Harrow and Oxford (Magdalen Coll.); *m.*, 18 Sep. 1928, Elsie Florence, da. of James Partridge TUCKER of co. Devon and widow of Sir Rupert Turner Havelock CLARKE, Bart. He *d.* 24 Oct. 1960. His widow *d.* 1972.

MARQUESSATE [I.] VI. VISCOUNTCY, Etc. [I.] VII. } 1960 6 and 7. THOMAS GEOFFREY CHARLES MICHAEL (TAYLOUR), MARQUESS OF HEADFORT, &c., only s. and h., *b.* 20 Jan. 1932; ed. at Stowe and Cambridge (Christ's Coll.); *m.* 1stly, 2 May 1958, Elizabeth Angela Veronica Rose, da. of Arthur Ronald (NALL-CAIN), 2nd BARON BROCKET. This marriage was diss. by divorce in 1969 and he *m.* 2ndly, 1972, Virginia, da. of Mr Justice NABLE of Manila.

[THOMAS MICHAEL RONALD CHRISTOPHER TAYLOUR, *styled* EARL OF BECTIVE, s. and h. ap., *b.* 10 Feb. 1959; *m.*, 1987, Susan Jane, 1st da. of C. Anthony VANDERVELL of Burnham, co. Buckingham.]

HEADLEY

page 429,
line 15, for 'Ferraby' read 'Ferriby'

page 431,
lines 5–6, delete from 'was living' to 'work' and replace by '*d.* Oct. 1928.'

V. 1913. 5. ROWLAND GEORGE (ALLANSON-WINN), LORD HEADLEY, &c., 1st cousin and h. male, being the eldest s. of Rowland ALLANSON-WYNN by Margaretta Stephana 2nd da. of George WALKER of Overhall, Essex, which Rowland was 2nd surv. s. of the abovenamed George Mark Arthur Way, father of the 3rd Lord; *b.* 19 Jan. 1855 [for further detail see note ([c])]. He *d.* 22, and was *bur.* 25 June 1935 in the Muslim Cemetery. His widow *d.* 6 Jan. 1947.

VI. 1935. 6. ROWLAND PATRICK JOHN GEORGE (ALLANSON-WINN), LORD HEADLEY, &c., 1st s. and h., *b.* 22 May 1901; *m.*, 18 Aug. 1936, Edith Jane, yst. da. of Rev. George DODS. He *d. s.p.* 17 Dec. 1969.

VII. 1969. 7. CHARLES ROWLAND (ALLANSON-WINN), LORD HEADLEY, BARON ALLANSON AND WINN OF AGHADOE [I.], br. and h., *b.* 19 May 1902; ed. at Bedford Sch.; *m.*, 8 Feb. 1927, Hilda May, 1st da. of Thomas Wells THORPE. He *d. s.p.m.s.* 23 Feb. 1994 when all his titles became *extinct*.

[JOHN ROWLAND ALLANSON-WINN, s. and h. ap., *b.* 14 Oct. 1934; ed. at Canford Sch. He *d. v.p.* and unm., 1990]

HENEAGE

page 434,
line 22, line to read as follows

II. 1922. 2. GEORGE EDWARD (HENEAGE), BARON HENEAGE OF HAINTON, 1st s. and h., *b.* 3 July 1866

lines 25–6, delete from 'Having' to 'work.]' and replace by 'He *d.* unm. 26 Jan. 1954.'

III. 1954. 3. THOMAS ROBERT (HENEAGE), BARON HENEAGE OF HAINTON, 3rd and only surv. br. and h., *b.* 24 July 1877; ed. at Cambridge (Trin. Hall); Clerk in Holy Orders, 1903. He *d.* unm. 19 Feb. 1967 when his title became *extinct*.

HENLEY

page 436,
note ([d]), line 5, for 'see vol. vii, Appendix F' read 'see note *sub* LEICESTER OF HOLKHAM'

page 437,
lines 3–4, delete from 'He was' to 'work([a])'

V. 1923. 5. ANTHONY ERNEST (HENLEY), BARON HENLEY OF CHARDSTOCK, &c., only brother and h. of the whole blood, *b.* 3 July 1858; [for marriages see note ([a])]. He *d. s.p.m.* 23 Oct. 1925. His widow *d.* 22 Nov. 1933.

VI. 1925. 6. FRANCIS ROBERT (HENLEY, *later* (1925) EDEN), BARON HENLEY OF CHARDSTOCK, &c., only brother of the half-blood, being only s. of 3rd Baron Henley by his 2nd wife. He was *b.* 11 Apr. 1877; ed. at Harrow and Oxford (Balliol Coll.); assumed, by deed poll, 11 Dec. 1925, the name EDEN in place of HENLEY for himself and his descendants. He *m.* 14 Oct. 1913, Lady Dorothy

Georgiana, da. of George James (HOWARD), 9th EARL OF CARLISLE. He *d.* 21 Apr. 1962. His widow *d.* 14 Sep. 1968.

VII. 1962. 7. MICHAEL FRANCIS (EDEN), BARON HENLEY OF CHARDSTOCK, &c., 1st s. and h., *b.* 13 Aug. 1914; ed. at Eton and Oxford (Balliol Coll.); *m.* 1stly, 19 Nov. 1943, Elizabeth, 1st da. of Sir Arthur Lawrence HOBHOUSE of Hadspen House, co. Somerset. This marriage was diss. by divorce in 1947 and he *m.* 2ndly, 31 Aug. 1949, Nancy Mary, da. of Stanley WALTON of Gilsland, Carlisle. This marriage was also diss. by divorce in 1975 (she was still living 1995). He *d.* 20 Dec. 1977.

VIII. 1977. 8. OLIVER MICHAEL ROBERT (EDEN), BARON HENLEY OF CHARDSTOCK, &c., 1st s. and h., *b.* 22 Nov. 1953; ed. at Clifton and Durham Univ.; *m.*, Caroline Patricia, da. of A.G. SHARP of Mackney, co. Oxford.

[JOHN MICHAEL OLIVER EDEN, 1st s. and h. ap., *b.* 30 June 1988.]

HENNIKER

page 437,
note (b), lines 4–5, delete from 'An' to 'publications.' [This applies to the 2nd Baron.]

page 439,
line 24, line to read as follows

VI. 1902. 6. CHARLES HENRY CHANDOS (HENNIKER-MAJOR), BARON HENNIKER OF STRATFORD UPON SLANEY, &c., 3rd(a) but 1st surv. s. and h.,

lines 29–30, delete from 'Having' to 'work.]' and replace by 'He *d.* unm. and *s.p.* 4 Feb. 1956.'

VII. 1956. 7. JOHN ERNEST DE GREY (HENNIKER-MAJOR), BARON HENNIKER OF STRATFORD UPON SLANEY, &c., br. and h. being 6th and only surv. s. of 5th Baron Henniker. He was *b.* 18 Jan. 1883; ed. at Radley and R.A.C., Cirencester; *m.*, 5 Dec. 1914, Molly, yr. da. of Sir Robert William BURNET, K.C.V.O. She *d.* 21 Oct. 1953. He *d.* 9 Feb. 1980.

VIII. 1980. 8. JOHN PATRICK EDWARD CHANDOS (HENNIKER-MAJOR), BARON HENNIKER OF STRATFORD UPON SLANEY, &c., 1st s. and h., *b.* 19 Feb. 1916; ed. at Stowe and Cambridge (Trin. Coll.); *m.* 1stly, 18 Dec. 1946, Margaret Osla, da. of James William BENNING of Montreal, Canada. She *d.* 1974, and he *m.* 2ndly, 1976, Julia Marshall (Mrs POLAND), 1st da. of George M. MASON of Kew, co. Surrey.

[MARK IAN PHILIP CHANDOS HENNIKER-MAJOR, 1st s. and h. ap. by 1st wife, *b.* 29 Sep. 1947; ed. at Eton and Cambridge (Trin. Coll.); *m.*, 1973, Lesley Antoinette (Mrs

MASTERTON-SMITH), da. of Wing Cmdr. G.W. FOSKETT of Fernvale, Queensland, Australia.]

HERBERT

page 442,
line 1, after 'in' add 'Sep.'

HEREFORD

page 447,
note (f), lines 1–3, delete from 'but' to '*seq.*).' and replace by 'as was his son William, who is described as "dapifer" in two charters quoted by C.H. Haskins, *Norman Institutions*, 1918, p. 58, note 289.'
note (h), before '*Gesta*' add 'William of Poitiers,'
note (i), after '*France*' add 'no. 75'

page 448,
line 13, for '20' read '18'
line 14, after 'She' add '*d.* 5 Oct. ?1070.'
line 18, delete from 'Renier' to 'Hainault' and replace by 'the Count of Egisheim (Alsace)'
note (e), before *Gesta*' add 'William of Poitiers'
note (h), for 'Ad ludum' read 'alacriter quasi ad ludum in Flandriam acessit'
note (i), delete all detail and replace by 'The obituary of the Abbey of Lire, of which he was the founder, gives his death as 18 Feb., "xij Kal. Mart. O Guilelmi Comitis institutoris hujus loci", Guèry, *Histoire de l'abbaye de Lire*, 1917, p. 585.'
note (k), line 2, after 'B).' add 'See also Guèry, *op. cit.*, "iij Non. Oct. O Dna. Adeliz. hujus loci fundatrix", p. 593.'

page 449,
line 8, after 'Ralph' add 'de Gael'
note (h), line 1, for 'Britolis' read 'Britolo'
line 2, for 'manifestum' read 'manifestam'

page 450,
note (d), line 7, after '536A).' add 'Another son "Willielmo filio Rogeri comitis" is a witness to a charter, see Le Prevost, *Notes . . . sur L'Eure*, vol. ii, p. 515.'

page 451,
line 11, delete '(c)'
note (c), delete all detail
note (g), line 3 (on page 452), after 'p. 79).' add 'See also "The Constable under the Norman Kings", G.H. White, *Genealogist*, N.S., vol. xxxviii, 1922, pp. 113–27.'

page 452,
note (b), lines 1–4, delete from 'This' to '7).' and replace by 'The charter granting to Miles of

Gloucester his father's lands with the office of Constable is BL Cott. Charter xvi, 33 (much decayed). There is a note of its contents by Camden in Lansdowne MS. 229, f. 124, where Miles is described as "filius Walteri Glos. constabularii mei" and the office granted is "Constabularium curie mei".'

page 453,
note ([h]), lines 2–3, delete from 'but' to 'doubtful' and replace by 'but is perhaps more likely Nest, da. of Osbern FitzRichard and Nest, da. of Gruffydd ap Llewellyn. See below *sub* Mortimer; Wagner, *Pedigree and Progress*, 1975, p. 207, and J.E. Lloyd, *History of Wales*, vol. 2, 1911, pp. 395, n. 123 and 397, n. 135.'

page 456,
line 3, after '([a])' add 'In 1192 she was widow of William de Poitou.' [Bracton's *Note Book*, no. 671]

page 462,
line 10, after 'h.,' add 'by 1st wife'

page 462,
line 1, for '(__)' read 'Isobel, sister'
line 2, after 'Hainault' add 'da. of Nicholas I, SEIGNEUR DE CONDÉ, by Isobel, DAME DE MORIALMÉ' [Joseph Noel, *Grands Seigneur d'Autrefois. Les Haut-Voués et Dames-Avoueresses de Fosse*, 1957, p. 31. *Ex inform.* Andrew Moriarty.]

page 472,
line 14, after 'AMPTON,' add ','
line 15, after 'Wigmore,' add '1st' and after 'and' add '3rd'
line 16, after 'BADLESMERE' add '[1st and 2nd LORDS BADLESMERE]'

page 475,
line 15, after '1stly,' add 'Thomas, 3rd EARL OF STAFFORD, and 2ndly'
line 15, for '(Stafford), Earl of Stafford' read '(STAFFORD), 5th EARL OF STAFFORD'

page 477,
note ([b]), line 10, after '*Rolls*).' add 'See also vol. vii, p. 418, note ([a]), *sub* LANCASTER.'
note ([c]), line 2, after '*Pedigree*,' add 'vol. i,'

page 481,
line 32, for 'Nantaribba' read 'Nantcribba'
line 34, for 'Nantaribba' read 'Nantcribba'

page 483,
line 21, after '81.' add 'He *d.* 27 and was *bur.* 31 Mar. 1930 in the churchyard of St. Peter's Church, Glasbury on Wye, Breconshire.'
line 22, line to read as follows

XVII. 1930. 17. ROBERT CHARLES (DEVEREUX), VISCOUNT HEREFORD, s. and h., *b.* 11 Aug. 1865;

line 26, for ']' read 'She *d.* 2 June 1945. He *d. s.p.m.s.* 16 Apr. 1952.'

[ROBERT GODFREY DE BOHUN DEVEREUX, only s. and h. ap., *b.* 24 Nov. 1894. He *m.*, 5 Dec. 1923, Audrey Maureen Leslie, yst. da. of James MEAKIN, of Westwood Manor, Staffs, by Emma Beatrice (*later* COUNTESS SONDES), 1st da. of Percy Hale WALLACE, of Muckamore Abbey, co. Antrim. He fought in WW1([d]) as Lieut. Welsh Guards. He *d. v.p.* 13 July 1934. His widow *m.* 2ndly, 14 Nov. 1961, Ernest Edmund Henry Malet (VAUGHAN), 7th EARL OF LISBURNE, who *d.* 30 June 1965. She *d.* 1978.]

XVIII. 1952. 18. ROBERT MILO LEICESTER (DEVEREUX), VISCOUNT HEREFORD, grandson and h., being only s. and h. of Robert Godfrey de Bohun DEVEREUX and Emma Beatrice abovenamed. He was *b.* 4 Nov. 1932; ed. at Eton; *m.*, 11 Dec. 1969, Susan Mary, da. of Major Maurice GODLEY of Ide Hill, co. Kent. This marriage was diss. by divorce in 1982.

[CHARLES ROBIN DE BOHUN DEVEREUX, 1st s. and h. ap., *b.* 11 Aug. 1975.]

note ([d]), lines 1–5, delete from 'Their' to '(wounded)'

HERON

page 493,
line 5, after 'SAY' add '[4th LORD SAY],'
line 7, after 'She,' add 'da. of Sir Thomas DE BREOSE [1st LORD BREWOSE],'
note ([f]), line 14, after '15 Edw. III,' add '(1341–2)'
line 26, after 'd).' add 'For a discussion of the heirs of William Heron, see G.W. Watson, *Misc. Geneal. et Her.*, vol. 9, 5th ser., 1935–7, pp. 241–3.'

HERRIES

page 496,
after line 24 add

* * * * * *

XIV. 1975. 14. ANNE ELIZABETH FITZLAN-HOWARD, *suo jure* BARONESS HERRIES OF TERREGLES [S.], 1st da. and heir of line of Bernard Marmaduke (FITZALAN-HOWARD), 16th DUKE OF NORFOLK, see *sub* NORFOLK below. She was *b.* 12 June 1938; *m.*, 1985, Sir Michael Colin COWDREY.

note ([b]), for '90' read '64'

HERSCHELL

page 498,
line 27, after '([c])' add 'He *m.*, 1 Nov. 1919, Annie Vera Violet, da. of Sir Arthur Thomas

Bennett Robert NICOLSON, Bart., of the ilk and Lasswade, Midlothian. He *d.* 14 Oct. 1929 at Ardington House, Wantage, Berks. His widow *d.* 31 Mar. 1961.

III. 1929. 3. ROGNVALD RICHARD FARRER (HERSCHELL), BARON HERSCHELL OF THE CITY OF DURHAM, only s. and h., *b.* 13 Sep. 1923; ed. at Eton; *m.*, 1 May 1948, Lady Heather Mary Margaret, da. of Humphrey (LEGGE), 8th EARL OF DARTMOUTH.

HERTFORD

page 500,
note (a), line 1, before 'One' add 'He does in fact seem to have become Earl immediately on the death of his brother, since he is *styled* Earl of Clare in Stephen's writ to Abbot Ording of Bury, giving him custody of the son of Baldwin FitzGeoffrey (D.C. Douglas, *Feudal Documents*, vol. i, p. 91, printing Campbell Charter xxix, 3, in the BL).'

page 502,
line 20, delete '(DE BEAUMONT),'

page 505,
line 25, after 'being' add ', it was said,'
note (d), line 8, after 'of' add 'Henry (or Thomas) Keys, the Queen's'

page 506,
note (a), line 3, after 'p. 173.' add '; in the record of the trial it appears that the Book of Common Prayer was used in the marriage, in which case the suggestion that the marriage was by a Roman Catholic priest appears impossible. See BL., Harl. MS. 6286 and Cambridge Univ. Lib. MS. Dd.3. 84.'

page 507,
line 16, delete from 'was' to '1607/8' and replace by 'dated her will 5 Dec. 1615, pr. 21 Dec. 1615 at Salisbury, and was *bur.* St. Edmunds, Salisbury, 17 Dec.'

page 515,
line 25, line to read as follows

MARQUESSATE. X. EARLDOM. XXII. 1912. 7. GEORGE ALEXANDER FRANCIS (SEYMOUR), MARQUESS OF HERTFORD, &c., s. and h., *b.* 20 Oct. 1871; *styled* EARL OF YARMOUTH 1884–1912;

line 27, after 'Watch.' add '(c)'
lines 30–2, delete from 'Having' to 'work.(c)]' and replace by 'He *d. s.p.* 16 Feb. 1940.'

MARQUESSATE. XI. EARLDOM. XXIII. 1940. 8. HUGH EDWARD CONWAY (SEYMOUR), MARQUESS OF HERTFORD, &c., nephew and h., being s. of Henry Charles SEYMOUR (*d.* 18 June 1939), by Lady Helen Frances, yst. da. of Hugh Lupus (GROSVENOR), 1st DUKE

OF WESTMINSTER, which Henry Charles was 2nd s. of 6th Marquess of Hertford. He was *b.* 29 Mar. 1930; ed. at Eton; *m.*, COUNTESS PAMELA THÉRÈSE LOUISE DE CARAMAN-CHIMAY, da. of Lieut. Col. PRINCE ALPHONSE DE CHIMAY.

[HENRY JOCELYN SEYMOUR *styled* EARL OF YARMOUTH, s. and h. ap., *b.* 6 July 1958; *m.*, 1990, Beatriz, da. of Jorge KARAM of Copacabana, Rio de Janeiro, Brazil.]

HEYTESBURY

page 518,
lines 33–4, delete from 'He was' to 'work'

IV. 1903. 4. LEONARD (HOLMES-A'COURT), BARON HEYTESBURY, next brother and h., *b.* 11 June 1863. He *m.* 9 Sep. 1896, Sybil Mary, da. of Frank B. MORRIS, Capt. Bengal Army. Etc. She *d.* 20, and was *bur.* 23 Apr. 1937, at Longbridge-Deverell, Warminster, Wilts. He *d.* 2 Feb. 1949.

V. 1949. 5. WILLIAM LEONARD FRANK (HOLMES-A'COURT), BARON HEYTESBURY, 1st s. and h., *b.* 17 Apr. 1906; ed. at Cambridge (Pembroke Coll.); *m.*, 11 May 1926, Beryl yst. da. of Albert Edward Bredin CRAWFORD of Aston Clinton House, co. Buckingham. She *d.* 8 Oct. 1968. He *d.* 27 Nov. 1971.

VI. 1971. 6. FRANCIS WILLIAM (HOLMES-A'COURT), BARON HEYTESBURY, only s. and h., *b.* 8 Nov. 1931; ed. at Bryanston and Cambridge (Pembroke Coll.); *m.*, 22 Sep. 1962, Alison J., 1st da. of Michael Graham BALFOUR, C.B.E.

[JAMES WILLIAM HOLMES-A'COURT, s. and h. ap., *b.* 30 July 1967.]

note ([d]), delete all detail

HILL

page 522,
lines 22–3, delete from 'He was' to 'work' and replace by 'His widow *d.* 10 and was *bur.* 14 Jan. 1937 at Hodnet, co. Salop.'

V. 1923. 5. FRANCIS WILLIAM (CLEGG-HILL), VISCOUNT HILL OF HAWKESTONE AND OF HARDWICKE, &c., brother and h., *b.* 4 Nov. 1866. He *m.*, 5 Sep. 1905, Caroline, 2nd da. of Frank CORBETT, of Greenfield, Presteign, co. Radnor. He *d. s.p.*, 6 July 1924. His widow *d.* 29 June 1941.

VI. 1924. 6. CHARLES ROWLAND (CLEGG-HILL), VISCOUNT HILL OF HAWKESTONE AND OF HARDWICKE, &c., eldest half-brother by the 2nd wife of the 3rd Viscount, *b.* 5 May 1876. Served in the South African War 1899–1902, wounded, D.S.O., and in WW1. He *m.*, 6 Jan. 1903, Mildred, da. of Thomas BULTEEL of Radford, Devon. She *d.* 29 Jan. 1934 and he *m.* 2ndly, 18 Jan. 1936, at St. George's, Camden Hill, Berthe Marie Emilie, da. of A. SCHMIDT-IMMER of Alsace Lorraine. He *d.* 3 May 1957. His widow *d.* 31 Dec. 1959.

VII. 1957. 7. GERALD ROWLAND (CLEGG-HILL), VISCOUNT HILL OF HAWKESTONE AND OF HARDWICKE, &c., 1st and only surv. s. and h., *b.* 31 Mar. 1904; ed. at Shrewsbury; *m.* 1stly, 7 Oct. 1930, Elisabeth Flora, 2nd da. of Brig. Gen. George Nowell Thomas SMYTH-OSBOURNE, C.B., C.M.G., D.S.O., of Ash, Iddesleigh, co. Devon. This marriage was diss. by divorce in 1942 (she *d.* 19 Mar. 1967), and he *m.* 2ndly, 30 Nov. 1942, Catherine Mary, da. of Dr Rowland Venables Lloyd WILLIAMS of Malford, Denbigh. He *d.* 11 May 1974. His widow was living 1995.

VIII. 1974. 8. ANTHONY ROWLAND (CLEGG-HILL), VISCOUNT HILL OF HAWKESTONE AND OF HARDWICKE, &c., 1st s. and h. by 1st wife, *b.* 19 Mar. 1931; ed. at Kelly Coll. and R.M.A., Sandhurst; *m.*, 10 Aug. 1963, Juanita Phyllis, da. of John W. PERTWEE. This marriage was diss. by divorce in 1976 and he *m.* 2ndly, 1989, Elizabeth Harriett, da. of Ronald OFFER of Salisbury, Wilts.

note ([d]), delete all detail

HILLINGDON

page 524,
line 4, line to read as follows

III. 1919. 3. ARTHUR ROBERT (MILLS), BARON HILLINGDON OF HILLINGDON [1886], 3rd and yst.([b]) but only surv s. and h.,

lines 11–12, delete from 'Having' to 'work.]' and replace by 'He *d.* 5 Dec. 1952. His widow *d.* 4 June 1969.'

IV. 1952. 4. CHARLES HEDWORTH (MILLS), BARON HILLINGDON OF HILLINGDON, 1st and only surv. s., *b.* 12 June 1922; ed. at Eton; *m.*, 9 Aug. 1947, Lady Sarah Gray, 2nd da. of Francis Douglas (STUART), 18th EARL OF MORAY. He *m.* 2ndly, 1978, Phoebe Maxwell, da. of Capt. Mervyn James Hamilton of Cornacassa, co. Monaghan and formerly wife of John Sholto Fitzpatrick COOKE, Lieut. Cmdr., R.N.V.R., and of John COOPER. He *d. s.p.m.* 6 May 1978. His widow was living 1995.

[CHARLES JAMES MILLS, s. and h., ap., *b.* 8 Mar. 1951; ed. at Radley. He *d. v.p.* and unm. 1976.]

V. 1978. 5. PATRICK CHARLES (MILLS), BARON HILLINGDON OF HILLINGDON, distant cousin and h., being 3rd s. of Geoffrey Edward MILLS, Cmdr., R.N.V.R. (*d.* 14 Aug. 1917), by his 1st wife, Grace Victoria, da. of Hungerford BODDAM, which Geoffrey Edward was 6th s. of 1st Baron HILLINGDON. He was *b.* 4 Nov. 1906; ed. at Lancing and Cambridge (St. Catharine's Coll.); *m.* 1stly, 11 June 1931, Nancy Elizabeth, da. of Brinsley NIXON of Westward Ho!, co. Devon. This marriage was diss. by divorce in 1939 and he *m.* 2ndly, 31 Mar. 1945, Mary Miriam, da. of W. Hoare WARD. She *d.* 1976. He *d. s.p.m.* 1 Sep. 1982 when his title became *extinct*.

HINDLIP

page 526,
lines 20–1, for 'was living 1925' read '*d.* 15 Jan. 1939.'
line 32, after 'Bart.' add 'He *d.* 2 and was *bur.* 5 Dec. 1931 in Hindlip Church. His widow *d.* 11 Dec. 1962.'
line 33, delete all detail and replace as follows

IV. 1966. 4. CHARLES SAMUEL VICTOR (ALLSOPP), BARON HINDLIP OF HINDLIP AND OF ALSOP-EN-LE-DALE [1886], &c., 1st s. and h., *b.* 5 Nov. 1906; ed. at Eton; *m.*, 23 Feb. 1932, Bridget, da. of Harold NICKOLS. This marriage was diss. by divorce in 1934 and he *m.* 2ndly, 16 Feb. 1939, Hansina Elfrida Cecilia Tulla Karr-Harris, da. of Frederick William HARRIS. He *d. s.p.m.* 30 Mar. 1966. His widow *d.* 1988.

V. 1966. 5. HENRY RICHARD (ALLSOPP), BARON HINDLIP OF HINDLIP AND OF ALSOP-EN-LE-DALE, br. and h., *b.* 1 July 1912; *d.* at Eton and R.M.C., Sandhurst; *m.*, 12 Apr. 1939, Cecily Valentine Jane, da. of Lieut. Col. Malcolm BORWICK, D.S.O., of Hazelbech Hill, Northampton. He *d.* 19 Dec. 1993. His widow was living 1995.

VI. 1993. 6. CHARLES HENRY (ALLSOPP), BARON HINDLIP OF HINDLIP AND OF ALSOP-EN-LE-DALE, 1st s. and h., *b.* 5 Aug. 1940; ed. at Eton; *m.*, 18 Apr. 1968, Fiona Victoria Jean, da. of William Johnston MCGOWAN.

[HENRY WILLIAM ALLSOPP, s. and h. ap., *b.* 8 June 1973.]

HOLAND

page 528,
note (1), line 1, for 'Azure fleurette' read 'Azure semy of fleurs de lys argent'
line 2, after '287.' add 'See H. Stanford London, "Holand Heraldry", *N&Q*, vol. 195, pp. 24–8.'

page 530,
line 10, after 'Maud,' add '1st'

page 533,
line 9, for '3rd' read '6th'

HOLDERNESS

page 537,
line 8, for 'illegit.' read 'morganatic'

HOLLAND

page 541,
line 15, after '1713' add '–18'

line 16, after '1720;' add 'adm. Student Inner Temple 16 May 1723;'

page 542,
line 2, for 'Millwick' read 'Milwick'

HOLMES

page 548,
line 15, for 'APSLEY read 'ASPLEY

HOLMPATRICK

page 549,
line 16, for 'was living 1925' read '*d.* 31 July 1933 at Longthorpe House, Peterborough, co. Northampton.'
line 21, after 'Ireland.' add 'He *m.*, 27 Oct. 1925, in the Savoy Chapel, Lady Edina Dorothy Hope, da. of Henry Francis (CONYNGHAM), 4th MARQUESS CONYNGHAM and formerly wife of Sir Thomas AINSWORTH, Bart. He *d.* 5 Sep. 1942. His widow *d.* 13 Apr. 1964.'

III. 1942. 3. JAMES HANS (HAMILTON), BARON HOLMPATRICK, only s. and h., *b.* 29 Nov. 1928; ed. at Eton; *m.*, 22 May 1954, Anne Loys Roche, da. of John Ernest Padwick BRASS, Cmdr., R.N., of Haverfordwest, co. Pembroke. He *d.* 15 Feb. 1991. His widow was living 1995.

IV. 1991. 4. HANS JAMES DAVID (HAMILTON), BARON HOLMPATRICK, 1st s. and h., *b.* 15 Mar. 1955; ed. at Harrow; *m.*, 1984, Gill Francesca Ann (Mrs DU FEU), da. of Kenneth James Toby HARDING, Sqn. Ldr., R.A.F., of Binisafua, Minorca.

[JAMES HANS STEPHEN HAMILTON, s. and h. ap., *b.* 1982.]

HOME

page 552,
line 11, after 'MONTGOMERIE' add '(s. and h. ap. of Alexander, 1st LORD MONTGOMERIE)' and for 'Hales' read 'Hailes'

page 559,
line 20, for 'Scrotty' read 'Scratby'

page 560,
line 40, line to read as follows

EARLDOM [S.] XIII. BARONY [S]. XVIII. } 1918 13 and 18. CHARLES COSPATRICK ARCHIBALD (DOUGLAS-HOME), EARL OF HOME, &c., only s. and h., *b.* 29 Dec. 1873, *styled* LORD DUNGLAS from 1881–1918,

page 561,
line 2, after 'LAMBTON,' add '(*later* 4th EARL OF DURHAM),'
lines 3–4, delete from 'Having' to 'work.]' and replace by 'He *d.* 11 July 1951. His widow *d.* 26 Sep. 1966.'

EARLDOM [S.] XIV. BARONY [S]. XIX. } 1951

14 and 19. ALEXANDER FREDERICK (DOUGLAS-HOME), EARL OF HOME, &c., 1st s. and h., *b.* 2 July 1903; ed. at Eton and Oxford (Ch. Ch.); disclaimed his titles for life, 23 Oct. 1963, under the Peerage Act 1963; *cr.* BARON HOME OF THE HIRSEL of Coldstream, co. Berwick (a Life Peerage), 1974. He *m.*, 3 Oct. 1936, in Durham Cathedral, Elizabeth Hester, 2nd da. of Very Rev. Cyril Argentine ALINGTON, Dean of Durham. She *d.* 1990. He *d.* 10 Oct. 1995.

EARLDOM [S.] XV. BARONY [S]. XX. } 1995

15 and 20. DAVID ALEXANDER COSPATRICK (DOUGLAS-HOME), EARL OF HOME, &c., only s. and h., *b.* 20 Nov. 1943; ed. at Eton and Oxford (Ch. Ch.). *Styled* LORD DUNGLASS 1951–63 when he discontinued its use. He *m.*, 1972, Jane Margaret, da. of Col. John Francis WILLIAMS-WYNNE, C.B.E., D.S.O.

[MICHAEL DAVID ALEXANDER DOUGLAS-HOME, s. and h. ap., *b.* 30 Nov. 1987.]

HOOD

page 571,
line 11, line to read as follows

VISCOUNTCY, &c. [G.B.] V. BARONY [I]. V. } 1907

5. GROSVENOR ARTHUR ALEXANDER (HOOD), VISCOUNT HOOD OF WHITLEY, &c., 2nd but 1st surv. s. and h.,

lines 20–1, delete from 'Having' to 'work.]' and replace by 'He *m.* 2ndly, 2 June 1928, Marguerite Jenny, yr. da. of Albert HOOD (2nd s. of Samuel, 3rd VISCOUNT HOOD). He *d. s.p.* 26 Apr. 1933. His widow *d.* 10 May 1966.'

VISCOUNTCY, &c. [G.B.] VI. BARONY. V. } 1933

6. SAMUEL (HOOD), VISCOUNT HOOD OF WHITLEY, &c., nephew and h., being s. and h. of Horace Lambert Alexander HOOD, Rear Adm., R.N. (*d.* 31 May 1916, being *k.* at Jutland), by Ellen, da. of A.E. TOUZALIN and widow of George Augustus NICKERSON of Dedham, Massachusetts, U.S.A., which Horace Lambert was 3rd s. of the 4th Viscount Hood. He was *b.* 15 Oct. 1910; ed. at Eton and Cambridge (Trin. Coll.). He *d.* unm. and *s.p.* 13 Oct. 1981.

VISCOUNTCY, &c. [G.B.] VII. BARONY. VI. } 1981

7. ALEXANDER LAMBERT (HOOD), VISCOUNT HOOD OF WHITLEY, &c., br. and h., *b.* 11 Mar. 1914; ed. at R.N.C., Dartmouth and Cambridge (Trin. Coll.) and Harvard Univ.; *m.*, 30 Apr. 1957,

Diana Maud, 1st da. of George William LYTTELTON of Findale House, Grundisburgh, co. Suffolk.

[HENRY LYTTELTON ALEXANDER HOOD, 1st s. and h. ap., *b.* 16 Mar. 1958; *m.*, 1991, Flora Susan, yr. da. of Michael Bernard CASEMENT, Cmdr., R.N.]

HOPETOUN

page 575,
line 10, after 'illegit.' add '(but legitimated)([a])'
note ([a]) By decree of the Court of Session 4 June 1910 her brother A.W.R. Macdonald was adjudged to be lawfully born by the law of Scotland.
line 16, for 'Sep. 1802' read ', *bap.* 29 Dec. 1802 at Notting Hill' [See Alice Macdonald, *A Romantic Chapter in Family History*, p. 13, *ex inform.* C.R. Hudleston.]
line 27, for 'Erthig' read 'Erddig'

page 576,
line 11, for 'is' read 'was' and for 'was living 1925' read '*d.* in a nursing home in Lausanne, 3, and was *bur.* 8 Apr. 1937, at Hopetoun.'
line 12, line to read as follows

MARQUESSATE [U.K.] II.
EARLDOM [S.] VIII.
BARONY [U.K.] VI. } 1908

2, 8 and 6. VICTOR ALEXANDER JOHN (HOPE), MARQUESS OF LINLITHGOW, EARL OF HOPETOUN, &c., s. and h., *b.* 24 Sep. 1887; MASTER OF HOPETOUN and *styled* LORD HOPE till 1908.

lines 19–20, delete from 'Having' to '([d])]' and replace by 'He *d.* 5 Jan. 1952. His widow *d.* 2 Aug. 1965.'

MARQUESSATE [U.K.] III.
EARLDOM [S.] IX.
BARONY [U.K.] VII. } 1952

3, 9 and 7. CHARLES WILLIAM FREDERICK (HOPE), MARQUESS OF LINLITHGOW, EARL OF HOPETOUN, &c., 1st s. and h., *b.* 7 Apr. 1912; ed. at Eton and Oxford (Ch. Ch.); *styled* EARL OF HOPETOUN 1912–52; *m.* 1stly, 24 July 1939, Vivien, 1st da. of Major Robert Orlando Rodolph KENYON-SLANEY of Hatton Grange, Shifnal, co. Salop. She *d.* 23 Sep. 1963 and he *m.* 2ndly, 18 Feb. 1965, Judith, da. of Stanley Matthew LAWSON, of Cincinnati, Ohio, U.S.A., widow of Lieut. Col. Esmond Charles BARING, O.B.E., and formerly wife of John Symonds RADWAY. He *d.* 7 Apr. 1987. His widow *d.* 1991.

MARQUESSATE [U.K.] IV.
EARLDOM [S.] X.
BARONY [U.K.] VIII. } 1987

4, 10 and 8. ADRIAN JOHN CHARLES (HOPE), MARQUESS OF LINLITHGOW, &c., only s. and h., *b.* 1 July 1946; ed. at Eton; *m.* 1stly, 9 Jan. 1968, Anne Pamela, 1st da. of Arthur Edmund LEVESON of Hall Place, Popley, co. Hertford. This marriage was diss. by divorce in 1978 and he *m.* 2ndly, 1980, Peta Carol, da. of Charles Victor Ormonde BINDING of Congresbury, co. Somerset.

[ANDREW VICTOR ARTHUR CHARLES HOPE, *styled* EARL OF HOPETOUN, 1st s. and h. ap., *b.* 22 May 1959; ed. at Eton and Oxford (Exeter Coll.); *m.*, 1993, Skye Laurette, 1st da. of Major Bristow Charles BOVILL of Shipston on Stour, co. Warwick.]

note ([d]), delete all detail

HOTHAM

page 577,
line 2, for 'Scarborough' read 'Scorborough, near Beverley,'

page 579,
lines 25–6, delete from 'He was' to 'work.([a])'

VI. 1907. 6. FREDERICK WILLIAM (HOTHAM), BARON HOTHAM OF SOUTH DALTON [I.], &c., cousin and h, male, being only. s. and h. of Rev. William Francis HOTHAM by Emma, 5th da. of John CHARBONELL, which William Francis was 5th s. of Rev. William HOTHAM by Anne Elizabeth, eld. da. of Thomas Hallett HODGES of Hemsted Place, Kent, the Rev. William being 2nd s. of the 2nd Baron. He was *b.* 19 Mar. 1863. He *m.*, 9 July 1902, Eliza Benite, da. of Thomas SANDERS, of Sanders Park, Charleville, co. Cork. He *d. s.p.m.* at Dalton Hall, Beverley, 7, and was *bur.* 10 Oct. 1923, at Dalton Holme. Will pr. Dec. 1923 at £98,730 gross and £58,449 net. His widow *d.* 14 Dec. 1954.

VII. 1923. 7. HENRY FREDERICK (HOTHAM), BARON HOTHAM OF SOUTH DALTON [I.], also a Baronet [1622], cousin and h. male, being 1st s. and h. of Henry Edward HOTHAM, by Ethel Lindsay, da. of Collingwood Lindsay WOOD of Freeland, Perthshire, which Henry Edward was 1st s. and h. of Rev. Frederick Harry HOTHAM, by Eleanor, 4th da. of Robert GOSLING, of Botleys Park, Surrey, this Frederick Harry in turn being 2nd s. and h. of Vice Admiral of the Red Sir Henry HOTHAM, 3rd s. of the 2nd Baron. He was *b.* 13 Aug. 1899; ed. at Winchester and R.M.C., Sandhurst; *m.*, 16 Dec. 1937, Lady Letitia Sibell Winifred, 1st da. of William Thomas Brownlow (CECIL), 5th MARQUESS OF EXETER. He *d.* 18 Nov. 1967. His widow *d.* 1992.

VIII. 1967. 8. HENRY DURAND (HOTHAM), BARON HOTHAM OF SOUTH DALTON, 3rd but 1st surv. s. and h., *b.* 3 May 1940; ed. at Eton and R.A.C., Cirencester; *m.*, 1972, Alexandra Mary, 2nd da. of Major Andrew Charles Stirling Home Drummond MORAY.

[WILLIAM BEAUMONT HOTHAM, 1st s. and h. ap., *b.* 13 Oct. 1972.]

note ([a]), delete all detail

HOTHFIELD

page 580,
line 16, after 'afsd.' add 'He *d.* 29 Oct. 1926.'
line 17, line to read as follows

II. 1926. 2. JOHN SACKVILLE RICHARD (TUFTON), BARON HOTHFIELD OF HOTHFIELD, 1st s. and h., *b.* 8 Nov. 1873;

line 23, for '(e)]' read 'She *d.* 5 and was *bur.* 9 Jan. 1935 at Appleby and he *m.* 2ndly, 31 Dec. 1935, Sybil Augusta, da. of John SANT of South Wales. She *d.* 7 June 1950. He *d.* 21 Sep. 1952.'

III. 1952. 3. HENRY HASTINGS SACKVILLE (TUFTON), BARON HOTHFIELD OF HOTHFIELD, 1st s. and h., *b* 16 Mar. 1897; *m.*, 18 June 1918, Dorothy, 1st da. of William George RAPHAEL. He *d. s.p.* 20 Aug. 1961. His widow *d.* 1981.

IV. 1961. 4. THOMAS SACKVILLE (TUFTON), BARON HOTHFIELD OF HOTHFIELD, cousin and h., being s. of Sackville Philip TUFTON (*d.* 24 Jan. 1936), by his 2nd wife Winifred Mary Ripley, 1st da. of Edward Ripley DALTON, which Sackville Philip was 2nd s. of 1st Baron Hothfield. He was *b.* 20 July 1916; ed. at Eton and Cambridge. He *d.* unm. and *s.p.*, 16 May 1986.

V. 1986. 5. GEORGE WILLIAM ANTHONY (TUFTON), BARON HOTHFIELD OF HOTHFIELD, cousin and h., being 1st s. of Charles Henry TUFTON (*d.* 23 Sep. 1923), by Stella Josephine Faudel, yst. da. of Sir George FAUDEL-PHILLIPS, Bart., which Charles Henry was 3rd s. of 1st Baron Hothfield. He was *b.* 28 Oct. 1904; ed. at Eton and Oxford (Hertford Coll.); *m.*, 3 Dec. 1936, Evelyn Margarette, 1st da. of Eustace MORDAUNT. She *d.* 1989. He *d.* 5 Feb. 1991.

VI. 1991. 6. ANTHONY CHARLES SACKVILLE (TUFTON), BARON HOTHFIELD OF HOTHFIELD, 1st s. and h., *b.* 21 Oct. 1939; ed. at Eton and Cambridge (Magdalene Coll.); *m.*, 1975, Lucinda Marjorie, da. of Capt. Timothy John GURNEY and formerly wife of Capt. Graham Morison Vere NICHOLL.

[WILLIAM SACKVILLE TUFTON, s. and h. ap., *b.* 14 Nov. 1977; ed. at Eton.]

note (e), delete all detail

HOWARD

page 583,
line 3, after 'was' add '*cr.* LORD HOWARD between 29 Dec. 1469 and 12 Feb. 1470 and was' [See Anne Crawford, *Howard Household Books*, 1992, p. xxx, note 62.]
line 7, delete all detail

HOWARD OF BINDON

page 585,
note ([a]), line 3, for '1606' read '10 Oct. 1600' [R. Davies, *Chelsea Old Church*, 1904, p. 122.]

HOWARD OF GLOSSOP

page 589,
line 18, line to read as follows

III. 1924. 3. BERNARD EDWARD (FITZALAN-HOWARD), BARON HOWARD OF GLOSSOP, 1st s. and h., by 1st wife

lines 22–4, delete from 'Having' to 'work.]' and replace by 'She *d.* 31 Aug. 1971. He *d.* 24 Aug. 1972.'

IV. 1972. 4. MILES FRANCIS (FITZALAN-HOWARD), BARON HOWARD OF GLOSSOP, s. and h., *b.* 21 July 1915. He *suc.* to the Barony of Beaumont, 1971, on the death of his mother and to the Dukedom of Norfolk on the death of his distant cousin, Bernard Marmaduke (FITZALAN-HOWARD), 16th DUKE OF NORFOLK. See that title, below.

note ([d]), delete all detail

HOWARD DE WALDEN

page 593,
line 37, after 'Leicester.' add 'He *d.* 5 July 1946. His widow *d.* 1974.'
line 38, delete all detail and replace as follows

IX. 1946. 9. JOHN OSMAEL (SCOTT-ELLIS), LORD HOWARD (of Walden) [1597], s and h., *b.* 27 Nov. 1912; ed. at Eton and Cambridge (Magdalene Coll.); *m.*, 22 Aug. 1934, at Dreifaltigkeite Kirche, Munich (civil ceremony, Munich Register Office, 21 Aug. 1934), COUNTESS IRENE, yst. da. of COUNT HANS ALBRECHT HARRACH of Munich. She *d.* 1975 and he *m.* 2ndly, 1978, Gillian Margaret, da. of Cyril Francis Stuart BUCKLEY and formerly wife of Richard Henry Piers (BUTLER), 17th VISCOUNT MOUNTGARRET.

HOWDEN

page 594,
line 9, after '1774' add 'and to the Middle Temple 9 Feb. 1776'

HOWE

page 596,
line 5, after '11th' add 'BARON SCROPE (of Bolton) and 1st'

page 597,
line 12, after '(c)' add 'Ed. at Eton *c*. 1734;'
note (a), line 3, after '*Queen*' add ', (see also *sub* DARLINGTON above)

page 598,
line 2, after '1725/6' add '; ed. at Westm. Sch., 1731–5;'
line 12, after 'Eton' add 'from 1742'
line 23, after '1804;' add 'Lieut.-Gov. of the Isle of Wight 1768–95.'

page 599,
line 8, after 'school' add '1731–5'
line 9, after 'in' add '16 July'

page 601,
line 8, for ', co. Worcester' read 'Hall'

page 603,
line 13, after 'afsd.' add 'He *m* 3rdly, 4 Aug. 1927, Lorna Katherine, da. of Capt. Ernest Charles Penn CURZON, by Edith, da. of Charles Henry BASSETT of Pilton House, Barnstaple, Devon. He *d*. 10, of heart failure and was *bur*. at Penn Street, co. Buckingham, 16 Jan. 1929.'
line 14, line to read as follows

EARLDOM. VI. BARONY. VII. } 1929 5 and 7. FRANCIS RICHARD HENRY PENN (CURZON-HOWE), EARL HOWE, &c., 1st s. and h., *b*. 1 May 1884, from 1900 *styled* VISCOUNT CURZON

line 21, for '(a)]' read 'This marriage was diss. by divorce in 1937 (she *d*. 1 Sep. 1962), and he *m*. 2ndly, 8 Feb. 1937, Joyce Mary McLean, da. of Charles McLean JACK of Johannesburg, South Africa. This marriage was in turn diss. by divorce in 1943 and he *m*. 3rdly, 8 Feb. 1944, Sybil Boyter, da. of Capt. Francis JOHNSON of Edinburgh and formerly wife of Major Ernest Duncombe SHAFTO. He *d*. 26 July 1964. His widow was living 1995.

EARLDOM. VII. BARONY. VIII. } 1964 6 and 8. EDWARD RICHARD ASSHETON PENN (CURZON), EARL HOWE, &c., s. and h., *b*. 7 Aug. and *bap*. 6 Oct. 1908 at Gopsall House, Edward VII being one of his sponsors; ed. at Eton and Cambridge (Corpus Christi Coll.); *m*. 1stly, 23 July 1935, Priscilla Crystal Frances Blundell, da. of Sir William Ernest George Archibald WEIGALL, Bart., in the Chapel of the Order of St. Michael and St. George, in St. Paul's Cathedral. This marriage was diss. by divorce in 1943 and he *m*. 2ndly, 30 Apr. 1946, Grace Lilian, da. of Stephen Frederick WAKELING of Durban, South Africa and formerly wife of Capt. A.N. BARKER of Durban afsd. He *d*. *s.p.m*. 29 May 1984. His widow *d*. 1985.

EARLDOM. VIII. BARONY. IX. } 1984 7 and 9. FREDERICK RICHARD PENN (CURZON), EARL HOWE, &c., distant cousin and h., being s. of Chambré George William Penn CURZON, Cmdr., R.N., by his 2nd wife Jane Victoria, da. of Malcolm Mackenzie FERGUSON of Toronto, Canada, which Chambré was s. of Frederick Graham CURZON (*d.* 4 Nov. 1920), by Minnie Ellis Gertrude, da. of Capt. Dodsworth JEFFREYS, which Frederick was 2nd s. of 3rd Earl Howe. He was *b.* 29 Jan. 1951; ed. at Rugby and Oxford (Ch. Ch.); *m.*, 1983, Elizabeth Helen, 1st da. of Capt. Burleigh Edward St. Lawrence STUART.

note ([a]), delete all detail

HOWTH

page 605,
line 18, for '2nd' read '1st'
note ([a]), line 4, for 'grandfather' read 'father'

HUNGERFORD

page 615,
line 9, after '1stly' add 'shortly after 8 Oct. 1396' [The date of the marriage settlement, *Hist. MSS. Com.*, Hastings MSS., part 1, p. 299.]

page 616,
line 2, for '14 June 1426' read '12 Nov. 1432'
line 7, after 'POYNINGS' add '(s. and h. ap. of Robert, 4th LORD POYNINGS)'
note ([b]), delete all detail and replace by '*Hist. MSS. Com.*, Hastings MSS., part 1, p. 259.'

page 617,
line 6, after '*m.*' add 'about 1420([ea])'
note ([ea]) An indented agreement for their marriage "to take place at Aller [Somerset] upon 6 or 7 of July next following" (*Hist. MSS. Com.*, Hastings MSS., part 1, pp. 287–8). In this agreement she is called eldest daughter of Lord Botreaux.

page 621,
line 6, for '3rd' read '2nd'

page 625,
line 13, for '30' read '28'

page 627,
line 1, for 'Congleton, Worc.' read 'Coughton, co. Warwick'
note ([e]), line 6, for '1520/1' read '1519/20' [*L. and P. Hen. VIII*, vol. iii, p. 1539]
line 7, after 'son'. add 'For a discussion of this possibility, see Anthony Hoskins, *Geneal. Mag.*, vol. 25, 1997, pp. 346–52.'

HUNTERCOMBE

page 636,
line 3, after 'HYLTON, add '[2nd LORD HILTON]'

HUNTINGDON

page 639,
note (f), lines 8–11, delete from '(3)' to 'below).'

page 643,
line 20, delete '(DE BEAUMONT)'
lines 21–2, delete from 'Ralph' to 'BRITTANY and replace by 'Ralph DE GAEL II, Seigneur of Gael and Montfort-sur-Meu'

page 645,
line 8, for 'Comte' read 'Vicomte'
line 18, for 'GAND read 'GANT'

page 647,
line 9, after 'Maud,' add 'sister and coh. of Ranulph, 4th EARL OF CHESTER,'

page 649,
line 8, for '1336/7' read '1337/8'
line 19, after 'Juliane,' add '*de jure suo jure* (according to modern doctrine), BARONESS LEYBURN,'
line 20, after 'BLOUNT' add '[1st LORD BLOUNT],'
line 21, for '(*d.* 1325)' read '[2nd LORD HASTINGS] (*d.* 20 Jan. 1324/5)'
line 21, after 'LEYBURNE' add '(s. and h. of William 1st LORD LEYBURN),'
line 22, after 'Alice,' add 'sister and h. ap. of Sir Robert DE TONI [1st LORD TONY],'

page 655,
line 2, for 'about' read '10 July'
note (e), line 1, after 'Molens,"' add ' (notably not Lord Hungerford),'
note (f), line 2, after 'however, of' add '9 Aug. for the Parliament which was to meet on'

page 656,
line 11, delete 'dat. 10 June 1544,'
note (g), delete all detail and replace by 'A will of 10 June 1544 (see BL Harl. MS. 3881, f. 41), a disposition of manors and land only, was revoked by the later will, pr. in 1561. (See also *Hist. MSS. Com.*, Hastings MSS., part 1, p. 315.)'

page 658,
line 23, for '1601' read '1600/1, at Stonely, co. Stafford'

page 660,
line 5, after '1685–8;' add 'Cupbearer to the King at the Coronation, 23 Apr. 1685;'
line 31, after '1701;' add 'ed. at Eton till June 1692 and then at Tamworth;'

page 661,
line 9, for 'but never matric. there' read '1712 after matric.'
line 20, for 'pr.' read 'dat. 11 Jan. 1790, with var. cod., pr. 6 July.' [*ex inform.* R.M. Glencross]

page 662,
line 8, for 'pr. 8' read 'dat. 9 Aug. 1779, cod. dat. 5 Feb., pr. 10([ea])'
line 29, after 'Osgathorpe' add '(1764–95)'
note ([ea]) The contents of the will are given in H.N. Bell, *Huntingdon Peerage*, 1820, p. 165, and some corrections of that account are in *Hist. MSS. Com.*, Hastings MSS., part 1, p. 322.

page 663,
line 1, for '(1764)' read '(1764–95)'
line 2, after 'Notts.' add '(1795–8)'
line 3, for 'in 1798 (when in his 70th year)' read 'West Leake afsd., 25 Apr. 1797 (when in his 69th year)'
line 4, after 'intestate' add '(admon. 26 Sep. 1804 (under £300) and 17 Aug. 1812 (under £100))'
line 5, after '75' add 'His widow *d.* at Loughborough, 17 Aug. 1810. Admon. 7 Feb. 1811 (under £800).'
line 10, after 'da.' add 'of Col. Thomas Hodges, Col. in the Guards, by Sarah' [*ex inform.* Rupert Willoughby]

page 664,
line 24, after 'Colony.' add 'He *d.* 5 Apr. 1939. His widow *d.* 26 Dec. 1953.'
lines 25–7, delete all detail and replace as follows

XXXIII. 1939. 16. FRANCIS JOHN CLARENCE WESTENRA PLANTAGENET (HASTINGS), EARL OF HUNTINGDON, only s. and h., *b.* 20 Jan., and *bap.* Mar. 1901, at 10 Grosvenor Sq., W. *Styled* VISCOUNT HASTINGS([c]) 1901–39; ed. at Eton and Oxford (Ch. Ch.); *m.* 1stly (and secretly), 21 Oct. 1925, at a London Registry Office, Cristina, da. of MARCHESE CASATI of Rome. This marriage was diss. by divorce in 1943 (she *d.* 22 Mar. 1953) and he *m.* 2ndly, 1 Feb. 1944, Margaret, da. of Harry George LANE, of Vernham Dean, Andover, Hants. and formerly wife of Bryan WALLACE. He *d. s.p.m.* 24 Aug. 1990. His widow *d.* 1994.

XXXIV. 1990. 17. WILLIAM EDWARD ROBIN HOOD (HASTINGS-BASS), EARL OF HUNTINGDON, cousin and h., being 1st s. of Capt. Peter Robin Hood HASTINGS-BASS (*d.* 4 June 1964), by Priscilla, da. of Capt. Sir Malcolm BULLOCK, Bart., which Peter Robin Hood was 1st s. of Aubrey Craven Theophilus Robin Hood HASTINGS, (*d.* 25 May 1929), by Winifred, da. of Thomas FORSYTH-FOREST, of Cirencester, co. Gloucester, which Aubrey Craven was 3rd s. of 13th Earl of Huntingdon. He was *b.* 30 Jan. 1948; ed. at Winchester and Cambridge (Trin. Coll.); *m.*, 1989, Susan Mary Gavin, da. of John Jellicoe Pelham Francis WARNER.

HUNTINGFIELD

page 665,
line 10, after 'GREY' add ', of Shirland, co. Derby,'

page 666,
line 14, after 'Hallaton' add ', co. Leicester'

page 667,
line 6, after 'Isabel,' add '1st'
lines 6–7, for '(DE VALENCE)' read 'DE VALENCE, sometimes *styled*'
line 10, after 'Sybil' add 'sister and (in her issue) coh. of William DE FOURNEAUX, of Carlton in Lindrick, Kingston, Notts, 2nd da. of Sir Richard DE FOURNEAUX'

page 668,
line 6, after 'da.' add 'and (in her issue) coh. of'
line 6, after 'NORWICH' add 'by Catherine, da. of John DE HEDERSETE

page 670,
line 1, after 'h.' add 'ap.'
line 9, for 'Alice' read 'Eleanor'
lines 10–21, delete from 'The' to 'Kny[vett],' and replace by 'The name Alice is an error for Eleanor, da. of Richard Fraunceys, by Elizabeth, sister and h. of William, 1st Lord Huntingfield.(f)'
note (f), delete all detail and replace by 'See NORWICH, vol. ix, p. 766, note (e).'
note (g), delete all detail
note (h), delete all detail

page 671,
lines 1–3, delete from 'Chancellor' to '(a)'

HUNTINGFIELD OF HEVENINGHAM HALL

page 675,
line 1, line to read as follows

V. 1915. 5. WILLIAM CHARLES ARCEDECKNE (VANNECK), BARON HUNTINGFIELD OF HEVENINGHAM HALL [I.], nephew and h., being 1st(a) s. and h.

line 4, after 'Baron' add 'was *b.* 30 Oct. 1845,' and after '1883' add 'at Gatton, Queensland; ed. at Wellington, 1898–1901.'
lines 6–7, delete from 'Having' to 'work.(b)]' and replace by 'She *d.* 1 Mar. 1943 and he *m.* 2ndly, 24 May 1944, Muriel Mary Georgina, da. of Col. Jemmet DUKE and widow of George Douglas Cochrane (NEWTON), 1st and last BARON ELTISLEY. She *d.* 13 May 1953. He *d.* 20 Nov. 1969.'

VI. 1969. 6. GERARD CHARLES ARCEDECKNE (VANNECK), BARON HUNTINGFIELD OF HEVENINGHAM HALL [I.], s. and h., *b.* 29 May 1915; ed. at Stowe and Cambridge (Trin. Coll.); *m.*, 27 Oct. 1941, Janetta Lois, 1st da. of Reginald Hugh ERRINGTON, Capt., R.N., of Bury St. Edmunds, co. Suffolk. He *d.* 1 May 1994. His widow was living 1995.

VII. 1994. 7. JOSHUA CHARLES (VANNECK), BARON HUNTINGFIELD OF HEVENINGHAM HALL, only s. and h., *b.* 10 Aug. 1954; ed. at Eton and Cambridge (Magdalene Coll.); *m.*, 1982, Arabella Mary, 1st da. of Major Alastair Hugh Joseph FRASER, M.C., of Moniack Castle, Kirkhill, co. Inverness.

[GERARD CHARLES ALASTAIR VANNECK, 1st s. and h. ap., *b.* 12 Mar. 1985.]

note (b), delete all detail

HUNTLY

page 676,
line 13, after '1439–54' add ', by his wife Agnes'

page 684,
note (f), line 2, for 'vol. i, p. 3.' read 'vol. iii, p. 111'

page 685,
line 1, for 'BISSOPP' read 'BISSHOPP'

page 686,
line 7, after 'U.S.A.' add 'He *d. s.p.* 20 Feb. 1937, aged nearly 90 and was *bur.* 26 Feb. at Aboyne. His widow *d.* 17 May 1939.'

XII. 1937. 12. DOUGLAS CHARLES LINDSEY (GORDON), MARQUESS OF HUNTLY, &c., great-nephew and h., being 1st s. of Lieut. Col. Granville Cecil Douglas GORDON (*d.* 3 Oct. 1930), by Violet Ida, da. of Gerard STREATFEILD, which Granville Cecil was 2nd s. of Granville Armyne GORDON (*d.* 14 June 1907), by his 1st wife Charlotte D'Olier, da. of Henry ROE of Mount Anneville Park, co. Dublin, which Granville Armyne was 6th s. of 10th Marquess of Huntly. He was *b.* 3 Feb. 1908; *m.*, 15 Mar. 1941, Mary Pamela, da. of James Gomer (BERRY), 1st VISCOUNT KEMSLEY. This marriage was diss. by divorce in 1965 and he *m.* 2ndly, 1977, Elizabeth Haworth, da. of Frederick Haworth LEIGH, Lieut. Cmdr., R.N.R. He *d.* 26 Jan. 1987. His widow was living 1995.

XIII. 1987. 13. GRANVILLE CHARLES GOMER (GORDON), MARQUESS OF HUNTLY, &c., only s. and h., *b.* 4 Feb. 1944; ed. at Gordonstoun; *m.* 1stly, 1972, Jane Elizabeth Angela, da. of Lieut. Col. Alastair Monteith GIBB. This marriage was diss. by divorce in 1990 and he *m.* 2ndly, 1991, Catheryn (Mrs MILLBOURN), da. of (__) KINDERSLEY.

[ALASTAIR GRANVILLE GORDON, *styled* EARL OF ABOYNE, *b.* 26 July 1973; ed. at Harrow.]

APPENDIXES

APPENDIX B

page 694,
line 21, for 'George' read 'Richard'

page 695,
line 15, after 'Hastings' add '?'

APPENDIX F

page 706,
note (a), after 'Charles II' add 'Two of the fourteen listed here, Anne Palmer and Barbara (Benedicta) FitzRoy, are queried in *Geneal. Mag.*, vol. 22, 1987, p. 246.'

VOLUME 7

HUSSEE

page 5,
line 1, after 'h.' add 'ap.'
line 5, after 'MORTIMER,' add '[1st LORD MORTIMER]'

page 6,
line 2, after 'Notts.' add ', who *d.* 3 July 1383.'

HYLTON

page 26,
line 17, for 'Margaret' read 'Constance, da. of Piers, 4th LORD MAULEY, by Constance,'
line 19, after 'Holderness' add '[3rd LORD SUTTON OF HOLDERNESS]'

page 29,
line 6, for 'elder 'read 'yr.(aa)'
note (aa) She was not her father's elder da. despite his *Inq. p. m.*, see F.W. Ragg, in *Trans. Cumb. and Westm. Arch. Soc.*, N.S., vol. xiii, p. 226.
note (c), after '48' add 'in which the marriages of his das. are reversed'

page 30,
note (b), line 6, after '226).' add 'William Hylton, apparently without success, tried several times to divorce Margery on the grounds of consanguinity (*Cal. Papal Reg.*, vol. xiii, part 2, 1471–84, 1955, pp. 661–2. *Ex inform.* W.E. Hampton.)'

page 34,
line 29, after 'intestate' add '(Admon. 8 Apr. 1708)' and for '16 Apr. 1712(d)' read '25 Nov. 1707'
note (d), delete all detail

page 35,
line 2, after 's. and h.' add '*bap.* 6 Jan. 1696/7' [Washington Parish Register]
line 5, for '27 Apr. 1699' read '10 Apr. 1701' [Washington Parish Register. His elder br. John was *bur.*, aged 5, 12 Jan. 1699/1700]
note (a), line 1, for '(1)' read '(1) Dorothy, *bap.* 1 Jan. 1695/6, who *d.* unm. Aug. 1753.'
line 2, for 'who *m.*' read '17 Feb. 1697/8, who *m.*, 13 Jan. 1723/4'
line 4, after '*m.*' add '(bond, 20 May 1726)'
line 7, after 'Cumberland' add 'She *d.* at Croft Hall, Cumberland, 8 June and was *bur.* at Thursby, Cumberland, 11 June 1756, aged 50.'
note (b), line 2, for '1st' read '2nd'

page 37,
line 7, after '(a)' add 'He *d.* 26 May 1945. His widow *d.* 27 Aug. 1962.'

line 8, line to read as follows

IV. 1945. 4. WILLIAM GEORGE HERVEY (JOLIFFE), BARON HYLTON OF HYLTON AND OF PETERSFIELD, 1st s. and h., *b.* 2 Dec. 1898

line 12, for ']' read 'He *m.*, 14 Jan. 1931, Lady Perdita Rose Mary, da. of Raymond ASQUITH and sister of Julian Edward George (ASQUITH), 2nd EARL OF OXFORD AND ASQUITH. He *d.* 14 Nov. 1967. His widow was living 1995.'

V. 1967. 5. RAYMOND HERVEY (JOLIFFE), BARON HYLTON OF HYLTON AND OF PETERSFIELD, 1st s. and h., *b.* 13 June 1932; ed. at Eton and Oxford (Trin. Coll.); *m.*, 29 June 1966, Joanna Ida Elizabeth, 1st da. of Andrew de Ramon Dalzell BERTODANO.

[WILLIAM HENRY MARTIN JOLIFFE, 1st s. and h. ap., *b.* 1 Apr. 1967; ed. at Ampleforth and R.A.C., Cirencester.]

IDDESLEIGH

page 43,
line 3, delete '([a])'
line 15, after 'Pyne' add 'His widow *d.* 20 at Prince's Gate and was *bur.* 24 Sep. 1936 at Upton Pyne afsd.'
after line 15 add as follows

III. 1927. 3. HENRY STAFFORD (NORTHCOTE), EARL OF IDDESLEIGH, &c., nephew and h. being eldest surv. s. and h. male of Rev. John STAFFORD, by Hilda Cardew, 2nd da. of Very Rev. Frederic William FARRAR, Dean of Canterbury, which John was 3rd s. of the 2nd Earl, *b.* 19 Nov. 1901; ed. at Rugby and Oxford (Magdalen Coll.); *m.*, 14 May 1930, at Westm. Cath., Elizabeth Susan Angela Mary, 1st da. of Frederic Sawrey Archibald LOWNDES He *d.* 16 Feb. 1970. His widow *d.* 1991.

IV. 1970. 4. STAFFORD HENRY (NORTHCOTE), EARL OF IDDESLEIGH, &c., 1st s. and h., *b.* 14 July 1932; ed. at Downside; *m.*, 29 July 1955, Maria Luisa, CONDESA DEL REAL AGRADO, da. of Don Gonzalez ALVAREZ-BUILLA Y ALVERA.

[JOHN STAFFORD NORTHCOTE, *styled* VISCOUNT ST. CYRES, s. and h. ap., *b.* 15 Feb. 1957; ed. at Downside and R.A.C., Cirencester; *m.*, 1983, Fiona Caroline Elizabeth, da. of Paul Alan Campbell WAKEFIELD of Barcelona, Spain.]

note ([a]), delete all detail

ILCHESTER

page 48,
line 35, for 'was living 1928' read '*d.* 25 Oct. 1935.'

line 36, line to read as follows

VI. 1905. 6. GILES STEPHEN HOLLAND (FOX-STRANGWAYS), EARL OF ILCHESTER, &c., *b.* 31 May 1874, *styled* LORD STAVORDALE 1874–1905;

page 49,
lines 4–5, delete from 'Having' to 'work.([a])]' and replace by 'She *d.* 14 Jan. 1956. He *d.* 29 Oct. 1959.'

VII. 1959. 7. EDWARD HENRY CHARLES JAMES (FOX-STRANGWAYS), EARL OF ILCHESTER, &c., 1st s. and h., *b.* 1 Oct. 1905, *styled* LORD STAVORDALE 1905–59; ed. at Eton and Oxford (Ch. Ch.); *m.*, 27 Apr. 1931, Helen Elizabeth, twin da. of Cyril Augustus WARD, Capt., R.N. He *d. s.p.m.s.* 21 Aug. 1964. His widow *d.* 1970.

[GILES HENRY HOLLAND FOX-STRANGWAYS, *styled* LORD STRANGWAYS, 1st s. and h. ap., *b.* 7 May 1934. He *d.* as a result of an accident, 2 Sep. 1947.]

[CHARLES STEPHEN FOX-STRANGWAYS, *styled* LORD STRANGWAYS from 1947, 2nd surv. s. and h. ap., *b.* 6 May 1938; ed. at Eton. He was *k.* on active service in Cyprus 8 July 1958.]

VIII. 1964. 8. WALTER ANGELO (FOX-STRANGWAYS), EARL OF ILCHESTER, &c., distant cousin and h., being 1st s. of Maurice Walter F-S (*d.* 27 May 1938), by Louisa Blanche, da. of Major Gen. George R. PHILLIPS, which Maurice Walter was 2nd s. of Col. Walter Aston F-S (*d.* 26 Feb. 1885), by Harriet Elizabeth, 2nd da. of John Edward BULLER of Enfield, co. Midx., which Walter Aston was 2nd s. of Rev. Henry F-S (*d.* 25 Feb. 1860), by Hester Eleonora, da. of James BULLER, which Henry was 3rd s. of Rev. Charles Redlynch FOX-STRANGWAYS (*d.* 4 Nov. 1836), by Jane, da. of Rev. Dr HAINES, which Charles was 3rd s. of 1st Earl of Ilchester. He was *b.* 24 Sep. 1887; ed. at Charterhouse and Cambridge (Pembroke Coll.); *m.*, 8 Apr. 1916, Laure Georgine Emilie, da. of Evanghelos Georgios MAZARAKI. She *d.* 1970. He *d.* 4 Oct. 1970.

IX. 1970. 9. MAURICE VIVIAN DE TOUFFREVILLE (FOX-STRANGWAYS), EARL OF ILCHESTER, &c., 1st s. and h., *b.* 1 Apr. 1920; ed. at Kingsbridge Sch.; *m.*, 29 Nov. 1941, Diana Mary Elizabeth, 1st da. of George Frederick SIMPSON of Cassington, Oxford.

note ([a]), delete all detail

INCHIQUIN

page 57,
line 8, after 'afsd.' add 'He *d.* 9 at Dromoland Castle, co. Clare, and was *bur.* 13 Dec. 1929 at Kilnasoolagh, co. Clare. His widow *d.* 5 June 1940.'
line 9, line to read as follows

XVI. 1929. 16. DONOUGH EDWARD FOSTER (O'BRIEN), BARON INCHIQUIN, 1st s. and h., *b.* 5 Jan. 1897;

line 17, for ']' read 'He *d. s.p.m.* 19 Oct. 1968. His widow *d.* 1973.'

XVII. 1968. 17. PHAEDRIG LUCIUS AMBROSE (O'BRIEN), BARON INCHIQUIN, br. and h., *b.* 4 Apr. 1900; ed. at Eton and Oxford (Magdalen Coll.) and London Univ., Royal Sch. of Mines; *m.*, 19 Feb. 1945, Vera Maud, da. of Rev. Clifton Samuel WINTER of Winton House, Dawlish, co. Devon. He *d. s.p.* 20 May 1982. His widow was living 1995.

XVIII. 1982. 18. CONOR MYLES JOHN (O'BRIEN), BARON INCHIQUIN, nephew and h., being s. and h. of Fionn Myles Maryons O'BRIEN, by Josephine Reine, da. of Joseph Eugene BEMBARON of Long Ditton, co. Surrey, which Fionn was 3rd s. of 15th Baron Inchiquin. He was *b.* 17 July 1943; ed. at Eton; *m.*, 1988, Helen O'Farrell, da. of Gerald Fitzgerald O'FARRELL of Longford, co. Longford.

INGHAM

page 60,
line 16, after 'h.' add 'ap.'

page 61,
line 1, after 'h.' add 'ap.'

page 64,
line 24, after 'Howard' add '(yr. s. of Thomas 2nd Duke of Norfolk)'

INVERCLYDE

page 67,
line 26, line to read as follows

III. 1905. 3. JAMES CLELAND (BURNS), BARON INVERCLYDE, &c., br. and h., *b.* 14 Feb. 1864;

lines 32–3, delete from 'Having' to 'son.([d])]'

IV. 1919. 4. JOHN ALAN (BURNS), BARON INVERCLYDE, and a Baronet, only s. and h., *b.* 12 Dec. 1897; ed. at Eton and R.M.C., Sandhurst. Served in WW1 as Lieut. Scots Guards. He *m.* 23 Nov. 1926, at St. Margaret's, Westm., Olive Sylvia, yr. da. of Arthur SAINSBURY, of 2 Gloucester House, Park Lane. This marriage was diss. by divorce in 1928 and he *m.* 2ndly, 21 Mar. 1929, June, da. of Walter Howard TRIPP. This marriage was in turn diss. by divorce in 1933. He *d. s.p.* 17 June 1957 when his titles became *extinct*.

note ([d]), delete all detail

ISLES

page 77,
note ([d]), line 9 (on page 78), delete from 'The' to 'are heirs male' and replace by 'Following the decision of the Court of Session in 1910, the Baronets Bosville Macdonald of Sleat are heirs male. See vol. vii, p. 339, note ([a]), *sub* MACDONALD OF SLEAT.'

IVEAGH

page 79,
line 1, line to read as follows

II. 1927. 2. RUPERT EDWARD CECIL LEE (GUINNESS), EARL OF IVEAGH, 1st s. and h., *b.* 29 Mar. 1874 at 5 Berkeley Sq., *styled* VISCOUNT ELVEDEN 1919–27;

lines 13–14, delete from 'Having' to 'work.]' and replace by 'She *d.* 16 Feb. 1966. He *d.* 14 Sep. 1967.'

[ARTHUR ONSLOW EDWARD GUINNESS, *styled* Viscount Elveden, 2nd but 1st surv s. and h. ap., *b.* 8 May 1912; ed. at Eton and Cambridge (Trin. Coll.); *m.*, 22 July 1936, at St. Margaret's, Gdns., Lady Elizabeth Cecilia, yr. da. of Richard Granville (HARE), 4th EARL OF LISTOWEL. He *d. v.p.* 8 Feb. 1945, being *k.* in action in Holland. His widow *m.* 2ndly, 30 Sep. 1947, Edward Rory More O'FARRELL, who *d.* 1990. She *d.* 1990.]

III. 1967. 3. ARTHUR FRANCIS BENJAMIN (GUINNESS), EARL OF IVEAGH, &c., grandson and h., being only s. and h. of Arthur Onslow Edward GUINNESS and Lady Elizabeth abovenamed. He was *b.* 20 May 1937; ed. at Eton and Cambridge (Trin. Coll.); *m.*, 12 Mar. 1963, Miranda Daphne Jane, da. of Major Michael SMILEY of Castle Fraser, Kemnay, co. Aberdeen. This marriage was diss. by divorce in 1984 (she was still living in 1995). He *d.* 18 June 1992.

IV. 1992. 4. ARTHUR EDWARD RORY (GUINNESS), EARL OF IVEAGH, &c., 1st s. and h., *b.* 10 Aug. 1969.

JEFFREYS

page 83,
line 14, for 'Bewsay' read 'Bewsey'
line 15, for '1648' read '1644' [*TLS.*, Aug. 1929, p. 607.]

page 84,
line 7, for 'Funmon' read 'Fonmon'

JERSEY

page 93,
line 24, for 'was living 1928' read '*d.* 22 May 1945'

line 25, line to read as follows

VIII. 1915. 8. GEORGE HENRY ROBERT (CHILD-VILLIERS), EARL OF JERSEY, &c., 1st s. and h., *b.* at 7 Norfolk Cresecent, London, 2 June, and *bap.* 3 Aug. 1873 at all Saints, Middleton Stoney; *styled* VISCOUNT VILLIERS 1873–1905;

line 34, after 'Stoney.' add '(b)'
lines 34–5, delete from 'Having' to 'work.(b)'

page 94,
line 3, for ']' read 'He *d.* 14 Apr. 1945. She *d.* 12 Jan. 1947.'
line 4, line to read as follows

IX. 1923. 9. GEORGE FRANCIS (CHILD-VILLIERS), EARL OF JERSEY, &c., 1st s. and h.,

lines 6–7, delete from 'Having' to 'work.]' and replace by '*Styled* VISCOUNT GRANDISON, 1915–23; ed. at Eton and Oxford (Ch. Ch.); *m.* 1stly, 12 Jan. 1932, at St. Margaret's, Gdns., Patricia Kenneth, da. of Kenneth RICHARDS of Cowcumbla, Cootamundra, New South Wales. This marriage was diss. by divorce in 1937 and he *m.* 2ndly, 30 July 1937, Virginia, da. of James E. CHERRILL of the U.S.A. and formerly wife of Archibald Alexander LEACH (Cary Grant). This marriage was in turn diss. by divorce in 1946 and he *m.* 3rdly, 16 Oct. 1947, Bianca Maria Luciana Adriana, 1st da. of Enrico MOTTIRONI of Via Goffredo Casalis, Turin.'

[GEORGE HENRY CHILD-VILLIERS, *styled* VISCOUNT VILLIERS, s. and h. ap. by 3rd wife, *b.* 29 Aug. 1948; ed. at Eton and Millfield; *m.* 1stly, 22 Dec. 1969, Verna, 2nd da. of Kenneth A. STOTT, of St. Mary, Jersey. This marriage was diss. by divorce in 1973 and he *m.* 2ndly, 1974, Sacha Jane Hooper, da. of Peter Hooper VALPY of Jersey and formerly wife of K.F. LAUDER. This marriage was in turn diss. by divorce in 1988 and he *m.* 3rdly, 1992, Stephanie Louise, da. of John Ian PENMAN.]

KEITH

page 98,
lines 3–4, delete from 'possibly' to '1439/40' and replace by 'before 1451'
lines 4–5, for 'His 2nd s. William' read 'He'

KELLIE

page 105,
line 10, for 'Col. (__) YOUNGSON' read 'Lieut. Col. William YOUNGSON, 6th Madras Native Infantry'
line 12, after 'widow' add ', who was *b.* 25 Nov. 1813,' and after '81' add 'and was *bur.* 18 July at Alloa' [She was called Eliza in her father's will. All *ex inform.* C. Roy Hudleston]

page 106,
line 16, after '1868.' add 'She *d.* 16 Dec. 1938. He *d.* 3 June 1955.'
line 25, after 'WYTHES' add 'He *d. v.p.* 3 May 1953. His widow *d.* 22 Nov. 1967.'

XV. 1955. 15. JOHN FRANCIS HERVEY (ERSKINE), EARL OF MAR [1565], EARL OF KELLIE [1619] &c., grandson and h., being 1st s. and h. of John Francis Ashley ERSKINE and Marjorie abovenamed, *b.* 15 Feb. 1921; ed. at Eton and Cambridge (Trin. Coll.); *m.*, 24 Apr. 1948, Pansy Constance, yst. da. of Gen. Sir Andrew Nichol THORNE, K.C.B., C.M.G., D.S.O. of Reading, Berks. He *d.* 22 Dec. 1993. His widow was living 1995.

XVI. 1993. 16. JAMES THORNE (ERSKINE), EARL OF MAR [1565], EARL OF KELLIE [1619], &c., 1st s. and h., *b.* 10 Mar. 1949; ed. at Eton; *m.*, 1974, Mary Irene, yr. da. of Dougal MacDougall KIRK of Edinburgh and formerly wife of Roderick James MOONEY.

note ([c]), delete all detail

KENDAL

page 108,
line 21, for 'D'ALBRECHT, his wife' read 'da. of Arnald AMANJEU, SIRE OF ALBRET' [See vol. viii, p. 128, *sub* LONGUEVILLE.]

page 110,
line 11, after '*m.*' add '*c.* 1447'
lines 12–13, delete from 'and said' to 'POLE' and replace by 'da. of Sir Thomas KERDESTON by Elizabeth, da. of Michael DE LA POLE, 2nd EARL OF SUFFOLK'
note ([c]), delete all detail and replace by 'Charles M. Hansen, *Geneal. Mag.*, vol. 22, 1988, pp. 373–7.'

page 111,
note ([d]), line 9 (on page 112), after 'Darlington.' add 'In fact half-sister to George I, see *sub* DARLINGTON'

page 112,
note ([a]), delete all detail and replace by 'She had three daughters by the king, *viz*, (1) Anna Louise Sophie, *b.* 1692, *m.*, 1707, Ernst August Philip von der Bussche-Ippenburg, divorced before 1714; 1722, Reichsgraffin von Delitz, *d.* 11 Nov. 1773, being then called "the Hon. Lady Dallet" (*i.e.* Delitz) in the *London Mag.* of 1773; (2) Petronille Melusine, *b.* 1693, *suo jure* Countess of Walsingham (so *cr.* 1722), who *m.* Philip (Stanhope), Earl of Chesterfield; (3) Margaret Gertrude, *b.* 1701, *m.* Albrecht Wolfgang, Graf von Schaumberg-Lippe, she *d.* 1726.'

KENMARE

page 116,
line 24, line to read as follows

EARLDOM, Etc. [I.]
V.
BARONY [U.K.]
IV.
1905

5 and 3. VALENTINE CHARLES (BROWNE), EARL OF KENMARE, &c., 1st s. and h., *b.* 1 Dec. 1860, in Belgrave Sq., *styled* VISCOUNT CASTLEROSSE 1871–1905;

lines 32–3, delete from 'Having' to 'work.]' and replace by 'He *d.* 14 Nov. 1941. His widow *d.* 21 May 1944.'

EARLDOM, Etc. [I.]
VI.
BARONY [U.K.]
V.
1941

6 and 4. VALENTINE EDWARD CHARLES (BROWNE), EARL OF KENMARE, &c., 1st s. and h., *b.* 29 May 1891; ed. at Cambridge (Trin. Coll.); *m.* 1stly, 16 May 1928, Doris, da. of Edward DE LAVIGNE. This marriage was diss. by divorce in 1938 (she *d.* 12 Dec. 1942) and he *m.* 2ndly, 26 Jan. 1943, Enid Maude, da. of Charles LINDEMAN of Sydney, Australia and widow of, 1stly, Roderick CAMERON, 2ndly of Brig. Gen. Frederick Hart CAVENDISH and 3rdly of Marmaduke (FURNESS), 1st VISCOUNT FURNESS. He *d. s.p.* 20 Sep. 1943.

EARLDOM, Etc. [I.]
VII.
BARONY [U.K.]
VI.
1943

7 and 5. GERALD RALPH DESMOND (BROWNE), EARL OF KENMARE, &c., surv. br. and h., *b.* 20 Dec. 1898; ed. at Oratory Sch. He *d.* unm. and *s.p.* 14 Feb. 1952 when all his titles became *extinct*.

KENMURE

page 120,
line 8, after 'WILLIAM' add 'EDWARD'
lines 8–9, for '*b.* about 1748' read '*bap.* 1 May 1748 at his father's house Greenlaw, Kirk Andrews on Eden, co. Cumberland'
line 18, for '*b.* 1750' read '*bap.* 23 June 1749 at Greenlaw afsd.' [*ex inform.* C. Roy Hudleston]

KENSINGTON

page 124,
line 11, after '1878.' add 'She *d.* 25 and was *bur.* 29 Mar. 1934 at St. Bride's, co. Pembroke. He *d.* 4 Mar. 1938.'
line 12, delete all detail and replace as follows

BARONY [I.]
VII.
BARONY [U.K.]
IV.
1938

7 and 4. WILLIAM (EDWARDES), BARON KENSINGTON, &c., 1st s. and h., *b.* 15 May 1904; ed. at Eton and R.M.C., Sandhurst. He *d.* unm. and *s.p.* 19 Aug. 1981.

BARONY [I.]
VIII.
BARONY [U.K.]
V.
1981

8 and 5. HUGH IVOR (EDWARDES), BARON KENSINGTON, &c., nephew and h., being s. of Hugh Owen EDWARDES (*d.* 29 June 1937), by Angela Dorothea, da. of Lieut. Col. Eustace SHEARMAN, which Hugh Owen was 2nd s. of 6th Baron Kensington. He was *b.* 24 Nov.

1933; ed. at Eton; *m.*, 18 Mar. 1961, Juliet Elizabeth Massy, da. of Alexander Massy ANDERSON.

[WILLIAM OWEN ALEXANDER EDWARDES, 1st s. and h. ap., *b.* 21 July 1964; *m.*, 1991, Marie Hélène Anne Véronique, 1st da. of Jean-Alain LALOUETTE of Vacoas, Mauritius.]

KENT

page 149,
line 7, for '1347/8' read '1348/9' and for '21 Edw. III' read '22 Edw. III'
line 14, after 'Guillaume,' add '1st EARL OF CAMBRIDGE, also'
note (e), after 'guardant' add 'or'

page 150,
line 11, for 'in or before 1339' read 'spring 1340'
note (f), before 'See' add 'Karl P. Wentersdorf, *J. Med. Hist.*, vol. 5, 1979, p. 210.'

page 151,
line 15, for '1346' read 'before 10 Feb. 1340/1'
note (j), line 7, after 'Library.)' add 'See below, *sub* SALISBURY, vol. xi, p. 390, note (a). For a full discussion of the marriages of Joan of Kent, see Karl P. Wentersdorf, *J. Med. Hist.*, vol. 5, 1979, pp. 203–31.'

page 154,
note (e), line 7, after 'arms.' add 'See also "Holand Heraldry", H.S. London, *N&Q*, vol. 195, pp. 24–8.'

page 155,
note (b), for '71' read '11'

page 165,
line 10, for 'before Jan. 1458/9' read 'probably before 1440'
note (g), delete all detail and replace by 'PRO, SC 6/1119/4, m. 3d and SC 6/1119/5, dated 1444, where their "sons" and two daughters are mentioned.'

page 166,
line 7, for 'Joan, da.' read 'Joan, sister of Elizabeth, the Queen Consort, da., and (in her issue) coh.', and for 'WIDEVILE read 'Widevill'
line 10, for '27 Nov.' read '26 June'
note (f), line 17, after 'See' add 'R. Ian Jack, "The alleged daughter of Sir Anthony Grey", *Geneal. Mag.*, vol. 14, 1962, pp. 56–9, and'
note (g), delete all detail and replace by '*Cal. Pat. Rolls, 1476–85*, p. 567; *Privy Purse Expenses*, Nicolas, p. 157 (where his brother George is described as heir to their father)'

page 167,
line 16, for 'in or after 1483' read 'June 1480, when he was given clothes against his marriage by Edward IV, 26 June 1480.' [See note (g), above.]
line 18, for 'after '12 Feb. 1482/3' read 'before 8 Feb. 1480' [*Cal. Fine Rolls, 1476–85*, no. 517]
line 19, for 'WIDEVILE' read 'WIDEVILL' and after 'by' add 'Jacqueline or'

line 20, for 'ADD' read ',' and after 'CONVERSANO' add 'AND BRIENNE'
line 23, for 'da. of Sir Walter DEVEREUX' read 'sister of Walter (DEVEREUX), 1st LORD FERRERS, da. of Sir Walter DEVEREUX, of Weobley, co. Hereford'

page 171,
line 9, for 'about 1533' read '1553–4' [See WILLOUGHBY D'ERESBY, vol. xii, part 2, p. 674.]

page 185,
after line 9 add as follows

DUKEDOM. III. } 1934 1. *H.R.H.* GEORGE EDWARD ALEXANDER EDMUND, Prince of the United Kingdom of Great Britain and Ireland, 4th s. of KING GEORGE V, by Victoria Mary Augusta Louise Olga Pauline Claudine Agnes, only da. of *H.H.* the DUKE OF TECK. He was *cr.*, 12 Oct. 1934, DUKE OF KENT, &c. See vol. xiii, p. 541 and below, p. 720.

KENYON

page 188,
line 8, for 'was living 1928' read '*d.* 25 Nov. 1927.'
line 21, after '1927.' add 'She *d.* 26 Feb. 1965.'
lines 22–4, delete all detail and replace as follows

V. 1927. 5. LLOYD (TYRELL-KENYON), LORD KENYON, BARON OF GREDINGTON, &c., 1st s. and h., *b.* 13 Sep. 1917; ed. at Eton and Cambridge (Magdalene Coll.); *m.*, 3 June 1946, Leila Mary, da. of John Wyndham COOKSON, Cmdr. R.N., of Winchelsea, co. Sussex and widow of Hugh William Jardine Ethelston PEEL. He *d.* 16 May 1993. His widow was living 1995.

VI. 1993. 6. LLOYD (TYRELL-KENYON), LORD KENYON, &c., 1st s. and h., *b.* 13 July 1947; ed. at Eton and Cambridge (Magdalene Coll.); *m.*, 1971, Sally Carolyn, 1st da. of Jack Frank Page MATTHEWS of Bury St. Edmunds, co. Suffolk.

[LLOYD NICHOLAS TYRELL-KENYON, 1st s. and h. ap., *b.* 9 Apr. 1972; ed. at Eton and Manchester Univ.]

KERDESTON

page 193,
line 7, after 'FELTON,' add '[3rd LORD FELTON]'

page 198,
note (b), line 3, after 'Robsart' add 'The first wife of Thomas Kerdeston was Elizabeth, widow of Sir Edward Burnell and da. of Michael (de la Pole), 2nd Earl of Suffolk, by whom he had a daughter, Margaret, wife of Jean de la Foix, Captal de Buch and Earl of Kendal (which see)' [*ex. inform.* Charles M. Hansen]

page 199,
line 7 of chart, for '. . . .' read 'Margaret'
line 8 of chart, for '1447' read '1446'

KERRY

page 206,
line 17, after 'GERALDINE, add '(FITZGERALD), 4th EARL OF DESMOND [I.],'

page 208,
line 31, after 'Carbery.' add 'She *m.* 3rdly before 27 July 1551, Edmund (BUTLER), 1st BARON DUNBOYNE [I.], who *d.* May 1567, and 4thly, in 1568, as his 3rd wife, Richard (BOURKE), 2nd EARL OF CLANRICARDE [I.]. She was living *circa* 1580.' [See *Irish Genealogist*, vol. ii, p. 136.]

KESTEVEN

page 217,
lines 4–5, delete from 'He was' to 'work.([b])' and replace by 'His widow *d.* 13 Apr. 1941.'

III. 1915. 3. THOMAS CAREW (TROLLOPE), BARON KESTEVEN OF CASEWICK [1868], and a Baronet [1642], nephew and h. male, being 1st s. of Robert Cranmer TROLLOPE (who was 2nd s. of the 1st Baron), by Ethel Mary, da. of G.H.W. CAREW, of Crowcombe Court, Somerset, *b.* 1 May 1891; served in WW1([b]) as Capt., Lincolnshire Yeomanry. He *d.* unm., 5 Nov. 1915, of wounds received in action on a transport off the Algerian coast, when the peerage became *extinct*, but the Baronetcy devolved on his cousin.

note ([b]), lines 1–5, delete from 'Thomas' to 'cousin.'

KILDARE

page 219,
note ([c]), line 4, for '*Foedera*' read 'Rymer'
lines 22–4, delete from 'According' to 'he' and replace by 'He'
line 25, after 'dated)' add 'although this surrender is unlikely to have been due to this dispute. See VESCY, vol. xii, part 2, p. 282, note ([a])'

page 221,
line 7, for 'of John' read 'or sister of Alexander'

page 222,
line 20, after 'Justiciar' add '[1st LORD DARCY]'

page 223,
line 7, after 'h.,' add ', *b.* 7 June 1321([ca])'
note ([ca]) See G.W. Watson, "Ormond and Kildare", *Misc. Gen. et Heraldica*, 5th ser., vol. 8, 1932–4, p. 230.

page 224,
line 20, after '*m.*,' add '[mar. cont. 12 Nov.],'

page 225,
line 1, for 'in' read '15 Aug.' [G.W. Watson, *op. cit.*]

page 227,
line 12, delete from '11 Dec. 1432' and replace by '13 Oct. 1432'
note (h), line 1, before 'Inquisition' add '*Cal. Ormond Deeds*, vol. 3, 1413–1509, 1935, pp. 83–9, an inquisition made at his death. An'
line 2, after 'f. 22' add 'gives 11 Dec.'

page 228,
lines 9–13, delete from 'John' to 'dead' and replace by 'It seems possible that John, 6th Earl, survived until the succession of Thomas, 7th Earl. A John FitzMorris, of Castletown and Kildrought, was certainly carrying out land transactions in 1436. [Leinster Papers, P.R.O. Northern Ireland, vol. 3, D3078/1/1/3, ff. 7–7a.]'
line 22, delete from ', but' to '(d)'
note (d), delete all detail

page 229,
note (o), after 'dispensation' add 'This is possibly corroborated by a statute (Irish Statute Rolls), showing that he was not yet 21 in 1470 (Donough Bryan, *Gerald FitzGerald, the Great Earl of Kildare*, 1933, p. 267).'

page 232,
line 7, delete 'Sir'
line 9, for 'BARON' read 'LORD'
note (f), line 8, delete 'Sir'

page 239,
line 11, for 'Mary' read 'Katherine' [M.I., Westm. Abbey]
note (f), line 6, for '29 July' read '26 June'
line 7, for 'by Privy Seal, *cr.*' read 'in a Privy Seal, recognised as'

page 242,
line 19, for '29 July' read '26 June'

page 243,
note (b), line 3, after 'text.' add 'See vol. x, p. 18, note (e).'

KILLANIN

page 247,
line 12, line to read as follows

II. 1901. 2. MARTIN HENRY FITZPATRICK (MORRIS), BARON KILLANIN, 1st s. and h., *b.* 22 July 1867;

lines 16–18, delete from 'Having' to 'nephew.(c)]'

III. 1927. 3. MICHAEL (MORRIS), BARON KILLANIN, nephew and h., being 1st and only s. of George Henry MORRIS, 2nd s. of the 1st Baron (*d.* 1 Sep. 1914, near Villers Cotteret), by Dora Maryan, 2nd da. of James Wesley HALL of Melbourne, Victoria, Australia. He was *b.* 30 July 1914; ed. at Eton, the Sorbonne and Cambridge (Magdalene Coll.); *m.*, 17 Dec. 1945, Mary Sheila Cathcart, da. of Rev. Canon Douglas Lyall Cathcart DUNLOP of Oughterard, co. Galway.

[GEORGE REDMOND FITZPATRICK MORRIS, 1st s. and h. ap., *b.* 26 Jan. 1947; ed. at Gonzaga Coll., Dublin, Ampleforth and Trin. Coll., Dublin; *m.*, 1972, Pauline, da. of Geoffrey HORTON of Cabinteely, co. Dublin.]

KILMAINE

page 256,
line 34, line to read as follows

VI. 1907. 5. JOHN EDWARD DEAN (BROWNE), BARON KILMAINE, &c., only child and h. male, *b.* 18 Mar. 1878,

page 257,
line 2, delete '(a)'
lines 3–4, delete from 'Having' to 'work.]' and replace by 'He *d.* 27 Aug. 1946. His widow *d.* 1 July 1957.'

VII. 1946. 6. JOHN FRANCIS ARCHIBALD (BROWNE), BARON KILMAINE [I.], also a Baronet [N.S.], 1st and only surv. s. and h., *b.* 22 Sep. 1902; ed. at Winchester and Oxford (Magdalen Coll.); *m.*, 12 July 1930, Wilhelmina Phyllis, da. of Scott ARNOTT of Brasted, co. Kent. He *d.* 26 July 1978. His widow was still living 1995.

VIII. 1978. 7. JOHN DAVID HENRY (BROWNE), BARON KILMAINE, s. and h., *b.* 2 Apr. 1948; ed. at Eton; *m.*, 1978, Linda, yr. da. of Dennis ROBINSON of Budleigh Salterton, co. Devon.

[JOHN FRANCIS SANDFORD BROWNE, s. and h. ap., *b.* 4 Apr. 1983.]

KILMARNOCK

page 259,
after line 19 add as follows

VI. 1941. 6. GILBERT ALAN ROWLAND (HAY, *later* BOYD), BARON KILMARNOCK, br. and h. male of Josslyn Victor (HAY), 22nd EARL OF ERROLL (see above, *sub* ERROLL). He was *b.* 15 Jan. 1903; ed. at Cheltenham. By warrant of the Lord Lyon, 1941, he assumed the name of Boyd in lieu of that of Hay; *m.* 1stly, 12 July 1926, Rosemary Sibell, 1st da. of Ivor Churchill (GUEST), 1st VISCOUNT WIMBORNE. This marriage was diss. by divorce in 1955 and he *m.* 2ndly, 17 May 1955, Denise Aubrey Doreen, da. of Major Lewis COKER. He *d.* 15 May 1975. His widow *d.* 1989.

VII. 1975. 7. ALASTAIR IVOR GILBERT (BOYD), BARON KILMARNOCK, s. and h., *b.* 11 May 1927; ed. at Bradfield and Cambridge (King's Coll.); *m.* 1stly, 10 Sep. 1954, Diana Mary Grant (Mrs Hawkins), da. of Donald Grant GIBSON. This marriage was diss. by divorce in 1969 (she *d.* 1975), and he *m.* 2ndly, 1977, Hilary Ann, formerly wife of Sir Kingsley Amis, da. of Leonard SIDNEY.

[CHARLES JAMES EDWARD BOYD, s. and h. ap. by 2nd wife, was *b.* 1972.]

KILMOREY

page 264,
line 28, line to read as follows

EARLDOM [I.] IV. VISCOUNTCY [I.] XV. } 1915 4 and 15. FRANCIS CHARLES ADELBERT HENRY (NEEDHAM), EARL OF KILMOREY, &c., 1st s. and h., *b.* 26 Nov. 1883, at Gordon House, Isleworth, Midx, *styled* VISCOUNT NEWRY AND MORNE 1883–1915;

page 265,
lines 3–4, delete from 'Having' to 'work.]' and replace by 'He *d. s.p.m.* 11 Jan. 1961. His widow *d.* 1985.'

EARLDOM [I.] V. VISCOUNTCY [I.] XVI. } 1961 5 and 16. FRANCIS JACK RICHARD PATRICK (NEEDHAM), EARL OF KILMOREY, &c., nephew and h., being 1st s. of Francis Edward NEEDHAM (*d.* 24 Oct. 1955), by Blanche Esther, da. of Richard COMBE of Farnham, Surrey, which Francis Edward was 2nd s. of 3rd Earl of Kilmorey. He was *b.* 4 Oct. 1915; ed. at Stowe and R.M.C., Sandhurst; *m.*, 28 Apr. 1941, Helen Bridget, yst. da. of Sir Lionel FAUDEL-PHILLIPS, Bart. He *d.* 11 Apr. 1977. His widow *m.* 2ndly, Harold William ELLIOTT of Godalming, Surrey. This marriage was diss. in 1990. She was still living 1995.

EARLDOM [I.] VI. VISCOUNTCY [I.] XVII. } 1977 6 and 17. RICHARD FRANCIS (NEEDHAM), EARL OF KILMOREY, &c., 1st s. and h., *b.* 29 Jan. 1942; ed. at Eton; M.P., does not use title nor used courtesy title; *m.*, 5 June 1965, Sigrid Julianne, da. of Ernst THIESSEN of Hamburg, Germany.

[ROBERT FRANCIS JOHN NEEDHAM, *styled* VISCOUNT NEWRY AND MOURNE, 1st s. and h. ap., *b.* 30 May 1966; ed. at Eton and Oxford (Lady Margaret Hall) and Imperial Coll., London; *m.*, 1991, Laura Mary, only da. of Michael TREGASKIS of Cosham, Hants.]

KIMBERLEY

page 270,
line 17, for '1867' read '1866'
line 28, line to read as follows

EARLDOM. II. BARONY IV.	1902	2 and 4. JOHN (WODEHOUSE), EARL OF KIMBERLEY, &c., s. and h., *b.* 10 Dec. 1848, in Montagu Sq., Marylebone, *styled* LORD WODEHOUSE 1866–1902.

lines 33–4, delete from 'Having' to 'work.(c)]' and replace by 'He *d.* 7 Jan. 1932.'

EARLDOM. III. BARONY V.	1932	3 and 5. JOHN (WODEHOUSE), EARL OF KIMBERLEY and BARON WODEHOUSE OF KIMBERLEY, 1st and only surv. s. and h., *b.* 11 Nov. 1883; *styled* 1903–32 LORD WODEHOUSE; ed. at Eton and Cambridge (Trin. Coll.). Served in WW1(c) as Capt. 16th Lancers; M.C. He *m.*, 5 May 1922, at Princes Row

Reg. Office, Frances Margaret, da. of Leonard Howard IRBY, and formerly wife of James Fontayne MONTAGU. He *d.* 16 Apr. 1941, being *k.* in an air raid. His widow *d.* 4 Jan. 1950.

EARLDOM. IV. BARONY VI.	1941	4 and 6. JOHN (WODEHOUSE), EARL OF KIMBERLEY, &c., only s. and h., *b.* 12 May 1924; ed. at Eton and Cambridge (Magdalene Coll.); *m.* 1stly, 27 Oct. 1945, Diana Evelyn, da. of Lieut. Col. Sir Piers LEGH, G.C.V.O. This marriage was diss. by divorce in 1952 and he *m.* 2ndly, 9 Feb. 1949,

Carmel June, 3rd da. of Michael Joseph MACGUIRE of Melbourne, Victoria, Australia. This marriage was in turn diss. by divorce in 1952 and he *m.* 3rdly, 15 Sep. 1953, Cynthia Abdy, yr. da. of Eric Abdy COLLINS of Saxmundham, co. Suffolk. This marriage was also diss. by divorce in 1961 and he *m.* 4thly, 7 July 1961, Margaret, da. of Albert SIMONS. In turn this marriage was diss. by divorce in 1965 and he *m.* 5thly, 1970, Gillian, da. of Col. Norman IRELAND-SMITH and formerly wife of John RAW. After yet another divorce in 1982 he *m.* 6thly, 1982, Sarah Jane Hope, 1st da. of Lieut. Col. Christopher D'Arcy Preston CONSETT, D.S.O., M.C.

[JOHN ARMINE WODEHOUSE, *styled* LORD WODEHOUSE, 1st s. and h. ap. by 2nd wife, *b.* 15 Jan. 1951; ed. at Eton and Univ. of East Anglia; *m.*, 1973, Carol Lylie, 1st da. of Raymond Cecil (PALMER), 3rd BARON PALMER.]

note (a), delete all detail and replace by 'Modern historians have a high opinion of Kimberley as a diplomat, as did such an acute observer as Charles Greville, clerk to the Privy Council. Lord Redesdale's low opinion of Kimberley in his *Further Memories*, written 40 years after the event, can now be dismissed. See John Powell, *Liberal by Principle*, 1996, p. 281. I am grateful to Prof. Powell for drawing my attention to this.'

note (b), line 4, after 'Irishwoman' add ' (see A.M.W. Stirling, *The Letter Bag of Lady Elizabeth Spencer-Stanhope*, vol. 2, 1913, p. 217)'

note (c), delete lines 1–3 and (on page 271), lines 1–2, from 'da.' to '1924.'

KINGSALE

page 290,
line 4, for '(__)' read 'Palsgrave' [G.A. Moriarty, *Irish Geneal.*, vol. 2, 1947, pp. 137–40]

page 292,
line 16, for 'Alençons' read 'Alençon'

page 293,
line 4, add at end 'He *d.* 24 Jan. 1931.'
line 5, line to read as follows

XXIX. 1931. 29. MICHAEL WILLIAM ROBERT (DE COURCY), LORD KINGSALE [I.], s. and h., *b.* 26 Sep. 1882.

line 11, delete '(d)'
line 13, for ']' read 'She *d.* 12 Aug. 1946 and he *m.* 2ndly, June 1947, Ruth, da. of Herbert Thomas HOLMES of Reigate, co. Surrey. This marriage was diss. by divorce in 1957. He *d. s.p.m.* 7 Nov. 1969.

[MICHAEL JOHN RANCÉ DE COURCY, 1st s. and h. ap., *b.* 30 Sep. 1907; *m.* 1stly, 31 Aug. 1929, Glory Elizabeth, da. of Alfred Claremont EVANS, Eng. Cmdr., R.N. This marriage was diss. by divorce in 1933 and he *m.* 2ndly, 11 July 1936, Joan, yr. da. of Robert REID of Beckwithshaw, Harrowgate, co. York. He *d.* 18 Aug. 1940, being *k.* by enemy action. His widow *d.* 5 Aug. 1967.]

XXX. 1969. 30. JOHN (DE COURCY), LORD KINGSALE, &c., grandson and h., being s. and h. (posthumous) of Michael John Rancé DE COURCY and his 2nd wife Joan abovenamed. He was *b.* 27 Jan. 1941; ed. at Stowe.

note (d), delete all detail

KINGSTON

page 298,
line 7, after '(b)' add 'Will dat. 27 July (with codicil 17 Dec.), 1689.'

page 301,
note (b), line 1, after 'with' add 'indecent assault with intent to commit'

page 302,
line 2, after 'Corner' add ', and was *bur.* at Brompton Cemetery' [*ex inform.* C. Roy Hudleston]
line 30, after '1872.' add 'He *d.* 11 Jan. 1946. His widow *d.* 18 Apr. 1949.'
line 31, line to read as follows

X. 1946. 10. ROBERT HENRY ETHELBERT (KING-TENISON), EARL OF KINGSTON, &c., s. and h., *b.* 27 Nov. 1897, *styled* VISCOUNT KINGSBOROUGH 1897-1946;

line 34, for ']' read 'He *m.* 1stly, 24 Dec. 1937, Gwyneth Joan, da. of William Howard EVANS of Tenby. co. Pembroke. This marriage was diss. by divorce in 1947 (she *d.* 1987) and he *m.* 2ndly, 29 May 1947, Jean Sinclair, da. of James Lascelles ALEXANDER of Orkney and Aberdeen. He *d.* 17 July 1948. His widow *m.* 2ndly, 1953, Cecil Geoffrey MONSON, who *d.* 1974. She *d.* 1983.

XI. 1948. 11. BARCLAY ROBERT EDWIN (KING-TENISON), EARL OF KINGSTON, &c., only s. and h., *b.* 23 Sep. 1943; ed. at Winchester; *m.* 1stly, 20 Mar. 1965, Patricia Mary, da. of Ernest Charles KILLIP of Uttoxeter, co. Stafford. This marriage was diss. by divorce in 1974 and he *m.* 2ndly, 1974, Victoria, da. of D.C. EDMONDS. This marriage was diss. by divorce in 1979 and he *m.* 3rdly, 1990, Corleen Jennifer RATHBONE.

[ROBERT CHARLES HENRY KING-TENISON, *styled* VISCOUNT KINGSBOROUGH, s. and h. ap. by 1st wife, *b.* 20 Mar. 1969.]

page 304,
note (e), line 4, delete from 'appears' to 'Doctor' and replace by ', with Lord Ochiltree (see vol. x, p. 8, note (g)) appears, before more modern times, to be the only peers who practised as Doctors'

page 307,
line 22, delete from 'between' to '16' and replace by '20'
line 23, for 'Sep.' read '7 Apr.'
line 26, after '*d. v.p.*,' add '1 July,'
note (g), after '300.' add 'The corrected dates are from a Thoresby Park estate book (on the inside cover), now one of the BL Egerton MSS. (*ex inform.* G.J. Hales, BM MSS. Dept., 1943.)'

KINLOSS

page 312,
line 20, after '£3,584.' add 'She *d.* 17 Oct. 1944.'
line 29, after 'Stowe' add 'He *d. v.m. s.p.m.* 2 Aug. 1944. His widow *d.* 1 June 1960.'

XII. 1944. 12. BEATRICE MARY GRENVILLE, *suo jure* BARONESS KINLOSS [S.], granddaughter and h., being daughter and h. of Luis Chandos Francis Grenville MORGAN-GRENVILLE and Katherine Beatrice abovenamed. She was *b.* 18 Aug. 1950; *m.*, 29 Aug. 1950, Greville Stewart Parker FREEMAN, F.S.A. Their assumption of the name FREEMAN-GRENVILLE in lieu of FREEMAN was recognised by the Lord Lyon, 1950.

[BEVIL DAVID STEWART FREEMAN-GRENVILLE, MASTER OF KINLOSS, s. and h. ap., *b.* 20 June 1953.]

KINNAIRD

page 314,
line 23, after '*m.*' add '9 Aug. 1745 at Stanwix,' [from the church register, *ex inform.* C. Roy Hudleston]
line 32, after 'h.;' add '*bap.* 26 July 1748;' [Register of Kirkandrews upon Eden, co. Cumberland, *ex inform.* C. Roy Hudleston]

page 317,
line 19, line to read as follows

BARONY [S.] XII. BARONY [U.K.] IV. } 1923 12 and 4. KENNETH FITZGERALD (KINNAIRD), LORD KINNAIRD OF INCHTURE, &c., 2nd but 1st surv. s. and h., *b.* 31 July 1880, MASTER OF KINNAIRD 1914–23

lines 25–6, delete from 'Having' to 'work.([c])]' and replace by 'She *d.* 27 July 1960. He *d.* 5 July 1972.'

BARONY [S.] XIII. BARONY [U.K.] V. } 1972 13 and 5. GRAHAM CHARLES (KINNAIRD), LORD KINNAIRD OF INCHTURE, &c., 1st s and h., *b.* 15 Sep. 1912; MASTER OF KINNAIRD 1923–72; ed. at Eton; *m.* 1stly, 6 May 1938, Nadia, da. of Harold Augustus FORTINGTON of Isle of Jethou, Channel Islands. This marriage was diss. by divorce in 1940 and he *m.* 2ndly, 4 Oct. 1940, Diana Margaret Elizabeth, yr. da. of Robert Shuckburgh COPEMAN of Diss. co. Norfolk.

[NICHOLAS CHARLES KINNAIRD, s. and h. ap. by 2nd wife, *b.* 27 Aug. 1946. He *d. v.p.* 15 Mar. 1951.]

note ([c]), delete all detail

KINNOULL

page 326,
line 17, for 'Luiz' read 'Luz'
line 19, after '23' add 'His widow *d.* 28 Jan. and was *bur.* 1 Feb. 1932 at Dupplin, Perth.'
line 20, line to read as follows

XIV. 1916. 14. GEORGE HARLEY (HAY), EARL OF KINNOULL, &c., grandson and h., being only s. and h. of

line 22, delete 'from 1903' and after 'DUPPLIN' add '1903–16'
lines 29–30, delete from '. Having' to 'work.]' and replace by 'and of Ferdinand Richard Holmes MEYRICK M.D. He *d.* 18 Mar. 1938. His widow *d.* 15 Dec. 1938.'

XV. 1938. 15. ARTHUR WILLIAM GEORGE PATRICK (HAY), EARL OF KINNOULL, &c., 3rd surv. s. and h. being 2nd surv. s. and h. by 2nd wife, *b.* 26 Mar. 1935; ed. at Eton; *m.*, 1 June 1961, Gay Ann, 1st da. of Sir Denys Colquhoun Flowerdew LOWSON, Bart.

[CHARLES WILLIAM HARLEY HAY, *styled* VISCOUNT DUPPLIN, s. and h. ap., *b.* 20 Dec. 1962; ed. at Eton and Oxford (Ch. Ch.).]

note (b), line 1, for 'half-br.' read 'br.'
note (c), line 2, after '1925.' add 'The 2nd s. of the Earl, his 1st by his 2nd wife, was *b.* 9 and *d.* 19 May 1931.'

KINTORE

page 331,
line 3, after '(Ch. Ch.)' add ', having matric. from St. Mary Hall in 1812'

page 332,
line 7, after '1851.' add 'He *d.* 3 and was *bur.* 7 Mar. 1930 at Keith Hall, Inverurie, co. Aberdeen. His widow *d.* 21 Sep. 1932 at Keith Hall afsd.'
line 13, line to read as follows

EARLDOM [S.] X. BARONY [U.K.] IV. } 1930 10 and 4. ARTHUR GEORGE (KEITH-FALCONER), EARL OF KINTORE, &c., 2nd and yst. but only surv. s. and h., *b.* 5 Jan. 1879, *styled* LORD FALCONER 1897–1930

line 17, for ']' read 'He *m.*, 23 Nov. 1937, Helena, da. of Eugene ZIMMERMAN, of Cincinnati, U.S.A. and formerly wife of William Angus Drogo (MONTAGU), 9th DUKE OF MANCHESTER. He *d. s.p.* 26 May 1966 when Barony of Kintore [U.K.], became *extinct* and the Lordship of Falconer of Halkertoun [S.] became *dormant*, due to being removed from the Union Roll by accident in 1844 (the Earls of Kintore had not voted as Lords Falconer for over 40 years at that time). It will presumably be restored to the next heir to the Lordship to petition for its restoration to the Roll. The Earl was *suc.* in his other titles by his sister.'

XI. 1966. 11. ETHEL SYDNEY KEITH-FALCONER, sister and h., *suo jure* COUNTESS OF KINTORE and BARONESS KEITH. She *m.*, 15 Feb. 1905, John Lawrence BAIRD, later *cr.*, 12 June 1925, BARON STONEHAVEN of Ury, co. Kincardine, and, 27 June 1938, VISCOUNT STONEHAVEN [see vol. xiii, p. 412]. He *d.* 20 Aug. 1941. She *d.* 21 Sep. 1974.

XII. 1974. 12. JAMES IAN (BAIRD, *later* KEITH), EARL OF KINTORE, &c., s. and h., *b.* 25 July 1908; ed. at Eton. He *suc.* to the Viscountcy of Stonehaven on the death of his father, 20 Aug. 1941, and to his other titles on the death of his mother. Changed his name from BAIRD to KEITH, 28 June 1967. He *m.*, 5 Mar. 1935, Delia, da. of William Lewis Brownlow LOYD of Guildford, Surrey. He *d.* 1 Oct. 1989. She was still living 1995.

XIII. 1989. 13. MICHAEL CANNING WILLIAM JOHN (KEITH), EARL OF KINTORE, &c., s. and h., *b.* 22 Feb. 1939; ed. at Eton and R.M.A. Sandhurst; *m.* 1972, Mary, da. of Elisha Gaddis PLUM, of Rumson, New Jersey, U.S.A.

[JAMES WILLIAM FALCONER KEITH, MASTER OF KINTORE, *styled* LORD INVERURIE, 1st s. and h. ap., was *b.* 15 Apr. 1976, ed. at Gordonstoun.]

KITCHENER

page 343,
lines 10–11, delete from 'Under' to 'work.'

II. 1916. 2. HENRY ELLIOTT CHEVALLIER (KITCHENER), EARL KITCHENER OF KHARTOUM AND OF BROOME, also VISCOUNT BROOME and BARON DENTON, eldest and only surv. br. under the special rem., *b.* 5 Oct. 1846; Col. Duke of Cornwall's L.I. Served in WW1.([c]) He *m.*, 9 Oct. 1877, Eleanor Fanny, only child of Franklin LUSHINGTON, C.B., Col. Scots Fus. Guards, by Anne Dobree, da. of Gen. Sir Philip Bainbrigge, K.C.B. She *d.* 1 June 1898. He *d. s.p.s.* 27 Mar. 1937.

[HENRY FRANKLIN CHEVALLIER KITCHENER, only s. and h. ap., *b.* 17 Oct. 1878, *styled* VISCOUNT BROOME from 1916; Commander R.N.; served in WW1.([c]) He *m.*, 11 Sep. 1916, at Ringwould, Kent, Adela Mary Evelyn, 1st da. of John Henry MONINS, of Ringwould House, near Deal. He *d. v.p.* at Maydeken, Denton, near Canterbury, 13, and was *bur.* 16 June 1928, at Barham, Kent.]

III. 1937. 3. HENRY HERBERT (KITCHENER), EARL KITCHENER OF KHARTOUM AND OF BROOME, &c., grandson and h., being s. and h. of Henry Franklin Chevallier KITCHENER and Eleanor Fanny abovenamed. He was *b.* 24 Feb. 1919, *styled* VISCOUNT BROOME 1928–37; ed. at Winchester and Cambridge (Trin. Coll.).

note ([c]), lines 1–4, delete all detail
lines 1–6 (on page 343), delete from 's.' to '1919.'

KNUTSFORD

page 351,
line 1, line to read as follows

II. 1914. 2. SYDNEY GEORGE (HOLLAND), VISCOUNT KNUTSFORD OF KNUTSFORD [1895], BARON KNUTSFORD [1888], 1st s. (twin) and h., *b.* 19 Mar. 1855,

lines 10–11, delete from 'Having' to 'work.]' and replace by 'He *d. s.p.m.* 27 July 1931. His widow *d.* 3 May 1947.'

III. 1931. 3. ARTHUR HENRY (HOLLAND, *later* HOLLAND-HIBBERT), VISCOUNT KNUTSFORD OF KNUTSFORD, &c., twin br. and h., *b.* 19 Mar. 1855; took, 17 May 1876, by Royal licence, in accordance with the will of his grandmother, the additional surname of HIBBERT. He *m.*, 5 Nov. 1884, Ellen, da. of Sir Wilfred LAWSON, Bart. He *d.* 16 Jan. 1935. His widow *d.* 5 June 1949.

IV. 1935. 4. THURSTAN (HOLLAND-HIBBERT), VISCOUNT KNUTSFORD OF KNUTSFORD, &c., 1st s. and h., *b.* 19 June 1888; ed. at Eton and Cambridge (Trin. Coll.); *m.*, 24 July 1912, Viola Mary, da. of Thomas Meadows CLUTTERBUCK of Rickmansworth, co. Hertford. She *d.* 12 Jan. 1964. He *d.* 17 Feb. 1976.

V. 1976. 5. JULIAN THURSTAN (HOLLAND-HIBBERT), VISCOUNT KNUTSFORD OF KNUTSFORD, &c., only s. and h., *b.* 3 May 1920; ed. at Eton and Cambridge (Trin. Coll.). He *d.* unm. and *s.p.* 8 Mar. 1986.

VI. 1986. 6. MICHAEL (HOLLAND-HIBBERT), VISCOUNT KNUTSFORD OF KNUTSFORD, &c., cousin and h. being s. of Wilfred HOLLAND-HIBBERT (*d.* 18 Feb. 1961), by Isabel Audrey, da. of Mark FENWICK of Stow-on-the-Wold, co. Gloucester, which Wilfred was 2nd s. of 3rd Viscount Knutsford. He was *b.* 27 Dec. 1926; ed. at Eton and Cambridge (Trin. Hall); *m.*, 8 May 1951, Sheila Constance, 1st da. of Edward Claud Berkeley (PORTMAN), 5th VISCOUNT PORTMAN.

[HENRY THURSTAN HOLLAND-HIBBERT, 1st s. and h. ap., *b.* 6 Apr. 1959; ed. at Eton and R.A.C., Cirencester; *m.*, 1988, Katherine, da. of Sir John Bruce Woolacott ROPNER, Bart.]

KNYVETT

page 351,
line 18, after 'James I;' add 'knighted between 27 April and Oct. 1601 (probably in May)'

KYME

page 355,
line 15, after 'BIGOD' add 'Justiciar of England,'

page 359,
line 4, for 'Henry' read 'Edmund'

LAMINGTON

page 371,
line 6, add at end 'He *d.* 16 Sep. 1940. His widow *d.* 18 Jan. 1944.'
line 7, line to read as follows

III. 1940. 3. VICTOR ALEXANDER BRISBANE WILLIAM (COCHRANE-BAILEY), BARON LAMINGTON, only s. and h., *b.* 23 July 1896.

line 11, for ']' read 'He *d. s.p.* 20 Sep. 1951 when his title became *extinct*.'

LANCASTER

page 386,
line 7, for '8 or 9' read '7' and after '1269' add '(ea)'
note (ea) The Liberate Roll (P.R.O. C62/45, m. 9), mentions the marriage feast of Edmund who "in quindena instantis pasche filiam comitis Abbemarl' ducet in uxorem", *i.e.* Sunday 7 April (*ex inform.* A.E. Stamp).
line 8, after 'Isabel,' add 'sister and coh. of Baldwin (DE REVIERS), 7th EARL OF DEVON,'
lines 12–13, delete from 'apparently' to '1276' and replace by 'between 18 Dec. 1275 and 18 Jan. 1275/6'
note (h), delete all detail
note (i), delete all detail and replace by 'See R. Somerville, *Duchy of Lancaster*, vol. i, p. 15, note 1.'

page 395,
line 25, after 'Alice,' add '*suo jure* COUNTESS OF LINCOLN and COUNTESS OF SALISBURY,'
line 27, delete from 'by' to 'SALISBURY

page 396,
line 2, after 'LESTRAUNGE,' add '[1st LORD STRANGE],'

page 409,
line 6, for '24' read '23' [*Inq. p.m.*, vol. xi, no. 118]
line 10, after 'him' add '?'

page 410,
line 9, for '14' read '20' [See *Inq. p.m.*, vol. xi, no. 118 (pp. 96 and 105), but *John of Gaunt's Register 1372–6*, vol. 2, p. 70, says she was 24 when she died (in 1368), and was thus 16 in 1361.]
line 14, for 'in the spring of' read 'Mar.' [Anthony Goodman, *John of Gaunt*, 1992, p. 28]

page 415,
line 13, for '1369' read '1368' [See Goodman, *John of Gaunt*, p. 46.]
line 17, delete 'or 4' [Goodman, *John of Gaunt*, p. 168]

page 418,
note (a), line 7, for 'Canterbury' read 'Leicester' [confirmed by the reference to Devon's *Issues of the Exchequer*, line 10 of the note, *ex inform.* C.R. Humphry-Smith]

LANDAFF

page 421,
note (b), line 8, for 'Orchard' read 'Richard'

LANESBOROUGH

page 424,
line 34, for 'da. and h. of William' read '2nd but only surv. da. of Richard'
line 35, after 'Westmeath' add ', by his wife Alice, da. of Thomas Smyth of Drumcree'

page 427,
line 22, line to read as follows

EARLDOM [I.] VII. VISCOUNTCY [I.] X. } 1905 — 7 and 8. CHARLES JOHN BRINSLEY (BUTLER), EARL OF LANESBOROUGH, &c., 1st s. and h., *b.* 12 Dec. 1865, at Devonport, *styled* LORD NEWTOWN-BUTLER 1866–1905,

lines 35–7, delete from 'Having' to 'work.]' and replace by 'He *d. s.p.m.s.* 18 at Swithland Hall near Loughborough and was *bur.* 22 Aug. 1929 at Swithland. His widow *d.* 6 Oct. 1935.'

EARLDOM [I.] VIII. VISCOUNTCY [I.] XI. } 1929 — 8 and 9. HENRY CAVENDISH (BUTLER), EARL OF LANESBOROUGH, &c., br. and h., *b.* 2 June 1868; *m.* 1stly, 27 Nov. 1894, Isobel. da. of Ralph Allen DANIELL. She *d.* 1905 and he *m.* 2ndly, 6 Dec. 1917, Grace Lillian, 1st da. of Sir Anthony Charles Sykes ABDY, Bart. He *d.* 22 Aug. 1950. His widow *d.* 1983.

EARLDOM [I.] IX. VISCOUNTCY [I.] XII. } 1950 — 9 and 10. DENIS ANTHONY BRIAN (BUTLER), EARL OF LANESBOROUGH, &c., 1st and only surv. s. and h. by 2nd wife,(d) *b.* 28 Oct. 1918; ed. at Stowe; *m.*, 20 Dec. 1939, Bettyne Ione, da. of Sir Lindsay EVERARD of Ratcliffe Hall, co. Leicester.

note (d) His yr. br., Patrick Henry Stanley Danvers Butler, was *b.* 27 Dec. 1920 and was *k.* in action at Anzio, *v.p.* and unm. 28 Feb. 1944.

LANGDALE

page 429,
line 11, for 'WHARTON' read 'WARTON

page 431,
line 19, for 'Painesley, co. York.' read 'Painsley, co. Stafford'

LANGFORD OF SUMMERHILL

page 434,
line 8, for 'was living 1929' read '*d.* 1976.'
lines 9–12, delete all detail and replace as follows

V. 1919. 5. JOHN HERCULES WILLIAM (ROWLEY), BARON LANGFORD OF SUMMERHILL [I.], 1st and only surv s., *b.* 16 Dec. 1894.([a]) He *d.* unm., after a short illness, 29 Sep. 1922.

VI. 1922. 6. WILLIAM CHAMBRÉ (ROWLEY), BARON LANGFORD OF SUMMERHILL [I.], uncle and h. male, being the second s. of the 3rd Baron, *b.* 30 Aug. 1849. Lieut. Col. R.A., served in the Afghan War 1879–80 and in WW1, 1914–18. He *m.* 25 July 1889, Mabel Maud, 2nd da. of WILLIAM JOHN (LEGH), 1st BARON NEWTON. He *d. s.p.* 22 Jan. 1931 in Corsica. She, who was *b.* 16 Sep. 1863, *d.*, aged 102, 12 May 1966.

VII. 1931. 7. CLOTWORTHY WELLINGTON THOMAS EDWARD (ROWLEY), BARON LANGFORD OF SUMMERHILL, nephew and h., being s. of Randolfe Thomas ROWLEY (*d.* 22 Dec. 1910), by Rosetta, da. of Thomas Henry FLETCHER of Kati Kati, New Zealand, which Randolfe Thomas was 3rd s. of 3rd Baron Langford. He was *b.* 1 June 1885; *m.*, 26 Apr. 1922, Florence Eileen O'Donovan, 2nd da. of Isaac SHIEL of Ballsbridge, Dublin. He *d. s.p.m.s.* 15 July 1952.([c]) His widow *d.* 1989.

VIII. 1952. 8. ARTHUR SHOLTO LANGFORD (ROWLEY), BARON LANGFORD OF SUMMERHILL, distant cousin and h., being 2nd s. of Col. Hercules Langford Boyle ROWLEY (*d.* 20 Mar. 1904), by Louisa Jane, da. of Archibald DOUGLAS, *later* CAMPBELL, and sister of Archibald (CAMPBELL), 1st BARON BLYTHSWOOD, which Hercules Langford Boyle was 2nd s. of 2nd Baron Langford. He was *b.* 10 Dec. 1870; *m.* 1stly, 23 June 1908, Margarita Ines, da. of Hugh Robert F. JAMISON of Iquiqui, Chile. She *d.* 1 Jan. 1928 and he *m.* 2ndly, 1929, 2nd da. of Henri LELACHEUR of Guernsey, Channel Islands. He *d. s.p.* 19 Aug. 1953. His widow *d.* 1958.

IX. 1953. 9. GEOFFREY ALEXANDER (ROWLEY-CONWY), BARON LANGFORD OF SUMMERHILL, distant cousin and h., being s. of Major Geoffrey Seymour ROWLEY-CONWY (*d.* 10 Aug. 1915, at Gallipoli), by Bertha Gabrielle, da. of Alexander COCHRAN, which Geoffrey Seymour was 3rd s. of Conwy Grenville Hercules Rowley, *later* Rowley-Conwy (*d.* 18 Jan. 1900), by Marian, 2nd da. of Frederick HARFORD of Down Place, Windsor, Berks., which Conwy Grenville Hercules was 1st s. of Col. Richard Thomas ROWLEY (*d.* 11 Nov. 1887), by his 1st wife Charlotte, da. of Lieut. Col. SHIPLEY, which Richard Thomas was 2nd s. of 1st Baron Langford. He was *b.* 8 Mar. 1912; ed. at Marlborough and R.M.A., Sandhurst; *m.* 1stly, 24 Jan. 1939, Ruth St. John, da. of Albert St. John MURPHY of Little Island, co. Cork. This marriage was diss. by divorce in 1956 (she *d.* 1991), and he *m.* 2ndly, 7 Feb. 1957, Grete, da. of Col. E.T.C. VON FRIESLEBEN of Snekkersten, Denmark. She *d.* 1973 and he *m* 3rdly, 1975, Susan Winifred, da. of C.H.C. DENHAM of Wrexham, co. Denbigh.

[OWAIN GRENVILLE ROWLEY-CONWY, s. and h. ap. by 2nd wife, *b.* 27 Dec. 1958; ed. at Marlborough and R.A.C. Cirencester; m., 1986, Joanna, da. of Jack FEATHERSTONE of Cae Sion, Trefnant, Clwyd. This marriage was diss. by divorce in 1993.]

note ([b]), delete all detail

note (c) His only child, Clotworthy Alexander Rowley, was *b.* 10 Dec. 1923 and *d.* 15 Mar. 1924.

LANSDOWNE

page 442,
line 18, for 'was living 1929' read '*d.* 21 and was *bur.* 25 Oct. 1932 at Derry Hill Church, near Chippenham, Wilts.'
line 19, line to read as follows

VI. 1927. 6. HENRY WILLIAM EDMOND (PETTY-FITZMAURICE), MARQUESS OF LANSDOWNE, &c., 1st s. and h., *b.* 14 Jan. 1872, *styled* Earl of Kerry, 1872–1927;

page 443,
lines 6–7, delete from 'Having' to 'work.(b)]' and replace by 'He *d.* 5 and was *bur.* 10 Mar. 1936 at Derry Hill afsd. His widow *m.* 2ndly, 14 Feb. 1940, Lord Colum CRICHTON-STUART (3rd s. of John Patrick (CRICHTON-STUART), 3rd MARQUESS OF BUTE, who *d.* 18 Aug. 1957. She *d.* 25 Mar. 1964.'

[HENRY MAURICE JOHN PETTY-FITZMAURICE, *styled* EARL OF KERRY from 1927, *b.* 7 Oct. 1913, *d.* unm. *v.p. s.p.* 12 Sep. 1933]

VII. 1936. 7. CHARLES HOPE (PETTY-FITZMAURICE), MARQUESS OF LANSDOWNE, &c., 2nd but 1st surv. s. and h., *b.* 9 Jan. 1917; ed. at Eton and Oxford (Balliol Coll.). He *d.* unm. and *s.p.* 20 Aug. 1944, being *k.* in action in Italy, when the Barony of Nairne was inherited by his sister Kathleen Evelyn Constance BIGHAM, VISCOUNTESS HALIFAX (see above, *sub* NAIRNE), but he was *suc.* in his other titles by his cousin.

VIII. 1944. 8. GEORGE JOHN CHARLES (MERCER-NAIRNE, *later* MERCER-NAIRNE-PETTY-FITZMAURICE), MARQUESS OF LANSDOWNE, &c., distant cousin and h., being s. of Charles George Francis PETTY-FITZMAURICE, *later* MERCER-NAIRNE (*d.* 30 Oct. 1914, being *k.* in action), by Lady Violet Mary, yst. da. of Gilbert John (ELLIOTT-MURRAY-KYNYNMOUND), 4th EARL OF MINTO, which Charles George Francis was 2nd s. of 5th Marquess of Lansdowne. He was *b.* 27 Nov. 1912; ed. at Eton and Oxford (Ch. Ch.); assumed additional surnames of PETTY-FITZMAURICE, recognised by decree of Lord Lyon, 1947. He *m.* 1stly, 18 Mar. 1938, Barbara, da. of Harold Stuart CHASE of Santa Barbara, Califonia, U.S.A. She *d.* 17 Feb. 1965 and he *m.* 2ndly, 22 Dec. 1969, Selina Polly Dawson, da. of David McAdam (ECCLES), 1st VISCOUNT ECCLES and formerly wife of Robin Duthac CARNEGIE. This marriage was diss. by divorce in 1978 and he *m.* 3rdly, 1978, Gillian Anna, da. of Alured MORGAN. She *d.* 1982.

[CHARLES MAURICE MERCER-NAIRNE-PETTY-FITZMAURICE, *styled* EARL OF SHELBURNE, 1st s. and h. ap. by 1st wife, *b.* 21 Feb. 1941; ed. at Eton; *m.*, 9 Oct. 1965, Lady Frances Helen Mary, da. of Nicholas Richard Michael (ELIOT), 9th EARL OF ST. GERMANS. This marriage was diss. by divorce in 1987 and he *m.* 2ndly, 1987, Fiona Mary, da. of Donald MERRITT.]

note ([b]), delete all detail

LATHOM

page 450,
line 13, after 'K.C.B.' add 'She *d.* 10 Feb. 1931.'
line 14, line to read as follows

III. 1910. 3. EDWARD WILLIAM (BOOTLE-WILBRAHAM), EARL OF LATHOM and LORD SKELMERSDALE, only s. and h., *b.* 16 May 1895.

lines 19–20, delete from 'Having' to 'work.]' and replace by 'He *d. s.p.* 6 Feb. 1930 when his Earldom became *extinct* but the Barony of Skelmersdale devolved on his cousin and h. male. See SKELMERSDALE.'

LATIMER

pages 452–3,
pedigree, lines 19–20, for '*suo jure* Baroness Lisle and Baroness Berkeley' read 'Beauchamp'

page 453,
line 21, after 'LA WARRE' add '[2nd LORD LA WARRE]'
line 22, delete from 'h. of' to 'Manchester' and replace by 'eventually h. of Thomas GRELLE [1st LORD GRELLE], lord of Manchester'

page 467,
line 3, for 'yr. da. and coh.' read 'h.'
line 4, after 'THWENG,' add 'elder br. of Marmaduke, 1st LORD THWENG,'

page 470,
line 10, for 's.' read 'LORD UFFORD, 1st s. and h. ap.'

page 477,
note ([i]), line 1, for '1st' read '4th'

page 483,
line 10, for '1526/27' read '1525/6' [See G.H. White, "The Sisters of John de Vere, 14th Earl of Oxford", *Geneal. Mag.*, vol. 12, pp. 293–4.]
line 11, for 'Hornby' read "Well'

page 484,
line 13, for 'K.G.' read 'Standard Bearer to Henry VII'

page 486,
line 8, after '1913' add '[See vol. xiii, p. 173 and below.]'

V. 1913. 5. FRANCIS BURDETT (MONEY-COUTTS, *later* COUTTS-NEVILL),

LORD LATIMER [1432], in whose favour the Barony was called out of *abeyance*, 11 Feb. 1913. He was *b.* 18 Sep. 1852; *m.*, 15 Apr. 1875, Edith Ellen, 1st da. of Charles CHURCHILL of Weybridge Park, Surrey. He *d.* 8 June 1923. His widow *d.* (as the result of an accident), 28 Apr. 1942.

VI. 1923. 6. HUGH BURDETT (MONEY-COUTTS), LORD LATIMER, only s. and h., *b.* 13 Aug. 1876; ed. at Radley and Oxford (New Coll.); *m.*, 11 June 1900, Hester Frances, 4th da. of Major Gen. John Cecil RUSSELL. He *d.* 23 Nov. 1949. His widow *d.* 1 Feb. 1961.

VII. 1949. 7. THOMAS BURDETT (MONEY-COUTTS), LORD LATIMER, 1st s. and h., *b.* 6 Aug. 1901; ed. at Radley and Oxford (Trin. Coll.); *m.*, 8 Jan. 1925, Patience Margaret, da. of William Courtenay THOMPSON. She *d.* 1982. He *d.* 24 May 1987.

VIII. 1987. 8. HUGO NEVILL (MONEY-COUTTS), LORD LATIMER, only s. and h., *b.* 1 Mar. 1926; ed. at Eton; *m.*, 28 July 1951, Penelope Ann Clare, yr. da. of Thomas Addis EMMET of Amberley Castle, Sussex. This marriage was diss. by divorce in 1965 and he *m.* 2ndly, 1965, Jinty Ann, 2nd da. of Peter George CALVERT.

[CRISPIN JAMES ALAN NEVILL MONEY-COUTTS, 1st s. and h. ap. by 1st wife, *b.* 8 Mar. 1955; ed. at Eton and Oxford (Keble Coll.); *m.*, 1978, Lucy Rose, yst. da. of William Francis (DEEDES), BARON DEEDES, a Life Peer.]

LAUDERDALE

page 498,
line 7, for 'was living 1929' read '*d.* 14 Sep. 1931. M.I. to both in Brompton Cemetery.
line 8, line to read as follows

XIV. 1929. 14. FREDERICK COLIN (MAITLAND), EARL OF LAUDERDALE, &c., s. and h. by 1st wife, *b.* 12 Apr. 1868, *styled* VISCOUNT MAITLAND 1884–1929

line 15, delete '(d)'
lines 19–20, delete from 'Having' to 'work.]' and replace by. 'He *d.* 14 Sep. 1931.'

XV. 1931. 15. IAN COLIN (MAITLAND), EARL OF LAUDERDALE, &c., only s. and h., *b.* 30 Jan. 1891, *styled* LORD THIRLESTANE AND BOULTON, 1924–31; ed. at Eton. Served in WW1 as Capt. 3rd Battn. Cameron Highlanders; A.D.C. to the Lord Lieut. of Ireland, 1916; Staff Lieut. 1917. REP. PEER [S.] 1931–45, when he retired. He *m.*, 11 Nov. 1912, Ethel Mary (Ivy), 1st da. of James Jardine BELL-IRVING, of Makerstoun, Kelso, by Eva Gertrude, 4th da. of Benjamin PIERCY, of Marchwiel Hall, co. Denbigh. She was *b.* 6 Oct. 1891. He *d. s.p.m.s.* 17 Feb. 1953. His widow *d.* 1970.

[IVOR COLIN JAMES MAITLAND, *styled* VISCOUNT MAITLAND, only s. and h. ap., *b.* 29

Aug. 1915, served in WW2. He *m.*, 29 Oct. 1936, at St. Margaret's Ch., Westminster, Helena Ruth, yr. da. of Col. Sir Herbert Charles PERROTT, Bart. He *d. v.p. s.p.m.* 18 Jan. 1943, being *k.* in action in North Africa. His widow was living 1995.]

XVI. 1953. 16. ALFRED SYDNEY FREDERICK (MAITLAND), EARL OF LAUDERDALE, &c., cousin and h., being 1st s. of Rev. Sydney George William MAITLAND (*d.* 21 Aug. 1946), by Ella Frances, da. of Rev. James RICHARDS, which Sydney George was 2nd s. of 13th Earl of Lauderdale. He was *b.* 17 Apr. 1904; ed. at Westminster and Cambridge (Sidney Sussex Coll.); Clerk in Holy Orders. He *m.* 1stly, 6 Aug. 1938, Norah Mary, da. of William Henry LA TOUCHE. She *d.* 3 Nov. 1938 and he *m.* 2ndly, 4 June 1940, Irene Alice May, da. of Rev. Charles Percy SHIPTON of Halsham, co. York. He *d. s.p.* 27 Nov. 1968. His widow was living 1995.

XVII. 1968. 17. PATRICK FRANCIS (MAITLAND), EARL OF LAUDERDALE, &c., br. and h., *b.* 17 Mar. 1911; ed. at Lancing and Oxford (Brasenose Coll.); *m.*, 20 July 1936, Stanka, 1st da. of Prof. Milivovye LOSANITCH of Belgrade.

[IAN MAITLAND, *styled* VISCOUNT MAITLAND, MASTER OF LAUDERDALE, 1st s. and h. ap., *b.* 4 Nov. 1937; ed. at Radley and Oxford (Brasenose Coll.); *m.*, 27 Apr. 1963, Ann Paula, da. of Geoffrey CLARK.]

note ([d]), delete all detail

LAWRENCE

page 502,
line 3, for 'was living 1929' read '*d.* 16 Nov. 1938.'
line 4, line to read as follows

III. 1913. 3. ALEXANDER GRAHAM (LAWRENCE), BARON LAWRENCE OF THE PUNJAUB AND OF GRATELY, 2nd but only surv. s. and h.,

lines 8–9, delete from 'Having' to 'work.]' and replace by 'She *d.* 1 Feb. 1935 and he *m.* 2ndly, 3 Sep. 1936, Jessie, da. of Col. Byron Gordon DANIELS and widow of William Frederick LAWRENCE of Cowesfield House, Wilts. She *d.* 29 Dec. 1936 and was *bur.* 1 Jan. 1937 at Whiteparish, near Salisbury, and he *m.* 3rdly, 29 June 1938, Catherine Louisa, da. of Charles FERNIHAUGH of Lichfield, co. Stafford and widow of William Burnet CRAIGIE. He *d.* 24 June 1947. His widow *d.* 24 Oct. 1965.'

IV. 1947. 4. JOHN ANTHONY (LAWRENCE), BARON LAWRENCE OF THE PUNJAUB AND OF GRATELY, only s. and h., *b.* 16 Oct. 1908; ed. at Haileybury; *m.* 1stly, 8 Aug. 1936, Margaret Jean, da. of Arthur DOWNER of Rotherfield, co. Kent. This marriage was diss. by divorce in 1947 and he *m.* 2ndly, 16 Oct. 1948, Joan Alice Mildred, da. of Col. Arthur John LEWER of Bonchurch, Isle of Wight. He *d.* 8 Oct. 1968. His widow *m.* 2ndly, 1969, John EDDISON of Ryde, Isle of Wight. He *d.* 1989. She was still living 1995.

V. 1968. 5. DAVID JOHN DOWNER (LAWRENCE), BARON LAWRENCE OF THE PUNJAUB AND OF GRATELY, only s. and h., *b.* 4 Sep. 1937; ed. at Bradfield Coll.

note ([d]), lines 1–2, delete from 'Their' to '1908'

LECONFIELD

page 506,
line 6, for 'was living 1929' read '*d.* 27 June 1939.'
line 13, after '1892.' add 'He *d.s.p.* 17 Apr. 1952. His widow *d.* 22 May. 1956.'

IV. 1952. 4. HUGH ARCHIBALD (WYNDHAM), BARON LECONFIELD, br. and h., *b.* 4 Oct. 1877; ed. at Eton and Oxford (New Coll.); *m.*, 25 Feb. 1908, Maud Mary, 1st da. of Charles George (LYTTELTON), 8th VISCOUNT COBHAM. She *d.* 22 July 1953. He *d. s.p.* 6 July 1963.

V. 1963. 5. EDWARD SCAWEN (WYNDHAM), BARON LECONFIELD, br. and h., *b.* 30 Apr. 1883; ed. at Eton; *m.*, 14 Oct. 1907, Gladys Mary, da. of FitzRoy James Wilberforce FARQUHAR, 5th s. of Sir Walter Rockcliffe FARQUHAR, Bart. He *d.* 17 Oct. 1967. His widow *d.* 1971.

[HENRY SCAWEN WYNDHAM, 1st s. and h. ap., *b.* 8 Nov. 1915; ed. at Eton. He *d. v.p.* and unm. 28 Oct. 1942, being *k.* at El Alamein.]

VI. 1967. 6. JOHN EDWARD REGINALD (WYNDHAM), BARON LECONFIELD, 2nd but 1st surv. s. and h., *b.* 5 June 1920; ed. at Eton and Cambridge (Trin. Coll.). He was *cr.*, 27 Nov. 1963, BARON EGREMONT of Petworth, co. Sussex. He *m.*, 24 July 1947, Pamela, yst. da. of Valentine WYNDHAM-QUIN, Capt., R.N. of Newbury, Berks. He *d.* 6 June 1972. His widow was living 1995.

VII. 1972. 7. JOHN MAX HENRY SCAWEN (WYNDHAM), BARON LECONFIELD and BARON EGREMONT, 1st s. and h., *b.* 21 Apr. 1948; ed. at Eton and Oxford (Ch. Ch.); *m.*, 1978, Audrey Caroline, 1st da. of Alexander Ronan NELSON of Taynuilt, Argyll.

[GEORGE RONAN VALENTINE, s. and h. ap., *b.* 31 July 1983.]

LEEDS

page 507,
line 6, for 'Dunkenhalg' read 'Dunkenhalgh'

page 519,
line 8, for 'was living 1929' read '*d.* 1952.'
line 9, line to read as follows

XI. 1927. 11. JOHN FRANCIS GODOLPHIN (OSBORNE), DUKE OF LEEDS, &c., s. and h., *b.* 12 Mar. 1901,

lines 10–11, delete from 'Having' to 'work.]' and replace by 'He *m.* 1stly, 27 Mar. 1933, Irma, da. of Iskender DE MALKHAZOUNY of Paris, formerly wife of Paul BREWSTER. This marriage was diss. by divorce in 1947 (in the U.S.A.), and she *m.* 2ndly, 21 June 1947, Frank Atherton HOWARD of New Jersey, U.S.A. He *m.* 2ndly, 21 Dec. 1948, Audrey, da. of Brig. Desmond YOUNG and formerly wife of A.E.B. WILLIAMS. This marriage was in turn diss. by divorce in 1955 and he *m.* 3rdly, 22 Feb. 1955, Caroline Fleur, da. of Col. Henry Monckton VATCHER of St. Brelade's, Jersey, Channel Islands. He *d. s.p.m.* 26 July 1963. His widow was living 1995.'

XII. 1963. 12. FRANCIS D'ARCY GODOLPHIN (OSBORNE), DUKE OF LEEDS, &c., distant cousin and h., being 1st s. of Sidney Francis Godolphin OSBORNE (*d.* 22 Oct. 1903), by Margaret Dulcibella, da. of Hugh HAMMERSLEY, which Sidney Francis was s. of Rev. Sydney Godolphin Osborne (*d.* 9 May 1889), by Emily Charlotte, da. of Pascoe GRENFELL, of Taplow House, Taplow, co. Buckingham, which Sydney Godolphin was 3rd s. of Francis Godolphin (OSBORNE), 1st BARON OSBORNE (*b.* 15 Feb. 1850), by Elizabeth Charlotte, da. of William (EDEN), 1st BARON AUCKLAND which Francis Godolphin was 2nd s. of 5th Duke of Leeds. He was *b.* 16 Sep. 1884; ed. at Haileybury. He *d.* unm. and *s.p.* 20 Mar. 1964 when all his titles became *extinct*.

LEICESTER

page 530,
line 2, after 'FITZOSBERN' add ', 1st EARL OF HEREFORD'

page 533,
line 1, for '1190' read '31 Aug. 1190, at sea near Brindisi, or in Romania on his way to Jerusalem' [See vol. x, Appendix I, p. 106, note (b).]

page 534,
note (f), line 8, after 'agreement.' add 'See also Vernier, *Facsimiles des Chartes Normandes*, no. 8 (p. 13), Equestrian seal.'

page 551,
line 7, for 'Mary' read 'Katherine' [M.I., Westm. Abbey]

page 559,
line 8, delete 'ed. at Turin Univ;'

page 563,
note (b), line 2, for '(Nevinson)' read 'Nevinson (Howard)' and after 'Andover' add 's. and h. of John (Howard), 15th Earl of Suffolk,'

LEICESTER OF HOLKHAM

page 565,
line 10, for 'was living 1929' read '*d.* at 8 Park Str., Mayfair, 26 Feb. and was *bur.* 2 Mar. 1937 at Holkham.'

line 11, line to read as follows

III. 1909. 3. THOMAS WILLIAM (COKE), EARL OF LEICESTER OF HOLKHAM, &c., 1st s. and h. by 1st wife, *b.* at Holkham 20 July and *bap.* there 17 Dec. 1848, *styled* VISCOUNT COKE 1848–1909,

line 19, after 'STUART' add '(d)'
lines 19–20, delete from 'Having' to 'work.(d)]' and replace by 'She *d.* 24 Apr. 1936. He *d.* 19 Nov. 1941.'

IV. 1941. 4. THOMAS WILLIAM (COKE), EARL OF LEICESTER OF HOLKHAM, &c., 1st s. and h., *b.* at 12 Augusta Gdns., Folkestone, 9 July, and *bap.* 22 Aug. 1880, at Holkham, *styled* VISCOUNT COKE 1909–41 [for further detail see note (d)]. He *d.* 21 Aug. 1949. His widow *d.* 23 Nov. 1955.

note (d), line 8, delete from 'Their' to '1908' and replace as follows

V. 1949. 5. THOMAS WILLIAM EDWARD (COKE), EARL OF LEICESTER OF HOLKHAM, &c., 1st and only surv. s.,(e) *b.* 16 May 1908; ed. at Eton and R.M.C., Sandhurst; *m.*, 1 Oct. 1931, Lady Elizabeth Mary, da. of Charles Alexander (YORKE), 8th EARL OF HARDWICKE. He *d.* 3 Sep. 1976. His widow *d.* 1985.

VI. 1976. 6. ANTHONY LOUIS LOVEL (COKE), EARL OF LEICESTER OF HOLKHAM, cousin and h., being s. of Arthur George COKE (*d.* 2 May 1915 in Dardenelles Bay), by Phyllis Hermione, da. of Francis Saxham Elwes DRURY, which Arthur George was 2nd s. of 3rd Earl of Leicester. He was *b.* 11 Sep. 1909; *m.* 1stly, 11 Sep. 1934, Moyra Joan, da. of Douglas CROSSLEY. This marriage was diss. by divorce in 1947 (she *d.* 1987) and he *m.* 2ndly, 1947, Vera, da. of Herbert William HAIGH of Durham. She *d.* 1984 and he *m.* 3rdly, 1985, Elizabeth Hope Smith, da. of Clifford Arthur JOHNSTONE of Cape Province, South Africa. He *d.* 19 June 1994. His widow was living 1995.

VII. 1994. 7. EDWARD DOUGLAS (COKE), EARL OF LEICESTER OF HOLKHAM, 1st s. and h., by 1st wife, was *b.* 6 May 1936; *styled* VISCOUNT COKE 1976–94; ed. at St. Andrew's Coll., Grahamstown, Cape Province; *m.*, 28 Apr. 1962, Valerie, 1st da. of Leonard A. POTTER of Berkhamstead, co. Hertford. This marriage was diss. by divorce in 1985 and he *m.* 2ndly, 1986, Sarah, da. of Noel Henry Boys FORDE of Wells-next-the-Sea, Norfolk and formerly wife of 1stly, (__) HANCOCK and 2ndly of Colin Graham Ramsay DE CHAIR.

[THOMAS EDWARD COKE, *styled* VISCOUNT COKE, 1st s. and h. ap. by 1st wife, *b.* 6 July 1965; ed. at Eton and Manchester Univ.]

note (e) His only br., David Arthur Coke, was *b.* 4 Dec. 1915, ed. at Eton, served as Flt. Lieut. R.A.F.V.R. in WW2, *k.* in action in Libya, 9 Dec. 1941.

LEIGH

page 569,
note (b), line 13, for 'H.K. Causton' read 'George Leigh'

page 571,
line 15, line to read as follows

VIII. 1905. 3. FRANCIS DUDLEY (LEIGH), BARON LEIGH OF STONELEIGH, 2nd but 1st surv. s. and h., *b.* 30 July 1855;

lines 22–3, delete from 'Having' to 'work.]' and replace by 'He *d. s.p.* 16 May 1938. His widow *d.* 13 Mar. 1949.'

IX. 1938. 4. RUPERT WILLIAM DUDLEY (LEIGH), BARON LEIGH OF STONELEIGH, nephew and h., being s. of Rupert LEIGH (*d.* 14 Aug. 1919), by Beatrice Mary, da. of Dudley Robert SMITH, which Rupert was 3rd s. of 2nd Baron Leigh. He was *b.* 14 Mar. 1908; ed. at Eton and R.M.C., Sandhurst; *m.*, 27 Apr. 1931, Anne, 2nd da. of Ellis HICKS-BEACH of Witcombe Park, co. Gloucester. She *d.* 1977. He *d.* 24 June 1979.

X. 1979. 5. JOHN PIERS (LEIGH), BARON LEIGH OF STONELEIGH, 1st s. and h., *b.* 11 Sep. 1935; ed. at Eton and London Univ; *m.* 1stly, 27 Apr. 1957, Cecilia Poppy, yst. da. of Robert Cecil JACKSON of Redlynch, Wilts. This marriage was diss. by divorce 1974 and he *m.* 2ndly, 1976, Susan, yst. da. of John Reginald CLEAVE of Leamington Spa, co. Warwick. This marriage was in turn diss. by divorce in 1982 and he *m.* 3rdly, 1982, Lea, da. of Col. Harry Noel Havelock WILD and formerly wife of Lieut. Col. Brian Gustavus HAMILTON-RUSSELL.

[CHRISTOPHER DUDLEY PIERS LEIGH, 1st s. and h. ap. by 1st wife, *b.* 20 Oct. 1960; ed. at Eton and R.A.C., Cirencester; *m.*, 1990, Sophy-Ann, da. of Richard BURROWS of Groby, co. Leicester.]

LEINSTER

page 577,
line 35, for '1554' read '1620'

page 578,
lines 3–6, delete from 'He was' to 'work.(b)' and replace as follows

VIII. 1922. 7. EDWARD (FITZGERALD), DUKE OF LEINSTER, &c., 3rd(a) but next surv. br., *b.* 6 May 1892; ed. at Eton; served in WW1 as Lieut. 8th Battn. Duke of Wellington's West Riding Regt. &c., served in WW2. He *m.*, at the Wandsworth Registry Office, 12 June 1913, May, da. of Jesse ETHERIDGE, an actress. This marriage was diss. by divorce (in the Scottish Courts, in 1930, she *d.* 11 Feb. 1935) and he *m.* 2ndly, 1 Dec. 1932, Agnes Raffaelle, da. of Robert Davidson KENNEDY and formerly wife of

Clare VAN NECK. This marriage was in turn diss. by divorce in 1946 (she *d.* 1993) and he *m.* 3rdly, 11 Mar. 1946, Jessie Denise Orme, da. of Alfred SMITHER and formerly wife of 1stly, John Reginald Lopes (YARDE-BULLER), 3rd BARON CHURSTON and 2ndly of Theodore William WESSEL. She *d.* 20 Oct. 1960 and he *m.* 4thly, Vivien Irene, da. of Thomas Albert FELTON and formerly wife of George William CONNOR. He *d.* 8 Mar. 1976. His widow *d.* 1992.

IX. 1976. 8. GERALD (FITZGERALD), DUKE OF LEINSTER, &c., 1st s. and h. by 1st wife, *b.* 27 May 1914; *styled* MARQUESS OF KILDARE 1922–76; ed. at Eton and R.M.C., Sandhurst; *m.* 1stly, 17 Oct. 1936, Joane, 1st da. of Major Arthur McMorrough KAVANAGH, M.C., of Borris House, co. Carlow. This marriage was diss. by divorce in 1946 and he *m.* 2ndly, 12 June 1946, Anne, yr. da. of Lieut. Col. Philip Eustace SMITH, M.C., of Morpeth, Northumberland.

[MAURICE FITZGERALD, *styled* MARQUESS OF KILDARE, 1st s. and h. ap. by 2nd wife, *b.* 7 Apr. 1948; ed. at Millfield; *m.*, 1972, Fiona Mary Francesca, da. of Harry HOLLICK of Sutton Courtenay, co. Oxford.]

note (b), delete all detail

LEITRIM

page 584,
line 4, add at end 'This marriage was diss. by divorce in 1932 (she *d.* 9 July 1943) and he *m.* 2ndly, 29 Apr. 1939, Anne Mary Challoner (Mrs BORRETT), da. of William Arcedeckne VANNECK and sister of William Charles Arcedeckne (VANNECK), 5th BARON HUNTINGFIELD. He *d. s.p.* 9 June 1952 when all his titles became *extinct*.'

LENNOX

page 589,
line 6, after 'MENTEITH' add '[S.]'

page 593,
line 4, after 'LENNOX' add '[S.]'

page 599,
line 8, for '18 Oct.' read '6 Oct.' [*L. and P. Hen. VIII*, vol. ii, part 1, pp. 274–5]

LEVEN

page 624,
line 24, after 'widow' add ', who was *b.* 16 Jan. 1806,'
line 25, after 'him.' add 'M.I. to them both.'

page 625,
line 7, after '72.(b)' add 'M.I. in Brompton Cemetery, with his parents.'

line 30, for 'was living 1929' read '*d.* 1 Mar. 1941.'
line 31, line to read as follows

XIV. 1906. 14. JOHN DAVID (LESLIE-MELVILLE), EARL OF LEVEN, EARL OF MELVILLE, &c., 1st s. and h., *b.* 5 Apr. 1886, at Portman House, Marylebone, *styled* LORD BALGONIE 1889–1906.

page 626,
lines 1–2, delete from 'Having' to 'brother.([a])]' and replace as follows

XV. 1913. 15. ARCHIBALD ALEXANDER (LESLIE-MELVILLE), EARL OF LEVEN, EARL OF MELVILLE, &c., br. and h., *b.* 6 Aug. 1890; ed. at Eton and R.M.C., Sandhurst. Served in WW1 as Lieut. 2nd Dragoons (Royal Scots Greys).([a]) He *m.* 3 Sep. 1918, at St. Geo. Hanover Sq., Rosamund Sylvia Diana Mary, da. of CECIL GEORGE SAVILE (FOLJAMBE), 1st EARL OF LIVERPOOL. He *d.* 15 Jan. 1947. His widow *d.* 1974.

XVI. 1947. 16. ALEXANDER ROBERT (LESLIE-MELVILLE), EARL OF LEVEN, EARL OF MELVILLE, &c., 1st s. and h., *b.* 13 May and *bap.* 9 June 1924, at St. James's, Sussex Gdns.; ed. at Eton; *m.*, 30 Apr. 1953, Susan, 1st da. of Lieut. Col. Ronald STEUART-MENZIES of Culdares, of Craigellachie, Banffshire.

[DAVID ALEXANDER LESLIE-MELVILLE, *styled* LORD BALGONIE, 1st s. and h. ap., *b.* 26 Jan. 1954; ed. at Eton; *m.*, 1981, Julia Clare, yr. da. of Col. Ian Ranald CRITCHLEY.]

note ([a]), lines 1–3, delete from 'Archibald' to 'Greys)'
lines 5–8, delete from 'The' to 'Gardens'

LEYBURN

page 630,
note ([n]), line 2, after 'Faye' add '(she *m.* 2ndly, Hugh de Neville, see vol. x, p. 480, *sub* Neville)'

page 634,
line 11, after 'Sybil' add '3rd'
line 12, after PEMBROKE' add ', sister of Walter, 8th EARL OF PEMBROKE'

page 638,
line 23, after 'BLOUNT' add '[1st LORD BLOUNT]'

page 642,
line 3, after 'CORBET,' add '[2nd LORD CORBET],'

LICHFIELD

page 649,
line 8, for 'was living 1929' read '*d.* 12 May 1941.'

line 9, line to read as follows

IX. 1918. 4. THOMAS EDWARD (ANSON), EARL OF LICHFIELD, &c., 1st s. and h., *b.* 9 Dec. 1883, *styled* VISCOUNT ANSON 1892–1918; ed. at Harrow and Cambridge (Trin. Coll.);

line 15, delete '(c)'

lines 14–16, delete from 'She' 'to 'work.]' and replace by 'She, who was *b.* 15 Apr. 1887, *d.* 16 Apr. 1945. He *m.* 2ndly, 23 Feb. 1949, Violet Margaret, yr. da. of Henry Dawson DAWSON-GREENE of Whittington Hall, Kirkby Lonsdale, co. Lancaster. He *d.* 14 Dec. 1960. His widow *d.* 1988.'

[THOMAS WILLIAM ARNOLD ANSON, 1st s. and h. ap., *styled* VISCOUNT ANSON from 1918, *b.* 4 May 1913; ed. at Harrow; *m.* 1stly, 28 Apr. 1938, Anne Ferelith Fenella, da. of John Herbert BOWES-LYON. This marriage was diss. by divorce in 1948 and he *m.* 2ndly, 12 May 1955, Monica, da. of Ralph NEVILLE, Cmdr., R.N., and formerly the wife of 1stly, Major Peter Holdsworth HUNT, M.C., and 2ndly of Robert Maxtone INGLIS. He *d. v.p.* 18 Mar. 1958. His widow *m.* 4thly, 29 July 1959, Lieut. Col. Eric Astley COOPER-KEY. She *d.* 8 Nov. 1969.]

X. 1960. 5. THOMAS PATRICK JOHN (ANSON), EARL OF LICHFIELD, &c., grandson and h., being only s. and h. of Thomas William Arnold ANSON and his 1st wife, Anne Ferelith Fenella abovenamed. He was *b.* 25 Apr. 1939; ed. at Harrow and R.M.A., Sandhurst; *m.*, 1975, Lady Leonora Mary, da. of Robert George (GROSVENOR), 5th DUKE OF WESTMINSTER. This marriage was diss. by divorce in 1975.

[THOMAS WILLIAM ROBERT HUGH ANSON, *styled* VISCOUNT ANSON, s. and h. ap., *b.* 19 July 1978.]

note (c), delete all detail

LIFFORD

page 653,
line 6, for 'Armagh' read 'Tuam'

page 654,
lines 8–10, delete from 'At his 'to 'work'

VI. 1913. 6. ARCHIBALD ROBERT (HEWITT), VISCOUNT LIFFORD, &c., br. and h., *b.* 14 Jan. 1844. Served in the Royal Navy, retiring with rank of Capt. in 1890. He *m.* 5 Dec. 1878, Helen Blanche, only da. of Charles S. GEACH. He *d.* 22 and was *bur.* 25 May 1925, at Lyndhurst, Hants. His widow *d.* 4 June 1942.

VII. 1925. 7. EVELYN JAMES (HEWITT), VISCOUNT LIFFORD, &c., 1st s. and h., *b.* 18 Dec. 1880; ed. at Haileybury. Served in the S. African War, 1899–1902 and in WW1,(a) Capt. Dorsetshire Regt., D.S.O. 1916 and bar 1918, Despatches. He *m.* 8 July 1919, Charlotte Rankine, widow of Capt. Edgar WALKER, and yr. da. of Sir Robert MAULE, of Edinburgh. She *d.* 2 Apr. 1954. He *d. s.p.* 5 Apr. 1954.

VIII. 1954. 8. ALAN WILLIAM WINGFIELD (HEWITT), VISCOUNT LIFFORD, &c., cousin and h., being 2nd and surv. s. and h. of George Wildbore HEWITT (*d.* 23 Apr. 1924), by Elizabeth Mary, 1st da. of Charles RAMPINI, which George Wildbore was 7th s. of 4th Viscount Lifford. He was *b.* 11 Dec. 1900; ed. at Winchester and R.M.C., Sandhurst; *m.*, 16 Jan. 1935, Alison Mary Patricia, 2nd da. of Thomas Wingrave ASHTON of Hursley, Winchester, Hants. He *d.* 6 Jan. 1987. His widow was living 1995.

IX. 1987. 9. EDWARD JAMES WINGFIELD (HEWITT), VISCOUNT LIFFORD, &c., s. and h., *b.* 27 Jan. 1949; *m.*, 1976, Alison Mary, da. of Robert LAW of Withersfield, co. Suffolk.

[JAMES THOMAS WINGFIELD HEWITT, s. and h. ap., *b.* 29 Sep. 1979.]

note (a), lines 1–8, delete from 'Archibald' to 'Edinburgh' and for 'The' read 'His'

LILFORD

page 659,
line 3, for 'was living 1929' read '*d.* 7 Apr. 1929.'
line 9, after 'Devon.' add 'She *d.* 8 Apr. 1940. He *d. s.p.m.s.* 17 Dec. 1945.

[THOMAS ATHERTON POWYS, s. and h. ap., *b.* 8 May 1896 and *d.* 3 Aug. 1909.]

between lines 12 and 13 add as follows

VI. 1945. 6. STEPHEN (POWYS), BARON LILFORD, br. and h., *b.* 8 Mar. 1869; ed. at Harrow and Cambridge (Trin. Coll.). He *d.* unm. and *s.p.* 19 Sep. 1949.

VII. 1949. 7. GEORGE VERNON (POWYS), BARON LILFORD, distant cousin and h., being s. and h. of Robert Horace POWYS (*d.* 28 Jan. 1940), by Vera Grace BRYANT, which Robert Horace was 1st s. of Robert Vernon POWYS (*d.* 6 Oct. 1933), by Wilhelmina HART, which Robert Vernon was 2nd s. of Robert Horace POWYS (*d.* 17 Sep. 1913), by Ellen Elizabeth, 1st da. of Lieut. Col. William Henry BUDD which Robert Horace was 1st s. of Robert Vernon POWYS (*d.* 26 May 1854), by Jane, 3rd da. of William BECKETT of Enfield, Middlesex, which Robert Vernon was 2nd s. of 2nd Baron Lilford. He was *b.* 8 Jan. 1931; ed. at Stonyhurst; *m.* 1stly, July 1954, Mrs Eveline BIRD, da. of (__). This marriage was diss. by divorce and he *m.* 2ndly, 29 June 1957, Anuta, da. of L.F. MERRITT of Johannesburg, South Africa. This marriage was in turn diss. by divorce in 1958 and he *m.* 3rdly, 12 Sep. 1958, Norma Yvonne, da. of V. SHELL of Johannesburg afsd. This marriage was also diss. by divorce in 1961 and he *m.* 4thly, 23 Dec. 1961, Muriel Norma, da. of (__) COOKE formerly wife of Nigel SPOTTISWOODE. Once again, this marriage was diss. by divorce, in 1969, and he *m.* 5thly, 7 Aug. 1969, Margaret, da. of A. PENMAN of Roslin, Midlothian. This last marriage has also been dissolved, in 1991.

[MARK VERNON POWYS, s and h. ap. by 5th wife, *b.* 16 Nov. 1975.]

LIMERICK

page 665,
line 40, after 'Limerick.' add 'He *d. s.p.m.* 18 Mar. 1929. His widow *d.* 11 Mar. 1943.'

page 666,
between lines 2 and 3 add as follows

VII. 1929. 5. EDMUND COLQUHOUN (PERY), EARL OF LIMERICK, &c., half-brother and h., being only s. of 3rd Earl by 2nd wife, *b.* 16 Oct. 1888; ed. at Eton and Oxford (New Coll.). Served in WW1 as Brigade Major, R.H.A.; D.S.O., Despatches. He *m.*, 1 June 1926, Angela Olivia, da. of Lieut. Col. Sir Henry TROTTER, K.C.M.G. He *d.* 4 Aug. 1967. His widow *d.* 1981.

VIII. 1967. 6. PATRICK EDMUND (PERY), EARL OF LIMERICK, &c., 1st s. and h., *b.* 12 Apr. 1930; ed. at Eton and Oxford (New Coll.); *m.*, 22 Apr. 1961, Sylvia Rosalind, 1st da. of Brig. Maurice Stanley LUSH.

[EDMUND CHRISTOPHER PERY, *styled* VISCOUNT GLENTWORTH, 1st s. and h. ap., *b.* 10 Feb. 1963; ed. at Eton, Oxford (New Coll.) and Pushkin Inst., Moscow; *m.*, 1990, Emily, da. of Michael Gavin Lynam THOMAS of Winchester, Hants.]

note (a), lines 1–2, delete from 'Edmund' to 'Despatches'

LINCOLN

page 672,
line 15, after 'Roger,' add '1st and 2nd'
note (b), line 2, for 'Count' read 'Lord'
line 21, delete from '; he' to 'p. 327)'
line 27, after '54 d.).' add 'For the origin of the Gant family, see G. Andrews Moriarty, "The parentage of Gilbert de Gant", *New England Gen. Hist. Reg.*, vol. 115, 1961, pp. 209–11.

page 676,
line 11, after '(d)' add 'She was still *styled* COUNTESS OF LINCOLN *circa* Easter 1234' [P.R.O. *Curia Regis Rolls*, 115B, m. 34 [*ad finem*], *ex inform.* Sir Cyril Howes]
line 11, for '(DE QUINCY),' read '(DE QUENCY), 1st'
line 12, for 'in London in 1217' read 'before 1232'
note (f), for '274' read '174' [see also *post*, vol. xii, part 2, p. 751, *sub* WINCHESTER [1209]]'

page 677,
line 9 of pedigree, for 'Robert FitzEustace' read 'Richard FitzEustace'

page 682,
line 1, delete '1st'
line 2, delete 'coh.'

page 688,
line 2, for 'became *extinct*' read 'was taken into the King's hands and bestowed on Henry "of Grosmont", Earl of Lancaster. The heir general was the heir of Maud, sister of Edmund de Lacy, 2nd Earl of Lincoln who *m.* Richard de Clare, Earl of Gloucester'

page 689,
line 16, for 'WYDVILLE' read 'WYDVILL'

page 693,
line 4, after 'wife' add '*b.* 6 June 1542' [N.J. O'Connors, *Godes Pece and the Queenes*, 1934, citing BL Egerton MS. 1991, f. 2]
line 7, for '1557' read 'probably in 1572'
note ([c]), after '146,' add 'This reference has '1557' which is probably a mistake for 1572, as Philip Sydney, mentioned in the same passage, was aged 3 in 1557, but is known to have gone to France in 1572 in the suite of the Earl of Lincoln.'

page 694,
line 9, for '1616' read '1615' [*Cal. S. P. Dom., 1611–18*, pp. 315, 344]

page 696,
note ([c]), line 12, for 'May 1635' read 'July 1634' [*ex inform.* G.A. Moriarty]

page 700,
after line 18 add

* * * * * *

XXXIII. *1988.* *18.* EDWARD HORACE (FIENNES-CLINTON), EARL OF LINCOLN, very distant cousin and h., (of the last Duke of Newcastle-under-Lyne, see that title), being 1st s. and h. of Edward Henry FIENNES-CLINTON (*d. circa* 1915), by Edith Annie, da. of Horace GUEST, which Edward Henry was s. of Charles Edward F-C (*d.* 11 Jan. 1888), by Alice Gertrude, da. of William WARING, M.D., which Charles Edward was 2nd s. of Rev. Henry F-C (*d.* 17 Oct. 1911), by Sarah Katherine, da. of Rev. John B. SMITH, D.D., which Henry was 1st s. of Clinton James F-C (*d.* 11 Apr. 1833), by Penelope, da. of Sir William Earle WELBY, Bart., which Clinton James was 2nd s. of Rev. Charles Fynes-Clinton (he having assumed the name Fynes-Clinton) (*d.* 13 Nov. 1827), by Emma, da. of Job BROUGH of Newark, co. Lincoln, which Charles was descended in the 4th generation from Norreys Fynes by his 3rd wife Margaret, which Norreys was 3rd s. of Sir Henry FYNES (*d.* 1641), by his 1st wife Eleanor, da. of Sir James HARRINGTON, which Sir Henry was 3rd s., (1st by his 2nd wife) of 2nd Earl of Lincoln. He was *b.* 23 Feb. 1913; *m.* 1stly, 1940, Leila Ruth, da. of John James MILLEN of Kalgoorlie, Western Australia. She *d.* 19 July 1947, and he *m.* 2ndly, 3 Dec. 1953, Linda Alice, da. of Charles CRED and widow of James O'BRIEN of Kalgoorlie afsd. No right to the Earldom has yet been established, which is accordingly *dormant*.

[EDWARD GORDON FIENNES-CLINTON, s. and h. ap., *b.* 7 Feb. 1943; *m.*, 1970, Julia, da. of William HOWSON.]

APPENDIXES

APPENDIX A

page 703,
line 20, for '1449' read '1450'

APPENDIX D

page 716,
note (e), line 3, after 'charters.' add 'This important discovery is due to the work of L.C. Loyd.'

APPENDIX E & F

page 718,
line 26, for '1449' read '1450'

APPENDIX I

page 737,
note (a), after 'White.' add 'See also vol. xii, part 2, pp. 829–37, *sub* WORCESTER.'

page 738,
note (m), line 7, delete '*s.p.*'
line 8, for 'inherited his lands' read 'was in possession of his lands, probably only as guardian for a missing nephew. Amauri left a s. Amauri, seigneur of La Queue, and a da. Helisende, who *m.* William de Tancarville, Chamberlain of Normandy (see G.W. Watson, "Fontenoy-le-Marmion", in *Misc. Gen. et Heral.*, 5th ser., vol. 8, pp. 285–6, and *C.P.*, vol. xii, part 2, p. 837, note (e))'
line 1 (on page 739), for 'Seigneur' read 'in possession'

page 739,
note (a), line 8, after '565)' add 'See G.H. White, N&Q, vol. 147, 1924, p. 101, for further comments on there being only one Robert.'

page 740,
line 21, delete full stop after '1207' and after '(k)' add ', on 21 Sep.(l)'
note (l) According to the obituary of Lyre, see C. Guéry, *Histoire de l'Abbaye de Lyre*, 1917, p. 416.

APPENDIX J

page 746,
note (b), lines 9–10, delete all detail and replace by 'That Lucy's father was Thorold the Sheriff and her mother da. of William Malet was shown conclusively by Dr Keats-Rohan in *Nottingham Med. Studies*, vol. xli, 1996, pp. 22–5.

VOLUME 8

LINDSAY

page 14,
line 28, for '18 July 1858' read '20 July 1858, at H.M. Legation at Frankfurt'

page 15,
line 14, line to read as follows

EARLDOM [S.] XII. BARONY [S.] XXI.	1917	12 and 21. REGINALD BETHUNE LINDESAY (BETHUNE, *later* LINDESAY-BETHUNE), EARL OF LINDSAY, &c., 1st s. and h., *b.* 18 May 1867, *styled* VISCOUNT GARNOCK 1894–1917;

lines 19–21, delete from 'Having' to 'work.]' and replace by 'He *d. s.p.* 14 Jan. 1939. His widow *d.* 9 Nov. 1944.'

EARLDOM [S.] XIII. BARONY [S.] XXII.	1939	13 and 22. ARCHIBALD LIONEL (LINDESAY), EARL OF LINDSAY, &c., br. and h., *b.* 14 Aug. 1872; *m.*, 31 Jan. 1900, Ethel, da. of William Austin TUCKER of Boston, Massachusetts, U.S.A. She *d.* 31 May 1942. He *d.* 15 Aug. 1943.

EARLDOM [S.] XIV. BARONY [S.] XXIII.	1943	14 and 23. WILLIAM TUCKER (LINDESAY, *later* LINDESAY-BETHUNE), EARL OF LINDSAY, &c., only s. and h., *b.* 28 Apr. 1901; assumed, 1939, the additional surname of BETHUNE; *m.*, 6 Jan. 1925, Marjory, da. of Arthur John Graham CROSS. He *d.* 19 Oct. 1985. His widow *d.* 1988.

EARLDOM [S.] XV. BARONY [S.] XXIV.	1985	15 and 24. DAVID BETHUNE (LINDESAY-BETHUNE), EARL OF LINDSAY, &c., 1st s. and h., *b.* 9 Feb. 1926; ed. at Eton and Cambridge (Magdalene Coll.); *m.* 1stly, 31 Oct. 1953, Mary-Clare, yst. da. of John Walter Edward (DOUGLAS-SCOTT-MONTAGU), 2nd BARON MONTAGU OF BEAULIEU. This

marriage was diss. by divorce in 1968 and he *m.* 2ndly, 9 June 1969, Penelope Georgina, da. of Anthony Crommelin CROSSLEY and formerly wife of Major Henry Ronald BURN-CALLANDER, M.C. He *d.* 1 Aug. 1989. His widow was living 1995.

EARLDOM [S.] XVI. BARONY [S.] XXV.	1989	16 and 25. JAMES RANDOLPH (LINDESAY-BETHUNE), EARL OF LINDSAY, &c., only s. and h., *b.* 19 Nov. 1955; ed. at Eton and Univs. of Edinburgh and California; *m.*, 1982, Diana Mary, 1st da. of Major Nigel Donald Peter CHAMBERLAYNE-MACDONALD.

[WILLIAM JAMES LINDESAY-BETHUNE, *styled* VISCOUNT GARNOCK, s. and h. ap., *b.* 30 Dec. 1990.]

LINDSEY

page 16,
line 14, after 'patent' add '(where he is *styled* LORD BERTIE),'

page 22,
line 13, for '1687' read '1687/8'

page 25,
line 16, after 'Sydney.' add 'He *d. s.p.m.* at 53 Eaton Sq., 2, and was *bur.* 5 Jan. 1938, at Uffington, near Stamford. His widow *d.* 17 Aug. 1931.'

XIII. 1938. 13. MONTAGU HENRY EDMUND CECIL (BERTIE), EARL OF LINDSEY, distant cousin and h., being descended from James (BERTIE), 1st EARL OF ABINGDON (which see), *suc.* his grandfather as 8th EARL OF ABINGDON and BARON NORREYS OF RYCOTE, 10 Mar. 1928, recognised as Earl of Lindsey 1951. He was *b.* 2 Nov. 1887; *m.*, 11 Aug. 1928, Elizabeth Valetta Bettine, da. of Major Gen. Edward James MONTAGU-STUART-WORTLEY, D.S.O., and formerly wife of Capt. Allastair Edward George GRANT. He *d. s.p.* 11 Sep. 1963. His widow *d.* 1978.

EARLDOM. XIV. EARLDOM. VIII. } 1963 14. RICHARD HENRY RUPERT (BERTIE), EARL OF LINDSEY, EARL OF ABINGDON and BARON NORREYS, cousin and h., being s. and h. of Arthur Michael BERTIE (*d.* 2 Feb. 1957), by his 1st wife Aline Rose, 1st da. of George ARBUTHNOT-LESLIE, which Arthur Michael was 2nd s. of 7th Earl of Abingdon. He was *b.* 28 June 1931; ed. at Ampleforth; *m.*, 5 Jan. 1957, Norah Elizabeth Farquahar-Oliver, yr. da. of Mark OLIVER of Edgerston, Jedburgh, co. Roxburgh.

[HENRY MARK WILLOUGHBY BERTIE, *styled* LORD NORREYS, 1st s. and h., *b.* 6 June 1958; ed. at Eton and Edinburgh Univ.; *m.*, 1989, Lucinda Sol, 2nd da. of Christopher Stewart MOORSOM.]

LINLITHGOW

page 33,
line 3, for 'See' read 'For 1st two Marquesses see'

MARQUESSATE. III. EARLDOM [S.] IX. BARONY [U.K.] VII. } 1952 3, 9 and 7. CHARLES WILLIAM FREDERICK (HOPE), MARQUESS OF LINLITHGOW, &c., 1st s. and h., *b.* 7 Apr. 1912; ed. at Eton and Oxford (Ch. Ch.); *m.* 1stly, 24 July 1939, Vivien, 1st da. of Major Robert Orlando Rodolph KENYON-SLANEY of Hatton Grange, Shifnal, Salop. She *d.* 23 Sep. 1963 and he *m.* 2ndly, 18 Feb. 1965, Judith, da. of Stanley Matthew LAWSON of Cincinnati, Ohio, U.S.A. and widow of Lieut. Col. Esmond Charles BARING, O.B.E., and formerly wife of John Symonds RADWAY. He *d.* 7 Apr. 1987. His widow *d.* 1991.

MARQUESSATE. IV. EARLDOM [S.] X. BARONY [U.K.] VIII. } 1987 — 4, 10 and 8, ADRIAN JOHN CHARLES (HOPE), MARQUESS OF LINLITHGOW, &c., only s. and h., *b.* 1 July 1946; ed. at Eton; *m.* 1stly, 9 Jan. 1968, Anne Pamela, 1st da. of Arthur Edmund LEVESON of Hall Place, Ropley, co. Hertford. This marriage was diss. by divorce in 1978 and he *m.* 2ndly, 1980, Peta Carol, da. of Charles Victor Ormonde BINDING of Congresbury, Somerset.

[ANDREW VICTOR ARTHUR CHARLES, *styled* EARL OF HOPETOUN, s. and h. ap., *b.* 22 May 1969; ed. at Eton and Oxford (Exeter Coll.); *m.*, 1993, Skye Laurette, 1st da. of Major Bristow Charles BOVILL of Shipston on Stour, co. Warwick.]

LISBURNE

page 35,
line 25, for 'in 1727' read '16 Mar. 1726/7 at Norham'

page 36,
line 4, for 'about 1730' read '*bap.* 9 Jan. 1727/8'

page 37,
line 39, for 'Sapieka' read 'Sapieha'

page 38,
line 12, for 'was living 1930' read '*d.* 30 Aug. 1931.'
line 25, after 'subject.' add 'She *d.* 22 Jan. 1944 and he *m.* 2ndly, 14 Nov. 1961, Audrey Maureen Leslie, yr. da. of James MEAKIN of Westwood Manor, Leek, co. Stafford and widow of Robert Godfrey de Bohun DEVEREUX. He *d.* 30 June 1965. His widow *d.* 1978.
lines 26–8, delete all detail and replace as follows

EARLDOM [I.] VIII. VISCOUNTCY [I.] XII. } 1965 — 8 and 11. JOHN DAVID MALET (VAUGHAN), EARL OF LISBURNE, &c. [I.], only s. and h., *b.* 1 Sep. 1918, at the Grove, Watford, Herts, and *bap.* in the private chapel there; *styled* VISCOUNT VAUGHAN till 1965. He was ed. at Eton and Oxford (Magdalen Coll.); *m.*, 4 Dec. 1943, Shelagh, 1st da. of Tinothy Alfred MACAULEY of Montreal, Canada.

[DAVID JOHN FRANCIS MALET VAUGHAN, *styled* VISCOUNT VAUGHAN, 1st s. and h. ap., *b.* 15 June 1945; ed. at Ampleforth; *m.*, 1973, Jennifer Jane, only da. of James Desiré John William Fraser CAMPBELL of Glengarry, co. Inverness.]

LISLE

page 42,
line 5, after 'DEVON' add ', by Agnes da. of John DE ST. JOHN, of Basing, Hants'

page 51,
line 7, after 'PEMBRUGGE' add '(who surv. her)'

page 58,
line 21, for 'Sep. 1466' read '19 Jan. 1466/7'
note (j), delete all detail and replace by 'P.R.O. Exchequer Accounts Various, KR E101/412/2, Account Book of John Fogge, Treasurer of the Household, Mich. 1466 to Mich. 1467, p. 13, *sub Dieta* Monday 19 Jan. 1467, "Isto die nuptus fuit Viscount Lile filiae domini Herberd" (marginal note).'

page 62,
note (l), lines 1–2, delete from 'Muriel' to '(1510),' and replace by 'Margaret, who *m.* Edward (STAFFORD), 2nd EARL OF WILTSHIRE,'

page 63,
line 9, for '1495' read '1501(aa)'
note (aa) Edmund Dudley's first wife, Anne Windsor, was still alive in 1500, since she is mentioned in the will of her father-in-law, John Dudley, dated 1 October 1500 (see vol. xii, part 1, p. 306, note (g)). Elizabeth Lisle's son by Edmund Dudley was *b.* in 1502.
note (b), line 1, before 'On' add 'He was probably *b. circa* 1470, garments for a "lord the Bastard" appear in the mid-1471 accounts of George Lovekyn, yeoman tailor to Edward IV (Anne F. Sutton, *Costume*, no. 15, 1981, p. 11).'

page 67,
note (f), line 3, after 'Office.' add 'Edited as *The Lisle Letters*, 6 vols., Muriel St. Clare Byrne, 1981.'

page 71,
line 8, after 'Warwick' add ', by Maud, da. and h. of Matthew DE LA MARE' [See vol. ix, p. 127, *sub* MONTFORT.]

page 78,
line 22, after 'was' add '*b.* in co. Limerick and'

LISLE OF MOUNTNORTH

page 79,
line 11, after 'wife;' add '*b.* in Dublin;'

page 80,
line 15, delete '(a)'

VII. 1919. 7. JOHN NICHOLAS HORACE (LYSAGHT), BARON LISLE OF MOUNTNORTH [I. 1758], grandson and h., being 1st s. and h. of the abovesaid Horace George LYSAGHT and Emily Catherine, *b.* 10 Aug. 1903; *m.* 1stly, 21 Apr. 1928, Vivienne, da. of Rev. M. BREW. This marriage was diss. by divorce in 1939 (she *d.* 1948) and he *m.* 2ndly, 14 Jan. 1939, Marie Helen, da. of Adolph D. PURGOLD of Gobowen, co. Salop.

note ([a]), delete all detail

LISTOWEL

page 85,
lines 14–15, for 'was living 1930' read '*d.* 27, at Kingston House, Princes Gate, and was *bur.* 31 Dec. 1936.'
line 16, line to read as follows

IV. 1924. 4. RICHARD GRANVILLE (HARE), EARL OF LISTOWEL, &c., s. and h., *b.* 12 Sep. 1866, *styled* VISCOUNT ENNISMORE 1866–1924;

line 23, delete '([d])'
lines 23–4, delete from 'Having' to 'work.]' and replace by 'He *d.* 16 Nov. 1931. His widow *d.* 10 Mar. 1968.'

V. 1931. 5. WILLIAM FRANCIS (HARE), EARL OF LISTOWEL, &c., eld. s. and h., *b.* 28 Sep. 1906, *styled* VISCOUNT ENNISMORE 1924–31; ed. at Cambridge (Magdalene Coll.); *m.*, 24 July 1933, in the Sigismund Chapel, Royal Castle, Budapest, Judith, only da. of Raoul DE MARFFY-MANTUANO formerly Min. Plenipot. of Budapest. This marriage was diss. by divorce in 1945 and he *m.* 2ndly, 1 July 1958, Stephanie Sandra Yvonne, da. of Sam WISE of Toronto, Canada and formerly wife of Hugh CURRIE. This marriage was in turn diss. by divorce in 1963 and he *m.* 3rdly, 4 Nov. 1963, Pamela Mollie, da. of Francis DAY of Croydon and formerly wife of John Alexander READ.

[FRANCIS MICHAEL HARE, *styled* VISCOUNT ENNISMORE, s. and h. ap., *b.* 28 June 1964.]

note ([d]), delete all detail

LIVERPOOL

page 87,
line 16, for 'BISSHOP read 'BISHOP'

page 89,
line 29, after 'LIVERPOOL' add 'For first two Earls of the creation of 1905 see'
line 30, delete 'See'

VI. 1941. 3. GERALD WILLIAM FREDERICK (SAVILE), EARL OF LIVERPOOL, VISCOUNT HAWKESBURY and BARON HAWKESBURY, br. and h. being 3rd surv. s., 1st by 2nd wife, was *b.* 12 May 1878; ed. at Eton; *m.*, 29 July 1909, Constance Isabelle, only surv. da. of John HOLDEN of Hawton. co. Nottingham. He *d. s.p.* 27 July 1962. His widow *d.* 1976.

VII. 1962. 4. ROBERT ANTHONY EDWARD ST. ANDREW (SAVILE), EARL OF LIVERPOOL, &c., br. and h., *b.* 3 Apr. 1887; ed. at Malvern Coll. He *d.* unm. 13 Mar. 1969.

VIII. 1969. 5. EDWARD PETER BERTRAM SAVILE FOLJAMBE (SAVILE), EARL OF LIVERPOOL, &c., great-nephew and h., being s. of Peter George William SAVILE (*k.* in action 2 Sep. 1944), by Elizabeth Joan, yr. da. of Major Eric Charles Montagu FLINT of Hembury Castle, Torrington, Devon, which Peter George was only s. of Major Bertram Marmaduke Osbert SAVILE (*d.* 13 Oct. 1955), by Joyce Norton, 1st da. of W.B. EDMONDSON, which Bertram Marmaduke was 6th s. of 1st Earl of Liverpool. He was*b.* (posthumously) 14 Nov. 1944; ed. at Shrewsbury; *m.*, 29 Jan. 1970, Lady Juliana Mary Alice, 1st da. of Anthony Gerard Edward (NOEL), 5th EARL OF GAINSBOROUGH. She was *b.* 27 Jan. 1949.

[LUKE MARMADUKE PETER SAVILE, *styled* VISCOUNT HAWKESBURY, 1st s. and h. ap., *b.* 25 Mar. 1972.]

LLANDAFF

page 97,
line 25, for 'Clehanger' read 'Clehonger'

LLANGATTOCK

page 98,
line 26, line to read as follows

II. 1912. 2. JOHN MACLEAN (ROLLS), BARON LLANGATTOCK, 1st. s. and h.,

page 99,
lines 4–5, delete from 'Having' to 'work.'
line 6, delete ']'

LLANOVER

page 99,
line 8, after 'Benjamin' add 'Richard Crawshay'
line 11, for 'William' read 'Richard'

LOCH OF DRYLAW

page 101,
line 3, for 'was living in 1930' read '*d.* at Chelsea 12, and was *bur.* 16 Mar. 1938, at Stoke-by-Clare, Suffolk.'
line 19, after 'ASHBURTON' add 'He *d.* 14 Aug. 1942. His widow *d.* 1970.'
line 20, delete all detail and replace as follows

III. 1942. 3. GEORGE HENRY COMPTON (LOCH), BARON LOCH OF DRYLAW, 1st s. and h., *b.* 3 Feb. 1916; ed. at Eton and R.M.C., Sandhurst; *m.* 1stly, 5 Oct. 1942, Leila Mary Grace Isabel Hill, da. of Robert Duncanson MACKENZIE of Montreal, Canada. This marriage was diss. by divorce in 1946 and he *m.* 2ndly, 26 Oct. 1946, Doreen Betty, da. of Frederick Ernest PARSONS of Sydney, New South Wales and formerly wife of, 1stly, Cyril Alfred Flux DUNDAS and 2ndly of Michael Castillon DU PERRON. This marriage was in turn diss. by divorce in 1952 and he *m.* 3rdly, 1952, Joan Dorothy Hawthorn BINNS. This marriage was also diss. by divorce and he *m.* 4thly, 1975, Mrs Sylvia Barbara BEAUCHAMP-WILSON, only da. of A.G. Beauchamp CAMERON of Delmahoy, Midlothian. He *d. s.p.m.* 15 Dec. 1982. She *m.* 3rdly, 1984, Richard G.P. HAWKINS and was still living 1995.

IV. 1982. 4. SPENCER DOUGLAS (LOCH), BARON LOCH OF DRYLAW, br. and h., *b.* 12 Aug. 1920; ed. at Wellington and Cambridge (Trin. Coll.); *m.*, 1 Apr. 1948, Rachel, yr. da. of Lieut. Col. Howard Lister COOPER, by Nan Ino, *suo jure* BARONESS LUCAS OF CRUDWELL and of DINGWALL. She *d.* 1976 and he *m.*, 1979, Davina Julia, da. of FitzHerbert WRIGHT and formerly wife of Sir Richard BOUGHEY, Bart. He *d. s.p.m.s.* 24 June 1991 when his title became *extinct.* His widow was living 1995.

LONDESBOROUGH

page 105,
line 15, for 'was living in 1930' read '*d.* 13 June 1933 at Mill Hill Cottage, Barnes Common.'
lines 16–19, delete all detail and replace as follows

EARLDOM. III. BARONY. IV. } 1917 3 and 4. GEORGE FRANCIS WILLIAM HENRY (DENISON), EARL OF LONDESBOROUGH, &c., 1st s. and h., *b.* 17 July 1892; *styled* VISCOUNT RAINCLIFFE 1900–17. He *d.* unm., 12, and was *bur.* 17 Sep. 1920 at Londesborough.

lines 20–3, delete all detail and replace as follows

EARLDOM. IV. BARONY. V. } 1920 4 and 5. HUGO WILLIAM CECIL (DENISON), EARL OF LONDESBOROUGH, &c., 2nd s. and h., *b.* 13 Nov. 1894; ed. at Wellington; Capt. 1st Life Guards; served in WW1.(b) He *m.* 4 Sep. 1935, Marigold Rosemary Joyce, 3rd da. of Edgar LUBBOCK. He *d. s.p.m.* of pneumonia in a London Nursing Home, 17, and was *bur.* 20 Apr. 1937, at Blankney, Lincs, aged 42. At his death the Earldom of Londesborough and Viscountcy of Raincliffe became *extinct* but he was *suc.* in the Barony of Londesborough by his cousin. His widow, having married 2ndly, *d.* 1976.

VI. 1937. 6. ERNEST WILLIAM (DENISON), BARON LONDESBOROUGH, cousin and h., being only s. of Albert Denison Somerville DENISON, Rear Adm. (*d.* 2 Sep. 1903), by Louisa Crichlow, yst. da. of Antonio FABRIS of Beckenham, Kent, which Albert Denison Somerville was 2nd s. of 1st Baron

Londesborough. He was *b.* 9 Aug. 1876; *m.*, 1 June 1905, Sybil May, da. of Capt. Henry Thomas ANLEY of Binstead, Isle of Wight. She *d.* 5 July 1963. He *d. s.p.* 31 Dec. 1963.

VII. 1963. 7. CONYNGHAM CHARLES (DENISON), BARON LONDESBOROUGH, cousin and h., being 1st s. of Conyngham Albert DENISON, Cmdr., R.N. (*d.* 25 May 1938), by Evelyn Maude, da. of Charles Fox WEBSTER, which Conyngham Albert was 4th s. of 1st Baron Londesborough. He was *b.* 6 Apr. 1885; ed. at H.M.S. Britannia; *m.* 1stly, 8 Feb. 1912, Vera, only da. of Francis Hugh BAXENDALE of Framfield Place, Sussex. This marriage was diss. by divorce in 1925 and he *m.* 2ndly, 18 June 1926, Mabel Violet, da. of Matthew George MEGAW. She *d.* 30 July 1951 and he *m.* 3rdly, 23 Jan. 1952, Jocelyn Helen, da. of Hugh Duppa COLLINS, Lieut. Cmdr., R.N., of Bembridge, Isle of Wight. He *d. s.p.* 31 Oct. 1967. His widow was living 1995.

VIII. 1967. 8. JOHN ALBERT LISTER (DENISON), BARON LONDESBOROUGH, cousin and h., being only s. of Harold Albert DENISON, Lieut., R.N. (*d.* 2 Jan. 1948), by Katherine, da. of Sir Thomas Villiers LISTER, K.C.M.G., which Harold Albert was 5th s. of 1st Baron Londesborough. He was *b.* 30 May 1901; ed. at Wellington and Cambridge (Trin. Coll.); *m.* 1stly, 8 Jan. 1949, Lesley Maxwell Gordon, da. of Lieut. Col. Herbert Forbes CHURCHILL. This marriage was diss. by divorce in 1953 and he *m.* 2ndly, 15 June 1957, Elizabeth Ann, da. of Edward Little SALE and formerly wife of Thomas Chambers Windsor ROE. He *d.* 5 Apr. 1968. His widow *d.* 1994.

IX. 1968. 9. RICHARD JOHN (DENISON), BARON LONDESBOROUGH, only s. and h. by 2nd wife, *b.* 2 July 1959; ed. at Wellington and Exeter Univ.; *m.*, 1987, Rikki, da. of J.E. MORRIS.

[JAMES FREDERICK DENISON, s. and h. ap., *b.* 4 June 1990.]

LONDONDERRY

page 110,
note (a), line 3, after 'V.G.' add 'For the early ancestry of this family see "Pedigree of Stewarts of Ballylawn, Co. Donegal", by W.A. Stewart, *Geneal. Mag.*, vol. ix, 1936, pp. 302–9, also pp. 516–20.'

page 117,
line 12, line to read as follows

MARQUESSATE [I.]
VII.
EARLDOM [I.]
XIV.
BARONY [I.]
X. } 1915 7. CHARLES STEWART HENRY (VANE-TEMPEST-STEWART), MARQUESS OF LONDONDERRY, &c., only s. and h.,

lines 24–5, delete from 'Having' to 'work.]' and replace by 'He *d.* 11 Feb. 1949. His widow *d.* 23 Apr. 1959.'

MARQUESSATE [I.] VIII. EARLDOM [I.] XV. BARONY [I.] XI.	1949	8. EDWARD CHARLES STEWART ROBERT (VANE-TEMPEST-STEWART), MARQUESS OF LONDONDERRY, &c., only s. and h., *b.* 18 Nov. 1902; ed. at Eton and Oxford (Ch. Ch.); *m.*, 31 Oct. 1931, Romaine, 1st da. of Major Boyce COMBE of Dockenfield, Surrey. She *d.* 19 Dec. 1951. He *d.* 17 Oct. 1955.

MARQUESSATE [I.] IX. EARLDOM [I.] XVI. BARONY [I.] XII.	1955	9. ALEXANDER CHARLES ROBERT (VANE-TEMPEST-STEWART), MARQUESS OF LONDONDERRY, &c., only s. and h., *b.* 7 Sep. 1937; ed. at Eton; *m.*, 16 May 1958, Nicolette, only da. of Michael HARRISON by his wife BARONESS MARIA MADELEINE BENITA, da. of BARON ALEXANDER KARL WILHELM VON KOSKULL. This marriage was diss. by divorce in 1971

and he *m.* 2ndly, 1972, Doreen WELLS.

[FREDERICK AUBREY VANE-TEMPEST-STEWART, *styled* VISCOUNT CASTLEREAGH, s. and h. ap., *b.* 6 Sep. 1972.]

LONGFORD

page 125,
line 22, for 'was living 1930' read '*d.* 21 Nov. 1933.'
line 23, line to read as follows

EARLDOM [I.] VIII. BARONY [I.] XI.	1915	6 and 7. EDWARD ARTHUR HENRY (PAKENHAM), EARL OF LONGFORD, &c., 1st s. and h., *b.* 29 Dec. 1902;

lines 26–7, delete from 'Having' to 'work.]' and replace by 'He *d. s.p.* 4 Feb. 1961. His widow *d.* 1980.'

EARLDOM [I.] IX. BARONY [I.] XII.	1961	7 and 8. FRANCIS AUNGIER (PAKENHAM), EARL OF LONGFORD, &c., br. and h., *b.* 5 Dec. 1905; ed. at Eton and Oxford (New Coll.); *m.*, 3 Nov. 1931, Elizabeth, 1st da. of Nathaniel Bishop HARMAN. He was *cr.*, 12 Oct. 1945, BARON PAKENHAM of Cowley, in the City of Oxford.

[THOMAS FRANK DERMOT PAKENHAM, 1st s. and h. ap., *b.* 14 Aug. 1933; ed. at Ampleforth and Oxford (Magdalen Coll.); *m.*, 23 July 1964, Valerie Susan, yst. da. of Major Ronald Guthrie McNair SCOTT of Huish House, Old Basing, Hants. by his wife Mary Cecilia, 1st da. of William Ewart (BERRY), 1st VISCOUNT CAMROSE.]

LONGUEÜIL

page 126,
line 18, after 'action.' add 'His widow *m.* 11 Sep. 1770 at Montreal, William GRANT of

St. Roch, who *d.* 5 Oct. 1805. She *d.* 25 Feb. 1795.' [*ex inform.* Charles Evans, from J.M. Le Maine, *Picturesque Quebec*, 1882]

page 127,
line 11, after '1927.' add 'He *d. s.p.* 3 Aug. 1931.'

JOHN MOORE DE BIENVILLE CHARLES (GRANT), BARON DE LONGUEÜIL, half-brother and h., being 4th surv. s. of Charles Irwin GRANT by his 2nd wife. He was *b.* 10 Jan. 1861 in Bath. He *m.* 1886, Mary, da. of Joseph BARRON. He *d.* 17 Oct. 1938 at Maison Boale, Pau, aged 77.

RONALD CHARLES (GRANT), BARON DE LONGUEÜIL, eld. s. and h., *b.* 13 Mar. 1888. He *m.* 4 Oct. 1918, Mrs Ernestine Hester Maud SCOTT, da. of Ernest BOWES-LYON, br. of the 14th EARL OF STRATHMORE.

[RAOUL CHARLES GRANT, 1st s. and h., *b.* 7 July 1919. He *m.*, 3 Dec. 1941, Marcelle Aileen Mary, only da. of Georges WATERKEYN of Egham, Surrey. He was *k.* in action, *s.p.* Feb. 1942.]

RAYMOND DAVID GRANT, BARON DE LONGUEÜIL, br. and h., *b.* 3 Sep. 1921. He *m.*, 10 Aug. 1946, Anne Patricia, da. of Patrick Brough MALTBY.

[MICHAEL CHARLES GRANT, s. and h. ap., *b.* 20 June 1947.]

LONSDALE

page 131,
line 11, for 'Hilsington' read 'Helsington'
note ([d]), lines 3–5, delete from 'There' to 'list' and replace by 'The Baronetcy was *cr.* in 1638, before 16 Sep., when he was described as Sir John Lowther, Knt. and Baronet, in an entry in the Lowther Parish records, concerning a gift of ground for a school. In his own accounts for 1639 he recorded the cost of £850 for "the Baronetcy put upon me".' [*Ex inform.* Capt. Hugh Owen, R.N., to whom I also owe the subsequent Lowther corrections.]

page 132,
line 14, for '1692' read '13 Mar. 1691/2 in London, and was *bap.* 29 Mar. in St. Martin's in the Fields.' and for '1' read '24'
line 15, after 'there' add '8 Jan. 1713/14'
note ([c]), line 1, for 'In 1685 he pulled down and rebuilt Lowther Hall' read 'In 1691 he pulled down and began rebuilding Lowther Hall.'
line 12, For a full account of his life based on his published and unpublished memoirs and other original accounts, see Hugh Owen, *Lowther Family*, 1990, chap. 16.

page 133,
line 3, for '1694' read '30 July at Lowther and was *bap.* there 13 Aug. 1694.'

line 9, for '6 or 7' read '7'

line 10, after 'York,' add 'and was *bur.* 18 Mar. follg. at Lowther,' [*ex inform.* C. Roy Hudleston]

line 22, for 'Wresal' read 'Wressle'

line 25, after 'in' add '7'

note ([a]), lines 1–2, delete from 'which' to rebuilt' and replace by 'was partially destroyed by fire in 1718 and the surviving wings converted for domestic use.'

note ([c]), line 3, after 'V.G.' add 'For his life, and in particular for his part in resisting the 1715 and 1745 Jacobite risings, see Owen, *Lowther Family*, chap. 17.'

note ([d]), delete all detail and replace by 'His younger brother Anthony, was M.P. for Cockermouth 1721–2 and for Westmorland 1722–41. He *d.* unm. 24 Nov. 1741.'

page 134,

line 1, for '£2,000,000' read 'a very large sum of money' and for '2 Jan. 1755' read '15 Apr. 1756.'

line 2, delete from 'Sir' to 'Whitehaven' and replace by 'Sir William Lowther, 3rd Bart. of Holker.'

note ([a]), delete all detail and replace by 'When the Baronetcy of Lowther of Holker [1697] became *extinct*.'

page 135,

note ([b]), delete from 'who' to '109).' and replace by 'he was M.P. for Westmorland 1759–61 and 1763. He *d.* 1777.'

note ([d]), line 2, for '81' read '80'

line 3, for '8th' read '7th'

line 4, for '65' read '66'

page 137,

line 33, after 'She' add ', who' and after '1854' add '*d.* 12 May 1941. He *d. s.p.* 13 Apr. 1944.'

VII. 1944. 6. LANCELOT EDWARD (LOWTHER), EARL OF LONSDALE, &c., br. and h., *b.* 25 June 1867; ed. at Cheltenham and Cambridge (Magdalene Coll.); *m.* 1stly, 24 Apr. 1889, Sophia Gwendoline Alice, 1st da. of Sir Robert SHEFFIELD, Bart. She *d.* 4 Nov. 1921 and he *m.* 2ndly, 8 Oct. 1923, Sybil Beatrix, da. of Major Gen. Edward FLEETHAM of Ascot, Surrey. He *d.* 11 Mar. 1953. His widow *d.* 10 Mar. 1966.

[ANTHONY EDWARD LOWTHER, *styled* VISCOUNT LOWTHER, s. and h. ap., *b.* 24 Sep. 1896; ed. at Wellington and R.M.C., Sandhurst; *m.*, 1 Feb. 1922, Muriel Frances, 2nd da. of Sir George FARRAR, Bart. He *d. v.p.* 6 Oct. 1949. His widow *d.* 25 Feb. 1968.]

VIII. 1953. 7. JAMES HUGH WILLIAM (LOWTHER), EARL OF LONSDALE, &c., grandson and h., being s. and h. of Anthony Edward LOWTHER and Muriel Frances abovenamed. He was *b.* 3 Nov. 1922; ed. at Eton; *m.* 1stly, 18 June 1945, Tuppina Cecily, da. of Capt. Geoffrey Henry BENNETT. This marriage was diss. by divorce in 1962 and he *m.* 2ndly, 9 Sep. 1954, Jennifer, da. of

Christopher LOWTHER. This marriage was in turn diss. by divorce in 1962 and he *m.* 3rdly, 6 Mar. 1963, Nancy Ruth, da. of Thomas F. COBBS of California, U.S.A. and formerly wife of (__) STEPHENSON. This marriage was also diss. by divorce and he *m.* 4thly, 1975, Caroline Sheila, yst. da. of Sir Gerald Gordon LEY, Bart.

[HUGH CLAYTON LOWTHER, *styled* VISCOUNT LOWTHER, 1st s. and h. ap. by 1st wife, *b.* 27 May 1949; *m.* 1stly, Pamela Colleen MIDDLETON. This marriage was diss. by divorce and he *m.* 2ndly, 1986, Angela M., da. of Peter WYATT, Capt., R.N. of Dartmouth, Devon.]

LORN

page 139,
line 15, for 'shortly before 23 June 1481' read 'before 16 Jan. 1477/8'
line 17, for '1st lord Keith' read '1st EARL MARISCHAL'

LOTHIAN

page 156,
line 23, after 'TALBOT. add 'She *d.* at Monteviot Ancrum 19, and was *bur.* 22 June 1938 at Newbattle Abbey, Dalkeith.'

page 157,
line 16, after '*d.*' add 'unm.'
line 17, delete '([a])'

MARQUESSATE [S.] XI. EARLDOM [S.] XIV. 1930

11 and 12. PHILIP HENRY (KERR), MARQUESS OF LOTHIAN, &c., cousin and h., being 1st s. of Major Gen. Ralph Drury KERR (*d.* 18 Sep. 1916), by Anne, da. of Henry Granville (FITZALAN-HOWARD), 14th DUKE OF NORFOLK, which Ralph was 3rd s. of 7th Marquess of Lothian. He was *b.* 18 Apr. 1882; ed. at Oxford (New Coll.). He *d.* unm. 12 Dec. 1940.

MARQUESSATE [S.] XII. EARLDOM [S.] XV. 1940

12 and 13. PETER FRANCIS WALTER (KERR), MARQUESS OF LOTHIAN, &c., distant cousin and h., being 1st s. of Andrew William KERR, Capt., R.N. (*d.* 28 Mar. 1929), by Marie Constance Annabel, da. of Capt. William Walter Raleigh Kerr (desc. from 5th Marquess of Lothian), which Andrew William was 2nd s. of Adm. Walter Talbot KERR, (*d.* 12 May 1927), by Amabel Frederica Henrietta, yst. da. of George Augustus Frederick (COWPER), 6th EARL COWPER, which Walter Talbot was 4th s. of 7th Marquess of Lothian. He was *b.* 8 Sep. 1922; ed. at Ampleforth and Oxford (Ch. Ch.); *m.*, 30 Apr. 1943, Antonella, da. of Major Gen. Sir Foster Reuss NEWLAND, K.C.M.G.

[MICHAEL ANDREW FOSTER JUDE, *styled* EARL OF ANCRAM, 1st s. and h., *b.* 7 July 1945; ed. at Ampleforth, Oxford (Ch. Ch.) and Edinburgh Univ.; *m.*, 1975, Theresa Jane, 4th da. of Bernard Marmaduke (FITZALAN-HOWARD), 16th DUKE OF NORFOLK.]

note ([a]), delete all detail

LOUDOUN

page 165,
lines 23–4, for 'passed to the heir of line' read 'devolved as under'
lines 24–6, delete from 'his' to 'work'
lines 28–9, delete from 'who' to '*extinct*' and replace by 'see under DONINGTON in the present volume'

between lines 29 and 30 add as follows

* * * * * *

EARLDOM [S.] XII. BARONY [S.] XIII. } 1920

12 and 13. EDITH MAUD *suo jure* COUNTESS OF LOUDOUN, BARONESS CAMPBELL OF LOUDOUN, AND BARONESS TARRINZEAN AND MAUCHLINE [S.], niece and heir of line, being eld. da. of Paulyn Francis Cuthbert RAWDON-HASTINGS, 2nd s. of the above Edith Maud (mother of the 11th Earl), *b.* 11 May 1883, *m.* 12 Dec. 1916, Reginald Mowbray Chichester HUDDLESTON (afterwards ABNEY-HASTINGS), Capt. Royal Scots, who assumed by Royal lic. (15 Jan. 1918), the name and arms of ABNEY-HASTINGS in lieu of HUDDLESTON. On 7 Mar. 1921 the *abeyance* in the Baronies of BOTREAUX, STANLEY and HASTINGS of Hastings was determined in her favour by letters patent. Her 1st marriage was diss. by divorce in 1947, and she *m.* 2ndly, 1 Sep. 1954, Capt. Arthur Alexander HUBBLE, s. of Arthur Whibley HUBBLE of Hunton, Kent. She *d.* 24 Feb. 1960 when the Peerages of Scotland were inherited by her eldest da., but the Baronies of Botreaux, Stanley and Hastings fell into *abeyance* between her daughters, nephew and nieces.

[IAN HUDDLESTON, only s. and h. ap., *b.* 23 Mar. 1918, *styled* LORD MAUCHLINE 1918–44. He was *k.* on active service in Italy, *v.m.* and unm. 11 July 1944.]

EARLDOM [S.] XIII. BARONY [S.] XIV. } 1960

13 and 14. BARBARA HUDDLESTON, *later* ABNEY-HASTINGS, *suo jure* COUNTESS OF LOUDOUN, &c., 1st da. and h., *b.* 3 July 1919; *m.* 1stly, 5 Sep. 1939, Capt. Walter Strickland LORD. This marriage was diss. by divorce in 1945 and she *m.* 2ndly, 21 Nov. 1945, Capt. Gilbert Frederick GREENWOOD. He *d.* 24 May 1951 and she *m.* 3rdly, 15 Sep. 1954, Peter GRIFFITHS. They assumed by deed poll, 1955, the name of ABNEY-HASTINGS in place of GRIFFITHS.

[MICHAEL EDWARD STRICKLAND LORD, *later* (1946) ABNEY-HASTINGS, *styled* LORD MAUCHLINE, 1st s. and h. ap., *b.* 22 July 1942; ed. at Ampleforth; *m.*, 1969, Noelene Margaret, da. of W.J. MCCORMICK of Barham, New South Wales, Australia.]

note ([c]), lines 1–6 (nos. 5–6 on page 167), delete from 'On' to '1918'
line 9 (on page 167), after '1921' add 'See vol. xiii, pp. 94, 346.'

LOUTH

page 171,
note (e), line 8, for '14 June' read '11 June'

page 177,
line 16, after 'Kildare' add 'She *d.* 1916.'
line 29, after 'Hampstead.' add 'She *d.* 21 Apr. 1941. He *d.* 28 Oct. 1941.'
lines 17–19, delete all detail and replace as follows

XV. 1941. 15. OTWAY RANDAL PERCY OLIVER (PLUNKETT), BARON LOUTH [I.], 1st s. and h., *b.* 26 Apr. 1892; ed. at Downside; fought in WW1 with the Canadian Forces. He *m.* 4 July 1927, at St. Saviour's, St. Helier, Jersey, Ethel Molly, da. of Walter John GALLICHAN, a railway worker. He *d.* 3 Feb. 1950. His widow *d.* 1992.

XVI. 1950. 16. OTWAY MICHAEL JAMES OLIVER (PLUNKETT), BARON LOUTH [I.], only s. and h., *b.* 19 Aug. 1929; ed. at Downside; *m.*, 9 Aug. 1951, Angela Patricia, da. of William CULLINANE of St. Helier, Jersey.

[JONATHAN OLIVER PLUNKETT, 1st s. and h. ap., *b.* 4 Nov. 1952; ed. at De la Salle Coll. and Hautlieu Sch., Jersey and Hull Univ.; *m.*, 1981, Jennifer, da. of Norman Oliver HODGETTS of Coventry.]

note (b), delete all detail

LOVAINE

page 178,
line 10, for '(__)' read 'Maud de Flamville, da. of (__)' [See Lionel Landon, *Essex Arch. Trans.*, vol. 19, 1930, pp. 174–9.]

LOVAT

page 198,
line 7, for 'K.G.' read 'K.T.'
line 24, for 'Eskdale' read 'Eskadale'
line 25, for 'was living 1930' read '*d.* 3 Jan. 1938.'

page 199,
line 6, after '1892' add 'He *d.* 18, and was *bur.* 22 Feb. 1933 at Eskadale afsd. His widow *d.* 24 Mar. 1965.'
lines 7–8, delete all detail and replace as follows

BARONY [S.] XV. BARONY [U.K.] III. } 1933 15 and 4. SIMON CHRISTOPHER JOSEPH (FRASER), LORD LOVAT [S.], also BARON LOVAT [U.K.], 1st s. and h., *b.* 9 July 1911, MASTER OF LOVAT 1911–33; ed. at

Ampleforth and Oxford (Magdalen Coll.); *m.*, 10 Oct. 1938, Rosamund, only da. of Major Sir Henry Delves BROUGHTON, Bart.

[SIMON AUGUSTINE LOVAT, MASTER OF LOVAT, 1st s. and h. ap., *b.* 28 Aug. 1939; ed. at Ampleforth; *m.*, 1972, Virginia, da. of David GROSE. He *d. v.p.* 26 Mar. 1994. His widow was living 1995.]

[SIMON LOVAT, MASTER OF LOVAT, grandson and h., being s. and h. of Simon Augustine LOVAT and Virginia abovenamed, *b.* 13 Feb. 1977; ed. at Harrow.]

LOVEL

page 210,
line 16, after 'BRÉTEUIL' add 's. and h. (in Normandy) of William FITZOSBERN, 1st EARL OF HEREFORD'

page 211,
line 18, for 'COUNTS read 'COUNT'

page 217,
line 9, for '[LORD ROS]' read 'of Helmsley'

page 223,
line 14, after 'Joan,' add 'sister and (in her issue), coh. of William, 2nd VISCOUNT BEAUMONT,'

page 225,
note (a), line 4, after 'p. 12' add 'See Sutton and Hammond, *The Coronation of Richard III*, 1983, pp. 206, 218'
note (f), line 2, after 'sisters' add '(Joan, *m.* Sir Brian Stapleton and Frideswide, *m.* Sir Edward Norris),'
line 6, after 'of 'add 'Thomas Stapleton,' and after 'coheir' add '(see *Dignity of a Peer*, vol. 2, pp. 302–4)

LOVELACE

page 228,
line 11, for 'was living 1930' read '*d.* 18 Apr. 1941.'
line 12, line to read as follows

III. 1906. 3. LIONEL FORTESCUE (KING), EARL OF LOVELACE, &c., half-brother and h., being only s. of the 1st Earl by his 2nd wife,

lines 20–2, delete from 'Having' to 'work.(c)]' and replace by 'His widow *d.* 8 Oct. 1932.'

IV. 1929. 4. PETER MALCOLM (KING), EARL OF LOVELACE, &c., s. and h., *b.* 30 Mar. 1905; ed. at Eton; *m.* 1stly, 30 Mar. 1939, Doris EVISON. She *d.* 20 Sep. 1940 and he *m.* 2ndly, 18 June 1951, Manon Lis, da. of Axel

Sigurd TRANSO of Copenhagen and widow of Fredrik Gustav, BARON BLIXEN-FINECKE. He *d.* 4 Dec. 1964. His widow *d.* 1990.

V. 1964. 5. PETER AXEL WILLIAM (KING), EARL OF LOVELACE, &c., only s. and h., *b.* 26 Nov. 1951; *m.* 1stly, 1980, Kirsteen Oihrig, da. of Calum KENNEDY of Leethland, co. Renfrew. This marriage was diss. by divorce in 1989 and he *m.* 2ndly, 1994, Kathleen Anne SMOLDERS of Melbourne, Australia.

note (c), delete all detail

LOVELACE OF HURLEY

page 231,
note (c), delete all detail [This Francis was not a Lovelace of Hurley, he was br. of Richard Lovelace, the poet, and of Bethersden, Kent.]

LUCAN

page 239,
line 13, for 'Foot Guards' read 'Foot'

page 240,
line 20, line to read as follows

V. 1914. 5. GEORGE CHARLES (BINGHAM), EARL OF LUCAN, &c., 1st s. and h., *b.* 13 Dec. 1860, at 51 Portland Place afsd., and *bap.* at All Souls, Langham Place, 2 Mar. 1861, *styled* Lord Bingham 1888–1914;

line 29, after '1924.' add 'He was *cr.*, 26 June 1934, BARON BINGHAM of Melcombe Bingham, co. Dorset [U.K.] [for further detail see vol. xiii, p. 537].'
lines 33–4, delete from 'Having' to 'work.]' and replace by 'He *d.* 20 Apr. 1949. His widow *d.* 1972.'

VI. 1949. 6. GEORGE CHARLES PATRICK (BINGHAM), EARL OF LUCAN, &c., s. and h. [for further detail see note (c)]. He *d.* 21 Jan. 1964. His widow *d.* 1985.

VII. 1964. 7. RICHARD JOHN (BINGHAM), EARL OF LUCAN, &c., 1st s. and h., *b.* 18 Dec. 1934; ed. at Eton; *m.*, 28 Nov. 1963, Veronica, 3rd da. of Major Charles Moorhouse DUNCAN, M.C. He disappeared 7 Nov. 1974 and has not been seen since.

[GEORGE CHARLES BINGHAM, *styled* LORD BINGHAM, s. and h. ap., *b.* 21 Sep. 1967; ed. at Eton and Cambridge (Trin. Hall).]

LUCAS

page 244,
line 9, line to read as follows

IX. 1905. 9. AUBERON THOMAS (HERBERT), BARON LUCAS OF CRUDWELL and

lines 21–2, delete from 'Having' to 'work.]'
line 23, line to read as follows

X. 1916. 10. NAN INO, *suo jure* BARONESS LUCAS OF CRUDWELL [1663], also

line 27, delete from 'Having' to 'work.]' and replace by 'She *d.* 3 Nov. 1958. Her widower *d.* 1972.'

XI. 1958. 11. ANNE ROSEMARY PALMER *suo jure* BARONESS LUCAS OF CRUDWELL, also BARONESS DINGWALL, 1st da. of Nan Ino and Howard Lister COOPER abovementioned. She was *b.* 28 Apr. 1919; *m.*, 11 May 1950, Major Robert Jocelyn PALMER, M.C., 3rd s. of Roundell Cecil (PALMER), 3rd EARL OF SELBORNE. He *d.* 30 Nov. 1991. She *d.* 31 Dec. 1991.

XII. 1991. 12. RALPH MATTHEW (PALMER), BARON LUCAS OF CRUDWELL and BARON DINGWALL, 1st s. and h., *b.* 7 June 1951; ed. at Eton and Oxford (Balliol Coll.); *m.*, 1978, Clarissa Marie, da. of George Vivian LOCKETT of Stratford St. Mary, Colchester, Essex.

[LEWIS EDWARD PALMER, s. and h. ap., *b.* 7 Dec. 1987.]

LUCY

page 248,
line 18, for '13 Aug. 1218' read '10 Mar. 1217/18' [See vol. ix, p. 401, *sub* MULTON.]

page 252,
line 11, for 'Parl.' read 'a Council'
line 12, delete from 'again' to death' and replace by 'to Parl.'

page 253,
line 6, after 'MULTON' add '[2nd LORD MULTON]'
line 7, after 'MULTON' add '[1st LORD MULTON]'

page 254,
line 8, after 'ANGUS' add '[S.]'
note (h), line 1, for 'Bintworth' read 'Bentworth'

page 256,
line 15, after 'HASTINGS,' add '*de jure* 10th Lord Hastings,'

page 258,
line 16, after 'Eve' add ', da. and h. of Eustace'
note (i), after 'DESPENSER' add ', vol. iv, p. 287, note (c)'

page 262,
line 18, after '1stly,' add 'Margaret NEVILL, kinswoman of the Earl of March, 2ndly,' [*Cal. Pat. Rolls, 1422–9*, pp. 322, 342, both dated 1426]
line 20, for '2ndly' read '3rdly'

page 263,
note (b), line 2, after 'Worcester.' add 'See also *Gregory's Chronicle* (Camden Soc. N.S., vol. xvii), p. 207, and W. Worcester, *Annales* (Stevenson, *Wars of the English*), R.S. vol. ii, part 2, pp. 773, 788.'

LUMLEY

page 268,
line 12, after 'brother' add ', the 4th Lord'

page 274,
note (e), delete from 'No evidence' to 'marriage' and replace by 'The evidence for this marriage is found in two sources. The earliest of these is Harl. MS. 1074, f. 306 (published in *Collect. Misc. et Geneal.*, vol. i, 1834, p. 304), which states that Thomas Lumley "wedded a bastard daughter of King Edward IV". This manuscript dates from *circa* 1505, and is thus virtually contemporary. The next piece of evidence is from Thomas Tonge's *Visitation of the North* in 1530. This says that Thomas Lumley, s. and h. of George Lord Lumley, married Elizabeth, bastard da. of Edward IV, by whom he had Richard, Lord Lumley, and other issue (College of Arms MS. E6, f. 5b, also in Harl. MS. 1499, f. 47b, see *Heraldic Visitation of the Northern Counties in 1530*, by Thomas Tonge, ed. W.H.D. Longestaffe, Surtees Society, 1863, p. 27, for the latter. This manuscript was owned by Thomas Wriothesley, Garter King of Arms, *d.* 1534). The assertion that there were any issue is certainly not true.'

LURGAN

page 283,
line 6, after '£8500' add 'He *d.* 9 Feb. 1937 in a London Nursing Home and was *bur.* at Culford.'
lines 7–8, delete all detail and replace as follows

IV. 1937. 4. WILLIAM GEORGE EDWARD (BROWNLOW), BARON LURGAN, s. and h., *b.* 22 Feb. 1902; ed. at Eton and Oxford; *m.*, 1979, Florence May, da. of Louis Francis Squire WEBSTER of Johannesburg, South Africa, and widow of Eric COOPER of Johannesburg afsd. He *d. s.p.* 30 Jan. 1984. His widow was living 1995.

V. 1984. 5. JOHN DESMOND CAVENDISH (BROWNLOW), BARON LURGAN, cousin and h., being 2nd but 1st surv. s. of Francis Cecil BROWNLOW (*d.* 21 Dec. 1932), by Angela, 1st da. of Samuel Radcliffe PLATT of Werneth Park, Oldham, co. Lancaster, which Francis Cecil was 3rd s. of 2nd Baron Lurgan. He was *b.* 26 June 1911; ed. at Eton. He *d.* unm. and *s.p.* 17 Sep. 1991 when his Barony became *extinct*.

LUTEREL

page 286,
note (h), before 'Thoroton' add 'A Master Henry Duket paid £20 for the marriage of Joan who was wife of Robert Luterel, P.R.O. *Pipe Roll*, 1303/4, 32 Edw. I;'

LYNEDOCH

page 301,
line 6, for 'Foi' read 'Foy'

LYTTELTON

page 311,
note (h), line 18 (on page 312), for 'Arnflett' read 'Amphlett'
line 19, for 'them each £5000' read 'two sisters each £5,000, the third £2,500'

page 314,
line 8, for '3 Mar.' read '4 Mar.'

LYTTON

page 317,
note (b), line 1, for 'Guestwich' read 'Guestwick'

page 319,
line 12, for 'was living 1930' read '*d.* 17, at Knebworth, and was *bur.* 21 Sep. 1936.'

page 320,
line 5, after 'Jerusalem' add 'He *d.* 25 Oct. 1947. His widow *d.* 1971.'
line 8, after 'godfather' add 'He was ed. at Eton and Oxford (Magdalen Coll.). He *d. v.p.* and unm. 1, as the result of an air accident at Hendon, and was *bur.* 5 May 1933 at Knebworth.'

[ALEXANDER EDWARD JOHN BULWER-LYTTON, *styled* VISCOUNT KNEBWORTH, 2nd but only surv. s. and h. ap., *b.* 11 Mar. 1910; ed. at Cambridge (Trin. Coll.). He was *k.* at El Alamein, 4 July 1942, *v.p.* and unm.]

EARLDOM. III. BARONY. IV. } 1947 3 and 4. NEVILLE STEPHEN (BULWER-LYTTON), EARL OF LYTTON, &c., br. and h., *b.* 6 Feb. 1879; ed. at Eton and École des Beaux Arts, Univ. of Paris; *m.* 1stly, 2 Feb. 1899, Judith Anne Dorothea, *suo jure* BARONESS WENTWORTH [for further detail see vol. xii, part 2, p. 516, note (d), from p. 515]. This marriage was diss. by divorce in 1923 (she *d.* 8 Aug. 1957) and he *m.* 2ndly, 1 May 1924, Alexandra FORTEL of Paris. He *d.* 9 Feb. 1951. His widow *d.* 1980.

EARLDOM. IV. BARONY. V. } 1951 4 and 5. NOEL ANTHONY SCAWEN (LYTTON, *afterwards* LYTTON-MILBANKE, *later* LYTTON), EARL OF LYTTON, &c., only s. and h. by 1st wife, *b.* 7 Apr. 1900; ed. at Downside and R.M.C., Sandhurst; inherited, 8 Aug. 1957, the Barony of Wentworth on the death of his mother [for further detail see note referred to above]. He *m.*, 30 Nov. 1946, Clarissa Mary, 1st da. of Brig. Gen. Cyril Eustace PALMER of Christchurch, Hants. He *d.* 18 Jan. 1985. His widow was living 1995.

EARLDOM. IV. BARONY. VI. } 1985 4 and 6. JOHN PETER MICHAEL SCAWEN (LYTTON-MILBANKE, *afterwards* LYTTON), EARL OF LYTTON [1880], VISCOUNT KNEBWORTH [1880], BARON WENTWORTH [E. 1529], and BARON LYTTON OF KNEBWORTH [1866]. 1st s. and h., was *b.* 7 June 1950; *styled* VISCOUNT KNEBWORTH till 1985; ed. at Downside and Reading Univ.; *m.*, 1980, Ursula, da. of Anton KOMOLY of Vienna, Austria.

[PHILIP ANTHONY SCAWEN LYTTON, *styled* VISCOUNT KNEBWORTH, s. and h. ap., *b.* 7 Mar. 1989.]

LYVEDEN

page 320,
line 30, after 'WILSON.' add ', both being children by Mrs Elizabeth WILSON. [*ex inform.* R.M. Glencross]

page 322,
lines 5–8, delete all detail and replace as follows

IV. 1926. 4. ROBERT FITZPATRICK COURTENAY (VERNON), BARON LYVEDEN, s. and h., *b.* 1 Feb. 1892; ed. at Harrow. Served in WW1, 1914–18 as Paymaster-Lieut. R.N.R.(b) He *m.* 28 Oct. 1949, Doris Violet, da. of Henry Francis Coghlan WHITE of Courlands, West Hoathly, Sussex. He *d. s.p.* 9 Jan. 1969. His widow *d.* 1985.

V. 1969. 5. SYDNEY MUNROE ARCHIBALD (VERNON), BARON LYVEDEN, distant cousin and h., being 1st s. of Cecil Sydney Archibald VERNON (*d.* 22 Oct. 1944), by Jessie Jane MUNROE, which Cecil Sydney was 2nd s. of Greville Richard VERNON (*d.* 19 Feb. 1909), by Susan Caroline, 2nd da. of Richard Howe COCKERELL, Cmdr., R.N., which Greville Richard was 4th s. of 1st Baron Lyveden. He was *b.* 21 Nov. 1888; ed. at Northland Private Boarding Sch.; *m.* 1stly, 2 July 1912, Ruby, da. of Robert John SHANDLEY. She *d.* 26 Jan. 1932 and he *m.* 2ndly, 1959, Gladys, widow of John CASSIDY. He *d.* 19 Sep. 1973. His widow *d.* 1986.

VI. 1973. 6. RONALD CECIL (VERNON), BARON LYVEDEN, only s. and h., *b.* 10 Apr. 1915; ed. at Te Aroha College, New Zealand; *m.*, 21 May 1938, Queenie Constance, da. of Howard ARDERN.

[JACK LESLIE VERNON, 1st s. and h. ap., *b.* 10 Nov. 1938; *m.*, 11 Nov. 1961, Lynette June, da. of William Herbert LILLEY of Auckland, New Zealand.]

MACAULAY

page 326,
note ([a]), line 5, for 'set' read 'sect'

MACCLESFIELD

page 330,
line 2, after '1659;' add 'ed. at Oxford (Ch. Ch.), matric. 1671'

page 331,
note ([e]), line 3, for 'Earl of' read 'Lord'

page 332,
line 12, for 'Nuneham' read 'Wincham'

page 333,
note ([e]), lines 3–4, delete from ', whose' to 'Earl'

page 337,
line 6, after '1895–6;' add 'ed. at Eton and'
line 9, delete '([b])' and replace by 'She *d.* 1974. He *d.* 20 Sep. 1975.'

XI. 1975. 11. GEORGE ROGER ALEXANDER THOMAS (PARKER), EARL OF MACCLESFIELD, &c., s. and h., *b.* 6 May 1914, *styled* LORD PARKER 1914–75; ed. at Stowe; *m.*, 18 June 1938, Valerie, only da. of Ralph Sheldon (MANSFIELD), 4th BARON MANSFIELD. He *d.* 7 Dec. 1992. His widow was living 1995.

XII. 1992. 12. RICHARD TIMOTHY GEORGE MANSFIELD (PARKER), EARL OF MANSFIELD, &c., 1st s. and h., *b.* 31 May 1943; ed. at Stowe and Oxford (Worcester Coll.); *m.* 1stly, 11 Aug. 1967, Tatiana Cleone Anne, only da. of Major Craig WHEATON-SMITH of Wenham, Massachusetts, U.S.A. This marriage was diss. by divorce in 1985 and he *m.* 2ndly, 1986, Sandra Hope (Mrs MEAD), da. of Silvio FIORE of Florida, U.S.A.

note ([b]), delete all detail

MACDONALD

page 341,
line 24, after 'Kilmore.' add 'He *d.* 20 Jan. 1947.'
line 31, after 'BANKES.' add 'His widow *d.* 7 Nov. 1928.'

page 342,
lines 1–3, delete all detail and replace as follows

VII. 1947. 7. ALEXANDER GODFREY (MACDONALD), BARON MACDONALD OF SLATE [I.], grandson and h., being 1st s. and h. of Godfrey Evan Hugh BOSVILLE-MACDONALD and Helen his wife next abovenamed. He was *b.* 27 June 1909; ed. at Eton and Cambridge (Magdalene Coll.). As Chief of the name and arms of Macdonald of Macdonald and inheritor of the feudal barony of Macdonald the ancient arms of Macdonald were restored to him, 1 May 1947, by the Lord Lyon. He *m.*, 14 June 1945, Anne, only da. of Alfred WHITAKER of Itchenor, Sussex. He *d.* 29 Nov. 1970. His widow *d.* 1988.

VIII. 1970. 8. GODFREY JAMES (MACDONALD), BARON MACDONALD OF SLATE, 1st s. and h., *b.* 28 Nov. 1947; ed. at Eton; *m.*, 14 June 1969, Claire, 1st da. of Thomas Noel CATLOW, Cmdr., R.N., of Tunstall, Carnforth, co. Lancaster.

[GODFREY EVAN HUGO THOMAS MACDONALD, s. and h. ap., *b.* 24 Feb. 1982.]

MADERTY

page 348,
line 23, for '20 Jan. 1691/2' read 'in or before 1694'
note (g), line 1, before 'It' add 'His autograph is in a volume of the Innerpeffray Library, the imprint of which is 1694, but it is not found in books of a later date.'

MAGHERAMORNE

page 355,
lines 15–16, delete from 'He was' to 'work'
line 18, after 'REVELSTOKE' add 'She *d.* 22 Jan. 1931. Her 2nd husband *d.* 20 Aug. 1949.'

III. 1903. 3. DUDLEY STUART (MCGAREL-HOGG), BARON MAGHERAMORNE, br. and h., *b.* 3 Dec. 1863. He *d.* unm. 14 Mar. 1946.

IV. 1946. 4. RONALD TRACY (MCGAREL-HOGG), BARON MAGHERAMORNE, br. and h., *b.* 28 July 1865. He *d.* unm. and *s.p.* 21 Apr. 1957 when his Barony and the Baronetcy became *extinct*.

note (c), delete all detail

MALMESBURY

page 358,
line 23, for 'WINCHENDEN' read 'WINCHENDON'
line 24, for 'WOBURN, co. Beds' read 'WOOBURN, co. Bucks.'

page 363,
line 3, after 'Jerusalem' add 'She *d*. 21, at Scots Hill House, Croxley Green, Herts. and was *bur*. 23 Nov. 1935 at All Saints', Broomfield, Bridgwater, Somerset.'
line 19, after 'there' add 'She *d*. 3 Apr. 1934'

page 364,
line 5, after 'Gate' add 'He *d*. 12 June 1950. His widow *d*. 1972.'
line 6, line to read as follows

VI. 1950. 6. WILLIAM JAMES (HARRIS), EARL OF MALMESBURY, &c., only s. and h.,

line 8, after 'sponsors' add '*styled* VISCOUNT FITZHARRIS 1907–50;'
line 11, for ']' read 'He *m*. 1stly, 7 July 1932, Diana Claudia Patricia, 1st da. of Dudley Massey Pigott (CARLETON), 2nd BARON DORCHESTER. She *d*. 1990 and he *m*. 2ndly, 1991, Margaret Fleetwood, yst. da. of Col. Robert William Pigott Clarke CAMPBELL-PRESTON of Ardchattan Priory, co. Argyll.

[JAMES CARLETON HARRIS, *styled* VISCOUNT FITZHARRIS, 1st s. and h. ap. by 1st wife, *b*. 19 June 1946; ed. at Eton and Univ. of St. Andrews; *m*., 14 June 1969, Sally Ann, yr. da. of Sir Richard Newton RYCROFT, Bart.]

MANCHESTER

page 379,
line 13, for 'EVANS' read 'GREEN. This marriage was diss. by divorce in 1931 (she *m*. 2ndly, 23 Nov. 1937, Arthur George (KEITH), 10th EARL OF KINTORE, and she *d*. 1971.), he *m*. 2ndly, 17 Dec. 1931, Kathleen, da. of W.H. DAWES. He *d*. 9 Feb. 1947. His widow *d*. 28 Mar. 1966.'
line 14, line to read as follows

DUKEDOM. X. EARLDOM. XIII. } 1947 10 and 13. ALEXANDER GEORGE FRANCIS DROGO (MONTAGU), DUKE OF MANCHESTER, &c., 1st s. and h.,

line 17, after 'sponsors' add '*styled* VISCOUNT MANDEVILLE 1902–47; ed. at R.N.C.S, Osborne and Dartmouth.'
line 19, for ']' read 'She *d*. 2 Sep. 1966 and he *m*. 2ndly, 7 Feb. 1969, Elizabeth, da. of Samuel Clyde FULLERTON of Miami, Oklahoma, U.S.A. and formerly wife of W.W. CROCKER. He *d*. 23 Nov. 1977. His widow was living 1995.

DUKEDOM. XI. EARLDOM. XIV. } 1977 11 and 14. SIDNEY ARTHUR ROBIN GEORGE DROGO (MONTAGU), DUKE OF MANCHESTER, &c., 1st s. and h., *b*. 5 Feb. 1929; *m*. 1stly, 5 Feb. 1955, Adrienne Valerie, 1st da. of John Kenneth CHRISTIE of Sedgerfield, Cape Province, South Africa. This marriage was diss. by divorce in 1978 (she *d*. 1988) and he *m*. 2ndly, 1978, Andrea, da. of Cecil Alexander JOSS of Johannesburg, South Africa and formerly wife of 1stly, Major S. WHITEHEAD and 2ndly of G.J.W. KENT. He *d. s.p.* 3 June 1985. His widow was living 1995.

DUKEDOM. XII. EARLDOM. XV. } 1985 12 and 15. ANGUS CHARLES DROGO (MONTAGU), DUKE OF MANCHESTER, &c., br. and h., *b.* 9 Oct. 1938; ed. at Gordonstoun; *m.* 1stly, 22 Nov. 1961, Mary Eveleen, da. of Walter Gillespie MCCLURE of Geelong, Australia. This marriage was diss. by divorce in 1970 and he *m.* 2ndly, 1971, Diane Pauline, da. of Arthur PLIMSAUL of Corfe Mullen, Dorset. This marriage was in turn diss. by divorce in 1985 and he *m.* 3rdly, 1989, Ann-Louise (Mrs BIRD), da. of Dr Alfred Butler TAYLOR of Cawthorne, co. York.

[ALEXANDER CHARLES DAVID DROGO MONTAGU, *styled* VISCOUNT MANDEVILLE, 1st s. and h. by 1st wife, *b.* 11 Dec. 1962.]

MANNERS

page 383,
line 18, line to read as follows

IV. 1927. 4. FRANCIS HENRY (MANNERS), BARON MANNERS OF FOSTON, 2nd and only surv. s. and h., *b.* 21 July 1897; ed. at Eton and Cambridge (Trin. Coll.).

page 384,
lines 1–2, delete from '([a])' to 'work.]' and replace by 'He *d.* 25 Nov. 1972. His widow *d.* 1994.'

V. 1972. 5. JOHN ROBERT (MANNERS), BARON MANNERS OF FOSTON, 1st s. and h., *b.* 13 Feb. 1923; ed. at Eton and Oxford (Trin. Coll.); *m.*, 6 Oct. 1949, Jennifer Selena, only da. of Stephen Ian FAIRBAIRN.

[JOHN HUGH ROBERT MANNERS, s. and h. ap., *b.* 5 May 1956; ed. at Eton. He *m.* 1983, Lanya Mary, da. of Dr H.E. HEITZ.]

note ([a]), delete all detail

MANSFIELD

page 392,
note ([b]), for 'Midlothian' read 'Middlesex'

page 394,
lines 1–2, delete from 'He was' to 'work.' and replace as follows

VI. and V. 1906. 6 and 5. ALAN DAVID (MURRAY), EARL OF MANSFIELD, &c., br. and h., *b.* 25 Oct. 1864; ed. at Charterhouse and R.M.C., Sandhurst. He *m.* 20 Apr. 1899, Margaret Helen Mary, da. of Rear Adm. Sir Malcolm MACGREGOR, Bart., by Helen Laura, da. of HUGH SEYMOUR (MCDONNELL), 4th EARL OF

ANTRIM. She *d.* 13 Feb. 1933 at Ard Choille, Perth. He *d.* 14, at Ard Choille, afsd. and was cremated and *bur.* privately, 16 Mar. 1935, at Scone.

VII. and VI. 1935. 7 and 6. MUNGO DAVID MALCOLM (MURRAY), EARL OF MANSFIELD, &c., only s. and h., *b.* 9 Aug. 1900, *styled* LORD SCONE 1906–35. Ed. at Oxford (Ch. Ch.). He *m.* 19 July 1928, Dorothea Helena, da. of Sir Lancelot Douglas CARNEGIE. He *d.* 2 Sep. 1971. His widow *d.* 1985.

VIII. and VII. 1971. 8 and 7. WILLIAM DAVID MUNGO JAMES (MURRAY), EARL OF MANSFIELD, &c., only s. and h., *b.* 7 July 1930; ed. at Eton and Oxford (Ch. Ch.); *m.*, 19 Dec. 1955, Pamela Joan, only da. of Wilfred Neill FOSTER.

[ALEXANDER DAVID MUNGO MURRAY, *styled* VISCOUNT STORMONT, 1st s. and h. ap., *b.* 17 Oct. 1956; ed. at Eton. He *m.*, 1985, Sophia Mary Veronica, only da. of Philip Biden Derwent ASHBROOKE of St. John, Jersey, Channel Islands.]

note (a), delete all detail

MANVERS

page 396,
line 32, after 'net' add 'His widow *d.* 11 Mar. 1939.'
lines 33–5, delete all detail and replace as follows

V. 1926. 5. EVELYN ROBERT (PIERREPONT), EARL MANVERS, &c., s. and h., *b.* 25 July 1888, *styled* VISCOUNT NEWARK 1900–26; ed. at Eton. He *d.* unm. 6 Apr. 1940.

VI. 1940. 6. GERVASE EVELYN (PIERREPONT), EARL MANVERS [1806], VISCOUNT NEWARK [1796], BARON PIERREPONT [1796], cousin and h., being 1st s. of Evelyn Henry PIERREPONT (*d.* 4 June 1926), by Sophia, da. of William ARKWRIGHT of Sutton Scarsdale, co. Derby, which Evelyn Henry was 2nd s. of 3rd Earl Manvers. He was *b.* 15 Apr. 1881; ed. at Winchester and R. Indian Eng. Coll., Cooper's Hill. He *m.*, 5 Feb. 1918, Marie-Louise Roosevelt, da. of Sir Frederick W.L. BUTTERFIELD. He *d. s.p.m.s.* 13 Feb. 1955 when all his titles became *extinct*.

[EVELYN LOUIS BUTTERFIELD PIERREPONT, *styled* VISCOUNT NEWARK, s. and h. ap., *b.* 8 May 1924. He *d. v.p.* 29 Sep. 1928.]

MAR

page 403,
line 10, after 'and' add 'said to have been'

page 406,
line 1, for 'SIR RICHARD TALBOT of Goodrich' read 'Richard (TALBOT), 2nd LORD TALBOT'

line 12, after 'Scotland.' add 'See fuller particulars *sub* TALBOT [1332 and 1346].'

page 430,
line 15, for 'Aug.' read 'July' [*Carlisle Patriot*, 6 Aug. 1825, *ex inform.* C. Roy Hudleston]

page 432,
line 26, line to read as follows

XXVIII. 1930. 27. JOHN FRANCIS HAMILTON SINCLAIR CUNLIFFE BROOKS FORBES (GOODEVE-ERSKINE), EARL OF MAR [S. 1393 or 1404], only s. and h., *b.* 27 Feb. 1868, at Bournemouth, Hants., *styled* LORD GARIOCH,(c) 1868–1930,

lines 32–3, delete from 'Having' to 'work.]' and replace by 'He *d. s.p.* 29 Sep. 1932 at Foveran, Aberdeenshire, aged 64. His widow *d.* 20 July 1958.'

XXIX. 1932. 28. LIONEL WALTER YOUNG (GOODEVE-ERSKINE, *later* ERSKINE), EARL OF MAR, distant cousin and h., being s. of Major Charles Walter ERSKINE (*d.* 1898), by Constance Barnes, da. of Rev. John Lovick JOHNSON, which Charles Walter was s. of Frances Jemima (*d.* 11 Aug. 1887), by Lieut. Gen. James Nowell YOUNG, which Frances Jemima was da. of Frances Jemima (*d.* 20 June 1842), by William James GOODEVE, who *d.* 22 Dec. 1861, which Frances Jemima was da. of 24th Earl of Mar and sister of 25th Earl. He was *b.* 13 June 1891. He assumed the surname of ERSKINE, 1932, registered at the Lyon Court. He *d.* unm. 27 Nov. 1965.

XXX. 1965. 29. JAMES CLIFTON (GOODEVE-ERSKINE, *later* OF MAR), EARL OF MAR, cousin and h., being s. of Charles Macdonald GOODEVE-ERSKINE (*d.* 30 Apr. 1956), by Jessie Helen, 1st da. of John Brown GRANT, which Charles Macdonald was s. of Alice (*d.* 25 Apr. 1951), by James Horsburgh LANE (*d.* 11 Dec. 1915), which Alice was da. of Francis Jemima and James Nowell YOUNG abovesaid. He was *b.* 22 Nov. 1914; ed. at Marlborough. Recognised, 1959, by warrant of the Lord Lyon, in the surname OF MAR. He *m.* 1stly, 1939, Millicent Mary, da. of William SALTON. This marriage was diss. by divorce in 1958 (she *d.* 1993) and he *m.* 2ndly, 1960, Marjorie Aileen, da. of John Reginald MILLER and widow of Major C.W.S. GRICE. He *d. s.p.m.s.* 21 Apr. 1975. His widow *d.* 1975.

[DAVID CHARLES OF MAR, *styled* LORD GARIOCH, s. and h. ap., *b.* 10 Aug. 1944; ed. at Gosfield Sch., Essex. He *d.* unm. and *v.p.* 8 Jan. 1967.]

XXXI. 1975. 30. MARGARET ALISON, *suo jure* COUNTESS OF MAR, 1st da. and h., *b.* 19 Sep. 1940. Recognised, 5 July 1967, in the surname OF MAR by warrant of the Lord Lyon, when she also ceased to use her 2nd name of Alison. She *m.* 1stly, 1959, Edwin Noel ARTISS, who was also recognised, 5 July 1967, by warrant of the Lord Lyon, in the style of Edwin Noel OF MAR. This marriage was diss. by divorce in 1976 and she *m.* 2ndly, 1976, John Leslie SALTON. He was recognised, 1976, by warrant of the Lord Lyon, in the surname OF MAR, when he also abandoned his name of

Leslie. This marriage was in turn diss. by divorce in 1981 and she *m.* 3rdly, 1982, John H. JENKIN.

MARCH

page 433,
note ([e]), after '558' add '; P.R.O. Exchequer K.R. E101 369/4; "with apparel tanquam filii baronis"'

page 439,
note ([h]), line 5, after 'descent' add 'of his wife'

page 441,
line 17, after 'da.' add 'and eventually coh.'

page 445,
line 7, after 'da.' add 'and (in her issue) coh.'

page 448,
line 1, for 'predeceased him' read '*d.* on or before 7 Jan. 1377/8' [See Lane, *Royal Daughters*, vol. 1, p. 233.]
lines 1–2, delete from 'Will' to '1381.([b])'
note ([b]), delete all detail
note ([e]), line 11, for 'Sir Thomas Poynings' read 'Thomas (de Poynings), 5th Lord St. John (of Basing)'

page 453,
lines 20–1, delete from ', but' to '1426' [See vol. xii, part 2, p. 906, note ([a]), *sub* YORK.]

MARE

page 464,
line 6, after 'and' add 'eventually'

MARISCHAL

page 473,
lines 11–12, delete from 'a' to 'da.' and replace by 'Jean, yst. da. of Robert II'

page 485,
note ([a]), line 2, for 'also attainted' read 'apparently not *attainted* (a letter in the possession of Lord Elphinstone, in 1915, from the Earl Marischal to his brother on 1 Aug. 1731, says "you are not attainted." See E.C. Cushell, *The Scottish Friend of Frederick the Great*, 1915, vol. 1, p. 160),'
line 3, for '13 Oct.' read '14 Oct.' [*ex inform.* Major A.W. Keith-Falconer]

MARLBOROUGH

page 491,
line 18, delete from 'sister' to 'BUCKINGHAM' and replace by da. and (eventually) coh. of John (BOTELER), 1st LORD BOTELER (of Brantfield)'

page 501,
line 9, after 'seat' add 'as Duke' and after '26 May' add '1807' [*ex inform.* Randolph S Churchill]

page 503,
line 12, after '1883' add ', she *d.* 7, in Park St., Grosvenor Sq., and was *bur.* 11 Jan. 1932 at Chenies Church, Bucks.'

page 504,
line 14, after 'C.M.G.' add 'She *d.* 6 Dec. 1964.'
line 16, after 'U.S.A.' add 'He *d.* 30 June 1934. She *d.* 1977.'
line 17, line to read as follows

X. 1934. 10. JOHN ALBERT EDWARD WILLIAM (SPENCER-CHURCHILL), DUKE OF MARLBOROUGH, &c., 1st s. and h.,

line 20, after 'sponsors' add '*Styled* MARQUESS OF BLANDFORD 1897–1934; ed. at Eton.'
line 25, for '(e)]' read 'She *d.* 23 May 1961 and he *m.* 2ndly, 1972, Frances Laura, 2nd da. of Capt. Guy Lawrence CHARTERIS, formerly wife of 1stly, Walter Francis David (LONG), 2nd VISCOUNT LONG, 2ndly of William Humble Eric (WARD), 3rd EARL OF DUDLEY and widow of Michael Temple CANFIELD. He *d.* 11 Mar. 1972. His widow *d.* 1990.'

XI. 1972. 11. JOHN GEORGE VANDERBILT HENRY (SPENCER-CHURCHILL), 1st s. and h., *b.* 13 Apr. 1926, *styled* EARL OF SUNDERLAND 1926–34, MARQUESS OF BLANDFORD 1934–72; ed. at Eton; *m.* 1stly, 19 Oct. 1951, Susan Mary, only da. of Michael Charles St. John HORNBY of Faringdon, Berks. This marriage was diss. by divorce in 1961 and he *m.* 2ndly, 23 Oct. 1961, Athina Mary, da. of Stavros G. LIVANOS and formerly wife of Aristotle Socrates ONASSIS. This marriage was in turn diss. by divorce in 1971 (she *d.* 1974) and he *m.* 3rdly, 1972, Dagmar Rosita Astri Libertas, da. of COUNT CARL LUDWIG DOUGLAS.

[CHARLES JAMES SPENCER-CHURCHILL, *styled* MARQUESS OF BLANDFORD, 1st s. and h. ap. by 1st wife, *b.* 24 Nov. 1955; ed. at Harrow; *m.*, 1990, Rebecca Mary, da. of Peter Few BROWN.]

note (e), delete all detail

MARMION

page 506,
lines 8–9, delete from 'whose' to 'unknown' and replace by 'da. of Hugh, COUNT OF RETHEL'

note (g), line 1, before 'She' add 'See G. Andrews Moriarty, *Geneal. Mag.*, 1944, vol. 9, pp. 424–6.

page 507,
pedigree, last line, under last '=' add '⅄'

page 509,
line 3, delete from 'da.' to 'RETHEL.' and replace by 'whose parentage is unknown.'

page 513,
note (d), line 8, after '312).' add 'There is good evidence that this claim that the manor of Scrivelsby was held by the service of acting as Champion at a Coronation was invented between the death of Philip Marmion, *circa* 1291, and the Coronation of Edward III. See G.H. White, "Coronation Claims", *Geneal. Mag.*, vol. 9, 1937, pp. 512–13.'

page 518,
line 14, for 'Robert DE DOVER' read 'Foubert DE DOUVRES' [See ATHOLL, vol. i, p. 305, in this volume.]

MARNY

page 523,
line 26, after 'London' add ', da. of Sir John CHEDWORTH,'

MARSHAL

page 527,
lines 7–8, delete from 'and after' to '(e)'
line 17, after '*m.*' add '1stly, Pernel, da. of Sir Henry ORTY' [See vol. x, p. 182, *sub* ORTY.]
line 17, delete from 'whose' to 'known' and replace by 'da. of Robert (DE FERRERS), 6th EARL OF DERBY(ia)'
note (ia) J.E. Lloyd, *History of Wales*, 1911, vol. 2, p. 259. She must have been very young at Marshal's death (1265), for her parents were *m.* only in 1249. Her 2nd marriage is recorded by Nicholas Trevet, *Annales* (Eng. Hist. Soc., 1845), p. 298, under the year 1277; "insuper et uxorem dedit filiam comitis Derbiae, quo nuper alio viro suo fuerat vidutae". *Ex inform.* Charles H. Evans.
note (e), delete all detail

page 529,
lines 6–8, delete from 'da.' to 'Lanvallei' and replace by 'da. of Robert (FITZWALTER), 1st LORD FITZWALTER, by his 1st wife, to whom she became sole h., Devorguille, 1st da. and coh. of Sir John DE BURGH, of Wakerley, Northants,' [See vol. v, p. 474, *sub* FITZWALTER.]

MARTIN

page 535,
line 6, after 'BRIAN' add 'of Laugharne, co. Carmarthen'

page 538,
line 15, after 'Hastinges' add ', 1st s. and h. ap. of John 1st Lord Hastings'

MASHAM

page 542,
line 15, line to read as follows

II. 1906. 2. SAMUEL CUNLIFFE (LISTER), BARON MASHAM OF SWINTON, 1st s. and h., *b.* 2 Aug. 1857;

lines 17–18, delete from 'Having' to 'work.(g)]'

III. 1917. 3. JOHN CUNLIFFE (LISTER), BARON MASHAM OF SWINTON, br. and h., *b.* 9 Aug. 1867. He *m.*, 7 Apr. 1906, Elizabeth Alice, 2nd da. of William Rippon BROCKTON, of Farndon, Newark-on-Trent. He *d. s.p.*, 4, and was *bur.* 8 Jan. 1924, at Masham Church, when his peerage became *extinct.* Will pr. 1 Oct. 1924, at £1,557,606. His widow *d.* 28 May 1924. Will pr. Sep. 1924, at £535,171.

note (g), delete all detail

MASSAREENE

page 543,
note (e), line 1, after 'Ulster' add '(probably)' and for 'Carrick, and Ormond' read 'and Carrick'
lines 2–3, delete from 'since the creation' to '1660)' and replace by 'since these it is believed that no patent (save that of Caher (1543) and this one of 1660)'

page 545,
line 14, delete 'probably'
line 15, for 'da.' read 'da. and coh.'
note (d), lines 7–8, delete from 'Lacy,"' to 'Matters' and replace by 'Lacy." It appears from the Visitation of Oxford (Harl. Soc., vol. v, pp. 268–9) that he was in fact her great-grandfather.'

page 548,
line 30, line to read as follows

XII. 1905. 12. ALGERNON WILLIAM JOHN CLOTWORTHY (SKEFFINGTON), VISCOUNT MASSAREENE, &c., 2nd but only surv. s. and h.,

page 549,
line 4, delete '(b)'
lines 4–5, delete from 'Having' to 'work.]' and replace by 'She *d.* 11 Dec. 1937 and he *m.* 2ndly,

17 Aug. 1940, Florence Clementina Vere, da. of Sydney William SKEFFINGTON, 3rd s. of 10th Viscount Massareene. He *d.* 20 July 1956. His widow *d.* 1978.'

XIII. 1956. 13. JOHN CLOTWORTHY TALBOT FOSTER WHYTE-MELVILLE (SKEFFINGTON), VISCOUNT MASSAREENE, &c., 2nd but 1st surv. s. and h.,(b) *b.* 22 Oct. 1914; ed. at Eton; *m.* 15 Mar. 1939, Annabelle Kathleen, 1st da. of Henry David LEWIS of Combwell Priory, Cranbrook, Kent. He *d.* 27 Dec. 1992. His widow was living 1995.

XIV. 1992. 14. JOHN DAVID CLOTWORTHY WHYTE-MELVILLE FOSTER (SKEFFINGTON), VISCOUNT MASSAREENE, &c., only s. and h., *b.* 3 June 1940; ed. at Millfield; *m.*, 1970, Anne Denise, da. of Norman ROWLANDSON.

[CHARLES JOHN FOSTER CLOTWORTHY WHYTE-MELVILLE SKEFFINGTON, s. and h. ap., *b.* 7 Feb. 1973.]

note (b), delete all detail and replace by 'The 1st s. was *b.* and *d.* 24 Apr. 1910.'

MASSY

page 550,
line 28, line to read as follows

VII. 1915. 7. HUGH SOMERSET JOHN (MASSY), BARON MASSY OF DUNTRILEAGUE [I.], only s. and h., *b.* 15 Feb. 1864.

line 32–3, delete from 'Having' to 'work.(b)]' and replace by 'His widow *d.* 1922.'

VIII. 1926. 8. HUGH HAMON CHARLES GEORGE (MASSY), BARON MASSY OF DUNTRILEAGUE [I.], 1st s. and h., *b.* 13 July 1894. He *m.*, in 1919, Margaret, widow of Dr MORAN, of Tara, co. Meath, and da. of Richard LEONARD, of Ashbourne, co. Limerick. He *d.* 20 Mar. 1958. His widow *d.* 1971.

IX. 1958. 9. HUGH HAMON SOMERSET JOHN (MASSY), BARON OF DUNTRILEAGUE [I.], only s. and h., *b.* 11 June 1921; ed. at Clongowes Wood Coll. and Clayesmere Sch.; *m.*, 18 Sep. 1943, Margaret Elizabeth, da. of John FLOWER of Barry, co. Meath.

[DAVID HAMON SOMERSET MASSY, 1st s. and h. ap., *b.* 4 Mar. 1947; ed. at St. George's Coll., Weybridge.]

note (b), delete all detail

MAULEY

page 565,
line 14, after 'LORD MAULEY' add 's. and h.'

page 567,
line 4, after 'LORD MAULEY' add 's. and h.'

page 568,
line 6, after 'SUTTON' add '[3rd LORD SUTTON OF HOLDERNESSE]'
line 15, after 'h.' add ', by 1st wife'
line 16, for 'yst.' read '2nd' and after 'SUTTON' add '[3rd LORD SUTTON OF HOLDERNESSE]'

page 570,
line 8, after 'WESTMORLAND' add 'by his 1st wife Margaret, da. of Hugh (DE STAFFORD), 2nd EARL OF STAFFORD' and for '*d. s.p.m.*' read '*d. s.p.*'

MAYO

page 609,
line 12, after 'Bristol' add 'and was *bur.* there on 17 Mar. 1807' [*ex inform.* C Roy Hudleston]

page 611,
lines 9–10, delete from 'He was' to 'work.([a])]' and replace by 'She *d.* 29 Nov. 1944.'

VIII. 1927. 8. WALTER LONGLEY (BOURKE), EARL OF MAYO, &c., cousin and h., being the only s. and h. of Rev. George Wingfield BOURKE, 5th s. of the 5th Earl, by Mary Henrietta, 1st da. of the Most Rev. Dr. Charles Thomas LONGLEY, ARCHBISHOP OF CANTERBURY, *b.* 28 Nov. 1859. He *m.* 1stly, 8 June 1887, Ethel Kathleen Jane, da. of John W. FREEMAN, Capt. 16th Regt. She *d.* 12 Feb. 1913. He *m.* 2ndly, 21 Dec. 1916, Margaret Anah, da. of John Harvey SCOTT, Major, Indian Army. He *d.* 6 May 1939. His widow *d.* 29 May 1964.

[EUSTACE GEORGE WALTER BOURKE, 1st s. and h. ap., *b.* 24 June 1888. He served in WW1([a]) as Capt. and Adj. 9th Battn. K.R.R.C., and was *k.* in action, *unm.* and *v.p.*, 16 June 1915.]

IX. 1939. 9. ULICK HENRY (BOURKE), EARL OF MAYO, &c., 2nd but 1st surv. s. and h., *b.* 13 Mar. 1890, *styled* LORD NAAS 1915–39; ed. at Wixenford and Uppingham; served in WW1. He *m.*, 31 July 1937, Noël Jessie Haliburton, yst. da. of William James WILSON of Kendal, Westmorland. He *d. s.p.* 19 Dec. 1962. His widow *d.* 1993.

X. 1962. 10. TERENCE PATRICK (BOURKE), EARL OF MAYO, &c., nephew and h., being s. of Bryan Longley BOURKE (*d.* 11 June 1961), by his 1st wife Violet Wilmot Heathcote, da. of Col. Charles Harcourt STISTED, which Bryan Longley was 3rd s. of 8th Earl of Mayo. He was *b.* 26 Aug. 1929; ed. at R.N.C., Dartmouth; *m.* 1stly, 5 Apr. 1952, Margaret Jane Robinson, only da. of Gerald Joseph Cuthbert HARRISON of Weatheral, Cumberland. This marriage was diss. by divorce in 1987 (she *d.* 1992) and he *m.* 2ndly, 1987, Sally Anne, only da. of F.G. MATTHEWS of Bampton, co. Oxford.

[CHARLES DIARMUIDH JOHN, *styled* LORD NAAS, 1st s. and h. ap., *b.* 11 June 1953; ed. at Queen's Univ., Belfast; *m.* 1stly, 1975, Marie Antoinette CRONNELLY. This marriage was diss. by divorce in 1979 and he *m.* 2ndly, 1985, Marie Veronica, da. of Francis MANNION of Clifden, co. Galway.]

note (a), lines 1–8, delete from 'Walter' to 'yr.' and replace by 'As did his yst.'

MEATH

page 618,
line 10, line to read as follows

XIII. 1929. 13. REGINALD LE NORMAND (BRABAZON), EARL OF MEATH, &c., 1st s. and h., *b.* 24 Nov. 1869, *styled* LORD ARDEE 1887–1929;

line 17, delete '(e)'
line 18, for ']' read 'He *d.* 10 Mar. 1949. His widow *d.* 25 Feb. 1962.'

XIV. 1949. 14. ANTHONY WINDHAM NORMAND (BRABAZON), EARL OF MEATH, &c., only s. and h. *b.* 3 Nov. 1910, *styled* LORD ARDEE 1929–49; ed. at Eton and R.M.C., Sandhurst; *m.*, 30 July 1940, Elizabeth Mary, only da. of Capt. Geoffrey Vaux Salvia BOWLBY.

[JOHN ANTHONY BRABAZON, *styled* LORD ARDEE, 1st s. and h. ap., *b.* 11 May 1941; ed. at Harrow; *m.*, 1973, Xenia, yr. da. of P. GOUDIME of Windlesham Park, Sunningdale, Surrey.]

note (e), delete all detail

MEINILL

page 628,
line 18, after 'da.' add 'and h.'

page 629,
line 1, after 'Kilton' add ', elder br. of Marmaduke, 1st LORD THWENG'

page 632,
line 8, after 'daughter' add 'and h.'
line 9, after 'Kilton' add ', elder br. of Marmaduke, 1st LORD THWENG'

MELVILLE [U.K.]

page 656,
lines 33–4, delete from 'He was' to 'work.' and replace by 'His widow *d.* 31 Mar. 1943.'

VI. 1904. 6. CHARLES SAUNDERS (DUNDAS), VISCOUNT MELVILLE, &c. [for further detail see note (d)]. His widow *d.* 2 Feb. 1961.

VII. 1926. 7. HENRY CHARLES CLEMENT (DUNDAS), VISCOUNT MELVILLE, &c., 1st s. and h., *b.* 25 June 1873; ed. at Trnity Coll., Glenalmond and Bath Coll. He served in WW1.(d) He *m.* 20 June 1899, Agnes Mary Florence, da. of Henry BROUNCKER, of Boveridge Park, Dorset. He *d.* 30 Jan. 1935 at Melville Castle of pneumonia. His widow *d.* 13 Sep. 1954.

VIII. 1935. 8. HENRY CHARLES PATRIC BROUNCKER (DUNDAS), VISCOUNT MELVILLE, &c., 1st s. and h., *b.* 5 Mar. 1909; ed. at King's Sch., Canterbury. He *d.* unm. and *s.p.* 26 Mar. 1971.

IX. 1971. 9. ROBERT DAVID ROSS (DUNDAS), VISCOUNT MELVILLE, &c., nephew and h., being only s. of Robert Maldred St. John Melville DUNDAS (*d.* on active service 5 June 1940), by Margaret Connell, 1st da. of Percy Cruden ROSS, which Robert David was 2nd s. of 7th Viscount Melville. He was *b.* 28 May 1937; ed. at Wellington; *m.*, 1982, Fiona Margaret, da. of Roger Kirkpatrick STILGOE of Derby House, Stogumber, Taunton, Somerset.

[ROBERT HENRY KIRKPATRICK DUNDAS, 1st s. and h. ap., *b.* 23 Apr. 1984.]

note (d), lines 7–11 (on page 657), delete from 'He was' to '1909'

MENTEITH

page 662,
note (b), line 5, after 'Hastinges' add '[1st Lord Hastinges (of Inchmahome)]'

METHUEN

page 682,
line 16, after 'Wilts' add 'He *d.* 30 Oct. and was *bur.* 2 Nov. 1932 at Corsham Parish Church, Wilts. His widow *d.* 11 May 1941.'
line 17, line to read as follows

IV. 1932. 4. PAUL AYSHFORD (METHUEN), BARON METHUEN OF CORSHAM, 1st s. and h., *b.* 29 Sep. 1886; ed. at Eton

lines 19–20, for ', da. of W.J. HENNESSY.]' read 'Norah, da. of William John HENNESSY of Rudgwick, Sussex. She *d.* 17 Dec. 1958. He *d. s.p.* 7 Jan. 1975.'

V. 1975. 5. ANTHONY PAUL (METHUEN), BARON METHUEN OF CORSHAM, br. and h., *b.* 26 June 1891; ed. at Wellington and Oxford (New Coll.); *m.*, 22 July 1920, Grace, 1st da. of Sir Richard Durning HOLT, Bart. She *d.* 1972. He *d.* 21 June 1975.

[ANTHONY RICHARD PAUL METHUEN, 1st s. and h. ap., *b.* 14 May 1923. He *d.* 8 Dec. 1934.]

VI. 1975. 6. ANTHONY JOHN (METHUEN), BARON METHUEN OF CORSHAM, 2nd but 1st surv. s. and h., *b.* 26 Oct. 1925; ed. at Winchester and R.A.C., Cirencester.

METHVEN

page 684,
line 32, for 'Heydon' read 'Hedon'

MEXBOROUGH

page 687,
lines 1–2, delete from 'He was' to 'work'
line 3, for '(b)' read 'She obtained a divorce from him in 1926, and *d.* 11 Feb. 1943'

VI. 1916. 6. JOHN HENRY (SAVILE), EARL OF MEXBOROUGH OF LIFFORD, &c., half-brother and h., being 1st s. by 2nd wife [for further detail see note (a)]. He *d.* 16 Sep. 1945. His widow *d.* 26 Jan. 1957.

VII. 1945. 7. JOHN RAPHAEL WENTWORTH (SAVILE), EARL OF MEXBOROUGH, &c., only s. and h., *b.* 11 Oct. 1906, *styled* VISCOUNT POLLINGTON 1916–80; ed. at Downside and Cambridge (Pembroke Coll.). He *m.*, 23 July 1930, at Westm. Cath., Josephine Bertha Emily, da. of Andrew Mansel Talbot FLETCHER, of Saltoun. He *d.* 15 May 1980. His widow *d.* 1992.

VIII. 1980. 8. JOHN CHRISTOPHER GEORGE (SAVILE), EARL OF MEXBOROUGH, &c., 1st s. and h., *b.* 16 May 1931; ed. at Eton and Oxford (Worcester Coll.); *m.* 1stly, 30 May 1958, Elizabeth Hariot, 1st da. of John (GRIMSTON), 6th EARL OF VERULAM. This marriage was diss. by divorce in 1972 and he *m.* 2ndly, 1972, Catherine Joyce, yst. da. of James Kenneth HOPE of West Park, Lanchester, co. Durham and formerly wife of Major Nicholas Crespigny Laurence VIVIAN, *later* 6th BARON VIVIAN.

[JOHN ANDREW BRUCE SAVILE, *styled* VISCOUNT POLLINGTON, 1st s. and h. ap. by 1st wife, *b.* 30 Nov. 1959.]

note (a), lines 4–7, delete from 'Their' to 'Saltoun'
note (b), delete all detail

MIDDLESEX

page 691,
line 8, for 'of Trebich [in St. Ives]' read 'Trebigh [in St. Ive]'

MIDDLETON

page 697,
note (e), lines 4–6 (on page 698), for 'heiress' read 'coheiress'; delete from 'Dorothy' to the second 'of' and replace by 'Bridget, da. of Sir Francis Willoughby (*d.* 1596), with Percival Willoughby, great-grandfather of the'

page 698,
line 2, for 'about 1670' read '9 Apr. 1672' [Lady Chandos' Register', *Geneal. Mag.*, vol. 10, 1948, p. 256]
line 11, for '17' read '2'
line 14, for '29 Sep. 1692' read '4, and *bap.* 14 Oct. 1692 at Wollaton'

page 701,
lines 9–10, delete from 'He was' to 'work.(c)'

X. 1922. 10. GODFREY ERNEST PERCIVAL (WILLOUGHBY), BARON MIDDLETON, br. and h., *b.* 18 June 1847; ed. at Eton. He *m.* 15 June 1881, Ida Eleanora Constance, da. of George William Holmes ROSS of Cromarty. She *d.* 7 Mar. 1924. He *d.* 11 Nov. 1924.

[HENRY ERNEST DIGBY HUGH WILLOUGHBY, 1st s. and h. ap., *b.* 1 July 1882. Cmdr. R.N.; *k.* in the naval action at Jutland, 31 May 1916.]

XI. 1924. 11. MICHAEL GUY PERCIVAL (WILLOUGHBY), BARON MIDDLETON, 2nd but 1st surv. s. and h., *b.* 21 Oct. 1887; ed. Wellington and R.M.C., Sandhurst; served in WW1(c) as Major, 10th Lancers, Indian Army; M.C. He *m.*, 28 Apr. 1920, Angela Florence Alfreda, da. of Charles HALL He *d.* 16 Nov. 1970. His widow *d.* 1978.

XII. 1970. 12. DIGBY MICHAEL GODFREY JOHN (WILLOUGHBY), BARON MIDDLETON, 1st s. and h., *b.* 1 May 1921; ed. at Eton and Cambridge (Trin. Coll.); *m.*, 14 Oct. 1947, Janet, only surv. da. of Gen. Sir James Handyside MARSHALL-CORNWALL.

[MICHAEL CHARLES JAMES WILLOUGHBY, 1st s. and h. ap., *b.* 14 July 1948; ed. at Eton; *m.*, 1974, Lucy Corinna Agneta, yst. da. of William Philip (SIDNEY), 1st VISCOUNT DE L'ISLE, V.C., K.G.]

note (c), delete from 'Godfrey' to '1921'

MIDLETON

page 701,
note (d), line 3, after '222–4.' add 'This was finally exposed as wholly fraudulent in an article entitled "The Brodrick Charters", in J.H. Round, *Family Origins*, 1930, pp. 103–8.'

page 705,
line 35, line to read as follows

IX. 1907. 9. WILLIAM ST. JOHN FREMANTLE (BRODRICK), VISCOUNT MIDLETON, &c., 1st s. and h., *b.* 14 Dec. 1856;

page 706,
line 5, delete 'WEMYSS-'
line 6, delete '-DOUGLAS'
lines 13–14, delete from 'Having' to 'work.([a])' and replace by 'He *d.* 13 Feb. 1942. His widow *d.* 2 June 1966.'

EARLDOM. II. VISCOUNTCY. X. } 1942 2 and 10. GEORGE ST. JOHN (BRODRICK), EARL OF MIDLETON [1920], VISCOUNT MIDLETON [1717], and BARON BRODRICK OF MIDLETON [1715], in the Peerage of Ireland, VISCOUNT DUNSFORD OF DUNSFORD [1920], also BARON BRODRICK OF PEPER HAROW [1796], 1st s. and h., only s. by 1st wife, *b.* 21 Feb. 1888, *styled* VISCOUNT DUNSFORD 1920–42; ed. at Eton and Oxford (Balliol Coll.). Served in WW1 as A.D.C. Personal Staff to Sir Ian Hamilton in Egypt and Gallipoli; Staff Officer 1918 (M.C., despatches). He *m.* 1stly, 23 June 1917, Margaret, da. of J. RUSH, of Cromer, Norfolk, an actress.([a]) She obtained a divorce in 1925. He *m.* 2ndly, 28 July 1925, at the American Presbyterian Church, Montreal, Canada, Guinevere, widow of George Jay GOULD, of New York, U.S.A., and da. of Alexander SINCLAIR of Dublin. She was an actress at the Gaiety Theatre. This marriage was diss. by divorce in 1975 (she *d.* 1978) and he *m.* 3rdly, 1975, Irene Lilian CREESE (Rene Ray, an actress). He *d. s.p.m.* 2 Nov. 1979 when his Earldom and the Viscountcy of Dunsford became *extinct* and he was *suc.* in his other titles by his distant cousin. His widow *d.* 1993.

XI. 1979. 11. TERRY LOWTHER (BRODRICK), VISCOUNT MIDLETON, and BARON BRODRICK OF MIDLETON, in the Peerage of Ireland, also BARON BRODRICK OF PEPER HAROW [G.B.], distant cousin and h., being 1st s. of William John Henry BRODRICK (*d.* 28 Oct. 1964), by Blanche Sophia Emily, 1st da. of F.A. HAWKER of Woodend, Wickham, Hants., which William John was 2nd s. of Rev. Alan BRODRICK (*d.* 6 May 1909), by Emily Hester, da. of Philip MELVILL, which Alan was 4th s. of 7th Viscount Midleton. He was *b.* 7 Mar. 1903; *m.*, 12 Aug. 1940, Sheila Campbell, da. of Charles Campbell MACLEOD of Cawthorpe House, Bourne, co. Lincoln. He *d. s.p.* 30 Oct. 1988. His widow was living 1995.

XII. 1988. 12. ALAN HENRY (BRODRICK), VISCOUNT MIDLETON, &c., nephew and h., being only s. of Alan Rupert BRODRICK (*d.* 1972). by Alice Elizabeth, da. of George R. ROBERTS of Purley, Surrey, which Alan Rupert was 2nd s. of William John Henry BRODRICK and Blanche Sophia Emily abovenamed. He was *b.* 4 Aug. 1949; ed. at St. Edmunds, Canterbury; *m.*, 1978, Julia Helen, da. of Michael PITT of Compton Dundon, Somerton, co. Somerset.

[ASHLEY RUPERT BRODRICK, 1st s. and h. ap., *b.* 25 Nov. 1980.]

note ([a]), lines 1–8, delete from 'His' to 'Theatre'

MINTO

page 716,
line 8, after '1858' add 'She *d.* 14 July 1940.'
line 9, line to read as follows

V. 1914. 5. VICTOR GILBERT LARISTON GARNET (ELLIOTT-MURRAY-KYNYNMOUND), EARL OF MINTO, &c., 1st s. and h., *b.* 12 Feb.

line 12, after 'sponsors' add '*styled* VISCOUNT MELGUND 1891–1914; ed. at Eton;'
line 15, delete '(c)'
lines 15–16, delete from 'Having' to 'work.]' and replace by 'She *d.* 1974. He *d.* 11 Jan. 1975.'

VI. 1975. 6. GILBERT EDWARD GEORGE LARISTON (ELLIOTT-MURRAY-KYNYNMOUND), EARL OF MINTO, &c., 1st s. and h., *b.* 19 June 1928, *styled* VISCOUNT MELGUND till 1975; ed. at Eton and R.M.C., Sandhurst. He *m.* 1stly, 26 Nov. 1952, Caroline, 1st da. of George Francis (CHILD-VILLIERS), 9th EARL OF JERSEY. This marriage was diss. by divorce in 1965 (and she *m.* 2ndly, 23 Sep. 1969, John Douglas STUART, yr. s. of James Gray (STUART), 1st VISCOUNT STUART OF FINDHORN), and he *m.* 2ndly, 10 July 1965, Mary Elizabeth, da. of Peter BALLANTINE of Gladstone, New Jersey, U.S.A. She *d.* 1983, and he *m.* 3rdly, 1991, Caroline Jane, da. of Stanley GODFREY of Ruislip, Middlesex and formerly wife of Christopher LARLHAM.

[GILBERT TIMOTHY GEORGE LARISTON ELLIOT-MURRAY-KYNYNMOUND, *styled* VISCOUNT MELGUND, 1st s. and h., ap., *b.* 1 Dec. 1953; ed. at Eton; *m.*, 1983, Diana Barbara, yr. da. of Brian S.L. TRAFFORD of Rudgwick, Sussex.]

note (c), delete all detail

APPENDIXES

APPENDIX F

page 823,
after WALERAN add as follows

WALLSCOURT (BLAKE)
Charles W.J.H., *b.* 1875 . . . . A. B.War; Vic.

VOLUME 9

CONTENTS

page iii,
APPENDIXES, 'K', delete all detail

INTRODUCTION

page viii,
line 11, for '*Genealogical*' read '*Genealogist's*'

MOELS

page 4,
note (g), line 3, for 'One of his daughters' read 'Maud'

page 5,
note (c), line 3, for 'perhaps a younger son of his' read 'probably a younger brother.'
line 7, for 'possibly son by an by an earlier wife' read 'and *d. v.p. s.p.*'
line 9, delete 'apparently by an earlier husband' [*Geneal. Mag.*, vol. 16, 1971, pp. 552–3]

page 6,
lines 12–13, for '[LORD LE DESPENSER]' read 'Justiciar of England'

page 7,
lines 23–4, delete from 'Sir Richard' to 'Somerset.(m)' and replace by 'Richard (LOVEL), 1st LORD LOVEL (of Castle Cary), by Muriel, da. and h. of Sir John DE SOULES'
note (m), delete all detail

MOHAUT

page 14,
line 6, after 'MOWBRAY' add 'by Maud, sister and (eventually) coh. of Simon DE BEAUCHAMP, 1st da. of William DE BEAUCHAMP, Baron of Bedford' [See vol. ix, p. 376, *sub* MOWBRAY.]

MOHUN

page 20,
line 15, after 'and' add 'eventually'

page 22,
line 18, after 'LORTY' add '1st LORD ORTY'

page 23,
line 8, delete '(*de Plessetis*) [LORD PLESSIS]'

page 24,
line 23, after 'daughters' add '(of which Philippe was the yst.)' [See *Cal. Fine Rolls, 1399–1405*, pp. 309, 321. *Ex inform.* Rosemary Horrox]

page 25,
line 2, for '1400/1' read '20 Sep. 1400'

MOLESWORTH

page 35,
line 36, line to read as follows

IX. 1906. 9. GEORGE BAGOT (MOLESWORTH), VISCOUNT MOLESWORTH OF SWORDS, &c. [I.], 1st s. and h., *b.* 6 June 1867; ed. at Wellington.

page 36,
line 1, delete '([a])'
lines 2–3, delete from 'Having' to 'work.]' and replace by 'He *d. s.p.m.s.* 20 Mar. 1947. His widow *d.* 25 Mar. 1958.'

[CHARLES WILLOUGHBY MURRAY MOLESWORTH, only s. and h. ap., *d. v.p.*; for further detail see note ([a]).]

X. 1947. 10. CHARLES RICHARD (MOLESWORTH), VISCOUNT MOLESWORTH OF SWORDS, &c., br. and h., *b.* 3 Jan. 1969; ed. at Cheltenham; *m.*, 4 Dec. 1906, Elizabeth Gladys, da. of Edward Martin LANGWORTHY. He *d.* 24 Feb. 1961. His widow *d.* 1974.

XI. 1961. 11. RICHARD GOSSETT (MOLESWORTH), VISCOUNT MOLESWORTH OF SWORDS, &c., 1st s. and h., *b.* 31 Oct. 1907; ed. at Lancing; *m.*, 29 Aug. 1958, Anne Florence, da. of John Mark Freeman COHEN of Purley, Surrey. She *d.* 1983.

[ROBERT BYSSHE KELHAM MOLESWORTH, 1st s. and h. ap., *b.* 4 June 1959; ed. at Cheltenham and Sussex Univ.]

MOLEYNS

page 39,
line 19, for 's. and h.' read '1st s. and h. ap.'
line 20, for 'da. of Sir Richard ROKESLEY' read '(__)'
line 21, for '6 May' read '16 May'

page 43,
lines 2–3, after 'HUNGERFORD' add '[3rd LORD HUNGERFORD]'
Note, line 13 (on page 44), for 'Bucks' read 'Hants'

MONCK OF BALLYTRAMMON

page 52,
line 19, line to read as follows

VI. 1927. 6 and 3. HENRY WYNDHAM STANLEY (MONCK), VISCOUNT MONCK OF BALLYTRAMON [I.] &c., grandson and h., being only s. and h.

lines 22–4, delete from 'Having' to 'work.]' and replace by 'He *m.*, 7 July 1937, Baroness Eva Maria VRETO, 2nd. da. of Prof. (__) ZAUNMULLER-FREUDENTHALER of Vienna. This marriage was diss. by divorce in 1951 and he *m.* 2ndly, 14 Dec. 1951, Brenda Mildred, da. of George William ADKINS of Harpenden, Herts. He *d.* 21 June 1982. His widow *m.* 2ndly, 1985, as his 2nd wife, Brig. Gerald Michael PALMER (who *d.* 1991). She was still living 1995.'

VII. 1982. 7 and 4. CHARLES STANLEY (MONCK), VISCOUNT MONCK OF BALLYTRAMON, 1st s. and h., *b.* 2 Apr. 1953; ed. at Eton.

MONCREIFF OF TULLIEBOLE

page 54,
lines 1–2, delete from ', and' to 'work([a])'

III. 1909. 3. ROBERT CHICHESTER (MONCREIFF), BARON MONCREIFF OF TULLIEBOLE, &c., br. and h., *b.* 24 Aug. 1843; ed. at Cambridge (Trin. Coll.). Took Holy Orders, 1870; Vicar of Tamworth, co. Warwick 1885–1913. He *m.*, 4 Jan. 1871, Florence Kate, da. of Col. Richard FITZHERBERT. He *d.* 14 May 1913. She *d.* 23 Nov. 1926.

IV. 1913. 4. JAMES HERBERT ARTHUR (MONCREIFF), BARON MONCREIFF OF TULLIEBOLE, &c., only s. and h., *b.* 19 July 1872; ed. at Oxford (New Coll.); *m.* 16 Dec. 1909, Lucy Vida., da. of David ANDERSON. He *d.* 8 Dec. 1942. His widow *d.* 1973.

V. 1942. 5. HARRY ROBERT WELLWOOD (MONCREIFF), BARON MONCREIFF OF TULLIEBOLE [1874], also a Baronet [S. 1626 and U.K. 1871], 1st s. and h., *b.* 4 Feb. 1915; ed. at Fettes Coll.; *m.*, 19 Jan. 1952, Enid Marion Watson, da. of Major Henry Watson LOCKE of Dollar, co. Clackmannan. She *d.* 1985.

[RHODERICK HARRY WELLWOOD MONCRIEFF, s. and h. ap., *b.* 22 Mar. 1954; ed. at Holt Sch., Norfolk; *m.*, 1982, Alison Elizabeth Anne, da. of James Duncan Alastair ROSS of Dollar, abovenamed.]

note ([a]), delete all detail

MONK BRETTON

page 55,
line 28, after '63.' add 'His widow *d.* 5 Aug. 1967.'
line 29, delete all detail and replace as follows

III. 1933. 3. JOHN CHARLES (DODSON), BARON MONK BRETTON, &c., s. and h., *b.* 17 July 1924; ed. at Westminster and Oxford (New Coll.); *m.*, 29 Jan. 1958, Zoë Diana Mary Alicia, da. of Ian Douglas Murray SCOTT.

[CHRISTOPHER MARK DODSON, 1st s. and h. ap., *b.* 2 Aug. 1958; ed. at Eton and Univ. of S. California; *m.*, 1988, Karen L., da. of B.J. MCKELVIN of Fairfield, Conn., U.S.A.]

MONKSWELL

page 57,
line 20, line to read as follows

III. 1909. 3. ROBERT ALFRED HARDCASTLE (COLLIER), BARON MONKSWELL, 1st s. and h., *b.* 13 Dec. 1875,

lines 29–30, delete from '(d)' to 'work.]' and replace by 'He *d. s.p.m.s.* 14 Jan. 1964. His widow *d.* 1985.'

[ROBERT DOUGLAS COLLLIER, only s. and h. ap., *b.* 8 Apr. 1926; Lieut. Hampshire Regt., accidentally drowned while on active service in Cyprus 5 Aug. 1946. He *d. v.p.* and unm.]

IV. 1964. 4. WILLIAM ADRIAN LARRY (COLLIER), BARON MONKSWELL, nephew and h., being 2nd surv. s.(d) of Gerard COLLIER (*d.* 26 Apr. 1923), 2nd s. of the 2nd Baron, by Lily Ermengarde Fanny, da. of Rt. Hon. Sir Mountstuart Elphinstone Grant DUFF, P.C., G.C.S.I. He was *b.* 25 Nov. 1913; ed. at Edinburgh Univ.; discl. his peerage for life, under the Peerage Act, 1963, 7 Apr. 1964. He *m.* 1stly, 21 Sep. 1939, Erika, da. of Dr. Edward KELLNER of Vienna. This marriage was diss. by divorce in 1945 and he *m.* 2ndly, 9 July 1945, Helen, da. of James DUNBAR of Edinburgh (she was still living 1995, as wife of Edward Edmund KEMP). This marriage was in turn diss. by divorce in 1950 and he *m.* 3rdly, 1951, Nora, da. of (__) SELBY. He *d.* 27 July 1984. His widow was still living 1995.

V. 1984. 5. GERARD (COLLIER), BARON MONKSWELL, 1st s. and h. by 2nd wife, *b.* 28 Jan. 1947; ed. at George Herriot's Sch., Edinburgh; *m.*, 1974, Ann Valeria, da. of James COLLINS of Liverpool.

[JAMES ADRIAN COLLIER, 1st s. and h. ap., *b.* 29 Mar. 1977.]

note (d), delete all detail and replace by 'His eld. brother was *b.* 16, and *d.* 22 June, 1922.'

MONSON

page 73,
line 30, for '2 Jan.' read '7 Jan.'

page 74,
line 12, for 'was living 1935' read '*d.* 21 May 1936.'
line 20, after 'Army' add 'He *d.* 10 Oct. 1940. His widow *d.* 1 Jan. 1943.'
lines 21–3, delete all detail and replace as follows

X. 1940. 10. JOHN ROSEBERY (MONSON), BARON MONSON OF BURTON, &c., only s. and h., *b.* 11 Feb. 1907; ed. at Eton and Oxford (Ch. Ch.). He *m.* 4 Aug. 1931, Bettie Northrup, da. of Col. E. Alexander POWELL. He *d.* 7 Apr. 1958. His widow *m.* 2ndly, 12 Feb. 1962, Capt. James Arnold PHILLIPS, who *d.* 1983. She was still living 1995.

XI. 1958. 11. JOHN (MONSON), BARON MONSON OF BURTON, &c., 1st s. and h., *b.* 3 May 1932; ed. at Eton and Cambridge (Trin. Coll.); *m.*, 2 Apr. 1955, Emma, da. of Anthony DEVAS.

[NICHOLAS JOHN MONSON, 1st s. and h. ap., *b.* 19 Oct. 1955; ed. at Eton; *m.*, 1981, Hilary, da. of Kenneth MARTIN of Kenya.]

MONTAGU

page 81,
line 12, after 'Verdun' add '(Lord Verdun)'
note (i), line 3, for 'younger son' read 'eldest son and heir'

page 82,
line 3, after 'wife' add ', da. and h. of Matthew DE LA MARE' [See MONTFORT, vol. ix, p. 127.]

page 89,
line 19, for '1456' read '31 Oct. or 1 Nov. 1454'
note (b), line 2, after 'Yorks]' add ', but see R.A. Griffiths, "Local Rivalries and National Politics", *Speculum*, vol. xliii, 1968, pp. 622, 623–4.'

page 90,
line 2, after 'was' add 'apparently sum. to the last Parliament of Henry VI, being *styled* "J. Montagu" on 28 Jan. 1461.' [*Procs. Privy Coun.*, vol. vi, p. 310, *ex inform.* Rosemary Horrox]

page 93,
note (i), line 2, after 'Hen. VII,' add 'vol. i,'
line 1 (on page 94), after 'Wentforth' add ', *de jure* (according to modern doctrine), 4th Lord le Despencer' and after 'Margaret' add ', aged 20 and more in 1486'

line 2 (on page 94), after 'Lucy' add ', aged 18 and more in 1486'
line 4 (on page 94), for 'Sir' read 'before 5 Nov. 1486, when she was aged 16 and more'
line 5 (on page 94), after 'Dacre' add ', pardon to William Smyth of Elford, Staffs., Esq., and Isobel his wife, late wife and executrix of William Huddylston, late of Millom, Cumb., and late wife and administratrix of Ranulph Dacre, late of Carlisle, Esq.' [*L. and P., Dom.*, new edn., vol. i, part 1, p. 232]

page 94,
line 4, for '1492' read 'Nov. 1488' [*ex inform.* Dr Hazel Pierce, see corrections *sub* SALISBURY]

page 97,
line 6, for 'MONTAGU' read 'MONTAGUE' [Entries for the Viscountcy of Montague, including page headings, should therefore all be altered correspondingly and the peerage should be inserted after line 4 on page 113.]
note (b), lines 13–14, delete from 'The' to 'Peerage' [See vol. ii, p. vi.]

page 98,
line 6, for 'MONTAGU' read 'MONTAGUE'
note (e), line 1, before 'On' add 'The spelling "Montague" is that in the original patent (See A.A. Dibben (to whom I am grateful for this reference), *The Cowdray Archives*, part 1, 1960, p. viii, note 7.)

page 103,
line 25, after '7 Jan. 1823' add '(e)'
note (e) Farley's *Bristol Journal* of Jan. 1823 has 10 Jan. 1823.

MONTAGU OF BEAULIEU

page 112,
line 6, line to read as follows

II. 1905. 2. JOHN WALTER EDWARD (DOUGLAS-SCOTT-MONTAGU), BARON MONTAGU OF BEAULIEU, 1st s. and h., *b.* 10 June 1866,

lines 21–2, delete from '(b)' to 'work'
line 23, for ']' read 'His widow *m.* 2ndly, 2 May 1936, Capt. Edward PLEYDELL-BOUVERIE, R.N., who *d.* 5 May 1951. She was still living 1995.'

III. 1929. 3. EDWARD JOHN BARRINGTON (DOUGLAS-SCOTT-MONTAGU), only s. and h., *b.* 20 Oct. 1926; ed. at Eton and Oxford (New Coll.); *m.* 1stly, 11 Apr. 1959, Elizabeth Belinda, da. of Capt. John de Bathe CROSSLEY. This marriage was diss. by divorce in 1974 and he *m.* 2ndly, 1974, Fiona Margaret, da. of Richard HERBERT.

[RALPH DOUGLAS-SCOTT-MONTAGU, 1st s. and h. ap. by 1st wife, *b.* 13 Mar. 1961.]

note (b), delete all detail

MONTEAGLE

page 119,
line 5, line to read as follows

III. 1926. 3. THOMAS AUBREY (SPRING-RICE), BARON MONTEAGLE OF BRANDON, 2nd but 1st surv. s. and h., *b.* 3 Nov. 1883;

lines 12–13, delete from '(c)' to 'work.]'

IV. 1934. 4. FRANCIS SPRING (RICE), BARON MONTEAGLE OF BRANDON, uncle and h., being 2nd s. of Stephen Edmond SPRING RICE afsd., *b.* 1 Oct. 1852; ed. St. Columba's Coll., co. Dublin and H.M.S. Britannia; Cmdr, R.N. He *m.* 28 Sep. 1882, Elizabeth Anne, da. of Sir Peter George FITZGERALD, Bart., 19th Knight of Kerry. She *d.* 11 Dec. 1922 and he *m.* 2ndly, 11 Sep. 1935, Julia Emma Isabella, 6th da. of Sir Peter George FitzGerald afsd. She *d.* 9 May 1936. He *d.* 21, at Coppa Foynes and was *bur.* 24 Dec. 1937 at Loughill.

V. 1937. 5. CHARLES SPRING (RICE), BARON MONTEAGLE OF BRANDON, 2nd but only surv. s.,(c) *b.* 28 Jan. 1887; ed. at Harrow and Cambridge (Trin. Coll.); *m.*, 14 Apr. 1925, Emilie DE KOSENKO. He *d.* 9 Dec. 1946. His widow *m.* 2ndly, 12 Nov. 1954, Col. Courtenay Fergus Ochoncar Grey FORBES. She *d.* 1981.

VI. 1946. 6. GERALD SPRING (RICE), BARON MONTEAGLE OF BRANDON, 1st s. and h., *b.* 5 July 1926; ed. at Harrow; *m.*, 28 May 1949, Anne, da. of Col. Guy James BROWNLOW of Ballywhite, Portaferry, co. Down.

[CHARLES JAMES RICE, s. and h. ap., *b.* 24 Feb. 1953; *m.*, 1987, Mary Teresa GLOVER.]

note (c), delete all detail and replace by 'His elder brother Francis Peter SPRING RICE was *b.* 13 Aug. and *d.* 2 Dec. 1883.'

MONTGOMERY

page 139,
line 6, for 'in Nov.' read 'before 20 Apr.'
lines 7–8, delete from 'before' to 'denization)' and replace by 'between 20 Apr. and 7 July 1625, in Scotland'
line 10, for 'William' read 'John'
line 11, delete from 'Catherine' to 'Newbottle' and replace by 'Agnes, *suo jure* BARONESS HERRIES OF TERREGLES [S.]' [See vol. xii, part 2, p. 636, *sub* WIGTOWN.]

note (e), for 'Fun. entry' read 'Lord Montgomery is said in *The Montgomery MSS.*, Hill (ed.), p. 110, to have been a widower for many months after her death. Her funeral entry, dated Nov. 1625, is'

MONTROSE

page 146,
line 16, for 'SCHAW, his wife' read ', da. of Sir James SHAW of Sauchie'

page 160,
line 8, after '73' add 'His widow *d.* 21 Nov. 1940.'
line 9, line to read as follows

DUKEDOM [S.] VI. MARQUESSATE [S.] IX. EARLDOM [S.] XIII. } 1925 — 6, 9 and 13. JAMES (GRAHAM), DUKE OF MONTROSE, &c., 1st s. and h., *b.* 1 May 1878, at 35 Chester Sq., Pimlico, *styled* MARQUESS OF GRAHAM 1878–1925,

lines 18–19, delete from '([a])' to 'work.]' and replace by 'He *d.* 20 Jan. 1954. His widow *d.* 21 Feb. 1957.'

DUKEDOM [S.] VII. MARQUESSATE [S.] X. EARLDOM [S.] XIV. } 1954 — 7, 10 and 14. JAMES ANGUS (GRAHAM), DUKE OF MONTROSE, &c., 1st s. and h., *b.* 2 May 1907, *styled* EARL OF KINCARDINE 1907–25 and MARQUESS OF GRAHAM 1925–54. Ed. at Eton and Oxford (Ch. Ch.). He *m.* 20 Oct. 1930, Isobel Veronica, da. of Lieut. Col. T.B. Sellar, C.M.G., D.S.O. This marriage was diss. by divorce in 1950 (she *d.* 1990) and he *m.* 2ndly, 17 Apr. 1952, Susan Mary Jocelyn, da. of Dr John Mervyn SEMPLE and widow of Michael Raleigh GIBBS. He *d.* 10 Feb. 1992. His widow was still living 1995.

DUKEDOM [S.] VIII. MARQUESSATE [S.] XI. EARLDOM [S.] XV. } 1992 — 8, 11 and 15. JAMES (GRAHAM), DUKE OF MONTROSE, &c., 1st s. and h., *b.* 6 Apr. 1935; ed. at Loretto; *m.*, 31 Jan. 1970, Catherine Elizabeth Macdonnell, yst. da. of Capt. Norman Andrew Thompson YOUNG of Ottawa, Canada.

[JAMES ALEXANDER NORMAN GRAHAM, *styled* MARQUESS OF GRAHAM, 1st s. and h. ap. by 1st wife, *b.* 16 Aug. 1973; ed. at Eton and Edinburgh Univ.]

note ([a]), delete all detail

MORAY

page 171,
line 2, delete 'She *d.* 1372.'

page 175,
note ([e]), line 27 (on p. 176), after 'found' add 'Andrew MacEwen (*The Geneal.*, vol. 3, 1982,

pp. 140–1), suggests that the Earl married Mariota of the Isles (see *post*, vol. 12, pt. 1, p. 546, *sub* SUTHERLAND) but in view of the evidence that her name was Margaret, this may be considered unproven.

page 192,
lines 28–9, delete from 'He was' to 'work.'

XXXI. 1901. 16. FRANCIS JAMES (STUART), EARL OF MORAY, &c., br. and h., *b.* 24 Nov. 1842; he *m.*, 24 June 1879, Gertrude Floyer, da. of Rev. Francis SMITH. He *d. s.p.* 20 Nov. 1909. His widow *d.* 15 Mar. 1928.

XXXII. 1909. 17. MORTON GRAY (STUART), EARL OF MORAY, &c., br. and h., *b.* 16 Apr. 1855; ed. at Cambridge (St. John's Coll.). He *m.*, 17 Dec. 1890, Edith Douglas, da. of Rear Adm. George PALMER. He *d.* 19 Apr. 1930. His widow *b.* 17 Apr. 1945.

XXXIII. 1930. 18. FRANCIS DOUGLAS (STUART), EARL OF MORAY, &c., 1st s. and h., *b.* 10 July 1892; ed. at Eton and Cambridge (Trin. Coll.). Served in WW1[b] as Capt. Scottish Horse, and R.A.F.; M.C. He *m.* 21 June 1924, Barbara, da. of J. Archibald MURRAY, of New York. He *d. s.p.m.* 9 July 1943. His widow was still living 1995.

XXXIV. 1943. 19. ARCHIBALD JOHN MORTON (STUART), EARL OF MORAY, &c., br. and h., *b.* 14 Nov. 1894; ed. at R.N.C.s, Osbourne and Dartmouth; *m.*, 28 Jan. 1922, Mabel Helen Maud, da. of Benjamin WILSON of S. Rhodesia. She *d.* 1 Oct. 1968. He *d.* 27 Mar. 1974.

XXXV. 1974. 20. DOUGLAS JOHN MORAY (STUART), EARL OF MORAY, &c., 1st s. and h., *b.* 13 Feb. 1928; ed. at Hilton Coll., Natal and Cambridge (Trin. Coll.); *m.*, 27 Jan. 1964, Lady Malvina Dorothea, 1st da. of Mungo David Malcolm (MURRAY), 7th EARL OF MANSFIELD.

[JOHN DOUGLAS STUART, *styled* LORD DOUNE, s. and h., *b.* 29 Aug. 1966.]

note ([b]), lines 1–2 (page 192), delete all detail, lines 1–5 (page 193) delete all detail.

MORDINGTON

page 206,
note ([f]), line 3, after 'register.' add 'See *Treasury Calendar*, vol. xxiii, 1949, p. 433 for Lord Mordington's denial of his marriage.'

MORLEY

page 214,
line 10, after 'MARSHAL' add '[1st LORD MARSHAL], by Christian, da. of Robert (FITZWALTER), 1st LORD FITZWALTER,'

page 217,
line 15, after '*d.*' add '6 Nov.'

page 234,
line 27, line to read as follows

IV. 1905. 4. EDMUND ROBERT (PARKER), EARL OF MORLEY, &c., 1st s. and h., *b.* 19 Apr. 1877; *styled* VISCOUNT BORINGDON;

line 28, for 'Coll.' read 'Hall'
lines 30–1, delete from 'Having' to 'work.]' and replace by 'He *d.* unm. 10 Oct. 1951.'

V. 1951. 5. MONTAGU BROWNLOW (PARKER), EARL OF MORLEY, &c., br. and h., *b.* 13 Oct. 1878; ed. at Eton. He *d.* unm. 28 Apr. 1962.

VI. 1962. 6. JOHN ST. AUBYN (PARKER), EARL OF MORLEY, &c., nephew and h., being 1st s. of John Holford PARKER (*d.* 27 Feb. 1955), by Marjory Katharine Elizabeth Alexandra St. Aubyn, da. of John Townsend (ST. AUBYN), 2nd BARON ST. LEVAN, which John Holford was 3rd s. of 3rd Earl of Morley. He was *b.* 29 May 1923; ed. at Eton; *m.*, 15 Oct. 1955, Johanna Katherine, 1st da. of Sir John MOLESWORTH-ST. AUBYN, Bart.

[MARK LIONEL PARKER, *styled* VISCOUNT BORINGDON, s. and h. ap., *b.* 22 Aug. 1956; ed. at Eton; *m.*, 1983, Carolyn Jell, da. of Donald MCVICAR of Meols, Wirral, Cheshire.]

MORNINGTON

page 235,
line 6, after '1690' add 'near 'Edenderry'

page 238,
line 10, for 'Carrollstown' read 'Carrolton'

MORTIMER

page 250,
lines 10–11, delete from 'THOMAS' to 'PARK' and replace by 'SIR THOMAS DE MORTIMER, s. and h. ap. He *m.* Mary, da. of Nicholas PARK.'
line 13, after 'widow' add '*m.* 2ndly, John FASTOLF, and 3rdly, John FARWELL.(h) She'
line 13, for 'him' read 'her 1st husband'
line 19, after 'Margery' add '(or Margaret)'
line 20, after 'Ellingham' add 'and (ii) Sir Philip Braunch'
note (h), before 'By' add 'James Gairdner, *Paston Letters*, vol. 3, pp. 155, 157. Thanks are due to Brice Clagett for drawing my attention to this.'
note (m), after 'Ellingham' add '*Paston Letters*' as above.

page 256,
lines 9–27, delete from 'The fact' to 'body.(d)' and replace by 'The younger John Mortimer

presented to the living of Tedstone Wafer on 20 Apr. 1347 and again in 1367, and "John le Mortimer" of Tedstone Wafer is mentioned as a subtenant of Humphrey de Bohun, 10th Earl of Hereford in 1361.([a]) In his will Humphrey bequeathed £100 for the purchase of land to be settled on John Mortimer and the heirs of his body.([b]) This John died before 4 Jan. 1395/6, when his son Roger presented to the living of Tedstone Wafer. Roger was married to Maud Herle, and died 13 Dec. 1402, when his son John was 14 (*b.* 13 Dec. 1388).([c]) The Mortimers of Chirk probably died out in the male line in 1513, when the last recorded John Mortimer died.([d])'

note ([a]), delete all detail and replace by '*Register of John de Trilleck*, Cant. and York Soc., vol. 8, 1912, p. 374; John Duncomb, *Herefordshire*, vol. 2, part 1, 1812, pp. 262–4; *Cal. Inq. p.m.*, vol. xiii, no. 167, p. 140. I am grateful to Dr Neil Thompson for giving me these and subsequent references to the later Mortimers.'

note ([b]), delete all detail and replace by '*Test. Vet.*, p. 68.'

note ([c]), delete all detail and replace by '*Register of John Trefnant*, Cant. and York Soc., vol. 20, 1914, p. 180; *Cal. Inq. p.m.*, vol. xvii, no. 1059; vol. xviii, no. 1094.'

note ([d]), delete all detail and replace by '*V.C.H. Worcester*, vol. 4, p. 282.'

page 257,

line 3, after '([b])' add 'He probably married Nest, da. of Gruffydd ap Llewellyn, King of Wales (*Dict. Welsh Biog.*, p. 312; J.E. Lloyd, *Hist. of Wales*, 1911, vol. 2, p. 395, note 123, and p. 397, note 135.)'

page 266,

line 3, after 'Talbot' add '(yr. br. of Gilbert, 1st LORD TALBOT)'

line 5, for 'by 1309' read 'before 12 Jan. 1308/9' [See vol. iv, p. 304, *sub* DEVEROIS.]

line 6, after 'Cornwall' add ', ancestor of John, 1st BARON FANHOPE,'

lines 6–7, for 'de Evereys' read '(DEVEROIS), 1st LORD DEVEROIS,'

page 271,

line 6, delete from ', after' to 'brother,'

page 280,

line 10, for 'Richard' read 'Walter'

line 11, after 'England' add ', da. of William, 4th EARL OF PEMBROKE, Marshal of England,'

page 281,

note ([c]), line 8, after 'Ferrers' add '[1st Lord Ferrers (of Chartley)],'

line 10, after 'de Vere' add '6th Earl of Oxford,'

page 283,

line 8, after '*m.*' add '1stly, (___)'

note ([m]), line 2, for 'three' read 'four'

line 4, after 'p. 335);' add 'He also had a da. Isolt by his first wife. See *ante*, vol. i, p. 347 (above, in present volume). Isolt, *m.* (1) Walter de Balun, (2) Hugh (AUDLEY), LORD AUDLEY (*ante*, vol. i, note ([e]))' [*ex inform.* Lord Sandon]

page 285,
line 3, after 'sister' add 'and coh.'
line 4, for 'shortly before 21 Jan. 1331/2' read '16 Dec. 1331'
line 8, for '8 June 1355' read 'June 1356' [See vol. ix, p. 667, *sub* NORTHAMPTON.]
note ([d]), line 1, delete from 'When' to 'issued.' and replace by 'The writs to the escheators were issued 21 Jan. 1331/2.'
line 3, after '387).' add 'The *Inqs. p. m.* differ as to the day of death.'

MORTON

page 302,
line 13, after 'Cheltenham.' add 'His widow *d.* 27 Aug. 1954.'
lines 14–16, delete all detail and replace as follows

XXI. 1935. 20. SHOLTO CHARLES JOHN HAY (DOUGLAS), EARL OF MORTON, &c., grandson and h., being only s. and h. of Sholto Charles DOUGLAS and Minnie his wife, both abovenamed, *b.* 12 April 1907; *styled* LORD ABERDOUR 1911–35; ed. at Oxford (Magdalen Coll.). He *d.* unm. 13 Feb. 1976.

XXII. 1976. 21. JOHN CHARLES SHOLTO (DOUGLAS), EARL OF MORTON, &c., cousin and h., being 2nd but 1st surv s. of Charles William Sholto DOUGLAS (*d.* 10 Oct. 1960), by his 2nd wife Florence, 1st da. of Major Henry Thomas TIMSON of Stydd House, Lyndhurst, co. Hants., which Charles William was 2nd s. of 19th Earl of Morton. He was *b.* 19 Mar. 1927; *m.*, 20 Sep. 1949, Sheila Mary, da. of Rev. Canon John Stanley GIBBS of Didmarton House, Badminton, co. Glos.

[JOHN STEWART SHOLTO DOUGLAS, *styled* LORD ABERDOUR, 1st s. and h. ap., *b.* 17 Jan. 1952; *m.*, 1985, Amanda Kirsten, yr. da. of David John Macfarlane MITCHELL of Kirkudbright.]

MOSTYN

page 304,
line 22, line to read as follows

IV. 1929. 4. EDWARD LLEWELYN ROGER (LLOYD-MOSTYN), BARON MOSTYN, &c., s. and h., *b.* 16 Mar. 1885; ed. at Eton.

lines 24–6, delete from '([c])' to 'work.]' and replace by 'He *d.* 2 May 1965. His widow *d.* 1976.'

V. 1965. 5. ROGER EDWARD LLOYD (LLOYD-MOSTYN), BARON MOSTYN, &c., 1st s. and h., *b.* 17 Apr. 1920; ed. at Eton and R.M.C., Sandhurst; *m.* 1stly, 3 Apr. 1943, Yvonne Margaret, yst. da. of Arthur Stuart JOHNSON, of Henshall Hall, Congleton, Cheshire. This marriage was diss. by divorce in 1957 and he *m.* 2ndly, Sheila Edmondson, da. of Major Reginald FAIRWEATHER of Stockwell Manor, Silverton, co. Devon.

[LLEWELLYN ROGER LLOYD LLOYD-MOSTYN, s. and h. ap., *b.* 26 Sep. 1948; ed. at Eton; *m.*, 1974, Denise Suzanne, da. of Roger DUVANEL.]

note ([c]), delete all detail

MOUNT EDGECUMBE

page 319,
line 4, line to read as follows

EARLDOM, Etc. V. BARONY. VII.	1917	5 and 7. PIERS ALEXANDER HAMILTON (EDGECUMBE), EARL OF MOUNT EDGECUMBE, &c., only s. and h., *b.* 2 July 1865, *styled* VISCOUNT VALLETOURT 1865–1917;

lines 10–11, delete from 'Having' to 'work.]' and replace by 'He *d. s.p.* 18 Apr. 1944.'

EARLDOM, Etc. VI. BARONY. VIII.	1974	6 and 8. KENELM WILLIAM EDWARD (EDGECUMBE), EARL OF MOUNT EDGECUMBE, &c., cousin and h., being only s. of Richard John Frederick EDGECUMBE (*d.* 3 Nov. 1937), by his 1st wife Mary Louisa, 2nd da. of John Bligh MONCK of Coley Park, co. Berks., which Richard John was 1st s. of George

EDGECUMBE (*d.* 18 Apr. 1882), by Fanny Lucy, 1st da. of Sir John SHELLEY, Bart., which George was 3rd s. of 2nd Earl of Mount Edgecumbe. He was *b.* 9 Oct. 1873; ed. at Harrow and Univ. Coll., London; *m.*, 19 July 1906, Lilian Agnes, da. of Col. Arthur Chandos ARKWRIGHT of Hatfield Place, Witham, Essex. She *d.* 28 Sep. 1964. He *d.* 10 Feb. 1965.

[PIERS RICHARD EDGECUMBE, only s. and h. ap., *b.* 22 Oct. 1914. He *d. v.p.* and unm. 27 May 1940, being *k.* in action near Wormhout.]

EARLDOM, Etc. VII. BARONY. IX.	1965	7 and 9. EDWARD PIERS (EDGECUMBE), EARL OF MOUNT EDGECUMBE, &c., distant cousin and h., being 1st s. of George Valletort EDGECUMBE (*d.* 1947), by Georgina Mildred, da. of Thomas Aubrey BELL, of Auckland, New Zealand, which George was 1st s. of Edward Mortimer EDGECUMBE (*d.* 29

June 1890), by Constance Bevin, yst. da. of Rev. Robert BURROWES of Auckland aforenamed, which Edward was 2nd s. of George EDGECUMBE, by Fanny Lucy, both abovenamed. He was *b.* 13 July 1903; ed. at Auckland Gram. Sch.; *m.*, 1944, Victoria Effie, yr. da. of Robert CAMPBELL. She *d.* 1979. He *d. s.p.* 9 Dec. 1982.

EARLDOM, Etc. VIII. BARONY. X.	1982	8 and 10. ROBERT CHARLES (EDGECUMBE), EARL OF MOUNT EDGECUMBE, &c., nephew and h., being 2nd but 1st surv. s. of George Aubrey Valletort EDGECUMBE (*d.* 1977), by his 1st wife Meta, da. of Charles Robert LHOYER of Nancy, France, which George was the yr. br. of the 7th Earl of Mount

Edgecumbe. He was *b.* 1 June 1939; ed. at Nelson Coll.; *m.*, 1960, Joan Ivy, da. of Ernest WALL of Otorohanga, New Zealand. She *d.* 1988.

MOUNTGARRET

page 328,
line 21, after 'O.B.E.' add 'She *d.* 13 Dec. 1944.'
line 22, line to read as follows

XV. 1912. 15. EDMUND SOMERSET (BUTLER), VISCOUNT MOUNTGARRET [I. 1550], 1st s. and h., being only s. by 1st wife, *b.* 1 Feb. 1875;

lines 26–8, delete from 'Having' to 'work'
line 28, after '1918' add ', suddenly at Ullswater Hotel, Patterdale, Westmorland, and was *bur.* on 26 June in Patterdale Churchyard'
line 28, delete '(d)', after 'widow' add '*m.* 2ndly, 12 July 1919, Lieut. Col. Charles Hervey GREY (who *d.* 24 July 1955). She, who' and for '.]' read ', *d.* 8 Apr. 1961.'

XVI. 1918. 16. PIERS HENRY AUGUSTINE (BUTLER), VISCOUNT MOUNTGARRET, &c., half-brother and h., being only s. by 2nd wife, *b.* 28 Aug. 1903; ed. at R.N.C.s, Osborne and Dartmouth, and Cambridge (Trin. Coll.). He *m.* 15 Oct. 1931, Eglantine Marie Elizabeth, da. of William Lorenzo CHRISTIE, of Jervaulx Abbey, co. York. This marriage was diss. by divorce in 1941 (she was still living 1995) and he *m.* 2ndly, 14 Nov. 1941, Elise Margarita, da. of Sir John Nicholson BARRAN, Bart., of Sawley Mill, Ripon, Yorks. He *d.* 2 Aug. 1966. His widow *d.* 8 Aug. 1968.

XVII. 1966. 17. RICHARD HENRY PIERS (BUTLER), VISCOUNT MOUNTGARRET, &c., only s. and h., *b.* 8 Nov. 1936; ed. at Eton and R.M.C., Sandhurst; *m.* 1stly, 20 May 1960, Gillian Margaret, da. of Cyril Francis Stuart BUCKLEY. This marriage was diss. by divorce in 1969 and he *m.* 2ndly, 1970, Jennifer Susan Melville, yr. da. of Capt. D.M. WILLS of Barley Wood, Wrington, Somerset and formerly wife of D.W. FATTORINI of Sawley Hall, Ripon, co. Yorks. This marriage was in turn diss. by divorce in 1983 and he *m.* 3rdly, 1983, Angela Ruth (Mrs WADDINGTON), da. of Major Thomas PORTER of Church Fenton, Tadcaster, co. Yorks.

[PIERS JAMES RICHARD BUTLER, s. and h. ap. by 1st wife, *b.* 15 Apr. 1961.]

note (d), delete all detail

MOUNTJOY

page 331,
note (b), lines 4–6, delete from 'See' to 'above'

page 337,
line 11, after 'COBHAM, ' add '*de jure* (according to modern doctrine), 5th LORD COBHAM (of Sherborough)
line 12, after 'CHIDIOK' add '[5th LORD FITZPAYN]'

page 338,
line 8, after 'ORMOND' add '[I.]'

MOUNTMORRES

page 357,
line 16, after 'Farnborough' add 'He *m.* 2ndly, 10 April 1934, Tempe Irene, only da. of Charles Frederick CROSS of the Hermitage, Totland Bay, Isle of Wight. He

d. s.p.m. 2, at a Nursing Home in Reading and was *bur.* 4 Dec. 1936 at Farnborough. She *d.* 4 Mar. 1937.'

VII. 1936. 7. ARTHUR HERVÉ ALBERIC BOUCHARD (DE MONTMORENCY), VISCOUNT MOUNTMORRES OF CASTLEMORRES, and BARON MOUNTMORRES OF CASTLEMORRES, both in the Peerage of Ireland, also a Baronet, cousin and h., being 2nd but 1st surv s. of Arthur Hill Trevor DE MONTMORENCY (*d.* 1 Jan. 1910), by Caroline, da. of Rev. George KEMMIS, of St. Helen's, Blackrock, which Arthur Hill was 4th s. of 4th Viscount Mountmorres. he was *b.* 6 Feb. 1879; ed. at Trin. Coll., Dublin; Clerk in Holy Orders; *m.*, 15 Apr. 1914, Katherine Sophia Clay, da. of T.A. WARRAND of Bridge of Allan, co. Stirling. He *d. s.p.m.* 15 Oct. 1951 when the Viscountcy and Barony became *extinct* but he was *suc.* in the Baronetcy by his distant cousin.

MOUNT SANDFORD

page 363,
note ([a]), line 5, after '*Mag.*).' add 'A less creditable version of the fight is given in a letter from Alfred Gatty, at Eton, to his father on 15 June 1828 (Birmingham Library, MS.1116). Mount Sandford apparently made himself 'obnoxious' in a gambling club and was thrown over the banisters, fracturing his skull in the fall'

MOWBRAY

page 367,
line 3, after 'BIGOD,' add 'probably' and after 'Alice,' add 'sister and coh. of William de TOSNY, Lord of Belvoir, da. of Robert de TOSNY, of the same,'

page 369,
note ([b]), line 3, for 'p. 24' read 'p. 137'

page 376,
line 10, after 'STRANGE add '(of Ellesmere)'

page 383,
line 7, after 'h.' add 'ap.'
line 9, after 'FITZPAYN, ' add 'sister and coh. of Giles 2nd LORD BADLESMERE'

page 384,
line 6, delete 'eventually'
lines 9–10, for 'is said to have become' read 'became'

page 388,
line 7, after '([b])' add 'He *d.* 29 July 1936.'

IX. 1936. [or *XXIII*] 9. WILLIAM MARMADUKE (STOURTON), LORD MOWBRAY, SEGRAVE and STOURTON, 1st s. and h., *b.* 31 Aug. 1895. He *d.* 7 May 1965. See STOURTON

X. 1965. [or *XXIV*] 10. CHARLES EDWARD (STOURTON), LORD MOWBRAY, SEGRAVE and STOURTON, only s. and h., *b.* 11 Mar. 1923. See STOURTON.

MULTON

page 398,
line 5, for 'Walingburg' read 'Wasingburg'

MUNCHENSY

page 411,
note ([a]), line 4, after 'Stokes' add 'see G. Edward Fowler, 'Montechensi of Edwardstone', *Misc. Gen. et Her.*, 5th Ser., vol. 10, 1938, pp. 1–10.

page 421,
line 17, after 'PEMBROKE, ' add 'by Isobel, *suo jure* COUNTESS OF PEMBROKE,'

page 422,
lines 2–3, delete from ', and was' to 'London'
note ([b]), line 1, for '554' read '1554'

page 424,
line 6, after '([d])' add 'She was *bur.* in the church of the Greyfriars in London. M.I' [See vol. xii, part 2, p. 254, *sub* VERE.]
line 18, for 'Aug.' read 'April'
note ([d]), lines 2–3, delete from ', where' to 'Canise'

MUNSTER

page 430,
note ([a]), line 5, after '£500.' add 'Another illegitimate son by an unknown mother, William Henry Courtney, died in H.M.S. *Blenheim* when she was sunk with all hands in 1806, see Hugh Owen, *Mariner's Mirror*, vol. 82, pp. 206–10.'

page 431,
line 8, line to read as follows

III. 1901. 3. GEOFFREY GEORGE GORDON (FITZCLARENCE), EARL OF MUNSTER, &c., 3rd but 1st surv. s. and h.;([a]) *b.* 18 July 1859, *styled* LORD TEWKESBURY 1870–1901,

lines 14–15, delete from 'Having' to 'work.]'

IV. 1902. 4. AUBREY (FITZCLARENCE), EARL OF MUNSTER, &c., br. and h., *b.* 7 June 1862. He *d.* unm. 1 Jan. 1928.

V. 1928. 5. GEOFFREY WILLIAM RICHARD HUGH (FITZCLARENCE), EARL OF MUNSTER, &c., cousin and h. [for further detail see note (b), line 2 *et seq.*]. He *d. s.p.* 27 Aug. 1975. His widow *d.* 1979.

VI. 1975. 6. EDWARD CHARLES (FITZCLARENCE), EARL OF MUNSTER, &c., distant cousin and h., being s. of Brig. Gen. Charles FITZCLARENCE, V.C. and bar (*d.* 12 Nov. 1914, being *k.* in action in France), by Violet, da. of Lord Alfred SPENCER-CHURCHILL, which Charles was 1st s. of Capt. George FITZCLARENCE, R.N. (24 Mar. 1894), by Lady Maria Henrietta, 1st da. of John Henry (SCOTT), 3rd EARL OF CLONMELL, which George was 3rd s. of 1st Earl of Munster. He was *b.* 3 Oct. 1899; ed. at Eton and R.M.C., Sandhurst; *m.* 1stly, 30 July 1925, Monica Sheila Harrington, 4th da. of Lieut. Col. Sir Henry Mulleneux GRAYSON, Bart., K.B.E. This marriage was diss. by divorce in 1930 (she *d.* 5 Oct. 1958) and he *m.* 2ndly, 28 Sep. 1939, Vivian (Mrs SCHOFIELD), da. of Benjamin SCHOFIELD of Rochdale. co. Lancs. He *d.* 15 Nov. 1983. His widow was still living 1995.

VII. 1983. 7. ANTHONY CHARLES (FITZCLARENCE), EARL OF MUNSTER, &c., only s. and h., *b.* 21 Mar. 1926; ed. at St. Edward's Sch., Oxford; *m.* 1stly, 28 July 1949, Louise Margaret Diane, da. of Louis DELVIGNE of Liège, Belgium. This marriage was diss. by divorce in 1966 and he *m.* 2ndly, 1966, Pamela Margaret (Mrs HYDE), da. of Arthur SPOONER. This marriage was in turn diss. by divorce in 1979 and he *m.* 3rdly, 1979, Dorothy Alexa, yst. da. of Lieut. Col. Edward Boyd MAXWELL, O.B.E., M.C. She *d.* 13 June 1995 and he *m.* 4thly, 3 May 1997, Dr Halina Winska.

note (b), lines 1–2, delete from 'He' to '1928'

MUSGRAVE

page 439,
line 20, for 'about 1680' read '19 May 1681, at Edenhall, Cumberland (settlement 16 May 1681)' [*ex inform.* C. Roy Hudleston]
line 23, for 'about 1682' read '*bap.* 19 May 1682 at Edenhall' [*ex inform.* C. Roy Hudleston]

MUSGRAVE

page 440,
line 17, after 'Dorset' add 'On his death any Barony which may be supposed to have been *cr.* by the writs to Thomas de Musgrave (see above), fell into abeyance between his daughters, Nora Mary Agnes and Kathleen Mary Eleanor, and their descendants.'

MUSKERRY

page 443,
line 6, after '1929.' add 'His widow *d.* 14 Mar. 1950.'
line 12, after 'MASSY.' add 'He *d.* 1 June 1923. She *d.* 12 Mar. 1958.'
lines 13–16, delete all detail and replace as follows

V. 1929. 5. ROBERT MATTHEW FITZMAURICE (DEANE-MORGAN), BARON MUSKERRY, 2nd but 1st surv. s. and h., *b.* 14 Nov. 1874. He *m.*, 1906,

Charlotte Jane, da. of John IRVINE, of Mervyn, co. Wexford. He *d. s.p.* 12 July 1952. She *d.* 27 July 1960.

VI. 1952. 6. MATTHEW CHICHESTER CECIL (DEANE-MORGAN), BARON MUSKERRY, br. and h., *b.* 3 Nov. 1875; *m.*, 8 June 1915, Helen Henrietta Blennerhassett, da. of Rodolph HARMAN, Surgeon Lieut. Col. She *d.* 11 Sep. 1952. He *d. s.p.* 3 May 1954.

VII. 1954. 7. MATTHEW FITZMAURICE TILSON (DEANE), BARON MUSKERRY, distant cousin and h., being s. of Matthew James Hastings Fitzmaurice DEANE (*d.* 1907), by Maria, da. of Rev. William BANBURY of Shandrum, co. Cork, which Matthew James was 3rd s. of 3rd Baron Muskerry. He was *b.* 30 July 1874; *m.* 1stly, 6 Oct. 1897, Mabel Kathleen Vivienne, da. of Charles Henry ROBINSON. She *d.* 15 Aug. 1954 and he *m.* 2ndly, 12 June 1964, Muriel Doreen Sellars, da. of Arthur Gibson SIMPSON of Carlisle. He *d.* 2 Nov. 1966. His widow was still living 1995.

VIII. 1966. 8. HASTINGS FITZMAURICE (DEANE), BARON MUSKERRY, 3rd but only surv. s. and h.,(b) *b.* 12 Mar. 1907; ed. at Trin. Coll., Dublin; *m.*, 29 Jan. 1944, Betty Fairbridge, da. of Wilfred George Reckless PALMER of Grahamstown, South Africa. She *d.* 20 Aug. 1988. He *d.* 14 Oct. 1988.

IX. 1988. 9. ROBERT FITZMAURICE (DEANE), BARON MUSKERRY, only s. and h., *b.* 26 Mar. 1948; ed. at Trin. Coll., Dublin; *m.*, 1975, Rita, da. of (__) BRINK of Pietermaritzburg, South Africa.

[JONATHAN FITZMAURICE DEANE, s. and h. ap., *b.* 7 June 1986.]

note (b) His two elder brothers were: (1) Matthew FitzMaurice Tilson Deane, 31 July 1898, served in WW1 in Canadian Gren. Guards, and *m.*, 12 May 1936, Dorothy, da. of Charles Cook of Liverpool. He *d. v.p. s.p.* 7 July 1956; (2) Victor Leslie FitzMaurice Deane, *b.* 26 June 1904, *d.* unm. 29 Oct. 1928.

NAIRNE

page 450,
line 6, after '1895.' add 'He *d.* 3 June 1927.'

VIII. 1927. 8. HENRY WILLIAM EDMUND KEITH (PETTY-FITZMAURICE), MARQUIS OF LANSDOWNE, &c., s. and h., *b.* 14 Jan. 1872. He *d.* 5 Mar. 1936 [for further detail see LANSDOWNE, Marquessate].

IX. 1936. 9. CHARLES HOPE (PETTY-FITZMAURICE), MARQUESS OF LANSDOWNE, &c., 2nd but 1st surv. s. and h.,(ax) *b.* 9 Jan. 1917. He was *k.* in action 20 Aug. 1944, and *d.* unm., being *suc.* in his titles by his cousin except for the Barony of Nairne in which he was *suc.* by his sister.

X. 1944. 10. KATHERINE EVELYN CONSTANCE BIGHAM, *suo jure* LADY NAIRNE, 1st da. and eventual h. (in the Barony) of Henry William Edmund Keith

(PETTY-FITZMAURICE), 6TH MARQUESS OF LANSDOWNE. She was *b.* 22 June 1912; *m.*, 24 July 1933, Edward Clive (BIGHAM), 3rd VISCOUNT MERSEY. He *d.* 2 Aug. 1979.

[RICHARD MAURICE CLIVE BIGHAM, MASTER OF NAIRNE 1944–79, *suc.* his father as 4th VISCOUNT MERSEY in 1979, which see.]

note ([ax]) His elder br., Henry Maurice John, *styled* Earl of Kerry, was *b.* 7 Oct. 1913 and *d. v.p.* and unm. 12 Sep. 1933.

NAPIER OF MAGDALA AND OF CARYNGTON

page 452,
lines 38–9, delete from 'He was' to 'peer,'

page 453,
line 1, delete from 'outside' to 'work.([a])'

III. 1921. 3. JAMES PEARSE (NAPIER), BARON NAPIER OF MAGDALA AND OF CARYNGTON, br. and h., *b.* 30 Dec. 1849; ed. at Cheltenham and Cambridge (Jesus Coll.); Col. late 10th Royal Hussars. He *m.* 25 July 1876, Mabel Elle, da. of Windsor PARKER, Lieut. Col. West Suffolk Militia, of Clopton Hall, Suffolk, who *d.* 16 July 1907. He *d. s.p.m.s.* at his home at Christchurch, Hants, 2, and was *bur.* 8 May 1935 at Wilby, Suffolk.

IV. 1935. 4. EDWARD HERBERT SCOTT (NAPIER), BARON NAPIER OF MAGDALA AND OF CARYNGTON, half-brother and h., being 1st s. of 1st Baron Napier by his 2nd wife, *b.* 16 Dec. 1861; ed. at Royal Indian Eng. Coll.; *m.*, 11 July 1900, Florence Martha, da. of Gen. John Maxwell PERCEVAL, C.B., of Dillon House, Downpatrick, co. Down. She *d.* 1 Dec. 1946. He *d.* 20 July 1948.

V. 1948. 5. ROBERT JOHN (NAPIER) BARON NAPIER OF MAGDALA AND OF CARYNGTON, only s. and h., *b.* 16 June 1904; ed. at Wellington; *m.*, 20 Sep. 1939, Elizabeth Marian, yst. da. of Edmund Henderson HUNT of Farnham, Surrey. He *d.* 29 Oct. 1987. His widow was still living 1995.

VI. 1987. 6. ROBERT ALAN (NAPIER), BARON NAPIER OF MAGDALA AND OF CARYNGTON, 1st s. and h., *b.* 6 Sep. 1940; ed. at Winchester and Cambridge (St. John's Coll.); *m.*, 4 Jan. 1964, Frances Clare, 1st da. of Alan Frank SKINNER of Woolpit, Suffolk.

[JAMES ROBERT NAPIER, s. and h. ap., *b.* 29 Jan. 1966; ed. at Winchester and Edinburgh Univ.; *m.*, 1992, Jacqueline, 1st da. of A. STEPHEN of Inverkeithing, Fife.]

note ([a]), delete all detail

NAPIER OF MERCHISTOUN

page 460,
line 26, line to read as follows

XII. 1913. 12. FRANCIS EDWARD BASIL (NAPIER), LORD NAPIER OF MERCHISTOUN, &c., 1st s. and h., *b.* 19 Nov. 1876.

page 461,
line 4, delete '([a])'
lines 4–5, delete from 'Having' to 'work.]' and replace by 'He *d.* 22 Mar. 1941. His widow *d.* 11 May 1951.'

XIII. 1941. 13. WILLIAM FRANCIS CYRIL JAMES (NAPIER), LORD NAPIER OF MERCHISTOUN, &c., 1st s. and h., *b.* 9 Sep. 1900, MASTER OF NAPIER 1913–41; ed. at Wellington and R.M.C., Sandhurst. Capt. 1st Battn. K.O.S.B. He *m.* 28 Sep. 1928, in St. John's Cathedral, Hongkong, Violet Muir, 1st da. of Sir Percy Wilson NEWSON. He *d.* 23 Aug. 1954. His widow *d.* 1992.

XIV. 1954. 14. FRANCIS NIGEL (NAPIER), LORD NAPIER OF MERCHISTOUN [S.], and BARON ETTRICK OF ETTRICK [U.K.], and a Baronet [S.], 1st s. and h., *b.* 5 Dec. 1930, MASTER OF NAPIER 1941–54; ed. at Eton and R.M.C., Sandhurst; *m.*, 30 Oct. 1958, Delia Mary, yr. da. of Major Archibald David Barclay PEARSON of Upper Sattenham, Milford, Surrey.

[FRANCIS DAVID CHARLES NAPIER, MASTER OF NAPIER, *b.* 3 Nov. 1962; *m.*, 1993, Zara Jane, da. of Hugh Dermot MCCALMONT.]

note ([a]), delete all detail

NELSON

page 466,
line 12, after 'Midx.' add 'She *d.* 24 May 1938.'
lines 13–15, delete all detail and replace as follows

EARLDOM. IV. BARONY. V. } 1913 4 and 5. THOMAS HORATIO (NELSON), EARL NELSON OF TRAFALGAR and OF MERTON, &c., 3rd([c]) but 1st surv. s. and h., *b.* 19 July 1854, at Trafalgar House, Wilts., *styled* VISCOUNT MERTON 1905–13. He *d.* unm. 30 Sep. 1947.

EARLDOM. V. BARONY. VI. } 1947 5 and 6. EDWARD AGAR HORATIO (NELSON), EARL NELSON OF TRAFALGAR and OF MERTON, &c., br. and h., *b.* 10 Aug. 1860; *m.*, 7 Aug. 1889, Geraldine, da. of Henry H. CAVE of Rugby, co. Warwick. She *d.* 20 July 1936. He *d.* 30 Jan. 1951.

EARLDOM. VI. BARONY. VII. } 1951 6 and 7. ALBERT FRANCIS JOSEPH HORATIO (NELSON), EARL NELSON OF TRAFALGAR and OF MERTON, &c., 1st s. and h., *b.* 2 Sep. 1890; ed. at Downside and at Maredsous, Belgium; *m.*, 16 Jan. 1924, Amelia, 4th da. of George Buchanan COOPER of California, U.S.A. and widow of John C. SCOTT. This marriage was diss. by divorce in 1925 (she *d.* 1937) and he *m.* 2ndly, 1927 (in Scotland)

and 1942 (in England), Marguerite Helen, da. of Capt. J.M. O'SULLIVAN of Dublin. He *d. s.p.* 23 June 1957. His widow *d.* 6 Feb. 1969.

EARLDOM. VII. BARONY. VIII. } 1957 — 7 and 8. HENRY EDWARD JOSEPH HORATIO (NELSON), EARL NELSON OF TRAFALGAR and OF MERTON, &c., br. and h., *b.* 22 Apr. 1894; ed. at Maredsous, Belgium. He *d.* unm. 8 Aug. 1972.

EARLDOM. VIII. BARONY. IX. } 1972 — 8 and 9. GEORGE JOSEPH HORATIO (NELSON), EARL NELSON OF TRAFALGAR and OF MERTON, &c., br. and h., *b.* 20 Apr. 1905; ed. at Ampleforth; *m.*, 29 Dec. 1945, Mary Winifred, da. of G. BEVAN of Swansea. He *d. s.p.m.* 21 Sep. 1981. His widow was still living 1995.

EARLDOM. IX. BARONY. X. } 1981 — 9 and 10. PETER JOHN HORATIO (NELSON), EARL NELSON OF TRAFALGAR and OF MERTON, &c., nephew and h., being 1st s. of John Marie Joseph Horatio NELSON, (*d.* 1970), by Kathleen Mary, da. of William BURR of Torquay, co. Devon, which John Marie was 5th s. of 5th Earl Nelson. He was *b.* 9 Oct. 1941; *m.*, 1969, Maureen Diana, da. of Patrick QUINN of Kilkenny. He *m.* 2ndly, 1992, Tracy, da. of (__) COWIE.

[SIMON JOHN HORATIO NELSON, *styled* VISCOUNT MERTON, s. and h. ap. by 1st wife, *b.* 21 Sep. 1971.]

NERFORD

page 470,
line 7, after 'BEREFORD,' add 'of Burton, co. Leicester, Chief Justice of the Common Pleas, by Margaret, da. of Hugh DE PLESEY,'

NEVILLE

page 486,
note (a), lines 3–5, delete from 'There' to 'p. 273).' [See vol. xii, part 2, p. 351 and note (i), *sub* WARD.]

page 491,
line 6, after '1366)' add ', by his wife Katherine'

page 501,
line 1, after 'LORD AUDLEY' add '(of Stratton)'
note (b), line 21, for 'Robert, s. of Robert, Lord Clifford' read 'Robert, 4th Lord Clifford, s. and h. of Robert, 3rd Lord Clifford'

page 503,
note (i), line 4, after 'Thomas' add ', Lord Furnivalle'

page 504,
line 4, after 'wife,' add 'sister and coh. of Edmund, 4th EARL OF KENT'

lines 17–18, delete from '3rd' to 'SALISBURY' and replace by '1st wife, Anne, da. of Edmund (STAFFORD), 5th EARL OF STAFFORD' [See vol. v, p. 215, note (a), *sub* EXETER and vol. xii, part 2, p. 550, *sub* WESTMORLAND.]

line 21, after 'DOUGLAS, ' add '[S.]'

NEWBOROUGH

page 510,
line 31, delete from 'He' to 'his' and replace by 'His widow *d.* 26 Nov. 1939.'

page 511,
lines 1–2, delete from 'brother' to 'work'

V. 1916. 5. THOMAS JOHN (WYNN), BARON NEWBOROUGH, 3rd but 1st surv. br.(a) and h., *b.* 22 Nov. 1878. He served in WW1 as Lieut. R.N.V.R. He *m.*, 30 Jan. 1907, at St. Peter's, Eaton Sq., Vera Evelyn Mary, widow of Henry WINCH, and da. of Philip MONTAGU, sometime Capt. 12th Lancers. This marriage was diss. by divorce in 1938 (she *d.* 30 Apr. 1940) and he *m.* 2ndly, 23 Mar. 1939, Denisa Josephine, da. of Lazar BRAUN of Yugoslavia and formerly wife of Jean MALPUECH, Gov. of Laos. This marriage was in turn diss. by divorce in 1947 and he *m.* 3rdly, 7 Aug. 1947, Katherine Rudkin, da. of Henry Stephen MURRAY of Melbourne, Australia. He *d. s.p.m.* 27 Apr. 1957. His widow *d.* 1979.

VI. 1957. 6. ROBERT VAUGHAN (WYNN), BARON NEWBOROUGH, cousin and h., being 1st s. of Charles Henry WYNN (*d.* 14 Mar. 1911), by Frances Georgiana, 2nd da. of Lieut. Col. (__) ROMER, which Charles Henry was 3rd s. of 3rd Baron Newborough. He was *b.* 17 July 1877; *m.*, 16 Dec. 1913, Ruby Irene, yst. da. of Edmund Wigley SEVERNE of Thenford, co. Northants and of Wallop, co. Salop. She *d.* 6 Nov. 1960. He *d.* 27 Oct. 1965.

VII. 1965. 7. ROBERT CHARLES MICHAEL VAUGHAN (WYNN), BARON NEWBOROUGH, 1st s. and h., *b.* 24 Apr. 1917; ed. at Oundle; *m.*, 1 Dec. 1945, Rosamund Lavington, yst. da. of Major Robert BARBOUR of Bolesworth Castle, Chester. This marriage was diss. by divorce in 1971 and he *m.* 2ndly, 1971, Jennifer Caroline Acton, yst. da. of Cecil C.A. ALLEN, Capt., R.N.

[ROBERT VAUGHAN WYNN, s. and h. ap. by 1st wife, *b.* 11 Aug. 1949; ed. at Milton Abbey; *m.*, 1981, Sheila Christine (Mrs WILSON), da. of William A. MASSEY, of Corsley, co. Wilts. This marriage was diss. by divorce and he *m.* 2ndly, 1988, Susan E. (Mrs HALL), da. of Andrew LLOYD of Malta.]

note (a), delete all detail and replace by 'The 2nd brother SPENCER PERCEVAL WYNN, was *b.* 16 May and *d.* 15 Aug. 1876.'

NEWBURGH

page 519,
line 25, line to read as follows

IX. 1908. 9. CHARLES (GIUSTINIANI-BANDINI), EARL OF NEWBURGH, &c., 2nd([b]) but 1st surv. s. and h., *b.* in Rome, 1 Jan. 1862, *styled* (since 1877)

lines 29–30, delete from 'Having' to 'work.([c])]' and replace by 'He *d.* 14 June 1941. His widow *d.* 22 Jan. 1949.'

[SIGISMONDO MARIA BANDINO GUISEPPE GIUSTIANI-BANDINI, *b.* in Rome, 20 June 1886; *styled* VISCOUNT KYNNAIRD and DUCA DI MONDRAGONE. He *m.* 4 Apr. 1910, Teresa, da. of PRINCIPE UGO BONCOMPAGNI-LUDOVISI. He *d. v.p. s.p.* 4 Nov. 1918.([c]) His widow, who was *b.* 24 Jan. 1889, *m.* 2ndly, 25 Aug. 1921, at Florence, Francesco Ambrò DE ADAMÓCZ. She *d.* 1 May 1969.]

X. 1941. 10. MARIA SOFIA GIUSEPPINA *suo jure* COUNTESS NEWBURGH, VISCOUNTESS OF KYNNAIRD and BARONESS LEVINGSTON OF FLACRAIG, in the Peerage of Scotland, also PRINCESS GIUSTINIANI BANDINI, &c., only surv. child, *b.* 4 May 1889; *m.* COUNT MANFREDI GRAVINA DI RAMACCA, HIGH CMDR. OF DANZIG. He *d.* 19 Sep. 1932. She *d. s.p.* 30 Apr. 1977.

XI. 1977. 11. GIULIO CESARE TADDEO COSIMO, EARL OF NEWBURGH, &c., PRINCE ROSPIGLIOSI, DUCA DI ZAGAROLO, cousin and h., being only s. of PRINCE GIAMBATTISTA PIO SIGISMONDO FRANCESCO (*d.* 5 Apr. 1956), by Ethel Julia, da. of Isaac BRONSON of New York, which Prince Giambattista was 1st s. of Lady Elena Maria Concetta Isabella Gioacchina Giuseppa GIUSTINIANI-BANDINI, PRINCESS CAMILLA ROSPIGLIOSI (*d.* 1 May 1950), and Camillo, PRINCE ROSPIGLIOSI, which Princess Elena was 3rd da. of 8th Earl of Newburgh. He was *b.* 26 Oct. 1907; ed. at Cambridge (Corpus Christi Coll.); *m.*, 25 Nov. 1940, Donna Giulia VISCONTI DI MODRONE, da. of Don Guido Carlo dei Duchi VISCONTI DI MODRONE, COUNT OF LONATE POZZOLO. He *d.* 18 Apr. 1986. His widow was still living 1995.

XII. 1986. 12. FILIPPO GIAMBATTISTA CAMILLO FRANCESCO ALDO MARIA ROSPGLIOSI, EARL OF NEWBURGH, &c., also PRINCE ROSPIGLIOSI, &c., 1st s. and h., *b.* 4 July 1942; *m.*, 1972, BARONESSA DONNA LUISA, da. of COUNT ANNIBALE CACCIA DOMINONI.

[BENEDETTA FRANCESCA MARIA, MISTRESS OF NEWBURGH, da. and h. ap., *b.* 4 June 1974.]

note ([c]), lines 1–2, delete all detail; lines 1–2 (on page 520), delete from '*d. s.p.*' to '2nd s,' and replace by 'His brother'

NEWCASTLE

page 521,
line 24, delete from 'and possibly BARON OGLE OF BOTHAL, '

page 522,
line 1, delete 'co. Northumberland.([a])'
note ([a]), delete all detail

page 527,
lines 2–3, delete from 'Anne' to 'CHEEKE' and replace by 'Elizabeth, only da. and h. of Sir Justinian LEWIN, of Otterden Place, Kent.(aa)'
note (aa) See T.E. Watson, *History and Pedigree of the Family of Lewin*, 1919, p. 7; Gyles Isham (ed.), *The Correspondence of Bishop Brian Duppa and Sir Justinian Isham 1650–60*, Northants Rec. Soc., vol. 47, 1955, p. 169, note 2.
line 3, for 'June' read '31 May'

NEWCASTLE-UNDER-LYNE

page 537,
line 14, delete '(b)'
line 15, for 'was living 1936' read 'His widow *d.* 1 June 1955.'

VIII. 1928. 8. HENRY FRANCIS HOPE (PELHAM-CLINTON-HOPE), DUKE OF NEWCASTLE-UNDER-LYNE, &c., br. and h., *b.* 3 Feb. 1866; by Roy. Lic. took further name and arms of Hope, 7 Apr. 1887 [for further detail see note (b), lines 2–6; line 4, after '1902.' add 'She *d.* 27 Aug. 1938]. He *d.* 20 Apr. 1938.

IX. 1938. 9. HENRY EDWARD HUGH (PELHAM-CLINTON-HOPE), DUKE OF NEWCASTLE-UNDER-LYNE, &c., only s. and h., *b.* 8 Apr. 1907, *styled* EARL OF LINCOLN 1928–38; ed. at Eton and Cambridge (Magdalene Coll.). He *m.*, 23 Mar. 1931, Mrs Jean Banks GIMBERNAT, yst. da. of David BANKS, of New York. This marriage was diss. by divorce in 1940 (she *d.* 2 Sep. 1968) and he *m.* 2ndly, 30 Nov. 1946, Lady Mary Diana, 2nd da. of Archibald Ralph (MONTAGU-STUART-WORTLEY-MACKENZIE), 3rd EARL OF WHARNCLIFFE. This marriage was in turn diss. by divorce in 1959 and he *m.* 3rdly, 23 Oct. 1959, Mrs Sally Ann Wemyss HOPE, 1st da. of Brig. John Henry ANSTICE of Kyrenia, Cyprus and formerly wife of Fikret JEMAL. He *d. s.p.m.* 4 Nov. 1988.

X. 1988. 10. EDWARD CHARLES (PELHAM-CLINTON), DUKE OF NEWCASTLE-UNDER-LYNE and EARL OF LINCOLN, distant cousin and h., being 1st s. of Capt. Guy Edward PELHAM-CLINTON (*d.* 18 Dec. 1934), by Hermione Edith Agnes, yst. da. of Arthur Frederick Churchill TOLLEMACHE, which Guy was 2nd s. of Henry William PELHAM-CLINTON (*d.* 18 Dec. 1927), by Mary, da. of Lieut. Gen. Frederick Green WILKINSON, which Henry was 2nd s. of Charles Pelham PELHAM-CLINTON (*d.* 15 Dec. 1894), by Elizabeth, da. of William GRANT of Congleton, Cheshire, which Charles was 2nd s. of 4th Duke of Newcastle. He was *b.* 18 Aug. 1920; ed. at Eton and Cambridge (Trin. Coll). He *d.* unm. 25 Dec. 1988 when his Dukedom became *extinct* and the Earldom of Lincoln became *dormant*. He was probably *suc.* in that title by his very distant cousin, see above.

note (b), lines 1–2, delete from 'He' to '1866'
lines 7–9, delete from 'Their' to 'York'

NEWLANDS

page 542,
line 7, line to read as follows

II. 1906 to 1929. 2. JAMES CECIL HENRY (HOZIER), BARON NEWLANDS OF NEWLANDS, &c., s. and h., *b.* 4 Apr. 1851;

lines 16–17, delete from 'Having' to 'work'

NEWMARCH

page 548,
note ([d]), line 2, after '356)' add 'for evidence tending to confirm this identification, see G. Andrews Moriarty, *Geneal. Mag.*, vol. 13, 1959, pp. 8–9.'

NEWTON

page 556,
line 31, after '1931' add 'He *d.* 21 Mar. 1942.'

page 557,
line 1, line to read as follows

III. 1942. 3. RICHARD WILLIAM DAVENPORT (LEGH), BARON NEWTON, 1st s. and h., *b.* 18 Nov. 1888;

line 7, after 'She' add ', who'; delete '([b])]' and replace by '*d.* 28 Dec. 1958. He *d.* 11 June 1960.'

IV. 1960. 4. PETER RICHARD (LEGH), BARON NEWTON, 1st s. and h., *b.* 6 Apr. 1915; ed. at Eton and Oxford (Ch. Ch.); *m.*, 6 July 1948, Priscilla, yr. da. of Capt. John EGERTON-WARBURTON of Arley Hall, Cheshire and widow of William Matthew PALMER, *styled* VISCOUNT WOLMER, s. and h. ap. of Roundell Cecil (PALMER), 3rd EARL OF SELBOURNE. He *d.* 16 June 1992. His widow was still living 1995.

V. 1992. 5. RICHARD THOMAS (LEGH), BARON NEWTON, 1st s. and h., *b.* 11 Jan. 1950; ed. at Eton and Oxford (Ch. Ch.); *m.*, 1978, Rosemary Whitfoot, yr. da. of Herbert Whitfoot CLARKE of Eastbourne, Sussex.

[PIERS RICHARD LEGH, s. and h. ap., *b.* 25 Oct. 1979.]

note ([b]), delete all detail

NORBURY

page 568,
line 11, after '1876' add 'He *d. s.p.* 20 Apr. 1943. His widow *d.* 26 May 1966'

EARLDOM [I.] V.
BARONY [I.] VI. } 1943 5 and 6. RONALD IAN MONTAGUE (GRAHAM-TOLER), EARL OF NORBURY, &c., distant cousin and h., being 2nd s. of James Otway GRAHAM-TOLER (*d.* 27 July 1913), by Emily Alexina, da. of Robert Balfour Wardlaw RAMSAY, of Whitehill, Midlothian,

which James Otway was 2nd s. of Otway Fortescue GRAHAM-TOLER (*d.* 23 Apr. 1884), by Henrietta Elizabeth, da. of Robert Campbell (SCARLETT), 2nd BARON ABINGER, which Otway was 2nd s. of 2nd Earl of Norbury. He was *b.* 11 Jan. 1893; ed. at H.M.S. Conway; *m.* 1stly, 7 Oct. 1919, Simone Evangeline Julie Caroline, da. of Hanes APENES, Norwegian Consul in France. This marriage was diss. by divorce in 1933 and he *m.* 2ndly, 24 May 1933, Margaret, da. of John Kevan GREENHALGH of Hoylake, Cheshire. He *d.* 24 May 1955. His widow *d.* 1984.

EARLDOM [I.] VI. / BARONY [I.] VII. — 1955 — 6 and 7. NOEL TERENCE (GRAHAM-TOLER), EARL OF NORBURY, &c., 2nd but 1st surv. (legit.) s. and h. by 2nd wife, *b.* 1 Jan. 1939; ed. at H.M.S. Conway; *m.*, 28 Oct. 1965, Rosamund Margaret Anne, 2nd da. of Francis MATHEW.

[RICHARD JAMES GRAHAM-TOLER, *styled* VISCOUNT GLANDINE, s. and h. ap., *b.* 5 Mar. 1967.]

NORFOLK

page 575,
note (b), line 5, after '(*Idem*)' add 'He undoubtedly came from the dept. of Calvados. See Lewis C. Loyd, *The Origins of Some Anglo-Norman Families*, Harl. Soc., 1951, pp. 14–15.'

page 585,
line 5, for 'dead in 1182' read '*d.* between 1145 and 1157'
note (c), line 1, before 'For' add 'She *m.* Walkelin I, not Walkelin II (who *d. s.p. circa* 1190), see Dugdale, *Monasticon*, vol. v, pp. 89, 97; *Annales Monastici*, *Rolls Series*, vol. iii, pp. 437, 440; *Pipe Roll*, 2 Ric. I, p. 151, 3 Ric. I, p. 146.'
line 2, for 'she granted' read 'Juliane granted'

page 590,
lines 2–3, for 'and Richard 2nd EARL' read '*suo jure* COUNTESS

page 599,
line 3, after 'h.' add 'ap.'
line 5, for '13 Sep. 1337' read 'Aug. 1334(da)'
note (da) See *Sir Christopher Hatton's Book of Seals*, L.C. Loyd and Doris Stenton (eds.), 1950, p. 249.
note (b), line 8, after 'Marshal.' add 'See vol. x, Appendix K, p. 126.'
note (e), lines 16–17, delete from ', and' to 'Pembroke'

page 601,
note (c), line 1, after 'p. 63' add ', limited to heirs male of his body'

page 604,
line 7, for '3 July 1414' read '18 Apr. 1411'
note (g), line 1, for '*Cal. Pat. Rolls, 1413–16*, p. 209.' read 'Bodleian Lib., Dodsworth MS. vol. 90, f. 150, in an indenture between Gerard Usflete and Elizabeth, Duchess of York.'

page 608,
line 9, after 'da.' add 'and (eventually) sole h.'

page 610,
line 13, after 'Abbey.' add '(ba)'
note (ba) Her body was subsequently moved (probably in 1502), when the Chapel of St. Erasmus was demolished to make way for the Henry VII Chapel, to the Abbey of the Minoresses, in the City of London. The coffin was subsequently discovered in a vault on the site of the Abbey in 1965. See *The Times*, 15 Jan. 1965; Museum of London, Joint Press Release on "Stepney Child Burial", 15 Jan. 1965. The discovery has never been properly reported.
note (c), line 5, after 'FERRERS.' add 'See vol. x, Appendix K, p. 126.'
note (d), line 4, after 'Ferrers,' add 's. and h. ap. of William, 5th Lord Ferrers (of Groby),'
note (e), delete all detail

page 611,
line 4, after 'was' add '*cr.* LORD HOWARD between 29 Dec. 1469 and 12 Feb. 1470 and was' [See Anne Crawford, *Howard Household Books*, 1992, p. xxx, note 62.]
note (k), after 'p. 191' add ', but see Sutton and Hammond, *Coronation of Richard III*, p. 246'

page 612,
note (c), line 2, delete from 'and' to '1490,'
line 3, after 'Club' add ', reprinted 1992'

page 613,
note (f), line 1, delete '(from the Tower)'

page 637,
line 29, after '1877' add 'and *d.* 28 Aug. 1945.'

page 638,
lines 5–8, delete all detail and replace as follows

DUKEDOM. XXI. EARLDOM. XXIX. } 1917

16 and 14. BERNARD MARMADUKE (FITZALAN-HOWARD), DUKE OF NORFOLK, &c., s. and h. by 2nd wife, *b.* at Arundel Castle, 31 May, and *bap.* 1 June 1908, in the chapel there, *styled* EARL OF ARUNDEL 1908–17; ed. at the Oratory Sch; made K.G. at the Coronation of George VI, 11 May 1937. On the 28 Aug. 1945, on the death of his mother, he succeeded her as BARON HERRIES of Terregles. He *m.*, 27 Jan. 1937, at the Brompton Oratory, Lavinia Mary, da. of Algernon Henry (STRUTT), 3rd BARON BELPER. He *d. s.p.m.* 31 Jan. 1975 when all his titles were inherited by his distant cousin except for the Barony of Herries of Terregles [S.], in which he was succeeded by his 1st da. and heir of line. See *sub* HERRIES OF TERREGLES, above. His widow was still living 1995.

DUKEDOM. XXII. EARLDOM. XXX. } 1975

17 and 15. MILES FRANCIS STAPLETON (FITZALAN-HOWARD), DUKE OF NORFOLK, &c., distant cousin and h., being 1st s. of Bernard Edward (FITZALAN-HOWARD), 3rd BARON HOWARD OF GLOSSOP, which see, by Mona Josephine Tempest Stapleton, *suo jure*, BARONESS BEAUMONT. He was *b.* 21 July 1915; ed. at Ampleforth and Oxford (Ch. Ch.). On the death of his

mother, 31 Aug. 1971, he *suc.* to the Barony of Beaumont (see *sub* BEAUMONT), and on the death of his father, 24 Aug. 1972, he *suc.* to the Barony of Howard of Glossop (see *sub* HOWARD OF GLOSSOP). He *m.*, 4 July 1949, Anne Mary Teresa, 1st da. of Wing Cmdr. Gerald Joseph CONSTABLE-MAXWELL of Alresford House, Alresford, co. Hants.

[EDWARD WILLIAM FITZALAN-HOWARD, *styled* EARL OF ARUNDEL AND SURREY, s. and h. ap., *b.* 2 Dec. 1956; ed. at Ampleforth and Oxford (Lincoln Coll.); *m.*, 1987, Georgina Susan, yr. da. of John Temple GORE.]

NORMANBY

page 641,
line 6, after '86.' add 'His widow *d.* 12 Mar. 1948.'
lines 7–10, delete all detail and replace as follows

MARQUESSATE. VI. VISCOUNTCY. V. } 1932 4 and 5. OSWALD CONSTANTINE JOHN (PHIPPS), MARQUESS OF NORMANBY, &c., s. and h., *b.* at Mulgrave castle, 29 July, and *bap.* 28 Aug. 1912, by his father, at St. Oswald's, Lythe, *styled* EARL OF MULGRAVE 1912–32; ed. at Eton and Oxford (Ch. Ch.); *m.*, 10 Feb. 1951, Grania Maeve Rosaura, da. of Walter Edward (GUINNESS), 1st BARON MOYNE. He *d.* 30 Jan. 1994. She, who was *b.* 14 Apr. 1920, was still living 1995.

MARQUESSATE. VII. VISCOUNTCY. VI. } 1994 5 and 6. CONSTANTINE EDMUND WALTER (PHIPPS), MARQUESS OF NORMANBY, &c., 1st s. and h., *b.* 24 Feb. 1954; ed. at Eton and Oxford (Worcester Coll.); *m.*, 1990, Nicola, da. of Milton SHULMAN and formerly wife of Edward ST. AUBYN.

NORMANTON

page 643,
line 10, after '68.' add 'His widow *d.* 29 Mar. 1961.'
lines 11–15, delete all detail and replace as follows

V. 1933. 5. EDWARD JOHN SIDNEY CHRISTIAN WELBORE ELLIS (AGAR), EARL OF NORMANTON, &c., s. and h., *b.* 29 Mar. 1910, and King Edward VII was sponsor at his baptism, *styled* VISCOUNT SOMERTON 1910–33. He was ed. at Eton and Cambridge (Trin. Coll.); *m.* 1stly, 5 July 1937, Barbara Mary, da. of Sir Frederick FRANKLAND, Bart., and of Mary Cecil, *suo jure* BARONESS ZOUCHE. This marriage was diss. by divorce in 1943 and he *m.* 2ndly, 30 Oct. 1944, Lady Fiona, yr. da. of John Charles (PRATT), 4th MARQUESS CAMDEN and formerly wife of Major Sir John Gerard Henry Fleetwood FULLER, Bart. He *d.* 28 Jan. 1967. His widow, who was *b.* 4 Mar. 1911, *d.* 1985.

VI. 1967. 6. SHAUN JAMES CHRISTIAN WELBORE ELLIS (AGAR), EARL OF NORMANTON, &c., 1st s. and h., *b.* 21 Aug. 1945; ed. at Eton. He *suc.* to the Barony of Mendip, 22 Dec. 1974, under the terms of the spec. rem to that title on the death of Arthur Victor (ELLIS), 8th and last VISCOUNT CLIFDEN, see *sub*

MENDIP. He *m.*, 29 Apr. 1970, Victoria Susan, da. of John H.C. BEARD of La Tourelle, St. Peter Port, Guernsey.

[JAMES SHAUN WELBORE ELLIS AGAR, *styled* VISCOUNT SOMERTON, *b.* 7 Sep. 1982.]

NORTH

page 649,
line 23, for 'widow of' read 'who afterwards *m.* Sir'
line 24, after 'WARREN' add (fa)
note (fa) This Sir Ralph was Lord Mayor in 1536 and part of 1543.

page 661,
line 15, line to read as follows

XII. 1932. 12. WILLIAM FREDERICK JOHN (NORTH), LORD NORTH, 1st s. and h., *b.* 13 Oct. 1860; ed. at the Oratory Sch.

lines 20–1, delete from 'Having' to 'work.(b)]' and replace by 'He *d.* 10 Dec. 1938. His widow *d.* 3 Aug. 1965, aged 98.'

[DUDLEY WILLIAM JOHN NORTH, s. and h. ap., *b.* 9 Aug. 1891; ed., at Eton and Oxford (Ch. Ch.). Served in WW1(b) as Lieut. 19th Hussars (M.C.; Desp.). He *m.*, 8 Aug. 1914, Dorothy, only child of Capt. John Robert DONNE, the Carabiniers. He *d. v.p.* 29 Mar. 1936.]

XIII. 1938. 13. JOHN DUDLEY (NORTH), LORD NORTH, grandson and h., being s. and h. of Dudley William John NORTH and Dorothy abovesaid, *b.* 7 June 1917; ed. at R.N.C., Dartmouth; *m*, 1940, Margaret, da. of Ronald W.H. GLENNIE of Cape Province, S. Africa. He was *k.* in action *s.p.*, 19 Dec. 1941, when his title fell into *abeyance* between his two sisters.(ba) His widow was living 1995.

note (ba) These, the two das. of the 12th Lord North, are: (1) Dorothy Anne, *b.* 4 May 1915; *m.* 1stly, 17 Sep. 1937, Major Robert Alexander Clive GRAHAM. This marriage was diss. by divorce in 1950 and she *m.* 2ndly, 23 Sep. 1950, Major John Edward Richard BOWLBY. She has issue by both marriages. (2) Susan Silence, *b.* 19 Jan. 1920; *m.*, Feb. 1943, Frederick Guy BEAUCHAMP, M.D. He *d.* 1981. She has issue by this marriage.
note (b), lines 1–4, delete from 'His' to '1917'

NORTHAMPTON

page 667,
line 14, after 'DE MORTIMER' add '[1st LORD MORTIMER],'
line 15, after 'BADLESMERE,' add '[2nd LORD BADLESMERE],'

page 689,
line 12, line to read as follows

MARQUESSATE. VII. EARLDOM. XXIII.	1913	6 and 14. WILLIAM BINGHAM (COMPTON), MARQUESS OF NORTHAMPTON, &c., 1st s. and h., *b.* 6 Aug. 1885, *styled* EARL COMPTON 1897–1915;

lines 19–21, delete from 'Having' to 'work.]' and replace by 'This marriage was diss. by divorce in 1942 (she *d.* 1980) and he *m.* 2ndly, 18 June 1942, Virginie Lucie, da. of David Rimington HEATON of Brookfield, Crownhilll, co. Devon. This marriage was in turn diss. by divorce in 1958 (she *m.* 2ndly, as his 3rd wife Thomas Andrew Hussey, Capt. R.N., who *d.* 1980, and was still living 1995) and he *m.* 3rdly, 2 Dec. 1958, Elspeth Grace, 1st da. of William Ingham WHITAKER of Pylewell Park, Lymington, co. Hants. and formerly wife of Christopher John Henry (ROPER-CURZON), 19th BARON TEYNHAM. She *d.* 1976. He *d.* 30 Jan. 1978.'

MARQUESSATE. VIII. EARLDOM. XXIV.	1978	7 and 15. SPENCER DOUGLAS DAVID (COMPTON), MARQUESS OF NORTHAMPTON, &c., 1st s. and h. by 2nd wife, *b.* 2 Apr. 1946; ed. at Eton; *m.* 1stly, 13 June 1967, Henriette Luisa Maria, da. of Adolph William Carel, BARON BENTINCK, Netherlands Ambassador to France.

This marriage was diss. by divorce in 1973 and he *m.* 2ndly, 1974, Annette Marie, da. of Charles Anthony Russell SMALLWOOD. This marriage was in turn diss. by divorce in 1977 and he *m.* 3rdly, 1977, Rosemary Ashley Morritt, da. of P.G.M. HANCOCK of Truro and formerly wife of Lionel John Charles Seymour DAWSON-DAMER. This marriage too was diss. by divorce in 1983 and he *m.* 4thly, 1985, Ellen Fritzi, da. of Hermann ERHARDT of Munich, Bavaria and formerly wife of Michael Orlando Weetman PEARSON. This 4th marriage was also diss. by divorce and he *m.* 5thly, 1990, Pamela Martina Raphaelo (Mrs KYPRIOS).

[DANIEL BINGHAM COMPTON, *styled* EARL COMPTON, s. and h. ap. by 1st wife, *b.* 16 Jan. 1973.]

NORTHBOURNE

page 690,
line 24, line to read as follows

III. 1923. 3. WALTER JOHN (JAMES), BARON NORTHBOURNE OF BETTESHANGER AND JARROW GRANGE, 1st s. and h., *b.* 2 Sep. 1869; ed. Harrow

lines 28–30, delete from 'Having' to 'work.([d])]' and replace by 'His widow *m.* 2ndly, 2 Aug. 1935, William Curtis GREEN, R.A., who *d.* 26 Mar. 1960. She *d.* 29 July 1952.'

IV. 1932. 4. WALTER ERNEST CHRISTOPHER (JAMES), BARON NORTHBOURNE OF BETTESHANGER AND JARROW GRANGE, s. and h., *b.* 18 Jan. 1896; ed. at Eton and Oxford (Magdalen Coll.). He served in WW1 as Lieut. Northumberland Fusiliers, and Machine Gun Corps (Desp.). He *m.*, 4 Mar. 1925, Katherine, da. of George NICKERSON, of Boston, U.S.A. She *d.* 1980. He *d.* 17 June 1982.

V. 1982. 5. CHRISTOPHER GEORGE WALTER (JAMES), BARON NORTHBOURNE OF BETTESHANGER AND JARROW GRANGE, s. and h., *b.* 18 Feb. 1926; ed. at Eton and Oxford (Magdalen Coll.); *m.*, 18 July 1959, Marie-Synge, 1st da. of Henri CLAUDEL of Chatou, Seine-et-Oise, France.

[CHARLES WALTER HENRI JAMES, 1st s. and h. ap., *b.* 14 June 1960; ed. at Eton and Oxford (Magdalen Coll.); *m.*, 1987, Catherine Lucy, da. of W. Ralph BURROWS of Prescot, co. Lancs.]

note ([d]), delete all detail

NORTHBROOK

page 692,
line 28, line to read as follows

EARLDOM. II. BARONY. III. } 1904 — 2 and 3. FRANCIS GEORGE (BARING), EARL OF NORTHBROOK, VISCOUNT BARING and BARON NORTHBROOK of Stratton, 1st s. and h., *b.* 8 Dec. 1850, *styled* VISCOUNT BARING 1876–1904;

page 693,
lines 6–7, delete from 'Having' to 'work'
line 7, after '*d.*' add '*s.p.*'
line 9, delete '([a])]' and replace by 'His widow *d.* 4 Dec. 1946.'

IV. 1929. 4. FRANCIS ARTHUR (BARING), BARON NORTHBROOK of Stratton, cousin and h., being the 1st s. by the 2nd wife of the 1st Baron, *b.* 20 July 1882; ed. at Eton and Oxford (Trin. Coll.). He *m.*, 30 Apr. 1914, Evelyn Gladys Isabella, da. of John George CHARLES by his wife Lady Edith Hester, da. of Henry Ulick (BROWNE), 5th MARQUESS OF SLIGO. She *d.* 20 Feb. 1919 and he *m.* 2ndly, 1 Dec. 1941, Constance Maude, da. of Frank GRIFFIN of Kew Gdns., co. Surrey. He *d.* 15 Dec. 1947. His widow *d.* 1976.

V. 1947. 5. FRANCIS JOHN (BARING), BARON NORTHBROOK of Stratton, s. and h., *b.* 31 May 1915; ed. at Winchester and Oxford (Trin. Coll.); *m.*, 27 Jan. 1951, Rowena Margaret, 2nd da. of Brig. Gen. Sir William Henry MANNING, G.C.M.G., K.B.E. He *d.* 4 Dec. 1990. His widow was still living 1995.

VI. 1990. 6. FRANCIS THOMAS (BARING), BARON NORTHBROOK, only s. and h., *b.* 21 Feb. 1954; ed. at Winchester and Bristol Univ.; *m.*, 1987, Amelia Sharon Elizabeth, 1st da. of Dr. Reginald David TAYLOR of Hursley, Winchester, co. Hants.

note ([a]), delete all detail

NORTHESK

page 698,
line 14, after '1921' add 'His widow *d.* 28 Jan. 1950.'
line 15, line to read as follows

XI. 1921. 11. DAVID LUDOVIC GEORGE HOPETOUN (CARNEGIE), EARL OF NORTHESK, &c., s. and h., *b.* 24 Sep. 1901, *styled* LORD ROSEHILL 1901–21; ed. at Gresham's Sch., Holt;

lines 20–1, delete from 'Having' to 'work.]' and replace by 'He *d. s.p.m.* 7 Nov. 1963. His widow *d.* 1991.'

XII. 1963. 12. JOHN DOUGLAS (CARNEGIE), EARL OF NORTHESK, &c., cousin and h., being 1st s. of Douglas George CARNEGIE (*d.* 27 Feb. 1937), by Margaret Jean, 2nd da. of Arthur Henry Johnstone DOUGLAS of Comlongon Castle, Ruthwell, co. Dumfries, which Douglas George was 2nd s. of 9th Earl of Northesk. He was *b.* 16 Feb. 1895; ed. at Gresham's Sch., Holt and Cambridge (King's Coll.); *m.*, 20 July 1920, Dorothy Mary, 1st da. of Col. Sir William Robert CAMPION, K.C.M.G., of Danny, Hassocks, Sussex. She *d.* 29 Aug. 1967. He *d.* 22 July 1975.

XIII. 1975. 13. ROBERT ANDREW (CARNEGIE), EARL OF NORTHESK, &c., 2nd but 1st surv. s. and h.,[ca] *b.* 24 June 1926; ed. at Nautical Coll., Pangbourne and U.S.A.; *m.* 1stly, 20 July 1949, Jean Margaret, yr. da. of Capt. John Duncan George MACRAE of Ballimore, Otter Ferry, Argyll. She *d.* 1989 and he *m.* 2ndly, 1989, Brownie Elizabeth, da. of Scott GRIMASON and widow of Carl. L. HEIMAN. He *d.* 26 Jan. 1994. His widow was still living 1995.

XIV. 1994. 14. DAVID JOHN MACRAE (CARNEGIE), EARL OF NORTHESK, &c., 2nd but only surv. s. and h.,[cb] *b.* 3 Nov. 1954; ed. at Eton; *m.*, 1979, Jacqueline May, 1st (adopted) da. of David Lorne Dundas REID of Portugal.

[ALEXANDER ROBERT MACRAE CARNEGIE, *styled* LORD ROSEHILL, s. and h. ap., *b.* 16 Nov. 1980.]

note [ca] His elder br., David John Carnegie, was *b.* 4 Dec. 1922 and *d. v.p.* 21 Nov. 1942.

note [cb] His elder br., Ian Robert MacRae Carnegie, was *b.* 9 Apr. 1950 and accidentally drowned, *v.p.*, 19 Nov. 1951.

NORTHUMBERLAND

page 707,

line 13, for 'DE PUISET' read 'DU PUISET'

line 24, after 'wife' add 'possibly' [see M.L. Bierbriar, *Geneal. Mag.*, vol. 19, 1978, pp. 176, 257.]

page 708,

line 4, after 'Bardolf.' add 'He *m.* Alice, illegit. da. of William DE PERCY II. Alice *m.* also Richard DE MORVILLE.' [see vol. x, p. 442, note [c], *sub* PERCY], and after '1194/5' add '[aa]'

note [aa] He had a s., Henry, founder of Finchale Abbey, Durham, for whom see vol. x, p. 442, note [c], *sub* PERCY.

page 712,
line 14, after 'LORD AUDLEY' add '(of Stratton)'
line 16, after 'ANGUS' add '[S.]'

page 718,
lines 16–17, for 'before 27 July 1485' read 'between 16 Mar. 1486 and 24 Feb. 1489 (and probably nearer the former) (ga)'
note (ga) *York City Chamberlain's Acct. Rolls*, 1396–1500, ed. R.B. Dobson, Surtees Soc., 1980, p. 186 and note 25, and *Test. Ebor.*, vol. 3, p. 306.

page 720,
note (c), line 1, for 'Eleanor' read 'Margaret'
note (h), line 3 (on page 721), after 'to' add 'James s. of'

page 742,
line 6, for 'WOBURN' read 'WOOBURN'

page 750,
line 26, line to read as follows

DUKEDOM. X. EARLDOM. XXV. } 1918 — 8 and 9. ALAN IAN (PERCY), DUKE OF NORTHUMBERLAND, &c., 4th but 1st surv. s. and h.,(c) *b.* 17 Apr. 1880;

page 751,
lines 4–5, delete from 'Having' to 'work.(a)]' and replace by 'His widow *d.* 13 June 1965.'

DUKEDOM. XI. EARLDOM. XXVI. } 1930 — 9 and 10. HENRY GEORGE ALAN (PERCY), DUKE OF NORTHUMBERLAND, &c., 1st s. and h., *b.* 15 July 1912, *styled* LORD PERCY 1913–30; ed. at Eton. He *d.* unm. 21 May 1940, being *k.* in action.

DUKEDOM. XII. EARLDOM. XXVII. } 1940 — 10 and 11. HUGH ALGERNON (PERCY), DUKE OF NORTHUMBERLAND, &c., br. and h., *b.* 6 Apr. 1914; ed. at Eton and Oxford (Ch. Ch.); *m.*, 12 June 1946, Lady Elizabeth Diana, 1st da. of Walter John (MONTAGU-DOUGLAS-SCOTT), 8th DUKE OF BUCCLEUGH. He *d.* 11 Oct. 1988. His widow was still living 1995.

DUKEDOM. XIII. EARLDOM. XXIX. } 1988 — 11 and 12. HENRY ALAN WALTER RICHARD (PERCY), DUKE OF NORTHUMBERLAND, &c., 1st s. and h., *b.* 1 July 1953; ed. at Eton and Oxford (Ch. Ch.). He *d.* unm. 31 Oct. 1995.

DUKEDOM. XIV. EARLDOM. XXX. } 1995 — 12 and 13. RALPH GEORGE ALGERNON (PERCY), DUKE OF NORTHUMBERLAND, &c., br. and h., *b.* 16 Nov. 1956; ed. at Eton and Oxford (Ch. Ch.); *m.*, 1979, Isobel Jane, da. of John Walter Maxwell Miller RICHARD of Edinburgh.

[GEORGE DOMINIC PERCY, *styled* LORD PERCY, 1st s. and h. ap., *b.* 4 May 1984.]

note ([a]), delete all detail

NORTHWODE

page 756,
line 1, after 'da.' add 'and (eventually, in her issue), coh.'
line 2, after 'TREGOZ' add '[LORD TREGOZ]'
line 19, after 'FOLIOT' add '[3rd LORD FOLIOT]'

NORTON

page 761,
line 16, line to read as follows

II. 1905. 2. CHARLES LEIGH (ADDERLEY), BARON NORTON, 1st s. and h., *b.* in Portman Sq., 10 Mar. 1846;

lines 26–8, delete from 'Having' to 'work.([b])]'

III. 1926. 3. RALPH BOWYER (ADDERLEY), BARON NORTON, 1st s. and h. [for further detail see note ([b])]. His widow *d.* 30 July 1939.

IV. 1933. 4. RONALD WOOLSTAN FLEETWOOD (ADDERLEY), BARON NORTON, br. and h., being the 5th s. of the 2nd Baron,([ba]) *b.* 15 Oct. 1885; He served in WW1.([b]) He *m.*, 20 Aug. 1931, Hylda, da. of Robert William TOVEY of Cheltenham. co. Glos. and widow of Hilary George DUNBAR of Glasgow. He *d. s.p.* 4 Jan. 1944. She *d.* Feb. 1952.

V. 1944. 5. HENRY ARDEN (ADDERLEY), BARON NORTON, uncle and h., being 2nd s. of 1st Baron Norton. He was *b.* 26 Sep. 1854; ed. at Eton and Oxford (Ch. Ch.); *m.*, 30 Aug. 1881, Grace, yst. da. of William Bruce Stopford SACKVILLE of Drayton House, Northants. She *d.* 16 Feb. 1944. He *d.* 1 Jan. 1945.

VI. 1945. 6. HUBERT BOWYER ARDEN (ADDERLEY), BARON NORTON, only s. and h., *b.* 21 Feb. 1886; ed. at Eton and R.M.C., Sandhurst; *m.*, 9 Jan. 1912, Elizabeth, da. of William John BIRKBECK of Stratton-Strawless, Norfolk. She *d.* 5 May 1952. He *d.* 17 Feb. 1961.

VII. 1961. 7. JOHN ARDEN (ADDERLEY), BARON NORTON, 1st s. and h., *b.* 24 Nov. 1915; ed. at Radley and Oxford (Magdalen Coll.); *m.*, 23 July 1946, Betty Margaret, da. of James McKee HANNAH of Domaine de Fontvielle, Aix-en-Provence, France. He *d.* 24 Sep. 1993. His widow was still living 1995.

VIII. 1993. 8. JAMES NIGEL ARDEN (ADDERLEY), BARON NORTON, 1st s. and h., *b.* 2 June 1947; ed. at Downside; *m.*, 1971, Jacqueline Julie, 1st da. of Guy W. WILLETT of Sundial House, Alderney.

[EDWARD JAMES ARDEN ADDERLEY, s. and h. ap., *b.* 19 Oct. 1982.]

note [b], lines 3–5, delete from 'He' to '1914–18'

note [ba] The 2nd s., Charles Arthur Reginald Kenelm Adderley, *b.* 17 May 1881, *d.* unm. and *v.p.*, 10 May 1905; the 3rd s., Humphrey James Arden Adderley, *b.* 16 Oct. 1882, Rifleman London Regt., *d.* unm. and *v.p.* of wounds received in action, 17 June 1917; the 4th s., Randolph Adderley, *b.* 16 April 1884, *d.* unm. 23 Oct. 1928.

NORWICH

page 764,
last line of pedigree, for 's. of Richard Playz' read '5th Lord Plaiz'

page 766,
note [f], line 3, 'for 1st nos., no. 52' read '(*Cal. Inq. P. M.*, vol. xiv, 1952, no. 46). His heir was found to be Katherine de Breuse, his cousin.'
line 6, 'after '*d. v.p.*' add 'Katherine, his heir, became a nun at Dartford, 2 Feb. 1378/9, and her heir was then found to be William de Ufford, Earl of Suffolk (*Cal. Inq. P. M.*, vol. xv, 1970, nos. 210, 211).'

APPENDIXES

APPENDIX A

page 3,
For comments on the relationship between the Warennes and the Mortimers see K.S.B. Keats-Rohan, *Nottingham Med. Studies*, vol. 37, 1993, pp. 21–4.

APPENDIX B

page 18,
lines 14–17, delete all detail and replace by 'He was second of the *Barones* who signed the letter to the Pope (*L. and P. Hen. VIII*, vol. iv, no. 6513), although this does not necessarily mean that he was Lord Rochford by this date (see Helen Miller, *Henry VIII and the English Nobility*, 1986, p. 25, note 102), and he was therefore probably *cr.* a Baron by the abovenamed writ.'

APPENDIX D

page 29,
line 27, after '(g)' add 'There is also evidence that there were Montagus at Hanging Houghton in the last years of the thirteenth century. These may possibly be connected with the Montagus referred to above, as well as the Ladde family.[h]

note [h] Northamptonshire Record Society, Gyles Isham collection, IL 1195, charter of Simon de Montecute, end of 13th century.

VOLUME 10

OFFALY

page 16,
line 11, after 'VALENCE),' add 'sometimes *styled*'
line 13, after '(*d.* 1247)' add ', da. of Warin DE MUNCHENSY, Lord of Swanscombe'

page 17,
line 8, delete 'as is commonly stated'
line 9, after 'JOINVILLE, ' add '[1st LORD GENEVILLE]
line 10, after '(g)' add 'She *m.* 2ndly, by 1294, John I, COUNT OF OBER-SALM. He was living 26 Feb. 1325/6.' [See *Genealogist*, vol. xxi, 1905, pp. 16, 76.]

O'HAGAN

page 46,
line 5, after 'Ross' add 'He *d.* 18 Dec. 1961. His widow *d.* 26 Nov. 1965.'
line 8, after '1935' add 'He assumed the additional Christian name of Towneley and the surname of STRACHEY by deed poll, 13 Sep. 1938. He *m.*, 11 Nov. 1944, Lady Mary Sophia, da. of Roundell Cecil (PALMER), 3rd EARL OF SELBOURNE. He *d. v.p.* 23 Dec. 1955. His widow (who *m.* 2ndly, 1981, as his 2nd wife, Francis St. John GORE), was still living 1995.

IV. 1961. 4. CHARLES TOWNELEY (STRACHEY), LORD O'HAGAN, grandson and h., being 1st s. and h. of Thomas Anthony Edward and Lady Mary Sophia abovenamed. He was *b.* 6 Sep. 1945; ed. at Eton and Oxford (New Coll.); *m.* 1stly, 13 July 1967, *H.S.H.* PRINCESS TAMARA, da. of Sqn. Ldr. *H.S.H.* PRINCE MICHAEL IMERTERINSKY of Menton, France and formerly wife of Lieut. Cmdr. Thomas Mervyn SMITH-DORRIEN-SMITH, R.N., of Tresco Abbey, Isles of Scilly. This marriage was diss. by divorce 1984 and he *m.* 2ndly, 1985, Mary Claire, da. of Rev. Leslie ROOSE-FRANCIS of Bodmin, Cornwall, formerly wife of (__) PARSONS.

page 61,
between lines 2 and 3 add new entries OLLERTON and O'MALLUN from page xi

O'NEILL

page 64,
line 9, after '1928(a)' add 'His widow *d.* 10 Aug. 1942.'
line 23, after 'Yeomanry.' add 'She *d.* 14 June 1948.'
line 24, line to read as follows

III. 1928. 3. SHANE EDWARD ROBERT (O'NEILL), BARON O'NEILL OF SHANE'S CASTLE, grandson and h., being 1st s. and h.

lines 27–8, delete from 'Having' to 'work.(c)]' and add 'He *m.*, 6 Oct. 1932, Ann Geraldine Mary,

1st da. of Guy Lawrence CHARTERIS. He *d.* 24 Oct. 1944, being *k.* in action. His widow *m.* 2ndly, 28 June 1945, Esmond Cecil (HARMSWORTH), 2nd VISCOUNT ROTHERMERE. This marriage was diss. by divorce 1952 and she *m.* 3rdly, 24 Mar. 1952, Ian Lancaster FLEMING (the author, who *d.* 12 Aug. 1964). She *d.* 1981.'

IV. 1944. 4. RAYMOND ARTHUR CLANABOY (O'NEILL), BARON O'NEILL OF SHANE'S CASTLE, only s. and h., *b.* 1 Sep. 1933; ed. at Eton and R.A.C., Cirencester; *m.*, 10 June 1963, Georgina Mary, da. of Lord George Francis John Montagu Douglas SCOTT.

[SHANE SEBASTIAN CLANABOY O'NEILL, s. and h. ap., *b.* 25 July 1965.]

note (c), delete all detail

ONSLOW

page 74,
line 4, line to read as follows

EARLDOM. V. BARONY. VIII. } 1911 — 5 and 8. RICHARD WILLIAM ALAN (ONSLOW), EARL OF ONSLOW, &c., 1st s. and h., *b.* at Clandon Park 23 Aug.,

line 26, delete '(b)'
lines 30–1, delete from 'Having' to work.]' and replace by 'He *d.* 9 June 1945. His widow *d.* 23 Oct. 1954.'

EARLDOM. VI. BARONY. IX. } 1945 — 6 and 9. WILLIAM ARTHUR BAMPFYLDE (ONSLOW), EARL OF ONSLOW, &c., s. and h., *b.* 11 June 1913, *styled* VISCOUNT CRANLEY 1911–71; ed. at Winchester and R.M.C., Sandhurst; *m.*, 4 Aug. 1936, at St. Kenelm's, Enstone, Oxon., Pamela Louisa Eleanor, only da. of Eric FitzGerald (DILLON), 19th VISCOUNT DILLON [I.] This marriage was diss. by divorce 1962 (she *d.* 1992) and he *m.* 2ndly, 30 June 1962, Nina Edith, da. of Thomas Percival STURDEE. He *d.* 3 June 1971. His widow was still living 1995.

EARLDOM. VII. BARONY. X. } 1971 — 7 and 10. MICHAEL WILLIAM COPLESTONE DILLON (ONSLOW), EARL OF ONSLOW, &c., *b.* 28 Feb. 1938; ed. at Eton and the Sorbonne; *m.*, 17 July 1964, Robin Lindsay, da. of Major Robert Lee BULLARD of Atlanta, Georgia, U.S.A.

[RUPERT CHARLES WILLIAM BULLARD, *styled* VISCOUNT CRANLEY, s. and h. ap., *b.* 16 June 1967.]

note (b), delete all detail

ORANMORE AND BROWNE

page 76,
line 17, line to read as follows

IV. 1927. 4. DOMINICK GEOFFREY EDWARD (BROWNE), BARON ORANMORE AND BROWNE [I.], 1st s. and h., *b.* 21 Oct. 1901,

line 20, delete '([a])'

lines 22–3, delete from 'Having' to 'work.]' and replace by 'She obtained a divorce in 1936 (and *d.* 1980). He *m.*, 2ndly, Oonagh, formerly wife of Philip Leyland KINDERSLEY (who obtained a divorce in 1936), and 3rd da. of Arthur Ernest GUINNESS, by Marie Clotilde, da. of Sir George RUSSELL, 4th Bart. This marriage was diss. by divorce 1950 and he *m.* 3rdly, 1 Dec. 1951, Constance Vera,([a]) da. of Charles Edward Stevens.'

[DOMINICK GEOFFREY THOMAS BROWNE, 1st s. and h. ap., *b.* 1 July 1929; *m.*, 25 Oct. 1957, Sara Margaret, da. of Dr. Herbert WRIGHT of Dublin. This marriage was diss. by divorce 1974.]

note ([a]), delete all detail and replace by 'She was known as Sally Grey, an actress.'

O'REILLY

page 77,
line 10, for 'for life' read 'in tail male, as was TYRCONNELL, see that title'

ORFORD

page 91,
line 7, after 'Walpole' add 'see *sub* WALPOLE for further details. His widow *d.* 1988.'

ORKNEY

page 93,
line 20, after 'STRATHEARN,' add 'AND EARL OF'

page 111,
line 33, after 'engineer' add 'She *d.* 9 May 1946. He *d. s.p.m.* 21 Aug. 1951.'

XIII. 1951. 8. CECIL O'BRYEN (FITZMAURICE), EARL OF ORKNEY, &c., distant cousin and h., being 2nd but 1st surv. s. and h. of Douglas Frederick Harold FITZMAURICE (*d.* 29 May 1937), and Dorothy Jeanette, da. of Capt. Robert DICKIE, R.N., which Douglas Frederick was 1st s. of Douglas Commerell Menzies FITZMAURICE (*d.* 13 Jan. 1932), by Esther, da. of W.G. DAVIES, which Douglas Commerell was 2nd but 1st surv. s. of Frederick O'Bryen FITZMAURICE (*d.* 26 Oct. 1867), by Mary Anne Taylor, da. of Robert Taylor Spooner ABRAHAM of Crewkerne, Somerset, which Frederick O'Bryen was 3rd s. of 5th Earl of Orkney. He was *b.* 3 July 1919; *m.*, 27 Nov. 1953, Rose Katherine Durke, da. of Joseph William Durke SILLEY of Brixham, Devon.

note ([c]), lines 5–6 (on page 112), delete from 'She' to 'Orkney' and replace by 'She *d. v.p. s.p.*, 6 Oct. 1950.'

ORMATHWAITE

page 113,
line 4, line to read as follows

III. 1920. 3. ARTHUR HENRY JOHN (WALSH), BARON ORMATHWAITE, 1st s. and h., *b.* 10 Apr. 1859;

lines 16–17, delete from 'Having' to 'work.(c)]' and replace by 'His wife *d.* 13 Jan. 1921. He *d. s.p.* 13 Mar. 1937.'

IV. 1937. 4. GEORGE HARRY WILLIAM (WALSH), BARON ORMATHWAITE, brother and h., *b.* 3 Dec. 1863; ed. at Wellington; Capt. Grenadier Guards; M.V.O. He *d.* unm. 27 Oct. 1943.

V. 1943. 5. REGINALD (WALSH), BARON ORMATHWAITE, br. and h., *b.* 17 July 1968; *m.*, 10 Dec. 1908, Lady Jane Margaret, 3rd da. of Charles Alexander (DOUGLAS-HOME), 12th EARL OF HOME. He *d.* 13 Feb. 1944. His widow *d.* 9 Sep. 1955.

VI. 1944. 6. JOHN ARTHUR CHARLES (WALSH), BARON ORMATHWAITE, only s. and h., *b.* 25 Dec. 1912; ed. at Eton and Cambridge (Trin. Coll.); *d.* unm. 8 Mar. 1984 when his Barony became *extinct*.

note (c), delete all detail

ORMOND

page 121,
line 6, after 'Ulster' add '[I.]'

page 125,
line 3, after 'Joan,' add 'sister and (eventually), coh. to Thomas (FITZALAN), 12th EARL OF ARUNDEL, '

page 128,
line 13, after 'STAFFORD, ' add 'of Southwick, Wilts.,'
line 16, after 'Elizabeth' add '(da. and h. of Sir Guy de BRYAN)' [See vol. ii, p. 361, *sub* BRYAN.]

page 133,
note (b), line 5, after '160' add ', see also *Visitation of Yorkshire, 1563 and 1564*, Har. Soc., vol. xvi, pp. 81–2, 346.'

page 136,
line 4, after 'da.' add 'and coh.'

page 139,
line 17, after 'TYLNEY' add 'of Askwellthorpe, Norfolk,'

page 140,
lines 12–15, delete from 'It' to 'divorce' and replace by 'He was *cr.* LORD ROCHFORD, 7 Feb. 1533.'
note (k), delete all detail and replace by 'It is unlikely that his name as "Rochford" on the Baron's letter to the Pope (*idem*, vol. iv, p. 6,513) shows that he had been *cr.* a peer by then (see H. Miller, *Henry VIII and the English Nobility*, 1988, p. 25, note 102). The writ of 7 Feb. 1533 (see vol. ix, Appendix F, p. 18), therefore, presumably *cr.* him Lord Rochford.'

page 167,
line 8, line to read as follows

MARQUESSATE [I.] VIII.
EARLDOM [I.] XXII.
BARONY [U.K.] IV.
1919

4, 22 and 4, JAMES ARTHUR WELLINGTON FOLEY (BUTLER), MARQUESS OF ORMONDE, &c., br. and h., *b.* 23 Sep. 1849;

lines 12–13, delete from 'Having' to 'work.(a)]' and replace by 'He *d.* 4 July 1943. His widow *d.* 17 June 1951.'

MARQUESSATE [I.] IX.
EARLDOM [I.] XXIII.
BARONY [U.K.] V.
1943

5, 23 and 5. JAMES GEORGE ANSON (BUTLER), 1st s. and h., *b.* 18 Apr. 1890 [for further detail see note (a)]. She, who was *b.* 24 Oct. 1888, *d.* 18 May 1948. He *d. s.p.m.s.* 21 June, 1949.

[JAMES ANTHONY BUTLER, s. and h. ap., *b.* 18 Aug. 1916, *styled* VISCOUNT THURLES from 1919. He *d.* unm. and *v.p.* 8 May 1940.]

MARQUESSATE [I.] X.
EARLDOM [I.] XXIV.
BARONY [U.K.] VI.
1949

6, 24 and 6. JAMES ARTHUR NORMAN (BUTLER), MARQUESS OF ORMONDE, EARL OF ORMONDE, EARL OF OSSORY, and VISCOUNT THURLES [I.], also BARON ORMONDE OF LANTHONY [U.K.], Chief Butler of Ireland, br. and h., *b.* 25 Apr. 1893; ed. at Harrow and R.M.C., Sandhurst; *m.*, 26 Jan. 1924, Jessie Carlos, da. of Charles Carlos CLARKE of Sunninghill, co. Berks. He *d. s.p.m.* 17 Apr. 1971. His widow *d.* 3 Dec. 1969.

MARQUESSATE [I.] XI.
EARLDOM [I.] XXV.
BARONY [U.K.] VII.
1971

7, 25 and 7. JAMES HUBERT THEOBALD CHARLES (BUTLER), MARQUESS OF ORMOND, &c., cousin and h., being 2nd but 1st surv. s. and h. of Rev. James Theobald Bagot John BUTLER (*d.* 16 June 1929), by Annabella Brydon, da. of Rev. Cosmo Reid GORDON, which James Theobald was 4th s. of the 2nd Marquess of Ormonde. He was *b.* 19 Apr. 1899; ed. at Haileybury and R.M.C., Sandhurst; *m.* 1stly, 2 Mar. 1935, Nan, da. of Garth GILPIN. She *d.* 1973 and he *m.* 2ndly, 1976, Elizabeth, da. of Charles B. RARDEN. She *d.* 1980.

note (a), lines 7–8, delete from 'His' to '1919'

after line 27 insert new entries ORONSAY and O'ROURKE from page xi

ORREBY

page 171,
line 17, after 'TATESHAL' add '[1st LORD TATESHALE]'

page 172,
line 1, delete 'great' and after 'Tateshal,' add 'the 3rd Lord,'

page 174,
line 12, after 'She' add '*m.* 2ndly Richard Stury and' [See vol. x, p. 463, *sub* PERCY.]

OXFORD

page 213,
note (b), line 5, after 'note' add ', an identification confirmed by Claude Blair, *Church Monuments*, vol. 8, 1993, p. 10, note 3. Blair dates the effigy to 1315'

page 221,
line 14, for 'TIBETOT (*d.* before 18 July' read '1st LORD TIBETOT, *d.* 24 June'
line 15, for 'of Hamlake' read '[1st LORD ROS OF HELMSLEY]', and for '1st' read 'yr.'

page 225,
line 3, for '10th' read 'Xth'

page 230,
note (f), line 2, for 'Myers' read 'Myres'

page 238,
note (j), line 4, after '87/7/131.' add 'The circumstances surrounding this surrender, and the documents, were discussed by M. Hicks, "The Last Days of Elizabeth Countess of Oxford", *Eng. Hist. Review*, vol. 100, 1988, pp. 76–95.'

page 245,
line 4, after 'TYLNEY' add ', of Boston, Lincs.'
note (h), line 1, before 'A' add 'These sisters are discussed in Geoffrey White, 'The Sisters of John De Vere, 14th Earl of Oxford', *Geneal. Mag*, vol. 12, 1957, pp. 293–5 and 347.'

page 256,
line 10, after 'male' add 'being s. and h. of Hugh de Vere, by Eleanor, da. of William

WALSH, which Hugh was s. and h. of Aubrey de Vere, 1st s. by 2nd wife of John, 15th Earl of Oxford (by Margaret da. of John SPRING of Lavenham, Suffolk)'

page 260,
note ([e]), line 15, after 'Hoet' add '(called "Foot" in the original application for the marriage licence, 4 July 1703, *ex inform.* Colin Mills). See also Robert Garrett, *Geneal. Mag.*, vol. 20, 1982, p. 298.'

OXFURD

page 273,
line 12, for 'extinct or' read 'also'
note ([g]), line 1, (on page 274), after 'Viscount.' add 'He was recognised as Baronet in 1906, the year he died.'

after line 24 add

VI. 1977. 6. JOHN DONALD ALEXANDER ARTHUR (MAKGILL), VISCOUNT OXFURD and LORD MAKGILL OF COUSLAND [S.], also a Baronet [S.], 1st s. and h. of Sir George MAKGILL, heir male of Sir James MAKGILL, great grandfather, through David, his 3rd s., of the first Lord Oxfurd. He received a writ of Summons, 1977, as a result of a decision by the Committee for Privileges ([e]). He was *b.* 31 Dec. 1899; ed. at Eton and R.M.C. Sandhurst; *m.*, 1stly, 5 July 1927, Esther Lilian, 2nd da. of Sir Robert BROMLEY, Bt. This marriage was diss. by divorce in 1943 and he *m.*, 2ndly, 6 Oct. 1955, Maureen, 2nd da. of Lieut. Col. Arthur Tilson Shaen MAGAN, C.M.G., of Killyon Manor, Hill of Down, co. Meath and formerly wife of Col. John Herbert GILLINGTON. He *d. s.p.m.* 24 Jan. 1986. His widow was still living 1995.

VII. 1986. 7. GEORGE HUBBARD (MAKGILL), VISCOUNT OXFURD &c., nephew and h., being s. and h. of Richard James Haldane MAKGILL, (*k.* 9 Aug. 1948), by Elizabeth Lyman, da. of Gorham HUBBARD of Boston, U.S.A., which Richard James was 2nd s. of Sir George MAKGILL abovenamed. He was *b.* 7 Jan. 1934; *m.*, 1stly, 11 Feb. 1967, Alison Campbell, 1st da. of Neils Max JENSEN of Randers, Denmark. This marriage was diss. by divorce in 1977 and he *m.* 2ndly, 1980, Valerie Cunitia Mary, only da. of Charles Anthony STEWARD of Farnham, Surrey.

[IAN ARTHUR ALEXANDER MAKGILL, MASTER OF OXFURD, 1st s. and h., by 1st wife, was *b.* 14 Oct. 1969.]

note ([e]) The Committee for Privileges agreed that the petitioner had made out his case that the bond of tailzie executed by the 2nd Viscount in 1703 and the subsequent Charter of 1706, under which his daughter Christian claimed both the estates and the title, was not valid in law, and that the provision in the Patent of 1651 for a remainder to heirs male was operative. Since all collateral heirs male had failed, the petitioner, as the sole remaining heir male, was entitled to the Viscountcy and Barony. See Committee for Privileges Report, 1977 (H.L. 172–1) and G.W. Iredell, *Geneal. Mag.*, vol. 19, 1977, pp. 165–9. For Sir George Makgill, see page 273, note ([g]), line 2, (on page 274).

PAGET

page 276,
note (b), line 1, delete from 'His' to 'been' and replace by 'He was'
line 6, after 'f. 7)' add 'See *N&Q*, vol. 199, 1954, pp. 98–9.'

PAYNEL

page 318,
note (b), line 3 (on page 319), after 'Society' add 'and to Mr Clay'

page 319,
line 20, after 'Alice.' add 'Avice *m.* 3rdly, Walter DE PERCY.' [See vol. x, p. 439, note (e), *sub* Percy.]

PEEL

page 345,
line 15, line to read as follows

VISCOUNTCY. II. 1912. EARLDOM. I. 1929 — 1 and 2. WILLIAM ROBERT WELLESLEY (PEEL), VISCOUNT PEEL OF SANDY, s. and h., *b.* 7 Jan. 1867;

lines 27–8, delete from 'Having' to 'work.(c)]' and for further details see note (c)

EARLDOM. II. VISCOUNTCY. III. } 1937 — 2 and 3. ARTHUR WILLIAM ASHTON (PEEL), EARL PEEL, &c., s. and h., *b.* 29 May 1901; ed. at Eton and Oxford (Balliol College), B.A. 1924; Asst. Sec. Royal Commission on Land Drainage, 1927; attached to Indian Statutory Commission, 1928; *styled* VISCOUNT CLANFIELD 1929–37; Chairman of James Williamson & Son Ltd; a Director of Sea Insurance Co. Ltd, and of the London, Midland & Scottish Railway Co.; Chairman of the Lancashire and Cheshire Association of Boys Clubs and of the Lancaster Parliamentary Div. of the Conservative and Unionist Association. He *m.* 11 Mar. 1946, Kathleen, da. of Michael MCGRATH of Ballyculane, co. Cork. He *suc.* to the Baronetcy of Peel of Drayton Manor [1800] on the death of his kinsman, 10 Apr. 1942. He *d.* 22 Sep. 1969. His widow *d.* 1972.

EARLDOM. III. VISCOUNTCY. IV. } 1969 — 3 and 4. WILLIAM JAMES ROBERT (PEEL), EARL PEEL, VISCOUNT PEEL OF SANDY, VISCOUNT CLANFIELD, also a Baronet, 1st s. and h., *b.* 3 Oct. 1947; ed. at Ampleforth and R.A.C., Cirencester; *m.* 1stly, 1973, Veronica Naomi Livingston, da. of Major John Alastair Livingston TIMPSON. This marriage was diss. by divorce 1987 and he *m.* 2ndly, 1989, Charlotte Clementine, 2nd da. of Arthur Christopher John (SOAMES), BARON SOAMES (life peer) and formerly wife of Alexander Richard HAMBRO.

[ASHTON ROBERT GERARD PEEL, *styled* VISCOUNT CLANFIELD, s. and h. ap., *b.* 16 Sep. 1976.]

note (c), lines 5–12 (page 346), delete from 'and was' to 'Association'

PEMBROKE

page 354,
note (i), line 2, after '-17)', add 'For a discussion of the *Expugnatio* reference see *Coat of Arms*, N.S., vol. xi, no. 171, 1995, p. 132.

page 356,
line 3, delete '(it is said)' and 'alleged to have been either a'
line 4, delete 'brother of' and replace by 'and half sister'
line 5, delete 'or their sister'
note (b), lines 1–2, delete from 'but to all' and replace by 'David H. Kelly, *The Geneal.*, vol. 1, 1980, pp. 5, 24, (citing the "Ban Shenchus" and the *Book of Leinster*.)

page 367,
line 7, after 'da.' add 'and probably h.'

page 373,
note (h), for 'oe' read 'or'

page 375,
line 10, for 'coh.' read 'h.'
line 12, for '24 Nov. 1245' read 'before 12 Mar. 1244/5'
note (p), line 1, for 'M. Paris' read '*Cal. of Charter Rolls*, vol. 1, p. 281. Matthew Paris has 24 Nov. 1245'.

page 380,
note (j), line 3 (on page 381), after 'Pembroke.' add 'He was, however, *styled* Earl of Pembroke in the Memoranda Rolls of the Lord Treasurer's Remembrancer in Michaelmas, 1251 (H.S. Sweetman, *Calendar of Documents relating to Ireland*, vol. I, 1875.)'

page 388,
line 6, after 'Juliane' add '*de jure* (according to modern doctrine), BARONESS LEYBURN,'
line 7, after 'BLOUNT' add '[1st LORD BLOUNT],'

page 390,
line 13, after 'Joan' add ', *de jure* (according to modern doctrine), BARONESS GENEVILLE'

page 397,
line 5, for '1428' read '7 Mar. 1428/9'

page 398,
line 2, delete from 'Before' to 'he' and replace by 'He'

line 3, after 'PEMBROKE' add '23 Nov. 1452.'

note (e), line 1, before 'The' add 'R.S. Thomas, "The political career . . . of Jasper Tudor, Earl of Pembroke and Duke of Bedford", unpub. Ph.D. thesis, Univ. of Wales, 1971, p. 32 and note 4.'

line 3, for '; but' read ', this was their investiture (Thomas, *op. cit.* p. 34)' and after 'Edmund' add 'also'

page 402,

line 18, for 'Sep. 1466' read '20 Jan. 1466/7(ja)'

note (ja) Account Book of Sir John Fogge, Treasurer of the Household, Mich. 1466 to Mich. 1467, p. 13 (P.R.O. Exchequer Accts. Var. E101 412/2), *sub Dieta*, "Iste die nuptus fuit dominus Donnester filie comitus Rivers".

note (g), after '115.' add 'See Sutton and Hammond, *Coronation of Richard III*, 1983, pp. 249, 276.'

page 403,

note (c), lines 4–6, delete from 'Under' to 'July'

note (e), line 4, after '315)' add 'The year 1507 seems most likely, James Gairdner suggested this in the *Dict. Nat. Biog.* and defended the date later, *Eng. Hist. Review*, vol. 10, 1895, p. 104 [*ex inform* Dr R. Hetherington]. See also Anthony Hoskins, *Geneal. Mag.*, vol. 25, 1997, p. 346.'

page 405,

line 3, for 's. and h.' read '2nd s.'

page 425,

line 24, for 'North Ludlow' read 'Thomas'

line 25, delete ', Major of Dragoons'

page 430,

line 18, after 'net' add 'His widow *d.* 12 Mar. 1944.'

line 19, line to read as follows

XXXIV. 1913. 15. REGINALD (HERBERT), EARL OF PEMBROKE, &c., 1st s. and h., *b.* 8 Sep. 1880; ed. at Eton 1893–8; *styled* LORD HERBERT 1893–8;

lines 26–8, delete from 'Having' to 'work.(d)]' and replace by 'Hereditary Visitor, Jesus Coll. Oxford; Mayor of Wilton 1932 and 1933; had the Orders of the Rising Sun and Sacred Treasure of Japan, St. Stanislaus of Russia, Crown of Italy, and Legion of Honour. He *d.* 13 Jan. 1960. His widow *d.* 1973.'

XXXV. 1960. 16. SYDNEY CHARLES (HERBERT), EARL OF PEMBROKE, &c., 1st s. and h., *b.* 9 Jan. 1906; *styled* LORD HERBERT 1913–60; ed. at Eton and Oxford (Pembroke Coll.); Equerry to *H.R.H.* the Duke of Kent 1935–42. He *m.*, 27 July 1936, Mary Dorothea, yr. da. of John Adrian Louis (HOPE), 1st MARQUESS OF LINLITHGOW. She was Lady-in-Waiting to *H.R.H.* the Duchess of Kent 1934–49. He *d.* 16 Mar. 1969. His widow was still living 1995.

XXXVI. 1969. 17. HENRY GEORGE CHARLES (HERBERT), EARL OF PEMBROKE, &c., only s. and h., *b.* 19 May 1939; ed. at Eton and Oxford (Ch. Ch.); *m.* 1stly, 20 Jan. 1966, Claire Rose, da. of Douglas Gurney PELLY of Swaynes Hall, Saffron Walden, Essex. This marriage was diss. by divorce 1981 and he *m.* 2ndly, 1988, Miranda Juliet, da. of Cmdr. John Somerville Kendal ORAM, R.N., of Wilton, co. Wilts.

[WILLIAM ALEXANDER SIDNEY HERBERT, *styled* LORD HERBERT, s. and h. ap., was *b.* 18 May 1978.]

note (d), delete all detail

PENRHYN OF LLANDEGAI

page 433,
line 3, after '£250,000' add 'His widow *d.* 20 Feb. 1940.'
line 4, line to read as follows

III. 1907. 3. EDWARD SHOLTO (DOUGLAS-PENNANT), BARON PENRHYN OF LLANDEGAI, 1st s. and h., being only s. by 1st wife,

lines 12–13, delete from 'Having' to 'work.(b)]' and replace by 'His widow *d.* 28 Nov. 1944.'

[ALAN GEORGE SHOLTO DOUGLAS-PENNANT, 1st s. and h. ap., *b.* 11 June 1890; Lieut. Grenadier Guards; A.D.C. to the Gov. of Bengal, 1914; served in WW1,(b) and was *k.* in action, *v.p.* and unm. 29 Oct. 1914.]

IV. 1927. 4. HUGH NAPIER (DOUGLAS-PENNANT), BARON PENRHYN OF LLANDEGAI, 2nd but 1st surv. s. and h., *b.* 6 Aug. 1894; ed. Eton and R.M.C., Sandhurst; Lieut. Royal Scots Greys, served in WW1 in France and Belgium; Hon. Col. 6th Battn. Royal Welsh Fusiliers 1932; Lord Lieut. Carnarfonshire, 1933; O.St.J. He *m.*, 25 Apr. 1922, Sybil Mary, yr. da. of HENRY CHARLES (HARDINGE). 3rd VISCOUNT HARDINGE, by Mary Francis, 3rd da. of Ralph Pelham NEVIL, yr. br. of William (NEVIL), 5th EARL and 1st MARQUESS OF ABERGAVENNY. This marriage was diss. by divorce 1941. He *d. s.p.* 26 June 1949.

V. 1949. 5. FRANK (DOUGLAS-PENNANT), BARON PENRHYN OF LLANDEGAI, distant cousin and h., being 2nd s. of Lieut. Col. Archibald Charles Henry DOUGLAS-PENNANT (*d.* 7 Sep. 1884), by Harriet Ella, 2nd da. of Robert Francis (GIFFORD), 2nd BARON GIFFORD, which Archibald Charles was 2nd s. of the 1st Baron Penrhyn. He was *b.* 21 Nov. 1865; ed. at Eton and R.M.C., Sandhurst; *m.* 1stly, 25 Apr. 1892, Maud Eleanora, 1st da. of Col. John HARDY. This marriage was diss. by divorce 1903 (she *d.* 12 Dec. 1936), and he *m.* 2ndly, 18 Apr. 1905, Alice Nellie, da. of Sir William Charles COOPER, Bart. She *d.* 17 Dec. 1965. He *d.* 3 Feb. 1967.

[CYRIL EUSTACE DOUGLAS-PENNANT, 1st s. and h. ap. by 1st wife, *b.* 7 Apr. 1894; ed. at R.N.C.s, Osborne and Dartmouth; K.C.B., Adm. He *m.* 1stly, 6 Jan. 1917, Phyllis Constance, da. of Col. Oswald Mosley LEIGH of Belmont Hall, Northwich, Cheshire. This marriage was diss. by divorce 1936 and he *m.* 2ndly, 5 Apr. 1937, Sheila, 2nd. da. of Stanley BROTHERHOOD of Thornhaugh Hall, Peterborough. He *d. v.p.* and *s.p.m.* 3 Apr. 1961.]

VI. 1967. 6. MALCOLM FRANK (DOUGLAS-PENNANT), BARON PENRHYN OF LLANDEGAI, 2nd but 1st surv. s. and h., being 1st s. by 2nd wife, *b.* 11 July 1908; ed. at Eton and R.M.C., Sandhurst; *m.* 9 June 1954, Elizabeth Rosemary, da. of Brig. Sir Percy Robert LAURIE of Wavendon Lodge, Bletchley, co. Bucks.

note ([b]), lines 1–4, delete from 'His' to '1914'
lines 5–11, delete all detail

PERCY

page 442,
note ([c]), line 25, after 'married' add '(1) Hugh Bardolf, and (2)'
line 34, after '171' add 'and was thus the mother of Richard Malebise, instigator of the massacre of the Jews in York, 1190. (Hugh M. Thomas, *J. Haskins Soc.*, vol. 5, 1993, p. 2)'

page 461,
line 16, delete 'da. of'

page 462,
line 1, for 'Thomas DE CLARE' read 'aunt and coh. of Thomas DE CLARE, sister of Richard, 1st Lord Clare, Lord of Thomond (2nd s. of Richard DE CLARE), 5th EARL OF GLOUCESTER AND HEREFORD'

PERTH

page 463,
line 11, for 'Richard' read 'Patrick'
line 12, for 'CHAWORTH read 'DE CHAWORTH, of Kidwelly,'
line 13, after 'Joan' add '*de jure* (according to modern doctrine), BARONESS ORREBY and BARONESS MARE,'

page 491,
note ([b]), line 4, after '1933' add 'For details of the 7th Earl of Perth, see note ([c]), vol. xii, part 1, p. 376. For the 8th Earl, see below.'

EARLDOM [S.] VIII.
VISCOUNTCY [S.] XIII. } 1951

8 and 13. JOHN DAVID (DRUMMOND), EARL OF PERTH, &c., s. and h., *b.* 13 May 1907; ed. at Downside and Cambridge (Trin. Coll.); *styled* VISCOUNT STRATHALLAN 1937–51; served in WW2 as Lieut. Intelligence Corps.; seconded to War Cabinet Offices, 1942–3, and to the Ministry of Production, 1944–5; Rep. Peer [S.], 1952–63; Min. of State for Colonial Affairs, 1957–62; First Crown Estate Commissioner, 1962; P.C. He *m.*, 4 Aug. 1934, Nancy Seymour, da. of Reginald FINCKE, of New York City.

[JOHN ERIC DRUMMOND, *styled* VISCOUNT STRATHALLAN, 1st s. and h. ap., *b.* 7 July 1935;

ed. at Downside and Cambridge (Trin. Coll.); *m.* 1stly, 7 Jan. 1963, Margaret Anne, da. of Robin GORDON. This marriage was diss. by divorce 1972 and he *m.* 2ndly, 1988, Mrs Marion ELLIOT.]

PETRE

page 509,
line 11, after 'WALMSLEY' add 'or WALMESLEY'

page 512,
lines 14–15, delete from 'Having' to 'work.' and replace by 'His widow *d.* 4 Nov. 1959.'

XV. 1908. 15. PHILIP BENEDICT JOSEPH (PETRE), BARON PETRE, &c., br. and h.,[aa] *b.* 21 Aug. 1864; Lieut. 3rd Battn. East Lancs. Regt. He *m.*, 19 July 1888, Julia Mary, da. of George CAVENDISH-TAYLOR of 42 Elvaston Place, London. He *d.* 6 Dec. 1908. His widow *d.* 23, and was *bur.* 28 Oct. 1931.

note [aa] His younger br. Joseph Lucius Henry Petre, *b.* 22 Apr. 1866, Capt. Suffolk Yeo. Cav., was *k.* in action at Spion Kop, 24 Jan. 1900.

XVI. 1908. 16. LIONEL GEORGE CARROLL (PETRE), BARON PETRE, of Writtle [1603], s. and h., *b.* 3 Nov. 1890; ed. Oratory Sch., Birmingham and R.M.C., Sandhurst; Capt. Coldstream Guards. He *m.*, 28 June 1913, Catherine Margaret, da. of John Richard de Clare BOSCAWEN, 3rd s. of Evelyn (BOSCAWEN), 6th VISCOUNT FALMOUTH. Served in WW1,[b] and *d.* 30 Sep. 1915 in France of wounds received in action. His widow, *m.* 2ndly, 21 July 1921, Sir Frederick Carne RASCH, Bart. (who *d.* 12 June 1962) and *d.* 1983.

XVII. 1915. 17. JOSEPH WILLIAM LIONEL (PETRE), BARON PETRE, s. and h., *b.* 5 June 1914; ed. at Eton; *m.*, 25 Oct. 1941, Marguerite Eileen, da. of Ion Wentworth HAMILTON of Nettlebed, co. Oxon. He *d.* 1 Jan. 1989. His widow was still living 1995.

XVIII. 1989. 18. JOHN PATRICK LIONEL (PETRE), BARON PETRE, only s. and h., *b.* 4 Aug. 1942; ed. at Eton and Oxford (Trin. Coll.); *m.*, 16 Sep. 1965, Marcia Gwendolyn, da. of Alfred PLUMPTON of Portsmouth.

[DOMINIC WILLIAM PETRE, s. and h. ap., *b.* 9 Aug. 1966; ed. at Worth Abbey and Exeter Univ.]

note [b], lines 1–5, delete from 'Philip' to 'France'
lines 6–9, delete from 'For' to 'Regt.'

PEYVRE

page 517,
line 10, for '20' read '19'
line 12, for '14 Aug.' read '26 July'
line 25, after '529).' add 'See also pedigree of Broughton, *ante* vol. v, p. 80.'

PINKENEY

page 523,
lines 16–18, delete from 'Gerard' to 'SCOTLAND.' and replace by 'her brothers and da. and (eventual) h. of David LINDSAY of Crawford by Marjory, possibly da. of one of the two Henrys, natural sons of David, EARL OF HUNTINGDON.'

note (m), lines 1–2, delete all detail; line 1 (on page 524), for '*shire*, 1765 ed., p. 239).' read '*Scots Peerage*, vol. iii, p. 7.'

page 524,
line 9, for '(__)' read 'Agnes, da. of John de Wahull (*d.* 1296).' [Baker, *Hist. Northants*, vol. 1, pp. 11–12]

PIPARD

page 533,
line 16, after '1285)' add ', by Joan, sister and coh. of Richard (FITZJOHN), 1st LORD FITZJOHN, da. of Sir John FITZGEOFFREY'

PLAIZ

page 541,
line 9, after 'Margery),' add 'sister and (in 1361), coh. of John (DE ST. PHILIBERT), 1st LORD ST. PHILIBERT,' [See that title and WALEYS.]

page 542,
line 1, after 'Margaret,' add 'sister of John (DE NORWICH), 2nd LORD NORWICH,'

PLESCY

page, 548,
lines 3–4, delete from ', who' to MARSHAL).'

page, 551,
line 18, after '*d. s.p.*' add ', 26 Oct. 1379'

PLUNKETT

page 558,
line 24, after 'Fusiliers' add '(who *d.* 23 Dec. 1952). She *d.* 11 Feb. 1968.'
line 25, line to read as follows

VI. 1920. 6. TERENCE CONYNGHAM (PLUNKET), BARON PLUNKET OF NEWTON, 1st s. and h., *b.* 12 July 1899,

lines 31–2, delete from 'Having' to 'work.(d)]' and replace by 'He and Lady Plunket were *k.* in an aeroplane accident in California, 24 Feb. 1938.'

VII. 1938. 7. PATRICK TERENCE WILLIAM SPAN (PLUNKET), BARON PLUNKET OF NEWTON, 1st s. and h., *b.* 8 Sep. 1923; ed. at Eton and Cambridge (Magdalene Coll.). He *d.* unm. 28 May 1975.

VIII. 1975. 8. ROBIN RATHMORE (PLUNKET), BARON PLUNKET OF NEWTON, br. and h., *b.* 3 Dec. 1925; ed. at Eton; *m.*, 8 Nov. 1951, Jennifer, 2nd da. of Bailey SOUTHWELL of Crocodile Leap Farm, Olivenhoutpoort, South Africa.

note (d), delete all detail

PLYMOUTH

page 565,
between lines 8 and 9 add

* * * * * *

X. 1905. 1. ROBERT GEORGE (WINDSOR-CLIVE), LORD WINDSOR (of Stanwell) [1529], grandson and h. of Lady Harriet WINDSOR, *afterwards* CLIVE *afterwards* WINDSOR-CLIVE, yr. sister and, in 1833, coh. of Other Archer, last Earl of Plymouth [1682]. He was *cr.*, 18 Dec. 1905, EARL OF PLYMOUTH, co. Devon, and VISCOUNT WINDSOR, of St. Fagan's, co. Glamorgan. For fuller particulars see vol. xii, part 2, *sub* WINDSOR.

[OTHER ROBERT WINDSOR-CLIVE, 1st s. and h. ap., *b.* 23 Oct. 1884; *styled* VISCOUNT WINDSOR from 1905. He *d.* unm. and *v.p.* 23 Dec. 1908. For fuller particulars see vol. xii, part 2, *sub* WINDSOR.]

XI. 1923. 2. IVOR MILES (WINDSOR-CLIVE), EARL OF PLYMOUTH, &c., and LORD WINDSOR (of Stanwell), 2nd but only surv. s. and h., was *b.* 4 Feb. 1889; *styled* VISCOUNT WINDSOR 1908–23. He *d.* 1 Oct. 1943. For fuller particulars see vol. xii, part 2, *sub* WINDSOR.

XII. 1943. 3. OTHER ROBERT IVOR (WINDSOR-CLIVE), EARL OF PLYMOUTH and VISCOUNT WINDSOR, also LORD WINDSOR (of Stanwell), 1st s. and h., *b.* 9 Oct. 1923; *styled* VISCOUNT WINDSOR till 1943; ed. at Eton and Cambridge (Trin. Coll.); served in WW2, 1941–5, as Capt., Coldstream Guards; F.R.S.A. 1953; C. St. J. He *m.*, 11 Oct. 1950, Caroline Helen, only da. of Edward Denis RICE, of Dane Court, Eastry, Kent.

[IVOR EDWARD OTHER WINDSOR-CLIVE, *styled* VISCOUNT WINDSOR, 1st s. and h. ap., *b.* 19 Nov. 1951; ed. at Harrow; *m.*, 1979, Caroline Anne, da. of Frederick NETTLEFOLD.]

POLTIMORE

page 568,
line 24, line to read as follows

III. 1908. 3. COPLESTONE RICHARD GEORGE WARWICK (BAMPFYLDE), BARON POLTIMORE, &c., 1st s. and h., *b.* 29 Nov. 1859,

lines 29–30, delete from 'Having' to 'work.(c)]' and replace by 'He *d.* 2 Nov. 1918. His widow *d.* 4 Aug. 1931.'

IV. 1918. 4. GEORGE WENTWORTH WARWICK (BAMPFYLDE), BARON POLTIMORE, &c., 1st s. and h., *b.* 23 Sep. 1882 [for further detail see note (c)]. She *d.* 6 Sep. 1961. He *m.* 2ndly, 1962, Barbara Pitcairn, widow of James David WALKER, da. of Peter NICOL of Kirkintilloch, co. Dumbarton. He *d. s.p.m.s.* 13 July 1965. His widow *d.* May 1969.

[COPLESTONE JOHN DE GREY WARWICK BAMPFYLDE, *b.* 24 Mar. 1914; 2nd Lieut. Royal Horse Guards; *d. v.p.* and unm., 3 Oct. 1936.]

V. 1965. 5. ARTHUR BLACKETT WARWICK (BAMPFYLDE), BARON POLTIMORE, &c., br. and h., *b.* 29 Nov. 1883; ed. at Eton; *m.* 1stly, 28 Nov. 1916, Catherine Francis Graham, da. of Gen. Sir David Macdowall FRASER. She *d.* 9 Apr. 1938 and he *m.* 2ndly, 4 May 1939, Mabel Violet Blanche, 1st da. of Col. Arthur Hill Sandys MONTGOMERY of Grey Abbey, co. Down and formerly wife of Walter Thomas MEYRICK. This marriage was diss. by divorce in 1948, and she *d.* 12 Jan. 1957. He *d. s.p.* 10 June 1967.

VI. 1967. 6. HUGH DE BURGH WARWICK (BAMPFYLDE), BARON POLTIMORE, br. and h., *b.* 25 Mar. 1888; ed. at Winchester and Oxford (New Coll.); *m.*, 12 Aug. 1918, Margaret Mary, 3rd da. of 4th MARQUIS DE LA PASTURE. He *d. s.p.m.s.* 27 Mar. 1978. His widow *d.* 1981.

[ANTHONY GERARD HUGH BAMPFYLDE, 1st s. and h. ap., *b.* 2 Jan. 1920; ed. at Winchester and R.M.C., Sandhurst; *m.*, 25 Oct. 1947, Brita Yvonne, da. of BARON RUDOLPH CEDERSTRÖM. He *d. v.p.* 2 Jan. 1969. His widow *m.* 2ndly, 1975, Guy ELMES.]

VII. 1978. 7. MARK COPLESTONE (BAMPFYLDE), BARON POLTIMORE, grandson and h., being only s. of Anthony Gerard and Brita Yvonne abovenamed; *b.* 8 June 1957; ed. at Radley; *m.*, 1982, Sally Anne, da. of Dr Norman MILES of Caythorpe, co. Lincs.

[HENRY ANTHONY WARWICK BAMPFYLDE, s. and h. ap., *b.* 3 June 1985.]

note (c), lines 1–2, delete from 'He' to '1882'
lines 7–9, delete from 'His' to '1936'

POLWARTH

page 572,
line 15, line to read as follows

IX. 1920. 9. WALTER GEORGE (HEPBURNE-SCOTT), LORD POLWARTH [S. 1690], 1st s. and h., *b.* 7 Feb. 1864,

line 22, after '1919' add '; Rep. Peer [S.], 1929–44; hon. LLD. Edinburgh, 1937.'
lines 25–6, delete from 'Having' to 'work.(c)]' and replace by 'His wife *d.* 25 Mar. 1930. He *d.* 24 Aug. 1944.'

[WALTER THOMAS HEPBURNE-SCOTT, MASTER OF POLWARTH, 1st s. and h. ap., *b.* 22 Apr. 1890 [for further detail see note (c)]. He *d. v.p.* 7 Sep. 1942. His widow *d.* 5 Aug. 1964.]

X. 1944. 10. HENRY ALEXANDER (HEPBURNE-SCOTT), LORD POLWARTH [S.], grandson and h., being s. and h. of Walter Thomas HEPBURNE-SCOTT, MASTER OF POLWARTH, and Elspeth his wife, both abovenamed [in note (c)], *b.* 17 Nov. 1916; ed. at Eton and Cambridge (King's Coll.); *m.* 1stly, 4 June 1943, Caroline Margaret, 2nd da. of Capt. Robert Athole HAY of Marlesfield, co. Roxburgh. This marriage was diss. by divorce 1969 (she *d.* 1982) and he *m.* 2ndly, 8 Aug. 1969, Jean, da. of Adm. Sir Angus Edward Malise Bontine Cunninghame GRAHAM of Gartmore and formerly wife of Charles Eliot JAUNCEY.

[ANDREW WALTER HEPBURNE-SCOTT, MASTER OF POLWARTH, s. and h. ap., *b.* 30 Nov. 1947; ed. at Eton and Cambridge (Trin. Hall); *m.*, 1971, Isabel Anne, da. of Major John Freville Henry SURTEES of Down House, Wylye, co. Wilts.]

PORTARLINGTON

page 581,
line 32, after 'Place' add 'He *d. s.p.m.s.* 4 July 1959. His widow *d.* 1975.'
line 33, after 'Carlow' add 'from 1907'
line 39, after 'Toronto' add 'He was *k.* on active service, *v.p.*, 17 Apr. 1944. His widow, *m.* 2ndly, 14 Nov. 1945, Peter George Hodges, s. of Col. George Hodges NUGENT, of Churt, co. Surrey. They were div. in 1956. She *d.* 1 Nov. 1963.'

VII. 1959. 7. GEORGE LIONEL SEYMOUR (DAWSON-DAMER), EARL OF PORTARLINGTON, &c., grandson and h., being s. and h. of George Lionel and Peggy abovenamed. He was *b.* 10 Aug. 1938; ed. at Eton; *m.*, 26 July 1961, Davina, 1st da. of Sir Edward Henry WINDLEY of Quenington, co. Glos.

[CHARLES GEORGE YUILL SEYMOUR DAWSON-DAMER, *styled* VISCOUNT CARLOW, s. and h. ap., *b.* 6 Oct. 1965; ed. at Eton.]

PORTLAND

page 582,
line 13, after 'Mary,' add '(*bur.* at Roxwell 6 Oct. 1593),'
note (a), line 3, after 'disparaged.' add 'See also *New England Hist. Gen. Reg.*, vol. 74, 1920, pp. 134–40.'

page 597,
line 35, after 'Perth' add 'etc'

page 597,
line 35, after '(c)' add 'He *d.* 26 Apr. 1943.', after 'She' add ', who' and after 'Perth' add ', *d.* 30 July 1954.'

page 598,
line 1, line to read as follows

DUKEDOM. VII. EARLDOM. XII. } 1943 — 7 and 8. WILLIAM ARTHUR HENRY (CAVENDISH-BENTINCK), DUKE OF PORTLAND, &c., 1st s. and h.,

line 3, after 'Welbeck' add '*styled* MARQUESS OF TITCHFIELD till 1943;'
line 8, for 'from 1939' read '1939–62'
line 12, for ']' read 'He *d. s.p.m.* 21 Mar. 1977. His widow *d.* 1982.'

DUKEDOM. VIII. EARLDOM. XIII. } 1977 — 8 and 9. FERDINAND WILLIAM (CAVENDISH-BENTINCK), DUKE OF PORTLAND, &c., distant cousin and h., being 1st s. of William George Frederick CAVENDISH-BENTINCK (*d.* 13 Nov. 1948), by Ruth Mary, da. of EDWARD ST. MAUR, *styled* EARL ST. MAUR, which William George was 2nd s. of George Augustus Frederick C-B (*d.* 9 Apr. 1891), by Prudence Penelope, da. of Col. Charles Powell LESLIE, which George was only s. of Major Gen. Frederick CAVENDISH-BENTINCK (*d.* 11 Feb. 1828), by Mary, da. of William (LOWTHER), 1st EARL OF LONSDALE, which Frederick was 4th s. of the 3rd Duke of Portland. He was *b.* 4 July 1888; ed. at Eton and R.M.C., Sandhurst; *m.* 1stly, 9 May 1912, Wentworth Frances, da. of William James HOPE-JOHNSTONE. This marriage was diss. by divorce 1950 (she *d.* 25 June 1964) and he *m.* 2ndly, Gwyneth Ethel, da. of John Wesley EDWARD and widow of Col. David Alexander John BOWIE. He *d. s.p.* 13 Dec. 1980. His widow was still living 1995.

DUKEDOM. IX. EARLDOM. XIV. } 1980 — 9 and 10. VICTOR FREDERICK WILLIAM (CAVENDISH-BENTINCK), DUKE OF PORTLAND, [1716], MARQUESS OF TITCHFIELD [1716], EARL OF PORTLAND [1689], VISCOUNT WOODSTOCK [1689], and BARON CIRENCESTER [1689] br. and h., *b.* 18 June 1897; ed. at Wellington; *m.* 1stly, 16 Feb. 1924, Clothilde Bruce, da. of James Bruce QUIGLEY of Dallas, Texas, U.S.A. This marriage was diss. by divorce 1948 and he *m.* 2ndly, 27 July 1948, Kathleen Elsie, da. of Arthur BARRY of Montreal, Canada and formerly wife of Arthur Richie TILLOTSON. He *d. s.p.m.* 30 July 1990 when the Dukedom of Portland and the Marquessate of Titchfield became *extinct* but he was *suc.* in his other titles by his distant cousin. His widow was still living 1995.

XIV. 1990. 11. HENRY NOEL (BENTINCK), EARL OF PORTLAND, VISCOUNT WOODSTOCK and BARON CIRENCESTER all in the peerage of England, also a COUNT OF THE HOLY ROMAN EMPIRE, distant cousin and h., being s. and h. of Robert Charles BENTINCK (*d.* 12 Mar. 1932), by Lady Nora Ida, da. of Charles William Francis (NOEL), 3rd EARL OF GAINSBOROUGH, which Robert Charles was great-great-great-grandson of Hans William BENTINCK, 1st EARL OF PORTLAND, abovenamed. He was *b.* 2 Oct. 1919; ed. at Harrow; *m.* 1stly, 13 Oct. 1940, Pauline Ursula, da. of Frederick William MELLOWES She *d.* 11 Jan. 1967 and he *m.* 2ndly, 1974, Jennifer, da. of Reginald HOPKINS.

[TIMOTHY CHARLES ROBERT BENTINCK, COUNT OF THE HOLY ROMAN EMPIRE, *styled* VISCOUNT WOODSTOCK, s. and h. ap., *b.* 1 July 1953; ed. at Harrow and East Anglia Univ.; *m.*, 1979, Judith Ann, da. of John Robert EMERSON.]

PORTMAN

page 600,
note (b), line 7, for 'Jenico' read 'Dartas'

page 602,
line 10, line to read as follows

III. 1911. 3. HENRY BERKELEY (PORTMAN), VISCOUNT PORTMAN OF BRYANSTON, &c., 3rd but 1st surv. s. and h.,

lines 16–17, delete from 'Having' to 'work.(b)]' and replace by note (b), lines 1–3.

IV. 1923. 4. CLAUD BERKELEY (PORTMAN), VISCOUNT PORTMAN, &c., br. and h. male, being 4th s. of the 2nd Viscount [for further detail see note (b), lines 4–11].

V. 1929. 5. EDWARD CLAUD BERKELEY (PORTMAN), VISCOUNT PORTMAN, &c., s. and h., *b.* 8 July 1898 [for further detail see note (b), lines 12–15]. He *d. s.p.m.* 14 July 1942. His widow *d.* 1975.

VI. 1942. 6. SEYMOUR BERKELEY (PORTMAN), VISCOUNT PORTMAN, &c., uncle and h., being 5th s. of the 2nd Viscount Portman. He was *b.* 19 Feb. 1868 and *d.* unm. 2 Nov. 1946.

VII. 1946. 7. GERALD BERKELEY (PORTMAN), VISCOUNT PORTMAN, &c., br. and h., *b.* 23 Jan. 1875; ed. at Eton and R.M.C., Sandhurst; *m.*, 16 July 1902, Dorothy Marie Isolde, da. of Sir Robert SHEFFIELD, Bart. He *d.* 3 Sep. 1948. His widow *d.* 21 May 1964.

VIII. 1948. 8. GERALD WILLIAM BERKELEY (PORTMAN), VISCOUNT PORTMAN, &c., s. and h., *b.* 20 Aug. 1903; ed. at Eton and R.M.C., Sandhurst; *m.* 1stly, 27 Jan. 1926, Marjorie Josephine Bentley, da. of George Bentley GERARD of Montreal, Canada. This marriage was diss. by divorce 1946 and he *m.* 2ndly, 11 Apr. 1946, Nancy Maureen, 4th da. of Capt. Percy Herbert FRANKLIN, R.N., of Ropley, co. Hants. he *d. s.p.* 3 Nov. 1967. His widow was still living 1995.

IX. 1967. 9. EDWARD HENRY BERKELEY (PORTMAN), VISCOUNT PORTMAN, &c., nephew and h., being s. and h. of Michael Berkeley PORTMAN (*d.* 25 Oct. 1959), by his 1st wife, Madeleine June, da. of David CHARLES, which

Michael was 2nd s. of the 7th Viscount Portman. He was *b.* 22 Apr. 1934; ed. at Canford and R.A.C., Cirencester; *m.* 1stly, 26 Sep. 1956, Rosemary Joy, da. of Charles FARRIS of Combe Bissett, co. Wilts. This marriage was diss. by divorce 1966 and he *m.* 2ndly, 31 Mar. 1966, Penelope Anne Hassard, da. of Trevor Robert William ALLIN of North Moreton, co. Berks.

[CHRISTOPHER EDWARD BERKELEY PORTMAN, 1st s. and h. ap. by 1st wife, *b.* 30 July 1958; *m.* 1stly, 1983, Caroline, da. of Terence Ivan STEENSON of Caversham, co. Berks. This marriage was diss. by divorce and he *m.* 2ndly, 1987, Patricia Martins, da. of Bernardino PIM of Rio de Janeiro, Brazil.]

PORTSMOUTH

page 614,
line 22, line to read as follows

VII. 1917. 7. JOHN FELLOWES (WALLOP), EARL OF PORTSMOUTH, &c., *b.* 27 Dec. 1859;

lines 25–6, delete from 'Having' to 'work.(g)]'

VIII. 1925. 8. OLIVER HENRY (WALLOP), EARL OF PORTSMOUTH, &c., br. and h., *b.* 13 Jan. 1861; ed. at Eton and Oxford (Balliol Coll.); served in WW1(g) with the Red Cross. He *m.*, Apr. 1897, Marguerite, da. of Samuel Johnson WALKER, of Frankfort, Kentucky, U.S.A. She *d.* 9 May 1938, at Barton House, Morchard Bishop, N. Devon, and was *bur.* 12 May, at Farleigh Wallop. He *d.* 10 Feb. 1943.

IX. 1943. 9. GERARD VERNON (WALLOP), EARL OF PORTSMOUTH, &c., 1st s. and h., *b.* 16 May 1898; ed. at Winchester and Oxford (Balliol Coll.); *styled* VISCOUNT LYMINGTON 1925–43; served in WW1 as a Lieut. in the 2nd Life Guards and Guards Machine Gun Regt.; M.P. (Conservative) for the Basingstoke Div. of Hants, 1929–34. He *m.* 1stly, 31 July 1920, Mary Lawrence, da. of Waldron Kintzing POST, of Bayport, Long Island, U.S.A. (she obtained a divorce in 1936 and *m.* 2ndly, 12 Feb. 1938, Everard John Boothby HOW. She *d.* 6 Aug. 1964). He *m.* 2ndly, 14 Aug. 1936, Bridget Cory, only da. of Capt. Patrick Bermingham CROHAN, of Owlpen Old Manor, Uley, co. Glos. She *d.* 1979. He *d.* 28 Sep. 1984.

[OLIVER KINTZING WALLOP, *styled* VISCOUNT LYMINGTON, 1st s. and h. ap. by 1st wife, *b.* 14 Jan. 1923; ed. at Eton; *m.* 1stly, 26 June 1952, Maureen, da. of Lieut. Col. Kenneth Bridges STANLEY. This marriage was diss. by divorce 1954 and he *m.* 2ndly, 1954, Ruth Violet, da. of yst. da. of Brig. Gen. Gerald Carew SLADEN and formerly wife of R.D.M. MASON This marriage was in turn diss. by divorce 1974 and he *m.* 3rdly, Julia, 1974, da. of W. Graeme OGDEN of Frome, Somerset and formerly wife of Peter Robin KIRWEN-TAYLOR. He *d. v.p.* 5 June 1984. His widow was still living 1995.]

X. 1984. 10. QUENTIN GERARD CAREW (WALLOP), EARL OF PORTSMOUTH,

&c., grandson and h., being s. and h. of Oliver Kintzing and his 2nd wife Ruth Violet abovenamed. He was *b.* 25 July 1954; ed. at Eton and Millfield; *m.* 1stly, 1981, Candia Frances Juliet, da. of Colin MCWILLIAM of Edinburgh. This marriage was diss. by divorce 1985 and he *m.* 2ndly, 1990, Annabel, 1st da. of Dr Ian FERGUSON of Richmond, Surrey.

[OLIVER HENRY RUFUS WALLOP, *styled* VISCOUNT LYMINGTON, *b.* 22 Dec. 1981.]

note ([b]), delete all detail and replace by 'For a list of peers and sons of peers who served in this war, see vol. viii, Appendix F.'

POULETT

page 615,
note ([b]), line 5, for 'great-grandson' read 's.'

page 624,
lines 22–5, delete all detail and replace as follows

EARLDOM. VIII. BARONY. XI. } 1918 — 8 and 11. GEORGE AMIAS FITZWARRINE (POULETT), EARL POULETT, VISCOUNT HINTON ST GEORGE and BARON POULETT OF HINTON ST GEORGE, s. and h., *b.* 23 June 1909; *styled* VISCOUNT HINTON till 1918; ed. at Eton; served in WW2 as Tech. Asst. in Chief Mechanical Engineers Dept, Woolwich Arsenal, 1940–1, Tech. Asst. at the Min. of Supply (Small Arms Section), 1941–3. He *m.* 1stly, 21 June 1935, Oriel Ross, da. of John Howard SWINSTEAD, from whom he was div. 1941, 2ndly, 17 Dec. 1941, Olga Lorraine, da. of Waklin LAWRENCE, of Svendborg, Denmark. She *d.* 18 May 1961 and he *m.* 3rdly, 12 Sep. 1968, Margaret Christine, da. of Wilfred John Peter BALL of Reading. He *d. s.p.* 1 Mar. 1973 when the Earldom [1706] and the Viscountcy of Hinton St. George [1706] became *extinct*, and the Barony of Poulett of Hinton St. George [1627] became *extinct* or *dormant*. His widow was still living 1995.

POWER

page 634,
line 8, line to read as follows

XIX. 1915. *19.* JOHN WILLIAM RIVALLON DE LA POER of Gurteen afsd.

lines 17–19, delete from 'Having' to 'him.]' and replace by 'He *m.*, 1907, Muriel Henrietta Louisa, only da. of Capt. Robert BEST. She *d.* 19 Jan. 1936. He *d.* 27 Mar. 1939. In his son would have been vested any right to the Barony of Le Power and Coroughmore, in the Peerage of Ireland.'

POWERSCOURT

page 640,
line 8, line to read as follows

VISCOUNTCY [I.] X. BARONY [U.K.] II.	1904	8 and 2. MERVYN RICHARD (WINGFIELD), VISCOUNT POWERSCOURT and BARON WINGFIELD in the Peerage of Ireland and BARON POWERSCOURT in the Peerage of the United Kingdom, 1st s. and h.,

lines 19–21, delete from 'Having' to 'work.([c])' and after '1878' replace by 'and *d.* 6 Dec. 1946. He *d.* 21 Mar. 1947.'

VISCOUNTCY [I.] XI. BARONY [U.K.] III.	1947	9 and 3. MERVYN PATRICK (WINGFIELD), VISCOUNT POWERSCOURT, &c., 1st s. and h., *b.* 22 Aug. 1905; ed. at R.M.C., Sandhurst; Lieut. late 8th Hussars. He *m.*, 16 Dec. 1932, Sheila Claude, da. of Lieut. Col. Claude BEDDINGTON, of Grosvenor Str., London. He *d.* 3 Apr.

1973. His widow *d.* 1992.

VISCOUNTCY [I.] XII. BARONY [U.K.] IV.	1973	10 and 4. MERVYN NIALL (WINGFIELD), VISCOUNT POWERSCOURT, &c., 1st s. and h. ap., *b.* 3 Sep. 1935; ed. at Stowe; *m.* 1stly, 15 Sep. 1962, Wendy Anne Pauline, da. of Ralph C.G. SLAZENGER of Powerscourt, Enniskerry, co. Wicklow. This marriage was diss. by

divorce 1974 and he *m.* 2ndly, 1979, Pauline, da. of W.P. VAN of San Francisco, California.

[MERVYN ANTHONY WINGFIELD, s. and h. ap., *b.* 21 Aug. 1963.]

note ([c]), delete all detail

POWIS

page 645,
note ([c]), line 1, for 'Cornwall' read 'co. Montgomery'

page 655,
line 15, after '([a])' add 'He *d.* 9 Nov. 1952.'
line 30, after '([b])' add 'Served in WW2 as a Sqn. Ldr. R.A.F.V.R., *k.* on active service *v.p.*, Mar. 1943. The Barony of Darcy de Knayth was inherited by his only child, his da. Davina Marcia. See that title. His widow *m.* 2ndly, 24 Oct. 1945, Brig. Derek Schuldam SCHREIBER, who *d.* 1972. His widow was still living 1995.'

EARLDOM. X. BARONY. XII.	1952	5. EDWARD ROBERT HENRY (HERBERT), EARL OF POWIS, &c., distant cousin and h., being 1st s. and h. of Edward William HERBERT (*d.* 28 Dec. 1924), by Beatrice Anne, da. of Sir Hedworth WILLIAMSON, Bart., which Edward William

was 1st s. of Robert Charles HERBERT (*d.* 31 Oct. 1902), by Anne Maria, da. of Edward CLUDDE of Orleton, which Robert Charles was 4th s. of the 2nd Earl of Powis. He was *b.* 19 May 1889; ed. at Eton and Oxford (Ch. Ch.); *m.*, 12 Mar. 1932, Ella Mary, 5th da. of Col. William Hans RATHBORNE of Kilcogy, co. Cavan. He *d. s.p.m.* 15 Jan. 1974. His widow *d.* 1987.

EARLDOM. XI. BARONY. XIII. } 1974

6. CHRISTIAN VICTOR CHARLES (HERBERT), EARL OF POWIS, &c., br. and h., *b.* 28 May 1904; ed. at Oundle, Cambridge (Trin. Coll.) and Univ. Coll., London. He *d.* unm. 7 Oct. 1988.

EARLDOM. XII. BARONY. XIV. } 1988

7. GEORGE WILLIAM (HERBERT), EARL OF POWIS, &c., distant cousin and h., being 1st s. and h. of Rt. Rev. Percy Mark HERBERT, Bishop of Norwich, (*d.* 22 Jan. 1968), by Elaine Letitia Algitha, da. of William George Algar (ORDE-POWLETT), 5th BARON BOLTON, which Percy Mark was 2nd s. of William Henry Herbert (*d.* 29 Jan. 1909), by Sybella Augusta, da. of Mark William Vane MILBANK, which William Henry was 5th s. of the 2nd Earl of Powis. He was *b.* 4 June 1925; ed. at Eton and Cambridge (Trin. Coll.); *m.*, 26 July 1949, Katherine Odeyne, yst. da. of George (DE GREY), 8th BARON WALSINGHAM. He *d.* 13 Aug. 1993. His widow was still living 1995.

EARLDOM. XIII. BARONY. XV. } 1993

8. JOHN GEORGE (HERBERT), EARL OF POWIS, &c., 1st s. and h., *b.* 19 May 1952; ed. at Wellington and McMaster Univ., Ontario, Canada; *m.*, 1977, Marijke Sophia, 1st da. of Maarten N. GUNTHER of Ontario, Canada.

[JONATHAN NICHOLAS WILLIAM HERBERT, *styled* VISCOUNT CLIVE, *b.* 5 Dec. 1979.]

POYNINGS

page 660,
note (g), line 6, after 'Luke' add ', who *m.* the St. John heiress and was summ. to Parliament as Lord Poynings, see vol. x, pp. 665.'

page 661,
line 14, for 'John (DE MOLEYNS)' read 'Sir John DE MOLEYNS
line 15, delete 'LORD MOLEYNS'

page 663,
lines 10–11, delete from 'Elizabeth' to 'BRYAN' and replace by 'Isobel, da. of Sir John DE CLIFFORD'

page 664,
line 15, for '(__)' read 'before 22 Oct. 1397, Elizabeth, da. of Reynold (GREY), Lord GREY OF RUTHYN by his 1st wife Margaret, da. of Thomas (ROS), 4th Lord

ROS OF HELMSLEY.' [Devon, *Issues of the Exchequer*, 1837, p. 265; *Sussex Arch. Colls.*, vol. xv, 1863, p. 16]
line 21, after '*m.*,' add '*circa* 1423,'

page 674,
line 15, for 'Eudes' read 'Eon'
line 16, for 'MONTALT read 'MOHAUT'
lines 17–18, delete from 'CANTELOU' to CANTELOU' and replace by 'CAUNTELO, Lord of Abergavenny (*d.* 1273), and da. of Sir William de CAUNTELO, of Calne, Wilts.,'
line 19, after 'BRIOUZE' add 'of Abergavenny,'

page 675,
line 3, after '1315' add 'as his 2nd wife' and after CHAUNDOS' add '[1st LORD CHAUNDOS]'

POYNTZ

page 676,
line 1, for '(__)' read 'da. of Sir Walter Pavole, co. Wilts.'

QUEENSBURY

page 704,
line 32, after '1777' add 'and *bap.* 9 Mar. 1777 at Plumbland, co. Cumberland' [*ex inform.* C. Roy Hudleston]

page 705,
line 18, after 'Kelhead' add 'and *bap.* 22 Aug. 1779 at Plumbland afsd.'

page 707,
line 24, after '(c)' add 'His widow *d.* 4 Apr. 1956.'
line 25, line to read as follows

MARQUESSATE [S.] XI. EARLDOM [S.] XIII.	1920	11 and 13. FRANCIS ARCHIBALD KELHEAD (DOUGLAS), MARQUESS OF QUEENSBERRY, &c., [S.], s. and h., *b.* 17 Jan. 1896;

line 28, after 'twice)' add '; Rep. Peer [S.] 1920–9'

page 707,
note (b), line 5, after '280.)' add 'See also Alan Sinfield, *The Wilde Century*, 1994, p. 73'

page 708,
lines 6–7, delete from 'Having' to 'work.]' and replace by 'This marriage was also diss. by divorce 1946 (she *d.* 9 Sep. 1959) and he *m.* 3rdly, 23 Apr. 1947, Muriel

Beatrice Margaret, da. of Arthur John Rowe THORNETT and formerly wife of Albert Sydney Gore CHUNN. He *d.* 27 Apr. 1954. His widow *d.* 1992.'

MARQUESSATE [S.] XII. EARLDOM [S.] XIV. } 1954 — 12 and 14. DAVID HARRINGTON ANGUS (DOUGLAS), MARQUESS OF QUEENSBERRY, &c., 1st s. and h., *b.* 19 Dec. 1929; ed. at Eton; *m.* 1stly, 18 July 1956, Ann, da. of Maurice Sinnett JONES and formerly wife of George Arthur RADFORD. This marriage was diss. by divorce 1969 and he *m.* 2ndly, 10 July 1969, Alexandra Mary Clare Wyndham, da. of Guy Wyndham SICH of Chiswick. This marriage was in turn diss. by divorce, 1986.

[SHOLTO FRANCIS GUY DOUGLAS, *styled* VISCOUNT DRUMLANRIG, s. and h. ap., *b.* 1 June 1967.]

RADNOR

page 721,
line 29, after 'Britford' add 'His widow *d.* 5 Jan. 1946.'
line 30, line to read as follows

XI. 1930. 7. WILLIAM (PLEYDELL-BOUVERIE), EARL OF RADNOR, , &c., 1st s. and h., *b.* 18 Dec. 1895;

lines 37–8, delete from 'Having' to 'work.([c])]' and replace by 'This marriage was diss. by divorce 1942 (she *m.* 2ndly, 9 Oct. 1943, Brig. Montacute William Worrell SELBY-LOWNDES, who *d.* 1972, she *d.* 1985) and he *m.* 2ndly, 9 Oct. 1943, Anne Isobel, 1st da. of Lieut. Col. Richard OAKLEY of Lawrence End, Luton, co. Beds. He *d.* 23 Nov. 1968. His widow was still living 1995.'

XII. 1968. 8. JACOB (PLEYDELL-BOUVERIE), EARL OF RADNOR, &c., 1st s. and h., *b.* 10 Nov. 1927; ed. at Harrow and Cambridge (Trin. Coll.); *m.* 1stly, 8 July 1953, Anne Garden Farquharson, da. of Donald Farquharson SETH-SMITH of Whitsbury Cross, Fordingbridge, co. Hants. This marriage was diss. by divorce 1962 and he *m.* 2ndly, 29 June 1963, Margaret Robin, da. of Robin FLEMING of Drymen, co. Stirling. This marriage was in turn diss. by divorce 1985 and he *m.* 3rdly, 1986, Mary Jillean Gwenellan, da. of (__) and formerly wife of Anthony PETTIT.

[WILLIAM PLEYDELL-BOUVERIE, *styled* VISCOUNT FOLKESTONE, s. and h. ap. by 1st wife, *b.* 5 Jan. 1955; ed. at Harrow and R.A.C., Cirencester.]

note ([c]), delete all detail

RADSTOCK

page 723,
line 21, line to read as follows

IV. 1913. 4. GRANVILLE GEORGE (WALDEGRAVE), BARON RADSTOCK OF CASTLETOWN [I.], 1st s. and h., *b.* 1 Sep. 1859,

lines 26–7, delete from 'Having' to 'work.(d)]'

V. 1937 to 1953. 5. MONTAGU (WALDEGRAVE), BARON RADSTOCK OF CASTLETOWN [I.], br. and h., *b.* 15 July 1867, in London [for further detail see note (d)]. He *d. s.p.m.s.* 17 Sep. 1953, when his title became *extinct.*

[JOHN MONTAGU GRANVILLE WALDEGRAVE, s. and h. ap., *b.* 29 Aug. 1905; Cmdr. R.N., D.S.C. He *m.*, 29 June 1940, Hersey Margaret, 2nd da. of Patrick James (BOYLE), 8th EARL OF GLASGOW, served in WW2, *k.* on active service in H.M.S. Penelope, *v.p.* and *s.p.m.*, 18 Feb. 1944. His widow *m.* 2ndly, 24 July 1947, John GORING, s. of Charles GORING of Wiston, Sussex, who *d.* 1990. She *d.* 1993.]

RAGLAN

page 727,
line 5, line to read as follows

IV. 1921. 4. FITZROY RICHARD (SOMERSET), BARON RAGLAN, 1st s. and h., *b.* 10 June 1885;

lines 13–14, delete from 'Having' to 'work.(c)]' and replace by 'He *d.* 14 Sep. 1964. His widow *d.* 1971.'

V. 1964. 5. FITZROY JOHN (SOMERSET), BARON RAGLAN [1852], 2nd(c) but 1st surv s. and h., *b.* 8 Nov. 1927; ed. at Westminster and Oxford (Magdalen Coll.), and R.A.C., Cirencester; *m.* 1stly, 1973, Alice, da. of Peter BAILY of Great Whittington, Northumberland. This marriage was diss. by divorce 1981.

note (c), line 2, delete from 'His' to '1927'

RANELAGH

page 734,
line 7, for 'Earldom of Ranelagh' read 'all his titles'

page 735,
lines 8–9, for 'remained *dormant*' read 'apparently remained *dormant*, but was actually *extinct*.'
lines 12–31, delete all detail and replace as follows

VISCOUNTCY? [I.]
I. 1759. 1. CHARLES (JONES, *later* WILKINSON), VISCOUNT RANELAGH and BARON JONES [I.], s. and h. of Charles JONES of Lidlington, co. Beds. (being 3rd cousin of Richard (JONES), 3rd VISCOUNT

RANELAGH, abovenamed), by Elizabeth, da. of James DOUGLAS, Notary Public of Haddington, East Lothian, which Charles was only s. and h. of Roger JONES of Winchester, by Martha, da. of Joseph GULSTON, D.D., Dean of Chichester, which Roger was 1st s. of Richard JONES of Lidlington, co. Beds. by Christian HACKETT. Charles JONES was *b. post.* 1720 (his parents having been *m.* 28 Mar. 1720 at Dalkeith, Midlothian), and was not in the direct line of *suc.* to the titles of Viscount Ranelagh and Baron Jones, his grandfather, Roger Jones, being descended from an uncle of the 1st Viscount, and not from Thomas Jones, alleged 2nd s. of the 1st Viscount, who did not exist. The terms of the original letters patent quite clearly state that the dignities were to descend to the heirs male of the body of the 1st Viscount.([aa]) The true facts of his descent appear to have been concealed by Charles Jones, or his supporters, and he was allowed to take his seat in the Irish House of Lords, under the above titles, 16 Oct. 1759.([ab]) The following year a pedigree chart was drafted and deposited in the Office of the Ulster King of Arms, to the effect that the claimant was a great-grandson of the Honorable Thomas Jones and his wife Elizabeth Harris, which Thomas was the 2nd s. of the 1st Viscount. The same pedigree was placed in the College of Arms in 1805.([b]) No documentary proof appears to have been submitted to substantiate this claim. He was Chairman of several committees in the Irish House of Lords, receiving (1760–87) various grants and pensions to the amount of around £13,000. He was Constable of Athlone Castle, 1765 till his death, a Commissioner of the Paving Board and director of many charitable institutions. He assumed the name of WILKINSON and the lands and estates of Samuel WILKINSON of Epsom, co. Surrey and the City of Dublin, by the terms of the latter's will, dat. 31 Mar. 1785, pr. 24 Dec. 1791, in the Prerog. Ct. [I.]. He *m.* (lic. 25 Apr. 1761), Sarah, da. of Thomas MONTGOMERY, sometime M.P. [I.] for Lifford. He *d.* in Dublin, 20, and was *bur.* 23 Apr. 1797 at St. Patrick's, Dublin. Will dat. 31 Mar. 1797, pr. 9 May 1797, Prerog. Ct. [I.]. His widow was *bur.* at St. Patrick's, afsd., 3 Jan. 1812.

note ([aa]) See letters patent, House of Lords' Journals [I.], vol. 1, 1634–98, p. 81, "et heredibus mesculis de corpore legitime." There is no record of a further remainder being granted (or a new grant being made) to include descendants of the grandfather of the grantee.

note ([ab]) This article was contributed by Roger Powell, as is the following note. 'The implications which follow from the discovery that Charles Jones was not entitled to the dignities of Viscount Ranelagh and Baron Jones by hereditary right are very interesting. As none of the holders of the title up to 1712 left more than one s. and h. both titles became *extinct* and not *dormant* on the death of the 3rd Viscount in 1712. It could therefore be argued that by issuing a writ of summons to Charles Jones and allowing him to take his seat, a barony by writ was unwittingly created. It has hitherto been accepted that no Irish titles were ever created by writ, but only by tenure or patent (see vol. xi, Appendix A), but it is difficult to see how Charles Jones sat in the House of Lords [I.] unless there was a new creation in 1759, as he did not do so by hereditary right. If a hereditary barony by writ and sitting, descendible to heirs general were created, it could possibly be claimed by one of the descendants of Barbara Grafin von Rechberg und Rothenloren zu Hohenrechberg, the only surv. sister of the '7th' Viscount. The question of the Viscountcy is another and even more difficult matter, since current peerage law allows no title higher than a barony to have been created by writ in England or Ireland.'

line 32, for 'V' read 'II' and for '5' read '2'

page 736,
line 4, for 'VI' read 'III' and for '6' read '3'
line 15, for 'VII' read 'IV' and for '7' read '4'

RANFURLEY

page 740,
line 6, line to read as follows

VI. 1933. 6. THOMAS DANIEL (KNOX), EARL OF RANFURLEY, Etc. [I.], grandson and h., being 1st s. of Thomas Uchter and Hilda his wife next abovenamed, *b.* 29 May 1913; *styled* VISCOUNT NORTHLAND 1915–33;

lines 13–15, delete from 'Having' to 'work.]' and replace by 'He *d. s.p.m.* 6 Nov. 1988. His widow was still living 1995.'

VII. 1988. 7. GERALD FRANCOYS NEEDHAM (KNOX), EARL OF RANFURLEY, &c., distant cousin and h., being 1st s. of Capt. John Needham KNOX, R.N. (*d.* 5 Apr. 1967), by Monica, da. of Major Gen. Sir Gerald KITSON, which John was 1st s. of Edward Knox (*d.* 13 July 1950), by Mabel, da. of John Edward WADE of Brantingham Thorpe, co. Yorks., which Edward was 1st s. of Capt. Henry Needham Knox, R.N. (*d.* 18 June 1960), by Alexandrina Henriette Wilhelmina, da. of Jean-Jacques LAVIT, which Henry was 1st s. of John Henry KNOX (*d.* 27 Aug. 1872), by Lady Mabella Josephine, da. of Francis (NEEDHAM), 1st EARL OF KILMOREY, which John Henry was 3rd s. of the 1st Earl of Ranfurley. He was *b.* 4 Jan. 1929; ed. at Wellington; *m.*, 22 Jan. 1955, Rosemary Beatrice Vesey, da. of Air Vice Marshal Felton Vesey HOLT.

[EDWARD JOHN KNOX, *styled* VISCOUNT NORTHLAND, 1st s. and h. ap., *b.* 21 May 1957; ed. at Leys Sch. and Loughborough Univ.; *m.* 1stly, 1980, Rachel Sarah, da. of Frank Hilton LEE. This marriage was diss. by divorce 1984 and he *m.* 2ndly, 1994, Johanna Humphrey, da. of Sqn. Ldr. Harry Richard WALTON.]

RATHDONNELL

page 741,
note ([b]), line 1, delete 'hitherto [1941] the'

page 742,
line 11, line to read as follows

III. 1929. 3. THOMAS LEOPOLD (McCLINTOCK-BUNBURY), BARON RATHDONNELL [I.], 2nd but 1st surv. s. and h.

lines 20–1, delete from 'Having' to 'work.([c])'

IV. 1937. 4. WILLIAM ROBERT (MCCLINTOCK-BUNBURY), BARON RATHDONNELL [I.], s. and h., *b.* 23 Nov. 1914 [for further detail see note (c)]. He *d.* 13 Oct. 1959. His widow *m.* 2ndly, 27 May 1961, Major Hugh Caruthers MASSY, who *d.* 1987. She *d.* 1989.

V. 1959. 5. THOMAS BENJAMIN (MCCLINTOCK-BUNBURY), BARON RATHDONNELL, only s. and h., *b.* 17 Sep. 1938; ed. at Charterhouse and R.N.C., Dartmouth; *m.*, 2 Oct. 1965, Jessica Harriet, da. of George Gilbert BUTLER of Bennetsbridge, co. Kilkenny.

[WILLIAM LEOPOLD MCCLINTOCK-BUNBURY, s. and h. ap., *b.* 6 July 1966.]

RAVENSDALE

page 744,
between lines 14 and 15 add as follows

BARONY [U.K.] I. 1911. 1. GEORGE NATHANIEL CURZON, of Kedleston, s. and h. of Alfred Nathaniel (CURZON), 4th BARON SCARSDALE, was *cr.* BARON CURZON OF KEDLESTON, co. Derby [I.], 11 Nov. 1898, EARL CURZON OF KEDLESTON, co. Derby, VISCOUNT SCARSDALE OF SCARSDALE, co. Derby, and BARON RAVENSDALE OF RAVENSDALE, co. Derby, all with different rem. (for full details see vol. iii, *sub* CURZON and vol. xi, *sub* SCARSDALE) on 2 Nov. 1911, and finally MARQUESS CURZON OF KEDLESTON, 28 June 1921, to heirs male of his body. He *d. s.p.m.* 20 Mar. 1925, when his Marquessate, Earldom and Irish Barony became *extinct*. The Viscountcy of Scarsdale devolved, under a spec. rem., on his nephew, see SCARSDALE, above, who, as heir male also inherited the Barony of Scarsdale and two Baronetcies. The Barony of Ravensdale, devolved on his eldest da. (the rem. being, in default of male issue, to her and her issue male, with a like rem. to his 2nd and every other younger da.).

II. 1925. 2. MARY IRENE CURZON, 1st da. and h., *suo jure* BARONESS RAVENSDALE OF RAVENSDALE under the spec. rem. She was *b.* 20 Jan. 1896; *cr.* BARONESS RAVENSDALE OF KEDLESTON, of Kedleston, co. Derby, for life, 1958. She *d.* unm. 9 Feb. 1966.

III. 1966. 3. NICHOLAS (MOSLEY), BARON RAVENSDALE OF RAVENSDALE under the spec. rem., being 1st s. and h. of Cynthia Blanche (*d.* 16 May 1933), 2nd da. of George Nathaniel (CURZON), 1st and last MARQUESS CURZON abovenamed, by Sir Oswald Ernald MOSLEY, Bart. He was *b.* 25 June 1923; ed. at Eton and Oxford (Balliol Coll.); *m.* 1stly, 14 Nov. 1947, Rosemary Laura, da. of Marshal of the R.A.F. Sir John Maitland SALMOND. This marriage was diss. by divorce 1974 and he *m.* 2ndly, 1974, Verity Elizabeth, 2nd da. of John RAYMOND of Basingstoke, co. Hants. and formerly wife of John Adrian BAILEY.

[SHAUN NICHOLAS MOSLEY, 1st s. and h. ap., *b.* 5 Aug. 1949; ed. at Bryanston and Oxford (Hertford Coll.); *m.*, 1978, Theresa, da. of (__) CLIFFORD.]

RAVENSWORTH

page 748,
between lines 2 and 3 add as follows

EARLDOM. III. BARONY. V. } 1903. 3 and 4. ATHOLL CHARLES JOHN (LIDDELL), EARL OF RAVENSWORTH, &c., br. and h., *b.* 6 Aug. 1833 [for further detail see note (c), page 747].

BARONY. VI. 1904. 5. ARTHUR THOMAS (LIDDELL), BARON RAVENSWORTH, cousin and h., being 1st s. and h. of Rev. Robert LIDDELL (*d.* 29 June 1888), by Emily Ann Charlotte, da. of Rev. Gerald Valerian WELLESLEY, which Robert was 4th s. of the 1st Baron Ravensworth. He was *b.* 28 Oct. 1837; *m.*, 9 Oct. 1866, Sophia Harriet, 2nd da. of Sir Thomas Wathen WALLER, Bart. She *d.* Sep. 1918. He *d.* 12 Nov. 1919.

VII. 1919. 6. GERALD WELLESLEY (LIDDELL), BARON RAVENSWORTH, 1st s. and h., *b.* 21 Mar. 1869; ed. at Winchester; *m.*, 11 Oct. 1899, Isolda Blanche, da. of Charles Glynn PRIDEAUX-BRUNE. He *d.* 15 June 1932. His widow *d.* 26 Mar. 1938.

VIII. 1932. 7. ROBERT ARTHUR (LIDDELL), BARON RAVENSWORTH, only s. and h., *b.* 2 Jan. 1902; ed. at Winchester and Oxford (Ch. Ch.). He *d.* unm. 4 Aug. 1950.

IX. 1950. 8. ARTHUR WALLER (LIDDELL), BARON RAVENSWORTH, cousin and h., being only s. of Cyril Arthur LIDDELL (*d.* 4 Mar. 1932), by Dorothy Lindop, da. of William BROWN of Morpeth, Northumberland, which Cyril was 2nd s. of the 5th Baron Ravensworth. He was *b.* 25 July 1924; ed. at Harrow; *m.*, 1950, Wendy, adop. da. of J. Stuart BELL of Cookham, co. Berks.

[THOMAS ARTHUR HAMISH LIDDELL, s. and h. ap., *b.* 27 Oct. 1954; ed. at Gordonstoun; *m.*, 1983, Linda, da. of H. THOMPSON of Gosworth, Newcastle-upon-Tyne.]

RAYLEIGH

page 750,
line 17, line to read as follows

IV. 1919. 4. ROBERT JOHN (STRUTT), BARON RAYLEIGH OF TERLING PLACE, 1st s. and h., *b.* 28 Aug. 1875,

line 20, after '1929' add '–34'
line 23, after 'Science;' add 'Pres. of the Royal Inst. 1945;'
line 31, delete 'Having *suc.*'

page 751,
lines 1–2, delete from 'to the' to 'work.]' and replace by 'He *d.* 13 Dec. 1947. His widow *d.* 1980.'

V. 1947. 5. JOHN ARTHUR (STRUTT), BARON RAYLEIGH OF TERLING PLACE, 1st s. and h., *b.* 12 Apr. 1908; ed. at Eton and Cambridge (Trin. Coll.); *m.*, 1 Dec. 1934, Ursula Mary, da. of Lieut. Col. Richard Hugh Royds BROCKLEBANK. She *d.* 1982. He *d. s.p.* 21 Apr. 1988.

VI. 1988. 6. JOHN GERALD (STRUTT), BARON RAYLEIGH OF TERLING PLACE, nephew and h., being only s. of Charles Richard STRUTT (*d.* 11 Dec. 1981), by Jean Elizabeth, da. of John Colin Campbell (DAVIDSON), 1st VISCOUNT DAVIDSON, which Charles was 2nd s. of the 4th Baron Rayleigh. He was *b.* 4 June 1960; ed. at Eton and R.M.C., Sandhurst and R.A.C., Cirencester; *m.*, 1991, Annabel Kate, da. of Major William Garry PATTERSON.

[JOHN FREDERICK STRUTT, s. and h. ap., *b.* 29 Mar. 1993.]

REAY

page 759,

XII. 1921. 12. ERIC (MACKAY), LORD REAY, &c., cousin and h., being s. and h. of BARON AENEAS MACKAY D'OPHEMERT (*d.* 13 Nov. 1909), by BARONESS ELIZABETH WILLEMINA VAN LYNDEN (who *d.* 29 Apr. 1907), which Aeneas was s. and h. of John Francis Hendrik Jacob Ernestus MACKAY, br. of Aeneas, 10th LORD MACKAY abovenamed. He was *b.* 2 Apr. 1870. He never established his claim to the Scottish title. He *m.*, 7 Nov. 1901, BARONESS MARIA JOHANNA BERTHA CHRISTINA, da. of BARON ALEXANDER VAN DEDEM. He *d.* 1 Nov. 1921. His widow *d.* 1 Apr. 1932.

XIII. 1921. 13. AENEAS ALEXANDER (MACKAY), LORD REAY, &c., 1st s. and h., *b.* 25 Dec. 1905; ed. at Utrecht Univ; naturalised a British subject, 1938; *m.*, 14 Apr. 1936, Charlotte Mary, da. of William YOUNGER of Ravenswood, Melrose, co. Roxburgh. He *d.* 10 Mar. 1963. His widow was still living 1995.

XIV. 1963. 14. HUGH WILLIAM (MACKAY), LORD REAY, only s. and h., *b.* 14 July 1937; ed. at Eton and Oxford (Ch. Ch.); *m.* 1stly, 14 Sep. 1964, Annabel Thérèse, da. of Simon Christopher Joseph (FRASER), 17th BARON LOVAT. This marriage was diss. by divorce 1978 and he *m.* 2ndly, 1980, Victoria Isabella, da. of Victor Alexander George Anthony (WARRENDER), 1st BARON BRUNTISFIELD.

[AENEAS SIMON MACKAY, MASTER OF REAY, s. and h. ap., *b.* 20 Mar. 1965; ed. at Westminster and Brown Univ., U.S.A.]

note ([b]), delete all detail

REDESDALE

page 762,
note ([a]), line 6, after '-Mitford' add 'See vol. xiii, p. 21.'

RENDLESHAM

page 768,
line 20, line to read as follows

VI. 1911. 6. FREDERICK ARCHIBALD CHARLES (THELLUSSON), BARON RENDLESHAM, 1st s. and h., *b.* 8 June 1868;

lines 31–2, delete from 'Having' to 'work.(b)]' and replace by 'His widow *d.* 5 Aug. 1959.'

VII. 1938. 7. PERCY EDWARD (THELLUSSON), BARON RENDLESHAM, br. and h., *b.* 30 Oct. 1874 [for further detail see note (b)]. She *d.* 6 Nov. 1933. He *d. s.p.* 11 Dec. 1943.

VIII. 1943. 8. CHARLES ANTHONY HUGH (THELLUSSON), BARON RENDLESHAM [I. 1806], nephew and h., being 1st s. and h. of Hugh Edmund THELLUSSON (*d.* 10 July 1926), 3rd s. of the 5th Baron, by Gwynnydd Colleton, 5th da. of Brig. Gen. Sir Robert Augustus William COLLETON, Bart. He was *b.* 15 Mar. 1915; ed. at Eton; *m.* 1stly, 27 Apr. 1940, Margaret Elizabeth, da. of Lieut. Col. Robin Cowper ROME of Woolpit, Bury St. Edmunds, Suffolk. This marriage was diss. by divorce 1947 and he *m.* 2ndly, 3 Nov. 1947, Claire, da. of Lieut. Col. Douglas Howard Gwyn MCCRIRICK of Wiveliscombe, Somerset. She *d.* 1987.

[CHARLES WILLIAM BROOKE THELLUSSON, s. and h. ap., *b.* 10 Jan. 1954; ed. at Eton; *m.*, 1983, Susan, da. of E.R. FIELDING of Monte Carlo.]

REVELSTOKE

page 770,
after line 20 add as follows

III. 1929. 3. CECIL (BARING), BARON REVELSTOKE OF MEMBLAND, br. and h., *b.* 12 Sep. 1864 [for further detail see note (g)].

IV. 1934. 4. RUPERT (BARING), BARON REVELSTOKE OF MEMBLAND, s. and h., *b.* 8 Feb. 1911; ed. at Eton; 2nd Lieut. Roy. Armoured Corps; served in WW2 as officer in charge of B.R.C. Prisoners of War Food Supplies. He *m.*, 2 Mar. 1934, at Easton Neston, Towcester, co. Northants., Florence, 2nd. da. of THOMAS (FERMOR-HESKETH), 1st BARON HESKETH. They were divorced in 1944. She *d.* 1971. He *d.* 18 July 1994.

V. 1994. 5. JOHN (BARING), BARON REVELSTOKE OF MEMBLAND, 1st s. and h., *b.* 2 Dec. 1934; ed. at Eton.

note (g), lines 5–8 (page 771), delete from 'His' to 'Hesketh'

RICHMOND

page 793,
line 7, after 'Margaret' add 'of Scotland'

page 817,
note ([a]), lines 13–14, for 'Count of Moravia' read 'Earl of Moray'

page 824,
line 2, after 'WALES, ' add 'sister and h. of John 3rd EARL OF KENT, '

page 827,
note ([g]), lines 1–2, delete from 'The' to 'accordingly.'

page 835,
line 3, for 'June' read '31 May'
line 4, for 'Anne, da. of Sir Thomas CHEEKE' read 'Elizabeth, only da. of Sir Justinian Lewin, (*d.* 1620) of Otterden Place, Kent([ba])'
note ([ba]) T.E. Watson, *History and Pedigree of the Family of Lewin*, 1919, p. 7; Gyles Isham, (ed.), *The Correspondence of Bishop Brian Duppa and Sir Justinian Isham*, 1650–60, Northants Rec. Soc., vol. 47, 1955, p. 169, note 2.

page 836,
note ([b]), line 14, after '473).' add 'See also *N&Q*, vol. 193, p. 284.'

page 838,
line 1, for 'James' read 'Thomas'

page 844,
line 17, for 'Waterloo silver medal with eight clasps, 1816' read 'Peninsular medal with eight clasps, and in 1816, the Waterloo medal'

page 847,
line 3, line to read as follows

DUKEDOM [S.]
XII.
DUKEDOM [U.K.]
II.
} 1903

7 and 2. CHARLES HENRY (GORDON-LENNOX), DUKE OF RICHMOND &c., also DUKE OF LENNOX &c., [S.], and DUKE OF GORDON, [U.K.], also DUKE OF AUBIGNY in France, 1st s. and h., *b.* 27 Dec. 1845 in Portland Place afsd.; styled EARL OF MARCH 1860–1903;'

line 11, after 'George V,' add 'carried the sceptre with the dove at the Coronation of George V, 22 June 1911,'
lines 22–3, delete from 'Having' to 'work.([b])]'

DUKEDOM [S.]
XIII.
DUKEDOM [U.K.]
III.
} 1928

8 and 3. CHARLES HENRY (GORDON-LENNOX), DUKE OF RICHMOND &c., 1st s. and h. by 1st wife, *b.* 30 Dec. 1870. [For futher detail see note ([b])] His widow *d.* 1971.

DUKEDOM [S.] XIV. DUKEDOM [U.K.] IV.	1935	9 and 4. FREDERICK CHARLES (GORDON-LENNOX), DUKE OF RICHMOND &c., 3rd but 1st surv.([b]) s. and h., *b.* 5 Feb. 1904; ed. Eton 1917–20; matric. at Oxford (Ch. Ch.); Lieut. 98th (Surrey and Sussex Yeo.) Brigade R.F.A., 1925; 22nd (London) Armoured Car Co. 1926–8; served in

WW2 as Flt Lieut. R.A.F. Carried the sceptre with the dove at the Coronation of George VI, 12 May 1937, and of Elizabeth II, 2 June 1953. He *m.*, 15 Dec. 1927, at Holy Trinity, Sloane Str., Elizabeth Grace, yst. da. of the Rev. Thomas William HUDSON, Vicar of Wendover, Bucks. He *d.* 2 Nov. 1989. His widow *d.* 1992.

DUKEDOM [S.] XV. DUKEDOM [U.K.] V.	1989	10 and 5. CHARLES HENRY (LENNOX-GORDON), DUKE OF RICHMOND &c., 1st s. and h., *b.* 19 Sep. 1929; ed. at Eton and William Temple Coll., Rugby; *m.*, 26 May 1951, Susan Monica, d. of Col. Cecil Everard GRENVILLE-GREY of Blewbury, co. Berks.

[CHARLES HENRY LENNOX-GORDON, *styled* EARL OF MARCH AND KINRARA, was *b.* 8 Jan. 1955; ed. at Eton; *m.* 1stly, 1976, Sally da. of Maurice CLAYTON. This marriage was diss. by divorce 1989 and he *m.* 2ndly, 1991, Janet Elizabeth, da. of William (WALDORF), 3rd VISCOUNT ASTOR.]

note ([b]), lines 11–16, delete from 'He' to '1929'

APPENDIXES

APPENDIX F

page 50,
line 10, for 'more' read 'almost certain'

page 62,
line 4, for '20 Dec.' read '30 or 31 Dec.'
note ([e]), line 11, (on p. 63), after 'Chamberlain' add 'See also Sutton and Hammond, *Coronation of Richard III*, 1983, pp. 246–7, 251–2.'

page 63,
note ([a]), line 2, after 'Latimer' add 'For a discussion of the question of who was actually the eldest sister, see G.H. White, *Geneal. Mag.*, vol. 12, 1957, pp. 293–5, 347.'

page 74,
Table 2, line 4, for 'Ursula *d. s.p.*' read 'Ursula *d. s.p.s.*'

page 75,
note ([a]), line 5, for 'Charles' read 'Edward'

APPENDIX H

page 100,
line 15, after 'FitzMaurice' add '1st Baron of Offaly'

APPENDIX J

page 113,
line 18, for 'Ellis' read 'Ingram'

page 120,
note ([a]), line 1, for 'Henry' read 'Theinard'

APPENDIX K

page 122,
line 10, for '13 May' read '10 May'

APPENDIX L

page 129,
note ([d]), line 2, after '679–80.' add 'See also Geoffrey Ellis, *Earldoms in Fee*, 1963, pp. 181–95, in particular pp. 194–5.'

VOLUME 11

RIDLEY

page 1,
line 33, line to read as follows

II. 1904. 2. MATTHEW WHITE (RIDLEY), VISCOUNT RIDLEY, &c., 1st s. and h., *b.* 6 Dec. 1874;

page 2,
lines 7–8, delete from 'Having' to 'work.]' and replace by 'His widow *d.* 2 Dec. 1947.'

III. 1916. 3. MATTHEW WHITE (RIDLEY), VISCOUNT RIDLEY and BARON WENSLEYDALE OF BLAGDON AND BLYTH, 1st s. and h., *b.* 16 Dec. 1902; ed. at Eton and Oxford (Balliol Coll.). He *m.*, 13 Oct. 1924, Ursula, 2nd da. of Sir Edward LUTYENS, R.A., by Emily, da. of Edward Robert (LYTTON-BULWER), 1st EARL OF LYTTON. He *d.* 25 Feb. 1964. His widow *d.* 28 Dec. 1967.

IV. 1964. 4. MATTHEW WHITE (RIDLEY), VISCOUNT RIDLEY, &c., 1st s. and h., *b.* 29 July 1925; ed. at Eton and Oxford (Balliol Coll.); *m.*, 3 Jan. 1953, Lady Anne Katherine Gabrielle, da. of Lawrence Roger (LUMLEY), 11th EARL OF SCARBROUGH.

[MATTHEW WHITE, s. and h., ap., *b.* 7 Feb. 1958; *m.*, 1989, Anya Christine, da. of Dr Robert HURLBERT of Houston, Texas.]

note ([a]), delete all detail

RIPON

page 5,
line 18, line to read as follows

MARQUESSATE. II. EARLDOM. III. } 1909 2 and 3. FREDERICK OLIVER (ROBINSON), MARQUESS and EARL OF RIPON, EARL DE GREY, VISCOUNT GODERICH and BARON GRANTHAM, only s. and h., *b.* 29 Jan. 1852,

page 6,
line 4, delete ']'

RITHER

page 8,
line 9, after 'Lucy,' add 'the widow of Henry of Aldithley' [see vol. i, p. 338, *sub* AUDLEY] and after 's. of' add 'Sir'
line 10, for '1st LORD ROS of Helmsley' read 'DE ROS'

page 10,
line 14, after 'Umfreville' add '[5th and 6th LORDS UMFREVILLE]'
line 19, after 'Gascoigne' add ', of Gawthorpe'

RIVERS

page 16,
line 18, after 'Isabel' add 'GODARD'
note (k), line 3, after '400/22)' add 'Isabel Godard (probably of Swanbourne, co. Bucks.) has been identified on heraldic evidence, see Charles Hansen and Neil Thompson, *Coat of Arms*, N.S., vol. ix, 1992, pp. 179, 184.'

page 17,
note (g), line 2, delete from 'presumably' to 'marriage' and replace by 'a property leased in 1428 for 50 years by Richard and his wife Joan from Archbishop Chichele (*Hist. MSS. Comm.*, 9th Ann. Rpt., p. 113.' [*Ex inform.* Charles M. Hansen, to whom I am indebted for the subsequent corrections to the Rivers entries.]

page 19,
lines 3–4, delete from '__,' to Wellington' and replace by 'Joan, da. of Thomas BITTELSGATE of Knighteston, co. Devon, by his wife Joan, da. of Sir John Beauchamp of Lillesdon'
note (d), delete all detail and replace by '*Arch. Cant.*, vol. 64, pp. 120–4, reproducing their memorial brass from the Church Notes of Sir Edward Dering (*circa* 1630) and an extract from a petition of 1475 by Anthony, Earl Rivers, naming Joan's father as Thomas Bittlesgate (see also *Coat of Arms*, N.S., vol. 9, 1992, p. 182).'

page 20,
note (d), lines 8–10, delete all detail and replace by 'The reason for the choice of the title of Rivers is undoubtedly due to a claimed descent from the Rivers, Earls of Devon, as is shown from the arms used by the Earls. See A.R. Wagner, *N&Q*, vol. 194, pp. 512–13; Charles M. Hanson and Neil Thompson, *Coat of Arms*, N.S., vol. 9, 1992, pp. 179–87.'

page 25,
line 18, after 'RIVERS' add '(ga)'
note (ga) It has been suggested that Sir Thomas Darcy may have wished to receive the title of Rivers because of a descent of his heir Sir Thomas Savage, from the Widevills, the previous holders of the title. See Montague-Smith, *N&Q*, vol. 199, pp. 198–9.

RIVERS OF SUDELEY

page 30,
note (f), line 4, after '412–15)' add 'This letter was written during the Rockingham administration' [*ex inform.* Sir Lewis Namier]

ROBERTS

page 39,
line 9, after 'M.I.' add 'On his death the Barony of Roberts of Kandahar and the Baronetcy became *extinct*, his other titles were inherited under the *spec. rem.* by his da.'

after line 26 add as follows

II. 1913. 2. AILEEN MARY ROBERTS, 3rd but 1st surv. da., *suo jure* COUNTESS ROBERTS, &c., under the *spec. rem.*, *b.* 20 Sep. 1870; D.B.E. 1918. She *d.* unm. 9 Oct. 1944.

III. 1944. 3. ADA EDWINA STEWART ROBERTS, 4th and only surv. sister, COUNTESS ROBERTS, and VISCOUNT ST PIERRE under the *spec. rem.*, *b.* 28 Mar. 1875; Acting Cmdt. Ascot Mil. Hosp. during WW1; O.B.E. 1918. She *m.*, 26 Feb. 1913, Brig. Gen. Henry Frederick Elliott LEWIN, C.B., C.M.G., R.A. He *d.* 1 Dec. 1946. She *d. s.p.s.* 21 Feb. 1955, when all her titles became *extinct.*

[FREDERICK ROBERTS ALEXANDER LEWIN, only s. and h. ap., *b.* 18 Jan. 1915; Lieut. Irish Guards, served in WW2, *k.* in action in Norway, and *d. v.m.* and unm., May 1940.]

ROCHE

page 44,
line 3, for '_____' read 'poss. Maud da. of Roger, 1st LORD GREY OF RUTHYN by Elizabeth, da. of John 1st LORD HASTINGES' [R.I. Jack, 'The Greys of Ruthyn,' PhD thesis, London, 1961, p. 430.]
line 22, for 'sisters' read 'das.'

ROCHFORD

page 51,
line 25, for '*ante* 13 July 1530' read '7 Feb. 1533'
note (a), after 'p. 18' add '(see correction above)'

page 54,
line 13, for '1740' read '1742'
line 15, for 'Queen Caroline when' read 'the'
line 16, after 'Wales' add '(g)'
note (g) Walpole, *Letters*, ed. Toynbee, vol. 1, p. 227.
line 16, for 'aged 50' read 'she was *b.* 1715(h)
note (h) See pedigree of Young of Durnford, in R.C. Hoare, *Wiltshire*, vol. 2, part 2, p. 125.

RODEN

page 66,
lines 15–16, delete from 'He' to 'work.(b)'

VII. 1910. 7. ROBERT JULIAN ORDE (JOCELYN), EARL OF RODEN, &c., br. and h., *b.* 19 Apr. 1845 [for further detail see note (b)].

VIII. 1915. 8. ROBERT SOAME (JOCELYN), EARL OF RODEN, &c., 1st s. and h., *b.* 8 Sep. 1883; Capt. North Irish Horse; served in WW1; Rep. Peer [I.], 1919–56. He *m.*, 19 July 1905, Elinor Jessie, 2nd da. of Joseph Charlton PARR, Grappenhall Hayes, Cheshire, and Staunton Park, Staunton-on-Arrow, co. Hereford. He *d.* 30 Oct. 1956. His widow *d.* 11 Feb. 1962.

IX. 1956. 9. ROBERT WILLIAM (JOCELYN), EARL OF RODEN, &c., s. and h., *b.* 4 Dec. 1909; *m.*, 21 Oct. 1937, Clodagh Rose, da. of Edward Robert KENNEDY of Straffan, co. Kildare. She *d.* 1989. He *d.* 18 Oct. 1993.

X. 1993. 10. ROBERT JOHN (JOCELYN), EARL OF RODEN, &c., s. and h., *b.* 25 Aug. 1938; ed. at Stowe; *m.* 1stly, 1970, Sara Cecilia, da. of Brig. Andrew DUNLOP of Zimbabwe. They were divorced in 1982 and he *m.* 2ndly, 1989, Ann Margareta Maria, da. of Dr. Gunnar HENNING of Göteborg, Sweden.

[SHANE ROBERT HENNING JOCELYN, *styled* VISCOUNT JOCELYN, *b.* 9 Dec. 1989.]

note ([b]), lines 5–9, delete all detail

RODNEY

page 67,
line 2, for '*bap.*' read '*b.*'
line 3, for '1730' read '1730–2'
line 5, for '14 Oct.' read '17 Oct.'
line 15, after '1778' add '; app. Vice-Admiral of G.B., 1781'
note ([a]), lines 1–3, delete from '*Dict.*' to '"b").'

page 68,
line 10, for '24 May' read '23 May'

page 70,
line 18, line to read as follows

VIII. 1909. 8. GEORGE BRIDGES HARLEY GUEST (RODNEY), BARON RODNEY, &c., 1st s. and h. by 1st wife, *b.* 2 Nov. 1891; ed. at Eton and Oxford (Oriel Coll.);

lines 21–2, delete from '([a])' to 'work.]' and replace by 'She *d.* 29 July 1968. He *d.* 18 Dec. 1973.'

IX. 1973. 9. JOHN FRANCIS (RODNEY), BARON RODNEY, 2nd surv. s. and h., *b.* 28 June 1920; ed. at Stowe and McGill Univ., Canada; *m.* 3 Nov. 1951, Thérèse Marie Ghislaine, yr. da. of Chevalier Robert Egide Marie Ghislain PANGEAERT D'OPDORP of Chateau Rullingen, Looz, Belgium. He *d.* 13 Oct. 1992. His widow was still living in 1995.

X. 1992. 10. GEORGE BRYDGES (RODNEY), BARON RODNEY, s. and h., was *b.* 3 Jan. 1953; ed. at Eton.

note ([a]), for 'Their 1st s. and h.' read 'His elder br.'

ROLLO

page 80,
line 26, line to read as follows

XI. 1916. 11. WILLIAM CHARLES WORDSWORTH (ROLLO), LORD ROLLO OF DUNCRUB [S.] and BARON DUNNING [U.K.], s. and h., *b.* 8 Jan. 1860; MASTER OF ROLLO till 1916.

line 31, delete from 'Having' to 'work.]' and replace by 'He *d. s.p.* 3 Mar. 1946.'

XII. 1946. 12. JOHN ERIC HENRY (ROLLO), LORD ROLLO OF DUNCRUB, &c., nephew and h., being s. and h. of Eric Norman ROLLO (*d.* 12 Apr. 1930), by Constance Maud, yst. da. of Henry Booth HOHLER of Fawkham Manor, Kent, which Eric Norman was 2nd s. of the 10th Lord Rollo. He was *b.* 8 Jan. 1889; ed. at Eton; *m.* 1stly, 15 Feb. 1915, Helen Maude, da. of Frederick CHETWYND-STAPYLTON of Englefield Green, Surrey. She *d.* 15 Aug. 1928. He *m.* 2ndly, 24 Mar. 1930, Phyllis Carina, da. of Bernard SANDERSON. They were divorced in 1936 and he *m.* 3rdly, 5 June 1937, Lily Marie, da. of Max SEIFLOW of Hatch End, Middlesex, widow of (__) COCKSHUT. He *d.* 3 Sep. 1947. His widow *m.* 3rdly, 17 May 1949, Richard Andrew Percival LEACH, who *d.* 1981. She *d.* 1989.

XIII. 1947. 13. ERIC JOHN STAPYLTON (ROLLO), LORD ROLLO OF DUNCRUB, &c., 1st s. and h. by 1st wife, *b.* 3 Dec. 1915; ed. at Eton; *m.*, 17 Sep. 1938, Suzanne, 2nd da. of William Howard Brinton HATTON of Clent, co. Worcs.

[DAVID ERIC HOWARD ROLLO, MASTER OF ROLLO, 1st s. and h. ap., *b.* 31 Mar. 1943; ed. at Eton; *m.*, 1971, Felicity Anne Christian, da. of Lieut. Cmdr. John Bruce LAMB, R.N., of Tywardreath, Cornwall.]

ROMILLY

page 82,
line 26, line to read as follows

IV. 1905 to 1983. 4. WILLIAM GASPARD GUY (ROMILLY), BARON ROMILLY, only s. and h., *b.* 8 Mar. 1899;

lines 31–2, delete from 'Having' to 'work.]' and replace by 'This marriage was diss. by divorce 1944 and he *m.* 2ndly, 19 Dec. 1944, Dora Sybil, da. of Reginald MORRIS of Chelsea. She *d.* 24 Apr. 1960 and he *m.* 3rdly, 18 July 1966, Marion Elizabeth Jessie, 1st da. of Charles M. CLOVER of Blewbury, Berks., formerly wife of Geoffrey ADAMS and widow of Capt. Lionel CECIL. He *d. s.p.* 29 June 1983 when the Barony of Romilly of Barry [1866] became *extinct*. His widow *m.* 4thly, 1986, as his 2nd wife, Col. Edward John Sutton WARD. She was still living 1995.'

ROMNEY

page 88,
line 7, line to read as follows

EARLDOM. VI. BARONY. VII. } 1905 5 and 7. CHARLES (MARSHAM), EARL OF ROMNEY, &c., 1st s. and h., *b.* 25 Oct. 1864,

line 9, after 'Gardens' add '*styled* VISCOUNT MARSHAM till 1905;'
line 14, delete '([a])'
lines 14–15, delete from 'Having' to 'work.]'

EARLDOM. VII. BARONY. VIII. } 1933 — 6 and 8. CHARLES (MARSHAM), EARL OF ROMNEY, &c., s. and h., *b.* 8 July 1892 [for further detail see note ([a])]. He *d. s.p.* 6 Sep. 1975. His widow *d.* 1976.

EARLDOM. VIII. BARONY. IX. } 1975 — 7 and 9. MICHAEL HENRY (MARSHAM), EARL OF ROMNEY, , &c., cousin and h., being s. and h. of Lieut. Col. Reginald Hastings MARSHAM (*d.* 8 Nov. 1922), by Dora Hermione, 4th da. of Charles NORTH of Rougham, Norfolk, which Reginald Henry was 2nd s. of 4th Earl of Romney. He was *b.* 22 Nov. 1910; ed. at Sherborne; *m.*, 28 June 1939, Frances Aileen, da. of Lieut. Col. James Russell LANDALE.

ROS

page 100,
line 6, after 'LORD AUDLEY' add '(of Stratton)'

page 101,
line 4, after 'DESMOND' add '[I.]'

page 102,
line 1, after 'Mary' add '*de jure* (according to modern doctrine) BARONESS ORREBY and BARONESS MARE'
line 3, after 'Joan' add '*de jure* (acording to modern doctrine) BARONESS ORREBY and BARONESS MARE'
line 8, after 'York' add ', when any Baronies of ORREBY and MARE which may be supposed to have been *cr.* by writs of summons to members of these families, became *extinct*.'

page 103,
line 4, after 'ARUNDEL' add '[1st LORD ARUNDEL]'
note ([e]), line 6, delete 's. of John'

page 104,
line 2, for 'Margery' read 'Margaret'
note ([e]), lines 3–5, delete from 'Possibly' to '307).'

page 106,
note ([f]), line 1, for 'p. 32' read 'p. 33'

page 115,
line 25, line to read as follows

XXIV. 1907. 24. MARY FRANCES, BARONESS DE ROS, da. and h., being only child by 1st wife,

page 117,
between lines 10 and 11 add as follows

XXV. 1943. 25. UNA MARY ROSS, born DAWSON, eldest da. of the afsd. Mary Frances, *suo jure* BARONESS DE ROS, the title being called out of *abeyance* in her favour as abovesaid, *b.* 5 Oct. 1879; *m.*, 30 June 1904, Arthur John ROSS of Strangford, co. Down. He *d.* Aug. 1917, being *k.* in action. She *d.* 9 Oct. 1956 when the Barony again fell into *abeyance* between her two grand daughters until called out of *abeyance* as below.

[PETER ROSS, 1st s. and h. ap., *b.* 8 Aug. 1906; *m.*, 10 Sep. 1929, Angela Ierne Evelyn, 1st da. of Herbert (DIXON), 1st BARON GLENTORAN. He *d. v.m. s.p.m.* Oct. 1940, being *k.* in action. His widow *m.* 2ndly, 12 Nov. 1943, Lieut. Col. Trevor Langdale HORN, M.C. (*d.* 1966). His widow was living 1995.]

XXVI. 1956. 26. GEORGIANA ANGELA MAXWELL, born ROSS, eldest da. of the aforesaid Peter ROSS, *suo jure* BARONESS DE ROS, in whose favour the *abeyance* was terminated by letters patent in Aug. 1958. She was *b.* 2 May 1933; *m.*, 24 July 1954, Cmdr. John David MAXWELL, R.N. She *d.* 21 Apr. 1983. He *m.* 2ndly, 1984, Patricia Carolyn, da. of (__) ASH, widow of (__) COVENEY.

XXVII. 1983. 27. PETER TREVOR (MAXWELL), LORD DE ROS [1299], s. and h., *b.* 23 Dec. 1958; ed. at Headfort Sch, Kells, co. Meath, Stowe and Down High Sch., Downpatrick, co. Down; *m.*, 1987, Angela Siän, da. of Peter Campbell ROSS.

[FINBAR JAMES ROSS, s. and h. ap., *b.* 14 Nov. 1988.]

ROS OF WARK

page 121,
note (c), line 5, after 'p. 214).' add 'See vol. xii, part 1, pp. 740–1, *sub* THWENG.'

ROSEBERY

page 138,
line 10, line to read as follows

EARLDOM [S.] VI.
BARONY [U.K.] III. } 1929 6 and 3. ALBERT EDWARD HARRY MEYER ARCHIBALD (PRIMROSE), EARL OF ROSEBERY, &c., also EARL OF MIDLOTHIAN, VISCOUNT MENTMORE and BARON EPSOM [U.K. 1911], 1st s. and h., *b.* 8 Jan. 1882.

line 12, after 'James's;' add '*styled* LORD DALMENY till 1929;'
lines 27–8, delete from 'Having' to 'work.(d)]' and replace by 'He *d.* 31 May 1974. His widow *d.* 1987.'

EARLDOM [S.] VII.
BARONY [U.K.] IV. } 1974 7 and 4. NEIL ARCHIBALD (PRIMROSE), EARL OF ROSEBERY, &c., 2nd but only surv. s., being only s. by 2nd wife,(d) *b.* 11 Feb. 1929; ed. at Stowe and Oxford (New Coll.); *m.*, 22 Jan. 1955, Alison Mary Deirdre, 1st da. of Ronald William REID of Colchester, Essex.

[HARRY RONALD NEIL PRIMROSE, *styled* LORD DALMENY, s. and h. ap., *b.* 20 Nov. 1967; *m.*, 1994, Caroline, 1st da. of Ronald DAGLISH.]

note ([d]), lines 1–2 (on page 139), delete from 'By' to '1929'

ROSSE

page 171,
line 8, line to read as follows

VII. 1908. 5. WILLIAM EDWARD (PARSONS), EARL OF ROSSE, &c., 1st s. and h., *b.* 14 June 1873, in London; *styled* LORD OXMANTOWN till 1908;

line 20, delete '([d])'
lines 21–2, delete from 'Having' to 'work.'
line 24, for ']' read 'His widow *d.* 1992.'

VIII. 1918. 6. LAWRENCE MICHAEL HARVEY (PARSONS), EARL OF ROSSE, &c., 1st s. and h., *b.* 28 Sep. 1906; ed., Eton and Oxford (Ch. Ch.); Lieut. and temp. Capt. Irish Guards. He *m.*, 19 Sep. 1935, Mrs Anne ARMSTRONG-JONES, only da. of Lieut.-Col. Leonard Charles Rudolph MESSEL, of Nymans, Staplefield, Sussex. He *d.* 1 July 1979. His widow *d.* 1992.

IX. 1979. 7. WILLIAM BRENDAN (PARSONS), EARL OF ROSSE, &c., 1st s. and h., *b.* 21 Oct. 1936; ed. at Eton, Aiglon Coll., Switzerland, Grenoble Univ. and Oxford (Ch. Ch.); *m.*, 15 Oct. 1966, Alison Margaret, da. of Major John Davey COOKE-HURLE, of Barnard Castle, co. Durham.

[LAURENCE PATRICK PARSONS, *styled* LORD OXMANTOWN, 1st s. and h. ap., *b.* 31 Mar. 1969; ed. at Aiglon Coll., Switzerland.]

note ([d]), delete all detail

ROSSLYN

page 178,
line 11, after '([c])' add 'She *d.* 17 Feb. 1945.'

page 179,
line 2, after '([a])' add 'His widow *d.* 1975.'
line 11, after '([c])' add 'She *d.* 13 Oct. 1969.'

VI. 1939. 6. ANTHONY HUGH FRANCIS HARRY (ST. CLAIR-ERSKINE), EARL OF ROSSLYN, &c., eldest grandson and h., being 1st s. and h. of Francis Edward and Margaret abovenamed, *b.* 18 May 1917; ed. Eton and Oxford (Magdalen Coll.); *m.* 1stly, 3 Aug. 1955, Athenaís, da. of Louis Victor (DE MORTEMART), DUC DE VIVONNE. He *d.* 22 Nov. 1977. His widow was living 1995.

VII. 1977. 7. PETER (ST. CLAIR-ERSKINE), EARL OF ROSSLYN, &c., s. and h., *b.* 31 Mar. 1958; ed. at Eton and Bristol Univ.; *m.*, 1982, Helen, da. of C.R. WATTERS of Christ's Hosp., Sussex.

[JAMIE WILLIAM ST. CLAIR-ERSKINE, *styled* LORD LOUGHBOROUGH, s. and h. ap., *b.* 28 May 1986.]

note (c), lines 2–4, delete from 'His' to '1939'

ROSSMORE

page 183,
line 16, after '(c)' add 'His widow *d.* 8 Feb. 1953.'
line 17, line to read as follows

BARONY [I.] VI. BARONY [U.K.] V. } 1921 6 and 5. WILLIAM (WESTENRA), BARON ROSSMORE OF MONAGHAN, &c., 1st s. and h., *b.* 12 July 1892; ed. at Wellington;

lines 21–2, delete from 'Having' to 'work.]' and replace by 'He *d.* 17 Oct. 1958. His widow *d.* 1981.'

BARONY [I.] VII. BARONY [U.K.] VI. } 1958 7 and 6. WILLIAM WARNER (WESTENRA), BARON ROSSMORE OF MONAGHAN, &c., s. and h., *b.* 14 Feb. 1931; ed. at Eton and Cambridge (Trin. Coll.); *m.*, 1982, Valerie Marion, da. of Brian TOBIN of Birr, co. Offaly.

[BENEDICT WILLIAM WESTENRA, s. and h. ap., *b.* 6 Mar. 1983.]

ROTHES

page 207,
line 26, after 'Preston' add ', he *d.* 23 Dec. 1963. She *d.* 12 Sep. 1956.'
line 27, line to read as follows

XX. 1927. 20. MALCOLM GEORGE DYER-EDWARDES (LESLIE), EARL OF ROTHES, &c., 1st s. and h., *b.* 8 Feb. 1902;

lines 31–2, delete from 'Having' to 'work.]' and replace by 'He *d.* 7 May 1975. His widow *d.* 1994.'

XXI. 1975. 21. IAN LIONEL MALCOLM (LESLIE), EARL OF ROTHES, &c., only s. and h., *b.* 10 May 1932; ed. at Eton; *m.*, 8 July 1955, Marigold, da. of Sir David Martyn EVANS-BEVAN, Bart.

[JAMES MALCOLM DAVID LESLIE, *styled* LORD LESLIE, s. and h. ap., *b.* 4 June 1958.]

ROTHESAY

page 208,
lines 13–14, delete from 'by Jean' to 'Moray' and replace by 'By Joan, only child and h. of Maurice (MORAY), EARL OF STRATHEARN [S.]' [See vol. iv, p. 433, *sub* DOUGLAS; *Scots Peerage*, vol. iii, p. 162.]

ROTHSCHILD

page 212,
line 17, line to read as follows

II. 1915. 2. LIONEL WALTER (ROTHSCHILD), BARON ROTHSCHILD, a Baron of the Austrian Empire and a Baronet., 1st s. and h., *b.* 8 Feb. 1868;

page 213,
lines 5–6, delete from 'Having' to 'work.]'

III. 1937. 3. NATHANIEL MAYER VICTOR (ROTHSCHILD), BARON ROTHSCHILD, &c., cousin and h., being s. and h. of Nathaniel Charles ROTHSCHILD, 2nd s. of the 1st Baron, by Rozalka, 3rd da. of Capt. Alfred VON WERTHEIMSTEIN, of Nagyvarad, Hungary. He was *b.* 31 Oct. 1910; ed. at Harrow and Cambridge (Trin. Coll.). He *m.* 1stly, 28 Dec. 1933, Barbara Judith, only da. of St. John HUTCHINSON, K.C., by Mary, only da. of Sir Hugh BARNES, K.C.S.I. They were divorced in 1946 (she *d.* in 1989 having *m.* twice more), and he *m.* 2ndly, 14 Aug. 1946, Teresa Georgina, 2nd da. of Robert John Grote MAYOR. He *d.* 20 Mar. 1990. His widow was living 1995.

IV. 1990. 4. NATHANIEL CHARLES JACOB (ROTHSCHILD), BARON ROTHSCHILD, &c., 1st s. and h. by 1st wife, *b.* 29 Apr. 1936; ed. at Eton and Oxford (Ch. Ch.); *m.* 20 Oct. 1961, Serena Mary, da. of Sir Philip Gordon DUNN, Bart.

[NATHANIEL PHILIP VICTOR JAMES ROTHSCHILD, s. and h. ap., *b.* 12 July 1971; ed. at Oxford (Wadham Coll.).]

note ([a]), delete all detail

ROXBURGHE

page 229,
line 28, line to read as follows

DUKEDOM [S.] IX. EARLDOM [S.] XIII. } 1932 9 and 13. GEORGE VICTOR ROBERT JOHN (INNES-KER), DUKE OF ROXBURGHE, &c., only s. and h., *styled* MARQUESS OF BOWMONT till 1932, *b.* 7 Sep. 1913;

line 29, after 'at' add 'Eton and'

lines 35–6, delete from 'Having' to 'work.]' and replace by 'This marriage was diss. by divorce 1953 and he *m.* 2ndly, 5 Jan. 1954, Margaret Elisabeth, da. of Capt. Frederick Bradshaw MCCONNEL of Colmonell, Ayrshire formerly wife of Lieut. Col. James Cunningham CHURCH. He *d.* 26 Sep. 1974. His widow *m.* 3dly, 1976, Jocelyn Olaf HAMBRO. She *d.* 1983.'

DUKEDOM [S.] X. EARLDOM [S.] XIV. } 1974 10 and 14. GUY DAVID (INNES-KER), DUKE OF ROXBURGHE, &c., 1st s. and h., *b.* 18 Nov. 1954; ed. at Eton and Cambridge (Magdalene Coll.); *m.* 1stly, Lady Jane Meriel, da. of Robert George (GROSVENOR), 5th DUKE OF WESTMINSTER. They were divorced in 1990 and he *m.* 2ndly, 1992, Virginia Mary, da. of David WYNN-WILLIAMS.

[CHARLES ROBERT GEORGE INNES-KER, *styled* MARQUESS OF BOWMONT AND CESSFORD, 1st s. and h. ap., by 1st wife, was *b.* 18 Feb. 1981.]

RUSSELL

page 238,
line 17, delete '(d)'

page 239,
between lines 2 and 3 add as follows

III. 1931. 3. BERTRAND ARTHUR WILLIAM (RUSSELL), EARL RUSSELL, &c., br. and h., *b.* 18 May 1872 [for further detail see note (d) on page 238, in addition, on line 1 (page 239), after '1921' add 'She *d.* 21 Jan. 1951', on line 3, after '1935.' add 'She *d.* 1986.']. This marriage was in turn diss. by divorce in 1952 and he *m.* 4thly, 15 Dec. 1952, Edith, da. of Edward Bronson FINCH of New York. He *d.* 2 Feb. 1970. His widow *d.* 1978.

IV. 1970. 4. JOHN CONRAD (RUSSELL), EARL RUSSELL, &c., 1st s. and h. by 2nd wife, *b.* 16 Nov. 1921; ed. at Dartington Hall Sch., the Univ. of California and Harvard Univ.; *m.*, 28 Aug. 1946, Susan Doniphan, da. of Nicholas Vachel LINDSAY. They were divorced in 1955. He *d. s.p.* 16 Dec. 1987.

V. 1987. 5. CONRAD SEBASTIAN ROBERT (RUSSELL), EARL RUSSELL, &c., br. of the half-blood and h., being 2nd s. (only s. by 3rd wife), *b.* 15 Apr. 1937; ed. at Eton and Oxford (Merton Coll.); *m.*, 11 Aug. 1962, Elizabeth Franklin, 1st da. of Horace SANDERS of Harborne, Birmingham.

[NICHOLAS LYULPH RUSSELL, *styled* VISCOUNT AMBERLEY, 1st s. and h. ap., *b.* 12 Sep. 1968; ed. at William Ellis Sch., Camden.]

RUTHVEN

page 246,
line 11, after 'Riccarton' add '3rd s. of Patrick, 1st LORD HAILES [S.]'

page 251, note (e), line 4 (on page 252), after 'Thomson),' add 'This title was recognised, 1967, by the Lyon Court. See *sub* CARLISLE.'

RUTLAND

page 252,
line 16, after 'RUTLAND' add 'by 25 Sep. 1445'
note (e), line 1, before 'No' add 'BN n.a. fr. 5848 no. 389 (with thanks to Prof. Ralph A. Griffiths for this reference).'

page 274,
line 1, line to read as follows

DUKEDOM. VIII. EARLDOM. XVIII. } 1906 — 8 and 16. HENRY JOHN BRINSLEY (MANNERS), DUKE OF RUTLAND, &c., 1st s. and h.,

line 3, after 'Place' add '*styled* MARQUESS OF GRANBY 1888–1906;'
lines 16–17, delete from 'Having' to 'work.(b)'
line 19, delete ']'

DUKEDOM. IX. EARLDOM. XIX. } 1925 — 9 and 17. JOHN HENRY MONTAGU (MANNERS), DUKE OF RUTLAND, &c., 2nd(b) but 1st surv s. and h., *b.* 21 Sep. 1886; *m.*, 27 Jan. 1916; Kathleen, 3rd da. of Francis John TENNANT. He *d.* 21 Apr. 1940. His widow *d.* 1989.

DUKEDOM. X. EARLDOM. XX. } 1940 — 10 and 18. CHARLES JOHN ROBERT (MANNERS), DUKE OF RUTLAND, &c., 1st s. and h., *b.* 28 May 1919; ed. at Eton and Cambridge (Trin. Coll.); *m.* 1stly, 27 Apr. 1946, Anne Bairstow, da. of Major William Cumming BELL of Edgerton, Huddersfield. They were divorced in 1956 and he *m.* 2ndly, 15 May 1958, Frances Helen, da. of Charles SWEENEY by Margaret, DUCHESS OF ARGYLL.

[DAVID CHARLES ROBERT MANNERS, *styled* MARQUESS OF GRANBY, 1st s. and h. ap. by 2nd wife, *b.* 8 May 1959; *m.*, 1992, Emma, da. of John WATKINS of Powys.]

note (b), delete all detail and replace by 'His eld. s., Robert Charles John Manners, was *b.* 8 Aug. 1885, *styled* LORD HADDON, *d.* 28 Sep. 1894.'

page 275,
after line 8 add 'RYVERS see RIVERS'

SACKVILLE

page 281,
between lines 6 and 7 add as follows

III. 1908. 3. LIONEL EDWARD (SACKVILLE-WEST), BARON SACKVILLE OF KNOLE, nephew and h. male under the spec. rem. in the patent, being the 1st s. and h. of William Edward SACKVILLE-WEST, 6th and next br. of the 1st Baron, by Georgina, yst. da. of George DODSWELL of Kevinsfort. He was *b.* 15 May 1867; ed. at Wellington and Oxford (Ch. Ch.); *m.*, 17 June 1890 [see note (b)]. He *d. s.p.m.* 28 Jan. 1928. His widow *d.* 30 Jan. 1936.

IV. 1928. 4. CHARLES JOHN (SACKVILLE-WEST), BARON SACKVILLE OF KNOLE, br. and h., *b.* 10 Aug. 1870; ed. at Winchester and R.M.C., Sandhurst; *m.* 1stly, 5 Jan. 1897, Maud Cecilia, da. of Capt. Matthew John BELL. She *d.* 7 Dec. 1920 and he *m.* 2ndly, 30 Jan. 1924, Anne, da. of William MEREDITH of New York. She *d.* 8 Jan. 1961. He *d.* 8 May 1962.

V. 1962. 5. EDWARD CHARLES (SACKVILLE-WEST), BARON SACKVILLE OF KNOLE, s. and h., *b.* 13 Nov. 1901; ed. at Eton and Oxford (Ch. Ch.). He *d.* unm. 4 July 1965.

VI. 1965. 6. LIONEL BERTRAND (SACKVILLE-WEST), BARON SACKVILLE OF KNOLE, cousin and h. under spec rem. in the patent, being 1st s. and h. of Bertrand George SACKVILLE-WEST (*d.* 23 Aug. 1959), by Eva Adela Mabel Inigo, da. of Major Gen. Inigo Richmund JONES, which Bertrand George was 3rd s. of Lieut. Col. William Edward SACKVILLE-WEST (*d.* 30 Sep. 1905), by Georgina, da. of George DODWELL of Kevinsfort, co. Sligo, which William Edward was yst. br. of the 1st Baron Sackville. He was *b.* 30 May 1913; ed. at Winchester and Oxford (Magdalen Coll.); *m.*, 9 Oct. 1953, Jacobine Napier, da. of James Robert MENZIES-WILSON, widow of Capt. John HITCHENS. She *d.* 1971 and he *m.* 2ndly, 1974, Arlie Roebuck, da. of Charles WOODHEAD of Brisbane, Australia and widow of Major Hugh Dalzell STEWART and formerly wife of Major Gen. Sir Francis Wilfred DE GUINGAND. This marriage was in turn diss. by divorce and he *m.* 3rdly, 1983, Jean. da. of Arthur Stanley GARTON of Marlow, co. Bucks. and widow of Major Sir Edward Henry Bouhier IMBERT-TERRY, Bart.

SAINT ALBANS

page 287,
note (b), after 'p. 512)' add ', but no patent for this *cr.* appears to have passed the Great Seal'

page 294,
lines 17–19, delete from 'He was' to 'work.(c)'

XII. 1934. 12. OSBORNE DE VERE (BEAUCLERK), DUKE OF ST. ALBANS, &c., br. of the half-blood, being s. and h. by 2nd wife, *b.* 16 Oct. 1874 [for further detail see note (c)]. She *d.* 5 Aug. 1953. He *d. s.p.* 2 Mar. 1964.

XIII. 1964. 13. CHARLES FREDERICK AUBREY DE VERE (BEAUCLERK), DUKE OF ST. ALBANS, &c., 2nd cousin and h., being s. and h. of Aubrey Topham BEAUCLERK (*d.* 14 Jan. 1933), by Gwendolen Loftus, da. of Capt. Sir

Frederic HUGHES of Barstown House, co. Wexford, which Aubrey was 3rd s. of Capt. Charles Beauclerk (*d.* 2 Nov. 1861), by Laura Maria Theresa, da. and h. of Col. Edward STOPFORD of Nottingham, which Charles was 5th s. of the 8th Duke of St. Albans. He was *b.* 16 Aug. 1915; ed. at Eton and Cambridge (Magdalene Coll.); *m.* 1stly, 21 Mar. 1938, Nathalie Chatham, da. of Percival Field WALKER of Thames Ditton, Surrey. They were divorced in 1947 (she *d.* 1985) and he *m.* 2ndly, 19 Mar. 1947, Suzanne Marie Adèle, da. of Emile William FESQ of Vence, France. He *d.* 8 Oct. 1988. His widow was living 1995.

XIV. 1988. 14. MURRAY DE VERE (BEAUCLERK), DUKE OF ST. ALBANS, &c., 1st s. and h., *b.* 19 Jan. 1939; ed. at Tonbridge; *m.* 1stly, 31 Jan. 1963, Rosemary Frances, da. of Dr Francis Harold SCOONES of Greenford, Middlesex. They were divorced in 1974 and he *m.* 2ndly, 1974, Cynthia Theresa Mary, da. of Lieut. Col. William James Holdsworth HOWARD and formerly wife of Sir Anthony Robin Maurice HOOPER, Bart.

[CHARLES FRANCES TOPHAM DE VERE BEAUCLERK, *styled* EARL OF BURFORD, 1st s. and h. by 1st wife, *b.* 22 Feb. 1965; ed. at Sherborne, Oxford (Hertford Coll.) and Edinburgh Univ.]

SAINT AMAND

page 297,
note (f), line 2, after 'Simon,' add '(afterwards 1st Lord Montague),'

page 302,
line 6, for '2 Jan. 1448/9' read '22 May 1449'
note (d), line 1, before 'In' add '*Cal. Close Rolls, 1447–54*, p. 106.'

SAINT GERMANS

page 307,
note (b), line 5, for 'Finch' read 'French'
line 6, after 'St. George' add ', which they did under a settlement of the 1st Lord St. George.' [*ex inform.* Gordon St. George Mark]

page 313,
line 37, line to read as follows

EARLDOM. VI. BARONY. VII. } 1911 6 and 7. JOHN GRANVILLE CORNWALLIS (ELIOT), EARL OF SAINT GERMANS, &c., 2nd but only surv. s. and h.,

page 314,
lines 5–7, delete from '(a)' to work.'
line 9, for ']' read 'She *d.* 30 Aug. 1968.'

EARLDOM. VII. BARONY. VIII.	1922	7 and 8. GRANVILLE JOHN (ELIOT), EARL OF SAINT GERMANS [1815], and BARON ELIOT OF SAINT GERMANS [1784], cousin and h., being 1st s. of Charles George Cornwallis ELIOT (who *d.* 22 May 1901 and was 6th s. of the 3rd Earl), by Constance Rhiannon, 4th da. of Sir Josiah John

GUEST, 1st Bart. He was *b.* 22 Sep. 1867; ed. at Charterhouse. He *d.* unm. 20 Nov. 1942.

EARLDOM. VIII. BARONY. IX.	1942	8 and 9. MONTAGUE CHARLES (ELIOT), EARL OF SAINT GERMANS, &c., br. and h., *b.* 13 May 1870; ed. at Charterhouse and Oxford (Exeter Coll.); *m.*, 22 June 1910, Helen Agnes, da. of Arthur POST of New York. He *d.* 19 Sep. 1960. His widow *d.* 1 Sep. 1962.

EARLDOM. IX. BARONY. X.	1960	9 and 10. NICHOLAS RICHARD MICHAEL (ELIOT), EARL OF ST. GERMANS, &c., 1st s. and h., *b.* 26 Jan. 1914; ed. at Eton; *m.* 1stly, 25 Apr. 1939, Helen Mary, yr. da. of Lieut. Col. Charles Walter VILLIERS. They were divorced in 1947 (she *d.* 6 Dec. 1951) and he *m.* 2ndly, 27 May 1948, Margaret Eleanor,

da. of Lieut. Col. William Francis George WYNDHAM of Midhurst, Sussex and formerly wife of Hugh Wharton EARL and after that of Basil Francis EYSTON. This marriage was in turn diss. in 1959 (she *d.* 2 Aug. 1967), and he *m.* 3rdly, 15 Nov. 1965, Mary Bridget, da. of Sir Thomas Shenton Whitelegge THOMAS, G.C.M.G. and formerly wife of Lieut. Col. Jack Leslie Larry LOTINGA. He *d.* 11 Mar. 1988. His widow was still living 1995.

EARLDOM. X. BARONY. XI.	1988	10 and 11. PEREGRINE NICHOLAS (ELIOT), EARL OF ST. GERMANS, &c., only s. and h., *b.* 2 Jan. 1941; ed. at Eton; *m.* 1stly, 9 Oct. 1964, Jacquetta Jean Fredericka, 3rd da. of Miles Wedderburn (LAMPSON), 1st BARON KILLEARN. They were divorced in 1990 and he *m.* 2ndly, 1991, Elizabeth Mary, da. of (__) WILLIAMS.

[JAGO NICHOLAS ALDO ELIOT, *styled* LORD ELIOT, 1st s. and h. ap. by 1st wife, *b.* 24 Mar. 1966; ed. at Millfield.]

note (a), delete all detail

SAINT JOHN OF BASING

page 327,
lines 20–1, delete from 'presumably' to 'Poynings' and replace by 'yr. br. of Michael (DE POYNINGS), 1st LORD POYNINGS, s. of Sir Thomas DE POYNINGS.(ma)'
(ma) See J.H. Round, "The Lords Poyning and St. John", *Sussex Arch. Colls.*, vol. lxii, pp. 1–20.'

page 328,
line 6, after 'widow' add 'She *m.* a 3rd husband.' [See J.H. Round ref., above.]

page 330,
line 4, for '26 Dec. 1426' read '*d.v.p.* before 10 Feb. 1427/8' [see vol. xii, part 2, p. 757, note (b)]

page 331,
line 4, after '1887' add 'Their descendants were traced in detail in the claim in 1914 of Francis William Forester to the Barony of St. John of Basing. The Committee for Privileges came to the conclusion that there was no evidence of any sitting in a Parliament following the issuing of the various writs. (St. John Peerage Claim, 1915, HL 472.)'

ST. JOHN

page 331,
note ([c]), line 7, after '14 Oct.' add '(actually 14 Nov., see Frank T. Smallwood, "Henry St. John the Elder and the Estcourt Murder", *Report of the Friends of Lydiard Tregoze*, no. 5, 1972, pp. 27, 28)'

page 333,
line 3, for 'about 1695' read '3 May 1702' [BL, Egerton MS. 2378, f. 37, *ex inform.* Canon Brian Carne, to whom I am indebted for the following St. John corrections.]
line 11, for 'June' read 'July'
lines 12–13, for '27 Feb. 1748/9' read '26 Nov. 1748' [Coffin plate in Lydiard Tregoze church, *ex inform.* Frank T. Smallwood.]
line 13, after 'Tregoze' add '19 Mar. 1748/9'
line 14, for '1749' read '4 Feb. 1748/9'
line 16, for '1749' read '1748'

SAINT JOHN OF BLETSO

page 340,
lines 5–6, delete all detail and replace as follows

XVIII. 1912. 18. HENRY BEAUCHAMP OLIVER (ST. JOHN), BARON SAINT JOHN OF BLETSO [1559], also a Baronet [1660], 1st s. and h., *b.* 24 June 1876; ed. at Wellington and Cambridge (Magdalene Coll.). He *d.* unm. 17 Oct. 1920.

XIX. 1920. 19. MOUBRAY ST. ANDREW THORNTON (ST. JOHN), BARON SAINT JOHN OF BLETSO, &c., *b.* 5 Nov. 1877 [for further detail see note ([b])]. His widow *d.* 1978.

XX. 1934. 20. JOHN MOUBRAY RUSSELL (ST. JOHN), BARON SAINT JOHN OF BLETSO, &c., s. and h., *b.* 3 Aug. 1917. He *d.* unm. 13 Apr. 1976.

XXI. 1976. 21. ANDREW BEAUCHAMP (ST. JOHN), BARON ST. JOHN OF BLETSO, &c., cousin and h., being 3rd s. of Lieut. Col. Rowland Tudor ST. JOHN (*d.* 17 Nov. 1948), by Katherine Madge, da. of Sir Frank LOCKWOOD, M.P., which Rowland Tudor was 3rd s. of the 17th Baron St. John. He was *b.* 23 Aug. 1918; ed. at Wellington; *m.*, 10 Dec. 1955, Katharine, yst. da. of Alfred VON BERG of London. He *d.* 11 Feb. 1978. His widow was living 1995.

XXII. 1978. 22. ANTHONY TUDOR (ST. JOHN). BARON ST. JOHN OF BLETSO, &c., s. and h., *b.* 16 May 1957; ed. at Diocesan Coll., Cape Town, Cape Town Univ. and London Univ.

note ([b]), lines 8–9, delete from 'His' to '1917'

SAINT JOHN OF LAGEHAM

page 347,
line 13, after 'and' add 'great'

SAINT LEONARDS OF SLAUGHAM

page 353,
after line 22 add as follows

III. 1908. 3. FRANK EDWARD (SUGDEN), BARON SAINT LEONARDS OF SLAUGHAM, nephew and h., 2nd but 1st surv. s. of Henry Frank SUGDEN by Edith, 1st da. of Abraham BOWMAN, of Stangrove, Edenbridge, co. Kent, the afsd. Henry Frank being the 2nd s. of Henry SUGDEN, 2nd s. of the 1st Baron and Marianne his wife, both abovenamed. He was *b.* 11 Nov. 1890 [for further detail see note ([d]), on page 354, lines 2–8]. He *d.* unm. 18 July 1972.

IV. 1972. 4. JOHN GERARD (SUGDEN), BARON ST. LEONARDS OF SLAUGHAM, distant cousin, being 5th s.([e]) of Arthur Herbert SUGDEN (*d.* 9 May 1958), by Julia Sheila, da. of Philip WYATT of Curragh, co. Kildare, which Arthur Herbert was 1st s. of Arthur Henry SUGDEN (*d.* 1947), by Edith Lilian, da. of Henry E. BUSH, which Arthur Henry was s. of the Rev. Arthur SUGDEN (*d.* 26 Oct. 1868), by Annie Jane, 2nd da. of the Rev. George ELTON, which Arthur was 3rd s. of the 1st Baron St. Leonards. He was *b.* 3 Feb. 1950 and *d.* unm. 1 June 1985 when his Barony became *extinct.*

note ([e]) He was 5th s. of his father but 1st legit. Three of his br. survived him.

SAINT LEVAN OF SAINT MICHAEL'S MOUNT

page 355,
line 1, line to read as follows

II. 1908. 2. JOHN TOWNSHEND (ST. AUBYN), BARON SAINT LEVAN OF SAINT MICHAEL'S MOUNT, 1st s. and h., *b.* 23 Sep. 1857,

lines 28–9, delete from 'Having' to 'work.([b])]'

III. 1940. 3. FRANCIS CECIL (ST. AUBYN), BARON SAINT LEVAN OF SAINT MICHAELS MOUNT, nephew and h., being 1st s. and h. of Arthur James Dudley Stuart ST. AUBYN (4th s.([b]) of the 1st Baron), by Helen Kate, da.

of Dr. J.C. PHILLIPO, of Jamaica. He was *b.* 18 Apr. 1895; ed. at Eton 1907–13 and R.M.C., Sandhurst; joined the Grenadier Guards 1914; Lieut. 1915; served in WW1 1914–15 (wounded); also served in WW2, Col. Cmdg. W. Cornwall Sector H.G., 1942–4. He *m.*, 6 Oct. 1916, Clementine Gwendolen Catharine, only da. of Arthur (NICOLSON), 1st BARON CARNOCK, by Mary Katharine, da. of Capt. Arthur Rowan HAMILTON, of Killylegh Castle, co. Down. He *d.* 10 July 1972. His widow was living 1995.

IV. 1972. 4. JOHN FRANCIS ARTHUR (ST. AUBYN), BARON ST. LEVAN OF ST. MICHAEL'S MOUNT, 1st s. and h., *b.* 23 Feb. 1919; ed. at Eton and Cambridge (Trin. Coll.); *m.*, 1970; Susan, yr. da. of Major Gen. Sir John Noble KENNEDY, G.C.M.G., K.C.V.O, K.B.E.

note ([b]), delete all detail and replace by 'The 2nd and 3rd sons *d.* unm. in 1915 and 1895 respectively.'

SAINT MAUR

page 361,
line 16, for 'subsequently' read '(in her issue)' and after 'PEYVRE' add '[4th LORD PEYVRE],'
line 17, for 'Jan.' read '6 Jan.'

page 362,
line 8, after '([d])' add 'She *d.* 21 July 1447.([da])'
note ([da]) This date is given on the reverse of an appropriated brass, a rubbing of which is now in the Society of Antiquaries, see *Trans. Mon. Brass Soc.*, vol. iii, pp. 187–91, cited *Geneal. Mag.*, 1960, vol. 13, p. 251.
note ([d]), line 1, delete 'after his wife's death,'

SAINT OSWALD OF NOSTELL

page 363,
line 32, line to read as follows

III. 1919. 3. ROWLAND GEORGE (WINN), BARON SAINT OSWALD OF NOSTELL, 1st s. and h., *b.* 29 July 1893;

page 364,
lines 5–6, delete from 'Having' to 'work.]' and replace by 'He *d.* 25 Feb. 1957. His widow *d.* 1976.'

IV. 1957. 4. ROWLAND DENYS GUY (WINN), BARON ST. OSWALD OF NOSTELL, 1st s. and h., *b.* 19 Sep. 1916; ed. at Stowe and Bonn and Freiburg Universities; *m.* 1stly, 8 May 1952, Laurian, da. of Sir Roderick JONES, K.B.E., of Rottingdean, Sussex. They were divorced in 1955 and he *m.* 2ndly, 24 June 1955, Marie Wanda, yr. da. of Sigismund JAXA-CHAMIEC of Warsaw. She *d.* 1981. He *d. s.p.* 19 Dec. 1984.

V. 1984. 5. DEREK EDWARD ANTHONY (WINN), BARON ST. OSWALD OF NOSTELL, br. and h., *b.* 9 July 1919; ed. at Stowe; *m.*, 10 June 1954, Denise Eileen Charlotte, da. of Wilfred Haig LOYD of the Isle of Wight.

[CHARLES ROWLAND ANDREW WINN, s. and h. ap., *b.* 22 July 1959; ed. at New Sch., King's Langley; *m.*, 1985, Louise Alexandra, da. of Stewart MacKenzie SCOTT.]

ST PHILIBERT

page 367,
line 13, after 'Margaret' add 'sister to John DE NORWICH to whose grandson John her issue ultimately became heirs'

ST VINCENT

page 373,
lines 9–10, delete from 'He was' to 'work.'

VI. 1908. 6. RONALD CLARGES (JERVIS), VISCOUNT SAINT VINCENT OF MEAFORD, br. and h., *b.* 3 Dec. 1859 [for further detail see note ([a])].

[JOHN CYRIL CARNEGIE JERVIS, 1st s, and h. ap., *b.* 10 July 1898. He *d. v.p.* and unm. 20 June 1929, being *k.* in a sea plane accident.]

VII. 1940. 7. RONALD GEORGE JAMES (JERVIS), VISCOUNT ST. VINCENT OF MEAFORD, 2nd but only surv. s. and h., *b.* 3 May 1905; ed. at Sherborne; *m.*, 2 Oct. 1945, Constance Phyllida Anne, da. of Lieut. Col. Robert Hector LOGAN.

[EDWARD ROBERT JAMES JERVIS, 1st s. and h. ap., *b.* 12 May 1951; ed. at Radley Sch.; *m.*, 1977, Victoria Margaret, da. of Wolton J. OLDHAM of Jersey.]

SALISBURY

page 374,
note ([g]), line 2, after 'Walter the Sheriff' add '(possibly Walter Huse: a collation of the evidence for the Sheriffs of Wiltshire (from the Charter Rolls, *Reg. Malmsburiense*, and BL Lansd. MS. 417, f. 23v, shows that a Walter Huse (Hosatus/Husat), also apparently Walter, son of Edward, was Sheriff in the first few years of the 12th century)'

page 377,
line 9, for 'OF' read 'OF'

page 379,
note ([f]), line 3, after 'writ' add 'Charles Evans argued (in *The Geneal.*, vol. 3, 1982, pp. 265–6), that the Earl's mother was possibly Ida of Lorraine, *suo jure* Countess of Boulogne.'

page 381,
note ([k]), line 15 (on page 382), after 'FitzRobert' add ', but actually Ralph de Somery, see vol. xii, part 1, p. 111,'

page 388,
note ([b]), line 8, after '*note*' add ', also vol. x, p. 236, note ([a])'

page 393,
line 1, after '1352–69' add ', by Agnes, da. and coh. of William Champnes' [*Visitations of Kent*, Harl. Soc., vol. lxxv, p. 31]

page 399,
line 30, for '1519' read '1539'
line 32, for 'probably in 1491' read 'probably by November 1487' [*ex inform.* Dr Hazel Pierce]

page 400,
line 1, delete 'and not later than 1494'
line 2, for '18 Dec. 1505' read '20 Oct. 1504, aged *circa* 45([aa])' and for 'Richard' read 'Edward'
note ([aa]) Loans for the burial of Sir Richard Pole are recorded in Henry VII's accounts 20 Oct. and 15 Nov. 1504 (*Exc. Hist.*, p. 132; BL Add. MS. 7099, f. 80). *Ex inform.* Dr Hazel Pierce.
note ([a]), line 1, delete 'Sir'
line 2, for 'pr. 21 Mar. 1474/5' read 'dat. 12 Oct. 1478, dead by 11 Jan. 1479: *P.C.C.*, 35 Wattys; *Cal. Fine Rolls, 1471–85*, no. 450.' [*ex inform.* Dr Hazel Pierce]
line 5, for '2nd cousin' read '1st cousin of the half-blood'

page 401,
note ([c]), line 5, after '1558' add '; (iii) Sir Arthur Pole, who *m.* Jane, da. of Sir Roger Lewknor, see vol. ix, p. 96, note ([c])'

page 414,
line 6, line to read as follows

MARQUESSATE. IV. EARLDOM. XXIV.	1903	4 and 10. JAMES EDWARD HUBERT (GASCOYNE-CECIL), MARQUESS OF SALISBURY, &c., 1st s. and h., *b.* 23 Oct. 1861;

page 415,
lines 1–2, delete from 'He' to 'work.([a])]' and replace 'He *d.* 4 Apr. 1947. His widow *d.* 5 Feb. 1955.'

MARQUESSATE. V. EARLDOM. XXV.	1947	5 and 11. ROBERT ARTHUR JAMES (GASCOYNE-CECIL), MARQUESS OF SALISBURY, &c., 1st s. and h., *b.* 27 Aug. 1893, at Hatfield House; *styled* VISCOUNT CRANBORNE 1903–47 [for further detail see note ([a])]. He *d.* 23 Feb. 1972. His widow *d.* 1982.

MARQUESSATE. VI. EARLDOM. XXVI. } 1972 — 6 and 12. ROBERT EDWARD PETER (GASCOYNE-CECIL), MARQUESS OF SALISBURY, &c., only s. and h., *b.* 24 Oct. 1916; ed. at Eton; *m.*, 18 Dec. 1945, Marjorie Olein, 2nd da. of Capt. Valentine Maurice WYNDHAM-QUIN, R.N.

[ROBERT MICHAEL JAMES GASCOYNE-CECIL, *styled* VISCOUNT CRANBORNE, 1st s. and h. ap., *b.* 30 Sep. 1946; ed. at Eton and Oxford (Ch. Ch.). He was called to the House of Lords in his father's Barony of Cecil of Essendon [1603], 1992. He *m.*, 7 Jan. 1970, Hannah Ann, 1st da. of Lieut. Col. William Joseph STIRLING of Dunblane.]

SALTOUN

page 424,
line 18, after '1890' add '–1933'
line 26, line to read as follows

XX. 1933. 20. ALEXANDER ARTHUR (FRASER), LORD SALTOUN OF ABERNETHY, 1st s. and h., *b.* 8 Mar. 1886; MASTER OF SALTOUN till 1933; ed. at Eton and Oxford (New Coll.);

line 29, after '1935' add '–63'
lines 33–4, delete from 'Having' to 'work.([d])]' and replace by 'He *d.* 31 Aug. 1979. His widow *d.* 1985.'

[ALEXANDER SIMON FRASER, s. and h. ap., *b.* 12 Dec. 1921; MASTER OF SALTOUN; *d.* Feb. 1944, being *k.* in action.]

XXI. 1979. 21. FLORA MARJORY FRASER, da. and h., *suo jure* BARONESS SALTOUN OF ABERNETHY [S.]. She was *b.* 18 Oct. 1930; *m.*, 6 Oct. 1956, Capt. Alexander Arthur Alfonso David Maule RAMSAY of Mar.

note ([d]), delete all detail

SANDHURST

page 429,
line 21, delete from ',([b])' to 'work'

III. 1921. 3. JOHN WILLIAM (MANSFIELD), BARON SANDHURST OF SANDHURST [1871], br. and h., *b.* 10 July 1857 [for further detail see note ([b])]. His widow *d.* 1 Nov. 1939.

IV. 1933. 4. RALPH SHELDON (MANSFIELD), BARON SANDHURST OF SANDHURST, s. and h., *b.* 19 July 1892; ed. at Winchester and Cambridge (Trin. Coll.); Lieut. Royal Engineers, 1914, served in WW1 in France four years (des. twice, O.B.E.); Lieut. Col. Royal Signals, served in WW2. He *m.*, 8 Feb. 1917, Victoria Morley, only child of Edward Berners UPCHER, of Kirby Cane, Norfolk. She *d.* 17 June 1961. He *d.* 28 Oct. 1964.

V. 1964. 5. JOHN EDWARD TERENCE (MANSFIELD), BARON SANDHURST OF SANDHURST, 1st s. and h., *b.* 4 Sep. 1920; ed. at Harrow; *m.* 1stly, 7 Nov. 1942, Priscilla Ann, 2nd da. of J. Fielder JOHNSON. They were divorced in 1946 (she *d.* 1970) and he *m.* 2ndly, 3 Apr. 1947, Janet Mary, 1st da. of John Edward LLOYD of New York.

[GUY RHYS JOHN MANSFIELD, s. and h. ap., *b.* 3 Mar. 1949; ed. at Harrow and Oxford (Oriel Coll.); *m.*, 1976, Philippa St. Clair, 1st da. of Digby Everard VERDON-ROE.]

note (b), lines 5–8, delete from 'He was' to 'Norfolk'

SANDWICH

page 438,
line 17, after 'Mary' add 'Henrietta'
line 16, delete from 'da. of' to 'Munn' and replace by 'presumably da. of Mary, who was probably widow of ?Richard NUNN' [*ex inform.* W.E.C. Cotton]

page 439,
note (b), line 6, after '39).' add 'For some interesting comments on her will (pr. Nov. 1863), see Penrith *Observer*, 28 Oct. 1873, p. 3.'

page 440,
line 27, delete from 'He' to 'work.(d)'

IX. 1916. 9. GEORGE CHARLES (MONTAGU), EARL OF SANDWICH, &c., nephew and h., being the s. and h. of Rear Adm. Victor Alexander MONTAGU, 2nd s. of the 7th Earl, by the Lady Agneta Harriet, da. of Charles Philip (YORKE), 4th EARL OF HARDWICKE, *b.* 20 Dec. 1874; [for further detail see note (d)]. She *d.* 23 Oct. 1951 and he *m.* 2ndly, 12 Dec. 1952, Ella Lilian, formerly wife of Seymour Douglas CORBIN and da. of George SULLY, of North Petherton, co. Somerset. He *d.* 15 June 1962. His widow *d.* 1986.

X. 1962. 10. ALEXANDER VICTOR EDWARD PAULET (MONTAGU), EARL OF SANDWICH, &c., 1st s. and h., *b.* 22 May 1906; *styled* VISCOUNT HINCHINGBROOKE 1916–62; ed. at Eton and Cambridge (Trin. Coll.); Private Sec. to Mr (later Earl) Baldwin 1932–4; Lieut. 5th Battn. Northamptonshire Regt. (1st T.A.); served in WW2; Major, Gen. Staff; M.P. (Cons.) for South Dorset 1941–62. Under the Peerage Act 1963 he disclaimed his titles for life, 24 July 1964. He *m.* 1stly, 27 July 1934, Rosemary Maud, only da. of Major Ralph Harding PETO (by his 1st wife, Frances Ruby Vera, only child of Col. Walter James LINDSAY). They were div. in 1958 and he *m.* 2ndly, 7 June 1962, Lady Anne, yst. da. of Victor Christian William (CAVENDISH), 9th DUKE OF DEVONSHIRE and widow of Christopher John HOLLAND-MARTIN, M.P. This marriage was annulled in 1965. He *d.* 25 Feb. 1995.

XI. 1995. 11. JOHN EDWARD HOLLISTER (MONTAGU), EARL OF SANDWICH, &c., s. and h., styled VISCOUNT HINCHINGBROOKE 1962–70, when he ceased to use the title; *b.* 11 Apr. 1943; ed. at Eton and Cambridge (Trin. Coll.); *m.*, 1 July 1968, Susan Caroline, da. of the Rev. Perceval Ecroyd Cobham HAYMAN of Petersfield, Hants.

[LUKE TIMOTHY CHARLES MONTAGU, s. and h. ap., *b.* 1969, *styled* Lord Hinchingbrooke.]

note ([d]), line 6, after '1937' add '–47'
lines 6–12, delete from 'His' to 'Lindsay'

SANDYS OF OMBERSLEY

page 453,
lines 18–19, delete from 'He was' to 'work.'

VII. 1904. 5. MICHAEL EDWIN MARCUS (SANDYS), LORD SANDYS OF OMBERSLEY, br. and h., *b.* 31 Dec. 1855. He *m.*, 1886, Marjorie Clara Pentreath, da. of John MORGAN of Brighton. She *d.* 8 Oct. 1929. He *d.* 4 Aug. 1948.

VIII. 1948. 6. ARTHUR FITZGERALD SANDYS (HILL), LORD SANDYS OF OMBERSLEY, distant cousin and h., being s. of Arthur Blundell George Sandys HILL (*d.* 16 June 1923), by Helen Emily, 3rd da. of Most Rev. Richard Chevenix TRENCH, Archbishop of Dublin, which Arthur Blundell was 1st s. of George Augustus HILL (*d.* 6 Apr. 1879), by Cassandra Jane, yst. da. of Edward KNIGHT of Godmersham Park, Kent, which George was 5th s. of Mary, Baroness Sandys and heir to the title under the spec. rem. He was *b.* 4 Dec. 1876; ed. at Haileybury; *m.*, 10 Apr. 1924, Cynthia Mary, da. of Col. Frederick Richard TRENCH-GASCOIGNE of Craigrush Castle, Argyll. He *d.* 24 Nov. 1961. His widow *d.* 1990.

IX. 1961. 7. RICHARD MICHAEL OLIVER (HILL), LORD SANDYS OF OMBERSLEY, only s. and h., *b.* 21 July 1931; ed. at R.N.C., Dartmouth; *m.*, 16 Sep. 1961, Patricia Simpson, 1st da. of Capt. Lionel HALL, M.C., of Lower Beeding, Sussex.

note ([a]), delete all detail

SAVILE

page 463,
lines 19–22, delete all detail and replace as follows

III. 1931. 3. GEORGE HALIFAX (LUMLEY-SAVILE), BARON SAVILE OF RUFFORD, 1st s. and h. by 2nd wife, *b.* 24 Jan. 1919; ed. at Eton; 2nd Lieut., Duke of Wellington's Regt.

SAY

page 467,
note ([c]), line 2, after 'p. 207).' add 'She possibly died as late as 1217, see vol. v, pedigree between pp. 116 and 117.'

page 470,
line 9, after 'Aug.,' add '(?19 Aug.)' [See vol. v, as above.]
line 12, after 'h.' add 'by 1st wife'

page 475,
note (g), line 4, after 'Northwode' add '[2nd Lord Northwode]'

page 477,
line 8, after 'Alice' add 'sister of Robert, 1st LORD TONY

page 478,
line 5, after 'BURN(c)' add 'also (from 1395), BARONESS BREWES, *b.* 24 Feb. 1365/6,'
line 6, after 'Northants' add '[1st LORD FALVESLE]'
line 8, for 'Nov. 1393' read 'soon after 23 Nov. 1392'
line 10, after '1404' add 'as LORD HERON'
line 11, after '*d.*' add '*s.p.*'
line 12, for 'Barony' read 'Baronies of Say and Leyburn'
line 13, after '*abeyance*' add 'but that of BREWES became *extinct.*'
note (c), after 'p. 640' add '; vol. ii, p. 310'
note (g), line 16, delete from 'William' to 'Idonea' and replace by 'William (de Clinton), 4th Lord Clinton, s. and h. of Sir William de Clinton, by his 1st wife, Idonea.'
line 23, after '(no.ix)' add 'For a discussion of Elizabeth's heirs see G.W. Watson, *Misc. Gen. et Her.*, 5th ser., vol. 9, 1935–7, pp. 238–40.'

SAYE AND SELE

page 483,
line 4, for '1460' read '1450'

page 486,
note (b), before 'Vicecomitem' add 'Buckingham and William Fiennes were loosely speaking brothers-in-law, in that Elizabeth Fiennes, half-sister to William by their father's 2nd marriage, married Sir William Villiers, half-brother to the Duke' [See David Fiennes, *Geneal. Mag.*, vol. 16, 1969–71, pp. 334–5.]

page 496,
line 8, line to read as follows

XVIII. 1907. 12. GEOFFREY CECIL (TWISTLETON-WYKEHAM-FIENNES), LORD SAYE AND SELE, 1st s. and h.,

lines 20–1, delete from 'Having' to 'work.(d)]' and replace by 'His widow *d.* 27 July 1946.'

XIX. 1937. 13. GEOFFREY RUPERT CECIL (TWISTLETON-WYKEHAM-FIENNES), LORD SAYE AND SELE, s. and h., *b.* 27 Dec. 1884; ed. at Harrow and Oxford (New Coll.), B.A. 1910; served in WW1. He *d.* unm. 18 Feb. 1949.

XX. 1949. 14. IVO MURRAY (TWISTLETON-WYKEHAM-FIENNES), LORD SAYE AND SELE, br. and h., *b.* 15 Dec. 1885; ed. at Harrow and R.M.A., Woolwich; *m.*, 16 Oct. 1919, Hersey Cecilia HESTER, da. of Capt. Sir Thomas Dacres BUTLER. He *d.* 21 Oct. 1968. His widow *d.* 31 Oct. 1968.

XXI. 1968. 15. NATHANIEL THOMAS ALLEN (TWISTLETON-WYKEHAM-FIENNES, *later* FIENNES), LORD SAYE AND SELE, 1st s. and h., *b.* 22 Sep. 1920; ed. at Eton and Oxford (New Coll.); *m.*, 4 Dec. 1958, Mariette Helena, da. of Major Gen. Sir Arthur Guy SALISBURY-JONES, G.C.M.G., C.B.E., M.C., of Hambledon, Hants.

[RICHARD INGEL FIENNES, 1st s. and h. ap., *b.* 19 Aug. 1959.]

note ([d]), delete all detail

SCALES

page 502,
line 17, after 'NORWICH' add 'da. of Walter DE NORWICH [1st LORD NORWICH], to whose grandson, John [2nd LORD NORWICH], her issue ultimately became heirs.'

page 503,
note ([q]), line 11 (on page 504), after '426.' add 'For further comments on whether or not Elizabeth was a Bardolph, see *Sussex Notes and Queries*, vol. 4, 1932–3, pp. 51–3.'

SCARBROUGH

page 516,
line 1, delete '([a])'

XI. 1945. 11. LAWRENCE ROGER (LUMLEY), EARL OF SCARBROUGH, &c., nephew and h., being the 2nd but 1st surv.([a]) s. and h. of Osbert Victor George Atheling LUMLEY, by Constance Ellinor, 1st da. of Capt. Eustace John Wilson PATTEN (s. of John Wilson (PATTEN), 1st BARON WINMARLEIGH), 3rd s. of the 9th Earl. He was *b.* 27 July 1896; ed. at Eton, Oxford (Magdalen Coll.) and R.M.C., Sandhurst; K.G., Gov. of Bombay, G.C.S.I., G.C.I.E., G.C.V.O. He *m.*, 12 July 1922, Katharine Isobel, da. of Robert Finnie MCEWEN of Bardrochat, Ayrshire. He *d.* 29 June 1969. His widow *d.* 1979.

XII. 1969. 12. RICHARD ALDRED (LUMLEY), EARL OF SCARBROUGH, &c., only s. and h., *b.* 5 Dec. 1932; ed. at Eton and Oxford (Magdalen Coll.); *m.*, 1970, Lady Elizabeth, da. of Simon (RAMSAY), 16th EARL OF DALHOUSIE.

[RICHARD OSBERT LUMLEY, *styled* VISCOUNT LUMLEY, 1st s. and h. ap., *b.* 18 May 1973.]

note ([a]), delete all detail and replace by 'His elder br., Richard John Lumley, *b.* 30 July 1894, 2nd Lieut., 11th Hussars, was *k.* in action *v.p.*, 17 Oct. 1914.'

SCARSDALE

page 522,
line 7, line to read as follows

V. 1916. 5. GEORGE NATHANIEL (CURZON), BARON SCARSDALE [1761], also a Baronet [S. 1636; E. 1641], 1st s. and h., *b.* 11 Jan. 1859.

lines 17–21, delete from ', when' to '354.]' and replace by '. For further detail see *sub* CURZON OF KEDLESTON [vols. iii and xiii, p. 354].'

VISCOUNTCY. II. BARONY. VI. 1925 2 and 6. RICHARD NATHANIEL (CURZON), VISCOUNT SCARSDALE OF SCARSDALE and BARON SCARSDALE, &c., nephew and h. male, being the s. and h. of Alfred Nathaniel CURZON (2nd s. of the 4th Baron), by Henrietta Mary, da. of Spencer Dudley MONTAGUE, 4th s. of Matthew (MONTAGU), 4th BARON ROKEBY. He was *b.* 3 July 1898; ed. at Eton and R.M.C., Sandhurst; *m.* 1stly, 14 Apr. 1923, Mildred Carson, da. of William Roland DUNBAR of Huyton, co. Lancs. They were divorced in 1946 (she *d.* 18 May 1969) and he *m.* 2ndly, 10 Aug. 1946, Ottilie Margarete Julie, 1st da. of Charles PRETZLIK of Crawley, Sussex. He *d. s.p.m.* 19 Oct. 1977. His widow was living 1995.

VISCOUNTCY. III. BARONY. VII. 1977 3 and 7. FRANCIS JOHN NATHANIEL (CURZON), VISCOUNT SCARSDALE OF SCARSDALE, &c., cousin and h., being s. of Francis Nathaniel CURZON (*d.* 8 June 1941), by Winifred Phyllis, da. of Capt. Christian COMBE of Muir of Ord, Ross-shire which Francis Nathaniel was 3rd s. of the 4th Baron Curzon. He was *b.* 28 July 1924; ed. at Eton; *m.* 1stly, 3 July 1948, Solange Yvonne Palmyre Ghislaine (who *d.* 1974), yr. da. of Oscar Ghislain HANSE. They were divorced in 1967 and he *m.* 2ndly, 5 June 1968, Helene Gladys Frances, da. of Major William George Ferguson THOMSON of Kinellar, Aberdeenshire.

[PETER GHISLAIN NATHANIEL CURZON, 1st s. and h. ap., *b.* 6 Mar. 1949; ed. at Ampleforth; *m.*, 1983, Mrs Karen OSBORNE.]

SCROPE

page 541,
line 6, after 'by' add 'his wife' and after 'Catherine' add '?DE NORWICH'
line 7, delete from ', da. of' to '([b])'
note ([b]), delete all detail

page 542,
line 5, after 'of' add 'Sir William DEINCOURT (s. and h. ap. of' and after 'LORD DEINCOURT' add ')'

page 543,
lines 32–3, for 'was living 20 Oct. 1498' read '*d.* 10 May 1504' [*Cal. Inq. P. M.*, Henry VII, vol. iii, nos. 880–1]

page 544,
line 11, for '1462' read '1464'

page 545,
line 18, for '6th' read '5th'
lines 18–19, for '14 Jan. 1467/8' read '25 Dec. 1462'
lines 20–1, delete from 'who was' to '1470'
line 21, for '1488' read '1489, and *d.* before 3 July 1494' [See vol. xii, part 2, p. 945, *sub* ZOUCHE.]
line 26, delete ', aged 63'

SCROPE (of Masham or Upsall)

page 566,
line 3, after 'DEVEREUX' add '[2nd LORD DEVEREUX]
line 9, after 'WILLOUGHBY),' add 'sister and coh. of Edmund (DE HOLLAND), 4th EARL OF KENT'

page 570,
line 27, after 'WENTWORTH' add '[4th LORD LE DESPENCER]'

page 572,
line 17, for '1596' read '1599' [*ex inform.* Dr Ian Atherton]
note (f), line 6, for 'Margery and Anne' read 'Joan and Mary'

SCUDAMORE

page 573,
line 2, after '1619' add '(*d.* 13 Apr.)' [*ex inform.* Warren Skidmore, to whom I am grateful for the succeeding corrections to Scudamore, unless otherwise attributed]
line 4, after '*b.*' add '24 or 28 Feb.'
line 14, after '1631' add '1646' and delete 'zealous'
line 22, for *d.*' read 'was *bur.*'
note (a), line 1, after 'He' add ', or possibly his father, Sir John,'
lines 1–2, delete '*Inq. p.m.*, (Bucks.), 20 Sep. 1611' and replace by 'PRO, C 142/404/114.' [*ex inform.* Dr Ian Atherton]
note (f), lines 6–7 (on page 574), delete from 'Portraits' to 'Biog.)' and replace by 'A portrait of the 1st Viscount is now in Kentchurch Court, co. Hereford.' [*ex inform.* Dr Ian Atherton]

page 574,
line 13, for '*b.* about 1650' read '*bap.* 19 Oct. 1649; ed. at Westminster Sch., 1663–5;'
line 19, for '29 Oct.' read '22 June'

note (b), line 1, for 'six' read 'seven' and after '*v.p.*' add '(*bap.* 12 Feb. 1681 and was *bur.* at Holme Lacy, 8 Aug. 1691.)'

page 575,
line 1, for '10 July' read '2 June'
line 6, for '15 July' read '16 July'
line 9, for '7 Mar.' read '5 Mar.'
line 12, after '*bur.*' add '11 Dec.'
line 15, after '*bur.*' add '17 May'
note (b), lines 4–5, for '*d.* unm. 9 Feb. 1713' read '*m.* Elizabeth (__), who *m.* 2ndly, William Dew, a yeoman of Sellack, co. Hereford (C.J. Robinson, *Mansions and Manors in Herefordshire*, 1873, p. 43.). He *d.* 9 Feb. and was *bur.* 12 Feb. 1713/14. His widow *d.* 2 and was *bur.* 28 Aug. 1760 at Sellack.'
line 5, after 'M.I.' add 'Will dat. 3 Feb. 1713/14 (referring to his wife Elizabeth), pr. 29 June 1714.'

SEAFIELD

page 580,
between lines 21 and 22 add as follows

XII. 1915. 12. NINA CAROLINE OGILVIE-GRANT, *suo jure* COUNTESS OF SEAFIELD [1701] &c., all in the peerage of Scotland, only child and h. of line. She was *b.* 17 Apr. 1906; *m.*, 24 Jan. 1930, at St. James's, Westm., Derek STUDLEY-HERBERT, s. of John Tatchell STUDLEY, of Scarborough Court, Dorset, who assumed, 1939, the additional surnames of Ogilvie-Grant before those of Studley-Herbert. They were div. 1957 (he *d.* 26 Mar. 1960). She *d.* 30 Sep. 1969.

XII. 1969. 13. IAN DEREK FRANCIS (STUDLEY-HERBERT, *later* by warrant of the Lord Lyon, 1971, OGILVIE-GRANT), EARL OF SEAFIELD, &c., only s. and h., *b.* 20 Mar. 1939; ed. at Eton; *m.* 1stly, 5 Oct. 1960, Mary Dawn Mackenzie, da. of Henry George Coats ILLINGWORTH. They were divorced in 1971 and he *m.* 2ndly, 1971, Leila, da. of Mahmoud REFAAT of Cairo.

[JAMES ANDREW OGILVIE-GRANT, MASTER OF SEAFIELD, *styled* VISCOUNT REIDHAVEN, 1st s. and h., *b.* 30 Nov. 1963; ed. at Harrow.]

note (d), line 4, after 'Grant' add 'See vol. xii, part 1, *sub* STRATHSPEY.'
lines 4–9, delete from 'Nina' to 'work.'

SEAFORTH

page 586,
line 1, for 'Coxhow' read 'Coxhoe'
line 2, for 'Northumberland' read 'co. Durham' [*ex inform.* D.L. Ramage]
line 4, after '1744.' add 'Admon. York 24 May 1755'

SEATON

page 591,
line 29, delete '(c)'

IV. 1933. 4. JAMES ULYSSES GRAHAM RAYMOND (COLBORNE *afterwards* COLBORNE-VIVIEN), BARON SEATON OF SEATON, only surv. br.(c) and h., *b.* 20 Apr. 1863; ed. at R.M.C., Sandhurst; *m.*, 21 June 1904, Caroline Mabel, 1st da. of Sir Arthur Pendarves VIVIEN, K.C.B. She *d.* 3 June 1948. He *d. s.p.* 12 Mar. 1955 when his title became *extinct*.

note (c), lines 1–2, delete from 'He' to '1863'

SEFTON

page 595,
between lines 29 and 30 add as follows

EARLDOM [I.] VI. BARONY [U.K.] V. } 1901 — 6 and 5. OSBERT CECIL (MOLYNEUX), EARL OF SEFTON, &c., *b.* 21 Feb. 1870; *m.*, 8 Jan. 1898, Lady Helena Mary, da. of George Cecil Orlando (BRIDGEMAN), 4th EARL OF BRADFORD. He *d.* 16 June 1930. His widow *d.* 27 Aug. 1947.

EARLDOM [I.] VII. BARONY [U.K.] VI. } 1930 — 7 and 6. HUGH WILLIAM OSBERT (MOLYNEUX), EARL OF SEFTON [1771], VISCOUNT MOLYNEUX OF MARYBOROUGH [1628], in the peerage of Ireland, also BARON SEFTON OF CROXTETH [U.K. 1831], also a Baronet [1611], only surv. s. and h., *b.* 22 Dec. 1898; ed. at Harrow and R.M.C., Sandhurst; *m.*, 9 Dec. 1941, Josephine, da. of George Nathan ARMSTRONG of Virginia, U.S.A., formerly wife of Erskine GWYNNE. He *d. s.p.* 13 Apr. 1972 when all his titles became *extinct*.

note (d), lines 1–2, delete from 'He' to '1930'

SEGRAVE

page 601,
line 8, after 'Despencer' add 'da. of Thomas DESPENCER' [See DESPENCER, vol. iv, p. 259.]

page 607,
line 23, after 'Christiane,' add 'sister of Hugh, 1st LORD PLESCY'

SELBOURNE

page 615,
line 11, after 'net.' add 'His widow *d.* 27 Apr. 1950.'
line 12, line to read as follows

III. 1942. 3. ROUNDELL CECIL (PALMER), EARL OF SELBOURNE, &c., 1st s. and h., *b.* 15 Apr. 1887, in London; *styled* VISCOUNT WOLMER 1895–1942;

line 25, for ']' read 'She *d.* 22 Sep. 1959. He *m.* 2ndly, 3 Mar. 1966, Valerie Irene, yr. da. of Joseph Anthony Nicholas DE THOMKA DE TOMKAHÀZA ET FOLKUSFALVA, Secretary of State, Hungary, formerly wife of Bryan Henry BEVAN, which marr. was annulled. She *d.* 5 Dec. 1968. He *d.* 3 Sep. 1971.'

[WILLIAM MATTHEW ROUNDELL PALMER, *styled* VISCOUNT WOOLMER, 1st. s. and h. ap. by his 1st wife, *b.* 27 May 1912; ed. at Winchester and Oxford (Balliol Coll.); *m.*, 16 July 1936, Priscilla, yr. da. of Capt. John Egerton WARBURTON, of Arley Hall, Cheshire. He *d. v.p.* accidentally, 2 Oct. 1942. His widow *m.* 2ndly, 6 July 1948, Major Peter Richard (LEGH), 4th BARON NEWTON, who *d.* 1992, and she *m.* 3rdly, 1994, as his 2nd wife, Frederick Charles Horace FRYER. She was still living 1995.]

VI. 1971. 4. JOHN ROUNDELL (PALMER), EARL OF SELBOURNE, &c., grandson and h., being s. and h. of the abovesaid Viscount Woolmer and Priscilla, *b.* 24 Mar. 1940; ed. at Eton and Oxford (Ch. Ch.); *m.*, 9 Dec. 1969, Joanna van Antwerp, yr. da. of Evan Maitland JAMES of Abingon, Berks.

[WILLIAM LEWIS PALMER, *styled* VISCOUNT WOOLMER, 1st s. and h. ap., *b.* 1 Sep. 1971; ed. at Eton and Oxford (Ch. Ch.).]

SELKIRK

page 620,
between lines 16 and 17 add as follows

VII. 1940. 7. GEORGE NIGEL (DOUGLAS-HAMILTON), EARL OF SELKIRK, LORD DAER AND SHORTCLEUGH [S. 1646], 2nd s. of the 13th Duke of Hamilton, and thus heir of the 6th Earl under the special proviso in the *novodamus* of 1688. He was *b.* 4 Jan. 1906; ed. at Eton, Oxford (Balliol Coll.) and Univs. of Edinburgh, Paris, Bonn and Vienna; *m.*, 6 Aug. 1949, Audrey Durell, only da. of Maurice DRUMMOND-SALE-BARKER. He *d. s.p.* 24 Nov. 1994. His widow *d.* 21 Dec. 1994.

VIII. 1994. 8. JAMES ALEXANDER (DOUGLAS-HAMILTON), EARL OF SELKIRK, LORD DAER OF SHORTCLEUGH, 2nd s. of the 15th Duke of Hamilton, and thus heir as above. He *suc.* to the titles on the death of his uncle although he disclaimed them 28 Nov. 1994 under the Peerage Act, 1963.([ba]) He was *b.* 31 July 1942; ed. at Eton, Oxford (Balliol Coll.), and Edinburgh Univ.; *m.*, 1974, Priscilla Susan, da. of John Norman Stuart (BUCHAN), 2nd Baron Tweedsmuir.

[JOHN ANDREW HAMILTON STUART, MASTER OF SELKIRK, was *b.* 1978.]

note ([ba]) The Earl, until then an M.P., disclaimed his titles to avoid causing a by-election, although who should succeed to the Earldom had then not actually been decided. His first cousin, son of the yr. br. of the 7th Earl, also claimed the title, but in accordance with the precedent set in the case of the 7th Earl, the Lord Lyon Court decided, 14 Mar. 1996, that Lord James was Earl of Selkirk. See *The Times*, 29 Nov. 1994, and 15 Mar. 1996, also note ([b]) above.

note ([b]), line 1, for 'has now been' read 'was'

SEMPILL

page 630,
line 25, line to read as follows

XVIII. 1906. 18. JOHN (FORBES *afterwards* FORBES-SEMPILL), LORD SEMPILL [S. 1488?], also a Bart. [S. 1630], 1st s. and h. by 2nd wife;

page 631,
lines 5–7, delete from 'Having' to 'work.([a])]' and replace by 'His widow *d.* 2 Mar. 1944.'

XIX. 1934. 19. WILLIAM FRANCIS (FORBES-SEMPILL), LORD SEMPILL, also a Bart. [S.], s. and h., *b.* 24 Sep. 1893; ed. at Eton. Rep. Peer [S.] 1935–63. Wing Commander late R.N.A.S. and Col. R.A.F. He *m.*, 20 Feb. 1919, Eileen Marion, only da. of Sir John LAVERY, R.A. She *d.* 18 July 1935. He *m.* 2ndly, 1 Feb. 1941, Cecilia Alice, da. of Bertram Edward DUNBAR-KILBURN of Sandford St. Martin, co. Oxon. He *d. s.p.m.* 30 Dec. 1965 when he was *suc.* in his barony by his 1st da. and in his baronetcy by his br. His widow *d.* 1984.

XX. 1965. 20. ANN MOIRA SEMPILL, *suo jure* BARONESS SEMPILL [S.], 1st da. and h. of line. She was *b.* 19 Mar. 1920 and *m.* 1stly, 25 Oct. 1941, Capt. Arthur Eric HOLT. They were divorced in 1945 and she *m.* 2ndly, 28 Oct. 1948, Lieut. Col. Stuart Whitemore CHANT (later by decree of the Lyon Court, 1966, CHANT-SEMPILL), O.B.E., M.C. He *d.* 1991.

[JAMES WILLIAM STUART WHITEMORE SEMPILL, MASTER OF SEMPILL, *b.* 25 Feb. 1949; ed. at the Oratory Sch. and Oxford (Hertford Coll.); *m.*, 1977, Josephine Ann Edith, da. of Joseph Norman REES of Johannesburg, South Africa.]

note ([a]), delete all detail

SETON AND TRANENT

page 637,
line 3, for '; forfeited 1715' read 'There is in fact no evidence of the creation of such a barony' [See vol. xii, part 2, *sub* WINTON.]

SHAFTESBURY

page 653,
line 19, for 'is' read 'was'
line 20, after 'Jerusalem' add 'She *d.* 8 July 1957. He *d.* 25 Mar. 1961.'

line 28, after 'Rouen' add 'He *d.* 8 Mar. 1947. His widow *m.* 2ndly, 12 Aug. 1947, Col. Francois GOUSSAULT, who *d.* 1984. She was still living 1995.

X. 1961. 10. ANTHONY (ASHLEY-COOPER), EARL OF SHAFTESBURY, &c., grandson and h., being1st s. and h. by 2nd wife of Anthony and Françoise abovesaid, *b.* 22 May 1938; ed. at Eton and Oxford (Ch. Ch.); *m.* 1stly, 21 July 1966, Bianca Maria, da. of Gino DE PAOLIS of Rome and formerly wife of Jack LE VIEN. They were divorced in 1976 and he *m.* 2ndly, 1976, Christina Eva, da. of Nils MONTAN, formerly wife of (__) CASELLA.

[ANTHONY NILS CHRISTIAN ASHLEY-COOPER, *styled* LORD ASHLEY, 1st s. and h.p. by 2nd wife, *b.* 24 June 1977.]

SHANNON

page 660,
line 21, line to read as follows

VII. 1906. 7. RICHARD BERNARD (BOYLE), EARL OF SHANNON, &c., 2nd but 1st surv. s. and h., *b.* 13 Nov. 1897;

lines 24–5, delete from '(b)' to 'work.]'

VIII. 1917. 8. ROBERT HENRY (BOYLE), EARL OF SHANNON, &c., *b.* 1 Feb. 1900 [for further detail see note (b)]. He *m.*, 27 Dec. 1923, at Ootacamund, Madras, Marjorie, da. of Septimus Augustus WALKER, of Ootacamund. He *d.* 29 Dec. 1963. His widow *d.* 1981.

IX. 1963. 9. RICHARD BENTINCK (BOYLE), EARL OF SHANNON, &c., only s. and h., *b.* 23 Oct. 1924; ed. at Eton; *m.* 1stly, 17 Sep. 1947, Donna Catherine Irene Helen, da. of MARQUIS DEMETRIO IMPERIALI DI FRANCAVILLA. They were divorced in 1955 and he *m.* 2ndly, 25 May 1957, Susan Margaret Rogers, da. of John P. Russell HOGG. They were also divorced in 1979 and he *m.* 3rdly, 1994, Almine, da. of Rocco Catorsia DE VILLIERS of Cape Town, South Africa.

[RICHARD HENRY JOHN BOYLE, *styled* VISCOUNT BOYLE, s. and h. ap. by 2nd wife, *b.* 19 Jan. 1960.]

note (b), lines 3–4, delete from 'He' to 'Walker'

SHELBURNE

page 670,
lines 1–2, for 'sister and h. (1726) of Sir John CLAVERING, 3rd Bart.' read 'yr. sister and coh. of Sir James, and da. of Sir John CLAVERING,' [See under 2nd Viscount Windsor of Blackcastle.]

SHERBORNE

page 678,
line 15, delete '(c)'

V. 1919. 5. FREDERICK GEORGE (DUTTON), BARON SHERBORNE, br. and h., *b.* 28 May 1840; ed. at Oxford (Ch. Ch.). In Holy Orders; Vicar of Sherborne 1870–4, and of Bibury 1874–1916. He *d.* unm. 3 Jan. 1920.

VI. 1920. 6. JAMES HUNTLY (DUTTON), BARON SHERBORNE, nephew and h., being 1st s. of Charles DUTTON (*d.* 6 Nov. 1909), by May Arbuthnott, da. of George Noble TAYLOR, which Charles was 5th s. of the 3rd Baron Sherborne. He was *b.* 5 Mar. 1873; ed. at Wellington and R.M.C., Sandhurst; *m.*, 27 Feb. 1908, Ethel Mary, da. of William BAIRD of Elie, Fife. He *d.* 17 Sep. 1949. His widow *d.* 30 Sep. 1969.

VII. 1949. 7. CHARLES (DUTTON), BARON SHERBORNE, 1st s. and h., *b.* 13 May 1911; ed. at Stowe; *m.*, 20 Feb. 1943, Joan Molesworth, 3rd da. of Sir James Hamett DUNN, Bart. and widow of John Anthony JENKINSON. She *d.* 1982. He *d. s.p.* 25 Dec. 1982.

VIII. 1982. 8. RALPH STAWELL (DUTTON), BARON SHERBORNE, distant cousin and h., being s. of Henry John DUTTON (*d.* 1 Jan. 1935), by Blanche Eleanor, 2nd da. of Laurence Trent CAVE, of Ditcham Park, Petersfield, co. Hants., which Henry John was 1st s. of John Thomas DUTTON (*d.* 22 June 1884), by Lady Lavinia Agnes, yst. da. of Thomas (PARKER), 5th EARL OF MACCLESFIELD, which John Thomas was 2nd s. of the 2nd Baron Sherborne. He was *b.* 25 Aug. 1898; ed. at Eton and Oxford (Ch. Ch.). He *d.* unm. 20 Apr. 1985 when his title became *extinct*

note (c), delete all detail

SHREWSBURY

page 685,
line 2, for '4 Dec.' read '24 Dec.'

page 688,
note (a), line 2, after 'Roger.' add 'He was probably dead by 1060 or 1062, see G.H. White, *Geneal. Mag.*, vol. 10, 1946, pp. 7–8.'

page 706,
line 22, for 'about 1467' read 'in (1457–8), 36 Hen. VI, in the chapel of Maxstoke Castle, co. Warwick' [Dugdale, *Antiq. of Warwickshire*, vol. ii, p. 995]

page 730,
line 15, after 'PENNOYER' add ', who *d.* 17 Nov. 1968. She *d.* 18 Apr. 1965.'
line 16, line to read as follows

XXIV. 1921. 21. JOHN GEORGE CHARLES HENRY ALTON ALEXANDER CHETWYND (CHETWYND-TALBOT), EARL OF SHREWSBURY, &c., grandson and h.,

lines 26–7, delete from 'Having' to 'work.(b)]' and replace by 'This marriage was diss. by divorce 1963 and he *m.* 2ndly, 18 Oct. 1963, Doris Aileen MORTLOCK. He *d.* 12 Nov. 1980.(b) His widow *d.* 1993.'

XXV. 1980. 22. CHARLES HENRY JOHN BENEDICT CROFTON CHETWYND (CHETWYND-TALBOT), EARL OF SHREWSBURY, &c., 1st s. and h. by 1st wife, *b.* 18 Dec. 1952; ed. at Harrow; *m.*, 1974, Deborah Jane, da. of Noel Staughton HUTCHINSON of Sambrook, co. Salop.

[JAMES RICHARD CHARLES JOHN CHETWYND-TALBOT, *styled* VISCOUNT INGESTRE, 1st s. and h. ap., *b.* 11 Jan. 1978.]

SIDMOUTH

page 736,
line 22, line to read as follows

IV. 1913. 4. GERALD ANTHONY PELLEW BAGNALL (ADDINGTON), VISCOUNT SIDMOUTH, 1st s. and h.,

line 27, for 'was living in 1946.]' read '*d.* 18 Dec. 1954.'
line 28, line to read as follows

V. 1915. 5. GERALD WILLIAM (ADDINGTON), VISCOUNT SIDMOUTH, 1st s. and h., *b.* 19 Aug. 1882;

lines 32–3, delete from 'Having' to 'work.]' and replace by 'He *d. s.p.* 4 Apr. 1953. His widow *d.* 1983.'

VI. 1953. 6. RAYMOND ANTHONY (ADDINGTON), VISCOUNT SIDMOUTH, br. and h., *b.* 24 Jan. 1887; ed. at Cheltenham and R.M.C., Sandhurst; *m.*, 26 Aug. 1913, Gladys Mary Dever, da. of Thomas Francis HUGHES. He *d.* 7 Feb. 1976. His widow *d.* 1983.

VII. 1976. 7. JOHN TONGE ANTHONY PELLEW (ADDINGTON), VISCOUNT SIDMOUTH, 1st s. and h., *b.* 3 Oct. 1914; ed. at Downside and Oxford (Brasenose Coll.); *m.* 1stly, 20 Jan. 1940, Barbara Mary Angela, 1st da. of Bernard ROCHFORT. She *d.* 1989 and he *m.* 2ndly, 1993, Marie Thérèse, da. of Sir Joseph Alfred SHERIDAN and widow of Francis Anthony Baring POLLEN.

[CHRISTOPHER JOHN ADDINGTON, 1st s. and h. ap., *b.* 10 Apr. 1941; ed. at Downside and Oxford (Brasenose Coll.); *m.*, 28 July 1963, Clio Mona, da. of Dr John PERISTIANY of Athens. She *d.* 8 Apr. 1986. He *d. v.p. s.p.* 2 June 1986.]

[JEREMY FRANCIS ADDINGTON, 2nd but 1st surv. s. and h. ap., *b.* 29 July 1947; ed. at Ampleforth; *m.* 1stly, 20 Mar. 1970, Grete, da. of (__) HENNINGSEN of Randers, Denmark. He *m.* 2ndly, 1986, Una, 1st da. of James COOGAN of Calne, Wilts.]

SINCLAIR

page 747,
line 36, line to read as follows

XVI. 1922. 7. ARCHIBALD JAMES MURRAY (ST. CLAIR), LORD SINCLAIR, 1st s. and h., *b.* 16 Feb. 1875;

page 748,
line 7, after 'She' add ', who' and after '1881' add ', 8 Nov. 1953.'
lines 7–9, delete from 'Having' to 'work.]' and replace by 'He *d.* 25 Nov. 1957.'

XVII. 1957. 8. CHARLES MURRAY KENNEDY (ST. CLAIR), LORD SINCLAIR, only s. and h., *b.* 21 June 1914; ed. at Eton and Cambridge (Magdalene Coll.); Portcullis Pursuivant, 1949–57, York Herald, 1957–68. He *m.*, 6 Jan. 1968, Anne Lettice, yr. da. of Lieut. Col. Sir Richard Charles Geers COTTERELL, Bart., C.B.E.

[MATTHEW MURRAY KENNEDY ST. CLAIR, MASTER OF SINCLAIR, s. and h. ap., *b.* 9 Dec. 1968.]

APPENDIXES

APPENDIX D

page 105,
note (d), line 8, after 'children.' add 'Another daughter, Elizabeth, said to be Henry's youngest illegitimate child, is mentioned in *Scots Peerage*, (vol. iv, p. 136), and there said to have married Fergus, Lord of Galloway. See also C. Warren Hollister, *Monarchy, Magnates and Institutions*, 1986, p. 251, n. 17. G.W.S. Barrow, *Robert Bruce*, 1988, p. 331, n. 26, corrects doubts as to the marriage in the *Scots Peerage*. *Ex inform.* Eric Thompson.

page 108,
line 5, for 'Beatrice' read '?Mabel' [Douglas Richardson, *The Geneal.*, vol. 9, 1988, p. 226.]
note (d), line 2, for '4' read '3'
line 3, after 'coheirs' add '(W.L. Sheppard, *Amer. Geneal.*, vol. 29, 1953, pp. 13–17; vol. 31, 1955, p. 118.)'

page 132,
note (d), line 2, after 'understanding.' add 'See also vol. xii, part 2, p. 396, note (c), *sub* WARWICK.'

VOLUME 12 PART 1

SKELMERSDALE

page 1,
line 31, delete '([d])' and after this line add

* * * * * *

V. 1930. 5. ARTHUR GEORGE (BOOTLE-WILBRAHAM), BARON SKELMERSDALE, kinsman of Edward William, 4th BARON SKELMERSDALE and 3rd EARL OF LATHOM (see LATHOM above), being s. and h. of Arthur BOOTLE-WILBRAHAM (*d.* 21 May 1897), which Arthur was s. and h. of Col. Edward BOOTLE-WILBRAHAM (*d.* 17 Dec. 1882), 2nd s. of the 1st Baron. He was *b.* 21 May 1876; ed. at Wellington and Freiburg (Saxony), Sch. of Mines. He *d.* unm. 9 Feb. 1969.

VI. 1969. 6. LIONEL (BOOTLE-WILBRAHAM), BARON SKELMERSDALE, cousin and h., being only s. and h. of Lionel BOOTLE-WILBRAHAM (21 May 1897), by Lavinia, da. of Abraham WILSON of Downshire House, Newry, co. Down, which Lionel was 2nd s. of Edward BOOTLE-WILBRAHAM abovementioned. He was *b.* 23 Sep. 1896; ed. at Wellington and Cheltenham; *m.*, 1 Oct. 1936, Anne, da. of Percy Cuthbert QUILTER. He *d.* 21 July 1973. His widow *d.* 1974.

VII. 1974. 7. ROGER (BOOTLE-WILBRAHAM), BARON SKELMERSDALE, s. and h., *b.* 2 Apr. 1945; ed. at Eton and Lord Wandsworth Coll.; *m.*, 1972, Christine Joan, da. of Philip Roy MORGAN, of Evercreech, Somerset.

[ANDREW BOOTLE-WILBRAHAM, s. and h. ap., *b.* 9 Aug. 1977.]

note ([d]), delete all detail

SLANE

page 16,
line 9, after (FLEMING) add LORD SLANE [I.]

SLATE

page 23,
after line 7 add as follows

SLATE OR SLEAT

Sir Donald Macdonald of Sleat, 1st s. and h. of Sir Donald MACDONALD, 3rd Bart. by Mary, 2nd da., and in her issue h. of Robert (DOUGLAS), 10th EARL OF MORTON, was *cr.* 23 Dec. 1716, by the *titular* King James III, BARON MACDONALD OF SLEAT or SLATE [S.], with rem. to his heirs male.([c]) For fuller particulars of him and his successors see Ruvigny's *Jacobite Peerage.*, 1904, pp. 166–8 and above *sub* MACDONALD OF SLATE [I.].

note ([c]) See vol. i, Appendix F for a list of Jacobite Peerages.

SLIGO

page 26,
lines 28–9, delete from 'He' to 'work.([e])'

V. 1903. 5. HENRY ULICK (BROWNE), MARQUESS OF SLIGO, &c., 5th and only surv. br., *b.* 14 Mar. 1831 [for further detail see note ([e])].

VI. 1913. EARLDOM [I.] V. 1916. 6 and 5. GEORGE ULICK (BROWNE), MARQUESS OF SLIGO, &c., EARL OF CLANRICARDE [I.], s. and h., *b.* 1 Sep. 1856 [for further detail see note ([e]), on page 27].

MARQUESSATE [I.] VII. EARLDOM [I.] VI. } 1935 7. and 6. ULICK DE BURGH (BROWNE), MARQUESS OF SLIGO [1800], EARL OF ALTAMONT [1771], EARL OF CLANRICARDE [1800], VISCOUNT WESTPORT [1768], and BARON MOUNT EAGLE OF WESTPORT [1760], all in the Peerage of Ireland, also BARON MONTEAGLE OF WESTPORT [U.K. 1806], s. and h., *b.* 30 Mar. 1898 [for further detail see note ([e]), on page 27].

MARQUESSATE [I.] VIII. EARLDOM [I.] VII. } 1941 8 and 7. ARTHUR HOWE (BROWNE), MARQUESS OF SLIGO, &c., uncle and h. [for further detail see note ([e]), on page 27]. He *d. s.p.* 28 May 1951. His widow *d.* 13 Aug. 1953.

MARQUESSATE [I.] IX. EARLDOM [I.] VIII. } 1951 9 and 8. TERENCE (BROWNE), MARQUESS OF SLIGO, , &c., br. and h., *b.* 28 Sep. 1873; Supt. Bengal Police, 1894–1907. He *d.* unm. 28 July 1952.

MARQUESSATE [I.] X. EARLDOM [I.] IX. } 1952 10 and 9. DENIS EDWARD (BROWNE), MARQUESS OF SLIGO, &c., nephew and h., being s. and h. of Alfred Eden BROWNE (*d.* 27 Aug. 1928, being *k.* in action), by Cicely, da. of Edward WORMALD which Alfred was 5th s. of the 5th Marquess. He was *b.* 13 Dec. 1908; ed. at Eton; *m.*, 12 Nov. 1930, José, da. of William GAUCHE. He *d.* 11 Sep. 1991. His widow was still living 1995.

MARQUESSATE [I.] XI. EARLDOM [I.] X. } 1991 11 and 10. JEREMY ULICK (BROWNE), MARQUESS OF SLIGO, &c., only s. and h., *b.* 4 June 1939; ed. at St. Columba's Coll. and R.A.C., Cirencester; *m.*, 26 Oct. 1961, Jennifer June, da. of Major Derek COOPER, M.C.

SOMERS

page 30,
note ([d]), line 2, delete 'Sir'

page 36,
lines 2–3, delete from 'He' to 'work.'

BARONY. VIII. } 1944 7. ARTHUR PERCY SOMERS (COCKS), BARON SOMMERS OF EVESHAM, &c., 4th and yst. s. of Arthur Herbert COCKS abovenamed, br. of the 5th Baron [for further detail see note (b)]. She *d.* 29 May 1950. He *d.* 8 Feb. 1953.

BARONY. IX. } 1953 8. JOHN PATRICK SOMERS (COCKS), BARON SOMMERS OF EVESHAM, &c., s. and h., *b.* 30 Apr. 1907; ed. at Royal Coll. of Music; etc. He *m.* 1stly, 15 Aug. 1935, Barbara Marianne, da. of Charles Henry SOUTHALL, of Norwich. She *d.* 11 Sep. 1959 and he *m.* 2ndly, 28 July 1961, Dora Helen, da. of John MOUNTFORT of Sydney, N.S.W., Australia. She *d.* 1993. He *d. s.p.* 15 Feb. 1995.

BARONY. X. } 1995 9. PHILIP SEBASTIAN SOMERS (COCKS), BARON SOMMERS OF EVESHAM, &c., kinsman and h., being 1st s. and h. of John Sebastian Somers COCKS (*d.* 25 May 1964), by Marjorie Olive, da. of Arthur Julius WELLER, which John was s. and h. of Philip Alphonso Somers Cocks (*d.* 26 Mar. 1940), by Gwenllian Blanche, da. of David WILLIAMS of Hirwain, co. Glamorgan, which Philip was s. and h. of John James Thomas Somers Cocks (*d.* 21 Sep. 1906), by Ann, da. of the Rev. Joseph SIMPSON, which John was 4th s. of Philip James COCKS (*d.* 1 Apr. 1857), by Frances, da. of Arthur HERBERT of Brewsterfield, Killarny, which Philip was 3rd s. of the 1st Baron. He was *b.* 4 Jan. 1948; ed. at Elston Hall, Newark, and Craig-y-Parc, Cardiff.

note (b), lines 7–9, delete from 'His' to 'Norwich'

SOMERSET

page 39,
note (f), line 6, after 'creation.' add 'For the probably mythical earldom of Somerset granted to Reynold de Mohun, see *ante* vol. ix, p. 20, note (l), and the references there cited.'

page 88,
line 22, delete '(e)'

page 89,

XX. 1923. 16. EDWARD HAMILTON (SEYMOUR), DUKE OF SOMERSET, &c., kinsman and h. male [for further detail see note (e), on page 88]. His widow *d.* 13 Nov. 1950.

XXI. 1931. 17. EVELYN FRANCIS EDWARD (SEYMOUR), DUKE OF SOMERSET, &c., s. and h., *b.* 1 May 1882 in Ceylon [for further detail see note (e), on page 88]. He *d.* 26 Apr. 1954. His widow *d.* 19 Apr. 1962.

[FRANCIS EDWARD SEYMOUR, 1st s. and h. ap., *b.* 28 Sep. 1906, *d. v.p.* an infant, 12 May 1907.]

[ALGERNON FRANCIS EDWARD SEYMOUR, 2nd s. and h. ap., *b.* 22 July 1908, *d. v.p.* 14 Feb. 1911.]

XXII. 1954. 18. PERCY HAMILTON (SEYMOUR), DUKE OF SOMERSET and BARON SEYMOUR [1547], also a Baronet [1611], 3rd but 1st surv. s. and h., *b.* 27 Sep. 1910; ed. at Blundell's Sch. and Cambridge (Clare Coll.); B.A. 1933; *styled* LORD SEYMOUR 1931–54; served in WW2 1939–45, in the Wiltshire Regt.; Major 1943. He *m.*, 18 Dec. 1951, Gwendoline Collette Jane, 2nd da. of Major John Cyril Collette THOMAS of Bude, Cornwall. He *d.* 15 Nov. 1984. His widow was still living in 1995.

XXIII. 1984. 19. JOHN MICHAEL EDWARD (SOMERSET), DUKE OF SOMERSET, &c., 1st s. and h., *b.* 30 Dec. 1952; ed. at Eton; *m.*, 1978, Judith-Rose, da. of John HULL of London.

[SEBASTIAN EDWARD SOMERSET, s. and h. ap., *b.* 3 Feb. 1982.]

note (e), from page 88, lines 26–9 (on page 89), delete from 'Percy' to '1943'

SOMERY

page 110,
line 4, after 'PAYNEL' add 'see PAYNELL'

page 111,
line 3, delete 'between'
line 4, delete 'and Michaelmas 1211'
line 7, after 'BEAUCHAMP' add 'OF BEDFORD'
note (b), lines 2–4, delete from 'These'

page 113,
line 20, after 'CHAUCOMBE' add 'of Chalcombe, Northants'

SONDES

page 118,
lines 5–6, delete from 'He' to 'work.'

EARLDOM. III. BARONY. VII. } 1907 3 and 7. LEWIS ARTHUR (MILLES), EARL SONDES OF LEES COURT, &c., br. and h., *b.* 3 Oct. 1866 [for further detail see note (b)].

EARLDOM. IV. BARONY. VIII. } 1941 4 and 8. GEORGE HENRY (MILLES-LADE),(ba) EARL SONDES OF LEES COURT, &c., nephew and h., being s. and h. of Henry Augustus MILLES-LADE (*d.* 30 July 1937), by Esther, da. of Col. Joseph Spencer BENYON, which Henry was 4th s. of the 1st Earl. He was *b.* 8 Feb. 1918 [for further detail see note (b)]. She *d.* 10 Nov. 1967. He *d.* 30 Apr. 1970.

EARLDOM. V. BARONY. IX. } 1970 — 5 and 9. HENRY GEORGE HERBERT (MILLES-LADE), EARL SONDES OF LEES COURT [1880], VISCOUNT THROWLEY [1880], and BARON SONDES of LEES COURT [1760], s. and h., *b.* 1 May 1940; *styled* VISCOUNT THROWLEY 1941–70; ed. at Eton and La Rosey; *m.* 1stly, 1 Jan. 1968, Primrose Ann, da. of Lawrence Stopford Llewellyn COTTER and formerly wife of Richard Hugh Nicholas CRESSWELL. This marriage was diss. by divorce in 1969 and he *m.* 2ndly, 1976, Silvia-Gabrielle, da. of Hans Otto SCHIED and widow of ALTGRAF HUGO ZU SALM-REIFFERSCHEIDT-RAITZ. This marriage was diss. by divorce in 1981 and he *m.* 3rdly, 1981, Sharon MCCLUSKEY, which marriage was also diss. by divorce in 1984 and he *m.* 4thly, 1986, Phyllis Kane SCHMERTZ. He *d. s.p.* 2 Dec. 1996 when his titles became *extinct* or *dormant*. His widow was still living in 1995.

note ([b]), lines 8–9, delete from 'His' to '1941'

note ([ba]) His father Henry Augustus Milles, 4th s. of the 1st Earl, assumed the additional name and arms of Lade in 1912.

SOUTHAMPTON

page 137,

line 33, after 'York' add 'She *d.* 19 May 1957. He *d.* 7 Dec. 1958.'

line 34, line to read as follows

V. 1958. 5. CHARLES (FITZROY), BARON SOUTHAMPTON, s. and h., *b.* 3 Jan. 1904;

page 138,

line 1, delete '([a])' and replace by 'On death of his father disclaimed his peerage for life, 16 Mar. 1964.'

line 6, delete ']' and replace by 'He *m.* 3rdly, 3 Feb. 1951, Rachel Christine, da. of Charles ZAMAN of Lille, France. She *d.* 1985. He *d.* 1989.'

VI. 1989. 6. CHARLES JAMES (FITZROY), s. and h. by 1st wife, *b.* 12 Aug. 1928; ed. at Stowe; *m.*, 29 May 1951, Pamela Anne, da. of Edward Percy HENRIKER of Yelverton, Devon.

[CHARLES FITZROY, 1st s. and h. ap., *b.* 18 Jan. 1954; ed. at Gresham's Sch., Holt; *m.*, 1975, Joanna Dana, da. of Chandos Robert Henry BRUDENELL-BRUCE. He *d.* 1975, being *k.* in a motor accident.]

[EDWARD CHARLES FITZROY, 2nd but 1st surv. s. and h. ap., *b.* 8 July 1955; ed. at Greshams Sch., Holt and R.A.C., Cirencester. He *m.*, 1978, Rachel Caroline Vincent, 2nd da. of Peter John Curnow MILLETT, of Drewsteignton, Devon.]

note ([a]), delete all detail

SOUTHESK

page 147,

line 27, line to read as follows

VII. 1905. 7. CHARLES NOEL (CARNEGIE), EARL OF SOUTHESK, &c., 1st s. and h. by 1st wife, *b.* 20 Mar. 1854 in Piccadilly; *styled* LORD CARNEGIE 1855–1905;

page 148,
lines 3–4, delete from 'Having' to 'work.([a])]'
line 5, delete ']'

VIII. 1941. 8. CHARLES ALEXANDER (CARNEGIE), EARL OF SOUTHESK, &c. [S.], BARON BALINHARD OF FARNELL [U.K.], 1st s. and h., *b.* 23 Sep. 1893 [for further detail see note ([a])]. He *m.* 2ndly, 16 May 1952, Evelyn Julia, 1st da. of Lieut. Col. Arthur Peere WILLIAMS-FREEMAN, D.S.O., O.B.E. and widow of Major Ian Edward FitzGerald CAMPBELL. He *d.* 16 Feb. 1992. His widow *d.* 30 Aug. 1992.

[JAMES GEORGE ALEXANDER BANNERMAN CARNEGIE, s. and h. ap., *b.* 23 Sep. 1929; MASTER OF CARNEGIE 1929–41, *styled*, LORD CARNEGIE, 1941–59. Was heir presumptive to the Dukedom of Fife in accordance with the spec. rem. in the creation (1900) of the dignity, and *suc.* his aunt in that dignity in 1959. See FIFE.]

note ([a]), lines 9–13, delete from 'His' to 'see'

SOUTHWELL

page 151,
line 39, after 'Newbury' add 'His widow *d.* 18 Sep. 1952.'

page 152,
line 1, line to read as follows

VISCOUNTCY [I.] VI. BARONY [I.] VIII. } 1944 6 and 8. ROBERT ARTHUR WILLIAM JOSEPH (SOUTHWELL), VISCOUNT SOUTHWELL OF CASTLE MATTRESS, &c., 1st s. and h., *b.* 5 Sep. 1898;

lines 9–10, delete from 'Having' to 'work.([c])]' and replace by 'He *d. s.p.m.* 18 Nov. 1960. His widow *d.* 1973.'

VISCOUNTCY [I.] VII. BARONY [I.] IX. } 1960 7 and 9. PYERS ANTHONY JOSEPH (SOUTHWELL), VISCOUNT SOUTHWELL OF CASTLE MATTRESS, &c., nephew ([c]) and h., being the s. and h. of Francis Joseph SOUTHWELL (*d.* 7 Jan. 1953, 2nd s. of the 5th Viscount), by Agnes Mary Annette, 1st da. of Charles William CLIFFORD of The Red House, Market Drayton. He was *b.* 14 Sep. 1930; ed. at Beaumont Coll., Old Windsor and R.M.C., Sandhurst. He *m.*, 3 Dec. 1955, Barbara Jacqueline, yr. da. of Andrew RAYNES of Harpenden, co. Herts.

[RICHARD ANDREW PYERS SOUTHWELL, s. and h. ap., *b.* 15 June 1956.]

note ([c]), lines 1–2, delete from 'The' to '1900'

SPENCER

page 158,
line 23, for 'See' read 'For Charles Robert and his s., Albert Edward John, 7th EARL SPENCER see'

EARLDOM. VIII. VISCOUNTCY. III. } 1975

8 and 3. EDWARD JOHN (SPENCER), EARL SPENCER AND VISCOUNT ALTHORP [G.B. 1765], &c., and VISCOUNT ALTHORP [U.K. 1905], 1st s. and h. [of 7th Earl Spencer, see vol. xiii, p. 39], *b.* 24 Jan. 1924. Queen Mary and the Prince of Wales were godparents at his baptism. Ed. at Eton, R.M.C., Sandhurst and R.A.C., Cirencester; *m.* 1stly, 1 June 1954, Frances Burke Ruth, yr. da. of Edmund Maurice (ROCHE), 4th BARON FERMOY. This marriage was diss. by divorce in 1969 and he *m.* 2ndly, Raine, da. of Alexander George MCCORQUODALE, of Speen, co. Bucks., formerly wife of Gerald Humphrey (LEGGE), 9th EARL OF DARTMOUTH. He *d.* 29 Mar. 1992. His widow, *m.* 3rdly, 1993, COUNT JEAN FRANCOIS DE CHAMBRUN. She was still living 1995.

EARLDOM. IX. VISCOUNTCY. IV. } 1992

9 and 4. CHARLES EDWARD MAURICE (SPENCER), EARL SPENCER, &c., 2nd but 1st surv. s. and h.,([b]) *b.* 20 May 1964; ed. at Eton and Oxford (Magdalen Coll.); *m.*, 1989, Catherine Victoria, da. of John LOCKWOOD. This marriage was diss. by divorce 1997.

[LOUIS FREDERICK SPENCER, *styled* VISCOUNT ALTHORP, s. and h. ap., *b.* 14 Mar. 1994.]

note ([d]) The 1st s., John, was *b.* and *d.* 12 Jan. 1960.

STAFFORD

page 171,
line 12, after 'MUCEGROS' add 'of Charlton, by Hawise, da. and coh. of Sir William MALET, of Curry Mallet. [See LISLE, vol. viii, p. 70.]
line 13, after '1242.' add 'Mabel *m.* 2ndly, Robert DE LISLE, who *d.* 1284.'

page 173,
lines 13–14, before 'LORD' add '1st' and delete from 'Joan' to 'Ruthin' and replace by 'Hawise.'
note ([k]), line 1, after 'Her.' add 'N.S.' and after 'iii,' add '1880',

page 182,
line 2, delete 'slain' and replace by 'wounded. He *d.* about 1458.'

page 198,
lines 1–12, delete from '([d])' to 'work.'

XXI. 1913. 6. FRANCIS HERBERT FITZHERBERT (STAFFORD-JERNINGHAM), BARON

STAFFORD, &c., nephew and h. gen., being the 1st s. and h. of Basil Thomas FITZHERBERT [for further detail see note ([d])]. His widow *d.* 15 Dec. 1958.

XXII. 1932. 7. EDWARD STAFFORD (FITZHERBERT), BARON STAFFORD [1640], 3rd but next surv. br. and h., *b.* 17 Apr. 1864 [for further detail see note ([d])].

XXIII. 1941. 8. BASIL FRANCIS NICHOLAS (FITZHERBERT), BARON STAFFORD, nephew and h., being the 1st s. and h. of Capt. Thomas Charles FITZHERBERT (*d.* 20 Sep. 1937, 4th and yst. br. of the 6th Baron), by Helen Beryl Frances, widow of Major Henry Brougham, R.A., 2nd da. of John Michael WATERS, of Hill House, Farnham, Surrey. He was *b.* 7 Apr. 1926; ed. at Ampleforth; served in WW2; Lieut. Scots Guards, 1945; *m.*, 16 June 1952, Morag Nada, yr. da. of Lieut. Col. Alastair CAMPBELL of Milltimber, Aberdeenshire. He *d.* 8 Jan. 1986. His widow was still living 1995.

XXIV. 1986. 9. FRANCIS MELFORT WILLIAM (FITZHERBERT), BARON STAFFORD, 1st s. and h., *b.* 13 Mar. 1954; ed. at Ampleforth; *m.*, 1980, Katharine Mary, 3rd da. of John CODRINGTON of Barnes.

[BENJAMIN JOHN BASIL FITZHERBERT, 1st s. and h. ap., *b.* 8 Nov. 1983.]

note ([d]), lines 27–30, delete from 'and was' to '1945'

page 200,
line 10, after '25' add ', *sic*'

STAIR

page 215,
line 13, line to read as follows

EARLDOM [S.] XI. / VISCOUNTCY [S.] XII. } 1903 — 11 and 12. JOHN HEW NORTH GUSTAVE HENRY HAMILTON (DALRYMPLE), EARL OF STAIR, &c., 1st s. and h., *b.* 12 June 1848 ;

line 25 (to line 2 on page 216), delete from 'Having' to 'work.]'

EARLDOM [S.] XII. / VISCOUNTCY [S.] XIII. } 1914 — 12 and 13. JOHN JAMES (DALRYMPLE), EARL OF STAIR, &c., and BARON OXENFOORD OF COUSLAND, *b.* 1 Feb. 1879 [for further detail see note ([c])]. He *d.* 4 Nov. 1961. His widow *d.* 22 Feb. 1968.

EARLDOM [S.] XIII. / VISCOUNTCY [S.] XIV. } 1961 — 13 and 14. JOHN AYMER (DALRYMPLE), EARL OF STAIR, &c., 1st s. and h., *b.* 9 Oct. 1906; *styled* VISCOUNT DALRYMPLE 1914–63 [for further detail see note ([c])]. He *m.*, 14 Jan. 1960, Davina Katharine, da. of Sir David BOWES-LYON, K.C.V.O.

[JOHN AYMER DALRYMPLE, *styled* VISCOUNT DALRYMPLE, 1st s. and h. ap., *b.* 4 Sep. 1961.]

STALBRIDGE

page 217,
line 1, line to read as follows

II. 1912. 2. HUGH (GROSVENOR), BARON STALBRIDGE, 1st s. and h., *b.* 5 May 1880;

lines 7–8, delete from 'Having' to 'work.(c)]' and replace by 'He *d. s.p.m.s.* 24 Dec. 1949, when his Barony became *extinct*.

[HUGH RAUFE GROSVENOR, s. and h. ap., *b.* 17 Aug. 1904 [for further detail see note (c)].]

STAMFORD

page 226,
line 16, after 'BILLAGE' add 'shoemaker of Blackamoor Yard, Bridge Street, Cambridge by Susan, da. of [__] King (*m.* 24 Dec. 1822).'
line 17, delete 'of Wincanton Somerset'
line 17, delete 'She *d. s.p.*' and replace by 'She, who was *b.* 1823, *d. s.p. legit.*(aa)'
note (a), delete all detail and replace by 'John Billage was son of John Billage, shoemaker, of King Str., Cambridge. John Billage the younger is also said to have been of Wincanton, Somerset. *Ex inform.* Mrs M.J. Solman.'
note (aa) She may have left an illegitimate daughter. (*Ex inform.* Mrs M.J. Solman)

page 228,
line 8, after '1920' add 'She *d.* 1 Sep. 1959.'
line 9, line to read as follows

X. 1910. 10. ROGER(c) (GREY), EARL OF STAMFORD [1628] and BARON GREY OF GROBY [1603], 1st s. and h.,

line 11, after 'James's;' add '*styled* LORD GREY OF GROBY till 1910;'
lines 15–17, delete from 'Having' to 'work.]' and replace by 'He *d.* unm. 18 Aug. 1976 when his titles became *extinct*.'

STANHOPE

page 238,
line 13, line to read as follows

VII. 1905. 7. JAMES RICHARD (STANHOPE), EARL STANHOPE [1718], VISCOUNT STANHOPE OF MAHON [1717] and BARON STANHOPE OF ELVASTON [1717], &c., 1st s. and h., *b.* 11 Nov. 1880 at 20 Grosvenor Place; *styled* VISCOUNT MAHON till 1905;

page 239,
line 5, after '1941–8' add '[note (a), lines 1–3, to 'Chesterfield.' After 'Chesterfield' add '(see tab. ped.)']

lines 9–10, delete from 'Having' to 'work.(a)]' and replace by 'He *d. s.p.* 15 Aug. 1967, when all his titles became *extinct*, including the Earldom of Chesterfield, with the exception of the Viscountcy of Stanhope of Mahon and the Barony of Stanhope of Elvaston which were, in accordance with the spec. rem. of those dignities, inherited by his kinsman the 11th EARL OF HARRINGTON [1742], which see.'

note (a), lines 3–8, delete from 'There' to 'above'

STANLEY

page 245,
line 6, delete '1170–90' and replace by '*circa* 1200' [W. Ferguson Irvine, "The Early Stanleys", *Trans. Hist. Soc. Lancs. and Ches.*, vol. 105, 1954, pp. 47–9]

STANLEY OF ALDERLEY

page 256,
line 3, delete '(b)'

IV. 1903. 4. EDWARD LYULPH (STANLEY), BARON STANLEY OF ALDERLEY, &c., 3rd but next surv. br. and h., *b.* 16 May 1839 [for further detail see note (b)].

V. 1925. 5. ARTHUR LYULPH (STANLEY), BARON STANLEY OF ALDERLEY, &c., s. and h., *b.* 14 Sep. 1875 [for further detail see note (a), lines 15–28]. His widow *d.* 12 Apr. 1964.

VI. 1931. 6. EDWARD JOHN (STANLEY), BARON STANLEY OF ALDERLEY, &c. [for further detail see note (a), lines 28–31, and page 257, lines 1–8]. This marriage was diss. by divorce in 1948 and he *m.* 3rdly, Thérèse da. of Gen. (__) HUSSON of Toulon, France. This marriage was in turn diss. by divorce in 1957 and he *m.* 4thly, 15 Sep. 1961, Kathleen Margaret, da. of Cecil Murray WRIGHT and widow of Sir Edmund Frank CRANE. He *d.* 5 Mar. 1971. His widow was still living 1995.

VII. 1971. 7. LYULPH HENRY VICTOR OWEN (STANLEY), BARON STANLEY OF ALDERLEY, &c., br. and h., *b.* 22 Oct. 1915; ed. at Eton and Oxford (Balliol Coll.). He *d.* unm. 23 June 1971.

VIII. 1971. 8. THOMAS HENRY OLIVER (STANLEY), BARON STANLEY OF ALDERLEY [U.K. 1839], BARON EDDISBURY OF WINNINGTON [U.K. 1848], BARON SHEFFIELD OF ROSCOMMON [I. 1783], also a Baronet [1660], cousin and h., being 3rd s. of Lieut. Col. Oliver Hugh STANLEY (*d.* 13 Feb. 1952), by Alice Kathleen Violet, da. of Thomas Henry (THYNNE), 5th MARQUESS OF BATH, which Oliver was 3rd s. of the 4th Baron. He was *b.* 28 Sep. 1927; ed. at Wellington; *m.*, 30 Apr. 1955, Jane Barrett, da. of Ernest George HARTLEY of Milton under Wychwood, co. Oxford.

[RICHARD OLIVER STANLEY, s. and h. ap., *b.* 24 Apr. 1956; ed. at St. Edward's Sch., Oxford and Univ. Coll., London. He *m.*, 1983, Carla Mary Angela, 1st da. of Dr. Kenneth Thomas Clyde MCKENZIE of Solihull.]

STANMORE

page 258,
line 24, line to read as follows

II. 1912. 2. GEORGE ARTHUR MAURICE (HAMILTON-GORDON), BARON STANMORE, only s. and h., *b.* 3 Jan. 1871;

page 259,
lines 3–4, delete from 'Having' to 'work.]' and replace by 'He *d.* unm. 13 Apr. 1957 when his Barony became *extinct*.'

STAPLETON

page 263,
lines 4–5, delete from 'da. and' to 'BRUS' and replace by 'da. of John DE BELLEW, by Laderance (to whom she was coh.), sister and coh. of Sir Piers DE BRUS III of Skelton and Danby in Cleveland and 4th da. of Sir Piers DE BRUS II, of the same.' [See FAUCONBERGE, FITZHENRY and LANCASTER (Barony).]

STAWELL

page 266,
line 3, for 'about 1640' read '*bap*. 10 Sep. 1640'
note (b), after 'M.I.' add 'gives 1640, the parish register gives 10 Sep.' [*ex inform*. Thomas Woodcock, Norroy and Ulster King of Arms]

page 269,
line 12, after 'M.I.' add 'Will dat. 4 Apr. 1764, pr. 10 Sep. 1764, cod. 21 May, 1764.' [*ex inform*. W.H. Chellen]

STORMONT

page 292,
line 26, for 'Isabel' read 'Mary'

STOURTON

page 303,
line 11, after 'CHIDIOCK' add '6th LORD FITZPAYN'
line 12, after 'LUMLEY' add '1st LORD LUMLEY'

page 315,
line 24, after 'there' add 'His widow *d.* 9 Dec. 1961.'
line 25, line to read as follows

XXII. 1936. 22. WILLIAM MARMADUKE (STOURTON), LORD MOWBRAY, &c., 1st s. and h., *b.* 31 Aug. 1895

lines 31–2, delete from 'Having' to 'work.(g)]' and replace by 'He *d.* 7 May 1965. His widow *d.* 1975.'

XXIII. 1965. 23. CHARLES EDWARD (STOURTON), LORD MOWBRAY [1295], LORD SEGRAVE [1295], and BARON STOURTON [1448], *b.* 11 Mar. 1923; ed. at Ampleforth and Oxford (Ch. Ch.); served in WW2 as Lieut., Gren. Guards, in France, 1944; wounded; a Knight of the Sov. Mil. Order of Malta. He *m.*, 28 June 1952, Jane Faith de Yarborough, only da. of Stephen Nicholas (BATESON), 5th BARON DERAMORE.

[EDWARD WILLIAM STEPHEN STOURTON, s. and h. ap., *b.* 17 Apr. 1953; ed. at Ampleforth and Oxford (Ch. Ch.); *m.*, 1980, Penelope Lucy, 1st da. of Dr Peter BRUNET, of Steeple Aston, co. Oxford.]

note (g), delete all detail

STRADBROKE

page 323,
line 31, after '(d)' add 'His widow *d.* 14 Apr. 1949.'

page 324,
line 1, line to read as follows

IV. 1947. 4. JOHN ANTHONY ALEXANDER (ROUS), EARL OF STRADBROKE, &c., 1st s. and h.,

line 2, after '1903;' add '*styled* VISCOUNT DUNWICH till 1947;'
lines 7–8, delete from 'Having' to 'work.(a)]' and replace by 'She *d.* 1977. He *d.* 14 July 1983.'

V. 1983. 5. WILLIAM KEITH (ROUS), EARL OF STRADBROKE, &c., br. and h., *b.* 10 Mar. 1907; ed. at Harrow and Geelong Gram. Sch., Australia; Lieut. R.N. He *m.* 1stly, Pamela Catherine Mabel (who *d.* 1972), da. of Capt. Edward James Kay SHUTTLEWORTH. This marriage was diss. by divorce in 1940 and he *m.* 2ndly, 19 July 1943, April Mary, da. of Brig. Gen. Arthur Melland ASQUITH, D.S.O. He *d.* 18 July 1983. His widow was still living 1995.

VI. 1983. 6. ROBERT KEITH (ROUS), EARL OF STRADBROKE, &c., s. and h. by 1st wife, *b.* 25 Mar. 1937; ed. at Harrow; *m.* 1stly, 3 Sep. 1960, Dawn Antoinette, da. of Thomas Edward BEVERLEY, of Brisbane, Australia. This marriage was diss. by divorce in 1977 and he *m.* 2ndly, 1977, Roseanna Mary Blanche, da. of Dr Francis REITMAN.

[ROBERT KEITH ROUS, s. and h. ap. by 1st wife, *b.* 15 Nov. 1961.]
note (a), delete all detail

STRAFFORD

page 337,
line 5, line to read as follows

BARONY. VI. EARLDOM. XI. } 1918 6. EDMUND HENRY (BYNG), EARL OF STRAFFORD, &c., 2nd but 1st surv. s. and h.,

lines 10–11, delete from 'Having' to 'work.(a)]' and replace by 'She *d.* 2 Oct. 1951. He *d.* 24 Dec. 1951.'

BARONY. VII. EARLDOM. XII. } 1951 7. ROBERT CECIL (BYNG), EARL OF STRAFFORD, &c., nephew and h., being 2nd but only surv. s. and h. of Ivo Francis BYNG, 4th s. of the 5th Earl (who *d.* 11 June 1949), being 2nd s. of the 2nd wife. He was 29 July 1904; *m.* 1stly, 1 Jan. 1934, Maria Magdalena Elizabeth, da. of Henry CLOETE of Alphen, South Africa. This marriage was diss. by divorce in 1947 (she *m.* 2ndly as his 2nd wife, James Henry ROYDS), and he *m.* 2ndly, 19 June 1948, Clara Evelyn, da. of Sir Nusserwanjee Nowrosjee WADIA, K.B.E., C.I.E. He *d.* 4 Mar. 1984. His widow *d.* 1985.

BARONY. VIII. EARLDOM. XIII. } 1984 8. THOMAS EDMUND (BYNG), EARL OF STRAFFORD, &c., 1st s. and h. by 1st wife, *b.* 26 Sep. 1936; ed. at Eton and Cambridge (Clare Coll.); *m.* 1stly, 2 Aug. 1963, Jennifer Mary Denise, 2nd da. of Rt. Hon. William Morrison MAY, M.P., of Holywood, co. Down. This marriage was diss. by divorce in 1981 and he *m.* 2ndly, 1981, Julia Mary, yr. da. of Sir Dennis PILCHER, C.B.E., of Pulborough, Sussex and formerly wife of Derek Nicholas HOWARD.

[WILLIAM ROBERT BYNG, 1st s. and h. by 1st wife, *b.* 10 May 1964; ed. at Winchester.]

note (a), delete all detail

STRANGE OR LESTRANGE (of Blackmere)

page 343,
line 2, for 'Brimsfield' read 'Brimpsfield'
line 3, after 'GIFFARD' add (1st and 2nd LORDS GIFFARD)'

page 344,
line 4, after 'Ferrers' add [4th LORD FERRERS (of Chartley)]
lines 6–14, delete all detail. [The two das. attrib. to Fulk, LORD STRANGE in this volume were in fact das. of Fulk LESTRANGE of Longnor and Betton, his uncle, yr. son

of Fulk, 1st LORD STRANGE. See J.K. L'Estrange, "The Barony of Strange of Blackmere", *N&Q*, vol. 199, p. 98.]

line 15, delete '1 or'

line 25, delete '2 or'

note (i), line 2, after '3059.' add 'Margaret Ashton, *Thomas Arundel*, 1967, FitzAlan Family Tree, p. 436, argues that Mary FitzAlan was da. of Edmund, 9th Earl of Arundel, not Richard, 10th Earl. If this was so, Mary would have been about forty years of age when her son John was born.'

page 345,

line 6, delete '3 or'

line 13, delete '4 or'

page 346,

line 2, delete '5 or'

STRANGE OR LESTRANGE (of Knokyn)

page 352,

lines 18–19, delete from 'He' to 'Maud(l)' and replace by 'He *m.* 1stly, between 13 Oct. 1275 and 1 June 1276, Alianore da. and h. of Eble DE MONTZ, Constable of Windsor Castle, by Joan, widow of Godfrey DE CRAUCOMBE and before this of Stephen DE SOMERY, perhaps da. of (__) DE BECHE. She *d.* before 14 Aug. 1282. He *m.*, 2ndly Maud, widow of John DE STRADLING, or STRUTTELINGAS (*d.* shortly before Feb. 1282/3), da. and h. of John DE WALTON, of Little Wellesbourne and Walton Deyville, co. Warwick (*d.* before 28 Dec. 1277), by his wife Isabel(k)'

notes (k) and (l), delete all detail from both and replace as follows

note (k) C. L'Estrange Ewen, *Observations on the Stranges*, 1946, pp. 4–8; *V.C.H. Warwicks*, vol. v, pp. 195–6; *Warwicks. Feet of Fines*, Dugdale Soc., 1284–1345, no. 1093, *ex inform.* W.G. Davis.

page 353,

lines 1–2, delete from 'His' to 1309' and replace by 'His widow *m.* between 30 Oct. 1309 and 28 Nov. 1310, as his 1st wife, Thomas DE HASTANG, of Chebsey, co. Stafford, who *d.* in or before 1348. She *d.* before July 1325.'

note (b), after 'p. 50' add ', *ante*, vol. vi, pp. 342–4 *sub* HASTANG'

page 354,

line 7, delete from 'who' to 'Roger,' [*Cal. Fine Rolls*, vol. v, p. 383.]

line 17, after 'WARENNE' add '(only s. and h. ap. of John, 7th EARL OF SURREY)'

page 356,

line 1, delete after 'widow' and replace by '*m.* 2ndly Sir Roger KYNASTON, of Hordley, co. Salop. She *d.* on or before 11 Feb. 1453/4.' [J.K. L'Estrange, 'L'Estrange of Knokyn', *N&Q*, vol. 199, pp. 325, 326]

line 8, after '(g)' add 'sister of Elizabeth, Queen Consort of EDWARD IV, da. of Richard

(WIDEVILL), 1st EARL RIVERS, by Jacquette, widow of John DUKE OF BEDFORD, da. of Pierre DE LUXEMBOURG, COUNT OF ST. POL, and 2ndly Anne.[h] She was probably da. of Sir Edward NEVILL, 2nd LORD BERGAVENNY (*d.* 1476)'

note ([g]), lines 1–3, delete from 'Dugdale' to 'she' and replace by 'She presumably'

page 357,
after line 35 add as follows

XIV. 1921. 14. ELIZABETH FRANCIS, VISCOUNTESS ST. DAVIDS, BARONESS STRANGE OF KNOKYN, HUNGERFORD and DE MOLEYNS [see note ([c]) and ST. DAVIDS in vol. xiii, p. 94 and below]. She *d.* 12 Dec. 1974.

XV. 1974. 15. JESTYN AUSTEN PLANTAGENET (PHILIPPS), VISCOUNT ST. DAVIDS, LORD STRANGE OF KNOKYN, s. and h., *b.* 19 Feb. 1917. [For further detail and for the 3rd VISCOUNT ST. DAVIDS, see vol. xiii, p. 95, below.]

STRATHALLAN

page 376,
lines 32–4, delete from 'He' to 'work.' and replace by 'His widow *d.* 3 Oct. 1957.'

X. 1937. 10. JAMES ERIC (DRUMMOND), EARL OF PERTH [1605], VISCOUNT STRATHALLAN [1686], &c., half-brother and h., that is 2nd s. of the 8th Viscount, being 1st s. by 2nd wife [for further detail see note ([c]); after line 8, 'from 1941' read '1941–51']. He *d.* 15 Dec. 1951. His widow *d.* 24 Apr. 1965.

XI. 1951. 11. JOHN DAVID (DRUMMOND), EARL OF PERTH, VISCOUNT STRATHALLAN, &c., s. and h., *b.* 13 May 1907 [for further detail see note ([c]); after '1944–5', line 8 (page 377) of that note, add 'Minister of State for Colonial Affairs, 1957–62; P.C. 1957,'].

[JOHN ERIC DRUMMOND, s. and h. ap., *b.* 7 July 1935; ed. at Downside and Cambridge (Trin. Coll.); *m.* 1stly, 7 Jan. 1963, Margaret Ann, da. of Robin GORDON. This marriage was diss. by divorce in 1972 and he *m.* 2ndly, 1988, Mrs Marion ELLIOTT.]

note ([c]), line 8, for 'from 1941' read '1941–51'
line 9 (on page 377), delete from 'His' to '1935'

STRATHCONA

page 379,
lines 3–6, lines to read as follows

II. 1914. 2. MARGARET CHARLOTTE (SMITH), *suo jure* BARONESS STRATHCONA AND MOUNT ROYAL [1900] in accordance with the spec rem. in the creation of that dignity, only child and h., *b.* 17 Jan. 1854 in Labrador.

lines 12–13, delete from 'Having' to 'work.(b)]'

III. 1926. 3. DONALD STERLING PALMER (HOWARD), BARON STRATHCONA AND MOUNT ROYAL, 1st s. and h., *b.* 14 June 1891 [for further detail see note (b)]. He *d.* 22 Feb. 1959. His widow *d.* 1985.

IV. 1959. 4. DONALD EUAN PALMER (HOWARD), BARON STRATHCONA AND MOUNT ROYAL, 1st s. and h., *b.* 26 Nov. 1923; ed. at Eton, Cambridge (Trin. Coll.) and McGill Univ., Montreal, Canada; served in WW2 1939–45, in Royal Navy; Ordinary Seaman, 1942, Midshipman, R.N.V.R., 1943, Lieut. 1945. He *m.* 1stly, 20 Feb. 1954, Jane Mary, da. of Geoffrey Noel (WALDEGRAVE), 12th EARL WALDEGRAVE. This marriage was diss. by divorce in 1978 and he *m.* 2ndly, 1978, Patricia, da. of Harvey Evelyn THOMAS and widow of John MIDDLETON.

[DONALD ALEXANDER SMITH HOWARD, 1st s. and h. ap. by 1st wife, *b.* 24 June 1961; ed. at Gordonstoun and London Business Sch.; *m.*, 1992, Jane Maree, da. of R. Shaun GIBB of Sydney, Australia.]

note (b), lines 13–16, delete from 'His' to '1945'

STRATHEARN

page 382,
note (n), add at end 'See *ante* vol. x, Appendix A, p. 29'

STRATHEDEN

page 394,
line 19, line to read as follows

IV. 1918. 4. ALISTAIR (CAMPBELL), BARON STRATHEDEN OF CUPAR, &c., grandson and h., being 1st s. and h. of John Beresford CAMPBELL and Alice Susan his wife,

lines 30–1, delete from 'Having' to 'work.(d)]' and replace by 'She *d.* 9 Aug. 1956. He *m.* 2ndly, 21 Dec. 1964, Noel Christabel, da. of Capt. Conrad VINER and formerly wife of George VINCENT. He *d.* 12 Dec. 1981. His widow was still living 1995.'

V. 1981. 5. GAVIN (CAMPBELL), BARON STRATHEDEN OF CUPAR and BARON CAMPBELL OF ST. ANDREWS, br. and h., *b.* 28 Aug. 1901; ed. at Eton and R.M.C., Sandhurst; late K.R.R.C. and King's African Rifles. He *m.*, 26 Apr. 1933, Evelyn Mary Austin, da. of Col. Herbert Austin SMITH, C.I.E. He *d.* 29 Oct. 1987. His widow *d.* 1989.

VI. 1987. 6. DONALD (CAMPBELL), BARON STRATHEDEN OF CUPAR, &c., only s. and h., *b.* 4 Apr. 1934; ed. at Eton; *m.*, 8 Nov. 1957, Hilary Ann Holland, da. of Lieut. Col. William Derrington TURNER of Simonstown, South Africa. She *d.* 1991.

[DAVID ANTHONY CAMPBELL, s. and h. ap., *b.* 13 Feb. 1963; ed. in Queensland, Australia; *m.*, 1993, Jennifer Margaret OWENS.]

note ([d]), delete all detail

STRATHMORE

page 400,
line 13, for '1749' read '1748/9'

page 401,
line 2, after 'parish' add 'For his mistress Sarah Hussey, COUNTESS OF TYRCONNELL [I.], see *sub* TYRCONNELL [1762]'

page 402,
line 28, line to read as follows

XII. 1904. EARLDOM. 1937. 12 and 1. CLAUDE GEORGE (BOWES-LYON), EARL OF STRATHMORE AND KINGHORNE, &c. [S.], 1st s. and h., *b.* 14 Mar. 1855 in Lowndes Sq.;

page 403,
lines 1–2, delete from 'Having' to 'work.([b])]'

EARLDOM [S.] XIII. EARLDOM. II. } 1944 — 13 and 2. PATRICK (BOWES-LYON), EARL OF STRATHMORE AND KINGHORNE, &c. [S.] and and EARL OF STRATHMORE AND KINGHORNE [U.K. 1937], *b.* 22 Sep. 1884 [for further detail see note ([b])]. He *d.* 25 May 1949.

[JOHN PATRICK BOWES-LYON, 1st s. and h. ap., *b.* 1 Jan. 1910; MASTER OF GLAMIS; ed. at Harrow; 2nd Lieut., Scots Guards, 1931; Lieut., 1934; served in WW2, 1939–41 in N. Africa, and was *k.* in action, *v.p.* and unm., 19 Sep. 1941 at Halfaya Pass.]

EARLDOM [S.] XIV. EARLDOM. III. } 1949 — 14 and 3. TIMOTHY (BOWES-LYON), EARL OF STRATHMORE AND KINGHORNE, &c. [S.], &c., 2nd but 1st surv. s. and h., *b.* 18 Mar. 1918; ed. at Stowe; served in WW2, 1939–45, as Lieut., The Black Watch; MASTER OF GLAMIS 1941–4, and *styled* LORD GLAMIS 1944–9. He *m.*, 18 June 1958, Mary Bridget, da. of Peter BRENNAN of co. Leix, Eire. She *d.* 8 Sep. 1967. He *d. s.p.m.* 13 Sep. 1972.

EARLDOM [S.] XV. EARLDOM. IV. } 1972 — 15 and 4. FERGUS MICHAEL CLAUDE (BOWES-LYON), EARL OF STRATHMORE AND KINGHORNE, &c., cousin and h., being 1st s. of Michael Claude Hamilton BOWES-LYON (*d.* 1 May 1953), by Elizabeth Margaret, da. of John CATOR, which Michael was 5th s. of the 12th Earl. He was *b.* 31 Dec. 1928; ed. at Eton and R.M.C., Sandhurst; *m.*, 10 Apr. 1956, Mary Pamela, yr. da. of Brig. Norman Duncan MCCORQUODALE, M.C., of St. Boswell's, Roxburghshire. He *d.* 18 Aug. 1987. His widow was still living 1995.

EARLDOM [S.] XVI. EARLDOM. V. } 1987 16 and 5. MICHAEL FERGUS (BOWES-LYON), EARL OF STRATHMORE AND KINGHORNE, &c., only s. and h., *b.* 7 June 1957; ed. at Aberdeen Univ.; *m.*, 1984, Isobel Charlotte, yr. da. of Capt. Anthony WEATHERALL of Cowhill, Dumfries.

[SIMON PATRICK BOWES-LYON, s. and h. ap., *b.* 18 June 1986.]

note ([b]), lines 7–13, delete from 'His' to '1944'

STRATHSPEY OF STRATHSPEY

page 405,
between lines 15 and 16 add as follows

BARONY. IV. } 1915 4. TREVOR (OGILVIE-GRANT), BARON STRATHSPEY OF STRATHSPEY, in the counties of Inverness and Moray, also a Baronet [S. 1625], and Chief of Clan Grant, br. and h. male, *b.* 2 Mar. 1879; ed. at Waitaki High Sch. and St. John's Coll., New Zealand; *m.* 1stly, 19 Dec. 1905, Alice Louisa, da. of T.M. HARDY-JOHNSTON of Christchurch, New Zealand. She *d.* 18 Nov. 1945. He *m.* 2ndly, Mar. 1947, Elfrida Minnie Fass, da. of Gordon William Alexander CLOETE, of Cape Province, South Africa and widow of Lieut. Col. George CAPRON. He *d.* 11 Nov. 1948. His widow *d.* 19 July 1949.

V. 1948. 5. DONALD PATRICK TREVOR GRANT (OGILVIE-GRANT), BARON STRATHSPEY OF STRATHSPEY, &c., s. and h., *b.* 18 Mar. 1912; ed. at Stowe. He was recognised in the name of Grant of Grant by decree of the Lord Lyon, 1950. He *m.* 1stly, 24 Sep. 1938, Alice, da. of Francis BOWE of Timaru, New Zealand. This marriage was diss. by divorce in 1951 and he *m.* 2ndly, 1 Sep. 1951, Olive, da. of Wallace Henry GRANT of Norwich. He *d.* 27 Jan. 1992. His widow was still living 1995.

VI. 1992. 6. JAMES PATRICK TREVOR (OGILVIE-GRANT), BARON STRATHSPEY OF STRATHSPEY, &c., s. and h. by 1st wife, *b.* 9 Sep. 1943; *m.* 1stly, 1966, Linda, da. of David PIGGOTT of Forfar. This marriage was diss. by divorce in 1984 and he *m.* 2ndly, 1985, Margaret, da. of Robert DRUMMOND of Fife.

note ([b]), lines 4–5, delete from 'who' to 'See' and replace by 'see below and'

SUDELEY

page 417,
line 1, after 'Maud' add 'sister and coh. of Piers 3rd LORD MONTFORT'
line 1, delete 's. of' and replace by '1st LORD'

page 418,
note ([c]), add at end 'Dugdale was wrong in supposing that there were two Williams. Joan Sudeley's husband was William 2nd LORD BOTELER (of Wem), Joan being his second wife. See Walter L. Sheppard, *Geneal. Mag.*, vol. 13, 1960, pp. 173–4

and Col. F.R. Twemlow, "Manor of Tyrley", Staffs. Rec. Soc., pp. 41–2. See BOTELER, *ante*, vol. ii, p. 232.'

page 419,
line 12, for '1714' read '1417'

SUDELEY OF TODDINGTON

page 423,
line 38, line to read as follows

V. 1922. 5. WILLIAM CHARLES FREDERICK (HANBURY-TRACY), BARON SUDELEY OF TODDINGTON, 1st s. and h., *b.* 10 Apr. 1870;

page 424,
lines 7–8, delete from 'Having' to 'work.(d)]'

VI. 1932. 6. RICHARD ALGERNON FREDERICK (HANBURY-TRACY), BARON SUDELEY OF TODDINGTON, nephew and h. [for further detail see note (d)]. His widow was still living 1995.

VII. 1941. 7. MERLYN CHARLES SAINTHILL (HANBURY-TRACY), BARON SUDELEY OF TODDINGTON [1838], 1st cousin once removed and h. [for further detail see note (d), lines 7–12]. Ed. at Eton and Oxford (Worcester Coll.); *m.*, 1980, Elizabeth Mairi, 1st da. of Derek William Charles (KEPPEL), VISCOUNT BURY and formerly wife of Alastair Michael Hyde VILLIERS.

note (b), line 2, after 'Oxon.' add 'She *d.* 1975.'
note (d), lines 12–14, delete from 'The' to '1910'

SUFFIELD

page 428,
line 1, line to read as follows

VI. 1914. 6. CHARLES (HARBORD), BARON SUFFIELD, &c., 1st s. and h., *b.* 14 June 1855 at Gunton

lines 13–14, delete from 'Having' to 'work.(b)]' and replace by 'His widow *d.* 6 Feb. 1951.'

VII. 1924. 7. VICTOR ALEXANDER CHARLES (HARBORD), BARON SUFFIELD, &c., s. and h., *b.* 12 Sep. 1897 [for further detail see note (b)].

VIII. 1943. 8. JOHN (HARBORD), BARON SUFFIELD [1786], also a Baronet [1746], br. and h., *b.* 1 July 1907 [for further detail see note (b)].

IX. 1945. 9. GEOFREY WALTER (HARBORD), BARON SUFFIELD, &c., 1st cousin once removed and h. [for further detail see note (b)].

X. 1946. 10. RICHARD MORDEN (HARBORD-HAMOND), BARON SUFFIELD, &c., cousin and h. [for further detail see note ([b])]. He *d.* 2 Feb. 1951. His widow *d.* 8 Nov. 1955.

XI. 1951. 11. ANTHONY PHILIP (HARBORD-HAMOND), BARON SUFFIELD, &c., s. and h., *b.* 19 Jun. 1922; ed. at Eton; served in WW2, 1941–5, in N. Africa and Italy, Capt. Coldstream Guards. He *m.*, 16 Jan. 1952, Elizabeth Eve, 1st da. of Judge Samuel Richard EDGEDALE of Crowthorne, Berks. She *d.* 1995.

[CHARLES ANTHONY ASSHETON HARBORD-HAMOND, s. and h. ap., *b.* 3 Dec. 1953; ed. at Eton; *m.*, 1983, Lucy, yr. da. of Cmdr. A.S. HUTCHINSON, R.N., of Lechlade, co. Glos. This marriage was diss. by divorce in 1990.]

note ([b]), lines 26–8, delete from 'His' to 'Guards'

SUFFOLK

page 432,
line 5, add at end '1st LORD NORWICH'
line 6, after 'John' add 'DE NORWICH, 2nd LORD NORWICH'

page 433,
line 17, delete '2nd or'

page 434,
line 8, after '([c])' add 'by his first wife Elizabeth, da. of William (DE BOHUN), 1st EARL OF NORTHAMPTON'
note ([d]), line 14, after 'known' add 'For the early history of the de la Poles, see Rosemary Horrox, *The de la Poles of Hull*, East Yorks. Local History Soc., 1983.

page 440,
lines 3–4, delete from 'and' to 'GLANVILE' and replace by 'of Sir Richard DE BREWS of Wingfield'
note ([c]), lines 2–4, delete from 'Her' to 'f. 54' and replace by 'For her ancestry, see G.A. Moriarty, *New England Hist. and Gen. Reg.*, vol. 103, 1949, p. 291.'

page 450,
line 1, for '24 Mar.' read '6 Mar.' (*Benet's Chron.*, p. 209, n. 180).

page 458,
line 5, for 'aunt of the said Anne' read 'sister of the said Anne's stepmother'

page 459,
line 2, for '3rd' read '1st'
lines 3–4, delete from 'Lucy' to 'named' and replace by 'by his 1st wife([ax])'
note ([ax]) Her identity is unknown. Browne's 2nd wife was Lucy, da. and coh. of John (Neville) Marquess of Montagu abovenamed, being sister of Margaret, Lady Mortimer, also abovenamed.

page 460,
line 1, for '1534' read '1533'

page 481,
line 12, after 'nil' add 'His widow *d.* 5 Mar. 1968.'
line 13, line to read as follows

XXX. 1917. 20. CHARLES HENRY GEORGE (HOWARD), EARL OF SUFFOLK, EARL OF BERKSHIRE, &c., 1st s. and h., *b.* 2 Mar. 1906 at Charlton;

line 24, delete from 'Having' to 'work.(g)]' and replace by 'His widow *d.* 22 Feb. 1966.'

XXI. 1941. 21. MICHAEL JOHN JAMES GEORGE ROBERT (HOWARD), EARL OF SUFFOLK, EARL OF BERKSHIRE, &c., s. and h. *b.* 27 Mar. 1935; *styled* VISCOUNT ANDOVER till 1941; ed. at Winchester; *m.* 1stly, 1 Oct. 1960, Mme. Simone, da. of Georges LITMAN of Paris and formerly wife of Michel PAULMIER. This marriage was diss. by divorce in 1967 and he *m.* 2ndly, 1973, Anita Robsahm, da. of Robin Robsahm FUGLESANG of Cuckfield, Sussex. This marriage was also diss. by divorce, in 1980, and he *m.* 3rdly, 1983, Linda Jacqueline, da. of Lieut. Col. Vincent Rudolph PARAVICINI of Basingstoke, formerly wife of Alexander Nelson (HOOD), 4th VISCOUNT BRIDPORT.

[ALEXANDER CHARLES MICHAEL WINSTON ROBSAHM HOWARD, *styled* VISCOUNT ANDOVER, s. and h. ap. by 2nd wife, *b.* 17 Sep. 1974.]

note (g), delete all detail

SURREY

page 491,
note (g), line 7, (on page 492), after 'son.' add 'The entries for Rodulf I and Rodulf II need considerable revision, see "Aspects of Robert of Torigny's Genealogies revisited", K.S.B. Keats-Rohan, *Nottingham Med. Studies*, vol. 37, 1993, pp. 21–4.'

page 492,
line 7, delete '1stly'
lines 8–9, delete from 'Gunnor' to 'Normandy' and replace by 'Gotmund Rufus DE VASCOEUIL, da. of Tesselin, Vicomte of Rouen.'
lines 10–11, delete from 'Rodulf' to '(i)'
note (f), delete all detail and replace by 'Keats-Rohan, *op. cit.* above, p. 24. Beatrice is there shown to have probably been a great-niece of Gunnor, 2nd wife of Richard I, Duke of Normandy.'
note (i), delete all detail.

page 493,
line 1, delete 'by 1st wife(b)'
line 4, replace 'brother' by 'son'
lines 5–6, delete from 'and as' to 'issue' and replace by 'he *m.* Emma, whose parentage is unknown'

lines 8–9, replace 'yr. s. of Rodulf I by 1st wife' and replace by '1st s. of Rodulf II'
note ([b]), delete all detail
note ([d]), delete all detail and replace by 'See Keats-Rohan, *op. cit.*, p. 22.'
note ([e]), delete all detail

page 499,
line 4, for 'HAMEL' read 'HAMELIN'

page 505,
line 10, for '1269' read '1270'
line 11, delete 'one of the justices'

page 506,
note ([d]), line 1, for 'Edward' read 'John'

SUTHERLAND

page 537,
above '1235?' should appear EARLDOM [S.]

page 546,
line 22, for '95' read '?80' [Andrew MacEwan, *The Geneal.*, vol. 3, 1982, pp. 136–7]
line 28, after '([i])' add 'He appears to have *m.*, as her 3rd husband, Mariota, da. of Donald, Lord of the Isles. She was dead by 20 Jul. 1448.' [MacEwan, *op. cit.*, pp. 139–42, vol. 5, p. 225.]
note ([g]), add at end 'There is some evidence that the Earl married 1stly, before Margaret Baillie, a Helen Sinclair, da. of (probably) Henry, 2nd Earl of Orkney, (*Ane Breve Cronicle of the Earlis of Ross*, Edin., 1850, p. 26. *Ex Inform.* Col. G.R. Gayre.'
note ([j]), line 2, (on page 547) after 'Dunbeath.' add 'It is argued by Andrew MacEwan, (*op. cit.*, pp. 131–53, vol. 5, 1984, p. 225), that this Alexander Sutherland was indeed Alexander, Master of Sutherland, but that he was also 2nd son of Robert, 6th Earl of Sutherland. MacEwan further argues that this Alexander was born *c.* 1395–1400.'

page 568,
line 9, after '1925' add 'She *d.* 20 Aug. 1955.'
line 10, line to read as follows

DUKEDOM [U.K.] V. EARLDOM [S.] XXIII.	1913	5 and 23. GEORGE GRANVILLE (SUTHERLAND-LEVESON-GOWER), DUKE OF SUTHERLAND, &c., 1st s. and h., *b.* 29 Aug. 1888 at Cliefden House afsd.;

page 569,
lines 4–5, delete from 'Having' to 'work([b])]' and replace by 'He *d.* 1 Feb. 1963 when he was *suc.* by his cousin and h. male in all his dignities except the Earldom of Sutherland [S.], in which he was *suc.* by his niece and h. of line. See below. His widow was still living 1995.'

DUKEDOM [U.K.] VI. MARQUESSATE. VII. } 1963 — 6 and 7. JOHN SUTHERLAND (EGERTON), DUKE OF SUTHERLAND [1833], MARQUESS OF STAFFORD [1786], EARL GOWER [1746], EARL OF ELLESMERE [1846], VISCOUNT TRENTHAM [1746], VISCOUNT BRACKLEY [1846] and BARON GOWER OF STITTENHAM [1703], also a Baronet [1620], distant cousin and h., being 1st s. and h. of John Francis Granville Scrope (EGERTON), 4th EARL OF ELLESMERE (*d.* 24 Aug. 1944), by Violet, 1st da. of Frederick William (LAMBTON), 4th EARL OF DURHAM, 3rd in descent from the 1st EARL OF ELLESMERE who was 2nd s. of the 1st DUKE OF SUTHERLAND. He was *b.* 10 May 1915 and *suc.* his father as EARL OF ELLESMERE in 1944 and his cousin as DUKE OF SUTHERLAND, Etc. in 1963. Ed. at Eton and Cambridge (Trin. Coll.); *m.* 1stly, 29 Apr. 1939, Lady Diana Evelyn, da. of Alan Ian (PERCY), 8th DUKE OF NORTHUMBERLAND. She *d.* 1978 and he *m.* 2ndly, 1979, Evelyn Mary, da. Major Robert MOUBRAY.

SUTHERLAND (COUNTY)

page 569,

EARLDOM [S.] 1963 — 24. ELIZABETH MILLICENT, *suo jure* COUNTESS OF SUTHERLAND [S. 1235?], only da. and h. of Lord Alastair St. Clair SUTHERLAND-LEVESON-GOWER (*d.* 28 Apr. 1921), 2nd s. of the 4th Duke. Chief of Clan Sutherland, adopted the name of Sutherland in 1963. She was *b.* 30 Mar. 1921; *m.*, 5 Jan. 1946, Capt. Charles Noel JANSON, late Welsh Guards, s. of Charles Wilfred JANSON of Wilton Crescent, S.W.1.

[ALASTAIR CHARLES ST. CLAIR SUTHERLAND,(b) MASTER OF SUTHERLAND, *styled* LORD STRATHNAVER, *b.* 7 Jan. 1947; ed. at Eton and Oxford (Ch. Ch.); *m.* 1stly, 29 Nov. 1968, Eileen Elizabeth, da. of Richard Wheeler BAKER of Princeton, U.S.A. This marriage was diss. by divorce and he *m.* 2ndly, 1980, Gillian Margaret St. Clair, 1st da. of Robert MURRAY of Gouroch, Renfrewshire.]

note (b), lines 1–10, delete from 'The' to 'and' and replace by 'He has a twin brother'
line 10, for 'See' read 'For comments on the succession to the Earldom of Sutherland see'

SUTTON

page 575,
line 15, after 'Agnes' add 'da. of Sir John DE HOTHAM, of Scarborough, co. York'

SWANSEA OF SINGLETON

page 577,
line 7, delete '(b)'

III. 1922. 3. ODO RICHARD (VIVIAN), BARON SWANSEA OF SINGLETON, br. and h., being 4th but 1st surv. br. of the half-blood, 1st surv. s. by 3rd wife of the 1st Baron. He was *b.* 22 Apr. 1875 [for further detail see note (b)].

IV. 1934. 4. JOHN HUSSEY HAMILTON (VIVIAN), BARON SWANSEA OF SINGLETON, s. and h., *b.* 1 Jan. 1925; ed. at Eton and Cambridge (Trin. Coll.); *m.* 1stly, 19 Apr. 1956, Miriam Antoinette, da. of A.W.F. CACCIA-BIRCH, M.C., of Marton, New Zealand. This marriage was diss. by divorce in 1973 and he *m.* 2ndly, 1982, Mrs Lucy TEMPLE-RICHARDS, da. of the Right Rev. Hugh Rowlands GOUGH of Stockbridge, Hants.

[RICHARD ANTHONY HUSSEY VIVIAN, *b.* 24 Jan. 1957; ed. at Eton and Durham Univ.]

note (b), lines 10–12, delete from 'he' to '(Trin. Coll.)'

SWYNNERTON

page 588,
note (k), line 1, for 'His' read 'It has been suggested that he died in 1386 (*Hist. Coll. Staffs.*, vol. vii, p. 44). If this was so, it is strange that this dower case was not brought until ten years after he died. Robert's'

TAAFE

page 601,
lines 9–10, delete all detail and replace by

XIII. *13.* EDWARD CHARLES (TAAFFE), who but for the abovementioned Order in Council would have been VISCOUNT TAAFFE OF CORREN and BARON OF BALLLYMOTE [I.], and in whom is/was vested the right to petition, under the Titles Deprivation Act (7&8 Geo. V, cap. 47), 1917, for restoration of his peerages.(b) He was 1st s. and h., being only s. by 1st wife, *b.* 20 Mar. 1898 at Ellischau.

note (b) See Burke's *Peerage*, 1953, pp. cli–cliii.

TALBOT OF MALAHIDE & TALBOT DE MALAHIDE

page 628,
lines 3–6, delete all detail and replace as follows

BARONY [I.] VI. BARONY [U.K.] III. } 1921 6 and 3. JAMES BOSWELL (TALBOT), BARON TALBOT OF MALAHIDE, &c., only s. and h., *b.* 18 May 1874; *m.*, 19 Sep. 1924, Joyce Gunning (*b.* 16 Apr. 1897), da. of Frederick KERR, by Lucy, da. of (__) DOWSON. He *d. s.p.* 22 Aug. 1948. She *m.* 2ndly, 3 Oct. 1951, Brig. John Smith MCCOMBE (*d.* 19 Oct. 1959), and *d.* 1980.

BARONY [I.] VII. BARONY [U.K.] IV. } 1948 7 and 4. MILO JOHN REGINALD (TALBOT), BARON TALBOT OF MALAHIDE [I. 1831], also BARON TALBOT DE MALAHIDE [U.K. 1856], cousin and h., being s. of Col. Milo George TALBOT, C.B. (*d.* 3 Sep. 1931), by Eva, da. of

Col. John JOICEY, M.P., which Milo George was 4th s. of the 4th Baron Talbot. He was *b.* 1 Dec. 1912; ed. at Winchester and Cambridge (Trin. Coll.). He *d.* unm. 14 Apr. 1973 when his U.K. Barony became *extinct* but he was *suc.* in his Irish Barony by his distant cousin.

VIII. 1973. 8. REGINALD STANILAUS VICTOR (TALBOT), BARON TALBOT OF MALAHIDE [I. 1831], distant cousin and h., being 2nd s. of John Reginald Charles TALBOT (*d.* 5 Feb. 1909), by Maria Josephine, da. of the 3rd DUC DE STACPOOLE, which John Reginald was s. and h. of John Reginald Francis George Talbot (*d.* 17 Jan. 1906), by Sarah Eliza, da. of the Rev. David JONES, which John Reginald was 1st s. of Adm. Sir John TALBOT, G.C.B. (*d.* 18 Dec. 1843), by Juliana, 3rd da. of James Everard (ARUNDELL), 9th BARON ARUNDELL OF WARDOUR, which Sir John was 3rd. s. of 1st Baroness Talbot de Malahide. He was *b.* 7 May 1897; ed. at Beaumont Coll., Old Windsor; *m.*, 24 Apr. 1924, Cecily Elizabeth, da. of Major Garstang HODGSON of Clevedon, Somerset. He *d. s.p.* 2 Apr. 1975. His widow *d.* 1976.

IX. 1975. 9. JOSEPH HUBERT GEORGE (TALBOT), BARON TALBOT OF MALAHIDE [I.], br. and h., *b.* 22 Apr. 1899; ed. at Beaumont Coll., Old Windsor; *m.* 1stly, 5 July 1924, Hélène, da. of M. GOULEY of Seine et Oise, France. She *d.* 1961. He *m.* 2ndly, 1962, Beatrice, da. of (__) BROS of Nice, France. This marriage was diss. by divorce in 1970. He *d. s.p.* 20 Feb. 1987.

X. 1987. 10. REGINALD JOHN RICHARD (ARUNDELL), BARON TALBOT OF MALAHIDE, 1st cousin once removed, being s. and h. of Reginald John Arthur (who assumed the name of ARUNDELL, by Royal Lic. in 1945, *d.* 24 Nov. 1953), by Winifred, da. of Richard Barrett Stanswick CASTLE, which Reginald John Arthur was 1st s. of Reginald Aloysius TALBOT (*d.* 19 May 1922), by Mabile Mary, da. of Robert Arthur ARUNDELL, 4th s. of 9th BARON ARUNDELL, which Reginald Aloysius was s. of John Reginald Francis George abovementioned. He was *b.* 9 Jan. 1931; ed. at Stoneyhurst and R.M.A., Sandhurst; *m.* 1stly, 24 Sep. 1955, Laura Duff, da. of Grp. Capt. Edward John TENNANT, D.S.O., M.C. She *d.* 1989. He *m.* 2ndly, 1992, Patricia Mary, 1st da. of John Cuthbert Widdrington RIDDELL of Swinburne Castle, Northumberland and formerly wife of Major Geoffrey Thomas BLUNDELL-BROWN.

[RICHARD JOHN TENNANT ARUNDELL, s. and h. ap. by 1st wife, *b.* 28 Mar. 1957; ed. at Stoneyhurst and R.A.C., Cirencester; *m.*, 1984, Jane Catherine, da. of Timothy Heathcote UNWIN.]

TANKERVILLE

page 634,
line 9, after '1716' add '(said in the Register to have been *bap.* 27 Aug. 1716 at All Saints, Newcastle upon Tyne)'

page 636,
line 27, after '(d)' add 'His widow, *d.* 15 Feb. 1949.'
line 28, line to read as follows

IX. 1931. 8. CHARLES AUGUSTUS KER (BENNET), EARL OF TANKERVILLE, &c., 1st s. and h., *b.* 16 Aug. 1897;

page 637,
line 6, delete from 'Having' to 'work.([d])' and replace by '[for further detail, see note ([d])]. He *d.* 1 Dec. 1971. His widow was still living 1995.'

X. 1971. 9. CHARLES AUGUSTUS GREY (BENNET), EARL OF TANKERVILLE, &c., 1st s. and h. by 1st wife, *b.* 28 July and *bap.* 15 Oct. 1921, at St. Margaret's, Westm.; *styled* LORD OSSULSTON 1931–71; served in WW2, 1939–45, as Flight-Lieut., R.A.F.V.R.; *m.* 1stly, 15 May 1943, Mrs Virginia Diether MORRIS, da. of Louis M. DIETHER, of Vancouver, B.C. This marriage was diss. by divorce in 1950 and he *m.* 2ndly, 22 June 1954, Georgiana Lilian Maude, da. of Gilbert WILSON of Vancouver, B.C. He *d.* 27 Apr. 1980. His widow was still living 1995.

XI. 1980. 10. PETER GREY (BENNET), EARL OF TANKERVILLE, &c., s. and h. by 2nd wife, *b.* 18 Oct. 1956; ed. at Grace Cathedral Sch., San Francisco, U.S.A., Oberlin Conservatory, Ohio, and San Francisco State Univ.

note ([d]), lines 3–7, delete from 'His' to 'B.C.'

TEIGNMOUTH

page 657,
lines 13–15, delete from 'and was' to 'work.([a])'

IV. 1915. 4. FREDERICK WILLIAM JOHN (SHORE), BARON TEIGNMOUTH, &c., br. and h., *b.* 27 Aug. 1844 [for further detail see note ([a])].

V. 1916. 5. HENRY NOEL (SHORE), BARON TEIGNMOUTH, &c., br. and h., *b.* 29 Aug. 1847; ed. at Edinburgh Acad. and H.M.S. Britannia [for further detail see note ([a])].

VI. 1926. 6. HUGH AGLIONBY (SHORE), BARON TEIGNMOUTH [I.], also a Baronet [1792], 1st s. and h., *b.* 12 July 1881; ed. at Wellington, 1895–9; sometime of the Indian P.W. Dept., Madras; served in WW1, 1914–18,([aa]) as Lieut. R.M.E.; *m.*, 27 July 1915, Anne Adelaide Caroline, only da. of Col. Willoughby Digby MARSH, R.E., of Brownsbarn, Thomastown, co. Kilkenny. He *d.* 13 Aug. 1964. His widow *d.* 1976.

[LIONEL CHARLES FREDERICK SHORE, 1st s. and h. ap., *b.* 3 Jan. 1918; ed. at Wellington from 1931; served in WW2, 1939–44, as Major, 2nd King Edward VII's Own, Gurkha Rifles. He *d. v.p.* and unm., being *k.* in action nr. Arezzo, 20 July 1944.]

VII. 1964. 7. FREDERICK MAXWELL AGLIONBY (SHORE), BARON TEIGNMOUTH [I.], also a Baronet [1792], 2nd but 1st surv. s. and h., *b.* 2 Dec. 1920; ed. at Wellington, 1934–9; served in WW2, 1939–45, as Lieut. R.N.V.R.; D.S.C. and bar, 1944. He *m.* 1stly, 20 Dec. 1947, Daphne Beryl, da. of W.H. FREKE-EVANS of Hove. This marriage was diss. by divorce in 1952 and he *m.* 2ndly, 1979, Mrs Pamela MYER, da. of H. EDMONDS-HEATH. He *d. s.p.* 7 July 1981 when his title became *extinct.*

note ([a]), lines 10–16, delete from 'Lionel' to '1944'

note ([aa]) His yr. br., Lionel Henry Shore, *b.* 18 Nov. 1882, Cmdr. R.N., also served and *d. v.p.* and unm. 31 May 1916, being *k.* in action at Jutland.

TEMPLE OF STOWE

page 661,
line 18, line to read as follows

V. 1902. 5. ALGERNON WILLIAM STEPHEN (TEMPLE-GORE-LANGTON), EARL TEMPLE OF STOWE, 1st s. and h., *b.* 9 Nov. 1871;

lines 23–4, delete from 'Having' to 'work.([b])]' and replace by '[for further detail see note ([b]), lines 1–5].'

VI. 1940. 6. CHANDOS GRENVILLE (TEMPLE-GORE-LANGTON), EARL TEMPLE OF STOWE, nephew and h. [for further detail see note ([b])]. He *d. s.p.* 14 Apr. 1966. His widow *d.* 1977.

VII. 1966. 7. RONALD STEPHEN BRYDGES (TEMPLE-GORE-LANGTON), EARL TEMPLE OF STOWE, br. and h., *b.* 5 Nov. 1910. A company representative in Australia who never used the title. He *d.* unm. 28 Aug. 1988.

VIII. 1988. 8. WALTER GRENVILLE ALGERNON (TEMPLE-GORE-LANGTON), EARL TEMPLE OF STOWE, cousin and h., being s. and h. of Cmdr. Evelyn Arthur TEMPLE-GORE LANGTON, R.N., (*d.* 1972), by Irene, da. of Brig. Gen. Cavendish Walter GARTSIDE-SPAIGHT, which Evelyn Arthur was 3rd s. of the 4th Earl Temple. He was *b.* 2 Oct. 1924; ed. at Nautical Coll., Pangbourne; *m.* 1stly, 24 July 1954, Zillah Ray, da. of James BOXALL of Petworth, Sussex. She *d.* 12 Oct. 1966. He *m.* 2ndly, 1 June 1968, Margaret Elizabeth Graham, da. of Col. Henry William SCARTH of Breckness, Orkney.

[JAMES GRENVILLE TEMPLE-GORE-LANGTON, s. and h. ap., *b.* 11 Sep. 1955; ed. at Winchester.]

TEMPLEMORE

page 662,
line 37, line to read as follows

III. 1906. 3. ARTHUR HENRY (CHICHESTER), BARON TEMPLEMORE, only s. and h., *b.* 16 Sep. 1854;

page 663,
lines 6–7, delete from 'Having' to 'work.([a])]' and replace by 'He *d.* 28 Sep. 1924. His widow *d.* 30 Sep. 1954.'

IV. 1924. 4. ARTHUR CLAUD SPENCER (CHICHESTER), BARON TEMPLEMORE,

s. and h., *b.* 12 Sep. 1880 [for further detail see note ([a])]. He *d.* 2 Oct. 1953. His widow *d.* 23 July 1969.

[ARTHUR PATRICK SPENCER CHICHESTER, 1st s. and h. ap., *b.* 23 Mar. 1914; for further detail see note ([a]).]

V. 1953. 5. DERMOT RICHARD CLAUD (CHICHESTER), BARON TEMPLEMORE [1831], 2nd but 1st surv. s. and h., *b.* 18 Apr. 1916 [for further detail see note ([a])]. He *suc.* his kinsman, 1975, as MARQUESS OF DONEGAL, which see.

TEMPLETOWN

page 665,
line 14, after 'Italy' add '(M.I. San Remo gives date of death as 9 Jan., clearly wrong)' [*ex inform.* C.R. Hudleston]

page 666,
line 6, line to read as follows

VISCOUNTCY [I.] IV. BARONY [I.] V.	1939	5 and 6. HENRY AUGUSTUS GEORGE MOUNTJOY HENEAGE (UPTON), VISCOUNT TEMPLETOWN, [I. 1806] and BARON TEMPLETON [I. 1776], 2nd but 1st surv s. and h., *b.* 12 Aug. 1894;

lines 11–12, delete from 'Having' to 'work.([b])]' and replace by 'She *d.* 1974. He *m.* 2ndly, 1975, Margaret Violet Louisa, da. of Lieut. Col. Henry Arthur CLOWES, widow of Sir Lionel George Archer CUST. He *d. s.p.m.s.* 10 Feb. 1981 when his titles both became *extinct.*

[HENRY ERIC PATRICK MOUNTJOY SPALDING UPTON, s. and h. ap., *b.* 20 May 1917; ed. at Stowe and at R.M.C., Sandhurst; Lieut. Indian Army; *m.*, Margaret, da. of Lieut. Col. the Rev. Thomas Hudson STEWART, M.C. This marriage was diss. by divorce in 1951. He *d. v.p. s.p.* Feb. 1957.]

note ([d]), delete all detail

TENNYSON OF ALDWORTH AND OF FRESHWATER

page 669,
line 16, line to read as follows

III. 1928. 3. LIONEL HALLAM (TENNYSON), BARON TENNYSON OF ALDWORTH AND OF FRESHWATER,([c]) s. and h., *b.* 7 Nov., 1889;

page 670,
line 9, after '1943.' add 'She *d.* 3 Sep. 1960.'

lines 9–10, delete from 'Having' to 'work.([b])]' and replace by '[for further detail see note ([b]), lines 1–4]. He *d.* 6 June 1951.'

IV. 1951. 4. HAROLD CHRISTOPHER (TENNYSON), BARON TENNYSON OF ALDWORTH AND OF FRESHWATER, 1st s. and h. by 1st wife, *b.* 25 Mar. 1919; ed. at Eton and Cambridge (Trin. Coll.). He *d.* unm. 19 Oct. 1991.

V. 1991. 5. MARK AUBREY (TENNYSON), BARON TENNYSON OF ALDWORTH AND OF FRESHWATER, br. and h., *b.* 28 Mar. 1920; ed. at R.N.C., Dartmouth; *m.*, 1964, Deline Celeste, da. of Arthur Harold BUDLER of Cradock, South Africa.

note ([b]), lines 4–6, delete from 'His' to '1940'

TEYNHAM

page 689,
line 21, line to read as follows

XIX. 1936. 19. CHRISTOPHER JOHN HENRY (ROPER-CURZON), BARON TEYNHAM, s. and h., *b.* 6 May 1896

lines 34–6, delete from 'Having' to 'work.([d])]' and replace by 'This marriage was diss. by divorce 1954 (she *m.* 2ndly, 1958, Walter Bingham (COMPTON), 6th MARQUESS OF NORTHAMPTON and *d.* 1976), and he *m.* 2ndly, 11 Feb. 1955, Anne Rita, da. of Capt. Leicester Charles Assheton St. John CURZON-HOWE, R.N. He *d.* 5 May 1972. His widow *m.* 2ndly, Dr Ian EDWARDS, who *d.* 1988. His widow was still living 1995.'

XX. 1972. 20. JOHN CHRISTOPHER INGHAM (ROPER-CURZON), BARON TEYNHAM, 1st s. and h., *b.* 25 Dec. 1928; ed. at Eton; *m.*, 31 Oct. 1964, Elizabeth, yst. da. of Lieut. Col. David SCRYMGEOUR-WEDDERBURN by Patricia, yst. da. of Lord Herbert MONTAGU-DOUGLAS-SCOTT, C.M.G., D.S.O.

[DAVID JOHN HENRY INGHAM ROPER-CURZON, 1st s. and h., *b.* 5 Oct. 1965; *m.*, 1985, Lydia Lucinda, 1st da. of Major Gen. Sir Christopher AIRY.]

note ([d]), delete all detail

THANET

page 694,
line 19, for '5' read '6'

page 698,
line 11, after '61' add 'having had a fit of apoplexy in Hothfield Church, dying soon after reaching home.' [*Cumberland Paquet*, 1 May 1832, *ex inform.* C.R. Hudleston]

note (c), add at end 'William, the yst. son of the 8th Earl was *b.* 16 Nov. 1777, and drowned in the Thames, 1786.' [*ex inform.* C.R. Hudleston]

THURLOW

page 732,
line 20, after '1814' add 'in FitzRoy Sq., London'

page 733,
line 38, after '*d.*' add '13 May' and after '1942' add 'She *d.* 29 Mar. 1954.'

page 734,
line 1, line to read as follows

VI. 1916. 6. CHARLES EDWARD (HOVELL-THURLOW-CUMMING-BRUCE), BARON THURLOW, 2nd but 1st surv. s. and h.,

line 17, delete from 'Having' to 'work.(a)]' and replace by 'He *d.* 23 Apr. 1952. His widow *d.* 16 Jan. 1959.'

VII. 1952. 7. HENRY CHARLES (HOVELL-THURLOW-CUMMING-BRUCE), BARON THURLOW [1792], *b.* 29 May 1910 [for further detail see note (a)]. He *d.* unm. 29 May 1971.

VIII. 1971. 8. FRANCIS EDWARD (HOVELL-THURLOW-CUMMING-BRUCE), BARON THURLOW, br. and h., *b.* 9 Mar. 1912; ed. at Shrewsbury and Cambridge (Trin. Coll.); *m.*, 11 Aug. 1949, Yvonne Diana, da. of Aubyn WILSON of St. Andrews, Fife. She *d.* 1990.

[ROUALEYN ROBERT HOVELL-THURLOW-CUMMING-BRUCE, s. and h. ap., *b.* 13 Apr. 1952; ed. at Milton Abbey; *m.*, 1980, Bridget Anne Julia, da. of Hugh Bruce Ismay CHEAPE of the Isle of Mull.]

THWENG

page 738,
line 2, for 'Kilton, Thorpe' read 'Kilton Thorpe, N. Riding'

page 739,
line 1, for 'da.' read 'sister'

page 743,
line 10, for 'by his 1st wife' read '[2nd Lord Daubeney], by his 2nd wife'

TOLLEMACHE OF HELMINGHAM

page 751,
line 5, delete 'of the same,'

note ([a]), line 2, for '1771' read '1770'

page 752,
line 11, line to read as follows

III. 1904. 3. BENTLEY LYONEL JOHN (TOLLEMACHE), BARON TOLLEMACHE OF HELMINGHAM [1876], grandson and h., being 1st s. and h.

line 22, delete from 'Having' to 'work.([c])]' and replace by 'He *d.* 13 Jan. 1955. His widow *d.* 1982.'

IV. 1955. 4. JOHN EDWARD HAMILTON (TOLLEMACHE), BARON TOLLEMCHE OF HELMINGHAM, cousin and h., being only s. of Major-Gen. Edward Devereux Hamilton TOLLEMACHE, D.S.O., M.C. (*d.* 27 Aug. 1947), s. and h. of Hamilton James TOLLEMACHE (*d.* 16 June 1893), 4th s. of the 1st Baron. He was *b.* 24 Apr. 1910; ed. at Eton and R.M.C., Sandhurst; *m.*, 16 Feb. 1939, Dinah Susan, da. of Sir Archibald Auldjo JAMIESON, K.B.E., M.C. He *d.* 27 May 1975. His widow was still living 1995.

V. 1975. 5. TIMOTHY JOHN EDWARD (TOLLEMACHE), BARON TOLLEMACHE OF HELMINGHAM, 1st s. and h., *b.* 13 Dec. 1939; ed. at Eton; *m.*, 24 Feb. 1970, Alexandra Dorothy Jean, da. of Col. Hugo MEYNELL, M.C., of Newborough, Burton-on-Trent.

[EDWARD JOHN HUGO TOLLEMACHE, 1st s. and h. ap., *b.* 12 May 1976.]

note ([c]), delete all detail

TONY

page 756,
note ([b]), line 14, after 'below.' add 'See "Tony of Belvoir", Charles Evans, *Geneal. Mag.*, vol. 15, 1968, pp. 616–18.'

page 760,
note ([e]), line 1, for '2' read '3' and after 'Ralph add 'and Richer (Orderic Vitalis, vol. 4, p. 67, quoted in *Dict. Hist. . . . de l'Eure*, 1868. *Ex inform.* Philip Daykin, to whom I an indebted for the following Tony corrections). This Richer may be the Richard who witnessed two charters, quoted by D.C. Douglas, *Studies in Social and Legal Hist.*, vol. ix, 1927, Appendix I, p. 254, no. 57.'

page 762,
note ([e]), line 8, after 'above' add 'Simon probably became Abbot of Coggeshall, Essex, 1167 and *d.* 17 Sep. 1184 as Bishop of Moray. The da. Isobel *m.* Walter FitzRichard (*Register of St. Osmund*, W.H. Rich-Jones (ed.), 1883, p. 266), i.e. Walter de Clifford, s. of Richard FitzPons (*Hereford Domesday*, 1166/70, Pipe Roll Soc., N.S., vol. 25, p. 94)'

page 764,
note ([h]), line 8, after '115).' add 'For the identity of Baldwin, see P.W. Daykin, *Family Hist.*, vol. 18, no. 146, 1996, p. 47 and note (5).'

note ([i]), after 'descent' add 'There were two other sons, Roger, seigneur de Acquiny, *m.* Ida de Chaumont (Pipe Roll Soc., vol. 35, p. 51) and Geoffrey, who entered the church, for whose son, Baldwin, see P.W. Daykin, *op. cit.*, above.'

page 769,
note ([e]), line 5, for '3' read '4'
line 6, after '298).' add 'The 4th son, William, is referred to as brother of Ralph VI in the *Chartulary of Ramsey Abbey*, 1884, vol. i, p. 86, no. 128; p. 93, nos. 281 and 304. The daughter Margaret *m.* Malcolm, Earl of Fife, see above.'

page 773,
note ([a]), after '393.' add 'A 2nd son Geoffrey held lands in London and co. Cambridge for his nephew Robert, Lord Tony.'

TORPHICHEN

page 783,
line 15, after 'her' add '(*d.* 1943)'
line 22, line to read as follows

XIII. 1915. 13. JOHN GORDON (SANDILANDS), LORD TORPHICHEN, 2nd but 1st surv. s. and h., *b.* 8 June 1886;

lines 25–7, delete from 'Having' to 'work.([b])]' and replace by 'He *m.* 2ndly, 19 Sep. 1950, Isobel Fernandez, da. of Richard Bowden DANIEL of Jacksonville, Florida, U.S.A. and widow of Richard Youel PHILIPS of Kenya. He *d.* 1 July 1973. His widow *d.* 1976.'

XIV. 1973. 14. JAMES BRUCE (SANDILANDS), LORD TORPHICHEN [S. 1564], s. and h., *b.* 26 Oct. 1917; MASTER OF TORPHICHEN till 1973; ed. at Eton and Oxford (Balliol Coll.). He *m.*, 15 Oct. 1943, at the Oratory, Birmingham, Mary Thurstan, da. of Randle Henry Neville VAUDREY, of Montague Rd., Edgebaston, Birmingham. This marriage was diss. by divorce in 1952 and he *m.* 2ndly, Aug. 1955, Margaret Jane, da. of George DAWSON, New York City. This marriage was also diss. by divorce and he *m.* 3rdly, 1973, Pamela Mary, da. of John Howard SNOW and widow of Thomas HODGSON-PRESSINGER. He *d.* 12 July 1973. His widow was still living 1995.

XV. 1973. 15. JAMES ANDREW DOUGLAS SANDILANDS, s. and h., ap., *b.* 27 Aug. 1946; *m.* 1976, Margaret Elizabeth, da. of William A. BEALE of Boston, Mass., U.S.A.

note ([b]), delete all detail

TORRINGTON

page 796,
line 36, for '([d])' read 'His widow *d.* 29 Jan. 1968.'

X. 1944. 10. ARTHUR STANLEY (BYNG), VISCOUNT TORRINGTON, &c., cousin and h., being 1st s. and h. of Sydney BYNG (*d.* 27 Feb. 1920), 3rd and yst. br. of the 8th Viscount [for further detail see note ([d]) (line 10, after '1936' add 'She *d.* 11 Oct. 1961')]. He *d.* 28 Nov. 1961.

[GEORGE BYNG, s. and h. ap., *b.* 18 Feb. 1918 [for further detail see note ([d]), on page 797, lines 11-16]. His widow remarr., 27 Jan. 1951, Howard Henry Masterton CARPENTER. He *d.* 1976, and she *m.*, 1991, Michael Ingram BOSTOCK.]

XI. 1961. 11. TIMOTHY HOWARD ST. GEORGE (BYNG), VISCOUNT TORRINGTON and BARON BYNG OF SOUTHILL, grandson and h., being only s. and h. of George Byng, by Anne Yvonne, his wife, both abovenamed. He was *b.* 13 July 1943; ed. at Harrow; *m.*, 1973, Susan Honour, da. of Michael George Thomas WEBSTER of Dummer, co. Hants.

note ([d]), lines 16–18 (on page 797), delete from 'Timothy' to '1943'

TOWNSHEND OF LYNN REGIS & TOWNSHEND OF RAYNHAM

page 815,
line 26, after 'Norfolk' add 'She *d.* 10 Oct. 1959.

page 816,
line 1, line to read as follows

MARQUESSATE. VII. VISCOUNTCY, ETC. X.	1921	7 and 10. GEORGE JOHN PATRICK DOMINIC (TOWNSHEND), MARQUESS TOWNSHEND OF RAYNHAM, &c., *b.* 13 May 1916.

line 3, after 'N.W.;' add '*styled* VISCOUNT RAYNHAM till 1921'
line 10, delete from 'Having' to 'work.([a])]' and replace by 'This marriage was diss. by divorce 1960 (she remarr., 1960, Brig. Sir James GAULT and *d.* 1989), and he *m.* 2ndly, 22 Dec. 1960, Ann Frances, da. of Arthur Pellew DARLOW. She *d.* 1988.'

[CHARLES GEORGE TOWNSHEND, *styled* VISCOUNT RAYNHAM, 1st s. and h. ap. by 1st wife, *b.* 26 Sep. 1945; ed. at Eton; *m.* 1stly, 1975, da. of Lieut. Cmdr. Robert Martin Dominic PONSONBY, R.N. She *d.* 1985. He *m.* 2ndly, Mrs Alison MARSHALL, yr. da. of Sir Willis Ide COMBS of Wadhurst Park, East Sussex.]

APPENDIXES

APPENDIX D

page 6,
note ([a]), line 2, after 'p. 161' add 'See also Frank McEvoy, "The Slane Peerage Claim", *J. Kilkenny Arch. Soc.*, 1982, pp. 352–62.'

APPENDIX H

Delete whole Appendix. See note in this volume, p. 595, *sub* STRANGE OF BLACKMERE.

APPENDIX K

page 30,
line 14, for 'him' read 'William'

APPENDIX L

page 37,
line 33, after 'authority' add 'The argument that the *Carmen* cannot be the lost poem of Guy, Bishop of Amiens, is accepted by Sir Frank Stenton (*The Bayeux Tapestry*, 1957, pp. 24, 87).

page 39,
note (j), line 6, after '*pleno*' add '*tam in bosio, quem in pleno*'

page 47,
note (c), line 7, after 'pp. 28–30)' add 'If there were any doubt as to whether they had identified the right body as Harold's, William would not have dared to sell the corpse to Harold's mother. She would certainly have discovered the fraud if the body was not the King's.'

VOLUME 12 PART 2

TREDEGAR

page 15,
lines 31–2, delete from ',(c)' to 'volume' and replace by 'see below.'

III. 1913. 3. COURTENAY CHARLES EVAN (MORGAN), BARON TREDEGAR [1859], 1st s. and h. of Frederick Courtenay MORGAN (*d.* 8 Jan. 1909), 3rd s. of the 1st Baron. He was *b.* 10 Apr. 1867, and was *cr.* 4 Aug. 1926, VISCOUNT TREDEGAR(c) [for further detail see vol. xiii, p. 422]. He *d.* 3 May 1934.

VISCOUNTCY. II. BARONY. IV. } 1934 2 and 4. EVAN FREDERIC (MORGAN), VISCOUNT TREDEGAR, &c., s. and h., *b.* 13 July 1893 [for further detail see vol. xiii, pp. 422–3]. He *m.* 2ndly, 13 Mar. 1939, Olga Sergievna, da. of Gen. PRINCE SERGE ALEXANDROVITCH DOLGOROUKY. This marriage was annulled in 1943. He *d. s.p.* 27 Apr. 1949, when his Viscountcy became *extinct* but his Barony was inherited by his uncle.

V. 1949. 5. FREDERICK GEORGE (MORGAN), BARON TREDEGAR, uncle and h., being 2nd s. of Frederick Courtenay MORGAN (*d.* 8 Jan. 1909), by Charlotte Ann, da. of Charles A. WILLIAMSON of Lawers, co. Perth, which Frederick was 3rd s. of the 1st Baron. He was *b.* 22 Nov. 1873; ed. at Eton and Oxford; *m.*, 14 Apr. 1898, Dorothy Syssyllt, da. of Ralph Thurstan Bassett, of Bonvilston, co. Glamorgan. This marriage was diss. by divorce in 1921, and she *d.* 1 Oct. 1929. He *d.* 21 Aug. 1954.

VI. 1954. 6. 1954. 6. FREDERICK CHARLES JOHN (MORGAN), BARON TREDEGAR [1859], also a Baronet [1792], s. and h., *b.* 26 Oct. 1908; ed. at Eton. He *m.*, 26 Oct. 1908, Joanna, formerly wife of Cmdr. A.B. RUSSELL, R.N., da. of W.H. LAW-SMITH of Adelaide, S. Australia. He *d. s.p.* 17 Nov. 1962 when his honours became *extinct*. His widow was still living 1995.

note (c), lines 1–2 and line 1 on page 16, delete from 'Courtenay' to 'Tredegar'

TREVOR

page 34,
lines 4–5, delete from 'He' to 'work.'

III. 1923. 3. CHARLES EDWARD (HILL-TREVOR), BARON TREVOR OF BRYNKINALT, br. and h., being the 2nd but 1st surv. s. by the 2nd wife of the 1st Baron, *b.* 22 Dec. 1863 [for further detail see note (b)]. His widow *d.* 1990.

IV. 1950. 4. CHARLES EDWIN (HILL-TREVOR), BARON TREVOR OF BRYNKINALT, 1st s. and h., *b.* 13 Aug. 1928; ed. at Shrewsbury. He *m.*, 4 Jan. 1967, Susan Janet Elizabeth, da. of Ronald Ivor BENCE, of Selly Oak, Birmingham.

[MARKE CHARLES HILL-TREVOR, s. and h. ap., *b.* 8 Jan. 1970.]

note ([b]), lines 7–10, delete from 'and was' to '1931'

TRIMLESTOWN

page 46,
line 3, line to read as follows

XIX. 1937. 19. CHARLES ALOYSIUS (BARNEWALL), BARON TRIMLESTOWN, 2nd but only surv. s. and h., by 1st wife, *b.* 2 June 1899; ed. at Ampleforth; *m.* 1stly, 16 June 1926, Muriel, da. of Edward Oscar SCHNEIDER, of Mansfield Lodge, Whalley Range, Manchester. She *d.* 22 June 1937 and he *m.* 2ndly, 7 May 1952, Freda Kathleen, da. of Alfred Allen WATKINS, of Ross-on-Wye, co. Hereford. She *d.* 1987. He *d.* 9 Oct. 1990.

lines 9–10, delete from 'Having' to 'work.([b])]'.

XX. 1990. 20. ANTHONY EDWARD (BARNEWALL), BARON TRIMLESTOWN, 1st s. and h., *b.* 2 Feb. 1928; ed. at Ampleforth; *m.*, 30 Sep. 1963, Lorna Margaret Marion, da. of Charles Douglas RAMSAY of Closglas, Sarnau, Cardigan. This marriage was diss. in 1973 (she *d.* 1988), and he *m.* 2ndly, 1977, Mary Wonderly, 1st da. of Judge Thomas F. MCALLISTER.

note ([b]), delete all detail

TWEEDDALE

page 84,
line 36, line to read as follows

MARQUESSATE [S.] XI. EARLDOM [S.] XII. BARONY [U.K.] II. } 1911 — 11, 12 and 2. WILLIAM GEORGE MONTAGU (HAY), MARQUESS OF TWEEDDALE, &c., 1st s. and h.,

page 85,
lines 12–13, delete from 'Having' to 'work.([b])]' and replace by 'He *d. s.p.m.s.* 30 Mar. 1967. His widow *d.* 1977.'

[Only s. and h. ap. by 1st wife, *b.* and *d.* 16 July 1928.]

MARQUESSATE [S.] XII. EARLDOM [S.] XIII. BARONY [U.K.] III. } 1967 — 12, 13 and 3. DAVID GEORGE MONTAGU (HAY), MARQUESS OF TWEEDDALE, &c., nephew and h., being only s. of Col. Lord Edward Douglas John HAY (*d.* 18 June 1944),([b]) 3rd s. of the 10th Marquess. He was *b.* 25 Oct. 1921; ed. at Eton; *m.* 1stly, 26 Oct. 1946, Sonia Mary, da. of Osbert (PEAKE), 1st VISCOUNT INGLEBY. This marriage was diss. by divorce in 1958. He *m.* 2ndly, 14 Jan. 1959, Nella Doreen, da. of M.M. DUTTON. He *d.* 23 Jan. 1979. His widow was still living 1995.

note ([b]), delete all detail and replace by 'Lord Edward Douglas John Hay, Gren. Guards., was *k*. by enemy action in the Guards Chapel, Wellington Barracks.'

MARQUESSATE [S.] XIII. EARLDOM [S.] XIV. BARONY [U.K.] IV.	1979	13, 14 and 4. EDWARD DOUGLAS JOHN (HAY), MARQUESS OF TWEEDDALE, &c., 1st s. and h., *b.* 6 Aug. 1947; ed. at Milton Abbey Sch. and Oxford (Trin. Coll.).

TWEEDMOUTH

page 87,
line 1, line to read as follows

III. 1909 to 1935. 3. DUDLEY CHURCHILL (MARJORIBANKS), BARON TWEEDMOUTH OF EDINGTON, only s. and h., *b.* 2 Mar. 1874;

lines 20–1, delete from 'Having' to 'work.]'

page 111,
note ([a]), delete all detail and replace by 'See correction to O'REILLY, *ante*, vol. x, p. 77'

ULSTER

page 176,
line 22, after 'Margaret' add '(poss. da. of Arnoul III, Count of Guisnes, by Alice, da. of Enguerrand III, Lord of Coucy)'
note ([k]), line 2, before '*Cal*.' add 'See J.C. Parsons, *Geneal Mag*., vol. 20, 1982, pp. 335–40;'
lines 3–6, delete all detail from 'In' to '(de'
lines 1–4 (on page 177), delete all detail

page 180,
line 22, for 'before him' read 'on or before 7 Jan. 1377/8'
line 23, delete from 'Will' to '1380/1.'

page 181,
after line 30 add as follows

i.e. "Ulster," Earldom [U.K.] (*H.R.H. Prince Henry William Frederick Albert*), *cr.* 31 Mar. 1928, with the BARONY OF CULLODEN and DUKEDOM OF GLOUCESTER, which last see, vol. xiii.

VALENTIA

page 213,
line 1, line to read as follows

VISCOUNTCY [I.] XIII. BARONY [U.K.] II.	1927 to 1949	12 and 2. CARYL ARTHUR JAMES (ANNESLEY), VISCOUNT VALENTIA, &c. [I.]([c]) and BARON ANNESLEY [U.K. 1917], 2nd but only surv. s. and h.,

line 11, delete '(b)'
lines 11–13, delete from 'Having' to 'work.]'

XIV. 1949. *13.* WILLIAM MONCKTON (ANNESLEY), VISCOUNT VALENTIA, &c. [I.], distant cousin and h. male,(c) being, it was said, 5th in descent from the Rev. Martin Annesley, D.D. (*d. v.p.* June 1749) [for further detail see note (b)]. His widow was living 1995.

XV. 1951. 14. FRANCIS DIGHTON (ANNESLEY), VISCOUNT VALENTIA [1622], and BARON MOUNTNORRIS [1629] in the peerage of Ireland, also a Baronet [I. 1620], cousin and h., being the only s. and h. of George Dighton ANNESLEY (*d.* 14 July 1931), 4th s. of the Rev. Henry Arthur ANNESLEY (*d.* 1 Sep. 1924), father of the 13th Viscount. He was *b.* 12 Aug. 1888 [for further detail see note (b), lines 16–24]. He established his succession to the Annesley honours, 9 June 1959, soon after *suc.* his cousin, the titles having in fact been *dormant* since 1949. He *d.* 16 Mar. 1983 and his widow *d.* 1986.

XVI. 1983. 15. RICHARD JOHN DIGHTON (ANNESLEY), VISCOUNT VALENTIA, &c., s. and h., *b.* 15 Aug. 1929; ed. at Marlborough and R.M.A., Sandhurst; *m.*, 10 Aug. 1957, Anita Phyllis, only da. of William Arthur JOY, of Bristol.

[FRANCIS WILLIAM DIGHTON ANNESLEY, s. and h. ap., *b.* 29 Dec. 1959; ed. at Falcons, Bulawayo, S. Rhodesia; *m.*, 1982, Shaneen, da. of (__) HOBBS.]

note (c), after 'above.' add 'The claim of the Rev. William Monckton Annesley to the title was never proved.'

VAUX OF HARROWDEN

page 230,
lines 14–15, delete from ', who is' to 'work.(b)'

VIII. 1938. 8. GRACE MARY ELEANOR GILBEY, *formerly* MOSTYN, 1st da. by 1st wife, *suo jure* BARONESS VAUX OF HARROWDEN after the *abeyance* of the Barony was terminated in her favour by letters patent on 8 July 1938. She was *b.* 22 May 1887; ed. at Hillside Convent, Farnborough. She *m.*, 15 July 1911, William Gordon GILBEY, of Denham, co. Bucks. She *d.* 11 May 1958. He *d.* 14 Feb. 1965.

IX. 1958. 9. PETER HUBERT GORDON (GILBEY), LORD VAUX OF HARROWDEN, 1st s. and h., *b.* 28 June 1914; ed. at Ampleforth and Oxford (St. Benet's Hall); ordained Priest, 1940; a member of the Order of St. Benedict at Ampleforth Abbey, co. York. He *d.* 1 Nov. 1977.

X. 1977. 10. JOHN HUGH PHILIP (GILBEY), LORD VAUX OF HARROWDEN, br. and h., *b.* 4 Aug. 1915; ed. at Ampleforth and Oxford (Ch. Ch.); *m.*, 5 July 1939, Maureen Pamela, da. of Hugh GILBEY of Dorking, Surrey.

[ANTHONY WILLIAM GILBEY, s. and h. ap., *b.* 25 May 1940; ed. at Ampleforth; *m.*, 4 July 1964, Beverley Anne, only da. of Charles Alexander WALTON, of Cooden, Sussex.]

note (b), delete all detail

VENTRY

page 240,
line 20, line to read as follows

V. 1914. 5. FREDERICK ROSSMORE WAUCHOPE (EVELEIGH-DE MOLEYNS), BARON VENTRY, &c., s. and h., *b.* 11 Dec. 1861 at Niddrie House;

page 241,
lines 1–2, delete all detail

VI. 1923. 6. ARTHUR WILLIAM (EVELEIGH-DE MOLEYNS), BARON VENTRY [I.], &c., br. and h., *b.* 6 Apr. 1864 [for further detail see note (a)]. His widow *d.* 29 Mar. 1966 in her 90th year.

VII. 1936. 7. ARTHUR FREDERICK DAUBENEY (EVELEIGH-DE MOLEYNS), BARON VENTRY [I. 1800], also a Baronet [I. 1797], 1st s. and h., *b.* 28 July 1898 [for further detail see note (a)]. He *d.* unm. 7 Mar. 1987.

VIII. 1987. 8. ANDREW WESLEY (DAUBENEY DE MOLEYNS, *formerly* EVELEIGH-DE MOLEYNS), BARON VENTRY, &c., nephew and h. being s. and h. of Francis Alexander Innys EVELEIGH-ROSS-DE MOLEYNS (*d.* 29 Apr. 1964), by his 2nd wife, Joan, 1st da. of Harold WESLEY of East Molesey, Surrey, and widow of Flt. Lieut. H.G. ADAMS, which Francis was 2nd s. of the 6th Baron. He was *b.* 28 May 1943; ed. at Aldenham Sch.; *m.* 1stly, 26 Feb. 1963, Nelly Eduoard Renée, da. of Abel CHAUMILLON of Malaga, Spain. This marriage was diss. by divorce in 1979 and he *m.* 2ndly, 1983, Jill Rosemary, da. of Cecil Walter ORAMON.

[FRANCIS WESLEY DAUBENEY DE MOLEYNS, s. and h. ap., *b.* 1 May 1965; ed. at Gordonstoun.]

note (a), lines 11–12, delete from 'The' to '1901'

VERNON

page 265,
line 7, delete all detail

IX. 1915. 9. FRANCIS LAWRANCE WILLIAM (VENABLES-VERNON), LORD VERNON, BARON OF KINDERTON, *b.* 6 Nov. 1889 [for further detail see note (b)]. He *d.* 18 Mar. 1963. His widow *d.* 1978.

X. 1963. 10. JOHN LAWRANCE (VENABLES-VERNON), LORD VERNON, BARON OF KINDERTON, only s. and h., *b.* 1 Feb. 1923 [for further detail see note (b)]. His marriage was diss. by divorce in 1982 and as her 3rd husband he *m.* 2ndly, Sally Anne, da. of Robin STRATFORD.

VERULAM

page 267,
line 16, line to read as follows

IV. 1924. 4. JAMES WALTER (GRIMSTON), EARL OF VERULAM, &c., only s. and h., *b.* 17 Apr. 1880;

page 268,
lines 2–4, delete from 'Having' to 'work.(a)]'

V. 1949. 5. JAMES BRABAZON (GRIMSTON), EARL OF VERULAM, &c., also VISCOUNT GRIMSTON, &c. [I.], also LORD FORRESTER OF CORSTORPHINE [S.], 1st s. and h., *b.* 11 Oct. 1910 [for further detail see note (a)]. He *d.* unm. 13 Oct. 1960.

VI. 1960. 6. JOHN (GRIMSTON), EARL OF VERULAM, &c., br. and h., *b.* 17 July 1912; ed. at Oundle and Oxford (Ch. Ch.); *m.* 2 June 1938. Marjorie Ray, 1st da. of Walter Atholl DUNCAN. He *d.* 15 Apr 1973. His widow *d.* 21 Dec. 1994.

VII. 1973. 7. JOHN DUNCAN (GRIMSTON), EARL OF VERULAM, &c., s. and h., *b.* 21 Apr. 1951; ed. at Eton and Oxford (Ch. Ch.). He *m.*, 1976, Dione Angela, 1st da. of Jeremy SMITH, of Balcombe, Sussex.

[JAMES WALTER GRIMSTON, 1st s. and h. ap., *b.* 6 Jan. 1978.]

note (b), lines 9–10, delete from 'The' to '1912'

VESCY

page 285,
note (g), line 3, after '[1371]).' add 'For the ancestry of Sir Edward see W.L. Sheppard, *Geneal. Mag.*, vol. 19, 1977, pp. 130–3.'

VIVIAN

page 292,
line 28, for 'is (1953)' read 'was' and after 'W.V.S.' add 'She *d.* 1970'
line 29, line to read as follows

V. 1941. 5. ANTHONY CRESPIGNY CLAUDE (VIVIAN), BARON VIVIAN OF GLYNN AND OF TRURO, 1st s. and h. by 1st wife, *b.* 4 Mar. 1906;

page 293,
lines 4–5, delete from 'Having' to 'work.(a)]' and replace by 'He *d.* 24 June 1991. His widow *d.* 1985.'

VI. 1991. 6. NICHOLAS CRESPIGNY LAURENCE (VIVIAN), BARON VIVIAN OF GLYNN AND OF TRURO, 1st s. and h., *b.* 11 Dec. 1935; ed. at Eton and Madrid Univ. He *m.* 1stly, 13 Dec. 1960, Catherine Joyce, yst. da. of James Kenneth HOPE. This marriage was diss. by divorce in 1972 and he *m.* 2ndly, 1972, Carol, 1st da. of F. Alan MARTINEAU.

[CHARLES HUSSEY CRESPIGNY, 1st s. and h. ap. by 1st wife, *b.* 20 Dec. 1966; ed. at Milton Abbey Sch.]

note ([a]), delete all detail

page 293,
after line 10 add as follows

VYNE

See "SANDYS (of the Vyne)," Barony (*Sandys*), *cr.* 1524 or 1529; in *abeyance* since 1683

WAHULL or WODHULL

page 294,
note ([a]), line 6, after '69–73.' add 'See also 'The Barons of Woodhull', Charles Hansen, *The Geneal.*, vol. 7–8, 1986–7, pp. 4–126.'

WAKE

page 302,
line 5, after 'Joan' add 'DE FIENNES'
note ([c]), lines 1–3, delete from 'She' to '318.' and replace by 'See John Parsons, *Geneal. Mag.*, vol. 20, 1982, p. 336.'

WALDEGRAVE

page 315,
line 29, line to read as follows

EARLDOM. X. BARONY. XI.	1930	10 and 11. WILLLIAM EDWARD SEYMOUR (WALDEGRAVE), EARL WALDEGRAVE, &c., only s. and h., *b.* 2 Oct. 1882;

page 316,
lines 1–2, delete from 'Having' to 'work.([a])]'

EARLDOM. XI. BARONY. XII.	1933	11 and 12. HENRY NOEL (WALDEGRAVE), EARL WALDEGRAVE, &c., uncle and h. male [for further detail see note ([a])]. His widow *d.* 21 Mar. 1962, aged 94.
EARLDOM. XII. BARONY. XIII.	1936	12 and 13. GEOFFREY NOEL (WALDEGRAVE), EARL WALDEGRAVE, &c., only s. and h., *b.* 21 nov. 1905 [for further detail see note ([a])]. He *d.* 23 May 1995. His widow was still living in 1995.
EARLDOM. XIII. BARONY. XIV.	1995	13 and 14. JAMES SHERBROOKE (WALDEGRAVE), EARL WALDEGRAVE, &c., 1st s. and h., *b.* 8 Dec. 1940, in Sherbrooke, Canada; ed. at Eton and Cambridge (Trin. Coll.). He *m.*, 1986, Mary Alison Anthea, da. of Sir Robert FURNESS of Little Shelford, co. Cambs.

[EDWARD ROBERT WALDEGRAVE, s. and h. ap., *b.* 10 Oct. 1986.]

note ([a]), lines 18–19, delete from 'His' to '1940'

WALLSCOURT

page 327,
line 18, line to read as follows

V. 1918 to 1920. 5. CHARLES WILLIAM JOSEPH HENRY (BLAKE), BARON WALLSCOURT OF ARDFRY [I. 1800], only s. and h., *b.* 12 Jan. 1875;

lines 22–3, delete from 'Having' to 'work.'
line 25, delete ']'

WALPOLE OF WALPOLE and WALPOLE OF WOLTERTON

page 330,
after line 2 add as follows

See note ([a]), lines 1–5, from 'On the' to 'Wolterton'

BARONY. IX. BARONY. VII. } 1931 9 and 7. ROBERT HENRY MONTGOMERIE (WALPOLE), BARON WALPOLE OF WALPOLE [1723] and WALPOLE OF WOLTERTON [1756], distant cousin and h. male [for further detail see note ([a])]. He *d.* 25 Feb. 1989. His widow was still living in 1995.

BARONY. X. BARONY. VIII. } 1989 10 and 8. ROBERT HORATIO (WALPOLE), BARON WALPOLE OF WALPOLE and BARON WALPOLE OF WOLTERTON, 1st s. and h., *b.* 8 Dec. 1938; ed. at Eton and Cambridge (King's Coll.); *m.* 1stly, 30 June 1962, Sybil Judith (*d.* 1993), da. of Theodore Thomas SCHOFIELD, of Harpenden, Herts. This marriage was diss. by divorce in 1979 and he *m.* 2ndly, 1980, Laura Celia, only da. of S.T. BALL of Swindon, Wilts.

[JONATHAN ROBERT HUGH WALPOLE, 1st s. and h. ap. by 1st wife, *b.* 16 Nov. 1967.]

WALSINGHAM

page 337,
lines 12–13, delete from ', being' to 'work'

VII. 1919. 7. JOHN AUGUSTUS (DE GREY), BARON WALSINGHAM, br. of the half-blood and h., being 2nd s. of the 5th Baron [for further information see note ([c])].

VIII. 1929. 8. GEORGE (DE GREY), BARON WALSINGHAM, 1st s. and h. by 1st wife, *b*. 9 May 1884 [for further detail see note ([c])]. He *d*. 29 Nov. 1965. His widow *d*. 1968.

IX. 1965. 9. JOHN (DE GREY), BARON WALSINGHAM, only s. and h., *b*. 21 Feb. 1925 [for further detail see note ([c]), on page 338]. He *m*, 30 July 1963, Wendy Elizabeth, 1st da. of Edward Sidney HOARE of Southwick, Sussex.

[ROBERT DE GREY, s. and h. ap., *b*. 21 June 1969; ed. at Exeter Univ. He *m*., 1995, Josephine Elizabeth, da. of Richard HARYOTT.]

WARWICK

page 361,
note ([k]), line 3, after 'p. 153.' add 'It is possible that he was in the Holy Land for part of the 1140s, see Emma Mason, *J. Med. Hist*., vol. 14, no. 2, 1988, p. 84.'

page 363,
note ([d]), line 2, after 'p. 289.' add 'See also Emma Mason, *J. Med. Hist*., vol. 14, no. 2, 1988, p. 84.'

page 366,
note ([d]), line 1, after 'The' add 'original'
line 2, for 'is' read 'was'

WATERFORD

page 425,
line 25, line to read as follows

VII. 1911. 7. JOHN CHARLES DE LA POER (BERESFORD), MARQUESS OF WATERFORD, &c., 1st s. and h., *b*. 6 Jan. 1901;

line 33, delete all detail

page 426,
line 1, delete 'this work.([a])' and replace by 'She *d*. 1987.'

VIII. 1934. 8. JOHN HUBERT DE LA POER (BERESFORD), MARQUESS OF WATERFORD, &c., 1st s. and h., *b*. 14 July 1933 and *bap*. 24 Aug. at the Church of the Annunciation, Bryanston Str.; *styled* EARL OF TYRONE 1933–4; ed. at Eton; 2nd Lieut., R. Horse Guards. He *m*, 23 July 1957, Lady Caroline Olein Geraldine, da. of Richard Southwell Windham Robert (WYNDHAM-QUINN), 6th EARL OF DUNRAVEN AND MOUNT EARL.

[HENRY NICHOLAS DE LA POER, 1st s. and h. ap., *styled* EARL OF TYRONE, *b*. 23 Mar. 1958; ed. at Harrow; *m*., 1986, Amanda, da. of Norman THOMPSON of Borris-in-Ossory, co. Leix.]

note ([a]), delete all detail

WATERPARK

page 428,
line 12, line to read as follows

V. 1912. 5. CHARLES FREDERICK (CAVENDISH), BARON WATERPARK, 2nd and only surv. s. and h., *b.* 11 May 1883;

lines 16–17, delete from 'Having' to 'work.(c)]'

VI. 1932. 6. HENRY SHEPPARD HART (CAVENDISH), BARON WATERPARK, 2nd cousin and h. male [for further detail see note (c)]. His widow *d.* 1968.

VII. 1948. 7. FREDERICK CARYLL PHILIP (CAVENDISH), BARON WATERPARK, nephew and h. male [for further detail see note (c)].

[RODERICK ALEXANDER CAVENDISH, s. and h. ap., *b.* 10 Oct. 1959; *m.*, 1989, Anne, da. of Luke ASQUITH.]

note (c), lines 24–5, delete from 'The' to '1908'

WELLES

page 439,
line 6, after '*d.s.p.*' add '21 Apr. 1288' [Chron. of Premonstratensian Abbey of Hagneby, Lincs., BL Cott. MS, Vesp. B xi, f. 32v. *Ex inform.* Mrs Juanita Knapp.]
note (b), line 1, for 'vol. ii, pp. 216–7; no. 429' read 'vol. ii, no. 381, (pp. 216–7); no. 429.'
note (c), line 2, for '1181' read '1281'

page 446,
line 2, delete from 'probably' to '1448/9' and replace by '26 Sep. 1435'
note (b), after 'vol.' add 'Two documents (the marriage settlement) in the Lincs. Rec. Office, Ancaster Deposit, 2 ANC 3/A/19 and 3 ANC 3/A/19, give the date of the marriage. *Ex inform.* Mrs Juanita Knapp.'

page 447,
note (f), line 2, after '(' add '*Rot. Parl.*, vol. 6, p. 287'

page 449,
line 17, after '*m.*' add 1stly', (___), 2ndly'
note (f), line 7, after '353).' add 'Sometime after June 1482, probably after the accession of Richard III, she was married to Ralph Scrope of Upsall, brother of Thomas Lord Scrope of Upsall. This marriage was dissolved in 1486, (Rosemary Horrox, *Richard III, A Study in Service*, 1989, p. 295.)'

page 450,
note (h), line 6, after '312–13.' add 'One of the children given in these pedigrees (*op. cit.*,

p. 313) was "Margaret". Her existence may possibly be confirmed by the reference in her will to her "Cosyn Margarett Keymes" by Lady Katherine Gordon, wife of Perkin Warbeck (*P.C.C.*, 10 Dyngeley, quoted in Michael Barrington, *A Mystery to this Day*, 1949, pp. 149–51). She would be a "cousin" through Katherine Gordon's own (Scots) royal blood.'

WELLINGTON

page 460,
line 41, line to read as follows

V. 1934. 5. ARTHUR CHARLES (WELLESLEY), DUKE OF WELLINGTON, &c., also EARL OF MORNINGTON, Etc. [I.], 1st s. and h., *b.* 9 June 1896;

page 461,
lines 7–9, delete from 'Having' to 'work.(c)]'
line 10, delete ']'

VI. 1941. 6. HENRY VALERIAN GEORGE (WELLESLEY), DUKE OF WELLINGTON, &c., only s. and h., *b.* 14 July 1912 [for further detail see note (c)].

At the death of the 6th Duke the Dukedom of Ciudad Rodrigo (but not the estates), in Spain, passed according to Spanish law, to his sister and h. gen., Lady Anne Maud, whose husband, David Reginald RHYS (3rd s. of the 7th Baron Dynevor), also, under the same law, became Duke of Ciudad Rodrigo and a Grandee of the First Class. However, she resigned her Spanish honours in 1949 in honour of her uncle, the 7th Duke, the h. male of the 6th Duke, who inherited the other titles.

VII. 1943. 7. GERALD (WELLESLEY), DUKE OF WELLINGTON, &c., uncle and h. male, 3rd but next surv. s. of the 4th Duke, *b.* 21 Aug. 1885 [for further detail see note (c)]. His wife *d.* 11 July 1956. He *d.* 4 Jan. 1972.

VIII. 1972. 8. ARTHUR VALERIAN WELLESLEY, only s. and h. ap., *b.* 2 July 1915 [for further detail see note (c)].

[ARTHUR CHARLES VALERIAN WELLESLEY, *styled* MARQUESS DOURO, 1st s. and h. ap., *b.* 19 Aug. 1945; ed. at Eton and Oxford (Ch. Ch.); *m.*, 1977, Antonia Brigid Elizabeth Louise, yr. da. of *H.R.H.* PRINCE FRIEDRICH GEORG WILHELM CHRISTOPH OF PRUSSIA.]

note (c), lines 7–12, delete from 'at' to 'Duke'

WEMYSS

page 478,
line 6, line to read as follows

EARLDOM [S.] IX. BARONY [U.K.] IV.	1914	9 and 4. HUGO RICHARD (CHARTERIS), EARL OF WEMYSS, &c., 4th but 1st surv. s. and h., by 1st wife, *b.* 25 Aug. 1857 in Edinburgh;

lines 17–19, delete from 'Having' to 'work.([c])'

[HUGO FRANCIS CHARTERIS, 1st s. and h. ap., *b.* 28 Dec. 1884 [for further detail see note ([c])].

EARLDOM [S.] X. BARONY [U.K.] V.	1937	10 and 5. FRANCIS DAVID (CHARTERIS), EARL OF WEMYSS, &c. [S.], also, probably, EARL OF MARCH, &c. [S.], also BARON WEMYSS OF WEMYSS [U.K.], grandson and h. [for further detail see note ([c])]. His wife *d.*1988.

[IAIN DAVID CHARTERIS, 1st s. and h. ap., *styled* LORD ELCHO, *b.* 20 June 1945. He *d. v.p.* 3 Apr. 1954, after a car crash.]

[JAMES DONALD CHARTERIS, 2nd but 1st surv. s. and h. ap., *styled* LORD NEIDPATH from 1954;([ca]) ed. at Eton and Oxford (Univ. Coll. and St. Anthony's Coll.); *m.*, 1983, Catherine Ingrid, 1st da. of Jonathan Bryan GUINNESS (s. and h. ap. of the 2nd Baron Moyne). This marriage was diss. by divorce in 1988.]

note ([c]), lines 19–22, delete from 'His' to '1954'
note ([ca]), transfer lines 23–4 of note ([c]), from 'The' to 'above', to this note

WENLOCK

page 488,
lines 1–2, delete from 'He' to 'work.'

IV. 1912. 4. RICHARD THOMPSON (LAWLEY), BARON WENLOCK, &c., br. and h. male, *b.* 21 Aug. 1856 [for further detail see note ([b])].

V. 1918. 5. ALGERNON GEORGE (LAWLEY), BARON WENLOCK, &c., br. and h. male, *b.* 25 Dec. 1857 [for further detail see note ([b])].

VI. 1931 to 1932. 6. ARTHUR (LAWLEY), BARON WENLOCK [1839], also a Baronet [1641], br. and h., *b.* 12 Nov. 1860 [for further detail see note ([b])].

[RICHARD EDWARD LAWLEY, only s. and h. ap., *b.* 9 May 1887; ed. H.M.S. *Britannia* and at Oxford. He *d.* unm. and *v.p.* 4 Sep. 1909, being *k.* in a hunting accident in India.]

note ([b]), lines 31–3, delete from 'Richard' to 'India'

WENTWORTH

page 501,
line 1, for '(__)' read 'Henry'

line 4, after '(d)' add 'He *m.* 3rdly, in or by 1582, Jane (*bap.* 13 Mar. 1541/2), da. of Sir John HARLESTON, by Mildred, da. of Sir John MUNDY.'

line 5, for '(f)' read 'His widow *m.* 2ndly, 8 Sep. 1589, as his 2nd wife, William Borough, the Navigator (*d.* by 28 Nov. 1598). She was *bur.* 14 Feb. 1615/16 in South Ockendon. Will pr., Commissary Court of London, 14 Feb. 1615/16.(f)'

note (f), delete all detail and replace by 'See Paul C. Reed, *The Geneal.*, vol. 9, 1988, pp. 175, 177–9, 288.'

page 515,
lines 24–5, for 'who' to 'work.(d)' read 'see below'

XIV. 1906. 14. ADA MARY, *suo jure* BARONESS WENTWORTH, also *de jure* BARONESS LE DESPENSER, only da. and h., *b.* 26 Feb. 1871, *d.* unm. 18 June 1917.

XV. 1917. 15. ANNE ISABELLA NOEL, *suo jure* BARONESS WENTWORTH, &c., aunt and h., being only da. of WILLIAM (KING, *afterwards* KING-NOEL), 1st Earl of Lovelace [for further detail see note (d)].

[WILFRED SCAWEN BLUNT, only s. and h. ap., *b.* and *d. v.m.* an infant, Nov. 1870.]

XVI. 1917. 16. JUDITH ANNE DOROTHEA, *suo jure* BARONESS WENTWORTH also *de jure* BARONESS LE DESPENSER, only da. and h., *b.* 1873 [for further detail see note (d), on page 516]. She *d.* 8 Aug. 1957.

XVII. 1957. 17. NOEL ANTHONY SCAWEN (LYTTON, *afterwards* LYTTON-MILBANKE *afterwards* LYTTON), *b.* 7 Apr. 1900; *suc.* his mother as BARON WENTWORTH also *de jure* BARON LE DESPENSER on her *d.* 1957 and his father as EARL OF LYTTON in 1951 [for further detail see note (d), on page 516]. He *d.* 18 Jan. 1985. His widow was still living 1995.

[For subsequent peers, see LYTTON, Earldom]

note (d), lines 1–4, delete from 'Ada' to 'Lovelace'
line 14, delete from 'Wilfred' to 'and'
lines 1–2 (on page 517), delete from '*d. v.m.*' to '1873'

page 525,
between lines 12 and 13 add as follows

IV. 1930. 4. RICHARD MORLAND TOLLEMACHE (BETHELL), BARON WESTBURY, grandson and h., being 1st s. and h. of Capt. Richard Bethell abovenamed, *b.* 9 Oct. 1914 [for further detail see note (b), on page 524]. He *d.* unm. in Geneva 26 June 1961.

V. 1961. 5. DAVID ALAN (BETHELL), BARON WESTBURY, br. and h., *b.* 16 July 1922; ed. at Harrow. He *m*, 21 Oct. 1947, Ursula Mary Rose, da. of Robert JAMES (3rd s. of 2nd Baron Northbourne).

[RICHARD NICHOLAS BETHELL, 1st s. and h. ap., *b.* 29 May 1950; ed. at Harrow; *m.*, 1975, Caroline Mary, da. of Richard John PALMER.]

note (b), lines 1–3, delete from 'He' to '1914'
lines 5–6, delete from 'The' to '1922'

WESTMEATH

page 536,
lines 36–7, delete from ', and' to 'work'

XII. 1933. 12. GILBERT CHARLES (NUGENT), EARL OF WESTMEATH, &c., only surv. br. and h., *b.* 9 May 1880; served in WW1, 1914–18, as Major R.A.; wounded twice; mentioned in dispatches. He *m.*, 20 Nov. 1915, Doris, 2nd da. of Charles IMLACH, of Liverpool. She *d.* 1968. He *d.* 20 Nov. 1971.

XIII. 1971. 13. WILLIAM ANTHONY (NUGENT), EARL OF WESTMEATH, &c., s. and h., *b.* 21 Nov. 1928; *styled* LORD DELVIN, 1933–71; ed. at Marlborough; Lieut. R.A. He *m.*, 31 July 1963, Susanna Margaret, only da. of James Charles Beresford Whyte LEONARD.

[SEAN CHARLES WESTON NUGENT, *styled* LORD DELVIN, 1st s. and h. ap., *b.* 16 Feb. 1965; ed. at Ampleforth.]

note (d), delete all detail

WESTMINSTER

page 543,
lines 6–7, delete from 'He' to 'work.(b)' and replace by 'His widow was still living 1995.'

between lines 12 and 13 add as follows

DUKEDOM. III. MARQUESSATE. V. } 1953 3 and 5. WILLIAM (GROSVENOR), DUKE OF WESTMINSTER, &c., cousin and h. male, being only s. of Lord Henry George GROSVENOR (*d.* 27 Dec. 1914), by Rosamund Angharad, da. of Edward LLOYD of Flint, which Henry George was 3rd s. of the 1st Duke. He was *b.* 23 Dec. 1894. He *d.* unm. 22 Feb. 1963.

DUKEDOM. IV. MARQUESSATE. VI. } 1963 4 and 6. GERALD HUGH (GROSVENOR), DUKE OF WESTMINSTER, &c., cousin and h., being 1st s. and h. of Hugh William GROSVENOR (*d.* 30 Oct. 1914, being *k.* in action), by Lady Mabel Florence Mary, yr. da. of John Henry (CRICHTON), 4th EARL OF ERNE, which Hugh was 6th s. of the 1st Duke. He was *b.* 13 Feb. 1907; ed. at Eton and R.M.A., Sandhurst; *m.*, 11 Apr. 1945, Sally, twin da. of George PERRY. He *d. s.p.* 25 Feb. 1967. His widow *d.* 1990.

DUKEDOM. V. MARQUESSATE. VII.	1967	5 and 7. ROBERT GEORGE (GROSVENOR), DUKE OF WESTMINSTER, &c., br. and h., *b.* 24 Apr. 1910; ed. at Eton; *m.*, 3 Dec. 1946, Viola Maud, da. of John Cavendish (LYTTELTON), 9th VISCOUNT COBHAM. She *d.* 1987, being *k.* in a motor accident. He *d.* 19 Feb. 1979.
DUKEDOM. VI. MARQUESSATE. VIII.	1979	6 and 8. GERALD CAVENDISH (GROSVENOR), DUKE OF WESTMINSTER, &c., s. and h., *b.* 22 Dec. 1951; ed. at Harrow and Sunningdale Sch.; *m.*, 1978, Natalia Ayesha, yst. da. of Lieut. Col. Harold Pedro Joseph PHILLIPS.

note ([b]), delete all detail

WESTMORLAND

page 562,

Tabular pedigree, line 3, for '*m.* Thomas Wentworth' read '*m.* (1) Sir William Gascoigne, (2) Sir James Harrington' [*ex inform.* Brice Clagett].

page 583,

line 9, after 'June' add 'His widow *d.* 1973.'

line 10, line to read as follows

XX. 1922. 14. VERE ANTHONY FRANCIS ST. CLAIR ERSKINE (FANE), EARL OF WESTMORLAND, &c., 1st s. and h., was *b.* 15 Mar. 1893

lines 24–5, delete from 'Having' to 'work.([c])]' and replace by 'His widow *d.* 1983.'

XXI. 1948. 15. DAVID ANTHONY THOMAS (FANE), EARL OF WESTMORLAND, &c., 1st s. and h., *b.* 31 Mar. 1924 [for further detail see note ([c])]. He *d.* 8 Sep. 1993. His widow was still living in 1995.

XXII. 1993. 16 ANTHONY DAVID FRANCIS HENRY (FANE), EARL OF WESTMORLAND, &c., 1st s. and h., *b.* 1 Aug. 1951; ed. at Eton; *m.*, 1985, Caroline, da. of Keon HUGHES, formerly wife of Charles FAIREY.

note ([c]), lines 7–8, delete from 'Their' to '1951'

WHARNCLIFFE

page 593,

line 39, line to read as follows

EARLDOM. III. BARONY. V.	1926	3 and 5. ARCHIBALD RALPH (MONTAGUE-STUART-WORTLEY-MACKENZIE), EARL OF WHARNCLIFFE, &c., 2nd but 1st surv. and h., was *b.* 17 Apr. 1892;

page 594,
lines 9–10, delete from 'Having' to 'work([b])]' and replace by 'His widow *d.* 1979.'

EARLDOM. IV. BARONY. VI. } 1953 4 and 6. ALAN JAMES (MONTAGUE-STUART-WORTLEY-MACKENZIE), EARL OF WHARNCLIFFE, &c., only s. and h., *b.* 23 Mar. 1935; *styled* VISCOUNT CARLTON till 1953; ed. at Eton; joined R.N.V.R., 1953; *m.*, 25 July 1957, Aline Margaret, da. of Robert Fernie Dunlop BRUCE of Wharncliffe Side, Sheffield. He *d.* 3 June 1987. His widow was living in 1995.

EARLDOM. V. BARONY. VII. } 1987 5 and 7. RICHARD ALAN (MONTAGUE-STUART-WORTLEY), EARL OF WHARNCLIFFE, &c., distant cousin and h., being 1st s. and h. of Alan Ralph MONTAGUE-STUART-WORTLEY (*d.* 1986), by Virginia Anne, da. of William Martin CLAYBAUGH, which Alan was 1st s. and h. of Ralph MONTAGUE-STUART-WORTLEY (*d.* 8 Feb. 1961), by Isabella, da. of George Edward WOOD, which Ralph was s. and h. of Ralph Granville MONTAGUE-STUART-WORTLEY (*d.* 1 Mar. 1927), by Virginia Maria, da. of Adm. Winfield Scott SCHLEY, U.S. Navy, which Ralph Granville was 3rd s. of Francis Dudley MONTAGU-STUART-WORTLEY (*d.* 21 Oct. 1893), by Maria Elizabeth, 1st da. of William Bennet MARTIN of Worsborough Hall, Yorks., which Francis was 2nd s. of the 2nd Baron Wharncliffe and br. and h. of the 1st Earl under the spec. rem. He was *b.* 26 May 1953; ed. at Wesleyan Univ., Conn., U.S.A.; *m.*, 1979, Mary Elizabeth, da. of Rev. Wellington REED, of Keene, New Hampshire.

[REED MONTAGUE-STUART-WORTLEY, *styled* VISCOUNT CARLTON, 1st s. and h. ap., *b.* 5 Feb. 1980.]

note ([b]), delete all detail

WHARTON

page 615,
between lines 2 and 3 add as follows

VII. 1916. 1. CHARLES THEODORE HASWELL (KEMEYS-TYNTE), BARON WHARTON [1916], being great-great-grandson of Col. Charles John KEMEYS-TYNTE, descended from Jane, elder s. and coh. of Philip, Duke of Wharton, and declared in 1845 by the Committee for Privileges to be h. to a one-third part of the Barony of Wharton, which it further decl. to be a Barony by Writ (see vol. xii, part 2, Appendix D, particularly p. 16). He was *b.* 18 Sep. 1876; summ. to Parl. 15 Feb. 1916; *m.*, 10 Aug. 1899, Dorothy, yst. da. of Major Gen. Sir Arthur Edward Augustus ELLIS. He *d.* 4 Mar. 1934. His widow *d.* 3 Aug. 1944.

VIII. 1934. 2. CHARLES JOHN HASWELL (KEMEYS-TYNTE), BARON WHARTON, s. and h., *b.* 12 Jan. 1908; ed. at Oxford (Ch. Ch.); *m.*, 1 Sep. 1967, Joanna, da. of Walter Henry LAW-SMITH of Adelaide, S. Australia, widow of Frederic John Charles (MORGAN), 6th and last BARON TREDEGAR, formerly wife of Cmdr. A.B. RUSSELL, R.N. He *d.* 11 July 1969. His widow married, 1971, Bruce YORKE.

IX. 1969. 3. ELIZABETH DOROTHY KEMEYS-TYNTE, *suo jure* BARONESS WHARTON, sister and h., *b.* 4 May 1906. She *m.* 1stly, 17 May 1933, David George ARBUTHNOT, s. and h. of Major John Bernard ARBUTHNOT. This marriage was diss. by divorce in 1946 and she *m.* 2ndly, 1946, St. John VINCENT. This marriage was diss. by divorce in 1958. She *d.* 4 May 1974, when the Barony fell into *abeyance* between her two das.

X. 1990. 4. MYRTLE OLIVE FELIX ARBUTHNOT, 1st da. of the aforesaid Elizabeth Dorothy, *suo jure* BARONESS WHARTON, the title being called out of abeyance in her favour by writ dated 4 Apr. 1990. She was *b.* 20 Feb. 1934 and *m.*, 17 Apr. 1958 Michael Macleod ROBERTSON.

[MYLES CHRISTOPHER DAVID ROBERTSON, 1st s. and h. ap. was *b.* 1 Oct. 1964; ed. at Kings Coll., Wimbledon]

WICKLOW

page 625,
line 10, after 'afsd.' add 'His widow *d.* 3 Dec. 1957.'
line 11, line to read as follows

VIII. 1946. 8. WILLIAM CECIL JAMES PHILIP JOHN PAUL (HOWARD), EARL OF WICKLOW, [I. 1793], VISCOUNT WICKLOW [I. 1785], and BARON CLONMORE [I. 1776], only s. and h. by 1st wife, was *b.* 30 Oct. 1902 at Shelton Abbey;

lines 17–18, delete from 'Having' to 'work.(b)]' and replace by 'He *m.*, 2 Sep. 1959, da. of Prof. Rudolph M. BUTLER, of Dublin. He *d. s.p.* 8 Feb. 1978 when the Earldom and Viscountcy of Wicklow and the Barony of Clonmore [I.] all became *extinct*. His widow was living 1995.

note (b), delete all detail

WILLOUGHBY DE ERESBY

page 682,
line 23, after 'ANCASTER' add '(*extinct* 1983)'

For further detail of the two subsequent Lords Willoughby de Eresby, see ANCASTER.

XXV. 1910. 25. GILBERT (HEATHCOTE-DRUMMOND-WILLOUGHBY), EARL OF ANCASTER, LORD WILLOUGHBY DE ERESBY, &c., s. and h., *b.* 29 July 1867. He *d.* 19 Sep. 1951.

XXVI. 1951. 26. GILBERT JAMES (HEATHCOTE-DRUMMOND-WILLOUGHBY), EARL OF ANCASTER, LORD WILLOUGHBY DE ERESBY, &c., s. and h., *b.* 8 Dec. 1907. He *d. s.p.m.* 29 Mar. 1983.

XXVII. 1983. 26. NANCY JANE MARIE HEATHCOTE-DRUMMOND-WILLOUGHBY, *suo jure* BARONESS WILLOUGHBY DE ERESBY, da. and h., *b.* 1 Dec. 1934.

WILLOUGHBY DE BROKE

page 700,
line 1, line to read as follows

XIX. 1902. 19. RICHARD GREVILLE (VERNEY), LORD WILLOUGHBY DE BROKE, &c., 1st s. and h., was *b.* 29 Mar. 1869;

lines 13–14, delete from 'Having' to 'work.([e])]'
line 16, delete ']'

XX. 1923. 20. JOHN HENRY PEYTO (VERNEY), LORD WILLOUGHBY DE BROKE, &c., only s. and h., was *b.* 21 May 1896 [for further detail see note ([e])]. He *d.* 25 May 1986. His widow *d.* 1991.

XXI. 1986. 21. LEOPOLD DAVID (VERNEY), LORD WILLOUGHBY DE BROKE, &c., only s. and h., *b.* 14 Sep. 1938, King Leopold III of the Belgians being a sponsor. Ed. at Le Rosey and Oxford (New Coll.); *m.*, 1 May 1965, Petra Daphne, 2nd da. of Col. Sir John Renton AIRD, Bart.

[RUPERT GREVILLE VERNEY, s. and h. ap., *b.* 4 Mar. 1966.]

note ([e]), lines 2–3 (on page 701), delete from 'Their' to 'sponsor'

WILLOUGHBY OF PARHAM

page 704,
lines 1–2, delete from 'between' to 'year' and replace by 'late in Dec. 1611 and was *bur.* 31 Dec. 1611 or 1 Jan. 1611/12([a])'
note ([a]), delete all detail and replace by 'P.J.W. Higson, *Geneal. Mag.*, vol. 17, 1972, p. 5.'
note ([b]), delete all detail

page 712,
lines 9–10, delete from 'of' to 'Lancaster' [P.J.W. Higson, *op. cit.*, p. 3]
line 23, delete from '1665' to '*(sic)*' and replace 'after 14 Nov. 1696'
note ([b]), line 2, after '–49).' add 'For an update to this article, see P.J.W. Higson, "The Barony of Willoughby of Parham: an epilogue", *Geneal. Mag.*, vol. 15, 1965, pp. 1–14, 121.'

page 713,
line 10, delete from '1 Aug. 1712 "aged 75" and was *bur.*' and replace by '3, and was *bur.* 9 July 1712' [P.J.W. Higson, *Geneal. Mag.*, vol. 17, 1972, p. 5]

page 714,
line 5, for 'Hester' read 'Ester'
line 18, for '21' read '22'
note ([c]), after '528.' add 'For the Willoughby's as dissenters, see P.J.W. Higson, *Northern History*, vol. 7, 1972, pp. 31–3. For a discussion of the career of Hugh, see Higson, *Antiquaries J.*, 1972, vol. 52, part 1, pp. 169–84.' Thanks are due to Dr Higson for drawing my attention to his work.

WILTON

page 726,
line 34, line to read as follows

VI. 1915. 6. SEYMOUR EDWARD FREDERIC (EGERTON), EARL OF WILTON, &c., only s. and h., was *b.* 1 Aug. 1896;

line 40, delete from 'Having' to 'after'

page 727,
line 1, delete from 'Jan.' to 'work.([a])'
line 3, delete ']'

VII. 1927. 7. SEYMOUR WILLIAM ARTHUR JOHN (EGERTON), EARL OF WILTON, &c., only s. and h., was *b.* 29 May 1921; *styled* VISCOUNT GREY DE WILTON untill 1927; ed. at Eton; Dep. Whip of the Lib. party in the House of Lords 1945. He *m.*, 24 Mar. 1962, Diana Elizabeth Lea, da. of Roy GALWAY of Ascot, Berks, formerly wife of David NAYLOR-LEYLAND.

note ([a]), delete all detail

WIMBORNE

page 744,
line 14, line to read as follows

II. 1914.
VISCOUNTCY.
I. 1918.
2. and 1. IVOR CHURCHILL (GUEST), BARON WIMBORNE OF CANFORD MAGNA, &c., 1st s. and h., was *b.* 16 Jan. 1873.

line 19, for '] ([b])' read 'He *d.* 14 June 1939. His widow *d.* 17 Apr. 1948.'

VISCOUNTCY.
II.
BARONY.
III.
1939
2 and 3. IVOR GROSVENOR (GUEST), VISCOUNT WIMBORNE, BARON ASHBY ST. LEDGERS and BARON WIMBORNE OF CANFORD MAGNA, only s. and h., was *b.* 21 Feb. 1903; ed. at Eton and Cambridge (Trin. Coll.); 2nd Lieut. Royal Tank Corps (T.A.); M.P. (national) for

Brecon and Radnor, 1935–9. He *m.*, 22 Nov. 1938, Lady Mabel Edith, da. of Giles Stephen Holland (FOX-STRANGEWAYS), 6th EARL OF ILCHESTER. He *d.* 7 Jan. 1967. His widow *d.* 11 Mar. 1995.

VISCOUNTCY. III. BARONY. IV. } 1967 — 3 and 4. IVOR FOX-STRANGWAYS (GUEST), VISCOUNT WIMBORNE, &c., 1st s. and h., was *b.* 2 Dec. 1939; ed. at Eton; *m.* 1stly, 20 Dec. 1966, Victoria Ann, da. of Col. Mervyn Doyne VIGORS. This marriage was diss. by divorce in 1981 and he *m.* 2ndly, 1983, Venetia Margaret, da. of Richard Bridges St. John QUARRY, formerly wife of Capt. Frederick G. BARKER. He *d.* 17 Dec. 1993. His widow was still living in 1995.

VISCOUNTCY. IV. BARONY. V. } 1993 — 4 and 5. IVOR MERVYN VIGORS (GUEST), VISCOUNT WIMBOURNE, &c., s. and h., *b.* 19 Sep. 1968; ed. at Eton.

note (b), delete all detail

WINCHESTER

page 773,
line 8, after 'Bombay' add 'He *d.* 28 June 1962. His widow *d.* 6 Sep. 1995.

XVII. 1962. 17. RICHARD CHARLES (PAULET), MARQUESS OF WINCHESTER, &c., distant cousin and h., being 1st s. and h. of Charles Standish PAULET (*d.* 18 Sep. 1953), by Lilian Jane Charlotte, da. of Major William Thomas Exham FOSBERY, which Charles was 1st s. and h. of Charles William Paulet (*d.* 8 Apr. 1897), by his 1st wife Susan Amelia Georgina, 4th da. of William Standish STANDISH, of Duxbury, Lancs., 1st s. and h. of the Rev. Charles PAULET (*d.* 23 July 1870), by his 1st wife Caroline Margaret, 3rd da. of Sir John RAMSDEN, Bart., which Charles was 2nd s. of the 13th Marquess. He was *b.* 8 July 1905; ed. at Eton. He *d.* unm. 5 Mar. 1968.

XVIII. 1968. 18. NIGEL GEORGE (PAULET), MARQUESS OF WINCHESTER, &c., distant cousin and h., being 1st s. and h. of George Cecil PAULET (*d.* 9 Aug. 1961), by Hazel Margaret, da. of Major Danvers WHEELER, which George was s. and h. of Cecil Henry Paulet (*d.* 26 Feb. 1916), by Ethel Frances, da. of Capt. Walter Frederick James COWAN of Alveston Lodge, co. Warwick, which Cecil was 2nd s. of Charles William PAULET abovementioned. He was *b.* 23 Dec. 1941; *m.*, 25 Nov. 1967, Rosemary Anne, da. of Major Aubrey John HILTON, of Harare, Zimbabwe.

[CHRISTOPHER JOHN HILTON PAULET, *styled* EARL OF WILTSHIRE, 1st s. and h. ap., *b.* 30 July 1969.]

WINCHELSEA

page 775,
line 1, after 'afsd.' add '18 Jan. 1614/15' [*ex inform.* Vincent Rendel, to whom the following corrections are also due]

page 776,
line 22, after 'afsd.' add 'on 12 Nov.'
line 23, after 'there' add '21 May'

page 779,
line 2, for 'soon after Aug. 1678.([a])' read '(of smallpox) and was *bur.* at Eastwell 8 May 1679.'
line 5, for '4 Sep.' read '10 Sep.'

page 780,
after line 12 add as follows

[THOMAS FINCH, *styled* VISCOUNT MAIDSTONE, 1st s. and h. ap., *b.* at Little Cholsey, Kent, July 1693 and *d.* at Eastwell on 19, and was *bur.* there 21 Jan. 1694/5.]

page 781,
line 18, for '24 Feb.' read '15 Feb. and *bap.* 6 Mar.'

page 791,
lines 10–11, delete from 'Having' to 'work.([b])]'

XIV. 1939. 14. CHRISTOPHER GUY HENEAGE (FINCH-HATTON), EARL OF WINCHELSEA, EARL OF NOTTINGHAM, &c., only s. and h., was *b.* 2 Aug. 1911 [for further detail see note ([b])]. His widow *d.* 22 June 1964.

XV. 1950. 15. CHRISTOPHER DENYS STORMONT (FINCH-HATTON), EARL OF WINCHELSEA, EARL OF NOTTINGHAM, &c., 1st s. and h. by 1st wife, was *b.* 17 Nov. 1936; *styled* VISCOUNT MAIDSTONE 1939–50; ed. at Eton and at Gordonstoun. He *m.*, 23 June 1962, Shirley, 1st da. of Bernard HATFIELD of Wylde Green, Sutton Coldfield.

[DANIEL JAMES HATFIELD FINCH-HATTON, *styled* VISCOUNT MAIDSTONE, s. and h. ap., *b.* 7 Oct. 1967.]

note ([b]), lines 7–11, delete from 'and was' to '1939'

WINDSOR

page 791,
after line 23 add as follows

i.e. WINDSOR, Dukedom (*Windsor*), *cr.* 8 Mar. 1937, see below, *sub* CORNWALL [1910].

page 803,
line 12, line to read as follows

XV. 1923. 15. IVOR MILES (WINDSOR-CLIVE), 2ND EARL OF PLYMOUTH and VISCOUNT WINDSOR, also LORD WINDSOR (of Stanwell) [1529], 2nd but only surv. s. and h., was *b*. 4 Feb. 1889;

lines 32–4, delete from 'Having' to 'work.(c)'
line 35, for ']' read 'She *d*. 1989.'

XVI. 1943. 16. OTHER ROBERT IVOR (WINDSOR-CLIVE), 3RD EARL OF PLYMOUTH, &c., and LORD WINDSOR (of Stanwell), 1st s. and h., was *b*. 9 Oct. 1923; *styled* VISCOUNT WINDSOR till 1943. [For further detail see note (c), lines 1–6.]

[IVOR EDWARD OTHER WINDSOR-CLIVE, *styled* VISCOUNT WINDSOR, 1st s. and h. ap., *b*. 19 Nov. 1951. For further detail see PLYMOUTH, above.]

WINTERTON

page 811,
line 1, line to read as follows

VI. 1907. 6. EDWARD (TURNOUR), EARL WINTERTON, &c., in the Peerage of Ireland, only child and h., was *b*. 4 Apr. 1883;

lines 26–7, delete from 'Having' to 'work.(d)]' and replace by 'He *d*. 26 Aug. 1962. At his *d*. the Barony of Turnour became *extinct* but his Irish titles devolved on his distant cousin and h. His widow *d*. 1974.'

VII. 1962. 7. ROBERT CHAD (TURNOUR), EARL WINTERTON, VISCOUNT TURNOUR and BARON WINTERTON, all in the Peerage of Ireland, distant cousin and h., being 1st s. and h. of Cecil TURNOUR (*d*. 1953), by Effie Annie, da. of Robert MCMILLAN of London, Ontario, Canada, which Cecil was s. and h. of Charles Chad Turnour (*d*. 30 June 1885), by Elizabeth Ethel, da. of William DOWNER of Petworth, Sussex, which Charles was s. and h. of Charles Chad Turnour (*d*. 21 Mar. 1878), by Frances Louisa, yst. da. of Lieut. Col. Harcourt MASTER, which Charles Chad was 1st s. of the Rev. Adolphus Augustus TURNOUR (*d*. 5 Mar. 1857), by Jessie, da. of John DEWAR, which Adolphus was 3rd s. of the 2nd Earl. He was *b*. 13 Sep. 1915; ed. at Nutana Coll., Canada; *m*. 1stly, 1941, Kathleen Ella, da. of D.B. WHITE of Saskatchewan, Canada. She *d*. 30 Apr. 1969. He *m*. 2ndly, 1971, Marion Eleanor, da. of Arthur PHILLIPS of Stirling, Ontario. He *d*. 2 June 1991 without establishing his claim to the peerages. His widow was still living 1995.

VIII. 1991. 8. DONALD DAVID (TURNOUR), EARL WINTERTON, &c., nephew and h., being 1st s. and h. of Cecil Noel TURNOUR (*d*. 1987), by Evelyn Isobel, da. of Dr C.A. OULTON, of Saskatoon, Saskatchewan, Canada, which Cecil

Noel was br. of the 7th Earl. He was *b.* 13 Oct. 1943; ed. at Waterloo Lutheran Univ., Ontario. He *m.* 14 Sep. 1968, Jill Pauline, da. of John Geddes ESPLEN, of Bala, Ontario. Since he has not established his claim to the titles they have thus been *dormant* since 1962.

note (d), delete all detail

WOLSELEY

page 826,
line 6, line to read as follows

II. 1913. 2. FRANCES GARNET (WOLSELEY), *suo jure* Viscountess Wolseley under the spec. rem., only da. and h., was *b.* 15 Sep. 1872 in Belgrave Rd., Pimlico.

lines 15–16, delete from 'Having' to 'work.]'

WOLVERTON

page 828,
line 25, line to read as follows

V. 1932. 5. NIGEL REGINALD VICTOR (GLYN), BARON WOLVERTON, 2nd but 1st surv. s. and h., was *b.* 23 June 1904;

lines 27–8, delete from 'Having' to 'work.(f)]' and replace by 'He *d.* unm. 18 Aug. 1986.'

VI. 1986. 6. JOHN PATRICK RIVERSDALE (GLYN), BARON WOLVERTON, distant cousin and h., being 5th s. of Maurice George Carr GLYN (*d.* 20 Aug. 1920), by Maud, 1st da. of Robert Wellesley (GROSVENOR), 2nd BARON EBURY, which Maurice was 3rd s. of Pascoe Charles GLYN (*d.* 3 Nov. 1904), by his 2nd wife, Caroline Henrietta, da. of Capt. William Amherst HALE, which Pascoe was 5th s. of the 1st Baron. He was *b.* 17 Apr. 1913; ed. at Eton and Oxford (New Coll.); *m.*, 3 Apr. 1937, Audrey Margaret, da. of Richard STUBBS of Haseley Manor, Oxford. He *d.* 4 July 1988. His widow was still living 1995.

VII. 1988. 7. CHRISTOPHER RICHARD (GLYN), BARON WOLVERTON, 1st s. and h., *b.* 5 Oct. 1938; ed. at Eton; *m.* 2ndly, 7 Dec. 1961, Carolyn Jane, 2nd da. of Anthony Noel HUNTER. This marriage was diss. by divorce in 1967 and he *m.* 2ndly, 1975, Mrs Francis Sarah Elizabeth Stuart BLACK, 1st da. of Robert Worboys SKENE. This marriage was diss. by divorce in 1989 and he *m.* 3rdly, 1990, Gillian KONIG.

note (f), delete all detail

WROTTESLEY

page 871,
lines 22–5, delete all detail and replace as follows

IV. 1910. 4. VICTOR ALEXANDER (WROTTESLEY), BARON WROTTESLEY, &c., 3rd(d) but 1st surv. s. and h., was *b.* 18 Sep. 1873, and for whom Queen Victoria stood Sponsor; ed. at Eton, and at Oxford (Ch. Ch.). He *d.* unm. 1 Sep. 1962.

V. 1962. 5. RICHARD JOHN (WROTTESLEY), BARON WROTTESLEY, nephew and h., being only child of Walter Bennet WROTTESLEY (4th s. of the 3rd Baron, *d.* 25 May 1962), by Kate May, only da. of Douglas Howard HARRIS of Capetown. He was *b.* 7 July 1918; ed. at Harrow and R.M.A., Sandhurst; *m.* 1stly, 25 Jan. 1941, Roshnara Barbara, da. of Capt. Esmé Cecil WINGFIELD-STRATFORD of Berkhamstead. This marriage was diss. by divorce in 1949 and he *m.* 2ndly, 9 Dec. 1949, Joyce Marion, da. of Frederick Alexander WALLACE, formerly wife of Major Sean RAINEY. This marriage was also diss. by divorce, 1953 and he *m.* 3rdly, 5 Mar. 1955, Mary Ada Van Echten, da. of Edgar Dryden TUDHOPE, of Cape Province, S. Africa. He *d.* 23 Oct. 1977. His widow was still living 1995.

[RICHARD FRANCIS GERARD WROTTESLEY, 1st surv. s. and h. ap. by 1st wife, *b.* 16 Aug. 1942. Ed. at Stowe and Cambridge (King's Coll.); *m.*, 6 Nov. 1967, Georgina Anne, 1st da. of Lieut. Col. Peter Thomas CLIFTON. He *d. v.p.* 1970. His widow *m.* 2ndly, 1982, Lieut. Col. Jonathan Lovett SEDDON-BROWN. She was still living 1995.]

VI. 1977. 6. CLIFTON HUGH LANCELOT DE VERDON (WROTTESLEY), BARON WROTTESLEY, grandson and h., being only s. of Richard Francis Gerard and Georgina Anne abovenamed. He was *b.* 10 Aug. 1968; ed. at Eton.

note (e), delete all detail

WYNFORD

page 883,
lines 6–7, delete from 'He' to 'work.(b)'

V. 1903. 5. GEORGE (BEST), BARON WYNFORD, cousin and h., being 1st s. and h. of the Rev. Samuel BEST (*d.* 20 Jan. 1873), 3rd s. of the 1st Baron, was *b.* 14 Dec. 1838 [for further detail see note (b)].

VI. 1904. 6. PHILIP GEORGE (BEST), BARON WYNFORD, 1st s. and h., was *b.* 27 Aug. 1871 [for further detail see note (b)]. His widow *d.* 1974.

VII. 1940. 7. SAMUEL JOHN (BEST), BARON WYNFORD [1829], br. and h. male, was *b.* 24 June 1874 [for further detail see note (b)]. His widow *d.* 28 Mar. 1966.

VII. 1943. 8. ROBERT SAMUEL (BEST), BARON WYNFORD, 1st s. and h. by 1st wife, was *b.* 5 Jan. 1917 [for further detail see note (b)].

[JOHN PHILIP ROBERT BEST, only s. and h. ap., *b.* 23 Nov. 1950; ed. at Radley, Keele

Univ. and R.A.C., Cirencester. He *m.*, 1981, Fenella Christian Mary, only da. of Arthur Reginald DANKS.]

note (b), line 28, delete all detail

YARBOROUGH

page 888,
line 9, line to read as follows

EARLDOM. V. BARONY. VI.	1936	5 and 6. SACKVILLE GEORGE (ANDERSON-PELHAM, *afterwards* PELHAM), EARL OF YARBOROUGH, &c., 2nd(b) but 1st surv. s. and h., was *b.* 17 Dec. 1888;

lines 28–9, delete from '(f) Having' to 'work.]' and replace by 'His widow was still living 1995.'

EARLDOM. VI. BARONY. VII.	1948	6 and 7. MARCUS HERBERT (ANDERSON-PELHAM, *afterwards* PELHAM), EARL OF YARBOROUGH, &c., only surv. br. and h. male, being 4th and yst. s. of the 4th Earl. He was *b.* 30 June 1893 [for further detail see note (f)]. He *d.* 2 Dec. 1966. His widow *d.* 31 Jan. 1968.

EARLDOM. VII. BARONY. VIII.	1966	7 and 8. JOHN EDWARD (PELHAM), EARL OF YARBOROUGH, &c., s. and h., was *b.* 2 June 1920 [for further detail see note (f), on page 889, line 3]. He *m.*, 12 Dec. 1957, Florence Ann Petronel, 3rd da. of John Herbert UPTON, formerly wife of Lieut. Charles John Riddell DUFFIN. He *d.* 21 Mar. 1991. His

widow was still alive 1995.

note (e), line 3, after 'W.R.N.S.' add 'She *m.*, 1959, Major Michael Hildesley LYCETT of Morpeth, Northumberland.'

YORK

page 899,
note (i), line 8 (on page 900), after '*passim*' add 'One source calls him "Edwardus Langeley", possibly by association with his father, see "*Historia vitae et regni Ricardi II*" (Hearne, 1729, p. 141).' [*Ex inform.* Dr Rosemary Horrox, to whom are also owed the following corrections to this entry.]

page 903,
note (l), line 3, after '574–5.' add 'The College was originally projected by his father, *Cal. Papal Reg.*, vol. vi, p. 190.'

page 904,
line 7, for 'shortly after July' read '29 Aug.' [P.E. Russell, *The English Intervention in Spain and Portugal*, 1955, p. 313]
lines 10–11, for 'between 27 Feb. 1396/7' read 'after 'Apr. 1397'
line 14, for '2nd da.' read '3rd da.' [*Cal. Fine Rolls, 1399–1405*, pp. 309, 321]
note (g), line 1, for 'When his' read 'His'
line 2, after 'negotiated' add '*m.* 27 Feb. 1396/7'

page 905,
lines 11–12, delete '*attainted* and'
line 12, after 'honours' add ', but not his right to succeed his uncle,'
line 19, for '21 Sep.' read '22 Sep.'
lines 19–20, delete ', despite his father's attainder,'
note (h), lines 1–3, delete from 'This' to 'latter' and replace by 'Neither the sentence passed on the Earl in August nor the confirmation passed in Parliament in November were attainders, see T.B. Pugh, *Henry V and the Southampton Plot*, 1988, p. 134. Nevertheless, there appear to be no grounds for the supposition that York'
note (j), line 2, for 'f. 55' read 'f. 58' and after 'U.S.A.)' add 'This source actually says "feast of St. Maurice" (22 Sep.), not the feast of St. Matthew (21 Sep.), see P.D. Johnson. *Duke Richard of York*, 1988, p. 1. *Ex inform.* Eric J. Thompson.'

page 909,
line 18, after 'resignation,' add 'probably in September, but possibly'
note (a), line 2, after 'time.' add 'For a discussion of the reburial and related ceremonies, see P.W. Hammond, *et al.*, *The Ricardian*, vol. x, 1994, pp. 122–65.'

page 913,
note (b), line 2, after 'Norfolk' add 'The body was subsequently removed (probably in 1502) to the Abbey of the Minoresses in the City of London. See NORFOLK in this volume.'

page 926,
between lines 7 and 8 add as follows

XIII. 1986. 1. *H.R.H.* ANDREW ALBERT CHRISTIAN EDWARD, PRINCE OF THE UNITED KINGDOM OF GREAT BRITAIN AND NORTHERN IRELAND, 2nd s. of *H.M.* QUEEN ELIZABETH II and *H.R.H.* PRINCE PHILIP, DUKE OF EDINBURGH, was *b.* at Buckingham Palace 19 Feb. 1960. He was *cr.*, 1986, BARON KILLYLEAGH, EARL OF INVERNESS, and DUKE OF YORK. He *m.*, 23 July 1986, at Westm. Abbey, Sarah Margaret, 2nd da. of Major Ronald Ivor FERGUSON. This marriage was diss. by divorce in 1996.

ZETLAND

page 929,
line 3, line to read as follows

MARQUESSATE. II. EARLDOM. IV. } 1929 — 2 and 4. LAWRENCE JOHN LUMLEY (DUNDAS), MARQUESS OF ZETLAND, EARL OF ZETLAND, EARL OF RONALDSHAY and BARON DUNDAS OF ASKE, 2nd but 1st surv. s. and h., was *b.* 11 June 1876 at 19 Arlington Str.; *styled* LORD DUNDAS, 1876–92, and EARL OF RONALDSHAY, 1892–1929;

lines 26–8, delete from 'Having' to 'work.(b)]' and replace by 'He *d.* 6 Feb. 1961. His widow *d.* 1973.'

MARQUESSATE. III. EARLDOM. V. } 1961 — 3 and 5. LAWRENCE ALDRED MERVYN (DUNDAS), MARQUESS OF ZETLAND, &c., 1st s. and h., was *b.* 12 Nov. 1908; *styled* LORD DUNDAS, 1908–29 and EARL OF RONALDSHAY, 1929–61 [for further detail see note (b)]. He *d.* 5 Oct. 1989. His widow was still living in 1995.

MARQUESSATE. IV. EARLDOM. VI. } 1989 — 4 and 6. LAWRENCE MARK (DUNDAS), MARQUESS OF ZETLAND, &c., 1st s. and h., *b.* 28 Dec. 1937; ed. at Harrow and Cambridge (Christ's Coll.); *m.*, 4 Apr. 1964, Susan Rose, 2nd da. of Guy Richard CHAMBERLIN of Wrington Hall, Bristol.

[ROBIN LAWRENCE DUNDAS, 1st s. and h. ap., *styled* EARL OF RONALDSHAY, *b.* 5 Mar. 1965; ed. at Harrow and R.A.C., Cirencester.]

note (b), lines 7–9, delete from 'His' to 'Harrow'

ZOUCHE

page 943,
note (m), line 2, after '114' add 'for a translation of her will see Paddy Payne and Caroline Barron, *Nottingham Med. Studies*, vol. xli, 1997, pp. 144–5.'

page 945,
line 10, for 'was living, Hil. 1430/1.' read '*d.* 21 July 1447.'
note (c), delete all detail and replace by 'This date is given on the reverse of an appropriated brass, a rubbing of which is now in the Society of Antiquaries, see *Trans. Mon. Brass Soc.*, vol. iii, pp. 187–91, cited in *Geneal. Mag.*, 1960, vol. 13, p. 251.'

page 951,
note (i), line 1, for 'nephew' read 'grandson'

page 956,
lines 22–3, delete from 'He was' to 'work'

XVI. 1914. 16. DAREA CURZON, *suo jure* BARONESS ZOUCHE OF HARYNGWORTH, only sister and h., was *b.* 13 Nov. 1860 and *d.* unm. 7 Apr. 1917 at 114 Eaton Sq., aged 56, and was *bur.* 11 Apr. at Parham.

XVII. 1917. 17. MARY CECIL CURZON, *suo jure* BARONESS ZOUCHE OF HARYNGWORTH, 1st cousin once removed and h. [for further detail see note (d)]. She *d.* 25 Sep. 1965.

[THOMAS WILLIAM ASSHETON FRANKLAND, 1st s. and h. ap., *b.* 18 Aug. 1902 [for further detail see note (d)]. His widow *m.* 3rdly, 29 June 1946, Michael BARCLAY, s. of Rev. Humphrey BARCLAY, of Southrepps Rectory, Norwich. This marriage was diss. by divorce in 1968.]

XVIII. 1965. 18. JAMES ASSHETON (FRANKLAND), BARON ZOUCHE OF HARYNGWORTH [1308], also a Baronet [1660], grandson and h., being only s. and h. of Sir Thomas William Assheton FRANKLAND and Pamela Catherine abovenamed, was *b.* 23 Feb. 1943; ed. at Lycée Jaccard, Lausanne. He *suc.* his father as 12th Baronet in 1944. He *m.*, 1978, Sally Olivia, 2nd da. of R.M. BARTON of Brook House, Pulham St. Mary, Norfolk.

[WILLIAM THOMAS ASSHETON FRANKLAND, s. and h. ap., *b.* 23 July 1984.]

note (d), lines 1–3, delete from 'Darea' to 'and h.,'
lines 4–6 (on page 957), delete from ', and was' to 'Haryngworth'

APPENDIXES

APPENDIX H

page 28,
line 15, after 'Penaranda' add '(b)'
note (b) This question was argued again by Godfrey W. Iredell in *Geneal. Mag.*, vol. 20, 1981, pp. 147–51, where it is concluded that Berwick probably was *attainted*.

APPENDIX J

page 35,
note (b), lines 5–6, delete from 'For' to 'Appendix I' and replace by 'For a recent discussion of the deaths of the Princes and of the bones from the Tower see P.W. Hammond and W.J. White, in P.W. Hammond (ed.), *Richard III: Loyalty, Lordship and Law*, 1986, pp. 104–47.'

VOLUME 13

MILNER

page 6,
line 17, after 'net' add 'His widow *d.* 10 Oct. 1958.'

KINROSS

page 13,
line 5, after 'Galloway' add 'He *d.* 28 July 1939. His widow *d.* 18 Feb. 1969.'
line 6, line to read

III. 1939. 3. JOHN PATRICK DOUGLAS (BALFOUR), BARON KINROSS, 1st s. and h., *b.* 25 June 1904; ed. at Winchester and Oxford (Balliol Coll.). He *m.*, 11 Feb. 1938, Angela Mary, da. of Capt. George CULME-SEYMOUR. This marriage was diss. by divorce in 1942. He *d. s.p.* 4 Jun. 1976.

lines 8–10, delete all detail and replace as follows

IV. 1976. 4. DAVID ANDREW (BALFOUR), BARON KINROSS, br. and h., *b.* 29 Mar. 1906; ed. at Sherborne and Edinburgh Univ.; *m.* 1stly, 10 June 1936, Araminta, 2nd da. of Lieut. Col. Willoughby Ewart PEEL of Eaglescarnie, Haddington. This marriage was diss. by divorce in 1941 and he *m.* 2ndly, 17 Apr. 1948, Helen Anne, da. of Alan Welwood HOG, of Edinburgh, and formerly wife of Lieut. Col. Patrick Cassan PERFECT. She *d.* 1969. He *m.* 3rdly, 1972, Ruth Beverley, da. of William Henry MILL of Edinburgh. He *d.* 20 July 1985. His widow was still living 1995.

V. 1985. 5. CHRISTOPHER PATRICK (BALFOUR), BARON KINROSS, s. and h. by his 2nd wife, *b.* 1 Oct. 1949; ed. at Eton, St. Andrews Univ. and Edinburgh Univ.; W.S.; *m.*, 1974, Susan Jane, da. of Ian Robert PITMAN.

[ALAN IAN BALFOUR, s. and h. ap., b. 4 Apr. 1978.]

SHUTTLEWORTH

page 14,
line 20, after '1924.' add 'He *d.* 20 Dec. 1939.'
line 35, after 'Kay-Shuttleworth' add 'She *d.* 23 June 1950.'
line 36, line to read as follows

II. 1939. 2. RICHARD UGHTRED PAUL (KAY-SHUTTLEWORTH), BARON SHUTTLEWORTH, &c., grandson and h.,

line 41, delete ']' and replace by 'He *d.* unm., being *k.* in action during the Battle of Britain on 8 Aug. 1940.'

III. 1940. 3. RONALD ORLANDO LAWRENCE (KAY-SHUTTLEWORTH), BARON SHUTTLEWORTH, also a Baronet, br. and h., was *b.* (posthumously) 7 Oct. 1917; ed. at Eton and Oxford (Balliol Coll.). He *d.* unm. 17 Nov. 1942, being *k.* in action in North Africa.

IV. 1942. 4. CHARLES UGHTRED JOHN (KAY-SHUTTLEWORTH), BARON SHUTTLEWORTH, cousin and h., being only s. and h. of Edward James KAY-SHUTTLEWORTH, 2nd s. of the 1st Baron (*d.* 10 July 1917). He was *b.* 24 June 1917; ed. at Eton and Cambridge (Magdalene Coll.). He *m.*, 5 Nov. 1947, Anne Elizabeth, 2nd da. of Col. Geoffrey PHILLIPS. He *d.* 5 Oct. 1975. His widow *d.* 1991.

V. 1975. 5. CHARLES GEOFFREY NICHOLAS (KAY-SHUTTLEWORTH), BARON SHUTTLEWORTH, 1st s. and h., *b.* 2 Aug. 1948; ed. at Eton; *m.*, 1975, Ann Mary, da. of James WATMAN of Shamley Green, Surrey and formerly wife of Daniel Henry BARCLAY.

[THOMAS EDWARD KAY-SHUTTLEWORTH, s. and. ap., *b.* 29 Sep. 1976.]

ALLERTON

page 15,

line 21, after '(3)' add 'His widow *d.* 25 May 1956.'

line 28, after '1934' add 'and *d.* at Thorp Arch, 6 May 1953.'

line 31, after 'ALLAN' add 'This marriage was diss. by divorce in 1947 and he *m.* 3rdly, 17 Sep. 1947, Anne Lorina, 1st da. of James Montagu FOUNTAYNE. He *d. s.p.m.s.* 1 July 1991, when his title became *extinct*.

[EDWARD LAWIES JACKSON, only s. and h. ap., *b.* 23 Mar. 1928; ed. at Eton. He *m.* 1stly, 14 Jan. 1953, Sally Moore, only da. of Ian Moore HEZLETT of Ascot, Berks. This marriage was diss. by divorce in 1971 and he *m.* 2ndly, 1971, Susannah Albinia, da. of Alfred Drewett CHAYTOR. He *d. v.p. s.p.m.* 1982. His widow was still living 1995.]

BARRYMORE

page 16,

line 20, after '(3)' add 'His widow *d.* 9 May 1930.'

GRENFELL

page 18,

line 2, after '1905;' add 'ed. at Eton;'

line 6, after 'U.S.A.' add 'This marriage was diss. by divorce in 1946 (she was still living 1995), and he *m.* 2ndly, 23 Jan. 1946, Irene Lilian, 1st da. of Harry Augustus George CARTWRIGHT of Buenos Aires, Argentina. He *d.* 24 Sep. 1976. She *d.* 1993.'

lines 7–8, delete all detail and replace as follows

III. 1976. 3. JULIAN PASCOE FRANCIS ST. LEGER (GRENFELL), BARON GRENFELL,

s. and h., *b.* 23 May 1935; ed. at Eton and Cambridge (King's Coll.); *m.* 1stly, 3 April 1961, Loretta Maria Olga Hildegard, da. of Alfredo REALI, of Florence, Italy. He *m.* 2ndly, 1970, Gabrielle, only da. of Ernst RAAB of Berlin. He *m.* 3rdly, 1987, Mrs Elizabeth PORTER, da. of Buford SCOTT of Richmond, Virginia, U.S.A. He *m.* 4thly, 1993, Mrs Dagmar Langbehn DEBREIL, da. of Carl LANGBEHN of Berlin.

KNOLLYS

page 19,
line 36, after 'Renfrewshire' add 'He *d.* 3 Dec. 1966. His widow *d.* 1987.'
line 37, delete all detail and replace as follows

III. 1966. 3. DAVID FRANCIS (KNOLLYS), VISCOUNT KNOLLYS, &c., s. and h., *b.* 12 June 1932; ed. at Eton; *m.*, 1 Oct. 1959, Sheelin Virginia, only da. of Lieut. Col. Somerset Arthur MAXWELL, M.P. (and sister of 12th BARON FARNHAM).

[PATRICK NICHOLAS MONK KNOLLYS, s. and h. ap., *b.* 11 Mar. 1967; ed. at Wymondham Coll., Norfolk and R.M.A., Sandhurst.]

REDESDALE

page 21,
line 23, after 'GORDON' add 'He *d.* 17 Mar. 1958. His widow *d.* 25 May 1963.'
line 25, after '1932' add 'He *d. v.p.*, unm., of wounds received in action in Burma, 30 May 1945.'

III. 1958. 3. BERTRAM THOMAS CARLYLE OGILVY (FREEMAN-MITFORD), BARON REDESDALE, br. and h., *b.* 2 June 1880. He *m.*, 24 Sep. 1925, Mary Margaret Dorothy, Thomas CORDES of Ascot, Berks. He *d. s.p.* 24 Dec. 1962. His widow *d.* 24 June 1967.

IV. 1962. 4. JOHN POWER BERTRAM OGILVY (FREEMAN-MITFORD), BARON REDESDALE, br. and h., *b.* 31 Jan. 1885. He *m.*, 5 Jan. 1914, Marie Anne, da. of Friedrich Viktor VON FRIEDLÄNDLER-FULD of Berlin. This marriage was annulled in 1914. He *d. s.p.* 31 Dec. 1963.

V. 1964. 5. CLEMENT NAPIER BERTRAM (FREEMAN-MITFORD), BARON REDESDALE, cousin and h., being the only s. and h. of Ernest Rupert Bertram Ogilvy FREEMAN-MITFORD (*d.* 7 Aug. 1939), 5th s. of the 1st Baron. He was *b.* 28 Oct. 1932; ed. at Eton; *m.*, 26 July 1958, Sarah Georgina Cranstoun, da. of Brig. Alston Cranstoun TODD, O.B.E., of Buxted, Sussex. He *d.* 3 Mar. 1991. His widow was living 1995.

VI. 1991. 6. RUPERT BERTRAM (MITFORD), BARON REDESDALE, only s. and h., *b.* 18 July 1967; ed. at Milton Abbey, Highgate and Newcastle Univ.

BURNHAM

page 26,
line 25, after '*extinct*' add 'His widow *d.* 20 Dec. 1939'
line 34, after 'K.C.M.G.' add 'She *d.* 3 May 1933. He *d.* 14 June 1943.'
line 35, line to read

IV. 1943. 4. EDWARD FREDERICK (LEVY-LAWSON), BARON BURNHAM, 1st s. and h., *b.* 16 June 1890;

line 40, delete ']' and replace by 'He *d.* 4 July 1963. His widow *d.* 1979.'

V. 1963. 5. WILLIAM EDWARD HARRY (LAWSON), BARON BURNHAM, s. and h., *b.* 22 Oct. 20; ed. at Eton; *m.*, 27 June 1942, Anne, 2nd da. of Major George Gerald PETHERICK, of St. Austell, Cornwall. He *d. s.p.m.* 18 June 1993. His widow was still living 1995.

VI. 1993. 6. HUGH JOHN FREDERICK (LAWSON), BARON BURNHAM, br. and h., *b.* 15 Aug. 1931; ed. at Eton and Oxford (Balliol Coll.); *m.*, 31 Dec. 1955, Hilary Mary, yr. da. of Alan HUNTER of Huntingtowerfield House, Almondbank, Perth.

[HARRY FREDERICK ALAN LAWSON, s. and h. ap., *b.* 22 Feb. 1968; ed. at Eton.]

BIDDULPH

page 27,
line 28, after 'LECONFIELD' add 'He *d.* 17 Dec. 1949. His widow *d.* 9 Nov. 1961.
line 29, line to read

III. 1949. 3. MICHAEL WILLIAM JOHN (BIDDULPH), BARON BIDDULPH, 1st s. and h., *b.* in London,

line 35, for ']' read 'He *d.* 21 July 1972. His widow *d.* 1983.'

IV. 1972. 4. ROBERT MICHAEL CHRISTIAN (BIDDULPH), BARON BIDDULPH, 1st s. and h., *b.* 6 Jan. 1931; ed. at Cranford and R.M.A., Sandhurst; *m.*, 9 Apr. 1958, Mary Helena, 1st da. of Ivor Colin James (MAITLAND), VISCOUNT MAITLAND, s. of 15th EARL OF LAUDERDALE. He *d.* 3 Nov. 1988. His widow was still living 1995.

V. 1988. 5. ANTHONY NICHOLAS COLIN (BIDDULPH, *later* MAITLAND-BIDDULPH), BARON BIDDULPH, 1st s. and h., *b.* 8 Apr. 1959; ed. at Cheltenham and R.A.C., Cirencester. He *m.*, 1993, Sian Diana, yr. da. of James David (GIBSON-WATT), BARON GIBSON-WATT (Life Peer).

[ROBERT JULIAN MAITLAND-BIDDULPH, s. and h. ap., *b.* 8 July 1994.]

ARMSTRONG

page 29,
line 31, after 'Worcester' add 'He *d.* 16 Oct. 1941. His widow *m.* 2ndly, 18 Feb. 1947, Lorne CAMPBELL-ROBSON. She *d.* 1970.'
line 32, line to read

II. 1941. 2. WILLIAM JOHN MONTAGU (WATSON-ARMSTRONG), BARON ARMSTRONG, 1st s. and h.,

line 40, for ']' read 'He *d.* 6 July 1972. His widow *d.* 1978.'

III. 1972. 3. WILLIAM HENRY CECIL JOHN ROBIN (WATSON-ARMSTRONG), BARON ARMSTRONG, s. and h., was *b.* 6 Mar. 1919, at Jesmond Dene, Newcastle-upon-Tyne; ed. at Eton and Cambridge (Trin. Coll.); *m.*, 16 Aug. 1947, Maria-Teresa, da. of Gen. Fabrizio Enea CHIODELLI-MANZONI, formerly wife of BARON JEAN MARIE GHISLAIN COLETTE ALPHONSE JULES DU FOUR. He *d.* 1 Oct. 1987 when his title became *extinct.* His widow was living in 1995.

note (2), lines 2–3, delete from 'His' to 'Tyne'

DUNEDIN

page 35,
line 30, after 'HENDERSON' add 'he *d.* 21 Aug. 1942 when the Barony of Dunedin became *extinct.* His widow *d.* 20 Mar. 1944.'

SELBY

page 37,
line 4, after '(5)' add 'His widow *d.* 22 July 1951.'
line 6, after '1911.' add 'He was ed. at Bradfield and Chillon Coll., Switzerland.'
line 18, after 'Yorkshire' add 'He *d.* 18 Sep. 1959. His widow was still living 1995.

IV. 1959. 4. MICHAEL GUY JOHN (GULLY), VISCOUNT SELBY, 1st s. and h., *b.* 15 Aug. 1942; ed. at Harrow; *m.*, 29 May 1965, Mary Theresa, da. of Capt. Thomas F. POWICK.

[EDWARD THOMAS WILLIAM GULLY, s. and h. ap., *b.* 21 Sep. 1967; ed. at Harrow; *m.*, 1992, Charlotte Catherine, da. of Rolph BREGE of Lomma, Switzerland.]

ALTHORP

page 39,
line 32, after '1937)' add 'She *d.* 4 Dec. 1972. He *d.* 7 June 1975.'
lines 33–5, delete all detail and replace by 'For the 3rd and subsequent Viscounts Althorp, see *sub* Earldom of Spencer.'

LIVERPOOL

page 41,
line 29, after 'vi' add 'and subsequently LIVERPOOL in the present volume.'

RITCHIE OF DUNDEE

page 42,
line 26, after 'JENNINGS' add 'He *d.* 19 July 1948. His widow *d.* 25 Nov. 1950 in Rye.'

page 43,
lines 3–4, delete all detail and replace as follows

III. 1948. 3. JOHN KENNETH (RITCHIE), BARON RITCHIE OF DUNDEE, 2nd but 1st surv. surv. s. and h., *b.* 22 Sep. 1902, and *bap.* at St. Jude's afsd; ed. at Winchester and Oxford (Magdalen Coll.); *m.*, 17 Feb. 1945, Joan Beatrice, only da. of the Rev. Henry Charles Lenox TINDALL. She *d.* 3 Aug. 1963. He *d. s.p.* 20 Oct. 1975.

IV. 1975. 4. COLIN NEVILLE OWER (RITCHIE), BARON RITCHIE OF DUNDEE, br. and h., *b.* 9 July 1908; ed. at Down House, Rottingdean and Oxford (Trin. Coll.); *m.*, Anne Petronill, da. of Henry Curteis BURRA, formerly wife of John Francis Burra HUNTLEY. He *d. s.p.* 16 Nov. 1975. His widow *d.* 1989.

V. 1978. 5. HAROLD MALCOLM (RITCHIE), BARON RITCHIE OF DUNDEE, br. and h., being the 4th but last surv. s. of the 2nd Baron, *b.* 29 Aug. 1919; ed. at Stowe and Oxford (Trin. Coll.); *m.*, 23 Aug. 1948, Anne, da. of Col. C.G. JOHNSTONE, M.C., of Durban, S. Africa.

[CHARLES RUPERT RENDELL RITCHIE, s. and h. ap., *b.* 15 Mar. 1958. He *m.* 1984, Tara, da. of Howard KOCH.]

WALERAN

page 44,
line 21, after 'Bradfield' add 'His widow *d.* 19 Feb. 1956 in Exmouth.'

page 45,
line 12, after 'Cardiff' add 'This marriage was diss. by divorce in 1954 and he *m.* 3rdly, 17 Dec. 1954, Mrs Valentine ROTHWELL, da. of Eric Oswald ANDERSON. He *d.* 4 Apr. 1966. At his death the Barony of Waleran and the Baronetcy became *extinct*. His widow was still living 1995.'

note (2), line 2, after '1925' add 'He *m.* May 1936, Edith Mary, da. of the Rev. Thomas Grey of Aboyne, Aberdeen. She *d.* 29 Dec. 1941. He *d. s.p.* 15 Apr. 1942.'

NORTHCLIFFE

page 48,
line 4, after 'Essex' add 'She *d.* 30 July 1963.'

MICHELHAM

page 49,
line 21, after '1900' add 'ed. at Malvern Coll.'
line 22, after 'Paris' add 'She *d.* 3 Nov. 1961. He *m.* 2ndly, 1980, Marie-José Dupas. He *d.* 19 Mar. 1984 when the Barony of Michelham and his Baronetcy became *extinct*. His widow was still living 1995.'

DESBOROUGH

page 51,
line 22, after 'COWPER' add 'He *d.* 9 Jan. 1945 when the Barony of Desborough became *extinct*. His widow *d.* 28 May 1962 in Panshanger, co. Hertford.'

ST. ALDWYN

page 55,
line 36, after '(1)' add 'His widow *d.* 17 Mar. 1940.'

page 56,
line 24, after '(T.A.)' add 'He *d.* 29 Jan. 1992. His widow *d.* 10 July 1992.'

III. 1992. 3. MICHAEL HENRY (HICKS-BEACH), EARL ST. ALDWYN, &c., 1st s. and h., *b.* 7 Feb. 1950; ed. at Eton and Oxford (Ch. Ch.); *m.*, 1982, Gilda Maria, only da. of Bárao SAARVEDRA of Rio de Janeiro, Brazil.

HEMPHILL

page 62,
line 26, after 'Dublin' add 'His widow *d.* 9 Jan. 1970.'

page 63,
line 4, after '1930' add 'His widow *d.* 25 Aug. 1958.'
line 8, after 'U.S.A.' add 'He *d.* 19 Mar. 1957. His widow *d.* 1990.'
line 9, delete all detail and replace as follows

V. 1957. 5. PETER PATRICK FITZROY MARTYN (HEMPHILL, *later* MARTYN-HEMPHILL), BARON HEMPHILL, s. and h., *b.* 5 Sep. 1928; ed. at Downside and Oxford (Brasenose Coll.); *m.*, 17 Apr. 1952, Olivia Ann, 1st da. of Major Robert Francis RUTTLEDGE of Cloonee, Ballinrobe, co. Mayo.

[CHARLES ANDREW MARTYN MARTYN-HEMPHILL, s. and h. ap., *b.* 8 Oct. 1954; ed. at Downside and Oxford (St. Benet's Hall); *m.* Sarah, 1st da. of Richard LUMLEY of Windlesham, Surrey.]

JOICEY

page 64,
line 28, after '(3)' add 'He *d. s.p.m.s.* 24 July 1940. His widow *d.* 4 Nov. 1952.'
after line 30 add as follows

III. 1940. 3. HUGH EDWARD (JOICEY), BARON JOICEY, br. and h., *b.* 21 Nov. 1981; ed. at Harrow; *m.*, 19 July 1921, Joan, da. of Frederick William (LAMBTON), 4th EARL OF DURHAM. He *d.* 14 Oct. 1966. His widow *d.* 4 Jan. 1967.

[DAVID HUGH JOICEY, 1st s. and h. ap., *b.* 21 Apr. 1922. He *d. v.p.* and unm. of wounds received at Salerno, Sep. 1943.]

IV. 1966. 4. MICHAEL EDWARD (JOICEY), BARON JOICEY, 2nd but 1st surv. s. and h., *b.* 28 Feb. 1925; ed. at Eton and Oxford (Ch. Ch.); *m.*, 27 Mar. 1952, Elizabeth Marion, da. of Lieut. Col. Ian Leslie MELVILLE. He *d.* 14 June 1993. His widow was living 1995.

V. 1993. 5. JAMES MICHAEL (JOICEY), BARON JOICEY, 1st s. and h., *b.* 28 June 1953; ed. at Eton and Oxford (Ch. Ch.). He *m.*, 1984, Agnes Harriet Frances Mary, da. of the Rev. William THOMPSON.

[WILLIAM JAMES JOICEY, 1st s. and h. ap., *b.* 21 May 1990.]

note (3), delete all detail

NUNBURNHOLME

page 65,
line 27, after 'Warter' add 'His widow *d.* 17 Jun. 1968.'
line 32, after 'Bart.' add 'This marriage was diss. by divorce in 1947 and he *m.* 2ndly, 2 Nov. 1953, Alex, only da. of Capt. Douglas HOCKLY, of Tenterden, Kent. He *d.* 1 Jan. 1974. His widow *m.* 2ndly, 1975, H.O.J.C. JONAS. She was still living 1995.'
line 33, delete all detail and replace as follows

IV. 1974. 4. BEN CHARLES (WILSON), BARON NUNBURNHOLME, 1st s. and h., *b.* 16 July 1928: ed. at Eton; *m.*, 8 Apr. 1958, Ines Dolores Jeanne, da. of Gérard WALRAVENS of Brussels.

COLEBROOKE

page 67,
line 21, after 'WYNDHAM' add 'He *d.* 28 Feb. 1939, when the Barony of Colebrooke and the Baronetcy [1759] became *extinct*.'

ALLENDALE

page 75,
line 7, after 'afsd,' add 'His widow *d.* 31 July 1945.'
line 19, after 'Cowes' add 'He *d.* 16 Dec. 1956. His widow *d.* 1979.'
lines 20–1, delete all detail and replace as follows

BARONY. IV. VISCOUNTCY. III. } 1956 4 and 3. WENTWORTH HUBERT CHARLES (BEAUMONT), VISCOUNT ALLENDALE, &c., 1st s. and h., was *b.* 12 Sep. 1922; ed. at Eton; *m.*, 10 Feb. 1948, Sarah Field, da. of Hastings Lionel (ISMAY), 1st BARON ISMAY.

[WENTWORTH PETER ISMAY BEAUMONT, s. and h. ap., *b.* 14 Nov. 1948 and ed. at Harrow. He was *m.*, 1975, Theresa Mary Magdalene, 2nd da. of Francis Ambrose More O'FERRALL.]

AIREDALE

page 80,
line 26, after 'Leeds' add 'She *d.* 8 July 1942. He *d. s.p.m.* 11 Mar. 1944.'

III. 1944. 3. ROLAND DUDLEY (KITSON), BARON AIREDALE, br. and h., being only s. of the 1st Baron by his 2nd wife, *b.* in Leeds 19 July 1882; ed. at Westminster and Cambridge (Trin. Coll.); served in WW1, 1914–18, as Capt. in the West Yorkshire Regt. He *m.* 1stly, 1 July 1913, Sheila Grace, yr. da. of Frank Edward VANDELEUR. She *d.* 8 Aug. 1935. He *m.* 2ndly, 16 Sep. 1937, Dorothy Christabel Rowland, da. of the Rev. Canon Raymond Percy PELLY. He *d.* 20 Mar. 1958. His widow *d.* 1970.

IV. 1958. 4. OLIVER JAMES VANDELEUR (KITSON), BARON AIREDALE, s. and h., *b.* 22 Apr. 1915; ed. at Eton and Cambridge (Trin. Coll.).

note (1), delete all detail

SWAYTHLING

page 81,
line 25, after '(5)' add 'His widow *d.* 8 Jan. 1965.'

page 82,
line 8, after 'BEARSTED' add 'This marriage was diss. by divorce in 1942 and he *m.* 2ndly, 13 Aug. 1945, Jean Marcia, da. of G.G. Leith MARSHALL and formerly wife of Sqn. Ldr. G.R.M. KNOX. He *d.* 5 Jan. 1990. His widow was living 1995.
line 9, delete all detail and replace as follows

IV. 1990. 4. DAVID CHARLES (SAMUEL-MONTAGU), BARON SWAYTHLING, 1st s. and h., *b.* 6 Aug. 1928; ed. at Eton and Cambridge (Trin. Coll.). He *m.*, 14 Dec. 1951, Christine Françoise Ninette, da. of Edgar DREYFUS of Paris.

[CHARLES EDGAR SAMUEL SAMUEL-MONTAGU, s. and h. ap., *b.* 20 Feb. 1954.]

BLYTH

page 83,
line 26, after 'DENNIS' add 'He *d. s.p.* 27 Feb. 1943. His widow *m.* 3rdly, Major Chave Charles Nainby LUXMOORE (who *d.* 1984), and *d.* 1977.'

III. 1943. 3. IAN AUDLEY JAMES (BLYTH), BARON BLYTH, nephew and h., being only s. and h. of Audley James BLYTH (*d.* 21 Mar. 1908), 2nd s. of the 1st Baron, was *b.* 28 Oct. 1905; *m.*, 30 May 1928, Edna Myrtle, da. of Ernest LEWIS of Wellington, New Zealand. She *d.* 1952. He *d.* 29 Oct. 1977.

IV. 1977. 4. ANTHONY AUDLEY RUPERT (BLYTH), BARON BLYTH, 1st s. and h., was *b.* 3 June 1931; *m.* 1stly, 1954, Elizabeth Dorothea, da. of Robert T. SPARROW of Vancouver, British Columbia, Canada. This marriage was diss. in 1962 and he *m.* 2ndly, 1963, Oonagh Elizabeth Ann, yr. da. William Henry CONWAY, of Dundrum, Dublin.

[RILEY AUDLEY BLYTH, s. and h. ap. by 1st wife, *b.* 4 Mar. 1955.]

note (2), delete all detail

WOLVERHAMPTON

page 89,
line 30, after 'LONDESBOROUGH' add 'He *d. s.p.* 9 Mar. 1943 when his peerage became *extinct*.'

MARCHAMLEY

page 92,
line 21, after 'Zealand' add 'He served in WW2. He *d.* 17 Nov. 1949. His widow *d.* 1974.'
lines 22–3, delete all detail and replace as follows

III. 1949. 3. JOHN WILLIAM TATTERSALL (WHITELEY), BARON MARCHAMLEY, s. and h., *b.* 24 Apr. 1922; *m.* 25 July 1967, Sonia Kathleen, da. of (__) PEDRICK. He *d.* 26 May 1994.

IV. 1994. 4. WILLIAM FRANCIS (WHITELEY), BARON MARCHAMLEY, only s. and h., *b.* 27 July 1968.

HOLDEN

page 93,
line 26, after 'Cemetery' add 'His widow *d.* 25 Jan. 1957.'
line 33, after '(1)' add 'He *d.* unm. 6 July 1951 when the Barony of Holden became

extinct but the Baronetcy was inherited by his 1st cousin once removed, the s. of the yr. br. of the 1st Baron.'

ST. DAVIDS

page 94,
line 34, after '£123,736 add 'His widow *d.* 12 Dec. 1974.'

page 95,
line 23, after 'Queensland' add 'This marriage was diss by divorce in 1954 (and she *d.* 19 Oct. 1956 in Australia), when he *m.* 2ndly, 15 Oct. 1954, Elizabeth Joyce, 1st da. of Dr E. Alec WOOLFF of Hove, Sussex. This marriage was also diss by divorce, in 1959, and he *m.* 3rdly, 19 Oct. 1959, Evelyn Marjorie, only da. of Dr John Edmund Guy HARRIS of Bray-on-Thames, Berks. On the *d.* of his mother (12 Dec. 1974) he *suc.* to the Baronies of STRANGE OF KNOKYN, HUNGERFORD and DE MOLEYNS (see also vol. xiii, p. 94). He *d.* 10 June 1991. His widow was living 1995.'

III. 1991. 3. COLWYN JESTYN JOHN (PHILIPPS), VISCOUNT ST. DAVIDS, &c., LORD STRANGE OF KNOKYN [1299], LORD HUNGERFORD [1426] and LORD MOLEYNS [1445], s. and h., *b.* 30 Jan. 1939; ed. at Sevenoaks Sch. and King's Coll., London; *m.*, 1965, Augusta Victoria Corea Larrain, da. of Don Estantislao Correa UGARTE of Santiago, Chile.

[RHODRI COLWYN PHILIPPS, 1st s. and h. ap., *b.* 16 Sep. 1966; ed. at Worth Sch.]

PENTLAND

page 99,
line 28, after 'A.M.I.C.E.' add 'He *m.*, 11 Sep. 1941, Elizabeth, 3rd da. of Sir Henry Babington SMITH. He *d. s.p.m.* 14 Feb. 1984 when the Barony of Pentland became *extinct*. His widow was still living 1995.'

GORELL

page 101,
line 21, after 'Police' add 'She *d.* 26 Apr. 1954. He *d.* 2 May 1963.'
line 22, delete all detail and replace as follows

IV. 1963. 4. TIMOTHY JOHN RADCLIFFE (BARNES), BARON GORELL, 1st s. and h., *b.* 2 Aug. 1927; ed. at Eton and Oxford (New Coll.); *m.*, 29 May 1955, Joan Marion, da. of John Edmund COLLINS M.C., of Sway, Hants.

SHAW

page 102,
line 31, after '(2)' add 'His widow *d.* 31 May 1939.'

CRAIGMYLE

page 103,
line 19, after 'Forfarshire' add 'He *d.* 29 Sep. 1944. His widow *d.* 31 May 1958.'
line 20, delete all detail and replace as follows

III. 1944. 3. THOMAS DONALD MACKAY (SHAW), BARON CRAIGMYLE, 1st s. and h., was *b.* 17 Nov. 1923; ed. at Eton and Oxford (Trin. Coll.); *m.*, 22 Sep. 1955, Anthea Ester Christine Theresa, da. of Edward Charles RICH.

[THOMAS COLUMBA RICH SHAW, 1st s. and h. ap., *b.* 19 Oct. 1960; *m.*, 1987, Alice, 2nd da. of David FLOYD, of Combe Down, Bath.]

DESART

page 104,
line 8, after '(1)' add 'See vol. iv, *sub* DESART'

FISHER

page 106,
line 9, after 'SHAPLEIGH' add 'She *d.* 29 Jan. 1955. He *d.* 11 May 1955.'
lines 10–11, delete all detail and replace as follows

III. 1955. 3. JOHN VAVASSEUR (FISHER), BARON FISHER, 1st s. and h., *b.* at Kilverstone, 24 July, and *bap.* there 26 Sep. 1921; ed. at Stowe and Cambridge (Trin. Coll.); *m.* 1stly, 25 July 1949, Elizabeth Ann Penelope, yr. da. of Herbert P. HOLT. This marriage was diss. by divorce in 1969 and ha *m.* 2ndly, 1970, Rosamund Ann, da. of Lewis Joseph Hugh (CLIFFORD), 12th BARON CLIFFORD OF CHUDLEIGH and formerly wife of Geoffrey Forrester FAIRBAIRN.

[PATRICK VAVASSEUR FISHER, 1st s. and h. ap., *b.* 14 June 1953; *m.*, 1977, Karen Jean, da. of Robert Andrew (CARNEGIE), 13th EARL OF NORTHESK.]

KILBRACKEN

p. 108,
line 3, after '1936.' add 'She *d.* 18 Feb. 1958.'
line 4, after 'Brighton' add 'She *d.* 23 Aug. 1948. He *d.* 13 Oct. 1950.'
lines 5–6, delete all detail and replace as follows

III. 1950. 3. JOHN RAYMOND (GODLEY), BARON KILBRACKEN, 1st s. and h. by 1st wife, was *b.* 17 Oct. 1920; ed. at Eton and Oxford (Balliol Coll.); *m.* 1stly, 22 May 1943, Penelope Anne, yst. da. of Rear Adm. Sir Cecil Nugent REYNE, K.B.E. This marriage was diss. by divorce in 1949 and he *m.* 2ndly, 1981, Susan Lee, da. of Norman HEAZLEWOOD, of Melbourne, Victoria, Australia. This marriage was diss. by divorce in 1989.

[CHRISTOPHER JOHN GODLEY, 1st s. and h. ap., by 1st wife, *b.* 1 Jan. 1945; ed. at Rugby and Reading Univ.; *m.*, 10 May 1969, Gillian Christine, da. of Lieut. Cmdr. S.W. BIRSE, O.B.E., R.N.]

GLADSTONE

page 111,
line 34, after '(3)' add 'His widow *d.* 20 June 1953.'

ASHBY ST. LEDGERS

page 112,
line 21, after 'ANNALY' add 'He *d.* 14 June 1939. His widow *d.* 17 Apr. 1948.'
lines 22–4, delete all detail and replace by 'For second and subsequent Viscounts Wimborne, see *sub* WIMBORNE.'

MERSEY

page 114,
line 26, after 'ROMILLY' add 'He *d.* 20 Nov. 1956. His widow *d.* 1973.'
line 27, line to read

III. 1956. 3. EDWARD CLIVE (BIGHAM), VISCOUNT MERSEY, &c., 1st s. and h., *b.* 5 June 1906, at

line 33, for ']' read 'She became BARONESS NAIRNE, *suo jure*, on the death of her br. the 7th MARQUESS OF LANSDOWNE, 20 Aug. 1944 (see *sub* LANSDOWNE and *sub* NAIRNE). He *d.* 2 Aug. 1979. His widow was still living 1995.'

IV. 1979. 4. RICHARD MAURICE CLIVE (BIGHAM), VISCOUNT MERSEY, &c., s. and h., *b.* 8 July 1934; ed. at Eton and Oxford (Balliol Coll.); *m.*, 6 May 1961, Joanna Dorothy, 1st da. of John Grey MURRAY, C.B.E.

[EDWARD JOHN HALLAM BIGHAM, s. and h., ap., *b.* 23 May 1966; ed. at Eton and Oxford (Balliol Coll.). He *m.*, 1994, Claire, da. of David HAIGH.]

CORNWALL

page 117,
line 29, after 'U.S.A.' add 'He *d. s.p.* 28 May in Paris and was *bur.* 5 June 1972 at Frogmore. His widow *d.* 24 Apr. in Paris and was also *bur.* 29 Apr. at Frogmore.'

See below, p. 800, for CHARLES PHILIP ARTHUR GEORGE, DUKE OF CORNWALL, &c.

ILKESTON

page 119,
line 36, after 'Taylor' add 'He *d. s.p.* 4 Jan. 1952 when his peerage became *extinct*.

DEVONPORT

page 120,
line 32, after 'Ayrshire' add 'He *d.* 29 Mar. 1973. His widow was still living 1995.'

III. 1973. 3. TERENCE (KEARLEY), VISCOUNT DEVONPORT, &c., s. and h., *b.* 29 Aug. 1944; ed. at Aiglon Coll., Switzerland and Cambridge (Selwyn Coll.); *m.*, 7 Dec. 1968, Elizabeth Rosemary, 2nd da. of John Gordon HOPTON of Chute Manor, Andover, co. Hants. This marriage was diss. by divorce in 1979.

COWDRAY

page 122,
line 9, after '(3)' add 'His widow *d.* 19 Feb. 1948.'
line 15, after 'T.A.' add 'He *m.* 1stly, 19 July 1939, Anne Pamela, da. of Orlando (BRIDGEMAN), 5th EARL OF BRADFORD. This marriage was diss. by divorce in 1950 and he *m.* 2ndly, 4 Mar. 1953, Elizabeth Georgiana, 2nd da. of Sir Anthony Henry Mather MATHER-JACKSON, Bart.

[MICHAEL ORLANDO WEETMAN PEARSON, s. and h. ap. by 1st wife, *b.* 17 June 1944; ed. at Gordonstoun; *m.*, 1977, Ellen, da. of Herman ERHARDT, of Munich. This marriage was diss. by divorce 1984 and he *m.* 2ndly, 1987, Marina Rose, 2nd da. of John Howard CORDLE, of Salisbury.]

ROTHERHAM

page 123,
line 34, for 'from 1922' read '1922–44'
line 35, after 'WRIGHT' add 'He *d. s.p.* 24 Jan. 1950 when the Barony of Rotherham and the Baronetcy became *extinct*. His widow *d.* 1971.

FURNESS

page 125,
line 3, after 'N.S.W.' add 'He *d.* 6 Oct. 1940. His widow *d.* 1973.'
line 5, after 'Officers' add 'He served in WW2, *k.* in action, *v.p.* and unm., 24 May 1940; V.C. (posthumous)

BARONY. III. VISCOUNTCY. II. } 1940 3 and 2. WILLIAM ANTHONY (FURNESS), VISCOUNT FURNESS, &c., 2nd surv. s. and h. being only s. by 2nd wife, *b.* 31 Mar. 1929; ed. at Downside. He is unm. 1995.

WILLINGDON

page 126,
line 37, after 'London.' add 'He *d.* 13 Feb. 1941. His widow *d.* 30 Jan. 1960.'

page 127,
line 6, line to read as follows

II. 1941. 2. INIGO BRASSEY (FREEMAN-THOMAS), MARQUESS OF WILLINGDON, EARL OF WILLINGDON, VISCOUNT WILLINGDON, VISCOUNT RATENDONE AND BARON WILLINGDON, 2nd but 1st surv. s. and h., was *b.* 25 July 1899, at Ratten, and *bap.* at Willingdon Church; *styled* VISCOUNT RATENDONE 1931–41;

line 15, delete ']' and replace by 'This marriage was diss. by divorce in 1939 and he *m.* 3rdly, 9 June 1943, Daphne, 2nd da. of Seymour CADWELL. He *d. s.p.* 19 Mar. 1979 when all his titles became *extinct*.'

HARDINGE OF PENSHURST

page 128,
line 30, after 'Kent' add 'He *d.* 2 Aug. 1944.'
line 37, line to read as follows

II. 1944. 2. ALEXANDER HENRY LOUIS (HARDINGE), BARON HARDINGE OF PENSHURST, 2nd but 1st surv. s. and h.,

page 129,
line 14, delete ']' and replace by 'He *d.* 29 May 1960. His widow *d.* 1979.'

III. 1960. 3. GEORGE EDWARD CHARLES (HARDINGE), BARON HARDINGE OF PENSHURST, only s. and h.; ed. at Eton; *m.*, 22 July 1944, Janet Christine Goschen, da. of Lieut. Col. Francis Cecil Campbell BALFOUR, M.C. This marriage was diss. by divorce in 1962 and he *m.* 2ndly, 1966, Mrs Margaret TRESIZE, da. of William Thomas JERRUM.

[JULIAN ALEXANDER HARDINGE, 1st s. and h. ap. by 1st wife, 23 Aug. 1945; ed. at Eton and Cambridge (Trin. Coll.).]

DE VILLIERS

page 131,
line 2, after '(2)' add 'His widow *d.* 28 Jan. 1968.'
line 5, after '1938' add 'He *m.*, 9 Nov. 1939, Edna Alexis Lovett, 1st da. of the Rev. Dr. A.D. MACKINNON of Peachland, British Columbia, Canada.

[ALEXANDER CHARLES DE VILLIERS only s. and h. ap., *b.* 29 Dec. 1940.]

GLENCONNER

page 137,
line 5, after 'London' add 'He *d.* 4 Oct. 1983. His widow was living 1995.'
lines 6–7, delete all detail and replace as follows

III. 1983. 3. COLIN CHRISTOPHER PAGET (TENNANT), BARON GLENCONNER, and a Baronet, 1st s. and h. by 1st wife, *b.* 1 Dec. 1926; ed. at Eton and Oxford (New Coll.); *m.*, 21 Apr. 1956, Anne Veronica, da. of Thomas William (COKE), 5th EARL OF LEICESTER.

[CHARLES EDWARD PEVENSEY TENNANT, 1st s. and h. ap., *b.* 15 Feb. 1957; *m.*, 1993, Shelagh, da. of Matthew Raymond SCOTT of Peebles.]

ABERCONWAY

page 139,
line 6, after 'SANDERSON' add 'He *d.* 23 May 1953. His widow *d.* 1974.'
line 7, line to read as follows

III. 1953. 3. CHARLES MELVILLE (MCLAREN), BARON ABERCONWAY, and a Baronet, 1st s. and h.,

line 9, delete ']' and replace by 'He *m.* 1stly, 6 Dec. 1941, Deirdre, da. of John KNEWSTUB. This marriage was diss. by divorce 1949 and he *m.* 2ndly, 15 Oct. 1949, Anne Lindsay, only da. of Alexander Lindsay AYMER and formerly wife of Maj. Robert Lee BULLARD.'

[HENRY CHARLES MCLAREN only s. and h. ap. by 1st wife, *b.* 26 May 1948; ed. at Eton and Sussex Univ. He *m.* 1981, Sally Ann, yr. da. of Capt. Charles Nugent LENTAIGNE, R.N., of Hawkley, Liss, co. Hants.]

ST. AUDRIES

page 140,
line 21, after '1917' add 'His widow *d.* 11 Oct. 1949.'
line 28, after '1917' add 'He *d.* 16 Oct. 1971. On his *d.* the Barony of St. Audries became *extinct* but the Baronetcies devolved on Alexander William FULLER-ACLAND-HOOD his distant cousin and h. These Baronetcies became *extinct* in 1990.'

MERTHYR

page 144,
line 15, after 'Northumberland' add 'He *d.* 5 Apr. 1977. His widow was living 1995.'
line 16, delete all detail and replace as follows

IV. 1977. 4. TREVOR OSWIN (LEWIS), BARON MERTHYR and a Baronet, 1st s. and h., *b.* 29 Nov. 1935; ed. at Eton, Oxford (Magdalen Coll.) and Cambridge (Magdalene Coll.); *m.*, 18 Apr. 1964, Susan Jane, da. of Arthur John BIRT-LLEWELLIN of Boulston Manor, Haverfordwest, co. Pembroke. He disclaimed, 26 Apr. 1977, his peerage for life under the Peerage Act, 1963.

[DAVID TREVOR LEWIS, s. and h. ap., *b.* 21 Feb. 1977.]

INCHCAPE

page 147,
line 7, after 'ESHER' add 'He *d.* 21 June 1939. His widow *d.* 10 Nov. 1957.'
lines 8–9, delete all detail and replace as follows

III. 1939. 3. KENNETH JAMES WILLIAM (MACKAY), EARL OF INCHCAPE, &c., 1st s. and h., *b.* 27 Dec. 1917; *styled* VISCOUNT GLENAPP 1932–9; ed. at Eton and Cambridge (Trin. Coll.); *m.* 1stly, 12 Feb. 1941, Aline Thorn, only da. of Sir Richard Arthur PEASE, Bart. This marriage was diss. by divorce in 1954 and he *m.* 2ndly, 13 Feb. 1965, Caroline, 1st da. of Cholmeley Dering HARRISON. He *d.* 17 Mar. 1994. His widow was still living 1995.

IV. 1994. 4. KENNETH PETER LYLE (MACKAY), EARL OF INCHCAPE, &c., 1st s. and h., *b.* 23 Jan. 1943; ed. at Eton; *m.*, 7 June 1966, Georgina, da. of Sydney CRESSWELL.

[FERGUS JAMES KENNETH MACKAY, *styled* VISCOUNT GLENAPP, s. and h. ap., *b.* 9 July 1979.]

ROWALLAN

page 148,
line 18, after 'N.B.' add 'She *d.* 1971. He *d.* 30 Nov. 1977.'
line 19, delete all detail and replace as follows

III. 1977. 3. ARTHUR CAMERON (CORBETT), BARON ROWALLAN, 1st s. and h., *b.* 17 Dec. 1919; ed. at Eton and Oxford (Balliol Coll.); *m.* 1stly, 23 June 1945, Eleanor Mary, da. of George Frederic BOYLE. This marriage was diss. by divorce 1962, and he *m.* 2ndly, 10 Sep. 1963, April ASHLEY. This marriage was annulled in 1963. He *d.* 24 June 1993.

IV. 1993. 4. JOHN POLSON CAMERON (CORBETT), BARON ROWALLAN, s. and h. by 1st wife, *b.* 8 Mar. 1947; ed. at Eton and R.A.C., Cirencester; *m.* 1stly, 1971, Susan Jane Dianne, da. of James A. GREEN of Longhorsley, Northumberland. This marriage was diss. by divorce in 1983 and he *m.* 2ndly, 1984, Sandrew Filomena, da. of William BRYSON of Kilmaurs, Ayrshire.

[JASON POLSON CAMERON CORBETT, s. and h. ap. by 1st wife, *b.* 21 Apr. 1972; ed. at Glenalmond and R.A.C., Cirencester.]

ASHTON OF HYDE

page 149,
line 30, after 'THOMAS' add 'He *d.* 21 Mar. 1983. His widow *d.* 1993.'
line 31, delete all detail and replace as follows

III. 1983. 3. THOMAS JOHN (ASHTON), BARON ASHTON OF HYDE, s. and h., *b.* 19 Nov. 1926; ed. at Eton and Oxford (New Coll.); *m.*, 18 May 1957, Pauline Trewlove, 1st da. of Lieut. Col. Robert Henry Langton BRACKENBURY, O.B.E., of Shipston-on-Stour, co. Warwicks.

[THOMAS HENRY ASHTON, 1st s. and h. ap., *b.* 18 July 1958; ed. at Eton and Oxford (Trin. Coll.); *m.*, 1987, Emma Louise, da. of Colin ALLINSON of Bath.]

CHARNWOOD

page 150,
line 17, after 'M.P.' add 'She *d.* 20 Apr. 1942. He *d.* 3 Feb. 1945.'
line 18, line to read as follows

II. 1945. 2. JOHN ROBY (BENSON), BARON CHARNWOOD, 1st but only surv. s. and h.,

line 20, after '(T.A.).' add 'He was ed. at Eton and Oxford (Balliol Coll.).'
line 22, delete ']' and replace by 'He *d. s.p.* 1 Feb. 1955, when his peerage became *extinct.*'

CREWE

page 151,
line 29, after '11' add 'He *d. s.p.m.s.* 20 June 1945 when all his honours became *extinct.* His widow *d.* 13 Mar. 1967.'

ELIBANK

page 152,
line 28, after 'MAGDALA' add 'He *d. s.p.* 12 Mar. 1951. For his successors, see ELIBANK above, p. 301. His widow *d.* 22 Mar. 1955.'

CHILSTON

page 155,
line 10, after 'Kent' add 'He *d.* 25 July 1947. His widow *d.* 11 Aug. 1962.'
line 14, after 'RICHARD' add 'He *m.* 2ndly, 1939, Marcia Victoria, da. of John Myddleton BRACE of Ceylon. He *d.* following a motor accident, *v.p. s.p.* 28 Feb. 1940. His widow *d.* 3 Nov. 1945.

III. 1947. 3. ERIC ALEXANDER (AKERS-DOUGLAS), VISCOUNT CHILSTON, 2nd but 1st surv. s. and h., *b.* 17 Dec. 1910; ed. at Eton and Oxford (Trin. Coll.); *m.*, 15 Feb. 1955, Marion, da. of Capt. Charles William HOWARD. He *d. s.p.* 10 Apr. 1982. His widow *d.* 1970.

IV. 1982. 4. ALASTAIR GEORGE (AKERS-DOUGLAS), VISCOUNT CHILSTON, &c., cousin and h., being s. of Capt. Ian Stanley AKERS-DOUGLAS (*d. v.p.* 16 Dec. 1952), by his 2nd wife Phyllis Rosemary, da. of Arthur David Clere PARSONS, which Ian was 1st s. and h. of Lieut. Col. George Alexander AKERS-DOUGLAS (*d.* 11 July 1955), by Doris, da. of Stanley CHRISTOPHERSON, which George was 2nd s. of the 1st Viscount. He was *b.* 5 Sep. 1946; ed. at Eton; *m.*, 1971, Juliet Anne, da. of Lieut. Col. Nigel LOVETT of Okehampton, Devon.

[OLIVER IAN AKERS-DOUGLAS, 1st s. and h. ap., *b.* 13 Oct. 1973.]

EMMOTT

page 156,
line 23, after '£91,756' add 'His widow *d.* 24 Nov. 1954.'

STRACHIE

page 157,
line 18, after '(2)' add 'His widow *d.* 22 Dec. 1936'
line 27, after 'PATON' add 'She *d.* 27 Feb. 1962. He *d. s.p.* 17 May 1973 when his Barony became *extinct* but his Baronetcy was inherited by his cousin Sir Charles STRACHEY.'

HOLLENDEN

page 163,
line 15, after 'Tonbridge.' add 'His widow *d.* 28 Oct. 1945.'
line 28, after 'Hants' add 'She *d.* 6 June 1962 and he *m.* 3rdly, 7 Jan. 1963, Violet Norris, da. of Alfred LEVERTON of Glaythorn, Peterborough and widow of Frank Ditch HOWITT, C.V.O. He *d.* 19 Oct. 1977. His widow was still living in 1995.

III. 1977. 3. GORDON HOPE (HOPE-MORLEY), BARON HOLLENDON, nephew and h., being only s. and h. of Capt. Claude Hope HOPE-MORLEY (*d.* 8 Apr. 1968), by Lady Dorothy Edith Isabel, 1st da. of Sidney Carr (HOBART-HAMPDEN-MERCER-HENDERSON), 7th EARL OF BUCKINGHAMSHIRE, which Claude was 2nd s. of the 1st Baron. He was *b.* 8 Jan. 1914; ed. at Eton; *m.*, 27 Oct. 1945, Sonja, da. of Thorolf SUNDT of Bergen, Norway.

[IAN HAMPDEN HOPE-MORLEY, s. and h. ap., *b.* 23 Oct. 1946; ed. at Eton; *m.* 1stly, 1972, Beatrice Saulnier, da. of BARON PIERRE D'ANCHALD of Paris. This marriage was diss.

by divorce and he *m.* 2ndly, 1988, Caroline, only da. of Kim ASH of Johannesburg, S. Africa.]

BUTLER

page 165,
line 18, after 'Florida.' add 'His widow *d.* 15 June 1946.'
line 26, after 'U.S.A.' add 'She *d.* 24 July 1954 and he *m.* 3rdly, 21 Oct. 1954, Ruth, da. of Francis T.M. MCENERY of Chicago, Illinois, U.S.A. He *d.* 31 July 1957. His widow *d.* 1972.'
lines 27–8, delete all detail and replace by 'For 3rd and subsequent Barons Butler see CARRICK [I.], above.'

WHITBURGH

page 169,
line 10, after 'Midlothian' add 'He *d.* unm. 29 Sep. 1967 when his Barony became *extinct* but his Baronetcy was inherited by his nephew, John Thomas BORTHWICK, 2nd s. of the 1st Baronet.'

LATIMER

page 173,
after line 12 add as follows

For 5th and subsequent Barons Latimer, see above, *sub* LATIMER.

SYDENHAM OF COMBE

page 174,
line 13, after '(1)' add 'His widow *d.* 6 June 1952 at the Priory, Lamberhurst, Kent.'

ROCHDALE

page 175,
line 22, after 'NORMANBY' add 'He *d.* 24 Mar. 1945. His widow *d.* 1966.'
line 23, line to read as follows

II. 1945. 2 and 1. JOHN DURIVAL (KEMP), BARON ROCHDALE, s. and h., *b.* 5 June 1906, at Beechwood,
VISCOUNTCY.
I. 1960

line 27, for ']' read 'He was *cr.*, 20 June 1960, VISCOUNT ROCHDALE of Rochdale in the County Palatine of Lancaster. He *d.* 24 May 1993. His widow was still living 1995.'

VISCOUNTCY. II. BARONY. III. } 1993 2 and 3. ST. JOHN DURIVAL (KEMP), VISCOUNT ROCHDALE, &c., only s. and h., *b.* 15 Jan. 1938; ed. at Eton; *m.* 1stly, 5 Jan. 1960, Serena Jane, da. of James Edward Michael CLARK-HALL, of Bethersden, Kent. This marriage was diss. by divorce 1974 and he *m.* 2ndly, 1976, Elizabeth, da. of Robert Norman Rossiter BOLDEN, and formerly wife of James Michael ANDERTON.

[JONATHAN HUGO DURIVAL KEMP, 1st s. and h. ap. by 1st wife, *b.* 10 June 1961; ed. at Stowe; *m.*, 1994, Ming Xian, only da. of (__) ZHU of Singapore.]

FURNIVALLE

page 176,
line 29, after 'China' add 'For further details see vol. v, *sub* FURNIVALLE and above.'

READING

page 182,
line 16, after 'GOETZE' add 'He *d.* 19 Sep. 1960. His widow *d.* 14 Aug. 1973.'
line 17, delete all detail and replace as follows

III. 1960. 3. MICHAEL ALFRED RUFUS (ISAACS), MARQUESS OF READING, &c., 1st s. and h., *b.* 9 Mar. 1916; *styled* VISCOUNT ERLEIGH 1935–60; ed. at Eton and Oxford (Balliol Coll.); *m.*, 7 June 1941, Margot Irene, yr. da. of Percy DUKE, O.B.E. He *d.* 2 July 1980. His widow was still living 1995.

IV. 1980. 4. SIMON HENRY RUFUS (ISAACS), MARQUESS OF READING, &c., s. and h., *b.* 18 May 1942; ed. at Eton and Tours Univ., France; *m.*, 1979, Melinda Victoria, yr. da. of Richard J.G. DEWAR of Seale, Surrey.

[JULIAN MICHAEL ISAACS, *styled* VISCOUNT ERLEIGH, s. and h. ap., *b.* 26 May 1986.]

PARMOOR

page 184,
line 28, for 'Gloucester' read 'Lancaster' (twice)
line 35, after 'ROWNTREE' add 'He *d.* 30 June 1941. His widow *d.* 6 July 1952.'
line 36, line to read as follows

II. 1941. 2. ALFRED SEDDON HENRY (CRIPPS), BARON PARMOOR, 1st s. and h., by 1st wife,

page 185,
line 4, delete ']' and replace by 'He *d.* unm. 12 May 1977.'

III. 1977. 3. FREDERICK HEYWORTH (CRIPPS), BARON PARMOOR, br. and h., *b.* 4 July 1885; ed. at Winchester and Oxford (New Coll.). He *m.* 8 Oct. 1927, Violet Mary Geraldine, da. of Sir William NELSON, Bart., formerly wife of George Richard Francis ROWLEY and then of the 2nd DUKE OF WESTMINSTER. This marriage was diss. by divorce in 1951. She *d.* 1983. He *d.* 5 Oct. 1977.

IV. 1977. 4. FREDERICK ALFRED MILO (CRIPPS), BARON PARMOOR, s. and h., *b.* 18 June 1929; ed. at Ampleforth and Oxford (Corpus Christi Coll.).

ROTHERMERE

page 186,
line 19, after 'Green.' add 'He *d.* 26 Nov. 1940.'
line 26, line to read as follows

II. 1940. 2. ESMOND CECIL (HARMSWORTH), VISCOUNT ROTHERMERE, &c., 3rd but only surv. s. and h.,(2)

line 34, delete ']' and replace by 'She *d.* 1991. He *m.* 2ndly, 28 June 1945, Anne Geraldine May, 1st da. of Guy Lawrence CHARTERIS and widow of Shane Edward Robert (O'NEILL), 3rd BARON O'NEILL. This marriage was diss. by divorce in 1952 and he *m.* 3rdly, 28 Mar. 1966, Mary, 1st da. of Kenneth MURCHISON of Dallas, Texas, U.S.A., formerly wife of Richard OHRSTROM of The Plains, Virginia, U.S.A. He *d.* 12 July 1978. His widow *d.* 1993.'

III. 1978. 3. VERE HAROLD ESMOND (HARMSWORTH), 1st s. and h. by 1st wife, *b.* 27 Aug. 1925; ed. at Eton and Kew Sch., Connecticut, U.S.A.; *m.* 1stly, 21 Mar. 1957, Patricia Evelyn Beverley, 1st da. of John William MATTHEWS and formerly wife of Capt. Christopher John BROOKS. She *d.* 1992. He *m.* 2ndly, 1993, Maiko Joeong-shun LEE, of Kyoto, Japan.

[HAROLD JONATHAN ESMOND VERE HARMSWORTH, s. and h. ap. by 1st wife, *b.* 3 Dec. 1967; *m.* Claudia, da. of T.J. CLEMENCE.]

BRYCE

page 187,
line 31, after '(3)' add 'His widow *d.* 27 Dec. 1939.'

BUXTON

page 189,
line 10, after '(5)' add 'His widow *d.* 7 Dec. 1955 in Hassocks, Sussex.'

COZENS-HARDY

page 190,
line 31, after 'Norfolk.' add 'His widow *d.* 17 Oct. 1957.'

page 191,
line 3, after 'Trent' add 'He *d.* 22 Oct. 1956. His widow *d.* 1975.'
line 4, delete all detail and replace as follows

IV. 1956. 4. HERBERT ARTHUR (COZENS-HARDY), BARON COZENS-HARDY, s. and h., was *b.* 8 June 1907; ed. at Winchester and Oxford (Worcester Coll.). He *d.* unm. 11 Sep. 1975 when his title became *extinct.*'

D'ABERNON

page 192,
line 33, after 'Bart.' add 'He *d. s.p.* 1 Nov. 1941 when his titles became *extinct.* His widow *d.* 16 May 1954, at Stoke D'Abernon.'

LYELL

page 194,
line 28, after '1918.' add 'His widow *d.* 22 May 1957.'
line 35, after 'ABINGDON' add 'He *d.* 27 Apr. 1943. His widow was living 1995.'

III. 1943. 3. CHARLES (LYELL), BARON LYELL, s. and h., *b.* 27 Mar. 1939; ed. at Eton and Oxford (Ch. Ch.).

CUNLIFFE

page 196,
line 21, after 'Headley' add 'His widow *d.* 22 Nov. 1965.'
line 30, after 'Westminster' add 'This marriage was diss. by divorce 1952, and he *m.* 2ndly, 23 Dec. 1952, Kathleen Elsie, widow of Phillip ROBINSON and da. of Ernest Bromfield POPE of Wargrave, Berks., at Caxton Hall Register office. He *d.* 24 Nov. 1963. His widow *d.* 1990.'
line 31, delete all detail and replace as follows

III. 1963. 3. ROGER (CUNLIFFE), BARON CUNLIFFE, s. and h., *b.* 12 Jan. 1932; ed. at Eton and Cambridge (Trin. Coll.); *m.*, 27 Apr. 1957, Clemency Ann, 1st da. of Maj. Geoffrey Binyon HOARE of Aldeburgh, Suffolk.

[HENRY CUNLIFFE, s. and h. ap., *b.* 9 Mar. 1962; ed. at Eton.]

WRENBURY

page 199,
line 22, after '(2)' add 'His widow *d.* 23 Nov. 1960.'

page 200,
line 7, after 'Stirling' add 'He *d.* 30 May 1940. His widow *d.* 1981.'
line 8, delete all detail and replace as follows

III. 1940. 3. JOHN BURTON (BUCKLEY), BARON WRENBURY, 1st s. and h., *b.* 18 June 1927; ed. at Eton and Cambridge (King's Coll.); *m.* 1stly, 10 Mar. 1956, Carolyn Joan Maule, da. of Lieut. Col. Ian BURN-MURDOCH, of Gartincaber, Doune, Perthshire. This marriage was diss. by divorce in 1961 and he *m.* 2ndly, 6 Oct. 1961, Penelope Sarah Frances, da. of Edward Dimond FORT of The White House, Sixpenny Handley, Dorset.

[WILLIAM EDWARD BUCKLEY, s. and h. ap., *b.* 19 June 1966.]

BUCKMASTER

page 202,
line 4, after 'W.' add 'This marriage was diss. by divorce 1944 and he *m.* 2ndly, 23 Jan. 1961, Diana Constance, da. of Major Arthur SETH-SMITH, of Haydon Bridge, Northumberland, and formerly wife of Charles Stewart M'Donnell VANE-TEMPEST.

[MARTIN STANLEY BUCKMASTER, 1st s. and h. ap., *b.* 17 Apr. 1923; ed. at Stowe.]

BERTIE OF THAME

page 203,
line 32, after 'WELLS' add 'He *d. s.p.* 29 Aug. 1954 when his titles became *extinct.*'

FRENCH (YPRES)

page 208,
line 10, after '£8,450' add 'His widow *d.* 21 June 1941.'
line 18, after 'London' add 'He *m.* 2ndly, 4 Oct. 1941, Violet Laird, da. of Col. James Laird IRVINE, C.B. He *d.* 5 Apr. 1958. His widow *d.* 1 Feb. 1970.'
lines 19–20, delete all detail and replace as follows

III. 1958. 3. JOHN RICHARD CHARLES LAMBART (FRENCH), EARL OF YPRES [1922], and VISCOUNT FRENCH [1916], 1st s. and h., *b.* 30 Dec. 1921; *styled* VISCOUNT FRENCH 1925–58; ed. at Winchester and Trin. Coll., Dublin; *m.*, 5 June 1943, Maureen Helena, da. of Henry John Piers KELLY of Attleborough, Norfolk. This marriage was diss. by divorce 1972 and he *m.* 2ndly, 1972, Deborah, da. of R. ROBERTS of Liverpool. He *d. s.p.m.* 4 Mar. 1988 when his titles became *extinct.* His widow was still living 1995.

ABERDEEN AND TEMAIR

page 209,

line 26, after '1937.' add 'He *d.* 6 Jan. 1965.'

For further detail and for the 3rd and subsequent Marquesses of Aberdeen, see above (*sub* corrections to vol. i).

FARINGDON

page 213,
line 5, after 'Buscot' add 'His widow *d.* 1 Oct. 1956.'
line 13, after 'PILKINGTON' add ', and *d.* 18 July 1961. He *d. s.p.* 29 Jan. 1977.'

III. 1977. 3. CHARLES MICHAEL (HENDERSON), BARON FARINGDON, nephew and h., being 2nd s. of Lieut. Col. Michael Thomas HENDERSON (*d.* 19 Nov. 1953), by Oonagh Evelyn, 2nd da. of Lieut. Col. Harold Ernest BRASSEY, which Michael Thomas was 2nd s. of Harold Greenwood abovenamed. He was *b.* 3 July 1937; ed. at Eton and Cambridge (Trin. Coll.); *m.* 30 June 1959, Sarah Caroline, da. of Maj. John Marjoribanks ASKEW of Ladykirk, Berwick-on-Tweed.

[JAMES HAROLD HENDERSON, 1st s. and h. ap., *b.* 14 July 1961; *m.*, 1986, Lucinda Maria, yst. da. of Desmond HANSON of Grantham, Lincs.]

SHAUGHNESSY

page 214,
line 33, after '1922' add 'He was ed. at Bishop's Coll. Sch. and Bishop's Univ., Quebec; *m.*, 18 Mar. 1944, Mary, only da. of John WHITLEY of Letchworth, Herts.

[PATRICK JOHN SHAUGHNESSY, 1st s. and h. ap., *b.* 22 Oct. 1944.]

ASTOR

page 216,
line 3, after 'KEEN' add 'He *d.* 30 Sep. 1952. His widow *d.* 2 May 1964.'
line 4, line to read as follows

III. 1952. 3. WILLIAM WALDORF (ASTOR), VISCOUNT ASTOR, &c., 1st s. and h., *b.* 13 Aug. 1907;

line 8, delete ']' and replace by 'He *m.* 1stly, 14 June 1945, Sarah Katharine Elinor, da. of Richard Henry Brinsley (NORTON), 6th BARON GRANTLEY. This marriage was diss. by divorce in 1953 and he *m.* 2ndly, 26 Apr. 1955, Philippa Victoria, 1st da. of Lieut. Col. Henry Philip HUNLOKE of Pendower House, Ruan High Lanes, Cornwall. This marriage was also diss. by divorce in

1960 and he *m.* 3rdly, 14 Oct. 1960, Janet Bronwen Alun, yst. da. of Sir John Alun PUGH of Dunsfold, Surrey. He *d.* 8 Mar. 1966. His widow was living 1995.'

IV. 1966. 4. WILLIAM WALDORF (ASTOR) VISCOUNT ASTOR, &c., s. and h. by 1st wife, *b.* 27 Dec. 1951; ed. at Eton. He *m.* 1976, Anabel Lucy Veronica, da. of Timothy Angus JONES, formerly wife of Sir Reginald Adrian Berkeley SHEFFIELD.

[WILLIAM WALDORF ASTOR, 1st s. and h. ap., *b.* 18 Jan. 1979.]

RATHCREEDAN

page 217,
line 21, after '(2)' add 'His widow *d.* 26 May 1955.'
line 26, after 'Infantry' add 'He *m.*, 7 Aug. 1946, Anne Pauline, 2nd da. of Surg. Capt. William BASTIAN, R.N.

[CHRISTOPHER JOHN NORTON, s. and h. ap., *b.* 3 June 1949; ed. at Wellington.]

RHONDDA

page 218,
line 24, after 'heir' add 'His widow *d.* 11 Mar. 1941.'

page 219,
line 10, after '(6)' add 'In 1922 she claimed the right of a writ of summons to Parliament in right of her Viscountcy. This was rejected.(7) She *d. s.p.* 20 July 1958 when her title became *extinct*.'

note (7) Viscountess Rhondda claimed that the Sex Disqualification (Removal) Act, 1919, which, provided that there should be no disqualification by sex from the exercise of any public function, was a clear and unambiguous statement of the law and that she should therefore receive a writ of summons to the House of Lords and be allowed to sit and vote. The Committee for Privileges discussed the matter at length but finally decided that her claim had not been made out. The Lord Chancellor, Lord Birkenhead, expressed their decision by explaining that the exclusion of women was of the very nature of a peerage grant and had nothing to do with any incapacity of women *as* women. This odd decision was not corrected until the passing of the Peerage Act, 1963. See R.P. Gadd, *Peerage Law*, 1985, pp. 73–5 and L.G. Pine, *New Extinct Peerage*, 1972, p. 230.

BURGH

page 220,
note (1), line 13, after 'U.S.A.' add 'This marriage was diss. by divorce 1943 and he *m.* 2ndly, 19 May 1947, Joyce Watts, 2nd da. of William Wilson WATSON of Hoylake, Cheshire. He *d.* 26 May 1959. His widow *m.* 2ndly, 14 June 1960, Rupert Walter WESTMACOTT. She was still living 1995.'

lines 13–14, delete from 'His' to '1934.'

For the 7th and subsequent Barons Burgh, see above, *sub* BURGH.

DUDLEY

page 221,
line 10, after 'Duxford.' add 'See DUDLEY above.'

STRABOLGI

page 221,

I. 1916. 1. CUTHBERT MATTHIAS (KENWORTHY), BARON STRABOLGI, *sum.* to Parliament, 1916, on the 'termination' of the *abeyance* in this 'Barony' in his favour, thus in fact *cr.* a new Barony.(1) He was *b.* 24 Feb. 1853; ed. at Rossall Sch. and Cambridge (Pembroke Coll.); *m.*, 15 Aug. 1884, Elizabeth Florence, 5th da. of George Buchanan COOPER of Sacramento City, California, U.S.A. He *d.* 12 Feb. 1934. His widow *d.* 23 Oct. 1951.

II. 1934. 2. JOSEPH MONTAGUE (KENWORTHY), BARON STRABOLGI, 1st s. and h., *b.* 7 Mar. 1886; ed. at H.M.S. *Britannia*; *m.* 1stly, 27 Nov. 1943, Doris Whitley, da. of Sir Frederick Whitley WHITLEY-THOMSON, M.P. This marriage was diss. by divorce in 1941 (she *d.* 1988) and he *m.* 2ndly, 1 Feb. 1941, Geraldine Mary, da. of Maurice FRANCIS and formerly wife of (__) HAMILTON. He *d.* 8 Oct. 1953. His widow *d.* 1970.

III. 1953. 3. DAVID MONTAGUE DE BURGH (KENWORTHY), BARON STRABOLGI, 1st s. and h. by 1st wife, *b.* 1 Nov. 1914; ed. at Gresham's Sch., Holt; *m.* 1stly, 22 July 1939, Denise, yr. da. of Jocelyn William GODEFROI, M.V.O. This marriage was diss. by divorce in 1946 and he *m.* 2ndly, 20 Sep. 1947, Angela, da. of George Victor STREET of Barton Lawn, co. Herts. This marriage was also diss. by divorce in 1951 and he *m.* 3rdly, 5 Nov. 1955, Myra Sheila, da. of Jack LITEWKA. This marriage was in turn diss. by divorce in 1961 and he *m.* 4thly, 3 June 1961, Doreen Margaret, 2nd da. of Alexander MORGAN of Ashton-under-Lyne, Lancs.

note (1) The modern peerages number this Baron the '9th'. For objections to this, see above, vol. iv, pp. 747–50 and vol. xii, part 1, *sub* STRABOLGI, note (d).

CHAPLIN

page 223,
line 10, after 'WELLESLEY' add 'He *d.* 12 Sep. 1949.'
line 11, line to read as follows

III. 1949. 3. ANTHONY FRESKIN CHARLES HAMBY (CHAPLIN), VISCOUNT CHAPLIN, 1st s. and h., *b.* 14 Dec. 1906; ed. at Radley.

line 14, after 'Perth' add 'This marriage was diss. by divorce 1950 and he *m.* 2ndly, 16 Mar. 1951, Rosemary, da. of Oliver (LYTTELTON), 1st VISCOUNT CHANDOS. He *d. s.p.m.* 18 Dec. 1981 when his title became *extinct*. His widow was living 1995.'

SOMERLEYTON

page 224,
line 25, after '(3)' add 'His widow *d.* 22 Nov. 1948.'
line 32, after 'Herts' add 'He *d.* 15 July 1959. His widow *d.* in 1983.'
line 33, delete all detail and replace as follows

III. 1959. 3. SAVILE WILLIAM FRANCIS (CROSSLEY), BARON SOMERLEYTON, &c., 1st s. and h., *b.* 17 Sep. 1928; ed. at Eton; *m.*, 14 Oct. 1963, Belinda Maris, da. of Vivian Graham LOYD, of Ascot co. Berks.

CARNOCK

page 225,
line 33, after '(1)' add 'His widow *d.* 23 Mar. 1951.'

page 227,
line 8, after '(2)' add 'He *d.* unm. 31 May 1952.'

III. 1952. 3. ERSKINE ARTHUR (NICOLSON), BARON CARNOCK, and a Baronet [S.], br. and h., *b.* 26 Mar. 1884; *m.*, 9 Oct. 1919, Katherine Frederica Alberta, da. of Henry Yarde Buller (LOPES), 1st BARON ROBOROUGH. She *d.* 24 Aug. 1968. He *d.* 2 Oct. 1982.

IV. 1982. 4. DAVID HENRY ARTHUR (NICOLSON), BARON CARNOCK, 1st (but only surv.) s. and h., *b.* 10 July 1920; ed. at Winchester and Oxford (Balliol Coll.). Recognised by Lord Lyon, 3 Sep. 1984, as holder of the Baronetcy of Nicolson of Lasswade, Chief of Clan Nicolson and Nicolson of that ilk.

GLENTANAR

page 228,
line 24, after 'Oslo' add 'He *d. s.p.m.* 28 June 1971 when his title became *extinct*.'

ROUNDWAY

page 229,
line 37, after 'Hong Kong' add 'he *d. s.p.m.* 29 Mar. 1944 when his title became *extinct*. His widow 8 July 1969.'

COBHAM

page 231,
line 14, after '*m.*' add '1stly, 1923, Christina Jean, da. of Albert Edward HONEYBONE. This marriage was diss. by divorce in 1934 and he *m.* 2ndly,'
line 18, after '1937' add 'He *m.* 3rdly, 1949, (his former wife), Christina Jean. He *d. s.p.m.* 21 Feb. 1951 when the barony fell into *abeyance* between his two das.(1)'

note (1) These were: (1) Mary Isobel, *b.* 11 June 1882, *m.* 1stly, 27 Apr. 1916, John Leslie Morton SHAW, who *d.* 18 Dec. 1925. She *m.* 2ndly, 21 May 1927, John BAZLEY-WHITE, M.C. She *d.* 1978, leaving issue by her 2nd husband. (2) Muriel Helen, *b.* 15 Mar. 1887; *m.*, 4 Mar. 1916, John Edmund Burnet THORNELY. She *d.* 1978, leaving issue.

FINLAY

page 233,
line 15, after 'Stafford' add 'He *d. s.p.m.* 30 June 1945 when his title became *extinct*. His widow *d.* in 1942.'

BEAVERBROOK

page 239,
line 22, after 'London.' add 'He *m.* 2ndly, 7 June 1963, Marcia Anastasia, da. of John CHRISTOFORIDES of Groombridge, Sussex, widow of Sir James Hamet DUNN, Bart. He *d.* 9 June 1964. His widow was living 1995.
line 23, line to read as follows

II. 1964. 2. JOHN WILLIAM MAXWELL (AITKEN), BARON BEAVERBROOK, also a Baronet, 1st s. and h., *b.* 15 Feb. 1910;

line 25, after 'Force' add 'He *m.* 1stly, 26 Aug. 1939, Cynthia Helen Glencairn, da. of Col. Hugh Glencairn MONTEITH, D.S.O., O.B.E. This marriage was diss. by divorce in 1944 and he *m.* 2ndly, Ursula Jane, yr. da. of Capt. Robert Orlando Rodolph KENYON-SLANEY of Shifnal, co. Salop., and formerly wife of Peter LINDSAY. This marriage was also diss. by divorce in 1950 and he *m.* 3rdly, 1 Jan. 1951, Violet, 3rd da. of Sir Humphrey Edmund DE TRAFFORD, Bart. He disclaimed his peerage, 12 June 1964, under the Peerage Act, 1963. He *d.* 30 Apr. 1985. His widow was still living 1995.

III. 1985. 3. MAXWELL WILLIAM HUMPHREY (AITKEN), BARON BEAVERBROOK, s. and h. by his 3rd wife, *b.* 29 Dec. 1951; ed. at Charterhouse and Cambridge (Pembroke Coll.); *m.*, 1974, Susan Angela, da. of Francis Ambrose Joseph More O'FARRELL.

[MAXWELL FRANCIS AITKEN, 1st s. and h. ap., *b.* 17 Mar. 1977.]

HARCOURT

page 240,
line 29, after 'Park' add 'His widow *d.* 7 Jan. 1961.'

page 241,
line 7, after 'GLASSON' add 'This marriage was diss. by divorce 1942 and he *m.* 2ndly, 23 Jan. 1946, Elizabeth Sonia, 2nd da. of Sir Harold Edward SNAGGE, K.B.E. She *d.* 30 Oct. 1959. He *d. s.p.m.* 3 Jan. 1979 when his title became *extinct*.'

GAINFORD

page 242,
line 24, after 'DUCIE' add 'She *d.* 22 Oct. 1941. He *d.* 15 Feb. 1943.'
line 25, line to read as follows

II. 1943. 2. JOSEPH (PEASE), BARON GAINFORD, 1st s. and h., *b.* 8 Mar. 1889, at Headlam Hall;

line 30, delete ']' and replace by 'ed. at Eton; *m.*, 3 Feb. 1921, Veronica Margaret, da. of Sir George John William NOBLE, Bart. He *d.* 23 Sep. 1971. His widow was still living 1995.'

III. 1971. 3. JOSEPH EDWARD (PEASE), BARON GAINFORD, 1st s. and h., *b.* 25 Dec. 1921; ed. at Eton and Gordonstoun; *m.*, 21 Mar. 1953, Margaret Theophilia Radcliffe, da. of Henry Edmund Fuise TYNDALE.

FORTEVIOT

page 243,
line 15, after '(1)' add 'His widow *d.* 22 Mar. 1940.'
line 26, after 'Wales' add 'She *d.* 6 Sep. 1945. He *m.* 2ndly, 20 Aug. 1946, Muriel Cecil Harriette, 1st da. of Lieut. Col. Sir Charles Henry Brabazon HEATON-ELLIS afsd. and widow, 1stly, of Richard Charles GRAVES-SAWLE and, 2ndly, Major Alwyn CAVENDISH. He *d. s.p.* 24 Oct. 1947. His widow *d.* 1975.'

III. 1947. 3. HENRY EVELYN ALEXANDER (DEWAR), BARON FORTEVIOT, also a Baronet, br. and h., being only s. of 1st Baron by 2nd wife, *b.* 23 Feb. 1906; ed. at Eton and Oxford (St. John's Coll.); *m.*, 25 Apr. 1933, Cynthia Monica, 1st da. of Piers Cecil Le Gendre STARKIE of Hartfield, Sussex. She *d.* 1986. He *d.* 25 Mar. 1993.

IV. 1993. 4. JOHN JAMES EVELYN (DEWAR), BARON FORTEVIOT, 1st s. and h., *b.* 5 Apr. 1938; ed. at Eton; *m.*, 17 Oct. 1963, Elisabeth Jeronima, 3rd da. of Geoffrey Noel (WALDEGRAVE), 12th EARL WALDEGRAVE.

[ALEXANDER JOHN EDWARD DEWAR, s. and h. ap., *b.* 4 Mar. 1971; ed. at Eton and Newcastle Univ.]

DOVERDALE

page 245,
line 33, after '1934.' add 'She *d.* 22 Dec. 1945.'

page 246,
line 8, after 'Australia' add 'He *d. s.p.* 18 Jan. 1949, when his title became *extinct*. His widow *m.* 2ndly, 21 Jan. 1950, Major Ernest Nathan ROWAT and *d.* 17 July 1970.'

LEVERHULME

page 253,
line 3, after 'Cheshire' add 'He *d.* 27 May 1949. His widow *d.* 19 Feb. 1966.'
line 4, line to read as follows

II. 1949. 3. PHILIP WILLIAM BRYCE (LEVER), VISCOUNT LEVERHULME, &c., only s. and h., *b.* at Bebington, Cheshire,

line 8, delete ']'

COLWYN

page 254,
line 18, after 'Manchester' add 'She *d.* 26 Jan. 1945. He *d.* 26 Jan. 1946.'
line 25, after 'Cirencester.' add 'She *d.* 4 Sep. 1964.'
line 26, line to read as follows

II. 1946. 2. FREDERICK JOHN VIVIAN (SMITH), BARON COLWYN, grandson and h.,

line 28, delete ']' and replace by '; ed. at Malvern; *m.* 1stly, 21 Dec. 1940, Miriam Gwendoline, da. of Victor Bruce FERGUSON, of Charlton Kings, Cheltenham, co. Gloucester (she was still living 1995). This marriage was diss. by divorce in 1951 and he *m.* 2ndly, 18 July 1952, Hermione Sophia O'Bryen, da. of Cyril Bertie Edward O'Bryen HOARE of Hove, Sussex. This marriage was also diss. by divorce in 1954 and he *m.* 3rdly, 8 Jan. 1955, Beryl, da. of Harvey WALKER, of Heathgates, co. Salop., widow of Mortimer Philip REDDINGTON and previously wife of Edward Chorley COOKSON, M.B.E. He *d.* 29 May 1966. His widow *d.* 1987.'

III. 1966. 3. IAN ANTHONY HAMILTON (SMITH), BARON COLWYN, s. and h. by 1st wife, *b.* 1 Jan. 1942; ed. at Cheltenham and London (Royal Dental Hosp.); *m.*, 30 May 1964, Sonia Jane, 2nd da. of Peter Henry Geoffrey MORGAN of Upton-upon-Severn co. Worcs.

[CRAIG PETER SMITH, s. and h. ap., *b.* 13 Oct. 1968.]

GISBOROUGH

page 255,
line 26, after '(1)' add 'His widow *d.* 27 Aug. 1941.'

page 256,
line 8, after 'Yorkshire' add 'He *d.* 11 Feb. 1951. His widow *d.* 1970.'
lines 9–10, delete all detail and replace as follows

III. 1951. 3. THOMAS RICHARD JOHN LONG (CHALONER), BARON GISBOROUGH, only s. and h., *b.* 1 July 1927; ed. at Eton; *m.* 26 Apr. 1960, Shane, 1st da. of Sidney Arthur NEWTON.

[THOMAS PEREGRINE LONG CHALONER, 1st s. and h. ap., *b.* 17 Jan. 1961.]

CAMBRIDGE

page 257,
line 34, after 'Castle' add 'His widow *d.* 27 Mar. 1929.'
line 38, after 'London;' add 'ed. at Eton and Oxford (Magdalen Coll.);'
line 43, after 'Argyll' add 'He *d.* 16 Apr. 1981 when his titles all became *extinct.*'

ATHLONE

page 258,
line 39, after 'PYRMONT' add 'He *d. s.p.m.s.* 16 Jan. 1957 when his titles became *extinct*. His widow *d.* 3 Jan. 1981.'

MILFORD HAVEN

page 260,
line 36, after 'Abbey' add 'His widow *d.* 24 Sep. 1950.'

page 261,
line 17, after '(2)' add 'His widow *d.* 22 Jan. 1963.'
line 21, after '1919.' add 'He was ed. at R.N.C., Dartmouth; *m.* 1stly, 4 Feb. 1950, Romaine Dahlgren, da. of Vinton Ulric Dahlgren PIERCE of the U.S.A. and formerly wife of William SIMPSON. This marriage was diss. by divorce in 1960 and he *m.* 2ndly, 17 Nov. 1960, Janet Mercedes, da. of Major Francis BRYCE, O.B.E., of Hamilton, Bermuda. He *d.* 14 Apr. 1970. His widow was still living 1995.

IV. 1970. 4. GEORGE IVAR LOUIS (MOUNTBATTEN), MARQUESS OF MILFORD HAVEN, &c., 1st s. and h. by his 2nd wife, *styled* EARL OF MEDINA till 1970, *b.* 6 June 1961; *m.*, 1989, Sarah Georgina, da. of George Alfred WALKER.

[HENRY DAVID LOUIS MOUNTBATTEN, *styled* EARL OF MEDINA, s. and h. ap., *b.* 19 Oct. 1991.]

CARISBROOKE

page 262,
line 27, after 'WESTMORLAND' add 'She *d.* 16 July 1956. He *d. s.p.m.* 23 Feb. 1960 when his titles became *extinct*.

SOUTHBOROUGH

page 263,
line 30, after 'Ayrshire' add 'She *d.* 8 June 1940. He *d.* 17 Jan. 1947.'

page 264,
line 1, line to read as follows

II. 1947. 2. JAMES SPENCER NEILL (HOPWOOD), BARON SOUTHBOROUGH, s. and h., by 1st wife,

line 6, delete ']' and replace by 'He *d. s.p.* 25 Feb. 1960. His widow *d.* in 1972.'

III. 1960. 3. FRANCIS JOHN (HOPWOOD), BARON SOUTHBOROUGH, br. and h., being s. of 1st Baron by 2nd wife, was *b.* 7 Mar. 1897; ed. at Westminster and Oxford (Ch. Ch.); *m.*, 23 Nov. 1918, Audrey Evelyn Dorothy, da. of Edgar George MONEY. He *d.* 4 Feb. 1982. His widow was still living 1995.

IV. 1982. 4. FRANCIS MICHAEL (HOPWOOD), BARON SOUTHBOROUGH, s. and h., *b.* 3 May 1922; ed. at Wellington and Oxford (Ch. Ch.); *m.*, 14 Nov. 1945, Moyna Kemp, da. of Robert John Kemp CHATTEY of Bexhill-on-Sea, Sussex. He *d.* 15 June 1992 when his title became *extinct*.

JELLICOE

page 268,
line 21, after '(3)' add 'His widow *d.* 12 May 1964.'

page 269,
line 4, after '1925–35;' add 'ed. at Winchester and Cambridge (Trin. Coll.);'
line 5, after '1937' add 'He *m.* 1stly, 23 Mar. 1944, Patricia Christine, da. of Jeremiah O'KANE of Vancouver, Canada. This marriage was diss. by divorce in 1966 and he *m.* 2ndly, 1966, Phillipa Ann, da. of Philip DUNNE of Leominster, co. Hereford and formerly wife of Christopher Charles Cyprian BRIDGE.

[PATRICK JOHN BERNARD JELLICOE, *styled* VISCOUNT BROCAS, 1st s. and h. by 1st wife, *b.* 29 Aug. 1950; ed. at Eton.]

MORRIS

page 270,
line 6, after 'Hereford' add 'She *d.* 1989. This marriage was diss. by divorce in 1946 and he *m.* 2ndly, 12 July 1960, Mary, yr. da. of the Rev. Alexander Reginald LANGHORNE of Neston, Cheshire and formerly wife of Anthony Robert AGATE. He *d.* 11 Mar. 1975. His widow *d.* 1991.'
line 7, delete all detail and replace as follows

III. 1975. 3. MICHAEL DAVID (MORRIS), BARON MORRIS, 1st (twin) s. and h., *b.* 9 Dec. 1937; ed. at Downside; *m.* 1959, Denise Eleanor, da. of Morley RICHARDS. This marriage was diss. by divorce in 1961 and he *m.* 2ndly, 1961, Jennifer, da. of Sqn. Ldr. Tristram GILBERT of Cirencester, co. Glos. This marriage was also diss. by divorce in 1969 and he *m.* 3rdly, 1980, Juliet Susan, da. of Anthony BUCKINGHAM.

[THOMAS ANTHONY SALMON MORRIS, 1st s. and h. ap. by his 3rd wife, *b.* 2 July 1982.]

CAWLEY

page 271,
line 25, after 'BANCROFT' add 'He *d.* 24 Sep. 1954. His widow *d.* 1978.'
line 26, delete all detail and replace as follows

III. 1954. 3. FREDERICK LEE (CAWLEY), BARON CAWLEY, &c., 1st s. and h., *b.* 27 July 1913; ed. at Eton and Oxford (New Coll.); *m.*, 12 Dec. 1944, Rosemary Joan, yst. da. Reginald Edward MARSDEN.

[JOHN FRANCIS CAWLEY, 1st s. and h. ap., *b.* 28 Sep. 1946; ed. at Eton; *m.*, 1979, Regina Sarabia, 1st da. of MARQUÉS DE HAZAS of Madrid.]

QUEENBOROUGH

page 273,
line 27, after '(2)' add 'She *d.* Jan. 1933. He *d. s.p.m.* 22 Sep. 1949 when his title became *extinct*.'

TERRINGTON

page 274,
line 20, after 'Giles' add 'His widow *d.* 25 May 1942.'
line 31, after 'Wexford' add 'He *d. s.p.* 19 Nov. 1940. His widow *d.* 1973.'

III. 1940. 3. HORACE MARTON (WOODHOUSE), BARON TERRINGTON, br. and h., *b.* 27 Oct. 1887; ed. at Winchester and Oxford (New Coll.); *m.* 1stly, 28 May 1914, Valerie, da. of George Allen PHILLIPS of Edenbridge, Kent. She *d.* 16 Nov. 1958 and he *m.* 2ndly, 22 Oct. 1959, Phyllis Mary, 2nd da. of William Wilson

DREW and formerly wife of Major Charles HAGGARD. He *d.* 7 Jan. 1961. His widow *d.* 1971.

IV. 1961. 4. JAMES ALLAN DAVID (WOODHOUSE), BARON TERRINGTON, 1st s. and h., *b.* 30 Dec. 1915; ed. at Winchester and R.M.C., Sandhurst; *m.*, 7 Nov. 1942, Suzanne, yst. da. of Col. Thomas Strutt IRWIN of Justicetown, Carlisle, Cumberland.

WEIR

page 276,
line 26, after 'Glasgow' add 'He *d.* 2 July 1959. His widow *d.* 9 Nov. 1959.'
line 27, line to read as follows

II. 1959. 2. JAMES KENNETH (WEIR), VISCOUNT WEIR, &c., 1st s. and only surv. h., *b.* 10 Sep. 1905;

line 31, after 'Ottawa,' add 'Dorothy Isobel'
line 32, delete ']' and replace by 'She *d.* 1972 and he *m.* 2ndly, 1973, Dorothy, da. of William Yerrington DEAR and widow of Edward F. HUTTON. He *d.* 16 Aug. 1975. His widow was still living 1995.'

III. 1975. 3. WILLIAM KENNETH JAMES (WEIR), VISCOUNT WEIR, &c., *b.* 9 Nov. 1933; ed. at Eton and Cambridge (Trin. Coll.); *m.* 1stly, 25 Apr. 1964, Diana Lucy, da. of Peter Lewis MACDOUGALL of Montreal, Canada. This marriage was diss. by divorce in 1974, and he *m.* 2ndly, Jacqueline Mary, 1st da. of BARON LOUIS DE CHOLLET of Fribourg, Switzerland and formerly wife of Donal Alexander CAMERON. This marriage was also diss. by divorce and he *m.* 3rdly, 1989, Marina, da. of Marc SEVASTOPOULO of New York.

[JAMES WILLIAM HARTLAND WEIR, 1st s. and h. ap. by 1st wife, *b.* 6 June 1965.]

GLENARTHUR

page 277,
line 19, after 'Troon' add 'His widow *d.* 3 Oct. 1946.'
line 26, after 'Canada' add 'He *d.* 11 Dec. 1942. His widow *d.* 9 May 1959.'
line 27, line to read as follows

III. 1942. 3. MATTHEW (ARTHUR), BARON GLENARTHUR, &c., only s. and h., *b.* 12 May 1909;

line 27, after '1909' add '; ed. at Winchester and Oxford (Magdalen Coll.)'
line 29, delete ']' and replace by 'This marriage was diss. by divorce 1939 and he *m.* 2ndly, 1 Sep. 1939, Margaret Risk, da. of Capt. Henry James HOWIE of Stairaird, Mauchline, Ayrshire. He *d.* 19 May 1976. His widow *d.* 1993.'

IV. 1976. 4. SIMON MARK (ARTHUR), BARON GLENARTHUR, also a Baronet, only s. and h. by 2nd wife, *b.* 7 Oct. 1944; ed. at Eton; *m.*, 12 Nov. 1969, Susan, yr. da. of Cmdr. Hubert Wyndham BARRY, R.N.

[EDWARD ALEXANDER ARTHUR, s. and h. ap., *b.* 9 Apr. 1973; ed. at Eton.]

GLANELY

page 278,
line 17, after 'Cemetery' add 'He *d. s.p.m.s.* 28 June 1942 when his peerage and his Baronetcy became *extinct.*'

PHILLIMORE

page 282,
line 20, after 'MALAHIDE' add 'He *d.* 28 Nov. 1947. His widow *d.* 22 Feb. 1950.'
line 27, after 'York' add 'He was *k.* in action in France, *v.p.*, *c.* 23 May 1940.

III. 1947. 3. ROBERT GODFREY (PHILLIMORE), BARON PHILLIMORE, grandson and h., being s. and h. of Anthony Francis and Julia abovenamed, *b.* 24 Sep. 1939; ed. at Winchester and R.M.A., Sandhurst; *m.* 1stly, 1974, Amanda, da. of Carlo Hugo GONZALES-CASTILLO. This marriage was diss. by divorce in 1982, and he *m.* 2ndly, 1983, Maria, da. of Ilya SLONIM. He *d. s.p.* 26 Feb. 1990. His widow was still living 1995.

IV. 1990. 4. CLAUD STEPHEN (PHILLIMORE), BARON PHILLIMORE, uncle and h., being 2nd s. of the 2nd Baron Phillimore. He was *b.* 15 Jan. 1911; ed. at Winchester and Cambridge (Trin. Coll.); *m.*, 17 Feb. 1944, Anne Elizabeth, 1st da. of Major Algernon SMITH-DORRIEN-SMITH, D.S.O., of Tresco Abbey, Isles of Scilly. He *d.* 29 Mar. 1994. His widow was still living 1995.

V. 1994. 5. FRANCES STEPHEN (PHILLIMORE), BARON PHILLIMORE, s. and h., *b.* 25 Nov. 1944; ed. at Eton and Cambridge (Trin. Coll.); *m.*, 1971, Nathalie, da. of Michael Anthony PEQUIN of Paris.

[TRISTAN ANTHONY PHILLIMORE, 1st s. and h. ap., *b.* 18 Aug. 1977.]

LEE OF FAREHAM

page 284,
line 5, after 'U.S.A.' add 'He *d. s.p.* 21 July 1947 when his titles became *extinct*. His widow *d.* 2 July 1966.'

BLEDISLOE

page 286,
line 6, after 'DANIEL' add 'She *d.* 6 Feb. 1956. He *d.* 3 July 1958.'

line 7, line to read as follows

II. 1958. 2. BENJAMIN LUDLOW (BATHURST), VISCOUNT BLEDISLOE, 1st s. and h., *b.* 2 Oct. 1899,

line 4, for 'O. KRISHABER]' read 'Otto KRISHABER. He *d.* 17 Sep. 1979. His widow was still living 1995.'

III. 1979. 3. CHRISTOPHER HILEY LUDLOW (BATHURST), VISCOUNT BLEDISLOE, 1st s. and h., *b.* 24 June 1934; ed. at Eton and Oxford (Trin. Coll.); *m.*, 29 Aug. 1962, Elizabeth Mary, 2nd da. of Sir Edward Walter THOMPSON, of Bridgenorth, co. Salop.

[RUPERT EDWARD LUDLOW BATHURST, 1st s. and h. ap., *b.* 13 Mar. 1964.]

BIRKENHEAD

page 293,
line 34, after '(4)' add 'His widow *d.* 8 Sep. 1968.'

page 294,
line 11, after '(5)' add 'He *d.* 10 June 1975.'
lines 12–13, delete all detail and replace as follows

III. 1975. 3. FREDERICK WILLIAM ROBIN (SMITH), EARL OF BIRKENHEAD, &c., 1st s. and h., *b.* 17 Apr. 1936; ed. at Eton and Oxford (Christchurch). He *d.* unm. 16 Feb. 1985 when his titles all became *extinct*.

INVERFORTH

page 297,
line 15, after 'Kirkaldy' add 'She *d.* 12 June 1941. He *d.* 7 Sep. 1955.'
line 16, line to read as follows

II. 1955. 2. ANDREW ALEXANDER MORTON (WEIR), BARON INVERFORTH, 1st s. and h., *b.* 12 Sep. 1897,

line 20, delete ']' and replace by 'He *d.* 17 Nov. 1975. His widow was still living 1995.'

III. 1975. 3. ANDREW CHARLES ROY (WEIR), BARON INVERFORTH, 1st s. and h., *b.* 6 June 1932; ed. at Malvern; *m.*, 26 Jan. 1966, Jill Elizabeth, da. of John Ward THORNEYCROFT, C.B.E., of Bembridge, Isle of Wight. He *d.* 6 June 1982. His widow was still living 1995.

IV. 1982. 4. ANDREW PETER (WEIR), BARON INVERFORTH, only s. and h., *b.* 16 Nov. 1966; ed. at Marlborough.

SINHA

page 298,
line 25, after 'Named' add 'He *d.* 11 May 1967.'
lines 26–7, delete all detail and replace as follows

III. 1967. 3. SUBHINDRO PROSANNA (SINHA), BARON SINHA, 1st s. and h. by 2nd wife, *b.* 29 Oct. 1920. He *m.*, 1945, Madhabi, da. of Monoranjan CHATTERJEE of Calcutta. He *d.* 1989. His widow was still living 1995.

IV. 1989. 4. SUSANTA PROSANNA (SINHA), BARON SINHA, s. and h., *b.* 1953. He *m.*, 1972, Patricia ORCHARD.

ASKWITH

page 300,
line 3, after '(2)' add 'He *d. s.p.m.* 2 June 1942 when his peerage became *extinct*. His widow *d.* 12 Jan. 1962.'

CHALMERS

page 301,
line 27, after '(2)' add 'His widow *d.* 24 June 1966.'

COCHRANE OF CULTS

page 303,
line 20, after 'ABERCROMBY' add 'She *d.* 12 Dec. 1950, and he *d.* 17 Jan. 1951.'
line 21, line to read as follows

II. 1951. 2. THOMAS GEORGE FREDERICK (COCHRANE), BARON COCHRANE OF CULTS, 1st s. and h., was *b.* 19 Mar. 1883;

line 28, delete ']' and replace by 'He *m.* 2ndly, 22 Oct. 1948, Millicent Agnes Mary, 1st da. of Dr Alexander DUCKHAM, formerly wife of Wilfred Neill FOSTER. He *d.* 8 Dec. 1968. His widow *d.* 1968.'

III. 1968. 3. THOMAS CHARLES ANTHONY (COCHRANE), BARON COCHRANE OF CULTS, 1st s. and h., *b.* 31 Oct. 1922. He *d.* unm. 15 June 1990.

IV. 1990. 4. RALPH HENRY VERE (COCHRANE), BARON COCHRANE OF CULTS, br. and h., *b.* 20 Sep. 1926; ed. at Eton and Cambridge (King's Coll.); *m.*, 18 Dec. 1956, Janet Mary Watson, da. of William Hunter Watson CHEYNE.

[THOMAS HUNTER VERE COCHRANE, 1st s. and h. ap., *b.* 7 Sep. 1957; ed. at Eton and Exeter Univ.]

WYFOLD

page 305,
line 5, after 'Oxfordshire' add 'He *d.* 14 Oct. 1942. His widow *d.* 1976.'
lines 6–7, delete all detail and replace as follows

III. 1942. 3. HERMON ROBERT FLEMING (HERMON-HODGE), BARON WYFOLD and a Baronet, only s. and h., *b.* 26 June 1915; ed. at Eton and Le Rosey, Switzerland.

CLWYD

page 305,
line 17, after 'Liverpool' add 'She *d.* 1 Jan. 1951. He *d.* 19 Dec. 1955.'
line 18, line to read as follows

II. 1954. 2. JOHN TREVOR (ROBERTS), BARON CLWYD, 1st s. and h., *b.* at Bryngwenallt afsd.,

line 22, delete ']' and replace by 'She *d.* 1985. He *d.* 30 Mar. 1987.'

III. 1987. 3. JOHN ANTHONY (ROBERTS), BARON CLWYD, s. and h., *b.* 2 Jan. 1935; ed. at Harrow and Cambridge (Trin. Coll.); *m.*, 1959, Linda Geraldine, da. of Charles Eugene CANNONS of Sanderstead, Surrey.

[JOHN MURRY ROBERTS, 1st s. and h. ap., *b.* 27 Aug. 1971.]

BEATTY

page 308,
lines 9–10, delete from '(__)' to 'T.F.' and replace by 'Harry Ester Reynolds HALL and da. of Thomas Sarsfield Kent'
line 10, after 'U.S.A.' add 'This marriage was diss. by divorce 1945 (she *d.* 11 May 1966), and he *m.* 2ndly, 7 Feb. 1946, Dorothy Rita, da. of Michael James FUREY of New Orleans, Louisiana, U.S.A. and widow of Richard Edward BRAGG. This marriage also was diss. by divorce 1950 and he *m.* 3rdly, 5 July 1951, Adelle, da. of M. DILLINGHAM of Oklahoma City, U.S.A. and formerly wife of William V. O'CONNOR of Los Angeles, California, U.S.A. This marriage in turn was diss. by divorce in 1958 and he *m.* 4thly, 3 Dec. 1959, Diane Kirk, da. of John BLUNDELL of Hayling Island, co. Hants. He *d.* 10 June 1972. His widow was still living 1995.

III. 1972. 3. DAVID (BEATTY), EARL BEATTY, &c., 1st s. and h. by 1st wife, *b.* 21 Nov. 1946; ed. at Eton; *m.* 1stly, 1971, Anne, da. of A. PLEASE of Wokingham, Berks. This marriage was diss. by divorce in 1983 and he *m.* 2ndly, 1984, Anoma Corinne, da. of Ray WIJEWARDENE of Columba, Sri Lanka.

[SEAN DAVID BEATTY, *styled* VISCOUNT BORODALE, 1st s. by 1st wife and h. ap., *b*. 12 June 1973.]

HAIG

page 310,
line 3, after '(2)' add 'His widow *d*. 18 Oct. 1939.'
line 6, after 'School' add 'and Oxford (Ch. Ch.) and after 'VI' add 'He *m*. 1stly, 19 July 1956, Adrienne Thérèse, da. of Derrick MORLEY of Quaives, Wickhambreux, Kent. This marriage was diss. by divorce in 1981 and he *m*. 2ndly, 1981, Donna Gerolama, da. of (__) LOPEZ Y ROYO.'

[ALEXANDER DOUGLAS DERRICK HAIG, *styled* VISCOUNT DAWICK, s. and h. ap. by 1st wife, *b*. 30 June 1961; ed. at Stowe.]

PLUMER

page 313,
line 2, after '(2)' add 'His widow *d*. 1941.'
line 11, after 'Gladsmuir' add 'He *d*. *s.p.m.* 24 Feb. 1944 when the Viscountcy and Barony of Plumer became *extinct*. His widow *d*. 2 May 1963.'

RAWLINSON

page 314,
line 42, after '(1)' add 'His widow *d*. 29 Sep. 1951'

ALLENBY OF MEGIDDO

page 316,
line 2, after '(3)' add 'His widow *d*. 20 Mar. 1942.'
line 16, after 'Kent' add 'This marriage was diss. by divorce 1949 and he *m*. 2ndly, 13 Apr. 1949, Daisy, da. of Charles Francis HANCOX formerly wife of Carl Arthur BENDIX. He *d*. 17 July 1984. His widow *d*. 1985.'
lines 17–18, delete all detail and replace as follows

III. 1984. 3. MICHAEL JEFFRAY HYNMAN (ALLENBY), VISCOUNT ALLENBY OF MEGIDDO, only s. and h., *b*. 20 Apr. 1931; ed. at Eton; *m*., 29 July 1965, Sara Margaret, da. of Lieut. Col. Peter Milnes WIGGIN of Newbury, Berks.

[HENRY JEFFREY HYNMAN ALLENBY, s. and h. ap., *b*. 29 July 1968.]

RUSSELL OF LIVERPOOL

page 321,
line 22, after 'Chichester' add 'This marriage was also diss. by divorce in 1946 and he

m. 3rdly, 27 May 1946, Alix, da. of MARQUIS DE BRÉVIAIRE D'ALAINCOURT and widow of COMTE BERNARD DE RICHARD D'IVRY. She *d.* 1971 and he *m.* 3rdly, 1972, Selma, da. of (__) and widow of A.W. BRAYLEY. She *d.* 1977. He *d.* 8 Apr. 1981.'

line 23, for '1st' read 'only'

line 25, after 'Folkestone' add 'He *m.*, 13 June 1951, Kiloran Margaret, da. of Sir Arthur Jared Palmer HOWARD, K.B.E., C.V.O. He *d. v.p.* 1975. His widow was still living 1995.'

III. 1981. 3. SIMON GORDON JARED (RUSSELL), BARON RUSSELL OF LIVERPOOL, grandson and h., being 1st s. and h. of Langley Gordon Haslingden RUSSELL, by Kiloran Margaret his wife, both abovenamed, was *b.* 30 Aug. 1952; ed. at Charterhouse and Cambridge (Trin. Coll.); *m.*, 1984, Gilda, yst. da. of F. ALBANO, of Salerno, Italy.

[EDWARD CHARLES STANLEY RUSSELL, 1st s. and h. ap., *b.* 2 Sep. 1985.]

WAVERTREE

page 322,

line 21, after '(2)' add 'His widow *m.* 2ndly, 1947, F.M.B. FISHER. She *d.* 27 Nov. 1952.'

RUTHVEN OF GOWRIE

page 324,

line 17, after 'Stirling' add 'She *d.* 8 Dec. 1952 and he *m.* 2ndly, 18 Nov. 1953, Judith Gordon, yr. da. of Bertie E. BELL of Knapp, Guernsey. 1965. He *d. s.p.m.* 16 Apr. 1956. He was suc. in the Barony of Ruthven of Gowrie by his great nephew the Earl of Gowrie (see GOWRIE below, p. 726), and in the Barony of Ruthven of Freeland [S.] by his 1st da. (see above, vol. iii, *sub* CARLISLE). His widow *m.* 2ndly, 1965, Major Digby R. PEEL (who *d.* 1971). She was still living 1995.'

note (4), line 1, delete '(1938)'

[For 3rd Lord Ruthven of Gowrie see GOWRIE *infra*, p. 560.]

SWINFEN

page 325,

line 18, after '(1)' add 'His widow *d.* 8 June 1946.'

line 24, after 'DALBY' add 'This marriage was diss. by divorce 1945 and he *m.* 2ndly, 10 Nov. 1950, Averil Kathleen Suzanne, da. of Major Marshall Hickman HUMPHREYS and formerly wife of Lieut. Col. Andrew KNOWLES. He *d.* 19 Mar. 1977. His widow was still living 1995.

III. 1977. 3. ROGER MYNORS (SWINFEN), BARON SWINFEN, 1st s. and h., *b*. 14 Dec. 1938; ed. at Westminster and R.M.A., Sandhurst; *m*., 24 Oct. 1962, Patricia Anne, da. of Ian J.D. BLACKMORE of Dundrum, co. Dublin.

[CHARLES ROGER PEREGRINE SWINFEN, s. and h. ap., *b*. 8 Mar. 1971.]

WESTER WEMYSS

page 326,
line 30, after '*extinct*' add 'His widow *d*. 22 Apr. 1945.'

MESTON

page 327,
line 26, after 'MACDONALD' add 'He *d*. 7 Oct. 1943. His widow *d*. 23 Dec. 1946.'
line 27, line to read as follows

II. 1943. 2. DOUGALL (MESTON), BARON MESTON, only s. and h., *b*. 17 Dec. 1894; ed. at

line 31, delete ']' and replace by 'He *m*., 12 July 1947, Diana Mary Came, da. of Capt. Otto Sigismund DOLL. He *d*. 2 Jan. 1984. His widow was still living 1995.'

III. 1984. 3. JAMES (MESTON), BARON MESTON, only s. and h., *b*. 10 Feb. 1950; ed. at Wellington and Cambridge (St. Catharine's Coll.) and Leicester Univ.; *m*., 1974, Jean Rebecca Anne, da. of John CARDER of Chalvington, Sussex.

[THOMAS JAMES DOUGALL MESTON, s. and h. ap., *b*. 21 Oct. 1977.]

FORSTER

page 328,
line 20, after '(3)' add 'His widow *d*. 12 Apr. 1962.'
note (2), line 1, for 'is' read 'was'

ASHFIELD

page 331,
line 21, after 'BATEMAN' add 'He *d*. *s.p.m.* 4 Nov. 1948 when his peerage became *extinct*. His widow *d*. 21 June 1962.'

DAWSON OF PENN

page 334,
line 29, after 'FRANKLIN add 'He *d*. 7 Mar. 1945 when his title became *extinct*.'

CULLEN OF ASHBOURNE

page 335,
line 23, after '(3)' add 'His widow *d.* 1971.'
line 27, after 'Eton' add 'He *m.* 1stly, 2 July 1942, Valerie Catherine Mary, only da. of William Henry COLLBRAN. This marriage was diss. by divorce in 1947 and he *m.* 2ndly, 21 June 1948, Patricia Mary, 1st da. of Lieut. Col. S. CLULOW-GRAY.

INVERNAIRN

page 342,
line 15, after '*extinct*' add 'His widow *m.* 2ndly, 19 Dec. 1951, Col. Ulric THYNNE and *d.* 25 Mar. 1955.'

BOTREAUX, STANLEY and HASTINGS (of Hastings)

page 346, 7 MARCH 1921

BOTREAUX, STANLEY, and HASTINGS (of Hastings), Baronies by Writ (*Abney-Hastings*). The *abeyance* in these baronies was terminated by Letters Patent, 7 Mar. 1921, in favour of Edith Maud, COUNTESS OF LOUDOUN. See HASTINGS, vol. vi, p. 382, note (a), and *sub* LOUDOUN in the present volume.

FITZALAN OF DERWENT

page 347,
line 25, line to read as follows

II. 1947. 2. HENRY EDMUND (FITZALAN-HOWARD), VISCOUNT FITZALAN OF DERWENT, only s. and h., *b.* 30 Oct. 1883,

line 35, delete ']' and replace by 'This marriage was diss. by divorce 1955 and she *m.* 2ndly, 3 Apr. 1956, William Thomas George (WENTWORTH-FITZWILLIAM), 10th EARL FITZWILLIAM, who *d. s.p.* 21 Sept. 1979. She was still living 1995. He *d. s.p.m.* 17 May 1962 when his Viscountcy became *extinct*.'

CARSON

page 348,
line 27, after '(2)' add 'His widow *d.* 7 Aug. 1966.'

CHELMSFORD

page 349,
lines 25–6, delete from 'His' to '1931' and replace by 'He *d.* 1 Apr. 1933. His widow *d.* 24 Sep. 1957. For the 3rd and subsequent Viscounts, see vol. iii, *sub* Chelmsford.'

LONG

page 351,
line 8, after 'M.P.' add '(*d.* 1 May 1960). She *d.* 23 Mar. 1958.'
line 16, after 'Morayshire' add 'This marriage was diss. by divorce 1942 (she *d.* 1990). He *d. s.p.m.* 23 Sep. 1944, being *k.* in action.

III. 1942. 3. RICHARD ERIC ONSLOW (LONG), VISCOUNT LONG, uncle and h., being 2nd s. of the 1st Viscount Long, *b.* 22 Aug. 1892; ed. at Harrow; *m.*, 21 Oct. 1916, Gwendolyne Hague, da. of Thomas Reginald Hague COOK. He *d.* 12 Jan. 1967. His widow *d.* 19 Jan. 1959.

IV. 1967. 4. RICHARD GERARD (LONG), VISCOUNT LONG, 1st s. and h., *b.* 30 Jan. 1929; ed. at Harrow; *m.* 1stly, 2 Mar. 1957, Margaret Frances, da. of Ninian B. FRAZER. This marriage was diss. by divorce in 1984 and he *m.* 2ndly, 1984, Catherine Patricia Elizabeth Mier, da. of Charles Terence MILES-EDE and widow of (__) WOOLF. This marriage was also diss. by divorce in 1990 and he *m.* 3rdly, 1990, Helen Millar Wright FLEMING-GIBBONS

[JAMES RICHARD LONG, s. and h. ap. by 1st wife, *b.* 31 Dec. 1960.]

ILLINGWORTH

page 352,
line 29, after 'MOODY' add 'He *d. s.p.* 23 Jan. 1942 when his peerage became *extinct.*'

BEARSTED

page 354,
line 6, after 'BEDDINGTON' add 'He *d.* 8 Nov. 1948. His widow *d.* 19 Dec. 1949.'
lines 7–8, delete all detail and replace as follows

III. 1948. 3. MARCUS RICHARD (SAMUEL), VISCOUNT BEARSTED, &c., also a Baronet, 1st s. and h., *b.* 1 June 1909; ed. at Eton and Oxford (New Coll.); Lieut. Warwickshire Yeomanry. He *m.* 1stly, 15 Jan. 1947, Elizabeth Heather, 1st da. of Geoffrey FIRMSTON-WILLIAMS. This marriage was diss. by divorce in 1966 and he *m.* 2ndly, 24 Jan. 1968, Jean Agnew, da. of R.A. WALLACE and formerly wife of Major John SOMERVILLE. She *d.* 1978. He *d. s.p.m.* 15 Oct. 1986.

IV. 1986. 4. PETER MONTEFIORE (SAMUEL), VISCOUNT BEARSTED, &c., br. and h., *b.* 9 Dec. 1911; ed. at Eton and Oxford (New Coll.); *m.* 1stly, 11 Oct. 1939, Deirdre Du Barry, da. of Thomas KENT. This marriage was diss. by divorce in 1942 and he *m.* 2ndly, 20 Mar. 1946, Elizabeth Adelaide, da. of Lionel Leonard (COHEN), BARON COHEN.

[NICHOLAS ALAN SAMUEL, 1st s. and h. ap. by 2nd wife, *b.* 22 Jan. 1950; ed. at Eton and Oxford (New Coll.); *m.* 1975, Caroline Jane, da. of Dr David SACKS.]

CURZON OF KEDLESTON

page 354,
line 27, after '1896' add 'His widow *d.* 29 June 1958. See RAVENSDALE, above, in the present volume.'

AILWYN

page 357,
line 5, after 'Ipswich' add 'His widow *d.* 9 July 1938.'
line 7, after 'HOGG' add 'He *d. s.p.* 23 Mar. 1976.'

IV. 1976. 4. CAROL ARTHUR (FELLOWES), BARON AILWYN, br. and h., *b.* 23 Nov. 1896; ed. at R.N.C.s, Osborne and Dartmouth; *m.*, 16 Nov. 1936, Caroline Alice, da. of Maynard COWAN of Victoria, British Columbia, Canada and formerly wife of Charles William CUDEMORE. He *d. s.p.* 27 Sep. 1988 when his Barony became *extinct*. His widow *d.* 1985.

note (2), lines 2–4, delete from 'His' to 'served'

ULLSWATER

page 358,
line 34, after 'SALISBURY' add 'She *d.* 16 May 1944. He *d.* 27 Mar. 1949.'

page 359,
line 20, after 'Ardgay' add 'He *d. v.* grandfather 25 Aug. 1942 in a flying accident. His widow *d.* 10 Nov. 1945.'

II. 1949. 2. NICHOLAS JAMES CHRISTOPHER (LOWTHER), VISCOUNT ULLSWATER, great-grandson and h., being s. and h. of John Arthur LOWTHER and Ina Majorie Gwendoline, both abovenamed. He was *b.* 9 Jan. 1942; ed. at Eton and Cambridge (Trin. Coll.); *m.*, 10 June 1967, Susan, da. of James Howard WEATHERBY of East Knoyle, Salisbury, Wilts.

[BENJAMIN JAMES LOWTHER, s. and h. ap., *b.* 26 Nov. 1975.]

note (5), line 2, after 'Cholmondeley' add 'She *d.* 9 July 1969.'
note (6), after 'M.C.' add ' She *m.* 4thly and *d.* 10 Nov. 1945.'

GLENAVY

page 360,
line 25, after 'Cemetery' add 'His widow *d.* 22 Jan. 1939.'

page 361,
line 7, after 'M.D.' add 'He *d.* 30 July 1963.'
line 8, delete all detail and replace as follows

III. 1963. 3. PATRICK GORDON (CAMPBELL), BARON GLENAVY, &c., only s. and h., *b.* 6 June 1913; ed. at Rossall and Oxford (Pembroke Coll.); *m.* 1stly, 7 Aug. 1941, Sylvia Alfreda, da. of Capt. Kenneth WILLOUGHBY-LEE, M.C. This marriage was diss. by divorce and he *m.* 2ndly, 1947, Cherry Margaret, da. of Major George Lowson MONRO. This marriage was in turn diss. by divorce and he *m.* 3rdly, 24 Nov. 1966, Vivienne, da. of Charles KNIGHT of Ipswich, and formerly wife of Hartley SHARPE and of Charles ORME. He *d. s.p.m.* 9 Nov. 1980.

IV. 1980. 4. MICHAEL MASSEN (CAMPBELL), BARON GLENAVY, also a Baronet, br. and h., *b.* 25 Oct. 1924; ed. at St. Columba's Coll., Rathfarnham and Trin. Coll., Dublin; He *d.* unm. June 1984 when his Barony and his Baronetcy became *extinct*.

TREVETHIN

page 363,
line 5, after 'HAILSHAM' add 'She *d.* 9 Oct. 1964.'
line 11, after '1935' add 'He *d.* unm. 25 June 1959.'

BARONY. III. } 1959
BARONY. I. } 1947

3. GEOFFREY (LAWRENCE), BARON TREVETHIN, br. and h., *b.* 2 Dec. 1880; ed. at Haileybury and Oxford (New Coll.). He was *cr.* BARON OAKSEY [U.K.], 13 Jan. 1947. He *m.*, 22 Dec. 1921, Marjorie Frances Alice, da. of Cmdr. Charles Napier ROBINSON, R.N. He *d.* 28 Aug. 1971. His widow *d.* 1984.

BARONY. IV.
BARONY. II. } 1971

4. and 2. JOHN GEOFFREY TRISTRAM (LAWRENCE), BARON TREVETHIN [U.K. 1921], BARON OAKSEY [U.K. 1947], s. and h., *b.* 21 Mar. 1929; ed. at Eton and Oxford (New Coll.); *m.* 1stly, 21 May 1959, Victoria Mary, da. of Major John DENNISTOUN of Letcombe Regis, co. Berks. This marriage was diss. by divorce 1987 and he *m.* 2ndly, Mrs Rachel CROCKER.

[PATRICK JOHN TRISTRAM LAWRENCE, s. and h. ap. by 1st wife, *b.* 29 June 1960; *m.*, 1987, Lucinda, 1st da. of Demetri MARCHESSINI.]

GLENDYNE

page 367,
line 20, after 'EDGAR' add 'He *d.* 10 June 1968. His widow *d.* 1983.'
line 21, delete all detail and replace as follows

III. 1968. 3. ROBERT (NIVISON), BARON GLENDYNE, s. and h., *b.* 27 Oct. 1926; ed. at Harrow; *m.*, 25 Apr. 1953, Elizabeth, da. of Sir Stephen Cecil ARMITAGE, C.B.E., of Hawksworth Manor, co. Notts.

[JOHN NIVISON, s. and h. ap., *b.* 18 Aug. 1960.]

MANTON

page 369,
line 17, after '(1)' add 'His widow *d.* 19 Jan. 1944.'
line 27, after 'Guards' add 'He *d.* 10 June 1968. His widow *d.* 1983.'
lines 28–9, delete all detail and replace as follows

III. 1968. 3. JOSEPH RUPERT ERIC ROBERT (WATSON), BARON MANTON, s. and h., *b.* 22 Jan. 1924, at Compton Verney, and *bap.* there; ed. at Eton; *m.* 9 Jan. 1951, Mary Elizabeth, twin da. of Major Thomas Dennehy HALLINAN of Ashbourn, Glounthaune, co. Cork.

[MILES RONALD MARCUS WATSON, 1st s. and h. ap., *b.* 7 May 1958; ed. at Eton; *m.*, 1984, Elizabeth Adams, 1st da. of Julian Russell STORY, of Westcott, Surrey.]

BARNBY

page 370,
line 24, after '(2)' add 'He *d. s.p.* 30 Apr. 1982 when his title became *extinct.*'

HEWART

page 371,
heading on left and margin to read as follows

BARONY. I.	1922
VISCOUNTCY. I.	1940

line 17, after '(3)' add 'He was *cr.*, 1 Nov. 1940, VISCOUNT HEWART of Bury, co. Lancs.'
line 19, after 'Zealand' add 'He *d.* 5 May 1940.'
line 20, delete all detail and replace as follows

II. 1940. 2. HUGH VAUGHAN (HEWART), VISCOUNT HEWART, s. and h., *b.* 11 Nov. 1896; ed. at Manchester Gram. Sch., St. Paul's Sch. and Oxford (Univ. Coll.). He *d.* unm. 23 July 1964 when his titles became *extinct*.

BALFOUR

page 373,
line 15, after 'VILLIERS' add 'She *d.* 28 Mar. 1942. He *d.* 14 Jan. 1945.'
line 16, line to read as follows

III. 1945. 3. ROBERT ARTHUR LYTTON (BALFOUR), EARL OF BALFOUR, &c., only s. and h., *b.* 31 Dec. 1902; *styled* Viscount Traprain 1930–42; ed. at Eton and Cambridge (Trin. Coll.); *m.*, 12 Feb. 1925, Jean Lily, 4th da. of Rev. Canon Cooke YARBOROUGH. He *d.* 28 Nov. 1968. His widow *d.* 1981.

IV. 1968. 4. GERALD ARTHUR JAMES (BALFOUR), EARL OF BALFOUR, &c., 1st s. and h., *b.* 23 Dec. 1925; ed. at Eton; *m.*, 14 Dec. 1956, Natasha Georgina, da. of Capt. George ANTON and formerly wife of J.C. LOUSADA.

WARING

page 374,
line 20, after 'Cheshire' add 'He *d. s.p.m.s.* 9 Jan. 1940 when his title became *extinct*.'

FORRES

page 375,
line 26, after 'Angus' add 'His widow *d.* 5 May 1942.'

page 376,
line 5, after 'Taunton' add 'He *d.* 26 June 1954. His widow *d.* 1972.'
lines 6–7, delete all detail and replace as follows

III. 1954. 3. JOHN ARCHIBALD HARFORD (WILLIAMSON), BARON FORRES and a Baronet, 1st s. and h., *b.* 30 Oct. 1922; ed. at Eton and Cambridge (Trin. Coll.); *m.* 1stly, 21 Aug. 1945, Gillian Ann Maclean, 1st da. of Major John Maclean GRANT. This marriage was diss. by divorce 1967 and he *m.* 2ndly, 22 Sep. 1969, Cecily Josephine, 1st da. of Major Sir Alexander Penrose GORDON-CUMMING, Bart. and formerly wife of Roger David (MARQUIS), 2nd EARL OF WOOLTON. He *d.* 22 Sep. 1978. His widow was still living 1995.

IV. 1978. 4. ALASTAIR STEPHEN GRANT (WILLIAMSON), BARON FORRES, only s. and h., *b.* 16 May 1946; ed. at Eton; *m.*, 2 May 1969, Margaret Ann, da. of George John MALLAM of Mullumbimby, N.S.W., Australia.

[GEORGE ARCHIBALD WILLIAMSON, 1st s. and h. ap., *b.* 16 Aug. 1972.]

VESTEY

page 376,
line 22, after 'America' add 'He *d.* 10 Dec. 1940. His widow *d.* 23 May 1941.'
line 23, line to read as follows

II. 1940. 2. SAMUEL (VESTEY), BARON VESTEY, and a Baronet, 1st s. and h.,(1) by 1st wife, *b.* 25 Dec. 1882,

line 26, delete ']' and replace by 'He *d.* 4 May 1954. His widow *d.* 1969.'

[WILLIAM HOWARTH VESTEY, s. and h. ap., *b.* 24 Apr. 1912; *m.*, 27 Sep. 1939, Pamela Helen Fullerton Melba, da. of George Nesbit ARMSTRONG. He *d. v.p.* 25 June 1944, being *k.* in action in Italy. His widow was still living 1995.]

III. 1954. 3. SAMUEL GEORGE ARMSTRONG (VESTEY), BARON VESTEY, grandson and h., being s. and h. of William Howarth VESTEY and Pamela Helen abovenamed. He was *b.* 19 Mar. 1941; ed. at Eton; *m.* 1stly, 1970, Kathryn Mary, 1st da. of John ECCLES of Moor Park, co. Herts. This marriage was diss. by divorce 1981 and he *m.* 2ndly, Celia Elizabeth, da. of Major Hubert Guy Broughton KNIGHT, M.C., of Lockinge Manor, Wantage, co. Oxon.

[WILLIAM GUY VESTEY, 1st s. and h. ap. by 2nd wife, *b.* 27 Aug. 1983.]

BORWICK

page 377,
line 24, after '1938' add 'He *d. s.p.* 27 Jan. 1941. His widow *d.* 1986.'

III. 1941. 3. ROBERT GEOFFREY (BORWICK), BARON BORWICK, &c., brother and h., *b.* 1 July 1886; *m.* 1stly, 8 July 1913, Irene Phyllis, da. of Thomas Maine PATTERSON of Canterbury, co. Kent. This marriage was diss. by divorce 1920 (she *d.* 1969) and he *m.* 2ndly, 20 July 1920, Margaret Elizabeth, da. of Gilbert Robertson SANDBACH of Rossett, co. Denbigh. He *d.* 30 Jan. 1961. His widow *d.* 4 Feb. 1969.

IV. 1961. 4. JAMES HUGH MYLES (BORWICK), BARON BORWICK, &c., 1st s. and h., being only s. by 1st wife, *b.* 12 Dec. 1917; ed. at Eton; *m.*, 14 Sep. 1954, Hyllarie Adalia Mary, da. of Lieut. Col. William Hamilton Hall JOHNSTON, D.S.O., M.C., of Bryn-y-Goes, Bala, co. Merioneth.

MILDMAY OF FLETE

page 378,
line 22, after 'Stirling' add 'He *d.* 8 Feb. 1947. His widow *d.* 22 Mar. 1960.'
lines 23–4, delete all detail and replace as follows

II. 1947. 2. ANTHONY BINGHAM (MILDMAY), BARON MILDMAY OF FLETE, s. and h., *b.* 14 April 1909, in London, and *bap.* there; ed. at Eton and Cambridge (Trin. Coll.). He *d.* unm. 12 May 1950 in a swimming accident when his title became *extinct.*

MACLAY

page 379,
line 14, after '(1)' add 'He *d.* 24 Apr. 1951.'
line 19, line to read as follows

II. 1951. 2. JOSEPH PATON (MACLAY), BARON MACLAY and a Baronet, 3rd but 1st surv.(2) s. and h., *b.* 31 May 1899;

line 24, delete ']' and replace by 'He *d.* 7 Nov. 1969. His widow was still living 1995.'

III. 1969. 3. JOSEPH PATON (MACLAY), BARON MACLAY, 1st s. and h., *b.* 11 Apr. 1949; ed. at Winchester; *m.*, 1976, Elizabeth Anne, da. of G.M. BUCHANAN of Delamere, Pokataroo, N.S.W., Australia.

[JOSEPH PATON MACLAY, 1st s. and h. ap., *b.* 6 Mar. 1977.]

BETHELL

page 381,
line 16, after 'Essex' add 'He *d.* 27 May 1945. His widow *d.* 8 May 1957.'
line 22, line to read as follows

II. 1945. 2. JOHN RAYMOND (BETHELL), BARON BETHELL and a Baronet, 2nd but 1st surv. s. and h.,

line 27, delete ']' and replace by 'This marriage was diss. by divorce 1948 (she *d.* 1981) and he *m.* 2ndly, 6 Aug. 1948, Joan, da. of Brig. Gen. Norman William WEBBER. He *d.* 30 Sep. 1965. His widow *d.* 22 Apr. 1966.'

III. 1965. 3. GUY ANTHONY JOHN (BETHELL), BARON BETHELL, &c., only s. and h., *b.* 17 Mar. 1928; ed. at Eton. He *d.* unm. 2 Dec. 1967.

IV. 1967. 4. NICHOLAS WILLIAM (BETHELL), BARON BETHELL, &c., cousin and h., being s. and h. of William Gladstone BETHELL (*d.* 17 Oct. 1964), by Ann, da. of Lieut. Col. Robert George BARLOW, which William was 3rd s. of the 1st Baron. He was *b.* 19 July 1938; ed. at Harrow and Cambridge (Pembroke Coll.); *m.* 1stly, 7 Apr. 1964, Cecilia Mary Lothian, da. of Alexander Mackie HONEYMAN of St. Andrews, Fife. This marriage was diss. by divorce 1971 (she *d.* 1977) and he *m.* 2ndly, 1992, Bryony Lea Morgan, da. of Brian David GRIFFITHS of Llanrchstyd.

[JAMES NICHOLAS BETHELL, 1st s. and h. ap. by 1st wife, *b.* 1 Oct. 1967.]

DARYNGTON

page 385,
line 18, after 'Lancashire' add 'She *d.* 24 Dec. 1948. He *d.* 10 May 1949.'
line 23, line to read as follows

II. 1949. 2. JOCELYN ARTHUR PIKE (PEASE), BARON DARYNGTON, 2nd but 1st surv. s. and h.,

line 25, delete ']' and replace by 'He *d.* unm. 5 Apr. 1994 when his title became *extinct*.'

KYLSANT

page 386,
line 28, after 'decease' add 'His widow *d.* 14 Dec. 1952.'

YOUNGER OF LECKIE

page 388,
line 7, after 'Canada' add 'He *d.* 4 Dec. 1946. His widow *d.* 28 Dec. 1957.'
line 8, line to read as follows

III. 1946. 3. EDWARD GEORGE (YOUNGER), VISCOUNT YOUNGER OF LECKIE, &c., 1st s. and h., *b.* 21 Nov. 1906;

line 13, delete ']' and replace as follows

[GEORGE KENNETH HOTSON YOUNGER, 1st s. and h. ap., *b.* 22 Sep. 1931; ed. at Winchester and Oxford (New Coll.); *m.*, 7 Aug. 1954, Diana Rhona, 1st da. of Capt. Gerald Seymour TUCK R.N. He was *cr.* BARON YOUNGER OF PRESTWICH (life peer), 1992.]

CROMWELL

page 388,
lines 24–5, delete from 'He' to '1929.' and replace by 'For this and subsequent Barons Cromwell see above, *sub* CROMWELL.'

HUNSDON OF HUNSDON

page 390,
line 33, after 'RITCHIE' add 'He *d.* 30 May. 1969. His widow *d.* 1978. For subsequent holders of this Barony, see above, *sub* ALDENHAM.'
line 34, delete all detail

BLANESBURGH

page 391,
line 18, after 'Music' add 'He *d.* unm. 17 Aug. 1946 when his life Barony became *extinct.*

CECIL OF CHELWOOD

page 392,
line 30, after '[I.]' add 'He *d. s.p.* 24 Nov. 1958 when his title became *extinct*. His widow *d.* 24 Apr. 1959.

JESSEL

page 395,
line 28, after 'Florence' add 'He *d.* 1 Nov. 1950. His widow *d.* 23 Oct. 1965.'

line 29, line to read as follows

II. 1950. 2. EDWARD HERBERT (JESSEL), BARON JESSEL and a Baronet, s. and h., *b.* 25 Mar. 1904,

line 34, delete ']' and replace by 'This marriage was diss. by divorce 1960 and he *m.* 2ndly, 20 Dec. 1960, Jessica Marion, da. of William DE WET of Cape Town, South Africa. He *d. s.p.m.s.* 13 June 1990 when his title became *extinct*. His widow was still living 1995.'

[TIMOTHY EDWARD JESSEL, s. and h. ap., *b.* 23 Dec. 1935; ed. at Eton; *m.* 1stly, 8 June 1961, Janet Ursula Calliope, da. of Maurice Winnington SMITH of Bidborough, Tunbridge Wells, Kent. This marriage was diss. by divorce 1964 and he *m.* 2ndly, 26 Aug. 1965, Jill Elizabeth, da. of George POWELL of Auckland, New Zealand. He *d. v.p.* and *s.p.m.* 27 Dec. 1969. His widow was still living 1995.]

DARLING

page 397,
line 4, after 'College' add 'He *m.*, 15 Aug. 1942, Bridget Rosemary Whishaw, da. of Rev. Francis Cyprian DICKSON of Lyndhurst, co. Hants.'

[ROBERT JULIAN HENRY DARLING, 1st s. and h. ap., *b.* 29 Apr. 1944; ed. at Wellington and R.A.C., Cirencester; *m.*, 1970, Janet Rachel, da. of Mrs D.M.E. MALLINSON of Richmond, Yorks.]

BANBURY OF SOUTHAM

page 398,
line 31, after 'O.B.E.' add '(he *d.* 9 July 1959).'

page 399,
line 5, for 'joined the Coldstream Guards' read 'ed. at Stowe; *m.*, 1 Nov. 1945, Hilda Ruth, 2nd da. of A.H.R. CARR of Cultra, co. Down. This marriage was diss. by divorce 1958. He *d.* 29 Apr. 1981. His widow (who *m.* twice more), was still living 1995.

III. 1981. 3. CHARLES WILLIAM (BANBURY), BARON BANBURY, only s. and h., *b.* 29 July 1953; ed. at Eton; *m.* 1stly, 1984, Lucinda Elizabeth, 1st da. of John Frederick Edward TREHEARNE. This marriage was diss. by divorce 1986 and he *m.* 2ndly, 1989, Mrs Inger Marianne NORTON, da. of (__) WIEGERT.

OLIVIER

page 399,
line 30, after 'SMITH' add 'He *d.* 15 Feb. 1943 when his title became *extinct*. His widow *d.* 6 Nov. 1953'

ARNOLD

page 401,
line 17, after '1938' add 'He *d.* unm. 3 Aug. 1945 when his title became *extinct*.

FITZWALTER

page 404,
line 11, for '*dormant*' read 'abeyant until it was called out in favour of FitzWalter Brook PLUMPTRE. See above, *sub*. FITZWALTER.

MERRIVALE

page 407,
line 24, after 'Exeter' add 'He *d.* 20 May 1939.'
line 25, line to read as follows

II. 1939. 2. EDWARD (MERRIVALE), BARON MERRIVALE, only s. and h., *b.* 22 May 1883, in London;

line 33, delete ']' and replace by 'This marriage was diss. by divorce 1939 and he *m.* 2ndly, 5 Apr. 1939, Meta Thérèse Amelia, da. of Joseph Herman WOLCZON of Danzig. He *d.* 8 June 1951. His widow *d.* 1980.'

III. 1951. 3. JACK HENRY EDMOND DUKE (MERRIVALE), BARON MERRIVALE, s. and h. by 1st wife, *b.* 27 Jan. 1917; ed. at Dulwich and Ecole des Sciences Politique, Paris; *m.* 1stly, 30 Sep. 1939, Colette, da. of John Douglas WISE of Bordeaux, France. This marriage was diss. by divorce 1974 and he *m.* 2ndly, 1975, Betty, da. of (__) and widow of Paul BARON.

[DEREK JOHN PHILIP MERRIVALE, s. and h. ap. by 1st wife, *b.* 16 Mar. 1948; Lycée Janson de Sailly, Paris and Faculté de Sciences d'Orsay, Paris.]

BRADBURY

page 408,
line 23, after 'KING' add 'She *d.* 6 June 1949. He *d.* 3 May 1950.'
line 24, line to read as follows

II. 1950. 2. JOHN (BRADBURY), BARON BRADBURY, 1st s. and h., *b.* in London, 7 Jan., and *bap.* 15 Mar. 1914,

line 26, delete ']' and replace by 'ed. at Westminster and Oxford (Brasenose Coll.); *m.* 1stly, 19 Aug. 1939, Joan, da. of Walter Dingle KNIGHT of Adlestone, Surrey. This marriage was diss. by divorce 1946 and he *m.* 2ndly, 2 Dec. 1946, Gwerfyl, da. of E. Stanton ROBERTS of Ruthin, co. Denbigh. He *d.* 31 Mar. 1994. His widow was still living 1995.'

III. 1994. 3. JOHN (BRADBURY), BARON BRADBURY, only s. and h., *b.* 17 Mar. 1940; ed. at Gresham's Sch., Holt and Bristol Univ.; *m.* 1stly, 28 Sep. 1968, Susan, da. of William LIDDIARD of East Shefford, co. Berks.

[JOHN BRADBURY, 1st s. and h. ap., *b.* 1973.]

OXFORD AND ASQUITH

page 410,
line 4, after '(3)' add 'His widow *d.* 28 July 1945.'

page 411,
line 7, after '1927' add 'He *m.*, 28 Aug. 1947, Anne Mary Celestine, da. of Sir Charles Michael PALAIRES, K.C.M.G.'

[RAYMOND BENEDICT ASQUITH, *styled* VISCOUNT ASQUITH, 1st s. and h. ap., *b.* 24 Aug. 1952; ed. at Ampleforth and Oxford (Balliol Coll.); *m.*, 1978, Clare, 1st da. of Francis Anthony Baring POLLEN.]

STONEHAVEN

page 412,
line 35, after 'MANCHESTER' add 'He *d.* 20 Aug. 1941. His widow *d.* 21 Sep. 1974.'
line 36, line to read as follows

II. 1941. 2. JAMES IAN (BAIRD), VISCOUNT STONEHAVEN, 1st s. and h., *b.* 25 July 1908 in Edinburgh,

line 39, delete ']'

For further information, see above, *sub* KINTORE.

LLOYD

page 414,
line 25, after 'K.C.B.' add 'He *d.* 4 Feb. 1941. His widow *d.* 21 Sep. 1974.'
line 26, line to read as follows

II. 1941. 2. ALEXANDER DAVID FREDERICK (LLOYD), BARON LLOYD, only s. and h., *b.* 30 Sep. 1912;

line 28, delete ']' and replace by 'He *m.*, 24 Jan. 1942, Lady Victoria Jean Marjorie Mabel, 1st da. of David (OGILVY) 9th EARL OF AIRLIE. He *d. s.p.m.s.* 5 Nov. 1985 when his title became *extinct*. His widow was still living 1995.'

[CHARLES GEORGE DAVID LLOYD, s. and h. ap., *b.* 4 Apr. 1949; ed. at Eton and Cambridge (Trin. Coll.). He *d.* unm. and *v.p.* 1974.]

IRWIN

page 415,
line 32, after 'UTTOXETER' add 'He *d.* 23 Oct. 1959. His widow *d.* 1976.'
lines 33–5, delete all detail and replace by 'For 2nd and subsequent Barons IRWIN and Viscounts HALIFAX see above, *sub* HALIFAX'

page 416,
lines 1–5, delete all detail

HANWORTH

page 420,
line 2, after '(2)' add 'His widow *d.* 16 Feb. 1954.'
line 18, after 'Reserve' add 'He *m.*, 27 Apr. 1940, Isolda Rosamund, da. of Ian Geoffrey PARKER.'

[DAVID STEPHEN GEOFFREY POLLOCK, 1st s. and h. ap., *b.* 16 Feb. 1946; ed. at Wellington and Sussex Univ.; *m.*, 19 Oct. 1968, Elizabeth, da. of Lawrence VAMBE of Enfield, co. Midx.]

TREDEGAR

page 422,
line 25, after '(2)' add 'His widow *d.* 4 Oct. 1949.'

page 423,
line 15, after 'Dorset' add 'He *m.* 2ndly, 13 Mar. 1939, PRINCESS OLGA SERGIEVNA DOLGOROUKY, da. of Gen. PRINCE SERGE ALEXANDROVITCH DOLGOROUKY. This marriage was annulled 1943. He *d. s.p.* 27 Apr. 1949 when the Viscountcy became *extinct* and he was *suc.* in the Barony and Baronetcy by his uncle. See vol. xii, part 2, *sub* TREDEGAR.

GREENWAY

page 427,
line 19, after '(1)' add 'His widow *d.* 24 Apr. 1940.'
line 30, after 'SMITH' add 'She *d.* 8 Oct. 1962. He *d.* 30 Apr. 1963.'
lines 31–2, delete all detail and replace as follows

III. 1963. 3. CHARLES PAUL (GREENWAY), BARON GREENWAY, &c., 1st s. and h., *b.* 31 Jan. 1917, at Bombay, and *bap.* there; ed. at Winchester and Cambridge (Trin. Coll.); *m.*, 22 Dec. 1939, Cordelia Mary, da. of Major Humfrey Campbell STEPHEN of Dormansland, Surrey. He *d.* 14 Sep. 1975. His widow was still living 1995.

IV. 1975. 4. AMBROSE CHARLES DREXEL (GREENWAY), BARON GREENWAY, &c., 1st s. and h., *b.* 21 May 1941; ed. at Winchester; *m.*, 1985,

Rosalynne, da. of Lieut. Col. Peter Geoffrey FRADGLEY, and widow of (__) SCHENK.

CRAIGAVON

page 428,
line 26, after 'DERING' add 'He *d.* 24 Nov. 1940. His widow *d.* 17 Mar. 1960.'
line 27, line to read as follows

II. 1940. 2. JAMES (CRAIG), VISCOUNT CRAIGAVON and a Baronet, 1st (twin) s. and h., *b.* 2 Mar. 1906,

line 29, delete ']' and replace by 'He *m.*, 22 Nov. 1939, Angela Fiona, da. of Percy TATCHELL. He *d.* 18 May 1974. His widow was still living 1995.'

III. 1974. 3. JANRIC FRASER (CRAIG), VISCOUNT CRAIGAVON, &c., s. and h., *b.* 9 June 1944; ed. at Eton and London Univ.

HAYTER

page 429,
line 18, after 'VANNER' add 'She *d.* 8 Nov. 1940. He *d.* 7 Nov. 1946.'
line 19, line to read as follows

II. 1946. 2. CHARLES ARCHIBALD (CHUBB), BARON HAYTER and a Baronet, 1st s.(1) and h., *b.* 11 Nov. 1871,

line 26, delete ']' and replace by 'She *d.* 4 June 1948 and he *m.* 2ndly, 23 Mar. 1949, Margaret Alison, da. of John Gimson PICKARD of Leicester. He *d.* 3 Mar. 1967. His widow *d.* 1986.'

III. 1967. 3. GEORGE CHARLES HAYTER (CHUBB), BARON HAYTER, &c., 1st s. and h., *b.* 25 Apr. 1911; ed. at Leys Sch., Cambridge and Cambridge (Trin. Coll.); *m.*, 28 Mar. 1940, Elizabeth Ann, da. of Thomas Arthur RUMBOLD.

[GEORGE WILLIAM MICHAEL (CHUBB), BARON HAYTER, 1st. s. and h. ap., *b.* 9 Oct. 1943; ed. at Marlborough and Nottingham Univ.; *m.*, 1983, Waltrand, da. of J. FLACKL of Sydney, Australia.]

CORNWALLIS

page 430,
line 18, after 'Kent' add 'His widow *d.* 6 Mar. 1957.'
line 34, after 'Essex' add 'She *d.* 10 Oct. 1943 and he *m.* 2ndly, 26 Feb. 1948, Esmé Ethel Alice, da. of Capt. Montmorency DE BEAUMONT and widow of Sir Robert James Milo WALKER, Bart. She *d.* 1969. He *d.* 4 Jan. 1982.'
lines 35–6, delete all detail and replace as follows

III. 1982. 3. FIENNES NEIL WYKEHAM (CORNWALLIS), BARON CORNWALLIS, 1st s. and h. by 1st wife, *b.* 29 June 1921; ed. at Eton; *m.* 1stly, 17 Oct. 1942, Judith, da. of Lieut. Col. Geoffrey Lacy SCOTT of Wadhurst, Sussex. This marriage was diss. by divorce 1948 and he *m.* 2ndly, 1 June 1951, Agnes Jean Russell, da. of Henderson Russell LANDALE of West Farleigh, Maidstone, Kent.

[FIENNES WYKEHAM JEREMY CORNWALLIS, 1st s. and h. ap. by 1st wife, *b.* 25 May 1946; ed. at Eton; *m.*, 29 Mar. 1969, Sara Grey de Neufville, da. of Lieut. Col. Nigel STOCKWELL of Benenden, Kent.]

DARESBURY

page 431,
line 16, after '£1,173,796' add 'His widow *d.* 19 Oct. 1953.'
line 29, after 'HARE' add 'She *d.* 13 Nov. 1958 and he *m.* 3rdly, 16 June 1966, Lady Helena Albreda Marie Gabriella, yst. da. of William Charles de Meuron (WENTWORTH-FITZWILLIAM), 7th EARL FITZWILLIAM and formerly wife of Chetwode Charles Hamilton Hilton GREEN. She *d.* 1970. He *d.* 15 Feb. 1990.'

lines 31–2, delete all detail and replace as follows

III. 1990. 3. EDWARD GILBERT (GREENALL), BARON DARESBURY, only s. and h. by 2nd wife, *b.* 27 Nov. 1928; ed. at Eton; *m.* 1stly, 7 Feb. 1952, Margaret Ada, yst. da. of Charles John CRAWFORD. This marriage was diss. by divorce 1986 and he *m.* 2ndly, 1986, Mary Patricia, da. of Lewis PARKINSON.

[PETER GILBERT GREENALL, 1st s. and h. ap. by 1st wife, *b.* 18 June 1953; ed. at Eton; *m.*, 1982, Clare Alison, da. of Christopher Nicholas WEATHERBY of Whaddon Hall, Whaddon, co. Bucks.]

CUSHENDUN

page 433,
line 25, after '(3)' add 'His widow *d.* 11 Dec. 1939.'

WRAXALL

page 437,
line 28, after '(3)' add 'His widow *d.* 1979.'

STRICKLAND

page 439,
line 27, after 'MOSELEY' add 'He *d. s.p.m.s.* 22 Aug. 1940 when his Barony became *extinct*, but he was *suc.* as COUNT OF DELLA CATENA by his grandson, Thomas Henry STRICKLAND, s. and h. of Mary Constance Elizabeth Christina, his eldest da. His widow *d.* 28 Sep. 1950.'

ATKIN

page 440,
line 27, after '(2)' add 'He *d. s.p.* 25 June 1944 when his life Barony became *extinct*.'

LUGARD

page 441,
line 32, after 'Abinger' add 'He *d. s.p.* 11 Apr. 1945 when his peerage became *extinct*.

GLOUCESTER

page 442,
line 38, after '1901' add 'He *d.* 10 June 1974. His widow was still living 1995.'

[*H.R.H.* WILLIAM HENRY ANDREW FREDERICK, PRINCE OF THE UNITED KINGDOM OF GREAT BRITAIN AND NORTHERN IRELAND, 1st s. and h. ap., *b.* 18 Dec. 1941; ed. at Eton and Cambridge (Magdalene Coll.). He *d.* unm. in a flying accident, 28 Aug. and was *bur.* at Frogmore 2 Sep. 1972.]

VIII. 1974. 2. *H.R.H.* RICHARD ALEXANDER WALTER GEORGE, PRINCE OF THE UNITED KINGDOM OF GREAT BRITAIN AND NORTHERN IRELAND, DUKE OF GLOUCESTER, &c., 2nd but 1st surv. s. and h., *b.* at Northampton 26 Aug. 1944; ed. at Eton and Cambridge (Magdalene Coll.); *m.*, at Barnwell Parish Church, co. Northants, 8 July 1972, Birgitte Eva, yr. da. of Asgar Preben Wissing HENRIKSEN, of Odense, Denmark.

[ALEXANDER PATRICK GREGERS RICHARD, *styled* EARL OF ULSTER, 1st s. and h. ap., *b.* at St. Mary's Hosp., Paddington, 24 Oct. 1974.]

HAILSHAM

page 443,
line 36, after 'HIVES' add 'He *d.* 16 Aug. 1950. His widow *d.* 9 Oct. 1964.'
line 37, line to read as follows

II. 1950. 2. QUINTIN MCGAREL (HOGG), VISCOUNT HAILSHAM, &c., 1st s. and h., *b.* 9 Oct. 1907;

page 444,
line 4, delete ']' and replace by 'This marriage was diss. by divorce 1943 and he *m.* 2ndly, 18 Apr. 1944, Mary Evelyn, da. of Richard MARTIN. He disclaimed his peerage under the Peerage Act, 1963, 20 Nov. 1963. He was *cr.*, 1970, a Baron for Life as BARON HAILSHAM OF ST. MARYLEBONE of Hurstmonceux, co. Sussex, under the Life Peerages Act, 1958.'

[DOUGLAS MARTIN HOGG, 1st s. and h. ap. by 2nd wife, *b.* 5 Feb. 1945; ed. at Eton and

Oxford (Ch. Ch.); *m.*, 6 June 1968, Sarah Elizabeth Mary, yr. da. of John Archibald (BOYD-CARPENTER) BARON BOYD-CARPENTER, a Baron for Life.]

MELCHETT

page 445,
line 24, after '(4)' add 'His widow *d.* 25 Sep. 1945.'

page 446,
line 7, after 'Africa' add 'He *d.* 22 Jan. 1949. His widow *d.* 1982.'
line 8, after '1922' add 'He *m.*, 18 July 1942, Yvonne Victoria, da. of Capt. T. Douglas SEARLE. He *d. v.p. s.p.* in a flying accident, 30 Apr. 1945. His widow *m.* 2ndly, 14 Sep. 1951, Richard Louis ROWE. She was still living 1995.

III. 1949. 3. JULIAN EDWARD ALFRED (MOND), BARON MELCHETT, &c., 2nd but 1st surv. s. and h., *b.* 9 Jan. 1925; *m.*, 26 Apr. 1947, Sonia Elizabeth 1st da. of Lieut. Col. Roland Harris GRAHAM of The Lodge, Bridge, Canterbury, Kent. He *d.* 15 June 1973. His widow was still living 1995.

IV. 1973. 4. PETER ROBERT HENRY (MOND), BARON MELCHETT and a Baronet, s. and h., *b.* 24 Feb. 1948; ed. at Eton and Cambridge (Pembroke Coll.).

REMNANT

page 447,
line 19, after '(1)' add 'His widow *d.* 23 June 1944.'
line 28, after 'C.S.I.' add 'He *d.* 4 Jun 1967. His widow *d.* 1990.'
line 29, delete all detail and replace as follows

III. 1967. 3. JAMES WOGAN (REMNANT), BARON REMNANT, &c., s. and h., *b.* 23 Oct. 1930; ed. at Eton; *m.*, 24 June 1953, Serena Jane, da. of Cmdr. Sir Clive LOEHNIS, K.C.M.G., R.N.

[PHILIP JOHN REMNANT, 1st s. and h. ap., *b.* 20 Dec. 1954; ed. at Eton and Oxford (New Coll.); *m.*, 1977, Caroline Elizabeth Clare, da. of Capt. Godfrey Herbert Richard CAVENDISH.]

EBBISHAM

page 448,
line 26, after 'Surrey' add 'He *d.* 24 May 1953. His widow *d.* 2 Nov. 1965.'
line 27, line to read as follows

II. 1953. 2. ROWLAND ROBERTS (BLADES), BARON EBBISHAM and a Baronet, s. and h., *b.* 3 Sep. 1912,

line 30, delete ']' and replace by 'He *m.*, 26 Oct. 1949, Flavia Mary, yst. da. of Charles Francis MEADE. He *d. s.p.m.* 12 Apr. 1991 when all his honours became *extinct*. His widow was still living 1995.'

TRENT

page 454,

line 12, after '(1)' add 'His widow *d.* 16 June 1952.'

line 21, after 'Yorkshire' add 'He *d. s.p.m.* 8 Mar. 1956 when his peerage and the Baronetcy became *extinct*.'

MOYNIHAN

page 456,

line 7, after 'Australia' add 'This marriage was diss. by divorce 1952 and he *m.* 2ndly, 28 Nov. 1952, June Elizabeth, da. of Arthur Stanley Covacic HOPKINS. He *d.* 30 Apr. 1965. His widow, who *m.* 2ndly, was still living 1995.'

lines 8–9, delete all detail and replace as follows

III. 1965. 3. ANTONY PATRICK ANDREW CAIRNES BERKELEY (MOYNIHAN), BARON MOYNIHAN, &c., 1st s. and h. by 1st wife, *b.* 2 Feb. 1936; ed. at Stowe; *m.* 1stly, 23 May 1955, Ann, da. of Reginald Stanley HERBERT of Therfield, Royston, co. Herts. This marriage was diss. by divorce 1958 and he *m.* 2ndly, 1958, Shirin Rosehan Berry, da. of Ahmed QUERESHI of Malaya. This marriage was in turn diss. by divorce 1967 and he *m.* 3rdly, May 1968, Luthgarda Maria Beltran della Rosa, da. of Alfonso FERNANDEZ of Caloocan City, Phillipines. This marriage was also diss. by divorce 1979 and he *m.* 4thly, 1981, Editha Eduarda, da. of Major Gen. Eduardo RUBEN of Bulacan, Phillipines. He *d.* 24 Nov. 1991, when his titles became *dormant*, the succession not (1996), having been proven. His widow and ex-wives appear to have been alive 1995.

FAIRHAVEN

page 457,

heading on left and in margin to read as follows

BARONY.
I. } 1929

BARONY.
I. } 1961

line 10, after '(3)' add 'He was further *cr.* BARON FAIRHAVEN of Anglesey Abbey, co. Cambridge, 25 July 1961, with a spec. rem. to his yr. br. and the heirs male of his body. He *d.* unm. 20 Aug. 1966 when the Barony of Fairhaven of Lode became *extinct*, but he was *suc* in his other Barony by his yr. br. under the spec. rem.'

II. 1966. 2. HENRY ROGERS (BROUGHTON), BARON FAIRHAVEN [1961], brother and h., *b.* 1 Jan. 1900; ed. at Harrow and R.M.C., Sandhurst; *m.* 1stly, 28

June 1932, Diana Rosamund, da. of Capt. Coulson Churchill FELLOWES. She *d.* 12 May 1937 and he *m.* 2ndly, 14 Mar. 1953, Joyce Irene, da. of Edward Arthur MILLER and widow of Lieut. Gerald Henry Charles DICKENS, R.N. He *d.* 6 Apr. 1973. His widow *m.* 3rdly, 1982, Vice Adm. Sir Geoffrey THISTLETON-SMITH. She *d.* 1989.

III. 1973. 3. AILWYN HENRY GEORGE (BROUGHTON), BARON FAIRHAVEN, only s. and h., *b.* 16 Nov. 1936; ed. at Eton and R.M.A., Sandhurst; *m.*, 23 Sep. 1960, Kathleen Patricia, 1st da. of Col. James Henry MAGILL, C.B.E., of Camberley, Surrey.

[JAMES HENRY AILWYN BROUGHTON, 1st s. and h., *b.* 25 May 1963; ed. at Harrow; *m.*, 1990, Sarah Olivia, da. of Harold Digby Fitzgerald CREIGHTON.]

THANKERTON

page 458,
line 23, after '(2)' add 'He *d.* 13 June 1948 when his life peerage became *extinct*. His widow *d.* 28 Oct. 1949.'

BRIDGEMAN

page 460,
line 27, after '£49,607' add 'His widow *d.* 26 Dec. 1961,'

page 461,
line 10, after 'HALIFAX' add 'He *d. s.p.m.* 17 Nov. 1982. His widow *d.* 1981.

III. 1982. 3. ROBIN JOHN ORLANDO (BRIDGEMAN), VISCOUNT BRIDGEMAN, nephew and h., being only s. of Brig. Geoffrey John Orlando BRIDGEMAN (*d.* 19 May 1972), by Mary Meriel Gertrude, da. of Rt. Hon. Sir George John TALBOT, P.C., which Geoffrey John was 2nd s. of the 1st Viscount Bridgeman. He was *b.* 5 Dec. 1930; ed. at Eton; *m.*, 10 Dec. 1966, Victoria Harriet Lucy, da. of Ralph Meredyth TURTON of Kildale Hall, Whitby, co. Yorks.

[WILLIAM ORLANDO CASPAR BRIDGEMAN, 1st s. and h. ap., *b.* 15 Aug. 1968; ed. at Eton and Bristol Univ.]

BAYFORD

page 462,
line 20, after 'Bart.' add 'He *d. s.p.m.s.* 24 Feb. 1940 when the Barony of Bayford and the Baronetcy became *extinct*. His widow *d.* 17 Sep. 1957.'

CAMROSE

page 463,
line 14, after 'W.' add 'He *d.* 15 June 1954. His widow *d.* 9 Oct. 1962.'

line 15, line to read as follows

II. 1954. 2. JOHN SEYMOUR (BERRY), BARON CAMROSE and a Baronet, 1st s. and h., *b.* 12 July 1909;

line 18, delete ']' and replace by 'He *m.*, 1986, Joan Barbara, 1st da. of John Reginald Lopes (YARDE-BULLER), 3rd BARON CHURSTON and formerly wife of 1stly, Wing Cmdr. Thomas Loel Evelyn Bulkeley GUINNESS, O.B.E., and 2ndly of PRINCE ALY KHAN.'

SANKEY

page 464,
line 24, after '(1)' add 'He *d.* unm. 6 Feb. 1948 when his Viscountcy and Barony became *extinct*.'

PASSFIELD

page 465,
line 20, after 'M.P.' add 'She *d.* 1943. He *d. s.p.* 13 Oct. 1947 when his peerage became *extinct*.'

BRENTFORD

page 466,
line 27, after '(3)' add 'His widow *d.* 17 Jan. 1952.'

page 467,
line 10, after 'Scotland' add 'She *d.* 27 Nov. 1954 and he *m.* 2ndly, 16 Sep. 1955, Grace Esther Amelia, da. of Arthur Ernest Alfred TOTHILL of Cape Town, South Africa and widow of Donald Sinclair Tait MCNELLAN. He *d. s.p.* 27 June 1958. His widow *d.* 1984.

III. 1958. 3. LANCELOT WILLIAM (JOYNSON-HICKS), VISCOUNT BRENTFORD, &c., brother and h., *b.* 10 Apr. 1902; ed. at Winchester and Oxford (Trin. Coll.); *m.*, 15 July 1931, Phyllis, only da. of Major Herbert Cyril ALLFEY of Tetbury, co. Glos. She *d.* 1979. He *d.* 25 Feb. 1983.

IV. 1983. 4. CRISPIN WILLIAM (JOYNSON-HICKS), VISCOUNT BRENTFORD, &c., s. and h., *b.* 17 Apr. 1933; ed. at Eton and Oxford (New Coll.); *m.*, 21 Mar. 1964, Gillian Evelyn, 1st da. of Gerard Edward SCHLUTER, O.B.E., of Nairobi, Kenya.

[PAUL WILLIAM JOYNSON-HICKS, s. and h. ap., *b.* 1971.]

DULVERTON

page 468,
line 22, after 'R.N.' add 'He *d.* 1 Dec. 1956. His widow *d.* 5 Apr. 1968.'
lines 23–4; delete all detail and replace as follows

II. 1956. 2. FREDERICK ANTHONY HAMILTON (WILLS), BARON DULVERTON, 1st s. and h., *b.* 19 Dec. 1915; ed. at Eton and Oxford (Magdalen Coll.); *m.* 1stly, 2 Sep. 1939, Judith Betty, 1st da. of Lieut. Col. Ian LESLIE-MELVILLE. This marriage was diss. by divorce in 1961 and he *m.* 2ndly, 28 Apr. 1962, Ruth Violet Mary, da. of Sir Walter Randolph FitzRoy FARQUHAR and formerly wife of Major Richard Glenys FANSHAWE. He *d.* 17 Feb. 1992. His widow was living 1995.

III. 1992. 3. GILBERT MICHAEL HAMILTON (WILLS), BARON DULVERTON, 1st s. and h., *b.* 2 May 1944; ed. at Gordonstoun; *m.*, 1980, Rosalind Johnny Maria, da. of J. VAN DE VELDE of Rozenburg, Holland.

[ROBERT ANTHONY HAMILTON WILLS, s. and h. ap., *b.* 20 Oct. 1983.]

LUKE

page 469,
line 24, after 'Bedfordshire' add 'She *d.* 2 Aug. 1941. He *d.* 23 Feb. 1943.'
line 25, line to read as follows

II. 1943. 2. IAN ST. JOHN (LAWSON-JOHNSTON), BARON LUKE, 1st s. and h., *b.* 7 June 1905,

line 33, delete ']'

[ARTHUR CHARLES ST. JOHN LAWSON-JOHNSTON, 1st s. and h. ap., *b.* 13 Jan. 1933; ed. at Eton and Cambridge (Trin. Coll.); *m.* 1stly, 6 Aug. 1959, Silvia Maria, da. of H.E. Don Rosario ROIGT, formerly Argentine Ambassador to The Netherlands. This marriage was diss. by divorce in 1971 and he *m.* 2ndly, 1971, Sarah Louise, da. of Richard HEARNE, O.B.E.]

ALVINGHAM

page 470,
line 23, for '(__) BRIGHT' read 'R.E. BRIGHT' and add 'He *d.* 27 Nov. 1955. His widow *d.* 1992.'
lines 24–5, delete all detail and replace as follows

II. 1955. 2. ROBERT GUY EARDLEY (YERBURGH), BARON ALVINGHAM, s. and h., by 1st wife, *b.* 16 Dec. 1926, at Chelsea, and *bap.* at Knightsbridge; ed. at Eton; *m.*, 31 Mar. 1952, Beryl Elliott, da. of William David WILLIAMS of Hindhead, Surrey.

[ROBERT RICHARD GUY YERBURGH, s. and h. ap., *b.* 10 Dec. 1956; ed. at Eton; *m.*, 1981, Vanessa Kelly, yr. da. of Capt. Duncan Kinloch KIRK. This marriage was diss. by divorce in 1993.]

AMULREE

page 472,
line 23, after 'there' add 'He *d.* 5 May 1942.'
line 24, line to read as follows

II. 1942. 2. BASIL WILLIAM SHOLTO (MACKENZIE), BARON AMULREE, only s. and h., *b.* 25 July 1900,

line 26, delete ']' and replace by 'He *d.* unm. 15 Dec. 1983 when his peerage became *extinct*.'

TYRRELL

page 473,
line 20, after 'FORTESCUE' add 'He *d. s.p.m.s.* 14 Mar. 1947 when his peerage became *extinct*.'

GREENWOOD

page 474,
line 28, after 'Hereford' add 'He *d.* 10 Sep. 1948. His widow *d.* 24 Apr. 1968.'
lines 29–30, delete all detail and replace as follows

II. 1948. 2. DAVID HENRY HAMAR (GREENWOOD), VISCOUNT GREENWOOD and a Baronet, 1st s. and h., *b.* 30 Oct. 1914.

BADEN-POWELL

page 475,
line 32, after 'W.' add 'He *d.* 8 Jan. 1941. His widow *d.* 25 June 1977.
line 33, line to read as follows

II. 1941. 2. ARTHUR ROBERT PETER (BADEN-POWELL), BARON BADEN-POWELL and a Baronet, 1st s. and h., *b.* 30 Oct. 1913,

line 35, delete ']' and replace by 'He *d.* 9 Dec. 1962. His widow *d.* 1993.'

III. 1962. 3. ROBERT CRAUSE (BADEN-POWELL), BARON BADEN-POWELL, &c., 1st s. and h., *b.* 15 Oct. 1936; ed. at Bryanston; *m.*, 1963, Patience Hélène Mary, da. of Major Douglas Myers BATTY of Milsetter, Zimbabwe.

RUSSELL OF KILLOWEN

page 476,
line 18, after '(4)' add 'He *d.* 20 Dec. 1946 when his life Barony became *extinct*. His widow *d.* 10 Nov. 1956. His s. was also *cr.* a Lord of Appeal in Ordinary and a Baron for Life in 1975, see below.'

MARLEY

page 479,
line 23, after 'Peterhead' add 'He *d.* 29 Feb. 1952. His widow *d.* 2 Sep. 1969.'
line 24, delete all detail and replace as follows

II. 1952. 2. GEOFFREY PELHAM LEIGH (AMAN), BARON MARLEY, s. and h., *b.* 6 Sep. 1913; ed. at Bedales Sch. and Grenoble Univ.; *m.* 1stly, 16 Aug. 1938, Lilian Mary, da. of James CHRYSTAL. This marriage was diss. by divorce in 1948 and he *m.* 2ndly, 12 June 1956, Catherine Doone, da. of Frank Angwyn BEAL of Eden, Cap D'Ail, France. He *d. s.p.* 31 Mar. 1990 when his title became *extinct*. His widow was living 1995.

PONSONBY OF SHULBREDE

page 480,
line 20, after 'P.C.' add 'He *d.* 24 Mar. 1946. His widow *d.* 11 July 1963.'
line 21, line to read as follows

II. 1946. 2. MATTHEW HENRY HUBERT (PONSONBY), BARON PONSONBY OF SHULBREDE, s. and h., *b.* 28 July 1904; ed. at Oxford (Balliol Coll.);

line 24, delete ']' and replace by 'He *d.* 29 Apr. 1976. His widow *d.* 1985.'

III. 1976. 3. THOMAS ARTHUR (PONSONBY), BARON PONSONBY OF SHULBREDE, 1st and only surv. s. and h., *b.* 23 Oct. 1930; ed. at Bryanston and Oxford (Hertford Coll.); *m.* 1stly, 21 July 1956, Ursula Mary, yr. da. of Cmdr. Thomas Stanley Lane Fox PITT, O.B.E., R.N., of Gidleigh, Newton Abbot, co. Devon. This marriage was diss. by divorce in 1973 (she was still living 1995) and he *m.* 2ndly, 1973, Maureen Estelle, da. of Alfred William WINDSOR and formerly wife of Dr Paul CAMPBELL-TEICH. He *d.* 13 June 1990. His widow was living 1995.

IV. 1990. 4. FREDERICK MATTHEW THOMAS (PONSONBY), BARON PONSONBY OF SHULBREDE, only s. and h., *b.* 27 Oct. 1958; ed. at Univ. Coll., Cardiff and Imperial Coll., London.

DICKINSON

page 481,
line 25, after 'Baroda' add 'He *d. s.p.m.s.* 31 May 1943. His widow *d.* 11 May 1967.'

line 35, after '1935.' add 'His widow was still living 1995.'
line 36, line to read as follows

II. 1943. 2. RICHARD CLAVERING HYETT (DICKINSON), BARON DICKINSON, grandson and h.,

line 27, delete '] and replace by 'He was ed. at Eton; *m.*, 31 Oct. 1957, Margaret Ann, 1st da. of Brig. Gilbert Reader MCMEEKAN, C.B., D.S.O., O.B.E., of Painswick, co. Glos. This marriage was diss and he *m.* 2ndly, 1980, Rita Doreen (Mrs MOIR).'

[MARTIN HYETT DICKINSON, 1st s. and h. ap. by 1st wife, *b.* 30 Jan. 1961.]

WAKEFIELD

page 482,
line 28, after 'Lancashire' add 'He *d. s.p.* 15 Jan. 1941 when his title became *extinct*.'

TRENCHARD

page 484,
line 33, after 'Wigton' add 'He *d.* 10 Feb. 1956. His widow *d.* 5 Mar. 1960.'
line 34, after '1921' add 'ed. at Eton. He *d. v.p.* and unm. Mar. 1943 being *k.* in action.'

II. 1956. 2. THOMAS (TRENCHARD), VISCOUNT TRENCHARD and a Baronet, 2nd but 1st surv. s. and h., *b.* 15 Dec. 1923; ed. at Eton; *m.*, 19 June 1948, Patricia, da. of Adm. Sir Sidney Robert BAILEY, K.B.E., C.B., D.S.O. He *d.* 29 Apr. 1987. His widow was living 1995.

III. 1987. 3. HUGH (TRENCHARD), VISCOUNT TRENCHARD, 1st s. and h., *b.* 12 Mar. 1951; ed. at Eton and Cambridge (Trin. Coll.); *m.*, 1975, Fiona Elizabeth, da. of James Ian MORRISH.

[ALEXANDER THOMAS TRENCHARD, 1st s. and h. ap., *b.* 26 July 1978; ed. at Eton.]

MACMILLAN

page 486,
line 8, after 'Greenock' add 'He *d. s.p.* 5 Sep. 1952 when his life barony became *extinct*.'

NOEL-BUXTON

page 487,
line 14, after 'S.W.' add 'He *d.* 12 Sep. 1948. His widow *d.* 9 Dec. 1960.'

lines 15–16, delete all detail and replace as follows

II. 1948. 2. RUFUS ALEXANDER (BUXTON, *formerly* NOEL ALEXANDER NOEL-BUXTON), BARON NOEL-BUXTON, 1st s. and h., *b.* 13 Jan. 1917; ed. at Harrow and Oxford (Balliol Coll.); *m.* 1stly, 22 Sep. 1939, Helena Nancy, yr. da. of Col. Kenneth Hugh Munro CONNAL, C.B., O.B.E., of Monkton, Ayrshire. This marriage was diss. by divorce in 1947 (she *d.* 16 June 1949) and he *m.* 2ndly, 25 Sep. 1948, Margaret Elizabeth, 1st da. of Stephanus Abraham CLOETE, of Pretoria, South Africa. She *d.* 1978. He *d.* 14 July 1980.

III. 1980. 3. MARTIN CONNAL (NOEL-BUXTON, *formerly* BUXTON), BARON NOEL-BUXTON, 1st s. and h., by 1st wife, *b.* 8 Dec. 1940; ed. at Bryanston and Oxford (Balliol Coll.); *m.* 1stly, 21 July 1964, Miranda Mary, 1st da. of Major Hugo Atherton CHISENHALE-MARSH, of Epping, Essex. This marriage was diss. by divorce in 1968 (she *d.* 1979) and he *m.* 2ndly, 1972, Sarah Margaret Surridge, da. of Neil Charles Wolseley BARRETT of Teddington, co. Midx. This marriage was in turn diss. by divorce in 1982 and he *m.* 3rdly, Abigail Marie (Mrs GRANGER), da. of Eric Philip Richard CLENT.

[CHARLES CONNAL NOEL-BUXTON, s. and h. ap., *b.* 17 Apr. 1975.]

SANDERSON

page 488,
line 13, after 'Berks.' add 'He *d. s.p.* 25 Mar. 1939 when his title became *extinct*. His widow *d.* 21 Nov. 1962.'

HOWARD OF PENRITH

page 489,
line 29, after 'MASSANI' add 'He *d.* 1 Aug. 1939. His widow *d.* 20 Jan. 1963.'
lines 33–4, delete all detail and replace as follows

II. 1939. 2. FRANCIS PHILIP (HOWARD), BARON HOWARD OF PENRITH, 2nd but 1st surv. s. and h., *b.* 5 Oct. 1905; ed. at Downside and Cambridge (Trin. Coll.); Barrister; *m.*, 1 July 1944, Anne, da. of John Beaumont HOTHAM of Coldstream, Berwickshire.

[PHILIP ESME HOWARD, 1st s. and h. ap., *b.* 1 May 1945; ed. at Ampleforth and Oxford (Ch. Ch.), *m.*, 1969, Sarah, da. of Barclay WALKER.]

PLENDER

page 493,
line 40, after 'LAURIE' add 'He *d. s.p.* 19 Jan. 1946 when his Barony and Baronetcy became *extinct*. His widow *d.* 12 June 1970.'

HYNDLEY

page 494,
heading on left and in margin to read as follows

BARONY. I. } 1931
VISCOUNTCY. I. } 1948

line 15, after 'Durham' add 'He was *cr.*, 2 Feb. 1948, VISCOUNT HYNDLEY, of Meads, co. Sussex. He *d. s.p.m.* 5 Jan. 1963 when all his titles became *extinct*.'

RUTHERFORD OF NELSON

page 495,
line 29, after '*extinct*' add 'His widow *d.* 21 Jan. 1954.'

ROCHESTER

page 496,
line 22, after 'Down' add 'He *d.* 13 Jan. 1955. His widow *d.* 1979.'
lines 23–4, delete all detail and replace as follows

II. 1955. 2. FOSTER CHARLES LOWRY (LAMB), BARON ROCHESTER, 1st s. and h., *b.* 7 June 1916; ed. at Mill Hill and Cambridge (Jesus Coll.); *m.*, 12 Dec. 1942, Mary Carlisle, yr. da. of Thomas Benjamin WHEELER, C.B.E., of Hartford, Cheshire.

[DAVID CHARLES LAMB, 1st s. and h. ap., *b.* 8 Sep. 1944; ed. at Shrewsbury and Sussex Univ.; *m.*, 9 Apr. 1969, Jacqueline, da. of John Alfred STAMP of Torquay, Devon.]

SNELL

page 497,
line 15, after '(2)' add 'He *d.* unm. 21 Apr. 1944 when his Barony became *extinct*.'

SNOWDEN

page 498,
line 18, for 'Barony' read 'Viscountcy' and after '(2)' add 'His widow *d.* 22 Feb. 1951.'

MAMHEAD

page 499,
line 9, after 'Devon' add 'He *d.* unm. 2 Nov. 1945 when his Barony became *extinct*. and his Baronetcy was inherited by his cousin.'

CONWAY OF ALLINGTON

page 500,
line 21, after '*extinct*' add 'His widow *d.* 14 Mar. 1953.'

MOUNT TEMPLE

page 503,
line 21, after 'Hereford' add 'He *d. s.p.m.* 3 July 1939, when his Barony became *extinct*. His widow *d.* 24 June 1954.

SELSDON

page 504,
line 29, after '(3)' add 'His widow *d.* 12 Apr. 1956.'
line 32, after '1913' add 'He was ed. at Winchester'
line 34, after 'Spain' add 'This marriage was diss. by divorce in 1944 (she *d.* 1991, having *m.* 2ndly, 1972, Charles LARKING) and he *m.* 2ndly, 29 Aug. 1944, Dorothy, 1st da. of Frederick John GREENISH of Honington Hall, Grantham, co. Lincs. He *d.* 7 Feb. 1963. His widow *d.* 1988.'
lines 35–6, delete all detail and replace as follows

III. 1963. 3. MALCOLM MCEACHARN (MITCHELL-THOMSON), BARON SELSDON, &c., only s. and h. by 1st wife, *b.* 27 Oct. 1937; ed. at Winchester; *m.*, 2 June 1965, Patricia Anne, da. of Donald Smith of Haslemere, Surrey.

[CALLUM MALCOLM MCEACHARN MITCHELL-THOMSON, s. and h. ap., *b.* 7 Nov. 1969.]

ALLEN OF HURTWOOD

page 505,
line 16, after 'GILL' add 'He *d. s.p.m.* 3 Mar. 1939 when his Barony became *extinct*. His widow *d.* 11 Apr. 1976.'

MOYNE

page 506,
line 22, after 'Coventry' add 'She *d.* 21 July 1939. He, as Resident Minister in the Middle East, was assassinated in Cairo, 6 Nov. 1944.'
line 23, line to read as follows

II. 1944. 2. BRYAN WALTER (GUINNESS), BARON MOYNE, 1st s. and h., *b.* 27 Oct. 1905; ed. at Eton and Oxford (Ch. Ch.);

line 29, delete ']' and replace by 'He *d.* 6 July 1992. His widow was living 1995.'

III. 1992. 3. JONATHAN BRYAN (GUINNESS), BARON MOYNE, 1st s. and h., *b.* 16 Mar. 1930; ed. at Eton and Oxford (Trin. Coll.); *m.* 1stly, 25 July 1951, Ingrid Georgia Olivia, yr. da. of Major Guy Richard Charles WYNDHAM. This marriage was diss. by divorce in 1963 and he *m.* 2ndly, 10 Jan. 1964, Suzanne, da. of Harold William Denis LISNEY of Cadaques, Spain and formerly wife of Timothy PHILLIPS.

[JASPER JONATHAN RICHARD GUINNESS, 1st s. and h. ap. by 1st wife, *b.* 9 Mar. 1954; ed. at Eton; *m.*, 1985, Camilla Alexandra, da. of Robbie David Corbett UNIACKE.]

RHAYADER

page 507,
line 11, after '(4)' add 'He *d.* unm. 26 Sep. 1939 when his Barony became *extinct*.'

WRIGHT

page 508,
line 20, after 'Coldfield' add 'He *d.* 27 June 1964 when his life Barony became *extinct*.'

WOODBRIDGE

page 509,
line 17, after 'Ipswich' add 'etc. He *d. s.p.m.s.* 3 Feb. 1949 when his Barony and his Baronetcy became *extinct*.'

ESSENDON

page 510,
line 21, after 'Hartlepool' add 'He *d.* 24 June 1944. His widow *d.* 5 June 1967.'
lines 22–3, delete all detail and replace as follows

II. 1944. 2. BRIAN EDMUND (LEWIS), BARON ESSENDON and a Baronet, only s. and h., *b.* 7 Dec. 1903; ed. at Malvern and Cambridge (Pembroke Coll.); *m.*, 16 Dec. 1938, Mary, da. of G.W. BOOKER of Los Angeles, California, U.S.A. and widow of Albert DUFFILL. He *d.* 18 July 1978 when his Barony became *extinct*.

DAVIES

page 511,
line 22, after 'Perthshire' add 'He *d.* 16 June 1944. His widow *d.* 27 Oct. 1948.'
lines 23–4, delete all detail and replace as follows

II. 1944. 2. DAVID MICHAEL (DAVIES), BARON DAVIES, 1st s. and h. by 1st wife, *b.* 16 Jan. 1915; ed. at Oundle and Cambridge (King's Coll.); *m.*, 21 Dec.

1939, Ruth Eldrydd, 3rd da. of Major William Marshall DUGDALE, C.B., D.S.O., of Llanfyllin, co. Montgomery. He was *k.* in action in Europe, Sep. 1944. His widow *d.* 22 July 1966.

III. 1944. 3. DAVID (DAVIES), BARON DAVIES, 1st s. and h., *b.* 2 Oct. 1940; ed. at Eton and Cambridge (King's Coll.); *m.*, 1976, Beryl, da. of W.J. OLIVER.

[DAVID DANIEL DAVIES, 1st s. and h. ap., *b.* 23 Aug. 1975.]

GLADSTONE OF HAWARDEN

page 512,
line 26, after '(1)' add 'His widow *d.* 23 July 1941.'

RANKEILLOUR

page 513,
line 17, after 'Sussex' add 'He *d.* 14 Feb. 1949.'
line 18, line to read as follows

II. 1949. 2. ARTHUR OSWALD JAMES (HOPE), BARON RANKEILLOUR, 1st s. and h., *b.* 7 May 1897;

line 29, delete ']' and replace by 'He *d. s.p.m.* 26 May 1958. His widow *d.* 1975.'

III. 1958. 3. HENRY JOHN (HOPE), BARON RANKEILLOUR, brother and h., *b.* 20 Jan. 1899; ed. at Oratory Sch. and Oxford (Ch. Ch.); *m.*, 19 Dec. 1933, Mary Sibyl, yr. da. of Col. Wilfred RICARDO, D.S.O., of Hook Hall, Surrey. He *d.* 2 Dec. 1967. His widow was living 1995.

IV. 1967. 4. PETER ST. THOMAS MORE HENRY (HOPE), BARON RANKEILLOUR, only s. and h., *b.* 29 May 1935; ed. at Ampleforth.

HUTCHISON OF MONTROSE

page 514,
line 19, after 'Montrose' add 'She *d.* 22 Apr. 1941 and he *m.* 2ndly, 28 Apr. 1942, Alma, da. of W.G. COWES of Buenos Aires and widow of J.C. DRYSDALE of Kilrie, co. Fife. He *d. s.p.* 13 June 1950 when his title became *extinct*. His widow *m.* 3rdly, 9 Dec. 1954, Brig. I.L.W.D. LAURIE.'

RUNCIMAN OF DOXFORD

page 518,
line 14, after 'Shields.' add 'He *d.* 14 Nov. 1949. His widow *d.* 28 Oct. 1956.'
line 15, line to read as follows

BARONY. III. VISCOUNTCY. II. } 1949 — 3 and 2. WALTER LESLIE (RUNCIMAN), VISCOUNT RUNCIMAN OF DOXFORD, BARON RUNCIMAN and a Baronet, 1st s. and h., was *b.* 26 Aug. 1900;

line 22, after '1928' add ', she *d.* 1990'
line 24, delete ']' and replace by 'He *d.* 1 Sep. 1989. His widow *d.* 1993.'

BARONY. IV. VISCOUNTCY. III. } 1989 — 4 and 3. WALTER GARRISON (RUNCIMAN), VISCOUNT RUNCIMAN OF DOXFORD, &c., only s. and h. by 2nd wife, *b.* 10 Nov. 1934; ed. at Eton and Cambridge (Trin. Coll.); *m.*, 17 Apr. 1963, Ruth, da. of Joseph HELLMAN of Johannesburg, South Africa.

[DAVID WALTER RUNCIMAN, s. and h. ap., *b.* 1 Mar. 1967; ed. at Eton and Cambridge (Trin. Coll.).]

BROCKET

page 519,
line 22, after '(2)' add 'His widow *d.* 18 Oct. 1949.'
line 35, after 'Hutton' add 'He *d. s.p.m.s.* 24 Mar. 1967. His widow *d.* 1975.'
line 37, after '1928' add 'He was ed. at Eton, R.M.A., Sandhurst and R.A.C., Cirencester; *m.*, 15 Dec. 1950, Elizabeth Mary, 2nd da. of Richard John STALLARD of Petersfield, co. Hants. He *d. v.p.* 15 Mar. 1961. His widow *m.* 2ndly, 10 July 1964, Colin John Richard TROTTER. She was still living 1995.

III. 1967. 3. CHARLES RONALD GEORGE (NALL-CAIN), BARON BROCKET, &c., grandson and h., being 1st s. and h. of RONALD CHARLES MANUS BROCKET and Elizabeth Mary his wife abovenamed. He was *b.* 12 Feb. 1952; ed. at Eton; *m.*, 1982, Isabell Maria, da. of Gustavo LORENZO of Long Island, New York.

[ALEXANDER CHRISTOPHER CHARLES NALL-CAIN, 1st s. and h. ap., *b.* 30 Sep. 1984.]

HORDER

page 520,
line 22, after 'Herts.' add 'She *d.* 15 Feb. 1954. He *d.* 13 Aug. 1955.'
line 23, delete all detail and replace as follows

II. 1955. 2. THOMAS MERVYN (HORDER), BARON HORDER and a Baronet, only s. and h., *b.* 8 Dec. 1910; ed. at Winchester and Cambridge (Trin. Coll.); *m.*, 6 July 1946, Mary Ross, yr. da. of William Scott MCDOUGALL, M.D., of Wallington, Surrey.

MILNE

page 521,
line 31, after 'RICKMAN' add 'He *d.* 23 Mar. 1948. His widow *d.* 1970.'
line 32, delete all detail and replace as follows

II. 1948. 2. GEORGE DOUGLASS (MILNE), BARON MILNE, only s. and h., *b.* 10 Feb. 1909; ed. at Winchester and Oxford (New Coll.); *m.*, 1 Apr. 1940, Cicely, 3rd da. of Ronald LESLIE.

[GEORGE ALEXANDER MILNE, 1st s. and h. ap., *b.* 1 Apr. 1941; ed. at Winchester.]

DUVEEN

page 522,
line 24, after 'U.S.A.' add 'He *d. s.p.m.* 25 May 1939 when his Barony and Baronetcy became *extinct*.' His widow *d.* 13 Mar. 1963.'

RENNELL

page 523,
line 29, after 'Australia' add 'He *d.* 26 July 1941. His widow *d.* 20 Sep. 1951.'
line 30, line to read as follows

II. 1941. 2. FRANCIS JAMES RENNELL (RODD), BARON RENNELL, 1st s. and h., *b.* 25 Oct. 1895;

page 524,
line 3, after ']' add 'He *d. s.p.m.* 14 Mar. 1978. His widow *d.* 1981.'

III. 1978. 3. JOHN ADRIAN TREMAYNE (RODD), BARON RENNELL, 2nd(3) but 1st surv. s. and h. of Gustav Guthrie RENNELL, 4th surv. s. of the 1st Baron, by Yvonne Mary, 1st da. of Sir Charles Murray MARLING. He was *b.* 28 June 1935; ed. at Downside and R.N.C., Dartmouth; *m.*, 1977, Phyllis Caroline, da. of Thomas David NEILL of Portadown, co. Armagh.

[JAMES RODERICK DAVID TREMAYNE RODD, s. and h. ap., *b.* 9 Mar. 1978.]

(3) His elder brother, Saul David Rennell, *b.* 24 Sep. 1933, *d.* unm. 17 Jan. 1966.

MOTTISTONE

page 525,
line 30, after 'Hants' add 'He *d.* 7 Nov. 1947. His widow *d.* 1976.'
line 35, line to read as follows

II. 1947. 2. HENRY JOHN ALEXANDER (SEELY), BARON MOTTISTONE, 2nd but 1st surv. s. and h., *b.* 1 May 1899;

line 38, delete ']' and replace by 'He *d.* unm. 18 Jan. 1963.'

III. 1963. 3. ARTHUR PATRICK WILLIAM (SEELY), BARON MOTTISTONE, brother and h., *b.* 18 Aug. 1905; ed. at Harrow and Cambridge (Trin. Coll.); *m.*, 2 Sep. 1939, Josephine Wilhelmina Philippa, da. of Jonkheer Frans Izaak VAN HAEFTEN of The Hague, Netherlands. This marriage was diss. by divorce 1949. He *d. s.p.* 4 Dec. 1966.

IV. 1966. 4. DAVID PETER (SEELY), BARON MOTTISTONE, brother and h., being only s. by 2nd wife of the 1st Baron, *b.* 16 Dec. 1920; *m.*, 16 Sep. 1944, Anthea Christine, 1st da. of Victor MCMULLAN.

[PETER JOHN PHILLIP SEELY, 1st s. and h. ap., *b.* 29 Oct. 1949; ed. at Uppingham.]

ILIFFE

page 526,
line 19, after 'afsd.' add 'He *d.* 25 July 1960. His widow *d.* 1972.'
line 20, line to read as follows

II. 1960. 2. EDWARD LANGTON (ILIFFE), BARON ILIFFE, 1st and only surv. s. and h., *b.* 25 Jan. 1908; ed. at Sherborne and Cambridge (Clare Coll.); *m.*, 8 Dec. 1938, Renée Merandon, 1st da. of René Merandon DU PLESSIS of Chamarel, Mauritius.

PALMER

page 527,
line 16, after 'WARNER, add 'She *d.* 28 Feb. 1947. He *d.* 8 Dec. 1948.'
line 17, line to read as follows

II. 1948. 2. ERNEST CECIL NOTTAGE (PALMER), BARON PALMER and a Baronet, 1st s. and h., *b.* 9 June 1882,

line 22, delete ']' and replace by 'He *d.* 6 June 1950. His widow *d.* 13 Sep. 1959.'

III. 1950. 3. RAYMOND CECIL (PALMER), BARON PALMER, &c., 1st s. and h., *b.* 24 June 1916; *m.*, 30 Jan. 1941, Victoria Ellen, da. of Capt. Joseph Arthur Ronald Weston STEVENS of Maidenhead, co. Berks. He *d.* 26 June 1990. His widow was living 1995.

IV. 1990. 4. ADRIAN BAILIE NOTTAGE (PALMER), BARON PALMER, s. and h., *b.* 8 Oct. 1951; ed. at Eton and Edinburgh Univ.; *m.*, 1977, Cornelia Dorothy Katherine, da. of Rohan WADHAM.

[HUGO BAILIE ROHAN PALMER, 1st s. and h. ap., *b.* 5 Dec. 1980.]

BINGLEY

page 528,
line 20, after 'DEVON' add 'He *d. s.p.m.* 11 Dec. 1947 when his Barony became *extinct.*' His widow *d.* 25 Mar. 1962.'

ROCKLEY

page 532,
line 2, after 'Northumberland' add 'He *d.* 1 Apr. 1941. His widow *d.* 14 Sep. 1941.'
line 3, line to read as follows

II. 1941. 2. ROBERT WILLIAM EVELYN (CECIL), BARON ROCKLEY, only s. and h.,

line 10, delete ']' and replace by 'He *d.* 6 Jan. 1976. His widow *d.* 1980.'

III. 1976. 3. JAMES HUGH (CECIL), BARON ROCKLEY, 1st s. and h., *b.* 5 Apr. 1934; ed. at Eton and Oxford (New Coll.); *m.*, 18 Nov. 1958, Lady Sarah Primrose Beatrix, 1st da. of William Gerald Charles (Cadogan), 7th EARL CADOGAN.

[ANTHONY ROBERT CECIL, s. and h. ap., *b.* 29 July 1961; ed. at Eton and Cambridge; *m.*, 1988, Katherine Jane, da. of G.A. WHALLEY.]

PORTSEA

page 533,
line 21, after 'U.S.A.' add 'He *d. s.p.* 1 Nov. 1948 when his Barony and his Baronetcy became *extinct.*'

NUFFIELD

page 535,
line 3, after 'HOSIER' add 'He *d. s.p.* 22 Aug. 1963 when the Viscountcy, Barony and Baronetcy became *extinct.*'

ELTISLEY

page 535,
line 24, after 'Lancers' add 'He *d. s.p.m.* 2 Sep. 1942 when his Barony became *extinct.*'

ELTON

page 536,
line 19, after 'Norway' add 'He *d.* 18 Apr. 1973. His widow *d.* 1977.'
line 20, line to read as follows

II. 1973. 2. RODNEY (ELTON), BARON ELTON, only s. and h., *b.* 2 Mar. 1930,

line 22, delete ']' and replace by 'He was ed. at Eton and Oxford (New Coll.); *m.*, 18 Sep. 1958, Anne Frances, 1st da. of Brig. Robert Adolphus George TILNEY, D.S.O., of Sutton Bonnington, co. Leics. This marriage was diss. by divorce in 1979 and he *m.* 2ndly, 1979, Susan Richenda, yst. da. of Sir Hugh GURNEY, K.C.M.G., M.V.O.'

[EDWARD PAGE ELTON, s. and h. ap. by 1st wife, *b.* 28 May 1966.]

BINGHAM

page 537,
line 12, after '1937.' add 'See LUCAN, above.'

ALNESS

page 538,
line 20, after 'Dinard' add 'He *d. s.p.* 6 Oct. 1955 when his Barony became *extinct*.'

HIRST

page 539,
line 20, after '1938' add 'He *d. s.p.m.s.* 22 Jan. 1943 when his Barony and his Baronetcy became *extinct*.'
line 25, after 'Mansions.' add 'This marriage was diss. by divorce in 1938. She *d.* 20 Mar. 1966.'
line 28, after '1919' add 'He *d. v.* grandfather, and unm., 1941, being *k.* on active service.'

WAKEHURST

page 540,
line 16, after '(1)' add 'His widow *d.* 15 Dec. 1958.'
line 27, after 'Malmesbury' add 'He *d.* 30 Oct. 1970. His widow was still living 1995.'
lines 28–9, delete all detail and replace as follows

III. 1970. 3. JOHN CHRISTOPHER DE VERE (LODER), BARON WAKEHURST, only s. and h., *b.* 23 Sep. 1925, and *bap.* at St. Margaret's, Westm.; ed. at Eton and Cambridge (Trin. Coll.); *m.*, 27 Oct. 1956, Ingeborg, da. of Walter KRUMBHOLZ. She *d.* 1977 and he *m.* 2ndly, 1983, Brigid, yr. da. of William NOBLE of Cirencester, co. Glos.

[TIMOTHY WALTER LODER, s. and h. ap. by 1st wife, *b.* 28 Mar. 1958; ed. at Millfield; *m.*, 1987, Susan Elaine HURST.]

KENT

page 541,
line 32, after 'RUSSIA' add 'He *d.* in an air crash while on active service, 25 Aug. 1942,

and was *bur.* at Frogmore. His widow *d.* 27 Aug. 1968 at Kensington Palace and was *bur.* at Frogmore.'

lines 33–5, delete all detail and replace as follows

IV. 1942. 2. *H.R.H.* EDWARD GEORGE NICHOLAS PAUL PATRICK, Prince of the United Kingdom of Great Britain and Northern Ireland, 1st s. and h., *b.* 9 Oct. 1935; ed. at Eton and R.M.A., Sandhurst; *m.* at York Minster, 8 June 1961, Katherine Lucy Mary, da. of Sir William Arthington WORSLEY, Bart.

[GEORGE PHILIP NICHOLAS, *styled* EARL OF ST. ANDREWS, 1st s. and h. ap., *b.* at Coppins, Iver, co. Bucks., 26 June 1962; ed. at Eton and Cambridge (Downing Coll.); *m.* at Leith, 9 Jan. 1988, Sylvana Palma, da. of Maximilian Karl TOMASELLI and formerly wife of John Paul JONES.]

RUSHCLIFFE

page 545,
line 17, after 'Leicestershire' add 'She *d.* 5 Oct. 1947 and he *m.* 2ndly, Apr. 1948, Inez Alfreda, da. of Alfred LUBBOCK and formerly wife of Sir Harold Edward SNAGGE. He *d. s.p.m.* 18 Nov. 1949 when his Barony and his Baronetcy became *extinct*. His widow *d.* 4 May 1955.'

HESKETH

page 546,
line 17, after 'city' add 'He *d.* 20 July 1944. His widow *d.* 4 Mar. 1956.'
lines 25–6, delete all detail and replace as follows

II. 1944. 2. FREDERICK (FERMOR-HESKETH), BARON HESKETH and a Baronet, 2nd but 1st surv. s. and h., *b.* 8 Apr. 1916; ed. at Eton and Cambridge (Magdalene Coll.); *m.*, 22 Nov. 1949, Christian Mary, da. of Sir John Helias Finnie MCEWAN, Bart. of Marchmont, co. Berwick. He *d.* 10 June 1955. His widow was living 1995.

III. 1955. 3. THOMAS ALEXANDER (FERMOR-HESKETH), BARON HESKETH, &c., 1st s. and h., *b.* 28 Oct. 1950; ed. at Ampleforth; *m.*, 1977, Claire Georgina, 1st da. of Joseph Rupert Eric Robert (WATSON), 3rd BARON MANTON.

[FREDERICK HATTON FERMOR-HESKETH, s. and h. ap., *b.* 13 Oct. 1988.]

PORTAL

page 547,
heading on left and in margin to read as follows

BARONY.
I. } 1935

VISCOUNTCY.
I. } 1945

line 16, after 'Southampton' add 'He was further *cr.*, 1 Feb. 1945, VISCOUNT PORTAL of Laverstoke, co. Southampton.'

line 19, after 'BERENS' add 'He *d. s.p.* 6 May 1949 when his Barony and Viscountcy became *extinct* and his Baronetcy was inherited by his uncle. His widow *d.* 7 May 1962.'

TWEEDSMUIR

page 548,
line 22, for 'from 1935' read '1935–40'
line 27, after 'STUART-WORTLEY' add 'He *d.* 11 Feb. 1940. His widow *d.* 21 Mar. 1977.'
line 28, line to read as follows

II. 1940. 2. JOHN NORMAN STUART (BUCHAN), BARON TWEEDSMUIR, 1st s. and h., *b.* 25 Nov. 1911;

line 30, delete ']' and replace by 'He *m.* 1stly, 27 July 1948, Priscilla Jean Fortescue, yr. da. of Brig. Alan Fortescue THOMSON, D.S.O., of Kennethmont, co. Aberdeen and widow of Major Sir Arthur Lindsay GRANT, Bart. She was *cr.*, 1 July 1970, a life peer as BARONESS TWEEDSMUIR OF BELHEVIE, of Potterton in the co. of Aberdeen. She *d.* 11 Mar. 1978. He *m.* 2ndly, 1980, Jean Margharita, da. of Humphrey Douglas TOLLEMACHE, Capt., R.N. and widow of Sir Francis Cullen GRANT, Bart.'

SYSONBY

page 549,
line 24, after '(1)' add 'His widow *d.* 2 June 1955.'
line 28, after '(3)' add 'ed. at Eton.;'
line 30, for '(__)' read 'George Edward'
line 31, after 'U.S.A.' add 'He *d.* 21 Jan. 1956. His widow *d.* 1979.'

III. 1956. 3. JOHN FREDERICK (PONSONBY), BARON SYSONBY, only s. and h., *b.* 5 Aug. 1945.

WIGRAM

page 550,
line 22, for 'from 1937' read '1937–45.'
line 29, after 'Corps' add 'She *d.* 5 Jan. 1956. He *d.* 3 Sep. 1960.'
line 30, line to read as follows

II. 1960. 2. GEORGE NEVILLE CLIVE (WIGRAM), BARON WIGRAM, 1st s. and h., *b.* 2 Aug. 1915,

line 31, after 'at' add 'Winchester and'

line 33, delete ']' and replace by 'He *m.*, 19 July 1941, Margaret Helen, yr. da. of Gen. Sir Augustus Francis Andrew Nicol THORNE, K.C.B., C.M.G., D.S.O. (two bars), of Knowle Hill House, Reading, Berks.'

[ANDREW FRANCIS CLIVE WIGRAM, s. and h. ap., *b.* 18 Mar. 1949; ed. at Winchester, R.M.A., Sandhurst and R.A.C., Cirencester; *m.* 1974, Gabrielle Diana, yr. da. of R.D. MOORE of Wellington, New Zealand.]

BLACKFORD

page 551,
line 11, after 'Dumfries' add 'He *d.* 21 July 1947. His widow *d.* 19 May 1958.'
line 12, line to read as follows

II. 1947. 2. GLYN KEITH MURRAY (MASON), BARON BLACKFORD and a Baronet, only s. and h., *b.* 29 May 1887;

line 18, delete ']' and replace by 'She *d.* 1972. He *d.* 31 Dec. 1972.'

[WILLIAM MURRAY MASON, 1st s. and h. ap., *b.* 31 Jan. 1921. He was *k.* in action, *v.p.* 23 Mar. 1942.]

III. 1972. 3. KEITH ALEXANDER HENRY (MASON), BARON BLACKFORD, 2nd but 1st surv. s. and h., *b.* 23 Feb. 1923; ed. at Eton; *m.*, 19 Dec. 1957, Sarah, 1st da. of Judge Sir William Shirley Worthington WORTHINGTON-EVANS, Bart. This marriage was diss. by divorce in 1971. She *m.* 2ndly, Eric Ivor HOPTON. He *d.* 21 Apr. 1977.

IV. 1977. 4. WILLIAM KEITH (MASON), BARON BLACKFORD, &c., only s. and h., *b.* 27 Mar. 1962; ed. at Harrow. He *d.* unm. and *s.p.* 15 May 1988, when the Barony and Baronetcy became *extinct*.

RIVERDALE

page 552,
line 32, after 'KEIGHLEY' add 'He *d.* 7 July 1957. His widow *d.* 1 July 1960.'
line 33, line to read as follows

II. 1957. 2. ROBERT ARTHUR (BALFOUR), BARON RIVERDALE and a Baronet, 1st s. and h., *b.* 1 Sep. 1901; ed. at Oundle;

line 37, delete ']'

[MARK ROBIN BALFOUR, 1st s. and h. ap. by 1st wife, *b.* 16 July 1927; ed. at Aysgarth Sch. and Trin. Coll. Sch., Port Hope, Canada; *m.*, 31 Mar. 1959, Susan Ann, 1st da. of Robert P. PHILLIPS of Sheffield.]

MAY

page 553,
line 13, after 'London' add 'He *d.* 10 Apr. 1946. His widow *d.* 15 Jan. 1955.'
line 14, line to read as follows

II. 1946. 2. JOHN LAWRENCE (MAY), BARON MAY and a Baronet, 1st s. and h., *b.* 15 Aug. 1904;

line 16, delete ']' and replace by 'He *d.* 9 Mar. 1950. His widow *m.* 2ndly, W.H. HALLAM. She was still living 1995.'

III. 1950. 3. MICHAEL ST. JOHN (MAY), BARON MAY, only s. and h., *b.* 26 Sep. 1031; ed. at Wycliffe Coll. and Cambridge (Magdalene Coll.); *m.* 1stly, 27 Dec. 1958, Dorothea Catherine Ann, da. of Charles MCCARTHY of Boston, Mass., U.S.A. This marriage was diss. by divorce in 1963 and he *m.* 2ndly, 5 July 1963, Jillian May, da. of Albert Edward SHIPTON of Banbury, co. Oxford.

[JASPER BERTRAM ST. JOHN MAY, s. and h. ap. by 2nd wife, *b.* 24 Oct. 1965; ed. at Harrow.]

ST JUST

page 554,
line 15, after 'Horsham' add 'He *d.* 26 Nov. 1941. His widow *d.* 1971.'
line 16, delete all detail and replace as follows

II. 1941. 2. PETER GORDON (GRENFELL), BARON ST. JUST, only s. and h., *b.* 22 July 1922, at 24 Charles St., W., and *bap.* at Hambledon, Bucks; ed. at Harrow; *m.*, 1 June 1949, Leslie, da. of Condé NAST of New York. This marriage was diss. by divorce in 1955 and he *m.* 2ndly, 25 July 1956, Maria, da. of Alexandra BRITNEV of St. Petersburg, Russia. He *d. s.p.m.* 14 Oct. 1984 when his title became *extinct*.

KENNET

page 555,
line 35, after 'Aleppo' add 'She *d.* 25 July 1947. He *d.* 11 July 1960.'
line 36, delete all detail and replace as follows

II. 1960. 2. WAYLAND HILTON (YOUNG), BARON KENNET, s. and h., *b.* 2 Aug. 1923; ed. at Stowe and Cambridge (Trin. Coll.); *m.*, 24 Jan. 1948, Elizabeth Ann, da. of Brian Fullerton ADAMS, Capt., R.N., D.S.O., of Woodbridge, co. Suffolk.

[WILLIAM ALDUS THOBY YOUNG, s. and h. ap., *b.* 24 May 1957; ed. at Marlborough and Sussex Univ.; *m.*, 1987, Josephine Mary, yr. da. of Roger George Bowlby (KEYES), 2nd BARON KEYES.]

MAUGHAM

page 556,
heading and left hand margin to read as follows

BARONY FOR LIFE. I.	1935
VISCOUNTCY. I.	1939

line 14, after '1938.' add 'He was further *cr.*, 22 Sep. 1939, VISCOUNT MAUGHAM of Hartfield co. Sussex [U.K.].'

line 15, after '(3)' add 'She *d.* 12 Oct. 1950. He *d.* 23 Mar. 1958 when his life Barony became *extinct* and his Viscountcy was inherited by his only son.'

II. 1958. 2. ROBERT CECIL ROMER (MAUGHAM), VISCOUNT MAUGHAM, only s. and h., *b.* 17 May 1916; ed. at Eton and Cambridge (Trin. Hall.). He *d.* unm. and *s.p.* 13 Mar. 1981 when his title became *extinct*.

ROCHE

page 557,

line 20, after '(2)' add 'His wife *d.* 1955. He *d.* 22 Dec. 1956 when his life Barony became *extinct*.'

(2), line 1, after '1903' add 'His 2nd s. Thomas Gabriel was *b.* 11 May 1909.'

SWINTON

page 558,
heading and left hand margin to read as follows

VISCOUNTCY. I.	1935
EARLDOM. I.	1955

line 21, after '1929' add 'He was further *cr.*, 5 May 1955, EARL OF SWINTON and BARON MASHAM of Ellington, co. York.'

line 23, after 'MASHAM' add 'He *d.* 27 July 1972. His widow *d.* 1974.'

line 27, after 'Newbury.' add 'He *d. v.p.* 14 Apr. 1943 of wounds received in action. His widow *m.* 2ndly, 3 Apr. 1944, Donald Phillott CHAPPLE-GILL of Cibau, co. Montgomery.'

II. 1972. 2. DAVID YARBURGH (CUNLIFFE-LISTER), EARL OF SWINTON, VISCOUNT SWINTON of Masham, and BARON MASHAM, of Ellington, grandson and h., being 1st s. and h. of John Yarburgh CUNLIFFE-LISTER and Anne Irvine abovenamed, *b.* 21 Mar. 1937; ed. at Winchester and R.A.C., Cirencester; *m.*, 8 Dec. 1959, Susan Lilian Primrose, yr. da. of Sir Ronald Norman John Charles Udney

SINCLAIR, Bart. She was *cr.*, 12 Feb. 1970, a life peer as BARONESS MASHAM OF ILTON of Masham in the North Riding of Yorkshire.

MONSELL

page 559,
line 23, after 'Yorks.' add 'This marriage was diss. by divorce in 1950 (she *d.* 25 Dec. 1959) and he *m.* 2ndly, 25 July 1950, Essex Leila Hilary, da. of Lieut. Col. Edward Gerald Fleming FRENCH, D.S.O., formerly wife of Capt. Vivyan DRURY of Annamoe, co. Wicklow. He *d.* 21 Mar. 1969. His widow was living 1995.
lines 24–5, delete all detail and replace as follows

II. 1969. 2. HENRY BOLTON GRAHAM (EYRES-MONSELL), VISCOUNT MONSELL, only s. and h. by 1st wife, *b.* 21 Nov. 1905; ed. at Eton. He *d.* unm. and *s.p.* 28 Nov. 1993 when his title became *extinct.*

GOWRIE

page 560,
left hand margin to read

BARONY. I. } 1935
EARLDOM. I. } 1945

line 24, after '1938' add 'He was further *cr.*, 8 May 1945, EARL OF GOWRIE.'
line 27, after '[I.]' add 'He *d.* 2 May 1955. His widow *d.* 19 July 1965.'
line 30, after '1937.' add 'He *d. v.p.* and unm. 24 Dec. 1942 of wounds received in leading a commando raid in Tripoli. His widow *m.* 2ndly, 30 July 1952, as his 2nd wife, Major George Derek COOPER, O.B.E., M.C. She was still living 1995.'

II. 1955.
BARONY.
III. 1956.

2 and 3. ALEXANDER PATRICK GREYSTEIL (RUTHVEN), EARL OF GOWRIE, &c., grandson and h., being 1st s. and h. of Alexander Hardinge Patrick HORE-RUTHVEN and Pamela Margaret abovenamed. He was *b.* 26 Nov. 1939; ed. at Eton, Oxford (Balliol Coll.) and Harvard Univ. He *suc.*, 16 Apr. 1956, his great-uncle as BARON RUTHVEN OF GOWRIE [see vol. xiii, p. 324, and above, p. 685]. He *m.* 1stly, 21 Dec. 1962, Alexandra, da. of Col. Robert Albert Glanville BINGLEY. This marriage was diss. by divorce in 1974 and he *m.* 2ndly, 1974, COUNTESS ADELHEID, yst. da. of Fritz-Dietlof, GRAF VON DER SCHULENBURG.

[PATRICK LEO BRER RUTHVEN, *styled* VISCOUNT RUTHVEN OF CANBERRA, s. and h. ap. by 1st wife, *b.* 4 Feb. 1964; *m.*, 1990, Julie GOLDSMITH.]

STRATHCARRON

page 563,
line 24, after 'BAS' add 'She *d.* 4 Aug. 1956.'

line 27, after 'Commons' add 'He was ed. at Eton and Cambridge (Jesus Coll.); *m.* 1stly, 10 Feb. 1947, Valerie, 1st da. of T.N. COLE. This marriage was annulled in July 1947 and he *m.* 2ndly, 18 May 1948, Diana Hawtrey, da. of Ralph Hawtrey DEANE, Cmdr., R.N. and formerly wife of John Noel Ormiston CURLE.

[IAN DAVID PATRICK MACPHERSON, 1st s. and h. ap., *b.* 31 Mar. 1949; ed. at Horris Hill, Newbury and Grenoble.]

KEMSLEY

page 566,
left hand margin to read

BARONY.
I. } 1936
VISCOUNTCY.
I. } 1945

line 16, after 'honour.' add 'He was further *cr.*, 12 Sep. 1945, VISCOUNT KEMSLEY, of Dropmore, co. Buckingham.'
line 21, after '1930' add 'He *d.* 6 Feb. 1968. His widow *d.* 1976.'
line 22, line to read as follows

II. 1968. 2. GEOFFREY LIONEL (BERRY), VISCOUNT KEMSLEY, BARON KEMSLEY, and a Baronet, 1st s. and h., *b.* 29 June 1909;

line 27, delete ']'

CATTO

page 567,
line 20, after 'REES' add 'He *d.* 23 Aug. 1959. His widow *d.* 1980.'
lines 21–2, delete all detail and replace as follows

II. 1959. 2. STEPHEN GORDON (CATTO), BARON CATTO, also a Baronet, 1st s. and h., *b.* 14 Jan. 1923, at Stanmore, Middlesex; ed. at Eton, 1936, and Cambridge (Trin. Coll.); *m.* 1stly, 28 July 1948, Josephine Innes, 1st da. of George Herbert PACKER of Alexandria, Egypt. This marriage was diss. by divorce in 1965 and he *m.* 2ndly, 27 Jan. 1966, Margaret, da. of James Stuart FORREST of Dilston, Tasmania.

[INNES GORDON CATTO, 1st s. and h. ap., *b.* 7 Aug. 1950.]

CAUTLEY

page 568,
line 16, after 'Leicestershire' add 'He *d. s.p.* 21 Sep. 1946 when his Barony and his Baronetcy became *extinct*.'

HAILEY

page 569,
line 25, after 'Rome' add 'She *d.* 30 Jan. 1939. He *d. s.p.m.s.* 1 June 1969 when his Barony became *extinct.*'
line 28, after '1931' add 'He *d.* unm. and *v.p.* Feb. 1943 on active service in the Middle East,'

AUSTIN

page 570,
line 22, after 'city' add 'He *d. s.p.m.* 23 May 1941 when his Barony became *extinct.*'

WARDINGTON

page 571,
line 17, after 'BEAULIEU' add 'He *d.* 7 Aug. 1950. His widow *d.* 1983.'
lines 18–19, delete all detail and replace as follows

II. 1950. 2. CHRISTOPHER HENRY BEAUMONT (PEASE), BARON WARDINGTON, 1st s. and h., *b.* at Wardington, 22 Jan., and *bap.* there 16 Mar. 1924; ed. at Eton; *m.*, 9 Sep. 1964, Margaret Audrey, da. of John WHITE and formerly wife of Jack DUNFEE.

[CHRISTOPHER WILLIAM BEAUMONT, s. and h. ap., *b.* 1970.]

WINDLESHAM

page 575,
line 25, after 'WINTER' add 'She *d.* 10 July 1951. He *d.* 8 Oct. 1953.'
line 26, line to read as follows

II. 1953. 2. JAMES BRYAN GEORGE (HENNESSEY), BARON WINDLESHAM and a Baronet, 1st s. and h., *b.* 4 Aug. 1903; ed. at Eton;

line 29, delete ']' and replace by 'She *d.* 13 Mar. 1956, and he *m.* 2ndly, 25 Mar. 1957, Pamela Joan, yr. da. of Francis KENNEDY and formerly wife of Dermot A. DINAN. He *d.* 16 Nov. 1962. His widow *m.* 3rdly, 9 Dec. 1966, William Marsden ELVERSTON-TRICKETT. She was still living 1995.'

III. 1962. 3. DAVID JAMES GEORGE (HENNESSY), BARON WINDLESHAM, only s. and h. by 1st wife, *b.* 28 Jan. 1932; ed. at Ampleforth and Oxford (Trin. Coll.); *m.*, 22 May 1965, Prudence Loveday, yr. da. of Lieut. Col. Rupert Trevor Wallace GLYNN, M.C., of Harlesford House, Tetworth, co. Oxford.

[JAMES RUPERT HENNESSY, s. and h. ap., *b.* 9 Nov. 1968; ed. at Eton and Bristol Univ.]

MANCROFT

page 577,
line 3, after 'HENGLER' add 'He *d.* 17 Aug. 1942. His widow *d.* 1969.'
line 4, line to read as follows

II. 1942. 2. STORMONT MANCROFT (SAMUEL *afterwards* MANCROFT), BARON MANCROFT and a Baronet, 1st s. and h.,

line 8, delete ']' and replace by 'He *m.*, 8 May 1951, Diana Elizabeth, da. of Lieut. Col. Horace LLOYD, D.S.O. and formerly wife of Richard Bridges St. John QUARRY. He *d.* 14 Sep. 1987. His widow was living 1995.'

III. 1987. 3. BENJAMIN LLOYD STORMONT (MANCROFT), BARON MANCROFT, only s. and h., *b.* 16 May 1957; ed. at Eton; *m.*, 1990, Emma, 1st da. of Thomas PEART.

McGOWAN

page 578,
line 15, after 'Paisley' add 'She *d.* 8 Apr. 1952. He *d.* 13 July 1961.'
line 16, line to read as follows

II. 1961. 2. HARRY WILSON (McGOWAN), BARON McGOWAN, 1st s. and h., *b.* 18 May 1906,

line 23, delete ']' and replace by 'He *d.* 5 July 1966. His widow was living 1995.'

III. 1966. 3. HARRY DUNCAN CORY (McGOWAN), BARON McGOWAN, 1st s. and h., *b.* 20 July 1938; ed. at Eton; *m.*, 16 May 1962, Lady Gillian Angela, da. of John Digby Thomas (PEPYS), 7th EARL OF COTTENHAM.

[HARRY JOHN CHARLES McGOWAN, s. and h. ap., *b.* 23 June 1971.]

ADDISON

page 580,
heading on left and in margin to read as follows

BARONY.
I. } 1937

VISCOUNTCY.
I. } 1945

line 25, after '(1)' add 'He was further *cr.*, 6 July 1945, VISCOUNT ADDISON, also of Stallingborough afsd.'
line 28, after 'Staines' add 'He *d.* 11 Dec. 1951. His widow *d.* 1982.'

line 29, line to read as follows

II. 1951. 2. CHRISTOPHER (ADDISON), VISCOUNT ADDISON [1945] and BARON ADDISON [1937], 1st s. and h., by 1st wife, *b.* 8 Dec. 1904 at Pretty Corner, Northwood; ed. at Univ. Coll. Sch., Hampstead and Newton Coll., Newton Abbot.

line 31, delete ']' and replace by 'He *d. s.p.m.* 18 Nov. 1976. His widow *d.* 1980.'

III. 1976. 3. MICHAEL (ADDISON), VISCOUNT ADDISON, &c., brother and h., *b.* 12 Apr. 1914; ed. at Hele's Sch., Exeter and Oxford (Balliol Coll.); *m.*, 22 Aug. 1936, Kathleen, da. of Rt. Rev. and Rt. Hon. John William Charles WAND, Bishop of London. He *d.* 23 Mar. 1992. His widow was living 1995.

IV. 1992. 4. WILLIAM MATTHEW WAND (ADDISON), VISCOUNT ADDISON, &c., only s. and h., *b.* 13 June 1945; ed. at King's Sch., Bruton and Essex Inst. of Agric.; *m.* 1stly, 1970, Joanna Mary, 1st da. of John Ivor Charles DICKINSON of Blyborough Grange, Gainsborough, co. Lincoln. This marriage was diss. by divorce and he *m.* 2ndly, 1991, Lesley Ann, da. of George Colin MAWER of Welton, co. Lincoln.

[PAUL WATSON ADDISON, s. and h. ap. by 1st wife, *b.* 18 Mar. 1973; ed. at Rannoch Sch., Perth.]

DENHAM

page 581,
line 22, after '[S.]' add 'He *d.* 30 Nov. 1948. His widow was living 1995.
line 24, after 'Eton' add 'He was *k.* in action, *v.p.* and unm., Jan. 1943.'

II. 1948. 3. BERTRAM STANLEY MITFORD (BOWYER), BARON DENHAM, also a Baronet [1933.], 2nd but 1st surv. s. and h., *b.* 3 Oct. 1927; ed. at Eton and Cambridge (King's Coll.); *suc.*, 1950, his distant cousin as 10th Baronet of Bowyer of Denham [1660]. He *m.*, 14 Feb. 1956, Jean, da. of Major Kenneth MCCORQUODALE of Fambridge Hall, White Notley, co. Essex.

[RICHARD GRENVILLE GEORGE BOWYER, s. and h. ap., *b.* 8 Feb. 1959; *m.*, 1988, Eleanor, da. of A. SHARPE of Truemans Heath, co. Worcester.]

BESSBOROUGH

page 582,
line 23, after 'O.St.J.' add 'He *d.* 10 Mar. 1956. His widow *d.* 1979.'

For the 2nd EARL OF BESSBOROUGH [U.K.], see above, *sub* BESSBOROUGH.

REA

page 583,
line 14, after 'EWING' add 'He *d.* 26 May 1948. His widow *d.* 19 June 1964.'

line 15, line to read as follows

II. 1948. 2. PHILIP RUSSELL (REA), BARON REA and a Baronet, 1st s. and h., by 1st wife, *b.* 7 Feb. 1900;

line 17, delete ']' and replace by 'She *d.* 1978. He *d. s.p.m.s.* 22 Apr. 1981.'

[PIERS RUSSELL REA, s. and h. ap., *b.* 9 Nov. 1925. He *d. v.p.* 2 Sep. 1934.]

III. 1981. 3. JOHN NICHOLAS (REA), BARON REA, &c., nephew and h., being only s. and h. of James Russell REA (*d.* 15 Aug. 1954), 2nd s. of the 1st Baron by his 1st wife, Betty Marion, da. of Dr Arthur BEVAN. He was *b.* 6 June 1928; ed. at Dartington Hall, Dauntsey's Sch. and Cambridge (Christ's Coll.); *m.* 1stly, 24 Mar. 1951, Elizabeth Anne, da. of William Hensman ROBINSON of Woking, co. Surrey. This marriage was diss. by divorce in 1991 and he *m.* 2ndly, 1991, Judith Mary, da. of Norman POWELL of Lytham St. Anne's, co. Lancaster.

[MATTHEW JAMES REA, 1st s. and h. ap. by 1st wife, *b.* 28 Mar. 1956; ed. at William Ellis Sch., and Sheffield Univ.]

CHATFIELD

page 584,
line 25, after 'LEWIS' add 'He *d.* 15 Nov. 1967. His widow *d.* 1977.'
line 26, line to read as follows

II. 1967. 2. ERNLE DAVID LEWIS (CHATFIELD), BARON CHATFIELD, only s. and h., *b.* 2 Jan. 1917,

line 29, delete ']' and replace by 'He *m.* 16 May 1969, Felicia Mary Elizabeth, da. of Dr John Roderick BULMAN of Hereford.'

CADMAN

page 585,
line 33, after 'Trinidad' add 'He *d.* 21 May 1941. His widow *d.* 9 Nov. 1963.'
lines 33–4, delete all detail and replace as follows

II. 1941. 2. JOHN BASIL COPE (CADMAN), BARON CADMAN, 1st s. and h., *b.* 23 Mar. 1909; ed. at Harrow and Grenoble Univ. He *m.* 3 Dec. 1936, Marjorie Elizabeth, da. of Byron William BUNNIS. He *d.* 5 Apr. 1966. His widow was living 1995.

III. 1966. 3. JOHN ANTHONY (CADMAN), BARON CADMAN, 1st s. and h., *b.* 3 July 1938; ed. at Harrow, Cambridge (Selwyn Coll.) and R.A.C., Cirencester; *m.*, 1975, Janet, da. of A. HAYES of Bare, Morecombe, co. Lancaster.

[NICHOLAS ANTHONY JAMES CADMAN, 1st s. and h. ap., *b.* 18 Nov. 1977.]

BALDWIN OF BEWDLEY

page 586,
line 35, after 'Sussex' add 'She *d.* 17 June 1945. He *d.* 14 Dec. 1947.'
line 36, line to read as follows

II. 1947. 2. OLIVER RIDSDALE (BALDWIN), EARL BALDWIN OF BEWDLEY and VISCOUNT CORVEDALE, 1st s. and h., *b.* 1 Mar. 1899; *styled* VISCOUNT CORVEDALE 1937–47;

page 587,
line 4, for ']' read 'He *d.* unm. and *s.p.* 10 Aug. 1958.'

III. 1958. 3. ARTHUR WINDHAM (BALDWIN), EARL BALDWIN OF BEWDLEY, &c., brother and h., *b.* 22 Mar. 1904; ed. at Eton and Cambridge (Trin. Coll.); *m.*, 25 Aug. 1936, Joan Elspeth, yst. da. of Charles Alexander TOMES of New York. He *d.* 5 July 1976. His widow *d.* 1980.

IV. 1976. 4. EDWARD ALFRED ALEXANDER (BALDWIN), EARL BALDWIN OF BEWDLEY, &c., only s. and h., *b.* 3 Jan. 1938; ed. at Eton and Cambridge (Trin. Coll.); *m.*, 1970, Sarah MacMurray, 1st da. of Evan JAMES of Upwood Park, Abingdon, Berks.

[BENEDICT ALEXANDER STANLEY BALDWIN, *styled* VISCOUNT CORVEDALE, 1st s. and h. ap., *b.* 28 Dec. 1973; ed. at Bryanston.]

SAMUEL

page 588,
line 25, after 'SAMUEL' add 'She *d.* 13 Sep. 1959. He *d.* 5 Feb. 1963.'
line 26, line to read as follows

II. 1963. 2. EDWIN HERBERT (SAMUEL), VISCOUNT SAMUEL, 1st s. and h., *b.* 11 Sep. 1898;

line 31, delete ']' and replace by 'He *d.* 14 Nov. 1978. His widow *d.* 1986.'

III. 1978. 3. DAVID HERBERT (SAMUEL), VISCOUNT SAMUEL, 1st s. and h., *b.* 8 July 1922; ed. at Oxford (Balliol Coll.); *m.* 1stly, 5 May 1950, Esther, yr. da. of Jacob BERELOWITZ of Cape Town, South Africa. This marriage was diss. by divorce in 1957 and he *m.* 2ndly, 14 Dec. 1960, Rinna, da. of Meir GROSSMAN of Herzliyah, Israel and formerly wife of Reuven DAFNI. This marriage was in turn diss. by divorce in 1980 and he *m.*, 1979, Veronica Engelhardt (Mrs Grimm), da. of Ernst ENGELHARDT of Toronto, Canada. This marriage was also diss. by divorce in 1993.

MARCHWOOD

page 589,
line 24, after 'Ballymacrea' add 'He *d.* 1 Jan. 1955. His widow *d.* 20 Apr. 1957.'
line 25, line to read as follows

II. 1955. 2. PETER GEORGE (PENNY), BARON MARCHWOOD and a Baronet, only s. and h., *b.* 7 Nov. 1912, at Singapore,

line 29, delete ']' and replace by 'He *d.* 6 Apr. 1979. His widow *d.* 1979.'

III. 1979. 3. DAVID GEORGE STAVELEY (PENNY), BARON MARCHWOOD, 1st s. and h., *b.* 22 May 1936; ed. at Winchester; *m.*, 26 Sep. 1964, Tessa Jane, 2nd da. of Wilfred Francis NORRIS of Midhurst, co. Sussex.

[PETER GEORGE WORSLEY PENNY, 1st s. and h. ap., *b.* 8 Oct. 1965.]

HORNE OF SLAMANNAN

page 590,
line 23, after 'Italy' add 'He *d.* unm. 3 Sep. 1940 when his Viscountcy became *extinct*.'

KENILWORTH

page 591,
line 18, after 'MERCER' add 'She *d.* 18 Oct. 1953. He *d.* 3 Nov. 1953.'
line 19, line to read as follows

II. 1953. 2. CYRIL DAVENPORT (SIDDELEY), BARON KENILWORTH, 1st s. and h., *b.* 27 Aug. 1894 at Coventry,

line 23, delete ']' and replace by 'He *d.* 11 Aug. 1971. His widow *d.* 1977.'

III. 1971. 3. JOHN DAVENPORT (SIDDELEY), BARON KENILWORTH, only s. and h., *b.* 24 Jan. 1924; ed. at Marlborough and Cambridge (Magdalene Coll.); *m.*, 28 Aug. 1948, Jacqueline Paulette, da. of Robert GELPI. He *d.* 1981. His widow was living 1995.

IV. 1981. 4. JOHN RANDLE (SIDDELEY), BARON KENILWORTH, only s. and h., *b.* 16 June 1954; ed. at London Coll. of Furniture; *m.*, 1983, Kim, da. of Danie SERFONTEIN of Newcastle upon Tyne. This marriage was diss. by divorce in 1990 and he *m.* 2ndly, 1991, Kiki, da. of (__) AXFORD and formerly wife of David MCDONOUGH.

[WILLIAM RANDLE SIDDELEY, 1st s. and h. ap. by 2nd wife, *b.* 24 Jan. 1992.]

DAVIDSON

page 592,
line 26, after 'C.I.E.' add 'He *d.* 11 Dec. 1970. His widow *d.* 25 Nov. 1985.'
line 27, line to read as follows

II. 1970. 2. JOHN ANDREW (DAVIDSON), VISCOUNT DAVIDSON, 1st s. and h., *b.* 22 Dec. 1928,

line 29, delete ']' and replace by 'Ed. at Westminster and Cambridge (Pembroke Coll.); *m.* 1stly, 30 June 1956, Margaret Birgitta, da. of Major Gen. Cyril Henry NORTON. This marriage was diss. by divorce in 1974 and he *m.* 2ndly, 1970, Pamela Joy (Mrs DOBB), da. of John VERGETTE.'

SOUTHWOOD

page 593,
line 15, after 'COLLARD' add 'He *d. s.p.* 10 April 1946 when his Barony and Viscountcy (see p. 773) became *extinct*. His widow *d.* 7 Mar. 1951.'

PENDER

page 594,
line 19, after 'Merionethshire' add 'She *d.* 29 May 1943. He *d.* 4 Dec. 1949.'
line 20, line to read as follows

II. 1949. 2. JOHN JOCELYN (DENISON-PENDER), BARON PENDER, 1st s. and h., *b.* 26 Jan. 1907;

line 23, delete ']' and replace by 'He *d.* 31 Mar. 1965. His widow *d.* 1988.'

III. 1965. 3. JOHN WILLOUGHBY (DENISON-PENDER), BARON PENDER, 1st s. and h., *b.* 6 May 1923; ed. at Eton; *m.*, 19 Nov. 1962, Julia, yr. da. of Richard Nevill CANNON, of Lewes, co. Sussex.

[HENRY JOHN RICHARD DENISON-PENDER, s. and h. ap., *b.* 19 Mar. 1968.]

ROMER

page 597,
line 18, after '(2)' add 'He *d.* 19 Aug. 1944 when his life Barony became *extinct*. His widow *d.* 3 Mar. 1948.'
note (2), line 2, after '1897' add 'He *d.* 15 Feb. 1969, leaving issue.'

ROBOROUGH

page 598,
line 19, after '£67,659' add 'His widow *d.* 25 Mar. 1941.'
line 27, after 'Highlanders' add 'He *d.* 30 Jun. 1992. His widow was living 1995.

III. 1992. 3. HENRY MASSEY (LOPES), BARON ROBOROUGH and a Baronet, 1st s. and h., *b.* 2 Feb. 1940; ed. at Eton; *m.* 1stly, 26 Oct. 1968, Robyn Zenda Carol, 1st da. of John BROMWICH of Bacchus Marsh, Victoria, Australia. This marriage was diss. by divorce in 1986 and he *m.* 2ndly, 1986, Sarah Ann Pipon, 2nd da. of Colin BAKER of Tavistock. co. Devon.

[MASSEY JOHN HENRY LOPES, 1st s. by 1st wife and h. ap., *b.* 22 Dec. 1969; ed. at Eton.]

BIRDWOOD

page 600,
line 8, after 'SMITH' add 'She *d.* 14 Nov. 1947. He *d.* 17 May 1951.'
line 9, line to read as follows

II. 1951. 2. CHRISTOPHER BROMHEAD (BIRDWOOD), BARON BIRDWOOD, only s. and h., *b.* 22 May 1899,

line 19, delete ']' and replace by 'This marriage was diss. by divorce in 1953 and he *m.* 2ndly, 22 Feb. 1954, Joan Pollock, da. of Christopher Norman GRAHAM. He *d.* 5 Jan. 1962. His widow was living 1995.'

III. 1962. 3. MARK WILLIAM OGILVIE (BIRDWOOD), BARON BIRDWOOD, only s. and h., *b.* 23 Nov. 1938; ed. at Radley and Cambridge (Trin. Coll.); *m.*, 21 July 1956, Judith Helen, 1st da. of Reginald Godon Seymour ROBERTS of Newton Aycliffe, co. Durham.

BRASSEY OF APETHORPE

page 601,
line 18, after 'Surrey' add 'She *d.* 19 Nov. 1946. He *d.* 22 Oct. 1958.'
line 23, after 'LONSDALE' add 'She *d.* 19 Nov. 1946. He *d. v.p. s.p.* 11 Sep. 1949.'

II. 1958. 2. BERNARD THOMAS (BRASSEY), BARON BRASSEY OF APETHORPE, and a Baronet, 5th but 1st surv. s. and h., *b.* 15 Feb. 1905; ed. at Eton; *m.* 1stly, 14 Apr. 1931, Crystal Gloria, yr. da. of Lieut. Col. Francis William George GORE. She *d.* 15 Mar. 1962 and he *m.* 2ndly, 4 Apr. 1963, Barbara, yr. da. of Leonard JORGENSON of West Tytherley, Hants. and formerly wife of Lieut. Col. Herbert Campbell WESTMORLAND. He *d.* 28 June 1967. His widow was living 1995.

III. 1967. 3. DAVID HENRY (BRASSEY), BARON BRASSEY OF APETHORPE, &c., 1st s. and h., *b.* 16 Sep. 1932; ed. at Stowe; *m.* 1stly, 15 Oct. 1958, Myrna Elizabeth, da. of Lieut. Col. John BASKERVYLE-GLEGG of Withington Hall. Cheshire. She *d.* 1974 and he *m.* 2ndly, 1978, Caroline, da. of Lieut. Col. Godfrey Ariel EVILL.

[EDWARD BRASSEY, s. and h. ap. by 1st wife, *b.* 9 Mar. 1964.]

note (2), line 3, after '1918' add 'The 4th s., John Leonard Brassey, was *b.* and *d.* in 1903.'

BELSTEAD

page 602,
line 17, after 'RIDLEY' add 'He *d.* 15 Aug. 1958. His widow *d.* 23 Feb. 1962.'
lines 18–19, delete all detail and replace as follows

II. 1958. 2. JOHN JULIAN (GANZONI), BARON BELSTEAD and a Baronet, only s. and h., *b.* 30 Sep. 1932, at Ipswich; ed. at Eton and Oxford (Ch. Ch.).

PERRY

page 603,
line 18, after 'Hull' add 'He *d. s.p.* 17 June 1956 when his Barony became *extinct*. His widow *d.* 19 Dec. 1956.'

PORTER

page 604,
line 13, after '1938' add 'He was *cr.* G.B.E., 1951 and *d.* unm. 13 Feb. 1956 when his life Barony became *extinct*.

STAMP

page 606,
line 8, after 'LIGHT' add 'Lord and Lady Stamp both *d.* 16/17 Apr. 1941, as the result of enemy action.'
line 9, line to read as follows

II. 1941. 2. WILFRED CARLYLE (STAMP), BARON STAMP, 1st s. and h., *b.* 28 Oct. 1904,

line 12, delete ']' and replace by 'He *d. s.p.m.* 16/17 Apr. 1941, as the result of enemy action (see above).(4)'

III. 1941. 3. TREVOR CHARLES (STAMP), BARON STAMP, brother and h., *b.* 13 Feb. 1907; ed. at Leys Sch., Cambridge (Gonville and Caius Coll.) and St. Bartholomew's Hosp.; *m.*, 5 Apr. 1932, Frances Dawes, da. of Charles Henry BOSWORTH of Evanston, Illinois, U.S.A. He *d.* 16 Nov. 1987. His widow was living 1995.

IV. 1987. 4. TREVOR CHARLES BOSWORTH (STAMP), BARON STAMP, s. and h., *b.* 18 Sep. 1935; ed. at Leys Sch., Cambridge (Gonville and Caius Coll.), Yale Univ. and St. Mary's Hosp.; *m.* 1stly, 21 Mar. 1963, Anne Carolyn, da. of John Kenneth CHURCHILL of Tunbridge Wells, co. Kent. This marriage was diss. by divorce in 1971 and he *m.* 2ndly, 1975, Carol Anne, da. of Robert Keith RUSSELL of Farnham, Surrey.

[NICHOLAS CHARLES TREVOR STAMP, s. and h. ap. by 2nd wife, *b.* 1978.]

(4) He died as a result of the same enemy action as his father and mother, and it was decided, 10 Sep. 1941, by the Committee for Privileges, that he had momentarily *suc.* his father. This was by analogy with the Law of Property Act, 1925, which, although it did not specifically apply to peerages, provides that where two people die in circumstances making it uncertain which of them has died first, then it shall be presumed that the elder did so. See *The Times*, 11 Sep. and 1 Oct. 1941. This decision was approved by H.M. King George VI.

BICESTER

page 607,
line 16, after 'GREY' add 'He *d.* 17 Feb. 1956. His widow *d.* 16 Apr. 1959.'
line 17, line to read as follows

II. 1956. 2. RANDALL HUGH VIVIAN (SMITH), BARON BICESTER, 1st s. and h., *b.* 9 Jan. 1898,

line 22, for ']' read 'He was *k.* in a motor accident, *s.p.m.* 15 Jan. 1968. His widow *d.* 1947.'

III. 1968. 3. ANGUS EDWARD VIVIAN (SMITH), BARON BICESTER, nephew and h., being the 2nd but 1st surv. s. and h. of Lieut. Col. Stephen Edward Vivian SMITH, 2nd s. of the 1st Baron (*d.* 9 June 1952), by his 1st wife Elenor Anderson, da. of Edward Shepard HEWITT of New York City. He was *b.* 20 Feb. 1932; ed. at Eton.

APPENDIXES

APPENDIX A

page 609,
line 4, after '727' add '*cf.* "An Ancestor of Lord Nuffield", *N&Q*, vol. 194, 1949, pp. 553–4.'

PEERAGES OF 1939

1 FEBRUARY

FAIRFIELD

BARONY. I. 1939 1. The Right Hon. SIR FREDERICK ARTHUR GREER, s. of Arthur GREER, of Liverpool, and of Ballasalla, Isle of Man, was *b.* 1 Oct. 1863. He was *cr.*, 1 Feb. 1939, BARON FAIRFIELD, of Caldy, co. Chester. He *m.* 1stly, 17 Aug. 1901, Katherine, da. of Emanuel VAN NOORDEN of Orangebury, South Carolina, U.S.A. She *d.* 19 Mar. 1937 and he *m.* 2ndly, Mabel Lily, da. of W.J. FRASER and widow of C.W. NEELE. He *d. s.p.m.* 4 Feb. 1945, when his Barony became *extinct*. His widow *d.* 1 June 1960.

2 FEBRUARY

MILFORD

BARONY. I. 1939. 1. SIR LAURENCE RICHARD PHILIPPS, 1st Bart. [1919], yr. br. of John Wynford, 1st VISCOUNT ST. DAVIDS, and of Owen Cosby, 1st BARON KYLSANT, 6th and yst. s. of the Rev. Sir James Erasmus PHILIPPS, 12th Bart., of Picton, co. Pembroke, was *b.* 24 Jan. 1874; ed. at Felsted and Royal Sch. of Mines. He was *cr.*, 2 Feb. 1939, BARON MILFORD,(1) of Llanstephan, co. Radnor. He *m.*, 10 Apr. 1901, Ethel Georgina, da. of Rev. Benjamin SPEKE. He *d.* 7 Dec. 1962. His widow *d.* 1971.

II. 1962. 2. WOGAN (PHILIPPS), BARON MILFORD, also a Baronet, 1st s. and h., *b.* 25 Feb. 1902; ed. at Eton and Oxford (Magdalen Coll.); *m.* 1stly, 21 Nov. 1928, Rosamund Nina, da. of Rudolph Chambers LEHMAN. This marriage was diss. by divorce in 1944 and he *m.* 2ndly, 17 Jan. 1944, Cristina, da. of MARQUESS CASATI of Rome and formerly wife of Frances John Clarence Westenra Plantagenet (HASTINGS), 15th EARL OF HUNTINGDON. She *d.* 22 Mar. 1953 and he *m.* 3rdly, 20 May 1954, Tamara, da. of (__) KRAVET and widow of William RUST. He *d.* 30 Nov. 1993. His widow was living 1995.

III. 1993. 3. HUGO JOHN LAWRENCE (PHILIPPS), BARON MILFORD, only s. and h., *b.* 27 Aug. 1929; ed. at Eton and Cambridge (King's Coll.); *m.* 1stly, 7 Sep. 1951, Margaret, da. of Ralph HEATHCOTE, Capt., R.N. This marriage was diss. by divorce in 1958 and he *m.* 2ndly, 11 July 1959, Mary, twin da. of Roger Mellor (MAKINS), 1st BARON SHERFIELD. This marriage was in turn diss. by divorce in 1984 and he *m.* 3rdly, 1989, Felicity (Mrs LEACH), da. of Murray BALLANTYNE, of Montreal, Canada.

[GUY WOGAN PHILIPPS, 1st s. and h. ap. by 2nd wife, *b.* 25 July 1961; ed. at Eton and Oxford (Magdalen Coll.); *m.*, 1988, Rebecca, yr. da. of Nigel NICOLSON of Sissinghurst Castle, Cranbrook, Kent.]

note (1) Two of his collateral ancestors had held similar titles. (i) Sir Richard Philipps, 7th Bart., was *cr.*, 22 July 1776, Baron Milford in Ireland [I.] and *d. s.p.* 28 Nov. 1823. (ii) Sir Richard Bulkeley Philipps Grant Philipps, *formerly* Grant, 1st Bart., cousin and testamentary h. of the above, was *cr.*, 21 Sep. 1847, Baron Milford of Picton Castle, co. Pembroke, and *d. s.p.* 3 Jan. 1857. See those titles in vol. viii.

3 FEBRUARY

HANKEY

BARONY. I. 1939. 1. SIR MAURICE PASCHAL ALERS HANKEY, G.C.B., G.C.M.G., G.C.V.C., 3rd s. of Robert Alers HANKEY, of Chesham Place, Brighton, was *b.* 1 Apr. 1877; ed. at Rugby and R.N.C., Greenwich. He was *cr.*, 3 Feb. 1939, BARON HANKEY, of The Chart, co. Surrey. He *m.*, 16 Sep. 1903, Adeline Hermine Gertrude Ernestine, da. of Abraham DE SMIDT of Limpsfield, co. Surrey. He *d.* 25 Jan. 1963. His widow *d.* 1979.

II. 1963. 2. ROBERT MAURICE ALERS (HANKEY), BARON HANKEY, 1st s. and h., *b.* 4 July 1905; ed. at Rugby and Oxford (New Coll.); *m.* 1stly, 27 Sep. 1930, Frances Beryl, 1st da. of Walter Erskine STUART-MENTETH. She *d.* 31 Dec. 1957 and he *m.* 2ndly, 2 Oct. 1962, Joanna Riddall, da. of Rev. James Johnston WRIGHT of co. Perth. She *d.* 1991. He *m.* 3rdly, 1992, Stephanie S. (Mrs LANGLEY), da. of Brig. Percy Paulet KING.

[DONALD ROBIN ALERS PHILIPPS, 1st s. and h. ap. by 1st wife, *b.* 12 June 1938; ed. at Rugby and London (Univ. Coll.); *m.* 1stly, 14 Dec. 1963, Margaretha, yr. da. Henrik THORNDAHL of Copenhagen. This marriage was diss. by divorce in 1974. He *m.* 2ndly, 1974, Eileen Désirée, yr. da. of Maj. Gen. Stuart Hedley Molesworth BATTYE of Ascot.]

4 FEBRUARY

HARMSWORTH

BARONY. I. 1939. 1. CECIL BISSHOPP HARMSWORTH, yr. br. of Alfred Charles William, 1st VISCOUNT NORTHCLIFFE, and of Harold Sidney, 1st VISCOUNT ROTHERMERE, 3rd s. of Alfred HARMSWORTH, Barrister of the Middle Temple, was *b.* 28 Sep. 1869; ed. at Trin. Coll., Dublin. He was *cr.*, 4 Feb. 1939, BARON HARMSWORTH, of Egham, co. Surrey. He *m.*, 28 Apr. 1897, Emile Alberta, 4th da. of William Hamilton MAFFETT of St. Helena, Finglas, co. Dublin. She *d.* 4 May 1942. He *d.* 13 Aug. 1948.

[CECIL ALFRED HAMILTON HARMSWORTH, 1st s. and h. ap., *b.* 20 Mar. 1898, *d. v.p.* an infant 8 Feb. 1899.]

II. 1948. 2. CECIL DESMOND BERNARD (HARMSWORTH), BARON HARMSWORTH, 2nd but 1st surv. s. and h., was *b.* 19 Aug. 1903; ed. at Eton and Oxford (Ch. Ch.); *m.*, 10 Dec. 1926, Dorothy Alexander, da. of Joseph Charles HEINLEIN of Bridgeport, Ohio, U.S.A. He *d.* 2 June 1990. His widow *d.* 1990.

III. 1990. 3. THOMAS HAROLD RAYMOND (HARMSWORTH), BARON HARMSWORTH, nephew and h., being s. and h. of Eric Beauchamp Northcliffe HARMSWORTH, 3rd and yst. s. of 1st Baron Harmsworth by his 1st wife Hélène Marie (who *d.* 21 June 1962), 1st da. of Col. Jules Raymond DEHOVE of Paris. He was *b.* 20 July 1939; ed. at Eton and Oxford (Ch. Ch.); *m.*, 1971, Patricia Palmer, da. of Michael Palmer HORSLEY of Brough, co. York.

[DOMINIC MICHAEL ERIC HARMSWORTH, 1st s. and h. ap., *b.* 18 Sep. 1973; ed. at Eton.]

4 JULY

BROOKE OF OAKLEY

BARONY. I. 1939. 1. SIR ARTHUR RICHARD DE CAPELL BROOKE, 5th Bart. [1803], 1st s. and h. of Sir Richard Lewis de Capell BROOKE, 4th Bart. (*d.* 3 Feb. 1892), of Oakley, co. Northampton, was *b.* 12 Oct. 1869. He was *cr.*, 4 July 1939, BARON BROOKE OF OAKLEY, of Oakley, co. Northampton. He *m.*, 1897, Fanny Cecil Talbot, da. of Capt. Duncan MCNEILL of Colonsay, co. Argyll. She *d.* 1 Nov. 1942. He *d. s.p.* 17 Nov. 1944, when his Barony became *extinct*, but the Baronetcy passed to his br. and h.

5 JULY

ROTHERWICK

BARONY. I. 1939. 1. SIR HERBERT ROBIN CAYZER, 1st Bart. [1924], 5th s. of Sir Charles William CAYZER, 1st Bart., of Gartmore, co. Perth, was *b.* July 1881; ed. at Rugby. He was *cr.*, 5 July 1939, BARON ROTHERWICK, of Tylney, co. Southampton. He *m*, 18 Jan. 1911, Freda Penelope, 4th da. of Col. William Hans RATHBOURNE of Scripplestown and Kilcory, co. Cavan. He *d.* 17 Mar. 1958. His widow *d.* 11 Feb. 1961.

II. 1958. 2. HERBERT ROBIN (CAYZER), BARON ROTHERWICK, also a Baronet, 1st s. and h., was b. 5 Dec. 1912; ed. at Eton and Oxford (Ch. Ch.); *m.*, 4 Apr. 1952, Sarah Jane, da. of Sir Michael Nial SLADE, Bart. She *d.* 1978.

[HERBERT ROBIN CAYZER, 1st s. and h. ap., *b.* 12 Mar. 1954; *m.*, 1982, Sara Jane, da. of Robert James MCALPINE of Tarporley, Cheshire.]

6 JULY

ENNISDALE

BARONY. I. 1939. 1. SIR HENRY EDWARD LYONS, 1st Bart. [1937], O.B.E., s. of John Edward LYONS, of Ennis, co. Clare, was *b.* 29 Aug. 1878. He was *cr.*, 6 July 1939, BARON ENNISDALE, of Grateley, co. Southampton. He *m.*, 17 Jan. 1905, Helen, da. of Frank BISHOP. He *d. s.p.* 17 Aug. 1963 when his title became *extinct*.

7 JULY

WOOLTON

BARONY. I. } 1939
VISCOUNTCY. I. } 1953
EARLDOM. I. } 1956

1. SIR FREDERICK JAMES MARQUIS, only s. of Thomas Robert MARQUIS, of Tarnbrick, Beech Lane, Liverpool, was *b.* 24 Aug. 1883; ed. at Manchester Gram. Sch. and Manchester Univ. He was *cr.*, 7 July 1939, BARON WOOLTON, of Liverpool, co. Lancaster. He was further *cr.*, 2 July 1953, VISCOUNT WOOLTON of Liverpool, co. Lancaster; and, 9

Jan. 1956, VISCOUNT WARBLETON, of Warbleton, co. Sussex, and EARL OF WOOLTON. He *m.* 1stly, 10 Oct. 1912, Maud, yr. da. of Thomas SMITH of Manchester. She *d.* 13 Sep. 1961 and he *m.* 2ndly, 19 Oct. 1962, Margaret Eluned, da. of Richard Thomas of North Wales. He *d.* 14 Dec. 1964. His widow *d.* 1983.

II. 1964. 2. ROGER DAVID (MARQUIS), EARL OF WOOLTON, &c., only s. and h., *b.* 16 July 1922; ed. at Rugby and Cambridge (Trin. Coll.); *m.* 1stly, 9 Nov. 1946, Lucia Edith, da. of Edward Frederick (LAWSON), 4th BARON BURNHAM. This marriage was diss. by divorce in 1953 and he *m.* 2ndly, 25 June 1957, Cecily Josephine, 1st da. of Major Sir Alexander Penrose GORDON-CUMMING, Bart., M.C. He *d.* 7 Jan. 1969. His widow married twice more, and was living 1995.

III. 1969. 3. SIMON FREDERICK (MARQUIS), EARL OF WOOLTON, &c., only s. and h., *b.* 24 May 1958; *m.*, 1987, Sophie Frederika, da. of Mark William Ogilvie (BIRDWOOD), 3rd BARON BIRDWOOD.

8 JULY

GLENTORAN

BARONY. I. 1939. 1. The Right Hon. HERBERT DIXON, O.B.E., 4th s. of the Right Hon. Sir Daniel DIXON, 1st Bart., of Ballymenoch, co. Down, was *b.* 23 Jan. 1880; ed. at Rugby and R.M.C., Sandhurst. He was *cr.*, 8 July 1939, BARON GLENTORAN, of Ballyalloly, co. Down. He *m.*, 25 Nov. 1905, Emily Ina Florence da. of John George Barry (BINGHAM), 5th BARON CLANMORRIS He *d.* 20 July 1950. His widow *d.* 25 Apr. 1957.

II. 1950. 2. DANIEL STEWART THOMAS BINGHAM (DIXON), BARON GLENTORAN, only s. and h., was *b.* 19 Jan. 1912; ed. at Eton and R.M.C., Sandhurst; *m.*, 20 July 1933, Lady Diana Mary, 1st da. of Henry Arthur Mornington (WELLESLEY), 3rd EARL COWLEY. She *d.* 1984.

[THOMAS ROBIN VALERIAN DIXON, 1st s. and h. ap., *b.* 21 Apr. 1935; ed. at Eton; *m.* 1stly, 12 Jan. 1959, Rona, da. of Capt. George COLVILLE of Bishop's Waltham, Hants. This marriage was diss. by divorce 1975 and he *m.* 2ndly, 1979, Alwyn, da. of Hubert A. MASON of Grove Lodge, Donaghadee, co. Down. He *m.* 3rdly, 1990, Mrs Margaret RAINEY.]

6 SEPTEMBER

CALDECOTE

VISCOUNTCY. I. 1939. The Right Hon. SIR THOMAS WALKER HOBART INSKIP, C.B.E., Lord Chancellor of Great Britain, 1939–40, 2nd s. of James INSKIP, Solicitor, of Clifton Park House, Bristol, was *b.* 5 Mar. 1876; ed. at Clifton and Cambridge (King's Coll.). He was *cr.*, 6 Sep. 1939, VISCOUNT CALDECOTE, of Bristol, co. Gloucester. He *m.*, 30 July 1914, Lady Augusta Helen Elizabeth, da. of David (BOYLE), 7th EARL OF GLASGOW and widow of Charles Lindsay ORR-EWING, M.P. He *d.* 11 Oct. 1947. His widow *d.* 12 May 1967.

II. 1947. 2. ROBERT ANDREW (INSKIP), VISCOUNT CALDECOTE, only s. and h., was *b.* 8 Oct. 1917; ed. at Eton and Cambridge (King's Coll.); *m.*, 22 July 1942, Jean Hamilton, da. of Rear Adm. Hugh Dundas HAMILTON of Haddenham, co. Buckingham.

[PIERS JAMES HAMPDEN INSKIP, s. and h. ap., *b.* 20 May 1947; ed. at Eton; *m.* 1stly, 1970, Susan Bridget, da. of W.P. MELLEN of Great Sampford, Essex. This marriage was diss. by divorce and he *m.* 2ndly, 1984, Kristine Elizabeth, da. of Harvey HOLBROOKE-JACKSON of Ramsey, co. Cambridge.]

22 SEPTEMBER

MAUGHAM

VISCOUNTCY. I. 1939. 1. FREDERIC HERBERT (MAUGHAM), 1st BARON MAUGHAM [Barony for Life 1935], was further *cr.*, 22 Sep. 1939, VISCOUNT MAUGHAM, of Hartfield, co. Sussex, He *d.* 23 Mar. 1958, when his life Barony became *extinct*. For fuller particulars of him see vol. xiii, p. 556.

II. 1958. 2. ROBERT CECIL ROMER (MAUGHAM), VISCOUNT MAUGHAM, only s. and h., was *b.* 17 May 1916; ed. at Eton and Cambridge (Trin. Hall.). He *d.* unm. and *s.p.* 13 Mar. 1981 when his peerage became *extinct*.

PEERAGES OF 1940

18 APRIL

TRYON

BARONY. I. 1940. 1. The Right Hon. GEORGE CLEMENT TRYON, only s. of Vice-Adm. Sir George TRYON, K.C.B., R.N. (who was drowned in his Flagship *Victoria*, while comdg. the Mediterranean Fleet, 22 June 1893), was *b.* 15 May 1871; ed. at Eton and R.M.C., Sandhurst. He was *cr.*, 18 Apr. 1940, BARON TRYON, of Durnford, co. Wilts. He *m.*, 28 Feb. 1905, Averil, da. of Henry Hussey (VIVIAN), 1st BARON SWANSEA He *d.* 24 Nov. 1940. His widow *d.* 1 Feb. 1959.

II. 1940. 2. CHARLES GEORGE VIVIAN (TRYON), BARON TRYON, 1st s. and h., was *b.* 24 May 1906; ed. at Eton and R.M.C., Sandhurst; *m.*, 3 Aug. 1939, Etheldreda Josephine, da. of Lieut. Col. Sir Merrick Raymond BURNELL, Bart. He *d.* 9 Nov. 1976. His widow was still living 1995.

III. 1976. 3. ANTHONY GEORGE MERRIK (TRYON), BARON TRYON, only s. and h., *b.* 26 May 1940; ed. at Eton; *m.*, 1973, Dale Elizabeth, 1st da. of Barry HARPER of Melbourne, Victoria, Australia.

[CHARLES GEORGE BARRINGTON TRYON, 1st s. and h. ap., *b.* 15 May 1976.]

20 MAY

SIMON

VISCOUNTCY. I. 1940. 1. The Right Hon. SIR JOHN ALSEBROOK SIMON, G.C.S.I., G.C.V.O., O.B.E., Lord Chancellor of Great Britain, 1940–5, only s. of the Rev. Edwin

SIMON, Congregational Minister, of Bath, was *b.* 28 Feb. 1873; ed. at Fettes Coll., Edinburgh and Oxford (Wadham Coll.). He was *cr.*, 20 May 1940, VISCOUNT SIMON, of Stackpole Elidor, co. Pembroke. He *m.* 1stly, 24 May 1899, Ethel Mary, da. of Gilbert VENABLES. She *d.* 12 Sep. 1902 and he *m.* 2ndly, 18 Dec. 1917, Kathleen, da. of Francis Eugene HARVEY of Wexford and widow of Thomas MANNING, M.D. He *d.* 11 Jan. 1954. His widow *d.* 27 Mar. 1955.

II. 1954. 2. JOHN GILBERT (SIMON), VISCOUNT SIMON, only s. and h., was *b.* 2 Sep. 1902; ed. at Winchester and Oxford (Balliol Coll.); *m.*, 22 Dec. 1930, James Christie, da. of William Stanley HUNT. He *d.* 5 Dec. 1993. His widow was living 1995.

III. 1993. 3. JAN DAVID (SIMON), VISCOUNT SIMON, only s. and h., *b.* 20 July 1940; ed. at Westminster, Southampton Univ. and Sydney Univ.; *m.*, 1969, Mary Elizabeth, da. of Joseph BURNS of Sydney, New South Wales, Australia.

28 MAY

CROFT

BARONY. I. 1940. 1. Brig-Gen. SIR HENRY PAGE CROFT, 1st Bart [1924], C.M.G., T.D., yr. s. of Lieut. Richard Benyon CROFT, R.N., of Fanhams Hall, Ware, was *b.* 22 June 1881; ed. at Eton, Shrewsbury and Cambridge (Trin. Hall.). He was *cr.*, 28 May 1940, BARON CROFT, of Bournemouth, co. Southampton. He *m.*, 10 July 1907, Nancy Beatrice, yst. da. of Robert Hudson (BORWICK), 1st BARON BORWICK. He *d.* 7 Dec. 1947. His widow *d.* 24 Jan. 1949.

II. 1947. 2. MICHAEL HENRY GLENDOWER PAGE (CROFT) BARON CROFT, also a Baronet, only s. and h., was *b.* 20 Aug. 1916; ed. at Eton and Cambridge (Trin. Hall); *m.*, 30 Oct. 1948, Lady Antoinette Fredericka, da. of Frederick William Burton (CONYNGHAM), 6th MARQUIS CONYNGHAM. She *d.* 15 June 1959.

[BERNARD WILLIAM HENRY PAGE CROFT, s. and h. ap., *b.* 28 Aug. 1949; ed. at Stowe and Univ. of Wales.]

26 JUNE

ABERTAY

BARONY. I. 1940, June to Dec. 1. SIR CHARLES COUPAR BARRIE, K.B.E., 1st s. of Sir Charles BARRIE, of Airlie Park, Broughty Ferry, was *b.* 1875; ed. at Blairlodge Sch., Polmont, co. Stirling. He was *cr.*, 26 June 1940, BARON ABERTAY, of Tullybelton, co. Perth. He *m.*, 1 June 1926, Ethel, da. of Sir James Thomson BROOM. He *d. s.p.m.* 6 Dec. 1940, when his Barony became *extinct*.

27 JUNE

TEVIOT

BARONY. I. 1940. 1. CHARLES IAIN KERR, D.S.O., M.C., 1st s. of Charles William Rudolph KERR (who *d. v.p.* 7 Feb. 1894; grandson of William, 6th Marquess of Lothian [S.]), was *b.* 3 May 1874. He was *cr.*, 27 June 1940, BARON TEVIOT, of Burghclere, co. Southampton. He *m.* 1stly, 24 Jan. 1911, Muriel Constance, da. of William Gordon CANNING of Hartpury, co. Gloucester. This marriage was diss. by divorce in 1930 and he *m.* 2ndly, 31 July 1930, Florence Angela, 1st da. of Lieut. Col. Charles Walter VILLIERS, C.B.E., D.S.O. He *d.* 7 Jan. 1968. His widow *d.* 1979.

II. 1968. 2. CHARLES JOHN (KERR), BARON TEVIOT, only s. and h., *b.* 16 Dec. 1934; ed. at Eton; *m.*, 25 Sep. 1965, Mary, da. of Alexander HARRIS.

[CHARLES ROBERT KERR, s. and h. ap., *b.* 19 Sep. 1971.]

28 JUNE

NATHAN

BARONY. I. 1940. 1. HARRY LOUIS NATHAN, s. of Michael Henry NATHAN, of Manchester and London, was *b.* 2 Feb. 1889; ed. at St. Paul's Sch. He was *cr.*, 28 June 1940, BARON NATHAN, of Churt, co. Surrey. He *m.*, 27 Mar. 1919, Eleanor Joan Clara, da. of Carl STETTAUER. He *d.* 6 June 1972. His widow *d.* 1972.

II. 1972. 2. ROGER CAROL MICHAEL (NATHAN), BARON NATHAN, only s. and h., *b.* 5 Dec. 1922; ed. at Stowe and Oxford (New Coll.); *m.*, 14 Nov. 1950, Philippa Gertrude, 1st da. of Major Joseph Bernard SOLOMON of the Old Poorhouse, Sutton End, Pulborough, Sussex.

[RUPERT HENRY BERNARD NATHAN, s. and h. p., *b.* 26 May 1957; ed. at Charterhouse and Durham Univ.; *m.*, 1987, Ann, da. of A.S. HEWITT of Aldingbourne, Chichester, Sussex.]

21 OCTOBER

REITH

BARONY. I. 1940. 1. The Right Hon. SIR JOHN CHARLES WALSHAM REITH, G.C.V.O., G.B.E., 5th s. of the Very Rev. George REITH, D.D., of Glasgow, was *b.* 20 July 1889; ed. at Glasgow Acad. and Royal Tech. Coll., Glasgow. He was *cr.*, 21 October 1940, BARON REITH, of Stonehaven, co. Kincardine. He *m.*, 14 July 1921, Muriel Katharine, yr. da. of John Lynch ODHAMS. He *d.* 16 June 1971. His widow *d.* 1977.

II. 1971. 2. CHRISTOPHER JOHN (REITH), BARON REITH, only s. and h., *b.* 27 May 1928; ed. at Eton and Oxford (Worcester Coll.). He disclaimed, 21 Apr. 1972, his peerage for life under the Peerage Act, 1963. He *m.*, 28 May 1969, Penelope Margaret Ann, 1st da. of Henry Rowland MORRIS of Beeston. co. Nottingham.

[JAMES HARRY JOHN REITH, s. and h. ap., *b.* 2 June 1971.]

1 NOVEMBER

HEWART

VISCOUNTCY. I. 1940. 1. GORDON (HEWART) 1st BARON HEWART [1922], was further *cr.*, 1 Nov. 1940, VISCOUNT HEWART, of Bury, co. Lancaster. He *d.* 5 May 1943. For further particulars of him see vol. xiii, p. 371.

II. 1940. 2. HUGH VAUGHAN (HEWART), VISCOUNT HEWART [1940] and BARON HEWART [1922], only s. and h., was *b.* 11 Nov. 1896. For further detail see corrections *sub* HEWART, vol. xiii, p. 371.

PEERAGES OF 1941

9 JANUARY

SELBORNE

The Right Hon. ROUNDELL CECIL PALMER, *styled* VISCOUNT WOLMER, 1st s. and h. ap. of William Waldegrave (PALMER), 2nd EARL OF SELBORNE, was sum. to Parl. *v.p.* in his father's Barony as LORD SELBORNE, 9 Jan. 1941, taking his seat, 22 Jan. follg. He *suc.* his said father as EARL OF SELBORNE, 26 Feb. 1942. See that title in vol. xi.

20 JANUARY

CAMROSE

VISCOUNTCY. I. 1941. 1. WILLIAM EWERT (BERRY), 1st BARON CAMROSE [1929], also a Baronet [1921], was further *cr.*, 20 Jan. 1941, VISCOUNT CAMROSE, of Hackwood Park, co. Southampton. He *d.* 15 June 1954. For fuller particulars of him see vol. xiii, p. 463.

II. 1954. 2. JOHN SEYMOUR THOMAS (BERRY), VISCOUNT CAMROSE [1941] and Baron Camrose [1929], also a Baronet, was *b.* 12 July 1909. He was ed. at Eton and Oxford (Ch. Ch.); He *m.* 1986, Joan, 1st da. of John Reginald Lopes (YARDE-BULLER), 3rd BARON CHURSTON and formerly wife 1stly of Wing Cmdr. Thomas Loel Evelyn Bulkeley GUINNESS, and 2ndly of PRINCE ALY KHAN.

21 JANUARY

CECIL

The Right Hon. ROBERT ARTHUR JAMES GASCOYNE-CECIL, *styled* VISCOUNT CRANBORNE, s. and h. ap. of James Edward Hubert (GASCOYNE-CECIL), 4th MARQUESS OF SALISBURY, was sum. to Parl. *v.p.* in his father's Barony as LORD CECIL, 21 Jan. 1941, taking his seat, 22 Jan. follg. He *suc.* his said father as MARQUESS OF SALISBURY, 4 Apr. 1947. See that title in vol. xi.

25 JANUARY

QUICKSWOOD

BARONY. I. 1941. 1. The Right Hon. LORD HUGH RICHARD HEATHCOTE GASCOYNE-CECIL, 5th s. of Robert Arthur Talbot (GASCOYNE-CECIL), 3rd MARQUESS OF SALISBURY, was *b.* 14 Oct. 1869; ed. at Eton and Oxford

(Univ. Coll.). He was *cr.*, 25 Jan. 1941, BARON QUICKSWOOD, of Clothall, co. Hertford. He *d.* unm. 10 Dec. 1956, when his Barony became *extinct*.

27 JANUARY

MERRIMAN

BARONY. I. 1941. 1. The Right Hon. SIR FRANK BOYD MERRIMAN, O.B.E., Pres. of the Probate, Divorce and Admiralty Div. of the High Court of Justice from 1933, 1st s. of Frank MERRIMAN, of Hollingford House, Knutsford, co. Chester, was *b.* 28 Apr. 1880; ed. at Winchester. He was *cr.*, 27 Jan. 1941, BARON MERRIMAN, of Knutsford, co. Chester. He *m.* 1stly, 11 Sep. 1907, Eva May, da. of Rev. H.C. FREER. She *d.* 1 May 1919 and he *m.* 2ndly, 18 Dec. 1920, Olive McLaren, da. of F.W. CARVER. She *d.* 14 Mar. 1952 and he *m.* 3rdly, 1 Jan. 1953, Jane Lamb, da. of James STORMOUTH of Belfast. He *d. s.p.m.* 18 Jan. 1962 when his Barony becamr *extinct*. His widow was living 1995.

28 JANUARY

KINDERSLEY

BARONY. I. 1941. 1. SIR ROBERT MOLESWORTH KINDERSLEY, G.B.E., 2nd s. of Edward Nassau Molesworth KINDERSLEY, of Sherborne, Dorset, was *b.* 21 Nov. 1871; ed. at Repton. He was *cr.*, 28 Jan. 1941, BARON KINDERSLEY, of West Hoathly, co. Sussex. He *m.*, 3 Nov. 1896, Gladys Margaret, da. of Major Gen. James Princep BEADLE of Worton Grange, Wilts. He *d.* 20 July 1954. His widow *d.* 17 Jan. 1968.

[LIONEL NASSAU KINDERSLEY, 2nd Lieut., 15th Hussars, 1st s. and h. ap., *b.* 6 Aug. 1897. He *d.* unm. and *v.p.*, being *k.* in action in France, 24 Nov. 1917.]

II. 1954. 2. HUGH KENYON MOLESWORTH (KINDERSLEY), BARON KINDERSLEY, 2nd but 1st surv. s. and h., was *b.* 7 May 1899; ed. at Eton; *m.*, 12 Oct. 1921, Nancy Farnsworth, da. of Dr Geoffrey BOYD of Toronto, Canada. He *d.* 6 Oct. 1976. His widow *d.* 1977.

III. 1976. 3. ROBERT HUGH MOLESWORTH (KINDERSLEY), BARON KINDERSLEY, only s., *b.* 18 Aug. 1929; ed. at Eton and Oxford (Trin. Coll.); *m.* 1stly, 4 Sep. 1954, Venice Marigold Rosie, 1st da. of Lord Francis HILL of The White House, Ringmer, Sussex. This marriage was diss. by divorce in 1989 and he *m.* 2ndly, 1989, Patricia Margaret, only da. of Brig. Hugh Ronald NORMAN, D.S.O., of Kemsing, Kent and formerly wife of Henry Colum CHRICHTON-STUART.

[RUPERT JOHN MOLESWORTH, s. and h. ap. by 1st wife, *b.* 11 Mar. 1955; ed. at Eton; *m.*, 1975, Sarah Anne, da. of John D. WARDE.]

29 JANUARY

IRONSIDE

BARONY. I. 1941. 1. Field Marshal SIR WILLIAM EDMUND IRONSIDE, G.C.B., C.M.G., D.S.O., only s. of Surgeon-Major William IRONSIDE,

R.H.A., of Ironside, co. Aberdeen, was *b.* 6 May 1880; ed. at Tonbridge. He was *cr.*, 29 Jan. 1941, BARON IRONSIDE, of Archangel and Ironside, co. Aberdeen. He *m.*, 26 June 1915, Mariot Ysobel, da. of Charles CHEYNE. He *d.* 23 Sep. 1959. His widow *d.* 1984.

II. 1959. 2. EDMUND OSLAC (IRONSIDE), BARON IRONSIDE, only s. and h., was *b.* 21 Sep. 1924; ed. at Tonbridge; *m.*, 29 Apr. 1950, Audrey Marigold, yst. da. of Col. Thomas George Breadalbane MORGAN-GRENVILLE, D.S.O., M.C., of Wootton, co. Bedford.

[CHARLES EDMUND GRENVILLE IRONSIDE, s. and h. ap., *b.* 1 July 1956; *m.*, 1985, Elizabeth Mary, 1st da. of James Martin Bonar (LAW), 2nd BARON CHURSTON.]

19 MAY

LEATHERS

BARONY. I. 1941
VISCOUNTCY. I. 1954

1. FREDERICK JAMES LEATHERS, s. of Robert LEATHERS, of Stowmarket, Suffolk, was *b.* 21 Nov. 1883; ed. at Univs. of Birmingham and Leeds. He was *cr.*, 19 May 1941, BARON LEATHERS, of Purfleet, co. Essex; and was further *cr.*, 18 Jan. 1954. VISCOUNT LEATHERS, of Purfleet, co. Essex. He *m.*, 1 June 1907, Emily Ethel, da. of Henry BAXTER of Southend, Essex. He *d.* 19 Mar. 1965. His widow *d.* 1971.

II. 1965. 2. FREDERICK ALAN (LEATHERS), VISCOUNT LEATHERS, &c., 1st s. and h., was *b.* 4 Apr. 1908; ed. at Brighton Coll. and Cambridge (Emmanuel Coll.); *m.* 1stly, 22 June 1940, Elspeth Graeme, yr. da. of Sir Thomas Alexander STUART, K.C.S.I., K.C.I.E. This marriage was diss. by divorce in 1983 and he *m.* 2ndly, 1983, Lorna May, da. of A.K. MARSHALL and widow of Arthur A.C. BARNETT.

[CHRISTOPHER GRAEME LEATHERS, 1st s. and h. ap. by 1st wife, *b.* 31 Aug. 1941; ed. at Rugby; *m.*, 27 June 1964, Maria Philomena, yr. da. of Michael MERRIMAN of Charlestown, co. Mayo.]

3 JULY

VANSITTART

BARONY. I. 1941. 1. The Right Hon. SIR ROBERT GILBERT VANSITTART, G.C.B., G.C.M.G., M.V.O., 1st s. of Robert Arnold VANSITTART, M.B.E., F.R.C.S., of Foots Cray Place, Kent, was *b.* 25 June 1881; ed. at Eton. He was *cr.*, 3 July 1941, BARON VANSITTART, of Denham, co. Buckingham. He *m.* 1stly, 7 Sep. 1921, Gladys Robinson (Mrs DUFF), only da. of Glen W.C. HEPPENHEIMER of New Jersey, U.S.A. She *d.* 3 July 1928 and he *m.* 2ndly, 29 July 1931, Sarita ENRIQUETTA, da. of Herbert WARD of Paris and widow of Sir Colville Adrian de Rune BARCLAY, K.C.M.G. He *d. s.p.m.* 14 Feb. 1957, when his Barony became *extinct*.

4 JULY

CHERWELL

BARONY. I. 1941.
VISCOUNTCY. I. 1956.

1. FREDERICK ALEXANDER LINDEMANN, s. of Adolphus Frederick LINDEMANN, of Sidholme, Sidmouth, was *b.* 5 Apr. 1886. He was *cr.*, 4 July 1941, BARON CHERWELL, of Oxford, co. Oxford, and further *cr.*, 25 June 1956 VISCOUNT CHERWELL, of Oxford. He *d.* unm. 3 July 1957, when all his honours became *extinct.*

16 JULY

BENNETT

VISCOUNTCY. I. 1941.

1. The Right Hon. RICHARD BEDFORD BENNETT, 1st s. of Henry J. BENNETT, of Hopewell, New Brunswick, was *b.* 3 July 1870; ed. at Dalhousie Univ., Canada. He was *cr.*, 16 July 1941, VISCOUNT BENNETT, of Mickleham, co. Surrey, and of Calgary and Hopewell, in the Dominion of Canada. He *d.* unm. 27 June 1947, when his Viscountcy became *extinct.*

16 JULY

GREENE

BARONY. I. 1941.

1. The Right Hon. SIR WILFRED ARTHUR GREENE, O.B.E., Master of the Rolls, 1937–9, s. of Arthur Weguelin GREENE, of Beckenham, Kent, was *b.* 30 Dec. 1883; ed. at Westminster and Oxford (Ch. Ch.). He was *cr.*, 16 July 1941, BARON GREENE, of Holmbury St. Mary, co. Surrey. He *m.*, 28 May 1909, Nancy, da. of Francis WRIGHT of Nottingham. He *d. s.p.* 16 Apr. 1952, when his Barony became *extinct.*

6 AUGUST

SOULBURY

BARONY. I. 1941
VISCOUNTCY. I. 1954

1. The Right Hon. HERWALD RAMSBOTHAM, O.B.E., M.C., 1st s. of Herwald RAMSBOTHAM, of Crowborough Warren, Sussex, was *b.* 6 Mar. 1887; ed. at Uppingham and Oxford (Univ. Coll.). He was *cr.*, 6 Aug. 1941, BARON SOULBURY, of Soulbury, co. Buckingham; and was further *cr.*, 16 July 1954, VISCOUNT SOULBURY, of Soulbury, co. Buckingham. He *m.* 1stly, 11 Nov. 1911, Doris Violet, da. of Sigmund DE STEIN of Antwerp. She *d.* 20 Feb. 1954 and he *m.* 2ndly, 10 Nov. 1962, Ursula, da. of Armand JEROME and widow of Frederick WAKENHAM. She *d.* 12 Nov. 1964. He *d.* 30 Jan. 1971.

II. 1971.

2. JAMES HERWALD (RAMSBOTHAM), VISCOUNT SOULBURY, &c., 1st s. and h., was *b.* 21 Mar. 1915; ed. at Eton and Oxford (Magdalen Coll.); *m.*, 5 Apr. 1949, Anthea Margaret, da. of David WILTON. She *d.* 26 June 1950.

14 AUGUST

SHERWOOD

BARONY. I. 1941. 1. SIR HUGH MICHAEL SEELY, 3rd Bart. [1896], 2nd but 1st surv. s. and h. of Sir Charles Hilton SEELY, 2nd Bart., was *b.* 2 Oct. 1898; ed. at Eton. He was *cr.*, 14 Aug. 1941, BARON SHERWOOD, of Calverton, co. Nottingham. He *m.* 1stly, 23 Mar. 1942, Molly Patricia, da. of William Ewert (BERRY), 1st VISCOUNT CAMROSE and widow of Capt. Roger C.G. CHETWODE. This marriage was diss. by divorce in 1948 and he *m.* 2ndly, 16 Mar. 1970, Catherine Thornton, widow of John Osborne RANGER. He *d. s.p.* 1 Apr. 1970 when his Barony became *extinct* but he was *suc.* in his Baronetcy by his brother.

PEERAGES OF 1942

12 JANUARY

STANSGATE

VISCOUNTCY. I. 1942. 1. The Right Hon. WILLIAM WEDGWOOD BENN, D.S.C., D.F.C., 2nd s. of Sir John Williams BENN, 1st Bart., was *b.* 10 May 1877; ed. at Univ. Coll., London. He was *cr.*, 12 Jan. 1942, VISCOUNT STANSGATE, of Stansgate, co. Essex. He *m.*, 17 Nov. 1920, Margaret Eadie, da. of Daniel Turner HOLMERS. He *d.* 17 Nov. 1960. His widow *d.* 1991.

II. 1960. 2. ANTHONY NEIL WEDGWOOD (BENN), VISCOUNT STANSGATE, 1st s. and h., was *b.* 3 Apr. 1925; ed. at Westminster and Oxford (New Coll.); disclaimed, 31 July 1963, his peerage for life under the Peerage Act, 1963. He *m.*, 17 June 1949, Caroline Middleton, 1st da. of James Milton DE CAMP of Cincinnatti, Ohio, U.S.A.

[STEPHEN MICHAEL WEDGWOOD BENN, 1st s. and h. ap., *b.* 21 Aug. 1951; *m.*, 1988, Ishika Nita, da. of Stuart Ashley BOWES of Israel.]

16 JANUARY

LATHAM

BARONY. I. 1941. 1. CHARLES LATHAM, s. of George LATHAM, of Norwich, was *b.* 26 Dec. 1888. He was *cr.*, 16 Jan. 1942, BARON LATHAM, of Hendon, co. Middlesex. He *m.* 1stly, 14 June 1913, Maya Helen, da. of Louis George ALLMAN of Hendon. This marriage was diss. by divorce in 1957 and he *m.* 2ndly, 28 Mar. 1957, Sylvia May, da. of Alexander NEWMARK. He *d. s.p.m.s.* 31 Mar. 1970. His widow *d.* 1985.

[FRANCIS CHARLES ALLMAN LATHAM, s. and h. ap., *b.* 24 Jan. 1917; ed. at Dauntsey's Sch., Devizes; *m.* 1stly, July 1942, Margaret, da. of Ernest FULLER of Maidstone. She *d.* 28 Jan. 1944 and he *m.* 2ndly, Aug. 1944, Eleanor Roma, da. of Isadore ROSEMAN. This marriage was diss. by divorce in 1950 and he *m.* 3rdly, 1951, Gabrielle, da. of Dr S.M. O'RIORDAN. He *d. v.p.* Nov. 1959. His widow *d.* 1987.]

II. 1970. 2. DOMINIC CHARLES (LATHAM), BARON LATHAM, grandson and h., being 1st s. and h. of Francis Charles Allman LATHAM and Gabrielle, his 3rd wife, abovenamed. He was *b.* 20 Sep. 1954; ed. at New South Wales Univ.

21 JANUARY

WEDGWOOD

BARONY. I. 1942. 1. The Right Hon. JOSIAH CLEMENT WEDGWOOD, D.S.O., 3rd s. of Clement Francis WEDGWOOD, of Barlaston Lea, co. Stafford, Master Potter of Etruria, in that co., was *b.* 16 Mar. 1872; ed. at Clifton and R.N.C., Greenwich. He was *cr.*, 21 Jan. 1942, BARON WEDGWOOD, of Barlaston, co. Stafford. He *m.* 1stly, 3 July 1894, Ethel Kate, only da. of Charles Synge Christopher (BOWEN), BARON BOWEN (life peer, *cr.* 1882, see vol. ii above). This marriage was diss. by divorce in 1919 (she *d.* 26 Nov. 1952) and he *m.* 2ndly, 25 June 1919, Florence Ethel, da. of Edward Guy WILLETT. He *d.* 26 July 1943. His widow *d.* 1 July 1969.

II. 1943. 2. FRANCIS CHARLES BOWEN (WEDGWOOD), BARON WEDGWOOD, 1st s. and h., was *b.* 20 Jan. 1898; ed. at Bedales Sch. and Slade Sch. of Art. He *m.*, 28 May 1920, Edith May, da. of William TELFER of Glasgow. He *d.* 22 Apr. 1959. His widow *d.* 1977.

III. 1959. 3. HUGH EVERARD (WEDGWOOD), BARON WEDGWOOD, only s. and h. by 2nd wife, was *b.* 20 Apr. 1921; ed. at Bedales Sch. and Cambridge (Trin. Coll.); *m.* 20 Mar. 1945, Jean Annette Heather, only child of Ralph S. LEAKE of Bournemouth. This marriage was annulled in 1947 and he *m.* 2ndly, 5 Oct. 1949, Jane Weymouth, 2nd da. of William James POULTON of Kenya. He *d.* 18 Apr. 1970. His widow was living 1995.

IV. 1970. 4. PIERS ANTHONY WEYMOUTH (WEDGWOOD), BARON WEDGWOOD, only s. and h., was *b.* 20 Sep. 1954; ed. at Marlborough; *m.*, 1985, Mary Regina Margaret Kavanagh, da. of Edward QUINN of Philadelphia, U.S.A.

28 JANUARY

GEDDES

BARONY. I. 1942. 1. The Right Hon. SIR AUCKLAND CAMPBELL GEDDES, G.C.M.G., K.C.B., 2nd s. of Auckland Campbell GEDDES, C.I.E., of Edinburgh, was *b.* 21 June 1879; ed. at George Watson's Coll., Edinburgh and Univ. of Edinburgh. He was *cr.*, 28 Jan. 1942, BARON GEDDES, of Rolvenden, co. Kent. He *m.*, 8 Sep. 1906, Isabella Gamble, 3rd da. of William Adolphus ROSS of Staten Island, New York, U.S.A. She *d.* 8 Jan. 1917. He *d.* 8 Jan. 1954.

II. 1954. 2. ROSS CAMPBELL (GEDDES), BARON GEDDES, 1st s. and h., was *b.* 20 July 1907; ed. at Rugby and Cambridge (Gonville and Caius Coll.); *m.*, 26 Jan. 1931, Enid Mary, only child of Clarence Howell BUTLER of Tenterden, Kent. He *d.* 2 Feb. 1975. His widow was living 1995.

II. 1960. 3. EUAN MICHAEL ROSS (GEDDES), BARON GEDDES, 2nd but 1st surv. s.(1) and h., was *b.* 3 Sep. 1937; ed. at Rugby and Cambridge (Gonville and Caius Coll.); *m.*, 7 May 1966, Gillian, da. of William Arthur BUTLER of Henley on Thames, co. Oxford.

[JAMES GEORGE NEIL GEDDES, s. and h. ap., *b.*, 10 Sep. 1969.]

note (1) The 1st s. was *b.* 20 Sep. and *d.* 12 Oct. 1932.

4 FEBRUARY

WINSTER

BARONY. I. 1942. 1. REGINALD THOMAS HERBERT FLETCHER, 2nd but only surv. s. of Nicholas FLETCHER, of Rampholme, Windermere, Professor of Mathematics at the R.N.C., Greenwich, was *b.* 27 Mar. 1885. He was *cr.*, 4 Feb. 1942, BARON WINSTER, of Witherslack, co. Westmorland. He *m.*, 13 Oct. 1909, Elspeth, da. of Rev. H.J. LOMAX of Abbotswood, co. Gloucester. He *d. s.p.* 7 June 1961 when his Barony became *extinct*.

20 FEBRUARY

CLAUSON

BARONY. I. 1942. 1. The Right Hon. SIR ALBERT CHARLES CLAUSON, C.B.E., one of the Lords Justices of Appeal, 1938–42, yr s. of Charles Adhemar Roselli CLAUSON, was *b.* 14 Jan. 1870; ed. at Merchant Taylors' Sch. and Oxford (St. John's Coll.). He was *cr.*, 20 Feb. 1942, BARON CLAUSON, of Hawkshead, co. Hertford. He *m.*, 1902, Kate, da. of J.T. HOPWOOD of Lincoln's Inn and widow of Lucas THOMASSON. He *d. s.p.* 15 Mar. 1946, when his Barony became *extinct*.

9 MARCH

BRUNTISFIELD

BARONY. I. 1942. 1. SIR VICTOR ALEXANDER GEORGE ANTHONY WARRENDER, 8th Bart. [1715], M.C., s. and h. of Sir George John Scott WARRENDER, 7th Bart., was *b.* 23 June 1899; ed. at Eton. He was *cr.*, 9 Mar. 1942, BARON BRUNTISFIELD, of Boroughmuir, in the City of Edinburgh. He *m.* 1stly, 1 June 1920, Dorothy, da. of Col. Richard Hamilton RAWSON, M.P. This marriage was diss. by divorce in 1945 and he *m.* 2ndly, 22 June 1948, Tania Vjekoslava, yr. da. of Dr Michael KOLIN of Saint Jacob, Dubrovnik, Yugoslavia. He *d.* 14 Jan. 1993. His widow was living 1995.

II. 1993. 2. JOHN ROBERT (WARRENDER), BARON BRUNTISFIELD, 1st s. and h., *b.* 7 Feb. 1921; ed. at Eton and R.M.C., Sandhurst; *m.*, 15 Apr. 1948, Ann Moireen, 2nd da. of Lieut. Col. Sir Walter Fendall CAMPBELL. She *d.* 1976 and he *m.* 2ndly, 1977, Shirley, da. of J.L. ROSS and formerly wife of Jonathan James CRAWLEY. She *d.* 1981 and he *m.* 3rdly, 1985, Joanna Kathleen Campbell (Mrs GRAHAM).

[MICHAEL JOHN VICTOR WARRENDER, 1st s. and h. by 1st wife, *b.* 9 June 1949; ed. at Downside and R.M.A., Sandhurst; *m.*, 1978, Walburga, yr. da. of BARON JOHANNES VON TWICKEL of Schloss Lembeck, Lembeck, Germany.]

2 APRIL

LANG OF LAMBETH

BARONY. I. 1942. 1. The Most Rev. and Right Hon. COSMO GORDON LANG, G.C.V.O., D.D., Archbishop of Canterbury, 1928–42, s. of the Very Rev. John Marshall LANG, C.V.O., D.D., of Chanonry Lodge, Old Aberdeen, Principal of Aberdeen Univ., was *b.* 31 Oct. 1864; ed. at Glasgow Univ. and Oxford (Balliol Coll.). He was *cr.*, 2 Apr. 1942, BARON LANG OF LAMBETH, of Lambeth, co. Surrey. He *d.* unm. 5 Dec. 1945, when his Barony became *extinct.*

27 APRIL

MARGESSON

VISCOUNTCY. I. 1942. 1. The Right Hon. HENRY DAVID MARGESSON, M.C., 1st s. of Sir Mortimer Reginald MARGESSON, was *b.* 26 July 1890; ed. at Harrow and Cambridge (Magdalene Coll.). He was *cr.*, 27 Apr. 1942, VISCOUNT MARGESSON, of Rugby, co. Warwick. He *m.*, 29 Apr. 1916, Frances, da. of Francis Howard LEGGETT of New York, U.S.A. This marriage was diss. by divorce in 1940 (she *d.* 1940). He *d.* 24 Dec. 1965.

II. 1965. 2. FRANCIS VERE HAMPDEN (MARGESSON), VISCOUNT MARGESSON, only s. and h., was *b.* 17 Apr. 1922; ed. at Eton and Oxford (Trin. Coll.); *m.*, 18 Sep. 1958, Helena, da. of Heikki BACKSTROM of Oulu, Finland.

[RICHARD FRANCIS DAVID MARGESSON, only s. and h. ap., *b.* 25 Dec. 1960; *m.*, 1990, Wendy Maree, da. of James HAZELTON, of Kempsey, New South Wales, Australia.]

27 APRIL

BRABAZON OF TARA

BARONY. I. 1942. 1. The Right Hon. JOHN THEODORE CUTHBERT MOORE-BRABAZON, M.C., 2nd s. of John Arthur Henry MOORE-BRABAZON, of Tara House, co. Meath, and of Tallyallen, co. Louth, was *b.* 8 Feb. 1884; ed. at Harrow and Cambridge (Trin. Coll.). He was *cr.*, 27 Apr. 1942, BARON BRABAZON OF TARA, of Sandwich, co. Kent. He *m.*, 27 Nov. 1906, Hilda Mary, only da. of Charles Henry KRABBÉ of Buenos Aires, Argentine. He *d.* 17 May 1964. His widow *d.* 1977.

III. 1975. 2. DEREK CHARLES (MOORE-BRABAZON), BARON BRABAZON OF TARA, 1st s. and h., was *b.* 24 Dec. 1910; ed. at Harrow and Cambridge (Trin. Coll.); *m.*, 1 Sep. 1939, Henrietta Mary, da. of Sir Alfred Rowland CLEGG of Brynsiencyn, Anglesey and formerly wife of Ivor KRABBÉ. He *d.* 11 Dec. 1974. His widow *d.* 1985.

III. 1974. 3. IVOR ANTHONY (MOORE-BRABAZON), BARON BRABAZON OF TARA, only s. and h., was *b.* 20 Dec. 1946; ed. at Harrow; *m.*, 1979, Harriet Frances, da. of Mervyn Peter de Courcy HAMILTON of Harare, Zimbabwe.

[BENJAMIN RALPH MOORE-BRABAZON, s. and h. ap., *b.* 15 Mar. 1983.]

6 JULY

KEYNES

BARONY. I. 1942. 1. JOHN MAYNARD KEYNES, C.B., 1st s. of John Neville KEYNES, Registrar of Cambridge Univ., was *b.* 5 June 1883; ed. at Eton and Cambridge (King's Coll.). He was *cr.*, 6 July 1942, BARON KEYNES, of Tilton, co. Sussex. He *m.*, 7 Aug. 1925, Lydia, da. of Vassili LOPPKOFF of Leningrad, Russia. He *d. s.p.* and *v.p.* 21 Apr. 1946, when his Barony became *extinct*.

PEERAGES OF 1943

22 JANUARY

KEYES

BARONY. I. 1943. 1. Admiral of the Fleet SIR ROGER JOHN BROWNLOW KEYES, 1st. Bart. [1919], G.C.B., K.C.V.O., C.M.G., D.S.O., 1st s. of Gen. SIR CHARLES PATTON KEYES, G.C.B., of Croghan, co. Donegal, was *b.* 4 Oct. 1872. He was *cr.*, 22 Jan. 1943, BARON KEYES, of Zeebrugge and of Dover, co. Kent. He *m.*, 10 Apr. 1906, Eva Mary Salvin, da. of Edward Salvin BOWLBY of Gilston Park, co. Hertford and of Knoydart, co. Inverness. He *d.* 26 Dec. 1945. His widow *d.* 1973.

[Lieut. Col. GEOFFREY CHARLES TASKER KEYES, V.C. (posthumous), M.C., Royal Scots Greys, 1st s. and h. ap., *b.* 18 May 1917. He *d.* unm. and *v.p.*, being *k.* in action, 18 Nov. 1941, while leading a Commando raid on Gen. Rommell's H.Q.]

I. 1945. 2. ROGER GEORGE BOWLBY (KEYES), BARON KEYES, also a Baronet, 2nd but 1st surv. s. and h., was *b.* 14 Mar. 1919; ed. at R.N.C., Dartmouth; *m.*, 6 Dec. 1947, Grizelda Mary, 2nd da. of Lieut. Col. William Vere PACKE, D.S.O., of Bromley Common, Kent.

[CHARLES WILLIAM PACKE KEYES, 1st s. and h. ap., *b.* 8 Dec. 1951; ed. at Eton; *m.* 1stly, 1978, Sadiye Yasmin, da. of Mahir COSKUN of Istanbul. This marriage was diss. by divorce and he *m.* 2ndly, 1984, Sally, da. of Thomas JACKSON.]

1 FEBRUARY

HEMINGFORD

BARONY. I. 1943. 1. The Right Hon. SIR DENNIS HENRY HERBERT, K.B.E., 1st s. of the Rev. Henry HERBERT, Rector of Hemingford Abbots, co. Huntingdon, was *b*. 25 Feb. 1869; ed. at King's Sch., Ely and Oxford (Wadham Coll.). He was *cr*., 1 Feb. 1943, BARON HEMINGFORD, of Watford, co. Hertford. He *m*., 9 June 1903, Mary Graeme, da. of Valentine Graeme BELL He *d*. 10 Dec. 1947. His widow *d*. 24 July 1966.

II. 1947. 2. DENNIS GEORGE RUDDOCK (HERBERT), BARON HEMINGFORD, 1st s. and h., was *b*. 25 Mar. 1904; ed. at Oundle and Oxford (Brasenose Coll.); *m*., 25 June 1932, Elizabeth McClare, only da. of Col. John McClare CLARK of Haltwhistle, Northumberland. She *d*. 1979. He *d*. 19 June 1982.

III. 1982. 3. DENNIS NICHOLAS (HERBERT), BARON HEMINGFORD, only s. and h., was *b*. 25 July 1934; ed. at Oundle and Cambridge (Clare Coll.); *m*., 8 Nov. 1958, Jennifer Mary Toresen, da. of Frederick William BAILEY of Harrogate.

[CHRISTOPHER DENNIS CHARLES HERBERT, s. and h. ap., *b*. 4 July 1973; ed. at Oundle and Victoria Univ., Manchester.]

8 MARCH

MORAN

BARONY. I. 1943. 1. SIR CHARLES MCMORAN WILSON, M.C., 2nd s. of John Forsythe WILSON, M.D., was *b*. 10 Nov. 1882; ed. at Pocklington Gram. Sch. and St. Mary's Hosp., London. He was *cr*., 8 Mar. 1943, BARON MORAN, of Manton, co. Wilts. He *m*., 15 July 1919, Dorothy, da. of Samuel Felix DUFTON. He *d*. 12 Apr. 1977. His widow *d*. 1983.

II. 1977. 2. RICHARD JOHN MCMORAN (WILSON), BARON MORAN, 1st s. and h., was *b*. 22 Sep. 1924; ed. at Eton and Cambridge (King's Coll.); *m*., 29 Dec. 1948, Shirley Rowntree, 1st da. of George James HARRIS of Bossall Hall, York.

[JAMES MCMORAN WILSON, 1st s. and h. ap., *b*. 6 Aug. 1952; ed. at Eton and Cambridge (Trin. Coll.); *m*., 1980, Mary Jane, yst. da. of Henry Alexander (HEPBURNE-SCOTT), 10th LORD POLWARTH.]

6 MAY

DAVENTRY

VISCOUNTCY. I. 1943. 1. MURIEL FITZROY, C.B.E., widow of Capt. the Right Hon. Edward Algernon FITZROY, M.C., Speaker of the House of Commons, 1928–43 (who *d*. 3 Mar. 1943; yr. s. of Charles, 3rd BARON SOUTHAMPTON), 1st da. of Lieut. Col. Archibald Charles Henry DOUGLAS-PENNANT (yr. s. of Edward Gordon, 1st BARON PENRHYN), was *b*. 8 Aug. 1869. She was *cr*., 6 May 1943, VISCOUNTESS DAVENTRY, of Daventry co. Northampton, with rem. to her sons by the abovenamed Edward Algernon. She *d*. 8 July 1962.

II. 1962. 2. ROBERT OLIVER (FITZROY), VISCOUNT DAVENTRY, 1st s. and h., was *b*. 10 Jan. 1893; ed. at R.N.C.s, Osborne and Dartmouth; *m*., 5 Sep.

1916, Grace Zoë, da. of Claude Hugh Campbell GUINNESS, 4th s. of Richard Samuel GUINNESS. She *d.* 1978. He *d.* 19 Jan. 1986.

III. 1986. 3. FRANCIS HUMPHREY MAURICE (FITZROY-NEWDEGATE), VISCOUNT DAVENTRY, nephew and h., being only s. of John Maurice FITZROY-NEWDEGATE, Cmdr., R.N. (*d.* 1976), by Lucia Charlotte Susan, 1st da. and coh. of Sir Francis Alexander Newdigate NEWDEGATE, G.C.M.G., which John Maurice was 3rd s. of Viscountess Daventry. He was *b.* 17 Dec. 1921; ed. at Eton; *m.*, 20 Oct. 1959, Rosemary, 1st da. of Lieut. Gen. Sir Charles Willoughby Moke (NORRIE), 1st BARON NORRIE, G.C.M.G., G.C.V.O., M.C.

[JAMES EDWARD FITZROY-NEWDEGATE, 1st s. and h. ap., *b.*, 27 July 1960; ed. at Milton Abbey and R.A.C., Cirencester.]

MAY

DE ROS

ROS, or DE ROS, Barony by Writ (*Ross*, formerly *Dawson*, and before that *Fitzgerald De Ros*). The *abeyance* in this Barony was terminated, May 1943, in favour of the eldest coh., UNA MARY ROSS, widow of Arthur John ROSS, who was *k.* in action, Aug. 1917. See vol. xi, *sub* ROS or ROOS OF HELMSLEY. She *d.* 9 Oct. 1956, when the Barony again fell into *abeyance*. This *abeyance* was terminated, Aug. 1958, in favour of her eldest grand-daughter and coh., GEORGIANA ANGELA MAXWELL, wife of Lieut. John David MAXWELL, R.N., 1st da. and coh. of Lieut. Cmdr. Peter ROSS, R.N. (who *d. v.m.*, being *k.* in action, Oct. 1940), which Peter was 1st s. and h. ap. of Una Mary, BARONESS DE ROS, abovenamed. See above, in present volume, p. 554.

17 MAY

KILLEARN

BARONY. I. 1943. 1. The Right Hon. SIR MILES WEDDERBURN LAMPSON, G.C.M.G., C.B., M.V.O., 2nd s. of Norman George LAMPSON (3rd s. of Sir Curtis Miranda LAMPSON, 1st Bart.), was *b.* 24 Aug. 1880; ed. at Eton. He was *cr.*, 17 May 1943, BARON KILLEARN, of Killearn, co. Stirling. He *m.* 1stly, 6 July 1912, Rachel Mary Helen, yr. da. of William Wilton PHIPPS. She *d.* 23 Jan. 1930 and he *m.* 2ndly, 18 Dec. 1934, Jacqueline Aldine Leslie, only da. of MARCHESE SENATOR ALDO CASTELLANI, K.C.M.G. He *d.* 18 Sep. 1964. His widow was living 1995.

II. 1964. 2. GRAHAM CURTIS (LAMPSON), BARON KILLEARN, 1st s. and h., was *b.* 28 Oct. 1918; ed. at Eton and Oxford (Magdalen Coll.); *m.*, 15 May 1946, Nadine Marie Cathryn, only da. of Cecil Horace PILCHER, Vice Adm., D.S.O.

5 JULY

DOWDING

BARONY. I. 1943. 1 Air Chief Marshal SIR HUGH CASWALL TREMENHEERE DOWDING, G.C.B., G.C.V.O., C.M.G., 1st s. of Arthur John Caswall

DOWDING, of St. Ninian's, Moffat, was *b.* 24 Apr. 1882; Winchester and R.M.C., Sandhurst. He was *cr.*, 5 July 1943, BARON DOWDING, of Bentley Priory, co. Middlesex. He *m.* 1stly, 16 Feb. 1918, Clarice Maud, da. of Capt. John WILLIAMS and widow of (__) VANCOURT. She *d.* 28 June 1920 and he *m.* 2ndly, 25 Sep. 1951, Muriel, da. of John ALBINO of Richmond, Surrey and widow of Pilot Off. Jack Maxwell WHITING. He *d.* 15 Feb. 1970. His widow *d.* 1993.

II. 1970. 2. DEREK HUGH TREMENHEERE (DOWDING), BARON DOWDING, only s. and h. by 1st wife, was *b.* 9 Jan. 1919; ed. at Winchester and Cranwell; *m.* 1stly, 17 Feb. 1940, Joan Myrtle, da. of Donald James STUART of Nairn. This marriage was diss. by divorce in 1946 and he *m.* 2ndly, 7 May 1947, Alison Margaret, da. of James BANNERMAN and widow of Major R.W.H. PEEBLES. This marriage was in turn diss. by divorce in 1960 and he *m.* 3rdly, 17 Dec. 1961, Odette Lucie Marie Sophie, da. of Louis Joseph HOULES of Toulouse, France and formerly wife of Brian HUGHES. He *d.* 22 Nov. 1992. His widow was living 1995.

III. 1992. 3. PIERS HUGH TREMENHEERE (DOWDING), BARON DOWDING, 1st s. and h. by 2nd wife, was *b.* 18 Feb. 1948; ed. at Fettes and Amherst Coll., Massachusetts, U.S.A.; *m.*, 1973, Noriko Shiho of Japan.

22 JULY

WAVELL

VISCOUNTCY. I. } 1943
EARLDOM. I. } 1947

1. Field Marshal SIR ARCHIBALD PERCIVAL WAVELL, G.C.B., C.M.G., M.C., only s. of Major-Gen. Archibald Graham WAVELL, C.B., of Little Somborne, near Ringwood, Hants, was *b.* 5 May 1883; ed. at Winchester and R.M.C., Sandhurst. He was *cr.*, 22 July 1943, VISCOUNT WAVELL of Cyrenaica, and of Winchester, co. Southampton and was further *cr.*, 1 May 1947, VISCOUNT KEREN of Eritrea, of Winchester, co. Southampton, and EARL WAVELL. He *m.*, 22 Apr. 1915, Eugenie Marie, only da. of Col. J.O. QUIRK. He *d.* 24 May 1950.

II. 1950. 2. ARCHIBALD JOHN ARTHUR (WAVELL), EARL WAVELL [1947], VISCOUNT WAVELL [1943] and VISCOUNT KEREN [1947], only s. and h., was *b.* 11 May 1916; *styled* VISCOUNT KEREN, 1947–50; ed. at Winchester. He *d.* unm. 24 Dec. 1953, when all his honours became *extinct*.

PEERAGES OF 1944

27 JANUARY

GRETTON

BARONY. I. 1944.

1. The Right Hon. JOHN GRETTON, C.B.E., 1st s. of John Gretton, of Stapleford Park, co. Leicester, was *b.* 1 Sep. 1867; ed. at Harrow. He was *cr.*, 27 Jan. 1944, BARON GRETTON, of Stapleford, co. Leicester. He *m.*,

19 Apr. 1900, Maud Helen, 4th da. of Dayrolles Blakeney (EVELEIGH-DE-MOLEYNS) 4th BARON VENTRY. She *d.* 29 July 1934. He *d.* 2 June 1947.

II. 1947. 2. JOHN FREDERIC (GRETTON), BARON GRETTON, only s. and h., was *b.* 15 Aug. 1902; ed. at Eton. He *m.*, 6 May 1930, Anna Helena Margaret, elder da. of Capt. Henrik Loeffler. He *d.* 7 Mar. 1982. His widow was living 1995.

III. 1982. 3. JOHN HENRIK (GRETTON), BARON GRETTON, 1st s. and h., *b.* 9 Feb. 1941; ed. at Eton. He *m.*, 1970, Jennifer Ann, only da. of Edmund Sandford MOORE of York. He *d.* 4 Apr. 1989. His widow was living 1995.

IV. 1989. 4. JOHN LYSANDER (GRETTON), BARON GRETTON, only s. and h., *b.* 17 Apr. 1975; ed. at Shrewsbury.

28 JANUARY

ROYDEN

BARONY. I. 1944. 1. SIR THOMAS ROYDEN, 2nd Bart. [1905], C.H., 1st s. and h. of Sir Thomas Bland ROYDEN, 1st Bart., was *b.* 22 May 1871; ed. at Winchester and Oxford (Magdalen Coll.). He was *cr.*, 28 Jan. 1944, BARON ROYDEN, of Frankby, co. Chester. He *m.*, 22 Apr. 1922, Quenelda Mary, da. of Harry CLEGG and widow of Charles J. WILLIAMSON. He *d. s.p.* 6 Nov. 1950, when his Barony became *extinct*, but the Baronetcy passed to his br. and h.

29 JANUARY

WESTWOOD

BARONY. I. 1944. 1. WILLIAM WESTWOOD, O.B.E., s. of William WESTWOOD, of Broughty Ferry, near Dundee, was *b.* 28 Oct. 1880; ed. at Elementary Sch., Dundee. He was *cr.*, 29 Jan. 1944, BARON WESTWOOD, of Gosforth, co. Northumberland. He *m.* 1stly, June 1905, Margaret Taylor, da. of William YOUNG of Dundee. She *d.* Oct. 1916. He *m.* 2ndly, 26 Apr. 1918, Agnes Helen Flockhart, da. of James DOWNIE of Dundee. She *d.* 28 Jan. 1952. He *d.* 13 Sep. 1953.

II. 1953. 2. WILLIAM (WESTWOOD), BARON WESTWOOD, 1st s. and h., was *b.* 25 Dec. 1907; ed. at Queen's Park Acad., Glasgow. He *m.*, 9 June 1937, Marjorie, only child of Arthur BONWICK of Heaton, Newcastle upon Tyne. He *d.* 8 Nov. 1991. His widow was living 1995.

III. 1991. 3. WILLIAM GAVIN (WESTWOOD), BARON WESTWOOD, 1st s. and h., *b.* 30 Jan. 1944; ed. at Fettes. He *m.*, 21 June 1969, Penelope, elder da. of Dr Charles Edgar SHAFTO of Newcastle upon Tyne.

[WILLIAM FERGUS WESTWOOD, s. and h ap., *b.* 24 Nov. 1972; ed. at Royal Gram. Sch., Newcastle upon Tyne.]

31 JANUARY

AMMON

BARONY.
I. 1944.

1. CHARLES GEORGE AMMON, s. of Charles George AMMON, of London, was *b.* 22 Apr. 1873; ed. at state elementary schools and by private study. He was *cr.*, 31 Jan. 1944, BARON AMMON, of Camberwell, co. Surrey. He *m.*, 14 Sep. 1898, Ada Ellen, da. of David MAY of Walworth, London. She *d.* 1958. He *d. s.p.m.s.* 2 Apr. 1960 when his Barony became *extinct*.

1 FEBRUARY

COURTAULD-THOMSON

BARONY.
I. 1944.

1. SIR COURTAULD GREENWOOD COURTAULD-THOMSON, *formerly* THOMSON, K.B.E., C.B., 2nd s. of Robert William THOMSON, of Edinburgh and Stonehaven, co. Kincardine, was *b.* 16 Aug. 1865; ed. at Eton and Oxford (Magdalen Coll.). He was *cr.*, 1 Feb. 1944, BARON COURTAULD-THOMSON, of Dorneywood, co. Buckingham. He *d.* unm. 1 Nov. 1954, when his Barony became *extinct*.

18 APRIL

SIMONDS

BARONY FOR LIFE. I. } 1944
BARONY. I. } 1952
VISCOUNTCY. I. } 1954

1. The Right Hon. SIR GAVIN TURNBULL SIMONDS, one of the Judges of the Chancery Div. of the High Court of Justice, s. of Louis de Luze SIMONDS, of Audleys Wood, Basingstoke, was *b.* 25 Nov. 1881; ed. at Winchester and Oxford (New Coll.). On 18 Apr. 1944 he was app. a Lord of Appeal in Ordinary under the Appellate Jurisdiction Act of 1876, and *cr.* a Baron for Life by the style of BARON SIMONDS, of Sparsholt, co. Southampton. He was further *cr.*, 24 June 1952, BARON SIMONDS, of Sparsholt, co. Southampton, with the usual rem.; and, 18 Oct. 1954, VISCOUNT SIMONDS, of Sparsholt, co. Southampton. He *m.*, 28 Mar. 1912, Mary Hope, da. of Judge Francis Hope MELLOR. He *d. s.p.m.s.* (1) 28 June 1971 when his titles became *extinct*.

note (1) His eldest son, Gavin Alexander, *b.* 1 Aug. 1915, *d. v.p.* and unm. 19 Mar. 1951; his 2nd son (twin of Gavin Alexander), *m.* 12 Aug. 1944, Barbara, da. of T. ROBINSON of St Helens, and *d. v.p.*, being k. in action at Arnhem, 23 Sep. 1944.

26 JUNE

SCHUSTER

BARONY.
I. 1944.

1. SIR CLAUD SCHUSTER, G.C.B., C.V.O., s. of Frederick Leo SCHUSTER, of Heysham House, The Park, Cheltenham, was *b.* 22 Aug. 1869; ed. at Winchester and Oxford (New Coll.). He was *cr.*, 26 June 1944, BARON SCHUSTER, of Cerne, co. Dorset. He *m.*, 1 July 1896, Mabel Elizabeth, da.

of Rev. W.W. MERRY, Rector of Lincoln Coll., Oxford. She *d.* 6 Aug. 1936. He *d.* (1) *s.p.m.s.* 28 June 1956, when his Barony became *extinct*.

note (1) His only son Christopher John Claud, was *b.* 13 Jan. 1899, and *d. v.p.* and unm. 10 Aug. 1918, being *k.* in action at La Bohème.

11 JULY

HALIFAX

EARLDOM. I. 1944. 1. EDWARD FREDERICK LINDLEY (WOOD), 3rd VISCOUNT HALIFAX [1866] and 1st BARON IRVIN [1925], also a Baronet [1784], was further *cr.*, 11 July 1944, EARL OF HALIFAX. For fuller particulars of him see vol. vi, *sub* HALIFAX, and vol. xiii, p. 415, *sub* IRWIN.

14 JULY

TEMPLEWOOD

VISCOUNTCY. I. 1944. 1. The Right Hon. SIR SAMUEL JOHN GURNEY HOARE, 2nd Bart [1899], G.C.S.I., G.B.E., C.M.G., 1st s. and h. of Sir Samuel HOARE, 1st Bart. of Sidestrand Hall, Norfolk, and Hampstead, Midx., was *b.* 24 Feb. 1880; ed. at Harrow and Oxford (New Coll.). He was *cr.*, 14 July 1944, VISCOUNT TEMPLEWOOD, of Chelsea, co. Middlesex. He *m.*, 17 Oct. 1909, Lady Maud, 5th da. of Frederick (LYGON), 6th EARL BEAUCHAMP. He *d. s.p.* 7 May 1959 when his titles became *extinct*. His widow *d.* 27 Dec. 1962.

19 JULY

GODDARD

BARONY FOR LIFE. I. 1944. 1. The Right Hon. SIR RAYNER GODDARD, one of the Lords Justices of Appeal, s. of Charles GODDARD, of 3 South Square, Gray's Inn, London, was *b.* 10 Apr. 1877; ed. at Marlborough and Oxford (Trin. Coll.). On 19 July 1944 he was app. a Lord of Appeal in Ordinary under the Appellate Jurisdiction Act of 1876, and *cr.* a Baron for Life by the style of BARON GODDARD, of Aldbourne, co. Wilts. He *m.*, 31 May 1906, Mary Linda, da. of Sir Felix Otto (SCHUSTER), 1st Bart. She *d.* 16 May 1928. He *d. s.p.m.* 29 May 1971, when his Life Barony became *extinct*.

13 OCTOBER

NORMAN

BARONY. I. 1944. 1. The Right Hon. MONTAGU COLLET NORMAN, D.S.O., 1st s. of Frederick Henry NORMAN, of Moor Place, Much Hadham, co. Hertford, was *b.* 6 Sep. 1871; ed. at Eton and Cambridge (King's Coll.). He was *cr.*, 13 Oct. 1944, BARON NORMAN, of St. Clere, co. Kent. He *m.*, 21 Jan. 1933, Priscilla Cecilia Maria Worsthorne, da. of Major Robert REYNTIENS of Belgium by his wife Lady Alice Josephine, da. of Montagu Arthur (BERTIE), 7th EARL OF ABINGDON. He *d. s.p.* 4 Feb. 1950, when his Barony became *extinct*. His widow was living 1995.

PEERAGES OF 1945

8 JANUARY

GOWRIE, Earldom, RUTHVEN OF CANBERRA, Viscountcy

EARLDOM. I. 1945. 1. ALEXANDER GORE ARKWRIGHT (HORE-RUTHVEN), 1st BARON GOWRIE [1935], was further *cr.*, 8 Jan. 1945, VISCOUNT RUTHVEN OF CANBERRA, of Dirleton, co. East Lothian, and EARL OF GOWRIE. He *d.* 2 May 1955. For fuller particulars of him see vol. xiii, p. 560, *sub* GOWRIE.

[Major ALEXANDER HARDINGE PATRICK HORE-RUTHVEN, The Rifle Brigade, attd. S.A.S., 1st s. and h. ap., *b.* 30 Aug. 1913. He *m.*, 5 Jan. 1939, Pamela Margaret, 2nd da. of Rev. Arthur Henry FLETCHER. He *d. v.p.* 24 Dec. 1942 of wounds received in action in Libya.]

II. 1955. 2. ALEXANDER PATRICK GREYSTEIL (HORE-RUTHVEN), EARL OF GOWRIE [1945], VISCOUNT RUTHVEN OF CANBERRA [1945] and BARON GOWRIE [1935], grandson and h. being 1st s. and h. of Major Alexander Hardinge Patrick HORE-RUTHVEN abovenamed, was *b.* 26 Nov. 1939; *styled* VISCOUNT RUTHVEN, 1945–55. On 16 Apr. 1956 he *suc.* his great-uncle (who *d. s.p.m.*) as 3rd BARON RUTHVEN OF GOWRIE [1919]. See that title in vol. xiii, p. 323, and p. 726 above.

1 FEBRUARY

PORTAL

VISCOUNTCY. I. 1945 1. Sir WINDHAM RAYMOND (PORTAL), 1st BARON PORTAL [1935], also a Baronet [1901], was further *cr.*, 1 Feb. 1945, VISCOUNT PORTAL, of Laverstoke, co. Southampton. He *d. s.p.* 6 May 1949, when the Viscountcy and Barony became *extinct*, but the Baronetcy passed to his uncle and h. male. For fuller particulars of him see vol. xiii, p. 547 and above, p. 721.

12 FEBRUARY

LLOYD-GEORGE OF DWYFOR, Earldom, GWYNEDD, Viscountcy

EARLDOM. I. 1945 1. The Right Hon. DAVID LLOYD-GEORGE, O.M., s. of William GEORGE, of Bulford, co. Pembroke, Master of Hope St. Unitarian Schools, Liverpool, was *b.* 17 Jan. 1863; ed. at Llanystymdwy Church Sch. and privately. He was *cr.*, 12 Feb. 1945, VISCOUNT GWYNEDD, of Dwyfor, co. Caernarvon, and EARL LLOYD-GEORGE OF DWYFOR. He *m.* 1stly, Jan. 1888, Margaret, da. of Richard Owen of Mynydd Ednyfed, Criccieth, Caernarvon. She *d.* 20 Jan. 1941. He *m.*

2ndly, 23 Oct. 1943, Frances Louise, da. of John STEVENSON of Wallington, Surrey. He *d.* 26 Mar. 1945. His widow *d.* 1972.

II. 1945, Mar. 2. RICHARD (LLOYD-GEORGE), EARL LLOYD-GEORGE OF DWYFOR and VISCOUNT GWYNEDD, 1st s. and h., was *b.* 15 Feb. 1889; ed. at Portmadoc and Cambridge (Christ's Coll.); *styled* VISCOUNT GWYNEDD, Feb. to Mar. 1945. He *m.* 1stly, 7 Apr. 1917, Roberta Ida Freeman, 5th da. of Sir Robert MCALPINE, 1st Bart. This marriage was diss. by divorce in 1933, and she *d.* 10 Mar. 1936. He *m.* 2ndly, 1935, Winifred Emily, da. of Thomas William PEEDLE and formerly wife of Henry Malcolm CALVE. He *d.* 1 May 1968. His widow *d.* 1982.

II. 1968. 3. OWEN (LLOYD-GEORGE), EARL LLOYD-GEORGE OF DWYFOR and VISCOUNT GWYNEDD, only s. and h., *b.* 28 Apr. 1924; ed. at Oundle. He *m.* 1stly, 8 Sep. 1949, Ruth Margaret, only da. of Richard COIT; this marriage was diss. by divorce in 1982. He *m.* 2ndly, 1982, Cecily Josephine, elder da. of Major Sir Alexander Penrose Gordon CUMMING, M.C., 5th Bart., widow of Roger David (MARQUIS) 2nd EARL OF WOOLTON and formerly wife of John Archibald Harford (WILLIAMSON), 3rd BARON FORRES.

[DAVID RICHARD OWEN LLOYD-GEORGE, 1st s. by 1st marriage and h. ap., *b.* 22 Jan. 1951; ed. at Eton. He *m.*, 1985, Pamela Alexandra, only da. of Alexander KLEYFF.]

12 FEBRUARY

HAZLERIGG

BARONY. I. 1945. 1. SIR ARTHUR GREY HAZLERIGG, 13th Bart. [1622], only s. and h. of Lieut. Col. Arthur Grey HAZLERIGG, R. Scots. Fus. (who *d. v.p.* 16 July 1880; 1st s. and h. ap. of Sir Arthur Grey HAZLERIGG, 12th Bart.), was *b.* 17 Nov. 1878; ed. at Eton and Cambridge (Trin. Coll). He was *cr.*, 12 Feb. 1945, BARON HAZLERIGG, of Noseley, co. Leicester. He *m.*, 14 July 1903, Dorothy Rachel, elder da. of John Henry BUXTON of Ware, Herts. He *d.* 25 May 1949. His widow *d.* 1972.

II. 1949. 2. ARTHUR GREY (HAZLERIGG), BARON HAZLERIGG, also a Baronet, 1st. s. and h., was *b.* 24 Feb. 1910; ed. at Eton and Cambridge (Trin. Coll.). He *m.*, 19 Sep. 1945, Patricia, elder da. of John PULLAR of Durban, Natal. She *d.* 1972.

[ARTHUR GREY HAZLERIGG, only s. and h. ap., *b.* 5 May 1951. He *m*, 1986, Laura, elder da. of Sir William Stratford (DUGDALE), 2nd BART.]

2 JULY

ADDISON

VISCOUNTCY. I. 1945. 1. CHRISTOPHER (ADDISON), 1st BARON ADDISON [1937], was further *cr.*, 2 July 1945, VISCOUNT ADDISON, of Stallingborough, co. Lincoln. He *d.* 11 Dec. 1951. For further particulars of him see vol. xiii, p. 580.

II. 1951. 2. CHRISTOPHER (ADDISON), VISCOUNT ADDISON [1945] and BARON ADDISON [1937], 1st s. and h., was *b.* 8 Dec. 1904. For further particulars and for subsequent Viscounts Addison see above, *sub* ADDISON in main sequence, p. 729.

2 JULY

HACKING

BARONY. I. 1945. 1. The Right Hon. SIR DOUGLAS HEWITT HACKING, 1st Bart. [1938], O.B.E., s. of Joshua HACKING, of Henfield House, Clayton-le-Moors, co. Lancaster, was *b.* 4 Aug. 1884; ed. at Giggleswick and Manchester Univ. He was *cr.*, 2 July 1945, BARON HACKING, of Chorley, co. Lancaster. He *m.*, 15 Apr. 1909, Margery Allen, elder da. of Henry Hargreaves BOLTON of Newchurch-in-Rossendale, Lancs. He *d.* 29 July 1950. His widow *d.* 1984.

II. 1950. 2. DOUGLAS ERIC HACKING, BARON HACKING, also a Baronet, 1st s. and h., was *b.* 7 Dec. 1910; ed. at Charterhouse and Cambridge (Clare Coll.). He *m.*, 19 Feb. 1936, Daphne Violet, elder da. of Robert Leslie Finnis of Kensington. He *d.* 7 Nov. 1971. His widow was living 1995.

III. 1971. 3. DOUGLAS DAVID (HACKING), BARON HACKING, also a Baronet, 1st s. and h., *b.* 17 Apr. 1938; ed. at Charterhouse and Cambridge (Clare Coll.). He *m.* 1stly, 31 July 1965, Rosemary Anne, elder da. of Frank Penrose FORREST of Lytchett Matravers, Dorset. He *m.* 2ndly, 1982, Tessa Margaret, da. of Roland HUNT of Whitchurch Hill, Reading.

[DOUGLAS FRANCIS HACKING, 1st s. by 1st marriage and h. ap., *b.* 8 Aug. 1968.]

3 JULY

COURTHOPE

BARONY. I. 1945. 1. The Right Hon. SIR GEORGE LOYD COURTHOPE, 1st Bart. [1925], M.C., T.D., 1st s. of Lieut. Col. George John COURTHOPE, of Whiligh, Sussex, and Sprivers, Horsmonden, Kent, was *b.* 12 June 1877; ed. at Eton and Oxford (Christ C.). He was *cr.*, 3 July 1945, BARON COURTHOPE, of Whiligh, co. Sussex. He *m.* 1stly, 14 June 1899, Hilda Gertrude, only da. of Major Gen. Henry Pelham CLOSE. She *d.* 11 Nov. 1940. He *m.* 2ndly, 5 Sep. 1944, Margaret, da. of Frederick BARRY of Westbury, Bristol. He *d. s.p.m.* 2 Sep. 1955, when all his honours became *extinct*.

5 JULY

BALFOUR OF INCHRYE

BARONY. I. 1945. 1. The Right Hon. HAROLD HARINGTON BALFOUR, M.C., 2nd s. of Col. Nigel Harington Balfour, O.B.E., of Belton, Camberley, Surrey, was *b.* 1 Nov. 1897; ed. at Chilverton Elms Dover and R.N.C., Osborne. He was *cr.*, 5 July 1945, BARON BALFOUR OF INCHRYE, of Shefford, co. Berks. He *m.* 1stly, 15 Dec. 1921, Diana Blanche, 2nd da. of Sir Robert Grenville HARVEY, 2nd Bart. This marriage was diss. by divorce in 1946 and she *d.* in 1982. He *m.* 2ndly, 2 Jan. 1947, Mary Ainslie, yr. da. of BARON ALBERT PETER ANTHONY PROFUMO of Avon Dassett, Warwicks. He *d.* 21 Sep. 1988. His widow was living 1995.

II. 1988. 2. IAN (BALFOUR), BARON BALFOUR OF INCHRYE, only s. and h., *b.* 21 Dec. 1924; ed. at Eton and Oxford (Magdalen Coll.). He *m.*, 28 Nov. 1953, Josephine Maria Jane, da. of Morogh Wyndham Percy BERNARD.

6 JULY

JACKSON

BARONY. I. 1945 1. WILLIAM FREDERICK JACKSON, s. of George JACKSON, of Edgbaston, Birmingham, was *b.* 29 Nov. 1893; ed. at King Edward VI High Sch., Birmingham. He was *cr.*, 6 July 1945, BARON JACKSON, of Glewstone, co. Hereford. He *m.*, 19 Apr. 1923, Hope Hardy Falconer, da. of B.W. GILMOUR of Glasgow. He *d. s.p.* 2 May 1954, when his Barony became *extinct.*

7 JULY

QUIBELL

BARONY. I. 1945. 1. DAVID JOHN KINSLEY QUIBELL, s. of David John QUIBELL, of Scunthorpe, Lincs, was *b.* 21 Dec. 1879; ed. at Messingham Church of England Sch. He was *cr.*, 7 July 1945, BARON QUIBELL, of Scunthorpe, co. Lincoln. He *m.* 1stly, 12 Sep. 1900, Edith Jane, da. of J. FOSTER, she *d.* 14 Mar. 1953. He *m.* 2ndly, 27 May 1954 Catherine Cameron, da. of J.C. RAE. He *d. s.p.m.* 16 Apr. 1962, when his Barony became *extinct.*

9 JULY

WALKDEN

BARONY. I. 1945. 1. ALEXANDER GEORGE WALKDEN, s. of Charles Henry Scrivener WALKDEN, of Ashwell, co. Hertford, was *b.* 11 May 1873; ed. at Merchant Taylors' Sch., Ashwell, Herts. He was *cr.*, 9 July 1945, BARON WALKDEN, of Great Bookham, co. Surrey. He *m.*, 1898, Jennie, da. of Jesse WILSON of Market Rasen, Lincs. She *d.* 1934. He *d. s.p.m.* 25 Apr. 1951, when his Barony became *extinct.*

10 JULY

CHETWODE

BARONY. I. 1945. 1. Field Marshal SIR PHILIP WALHOUSE CHETWODE, 7th Bart. [1700], G.C.B., O.M., G.C.S.I., K.C.M.G., D.S.O., 1st s. and h. of Sir George CHETWODE, 6th Bart. was *b.* 21 Sep. 1869; ed. at Eton. He was *cr.*, 10 July 1945, BARON CHETWODE, of Chetwode, co. Buckingham. He *m.*, 1 June 1899, Alice Hester Camilla, el. da. of Col. Richard COTTON. She *d.* 29 June 1946. He *d.* 6 July 1950.

[Capt. ROGER CHARLES GEORGE CHETWODE, 11th (City of London Yeomanry) Light

A.A. Bde., R.A. (T.A.), only s. and h. ap., *b.* 18 Apr. 1906. He *m.*, 19 May 1936, Molly Patricia, 3rd da. of William Ewert (BERRY), 1st VISCOUNT CAMROSE. He *d. v.p.* 14 Aug. 1940. His widow married 2ndly and 3rdly and was still living 1995.]

II. 1950. 2. PHILIP (CHETWODE), BARON CHETWODE, also a Baronet, grandson and h., being 1st s. and h. of Capt. Roger Charles George CHETWODE and Molly Patricia abovenamed, was *b.* 26 Mar. 1937; ed. at Eton. He *m.* 1stly, 10 Aug. 1967, Susan Janet, 1st da. of Capt. Voltelin James Howard VAN DER BYL, R.N., and formerly wife of Alwyn Richard Dudley SMITH of Alverstoke, co. Hants. This marriage was diss. by divorce in 1979 and he *m.* 2ndly, 1990, Fiona (Mrs Holt), da. of Christos TSINTARIS of Thessaloniki, Greece.

[ROGER CHETWODE, 1st s. and h. ap. by 1st wife, *b.* 29 May 1968.]

11 JULY

COPE

BARONY. I. 1945. 1. SIR WILLIAM COPE, 1st Bart. [1928], s. of Matthew COPE, of Quarry Hill, St. Mellons, near Cardiff, was *b.* 18 Aug. 1870. He was *cr.*, 11 July 1945, BARON COPE, of St. Mellons, co. Monmouth. He was *ed.* at Repton and Cambridge (Clare Coll.); *m.* 5 Sep. 1900, Helen, da. of Major Alexander SHULDHAM of Flowerfield, co. Londonderry. He *d. s.p.m.s.* (1) 15 July 1946, when all his honours became *extinct.* His widow *d.* 21 Jan. 1961.

note (1) His only s., William Shuldham was *b.* 21 May 1902 and *d. v.p.* and unm. 1942.

12 JULY

RAMSDEN

BARONY. I. 1945. 1. SIR EUGENE JOSEPH SQUIRE HARGREAVES RAMSDEN, 1st Bart. [1938], O.B.E., only s. of James RAMSDEN, of The Wheatleys, Gomersal, near Leeds, was *b.* 2 Feb. 1883; ed. in England, France and Germany. He was *cr.*, 12 July 1945, BARON RAMSDEN, of Birkenshaw, in the West Riding of co. York. He *m.*, 22 May 1919, Margaret, da. of Frank Eugene WITHEY of Michigan, U.S.A. and widow of Major George FARWELL of U.S. army. He *d. s.p.* 9 Aug. 1955, when all his honours became *extinct.* His widow *d.* 4 Nov. 1965.

13 JULY

CHATTISHAM

BARONY. I. 1945, July to Aug. 1. SIR WILLIAM BRASS, s. of William BRASS, was *b.* 11 Feb. 1886; ed. at Eton and Cambridge (Trin. Coll.). He was *cr.*, 13 July 1945, BARON CHATTISHAM, of Clitheroe, co. Lancaster. He *d.* unm. 24 Aug. 1945, when his Barony became *extinct.*

14 JULY

SANDFORD

BARONY. I. 1945. 1. SIR ALBERT JAMES EDMONDSON, s. of James EDMONDSON, was *b.* 29 June 1886; ed. at Univ. Coll. Sch. He was *cr.*, 14 July 1945, BARON SANDFORD, of Banbury, co. Oxford. He *m.*, 20 June 1911, Edith Elizabeth, da. of James George FREEMAN. She *d.* 19 Mar. 1946. He *d.* 16 May 1959.

II. 1959. 2. Rev. JOHN CYRIL (EDMONDSON), BARON SANDFORD, elder s. and h., *b.* 22 Dec. 1920; ed. at Eton, R.N.C., Dartmouth and Westcott House Theological Coll. He *m.*, 4 Jan. 1947, Catherine Mary, da. of Rev. Oswald Andrew HUNT of Itchen Abbas, Winchester.

[JAMES JOHN MOWBRAY EDMONDSON, 1st s. and h. ap., *b.* 1 July 1949; ed. at Eton and York Univ. He *m.* 1stly, 1973, Ellen Sarah, da. of Jack SHAPIRO of Toronto, Canada. This marriage was diss. by divorce in 1986 and he *m.* 2ndly, 1986, Linda, da. of Michael WHEELER of Nova Scotia.]

23 JULY

LAMBERT

VISCOUNTCY. I. 1945. 1. The Right Hon. GEORGE LAMBERT, only s. of George LAMBERT, of Spreyton, Devon, was *b.* 25 June 1866 and educated privately. He was *cr.*, 23 July 1945, VISCOUNT LAMBERT, of South Molton, co. Devon. He *m.*, 30 July 1904, Barbara, da. of G. STAVERS of Morpeth, Northumberland. He *d.* 17 Feb. 1958. His widow *d.* 6 June 1963.

II. 1958. 2. GEORGE (LAMBERT), VISCOUNT LAMBERT, 1st s. and h., was *b.* 27 Nov. 1909; ed. at Harrow and Oxford (New Coll.). He *m.*, 16 Sep. 1939, Patricia Mary, da. of Joseph Francis QUINN. He *d.* 24 May 1989. His widow *d.* 1991.

[GEORGE LAMBERT, only s. and h. ap., *b.* 18 Aug. 1941; ed. at Harrow. He *d. v.p.* and unm. 1970.]

III. 1989. 3. MICHAEL JOHN (LAMBERT), VISCOUNT LAMBERT, br. and h., *b.* 29 Sep. 1912; ed. at Harrow and Oxford (New Coll.). He *m.*, 5 Sep. 1939, Florence Dolores, da. of Nicholas Lechmere Cunningham MACASKIE.

1 AUGUST

ALTRINCHAM

BARONY. I. 1945. 1. The Right Hon. SIR EDWARD WILLIAM MACLEAY GRIGG, K.C.M.G., K.C.V.O., D.S.O., M.C., s. of Henry Bidewell GRIGG, C.I.E., I.C.S., Political Resident in the State of Travancore, was *b.* 8 Sep. 1879; ed. at Winchester and Oxford (New Coll.). He was *cr.*, 1 Aug. 1945, BARON ALTRINCHAM, of Tormarton, co. Gloucester. He *m.*, 31 Jan. 1923, Joan Alice Katherine, only child of John Poynder (DICKSON-POYNDER), 1st BARON ISLINGTON. He *d.* 1 Dec. 1955. She *d.* 1987.

II. 1955. 2. JOHN EDWARD POYNDER (GRIGG), BARON ALTRINCHAM, 1st s. and h., was *b.* 15 Apr. 1924; ed. at Eton and Oxford (New Coll.). He *m.*, 3 Dec. 1958, Marian Patricia, only da. of Harold Ernest CAMPBELL of Belfast. He disclaimed his peerage for life, 31 July 1963 under the Peerage Act, 1963.

2 AUGUST

JOWITT

BARONY. I. 1945.
VISCOUNTCY. I. 1947.
EARLDOM. I. 1951.

1. The Right Hon. SIR WILLIAM ALLEN JOWITT, Lord Chancellor of Great Britain, s. of the Rev. William JOWITT, Rector of Stevenage, co. Hertford, was *b.* 15 Apr. 1885; ed. at Marlborough and Oxford (New Coll.). He was *cr.*, 2 Aug. 1945, BARON JOWITT, of Stevenage, co. Hertford. He was further *cr.*, 20 Jan. 1947, VISCOUNT JOWITT, of Stevenage, co. Hertford; and, 24 Dec. 1951, VISCOUNT STEVENAGE, of Stevenage, co. Hertford, and EARL JOWITT. He *m.*, 19 Dec. 1913, Lesley, da. of James Patrick MCINTYRE. He *d. s.p.m.* 16 Aug. 1957, when all his honours became *extinct*. His widow *d.* 22 Feb. 1970.

16 AUGUST

PETHICK-LAWRENCE

BARONY. I. 1945. 1. The Right Hon. FREDERICK WILLIAM PETHICK-LAWRENCE, 2nd s. of Alfred LAWRENCE, of 42 Gloucester Gdns., Bayswater, London, was *b.* 28 Dec. 1871; ed. at Eton and Cambridge (Trin. Coll.). He was *cr.*, 16 Aug. 1945, BARON PETHICK-LAWRENCE, of Peaslake, co. Surrey. He *m.*, 2 Oct. 1901, Emmeline, da. of Henry PETHICK of Weston-super-Mare, Somerset. He *d. s.p.* 10 Sep. 1961, when his Barony became *extinct*.

12 SEPTEMBER

KEMSLEY

VISCOUNTCY. I. 1945. 1. JAMES GOMER (BERRY), 1st BARON KEMSLEY [1936], also a Baronet [1928], was further *cr.*, 12 Sep. 1945, VISCOUNT KEMSLEY, of Dropmore, co. Buckingham. For fuller particulars of him see vol. xiii, p. 566.

12 SEPTEMBER

LLEWELLIN

BARONY. I. 1945. 1. The Right Hon. JOHN JESTYN LLEWELLIN, C.B.E., M.C., T.D., 2nd s. of William LLEWELLIN, of Upton House, Dorset, was *b.* 6 Feb. 1893; ed. at Eton and Oxford (Univ. Coll.). He was *cr.*, 12 Sep. 1945,

BARON LLEWELLIN, of Upton House, co. Dorset. He *d.* unm. 24 Jan. 1957, when his Barony became *extinct.*

13 SEPTEMBER

MARCHWOOD

VISCOUNTCY. I. 1945. 1. FREDERICK GEORGE (PENNY), 1st BARON MARCHWOOD [1937], also a Baronet [1933], was further *cr.*, 13 Sep. 1945, VISCOUNT MARCHWOOD, of Penang and of Marchwood, co. Southampton. He *d.* 1 Jan. 1955. For further particulars of him see vol. xiii, p. 589.

II. 1955. 2. PETER GEORGE (PENNY), VISCOUNT MARCHWOOD [1945] and BARON MARCHWOOD [1937], also a Baronet, only s. and h., was *b.* 7 Nov. 1912. For further particulars and for subsequent Viscounts MARCHWOOD see vol. xiii, above.

13 SEPTEMBER

LYLE OF WESTBOURNE

BARONY. I. 1945. 1. SIR CHARLES ERNEST LEONARD LYLE, 1st Bart. [1932], s. of Charles LYLE, of Brooke Hall, Norwich (yr. br. of Sir Alexander Park LYLE, 1st Bart), was *b.* 22 July 1882; ed. at Harrow and Cambridge (Trin. Coll.). He was *cr.*, 13 Sep. 1945, BARON LYLE OF WESTBOURNE, of Canford Cliffs, co. Dorset. He *m.*, 14 Jan. 1904, Edith Louise, 2nd da. of John LEVY of Rochester. She *d.* 22 Dec. 1942. He *d.* 6 Mar. 1954.

II. 1954. 2. CHARLES JOHN LEONARD (LYLE), BARON LYLE OF WESTBOURNE, also a Baronet, only s. and h., was *b.* 8 Mar. 1905; ed. at Harrow and Cambridge (Pembroke Coll.). He *m.*, 24 Nov. 1927, Joyce Jeanne, elder da. of Sir John JARVIS, 1st Bart. He *d. s.p.* 1 Aug. 1976, when his titles became *extinct.*

14 SEPTEMBER

BROADBRIDGE

BARONY. I. 1945. 1. SIR GEORGE THOMAS BROADBRIDGE, 1st Bart. [1937], K.C.V.O., s. of Henry BROADBRIDGE, of Brighton, Sussex, was *b.* 13 Feb. 1869; ed. at Brighton. He was *cr.*, 14 Sep. 1945, BARON BROADBRIDGE, of Brighton, co. Sussex. He *m.* 1stly, Dec. 1894, Fanny Kathleen, da. of Richard BRIGDEN of Brighton, Sussex. She *d.* 8 Mar. 1928. He *m.* 2ndly, 1929, Clara Maud, da. of John SWANSBOURNE of Bognor, Sussex. She *d.* 17 May 1949. He *d.* 17 Apr. 1952.

II. 1952. 2. ERIC WILBERFORCE (BROADBRIDGE), BARON BROADBRIDGE, also a Baronet, 1st s. and h., was *b.* 22 Dec. 1895; ed. at Hurstpierpoint. He *m.*, 2 June 1924, Mabel Daisy, only da. of Arthur Edward CLARKE of Carshalton. She *d.* 14 Feb. 1966. He *d.* 18 Nov. 1972.

III. 1972. 3. PETER HEWETT (BROADBRIDGE), BARON BROADBRIDGE, also a Baronet, only s. and h., *b.* 19 Aug. 1938; ed. at Hurstpierpoint and Oxford (St Catherine's Coll.). He *m.* 1stly, 1 Apr. 1967, Mary, only da. of W.O. BUSCH of Germany. This marriage was diss. by divorce in 1980 and he *m.* 2ndly, 1989, Sally Frances FINN.

15 SEPTEMBER

CUNNINGHAM OF HYNDHOPE

BARONY. I. 1945
VISCOUNTCY. I. 1946

1. Admiral of the Fleet SIR ANDREW BROWNE CUNNINGHAM, 1st Bart. [1942], K.T., G.C.B., D.S.O., 2nd s. of David John CUNNINGHAM, D.C.L., LL.D., of Edinburgh and Dublin, was *b.* 7 Jan. 1883; ed. at Edinburgh Acad., Stubbington House, Fareham and H.M.S. *Britannia*. He was *cr.*, 15 Sep. 1945, BARON CUNNINGHAM OF HYNDHOPE, of Kirkhope, co. Selkirk; and was further *cr.*, 26 Jan. 1946, VISCOUNT CUNNINGHAM OF HYNDHOPE, of Kirkhope, co. Selkirk. He *m.*, 21 Dec. 1929, Nora Christine, da. of Horace BYATH of Midhurst, Sussex. He *d. s.p.* 12 June 1963, when his titles became *extinct*.

17 SEPTEMBER

PORTAL OF HUNGERFORD

BARONY. I. 1945
VISCOUNTCY. I. 1946

1. Marshal of the Royal Air Force SIR CHARLES FREDERICK ALGERNON PORTAL, G.C.B., D.S.O., M.C., 4th s. of Edward Robert PORTAL, of Sulham House, Pangbourne, Berks, formerly of Eddington House, Hungerford, in that co., was *b.* 21 May 1893; ed. at Winchester and Oxford (Ch. Ch.). He was *cr.*, 17 Sep. 1945, BARON PORTAL OF HUNGERFORD, of Hungerford, co. Berks, with a spec. rem., in default of male issue, to his eldest da. and the heirs male of her body, with like rem. to his 2nd and every other da. successively. He was further *cr.*, 28 Jan. 1946, VISCOUNT PORTAL OF HUNGERFORD, of Hungerford, co. Berks, with the usual rem. He *m.*, 22 July 1919, Joan Margaret, da. of Sir Charles Glynn WELBY, 5th Bart. He *d. s.p.m.s.* (1) 22 Apr. 1971 when his Viscountcy became *extinct* but his Barony was inherited by his 1st da. under the spec. rem. His widow was living 1995.

II. 1971. 2. ROSEMARY ANN PORTAL, 1st da. and h., *suo jure* BARONESS PORTAL under the spec. rem. She was *b.* 12 May 1923 and *d.* unm. 29 Sep. 1990 when her title became *extinct*.

note (1) His only son was *b.* and *d.* 12 Sep. 1921.

18 SEPTEMBER

ALANBROOKE

BARONY. I. 1945
VISCOUNTCY. I. 1946

1. Field Marshal SIR ALAN FRANCIS BROOKE, G.C.B., D.S.O., 6th s. of Sir Victor Alexander BROOKE, 3rd Bart., was *b.* 23 July 1883; ed. abroad and at R.M.A., Woolwich. He was *cr.*, 18 Sep. 1945, BARON ALANBROOKE, of

Brookeborough, co. Fermanagh; and was further *cr.*, 29 Jan. 1946, VISCOUNT ALANBROOKE, of Brookeborough, co. Fermanagh. He *m.* 1stly, 28 July 1914, Jane Mary, da. of Col. John Mervyn Ashdall Carleton RICHARDSON of Rossfad, co. Fermanagh. She *d.* 24 Apr. 1925. He *m.* 2ndly, 7 Dec. 1929, Benita Blanche, eldest da. of Sir Harold PELLY, 4th Bart., of Gillingham, Dorset and widow of Sir Thomas LEES, 2nd Bart. He *d.* 17 June 1963. She *d.* 4 May 1968.

II. 1963. 2. THOMAS (BROOKE), BARON ALANBROOKE and VISCOUNT ALANBROOKE, 1st s. by 1st marriage and h., *b.* 9 Jan. 1920; ed. at Wellington. He *d.* unm., 19 Dec. 1972.

III. 1972. 3. ALAN VICTOR HAROLD (BROOKE), BARON ALANBROOKE and VISCOUNT ALANBROOKE, half-brother and h., being only s. by 2nd wife. He was *b.* 24 Nov. 1932; ed. at Harrow and Bristol Univ.

19 SEPTEMBER

BROUGHSHANE

BARONY. I. 1945. 1. SIR WILLIAM HENRY DAVISON, K.B.E., s. of Richard DAVISON, of Beechfield, Ballymena, co. Antrim, formerly of Knockboy, Broughshane, was *b.* 1872; ed. at Shrewsbury and Oxford (Keble Coll.). He was *cr.*, 19 Sep. 1945, BARON BROUGHSHANE, of Kensington, co. London. He *m.* 1stly, 1898, Beatrice Mary, 2nd da. of Sir Owen ROBERTS of Henley Park, Surrey and Plas Dinas, Caernarvon. This marriage was diss. by divorce in 1929 and she *d.* in 1971. He *m.* 2ndly, 6 June 1929, Louisa Mary Constance, da. of Major Charles Frederick MARRIOTT. He *d.* 19 Jan. 1954. His widow *d.* 1971.

II. 1953. 2. PATRICK OWEN ALEXANDER (DAVISON), BARON BROUGHSHANE, 1st s. and h., was *b.* 18 June 1903; ed. at Winchester and Oxford (Magdalen Coll.). He *m.*, 9 Oct. 1929, Bettine, only da. of Sir Arthur Edward Ian Montague RUSSELL, 6th Bart.

[ALEXANDER DAVISON, s. and h. ap., *b.* 11 Jan. 1936; ed. at Eton. He *m.*, 15 July 1961, Teresa Clare, only da. of James Guy BRAMWELL of St-Jacques de-Grasse, France. This marriage was diss. by divorce in 1966. He *m.* 2ndly, 1970, Cecilia Ann, da. of J.W. INGRAMS of Patchings, Sussex. She *d.* in 1977 and he *m.* 3rdly, 1988, Daphne Bridget, only da. of Thomas Walter JONES of Cawston, Norfolk and formerly wife of Anthony John NELSON-SULLIVAN. He *d. v.p.* and *s.p.m.* in 1988. His widow *m.* 3rdly and was still living 1995.]

12 OCTOBER

PAKENHAM

BARONY. I. 1945. 1. The Hon. FRANCIS AUNGIER PAKENHAM, 2nd s. of Thomas (PAKENHAM), 5th EARL OF LONGFORD [I.], was *b.* 5 Dec. 1905. He was *cr.*, 12 Oct. 1945, BARON PAKENHAM, of Cowley, in the City of Oxford, for further detail see above, *sub* LONGFORD.

19 OCTOBER

HENDERSON

BARONY. I. 1945. 1. WILLIAM WATSON HENDERSON, 1st s. of the Right Hon. Arthur HENDERSON, M.P., of Transport House, Smith Sq., London, was *b.* 8 Aug. 1891; ed. at Queen Elizabeth's Gram. Sch., Darlington. He was *cr.*, 19 Oct. 1945, BARON HENDERSON, of Westgate, in the City and co. of Newcastle-on-Tyne. He *d.* unm. 4 Apr. 1984, when his Barony became *extinct*.

12 NOVEMBER

MOUNTEVANS

BARONY. I. 1945. 1. Adm. SIR EDWARD RATCLIFFE GARTH RUSSELL EVANS, K.C.B., D.S.O., s. of Frank EVANS, Barrister-at-Law, of 5 New Square, Lincoln's Inn, was *b.* 28 Oct. 1881; ed. at Merchant Taylors' Sch. and H.M.S. *Worcester*. He was *cr.*, 12 Nov. 1945, BARON MOUNTEVANS, of Chelsea, co. London. He *m.* 1stly, 13 Apr. 1904, Hilda Beatrice, da. of Thomas Gregory RUSSELL of Christchurch, New Zealand. She *d.* 18 Apr. 1913. He *m.* 2ndly, 22 Jan. 1916, Elsa, da. of Richard ANDVORD of Oslo, Norway. He *d.* 20 Aug. 1957. His widow *d.* 21 Oct. 1963.

II. 1957. 2. RICHARD ANDVORD (EVANS), BARON MOUNTEVANS, 1st s. and h., was *b.* 27 Aug. 1918; ed. at Cranbrook Sch., Sydney and Stowe. He *m.*, 6 Sep. 1940, Deirdre Grace, da. of John O'Connell of Buxton Hill, co. Cork. He *d.* 12 Dec. 1974. His widow was living 1995.

III. 1974. 3. EDWARD PATRICK BROKE ANDVORD (EVANS), BARON MOUNTEVANS, 1st s. and h., *b.* 1 Feb. 1943; ed. at Rugby and Oxford (Trin. Coll.). He *m.*, 1974, Johanna, da. of Antonius Franciscus KEYZER of The Hague.

13 NOVEMBER

LINDSAY OF BIRKER

BARONY. I. 1945. 1. ALEXANDER DUNLOP LINDSAY, C.B.E., 1st s. of the Rev. Thomas M. LINDSAY, D.D., of Glasgow, Principal of the United Free Coll., Glasgow, was *b.* 14 May 1879; ed. at Glasgow Acad., Glasgow Univ. and Oxford (Univ. Coll.). He was *cr.*, 13 Nov. 1945, BARON LINDSAY OF BIRKER, of Low Ground, co. Cumberland. He *m.*, 1907, Erica Violet, yst. da. of F. STORR. He *d.* 18 Mar. 1952. His widow *d.* 28 May 1962.

II. 1952. 2. MICHAEL FRANCIS MORRIS (LINDSAY), BARON LINDSAY OF BIRKER, 1st s. and h., was *b.* 24 Feb. 1909; ed. at Gresham's Sch., Holt and Oxford (Balliol Coll.). He *m.*, 25 June 1941, Hsiao Li, da. of Col. Li Wen-Chi of the Chinese Army. He *d.* 13 Feb. 1994. His widow was living 1995.

III. 1994. 3. JAMES FRANCIS (LINDSAY), BARON LINDSAY OF BIRKER, only s. and h., *b.* 29 Jan. 1945; ed. at Geelong Gram. Sch. and Keele Univ. He *m.*, 1966, Mary Rose, da. of W.G. THOMAS of Cwmbran, Monmouth.

14 NOVEMBER

PIERCY

BARONY. I. 1945. 1. WILLIAM PIERCY, C.B.E., s. of Augustus Edward PIERCY, was *b.* 7 Feb. 1886; ed. privately and at London Sch. of Economics. He was *cr.*, 14 Nov. 1945, BARON PIERCY, of Burford, co. Oxford. He *m.* 1stly, 14 Apr. 1915, Mary Louisa, da. of Thomas Henry William PELHAM. She *d.* 8 Jan. 1953. He *m.* 2ndly, 16 July 1964, Veronica, da. of John Hordley WARHAM of Wembley Park, Midx. He *d.* 7 July 1966. His widow was living 1995.

II. 1966. 2. NICHOLAS PELHAM PIERCY, BARON PIERCY, only s. and h., *b.* 23 June 1918; ed. at Eton and Cambridge (King's Coll.). He *m.*, 28 Oct. 1948, Oonagh Lavinia, da. of Major Edward John Lake BAYLAY. He *d.* 22 Mar. 1981. His widow was living 1995.

III. 1981. 3. JAMES WILLIAM (PIERCY), BARON PIERCY, 1st s. and h., *b.* 19 Jan. 1946; ed. at Shrewsbury and Edinburgh Univ.

15 NOVEMBER

MORRISON

BARONY. I. 1945. 1. ROBERT CRAIGMYLE MORRISON, s. of James MORRISON, of Aberdeen, was *b.* 29 Oct. 1881; ed. at elementary and higher grade schools in Aberdeen. He was *cr.*, 15 Nov. 1945, BARON MORRISON, of Tottenham, co. Middlesex. He *m.*, 27 July 1910, Grace, elder da. of Thomas GLOSSOP. He *d.* 25 Dec. 1953. His widow *d.* 1983.

II. 1953. 2. DENNIS (MORRISON), BARON MORRISON, 1st s. and h., was *b.* 21 June 1914; ed. at Tottenham County Sch. He *m.* 1stly, 1940, Florence Alice Helena, da. of Augustus HENNES of Tottenham. This marriage was diss. by divorce in 1958. He *m.* 2ndly, 21 Mar. 1959, Joan Eleanor, da. of William R. MEECH of Acton, Midx. This marriage was diss. by divorce in 1975.

16 NOVEMBER

CHORLEY

BARONY. I. 1945. 1. ROBERT SAMUEL THEODORE CHORLEY, s. of Richard Fisher CHORLEY, of Chapel Close, Kendal, was *b.* 29 May 1895; ed. at Kendal Sch. and Oxford (Queen's Coll.). He was *cr.*, 16 Nov. 1945, BARON CHORLEY, of Kendal, co. Westmorland. He *m.*, 15 Apr. 1925, Katharine Campbell, only da. of Edward HOPKINSON of Alderley Edge, Cheshire. He *d.* 27 Jan. 1978. His widow *d.* 1986.

II. 1953. 2. ROGER RICHARD EDWARD (CHORLEY), BARON CHORLEY, 1st s. and h., *b.* 14 Aug. 1930; ed. at Stowe and Cambridge (Gonville and Caius

Coll.). He *m.*, 31 Oct. 1964, Ann Elizabeth, yr. da. of Archibald Scott DEBENHAM, of Ingatestone, Essex.

[NICHOLAS RUPERT DEBENHAM, 1st s. and h. ap., *b.* 15 July 1966.]

17 NOVEMBER

CALVERLEY

BARONY. I. 1945. 1. GEORGE MUFF, s. of George MUFF, of Bradford, was *b.* 10 Feb. 1877. He was *cr.*, 17 Nov. 1945, BARON CALVERLEY, of the City of Bradford, in the West Riding of co. York. He *m.*, 27 July 1909, Ellen Eliza, elder da. of Charles William ORFORD of Bath. He *d.* 20 Sept. 1955. His widow *d.* 1965.

II. 1955. 2. GEORGE RAYMOND ORFORD (MUFF), BARON CALVERLEY, only s. and h., was *b.* 1 May 1914; ed. at Bradford Gram. Sch. He *m.*, 21 Dec. 1940, Mary, da. of Arthur FARRAR of Halifax. He *d.* 4 June 1971. His widow was living 1995.

III. 1971. 3. CHARLES RODNEY (MUFF), BARON CALVERLEY, 1st s. and h., *b.* 2 Oct. 1946; ed. at Moravian Sch. for Boys, Fulneck, Pudsey. He *m.*, 1972, Barbara Ann, da. of Jonathan BROWN.

[JONATHAN EDWARD MUFF, 1st s. and h. ap., *b.* 16 Apr. 1975.]

1 DECEMBER

RUSHOLME

BARONY. I. 1945. 1. ROBERT ALEXANDER PALMER, s. of William PALMER, of Manchester, was *b.* 29 Nov. 1890; ed. at St. Mary's Sch., Ashton-on-Mersey. He was *cr.*, 1 Dec. 1945, BARON RUSHOLME, of Rusholme, in the City of Manchester. He *d.* unm. 18 Aug. 1977, when his Barony became *extinct*.

PEERAGES OF 1946

9 JANUARY

UTHWATT

BARONY FOR LIFE. I. 1946. 1. SIR AUGUSTUS ANDREWES UTHWATT, one of the Justices of the High Court of Justice, 3rd s. of Thomas Andrewes UTHWATT, of Middleton-on-the-Hill, co. Hereford, and of Maids Moreton, co. Buckingham, was *b.* 25 Apr. 1879; ed. at Ballarat Coll., Victoria and Trin. Coll., Melbourne. On 9 Jan. 1946 he was app. a Lord of Appeal in Ordinary under the Appellate Jurisdication

Act of 1876, and *cr.* a Baron for Life by the style of BARON UTHWATT, of Lathbury, co. Buckingham. He *m.*, 6 Aug. 1927, Mrs Mary Baxter BONHOTE, da. of Rev. Charles Edwin MEERES, Vicar of Eastry, Kent. He *d. s.p.* 24 Apr. 1949, when his Life Barony became *extinct*.

23 JANUARY

BARONY. I. 1946. 1. SIR ARTHUR WILLIAM TEDDER, G.C.B., Marshal of the R.A.F., 2nd s. of Sir Arthur John TEDDER, C.B., of Hemyock, Devon; *b.* 11 July 1890; ed. at Whitgift Sch., Croydon and Cambridge (Magdalene Coll.). He was *cr.* 23 Jan. 1946, BARON TEDDER of Glenguin, co. Stirling. He *m.* 1stly, 1915, Rosalinde, da. of William McIntyre MACLARDY of Sidney, N.S.W. She was k. in an air accident near Cairo, 4 Jan. 1943 and he *m.* 2ndly, 26 Oct. 1943, Marie de Seton, formerly wife of Capt. Ian Reddie Hamilton BLACK, R.N., 2nd da. of Col. Sir Bruce Gordon SETON. She *d.* 3 Jan. 1965. He *d.* 3 June 1967.

II. 1967. 2. JOHN MICHAEL (TEDDER), BARON TEDDER, 2nd but 1st surv. s. and h. (1), *b.* 4 July 1926; ed. at Dauntsey's Sch., Cambridge (Magdalene Coll.) and Birmingham Univ; *m.*, 17 Apr. 1952, Peggy Eileen, 2nd da. of Samuel George GROWCOTT of Birmingham. He *d.* 18 Feb. 1994. His widow was still living 1995.

III. 1994. 3. ROBIN JOHN (TEDDER), BARON TEDDER, 1st s. and h., *b.* 6 Apr. 1955; *m.* 1stly, 1977, Jennifer Peggy, da. of John MANGAN of New Zealand. She *d.* 1978 and he *m.* 2ndly, 1980, Rita Aristeia, 2nd da. of John FRANGIDIS of Sidney, N.S.W.

[BENJAMIN JOHN TEDDER, 1st s. and h. ap. by 1st wife, was *b.* 1985.]

note (1) His 1st s., Arthur Richard Brian Tedder was *b.* 21 July 1916. He *d. v.p.* and unm., 3 Aug. 1940, being k. in action over France.

25 JANUARY

SOUTHWOOD

VISCOUNTCY. I. 1946, Jan. to Apr. 1. JULIUS SALTWOOD (ELIAS), 1st BARON SOUTHWOOD [1937], was further *cr.*, 25 Jan. 1946, VISCOUNT SOUTHWOOD, of Fernhurst, co. Sussex. He *d. s.p.* 10 Apr. 1946, when all his honours became *extinct*. For fuller particulars of him see vol. xiii, p. 593.

26 JANUARY

CUNNINGHAM OF HYNDHOPE

CUNNINGHAM OF HYNDHOPE, Viscountcy (*Cunningham*), *cr.*, 26 Jan. 1946. See CUNNINGHAM OF HYNDHOPE, Barony, *cr.* 15 Sep. 1945, p. 768.

28 JANUARY

PORTAL OF HUNGERFORD

PORTAL OF HUNGERFORD, Viscountcy (*Portal*), *cr.* 28 Jan. 1946. See PORTAL OF HUNGERFORD, Barony, *cr.* 17 Sep. 1945, p. 768.

28 JANUARY

COLGRAIN

BARONY. I. 1946. 1. COLIN FREDERICK CAMPBELL, 1st s. of George William CAMPBELL (6th s. of Colin CAMPBELL of Colgrain, co. Dumbarton), was *b.* 13 June 1866; ed. at Eton. He was *cr.*, 28 Jan. 1946, BARON COLGRAIN, of Everlands, co. Kent. He *m.*, 9 May 1890, Lady Angela Mary Alice, 2nd da. of Henry Dudley (RYDER), 4th EARL OF HARROWBY. She *d.* 10 Nov. 1939. He *d.* 3 Nov. 1954.

II. 1954. 2. DONALD SWINTON (CAMPBELL), BARON COLGRAIN, 1st s. and h., was *b.* 6 Nov. 1891; ed. at Eton and Cambridge (Trin. Coll.). He *m.*, 1 Aug. 1917, Margaret Emily, eldest da. of Percy William CARVER of West Hoathly, Sussex. He *d.* 20 Oct. 1973. His widow *d.* 1989.

III. 1973. 3. DAVID COLIN (CAMPBELL), BARON COLGRAIN, 1st s. and h., *b.* 24 Apr. 1920. He *m.* 1stly, 30 June 1945, Veronica Margaret, yr. da. of Col. William Leckie WEBSTER. This marriage was diss. by divorce in 1964 and he *m.* 2ndly, 1973, Sheila, da. of Robert McLeod MITCHELL and formerly wife of M.M. HUDSON.

[ALASTAIR COLIN LECKIE CAMPBELL, only s. by 1st wife and h. ap., *b.* 16 Sep. 1951; ed. at Eton and Cambridge (Trin. Coll.). He *m.*, 1979, Annabel Rose, yr. da. of Robin Hugh WARRENDER of Bath.]

29 JANUARY

ALANBROOKE

ALANBROOKE, Viscountcy (*Brooke*), *cr.* 29 Jan. 1946. See ALANBROOKE, Barony, *cr.* 18 Sep. 1945, p. 768.

30 JANUARY

INMAN

BARONY. I. 1946. 1. PHILIP ALBERT INMAN, of Philip INMAN, of Knaresborough, co. York, was *b.* 12 June 1892; ed. at Knaresborough, Headingley Coll., Leeds and Leeds Univ. He was *cr.*, 30 Jan. 1946, BARON INMAN, of Knaresborough, in the West Riding of co. York. He *m.*, 27 Aug. 1919, May Amelie, only da. of Edward DEW of Harrow. He *d. s.p.m.s.* 26 Aug. 1979, when his Barony became *extinct*.

[PHILIP JOHN COPE, s. and h. ap., *b.* 15 Mar. 1929; ed. at Lancing and Geneva Univ.; *m.* 1stly, 17 June 1952, Jennifer, da. of George CLARK. This marriage was diss. by divorce 1957, and he *m.* 2ndly, 1966, Judith, da. of Albert George James GIBBINS, of Langford, Bristol. He *d. v.p.* and *s.p.m.* 26 Apr. 1968.]

31 JANUARY

MONTGOMERY OF ALAMEIN

VISCOUNTCY.
I. 1946.

1. Field Marshal SIR BERNARD LAW MONTGOMERY, G.C.B., D.S.O., 3rd s. of the Right Rev. Henry Hutchinson MONTGOMERY, K.C.M.G., of New Park, Moville, co. Donegal, sometime Bishop of Tasmania, was *b.* 17 Nov. 1887; ed. at St. Paul's Sch. and R.M.C., Sandhurst. He was *cr.*, 31 Jan. 1946, VISCOUNT MONTGOMERY OF ALAMEIN, of Hindhead, co. Surrey. He *m.*, 27 July 1927, Elizabeth, da. of Robert Thompson HOBART of Tunbridge Wells and widow of Capt. Oswald Armitage CARVER. She *d.* 19 Oct. 1937. He *d.* 24 Mar. 1976.

II. 1976.

2. DAVID BERNARD (MONTGOMERY), VISCOUNT MONTGOMERY OF ALAMEIN, only s. and h., *b.* 18 Aug. 1928; ed. at Winchester and Cambridge (Trin. Coll.). He *m.* 1stly, 27 Feb. 1953, Mary Raymond, yr. da. of Sir Charles CONNELL. This marriage was diss. by divorce in 1967. He *m.* 2ndly, 1970, Tessa, da. of Lieut. Gen. Sir Frederick Arthur Montague BROWNING by his wife Daphne du Maurier, and formerly wife of Major Peter P.J. DU ZULVETA.

[HENRY DAVID MONTGOMERY, only s. by 1st marriage and h. ap., *b.* 2 Apr. 1954. He *m.*, 1980, Caroline J., da. of Richard ODEY of Hotham Hall, York.]

5 FEBRUARY

DU PARCQ

BARONY FOR LIFE.
I. 1946.

1. The Right Hon. SIR HERBERT DU PARCQ, one of the Lords Justices of Appeal, s. of Clement Pixley DU PARCQ, of St. Helier, Jersey, was *b.* 5 Aug. 1880; ed. at Victoria Coll., Jersey and Oxford (Exeter and Jesus Colls.). On 5 Feb. 1946 he was app. a Lord of Appeal in Ordinary under the Appellate Jurisdiction Act of 1876, and *cr.* a Baron for Life by the style of BARON DU PARCQ, of Grouville, in the Isle of Jersey. He *m.*, 8 Sep. 1911, Lucy, da. of John RENOUF of St. Helier, Jersey. He *d.* 27 Apr. 1949, when his Life Barony became *extinct*. His widow *d.* 1965.

8 FEBRUARY

GORT

VISCOUNTCY.
I. 1946, Feb. to Mar.

1. JOHN STANDISH SURTEES PRENDERGAST (VEREKER), 6th VISCOUNT GORT [I. 1816] and BARON KILTARTON OF GORT [I. 1810], was *cr.*, 8 Feb. 1946, VISCOUNT GORT, of Mamsterley, co. Durham [U.K.]. He *d. s.p.m.s.* 31 Mar. 1946, when his Viscountcy [U.K.] became *extinct*, but the Irish honours passed to his br. and h. male. For fuller particulars of him see above and vol. vi, *sub* GORT.

11 FEBRUARY

TOVEY

BARONY. I. 1946. Admiral of the Fleet SIR JOHN CRONYN TOVEY, G.C.B., K.B.E., D.S.O., s. of Lieut. Col. Hamilton TOVEY, R.E., was *b.* 7 Mar. 1885. He was *cr.*, 11 Feb. 1946, BARON TOVEY, of Langton Matravers, co. Dorset. He *m.*, 28 Mar. 1916, Aida, da. of John ROWE. He *d. s.p.* 12 Jan. 1971 when his Barony became *extinct.*

12 FEBRUARY

DARWEN

BARONY. I. 1946. 1. JOHN PERCIVAL DAVIES, s. of Thomas Pearce DAVIES, of Heatherfield, Darwen, and Pengarth, Grange over Sands, co. Lancaster, was *b.* 28 Mar. 1885; ed. at Sidcot and Bootham schools and Manchester Univ. He was *cr.*, 12 Feb. 1946, BARON DARWEN, of Heys-in-Bowland, in the West Riding of co. York. He *m.*, 18 Mar. 1914, Mary Kathleen, da. of Alfred Kemp BROWN of Golders Green. He *d.* 26 Dec. 1950. His widow *d.* 26 Jan. 1964.

II. 1950. 2. CEDRIC PERCIVAL (DAVIES), BARON DARWEN, 1st s. and h., was *b.* 18 Feb. 1915; ed. at Sidcot Sch. and Manchester Univ. He *m.*, 14 July 1934, Kathleen Dora, da. of George Sharples WALKER of Pendleton, Manchester. He *d.* 9 Dec. 1988. His widow was living 1995.

III. 1988. 3. ROGER MICHAEL (DAVIES), BARON DARWEN, 1st s. and h., *b.* 28 June 1938; ed. at Bootham Sch., York. He *m.*, 1961, Gillian Irene, da. of Eric G. HARDY of Bristol.

[PAUL DAVIES, 1st s. and h. ap., *b.* 1962.]

1 MARCH

ALEXANDER OF TUNIS

VISCOUNTCY. I. } 1946
EARLDOM. I. } 1952

1. Field Marshal the Hon. SIR HAROLD RUPERT LEOFRIC GEORGE ALEXANDER, G.C.B., G.C.M.G., C.S.I., D.S.O., M.C., 3rd s. of James (ALEXANDER), 4th EARL OF CALEDON [I.], was *b.* 10 Dec. 1891. He was *cr.*, 1 Mar. 1946, VISCOUNT ALEXANDER OF TUNIS, of Errigal, co. Donegal; and was further *cr.*, 11 Mar. 1952, BARON RIDEAU, of Ottawa and of Castle Dorg, co. Tyrone, and EARL ALEXANDER OF TUNIS. He *m.*, 14 Oct. 1931, Lady Margaret Diana, yr. da. of George Charles (BINGHAM), 5th EARL OF LUCAN. He *d.* 16 June 1969. She *d.* 1971.

II. 1969. 2. SHANE WILLIAM DESMOND (ALEXANDER), EARL ALEXANDER OF TUNIS, VISCOUNT ALEXANDER OF TUNIS, and BARON RIDEAU, 1st s. and h., *b.* 30 June 1935; ed. at Harrow and Ashbury Coll., Ottawa. He *m.* 1stly, 1971, Hilary, only da. of John VAN GEEST. This marriage was diss. by divorce in 1976 and he *m.* 2ndly, 1981, Davina Mary, yst. da. of James Allen David (WOODHOUSE), 4th BARON TERRINGTON.

12 MARCH

WILSON

BARONY. I. 1946. 1. Field Marshal SIR HENRY MAITLAND WILSON, G.C.B., G.B.E., D.S.O., 1st s. of Arthur Maitland WILSON, C.B.E., of Stowlandtoft Hall, Suffolk, was *b.* 5 Sep. 1881; ed. at Eton and R.M.C., Sandhurst. He was *cr.*, 12 Mar. 1946, BARON WILSON, of Libya and of Stowlangtoft, co. Suffolk. He *m.*, 15 Dec. 1914, Hester Mary, yst. da. of Philip James Digby WYKEHAM of Tythrop House, Oxon. He *d.* 31 Dec. 1964. His widow *d.* 1979.

II. 1964. 2. PATRICK MAITLAND (WILSON), BARON WILSON, only s. and h., *b.* 14 Sep. 1915; ed. at Eton and Cambridge (King's Coll.). He *m.*, 12 Jan. 1945, Storeen Violet, eldest da. of Major James Hamilton Douglas CAMPBELL by his wife Anna Leonora Beatrice, 4th da. of Lionel Edward (MASSEY), 5th BARON CLARINA. She *d.* 1990.

5 APRIL

INVERCHAPEL

BARONY. I. 1946. 1. The Right Hon. SIR ARCHIBALD JOHN KERR CLARK KERR, *formerly* CLARK, G.C.M.G., 5th s. of John Kerr CLARK, of Crossbasket Castle, Hamilton, co. Lanark, was *b.* 17 Mar. 1882; ed. privately. He was *cr.*, 5 Apr. 1946, BARON INVERCHAPEL, of Loch Eck, co. Argyll. He *m.*, 24 Apr. 1929, Maria Teresa Dia Salas, da. of Don Javier Diaz LIRA of Santiago de Chile. He *d. s.p.* 5 July 1951, when his Barony became *extinct*.

25 JUNE

BEVERIDGE

BARONY. I. 1946. 1. SIR WILLIAM HENRY BEVERIDGE, K.C.B., only s. of Henry BEVERIDGE, I.C.S., of Pitfold, Shottermill, Surrey, was *b.* 5 Mar. 1879; ed. at Charterhouse and Oxford (Balliol Coll.). He was *cr.*, 25 June 1946, BARON BEVERIDGE, of Tuggal, co. Northumberland. He *m.*, 15 Dec. 1942, Jessy Janet, da. of William PHILIP of Fife and widow of David B. MAIR. She *d.* in 1959. He *d. s.p.* 16 Mar. 1963, when his Barony became *extinct*.

26 JUNE

UVEDALE OF NORTH END

BARONY. I. 1946. 1. SIR AMBROSE EDGAR WOODALL, s. of the Rev. Samuel Russell WOODALL, of Victoria Park, Manchester, a Primitive Methodist Minister, was *b.* 24 Apr. 1885; ed. at Victoria Univ. of Manchester and St. Bartholomew's Hosp. He was *cr.* 26 June 1946, BARON UVEDALE OF NORTH END, of North End, co. Middlesex. He *m.*, 27 Apr. 1949, Joyce Eleanor, 2nd da. of Sidney Herbert HOLMAN of Highgate and St. Margaret's Bay, Kent, and widow of Rt. Hon. Hastings Bertrand LEES-SMITH. He *d. s.p.* 28 Feb. 1974 when his Barony became *extinct*.

27 JUNE

LUCAS OF CHILWORTH

BARONY. I. 1946. 1. GEORGE WILLIAM LUCAS, s. of Percy William LUCAS, of Oxford, was *b.* 29 Mar. 1896. He was *cr.*, 27 June 1946, BARON LUCAS OF CHILWORTH, of Chilworth, co. Southampton. He *m.*, 24 Feb. 1917, Sonia, da. of Marcus FINKELSTEIN of Latvia. He *d.* 11 Oct. 1967. His widow *d.* 1979.

II. 1967. 2. MICHAEL WILLIAM GEORGE (LUCAS), BARON LUCAS OF CHILWORTH, 1st s. and h., *b.* 26 Apr. 1926; ed. at Peter Symonds Sch., Winchester. He *m.*, 9 June 1955, Ann-Marie, only da. of Ronald William BUCK of Southampton.

[SIMON WILLIAM LUCAS, 1st s. and h. ap., *b.* 6 Feb. 1957; ed. at Leicester Univ. He *m.*, 1993, Fiona, yr. da. of Thomas MACKINTOSH of Vancouver, Canada.]

28 JUNE

SHEPHERD

BARONY. I. 1946. 1. GEORGE ROBERT SHEPHERD, s. of George Robert SHEPHERD, of Spalding, co. Lincoln, was *b.* 19 Aug. 1881; ed. at Spalding Board Sch. He was *cr.*, 28 June 1946, BARON SHEPHERD, of Spalding, co. Lincoln. He *m.*, 4 Aug. 1915, Ada, da. of Alfred NEWTON of Halstead, Essex. He *d.* 4 Dec. 1954. His widow *d.* 1975.

II. 1954. 2. MALCOLM NEWTON (SHEPHERD), BARON SHEPHERD, only s. and h., was *b.* 27 Sep. 1918; ed. at Friends' Sch., Saffron Walden. He *m.*, 15 Nov. 1941, Allison, da. of Patrick REDMOND of Edinburgh.

[GRAEME GEORGE SHEPHERD, 1st s. and h. ap., *b.* 6 Jan. 1949.]

16 JULY

CITRINE

BARONY. I. 1946. 1. The Right Hon. SIR WALTER MCLENNAN CITRINE, K.B.E., s. of Alfred CITRINE, of Wallasey, co. Chester, was *b.* 22 Aug. 1887; ed. at elementary school. He was *cr.*, 16 July 1946, BARON CITRINE, of Wembley, co. Middlesex. He *m.*, 28 Mar. 1913, Doris Helen, da. of Edgar SLADE of Pendleton, Manchester. She *d.* 1973. He *d.* 22 Jan. 1983.

II. 1983. 2. NORMAN ARTHUR (CITRINE), BARON CITRINE, 1st s. and h., *b.* 27 Sep. 1914; ed. at Univ. Coll. Sch. He *m.*, 4 Jan. 1939, Kathleen Alice, da. of George CHILVERS of Saxmundham, Suffolk.

17 JULY

BRAND

BARONY. I. 1946. 1. ROBERT HENRY BRAND, C.M.G., 4th s. of Henry Robert (BRAND), 2nd Viscount Hampden, was *b.* 30 Oct. 1878; ed. at

Marlborough and Oxford (New Coll.). He was *cr.*, 17 July 1946, BARON BRAND, of Eydon, co. Northampton. He *m.*, 9 June 1917, Phyllis, da. of Chiswell Dabney LANGHORNE of Virginia, U.S.A. She *d.* 1937. He *d. s.p.m.s.* 23 Aug. 1963, when his Barony became *extinct*.

[ROBERT JAMES BRAND, only s. and h. ap., *b.* 1923, *k.* on active service in Western Europe in 1945.]

18 JULY

NEWALL

BARONY. I. 1946. 1. Marshal of the Royal Air Force SIR CYRIL LOUIS NORTON NEWALL, G.C.B., O.M., G.C.M.G., C.B.E., A.M., s. of Lieut. Col. William Potter NEWALL, I.A., was *b.* 15 Feb. 1886; ed. at Bedford Sch. and R.M.C., Sandhurst. He was *cr.*, 18 July 1946, BARON NEWALL, of Clifton-upon-Dunsmoor, co. Warwick. He *m.* 1stly, 18 June 1922, May Dulcie WEDDELL, who *d.* 1924. He *m.* 2ndly, 18 Apr. 1925, Olive Tennyson, only da. of Horace Tennyson FOSTER of Boston, U.S.A. He *d.* 30 Nov. 1963. His widow *d.* 1988.

II. 1963. 2. FRANCIS STORER EATON (NEWALL), BARON NEWALL, only s. and h., *b.* 23 June 1930; ed. at Eton and R.M.C., Sandhurst. He *m.*, 29 Sep. 1956, Pamela Elizabeth, elder da. of Edward Hugh Lee ROWCLIFFE of Malmesbury, Wilts.

[RICHARD HUGH EATON NEWALL, 1st s. and h. ap., *b.* 19 Feb. 1961.]

23 AUGUST

MOUNTBATTEN OF BURMA

VISCOUNTCY. I. 1946
EARLDOM. I. 1947

1. Acting Adm. LORD LOUIS FRANCIS ALBERT VICTOR NICHOLAS MOUNTBATTEN, G.C.V.O., K.C.B., D.S.O., yr. s. of Louis Alexander (MOUNTBATTEN), 1st MARQUESS OF MILFORD HAVEN (*formerly H.S.H.* PRINCE LOUIS OF BATTENBERG) was *b.* 25 June 1900; ed. at R.N.C.s, Osborne and Dartmouth, and Cambridge (Christ's Coll.). He was *cr.*, 23 Aug. 1946, VISCOUNT MOUNTBATTEN OF BURMA, of Romsey, co. Southampton, with a spec. rem., in default of male issue, to his eldest da. and the heirs male of her body, with like rem. to his 2nd and every other da. successively. He was further *cr.*, 18 Oct. 1947, BARON ROMSEY, co. Southampton, and EARL MOUNTBATTEN OF BURMA, with a similar spec. rem. He *m.*, 18 July 1922, Edwina Cynthia Annette, elder da. of Wilfrid William (ASHLEY), 1st and last BARON MOUNT TEMPLE. She *d.* 21 Feb. 1960 in North Borneo on a tour on behalf of St. John's Ambulance Brigade of which she was Superintendent-in-Chief, and was buried at sea, from H.M.S. *Wakeful* off Portsmouth. He was assassinated 27 Aug. 1979 when he was suc. in his titles by his eldest da.

II. 1979. 2. PATRICIA EDWINA VICTORIA KNATCHBULL, *suo jure* COUNTESS MOUNTBATTEN OF BURMA, 1st da. and h., *b.* 14 Feb. 1924. She *m.*, 26 Oct. 1946, John Ulick (KNATCHBULL), 7th BARON BRABOURNE.

[NORTON LOUIS PHILIP KNATCHBULL, *styled* LORD ROMSEY, 1st s. and h. ap., *b.* 8 Oct. 1947; ed. at Gordonstoun and Univ. of Kent. He *m.*, 20 Oct. 1979, Penelope Meredith, only da. of Reginald EASTWOOD of Palma de Mallorca, Spain.]

19 SEPTEMBER

FRASER OF NORTH CAPE

BARONY. I. 1946. 1. Adm. SIR BRUCE AUSTIN FRASER, G.C.B., K.B.E., s. of Gen. Alexander FRASER, C.B., R.E., was *b.* 5 Feb. 1888; ed. at Bradfield. He was *cr.*, 1946, BARON FRASER OF NORTH CAPE, of Molesey, co. Surrey. He *d.* unm. 12 Feb. 1981, when his Barony became *extinct.*

28 OCTOBER

HALL

VISCOUNTCY. I. 1946. 1. The Right Hon. GEORGE HENRY HALL, s. of George HALL, of Marshfield, co. Gloucester, was *b.* 31 Dec. 1881; ed. at Penrhiwceiber Elementary Sch. He was *cr.*, 28 Oct. 1946, VISCOUNT HALL, of Cynon Valley, co. Glamorgan. He *m.* 1stly, 10 Oct. 1910, Margaret, da. of William JONES of Ynysybwl, Glam. She *d.* 24 July 1941. He *m.* 2ndly, 29 Jan. 1964, Alice Martha, da. of Ben WALKER of Brinklow, Rugby. He *d.* 8 Nov. 1965.

II. 1965. 2. WILLIAM GEORGE LEONARD (HALL), VISCOUNT HALL, 1st s. and h., *b.* 9 Mar. 1913; ed. at Christ Coll., Brecon and Univ. Coll. Hosp., London. He *m.* 1stly, 1 June 1935, Joan Margaret, da. of William GRIFFITHS of Coedeley, Glam. She *d.* in 1962. He *m.* 2ndly, 21 Apr. 1963, Constance Ann Gathorne, only da. of Rupert Gathorne HARDY of London. She *d.* in 1972. He *m.* 3rdly, 1974, Marie-Colette, da. of Col. Henri BACH. He *d. s.p.m.* 24 July 1985, when his Viscountcy became *extinct.* His widow was living 1995.

PEERAGES OF 1947

6 JANUARY

NORMAND

BARONY FOR LIFE. I. 1947. 1. The Right Hon. WILFRED GUILD NORMAND, Lord Justice Gen. of Scotland and Lord Pres. of the Court of Session, s. of Patrick Hill NORMAND, of Whitehill, Aberdour, co. Fife, was *b.* 6 May 1884; ed. at Fettes Coll., Edinburgh, Oxford (Oriel Coll.), Paris and Edinburgh Univs. On 6 Jan. 1947 he was app. a Lord of Appeal in Ordinary under the Appellate Jurisdiction Act of 1876, and *cr.* a Baron for Life by the style of BARON NORMAND, of Aberdour, co. Fife. He *m.* 1stly, 22 July 1913, Gertrude, da. of William LAWSON, she *d.* 8 Nov. 1923. He *m.* 2ndly, 27 Apr. 1927, Marion, da. of David CUNNINGHAM. He *d.* 5 Oct. 1962 when his Life Barony became *extinct.*

13 JANUARY

OAKSEY

BARONY. I. 1947. 1. The Right Hon. SIR GEOFFREY LAWRENCE, D.S.O., T.D., one of the Lords Justices of Appeal, 3rd s. of Alfred Tristram (LAWRENCE), 1st BARON TREVETHIN, was *b.* 2 Dec. 1880. He was *cr.*, 13 Jan. 1947, BARON OAKSEY, of Oaksey, co. Wilts. He *suc.* his br. as 3rd BARON TREVETHIN, see vol. xiii, p. 362, above.

14 JANUARY

ISMAY

BARONY. I. 1947. 1. SIR HASTINGS LIONEL ISMAY, G.C.B., C.H., D.S.O., yr. s. of Sir Stanley ISMAY, K.C.S.I., Chief Judge of Mysore Chief Court, was *b.* 21 June 1887; ed. at Charterhouse and R.M.C., Sandhurst. He was *cr.*, 14 Jan. 1947, BARON ISMAY, of Wormington, co. Gloucester. He *m.*, 4 Aug. 1921, Laura Kathleen, da. of H.G. Clegg of Wormington Grange, Broadway, Glos. He *d. s.p.m.* 17 Dec. 1965, when his Barony became *extinct.*

15 JANUARY

RUGBY

BARONY. I. 1947. 1. SIR JOHN LOADER MAFFEY, G.C.M.G., K.C.B., K.C.V.O., C.S.I., C.I.E., s. of Thomas MAFFEY, of Rugby, was *b.* 1 July 1877; ed. at Rugby and Oxford (Ch. Ch.). He was *cr.*, 15 Jan. 1947, BARON RUGBY, of Rugby, co. Warwick. He *m.*, 28 Aug. 1907, Dorothy Gladys, 2nd da. of Charles Lang HUGGINS of Hadlow Grange, Buxted, Sussex. He *d.* 20 Apr. 1969. His widow *d.* 1973.

II. 1969. 2. ALAN LOADER (MAFFEY), BARON RUGBY, 1st s. and h., *b.* 16 Apr. 1913; ed. at Stowe and Ecole Supérieure de Commerce, Neuchatel. He *m.*, 14 Apr. 1947, Margaret, da. of Harold BINDLEY of Burton-on-Trent. He *d.* 12 Jan. 1990. His widow was living 1995.

[JOHN RICHARD MAFFEY, 1st s. and h. ap., *b.* 28 Aug. 1949; ed. at Harrow; *d. v.p.* and unm. in Egypt, 1981.]

III. 1990. 3. ROBERT CHARLES (MAFFEY), BARON RUGBY, 2nd but 1st surviving s. and h., *b.* 4 May 1951. He *m.*, 1974, Anne Penelope, yr. da. of David HALE of Somerden, Chiddingstone, Kent.

[TIMOTHY JAMES HOWARD MAFFEY, 1st s. and h. ap., *b.* 23 July 1975.]

16 JANUARY

LAYTON

BARONY. I. 1947. 1. SIR WALTER THOMAS LAYTON, C.H., C.B.E., s. of Alfred John LAYTON, of The Chalet, Fulham Park Rd., London, was *b.* 15 Mar. 1884;

ed. at King's Coll. Sch., London, Westm. City Sch., Univ. Coll., London and Cambridge (Trin. Coll.). He was *cr.*, 16 Jan. 1947, BARON LAYTON, of Danehill, co. Sussex. He *m.*, 2 Apr. 1910, Eleanor Dorothea, da. of Francis Beresford Plumptre OSMASTON of Stoneshill, Limpsfield, Surrey. She *d.* 18 Mar. 1959. He *d.* 14 Feb. 1966.

II. 1966. 2. MICHAEL JOHN (LAYTON), BARON LAYTON, 1st s. and h., *b.* 28 Sep. 1912; ed. at St. Paul's Sch. and Cambridge (Gonville and Caius Coll.). He *m.*, 31 Jan. 1938, Dorothy, da. of Albert Luther CROSS of Rugby. He *d.* 23 Jan. 1989. His widow *d.* 1994.

III. 1989. 3. GEOFFREY MICHAEL (LAYTON), BARON LAYTON, only s. and h., *b.* 18 July 1947; ed. at St. Paul's Sch., Stanford Univ. and Univ. of Southern California. He *m.* 1stly, 1969, Viviane, da. of François Cracco of Louvain, Belgium. This marriage was diss. by divorce in 1970. He *m.* 2ndly, 1989, Caroline Jane, da. of William Thomas MASON of Fairford, Glos. and formerly wife of Adm. Spyros SOULIS of Athens.

17 JANUARY

SIMON OF WYTHENSHAWE

BARONY. I. 1947. 1. SIR ERNEST DARWIN SIMON, s. of Henry Simon, M.I.C.E., of Lawnhurst, Didsbury, Manchester, was *b.* 9 Oct. 1879; ed. at Rugby and Cambridge (Pembroke Coll.). He was *cr.*, 17 Jan. 1947, BARON SIMON OF WYTHENSHAWE, of Didsbury, in the City of Manchester. He *m.*, 22 Nov. 1912, Shena Dorothy, da. of John Wilson POTTER of Westm. He *d.* 3 Oct. 1960. His widow *d.* 1972.

II. 1960. 2. ROGER (SIMON), BARON SIMON OF WYTHENSHAWE (but does not use the title), 1st s. and h., *b.* 16 Oct. 1913; ed. at Gresham's Sch., Holt and Cambridge (Gonville and Caius Coll.). He *m.*, 18 July 1951, Anthea Daphne, only da. of Sidney George William MAY of Milford-on-Sea, Hants.

[MATTHEW SIMON, only s. and h. ap., *b.* 10 Apr. 1955; ed. at St. Paul's Sch. and Oxford (Balliol Coll.).]

20 JANUARY

JOWITT

JOWITT, Viscountcy (*Jowitt*), *cr.* 20 Jan. 1947. See JOWITT, barony, *cr.* 2 Aug. 1945, p. 766.

20 JANUARY

KERSHAW

BARONY. I. 1947. 1. FRED KERSHAW, O.B.E., s. of John Joseph KERSHAW, of Prestwich, co. Lancaster, was *b.* 6 Nov. 1881; ed. at Prestwich Church of England Sch. He was *cr.*, 20 Jan. 1947, BARON KERSHAW, of

Prestwich, co. Lancaster. He *m.*, 18 July 1903, Frances Edith, da. of James Thomas WIGMORE of Hereford. She *d.* 31 July 1960. He *d.* 5 Feb. 1961.

II. 1961. 2. HERBERT (KERSHAW), BARON KERSHAW, 1st s. and h., *b.* 21 Aug. 1904; ed. at Glendale County Sch., Wood Green. He *m.*, 1933, Cissie Burness, da. of Charles E. SMYTHE of Friern Barnet. He *d. s.p.* 18 July 1961. His widow was living 1995.

III. 1961. 3. EDWARD AUBREY (KERSHAW), BARON KERSHAW, br. and h., *b.* 29 Aug. 1906; ed. at Friern Barnet Gram. Sch. He *m.*, 1 June 1935, Katharine Dorothea, da. of Charles Harry STAINES of Clapham. He *d.* 22 Feb. 1962. His widow was living 1995.

IV. 1962. 4. EDWARD JOHN (KERSHAW), BARON KERSHAW, only s. and h., *b.* 12 May 1936; ed. at Selhurst Gram. Sch., Croydon. He *m.*, 20 July 1963, Rosalind Lilian, yr. da. of Ian Strachan RUTHERFORD of Richmond, Surrey.

[JOHN CHARLES EDWARD KERSHAW, only s. and h. ap., *b.* 23 Dec. 1971.]

21 JANUARY

TREFGARNE

BARONY. I. 1947. 1. GEORGE MORGAN GARRO-JONES later TREFGARNE, s. of the Rev. David GARRO-JONES, of Milford Haven, co. Pembroke, was *b.* 14 Sep. 1894; ed. at Caterham Sch. He was *cr.*, 21 Jan. 1947, BARON TREFGARNE, of Cleddau, co. Pembroke. He *m.*, 9 May 1940, Elizabeth, yr. da. of Charles Edward CHURCHILL, of Ashton Keynes, Wilts. He *d.* 27 Mar. 1960. His widow *m.* 2ndly, 3 March 1962, Anthony Tosswill COURTNEY; this marriage was diss. by divorce in 1966 and she *m.* 3rdly 1971, Hugh Cecil Howat KER and *d.* in 1987.

II. 1960. 2. DAVID GARRO (TREFGARNE), BARON TREFGARNE, eldest s. and h., *b.* 31 Mar. 1941; ed. at Haileybury and Princeton Univ. He *m.*, 1968, Rosalie, da. of Peter Stewart (LANE), BARON LANE OF HORSELL (Life Peer).

[GEORGE GARRO TREFGARNE, s. and h. ap., *b.* 4 Jan. 1970.]

18 MARCH

BRUCE OF MELBOURNE

BARONY. I. 1947. 1. The Right Hon. STANLEY MELBOURNE BRUCE, C.H., M.C., s. of John BRUCE, of Melbourne, Australia, was *b.* 15 Apr. 1883; ed. at Melbourne Gram. Sch. and Cambridge (Trin. Hall). He was *cr.*, 18 Mar. 1947, VISCOUNT BRUCE OF MELBOURNE, of Westminster Gdns., in the City of Westm. He *m.*, 1913, Ethel Dunlop, da. of Andrew George ANDERSON of Melbourne. She *d.* 16 Mar. 1967. He *d. s.p.* 25 Aug. 1967 when his Viscountcy became *extinct*.

1 APRIL

DUKESTON

BARONY. I. 1947. 1. CHARLES DUKES, C.B.E., was *b.* 1881. He was *cr.*, 1 Apr. 1947, BARON DUKESTON, of Warrington, co. Lancaster. He *d.* unm. 14 May 1948, when his Barony became *extinct.*

18 APRIL

MORTON OF HENRYTON

BARONY FOR LIFE. I. 1947. The Right Hon. SIR FERGUS DUNLOP MORTON, M.C., one of the Lords Justices of Appeal, 3rd s. of George MORTON, of Lochgreen, Troon, and Henryton, co. Ayr, was *b.* 17 Oct. 1887; ed. at Kelvinside and Cambridge (St John's Coll.) On 1 Apr. 1947 he was app. a Lord of appeal in Ordinary under the Appellate Jurisdiction Act of 1876, and *cr.* a Baron for Life by the style of BARON MORTON OF HENRYTON, of Henryton, co. Ayr. He *m.*, 17 Dec. 1914, Margaret Greenlees, elder da. of James BEGG. He. *d.* 18 July 1973, when his Life Barony became *extinct.*

23 APRIL

MACDERMOTT

BARONY FOR LIFE. I. 1947. 1. The Right Hon. JOHN CLARKE MACDERMOTT, M.C., one of the Justices of the High Court of Justice for Northern Ireland, s. of the Rev. John MACDERMOTT, D.D., of Belmont, Belfast, was *b.* 12 Apr. 1896; ed. at Campbell Coll., Belfast and Belfast Univ. On 23 Apr. 1947 he was app. a Lord of Appeal in Ordinary under the Appellate Jurisdiction Act of 1876, and *cr.* a Baron for Life by the style of BARON MACDERMOTT, of Belmont, in the City of Belfast. He *m.*, 26 June 1926, Louise Palmer, only da. of Rev. John Corry JOHNSTON of Dublin. He *d.* 13 July 1979, when his Life Barony became *extinct.* His widow was still living 1995.

1 MAY

WAVELL, Earldom, KEREN, Viscountcy

WAVELL, Earldom, KEREN, Viscountcy (*Wavell*), *cr.* 1 May 1947. See WAVELL, Viscountcy, *cr.* 22 July 1943, p. 756.

3 JULY

CROOK

BARONY. I. 1947. 1. REGINALD DOUGLAS CROOK, s. of Percy Edwin CROOK, was *b.* 2 Mar. 1901; ed. at Strand Sch. He was *cr.*, 3 July 1947, BARON CROOK, of Carshalton, co. Surrey. He *m.*, 7 Oct. 1922, Ida Gertrude, da. of Joseph George HADDON. She *d.* 1985. He *d.* 10 Mar. 1989.

II. 1989. 2. DOUGLAS EDWIN (CROOK), BARON CROOK, only s. and h., was *b.* 19 Nov. 1926; ed. at Whitgift Sch., Croydon and Imp. Coll. of Sci. and Tech.; *m.*, 15 Feb. 1954, Ellenor, da. of Robert ROUSE.

[ROBERT DOUGLAS EDWIN CROOK, s. and h. ap., *b.* 29 May 1955; *m.*, 1981, Suzanne Jane, da. of Harold ROBINSON of Farnsfield, co. Nottingham.]

15 JULY

ROBINSON

BARONY. I. 1947. 1. SIR ROY LISTER ROBINSON, O.B.E., s. of William ROBINSON, of Perth, Western Australia, was *b.* 8 Mar. 1883; ed. at St. Peter's Col. Adelaide, Sch. of Mines, Univ. of Adelaide and Oxford (Magdalen Coll.). He was *cr.*, 15 July 1947, BARON ROBINSON, of Kielder Forest, co. Northumberland, and of Adelaide, in the Commonwealth of Australia. He *m.*, 26 Nov. 1910, Charlotte Marion Cust, yr. da. of Henry Cust BRADSHAW, of Fair Oak Park, co. Hants. He *d. s.p.m.s.* (1) 5 Sep. 1952, when his Barony became *extinct.*

note (1) Michael Lister, his only son, was *b.* 8 May 1916. He *d. v.p.* and unm. 10 April 1942, presumed k. in action.

16 JULY

AMWELL

BARONY. I. 1947. 1. FREDERICK MONTAGUE, C.B.E., s. of John MONTAGUE, of 12 Sun Street, Amwell, London, was *b.* 8 Oct. 1876. He was *cr.*, 16 July 1947, BARON AMWELL, of Islington, co. London. He *m.*, 25 Nov. 1911, Constance Mary, da. of James CRAIG of Runcorn, Cheshire. She *d.* 28 Jan. 1964. He *d.* 15 Oct. 1966.

II. 1966. 2. FREDERICK NORMAN (MONTAGUE), BARON AMWELL, only s. and h., was *b.* 6 Nov. 1916; ed. at Highbury Gram. Sch. and Northampton Coll. of Tech.; *m.*, 29 July 1939, Kathleen Elizabeth, da. of Arthur Percival FOUNTAIN of Tooting Graveney, Wandsworth. He *d.* 12 Oct. 1990. His widow was still living 1995.

III. 1990. 3. KEITH NORMAN (MONTAGUE), BARON AMWELL, only s. and h., was *b.* 1 Apr. 1943; ed. at Ealing Gram. Sch. and Nottingham Univ.; *m.*, 1970, Mary, only da. of Frank PALFREYMAN of Potters Bar, co. Hertford.

[IAN MONTAGUE, 1st s. and h. ap., *b.* 1973.]

9 OCTOBER

MILVERTON

BARONY. I. 1947. 1. SIR ARTHUR FREDERICK RICHARDS, G.C.M.G., s. of William RICHARDS, of Bristol, was *b.* 21 Feb. 1885; ed. at Clifton Coll. and Oxford (Ch. Ch.). He was *cr.*, 9 Oct. 1947, BARON MILVERTON, of Lagos and of Clifton, in the City of Bristol. He *m.*, 6 Sep. 1927, Noelle Bendon, da. of Charles Basil WHITEHEAD of Torquay. He *d.* 27 Oct. 1978. His widow was still living 1995.

II. 1978. 2. FRASER ARTHUR RICHARD (RICHARDS), BARON MILVERTON, 1st s. and h., was *b.* 21 July 1930; ed. at Ridley Coll., Ontario, Canada, Clifton Coll., Egerton Agric. Coll., Njoro, Kenya and Bishop's Coll., Cheshunt, co. Hertford; ordained priest, 1958. He *m.*, 10 Aug. 1957, Mary Dorothy, only da. of Leslie FLY of Bath.

18 OCTOBER

MOUNTBATTEN OF BURMA, Earldom, ROMSEY, Barony

MOUNTBATTEN OF BURMA, Earldom, Romsey, Barony (*Mountbatten*), *cr.* 18 Oct. 1947. See MOUNTBATTEN OF BURMA, Viscountcy, *cr.* 23 Aug. 1946, p. 779.

20 NOVEMBER

EDINBURGH, Dukedom, MERIONETH, Earldom, GREENWICH, Barony

DUKEDOM. I. 1947. 1. *H.R.H.* SIR PHILIP MOUNTBATTEN, K.G., Lieut., R.N., only s. of *H.R.H.* PRINCE ANDREW OF GREECE AND DENMARK, G.C.V.O., was *b.* 10 June 1921; ed. at Cheam Sch. *et. al.* and R.N.C. Dartmouth. On 20 Nov. 1947 he *m.* *H.R.H.* ELIZABETH ALEXANDRA MARY, PRINCESS OF THE UNITED KINGDOM AND NORTHERN IRELAND, 1st da. of *H.M.* KING GEORGE VI, (later *H.M.* QUEEN ELIZABETH II). He was *cr.*, 20 Nov. 1947, BARON GREENWICH, of Greenwich, co. London, EARL OF MERIONETH and DUKE OF EDINBURGH.

PEERAGES OF 1948

2 FEBRUARY

HYNDLEY

VISCOUNTCY. I. 1948. 1. JOHN SCOTT (HINDLEY), 1st BARON HYNDLEY [1931], also a Baronet [1927], was further *cr.*, 2 Feb. 1948, VISCOUNT HYNDLEY, of Meads, co. Sussex. For fuller particulars of him see vol. xiii, p. 494.

6 FEBRUARY

MACKINTOSH OF HALIFAX

BARONY. I. } 1948
VISCOUNTCY. I. } 1957

1. SIR HAROLD VINCENT MACKINTOSH, 1st Bart. [1935], s. of John MACKINTOSH, of Greystones, Halifax, co. York, was *b.* 8 June 1891; ed. at New Sch., Halifax. He was *cr.*, 6 Feb. 1948, BARON MACKINTOSH OF HALIFAX, of Hethersett, co. Norfolk, and was further *cr.*, 10 July 1957, VISCOUNT MACKINTOSH OF HALIFAX, of Hethersett, co. Norfolk. He *m.*, 8 June

1916, Constance Emily, 2nd da. of Edgar Cooper STONEHAM, O.B.E. He *d.* 27 Dec. 1964. His widow *d.* 1975.

II. 1964. 2. JOHN (MACKINTOSH), VISCOUNT MACKINTOSH OF HALIFAX, also a Baronet, only s. and h., was *b.* 7 Oct. 1921; ed. at Bedales and Trin. Coll., Hertford, Connecticut, U.S.A. He *m.* 1stly, 6 Dec. 1946, Bronda, only da. of Louis John FIBIGER of South Shields, co. Durham. This marriage was diss. by divorce in 1956 and he *m.* 2ndly, 30 Aug. 1956, Gwynneth CHARLESWORTH, 2nd da. of Charles Henry GLEDHILL of Halifax. He *d.* 2 Nov. 1980. His widow was living 1995.

III. 1980. 3. JOHN CLIVE (MACKINTOSH), VISCOUNT MACKINTOSH OF HALIFAX, 1st s. and h., was *b.* 9 Sep. 1958; ed. at Leys Sch. and Oxford (Oriel Coll.); *m.*, 1982, Elizabeth, only da. of D.G. LAKIN. This marriage was diss. by divorce in 1993.

[THOMAS HAROLD GEORGE MACKINTOSH, 1st s. and h. ap., *b.* 8 Feb. 1985.]

7 FEBRUARY

DOUGLAS OF KIRTLESIDE

BARONY. I. 1948. 1. Marshal of the Royal Air Force SIR WILLIAM SHOLTO DOUGLAS, G.C.B., M.C., D.F.C., 1st s. of Professor Robert Langton DOUGLAS, of New York, U.S.A., was *b.* 23 Dec. 1893; ed. at Tonbridge and Oxford (Lincoln Coll.). He was *cr.*, 7 Feb. 1948, BARON DOUGLAS OF KIRTLESIDE, of Dornock, co. Dumfries. He *m.*, 7 Sep. 1933, Joan Leslie, only da. of Col. Henry Cuthbert DENNY. This marriage was diss. by divorce in 1955 and he *m.* 2ndly, 28 Feb. 1955, Hazel, 2nd da. of George Eric Maas WALKER. He *d. s.p.m.* 29 Oct. 1969 when his Barony became *extinct.* His widow was living 1995.

9 FEBRUARY

BRAINTREE

BARONY. I. 1948. 1. SIR VALENTINE GEORGE CRITTALL, s. of Francis Henry CRITTALL, of Manors, Silver End, Witham, Essex, was *b.* 28 June 1884; ed. at Uppingham. He was *cr.*, 9 Feb. 1948, BARON BRAINTREE, of Braintree, co. Essex. He *m.* 1stly, 29 June 1915, Olive Lillian, da. of Charles Landay MACDERMOTT of Comber, Ontario, Canada. She *d.* 1932 and he *m.* 2ndly, 1933, Lydia Mabel, da. of J.J. REVY and widow of Frank C.R. REED. She *d.* 1947 and he *m.* 3rdly, 23 Sept. 1955, Phyllis Dorothy, da. of Curtis CLOUTMAN of Bristol and widow of George Henry Nelson PARKER. He *d. s.p.m.* 21 May 1961 when his Barony became *extinct.*

26 FEBRUARY

CLYDESMUIR

BARONY. I. 1948. 1. The Right Hon. SIR DAVID JOHN COLVILLE, G.C.I.E., only s. of John COLVILLE, M.P. for N.E. Lanarkshire, was *b.* 13 Feb. 1894; ed. at Charterhouse and Cambridge (Trin. Coll.). He was *cr.*, 26 Feb. 1948,

BARON CLYDESMUIR, of Braidwood, co. Lanark. He *m.*, 6 Oct. 1915, Agnes Anne, elder da. of Sir William BILSLAND, 1st Bart. He *d.* 31 Oct. 1954. His widow *d.* 1970.

II. 1954. 2. RONALD JOHN BILSLAND (COLVILLE), BARON CLYDESMUIR, only s and h. was *b.* 21 May 1917; ed. at Charterhouse and Cambridge (Trin. Coll.). He *m.*, 10 Apr. 1946, Joan Marguerita, elder da. of Lieut. Col. Ernest Brabazon BOOTH.

[DAVID RONALD COLVILLE, 1st s. and h. ap., *b.* 8 Apr. 1949; ed. at Charterhouse. He *m.*, 1978, Aline Frances, elder da. of Peter MERRIAM of Holton Lodge, Holton St. Mary, Suffolk.]

22 JUNE

WEBB-JOHNSON

BARONY. I. 1948. 1. SIR ALFRED EDWARD WEBB-JOHNSON, *formerly* JOHNSON, 1st Bart. [1945], K.C.V.O., C.B.E., D.S.O., T.D., 2nd s. of Samuel JOHNSON, M.D., Medical Officer of Health, Stoke-on-Trent, was *b.* 4 Sep. 1880; ed. at Newcastle-under-Lyme High Sch. and Manchester Univ. He was *cr.*, 22 June 1948, BARON WEBB-JOHNSON, of Stoke-on-Trent, co. Stafford. He *m.*, 23 Nov. 1911, Cecilia Flora, da. of D.G. MACRAE of Norbiton, Surrey. He *d. s.p.* 28 May 1958, when his Barony became *extinct*.

23 JUNE

MAENAN

BARONY. I. 1948. 1. SIR WILLIAM FRANCIS KYFFIN TAYLOR, G.B.E., K.C., s. of the Ven. William Francis TAYLOR, D.D., LL.D., Archdeacon of Liverpool, was *b.* 9 July 1854; ed. at Liverpool Coll. and Oxford (Exeter Coll.). He was *cr.*, 23 June 1948, BARON MAENAN, of Ellesmere, co. Salop. He *m.*, 1883, Mary Fleming, da. of Robert CROOKS of Rosemount, Liverpool. He *d. s.p.m.* 22 Sep. 1951, when his Barony became *extinct*.

24 JUNE

WILLIAMS

BARONY. I. 1948. 1. THOMAS EDWARD WILLIAMS, s. of William WILLIAMS, of Ynyshir, co. Glamorgan, was *b.* 26 July 1892; ed. at secondary schools and Ruskin Coll., Oxford. He was *cr.*, 24 June 1948, BARON WILLIAMS, of Ynyshir, co. Glamorgan. He *m.*, 14 May 1921, Lavinia Mary, da. of Charles NORTHAM of Plumstead. He *d. s.p.m.* 18 Feb. 1966 when his Barony became *extinct*. His widow was living 1995.

6 OCTOBER

REID

BARONY FOR LIFE. I. 1948. 1. The Right Hon. JAMES SCOTT CUMBERLAND REID, K.C., formerly Lord Advocate [S.], 1st s. of James REID,

Writer to the Signet, of Drem, East Lothian, was *b.* 30 July 1890; ed. at Edinburgh Acad. and Cambridge (Jesus Coll.). On 6 Oct. 1948 he was app. a Lord of Appeal in Ordinary under the Appellate Jurisdiction Act of 1876, and *cr.* a Baron for Life by the style of BARON REID, of Drem, co. East Lothian. He *m.*, 1 June 1933, Esther May, da. of C.B. NELSON and widow of Gerard Frank BRIERLEY. He *d. s.p.* 29 Mar. 1975 when his Life Barony became *extinct.*

PEERAGES OF 1949

16 FEBRUARY

ADAMS

BARONY. I. 1949. 1. JOHN JACKSON ADAMS, O.B.E., 7th s. of Thomas ADAMS, of Arlecdon, Cumberland, was *b.* 12 Oct. 1890; ed. at County Sch., Arlecdon. He was *cr.*, 16 Feb. 1949, BARON ADAMS, of Ennerdale, co. Cumberland. He *m.*, 1914, Agnes Jane, da. of Thomas BIRNEY. He *d. s.p.s.* 23 Aug. 1960 when his Barony became *extinct.*

9 MARCH

BOYD-ORR

BARONY. I. 1949. 1. SIR JOHN BOYD-ORR, D.S.O., M.C., 1st s. of Robert Clark ORR, was *b.* 23 Sep. 1880; ed. at West Kilbride Public Sch. and Glasgow Univ. He was *cr.*, 9 Mar, 1949, BARON BOYD-ORR, of Brechin Mearn, co. Angus. He *m.*, 21 Feb. 1915, Elizabeth Pearson, da. of John Bainbridge CALLUM of West Kilbride, co. Ayr. He *d. s.p.m.s.* (1) 25 June 1971 when his Barony became *extinct.*

note (1) Donald Noel, his only s., *b.* 19 May 1921, *d. v.p.* Dec. 1941, being k. in action.

13 APRIL

MACDONALD OF GWAENYSGOR

BARONY. I. 1949. 1. SIR GORDON MACDONALD, K.C.V.O., s. of Thomas MACDONALD, of Ashton-in-Makerfield, near Wigan, was *b.* 27 May 1888; ed. at St. Luke's Elementary Sch., Stubshaw Cross and Ruskin Coll., Oxford. He was *cr.*, 13 Apr. 1949, BARON MACDONALD OF GWAENYSGOR, of Gwaenysgor, co. Flint. He *m.*, 1913, Mary, yst. da. of William LEWIS of Blaenau Festiniog, North Wales. He *d.* 20 Jan. 1966. His widow *d.* 1967.

II. 1966. 2. GORDON RAMSAY (MACDONALD), BARON MACDONALD OF GWAENYSGOR, 1st s. and h., *b.* 16 Oct. 1915; ed. at Upholland Gram. Sch. and Manchester Univ. He *m.*, 1941, Leslie Margaret, da. of John Edward TAYLOR of Rainford, Lancs.

1 JUNE

RADCLIFFE

BARONY FOR LIFE. I. 1949. 1. SIR CYRIL JOHN RADCLIFFE, G.B.E., K.C., s. of Capt. Alfred Ernest RADCLIFFE, of North Court, Finchampstead, Berks, was *b.* 30 Mar. 1899; ed. at Haileybury and Oxford (New Coll. and All Souls). On 1 June 1949 he was app. a Lord of Appeal in Ordinary under the Appellate Jurisdiction Act of 1876, and *cr.* a Baron for Life by the style of BARON RADCLIFFE, of Werneth, co. Lancaster. He was further *cr.*, 11 July 1962, VISCOUNT RADCLIFFE. of Hampton Lacy, co. Warwick. He *m.*, 11 Dec. 1939, Antonia Mary Roby, elder da. of Godfrey Rathbone (BENSON), 1st BARON CHARNWOOD and formerly wife of Major John TENNANT. He *d.* 1 Apr. 1977 when his Life Barony became *extinct.*

21 JUNE

BADELEY

BARONY. I. 1949. 1. SIR HENRY JOHN FANSHAWE BADELEY, K.C.B., C.B.E., s. of Henry BADELEY, of Guy Harlings, Essex, was *b.* 27 June 1874; ed. at Radley and Oxford (Trin. Coll.). He was *cr.*, 21 June 1949, BARON BADELEY, of Badley, co. Suffolk. He *d.* unm. 27 Sep. 1951, when his Barony became *extinct.*

7 JULY

DUGAN OF VICTORIA

BARONY. I. 1949. 1. Major-General SIR WINSTON JOSEPH DUGAN, G.C.M.G., C.B., D.S.C., s. of Charles Winston DUGAN, of Oxmantown Hall, Birr, Eire, was *b.* 8 May 1877; ed. at Lurgan Coll. and at Wimbledon. He was *cr.*, 7 July 1949, BARON DUGAN OF VICTORIA, of Lurgan, co. Armagh. He *m.*, 1912, Ruby Lilian, da. of Charles ABBOTT of Abbott Abbey, co. Cork. He *d. s.p.* 17 Aug. 1951, when his Barony became *extinct.*

12 JULY

ARCHIBALD

BARONY. I. 1949. 1. GEORGE ARCHIBALD, s. of George W. ARCHIBALD, of Glasgow, was *b.* 21 July 1898; ed. at St. George's Rd. Elementary Sch. and Allan Glen's High Sch., Glasgow. He was *cr.*, 12 July 1949, BARON ARCHIBALD, of Woodside, in the City of Glasgow. He *m.* 1stly, Feb. 1926, Dorothy Holroyd, da. of George Henry EDWARDS of Liverpool. She *d.* 22 July 1960, and he *m.* 2ndly, 15 Nov. 1961, Catherine Edith Mary, yr. da. of Rt. Hon. Andrew Bonar LAW and formerly wife of Kent COLWELL. He *d.* 25 Feb. 1975. His widow *d.* 1992.

II. 1975. 2. GEORGE CHRISTOPHER (ARCHIBALD), BARON ARCHIBALD, only s. and h., *b.* 30 Dec. 1926; ed. at Phillips Exeter Acad., U.S.A., Cambridge (King's Coll.) and London Sch. of Economics. He *m.* 1stly, 19 Oct. 1951, Liliana Leah, only da. of Dr Noah BAROU. This marriage was diss. by divorce in 1964, and he *m.* 2ndly, 1971, Daphne May Vincent, da. of George Henry HENMAN. He disclaimed his peerage for life under the Peerage Act, 1963, 7 Mar. 1975.

PEERAGES OF 1950

27 JANUARY

ALEXANDER OF HILLSBOROUGH

VISCOUNTCY. I. 1950. 1. The Right Hon. ALBERT VICTOR ALEXANDER, C.H., s. of Albert ALEXANDER, of Weston-super-Mare, Somerset, was *b.* 1 May 1885; ed. at Barton Hill Elementary Sch., Bristol. He was *cr.* 27 Jan. 1950, VISCOUNT ALEXANDER OF HILLSBOROUGH, of Hillsborough, in the City of Sheffield. He *m.*, 6 June 1908, Esther Ellen, da. of George CHAPPLE of Tiverton, Devon. He *d. s.p.m.* 11 Jan. 1965 when his Viscountcy became *extinct*. His widow *d.* 18 Oct. 1969.

30 JANUARY

WILMOT OF SELMESTON

BARONY. I. 1950. 1. The Right Hon. JOHN WILMOT, s. of Charles WILMOT, engraver, was *b.* 2 Apr. 1895. He was *cr.*, 30 Jan. 1950, BERON WILMOT OF SELMESTON, of Selmeston, co. Sussex. He *d.* unm. 22 July 1964 when his Barony became *extinct*.

31 JANUARY

BILSLAND

BARONY. I. 1950. 1. SIR ALEXANDER STEVEN BILSLAND, 2nd Bart. [1907], M.C., 2nd but 1st surv. s. and h. of Sir William BILSLAND, 1st Bart., was *b.* 13 Sep. 1892; ed. at Cambridge (St John's Coll.). He was *cr.*, 31 Jan. 1950, BARON BILSLAND, of Kinrara, co. Inverness. He *m.*, 16 Feb. 1922, Amy, da. of David COLVILLE of Motherwell. He *d. s.p.* 10 Dec. 1970 when his Barony and his Baronetcy became *extinct*.

1 FEBRUARY

BURDEN

BARONY. I. 1950. 1. THOMAS WILLIAM BURDEN, C.B.E., s. of Thomas BURDEN, of Mile End, London, was *b.* 29 Jan. 1885; ed. at London Sch. of Economics. He was *cr.*, 1 Feb. 1950, BARON BURDEN, of Wadebarrow, co. Derby. He *m.*, 11 July 1910, Augusta, da. of David SIME of Aberdeen. He *d.* 27 May 1970. His widow *d.* 1976.

II. 1970. 2. PHILIP WILLIAM (BURDEN), BARON BURDEN, only s. and h., *b.* 21 June 1916; ed. at Raines Foundation Sch. He *m.*, 8 Sep. 1951, Audrey Elsworth, da. of Major Wilfred Elsworth SYKES of Kirk Ella, Hull.

[ANDREW PHILIP BURDEN, 1st s. and h. ap., *b.* 20 July 1959.]

2 FEBRUARY

HADEN-GUEST

BARONY. I. 1950. 1. LESLIE HADEN HADEN-GUEST, M.C., s. of Alexander HADEN-GUEST of Manchester, was *b.*, 10 Mar. 1877; ed. at William Hulme's Gram. Sch., Manchester, Owen's Coll., Manchester and the London Hosp. He was *cr.*, 2 Feb. 1950, BARON HADEN-GUEST, of Saling, co. Essex. He *m.* 1stly, 1898, Edith, da. of Max LOW of London. This marriage was diss. by divorce in 1909 and she *d.* in 1944. He *m.* 2ndly, 1910, Muriel Carmel, da. of Col. Albert GOLDSMID. She *d.* in 1943. He *m.* 3rdly, 10 Jan. 1944, Edith Edgar, da. of George MACQUEEN of Montrose, Angus. He *d.* 20 Aug. 1960. His widow *d.* 1977.

II. 1960. 2. STEPHEN HADEN (HADEN-GUEST), BARON HADEN-GUEST, 1st s. and h., *b.* 7 June 1902; ed. at St. John's House Sch., Institut St. Cyr, Nevers, France and Univ. Coll., London. He *m.* 1stly, 1948, Barbara Ann, da. of James Harvey PINSON of West Virginia, U.S.A. This marriage was diss. by divorce in 1954, and he *m.* 2ndly, 1968, Dorothy, da. of Thomas Roseberry GOOD, late of Princeton, New Jersey. He *d. s.p.m.* 21 Dec. 1974. His widow was living 1995.

III. 1974. 3. RICHARD HADEN (HADEN-GUEST), BARON HADEN-GUEST, br. and h., *b.* 20 July 1904; ed. at Bembridge Sch. He *m.* 1stly, 1926, Hilda Edith, da. of Thomas RUSSELL-CRUISE. This marriage was diss. by divorce in 1934 and she *d.* 1944. He *m.* 2ndly, 1934, Olive Maria, da. of Anders Gotfrid NILSSON. He *m.* 3rdly, 1949, Marjorie Douglas, da. of Dr Douglas F. KENNARD of Clacton-on-Sea. He *d. s.p.m.s.* 26 May 1987. His widow was living 1995.

IV. 1987. 4. PETER HADEN (HADEN-GUEST), BARON HADEN-GUEST, half-br. and h., being 1st surviving s. of 2nd wife of 1st Baron, *b.* 29 Aug. 1913; ed. at City of London Sch. and Oxford (New Coll.). He *m.* 1stly, 1939, Mrs Elizabeth Louise Ruth COKER, eldest da. of Paul WOLPERT of Konnigsberg. This marriage was diss. by divorce in 1945, and he *m.* 2ndly, 1945, Jean Pauline, da. of Dr Albert George HINDES of New York City.

[CHRISTOPHER HADEN-GUEST, 1st legit. s. and h. ap., *b.* 5 Feb. 1948. He *m.*, 1984, Jamie Lee, da. of Tony CURTIS.]

3 FEBRUARY

HENDERSON OF ARDWICK

BARONY. I. 1950, 3 to 26 Feb. 1. JOSEPH HENDERSON was *b.* 1884. He was *cr.*, 3 Feb. 1950, BARON HENDERSON OF ARDWICK, of Norton Park, in the City of Carlisle. He *m.*, 1908, Janet Glendenning, da. of James BUYERS of Rowanburnfoot, Canonbie, co. Dumfries. He *d. s.p.m.* 26 Feb. 1950, when his Barony became *extinct*.

17 MARCH

LAWSON

BARONY. I. 1950. 1. The Right Hon. JOHN JAMES LAWSON, s. of John LAWSON, of Whitehaven, Cumberland, was *b.* 16 Oct. 1881. He was *cr.*, 17 Mar. 1950, BARON LAWSON, of Beamish, co. Durham. He *m.*, 1906, Isabella, da. of Robert SCOTT. He *d. s.p.m.* 3 Aug. 1965 when his Barony became *extinct.*

11 APRIL

DOUGLAS OF BARLOCH

BARONY. I. 1950. 1. SIR FRANCIS CAMPBELL ROSS DOUGLAS, K.C.M.G., only. s. of Francis James Boswall DOUGLAS, farmer and breeder, was *b.* 21 Oct. 1889; ed. at Grantown-on-Spey Gram. Sch., Glasgow Univ. and Royal Univ. of Malta. He was *cr.*, 11 Apr. 1950, BARON DOUGLAS OF BARLOCH, of Maxfield, co. Sussex. He *m.*, 1 July 1914, Minnie Findlay, da. of William SMITH of Kirriemuir, Angus. She *d.* 24 Apr. 1969. He *d. s.p.m.* 30 Mar. 1980 when his Barony became *extinct.*

4 JULY

SILKIN

BARONY. I. 1950. 1. The Right Hon. LEWIS SILKIN was *b.* 14 Nov. 1889; ed. at elementary and secondary schools and London Univ. He was *cr.*, 4 July 1950, BARON SILKIN, of Dulwich, co. London. He *m.* 1stly, Aug. 1915, Rosa NEFT. She *d.* 29 Dec. 1947. He *m.* 2ndly, 5 Oct. 1948, Frieda M., da. of Rev. Canon PILLING of Norwich and widow of J.F. Fielder JOHNSON. She *d.* 24 June 1963. He *m.* 3rdly, 26 Mar. 1964, Marguerite SCHLAGETER. He *d.* 11 May 1972. His widow *d.* 1975.

II. 1972. 2. ARTHUR (SILKIN), BARON SILKIN, 1st s. and h., *b.* 20 Oct. 1916; ed. at Dulwich Coll. and Cambridge (Peterhouse Coll.). He *m.*, 13 Sep. 1969, Audrey, da. of Thomas BENNETT of Newark, Notts. He disclaimed his peerage for life, 18 May 1972 under the Peerage Act, 1963.

5 JULY

HURCOMB

BARONY. I. 1950. 1. SIR CYRIL WILLIAM HURCOMB, G.C.B., K.B.E., s. of William HURCOMB, of Oxford, was *b.* 18 Feb. 1883; ed. at Oxford High Sch. and Oxford (St John's Coll.). He was *cr.*, 5 July 1950, BARON HURCOMB, of Campden Hill, in the Royal Borough of Kensington. He *m.*, 14 Aug. 1911, Dorothy Ethel, da. of Alfred BROOKE. She *d.* 21 Feb. 1947. He *d. s.p.m.* 7 Aug. 1975 when his Barony became *extinct.*

6 JULY

CAMPION

BARONY. I. 1950. 1. SIR GILBERT FRANCIS MONTRIOU CAMPION, G.C.B., 1st s. of John Montriou CAMPION, was *b.* 11 May 1882; ed. at Bedford Sch. and Oxford

(Hertford Coll.). He was *cr.*, 6 July 1950, BARON CAMPION, of Bowes, co. Surrey. He *m.*, 1920, Hilda Mary, da. of W.A. SPAFFORD. He *d. s.p.* 6 Apr. 1958, when his Barony became *extinct.*

7 JULY

HIVES

BARONY. I. 1950. 1. ERNEST WALTER HIVES, C.H., R.B.E., s. of John William HIVES, of Reading, Berks, was *b.* 21 Apr. 1886; ed. at Redlands Sch., Reading. He was *cr.*, 7 July 1950, BARON HIVES, of Duffield, co. Derby. He *m.*, Feb. 1913, Gertrude Ethel, 2nd da. of John A. WARWICK of Derby. She *d.* 20 Sep. 1961. He *d.* 24 Apr. 1965.

II. 1965. 2. JOHN WARWICK (HIVES), BARON HIVES, 1st s. and h., *b.* 26 Nov. 1913; ed. at Derby Sch. He *m.* 1stly, 1937, Olwyn Protheroe LLEWELLIN. She *d.* 1972. He *m.* 2ndly, 1972, Gladys Mary, da. of Alfred SEALS.

8 JULY

GREENHILL

BARONY. I. 1950. 1. ERNEST GREENHILL, O.B.E., s. of Maurice GREENHILL, was *b.* 23 Apr. 1887. He was *cr.*, 8 July 1950, BARON GREENHILL, of Townhead, in the City of Glasgow. He *m.*, 1914, Ida, da. of Mark GOODMAN. He *d.* 18 Feb. 1967. His widow *d.* 1985.

II. 1967. 2. STANLEY (GREENHILL), BARON GREENHILL, 1st s. and h., *b.* 17 July 1917; ed. at Kelvinside Acad., Glasgow and Universities of Glasgow, Toronto and California. He *m.*, 1946, Margaret Jean, da. of Thomas NEWLANDS of Hamilton, Ontario, Canada. He *d. s.p.m.* 28 Sep. 1989. His widow was still living 1995.

III. 1989. 3. MALCOLM (GREENHILL), BARON GREENHILL, br. and h., *b.* 5 May 1924; ed. at Kelvinside Acad., Glasgow and Glasgow Univ.

10 JULY

OGMORE

BARONY. I. 1950. 1. Lieut. Col. DAVID REES REES-WILLIAMS, T.D., only s. of William Rees WILLIAMS, F.R.C.V.S., of Garth-celyn, Bridgend, was *b.* 22 Nov. 1903; ed. at Mill Hill Sch. and Univ. of Wales. He was *cr.*, 10 July 1950, BARON OGMORE, of Bridgend, co. Glamorgan. He *m.*, 30 July 1930, Alice Alexandra Constance, elder da. of Alderman Walter Robert WILLS. He *d.* 30 Aug. 1976. His widow was living 1995.

II. 1976. 2. GWILYM REES (REES-WILLIAMS), BARON OGMORE, 1st s. and h., *b.* 5 May 1931; ed. at Mill Hill Sch. and St. Luke's Coll., Exeter. He *m.*, 1967, Gillian Mavis, da. of Maurice Keith SLACK of Hindley, Lancs.

11 JULY

MORRIS OF KENWOOD

BARONY. I. 1950. 1. Lieut. Col. HARRY MORRIS, 7th s. of Jacob Samuel MORRIS was *b.* 7 Oct. 1893; ed. at Tivoli House Sch., Gravesend and privately. He was *cr.* 11 July 1950, BARON MORRIS OF KENWOOD, of Kenwood, in the City of Sheffield. He *m.*, 11 June 1924, Florence, da. of Henry ISAACS of Leeds. He *d.* 1 July 1954. His widow *d.* 1982.

[ROGER JAMES MORRIS, 1st s. and h. ap., *b.* 17 Aug. 1925, *d. v.p.* 3 June 1938.]

II. 1954. 2. PHILIP GEOFFREY (MORRIS), BARON MORRIS OF KENWOOD, 2nd but only surv. s. and h., was *b.* 18 June 1928; ed. at Loughborough Col. He *m.*, 9 Sep. 1958, Ruth Joan Gertrude Rahle, only da. of Barnett (JANNER), BARON JANNER (Life Peer).

[JONATHAN DAVID MORRIS, only s. and h. ap., *b.* 5 Aug. 1968.]

29 SEPTEMBER

TUCKER

BARONY FOR LIFE. I. 1950. 1. The Right Hon. SIR FREDERICK JAMES TUCKER. one of the Lords Justices of Appeal, s. of Frederick Nugent TUCKER, member of the Legislative Assembly, Natal, was *b.* 22 May 1888; ed. at Winchester and Oxford (New Coll.). On 29 Sep. 1950 he was app. a Lord of Appeal in Ordinary under the Appellate Jurisdication Act of 1876, and *cr.* a Baron for Life by the style of BARON TUCKER, of Great Bookham, co. Surrey. He *m.*, 19 Mar. 1918, Elisabeth Benedicta Palmer, da. of Rev. Charles Powell BERRYMAN, Vicar of Camberley, Surrey. She *d.* 1972. He *d.* 17 Nov. 1975 when his Life Barony became *extinct*.

PEERAGES OF 1951

16 JANUARY

WILLOUGHBY DE ERESBY

GILBERT JAMES HEATHCOTE-DRUMMOND-WILLOUGHBY, *styled* LORD WILLOUGHBY DE ERESBY, 1st s. and h. ap. of Gilbert (HEATHCOTE-DRUMMOND-WILLOUGHBY), 2nd EARL OF ANCASTER, was sum. to Parl. *v.p.* in his father's Barony as LORD WILLOUGHBY DE ERESBY, 16 Jan. 1951, taking his seat, 7 Feb. follg. He *suc.* his said father as EARL OF ANCASTER and as JOINT HEREDITARY LORD GREAT CHAMBERLAIN, 19 Sep. 1951. See vol. i, *sub* ANCASTER, and vol. xii, part 2, note *sub* WILLOUGHBY DE ERESBY.

25 JANUARY

MACPHERSON OF DRUMOCHTER

BARONY. I. 1951. 1. THOMAS MACPHERSON, s. of James MACPHERSON, of Muirhead, Chryston, co. Lanark, was *b.* 9 July 1888; ed. at St. George's Rd. Sch., Glasgow. He was *cr.*, 25 Jan. 1951, BARON MACPHERSON OF DRUMOCHTER, of Great Warley, co. Essex. He *m.*, 29 Jan. 1920, Lucy, da. of Arthur BUTCHER of Heybridge Basin, Maldon, Essex. He *d.* 11 June 1965. His widow *d.* 1984.

II. 1965. 2. JAMES GORDON (MACPHERSON), BARON MACPHERSON OF DRUMOCHTER, only s. and h., *b.* 22 Jan. 1924; ed. at Loretto and Wells House, Malvern. He *m.* 1stly, 15 Apr. 1947, Dorothy Ruth, da. of Rev. Henry COULTER of Bellahouston, Glasgow. She *d.* 1974, and he *m.* 2ndly, 1975, Catherine Bridget, only da. of Dr Desmond MACCARTHY of Brentwood, Essex.

[JAMES ANTHONY MACPHERSON, only s. and h. ap., *b.* 27 Feb. 1979.]

7 FEBRUARY

HUNGARTON

BARONY. I. 1951. 1. ARCHIBALD CRAWFORD, s. of Robert CRAWFORD, of Highfields Farm, Lowesby, co. Leicester, was *b.* 12 Sep. 1890; ed. at Wyggeston Gram. Sch., Leicester. He was *cr.*, 7 Feb. 1951, BARTON HUNGARTON, of Hungarton, co. Leicester. He *m.*, 14 Jan. 1914, Jean, da. of David JOHNSTONE of Castle Douglas, co. Kirkcudbright. She *d.* 8 Mar. 1966. He *d. s.p.m.s.* 14 June 1966 when his Barony became *extinct*.

[DAVID ROBERT CRAWFORD, only s. and h. ap., *b.* 10 Dec. 1920; ed. at Denstone Coll., Staffs. He was *k.* in action over Germany 6 Feb. 1945.]

23 APRIL

ASQUITH OF BISHOPSTONE

BARONY FOR LIFE. I. 1951. 1. The Right Hon. SIR CYRIL ASQUITH, one of the Lords Justices of Appeal, 4th s. of Herbert Henry (ASQUITH), 1st EARL OF OXFORD AND ASQUITH, was *b.* 5 Feb. 1890; ed. at Winchester and Oxford (Balliol Coll.). On 23 Apr. 1951 he was app. a Lord of Appeal in Ordinary under the Appellate Jurisdiction Act of 1876, and *cr.* a Baron for Life by the style of BARON ASQUITH OF BISHOPSTONE, of Bishopstone, co. Sussex. He *m.*, 12 Feb. 1918, Anne Stephanie, da. of Sir Adrian Donald Wilde POLLOCK. He *d.* 24 Aug. 1954, when his Life Barony became *extinct*. His widow *d.* 19 Feb. 1964.

26 JUNE

McENTEE

BARONY. I. 1951. 1. VALENTINE LA TOUCHE MCENTEE, C.B.E., 1st s. of Dr. William Charles MCENTEE, of Dublin, was *b.* 16 Jan. 1871; ed. at elementary school and privately. He was *cr.*, 26 June 1951, BARON McENTEE, of

Walthamstow, co. Essex. He *m.* 1stly, 1892, Elizabeth, da. of Edward CRAWFORD of Dublin. Following her death he *m.* 2ndly, June 1920, Catherine, da. of Charles WINDSOR of Walthamstow. He *d. s.p.* 11 Feb. 1953, when his Barony became *extinct.*

27 JUNE

KENSWOOD

BARONY. I. 1951. 1. ERNEST ALBERT WHITFIELD, 2nd s. of John Henry Christopher WHITFIELD, of London, was *b.* 15 Sep. 1887; ed. at Univ. Coll. Sch., London and at Vienna and London Univs. He was *cr.*, 27 June 1951, BARON KENSWOOD, of St. Marylebone, co. London. He *m.* 1stly, 13 Dec. 1920, Sophie Madeline, only child of Ernest Walters HOWARD of London. She *d.* 23 Aug. 1961 and he *m.* 2ndly, 26 July 1962, Catherine, da. of Frank THRUXTON and widow of Charles CHILVER-STAINER. He *d.* 21 Apr. 1963. His widow *d.* 1992.

II. 1963. 2. JOHN MICHAEL HOWARD (WHITFIELD), BARON KENSWOOD, only s. and h., *b.* 6 Apr. 1930; ed. at Trinity Coll. Sch., Port Hope, Ontario, Harrow, Grenoble Univ. and Cambridge (Emmanuel Coll.). He *m.*, 16 June 1951, Deirdre Anna Louise, da. of Colin Malcolm METHVEN of Errol, Perthshire.

[MICHAEL CHRISTOPHER WHITFIELD, 1st s. and h. ap., *b.* 3 July 1955.]

16 OCTOBER

FREYBERG

BARONY. I. 1951. 1. Lieut. Gen. SIR BERNARD CYRIL FREYBERG, V.C., G.C.M.G., K.C.B., K.B.E., D.S.O., Gov. Gen. and Cmdr.-in-Chief of New Zealand, s. of James FREYBERG, of Wellington, New Zealand, was *b.* 21 Mar. 1889; ed. at Wellington Coll. New Zealand. He was *cr.* 16 Oct. 1951, BARON FREYBERG, of Wellington, New Zealand, and of Munstead, co. Surrey. He *m.*, 14 June 1922, Barbara, da. of Col. Sir Herbert JEKYLL of Munstead House, Godalming, Surrey, and widow of Francis Walter Stafford MCLAREN. He *d.* 4 July 1963. His widow *d.* 1973.

II. 1963. 2. PAUL RICHARD (FREYBERG), BARON FREYBERG, only s. and h., *b.* 27 May 1923; ed. at Eton. He *m.*, 23 July 1960, Ivy Perronelle Katherine, only da. of Cyril Harrower GUILD of Aspell Hall, near Debenham, Stowmarket, Suffolk. He *d.* 26 May 1993. His widow was still living 1995.

III. 1993. 3. VALERIAN BERNARD (FREYBERG), BARON FREYBERG, only s. and h., *b.* 15 Dec. 1970.

12 NOVEMBER

COHEN

BARONY FOR LIFE. I. 1951. 1. The Right Hon. SIR LIONEL LEONARD COHEN, one of the Lords Justices of Appeal, only s. of Sir Leonard Lionel COHEN,

K.C.V.O., was *b.* 1 Mar. 1888; ed. at Eton and Oxford (New Coll.). On 12 Nov. 1951 he was app. a Lord of Appeal in Ordinary under the appellate Jurisdication Act of 1876, and *cr.* a Baron for Life by the style of BARON COHEN, of Walmer, co. Kent. He *m.*, 9 Apr. 1918, Adelaide, da. of Sir Isidore SPIELMANN of London by his wife Emily, da. of Sir Joseph SEBAG-MONTEFIORE. She *d.* 29 Dec. 1961. He *d.* 9 May 1973 when his Life Barony became *extinct.*

14 DECEMBER

RUFFSIDE

VISCOUNTCY. I. 1951. 1. Col. the Right Hon. DOUGLAS CLIFTON BROWN, 4th s. of James Clifton BROWN, of Holmbush, Sussex, br. of Sir William Richmond BROWN, 2nd Bart. [1963], and of Sir Alexander Hargreaves BROWN, 1st Bart. [1903], was *b.* 16 Aug. 1879; ed. at Eton and Cambridge (Trin. Coll.). He was *cr.*, 14 December 1951, VISCOUNT RUFFSIDE, of Hexham, co. Northumberland. He *m.*, 24 June 1907, Violet Cicely Kathleen, only da. of Frederick Eustace Arbuthnott WOLLASTON of Shenton Hall, co. Leics. He *d. s.p.m.* 5 May 1958, when his Viscountcy became *extinct.*

20 DECEMBER

MILNER OF LEEDS

BARONY. I. 1951. 1. Major the Right Hon. JAMES MILNER, M.C. (and bar), T.D., 1st s. of James Henry MILNER, Solicitor, of Mount Farm, Alwoodley, Leeds, was *b.* 12 Aug. 1889; ed. at Leeds Modern and Easingwold Gram. Schools and Leeds Univ. He was *cr.*, 20 Dec. 1951, BARON MILNER OF LEEDS, of Roundhay, in the City of Leeds. He *m.*, 10 Feb. 1917, Lois Tinsdale, da. of Thomas BROWN of Roundhay, Leeds. He *d.* 16 July 1967. His widow *d.* 1982.

II. 1967. 2. ARTHUR JAMES MICHAEL (MILNER), BARON MILNER OF LEEDS, only s. and h., *b.* 12 Sep. 1923; ed. at Oundle and Cambridge (Trin. Hall). He *m.* 31 Mar. 1951, Sheila Margaret, da. of Gerard HARTLEY of Headingley, Leeds.

[RICHARD JAMES MILNER, only s. and h. ap., *b.* 16 May 1959; ed. at Charterhouse and Surrey Univ. He *m.*, 1988, Margaret Christine, yst. da. of Gerald Francis VOISIN of Jersey.]

22 DECEMBER

KIRKWOOD

BARONY. I. 1951. 1. The Right Hon. DAVID KIRKWOOD, s. of John KIRKWOOD, winding master in Brown's Mill, Bridgeton, Glasgow, was *b.* 8 July 1872; ed. at Parkhead Public School. He was *cr.*, 22 Dec. 1951, BARON KIRKWOOD, of Bearsden, co. Dunbarton. He *m.*, 30 June 1899, Elizabeth, da. of Robert SMITH of Parkhead, Glasgow. He *d.* 16 Apr. 1955. His widow *d.* 3 May 1956.

[JOHN KIRKWOOD, 1st s. and h. ap., *b.* 29 Mar. 1900; ed. at Ruskin Coll., Oxford. He *m.*, 22 Oct. 1932, Ellen Florence, da. of Thomas Peter HAGGAR of Witham, Essex. He *d. s.p.m.* and *v.p.* 8 Dec. 1942.]

[ROBERT SMITH KIRKWOOD, 2nd but 1st surv. s. and h. ap., *b.* 25 Oct. 1901; ed. at Eastbank Academy. He *m.*, 21 Oct. 1921, Annie Kerr, da. of John MARSHALL of Glasgow. He *d. s.p.m.* and *v.p.* 17 May 1950.]

II. 1955. 2. DAVID (KIRKWOOD), BARON KIRKWOOD, 3rd but 1st surv. s. and h., was *b.* 15 Oct. 1903; ed. at Eastbank Academy. He *m.*, 29 March 1931, Eileen Grace, da. of Thomas Henry BOALCH of Bristol. He *d.* 9 March 1970. His widow was living 1995.

III. 1970. 3. DAVID HARVIE (KIRKWOOD), BARON KIRKWOOD, 1st s. and h., was *b.* 24 Nov. 1931; ed. at Rugby and Cambridge (Trin. Hall). He *m.*, 31 July 1965, Judith Rosalie, da. of John HUNT of Leeds.

24 DECEMBER

JOWITT, Earldom, STEVENAGE, Viscountcy

JOWITT, Earldom, STEVENAGE, Viscountcy (*Jowitt*) *cr.* 24 Dec. 1951. See JOWITT, Barony, *cr.* 2 Aug. 1945, p. 766.

24 DECEMBER

WISE

BARONY. I. 1951. 1. Major FREDERICK JOHN WISE, 2nd s. of Edward WISE, of Bury St. Edmunds, Suffolk, was *b.* 10 Apr. 1887; ed. at King Edward VI School, Bury St. Edmunds. He was *cr.*, 24 Dec. 1951, BARON WISE, of King's Lynn, co. Norfolk. He *m.*, 25 Nov. 1911, Kate Elizabeth, da. of John Michael STURGEON of Bury St. Edmunds. He *d.* 20 Nov. 1968.

II. 1968. 2. JOHN CLAYTON (WISE), BARON WISE, only s. and h., was *b.* 11 June 1923; ed. at Bury School, Suffolk. He *m.*, 21 Sept. 1946, Margaret Annie, da. of Frederick Victor SNEAD of Banbury, Oxon.

[CHRISTOPHER JOHN CLAYTON WISE, 1st s. and h. ap., *b.* 19 March 1949; ed. at Norwich School and Southampton Univ.]

PEERAGES OF 1952

5 JANUARY

HUDSON

VISCOUNTCY. I. 1952. 1. The Right Hon. ROBERT SPEAR HUDSON, C.H., s. of Robert William HUDSON, of Villa Paloma, Monaco, High Sheriff of Bucks in 1903, was *b.* 15 Aug. 1886; ed. at Eton and Oxford (Magdalen Coll.). He was *cr.*, 5 Jan. 1952, VISCOUNT HUDSON, of Pewsey, co. Wilts. He *m.*, 1 Dec. 1918,

Hannah, da. of Philip Synge Physick RANDOLPH of Philadelphia, U.S.A. He *d.* 3 Feb. 1957. His widow *d.* 24 April 1969.

II. 1957. 2. ROBERT WILLIAM (HUDSON), VISCOUNT HUDSON, only s. and h., was *b.* 28 Apr. 1924; ed. at Eton and Cambridge (Trin. Coll.). He *m.*, 14 Oct. 1948, Marie Claire, da. of Adrien SCHMITT of Paris. This marriage was diss. by divorce 1961, (she *d.* 1969). He *d.* 28 Aug. 1963 when his Viscountcy became extinct.

6 JANUARY

CORNWALL, Dukedom [E.],(1) ROTHESAY, Dukedom [S.],(2) CARRICK, Earldom [S.], RENFREW, Barony [S.]

DUKEDOM. XXIV. 1952. *H.R.H.* CHARLES PHILIP ARTHUR GEORGE, Prince of the United Kingdom of Great Britain and Northern Ireland, DUKE OF CORNWALL, in the Peerage of England, also DUKE OF ROTHESAY, EARL OF CARRICK and BARON OF RENFREW, in the Peerage of Scotland, Lord of the Isles and Great Steward of Scotland, s. and h. ap. of *H.M.* QUEEN ELIZABETH II, was, on his mother's succession to the throne, 6 Feb. 1952, entitled to the abovenamed dignities. He was *cr.*, 26 July 1958, PRINCE OF WALES and EARL OF CHESTER.(3). He *m.*, 29 July 1981, at St. Paul's Cathedral, Lady Diana Frances, 3rd da. of Edward John (SPENCER), 8th EARL SPENCER.

[*H.R.H.* WILLIAM ARTHUR PHILLIP LOUIS, Prince of the United Kingdom and Northern Ireland, 1st s. and h. ap., although not as such h. to any of his father's dignities, was *b.* 21 June 1982.]

note (1) For the earlier Dukes of Cornwall see vols iii and xiii.
note (2) For the earlier Dukes of Rothesay [S.] see vols iii, xi, and xiii.
note (3) For the earlier Earls of Chester see vols iii and xiii.

7 JANUARY

BRACKEN

VISCOUNTCY. I. 1952. 1. The Right Hon. BRENDAN BRACKEN, s. of J.K.A. BRACKEN, of Ardvullen House, Kilmallock, *b.* 1901, ed. at Sydney and Sedbergh. He was *cr.*, 7 Jan. 1952, VISCOUNT BRACKEN, of Christchurch, co. Southampton. He *d.* unm. 8 Aug. 1958, when his Viscountcy became *extinct.*

28 JANUARY

WAVERLEY

VISCOUNTCY. I. 1952. 1. The Right Hon. SIR JOHN ANDERSON, G.C.B., G.C.S.I., G.C.I.E., s. of David Alexander ANDERSON, Publisher, of Westland House, Estbank, Midlothian, was *b.* 8 July 1882; ed. at George Watson's

College, Edinburgh, and Edinburgh and Leipzig Univs. He was *cr.*, 28 Jan. 1952, VISCOUNT WAVERLEY, of Westdean, co. Sussex. He *m.*, 1stly, 2 April 1907, Christina, da. of Andrew MACKENZIE of Edinburgh. She *d.* 9 May 1920. He *m.* 2ndly, 30 Oct. 1941, Ava, da. of John Edward Courtenay BODLEY and widow of Ralph Follett WIGRAM. He *d.* 4 Jan. 1958. His widow *d.* 1974.

II. 1958. 2. DAVID ALASTAIR PEARSON (ANDERSON), VISCOUNT WAVERLEY, only s. and h., was *b.* 18 Feb. 1911; ed. at Malvern and Cambridge (Pembroke Coll.). He *m.*, 13 Nov. 1948, Lorna Myrtle Ann, da. of Lieut. Col. Frederick Hill LEDGERWOOD. He *d.* 21 Feb. 1990. His widow was living 1995.

III. 1990. 3. JOHN DESMOND FORBES (ANDERSON), VISCOUNT WAVERLEY, only s. and h., was *b.* 31 Oct. 1949; ed. at Malvern. He *m.*, 1994, Her Excellency Dr Ursula Helen, da. of Raymond Hugh BARROW of Belize City.

30 JANUARY

MATHERS

BARONY. I. 1952. 1. The Right Hon. GEORGE MATHERS, s. of George MATHERS, of Newtown St. Boswells, co. Roxburgh, was *b.* 28 Feb. 1886; ed. at Newtown St Boswells School and evening classes, Carlisle and Edinburgh. He was *cr.*, 30 Jan. 1952, BARON MATHERS, of Newtown St. Boswells, co. Roxburgh. He *m.*, 1stly, 6 June 1916, Edith Mary, da. of William ROBINSON of Carlisle. She *d.* 5 June 1938. He *m.* 2ndly, 31 Jan. 1940, Jessie Newton, da. of George GRAHAM of Peebles and Edinburgh. He *d. s.p.*, 26 Sep. 1965 when his Barony became extinct.

31 JANUARY

TURNOUR

TURNOUR, Barony (*Turnour*), *cr.* 31 Jan. 1952. See WINTERTON, Earldom [I.], in vol. xii, part 2 and above, p. 638.

11 MARCH

ALEXANDER OF TUNIS, Earldom, RIDEAU, Barony

1952. See ALEXANDER OF TUNIS, Viscountcy, *cr.* 1 Mar. 1946, p. 775.

10 APRIL

THURSO

VISCOUNTCY. I. 1952. 1. The Right Hon. SIR ARCHIBALD HENRY MACDONALD SINCLAIR, 4th Bart. [1786], K.T., C.M.G., only s. and h. of Clarence Granville SINCLAIR (who *d. v.p.*; 1st s. and h. ap. of Sir John George Tollemache SINCLAIR, 3rd Bart.), was *b.* 22 Oct. 1890; ed. at Eton and R.M.C. Sandhurst. He was *cr.*, 10

Apr. 1952, VISCOUNT THURSO, of Ulbster, co. Caithness. He *m.*, 18 May 1918, Marigold, da. of Lieut. Col. James Stewart FORBES. He *d.* 15 June 1970. His widow *d.* 1975.

II. 1970. 2. ROBIN MACDONALD (SINCLAIR), VISCOUNT THURSO, 1st s. and h., was *b.* 24 Dec. 1922; ed. at Eton, Oxford (New Coll.) and Edinburgh University. He *m.*, 14 Feb. 1952, Margaret Beaumont, da. of Col. Josiah James ROBERTSON of Norwood Wick, Caithness, and widow of Lieut. Guy Warwick BROKENSHA, R.N.

[JOHN ARCHIBALD SINCLAIR, 1st s. and h. ap., was *b.* 10 Sept. 1953; ed. at Eton. He *m.*, 1976, Marion, da. of Louis SAGE of Connecticutt, U.S.A.]

24 JUNE

SIMONDS

SIMONDS, Barony (*Simonds*), *cr.* 24 June 1952. See SIMONDS, Barony for Life, *cr.* 18 Apr. 1944, p. 758.

1 JULY

BROOKEBOROUGH

VISCOUNTCY. I. 1952. 1. The Right Hon. SIR BASIL STANLAKE BROOKE, 5th Bart. [1822], C.B.E., M.C., 1st s. and h. of Sir Arthur Douglas BROOKE, 4th Bart., was *b.* 9 June 1888; ed. at Winchester and R.M.C. Sandhurst. He was *cr.*, 1 July 1952, VISCOUNT BROOKEBOROUGH, of Colebrooke, co. Fermanagh. He *m.*, 1stly, 3 June 1919, Cynthia Mary, 2nd da. and co-heir of Capt. Charles Warden SERGISON of Cuckfield Park, Sussex. She *d.* 1970. He *m.* 2ndly, 1971, Sarah Eileen Bell, da. of Henry HEALEY of Belfast and widow of Cecil Armstrong CALVERT. He *d.* 18 Aug. 1973. She *d.* 1989.

II. 1973. 2. JOHN WARDEN (BROOKE), VISCOUNT BROOKEBOROUGH, 2nd but only surv. s., (1) was *b.* 9 Nov. 1922; ed. at Eton. He *m.*, 4 March 1949, Rosemary Hilda, da. of Lieut. Col. Arthur O'Neill Cubitt CHICHESTER of Galgorm Castle, Ballymena, co. Antrim. He *d.* 5 March 1987. His widow was living 1995.

III. 1987. 3. ALAN HENRY (BROOKE), VISCOUNT BROOKEBOROUGH, 1st s. and h. was *b.* 30 June 1952; ed. at Harrow and Millfield. He *m.*, 1980, Janet Elizabeth, only da. of John COOKE of Ballyvoy Lodge, Doagh, co. Antrim.

note (1) BASIL JULIAN DAVID (BROOKE), 1st s., was *b.* 18 April 1920; ed. at Eton, killed in action March 1943.

5 JULY

NORWICH

VISCOUNTCY. I. 1952. 1. The Right Hon. SIR ALFRED DUFF COOPER, G.C.M.G., D.S.O., only s. of Sir Alfred COOPER, F.R.C.S., of Whiting Bay, Isle of Arran, was *b.* 22 Feb. 1890; ed. at Eton and Oxford (New Coll.). He was *cr.*, 5 July 1952, VISCOUNT NORWICH, of Aldwick, co. Sussex. He *m.*, 2 June 1919, Lady Diana Olivia Winifred, 3rd da. of Henry John Brinsley (MANNERS) 8th DUKE OF RUTLAND. He *d.* 1 Jan. 1954. She announced her intention of reverting to her former name of Lady Diana COOPER 8 Jan. 1954 and *d.* 16 June 1986.

II. 1954. 2. JOHN JULIUS (COOPER), VISCOUNT NORWICH, only s. and h., was *b.* 15 Sep. 1929; ed. at Eton and Oxford (New Coll.). He *m.*, 1stly, 5 Aug. 1952, Anne Frances May, eldest da. of Sir Bede Edmund Hugh CLIFFORD of Queen Anne's Farm, Jacob's Well, near Guildford. This marriage was diss. by divorce 1985, and he *m.* 2ndly, 1989, Mrs Mary PHILIPPS, twin da. of Roger Mellor (MAKINS), 1st BARON SHERFIELD.

[JASON CHARLES DUFF BEDE COOPER only s. and h. ap. (by 1st marriage), *b.* 27 Oct. 1959.]

12 JULY

JEFFREYS

BARONY. I. 1952. 1. Gen. SIR GEORGE DARELL JEFFREYS, K.C.B., K.C.V.O., C.M.G., only s. of the Right Hon. Arthur Frederick JEFFREYS, M.P., of Burkham, Hants., was *b.* 8 Mar. 1878; ed. at Eton and R.M.C. Sandhurst. He was *cr.*, 12 July 1952, BARON JEFFREYS, of Burkham, co. Southampton. He *m.*, 28 Feb. 1905, Dorothy, da. of John Postle HESELTINE of Walhampton, Lymington and widow of Lionel Charles Cranfield SACKVILLE, *styled* VISCOUNT CANTELUPE, 1st s. and h. ap. of Reginald Windsor (SACKVILLE), 7th EARL DE LA WARR. She *d.* 21 May 1953. He *d.* 19 Dec. 1960.

[CHRISTOPHER JOHN DARELL JEFFREYS, only s. and h. ap. was *b.* 30 Dec. 1907; ed. at Eton and R.M.C. Sandhurst. He *m.*, 23 April 1931, Lady Rosemary Beatrice, youngest da. of Sidney James AGAR, 4th EARL OF NORMANTON. He was killed in action at Dunkirk, 28 May 1940. His widow *d.* 1984.]

II. 1960. 2. MARK GEORGE CHRISTOPHER (JEFFREYS), BARON JEFFREYS, grandson and h. was *b.* 2 Feb. 1932; ed. at Eton and R.M.C. Sandhurst. He *m.*, 24 July 1956, Sarah Annabelle Mary, only da. of Major Henry Claude Lyon GARNETT. This marriage was diss. by divorce 1967 (she was living 1995) and he *m.* 2ndly, 14 March 1967, Anne Louise, younger da. of his Honour Judge Sir William Shirley WORTHINGTON-EVANS, 2nd Bart. This marriage was in turn diss. by divorce 1981, and he *m.* 3rdly, 1981, Mrs Suzanne GILBERT, da. of James STEAD of Goudhurst, Kent. He *d.* 13 Feb. 1986. His widow was living 1995.

III. 1986. CHRISTOPHER HENRY MARK (JEFFREYS), BARON JEFFREYS, 1st s. and h. was *b.* 22 May 1957; ed. at Eton. He *m.*, 1985, Anne Elizabeth, da. of Antoine DENARIE.

[ARTHUR MARK HENRY JEFFREYS, only s. and h. ap. was *b.* 18 Feb. 1989.]

31 JULY

DUDHOPE, Viscountcy, SCRYMGEOUR, Barony [S.]

DUDHOPE, Viscountcy, SCRYMGEOUR, Barony [S.] (*Scrymgeour-Wedderburn*). On 31 July 1952 it was resolved by the House of Lords that HENRY JAMES SCRYMGEOUR-WEDDERBURN of Wedderburn and Birkhill, Hereditary Royal Standard Bearer for Scotland, was entitled of right to the dignities of VISCOUNT DUDHOPE and LORD SCRYMGEOUR [S.], as h. male (collateral) of Sir John Scrymgeour of Dudhope, who was so *cr.*, 15 Nov. 1641, with rem. to his heirs male whatsoever. On 20 May 1953, it was further resolved by the House of Lords that he was also entitled of right to the dignities of EARL OF DUNDEE and LORD INVERKEITHING [S.], as h. male (collateral) of John (Scrymgeour), 3rd Viscount Dudhope [S.], who was so *cr.*, 8 Sep. 1660, with rem. to his heirs male whatsoever. See vol. iv, *sub* DUDHOPE and DUNDEE. He was *cr.*, 30 July 1954, BARON GLASSARY, of Glassary, co. Argyll [U.K.], with the usual rem. See below.

PEERAGES OF 1953

11 FEBRUARY

RATHCAVAN

BARONY. I. 1953. 1. The Right Hon. SIR ROBERT WILLIAM HUGH O'NEILL, 1st Bart. [1929], 3rd s. of Edward (O'NEILL), 2nd BARON O'NEILL, was *b.* 8 June 1883; ed. at Eton and Oxford (New Coll.). He was *cr.*, 11 Feb. 1953, BARON RATHCAVAN, of The Braid, co. Antrim. He *m.*, 11 Feb. 1909, Sylvia Irene, younger da. of Walter Albert SANDEMAN of Morden House, Royston, Hertfordshire. She *d.* 1972. He *d.* 28 Nov. 1982.

II. 1982. 2. PHELIM ROBERT HUGH (O'NEILL), BARON RATHCAVAN, 1st s. and h. was *b.* 2 Nov. 1909; ed. at Eton. He *m.* 1stly, 12 Feb. 1934, Clare Desirée, da. of Detmar Jellings BLOW of London and Stroud, co. Gloucester. This marriage was diss. by divorce 1944, and she *d.* 3 March 1956. He *m.* 2ndly, 3 June 1953, Bridget Doreen, da. of Major Richard COKE and formerly wife of Thomas Richard EDWARDS-MOSS.

[HUGH DETMAR TORRENS (O'NEILL), only s. (by 1st wife) and h. ap., was *b.* 14 June 1939; ed. at Eton. He *m.*, 1983, Mrs Sylvie Marie-Thérèse CHITTENDEN, da. of Georges WICHARD of Provence, France.]

12 FEBRUARY

PERCY OF NEWCASTLE

BARONY. I. 1953. 1. The Right Hon. LORD EUSTACE SUTHERLAND CAMPBELL PERCY, 7th s. of Henry George (PERCY), 7th DUKE OF NORTHUMBERLAND, was *b.* 21 Mar. 1887; ed. at Eton and Oxford (Ch. Ch.). He was *cr.*, 12 Feb.

1953, BARON PERCY OF NEWCASTLE, of Etchingham, co. Sussex. He *m.*, 4 Dec. 1918, Stella Katherine, da. of Major Gen. Lawrence DRUMMOND. He *d. s.p.m.* 3 Apr. 1958, when his Barony became *extinct.*

13 FEBRUARY

BAILLIEU

BARONY. I. 1953. 1. SIR CLIVE LATHAM BAILLIEU, K.B.E., C.M.G., 1st s. of William Lawrence BAILLIEU, of Sefton, Macedon, Upper Victoria, Australia, was *b.* 24 Sep. 1889; ed. at Trin. Coll., Melbourne Univ. and Oxford (Magdalen Coll.). He was *cr.*, 13 Feb. 1953, BARON BAILLIEU, of Sefton, in the Commonwealth of Australia, and of Parkwood, co. Surrey. He *m.*, 24 Feb. 1915, Ruby Florence Evelyn, da. of William CLARK of Windlesham, Surrey. She *d.* 21 Oct. 1962. He *d.* 18 June 1967.

II. 1967. 2. WILLIAM LATHAM (BAILLIEU), BARON BAILLIEU, 1st s. and h., was *b.* 10 Dec. 1915; ed. at Winchester and Oxford (Magdalen Coll.); *m.* 1stly, 11 Aug. 1945, Anne Bayliss, 1st da. of Leslie William PAGE of Southport, Queensland, Australia. This marriage was diss. by divorce in 1961 and he *m.* 2ndly, 10 Feb. 1962, Delia Muriel (Mrs CHAPMAN). He *d.* 18 Apr. 1973. His widow was still living 1995.

III. 1973. 3. JAMES WILLIAM LATHAM (BAILLIEU), BARON BAILLIEU, 1st s. and h., was *b.* 16 Nov. 1950; ed. at Radley, *m.* 1stly, 1974, Cornelia Masters, yst. da. of William Conkling LADD. This marriage was diss. by divorce in 1985 and he *m.* 2ndly, 1987, Clare, da. of Peter STEPHENSON.

[ROBERT LATHAM BAILLIEU, s. and h. ap. by 1st wife, *b.* 2 Feb. 1979.]

20 MAY

DUNDEE, Earldom, INVERKEITHING, Barony [S.]

DUNDEE, Earldom, INVERKEITHING, Barony [S.] (*Scrymgeour-Wedderburn*). On 20 May 1953 it was resolved by the House of Lords that HENRY JAMES (SCRYMGEOUR-WEDDERBURN), VISCOUNT DUDHOPE [S.], was entitled of right to the dignities of EARL OF DUNDEE and LORD INVERKEITHING [S.]. See vol. iv, *sub* DUNDEE and above.

28 MAY

FITZWALTER

FITZWALTER, Barony by Writ (*Plumptre*). The *abeyance* in this Barony, was terminated by the issue of a writ of summons to Parliament, 28 May 1953, to FITZWALTER BROOK PLUMPTRE, who took his seat, 24 June follg. See FITZWALTER in vols v and xiii and above.

29 JUNE

GLYN

BARONY. I. 1953. 1. SIR RALPH GEORGE CAMPBELL GLYNN, 1st Bart. [1934], only s. of the Right Rev. Edward Carr GLYN, D.D., Bishop of Peterborough (8th and yst. s. of George Carr (GLYNN), 1st BARON WOLVERTON) was *b.* 3 Mar. 1885; ed. at Harrow and R.M.C., Sandhurst. He was *cr.*, 29 June 1953, BARON GLYN, of Farnborough, co. Berks. He *m.*, 25 Apr. 1921, Sibell, da. of Francis (VANDEN-BEMPDE-JOHNSTONE), 2nd BARON DERWENT and widow of Brig. Gen. W. LONG. He *d. s.p.* 1 May 1960 when his Barony became *extinct.*

30 JUNE

GRANTCHESTER

BARONY. I. 1953. SIR ALFRED JESSE SUENSON-TAYLOR, O.B.E., s. of Alfred George TAYLOR, of Stowford, Sutton, Surrey, was *b.* 14 Aug. 1893; ed. at Epsom and Cambridge (King's Coll.). He was *cr.*, 30 June 1953, BARON GRANTCHESTER, of Knightsbridge, in the City of Westm. He *m.*, 26 May 1920, Maria Henrietta Mamie, 2nd da. of Albert SUENSON of Copenhagen. He *d.* 2 July 1976. She *d.* 1976.

II. 1976. 2. KENNETH BENT (SUENSON-TAYLOR), BARON GRANTCHESTER, only s. and h., was *b.* 18 Aug. 1921; ed. at Westminster and Cambridge (Christ's Coll.); *m.*, 12 Apr. 1947, Betty, 1st da. of John MOORES of Freshfield, co. Lancaster.

[CHRISTOPHER JOHN SUENSON-TAYLOR, s. and h. ap., *b.* 8 Apr. 1951; ed. at Winchester and London Sch. of Econ.; *m.*, 1973, Jacqueline, da. of Dr Leo JAFFE.]

1 JULY

BENNETT OF EDGBASTON

BARONY. I. 1953. 1. SIR PETER FREDERICK BLAKER BENNETT, O.B.E., s. of Frederick C. BENNETT, of Birmingham, was *b.* 16 Apr. 1880; ed. at King Edward's Sch., Birmingham and Birmingham Univ. He was *cr.*, 1 July 1953, BARON BENNETT OF EDGBASTON, of Sutton Coldfield, co. Warwick. He *m.*, 1905, Agnes, 1st da. of Joseph PALMER. He *d. s.p.* 29 Sep. 1957, when his Barony became *extinct*. His widow *d.* 17 Nov. 1969.

2 JULY

WOOLTON

WOOLTON, Viscountcy (*Marquis*), *cr.* 2 July 1953. See WOOLTON, Barony, *cr.* 7 July 1939, p. 740.

16 OCTOBER

SALTER

BARONY. I. 1953. 1. The Right Hon. SIR JAMES ARTHUR SALTER, G.B.E., K.C.B., s. of James Edward SALTER, of Isis House, Oxford, was *b.* 15 Mar. 1881; ed. at

Oxford (Brasenose Coll.). He was *cr.*, 16 Oct. 1953, BARON SALTER, of Kidlington, co. Oxford. He *m.*, 15 June 1940, Ethel, da. of John Sherman BAGG of Springfield, Massachusetts, U.S.A., and widow of Arthur BULLAND. She *d.* 1969. He *d. s.p.* 27 June 1975 when his Barony became *extinct.*

4 NOVEMBER

KEITH OF AVONHOLM

BARONY FOR LIFE. I. 1953. 1. JAMES KEITH, one of the Senators of the Coll. of Justice [S.], as Lord Keith, s. of Sir Henry Shanks KEITH, G.B.E., of Avonholm, Hamilton, was *b.* 20 May 1886; ed. at Hamilton Acad. and Glasgow Univ. On 4 Nov. 1953 he was app. a Lord of Appeal in Ordinary under the Appellate Jurisdiction Act of 1876, and *cr.* a Baron for Life by the style of BARON KEITH OF AVONHOLM, of St. Bernard's, in the City of Edinburgh. He *m.*, 7 July 1915, Jean Maitland, da. of Andrew BENNETT. He *d. s.p.* 29 June 1969, when his Life Barony became *extinct.*

PEERAGES OF 1954

14 JANUARY

HORE-BELISHA

BARONY. I. 1954. 1. The Right Hon. LESLIE HORE-BELISHA, *formerly* BELISHA, s. of Capt. Jacob Isaac BELISHA, R. Fus., was *b.* 7 Sep. 1893; ed. at Clifton Coll., Paris, Heidelberg and Oxford (St. John's Coll.). He was *cr.*, 14 Jan. 1954, BARON HORE-BELISHA, of Devonport, co. Devon. He *m.*, 1944, Cynthia, da. of Gilbert ELLIOTT of Sholden, Kent. He *d. s.p.* 16 Feb. 1957, when his Barony became *extinct.*

16 JANUARY

STRANG

BARONY. I. 1954. 1. SIR WILLIAM STRANG, G.C.B., G.C.M.G., M.B.E., 1st s. of James STRANG, of Englefield, Berks, was *b.* 2 Jan. 1893; ed. at Palmer's Sch., Grays, Univ. Coll., London and the Sorbonne, Paris. He was *cr.* 16 Jan. 1954, BARON STRANG, of Stonesfield, co. Oxford. He *m.* 1 Mar. 1920, Elsie Wynne, da. of Josiah Edward JONES of Addiscombe. She *d.* 1974. He *d.* 27 May 1978.

II. 1978. 2. COLIN (STRANG), LORD STRANG, only s. and h., was *b.* 12 June 1922; ed. at Merchant Taylors' Sch. and Oxford (St. John's Coll.); *m.* 1stly, 3 July 1948, Patricia Marie, da. of Meiert CAVIS of Johannesburg, South Africa. This marriage was diss. by divorce in 1955 and he *m.* 2ndly, 21 Apr. 1955, Barbara Mary Hope, da. of Frederick Albert CARR of Wimbledon. She *d.* 1982 and he married 3rdly, 1984, Mary Shewell, da. of Richard MILES of Sheffield.

18 JANUARY

LEATHERS

LEATHERS, Viscountcy (*Leathers*), *cr.* 18 Jan. 1954. See LEATHERS, Barony, *cr.* 19 May 1941, p. 747.

18 JANUARY

DOVERCOURT

BARONY. I. 1954. 1. SIR JOSEPH STANLEY HOLMES, s. of Horace G. HOLMES, was *b.* 31 Oct. 1878; ed. at City of London Sch. He was *cr.*, 18 Jan. 1954, BARON DOVERCOURT, of Harwich, co. Essex. He *m.*, 1905, Eva Gertrude, da. of Thomas Bowley. He *d. s.p.* 22 Apr. 1961 when his Barony became *extinct*. His widow *d.* 12 Feb. 1967.

30 JANUARY

MOORE

BARONY. I. 1954. 1. HENRY CHARLES PONSONBY (MOORE), 10th EARL OF DROGHEDA [I. 1661], VISCOUNT MOORE OF DROGHEDA [I. 1622] and BARON MOORE OF MELLEFONT [I. 1616], was *cr.*, 30 Jan. 1954, BARON MOORE, of Cobham, co. Surrey [U.K.]. He *d.* 22 Nov. 1957. For further particulars see vol. iv, *sub* DROGHEDA.

16 FEBRUARY

COLERAINE

BARONY. I. 1954. 1. The Right Hon. RICHARD KIDSTON LAW, 1st s. of the Right Hon. Andrew Bonar LAW, Prime Minister and First Lord of the Treasury, 1922–3, was *b.* 27 Feb. 1901; ed. at Shrewsbury and Oxford (St. John's Coll.). He was *cr.*, 16 Feb. 1954, BARON COLERAINE, of Haltemprice, in the East Riding of co. York. He *m.*, 26 Jan. 1929, Mary Virginia, da. of Abram Fox NELLIS of Rochester, New York. She *d.* 1978. He *d.* 15 Nov. 1980.

II. 1980. 2. JAMES MARTIN BONAR (LAW), BARON COLERAINE, 1st s. and h., was *b.* 8 Aug. 1931; ed. at Eton and Oxford (Trin. Coll.); *m.* 1stly, 30 Apr. 1958, Emma Elizabeth, only da. of Nigel RICHARDS. This marriage was diss. by divorce in 1966 and he *m.* 2ndly, 31 May 1966, Anne Patricia, yr. da. of Major Gen. Ralph Henry FARRANT of Wareham, Dorset. She was accidentally drowned in Portugal, 1993.

[JAMES PETER BONAR LAW, s. and h. ap. by 2nd wife, *b.* 23 Feb. 1975; ed. at Eton.]

3 JULY

HARVEY OF TASBURGH

BARONY. I. 1954. 1. SIR OLIVER CHARLES HARVEY, G.C.M.G., G.C.V.O., C.B., yr. br. of Sir Charles Robert Lambart Edward HARVEY, 3rd Bart. [1868], being only s. by the 2nd wife of Sir Charles HARVEY, 2nd Bart., was *b.* 26 Nov. 1893; ed. at Malvern and Cambridge (Trin. Coll.). He was *cr.* 3 July 1954, BARON HARVEY OF TASBURGH, of Tasburgh, co. Norfolk; and *suc.* his said elder br. (who *d. s.p.m.s.*) in the Baronetcy, 15 Nov. follg. He *m.*, 8 Apr. 1920, Maud Annora, 1st da. of Arthur Watkin WILLIAMS-WYNN. He *d.* 29 Nov. 1968. His widow *d.* 1970.

II. 1968. 2. PETER CHARLES OLIVER (HARVEY), BARON HARVEY OF TASBURGH, 1st s. and h., was *b.* 28 Jan. 1921; ed. at Eton and Cambridge (Trin. Coll.); *m.*, 25 Apr. 1957, Penelope Ann, yr. da. of Lieut. Col. Sir William Vivian MAKINS.

16 JULY

SOULBURY

SOULBURY, Viscountcy (*Ramsbotham*), *cr.* 16 July 1954, See SOULBURY Barony, *cr.* 6 Aug. 1941, p. 748.

30 JULY

GLASSARY

GLASSARY, Barony (*Scrymgeour-Wedderburn*), *cr.* 30 July 1954. See vol. iv, *sub* DUNDEE.

31 JULY

COOPER OF CULROSS

BARONY. I. 1954. 1. The Right Hon. THOMAS MACKAY COOPER, O.B.E., Lord Justice Gen. and Pres. of the Court of Session [S.], as Lord Cooper, 1st s. of John COOPER, C.E., Burgh Engineer, of Edinburgh, was *b.* 24 Sep. 1892; ed. at George Watson's Coll., Edinburgh and Edinburgh Univ. He was *cr.*, 31 July 1954, BARON COOPER OF CULROSS, of Dunnet, co. Caithness. He *d.* unm. 15 July 1955, when his Barony became *extinct*.

9 SEPTEMBER

CHANDOS

BARONY. I. 1954. 1. Capt. the Right Hon. OLIVER LYTTELTON, D.S.O., M.C., 2nd but 1st surv. s. of the Right Hon. Alfred Lyttelton, K.C., Sec. of State for the Colonies, 1903–5 (8th and yst. s. of George William, (LYTTELTON), 4th BARON LYTTELTON), was *b.* 15 May. 1893; ed. at Eton and Cambridge (Trin. Coll.). He was *cr.*, 9 Sep. 1954, VISCOUNT CHANDOS,(1) of Aldershot, co. Southampton. He *m.*, 30 Jan. 1920, Lady Moira Godolphin, 4th da. of George Godolphin (OSBOURNE), 10th DUKE OF LEEDS. He *d.* 21 Jan. 1972. His widow *d.* 1976.

II. 1972. 2. ANTHONY ALFRED (LYTTELTON), VISCOUNT CHANDOS, only s. and h., was *b.* 23 Oct. 1920; ed. at Eton and Cambridge (Trin. Coll.); *m.*, 20 May 1949, Caroline Mary, yr. da. of Rt. Hon. Sir Alan

Frederick LASCELLES. He *d.* 28 Nov. 1980. His widow *m.* 2ndly, 1985, as his 2nd wife, David Hervey ERSKINE of Felsham, Bury St. Edmunds, Suffolk and was still living 1995.

III. 1980. 3. THOMAS ORLANDO (LYTTELTON), VISCOUNT CHANDOS, 1st s. and h., was *b.* 12 Feb. 1953; ed. at Eton and Oxford (Worcester Coll.); *m.*, 1985, Arabella Sarah Lucy, da. of John Adrian BAILEY.

[OLIVER ANTHONY LYTTELTON, s. and h. ap., *b.* 21 Sep. 1986.]

note (1) His uncle, the 5th Lord Lyttelton, *suc.* in 1889, his distant kinsman, the 3rd and last Duke of Buckingham and Chandos, as 8th Viscount Cobham and Baron Cobham, under the spec. rem. in the creation of those dignities, which see. For the descent of the Duke from John (Brydges), 1st Baron Chandos of Sudeley, so *cr.*, 8 Apr. 1554, and from Sir Robert de Chaundos, who was sum. to Parl. in 1337, see CHANDOS and CHAUNDOS in vol. iii.

4 OCTOBER

SOMERVELL OF HARROW

BARONY FOR LIFE. I. 1954. 1. The Right Hon. SIR DONALD BRADLEY SOMERVELL, O.B.E., one of the Lords Justices of Appeal, 2nd s. of Robert SOMERVELL, Asst. Master and Bursar at Harrow Sch., was *b.* 24 Aug. 1889; ed. at Harrow and Oxford (Magdalen Coll.). On 4 Oct. 1954 he was app. a Lord of Appeal in Ordinary under the Appellate Jurisdication Act of 1876, and was *cr.* a Baron for Life by the style of BARON SOMERVELL OF HARROW, of Ewelme, co. Oxford. He *m.* 1933, Laelia, da. of Sir Archibald BUCHAN-HEPBURN, Bart. He *d.* 18 Nov. 1960 when his Life Barony became *extinct.*

18 OCTOBER

SIMONDS

SIMONDS, Viscountcy (*Simonds*), *cr.* 18 Oct. 1954. See SIMONDS, Barony for Life, *cr.* 18 Apr. 1944, p. 758.

19 OCTOBER

KILMUIR

VISCOUNTCY. I. 1954. 1. The Right Hon. SIR DAVID PATRICK MAXWELL FYFE, G.C.V.C., Lord Chancellor of Great Britain, 4th and yst. s., being only s. by the 2nd wife, of William Thomson FYFE, Head Master of the Gram. Sch., Old Aberdeen, was *b.* 29 May 1900; ed. at George Watson's Coll., Edinburgh and Oxford (Balliol Coll.). He was *cr.*, 19 Oct. 1954, VISCOUNT KILMUIR, of Creich, co. Sutherland. He was further *cr.*, 20 July 1962. BARON FYFE, of Dornoch, co. Sutherland, and EARL OF KILMUIR. He *m.*, 1925, Sylvia, da. of W.R. HARRISON of Liverpool. He *d. s.p.m.* 27 Jan. 1967 when his titles became *extinct.*

PEERAGES OF 1955

10 JANUARY

GRIDLEY

BARONY. I. 1955. 1. SIR ARNOLD BABB GRIDLEY, K.B.E., s. of Edward GRIDLEY, of Abbey Dore, co. Hereford, was *b.* 16 July 1878; ed. at Bristol Gram. Sch. He was *cr.*, 10 Jan. 1955, BARON GRIDLEY, of Stockport, co. Chester. He *m.* 10 Aug. 1905, Mabel, da. of Oliver HUDSON of Fakenham, Norfolk. She *d.* 5 July 1955. He *d.* 27 July 1965.

II. 1965. 2. ARNOLD HUDSON (GRIDLEY), BARON GRIDLEY, 1st s. and h., was *b.* 26 May 1906; ed. at Oundle; *m.* 4 Dec. 1948, Edna Lesley Winifred, da. of Leslie Richard WHEEN of Shanghai, China and Penselwood, Somerset.

[RICHARD DAVID ARNOLD GRIDLEY, s. and h. ap., *b.* 22 Aug. 1956; ed. at Monckton Combe and Portsmouth Polytechnic.; *m.* 1stly, 1979, Amanda, da. of Ian MACKENZIE of Felixstowe. This marriage was diss. by divorce and he *m.* 2ndly, Suzanne Elizabeth, da. of (__) RIPPER.]

28 JANUARY

ADRIAN

BARONY. I. 1955. 1. EDGAR DOUGLAS ADRIAN, C.M., s. of Alfred Douglas ADRIAN, C.B., M.C., of Hampstead, was *b.* 30 Nov. 1889; ed. at Westminster and Cambridge (Trin. Coll.). He was *cr.*, 28 Jan. 1955, BARON ADRIAN, of Cambridge, co. Cambridge. He *m.*, 14 June 1923, Hester Agnes, da. of Hume Chancellor PINSENT of Boar's Hill, Oxford. She *d.* 20 May 1966. He *d.* 4 Aug. 1977.

II. 1977. 2. RICHARD HUME (ADRIAN), BARON ADRIAN, only s. and h., was *b.* 16 Oct. 1927; ed. at Westminster and Cambridge (Trin. Coll.); *m.*, 1 Apr. 1967, Lucy, 1st da. of Alban Douglas Rendall CAROE of Hambledon, Godalming, Surrey.

18 FEBRUARY

STRATHALMOND

BARONY. I. 1955. 1. SIR WILLIAM FRASER, s. of William FRASER, of Glasgow, was *b.* 3 Nov. 1888; ed. at Glasgow Acad. He was *cr.*, 18 Feb. 1955, BARON STRATHALMOND, of Pumpherston, co. Midlothian. He *m.*, 7 Oct. 1913, Mary Robertson, da. of Thomson MCCLINTOCK of Glasgow. She *d.* 17 Oct. 1963. He *d.* 1 Apr. 1970.

II. 1970. 2. WILLIAM (FRASER), BARON STRATHALMOND, only s. and h., was *b.* 8 May 1916; ed. at Loretto and Cambridge (Clare Coll.); *m.*, 31 Mar.

1945, Letitia, only da. of Walter Martin KREMENTZ of Morristown, New Jersey, U.S.A. He *d*. 27 Oct. 1975. His widow was living 1995.

III. 1975. 3. WILLIAM ROBERTON (FRASER), BARON STRATHALMOND, only s. and h., was *b*. 22 July 1947; ed. at Loretto; *m*., 1973, Amanda Rose, yr. da. of Rev. Gordon Clifford TAYLOR.

[WILLIAM GORDON FRASER, s. and h. ap., *b*. 24 Sep. 1976.]

18 MARCH

MALVERN

VISCOUNTCY. I. 1955. 1. The Right Hon. SIR GODFREY MARTIN HUGGINS, C.H., K.C.M.G., Prime Minister of the Federation of Rhodesia and Nyasaland, s. of Godfrey HUGGINS, of Bexley, Kent, was *b*. 6 July 1883; ed. at Malvern and St. Thomas's Hosp. He was *cr*., 18 Mar. 1955, VISCOUNT MALVERN, of Rhodesia and of Bexley, co. Kent. He *m*. 21 Nov. 1921, Blanche Elizabeth, da. of James Slatter of Pietermaritzburg, Natal. He *d*. 8 May 1971. His widow *d*. 1976.

II. 1971. 2. JOHN GODFREY (HUGGINS), VISCOUNT MALVERN, 1st s. and h., was *b*. 26 Oct. 1922; ed. at Winchester; *m*., 1 Jan. 1949, Patricia Marjorie, da. of Frank Renwick BOWER of Durban, Natal. He *d*. 28 Aug. 1978. His widow was still living 1995.

III. 1978. 3. ASHLEY KEVIN GODFREY (HUGGINS), VISCOUNT MALVERN, s. and h., *b*. 26 Oct. 1949.

4 MAY

STRATHCLYDE

BARONY. I. 1955. 1. The Right Hon. THOMAS DUNLOP GALBRAITH, s. of William Brodie GALBRAITH, of Overton, Kilmalcolm, co. Renfrew, was *b*. 20 Mar. 1891; ed. at Glasgow Acad, and R.N.Cs. Osborne and Dartmouth. He was *cr*., 4 May 1955, BARON STRATHCLYDE, of Barskimming, co. Ayr. He *m*., 2 Dec. 1915, Ida Jean, 1st da. of Thomas GALLOWAY of Auchendrane, Ayrshire. He *d*. 12 July 1985. His widow *d*. 1985.

[THOMAS GALLOWAY DUNLOP GALBRAITH, 1st s. and h. ap., *b*. 22 Oct. 1927; ed. at Wellington, Oxford (Ch. Ch.) and Glasgow Univ.; K.B.E.; *m*., 11 Apr. 1956, Simone Clotilde Fernande Marie Ghislaine, 1st da. of Jean DU ROY DE BLICQUY of Bois d'Hautmont, Brabant. He *d. v.p.* 2 Jan. 1982.]

II. 1985. 2. THOMAS GALLOWAY DUNLOP DU ROY DE BLICQUY (GALBRAITH), BARON STRATHCLYDE, grandson and h., being 1st s. and h. of Thomas Galloway Dunlop GALBRAITH and Simone Clotilde abovenamed. He was *b*. 22 Feb. 1960; ed. at Wellington Coll., Univ. of East Anglia and Univ. of Aix-en-Provence; *m*. 1992, Jane, 1st da. of John SKINNER of Chenies, co. Hertford.

5 MAY

SWINTON, Earldom, MASHAM, Barony

EARLDOM. I. 1955. 1. PHILIP (CUNLIFFE-LISTER), 1st VISCOUNT SWINTON [1935], was further *cr.*, 5 May 1955, BARON MASHAM, of Ellington, co. York, and EARL OF SWINTON. For fuller particulars of him see vol. xiii, p. 558; *cf.* vol. viii, *sub* MASHAM OF SWINTON.

12 MAY

CONESFORD

BARONY. I. 1955. 1. HENRY GEORGE STRAUSS, Q.C., s. of Alphonse Henry STRAUSS, of 90 Lancaster Gate, London, was *b.* 24 June 1892; ed. at Rugby and Oxford (Ch. Ch.). He was *cr.*, 12 May 1955, BARON CONESFORD, of Chelsea, co. London. He *m.*, 29 Jan. 1927, Anne Sadelbia Mary, yr. da. of John Bowyer NICHOLS of Lawford Hall, Manningtree, Essex. He *d. s.p.* 28 Aug. 1974 when his Barony became *extinct*.

20 JUNE

CLITHEROE

BARONY. I. 1955. 1. The Right Hon. RALPH ASSHETON, only s. and h. ap. of Sir Ralph Cockayne ASSHETON, 1st Bart. [1945], was *b.* 24 Feb. 1901; ed. at Eton and Oxford (Ch. Ch.). He was *cr.*, 20 June 1955, BARON CLITHEROE, of Downham, co. Lancaster; and *suc.* his said father in the Baronetcy, 21 Sep. follg. He *m.*, 24 Jan. 1924, Sylvia Benita Frances, elder da. of Frederick William (HOTHAM) 6th BARON HOTHAM. He *d.* 18 Sep. 1984. His widow *d.* 1991.

II. 1984. 2. RALPH JOHN (ASSHETON), BARON CLITHEROE, also a Baronet, elder s. and h., *b.* 3 Nov. 1929; ed. at Eton and Oxford (Ch. Ch.). He *m.*, 2 May 1961, Juliet, only da. of Lieut. Col. Christopher Lionel HANBURY of Juniper Hall, Burnham, Bucks.

[RALPH CHRISTOPHER ASSHETON, s. and h. ap., *b.* 19 Mar. 1962; ed. at Eton.]

25 JULY

HEYWORTH

BARONY. I. 1955. 1. SIR GEOFFREY HEYWORTH, s. of Thomas Blackwell HEYWORTH, of Oxton, Birkenhead, was *b.* 18 Oct. 1894; ed. at Dollar Acad. He was *cr.*, 25 July 1955, BARON HAYWORTH, of Oxton, co. Chester. He *m.*, 30 Nov. 1924, Lois, da. of Stevenson DUNLOP of Woodstock, Ontario, Canada. He *d. s.p.* 15 June 1974 when his Barony became *extinct*.

4 AUGUST

McNAIR

BARONY. I. 1955. 1. SIR ARNOLD DUNCAN McNAIR, C.B.E., Q.C., s. of John McNAIR, of Court Lane, Dulwich Village, was *b.* 4 Mar. 1885; ed. at Aldenham and Cambridge (Gonville and Caius Coll.). He was *cr.*, 4 Aug. 1955, BARON McNAIR, of Gleniffer, co. Renfrew. He *m.*, 28 Mar. 1912, Marjorie, 2nd da. of Sir Clement Meacher BAILHACHE of Totteridge, Herts. She *d.* 1971. He *d.* 22 May 1975.

II. 1975. 2. CLEMENT JOHN (McNAIR), BARON McNAIR, only s. and h., *b.* 11 Jan. 1915; ed. at Shrewsbury and Oxford (Balliol). He *m.*, 16 Nov. 1941, Vera, da. of Theodore James FAITHFULL of Birmingham. He *d.* 7 Aug. 1989. His widow was living 1995.

III. 1989. 3. DUNCAN JAMES (McNAIR), BARON McNAIR, 1st s. and h., *b.* 26 June 1947; ed. at Bryanston. He *m.* Kodikaraarachige PERERA of Sri Lanka.

2 SEPTEMBER

McCORQUODALE OF NEWTON

BARONY. I. 1955. 1. The Right Hon. MALCOLM STEWART McCORQUODALE, 2nd s. of Norman McCORQUODALE, C.B.E., of Winslow Hall, Bucks, was *b.* 29 Mar. 1901; ed. at Harrow and Oxford (Ch. Ch.). He was *cr.*, 2 Sep. 1955, BARON McCORQUODALE OF NEWTON, of Newton-le-Willows, co. Lancaster. He *m.* 1stly, 6 Oct. 1931, Winifred Sophia Doris, da. of James Oscar Max CLARK of Glasgow. She *d.* 16 Nov. 1960. He *m.* 2ndly, 26 Jan. 1962, Daisy Yoskyl Consuelo, eldest da. of Weetman Harold Miller (PEARSON), 2nd VISCOUNT COWDRAY and widow of 1stly Robert Brampton GURDON and 2ndly of Lieut. Col. Alastair Monteith GIBB. He *d. s.p.m.* 25 Sep. 1971 when his Barony became *extinct*.

16 DECEMBER

ATTLEE, Earldom, PRESTWOOD, Viscountcy

EARLDOM. I. 1955. 1. The Right Hon. CLEMENT RICHARD ATTLEE, O.M., C.H., 4th s. of Henry ATTLEE, Solicitor, of Westcott, Putney, was *b.* 3 Jan. 1883; ed. at Haileybury and Oxford (Univ. Coll.). Prime Minister and First Lord of the Treasury, 1945–51. He was *cr.*, 16 Dec. 1955, VISCOUNT PRESTWOOD, of Walthamstow, co. Essex, and EARL ATTLEE. He *m.*, 10 Jan. 1922, Violet Helen, 10th child and yst. da. of Henry Edward MILLAR of Hampstead Heath. She *d.* 7 June 1964. He *d.* 8 Oct. 1967.

II. 1967. 2. MARTIN RICHARD (ATTLEE), EARL ATTLEE, and VISCOUNT PRESTWOOD, only s. and h., *b.* 10 Aug. 1927; ed. at Millfield and Southampton Nautical Coll. He *m.* 1stly, 16 Feb. 1955, Anne Barbara, eldest da. of James HENDERSON of Bath. This marriage was diss. by divorce in 1988. He *m.*

2ndly, 1988, Margaret Deane, only da. of Geoffrey GOURIET of Hampton Court, Midx. He *d.* 27 July 1991. His former wife and his widow were alive in 1995.

III. 1991. 3. JOHN RICHARD (ATTLEE), EARL ATTLEE &c., only s. and h., by 1st wife; *b.* 3 Oct. 1956; ed. at Stowe. He *m.*, 1993, Celia Jane, yst. da. of Dexter PLUMMER of Bishops Stortford, Herts.

PEERAGES OF 1956

9 JANUARY

WOOLTON, Earldom, WARBLETON, Viscountcy

WOOLTON, Earldom, WARBLETON, Viscountcy (*Marquis*), *cr.*, 9 Jan. 1956. See WOOLTON, Barony, *cr.* 7 July 1939, p. 740.

12 JANUARY

DE L'ISLE

VISCOUNTCY. I. 1956. 1. WILLIAM PHILIP (SIDNEY) 6th BARON DE L'ISLE AND DUDLEY [1835], also a Baronet [1818], only s. and h. of William, 5th BARON DE L'ISLE AND DUDLEY,(1) was *b.* 23 May 1909. He was *cr.*, 12 Jan. 1956, VISCOUNT DE L'ISLE, of Penshurst, co. Kent.

note (1) This William, who *d.* 18 June 1945, was br. and h. of Algernon, the 4th Baron (*d.* unm. 18 Apr. 1945), who was br. and h. of Philip, the 3rd Baron (*d. s.p.* 24 Dec. 1922), for whom see vol. iv, *sub* DE L'ISLE AND DUDLEY.

13 JANUARY

CROOKSHANK

VISCOUNTCY. I. 1956. 1. Capt. the Right Hon. HARRY FREDERICK COMFORT CROOKSHANK, C.H., only s. of Harry Maule CROOKSHANK, F.R.C.S., of Cairo, Brit. Cons.-Gen. of the Daira Sanieh Admin., Egypt, 1897–1907, was *b.* 27 May 1893; ed. at Eton and Oxford (Magdalen Coll.). He was *cr.*, 13 Jan. 1956, VISCOUNT CROOKSHANK, of Gainsborough, co. Lincoln. He *d.* unm. 17 Oct. 1961, when his title became *extinct.*

17 JANUARY

INGLEBY

VISCOUNTCY. I. 1956. 1. The Right Hon. OSBERT PEAKE, Barrister-at-Law, of Sutton Hall, Thirsk, was *b.* 30 Dec. 1897; ed. at Eton, R.M.C., Sandhurst and Oxford (Ch. Ch.). He was *cr.*, 17 Jan. 1955, VISCOUNT INGLEBY, of Snilesworth, in the North Riding of co. York. He *m.*, 19 June 1922, Lady Joan Rachel de Vere, yr. da. of George Devereux de Vere (CAPELL), 7th EARL OF ESSEX. z 11 Oct. 1966. His widow *d.* 1979.

II. 1966. 2. MARTIN RAYMOND (PEAKE), VISCOUNT INGLEBY, only s. and h., *b.* 31 May 1926; ed. at Eton and Oxford (Trin. Coll.); *m.*, 26 Jan. 1952, Susan Gladys, 1st da. of Capt. Henderson Russell LANDALE of Ewell Manor, West Farleigh, Maidstone, co. Kent.

[RICHARD MARTIN HERBERT PEAKE, s. and h. ap., *b.* 7 Aug. 1953; ed. at Eton. He *d. v.p.* and unm. 19 July 1975.]

18 JANUARY

CILCENNIN

VISCOUNTCY. I. 1956. 1. The Right Hon. JAMES PURDON LEWES THOMAS, s. of James Lewes THOMAS, of Caeglas, Llandilo, co. Carmarthen, was *b.* 13 Oct. 1903; ed. at Rugby and Oxford (Oriel Coll.). He was *cr.*, 18 Jan. 1956, VISCOUNT CILCENNIN, of Hereford, co. Hereford. He *d.* unm. 13 July 1960 when his peerage became *extinct*.

19 JANUARY

COLYTON

BARONY. I. 1956. 1. The Right Hon. HENRY LENNOX D'AUBIGNÉ HOPKINSON, C.M.G., 1st s. of Sir Henry Lennox HOPKINSON, K.C.V.O., of Duntesbourne Manor House, Cirencester, co. Gloucester, was *b.* 3 Jan. 1902; ed. at Eton and Cambridge (Trin. Coll.). He was *cr.*, 19 Jan. 1956, BARON COLYTON, of Farway, co. Devon, and of Taunton, co. Somerset. He *m.* 1stly, 10 Nov. 1927, Alice Labouisse, da. of Henry Lane ENO of Bar Harbour, Maine, U.S.A. She *d.* 30 Apr. 1953 and he *m.* 2ndly, 11 Dec. 1956, Barbara Estella, da. of Stephen BARB of New York City and formerly wife of Charles Samuel ADDAMS.

[NICHOLAS HENRY ENO HOPKINSON, s. and h. ap., *b.* 18 Jan. 1932; ed. at Eton and Cambridge (Trin. Coll.); *m.*, 10 Aug. 1957, Fiona Margaret, only da. of Sir Thomas Torquil MUNRO, 5th Bart. of Lindertis. He *d. v.p.* 1991. His widow was still living 1995.]

[ALISDAIR JOHN MUNRO HOPKINSON, grandson and h. ap., *b.* 7 May 1958. He *m.*, 1980, Philippa J., yr. da. of Peter J. BELL of Harefield, Itchen Abbas, co. Hants.]

20 JANUARY

EVERSHED

BARONY. I. 1956. 1. The Right Hon. SIR FRANCIS RAYMOND EVERSHED, Master of the Rolls, s. of Frank EVERSHED, of Burton-on-Trent, was *b.* 8 Aug. 1899; ed. at Clifton and Oxford (Balliol Coll.). He was *cr.*, 20 Jan. 1956, BARON EVERSHED, of Stapenhill, co. Derby. He *m.*, 19 Dec. 1928, Cecily Elizabeth Joan, da. of Sir Charles Alan BENNETT of Beaconsfield, co. Buckingham. He *d. s.p.* 3 Oct. 1966 when his title became *extinct*.

21 JANUARY

ASTOR OF HEVER

BARONY. I. 1956. 1. Col. JOHN JACOB ASTOR, 2nd s. of William Waldorf (ASTOR), 1st VISCOUNT ASTOR, was *b.* 20 May 1886; ed. at Eton. He was *cr.*, 21 Jan. 1956, BARON ASTOR OF HEVER, of Hever Castle, co. Kent. He *m.*, 28 Aug. 1916, Lady Violet Mary, yst. da. of Gilbert John (ELLIOT-MURRAY-KYNYNMOUND), 4th EARL OF MINTO and widow of Lord Charles George Francis Mercer NAIRNE. She *d.* 3 Jan. 1965. He *d.* 19 July 1971.

II. 1971. 2. GAVIN (ASTOR), BARON ASTOR OF HEVER, 1st s. and h., *b.* 1 June 1918; ed. at Eton and Oxford (New Coll.); *m.*, 4 Oct. 1945, Lady Irene Violet Freesia Janet Augusta, yst. da. of Douglas (HAIG), 1st EARL HAIG, K.T. He *d.* 28 June 1984. His widow was living 1995.

III. 1984. 3. JOHN JACOB (ASTOR), BARON ASTOR OF HEVER, 1st s. and h., *b.* 16 June 1946; ed. at Eton; *m.* 1stly, 1970, Fiona Diana Lennox, da. of Capt. Roger Edward Lennox HARVEY of Ramsbury, Wilts. This marriage was diss. by divorce in 1990 and he *m.* 2ndly, 1990, Elizabeth Constance (Mrs CHAGRIN), yr. da. of John (MACKINTOSH), 2nd VISCOUNT MACKINTOSH OF HALIFAX.

[CHARLES GAVIN JOHN ASTOR, s. and h. ap. by 2nd wife, *b.* 10 Nov. 1990.]

23 JANUARY

GODBER

BARONY. I. 1956. 1. SIR FREDERICK GODBER, s. of Edward GODBER, of Dulwich, was *b.* 6 Nov. 1888. He was *cr.*, 23 Jan. 1956, BARON GODBER, of Mayfield, co. Sussex. He *m.*, 29 Aug. 1914, Violet Ethel Beatrice, da. of George Albert LOVESY of Cheltenham, co. Gloucester. He *d. s.p.m.* 10 Apr. 1976, when his Barony became *extinct*.

26 JUNE

CHERWELL

CHERWELL, Viscountcy (*Lindemann*), *cr.* 26 June 1956. See CHERWELL Barony, *cr.* 4 July 1941, p. 748.

9 JULY

WEEKS

BARONY. I. 1956. 1. Lieut. Gen. SIR ROBERT MORCE WEEKS, K.C.B., C.B.E., D.S.O., M.C., T.D., s. of Richard Llewellyn WEEKS, of Broomhough, Riding Mill, Northumberland, was *b.* 13 Nov. 1890; ed. at Charterhouse and Cambridge (Gonville and Caius Coll.). He was *cr.*, 9 July 1956, BARON WEEKS, of Ryton, co. Durham. He *m.* 1stly, 21 Apr. 1922, Evelyn Elsie, da. of Henry HAYNES of Clifton, co. Nottingham.

This marriage was diss. by divorce in 1930 and he *m.* 2ndly, 3 Feb. 1931, Cynthia Mary, da. of J.W. IRVINE of Liverpool. He *d. s.p.m.* 19 Aug. 1960 when his Barony became *extinct.*

16 JULY

COHEN OF BIRKENHEAD

BARONY. I. 1956. 1. SIR HENRY COHEN, s. of Isaac COHEN, of Liverpool, was *b.* 21 Feb. 1900; ed. at St. John's and Birkenhead Inst., and Univs. of Liverpool, London and Paris. He was *cr.*, 16 July 1956, BARON COHEN OF BIRKENHEAD, co. Chester. He *d.* unm. 7 Aug. 1977 when his Barony became *extinct.*

PEERAGES OF 1957

21 JANUARY

SINCLAIR OF CLEEVE

BARONY. I. 1957. 1. SIR ROBERT JOHN SINCLAIR, K.C.B., K.B.E., s. of Robert Henry SINCLAIR, of 4 Whittingehame Gdns., Glasgow, was *b.* 29 July 1893; ed. at Glasgow Acad. and Oxford (Oriel Coll.). He was *cr.*, 21 Jan. 1957, BARON SINCLAIR OF CLEEVE, of Cleeve, co. Somerset. He *m.*, 18 Sep. 1917, Mary Shearer, da. of Robert Shearer BARCLAY of Randfontein, South Africa. He *d.* 4 Mar. 1979. His widow *d.* 1984.

II. 1979. 2. ROBERT JOHN KILGOUR (SINCLAIR), BARON SINCLAIR OF CLEEVE, 1st s. and h., *b.* 3 Nov. 1919; ed. at Winchester and R.M.C., Sandhurst; *m.*, 12 Apr. 1950, Patricia, da. of Lawrence HELLYER of Lockerbie, co. Dumfries. He *d.* 27 Aug. 1985. His widow was living 1995.

II. 1979. 3. JOHN LAWRENCE ROBERT (SINCLAIR), BARON SINCLAIR OF CLEEVE, only s. and h., *b.* 6 Jan. 1953; ed. at Winchester and Univs. of Bath and Manchester.

22 JANUARY

MILLS

BARONY. I. 1957. VISCOUNTCY. I. 1962. 1. The Right Hon. SIR HERBERT PERCY MILLS, 1st Bart. [1953], K.B.E., s. of D. MILLS, of Stockton-on-Tees, was *b.* 4 Jan. 1890. He was *cr.*, 22 Jan. 1957, BARON MILLS, of Studley, co. Warwick. He was further *cr.*, 22 Aug. 1962, VISCOUNT MILLS, of Kensington, co. London. He *m.*, 7 Aug. 1915, Winifred Mary, da. of George C. CONATY of Birmingham. He *d.* 10 Sep. 1968. His widow *d.* 1974.

II. 1968. 2. ROGER CLINTON (MILLS), VISCOUNT MILLS, &c., only s. and h., *b.* 14 June 1919; ed. at Canford and Cambridge (Jesus Coll.); *m.*, 6 Oct. 1945, Joan Dorothy, da. of James SHIRREFF. He *d.* 6 Dec. 1988. His widow was living 1995.

III. 1988. 3. CHRISTOPHER PHILIP ROGER (MILLS), VISCOUNT MILLS, &c., only s. and h., *b.* 20 May 1956; ed. at Oundle Sch. and London Univ.; *m.*, 1980, Lesley Alison, 1st da. of Alan BAILEY.

4 FEBRUARY

BRIDGES

BARONY. I. 1957. 1. The Right Hon. SIR EDWARD ETTINGDEAN BRIDGES, G.C.B., G.C.V.O., M.C., s. of Robert Seymour BRIDGES, O.M., the Poet Laureate, was *b.* 4 Aug. 1892; ed. at Eton and Oxford (Magdalen Coll.). He was *cr.*, 4 Feb. 1957, BARON BRIDGES, of Headley, co. Surrey, and of St. Nicholas at Wade, co. Kent. He *m.*, 1 June 1922, Katharine Dianthe, 2nd da. of Thomas Cecil (FARRER), 2nd BARON FARRER. He *d.* 27 Aug. 1969. His widow *d.* 1986.

II. 1969. 2. THOMAS EDWARD (BRIDGES), BARON BRIDGES, 1st s. and h., *b.* 27 Nov. 1927; ed. at Eton and Oxford (New Coll.); *m.*, 1 Sep. 1953, Rachel Mary, yst. da. of Sir Henry Noel BUNBURY, K.C.B.

[MARK THOMAS BRIDGES, 1st s. and h. ap., *b.* 25 July 1954; ed. at Eton and Cambridge (Corpus Christi Coll.); *m.*, 1978, Angela Margaret, da. of J.L. COLLINSON of Mansfield, co. Nottingham.]

11 FEBRUARY

MONCKTON OF BRENCHLEY

VISCOUNTCY. I. 1957. 1. The Right Hon. SIR WALTER TURNER MONCKTON, K.C.M.G., K.C.V.O., M.C., Q.C., s. of Frank William MONCKTON, of Ightham Warren, Kent, was *b.*, 17 Jan. 1891; ed. at Harrow and Oxford (Balliol Coll.). He was *cr.*, 11 Feb. 1957, VISCOUNT MONCKTON OF BRENCHLEY, of Brenchley, co. Kent. He *m.* 1stly, 18 July 1914, Mary Adelaide Somes, da. of Sir Thomas Colyer COLYER-FERGUSON, Bart. This marriage was diss. by divorce in 1947 (she *d.* 30 Apr. 1964) and he *m.* 2ndly, 13 Aug. 1947, Bridget Helen, *suo jure* BARONESS RUTHVEN OF FREELAND (see that title and also *sub* CARLISLE), and formerly wife of George Josselyn L'Estrange (HOWARD), 11th EARL OF CARLISLE. He *d.* 9 Jan. 1965. His widow *d.* 1982.

II. 1965. 2. GILBERT WALTER RIVERSDALE (MONCKTON), VISCOUNT MONCKTON OF BRENCHLEY, only s. and h., was *b.* 3 Nov. 1915; ed. at Harrow and Cambridge (Trin. Coll.); *m.*, 30 Dec. 1950, Marianna Laetitia, 3rd da. of Robert Tatton BOWER, Cmdr., R.N.

[CHRISTOPHER WALTER MONCKTON, 1st s. and h. ap., *b.* 14 Feb. 1952; ed. at Harrow, Cambridge (Churchill Coll.) and Univ. Coll., Cardiff; *m.*, 1990, Juliet Mary Anne, yst. da. of Jorgen Malherbe JENSEN.]

12 FEBRUARY

TENBY

VISCOUNTCY. I. 1957. 1. Major the Right Hon. GWILYM LLOYD-GEORGE, T.D., 2nd s. of David (LLOYD-GEORGE), 1st EARL LLOYD-GEORGE OF DWYFOR, was *b.*, 4 Dec. 1894; ed. Eastbourne Coll. and Cambridge (King's Coll.). He was *cr.*, 12 Feb. 1957, VISCOUNT TENBY, of Fulford, co. Pembroke. He *m.*, 14 June 1921, Edna Gwenfron, da. of David JONES of Gwnfa, Denbigh. He *d.* 14 Feb. 1967. His widow *d.* 1971.

II. 1967. 2. DAVID (LLOYD-GEORGE), VISCOUNT TENBY, 1st s. and h., was *b.* 4 Nov. 1922; ed. at Eastbourne Coll. and Cambridge (Jesus Coll.). He *d.* unm. 14 July 1983.

III. 1983. 3. WILLIAM (LLOYD-GEORGE), VISCOUNT TENBY, br. and h., was *b.* 7 Nov. 1927; ed. at Eastbourne Coll. and Cambridge (St. Catherine's Coll.); *m.*, 23 Apr. 1955, Ursula Diana Ethel, yst. da. of Lieut. Col. Henry Edward MEDLICOTT, D.S.O.

[TIMOTHY HENRY GWILYM LLOYD-GEORGE, s. and h. ap., *b.* 19 Oct. 1962; ed. at Downside and Univ. Coll. of Wales, Aberystwth.]

15 FEBRUARY

HAILES

BARONY. I. 1957. 1. Major the Right Hon. PATRICK GEORGE THOMAS BUCHAN-HEPBURN, 3rd and yst. s. of Sir Archibald BUCHAN-HEPBURN, 4th Bart., was *b.* 2 Apr. 1901; ed. at Harrow and Cambridge (Trin. Coll.). He was *cr.*, 15 Feb. 1957, BARON HAILES, of Prestonkirk, co. East Lothian. He *m.*, 7 June 1945, Diana, only da. of Brig. Gen. Charles LAMBTON and widow of Major William Hedworth WILLIAMSON. He *d. s.p.* 5 Nov. 1974 when his Barony became *extinct.*

24 APRIL

DENNING

BARONY FOR LIFE. I. 1957. 1. The Right Hon. SIR ALFRED THOMPSON DENNING, one of the Lords Justices of Appeal, s. of Charles DENNING, of Whitchurch, Hants, was *b.* 23 Jan. 1899: ed. at Oxford (Magdalen Coll.). On 24 Apr. 1957 he was app. a Lord of Appeal in Ordinary under the Appellate Jurisdiction Act of 1876, and *cr.* a Baron for Life by the style of BARON DENNING, of Whitchurch, co. Southampton. He *m.* 1stly, 28 Dec. 1932, Hilda Mary Josephine, da. of Rev. Frank Northam HARVEY, Rector of Fawley, Hants. She *d.* 22 Nov. 1941 and he *m.* 2ndly, 27 Dec. 1945, Joan Daria, da. of John Vinings ELLIOTT-TAYLOR and widow of John Matthew Blackwood STUART. She *d.* 1992.

1 JULY

EVANS

BARONY. I. 1957. 1. SIR HORACE EVANS, G.C.V.O., s. of Harry EVANS, of Liverpool, was *b.* 1 Jan. 1903; ed. at City of London Sch., London Hosp. and London Univ. He was *cr.*, 1 July 1957, BARON EVANS, of Merthyr Tydfil, co. Glamorgan. He *d.* unm. 26 Oct. 1963 when his Barony became *extinct.*

2 JULY

RANK

BARONY. I. 1957. 1. Capt. JOSEPH ARTHUR RANK, a Lieut. for the City of London, s. of Joseph RANK, of Colley Corner, Reigate Heath, Surrey, was *b.* 22 Dec. 1888; ed. at Leys Sch., Cambridge. He was *cr.*, 2 July 1957, BARON RANK, of Sutton Scotney, co. Southampton. He *m.*, 18 Oct. 1917, Laura Ellen, da. of Horace Brooks (MARSHALL), 1st and last BARON MARSHALL OF CHIPSTEAD. She *d.* 1971. He *d. s.p.m.* 29 Mar. 1972 when his Barony became *extinct.*

10 JULY

MACKINTOSH OF HALIFAX

MACKINTOSH OF HALIFAX, Viscountcy (*Mackintosh*), *cr.* 10 July 1957. See MACKINTOSH OF HALIFAX, Barony, *cr.* 6 Feb. 1948, p. 786.

22 AUGUST

NORRIE

BARONY. I. 1957. 1. Lieut. Gen. SIR CHARLES WILLOUGHBY MOKE NORRIE, G.C.M.G., G.C.V.O., C.B., D.S.O., M.C., s. of Major George Edward Moke NORRIE, of 62 Queen's Gate, London, was *b.* 26 Sep. 1893; ed. at Eton and R.M.C., Sandhurst. He was *cr.*, 22 Aug. 1957, BARON NORRIE, of Wellington, New Zealand, and of Hawkesbury Upton, co. Gloucester. He *m.* 1stly, 9 June 1922, Jocelyn Helen, da. of Richard Henry GOSLING of Bracknell, Berks. She *d.* 7 Mar. 1938 and he *m.* 2ndly, 28 Nov. 1938, Patricia Merryweather, da. of Emerson Muschamp BAINBRIDGE, M.P. He *d.* 25 May 1977. His widow was living 1995.

II. 1977. 2. GEORGE WILLOUGHBY MOKE (NORRIE), BARON NORRIE, 1st s. and h. by 1st wife, was *b.* 27 Apr. 1936; ed. at Eton and R.M.A., Sandhurst. He *m.*, 10 Apr. 1964, Celia Margaret, only da. of Major John Pelham MANN, M.C., of Brimpton, Reading, Berks.

[MARK WILLOUGHBY JOHN NORRIE, s. and h. ap., *b.* 31 Mar. 1972.]

PEERAGES OF 1958

30 JANUARY

BRECON

BARONY. I. 1958. 1. DAVID VIVIAN PENROSE LEWIS, s. of Alfred William LEWIS, of Craiglas, Talybont-on-Usk, co. Brecknock, was *b.* 14 Aug. 1905; ed. at Monmouth Sch. He was *cr.*, 30 Jan. 1958, BARON BRECON, of Llanfeigan, co. Brecknock. He *m.*, 19 Apr. 1933, Mabel Helen, 2nd da. of John McColville of Abergavenny. He *d. s.p.m.* 10 Oct. 1976 when his Barony became *extinct*. His widow was living 1995.

31 JANUARY

BIRKETT

BARONY. I. 1958. 1. The Right Hon. SIR WILLIAM NORMAN BIRKETT, one of the Lords Justices of Appeal, s. of Thomas BIRKETT, of Nithsdal, Ulverston, co. Lancaster, was *b.* 6 Sep. 1883; ed. at Barrow-in-Furness Gram. Sch. and Cambridge (Emmanuel Coll.). He was *cr.*, 31 Jan. 1958, BARON BIRKETT, of Ulverston, co. Lancaster. He *m.*, 25 Aug. 1920, Ruth, da. of Emil NILSSON of Sweden. He *d.* 10 Feb. 1962. His widow *d.* 1969.

II. 1962. 2. MICHAEL (BIRKETT), BARON BIRKETT, only s. and h., was *b.* 22 Oct. 1929; ed. at Stowe and Cambridge (Trin. Coll.). He *m.* 1stly, 13 Oct. 1960, Junia, da. of Harold ELLIOTT and formerly wife of (__) CRAWFORD. She *d.* 1973 and he *m.* 2ndly, 1978, Gloria, da. of Thomas TAYLOR.

[THOMAS BIRKETT, s. and h. ap. by 2nd wife, *b.* 25 July 1982.]

17 FEBRUARY

HARDING OF PETHERTON

BARONY. I. 1958. 1. Field Marshal SIR ALLAN FRANCIS HARDING (commonly called SIR JOHN HARDING), G.C.B., C.B.E., D.S.O., M.C., s. of Francis E. HARDING, of Compton Way, South Petherton, Somerset, was *b.* 10 Feb. 1896; ed. at Ilminster Gram. Sch. He was *cr.*, 17 Feb. 1958, BARON HARDING OF PETHERTON, of Nether Compton, co. Dorset. He *m.*, 21 Apr. 1927, Mary Gertrude Mabel, da. of Joseph Wilson ROOKE of Knutsford, Cheshire. She *d.* 1983. He *d.* 20 Jan. 1989.

II. 1989. 2. JOHN CHARLES (HARDING), BARON HARDING OF PETHERTON, only s. and h., was *b.* 12 Feb. 1928; ed. at Marlborough and Oxford (Worcester Coll.); *m.*, 20 June 1966, Harriet, 2nd da. of Major Gen. James Francis HARE, D.S.O.

[WILLIAM ALLAN JOHN HARDING, 1st s. and h. ap., *b.* 5 July 1969.]

10 JULY

ROBINS

BARONY. I. 1958. 1. SIR THOMAS ELLIS ROBINS, K.B.E., D.S.O., E.D. (Southern Rhodesia), Hon. Col. in the Army in Southern Rhodesia, s. of Major Robert Patterson ROBINS, of Philadelphia, U.S.A., was *b.* 31 Oct. 1884; ed. at Univ. of Philadelphia and Oxford (Ch. Ch.). He was *cr.*, 10 July 1958, BARON ROBINS, of Rhodesia and of Chelsea, co. London. He *m.*, 31 Oct. 1912, Mary St. Quintin, da. of Philip WROUGHTON of Wantage co. Berks. He *d. s.p.m.* 21 July 1962 when his Barony became *extinct*.

11 JULY

POOLE

BARONY. I. 1958. 1. Lieut. Col. (Hon. Col.) OLIVER BRIAN SANDERSON POOLE, C.B.E., T.D., s. of Donald Louis POOLE, of Lloyd's, was *b.* 11 Aug. 1911; ed. at Eton and Oxford (Ch. Ch.). He was *cr.*, 11 July 1958, BARON POOLE, of Aldgate, in the City of London. He *m.* 1stly, 6 Sep. 1933, Betty Margaret, da. of Capt. Dugald Stewart GILKISON. This marriage was diss. by divorce in 1950 (she *d.* 1988) and he *m.* 2ndly, 9 May 1952, Daphne Wilma Kenyon, only da. of Eustace BOWLES (*formerly* PARKER) of Market Drayton, co. Salop. and formerly wife of Brig. Algernon George William HEBER-PERCY. This marriage was in turn diss. by divorce in 1965 and he *m.* 3rdly, 4 Apr. 1966, Barbara Ann, da. of E.A. TAYLOR of Harpenden, co. Hertford. He *d.* 28 Jan. 1993. His widow was living 1995.

II. 1993. 2. DAVID CHARLES (POOLE), BARON POOLE, only s. and h., *b.* 6 Jan. 1945; ed. at Gordonstoun, Oxford (Ch. Ch.) and INSEAD, Fountainebleau; *m.* 1stly, 21 Sep. 1967, Fiona, da. of John DONALD of London, SW6. This marriage was diss. by divorce and he *m.* 2ndly, 1975, Philippa, da. of Mark REEVE of King's Somborne, co. Hants.

[OLIVER JOHN POOLE, s. and h. ap. by 1st wife, *b.* 30 May 1972; ed. at Eton and Oxford (St. Anne's Coll.).]

26 JULY

CHESTER

CHESTER, Earldom, *cr.* 26 July 1958. *H.R.H.* CHARLES PHILIP ARTHUR GEORGE, s. and h. ap. of H.M. QUEEN ELIZABETH II, was *cr.*, 26 July 1958, PRINCE OF WALES and EARL OF CHESTER. See CORNWALL, Dukedom, by inheritance, 6 Feb. 1952, p. 800.

AUGUST

DE ROS

ROS, or de ROS, Barony by Writ (*Maxwell*, formerly *Ross*, originally *de Ros*). The *abeyance* in this Barony was terminated by Letters Patent, Aug. 1958, in favour of GEORGIANA ANGELA MAXWELL. See ROS, or DE ROS, Barony by Writ, *abeyance* terminated May 1943, see vol. xi, *sub* ROS or ROOS OF HELMSLEY.

PEERAGES OF 1959

16 FEBRUARY

ROOTES

BARONY. I. 1959. 1. SIR WILLIAM EDWARD ROOTES, G.B.E., s. of William ROOTES, of Hawkhurst, co. Kent, was *b.* 17 Aug. 1894; ed. at Cranbrook Sch. He was *cr.*, 16 Feb. 1959, BARON ROOTES, of Ramsbury, co. Wilts. He *m.* 1stly, 15 Mar. 1916, Nora, da. of Horace PRESS of Great Yarmouth, Norfolk. This marriage was diss. by divorce in 1951 (she *d.* 19 Sep. 1964) and he *m.* 2ndly, 9 Aug. 1951, Ruby Joy Ann, da. of Capt. Gordon DUFF of Brighton, Sussex, formerly wife of Sir Francis Henry Grenville PEEK, Bart. and before that widow of Sir Charles Thomas Hewitt MAPPIN, Bart. He *d.* 12 Dec. 1964. His widow *d.* 28 Dec. 1968.

II. 1964. 2. WILLIAM GEOFFREY (ROOTES), BARON ROOTES, 1st s. and h., was *b.* 14 June 1917; ed. at Harrow and Oxford (Ch. Ch.); *m.*, 15 Aug. 1946, Marian, da. of Lieut. Col. Herbert Roche HAYTER, D.S.O., of Newbury, co. Berks. and widow of Wing Cmdr. James Hogarth SLATER. He *d.* 17 Jan. 1992. His widow was living 1995.

III. 1992. 3. NICHOLAS GEOFFREY (ROOTS), BARON ROOTES, only s. and h., was *b.* 12 July 1951; ed. at Harrow. He *m.*, 1976, Dorothy Anne, da. of Cyril WOOD of Swansea and formerly wife of Jonathan BURN-FORTI.

10 MARCH

NETHERTHORPE

BARONY. I. 1959. 1. JAMES TURNER, s. of Albert Edward Mann TURNER, of Auston, Sheffield, co. York, was *b.* 6 Jan. 1908; ed. at Knaresborough and Leeds Univ. He was *cr.*, 10 March 1959, BARON NETHERTHORPE, of Auston, co. York. He *m.*, 3 Oct. 1935, Margaret Lucy, da. of James Arthur MATTOCK of Sheffield. He *d.* 8 Nov. 1980. His widow was living 1995.

II. 1980. 2. JAMES ANDREW (TURNER), BARON NETHERTHORPE, 1st s. and h., was *b.* 23 July 1936; ed. at Rugby and Cambridge (Pembroke Coll.); *m.*, 3 Sep. 1960, Belinda, only da. Frederick Hedley NICHOLSON of Firbeck, Worksop, co. Nottingham. He *d.* in a motor accident, 4 Nov. 1982. His widow was living 1995.

III. 1982. 3. JAMES FREDERICK (TURNER), BARON NETHERTHORPE, only s. and h., was *b.* 7 Jan. 1964; ed. at Harrow; *m.*, 1989, Elizabeth Curran, da. of Edward William FAHAN of Redding, Connecticut, U.S.A.

[ANDREW JAMES EDWARD TURNER, s. and h. ap., *b.* 24 Mar. 1993.]

6 APRIL

JENKINS

BARONY FOR LIFE.
I. 1959.

1. The Right Hon. SIR DAVID LLEWELYN JENKINS, one of the Lords Justices of Appeal, 3rd s. of Sir John Lewis JENKINS, K.C.S.I., was *b.* 8 April 1899; ed. at Charterhouse and Oxford (Balliol Coll.). On 6 April 1959 he was app. a Lord of Appeal in Ordinary under the Appellate Jurisdiction Act of 1876, and *cr.* a Baron for Life by the style of BARON JENKINS, of Ashley Gdns., Westm. He *d.* unm. 6 Apr. 1969 when his Life Barony became *extinct*.

15 JULY

CRATHORNE

BARONY.
I. 1959.

1. The Right Hon. SIR THOMAS LIONEL DUGDALE, 1st Bart, T.D., s. of James Lionel DUGDALE, of Crathorne, co. Yorks, was *b.* 20 July 1897; ed. at Eton and R.M.C., Sandhurst. He was *cr.*, 15 July 1959, BARON CRATHORNE, of Crathorne, co. York. He *m.*, 22 Sep. 1936, Nancy, yst. da. of Sir Charles TENNANT, Bart., formerly wife of Sylvester Govett GATES. She *d.* 1969. He *d.* 26 Mar. 1977.

II. 1977.

2. CHARLES JAMES (DUGDALE), BARON CRATHORNE, 1st s. and h., was *b.* 12 Sep. 1939; ed. at Eton and Cambridge (Trin. Coll.); *m.*, 1970, Sylvia Mary, yr. da. of Brig. Arthur MONTGOMERY.

[THOMAS ARTHUR JOHN DUGDALE, s. and h. ap., *b.* 30 Sep. 1977.]

16 JULY

FORSTER OF HARRABY

BARONY.
I. 1959.

1. SIR JOHN FORSTER K.B.E., Q.C., yr. s. of John James FORSTER, of Carlisle, Cumberland, was *b.* 15 Sept. 1888; ed. at Sedburgh. He was *cr.*, 16 July 1959, BARON FORSTER OF HARRABY, of Beckenham, Kent. He *m.*, 4 Sep. 1917, Muriel, da. of Samuel VOSPER. He *d. s.p.m.* 24 July 1972 when his title became *extinct*.

20 AUGUST

SPENS

BARONY.
I. 1959.

1. The Right Hon. SIR WILLIAM PATRICK SPENS, K.B.E., Q.C., s. of Nathaniel SPENS, of Kensington, London, was *b.* 9 Aug. 1885; ed. at Rugby and Oxford (New Coll.). He was *cr.*, 20 Aug. 1959, BARON SPENS, of Blairsanquhar, co. Fife. He *m.* 1stly, 15 Sep. 1913, Hilda Mary, 1st da. of Lieut. Col. Wentworth Grenville BOWYER of Olney, co. Buckingham. She *d.* 5 Mar. 1962 and he *m.* 2ndly, 25 May 1963, Kathleen Annie Fedden, da. of Roger DODDS of Bath. He *d.* 15 Nov. 1973. His widow was living 1995.

II. 1973. 2. WILLIAM GEORGE MICHAEL (SPENS), BARON SPENS, 1st s. and h., was *b.* 18 Sep. 1914; ed. at Rugby and Oxford (New Coll.); *m.*, 30 June 1941, Joan Elizabeth, da. of Reginald GOODALL. He *d.* 23 Nov. 1984. His widow was living 1995.

III. 1984. 3. PATRICK MICHAEL REX (SPENS), BARON SPENS, 1st s. and h., was *b.* 22 July 1942; ed. at Rugby and Cambridge (Corpus Christi Coll.); *m.*, 12 Mar. 1966, Janet Lindsay, da. of Rear Adm. Ralph Lindsay FISHER, D.S.O., D.S.C., of Dalnacreoch, Gartmore, Stirling.

[PATRICK NATHANIEL GEORGE SPENS, s. and h. ap., *b.* 14 Oct. 1968; ed. at Rugby.]

12 NOVEMBER

DUNROSSIL

VISCOUNTCY. I. 1959. 1. The Right Hon. WILLIAM SHEPHERD MORRISON, M.C., Q.C., s. of John MORRISON, of Torinturk, co. Argyll, was *b.* 10 Aug. 1893; ed. at George Watson's Coll., Edinburgh and Edinburgh Univ. He was *cr.*, 12 November 1959, VISCOUNT DUNROSSIL, of Vallaquie, Isle of North Uist, co. Inverness. He *m.* 22 Apr. 1924, Catherine Allison, da. of Rev. William Swan. He *d.* 3 Feb. 1961. His widow *d.* 1983.

II. 1961. 2. JOHN WILLIAM (MORRISON), VISCOUNT DUNROSSIL, eldest s. and h., was *b.* 22 May 1926; ed. at Fettes and Oxford (Oriel Coll.). He *m.*, 3 July 1951, Mavis Dawn, da. of Arthur Llewellyn SPENCER-PAYNE of Cape Province, South Africa. This marriage was diss. by divorce in 1969 and he *m.* 2ndly, 1969, Diana Mary Cunliffe, da. of C.M. VISE.

[ANDREW WILLIAM REGINALD MORRISON, 1st s. and h. ap. by 1st wife, *b.* 15 Dec. 1953; ed. at Eton and Oxford (Univ. Coll.).]

20 NOVEMBER

STUART OF FINDHORN

VISCOUNTCY. I. 1959. 1. The Right Hon. JAMES GRAY STUART, C.H., M.V.O., M.C., 3rd s. of Morton Gray (STUART), 17th EARL OF MORAY, was *b.* 9 Feb. 1897; ed. at Eton. He was *cr.*, 20 November 1959, VISCOUNT STUART OF FINDHORN, of Findhorn, co. Moray. He *m.*, 4 Aug. 1923, Lady Rachel, 4th da. of Victor Christian William (CAVENDISH), 9th DUKE OF DEVONSHIRE. He *d.* 20 Feb. 1971. His widow *d.* 1977.

II. 1971. 2. DAVID RANDOLPH MORAY (STUART), VISCOUNT STUART OF FINDHORN, 1st s. and h., was *b.* 20 June 1924; ed. at Eton; *m.* 1stly, 1945, Grizel Mary Wilfreda, da. of David Theodore FYFE and widow of Michael GILLIAN. She *d.* 24 Apr. 1948 and he *m.* 2ndly, 31 May 1951, Marian Emilia, da. of Gerald H. WILSON of Kinbury, Berks. This marriage was diss. by divorce in 1979 and he *m.* 3rdly, 1979, Margaret Anne, yr. da. of Cmdr. Peter DU CANE, R.N.

[JAMES DOMINIC MORAY STUART, 1st son and h. ap., only s. by 1st wife, *b.* 25 Mar. 1948; ed. at Eton; *m.*, 1979, Yvonne Lucienne, da. of Edgar DESPRÉS of Ottawa, Canada.]

8 DECEMBER

MACANDREW

BARONY. I. 1959. 1. Colonel The Right Hon. SIR CHARLES GLEN MACANDREW, T.D., s. of F. Glen MACANDREW, of Knock Castle, Largs, co. Ayr, was *b.* 13 Jan. 1888; ed. at Uppingham and Cambridge (Trin. Coll.). He was *cr.*, 8 December 1959, BARON MACANDREW, of the Firth of Clyde. He *m.* 1stly, 7 Feb. 1918, Lilian Cathleen, da. of James Prendergast CURRAN of St. Andrews, Fife. This marriage was diss. by divorce in 1938 (she *d.* 1978) and he *m.* 2ndly, 2 Feb. 1941, Mona, da. of James Alexander Ralston MITCHELL of Irvine, Ayrshire. He *d.* 11 Jan. 1979. His widow *d.* 1994.

II. 1979. 2. COLIN NEVILL GLEN (MACANDREW), BARON MACANDREW, 1st and only surv. s., was *b.* 1 Aug. 1919; ed. at Eton and Cambridge (Trin. Coll.); *m.*, 15 Sep. 1943, Ursula Beatrice, yr. da. of Joseph STEEL of Lockerbie, co. Dumfries. She *d.* 1986. He *d.* 9 July 1989.

III. 1989. 3. CHRISTOPHER ANTHONY COLIN (MACANDREW), BARON MACANDREW, 1st s. and h., was *b.* 16 Feb. 1945; ed. at Malvern; *m.*, 1975, Sarah Helen, only da. of Lieut. Col. Peter Hendy BRAZIER of Marnhull, Dorset.

[OLIVER CHARLES JULIAN MACANDREW, s. and h. ap., *b.* 3 Sep. 1983.]

PEERAGES OF 1960

7 JANUARY

MORRIS OF BORTH-Y-GEST

BARONY FOR LIFE. I. 1960. 1. The Right Hon. SIR JOHN WILLIAM MORRIS, C.B.E., M.C., one of the Lords Justices of Appeal, s. of Daniel MORRIS, of Liverpool and Portmadoc, was *b.* 11 September 1896; ed. at Liverpool Inst. High Sch. and Cambridge (Trin Hall). On 7 January 1960 he was app. a Lord of Appeal in Ordinary under the Appellate Jurisdiction Act of 1876, and *cr.* a Baron for Life by the style of BARON MORRIS OF BORTH-Y-GEST, of Borth-y-Gest, co. Caernarron. He *d.* unm. 9 June 1979 when his Life Barony became *extinct*.

20 JANUARY

ROCHDALE

VISCOUNTCY. I. 1960. 1. JOHN DURIVAL KEMP, O.B.E., T.D., 2nd BARON ROCHDALE [1913], was further *cr.*, 20 January 1960, VISCOUNT ROCHDALE, of Rochdale, co. Palatine of Lancaster. See vol. xiii, p. 175, and above, p. 664.

20 JANUARY

NELSON OF STAFFORD

BARONY. I. 1960. 1. SIR GEORGE HORATIO NELSON, 1st Bart [1955], 1st s. of George NELSON, of London, was *b.* 26 Oct. 1887; ed. at City and Guilds Tech. Coll., London. He was *cr.* 20 January 1960, BARON NELSON OF STAFFORD, of Hilcote Hall, co. Stafford. He *m.*, 17 July 1913, Florence Mabel Jane, only da. of Henry ROWE. He *d.* 16 July 1962. His widow *d.* 14 Dec. 1962.

II. 1962. 2. HENRY GEORGE (NELSON), BARON NELSON OF STAFFORD, only s. and h., *b.* 2 Jan. 1917; ed. at Oundle and Cambridge (King's Coll.); *m.*, 8 June 1940, Pamela Roy, yr. da. of Ernest Roy BIRD, M.P., of Robertsbridge, Sussex.

[HENRY ROY GEORGE NELSON, 1st s. and h. ap., *b.* 26 Oct. 1943; ed. at Ampleforth and Cambridge (King's Coll.); *m.*, 1968, Dorothy, da. of Leslie CALEY, of Driffield, co. York.]

8 FEBRUARY

HOWICK OF GLENDALE

BARONY. I. 1960. 1. SIR EVELYN BARING G.C.M.G., K.C.V.O., O.C., s. of Sir Evelyn BARING, 1st Earl of Cromer, by his second wife, Lady Katharine Thynne, 2nd da. of 4th Marquess of Bath, was *b.* 29 Sept. 1903; ed. at Winchester and Oxford (New Coll.). He was *cr.*, 8 February 1960, BARON HOWICK OF GLENDALE, of Howick, co. Northumberland. He *m.*, 24 Apr. 1935, Lady Mary Cecil, 1st da. of Charles Robert (GREY), 5th EARL GREY. He *d.* 10 Mar. 1973. His widow was living 1995.

II. 1973. 2. CHARLES EVELYN (BARING), BARON HOWICK OF GLENDALE. only s. and h., was *b.* 30 Dec. 1937; ed. at Eton and Oxford (New Coll.); *m.*, 11 Apr. 1964, Clare Nicolette, yr. da. of Col. Cyril DARBY, M.C., of Tewkesbury, co. Gloucester.

[DAVID EVELYN CHARLES BARING, s. and h. ap., *b.* 26 Mar. 1975.]

12 APRIL

GLADWYN

BARONY. I. 1960. 1. SIR HUBERT MILES GLADWYN JEBB, G.C.M.G., G.C.V.O., C.B., s. of Sydney JEBB of Firbeck Hall, co. York, was *b.* 25 April 1900; ed. at Eton and Oxford (Magdalen Coll.). He was *cr.*, 12 April 1960, BARON GLADWYN, of Bramfield, co. Suffolk. He *m.*, 22 Jan. 1929, Cynthia, yr. da. of Sir Saxton William Armstrong NOBLE, Bart. She *d.* 1990.

[MILES ALVERY GLADWYN, s. and h. ap., *b.* 3 Mar. 1930; ed. at Eton and Oxford (Magdalen Coll.).]

4 JULY

SANDERSON OF AYOT

BARONY. I. 1960. 1. BASIL SANDERSON, M.C., s. of Harold Arthur SANDERSON of Jenkyn Place, Bentley, Hants., was *b.* 19 June 1894; ed. at Rugby and Oxford (Trin. Coll.). He was *cr.*, 4 July 1960, BARON SANDERSON OF AYOT, of Welwyn. co. Hertford. He *m.*, 27 Jan. 1927, Evelyn Constance, yr. da. of Joseph Bruce ISMAY of Costelloe, co. Galway. She *d.* 9 Aug. 1940. He *d.* 15 Aug. 1971.

II. 1971. 2. ALAN LINDSAY (SANDERSON), BARON SANDERSON OF AYOT, 1st s. and h., was *b.* 12 Jan. 1931; ed. at Uppingham; disclaimed, 28 Sep. 1971, his peerage for life under the Peerage Act, 1963. He *m.*, 1959, Gertrud, da. of Herman BOSCHLER.

[MICHAEL SANDERSON, s. and h. ap., *b.* 6 Dec. 1959; ed. at St. Paul's Sch. and York Univ.]

15 JULY

SLIM

VISCOUNTCY. I. 1960. 1. Field-Marshal SIR WILLIAM JOSEPH SLIM, K.G., G.C.B., G.C.M.G., G.C.V.O., G.B.E., D.S.O., M.C., s. of John SLIM of Bristol, was *b.*, 6 Aug. 1891; ed. at King Edward's Sch., Birmingham. He was *cr.*, 15 July 1960. VISCOUNT SLIM, of Yarralumla, Australian Capital Territory, and of Bishopston, City and co. of Bristol. He *m.*, 1 Jan. 1926, Aileen, da. of Rev. John Anderson ROBERTSON, of Edinburgh. He *d.* 14 Dec. 1970. His widow *d.* 1994.

II. 1970. 2. JOHN DOUGLAS (SLIM), VISCOUNT SLIM, only s. and h., was *b.* 20 July 1927; ed. at Prince of Wales R. Indian Mil. Coll., Dehra Dun. He *m.*, 18 July 1958, Elisabeth, da. of Arthur Rawdon SPINNEY.

[MARK WILLIAM RAWDON SLIM, 1st s. and h. ap., *b.* 13 Feb. 1960; *m.*, 1992, Laura, yr. da. of Jonathan HARRISON of co. Bedford.]

2 AUGUST

HEAD

VISCOUNTCY. I. 1960. 1. The Right Hon. ANTONY HENRY HEAD, C.B.E., M.C., only s. of Geoffrey HEAD, of London, was *b.* 19 Dec. 1906; ed. at Eton and R.M.C., Sandhurst. He was *cr.*, 2 August 1960, VISCOUNT HEAD, of Throope, co. Wilts. He *m.*, 23 July 1935, Lady Dorothea Louise, 2nd da. of Anthony (ASHLEY-COOPER), 9th Earl of SHAFTESBURY. He *d.* 29 Mar. 1983. His widow *d.* 1987.

II. 1983. 2. RICHARD ANTHONY (HEAD), VISCOUNT HEAD, 1st s. and h., was *b.* 27 Feb. 1937; ed. at Eton and R.M.A., Sandhurst. He *m.*, 1974, Alicia Brigid, 1st da. of Julian John William SALMOND, of Badminton, co. Gloucester.

[HENRY JULIAN HEAD, 1st s. and h., *b.* 30 Mar. 1980.]

22 AUGUST

NUGENT

BARONY. I. 1960. 1. SIR TERENCE EDMUND GASCOIGNE NUGENT, G.C.V.O., M.C., s. of Brig. Gen. George Colborne NUGENT, M.B.O., of London, was *b.*, 11 Aug. 1895; ed. at Eton and R.M.C., Sandhurst. He was *cr.*, 22 August. 1960, BARON NUGENT, of West Harling, co. Norfolk. He *m.*, 25 Apr. 1935, Rosalie, only da. of Brig. Gen. Charles Strathavon Heathcote Drummond WILLOUGHBY. He *d. s.p.* 27 Apr. 1973 when his Barony became *extinct*. His widow was living 1995.

1 SEPTEMBER

AMORY

VISCOUNTCY. I. 1960. 1. The Right Hon. DERICK HEATHCOAT-AMORY, T.D., s. of Sir Ian Murray HEATHCOAT-AMORY, 2nd Bart., of Tiverton, co. Devon, was *b.* 26 Dec. 1899; ed. at Eton and Oxford (Ch. Ch.). He was *cr.*, 1 September 1960, VISCOUNT AMORY, of Tiverton, co. Devon. He *d.* unm. 20 Jan. 1981 when his Viscountcy became *extinct*.

8 SEPTEMBER

BOYD OF MERTON

VISCOUNTCY. I. 1960. 1. The Right Hon. ALAN TINDAL LENNOX-BOYD, C.H., s. of Alan Walter LENNOX-BOYD, was *b.* 18 Nov. 1904; ed. at Sherborne and Oxford (Ch. Ch.). He was *cr.*, 8 September 1960, VISCOUNT BOYD OF MERTON, of Merton-in-Penninghame, co. Wigtown. He *m.*, 29 Dec. 1938, Patricia Florence Susan, 2nd da. of Rupert Edward Cecil Lee (GUINNESS), 2nd EARL OF IVEAGH. He *d.* 8 Mar. 1983. His widow was living 1995.

II. 1983. 2. SIMON DONALD RUPERT NEVILLE (LENNOX-BOYD), VISCOUNT BOYD OF MERTON, 1st s. and h., was *b.* 7 Dec. 1939; ed. at Eton and Oxford (Ch. Ch.); *m.*, 24 July 1962, Alice Mary, only da. of Major Mersey George Dallas CLIVE of Whitfield, co. Hereford.

[BENJAMIN ALAN LENNOX-BOYD, 1st s. and h. ap., *b.* 21 Oct. 1964; ed. at Millfield; *m.*, 1993, Sheila Mary Margaret, da. of Harold Emmanuel George WILLIAMS of Plymouth and formerly wife of Michael CARROLL of Saltash, Cornwall.]

1 OCTOBER

HODSON

BARONY FOR LIFE. I. 1960. 1. The Right Hon. SIR FRANCIS LORD CHARLTON HODSON, M.C., one of the Lords Justices of Appeal, s. of the Rev. Thomas HODSON, Rector of Oddington, co. Gloucester, was *b.* 17 Sept. 1895; ed. at Cheltenham and Oxford (Wadham Coll). On 1 October 1960 he was app. Lord of Appeal in Ordinary under the Appellate Jurisdiction Act of 1876, and *cr.* a Baron for Life by the style of BARON HODSON, of Rotherfield Greys, co. Oxford. He *m.*, Susan Mary, da. of Major William Greaves BLAKE of Eccleshall, Sheffield. She *d.* 14 Jan. 1965. He *d.* 11 Mar. 1984 when his Life Barony became *extinct.*

11 NOVEMBER

WARD OF WITLEY

VISCOUNTCY. I. 1960. 1. The Right Hon. GEORGE REGINALD WARD, s. of William Humble (WARD), 2nd Earl of Dudley, was *b.* 20 November 1907; ed. at Eton and Oxford (Ch. Ch.). He was *cr.*, 11 November 1960, VISCOUNT WARD OF WITLEY, of Great Witley, co. Worcester. He *m.* 1stly, 30 May 1940, Anne Diana Frances Ayesha, 1st da. of Capt. Arthur Edward CAPEL. This marriage was diss. by divorce in 1951 and he *m.* 2ndly, 15 Mar. 1962, Barbara Mary Colonsay, only da. of Capt. Ronald Frank Rous MCNEILL, formerly wife of Michael Langhorne ASTOR. He *d. s.p.m.* 15 June 1988 when his Viscountcy became *extinct.*

23 NOVEMBER

COBBOLD

BARONY. I. 1960. 1. The Right Hon. CAMERON FROMANTEEL COBBOLD, s. of Lieut. Col. Clement COBBOLD, of Southwold, co. Suffolk, was *b.* 14 Sept. 1904; ed. at Eton and Cambridge (King's Coll.). He was *cr.*, 23 November 1960, BARON COBBOLD, of Knebworth, co. Hertford. He *m.*, 3 Apr. 1930, Margaret Hermione Millicent, 1st da. of Victor Alexander George Robert (BULWER-LYTTON), 2nd EARL OF LYTTON. He *d.* 1 Nov. 1987. His widow was living 1995.

II. 1987. 2. DAVID ANTHONY FROMANTEEL (COBBOLD, *later* LYTTON-COBBOLD), BARON COBBOLD, only s. and h., was *b.* 14 July 1937; ed. at Eton and Cambridge (Trin. Coll.); took by Deed Poll, 4 Dec. 1960, the additional surname of LYTTON. He *m.*, 7 Jan. 1961, Christine Elizabeth, 3rd da. of Major Sir Dennis Frederick Bankes STUCLEY, Bart.

[HENRY FROMANTEEL LYTTON-COBBOLD, 1st s. and h. ap., *b.* 12 May 1962; ed. at Eton and Kent Univ.; *m.*, 1987, Martha Frances, da. of James Buford BOONE of Tuscalloosa, Alabama, U.S.A.]

PEERAGES OF 1961

20 JANUARY

GUEST

BARONY FOR LIFE. I. 1961. 1. CHRISTOPHER WILLIAM GRAHAM GUEST, one of the Senators of the Coll. of Justice in Scotland, s. of Edward Graham

GUEST, of Edinburgh, was *b.* 7 Nov. 1901; ed. at Merchiston Castle Sch., Cambridge (Clare Coll.), and Edinburgh Univ. On 20 Jan. 1961 he was app. a Lord of Appeal in Ordinary under the Appellate Jurisdiction Act of 1876, and *cr.* a Baron for Life by the style of BARON GUEST, of Graden, co. Berwick. He *m.* 1stly, 3 Sep. 1927, Constance Jessie, da. of Finlay RAMAGE, of Edinburgh. This marriage was diss. by divorce 1940 and he *m.* 2ndly, 28 June 1941, Catherine Geraldine, yst. da. of John Beaumont HOTHAM, of Coldstream, co. Berwick. He *d.* 25 Sep. 1984 when his Life Barony became *extinct*. His widow was living 1995.

3 FEBRUARY

FLECK

BARONY.
I. 1961. 1. SIR ALEXANDER FLECK, K.B.E., F.R.S., s. of Robert FLECK, of Glasgow, was *b.* 11 Nov. 1889; ed. at Saltcoats Public Sch., Hillhead High Sch. and Glasgow Univ. He was *cr.*, 3 Feb. 1961, BARON FLECK, of Saltcoats, co. Ayr. He *m.*, 17 July 1917, Isabella Mitchell, da. of Alexander KELLY of Campbelltown, Argyllshire. She *d.* 4 Jan. 1955. He *d. s.p.* 6 Aug. 1968 when his Barony became *extinct*.

29 JUNE

ROBERTSON OF OAKRIDGE

BARONY.
I. 1961. 1. Gen. SIR BRIAN HUBERT ROBERTSON, 2nd Bart., G.C.B., G.B.E., K.C.M.G., K.C.V.O., D.S.O., M.C., s. of Field Marshal Sir William Robert ROBERTSON, 1st Bart, G.C.B., G.C.M.G., G.C.V.O., D.S.O., of Welbourn, co. Lincoln, was *b.* 22 July 1896; ed. at Charterhouse and R.M.A., Woolwich. He was *cr.*, 29 June 1961, BARON ROBERTSON OF OAKRIDGE, of Oakridge, co. Gloucester. He *m*, 4 Aug. 1926, Edith Christina, da. of James Black MACINDOE of Glasgow. He *d.* 29 Apr. 1974. His widow *d.* 1982.

II. 1974. 2. WILLIAM RONALD (ROBERTSON), BARON ROBERTSON OF OAKRIDGE, &c., s. and h., *b.* 8 Dec. 1930; ed. at Charterhouse. He *m.*, 1972, Celia Jane, yr. da. of William ELWORTHY of Winterborne Monkton, Dorchester, Dorset.

[WILLIAM BRIAN ELWORTHY ROBERTSON, s. and h. ap., *b.* 15 Nov. 1975.]

10 JULY

MARKS OF BROUGHTON

BARONY.
I. 1961. 1. SIR SIMON MARKS, s. of Michael MARKS, of Manchester, was *b.* 8 July 1888; ed. at Manchester Gram. Sch. He was *cr.*, 10 July 1961, BARON MARKS OF BROUGHTON, of Sunningdale, co. Berks. He *m.*, 27 July 1915, Miriam, da. of Ephraim SIEFF. He *d.* 8 Dec. 1964. His widow *d.* 1971.

II. 1964. 2. MICHAEL (MARKS), BARON MARKS OF BROUGHTON, s. and h., *b.* 27 Aug. 1920; ed. at St. Paul's Sch. and Cambridge (Corpus Christi).

He *m.* 1stly, 10 Jan. 1949, Ann Catherine, da. of Major Richard James PINTO, M.C. This marriage was diss. by divorce in 1958. He *m.* 2ndly, 26 May 1960, Helene, da. of Gustav FISCHER. This marriage was diss. by divorce in 1965. He *m.* 3rdly, 1976, Toshiko SHIMURA of Japan. This marriage was diss. by divorce in 1985.

[SIMON RICHARD MARKS, s. and h., *b.* 3 May 1950; ed. at Eton and Oxford (Balliol). He *m.*, 1982, Marion, only da. of Peter F. NORTON of the Azores.]

12 JULY

AVON, Earldom, EDEN, Viscountcy

EARLDOM. I. 1961. 1. The Right Hon. SIR ROBERT ANTHONY EDEN, K.G., M.C., s. of Sir William EDEN, 7th Bart, of Windlestone, co. Durham, was *b.* 12 June 1897; ed. at Eton and Oxford (Christ Church). Prime Minister and First Lord of the Treasury, 1955–7. He was *cr.*, 12 July 1961, VISCOUNT EDEN of Royal Leamington Spa, co. Warwick, and EARL OF AVON. He *m.* 1stly, 5 Nov. 1923, Beatrice Helen, 3rd da. of Sir William Gervase BECKETT, IST BART. This marriage was diss. by divorce in 1950 and she *d.* 29 June 1957. He *m.* 2ndly, 14 Aug. 1952, Anne Clarissa, only da. of Major John Strange SPENCER-CHURCHILL. He *d.* 14 Jan. 1977. His widow was living 1995.

II. 1977. 2. NICHOLAS (EDEN), EARL OF AVON and VISCOUNT EDEN OF ROYAL LEAMINGTON SPA, co. Warwick, 2nd but 1st surviving s. and h., [1] *b.* 3 Oct. 1930; ed. at Eton. He *d.* unm. 17 Aug. 1985 when his titles became *extinct*.

note [1] His 1st s. Simon Gascoyn, *b.* 13 Nov. 1924; ed. at Eton, was killed on active service in Burma, 23 June 1945.

26 JULY

FAIRHAVEN

BARONY. I. 1961. 1. URBAN HUTTLESTON ROGERS (BROUGHTON), 1st BARON FAIRHAVEN [1929], 1st s. of Urban Hanlon BROUGHTON (who *d.* 30 Jan. 1929 before his intended elevation to the peerage), was *cr.*, 26 July 1961, BARON FAIRHAVEN, of Anglesey Abbey, co. Cambridge, with spec. rem., in default of male issue, to his younger brother, and the heirs male of his body. For fuller particulars of him see vol. xiii, p. 457, *sub* FAIRHAVEN.

6 OCTOBER

SNOWDON, Earldom, LINLEY, Viscountcy

EARLDOM. I. 1961. 1. ANTONY CHARLES ROBERT ARMSTRONG-JONES, s. of Ronald Owen Lloyd ARMSTRONG-JONES, M.B.E., Q.C., of Plas Dinas, co. Caernarvon, was *b.* 7 March 1930; ed. at Eton and Cambridge (Jesus Coll.) He was *cr.*, 6 October 1961, VISCOUNT LINLEY, of Nymans, co. Sussex, and EARL OF SNOWDON. He *m.* 1stly, 6 May 1960, *H.R.H.* the Princess Margaret Rose, yr. da. of H.M.

KING GEORGE VI. This marriage was diss. by divorce in 1978. He *m.* 2ndly, 1978, Lucy Mary, only da. of Donald Brook DAVIES of Enniskerry, co. Wicklow, and formerly wife of Michael LINDSAY-HOGG.

[DAVID ALBERT CHARLES (ARMSTRONG-JONES), *styled* VISCOUNT LINLEY, s. and h., *b.* 3 Nov. 1961; ed. at Bedales. He *m.*, 8 Oct. 1993, Serena Alleyne Stanhope, only da. of Charles Henry (LEICESTER), VISCOUNT PETERSHAM.]

11 OCTOBER

DEVLIN

BARONY FOR LIFE. I. 1961. 1. SIR PATRICK ARTHUR DEVLIN, one of the Lords Justices of Appeal, s. of William J. DEVLIN, was *b.* 25 Nov. 1905; ed. at Stonyhurst and Cambridge (Christ's Col.). On the 11 Oct. 1961 he was app. a Lord of Appeal in Ordinary under the Appellate Jurisdiction Act of 1876, and *cr.* a Baron for Life by the style of BARON DEVLIN of West Wick, co. Wilts. He *m.*, 12 Feb. 1932, Madeleine Hilda, yr. da. of Sir Bernard OPPENHEIMER, 1st Bart. He *d.* 9 Aug. 1992 when his Life Barony became *extinct*. His widow was living 1995.

PEERAGES OF 1962

25 JANUARY

LEIGHTON OF SAINT MELLONS

BARONY. I. 1962. 1. SIR GEORGE LEIGHTON SEAGER, 1st Bart, C.B.E., y. s. of Sir William Henry SEAGER, of Cardiff, co. Glamorgan, was *b.* 11 Jan. 1896; ed. at Queen's Coll., Taunton. He was *cr.*, 25 Jan. 1962, BARON LEIGHTON OF SAINT MELLONS, of Saint Mellons, co. Monmouth. He *m.*, 19 Jan. 1921, Marjorie, da. of William Henry GIMSON of Brecon. He *d.* 17 Oct. 1963. His widow *d.* 1992.

II. 1963. 2. JOHN LEIGHTON (SEAGER), BARON LEIGHTON OF SAINT MELLONS, s. and h., *b.* 11 Jan. 1922; ed. at Leys Sch., Cambridge. He *m.* 1stly, 31 Oct. 1953, Elizabeth Rosita, only da. of Henry HOPGOOD of Cardiff. She *d.* 1979. He *m.* 2ndly, 1982, Ruth Elizabeth, da. of (__) and widow of John HOPWOOD.

[ROBERT WILLIAM HENRY LEIGHTON SEAGER, s. and h., *b.* 28 Sep. 1955.]

26 JANUARY

BRAIN

BARONY. I. 1962. 1. SIR WALTER RUSSELL BRAIN, 1st Bart, D.M. Oxon, F.R.C.P., s. of Walter John BRAIN, of Reading, co. Berks, was *b.* 23 Oct. 1895; ed. at Mill Hill Sch. and Oxford (New Coll.). He was *cr.*, 26 Jan. 1962, BARON BRAIN, of Eynsham, co. Oxford. He *m.*, 8 Sep. 1920, Stella, elder da. of Reginald Langdon LANGDON-DOWN of Teddington, Midx. He *d.* 29 Dec. 1966. His widow *d.* 1993.

II. 1966. 2. CHRISTOPHER LANGDON (BRAIN), BARON BRAIN, s. and h., *b.* 30 Aug. 1926; ed. at Leighton Park Sch., Reading and Oxford (New Coll.). He *m.* 11 Apr. 1953, Susan Mary, 2nd da. of George Philip MORRIS of Over, co. Cambridge.

29 JANUARY

ALDINGTON

BARONY. I. 1962. 1. The Right Hon. SIR TOBY AUSTIN RICHARD WILLIAM LOW, K.C.M.G., C.B.E., D.S.O., T.D., s. of Col. Stuart LOW, D.S.O., of London, was *b.* 25 May 1914; ed. at Winchester and Oxford (New Coll.). He was *cr.*, 29 Jan. 1962, BARON ALDINGTON, of Bispham, in the co. Borough of Blackpool, co. Lancaster. He *m.*, 10 Apr. 1947, Felicité Ann Araminta, elder da. of Sir Harold Alfred MACMICHAEL of Folkestone, Kent and formerly wife of Capt. Paul Humphrey Armytage BOWMAN.

[CHARLES HAROLD STUART LOW, s. and h. ap., *b.* 22 June 1948; ed. at Winchester and Oxford (New Coll.). He *m.*, 1989, Regine, da. of Erwin von CSONGRADY-SCHOPF of Germany.]

2 FEBRUARY

INCHYRA

BARONY. I. 1962. 1. SIR FREDERICK ROBERT HOYER MILLAR, G.C.M.G., C.V.O., s. of Robert Hoyer MILLAR, of Blair Castle, Culross, Fife, was *b.* 6 June 1900; ed. at Wellington and Oxford (New Coll.). He was *cr.*, 2 Feb. 1962. BARON INCHYRA, of St. Madoes, co. Perth. He *m.*, 15 Apr. 1931, Anna Judith Elizabeth, da. of Jonkheer Reneke de Marees VAN SWINDEREN, sometime Netherlands Minister in London. He *d.* 16 Oct. 1989. His widow was living 1995.

II. 1989. 2. ROBERT CHARLES RENEKE HOYER (MILLAR), BARON INCHYRA, s. and h., *b.* 4 Apr. 1945; ed. at Eton and Oxford (New Coll.). He *m*, 1 Aug. 1961, Fiona Mary, yr da. of Edmund Charles Reginald SHEFFIELD of Sutton Park, Sutton on the Forest, co. York.

[CHRISTIAN JAMES CHARLES HOYER MILLAR, s. and h. ap., *b.* 12 Aug. 1962; ed. at Eton and Edinburgh Univ. He *m.*, 1992, Caroline J., da. of Robin SWAN of Lower Wield, Hants.]

26 MARCH

LAMBURY

BARONY. I. 1962. 1. SIR LEONARD PERCY LORD, K.B.E., s. of William LORD of Coventry. He was *b.* 15 Nov. 1896; ed. at Bablake Sch., Coventry. He was *cr.*, 26 March 1962, BARON LAMBURY, of Northfield, co. Warwick. He *m.*, 16 July 1921 Ethel Lily, da. of George HORTON of Coventry. He *d. s.p.m.* 13 Sep. 1967 when his Barony became *extinct*.

19 APRIL

PEARCE

BARONY FOR LIFE.
I. 1962.

1. The Right Hon. SIR EDWARD HOLROYD PEARCE, one of the Lords Justices of Appeal, s. of John William Ernest PEARCE, of Hampstead London, was *b.* 9 Feb. 1901; ed. at Charterhouse and Oxford (Corpus Christi). On 19 April 1962, he was app. a Lord of Appeal in Ordinary under the Appellate Jurisdiction Act of 1876 and *cr.* a Baron for Life by the style of BARON PEARCE, of Sweethaws, co. Sussex. He *m.*, 9 Apr. 1927, Erica, da. of Bertram PRIESTMAN. She *d.* 1985. He *d.* 26 Nov. 1990 when his Life Barony became *extinct*.

15 JUNE

MABANE

BARONY.
I. 1962.

1. The Right Hon. SIR WILLIAM MABANE, K.B.E., s. of Joseph MABANE of Leeds, was *b.* 12 Jan. 1895; ed. at Woodhouse Grove Sch. and Cambridge (Gonville and Caius Coll.). He was *cr.*, 15 June 1962, BARON MABANE, of Rye, co. Sussex. He *m.* 1stly, 1918, Louise, da. of Edward TANTON of London. This marriage was diss. by divorce in 1926 and she *d.* 1947. He *m.* 2ndly, 31 Mar. 1944, Stella Jane, da. of Julian DUGGAN of Buenos Aires. He *d. s.p.* 16 Nov. 1969 when his Barony became *extinct*. His widow was living 1995.

11 JULY

RADCLIFFE

RADCLIFFE, Viscountcy (*Radcliffe*) *cr.*, 11 July 1962. See RADCLIFFE, Barony for Life, *cr.*, 1 June 1949, p. 790.

17 JULY

DILHORNE

BARONY.
I. 1962.
VISCOUNTCY.
I. 1964.

1. The Right Hon. SIR REGINALD EDWARD MANNINGHAM-BULLER 4th Bart, Lord Chancellor of Great Britain, only s. of Lieut. Col. Sir Mervyn MANNINGHAM-BULLER, 3rd Bart, was *b.* 1 Aug. 1905; ed. at Eton and Oxford (Magdalen Col.). He was *cr.*, 17 July 1962, BARON DILHORNE, of Towcester, co. Northampton. He was further *cr.*, 7 Dec. 1964, VISCOUNT DILHORNE, of Greens Norton, co. Northampton. He *m.*, 18 Dec. 1930, Lady Mary Lilian, 4th da. of David Alexander Edward (LINDSAY), 27th EARL OF CRAWFORD. He *d.* 7 Sep. 1980. His widow was living 1995.

II. 1980.

2. JOHN MERVYN (MANNINGHAM-BULLER), VISCOUNT DILHORNE, s. and. h., *b.* 28 Feb. 1932; ed. at Eton and R.M.C., Sandhurst. He *m.* 1stly, 8 Oct. 1955, Gillian Evelyn, elder da. of Col. George Cochrane STOCKWELL of Cap Martin, France. This marriage was diss. by divorce in 1973. He *m.* 2ndly, 1981, Susannah Jane, da. of Cmdr. W.C. EYKYN, R.N., and formerly wife of Colin GILCHRIST.

[JAMES EDWARD MANNINGHAM-BULLER, s. and h. ap., *b.* 20 Aug. 1956; ed. at Harrow and R.M.C. Sandhurst. He *m.*, 1985, Nicola Marion, elder da. of Sven MACKIE of Downpatrick, co. Down.]

20 JULY

KILMUIR, Earldom, FYFE, Barony

KILMUIR, Earldom, FYFE, Barony (*Maxwell Fyfe*) *cr.*, 20 July 1962. See KILMUIR, Viscountcy, *cr.* 19 Oct. 1954, p. 810.

1 AUGUST

ECCLES

BARONY. I. 1962.
VISCOUNTCY. I. 1964.

1. SIR DAVID MCADAM ECCLES, 3rd but 1st surv. s. of William McAdam ECCLES, consulting surgeon, St Bartholomew's Hosp., *b.* 18 Sep. 1904; ed. at Winchester and Oxford (New Coll.). He was *cr.*, 1 Aug. 1962, BARON ECCLES, of Chute, co. Wilts. and further *cr.*, 14 Jan. 1964, VISCOUNT ECCLES, of Chute afsd. He *m.* 1stly, 10 Oct. 1928, Sybil Frances, 1st da. of Sir Bertram Edward (DAWSON), 1st (and last) VISCOUNT DAWSON OF PENN. She *d.* 1977 and he *m.* 2ndly, 1984, Mary, da. of (—) and widow of Donald HYDE of New Jersey, U.S.A.

[JOHN DAWSON, 1st s. by 1st wife and h. ap., was *b.* 20 Apr. 1931; ed. at Winchester and Oxford (Magdalen Coll.); *m.*, 29 Jan. 1955, Diana Catherine, 2nd da. of Raymond Wilson STURGE of Ashmore, Salisbury, co. Wilts.]

22 AUGUST

MILLS, Viscountcy (*Mills*) *cr.* 22 August 1962. See MILLS, Barony, *cr.* 22 Jan. 1957, p. 818.

PEERAGES OF 1963

18 JANUARY

SILSOE

BARONY. I. 1963.

1. SIR ARTHUR MALCOLM TRUSTRAM EVE, 1st Bart, G.B.E., M.C., Q.C., 1st s. of Sir Herbert Trustram EVE, of London, was *b.* 8 April 1894; ed. at Winchester and Oxford (Ch. Ch.). He was *cr.* 18 Jan. 1963, BARON SILSOE, of Silsoe, co. Bedford. He *m.* 1stly, 23 Aug. 1927, Marguerite, yst. da. of Sir Augustus Meredith NANTON of Winnipeg, Canada. She *d.* 25 Dec. 1945. He *m.* 2ndly, 31 Oct. 1946, Margaret Elizabeth, yst. da. of Henry Wallace ROBERTSON of Milbrae Ayton, co. Berwick. He *d.* 3 Dec. 1976. His widow *d.* 1993.

II. 1976. 2. DAVID MALCOLM (EVE), BARON SILSOE, elder s. and h., *b.* 2 May 1930; ed. at Winchester, Oxford (Ch. Ch.) and Columbia Univ., U.S.A. He *m.*, 15 June 1963, Bridget Min, only da. of Sir Rupert Charles HART-DAVIS of Marske-in-Swaledale, Yorks.

[SIMON RUPERT TRUSTRAM (EVE), s. and h. ap., *b.* 17 Apr. 1966.]

24 JANUARY

NORMANBROOK

BARONY. I. 1963. 1. The Right Hon. SIR NORMAN CRAVEN BROOK, G.C.B., s. of Frederick Charles BROOK, of Bristol, was *b.* 29 April 1902; ed. at Wolverhampton Gram. Sch. and Oxford (Wadham Coll.). He was *cr.*, 24 Jan. 1963, BARON NORMANBROOK of Chelsea, co. London. He *m.*, 30 Nov. 1929, Ida Mary, da. of Edwyn Alfred GOSHAWK of London. He *d. s.p.* 15 June 1967 when his Barony became *extinct*.

8 NOVEMBER

BLAKENHAM

VISCOUNTCY. I. 1963. 1. The Right Hon. JOHN HUGH HARE, O.B.E., 3rd s. of Richard Granville (HARE) 4th EARL OF LISTOWEL, was *b.* 22 Jan. 1911; ed. at Eton. He was *cr.*, 8 Nov. 1963 VISCOUNT BLAKENHAM, of Little Blakenham, co. Suffolk. He *m.*, 31 Jan. 1934, Beryl Nancy, 2nd da. of Weetman Harold Miller (PEARSON), 2nd VISCOUNT COWDRAY. He *d.* 7 Mar. 1982. His widow was living 1995.

II. 1982. 2. MICHAEL JOHN (HARE), VISCOUNT BLAKENHAM, s. and h., *b.* 25 Jan. 1938; ed. at Eton and Harvard Univ. He *m.*, 12 Jan. 1965, his cousin Marcia Persephone, only da. of Alan Victor HARE.

[CASPAR JOHN HARE, s. and h. ap., *b.* 8 Apr. 1972.]

9 NOVEMBER

DRUMALBYN

BARONY. I. 1963. 1. The Right Hon. NIALL MALCOLM STEWART MACPHERSON, 3rd s. of Sir Thomas Stewart MACPHERSON, C.I.E., LL.D., was *b.* 3 Aug. 1908; ed. at Edinburgh Acad., at Fettes and Oxford (Trin. Coll.). He was *cr.*, 9 Nov. 1963, BARON DRUMALBYN, of Whitesands, Royal Burgh of Dumfries. He *m.* 1stly, 27 July 1937, Margaret Phyllis, da. of Julius Joseph RUNGE of Sevenoaks, Kent. She *d.* 1979. He *m.* 2ndly, 1985, Rita, da. of (—), widow of Harry EDMISTON. He *d. s.p.m.* 11 Oct. 1987, when his Barony became *extinct*. His widow was living 1995.

15 NOVEMBER

WAKEFIELD OF KENDAL

BARONY. I. 1963. 1. SIR WILLIAM WAVELL WAKEFIELD, s. of Roger William WAKEFIELD, of Kendal, co. Westmorland, was *b.* 10 Mar, 1898; ed. at Sedbergh and Cambridge (Pembroke Coll.). He was *cr.*, 15 Nov. 1963, BARON WAKEFIELD OF KENDAL, of Kendal, co. Westmorland. He *m.*, 19 Nov. 1919, Rowena Doris, da. of Llewellyn LEWIS of Neath, South Wales. She *d.* 1981. He *d. s.p.m.* 12 Aug. 1983 when his Barony became *extinct*.

26 NOVEMBER

UPJOHN

BARONY FOR LIFE. I. 1963. 1. The Right Hon. SIR GERALD RITCHIE UPJOHN, C.B.E., one of the Lords Justices of Appeal, s. of William Henry UPJOHN, K.C., of Lyndhurst, co. Southampton, was *b.* 25 Feb. 1903; ed. at Eton and Cambridge (Trin. Coll.). On 26 November 1963, he was app. a Lord of Appeal in Ordinary under the Appellate Jurisdiction Act of 1876 and *cr.* a Baron for Life by the style of BARON UPJOHN, of Little Tey, co. Essex. He *m.*, 22 May 1947, Marjorie Dorothy Bertha, da. of Major Ernest Murray LUCAS of Lyndhurst, Hants. He *d. s.p.* 27 Jan. 1971 when his Life Barony became *extinct*.

26 NOVEMBER

EGREMONT

BARONY. I. 1963. 1. JOHN EDWARD REGINALD WYNDHAM, M.B.E., 2nd s. of Edward Scawen (WYNDHAM), D.S.O., 5th BARON LECONFIELD, was *b.* 5 June 1920. He was *cr.*, 27 Nov. 1963, BARON EGREMONT, of Petworth, co. Sussex. See above, *sub* Leconfield.

PEERAGES OF 1964

11 JANUARY

DONOVAN

BARONY FOR LIFE. I. 1964. 1. The Right Hon. SIR TERENCE NORBERT DONOVAN, P.C., one of the Lords Justices of Appeal, 2nd s. of Timothy Cornelius DONOVAN of Walthamstow, was *b.* 13 June 1898; ed. at Brockley Gram. Sch. and by private coaching. On 11 January 1964, he was app. a Lord of Appeal in Ordinary under the Appellate Jurisdiction Act of 1876 and *cr.* a Baron for Life by the style of BARON DONOVAN, of Winchester, co. Hants. He *m.*, 1925, Marjorie Florence, da. of Charles MURRAY of Winchester. He *d.* 12 Dec. 1971 when his Life Barony became *extinct*.

7 DECEMBER

DILHORNE

DILHORNE, Viscountcy, (*Manningham-Buller*) *cr.* 7 Dec. 1964. See DILHORNE, Barony, *cr.* 17 July 1962, p. 836.

19 DECEMBER

GRIMSTON OF WESTBURY

BARONY. I. 1964. 1. SIR ROBERT VILLIERS GRIMSTON, elder s. of Canon Robert GRIMSTON, 3rd s. of James Walter GRIMSTON, 2nd EARL OF

VERULAM, was *b.* 8 June 1897; ed. at Repton and London University. He was *cr.*, 11 March 1952, a Baronet and 11 Dec. 1964, BARON GRIMSTON OF WESTBURY, of Westbury, co. Wilts. He *m.*, 24 Oct. 1923, Sybil Rose, eldest da. of Sir Sigmund NEUMANN, 1st Bart. She *d.* 1977. He *d.* 8 Dec. 1979.

II. 1979. 2. ROBERT WALTER SIGISMUND GRIMSTON, 1st s. and h., was *b.* 14 June 1925; ed. at Eton. He *m.*, 21 June 1949, June Mary, elder da. of Hubert William (PONSONBY), 5th BARON DE MAULEY.

[ROBERT JOHN SYLVESTER GRIMSTON, 1st s. and h. ap., was *b.* 30 April 1951; ed. at Eton and Reading University. He *m.*, 1984, Emily Margaret, da. of Major John Evelyn SHIRLEY of the Isle of Man.]

19 DECEMBER

ERROLL OF HALE

BARONY. I. 1964. 1. FREDERICK JAMES ERROLL, only s. of George Murison ERROLL of Glasgow and London, was *b.* 27 May 1914; ed. at Oundle and Cambridge (Trin. Coll.). He was *cr.*, 19 Dec. 1964, BARON ERROLL OF HALE, of Kilmun, co. Argyll. He *m.*, 19 Dec. 1950, Elizabeth, da. of Richard Sowton BARROW of Exmouth, co. Devon.

23 DECEMBER

RENWICK

BARONY. I. 1964. 1. SIR ROBERT BURNHAM RENWICK, only s. and h. of Sir Harry Benedetto RENWICK, 1st Bart., was *b.* 4 Oct. 1904; ed. at Eton and Oxford (Trin. Coll.). He succeeded his father as 2nd Bart, 7 Jan. 1932 and was *cr.*, 23 Dec. 1964, BARON RENWICK, of Coombe, co. Surrey. He *m.* 1stly, 10 June 1929, Dorothy Mary, elder da. of Major Harold PARKES of Alveston, Stratford on Avon. This marriage was diss. by divorce 1953 (she *m.* 2ndly, 1953, John FitzAdam ORMISTON and was living 1995), and he *m.* 2ndly, 28 July 1953, Edith Joan, only child of Sir Reginald CLARKE of Sunningdale, Berkshire and widow of Major John Ogilvie SPENCER. He *d.* 30 Aug. 1973. His widow was living 1995.

II. 1973. 2. HARRY ANDREW (RENWICK), BARON RENWICK, &c., only s. and h., was *b.* 10 Oct. 1935; ed. at Eton. He *m.* 1stly, 27 April 1965, Susan Jane, only child of Capt. Stephen Bamfylde LUCKING. This marriage was diss. by divorce 1989 and he *m.* 2ndly, 1989, Homayoun, da. of Major Mahmoud Yazdanparst PAKZAD and formerly wife of Joe MAZANDI of California, U.S.A.

[ROBERT JAMES RENWICK, elder s. and h. ap., *b.* 19 Aug. 1966.]

30 DECEMBER

FRASER OF ALLANDER

BARONY. I. 1964. 1. HUGH FRASER, only s. of Hugh FRASER of Glasgow, was *b.* 15 Jan. 1903; ed. at Warriston and Glasgow Academy. He was *cr.*, 19 Jan. 1961, a

Baronet and 30 Dec. 1964, BARON FRASER OF ALLANDER. He *m.*, 2 April 1931, Kate Hutcheon, da. of Sir Andrew Jopp Williams LEWIS. He *d.* 6 Nov. 1966. His widow was living 1995.

II. 1966. 2. HUGH (FRASER), BARON FRASER OF ALLANDER, &c., only s. and h., was *b.* 18 Dec. 1936; ed. at St Mary's, Melrose and Kelvinside Academy. He disclaimed his Barony for life, 7 Dec. 1966. He *m.* 1stly, 26 April 1962, Patricia Mary, eldest da. of John BOWIE of Milngavie, Stirlingshire. This marriage was diss. by divorce 1971 and he *m.* 2ndly, 1973, Aileen Margaret, da. of George Paterson ROSS. She *d.* 1984. He *d. s.p.m.* 5 May 1987 when his titles became *extinct*.

31 DECEMBER

ST. HELENS

BARONY. I. 1964. 1. MICHAEL HENRY COLIN HUGHES-YOUNG, only s. of Brig.-Gen. Henry George YOUNG of Skeffington Lodge, co. Antrim, was *b.* 28 Oct. 1912; ed. at Harrow and R.M.C. Sandhurst. He was *cr.*, 31 Dec. 1964, BARON ST. HELENS, of St. Helens, co. Palatine of Lancaster. He *m.*, 31 July 1939, Elizabeth Agnes, younger da. of Richard BLAKISTON-HOUSTON of Orangefield and Ballywater, co. Down. She *d.* 2 Oct. 1956. He *d.* 27 Dec. 1980.

[PATRICK MICHAEL HUGHES-YOUNG, 1st s. and h. ap., was *b.* 30 April 1942; ed. at Eton. He *d.* unmarried as the result of a riding accident 11 March 1970.]

II. 1980. 2. RICHARD FRANCIS (HUGHES-YOUNG), BARON ST. HELENS, 2nd but 1st surv. s. and h., was *b.* 4 Nov. 1945; ed. at Nautical College, Pangbourne. He *m.*, 1983, Mrs Emma R. TALBOT-SMITH.

[HENRY THOMAS HUGHES-YOUNG, s. and h. ap., was *b.* 7 March 1986.]

1 OCTOBER

WILBERFORCE

BARONY FOR LIFE. I. 1964. 1. SIR RICHARD ORME WILBERFORCE, C.M.G., only s. of Samuel WILBERFORCE of Lavington, Surrey, was *b.* 11 Mar. 1907; ed. at Winchester and Oxford (New Coll.). On 1 October 1964 he was app. a Lord of Appeal in Ordinary under the Appellate Jurisdiction Act of 1876 and *cr.* a Baron for Life by the style of BARON WILBERFORCE, of the City and County of Kingston upon Hull. He *m.*, 1947, Yvette Marie, da. of Roger LENOAN of Paris.

14 JANUARY

ECCLES, Viscountcy

ECCLES (*Eccles*) *cr.* 14 Jan. 1964. See ECCLES, Barony, *cr.* 1 Aug. 1962, p. 837.

10 MARCH

THOMSON OF FLEET

BARONY. I. 1964. 1. SIR ROY HERBERT THOMSON, 1st s. of Herbert THOMSON of Toronto, Canada, was *b.* 5 June 1894; ed. at Jarvis Street Collegiate School, Toronto. He was *cr.*, 10 March 1964, BARON THOMSON OF FLEET, of Northbridge in the City of Edinburgh. He *m.*, 22 Feb. 1916, Edna Alice, da. of John IRVINE of Drayton, Ontario, Canada. She *d.* 22 Feb. 1951. He *d.* 4 Aug. 1976.

II. 1976. 2. KENNETH ROY (THOMSON) OF FLEET, only s. and h., was *b.* 1 Sept. 1923; ed. at Upper Canada College, Toronto, Canada and Cambridge Univ. He *m.*, 13 June 1956, Nora Marilyn, da. of Albert Vernard LAVIS of Toronto.

[DAVID KENNETH ROY THOMSON, 1st s. and h. ap., was *b.* 12 June 1957.]

13 MAY

MARTONMERE

BARONY. I. 1964. 1. JOHN ROLAND ROBINSON, 1st s. of Roland Walkden ROBINSON of Blackpool, was *b.* 22 Feb. 1907; ed. at Cambridge (Trin. Hall). He was *cr.*, 13 May 1964, BARON MARTONMERE, of Blackpool in the co. Palatine of Lancaster. He *m.*, 9 July 1930, Maysie, da. of Clarence Warren GASQUE of Hampstead. He *d. s.p.m.* 3 May 1989. His widow *d.* Oct. 1989.

[RICHARD ANTHONY GASQUE ROBINSON, only s. and h. ap., was *b.* 11 March 1935; ed. at Winchester, Cambridge (Selwyn Coll.) and Stanford University, U.S.A. He *m.*, 8 Aug. 1959, Wendy Patricia, da. of James Cecil BLAGDEN of Bapchild Court near Sittingbourne, Kent. He *d. v.p.* 1979. His widow was living 1995.]

II. 1989. 2. JOHN STEPHEN (ROBINSON), BARON MARTONMERE, 1st grandson and h. ap., being s. and h. of Richard Anthony and Wendy Patricia abovenamed. He was *b.* 10 July 1963; ed. at Lakefield College School and Senaca College.

26 JUNE

WATKINSON

VISCOUNTCY. I. 1964. 1. HAROLD ARTHUR WATKINSON, 1st s. of Arthur Gill WATKINSON of Walton on Thames, was *b.* 25 Jan. 1910; ed. at Queen's College, Taunton and King's College, London. He was *cr.*, 26 June 1964, VISCOUNT WATKINSON, of Woking, co. Surrey. He *m.*, 18 Nov. 1939, Vera, youngest da. of John LANGMEAD of Ford, West Sussex.

30 JUNE

INGLEWOOD

BARONY. I. 1964. 1. WILLIAM MORGAN FLETCHER-VANE, only s. of Col. William Lyonel VANE, youngest brother of 9th Baron Barnard, was *b.* 12 April

1909; ed. at Charterhouse and Cambridge (Trin. Coll.). He assumed the surname Fletcher-Vane in lieu of Vane by Deed Poll 9 April 1931. He was *cr.*, 30 June 1964, BARON INGLEWOOD, of Hutton-in-the-Forest, co. Cumberland. He *m.*, 28 July 1949, Mary, eldest da. of Sir Richard George PROBY, 1st Bart. She *d.* 1982. He *d.* 22 June 1989.

II. 1989. 2. WILLIAM RICHARD (FLETCHER-VANE), BARON INGLEWOOD, 1st s. and h., was *b.* 31 July 1951; ed. at Eton, Cambridge (Trin. Coll.), and Cumbria College of Agriculture and Forestry. He *m.*, 1986, Cressida, youngest da. of Alan Desmond Frederick PEMBERTON-PIGOTT of Fawe Park, Keswick.

[HENRY WILLIAM FREDERICK FLETCHER-VANE, only s. and h. ap., *b.* 24 Dec. 1990.]

15 JULY

SHERFIELD

BARONY. I. 1964. 1. SIR ROGER MELLOR MAKINS, 1st s. of Sir Ernest MAKINS, K.B.E., C.B., D.S.O., was *b.* 3 Feb. 1904; ed. at Winchester and Oxford (Ch. Ch.). He was *cr.*, 15 July 1964, BARON SHERFIELD, of Sherfield-on-Loddon, co. Southampton. He *m.*, 30 April 1934, Alice, da. of Dwight Filey DAVIS of Washington D.C. She *d.* 1985.

[CHRISTOPHER JAMES MAKINS, 1st s. and h. ap., *b.* 23 July 1942; ed. at Winchester and Oxford (New Coll.). He *m.*, 1975, Wendy, da. of (—) CORTESI.]

16 JULY

MUIRSHIEL

VISCOUNTCY. I. 1964. 1. JOHN SCOTT MACLAY, 5th s. of Joseph Paton MACLAY, 1st BARON MACLAY, was *b.* 26 Oct. 1905; ed. at Winchester and Cambridge (Trin. Coll.). He was *cr.*, 16 July 1964, VISCOUNT MUIRSHIEL, of Kilmacolm, co. Renfrew. He *m.*, 16 Oct. 1930, Betty L'Estrange, younger da. of Major Delaval Graham L'Estrange ASTLEY of Wroxham, Norfolk. She *d.* 1974. He *d. s.p.* 17 Aug. 1992, when his Viscountcy became *extinct*.

16 JULY

GLENDEVON

BARONY. I. 1964. 1. JOHN ADRIAN HOPE, younger twin s. of Victor Alexander John (HOPE), 2nd MARQUESS OF LINLITHGOW, was *b.* 7 April 1912; ed. at Eton and Oxford (Ch. Ch.). He was *cr.*, 16 July 1964, BARON GLENDEVON, of Midhope, co. Linlithgow. He *m.*, 21 July 1948, Elizabeth Mary, only da. of William Somerset MAUGHAM, and formerly wife of Vincent PARAVICINI.

[JULIAN JOHN SOMERSET HOPE, 1st s. and h. ap., was *b.* 6 March 1950; ed. at Eton and Oxford (Ch. Ch.)]

4 SEPTEMBER

ERSKINE OF RERRICK

BARONY. I. 1964. 1. SIR JOHN MAXWELL ERSKINE, 1st s. of John McMichan ERSKINE of Kirkcudbright, was *b.* 14 Dec. 1893; ed. at Kirkcudbright Academy and Edinburgh University. He was *cr.*, 5 July 1961, a Baronet of the United Kingdom and 4 Sept. 1964, BARON ERSKINE OF RERRICK, of Rerrick, Stewartry of Kirkcudbright. He *m.*, 15 Sept. 1922, Henrietta, da. of William DUNNETT of East Canisbay, Caithness. He *d.* 14 Dec. 1980. His widow was living 1995.

II. 1980. 2. IAIN MAXWELL (ERSKINE), BARON ERSKINE OF RERRICK, &c., only s. and h., was *b.* 22 Jan. 1926; ed. at Harrow. He *m.* 1stly, 20 July 1955, Marie Elizabeth Burton, da. of Major Richard Burton ALLEN. This marriage was diss. by divorce 1964, and he *m.* 2ndly, 1974, Marie Josephine, da. of Dr Josef KLUPT. This marriage was diss. by divorce 1989, and he *m.* 3rdly, 1993, Debra, da. of Gordon Owen KNIGHT of co. Northampton.

PEERAGES FOR 1965

18 FEBRUARY

PEARSON

BARONY FOR LIFE. I. 1965. 1. The Right Hon. SIR COLIN HARGREAVES PEARSON, C.B.E., P.C., one of the Lords Justices of Appeal, yr. s. of Ernest William PEARSON of Minnedosa, Manitoba, Canada, was *b.* 28 July 1899; ed. at St. Paul's Sch. and Oxford (Balliol Coll.). On 18 February 1965 he was app. a Lord of Appeal in Ordinary under the Appellate Jurisdiction Act of 1876 and *cr.* a Baron for Life by the style of BARON PEARSON, of Minnedosa in Canada and of the Royal Borough of Kensington. He *m*, 1931, Sophie Grace Hermann, da. of Arthur Hermann THOMAS. He *d.* 31 Jan. 1980 when his Life Barony became *extinct*.

PEERAGES FOR 1968

30 SEPTEMBER

DIPLOCK

BARONY FOR LIFE. I. 1968. 1. The Right Hon. SIR WILLIAM JOHN KENNETH DIPLOCK, P.C., one of the Lords Justices of Appeal, s. of William John Hubert DIPLOCK of Croydon, Surrey, *b.* 8 Dec. 1907; ed. at Whitgift and Oxford (Univ. Coll.). On 30 September 1968 he was app. a Lord of Appeal in Ordinary under the Appellate Jurisdiction Act of 1876 and *cr.* a Baron for Life by the style of BARON DIPLOCK, of Wansford, co. Huntingdon. He *m.*, 1938, Margaret Sarah, da. of George ATCHESON of Londonderry. He *d. s.p.* 14 Oct. 1985 when his Life Barony became *extinct*.

PEERAGES FOR 1971

12 MARCH

CROSS OF CHELSEA

BARONY FOR LIFE. I. 1971.

1. The Right Hon. SIR ARTHUR GEOFFREY NEALE CROSS, P.C., one of the Lords Justices of Appeal. s. of Arthur George CROSS of Chelsea, was *b.* 1 Dec. 1904; ed. at Westminster and Cambridge (Trin Coll.). On 12 March 1971 he was app. a Lord of Appeal in Ordinary under the Appellate Jurisdiction Act of 1876 and *cr.* a Baron for Life by the style of BARON CROSS OF CHELSEA, of the Royal Borough of Kensington and Chelsea. He *m.*, 1952, Mildred Joan, da. of Major Theodore Eardley WILMOT and widow of Thomas Walton DAVIS. He *d. s.p.m.* 4 Aug. 1989 when his Life Barony became *extinct*. His widow was still living 1995.

4 OCTOBER

KILBRANDON

BARONY FOR LIFE. I. 1971.

1. CHARLES JAMES DALRYMPLE SHAW, s. of James Edward SHAW of Ayrshire, was *b.* 15 Aug. 1906; ed. at Charterhouse, Oxford (Balliol Coll.) and Edinburgh Univ. On 4 October 1971 he was app. a Lord of Appeal in Ordinary under the Appellate Jurisdiction Act of 1876 and *cr.* a Baron for Life by the style of BARON KILBRANDON, of Kilbrandon, co. Argyll. He *m.*, 1937, Ruth Caroline, da. of F.M.S. GRANT of Knockie, Inverness. He *d.* 10 Sep. 1989 when his Life Barony became *extinct*. His widow was still living 1995.

PEERAGES OF 1972

10 JANUARY

SALMON

BARONY FOR LIFE. I. 1972.

1. The Right Hon. SIR CYRIL BARNET SALMON, P.C., J.P., one of the Lords Justices of Appeal, s. of Montague SALMON of London, was *b.* 28 Dec. 1903; ed. at Mill Hill and Cambridge (Pembroke Coll.). On 10 January 1972 he was app. a Lord of Appeal in Ordinary under the Appellate Jurisdiction Act of 1876 and *cr.* a Baron for Life by the style of BARON SALMON, of Sandwich, co. Kent. He *m.* 1stly, 1929, Rencie, da. of Sidney Gordon VANDERFELT. She *d.* in 1942 and he *m.* 2ndly, 1946, Jean Beatrice, da. of Lieut. Col. David Edward MAITLAND-MACKGILL-CRICHTON, and formerly wife of Michael (MORRIS), 2nd BARON MORRIS. He *d.* 7 Nov. 1991.

PEERAGES OF 1974

1 OCTOBER

EDMUND-DAVIES

BARONY FOR LIFE.
I. 1974.

1. The Right Hon. SIR HERBERT EDMUND DAVIES, P.C., one of the Lords Justices of Appeal, s. of Morgan John DAVIES of Swansea and Mountain Ash, Glam., was *b.* 15 July 1906; ed. at Mountain Ash Gram. Sch., King's Coll., London and Oxford (Exeter Coll.). On 1 October 1974 he was app. a Lord of Appeal in Ordinary under the Appellate Jurisdiction Act of 1876 and *cr.* a Baron for Life by the style of BARON EDMUND-DAVIES, of Aberpennar, co. Mid-Glam. He *m.*, 1935, Eurwen, da. of John WILLIAMS. He *d. s.p.m.* 27 Dec. 1992 when his Life Barony became *extinct.*

PEERAGES OF 1975

13 JANUARY

FRASER OF TULLYBELTON

BARONY FOR LIFE.
I. 1975.

1. The Right Hon. WALTER IAN REID FRASER, P.C., s. of Alexander Reid FRASER of Glasgow and Auchengore, Rhu, Dunbartonshire, was *b.* 3 Feb. 1911; ed. at Repton, Oxford (Balliol Coll.) and Univ. of Glasgow. On 13 January 1975 he was app. a Lord of Appeal in Ordinary under the Appellate Jurisdiction Act of 1876 and *cr.* a Baron for Life by the style of BARON FRASER OF TULLYBELTON, of Bankfoot, co. Perthshire. He *m.*, 1943, Mary Ursula Cynthia Gwendolen, da. of Col. I.H. MacDonnell, of Connel, Argyllshire. He *d.* 17 Feb. 1989 when his life Barony became *extinct.* His widow was still living 1995.

30 SEPTEMBER

RUSSELL OF KILLOWEN

BARONY FOR LIFE.
I. 1975.

1. The Right Hon. SIR CHARLES RITCHIE RUSSELL, P.C., one of the Lords Justices of Appeal, s. of Sir Francis (Frank) Xavier (RUSSELL), LORD RUSSELL OF KILLOWEN, of Walton on the Hill, Tadworth, Surrey; ed. at Beaumont Coll. and Oxford (Oriel Coll.). On 30 September 1975 he was app. a Lord of Appeal in Ordinary under the Appellate Jurisdiction Act of 1876 and *cr.* a Baron for Life by the style of BARON RUSSELL OF KILLOWEN, of Killowen in co. Down, the same title being held as a life peerage by his father and grandfather. He *m.* 1stly, 1933, Joan Elizabeth, da. of Dr. James Aubrey TORRENS of Wimpole Street, London. She *d.* 1976, and he *m.* 2ndly, 1979, Elizabeth Cecilia, da. of Air Vice-Marshall W.F. Macneece FOSTER and widow of Edward LAUGHTON-SCOTT, Q.C. He *d.* 23 June 1986 when his Life Barony became *extinct.* His widow was still living 1995.

PEERAGES OF 1977

10 JANUARY

KEITH OF KINKEL

BARONY FOR LIFE. I. 1977.

1. The Right Hon. HENRY SHANKS KEITH, P.C., only s. of James KEITH, BARON KEITH OF AVONHOLM of Edinburgh (a Life Peer), was *b.* 7 Feb. 1922; ed. at Edinburgh Acad., Oxford (Magdalen Coll.) and Edinburgh Univ. A Lord of Session as Lord Keith, 1971–6. On 10 January 1977 he was app. a Lord of Appeal in Ordinary under the Appellate Jurisdiction Act of 1876 and *cr.* a Baron for Life by the style of BARON KEITH OF KINKEL, of Strathtummel, co. Perthshire. He *m.*, 1955, Alison Hope Alan, yr. da. of Alan BROWN.

30 SEPTEMBER

SCARMAN

BARONY FOR LIFE. I. 1977.

1. The Right Hon.SIR LESLIE GEORGE SCARMAN, P.C., one of the Lords Justices of Appeal, s. of George Charles SCARMAN of London and Brighton, was *b.* 29 July 1911; ed. at Radley and Oxford (Brasenose Coll.). On 30 September 1977 he was app. a Lord of Appeal in Ordinary under the Appellate Jurisdiction Act of 1876 and *cr.* a Baron for Life by the style of BARON SCARMAN, of Quatt, co. Salop. He *m.*, 1947, Ruth Clement, da. of Clement WRIGHT.

PEERAGES OF 1979

28 SEPTEMBER

LANE

BARONY FOR LIFE. I. 1979.

1. The Right Hon. SIR GEOFFREY DAWSON LANE, P.C., one of the Lords Justices of Appeal, s. of Percy Albert LANE of Lincoln, was *b.* 17 July 1918; ed. at Shrewsbury and Cambridge (Trin. Coll.). On 28 September 1979 he was app. a Lord of Appeal in Ordinary under the Appellate Jurisdiction Act of 1876 and *cr.* a Baron for Life by the style of BARON LANE, of St. Ippollitts, co. Herts. He *m.*, 1944, Jan, da. of Donald MACDONALD of Tulloch, Inverness-shire.

PEERAGES OF 1980

15 APRIL

ROSKILL

BARONY FOR LIFE.
I. 1980.

1. The Right Hon. SIR EUSTACE WENTWORTH ROSKILL, P.C., one of the Lords Justices of Appeal, yst. s. of John Henry ROSKILL, K.C., was *b.* 6 Feb. 1911; ed. at Winchester and Oxford (Exeter Coll.). On 15 April 1980 he was app. a Lord of Appeal in Ordinary under the Appellate Jurisdiction Act of 1876 and *cr.* a Baron for Life by the style of BARON ROSKILL, of Newtown, co. Hants. He *m.*, 1947, Elisabeth Wallace, 3rd da. of Thomas Frame JACKSON of Buenos Aires. He *d.* 4 October 1996 when his Life Barony became *extinct*. His widow was living 1996.

29 SEPTEMBER

BRIDGE OF HARWICH

BARONY FOR LIFE.
I. 1980.

1. The Right Hon. SIR NIGEL CYPRIAN BRIDGE, P.C., one of the Lords Justices of Appeal, s. of Cmdr. Cyprian Dunscomb Charles BRIDGE, R.N., of Hitchin, Herts., was *b.* 26 Feb. 1917; ed. at Marlborough. On 29 September 1980 he was app. a Lord of Appeal in Ordinary under the Appellate Jurisdiction Act of 1876 and *cr.* a Baron for Life by the style of BARON BRIDGE OF HARWICH, of Harwich, co. Essex. He *m.*, 1944, Margaret, da. of Leonard Heseltine SWINBANK of Weybridge, Surrey.

PEERAGES OF 1981

24 SEPTEMBER

BRANDON OF OAKBROOK

BARONY FOR LIFE.
I. 1981.

1. The Right Hon. SIR HENRY VIVIAN BRANDON, P.C., one of the Lords Justices of Appeal, s. of Capt. Vivian Ronald BRANDON, R.N., of Kensington, was *b.* 3 June 1920; ed. at Winchester and Cambridge (King's Coll.). On 24 September 1981 he was app. a Lord of Appeal in Ordinary under the Appellate Jurisdiction Act of 1876 and *cr.* a Baron for Life by the style of BARON BRANDON OF OAKBROOK, of Hammersmith in Greater London. He *m.*, 1955, Jeanette Rosemary, el. da. of Julian Vivian Breeze Janvrin.

PEERAGES OF 1982

11 MARCH

BRIGHTMAN

BARONY FOR LIFE.
I. 1982.

1. The Right Hon. SIR JOHN ANSON BRIGHTMAN, P.C., one of the Lords Justices of Appeal, 2nd s. of William Henry BRIGHTMAN of St. Albans, co. Hertford, was *b.* 20 June 1911; ed. at Marlborough and Cambridge (St John's Coll.). On 11 Mar. 1982 he was app. a Lord of Appeal in Ordinary under the Appellate Jurisdiction Act of 1876 and *cr.* a Baron for Life by the style of BARON BRIGHTMAN, of Ibthorpe, co. Hants. He *m.*, 1945, Roxane, da. of Gerasimo AMBATIELO of Cephalonia.

1 OCTOBER

TEMPLEMAN

BARONY FOR LIFE.
I. 1982.

1. The Right Hon. SIR SYDNEY WILLIAM TEMPLEMAN, P.C., one of the Lords Justices of Appeal, s. of Herbert William TEMPLEMAN of Hammersmith, was *b.* 3 March 1920; ed. at Southall Gram. Sch. and Cambridge (St John's Coll.). On 1 Oct. 1982 he was app. a Lord of Appeal in Ordinary under the Appellate Jurisdiction Act of 1876 and *cr.* a Baron for Life by the style of BARON TEMPLEMAN, of White Lackington, co. Somerset. He *m.*, 1946, Margaret Joan, da. of Morton ROWLES of Tardebigge, co. Worcester. She *d.* 1988.

PEERAGES OF 1983

16 JUNE

WHITELAW

VISCOUNTCY.
I. 1983.

1. The Right Hon. SIR WILLIAM STEPHEN IAN WHITELAW, K.T., C.H., M.C., P.C., s. of William Alexander WHITELAW of Monkland, Nairn, was *b.* 28 June 1918; ed. at Winchester and Cambridge (Trin Coll.). On 16 June 1983 he was *cr.* a Viscount by the style of VISCOUNT WHITELAW, of Penrith, co. Cumbria. He *m.*, 1943, Cecilia Doriel, yr. da. of Major Mark SPROT of Riddell by Melrose, Roxburghshire.

11 JULY

TONYPANDY

VISCOUNTCY.
I. 1983.

1. The Right Hon. SIR THOMAS GEORGE THOMAS, P.C., s. of Zachariah THOMAS of Tonypandy, was *b.* 29 Jan. 1909; ed. at Tonypandy Gram. Sch.

and Univ. of Southampton. On 11 July 1983 he was *cr.* a Viscount by the style of VISCOUNT TONYPANDY, of Rhondda, co. Glam. Speaker of the House of Commons 1976 to 1983.

PEERAGES OF 1984

10 FEBRUARY

STOCKTON, Earldom, MACMILLAN OF OVENDEN, Viscountcy

EARLDOM. I. 1984. 1. The Right Hon. SIR MAURICE HAROLD MACMILLAN, K.G., G.C.M.G., G.C.V.O., P.C., 3rd and yst. s. of Maurice Crawford MACMILLAN, was *b.* 10 Feb. 1894; ed. at Eton and Oxford (Balliol Coll.). On 10 February 1984 he was *cr.* VISCOUNT MACMILLAN OF OVENDEN, of Chelwood Gate, co. Sussex and of Stockton-on-Tees, co. Cleveland, and EARL OF STOCKTON. He *m.*, 21 April 1920, Lady Dorothy Evelyn, 3rd da. of Victor Christian William (CAVENDISH), 9th DUKE OF DEVONSHIRE. She *d.* 21 May 1966. Prime Minister and First Lord of the Treasury 1957 to 1963. He *d.* 29 Dec. 1986.

[MAURICE VICTOR MACMILLAN, *styled* VISCOUNT MACMILLAN OF OVENDEN, only s. and h. ap., *b.* 27 Jan. 1921; ed. at Eton and Oxford (Balliol Coll.). He *m.*, 22 Aug. 1942, Katherine Margaret Alice, 2nd da. of William George Arthur (ORMSBY-GORE), 4th BARON HARLECH. He *d. v.p.* 10 Mar. 1984. His widow was still living 1995.]

II. 1986. 2. ALEXANDER DANIEL ALAN (MACMILLAN), EARL OF STOCKTON, &c., grandson and h., being eldest s. of Maurice Victor and Katherine Margaret abovenamed. He was *b.* 10 Oct. 1943; ed. at Eton, Univ. of Paris and Strathclyde Univ. He *m.*, 1970, Hélène Birgitte, da. of Alan Douglas Christie HAMILTON of Mitford, Northumberland. This marriage was diss. by divorce in 1991.

[DANIEL MAURICE ALAN MACMILLAN, *styled* VISCOUNT MACMILLAN OF OVENDEN, s. and h. ap. *b.* 9 Oct. 1974.]

PEERAGES OF 1985

23 MAY

GRIFFITHS

BARONY FOR LIFE. I. 1985. 1. The Right Hon. SIR WILLIAM HUGH GRIFFITHS, P.C., one of the Lords Justices of Appeal, s. of Sir Hugh Ernest GRIFFITHS of Cooden, Sussex, was *b.* 26 Sep. 1923; ed. at Charterhouse and Cambridge (St John's Coll.). On 23 May 1985 he was app. a Lord of Appeal in Ordinary under the Appellate Jurisdiction Act of 1876 and *cr.* a Baron for Life by the style of BARON GRIFFITHS, of Govilon, co. Gwent. He *m.*, 1949, Evelyn, da. of Col. Kristian A. KREFTING.

PEERAGES OF 1986

6 JANUARY

ACKNER

BARONY FOR LIFE.
I. 1985.

1. The Right Hon. SIR DESMOND JAMES CONRAD ACKNER, P.C., one of the Lords Justices of Appeal, s. of Dr Conrad Adolph ACKNER of Beaconsfield, Bucks., was *b.* 18 Sep. 1920; ed. at Highgate Sch. and Cambridge (Clare Coll.). On 6 January 1986 he was app. a Lord of Appeal in Ordinary under the Appellate Jurisdiction Act of 1876 and *cr.* a Baron for Life by the style of BARON ACKNER, of Sutton, co. West Sussex. He *m.* 1946, Joan, da. of John EVANS, and widow of K.B. SPENCE.

6 JANUARY

OLIVER OF AYLMERTON

BARONY FOR LIFE.
I. 1986.

1. The Right Hon. SIR PETER RAYMOND OLIVER, P.C., one of the Lords Justices of Appeal, s. of David Thomas OLIVER, Fellow of Trinity Hall, Cambridge, was *b.* 7 Mar. 1921; ed. at Leys Sch., Cambridge and Cambridge (Trin. Hall). On 6 January 1986 he was app. a Lord of Appeal in Ordinary under the Appellate Jurisdiction Act of 1876 and *cr.* a Baron for Life by the style of BARON OLIVER OF AYLMERTON, of Aylmerton, co. Norfolk. He *m.* 1stly, 1945, Mary Chichester, da. of Sir Eric Keightley RIDEAL. She *d.* 1985, and he *m.* 2ndly, 1987, Wendy Anne, widow of Ivon Lloyd Lewis JONES.

6 JANUARY

GOFF OF CHIEVELEY

BARONY FOR LIFE.
I. 1986.

1. The Right Hon. SIR ROBERT LIONEL ARCHIBALD GOFF, P.C., one of the Lords Justices of Appeal, s. of Lieut. Col. Lionel Trevor GOFF of Monk Sherborne, Basingstoke, co. Hants., was *b.* 12 Nov. 1926; ed. at Eton and Oxford (New Coll.). On 6 January 1986 he was app. a Lord of Appeal in Ordinary under the Appellate Jurisdiction Act of 1876 and *cr.* a Baron for Life by the style of BARON GOFF OF CHIEVELEY, of Chieveley in the Royal County of Berkshire. He *m.*, 1953, Sarah, elder da. of Capt. Gerald Roger Cousins, R.N., of Child Okeford, Dorset.

PEERAGES OF 1988

12 JANUARY

JAUNCEY OF TULLICHETTLE

BARONY FOR LIFE.
I. 1988.

1. SIR CHARLES ELIOT JAUNCEY, s. of Capt. John Henry JAUNCEY, R.N., of Tullichettle, Comrie, Perthshire, was *b.* 8 May 1925; ed. at Radley, Oxford (Ch. Ch.) and Glasgow Univ. On 12 January 1988 he was app. a Lord of Appeal in Ordinary under the Appellate Jurisdiction Act of 1876 and *cr.* a Baron for Life by the style of BARON JAUNCEY OF TULLICHETTLE, of Comrie in the District of Perth and Kinross. He *m.* 1stly, 1948, Jean, only da. of Admiral Sir Angus Edward Malise Bontine Cunninghame GRAHAM of Ardoch, Cardross, co. Dumbarton. This marriage was diss. by divorce in 1969 and he *m.* 2ndly, 1973, Elizabeth, da. of Capt. R.H.V. SIVEWRIGHT, R.N., and widow of Major John BALLINGAL, M.C. This marriage was diss. by divorce in 1977 and he *m.* 3rdly, 1977, Sarah Camilla, yst. da. of Lieut. Col. Charles Frederick CATHCART of Pitcairlie.

PEERAGES OF 1991

1 OCTOBER

BROWNE-WILKINSON

BARONY FOR LIFE.
I. 1991.

1. The Right Hon. SIR NICOLAS CHRISTOPHER HENRY BROWNE-WILKINSON, P.C., one of the Lords Justices of Appeal, s. of Rev. Canon Arthur Rupert BROWNE-WILKINSON, was *b.* 30 Mar. 1930; ed. at Lancing and Oxford (Magdalen Coll.). In 1991 he was app. a Lord of Appeal in Ordinary under the Appellate Jurisdiction Act of 1876 and *cr.* a Baron for Life by the style of BARON BROWNE-WILKINSON, of Camden in the London Borough of Camden. He *m.* 1stly, 1955, Ursula, da. of Cedric de Lacy BACON, she *d.* 1987, and he *m.* 2ndly, 1990, Mrs Hilary Isabella Jane TUCKWELL, da. of Prof. James Wilfred WARBURTON.

PEERAGES OF 1992

10 JANUARY

MUSTILL

BARONY FOR LIFE.
I. 1992.

1. The Right Hon. SIR MICHAEL JOHN MUSTILL, one of the Lords Justices of Appeal, s. of Clement William MUSTILL of

Pateley Bridge, co. York, was *b.* 10 May 1931; ed. at Oundle and Cambridge (St John's Coll.). On 10 Jan. 1992 he was app. a Lord of Appeal in Ordinary under the Appellate Jurisdiction Act of 1876 and *cr.* a Baron for Life by the style of BARON MUSTILL, of Pateley Bridge, co. of North Yorks. He *m.* 1stly, 1960, Beryl Reid, da. of John Alban DAVIES of Chandlers Ford, co. Hants. This *m.* was diss. by divorce in 1983 and he *m.* 2ndly, 1991, Caroline, (Mrs PHILLIPS), da. of (—).

11 MARCH

SLYNN OF HADLEY

BARONY FOR LIFE.
I. 1992.

1. The Hon. GORDON SLYNN, one of the Justices of Appeal, s. of John SLYNN, was *b.* 17 Feb. 1930; ed. at Goldsmiths Coll. and Cambridge (Trin. Coll.). On 11 Mar. 1992 he was app. a Lord of Appeal under the Appellate Jurisdiction Act of 1876 and *cr.* a Baron for Life by the style of BARON SLYNN OF HADLEY, of Eggington, co. Bedford. He *m.*, 1962, Odile Marie Henriette, da. of Pierre BOUTIN.

29 APRIL

CECIL

The Right Hon. ROBERT MICHAEL JAMES GASCOYNE-CECIL, *styled* VISCOUNT CRANBORNE, s. and h. ap. of Robert Edward Peter (GASCOYNE-CECIL), 6th MARQUESS OF SALISBURY, was sum. to Parl. *v.p.* in his father's Barony as LORD CECIL, 29 April 1992. See above, *sub* SALISBURY.

1 OCTOBER

WOOLF

BARONY FOR LIFE.
I. 1992.

1. The Right Hon. SIR HARRY KENNETH WOOLF, P.C., one of the Lords Justices of Appeal, s. of Alexander WOOLF, was *b.* 2 May 1933; ed. at Fettes and Univ. Coll., London. On 1 Oct. 1992 he was app. a Lord of Appeal in Ordinary under the Appellate Jurisdiction Act of 1876 and *cr.* a Baron for Life by the style of BARON WOOLF, of Barnes, London Borough of Richmond. He *m.*, 1961, Marguerite, da. of George SASSOON.

PEERAGES OF 1993

1 OCTOBER

LLOYD OF BERWICK

BARONY FOR LIFE.
I. 1993.

1. The Right Hon. SIR ANTHONY JOHN LESLIE LLOYD, P.C., one of the Lords Justices of Appeal, s. of Edward John Boydell LLOYD of Dallington, Sussex, was *b.* 9 May 1929; ed.

at Eton and Cambridge (Trin Coll.). On 1 Oct. 1993 he was app. a Lord of Appeal in Ordinary under the Appellate Jurisdiction Act of 1876 and *cr.* a Baron for Life by the style of BARON LLOYD OF BERWICK, of Ludlay, co. East Sussex. He *m.*, 1960, Jane Helen Violet, da. of Cornelius William SHELFORD of Chailey Place, near Lewes, Sussex.

PEERAGES OF 1994

11 JANUARY

NOLAN

BARONY FOR LIFE. I. 1994. 1. The Right Hon. SIR MICHAEL PATRICK NOLAN, P.C., one of the Lords Justices of Appeal, yr. s. of James Thomas NOLAN of London, was *b.* 10 Sep. 1928; ed. at Ampleforth and Oxford (Wadham Coll.). On 11 Jan. 1994 he was app. a Lord of Appeal in Ordinary under the Appellate Jurisdiction Act of 1876 and *cr.* a Baron for Life by the style of BARON NOLAN, of Brasted, co. Kent. He *m.*, 1953, Margaret, yr. da. of Alfred NOYES.

3 OCTOBER

NICHOLLS OF BIRKENHEAD

BARONY FOR LIFE. I. 1994. 1. The Right Hon. SIR DONALD JAMES NICHOLLS, one of the Lords Justices of Appeal, s. of William Greenhow NICHOLLS; *b.* 25 Jan. 1933; ed. at Birkenhead Sch., Liverpool Univ. and Cambridge (Trin. Hall). On 3 Oct. 1994 he was app. a Lord of Appeal in Ordinary under the Appellate Jurisdiction Act of 1876 and was *cr.* a Baron for Life by the style of BARON NICHOLLS OF BIRKENHEAD, of Stoke D'Abernon in co. Surrey. He *m.*, 1960, Jennifer Mary, 2nd da. of W.E.C. THOMAS.

PEERAGES OF 1995

11 JANUARY

STEYN

BARONY FOR LIFE. I. 1995. 1. The Hon. SIR JOHAN VAN ZYL STEYN, one of the Lords Justices of Appeal, was *b.* 15 Aug. 1932; ed. at Jan. van Riebeeck Sch., Cape Town, Univ. of Stellenbosch, S. Africa and Oxford (Univ. Coll.). In January 1995 he was app. a Lord of Appeal in Ordinary under the Appellate

Jurisdiction Act of 1876 and *cr.* a Baron for Life by the style of BARON STEYN, of Swafield, co. Norfolk. He has *m.*, Susan Leonore, da. of (—) Lewis.

21 FEBRUARY

HOFFMAN

BARONY FOR LIFE. I. 1995.

1. SIR LEONARD HUBERT HOFFMAN, one of the Lords Justices of Appeal, s. of B.W. HOFFMAN, *b.* 8 May 1934; ed. at S. African College Sch., Cape Town, Cape Town Univ. and Oxford (Queen's Coll.). On 21 February 1995 he was app. a Lord of Appeal in Ordinary under the Appellate Jurisdiction Act, 1876 and *cr.* BARON HOFFMAN, of Chedworth, co. Glos. He *m.*, 1960, Gillian Lorna, da. of (__) STERNER.

INDEX

This is a family name and title index to pages 645–855. These pages contain the corrections to volume XIII and the additions to that volume. They are all arranged chronologically under date of creation. Family names have only been indexed where they differ from the title. In cases of families with the same surname but different titles the title has been added in brackets.

Aberconway (Barony), 660
Aberdeen and Temair (Marquessate), 669
Abertay (Barony), 743
Ackner (Life Barony), 851
Acland, *see* Fuller-Acland-Hood
Adams (Barony), 789
Addison (Barony and Viscountcy), 729
Adrian (Barony), 811
Agar, 665
Ailwyn (Barony), 689
Airedale (Barony), 653
Aitken, 673
Akers-Douglas, 662
Alamein, *see* Montgomery of Alamein (Viscountcy)
Alanbrooke (Barony and Viscountcy), 768
Alderney (Viscountcy), *see* Milford Haven (Marquessate)
Aldington (Barony), 835
Alexander, 673
Alexander of Hillsborough (Viscountcy), 791
Alexander of Tunis (Viscountcy and Earldom), 775
Allander, *see* Fraser of Allander (Barony)
Allen of Hurtwood (Barony), 713
Allenby of Megiddo (Viscountcy), 684
Allendale (Barony and Viscountcy), 653
Allerton (Barony), 646
Allington, *see* Conway of Allington (Barony)
Alness (Barony), 720
Althorp (Viscountcy), 649
Altrincham (Barony), 765
Alvingham (Barony), 707
Aman, 709
Ammon (Barony), 758
Amory (Viscountcy), 830
Amulree (Barony), 780
Amwell (Barony), 785
Anderson, 800
Apethorpe, *see* Brassey of Apethorpe (Barony)
Archibald (Barony), 790
Ardwick, *see* Henderson of Ardwick (Barony)
Armstrong-Jones, 833
Armstrong (Barony), 649
Arnold (Barony), 697
Arthur, 679
Ashbourne, *see* Cullen of Ashbourne (Barony)
Ashby St. Ledgers (Barony), 657
Ashfield (Barony), 686
Ashley, 713
Ashton of Hyde (Barony), 662
Askwith (Barony), 682
Asquith (Viscountcy), *see* Oxford and Asquith (Earldom)
Asquith of Bishopstone (Life Barony), 796
Assheton, 813
Astor (Barony and Viscountcy), 669
Astor of Hever (Barony), 817
Athlone (Earldom), 676
Atkin (Life Barony), 702
Attlee (Earldom), 814
Austin (Barony), 728
Avon (Earldom), 833
Avonholm, *see* Keith of Avonholm (Barony)
Aylmerton, *see* Oliver of Aylmerton (Life Barony)
Ayot, *see* Sanderson of Ayot (Barony)

Baads, *see* Douglas of Baads
Badeley (Barony), 790
Baden-Powell (Barony), 708
Baillieu (Barony), 805
Baird, 698
Baldwin of Bewdley (Earldom), 732

Balfour (Earldom), 691
Balfour of Inchrye (Barony), 762
Balfour (Kinross), 645
Balfour (Riverdale), 723
Banbury of Southam (Barony), 696
Baring, 828
Barloch, *see* Douglas of Barloch (Barony)
Barnby (Barony), 691
Barnes, 655
Barrie, 743
Barry, 646
Barrymore (Barony), 646
Bathurst, 680
Bayford (Barony), 705
Beach, *see* Hicks-Beach
Beardmore, 687
Bearsted (Barony and Viscountcy), 688
Beatty (Barony and Earldom), 683
Beaumont, 653
Beaverbrook (Barony), 673
Belisha, *see* Hore-Belisha (Barony)
Belstead (Barony), 736
Benn, 749
Bennett (Viscountcy), 748
Bennett of Edgbaston (Barony), 806
Benson, 662
Berkhamsted (Earldom), *see* Carisbrooke (Marquessate)
Berry (Camrose), 705, 745
Berry (Kemsley), 727
Bertie of Thame (Barony and Viscountcy), 668
Berwick, *see* Lloyd of Berwick (Life Barony)
Bessborough (Earldom), 730
Bethell (Barony), 694
Betterton, 721
Beveridge (Barony), 777
Bewdley, *see* Baldwin of Bewdley (Earldom)
Bewicke-Copley, 695
Bicester (Barony), 737
Biddulph (Barony), 648
Bigham, 657
Bilsland (Barony), 791
Bingham (Barony), 720
Bingley (Barony), 719
Birdwood (Barony), 735
Birkenhead (Barony, Viscountcy and Earldom), 681
Birkenhead, *see* Cohen of Birkenhead (Barony)
Birkenhead, *see* Nicholls of Birkenhead (Life Barony)
Birker, *see* Lindsay of Birker (Barony)
Birkett (Barony), 822
Bishopstone, *see* Asquith of Bishopstone (Barony)
Blackford (Barony), 723
Blades, 703
Blakenham (Viscountcy), 838
Blanesburgh (Life Barony), 695
Bledisloe (Barony and Viscountcy), 680
Blyth (Barony), 654
Boot, 704
Borodale (Viscountcy), *see* Beatty (Barony and Earldom)
Borth-y-Gest, *see* Morris of Borth-y-Gest (Life Barony)
Borthwick, 664
Borwick (Barony), 693
Botreaux (Barony), 687
Bowyer, 730
Boyd, *see* Lennox-Boyd
Boyd of Merton (Viscountcy), 829–30
Boyd-Orr (Barony), 789
Brabazon of Tara (Barony), 752
Bracken (Viscountcy), 800
Bradbury (Barony), 697
Brain (Barony), 834
Braintree (Barony), 787
Brand (Barony), 778
Brandon of Oakbrook (Life Barony), 848
Brass, 764
Brassey of Apethorpe (Barony), 735
Brecon (Barony), 822
Brenchley, *see* Monckton of Brenchley (Viscountcy)
Brentford (Viscountcy), 706
Bridge of Harwich (Life Barony), 848
Bridgeman (Viscountcy), 705
Bridges (Barony), 819
Brightman (Life Barony), 849
Broadbridge (Barony), 767

Brocas (Viscountcy), *see* Jellicoe (Viscountcy and Earldom)
Brocket (Barony), 716
Brook, 838
Brooke (Alanbrooke), 802
Brooke (Brookeborough), 768
Brooke of Oakley (Barony), 740
Brookeborough (Viscountcy), 802
Broughshane (Barony), 769
Broughton, 704
Broughton, *see* Marks of Broughton (Barony)
Brown, 798
Browne-Wilkinson (Life Barony), 852
Bruce of Melbourne (Viscountcy), 783
Bruntisfield (Barony), 751
Bryce (Viscountcy), 666
Buchan, 722
Buchan-Hepburn, 820
Buckley, 668
Buckmaster (Barony and Viscountcy), 668
Buller, *see* Manningham-Buller
Burden (Barony), 791
Burgh (Barony), 670
Burma, *see* Mountbatten of Burma (Viscountcy and Earldom)
Burnham (Barony and Viscountcy), 648
Butler (Barony), 664
Buxton (Viscountcy and Earldom), 666
Buxton, *see* Noel-Buxton (Barony)

Cadman (Barony), 731
Cain, *see* Nall-Cain
Caldecote (Viscountcy), 741
Calverley (Barony), 772
Cambridge (Marquessate), 676
Campbell Colgrain), 774
Campbell Glenavy), 689
Campion (Barony), 793
Camrose (Barony), 705
Camrose (Viscountcy), 745
Canberra, *see* Ruthven of Canberra (Viscountcy)
Carisbrooke (Marquessate), 677
Carnock (Barony), 672
Carrick (Earldom [S.]), *see* Cornwall (Dukedom)
Carrick (Earldom), *see* Butler (Barony)
Carson (Life Barony), 687
Catto (Barony), 727
Cautley (Barony), 727
Cawley (Barony), 678
Cayzer, 740
Cecil (Barony), 745
Cecil, 719
see also Gascoyne-Cecil
Cecil of Chelwood (Viscountcy), 695
Chalmers (Barony), 682
Chaloner, 676
Chandos (Viscountcy), 809
Chaplin (Viscountcy), 671
Charnwood (Barony), 662
Chatfield (Barony), 731
Chattisham (Barony), 764
Chelmsford (Viscountcy), 687
Chelsea, *see* Cross of Chelsea (Life Barony)
Chelwood, *see* Cecil of Chelwood (Viscountcy)
Cherwell (Barony and Viscountcy), 748
Chester (Earldom), *see* Cornwall (Dukedom)
Chetwode (Barony), 763
Chieveley, *see* Goff of Chieveley (Life Barony)
Chilston (Viscountcy), 662
Chilworth, *see* Lucas of Chilworth (Barony)
Chorley (Barony), 771
Chubb, 700
Churchman, 714
Cilcennin (Viscountcy), 816
Citrine (Barony), 778
Clark, 777
Clarke, 664
Clauson (Barony), 751
Cleeve, *see* Sinclair of Cleeve (Barony)
Clitheroe (Barony), 813
Clwyd (Barony), 683
Clydesmuir (Barony), 787
Coats, 672
Cobbold (Barony), 831
Cobham (Barony), 673
Cochrane of Cults (Barony), 682
Cohen (Life Barony), 797
Cohen of Birkenhead (Barony), 818
Cokayne, 687
Colebrooke (Barony), 652
Coleraine (Barony), 808

Colgrain (Barony), 774
Colston, 672
Colville, 787
Colwyn (Barony), 675
Colyton (Barony), 816
Combe, *see* Sydenham of Combe (Barony)
Conesford (Barony), 813
Conway of Allington (Barony), 713
Cooper of Culross (Barony), 809
Cooper, 802
Cope (Barony), 764
Copley, *see* Bewicke-Copley
Corbett, 661
Cornwall (Dukedom), 800
Cornwallis (Barony), 700
Corvedale (Viscountcy), *see* Baldwin of Bewdley (Earldom)
Courtauld-Thomson (Barony), 758
Courthope (Barony), 762
Coutts, *see* Money-Coutts
Coutts-Nevill, 664
Cowdray (Barony and Viscountcy), 658
Cozens-Hardy (Barony), 667
Craig, 700
Craigavon (Viscountcy), 700
Craigmyle (Barony), 656
Cranborne (Viscountcy), 745
Crathorne (Barony), 825
Crawford, 796
Crewe (Marquessate), 662
Crewe-Milnes, 662
Cripps, 665
Crittall, 787
Croft (Barony), 743
Cromwell (Barony), 695
Crook (Barony), 784
Crookshank (Viscountcy), 815
Cross of Chelsea (Life Barony), 845
Crossley, 672
Cuffe, 656
Cullen of Ashbourne (Barony), 687
Culloden (Barony), *see* Gloucester (Dukedom)
Culross, *see* Cooper of Culross (Barony)
Cults, *see* Cochrane of Cults (Barony)
Cunliffe (Barony), 667
Cunliffe-Lister, 725
Cunningham of Hyndhope (Barony and Viscountcy), 768
Curzon of Kedleston (Marquessate), 689
Cushendun (Barony), 701

D'Abernon (Barony and Viscountcy), 667
Daresbury (Barony), 701
Darling (Barony), 696
Darwen (Barony), 775
Daryngton (Barony), 694
Daventry (Viscountcy), 754
Davidson (Viscountcy), 734
Davies (Barony), 714
Davies, 775
see also Edmund-Davies (Life Barony)
Davison, 769
Dawick (Viscountcy), *see* Haig (Barony and Earldom)
Dawson of Penn (Barony and Viscountcy), 686
De Villiers (Barony), 659
De L'Isle (Viscountcy), 815
De Ros (Barony), 755
Denham (Barony), 730
Denison-Pender, 734
Denning (Life Barony), 820
Dent, 665
Derwent, *see* Fitzalan of Derwent (Viscountcy)
Desart (Barony), 656
Desborough (Barony), 651
Devlin (Life Barony), 834
Devonport (Barony and Viscountcy), 658
Dewar, 674
Dickinson (Barony), 709
Dilhorne (Barony and Viscountcy), 836
Diplock (Life Barony), 844
Dixon, 741
Donovan (Life Barony), 839
Douglas of Barloch (Barony), 793
Douglas of Kirtleside (Barony), 787
Douglas, *see* Akers-Douglas
Douglas of Baads (Barony), *see* Chilston (Viscountcy)
Dovercourt (Barony), 808
Doverdale (Barony), 675
Dowding (Barony), 755

Downpatrick (Barony), *see* Kent (Dukedom)
Doxford, *see* Runciman of Doxford (Viscountcy)
Drumalbyn (Barony), 838
Drummond, *see* Heathcote-Drummond-Willoughby
Drumochter, *see* Macpherson of Drumochter (Barony)
Du Parcq (Life Barony), 775
Dudhope (Viscountcy), 804
Dudley (Barony), 671
Dugan of Victoria (Barony), 790
Dugdale, 825
Dukes, 784
Dukeston (Barony), 784
Dulverton (Barony), 707
Dundee (Earldom), *see* Dudhope (Viscountcy)
Dundee, *see* Ritchie of Dundee
Dunedin (Barony and Viscountcy), 649
Dunrossil (Viscountcy), 826
Duveen (Barony), 717
Dwyfor, *see* Lloyd-George of Dwyfor (Earldom)

Eady, 685
Ebbisham (Barony), 703
Eccles (Barony and Viscountcy), 837
Eden (Viscountcy), *see* Avon (Earldom)
Edgbaston, *see* Bennett of Edgbaston (Barony)
Edinburgh (Dukedom), 786
Edmondson, 765
Edmund-Davies (Life Barony), 846
Egremont (Barony), 839
Elias, 734
Elibank (Viscountcy), 662
Eltham (Earldom), *see* Cambridge (Marquessate)
Eltisley (Barony), 719
Elton (Barony), 719
Emmott (Barony), 663
Ennisdale (Barony), 740
Eresby, *see* Willoughby de Eresby (Barony)
Erleigh (Viscountcy), *see* Reading (Barony, Viscountcy, Earldom and Marquessate)
Erroll of Hale (Barony), 840
Erskine of Rerrick (Barony), 844
Essendon (Barony), 714
Evans (Barony), 821
Evans, 770
Eve, 837
Evershed (Barony), 816
Eyres-Monsell, 726

Fairfield (Barony), 738
Fairhaven (Barony), 704
Falle, 719
Fareham, *see* Lee of Fareham (Barony and Viscountcy)
Faringdon (Barony), 669
Fellowes, 689
Fermor-Hesketh, 721
Findhorn, *see* Stuart of Findhorn (Viscountcy)
Finlay (Barony and Viscountcy), 673
Fisher (Barony), 656
Fitzalan of Derwent (Viscountcy), 687
Fitzalan-Howard, 687
Fitzroy, 754
Fitzroy-Newdegate, 755
Fitzwalter (Barony), 697, 805
Fleck (Barony), 832
Fleet, *see* Thomson of Fleet (Barony)
Fletcher, 751
Fletcher-Vane, 842
Flete, *see* Mildmay of Flete (Barony)
Foljambe, 650
Forres (Barony), 692
Forster (Barony), 686
Forster of Harraby (Barony), 825
Forteviot (Barony), 674
Foster, 658
Fowler, 654
Fox, *see* Lane-Fox
Fraser of Allander (Barony), 840
Fraser of North Cape (Barony), 780
Fraser of Tullybelton (Life Barony), 846
Fraser, 811
Freeman-Thomas, 659
Freeman-Mitford, 647
French (Viscountcy), 668
Freyberg (Barony), 797
Fuller-Acland-Hood, 660
Furneaux (Viscountcy), *see* Birkenhead (Barony, Viscountcy and Earldom)

Furness (Barony and Viscountcy), 658
Furniss, 711
Furnivalle (Barony), 665
Fyfe (Barony), *see* Kilmuir (Viscountcy and Earldom)

Gainford (Barony), 674
Galbraith, 812
Ganzoni, 736
Garro-Jones, 783
Gascoyne-Cecil (Cecil of Chelwood), 745
Gascoyne-Cecil, 695
Geddes (Barony), 750
Gibbs (Hunsdon of Hunsdon), 695
Gibbs (Wraxall), 701
Gisborough (Barony), 676
Gladstone (Viscountcy), 657
Gladstone of Hawarden (Barony), 715
Gladwyn (Barony), 828
Glanely (Barony), 680
Glassary (Barony), *see* Dudhope (Viscountcy)
Glenapp (Viscountcy), *see* Inchcape (Barony, Viscountcy and Earldom)
Glenarthur (Barony), 679
Glenavy (Barony), 689
Glenconner (Barony), 660
Glendale, *see* Howick of Glendale (Barony)
Glendevon (Barony), 843
Glendyne (Barony), 690
Glentanar (Barony), 672
Glentoran (Barony), 741
Gloucester (Dukedom), 702
Glyn (Barony), 806
Godber (Barony), 817
Goddard (Life Barony), 759
Godley, 656
Goff of Chieveley (Life Barony), 851
Gordon, 669
Gorell (Barony), 655
Gort (Viscountcy), 775
Gowrie (Barony and Earldom), 726, 760
Gowrie, *see* Ruthven of Gowrie (Barony)
Grantchester (Barony), 806
Greenall, 701
Greene (Barony), 748
Greenhill (Barony), 794
Greenway (Barony), 699
Greenwich (Barony), *see* Edinburgh (Dukedom)
Greenwood (Barony and Viscountcy), 708
Greer, 738
Grenfell (Barony), 646
Grenfell (Desborough), 651
Grenfell (St Just), 724
Gretton (Barony), 756
Gridley (Barony), 811
Griffiths (Life Barony), 850
Grigg, 765
Grimston of Westbury (Barony), 839
Guest (Life Barony), 831
Guest, *see* Haden-Guest (Barony)
Guest, 657
Guinness, 713
Gully, 649
Gwaenysgor, *see* Macdonald of Gwaenysgor (Barony)
Gwynedd (Viscountcy), *see* Lloyd-George of Dwyfor (Earldom)

Hacking (Barony), 762
Haddo (Earldom), 669
Haden-Guest (Barony), 792
Hadley, *see* Slynn of Hadley (Life Barony)
Haig (Barony and Earldom), 684
Hailes (Barony), 820
Hailey (Barony), 728
Hailsham (Barony and Viscountcy), 702
Hailsham of St. Marylebone (Life Barony), 702
Hale, *see* Erroll of Hale (Barony)
Halifax (Earldom), 759
Halifax, *see* Mackintosh of Halifax (Barony and Viscountcy)
Hall (Viscountcy), 780
Hankey (Barony), 739
Hanworth (Barony and Viscountcy), 699
Harcourt (Viscountcy), 674
Harding of Petherton (Barony), 822
Hardinge of Penshurst (Barony), 659
Hardy, *see* Cozens-Hardy (Barony)
Hare, 838
Harmsworth (Barony), 739
Harmsworth (Northcliffe), 651
Harmsworth (Rothermere), 666

Harraby, *see* Forster of Harraby (Barony)
Harrow, *see* Somervell of Harrow (Barony)
Harvey of Tasburgh (Barony), 808
Harwich, *see* Bridge of Harwich (Life Barony)
Hastings of Hastings (Barony), *see* Botreaux (Barony)
Hawarden, *see* Gladstone of Hawarden (Barony)
Hawkesbury (Viscountcy), *see* Liverpool (Earldom)
Hayter (Barony), 700
Hazlerigg (Barony), 761
Head (Viscountcy), 829
Heathcoat-Amory, 830
Heathcote-Drummond-Willoughby, 795
Hemingford (Barony), 753
Hemphill (Barony), 651
Henderson (Barony), 770
Henderson of Ardwick (Barony), 792
Henderson, 669
Hennessy, 728
Henryton, *see* Morton of Henryton (Life Barony)
Hepburn, *see* Buchan-Hepburn
Herbert, 753
Hermon-Hodge, 683
Hesketh (Barony), 721
Hever, *see* Astor of Hever (Barony)
Hewart (Barony), 691
Hewart (Viscountcy), 744
Heyworth (Barony), 813
Hicks, *see* Joynson-Hicks
Hicks-Beach, 651
Hillsborough, *see* Alexander of Hillsborough (Viscountcy)
Hindley, 712
Hirst (Barony), 720
Hives (Barony), 794
Hoare, 759
Hodge, *see* Hermon-Hodge
Hodson (Life Barony), 830
Hoffman (Life Barony), 855
Hogg, 702
Holden (Barony), 654
Holland, 658
Hollenden (Barony), 663
Holmes, 808
Hood, *see* Fuller-Acland-Hood
Hope (Glendevon), 843
Hope (Rankeillour), 715
Hope-Morley, 663
Hopkinson, 816
Hopwood, 677
Horder (Barony), 716
Hore-Belisha (Barony), 807
Hore-Ruthven, 685, 726
Horne of Slamannan (Viscountcy), 733
Howard, *see* Fitzalan-Howard
Howard of Penrith (Barony), 711
Howick of Glendale (Barony), 828
Hudson (Viscountcy), 799
Huggins, 812
Hughes-Young, 841
Hungarton (Barony), 796
Hungerford (Barony), *see* St. Davids (Barony and Viscountcy)
Hungerford, *see* Portal of Hungerford (Barony and Viscountcy)
Hunsdon of Hunsdon (Barony), 695
Hurcomb (Barony), 793
Hurtwood, *see* Allen of Hurtwood (Barony)
Hutchison of Montrose (Barony), 715
Hyde, *see* Ashton of Hyde
Hyndhope, *see* Cunningham of Hyndhope (Barony and Viscountcy)
Hyndley (Barony and Viscountcy), 712

Ikerrin (Viscountcy [I.]), *see* Butler (Barony)
Iliffe (Barony), 718
Ilkeston (Barony), 658
Illingworth (Barony), 688
Ilton, *see* Masham of Ilton (Life Barony)
Inchcape (Barony, Viscountcy and Earldom), 661
Inchrye, *see* Balfour of Inchrye (Barony)
Inchyra (Barony), 835
Ingleby (Viscountcy), 815
Inglewood (Barony), 842
Inman (Barony), 774
Inskip, 741
Inverchapel (Barony), 777
Inverforth (Barony), 681

Inverkeithing (Barony [S.]), *see* Dudhope (Viscountcy)
Invernairn (Barony), 687
Ironside (Barony), 746
Irwin (Barony), 699
Isaacs, 665
Ismay (Barony), 781

Jackson (Barony), 763
Jackson, 646
Jauncey of Tullichettle (Life Barony), 852
Jebb, 828
Jeffreys (Barony), 803
Jellicoe (Viscountcy and Earldom), 677
Jenkins (Life Barony), 825
Jessel (Barony), 695
Johnson, *see* Webb-Johnson (Barony)
Johnston, *see* Lawson-Johnston
Joicey (Barony), 652
Jones, *see* Armstrong-Jones, Garro-Jones and Leif-Jones
Jowitt (Barony, Viscountcy and Earldom), 766
Joynson-Hicks, 706

Kay-Shuttleworth, 645
Kearley, 658
Kedleston, *see* Curzon of Kedleston (Marquessate)
Keith of Avonholm (Life Barony), 807
Keith of Kinkel (Life Barony), 847
Kemp, 664
Kemsley (Barony and Viscountcy), 727
Kendal, *see* Wakefield of Kendal (Barony)
Kenilworth (Barony), 733
Kennet (Barony), 724
Kenswood (Barony), 797
Kent (Dukedom), 720
Kenwood, *see* Morris of Kenwood (Barony)
Kenworthy, 671
Keren (Viscountcy), *see* Wavell (Viscountcy and Earldom)
Kerr (Inverchapel), 777
Kerr (Teviot), 743
Kershaw (Barony), 782
Keyes (Barony), 753
Keynes (Barony), 753
Kilbracken (Barony), 656
Kilbrandon (Life Barony), 845
Killearn (Barony), 755
Killowen, *see* Russell of Killowen (Life Barony)
Kilmuir (Viscountcy and Earldom), 810
Kindersley (Barony), 746
Kinkel, *see* Keith of Kinkel (Life Barony)
Kinross (Barony), 645
Kirkwood (Barony), 798
Kirtleside, *see* Douglas of Kirtleside (Barony)
Kitson, 653
Knatchbull, 779
Knollys (Barony and Viscountcy), 647
Kylsant (Barony), 695

Lamb, 712
Lambert (Viscountcy), 765
Lambeth, see Lang of Lambeth, (Barony)
Lambury (Barony), 835
Lampson, 755
Lane (Life Barony), 847
Lane-Fox, 719
Lang of Lambeth (Barony), 752
Latham (Barony), 749
Latimer (Barony), 664
Launceston (Viscountcy), *see* Carisbrooke (Marquessate)
Law, 808
Lawrence (Oaksey), 781
Lawrence (Trevethin), 690
see also Pethick-Lawrence (Barony)
Lawson (Barony), 793
Lawson, *see* Levy-Lawson
Lawson-Johnston, 707
Layton (Barony), 781
Leathers (Barony and Viscountcy), 747
Leckie, *see* Younger of Leckie (Viscountcy)
Lee of Fareham (Barony and Viscountcy), 680
Leeds, *see* Milner of Leeds (Barony)
Leif-Jones, 714
Leighton of Saint Mellons (Barony), 834
Leith, 670
Lennox-Boyd, 830
Lever, 675
Leverhulme (Barony and Viscountcy), 675

Levy-Lawson, 648
Lewis (Brecon), 822
Lewis (Essendon), 714
Lewis (Merthyr), 660
Lindemann, 748
Lindsay of Birker (Barony), 770
Linley (Viscountcy), *see* Snowdon (Earldom)
Lister, *see* Cunliffe-Lister
Liverpool (Earldom), 650
Liverpool, *see* Russell of Liverpool (Barony)
Llewellin (Barony), 766
Lloyd (Barony), 698
Lloyd of Berwick (Life Barony), 853
Lloyd-George of Dwyfor (Earldom), 760
Lloyd-George, 820
Loder, 720
Long (Viscountcy), 688
Lopes, 734
Lord, 835
Low, 835
Lowther, 689
Lucas of Chilworth (Barony), 778
Lugard (Barony), 702
Luke (Barony), 707
Lyell (Barony), 667
Lyle of Westbourne (Barony), 767
Lyons, 740
Lyttelton, 809
Lytton-Cobbold, 831

Mabane (Barony), 836
MacAndrew (Barony), 827
McCorquodale of Newton (Barony), 814
Macdermott (Life Barony), 784
McEntee (Barony), 796
Macdonald of Gwaenysgor (Barony), 789
McGowan (Barony), 729
Mackay, 661
Mackenzie, 708
Mackintosh of Halifax (Barony and Viscountcy), 786
McLaren, 660
Maclay (Barony), 693
Maclay, 843
Macmillan (Life Barony), 710
Macmillan of Ovenden (Viscountcy), *see* Stockton (Earldom)
McNair (Barony), 814
McNeill, 701
Macpherson of Drumochter (Barony), 796
Macpherson (Drumalbyn), 838
Macpherson (Strathhcarron), 726
Madeley (Earldom), *see* Crewe (Marquessate)
Maenan (Barony), 788
Maffey, 781
Maitland-Biddulph, 648
Makins, 843
Malvern (Viscountcy), 812
Mamhead (Barony), 712
Mancroft (Barony), 729
Manningham-Buller, 836
Manton (Barony) 691
Marchamley (Barony), 654
Marchwood (Viscountcy), 767
Marchwood (Barony), 733
Margesson (Viscountcy), 752
Marks of Broughton (Barony), 832
Marley (Barony), 709
Marquis, 740
Martonmere (Barony), 842
Martyn-Hemphill, 651
Masham (Barony), *see* Swinton (Viscountcy and Earldom)
Masham of Ilton (Life Barony), 726
Mason, 723
Mathers (Barony), 801
Maugham (Life Barony and Viscountcy), 725
Maugham (Viscountcy), 742
Maxwell, 755
May (Barony), 724
Medina (Earldom), *see* Milford Haven (Marquessate)
Megiddo, *see* Allenby of Megiddo (Viscountcy)
Melbourne, *see* Bruce of Melbourne (Viscountcy)
Melchett (Barony), 703
Merioneth (Earldom), *see* Edinburgh (Dukedom)
Merriman (Barony), 746
Merrivale (Barony), 697
Mersey (Barony and Viscountcy), 657
Merthyr (Barony), 660
Merton, *see* Boyd of Merton (Viscountcy)

Meston (Barony), 686
Michelham (Barony), 651
Mildmay of Flete (Barony), 693
Milford (Barony), 738
Milford Haven (Marquessate), 676
Millar, 835
Mills (Barony and Viscountcy), 818
Milne (Barony), 717
Milner (Barony and Viscountcy), 645
Milner of Leeds (Barony), 798
Milnes, *see* Crewe-Milnes
Milverton (Barony), 785
Mitchell-Thomson, 713
Mitford, *see* Freeman-Mitford
Moleyns (Barony,) *see* St. Davids (Barony and Viscountcy)
Monckton of Brenchley (Viscountcy), 819
Mond, 703
Money-Coutts, 664
Monsell (Viscountcy), 726
Montagu, *see* Samuel-Montagu
Montague, 785
Montgomery of Alamein (Viscountcy), 775
Montrose, *see* Hutchison of Montrose (Barony)
Moore (Barony), 808
Moore-Brabazon, 752
Moran (Barony), 754
Morgan, 699
Morley, *see* Hope-Morley
Morris (Barony), 678
Morris, 719
Morris of Borth-y-Gest (Life Barony), 827
Morris of Kenwood (Barony), 795
Morrison (Barony), 771
Morrison, 826
Morton of Henryton (Life Barony), 784
Mottistone (Barony), 717
Mount Temple (Barony), 713
Mountbatten of Burma, (Viscountcy and Earldom), 779
Mountbatten (Carisbrooke), 677
Mountbatten (Milford Haven), 676
Mountevans (Barony), 770
Moyne (Barony), 713
Moynihan (Barony), 704
Muff, 772
Muirshiel (Viscountcy), 843
Munro, 720
Murray (Dunedin), 649
Murray (Elibank), 662
Mustill (Life Barony), 852

Nall-Cain, 716
Nathan (Barony), 744
Nelson, *see* Rutherford of Nelson (Barony)
Nelson of Stafford (Barony), 828
Netherthorpe (Barony), 824
Nevill, *see* Coutts-Nevill
Newall (Barony), 779
Newcastle, *see* Percy of Newcastle (Barony)
Newdegate, *see* Fitzroy-Newdegate
Newman, 712
Newton, 719
Newton, *see* McCorquodale of Newton (Barony)
Nicholls of Birkenhead (Life Barony), 854
Nicolson, 672
Nivison, 690
Noel-Buxton (Barony), 710
Nolan (Life Barony), 854
Norman (Barony), 759
Normanbrook (Barony), 838
Normand (Life Barony), 780
Norrie (Barony), 821
North Cape, *see* Fraser of North Cape (Barony)
North End, *see* Uvedale of North End (Barony)
Northallerton (Viscountcy), *see* Cambridge (Marquessate)
Northcliffe (Barony and Viscountcy), 651
Norton, 670
Norwich (Viscountcy), 802
Nuffield (Barony and Viscountcy), 719
Nugent (Barony), 830
Nunburnholme (Barony), 652
Nuneham (Barony), *see* Harcourt (Viscountcy)

O'Neill, 804
Oakbrook, *see* Brandon of Oakbrook (Life Barony)
Oakley, *see* Brooke of Oakley (Barony)

Oakridge, *see* Robertson of Oakridge (Barony)
Oaksey (Barony), 781
Ogmore (Barony), 794
Oliver of Aylmerton (Life Barony), 851
Olivier (Barony), 696
Orr, *see* Boyd-Orr (Barony)
Ovenden, *see* Macmillan of Ovenden (Viscountcy)
Oxford and Asquith (Earldom), 698

Paget, 678
Pakenham (Barony), 769
Palmer (Barony), 718
Palmer, 772
Palmer (Selborne), 745
Parcq, *see* Du Parcq (Life Barony)
Parmoor (Barony), 665
Partington, 675
Passfield (Barony), 706
Peake, 815
Pearce (Life Barony), 836
Pearson (Life Barony), 844
Pearson, 658
Pease (Daryngton), 694
Pease (Gainford), 674
Pease (Wardington), 728
Pender (Barony), 734
Penn, *see* Dawson of Penn (Barony and Viscountcy)
Penny, 733
Penrith, *see* Howard of Penrith (Barony)
Penshurst, *see* Hardinge of Penshurst
Pentland (Barony), 655
Percy of Newcastle (Barony), 804
Perry (Barony), 736
Petherton, *see* Harding of Petherton (Barony)
Pethick-Lawrence (Barony), 766
Petre, 665
Philipps (Kylsant), 738
Philipps (Milford), 695
Philipps (St Davids), 655
Phillimore (Barony), 680
Piercy (Barony), 771
Plender (Barony), 711
Plumer (Barony and Viscountcy), 684
Plumptre, 697, 805
Pollock, 699
Ponsonby (Bessborough), 730
Ponsonby (Sysonby), 722
Ponsonby of Shulbrede (Barony), 709
Poole (Barony), 823
Portal (Barony and Viscountcy), 721
Portal of Hungerford (Barony and Viscountcy), 768
Porter (Life Barony), 736
Portsea (Barony), 719
Powell, *see* Baden-Powell (Barony)
Prestwich, *see* Younger of Prestwich (Life Barony)
Prestwood (Viscountcy), *see* Attlee (Earldom)

Queenborough (Barony), 678
Quibell (Barony), 763
Quickswood (Barony), 745

Radcliffe (Life Barony and Viscountcy), 790
Ramsbotham, 748
Ramsden (Barony), 764
Rank (Barony), 821
Rankeillour (Barony), 715
Ratendone (Viscountcy), *see* Willingdon (Barony, Viscountcy, Earldom and Marquessate)
Rathcavan (Barony), 804
Rathcreedan (Barony), 670
Rawlinson (Barony), 684
Rea (Barony), 730
Reading (Barony, Viscountcy, Earldom and Marquessate), 665
Redesdale (Barony), 647
Rees-Williams, 794
Reid (Life Barony), 788
Reith (Barony), 744
Remnant (Barony), 703
Renfrew (Barony [S.]), *see* Cornwall (Dukedom)
Rennell (Barony), 717
Renwick (Barony), 840
Rerrick, *see* Erskine of Rerrick (Barony)
Rhayader (Barony), 714
Rhondda (Barony and Viscountcy), 670

Richards, 785
Rideau (Barony), *see* Alexander of Tunis (Viscountcy and Earldom)
Ritchie of Dundee (Barony), 650
Riverdale (Barony), 723
Roberts, 683
Robertson of Oakridge (Barony), 832
Robins (Barony), 823
Robinson (Barony), 785
Robinson, 842
Roborough (Barony), 734
Rochdale (Barony and Viscountcy), 664
Roche (Life Barony), 725
Rochester (Barony), 712
Rockley (Barony), 719
Rodd, 717
Romer (Life Barony), 734
Romsey (Barony), *see* Mountbatten of Burma, (Viscountcy and Earldom)
Rootes (Barony), 824
Ros, *see* De Ros (Barony)
Roskill (Life Barony), 848
Ross, 755
Rotherham (Barony), 658
Rothermere (Barony and Viscountcy), 666
Rotherwick (Barony), 740
Rothesay (Dukedom [S]), *see* Cornwall (Dukedom)
Roundway (Barony), 672
Rowallan (Barony), 661
Royden (Barony), 757
Ruffside (Viscountcy), 798
Rugby (Barony), 781
Runciman of Doxford (Viscountcy), 715
Rushcliffe (Barony), 721
Rusholme (Barony), 772
Russell of Killowen (Life Barony), 709, 846
Russell of Liverpool (Barony), 684
Rutherford of Nelson (Barony), 712
Ruthven of Gowrie (Barony), 685
see also Gowrie (Barony and Earldom)
Ruthven of Canberra (Viscountcy), *see* Gowrie (Barony and Earldom)
Ruthven of Freeland, (Barony [S.]), *see* Ruthven of Gowrie (Barony)
Ruthven, *see* Hore-Ruthven
Saint Mellons, *see* Leighton of Saint Mellons (Barony)
Salmon (Life Barony), 845
Salter (Barony), 806
Samuel (Viscountcy), 732
Samuel (Bearsted), 688
Samuel (Mancroft), 729
Samuel-Montagu, 653
Sanders, 705
Sanderson (Barony), 711
Sanderson of Ayot (Barony), 829
Sandford (Barony), 765
Sankey (Barony and Viscountcy), 706
Scarman (Life Barony), 847
Schuster (Barony), 758
Scrymgeour-Wedderburn, 804
Scrymgeour (Barony [S.]), *see* Dudhope (Viscountcy)
Seager, 834
Seely (Mottistone), 717
Seely (Sherwood), 749
Selbourne (Barony and Earldom), 745
Selby (Viscountcy), 649
Selmeston, *see* Wilmot of Selmeston (Barony)
Selsdon (Barony), 713
Shaughnessy (Barony), 669
Shaw (Life Barony), 655
Shaw (Craigmyle), 656
Shaw (Kilbrandon), 845
Shepherd (Barony), 778
Sherfield (Barony), 843
Sherwood (Barony), 749
Shulbrede, *see* Ponsonby of Shulbrede
Shuttleworth (Barony), 645
Siddeley, 733
Sidney, 815
Silkin (Barony), 793
Silsoe (Barony), 837
Simon (Viscountcy), 742
Simon of Wythenshawe (Barony), 782
Simonds (Life Barony, Barony and Viscountcy), 758
Sinclair of Cleeve (Barony), 818
Sinclair (Pentland), 655
Sinclair (Thurso), 801
Sinha (Barony), 682
Slim (Viscountcy), 829

Slynn of Hadley (Life Barony), 853
Smith (Bicester), 737
Smith (Birkenhead), 681
Smith (Colwyn), 675
Smith (Dudley), 671
Snell (Barony), 712
Snowden (Viscountcy), 712
Snowdon (Earldom), 833
Somerleyton (Barony), 672
Somervell of Harrow (Life Barony), 810
Soulbury (Barony and Viscountcy), 748
Southam, *see* Banbury of Southam (Barony)
Southborough (Barony), 677
Southwood (Barony), 734
Southwood (Viscountcy), 773
Spencer, 649
Spens (Barony), 825
St. Aldwyn (Viscountcy and Earldom), 651
St. Andrews (Earldom), *see* Kent (Dukedom)
St. Audries (Barony), 660
St. Davids (Barony and Viscountcy), 655
St. Helens (Barony), 841
St. Just (Barony), 724
St. Marylebone, *see* Hailsham of St. Marylebone (Life Barony)
Stafford, *see* Nelson of Stafford (Barony)
Stamp (Barony), 736
Stanley (Barony), *see* Botreaux (Barony)
Stanley, 686
Stansgate (Viscountcy), 749
Stern, 651
Stevenage (Viscountcy), *see* Jowitt (Barony, Viscountcy and Earldom)
Steyn (Life Barony), 854
Stockton (Earldom), 850
Stonehaven (Barony and Viscountcy), 698
Strabolgi (Barony), 671
Strachey, 663
Strachie (Barony), 663
Strang (Barony), 807
Strange of Knokyn (Barony), *see* St. Davids (Barony and Viscountcy)
Strathalmond (Barony), 811
Strathcarron (Barony), 726
Strathclyde (Barony), 812
Strauss, 813
Strickland (Barony), 701
Stuart of Findhorn (Viscountcy), 826
Suenson-Taylor, 806
Swaythling (Barony), 653
Swinfen (Barony), 685
Swinton (Viscountcy and Earldom), 725
Sydenham of Combe (Barony), 664
Sysonby (Barony), 722

Tara, *see* Brabazon of Tara (Barony)
Tasburgh, *see* Harvey of Tasburgh (Barony)
Tatem, 680
Taylor, 788
Taylor, *see* Suenson-Taylor
Tedder (Barony), 773
Templeman (Life Barony), 849
Templewood (Viscountcy), 759
Tenby (Viscountcy), 820
Tennant, 660
Terrington (Barony), 678
Teviot (Barony), 743
Thame, *see* Bertie of Thame
Thankerton (Life Barony), 705
Thesiger, 687
Thomas (Cilcennin), 816
Thomas (Rhondda), 670
Thomas (Tonypandy), 849
Thomas, *see* Freeman-Thomas 659
Thomson of Fleet (Barony), 842
Thomson, *see* Courtauld-Thomson (Barony)
Thomson, *see* Mitchell-Thomson
Thurso (Viscountcy), 801
Tonypandy (Viscountcy), 849
Tovey (Barony), 775
Traprain (Viscountcy), *see* Balfour (Earldom)
Tredegar (Viscountcy), 699
Trefgarne (Barony), 783
Trematon (Viscountcy), *see* Athlone (Earldom)
Trenchard (Barony and Viscountcy), 710
Trent (Barony), 704
Trevethin (Barony), 690
Tryon (Barony), 742
Tucker (Life Barony), 795
Tullichettle, *see* Jauncey of Tullichettle (Life Barony)
Tullybelton, *see* Fraser of Tullybelton (Life Barony)

Tunis, *see* Alexander of Tunis (Viscountcy and Earldom)
Turner, 824
Turnour (Barony), 638
Tweedsmuir (Barony), 722
Tyrrell (Barony), 708

Ullswater (Viscountcy), 689
Ulster (Earldom), *see* Gloucester (Dukedom)
Upjohn (Life Barony), 839
Uthwatt (Life Barony), 772
Uvedale of North End (Barony), 777

Vane, *see* Fletcher-Vane
Vansittart (Barony), 747
Vereker, 775
Vestey (Barony), 692
Victoria, *see* Dugan of Victoria (Barony)
Villiers, *see* De Villiers
Vincent, 667

Wakefield (Barony and Viscountcy), 710
Wakefield of Kendal (Barony), 838
Wakehurst (Barony), 720
Waleran (Barony), 650
Walkden (Barony), 763
Walker, 685
Walrond, 650
Warbleton (Viscountcy), *see* Woolton (Barony, Viscountcy and Earldom)
Ward of Witley (Viscountcy), 831
Wardington (Barony), 728
Waring (Barony), 692
Warrender, 751
Watkinson (Viscountcy), 842
Watson (Manton), 691
Watson (Thankerton), 705
Watson-Armstrong, 649
Wavell (Viscountcy and Earldom), 756
Waverley (Viscountcy), 800
Wavertree (Barony), 685
Webb, 706
Webb-Johnson (Barony), 788
Wedderburn, *see* Scrymgeour-Wedderburn
Wedgwood (Barony), 750
Weeks (Barony), 817
Weir (Barony and Viscountcy), 679
Weir, 681
Wemyss, 686
Westbourne, *see* Lyle of Westbourne (Barony)
Westbury, *see* Grimston of Westbury (Barony)
Wester Wemyss (Barony), 686
Westwood (Barony), 757
Whitburgh (Barony), 664
Whitelaw (Viscountcy), 849
Whiteley, 654
Whitfield, 797
Wigram (Barony), 722
Wilberforce (Life Barony), 841
Wilkinson, *see* Browne-Wilkinson (Life Barony)
Willey, 691
Williams (Barony), 788
Williams, *see* Rees-Williams
Williamson, 692
Willingdon (Barony, Viscountcy, Earldom and Marquessate), 659
Willoughby de Eresby (Barony), 795
Wills, 707
Wilmot of Selmeston (Barony), 791
Wilson (Barony), 777
Wilson (Moran), 754
Wilson Nunburnholme), 652
Wimborne (Viscountcy), *see* Ashby St. Ledgers (Barony)
Windlesham (Barony), 728
Winster (Barony), 751
Wise (Barony), 799
Witley, *see* Ward of Witley (Viscountcy)
Wolmer (Viscountcy), *see* Selbourne (Barony and Earldom)
Wolverhampton (Viscountcy), 654
Wood (Halifax), 759
Wood (Irwin), 699
Woodall, 777
Woodbridge (Barony), 714
Woodhouse, 678
Woolf (Life Barony), 853
Woolton (Barony, Viscountcy and Earldom), 740
Wraxall (Barony), 701
Wrenbury (Barony), 668
Wright (Life Barony), 714

Wyfold (Barony), 683
Wyndham, 839
Wythenshawe, *see* Simon of Wythenshawe (Barony)

Yerburgh, 707
Young, 724
see also Hughes-Young
Younger of Prestwich (Life Barony), 695
Younger, 695
Younger of Leckie (Viscountcy), 695
Ypres (Earldom), 668